REDCOATS TO RED ROSES

A History of The Queen's Lancashire Regiment

1689-1899

Volume II – 1803 to 1815
The Napoleonic War

John Downham

Front Cover Illustration:
The 30th Foot scaling the San Vicente Bastion at the storming of Badajoz, 6th April 1812.

Table of Contents

Larga (47th) – Withdrawal to Salamanca (30th, 40th, 47th & 82nd) – Manoeuvres at Salamanca – Withdrawal to Portugal – Suffering of the Army – Winter Quarters 1812-13

Situation in the Peninsula, Spring 1813 – Wellington's offensive strategy – Diversion on the East Coast (81st) – Battle of Castalla 13th April (81st) – Siege of Tarragona – the Great Flank March (40th, 47th, 59th & 82nd) – Battle of Vitoria 21st June 1813 (40th, 47th, 59th & 82nd) – Advance to the Pyrenees – Blockade of Pamplona (40th) – Combat of Maya 25th July (82nd) – Combats of Roncesvalles & Lintzoain 25th & 26th July (40th) – First Battle of of Sorauren 28th July (40th) – Second Battle of of Sorauren 30th July (40th and 82nd) – Pursuit of Soult (40th) – Siege & Storming of San Sebastian 31st August (47th, 59th & detachment 40th) – Battle of San Marcial 31st August (detachments 40th & 82nd) – Catalonia (81st) – The Bidassoa Crossing 7th October (47th & 59th) – Battle of the Nivelle 10th November (40th, 47th, 59th & 82nd) – Battle of the Nive 9th-13th December (47th & 59th).

Winter Quarters before Bayonne – Crossing the Gaves – Battle of Orthez 27th February (40th & 82nd) – Liberation of Bordeaux (82nd) – Battle of Toulouse 10th April (40th) – Sortie from & Capitulation of Bayonne (47th & 59th) – the End in Eastern Spain (81st) – Last Days of the Peninsula Army – Campaign Statistical Summary – the War of 1812 – Siege of Fort Erie (82nd) – Defence of Canada (81st & 82nd) – 40th in Ireland – Wreck of the Baring & Voyage to America (40th) – Mississippi Excursion & Siege of Fort Bowyer (40th) – 2nd/81st Home Service 1809-14 – 2nd/30th Home Service 1813-14 – Holland 1814 (30th & 81st) – 2nd/47th Home Service and Disbandment – Occupation of the Low Countries (30th & 81st)

30th, 47th & 59th to India – Vellore Mutiny 1806 (59th) – Marine Service in Dutch East Indies 1806-7 (30th) – Travancore 1808-9 (30th) – Occupation of Portuguese Colonies of Macau, Diu & Daman (30th & 47th) – Persian Gulf 1809 (47th) – the White Mutiny 1809 (30th & 59th) – Capture of Mauritius 1810 (59th) – 47th in India 1811-15 – Expeditions to Navanagar, the Peishwa's territory & Baroda – 30th in India 1810-15 – Wynad rising – Capture of Batavia & Storming of the Lines of Cornelis, Java 1811 (59th) – Expeditions to Palembang, Sumatra, 1812, Yogyakarta 1812, Bali 1814 & Macassar, Celebes 1814 (59th)

Mobilisation & Concentration (30th, 40th, 59th & 81st) - 'an Infamous Army' - Battle of Quatre Bras (30th) – Withdrawal to Waterloo (30th) & Halle (59th) - 40th March to Waterloo – the Field of Waterloo – Opening Moves (30th & 40th) – French Cavalry Attack (30th & 40th) – Crisis in the Centre (30th & 40th) – Defeat of the Imperial Guard (30th) – General Allied Advance (30th & 40th) – After the Battle – Advance on Paris (30th, 40th & 59th) & Storming of Cambrai (59th)

ILLUSTRATIONS

MAPS

Dedication

Dedicated to All Ranks of the Queen's Lancashire Regiment and their forebearers since 1689

Loyally They Served

About the Author

Born and bred in Lancashire, John Downham was commissioned from the Royal Military Academy Sandhurst into The Lancashire Regiment (Prince of Wales's Volunteers), which subsequently merged into The Queen's Lancashire Regiment. He served for nearly 30 years, with overseas tours in Africa, the Middle East, the Mediterranean and Germany, earning an MBE for his services as Chief of Staff of a NATO-roled brigade. John read History at Durham University and, as 'hands-on' Director and Chairman of Trustees of his Regimental Museum for 27 years, he has a particular interest in military history, ranging from the Roman Army to the present day. However, his 'special interest' is the earlier periods covered in the present publication. He is a published author and a frequent lecturer on military history, presenting topics ranging over the past three centuries of warfare, and has led numerous battlefield tours. He was commissioned in 2005 as a Deputy Lieutenant for Lancashire and, in addition to his responsibilities as Regimental Secretary, he has served as County President for the Royal British Legion and County Chairman for the Army Benevolent Fund.

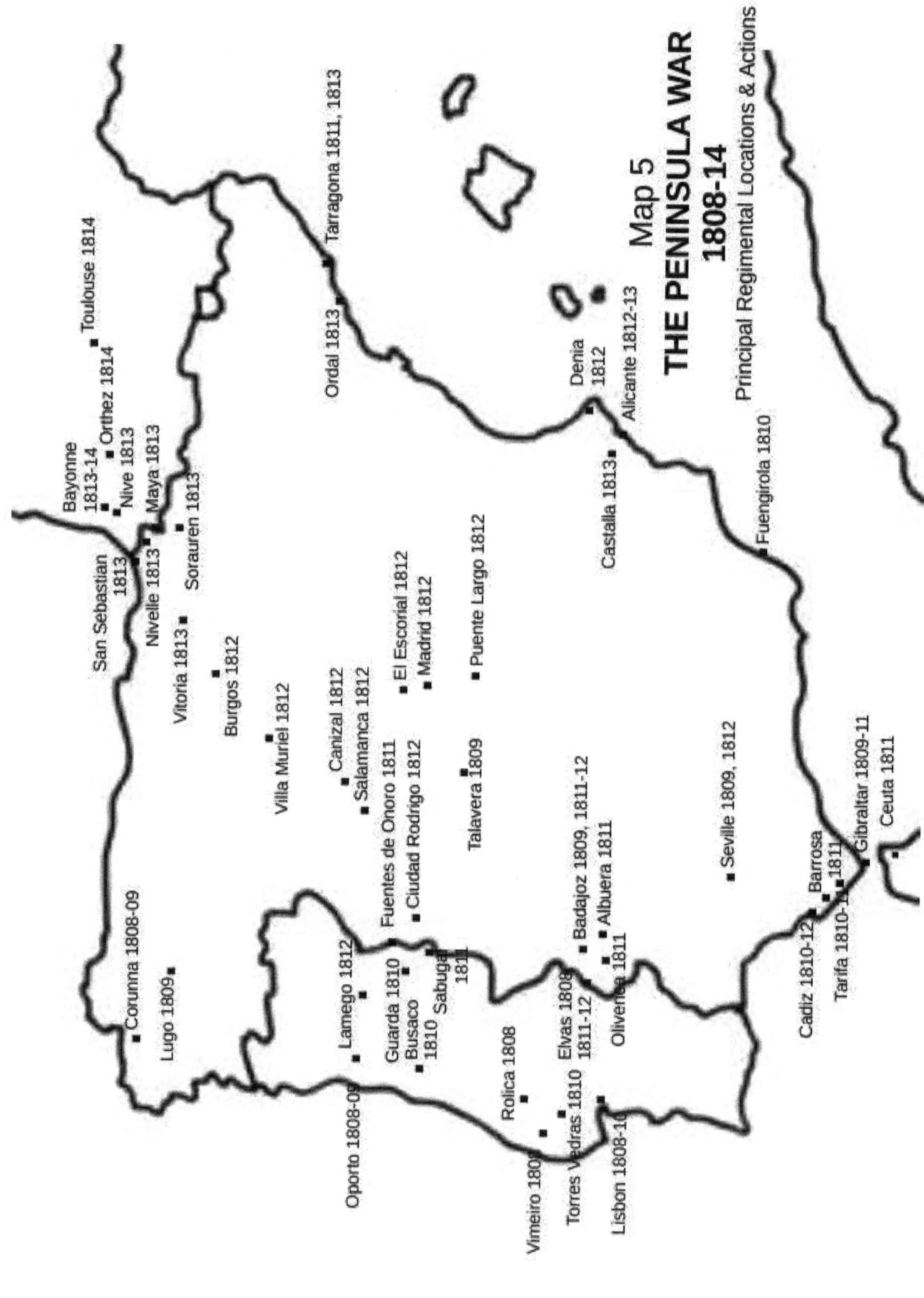

Toulouse 1814
Orthez 1814
Nive 1813
Maya 1813
Bayonne 1813-14
Sorauren 1813
San Sebastian 1813
Nivelle 1813
Vitoria 1813
Tarragona 1811, 1813
Ordal 1813
Burgos 1812
Villa Muriel 1812
Canizal 1812
Salamanca 1812
El Escorial 1812
Madrid 1812
Puente Largo 1812
Denia 1812
Alicante 1812-13
Castalla 1813
Corunna 1808-09
Lugo 1809
Fuentes de Onoro 1811
Ciudad Rodrigo 1812
Talavera 1809
Badajoz 1809, 1811-12
Albuera 1811
Fuengirola 1810
Seville 1809, 1812
Lamego 1812
Guarda 1810
Busaco 1810
Sabugal 1811
Elvas 1808, 1811-12
Olivenca 1811
Gibraltar 1809-11
Ceuta 1811
Barrosa 1811
Cadiz 1810-12
Tarifa 1810-11
Rolica 1808
Vimeiro 1808
Torres Vedras 1810
Lisbon 1808-10
Oporto 1808-09

Map 5
THE PENINSULA WAR
1808-14
Principal Regimental Locations & Actions

iii

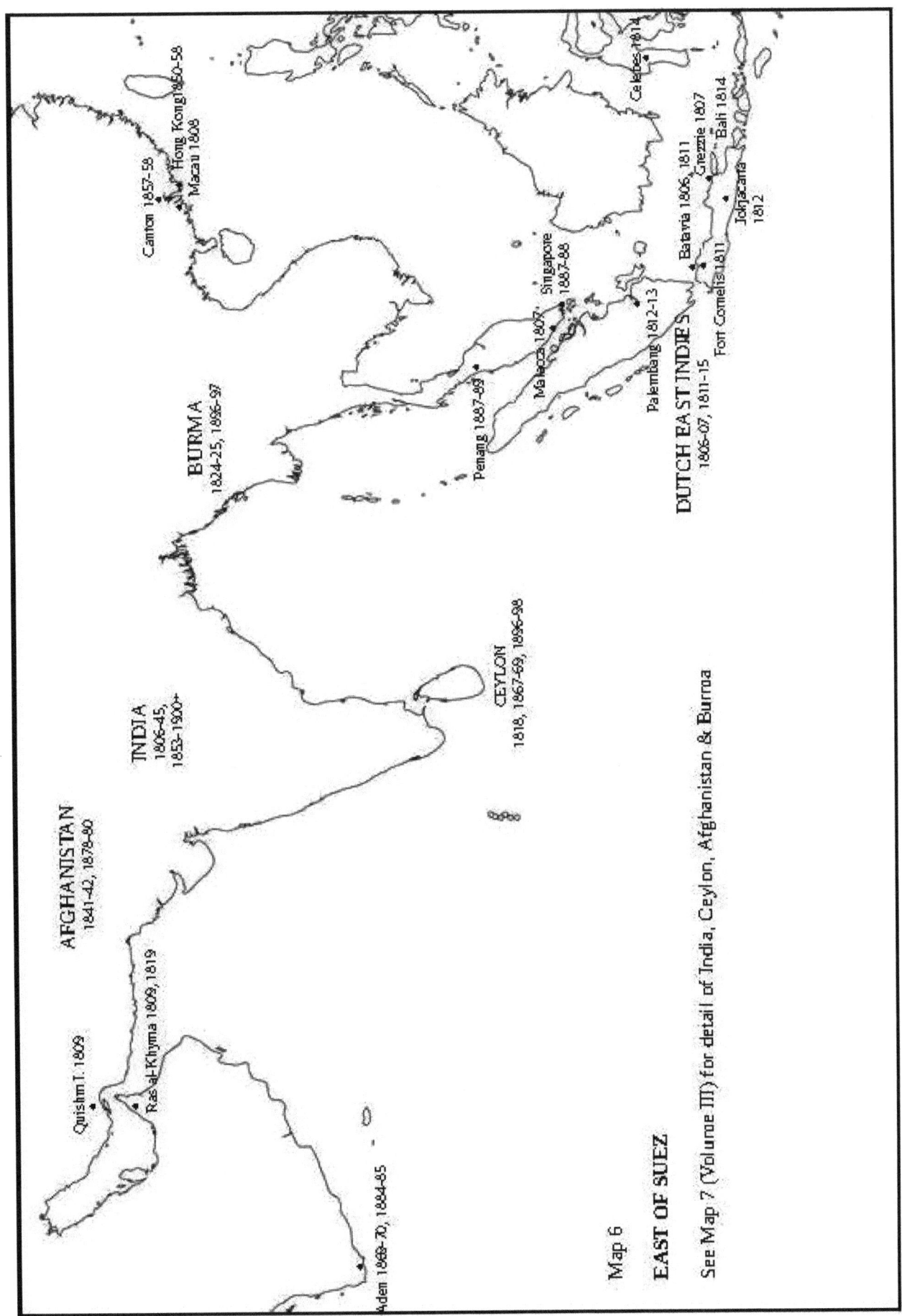

Map 6

EAST OF SUEZ

See Map 7 (Volume III) for detail of India, Ceylon, Afghanistan & Burma

AFGHANISTAN
1841-42, 1878-80

INDIA
1806-45,
1853-1900+

CEYLON
1818, 1867-69, 1896-98

BURMA
1824-25, 1856-97

DUTCH EAST INDIES
1806-07, 1811-15

Quishm I. 1809

Ras-al-Khyma 1809, 1819

Aden 1868-70, 1884-85

Penang 1867-69

Malacca 1807

Singapore
1867-68

Palembang 1812-13

Batavia 1806, 1811

Grezzie 1807

Fort Cornelis 1811

Djokjacarta
1812

Bali 1814

Celebes 1814

Canton 1857-58

Hong Kong 1850-58

Macau 1808

iv

Volume II Introduction

The central theme of the second volume of this history is the long struggle with the Napoleonic Empire in which the 30th, 40th, 47th, 59th, 81st and 82nd Regiments of Foot were among those who contended with Buonaparte's lieutenants, defeating them one by one until the 30th and 40th met the Emperor himself on the field of Waterloo. It is an epic story in which they played no small part. The 40th, notably, was one of just three regiments who fought throughout the six-year war in the Iberian Peninsula and was the only one of those who also took part in the crowning victory of Waterloo.

The Peninsula was indeed the main theatre of British military effort from 1808 until 1814. Overall, the 30th, 40th, 47th, 59th, 81st and 82nd took part in some fifty battles, sieges and lesser affairs in Spain, Portugal and the South of France, earning sixteen Battle Honours. The cost was heavy: 71 officers and nearly three thousand other ranks of those regiments lost their lives there, and thousands more were evacuated sick or wounded, a casualty toll which, for several battalions, was comparable to that suffered by their successors in the First World War.

The regimental accounts given in this volume, based very largely on the testimony of participants, add considerable detail, from a regimental perspective, to previously published histories of this campaign and, in several cases, offer revised interpretations of events.

Elsewhere in Europe, the 81st were victorious at Maida in Italy in 1806 and held Sicily from then until 1812, the 82nd participated in the siege and capture of Copenhagen in 1807, and the 30th took part in an abortive expedition to Germany in 1805-06, while the 30th, 40th, 47th, 59th and 81st all campaigned at various times in the Low Countries, at Walcheren in 1809, the siege of Antwerp in 1814, and the Waterloo campaign of 1815.

But the trial of strength between Britain and imperial France extended across the oceans, where the reverberations of that central contest carried the 40th and 47th to South America in 1806-07, the 47th to the Persian Gulf in 1809, the 59th to South Africa in 1806, Mauritius in 1810, Java from 1811 to 1815, Sumatra in 1812 and 1813, and Bali and the Celebes in 1814, and the 30th to China and the seas off Java, 1806-08. The 40th, 81st and 82nd also took part in the War of 1812 with the United States, the former serving off Louisiana and the latter two assisting in repelling invasion on the Canadian frontier in 1814.

We are very fortunate that a number of regimental participants have recorded vivid accounts of their experiences. Most notable among their many diaries, journals and letters are those of Lieutenant and Adjutant William Stewart, Lieutenant Parke Percy Nevill, Ensigns John Carter and Edward Macready, and Surgeon James Elkington of the 30th, Majors Fielding Browne and Sempronius Stretton, Lieutenants James Mill, William Neilley and Hugh Boyd Wray, Surgeon Charles Boutflower, and Sergeant William Lawrence of the 40th, Paymaster John Harley and Private Adam Reed of the 47th, and Lieutenant George Wood of the 82nd, but the experiences of many other individuals have been preserved, adding their rich and very human testimonies to the story of a momentous and ultimately victorious struggle.

The climax of this volume is the Waterloo campaign, in which the 30th and 40th Regiments played conspicuous parts, and the 59th and 81st also participated. Thanks largely to the efforts of Captain William Siborne of the 47th (Lancashire) Regiment, supplemented by those of Macready of the 30th, no fewer than twelve of the surviving officers of the 30th have left accounts of the campaign, providing an exceptional battalion-level perspective of the battles of Quatre Bras and Waterloo and a well-corroborated corrective to some persistent myths about those battles.

British troops including the 59th land in South Africa prior to the Battle of Blauuberg, 8th January 1806, and capture of Cape Town

Officer & Private 59th, 1806

Battle of Maida, 4th July 1806

Sir James Kempt commanded the 81st 1803-08 & was Colonel 81st 1819-29 & 40th 1829-34

The Maida Tortoise, shell presented by Sir James Kempt to the 81st Foot

Kempt's Light Battalion routing the French 1st Légère & 42nd Infantry at Maida

Chapter I:
The War Of The Third Coalition

The Peace of Amiens – Home from Malta (30th & 40th), Antigua (59th), Minorca (82nd), Bermuda (47th) & South Africa (81st) – An Audience with Bonaparte – Mobilisation 1803 – Formation of Second Battalions – Home Defence & Shorncliffe Camp (59th) – Cape of Good Hope & Battle of Blaauwberg 1806 (59th) – Expedition to the Weser and Wreck of the Jenny 1805-6 (30th) – Malta, Naples & Sicily 1805-6 (81st) – Battle of Maida 1806 (81st) – Siege of Scylla – Defence of Sicily 1806-12 (81st) – Capture of Ischia (81st) – Siege & Capture of Copenhagen 1807 (82nd).

The Peace of Amiens

By 1801 both sides in the long conflict following the French Revolution were war-weary. The two principal belligerents, Britain and France, had fought to a stale-mate; France, having demolished the Second Coalition, was dominant in Europe, while Britannia ruled the waves and had conquered many of her enemies' overseas possessions. Preliminary peace negotiations were hastily concluded, under French pressure, on 1st October 1801, the day before the news of the final British victory at Alexandria broke in London, and on 25th March 1802, a formal peace treaty between Britain and France was signed at Amiens. Under its terms, the gullible British ministry, under mounting domestic pressure for peace at almost any price, conceded a great deal for a relatively small advantage. Malta, Minorca and the Cape of Good Hope were to be evacuated, together with all maritime conquests in the West Indies and elsewhere except Ceylon and Trinidad. In return, French garrisons were to withdraw from Southern Italy but were left in effective possession of Holland, Switzerland, the left bank of the Rhine, and Northern Italy.

Napoleon Buonaparte, now First Consul and the effective ruler of France, had good reason for satisfaction with this settlement which gave him the opportunity to consolidate his power and to mature his continental and maritime ambitions. For the British Army, this temporary cessation of hostilities meant the withdrawal of overseas garrisons followed by over-hasty reductions, while Bonaparte continued to maintain vast armies and took advantage of the raising of the blockade to replenish his naval yards. Addington's reckless ministry abolished Pitt's income tax, disbanded the Volunteers, halved the Army and decommissioned nearly two-thirds of the Royal Navy's line-of-battle ships.

Homeward Bound

In November 1801, both battalions of the 40th Regiment[1] embarked at Valletta for Minorca. Their departure from Malta, at a late hour on the 26th, was, unfortunately, the occasion of some insobriety 'from the extraordinary cheapness of wine and the wish of having a farewell bout.' The 1st Battalion went aboard the *Haerlem*, 64, while five companies of the 2nd Battalion were shipped in the frigate *Ennis* and the balance on the transport *Charon*. Major Alexander Cosby Jackson of the 2nd Battalion had, as he termed it, a 'distressing' voyage aboard the *Ennis*:

'From the second day of our leaving Malta [there] was a continued series of gales of wind and such hurricanes as I believe were never before seen in these seas. The *Ennis* frigate was an old Dutch prize that, when she quitted England eighteen months before, was declared incapable of more than six months service. She had been, however, for the whole time with the troops in Egypt. Her seams were dried out with the sun so that she was wet at the best of times, but when the weather became worse we separated from the convoy and our situation

---

[1] The November strength returns for the 40th on Malta were: 1st Battalion: 29 officers, 35 sergeants, 13 drummers and 474 rank and file, with 117 sick. 2nd Battalion: 31 officers, 37 sergeants, 14 drummers and 459 rank and file, with 58 sick.

became truly alarming. Her night heads opened and closed like an oyster. Her stern frame was entirely loose so that we dreaded being pooped, we were in hourly expectation of the rudder being unshipped, which hung by a single pintle, and we had four feet of water in the hold, tho' our soldiers were continually pumping.

'At last, on the 23rd Dec'r in the afternoon, we made Minorca and so close to the harbour's mouth that I could discern the officer at the saluting battery. At this moment the wind suddenly blew a gale in our teeth and we reluctantly stood off. This night the carpenter came to Captain Cowan and reported a serious leak in the Gunner's store. Poor Cowan told [Lieutenant-Colonel] Clay and myself that he believed that if the wind lasted much longer we should founder. Towards morning, however, it moderated and veered in our favour. We made the harbour and, in spite of all the signals of the Naval Commandant to bring to, we proceeded to the top of the harbour and cast anchor close to the dockyard.

'A committee consisting of the Master Builder and two Captains of the Navy were desired to investigate and report the condition of the ship, and they declared they never saw one afloat in such a miserable condition. Captain Schomberg, who was one of the Committee, congratulated me on my escape. He said he took handfuls inside the head of the ship which was mere touchwood… Some blame must attach to those that could risk 600 of His Majesty's subjects in so crazy a vessel.'[2]

The 40th went into barracks at Port Mahon, where the 82nd Regiment was still stationed, and were soon absorbed in the usual round of guards, field days and reviews. Both Regiments remained there in garrison until the conclusion of general peace, when Minorca was ceded to Spain and, in late May, the British troops were ordered home.

The 30th Regiment had preceded them, leaving Malta on 13th January 1802[3] in several transports and reaching Spithead between the end of March and May 1802. As the companies were released from quarantine, they marched in succession from Portsmouth to Winchester. Then, on May 7th orders were received to march north, five companies to Newcastle-on-Tyne and Gateshead and five to Durham. By May 14th, the Regiment had reached Abingdon, where its strength included thirty-five sergeants, twenty drummers and 413 rank and file, 193 short of the establishment. On reaching Worksop, the 30th received new orders, sending them all to the Tyne; six companies were to proceed to Sunderland, where there was a large barracks, and four to Tynemouth.

There was a change of establishment in June, as a result of which two captains and eight lieutenants of the 30th were placed on half-pay, two more lieutenants were placed on ensign's pay, while eight sergeants were summarily discharged, three without pension, and another was permitted to continue to serve, but on a private's pay. Most oddly, this wholesale reduction of experienced officers and sergeants was accompanied by an increase in the number of private soldiers to 710.

Having landed at Portsmouth in July 1802, the 40th Regiment was quartered at Hilsea, where the 2nd Battalion was almost immediately reduced. Major Jackson was one of the many officers placed on half-pay. The surviving Battalion marched to Winchester in August before returning in October to Portsmouth. In June 1803, the 40th marched to Battle Barracks, and from there to Fairlight Camp in August, and then in November to Hastings, where they remained throughout 1804.

Also in July 1802, the 59th Regiment landed at Portsmouth from their long tour in the West Indies, marching from there to quarters around Trowbridge, Frome and Bradford-on-Avon.

The 82nd left Minorca at peace when the island was returned to Spain, and on 28th July, reached the Cove of Cork, where they were detained for twelve days in quarantine before disembarkation. On 9th August, they marched north to Newry. Arriving there fifteen days later. The Regiment mustered 580 rank and file, having lost 130 men in Minorca, chiefly from dysentery. The 82nd soon afterwards marched to Armagh, where they stayed less than a week before moving on to Omagh. By the end of 1802 a total of 180 men had been discharged, the greater part of whom had been enlisted for the duration of the war.

---

[2] Copy of manuscript Journal of Major Alexander Cosby Jackson, 40th, in the Regimental Archive.
[3] The Malta strength return for November 1801 shows the 30th Regiment with 32 Officers, 34 sergeants, 20 drummers, 325 rank and file, and 59 sick. William Lockhart commanded when they left Malta. Lieutenant Sam Bircham, Sergeant Major Peter Wallace and Sergeant Thompson remained behind, serving with the Maltese Regiment in which the latter two were later commissioned and of which Wallace became Adjutant in April 1805.

The 47th (Lancashire) Regiment of Foot had been in Bermuda since 1793. Their main body, under the command of Lieutenant-Colonel Thomas Backhouse, reached Portsmouth on 1st February 1803 and were then stationed at Gosport for three months.

It will be recalled that the 81st, or Loyal Lincoln Volunteers, were in garrison at Cape Town. On 15th December 1801, news of the preliminaries of peace reached the Cape, and it became known that one of the conditions was that the colony should be restored to the Batavian Republic. Part of the British garrison, the 22nd, 34th and 65th Regiments, was to be sent to India, while the 81st and 91st were to be 'drafted' for volunteers to bring those battalions up to strength and then returned to England. Private Robert Flockhart was one of the six to seven hundred rank and file of the 81st who volunteered for a sizable bounty, most of whom reinforced the 22nd Foot for service in India:

'Any man belonging to the two regiments that were ordered home was at liberty to volunteer into any of the three regiments that were going abroad and get two guineas of volunteer money. I think there were three days given for the volunteering. On the first day a great many of my comrades volunteered and got their bounty money. As I lay on my bed I thought that, after all my sufferings and privations, I was just as poor as when I left home. I resolved to volunteer into the 22nd Regiment the next day.'

In December 1802, Lieutenant-General Janssens arrived at the Cape with a party of Dutch troops to reoccupy the colony. On the 27th, the remnants of the 81st, largely a cadre of officers, NCOs and drummers, embarked in Table Bay on board HMS *Victorious*, 74, and the frigates *La Sybille*, *Orpheus* and *Undine*, who sailed on the 29th of the same month. It was to prove a particularly difficult and remarkably long voyage.

On 11th January 1803, the squadron anchored in St. James' Bay, St. Helena. The *Victorious* had become leaky and had to be hove down for repairs, which caused a delay of three weeks. Whilst they lay at St. Helena, HMS *Imogene* passed though bearing despatches from England directing General Dundas to delay the transfer of Cape Town to the Dutch. It seemed likely that the squadron might have to return to the Cape, but the new orders came too late, and when the repairs to *Victorious* had been completed, the ships resumed their northward course.

They were within a few day's sail of Land's End when, on 7th March, they encountered a violent gale that lasted eight days, during which *Victorious* became almost unmanageable. At length, having sprung all her masts and her bowsprit, she made water faster than the pumps could cope with, which obliged her to make for Lisbon 'in great distress' accompanied by the frigates *La Sybille* and *Undine*. On her arrival there, she was found to be unseaworthy and subsequently condemned to be broken up. As a consequence of this, *Undine* sailed for England with the headquarters of the 81st, leaving the companies which were on board *Victorious* and *La Sybille* at Lisbon. They subsequently embarked on a transport and reached England, only to meet with a violent gale off St. Helens, which drove the transport from her anchors. She was eventually, at considerable hazard, run ashore at Dover.

The headquarters of the Regiment had, in the meantime, landed at Portsmouth, where it was joined by Lieutenant Colonel Parry with a draft of 250 'able recruits' from Ireland. Unused to military discipline, 'they had not been remarkable for regularity either on their march or in quarters.' The Commanding Officer had, in consequence, become involved in a dispute with the General Officer Commanding which in turn resulted in his selling his commission.

The headquarters was ordered to Jersey and embarked on 24th March on HM Ships *Aurora* and *Déterminée*, 24, sloops of war. The ill luck of the Regiment at sea still pursued it, for the captain of *Déterminée* was unable to obtain a pilot and, attempting to follow *Aurora* into St. Aubin's Bay, Jersey, she struck broadside a sunken rock and was wrecked at 4.30 p.m. on 26th March. *Déterminée* immediately began to take in water, and although her cutter was launched, the ship fell on her beam ends, throwing many people into the water and leaving others clinging to the masts and rigging. Fortunately the weather was fine at the time, and *Aurora* was close at hand. Her boats and those of the *Camilla* rescued most of the passengers and crew over the next three and a half hours, but even so, nineteen lives were lost, including ten soldiers, three women and four children of the 81st Regiment. In May 1803, the Regiment was at last re-united in Jersey, where on 24th May, they were quartered in St. Aubin's Bay Barracks.

There, the misfortunes of the 81st continued, for on 11th July, Lieutenant-Colonel Lewis Mackenzie, who had been promoted to command the Regiment only that April, was riding through the market place at St. Heliers when he fell from his horse in a fit and immediately expired. He was succeeded by Lieutenant-Colonel John Hamilton.

It is more pleasant to recall that in that same year, 1803, the Royal Military Asylum for soldiers' orphans (the present Duke of York's Royal Military School) was established in the King's Road, Chelsea and that the first boy to enter was John Evans, son of Corporal Evans of the 81st Foot.

An Audience with Buonaparte

During the fourteen-month peace, or rather pause in hostilities, many British officers occupied their enforced idleness and satisfied their curiosity with a visit to France. Among the many who took this opportunity was Major Alexander Cosby Jackson, now on the half-pay of the 40th Regiment. He was not impressed by what he saw of the flower of the vaunted French Army:

'Having heard much of the fineness of the Consular Guard, I was induced frequently to attend guard mounting [at the Tuileries] but was disappointed with the sight, particularly as I understood the Guard was composed entirely of picked men of the French Army. If so, it must be, I apprehend, from their character rather than their stature as I am convinced that any eight companies taken indiscriminately of the British Army would produce much stouter men.[4] They were drawn up three deep with a very numerous and noisy band of musicians. I think I divest myself of all prejudice in declaring that every guard I have seen mounted by the British displayed more regular system and minute attention. The men were clean and their arms in good order. When off duty all these soldiers, officers not excepted, are far from considering uniformity of dress as at all requisite and I have frequently seen dirty and slovenly figures in the military garb... '[5]

On 4th January 1803, Jackson was introduced to Talleyrand, the machiavellian French Foreign Minister, whose 'frog-faced cadaverous countenance [and] spiral distorted legs strike your optics at the first glance,' through whom he was in turn admitted to an audience with Bonaparte. The First Consul was particularly attentive to the British officers, who were in uniform, and 'in a concise but unassuming manner' asked about their services.

'Their Great Man is of a diminutive size,' he recalled, 'I should think about 5 feet 3½ inches in height, straight and rather stoutly limbed He has a prominent nose, very intelligent, penetrating eyes and a sallow complection. His countenance has a melancholy expression; his voice is full and solemn. He wears his dark unpowdered hair combed negligently over his forehead.'

The First Consul's brows were soon to be adorned by rather more than a wayward lock, for on 18th May 1804, the former republican enthusiast completed his transition from Citoyen Buonaparte by crowning himself as the Emperor Napoleon.

Mobilisation, 1803

Appeasement seldom works for very long, and on 18th May 1803, Britain and France were once more at war. The immediate cause of renewed hostilities was British refusal to evacuate Malta in view of the continued French occupation of Southern Italy and the Ionian Islands and their evident ambitions in the Levant and East Indies; but in truth, there could be no real peace between nations which loathed and despised each other with such unrestrained visceral fury. For the French, Britain was 'perfidious Albion,' thwarting their legitimate aspirations to greatness, while Britons regarded the Corsican upstart as a monstrous, bloodthirsty tyrant.

In March 1803, Buonaparte had ordered the assembly of a flotilla of barges and gunboats for the invasion of Britain, and in June, he ordered the concentration of 120,000 troops, the 'Army of England,' in camps near the Channel ports. His initial plan was to push straight across the straits protected by gunboats, but by the end of January 1804, he accepted that he could not proceed without at least local naval superiority and bent his

---

[4] The average height of a French line infantry soldier at that time was 165cm (under 5foot 5inches), some two inches shorter than his English equivalent.

[5] Jackson, Letter home on 7th January 1803. In July 1803, on the renewal of hostilities, Jackson obtained a majority in the 67th Foot and went with them to the East Indies, where he served for many years. He died a Major-General at Dawlish on 29th January 1827, aged 54.

considerable energies towards achieving this. 'Let us be masters of the Channel for six hours,' he declaimed, 'and we shall be masters of the world.' This was a lot easier said than done. 'I do not say the French cannot come,' growled St. Vincent, the old First Lord of the Admiralty, 'I only say they cannot come by water!' Nevertheless, in 1804-05, the French and Spanish[6] combined fleets made repeated attempts to slip past the Royal Navy, and the danger was only removed by Nelson's crowning victory of Trafalgar, 21st October 1805.

Until the threat of invasion passed in the autumn of 1805, the British people took it very seriously. It was no longer 'Liberty, Equality and Fraternity' they were fighting, but the undisguised tyranny and aggression of 'the Corsican ogre,' who, as early as July 1803, was seen inspecting troops and barges at Boulogne. The atmosphere of alarm was heightened by the news that same month of Emmet's aborted republican rising in Dublin.

The Ministry hastily reversed its planned military reductions and, seeking to put the maximum number of men in uniform without delay or undue expense, appealed for able-bodied men to join the local Volunteer Associations, which sprang up throughout the realm. The nation rapidly became an armed camp, and by the autumn, 342,000 patriotic volunteers were in uniform, if not yet under arms, for the tailors and drill-book publishers were more prompt to deliver than the Ordnance Board. This spasm of popular enthusiasm for volunteering had the unfortunate effect of absorbing much of the manpower that might otherwise have been available to the Regular Army. Over fifty thousand Militia were also embodied, provoking a scramble for substitutes, which further dried up the sources of Regular Army recruitment.

Then, on 6th July 1803, Parliament passed the Additional Forces Act, which ordained that within the year, an Army of Reserve, numbering fifty thousand men between the ages of 18 and 40, was to be raised by compulsory ballot, in counties and parishes, and formed into second battalions for Regular infantry regiments. Serving for five years in the United Kingdom only, they might subsequently accept a bounty and volunteer for overseas service. The new battalions were originally intended for home service only, but as we shall see, this concept lasted no longer than most such schemes for Infantry reorganisation up to the present day.

Implementation of the Additional Forces Act was remarkably prompt. On 8th August, several officers and non-commissioned officers of the 47th (Lancashire) Regiment of Foot arrived in Norwich to receive the balloted men and substitutes of the Army of Reserve from Norfolk, whose training commenced the next day in Chapel Field.

Formation of the 2nd/30th

For the 30th Regiment, stationed at Tynemouth, the first overt signs of impending conflict came in April 1803, when the Admiralty began to press seamen, and Lieutenant-Colonel Wilkinson was ordered to support the naval impress officers on the Tyne. Soon after the declaration of war, the Regiment embarked at Shields for Harwich, where they landed on 17th June and marched to Ipswich. They were already actively recruiting, with thirteen officers' recruiting parties deployed to Doncaster, Lincoln, Nottingham, Sleaford and Wakefield (all old regimental recruiting grounds from the time of William III and Queen Anne), together with Cambridge, Alcester, Carlisle, Glasgow, Perth, Armagh, Sligo and Tuam.

The 30th were very prompt to form a second battalion, being ordered in June 1803 to fill their ranks with men chosen by ballot from the Army of Reserve of the County of Buckinghamshire.[7] Receiving parties of officers and NCOs were sent to Buckingham, High Wycombe and Aylesbury in that County in August 1803 to conduct these men to the Regiment. The standard height for those subject to the ballot had been lowered to 5 foot 2 inches, and to judge by the sickness and desertions in subsequent months, the recruits included some unpromising subjects as well as many who gave good service to the Iberian Peninsula, at Waterloo and beyond.

There was, of course, also a requirement for additional officers, and by January 1804, the 30th had sixty-six officers, of whom forty had joined the Regiment since the preceding July. Many came from half-pay, but few of these stayed for long; in truth, as a group, they tended to be too old for active service. The ensigns were newly commissioned.

---

[6] Spain too declared war on Britain, on 12th December 1804.
[7] The establishment of each battalion was to include 50 sergeants, 50 corporals, 22 drummers and 1,000 privates, but the full complement was never achieved.

Early in July, the 30th marched out some nine miles from Ipswich and encamped at Bromswell to await the arrival of the Army of Reserve. Whilst there, they were inspected by the Duke of York, Commander-in-Chief, accompanied by Lieutenant-General Sir James Craig, an old 30th man who at that time commanded Eastern District, and by Major-General Robert Manners, Colonel of the Regiment since 1799.

At the beginning of September, the 30th marched to Chelmsford, where an immense fortified camp had been built to defend London and occupied the old barracks.[8] Over the next few weeks, 1,600 recruits flowed in from Buckinghamshire and elsewhere, and presently, Lieutenant-Colonel William Lockhart and Sergeant-Major David Glass moved to the new barracks to form the 2nd Battalion. The existing companies were evenly divided, five and five, between the two battalions, and on 6th October, the 30th was formally established as a two-battalion regiment. It was impossible to provide the full establishment of NCOs, but every company had at least two sergeants and a dozen old soldiers in the ranks. The new recruits were soon clothed and armed, and it is notable that the new uniforms issued at this time were the first to indicate NCO rank with chevrons rather than epaulettes and shoulder knots.

In November 1803, both battalions of the 30th Regiment were ordered to march to Woodbridge, where in December, they were declared operational and issued with routes to proceed to Ireland. Later that month, they marched in several divisions to the neighbourhood of Northampton, from where they were carried by canal boats to Stockton Quay, on the Bridgewater Canal near Warrington, from where they marched on again to Liverpool for embarkation. Landing near Dublin between the 25th and 28th of January 1804, the Regiment was transferred to the Irish Command on the 25th of that month.

The 1st Battalion marched to King's County, where Headquarters and seven companies were stationed at Tullamore, with three companies under Major Vaumorel detached at Frankford. The 2nd Battalion was at first quartered in George Street Barracks, Dublin, but on March 23rd, they were ordered to Moate, Clara and Kilbeggan, only a few miles from Tullamore.

The assimilation of so many recruits, not all of whom were true volunteers, was far from easy, and there was a considerable wastage. Some were rejected as unsuitable, others immediately deserted, while a large sick list took a heavy toll on both battalions. There were numerous medical discharges, and many died in the crowded barracks, notably from smallpox, though vaccination was introduced in the Regiment at about this time. When the 2nd Battalion marched from Dublin, they left 150 sick there and a further 28 still in hospital in England. In the next three months, 57 men died. Drafts continued to arrive through 1805: for example, 98 men arrived in March, of whom 19 were at once rejected and 18 of the best were chosen by the 1st Battalion, the remainder going to the 2nd, which by the end of that year had lost 130 men – 70 discharges, 22 desertions and 38 deaths.

Indeed, the 2nd/30th soon became more of a depot for the 1st Battalion, and there was a major redistribution of both officers and men. The senior company officers in each rank were posted to the 1st Battalion, which also took the pick of the recruits and the best men from the 2nd and transferred all its undesirables and non-effectives in exchange, especially those who had not volunteered for foreign service. An unintended and unpredictable consequence of this redistribution was that four years later, the junior officers led a very young and inexperienced 2nd Battalion in the Iberian Peninsula while their regimental seniors sweltered on garrison duty in India.

Both battalions of the 30th marched to the Curragh for drill in July and August 1804 and then returned to their former quarters, except for the two light companies, which remained brigaded in Dublin. The latter were probably under Major Hamilton, who, early in 1805, was training a light battalion there.

Tragedy struck the 2nd Battalion that winter when Sergeant Edward Loughron[9] murdered his wife and was hanged for it in front of the jail at Mullingar. But whilst the Civil Power took its course with the unhappy sergeant, his Regiment looked after its own. Just before Edward Loughron's execution, his 10-year-old son John was enlisted into the 30th as a drummer and sent to the 2nd Battalion. This humane and practical measure bore fruit, for John Loughron served 32 years in the Regiment, rising to the rank of colour-sergeant.

---

[8] There had been an Officers' Mess in the 30th for many years, but at Chelmsford we are certain, for the first time, that a room in barracks was allocated for this purpose.
[9] Edward Loughron was one of the Irishmen who had joined the 30th in 1798, probably under duress, but he had made good and was promoted from the ranks in 1804 to fill one of the many NCO vacancies in the new 2nd Battalion.

The seasonal pattern of activity was repeated in the summer of 1805, with the 30th joining Regular Army and Militia battalions for training at the Curragh: 'On the 1st [of August], the troops destined to occupy this camp appeared on the ground in six divisions. The order to take up their positions being given by signal, the different points allotted to the several regiments were immediately occupied; and the command to pitch tents being announced by another signal, the whole camp was formed in little more than two minutes from the instant in which the signal was made.' As for the Light Infantry, 'the movements of these brigades to their posts to the sound of the bugle, the celerity of their manoeuvres, the brilliancy of their uniforms and the gay diversity of their various standards glancing across the hills – altogether produced a delightful effect…. Great was the galloping hither and thither of staff officers of every grade and denomination for nearly an hour, until at one o'clock bang went a signal gun… when the columns poured into the magnificent plain, or rather downs of the Curragh by all the roads leading to it, bands playing, colours flying, bugles screaming and all the pomp, pride and circumstance of military display.'

When the Curragh Camp broke up that year, the 1st Battalion marched to Limerick and the 2nd into the Royal Barracks, Dublin, where on 25th September 1805, Lieutenant-Colonel William Minet assumed command.[10]

Formation of the 2nd/40th

A second battalion was re-formed for the 40th Regiment at Taunton in August 1804 from men enrolled into the 10th Reserve Battalion under the Additional Forces Act in the West of England. Many of the officers were also gazetted to the 40th. The 2nd/40th served as a home or depot battalion for the Regiment from its formation until its disbandment in 1815.

The 2nd/40th had been authorised, together with other second battalions, to enlist ten boys per company, who were not to be over 16 years of age or under five feet in height. These lads were to be 'well limbed, open chested, and what is called long in the fork.' One hundred carbines (shortened muskets) were supplied to each battalion for their use. One of the boy recruits into the 2nd/40th at that time was William Lawrence, aged 14, who many years later recalled his enlistment. He had been apprenticed by his father to a builder in Studland, Dorset, but his master starved and thrashed him, and so he ran away. Entering a public house in the village of Winfrith, he met with a soldier, who promptly offered to enlist him into the 40th Regiment. Lawrence's new friend soon discovered that he was a runaway apprentice and consequently debarred from enlisting, but nevertheless took him home and hid him for a few days before bringing him before the Commanding Officer at Taunton. Lawrence enlisted before the local magistrates on 19th February 1805, receiving a bounty of £2 12s 6d. The soldier who had recruited him received two guineas.

Meanwhile, the 1st/40th remained at Hastings throughout the year 1804 as part of the anti-invasion force. Constant drill and target practice were the order of the day, and the troops at Hastings appear to have practised marching into the sea up to their waists to attack the French landing barges.

Among the young officers who joined at that time was William Hibbert, the first of three brothers from Ardwick Green, Manchester, to serve in the 40th. We have a family account of his introduction to the Regiment:

'When the war broke out again in 1803, the volunteering and enlisting had made an impression on his youthful soul, for he was then about seventeen; so a soldier he would be. His father said no; and at last the lad ran off to Liverpool, intending to enlist there, when Mr. Hibbert, seeing that it was useless to resist any longer the youth's inclination, wrote to his friend Dr. Charles Taylor, Chief Secretary of the Society of Arts, in London, who had considerable army interest, requesting that gentleman to arrange for the purchase of a commission. Dr. Taylor soon replied that he had settled with General Spencer, that on payment of the sum of £400, then the regulation price, William Hibbert should have an ensigncy in the 40th, "a regiment," observed Dr. Taylor, "which is one of the most eligible, both in point of officers and men, of any in the English service."

'The young officer joined the 40th at Hastings, in the summer of 1804, under what then appeared to be very good auspices; and Dr. Charles Taylor, when writing soon afterwards to Mr. Hibbert, said, "I do not think he could have been better placed than in his present regiment, which is unusually well spoken of. During my

---

[10] William Minet, who entered the Army in 1778, had served at the Great Siege of Gibraltar and had commanded a company of the 30th in the West Indies in 1783.

residence at Hastings I had the opportunity and introduced him to General Spencer and the colonels of his regiment, and to friends who will give him the best advice, whenever necessary. Colonel Brown[e] has promised to pay particular attention to his conduct. General Spencer and Colonel Brown[e] are excellent officers, and have seen much service, and keep the regiment in excellent discipline.'

Despite 'best advice,' it was difficult for an ensign to live on his net pay of about five pence a day, even with parental help, and it is hardly surprising that when his suspicious father paid William Hibbert an unexpected visit he found the young spark, on recruiting detachment at Frome, heavily in debt. Writing to his wife on 3rd October 1805 the perturbed father disclosed that William, 'has debts to pay to an amount I had no conception of, considering what he has had sent him. I understood he was short, but had no idea of the amount, until about a quarter of an hour before I set off, though I had asked for an account long before. I had no alternative but to give him a bill… for £140, for which he could get cash at Frome. It is a pity he was separated from his regiment, so inexperienced as he is.'

On 20th June 1805, the 1st/40th returned to Fairlight Camp, near Hastings, and on 26th September, the Battalion was part of Major-General Brent Spencer's brigade (14th, 40th and 88th Regiments) reviewed in Crowhurst Park by the Dukes of York and Cambridge. The encampment on Fairlight Down was broken up on 12th October, and the 40th marched into Bexhill Barracks, about six miles west of Hastings, where it spent the next ten months.

In June 1805, the newly-raised 2nd Battalion, with 389 effectives, marched from Taunton to Winchester, where it remained a month before moving, after a short stay in Portsmouth, to join the 1st Battalion at Bexhill. A number of men and boys, including young Private William Lawrence, were drafted from the 2nd/40th to the 1st Battalion, which was brought up to full strength for active service.

Formation of the 2nd/47th

Shortly after the outbreak of war, in June 1803, the 47th Regiment marched to Battle in Sussex, where they remained for three months. In September, the Regiment moved to Colchester, where a second battalion was raised from drafts enrolled under the Additional Forces Act in Norfolk. The 2nd/47th mustered for the first time in October with Lieutenant-Colonel Fielder King in command.[11] Among those who joined the 47th at that time was John Harley, an Irishman who transferred from the 54th as quartermaster and soon became paymaster.

Harley, a prolific and often indiscrete raconteur, tells the curious story of the subsequently notorious Captain Maurice St. Leger Farmer, of Poplar Hall, County Kildare, who was posted to the 2nd Battalion at Colchester in October 1803; although only seventeen, he was a senior captain, 'having obtained his commission while still in his cradle' and having been gazetted to a company in the 107th Foot at the age of nine. A man of some wealth, Farmer was eccentric and given to sudden caprices, with a temper so utterly uncontrolled that, it was said, even his brother officers could scarcely live with him. On arrival in the Battalion, he made it known that as a senior captain, he should have first choice of quarters in any garrison. Some of the officers determined to puncture Farmer's pretensions and informed him that there were no quarters in the barracks fit for him but that on the outskirts of town, there was a large house with apartments suitable for officers of his standing in the Army. Late at night, Farmer made his way to the house, only to discover that it was the residence of Lieutenant-General Sir James Craig, commanding the Eastern District. The bumptious 'senior captain' was peremptorily ushered out into the rain and spent the entire night walking the streets of Colchester.

Both battalions shortly moved to Woodbridge, Suffolk, from where in December, they marched to Liverpool for service in Ireland. Landing in Dublin in January 1804, within a month, the 1st Battalion moved to Kilkenny under Lieutenant-Colonel Thomas Backhouse and the 2nd to Clonmel, County Tipperary, under Lieutenant-Colonel Fielder King.

---

[11] Fielder King, aged 52, had been a lieutenant-colonel since 1797 and was brought in from the Cape Regiment to raise the 2nd Battalion. He remained under a year before being transferred to the 7th Foot, also to raise a 2nd Battalion, before being put out to grass as an Inspecting Field Officer of Yeomanry.

Whilst at Clonmel, the officers of the 47th became acquainted with Edmund 'Beau' Power, an irascible local landowner and dandy who rode hard to hounds, gambled recklessly, caroused all night with his cronies and was a terror to his family and neighbourhood. After a ball in Clonmel, his daughter Marguerite, a precocious girl of fourteen and a half, was proposed to by both Captains Maurice Farmer and James Murray of the 47th. She was forced by her impecunious parents to marry Farmer, who beat and swore at her and locked her up for days on end. When Farmer was ordered to the Curragh with the Regiment, she refused to follow him. Farmer was eventually required to leave the Regiment, having drawn his sword on Lord Caledon, Colonel of the Tyrone Militia. After service with the East India Company, Maurice Farmer died on 21st October 1817 in the King's Bench Prison, Southwark, having fallen from a window when drunk. Within months, his beautiful widow married the Earl of Blessington, and as Lady Blessington, she became a prolific novelist and journalist, an eminent society hostess, friend of Byron and Disraeli, and mistress of the exiled Louis Napoleon, future Emperor of France.

In March 1804, the 2nd/47th moved a short distance to Cahir, where Lieutenant-Colonel John Skerrett assumed command. Whilst at that station, there was a tragically unfortunate duel:

'Lieutenant [William Homman] Lennon and Lieutenant [Alexander] Wormall (or Wormald), two officers universally beloved in the Regiment, had some dispute late in the evening at the mess table, during which the latter used some irritating expressions. A hostile message was the consequence, which was accepted, and the following morning at five o'clock appointed for the meeting. Previous to the hour, poor Wormall, feeling that he had been the aggressor – for, though passionate, he had noble and generous principles – sent an apology by his second to Lennon; but the heartless scoundrel through whom it was sent, wishing for mischief, never delivered the apology which one of the parties cheerfully gave, and the other would as gladly have received. The meeting took place – Wormall was unfortunately wounded at the first discharge, and, having been conveyed to his barrack-room, was laid upon his bed, expressing the greatest anxiety to see Lennon. As soon as Lennon entered the room, he stretched out his hand to him, and said, "Shake hands with me; I know I am a dying man; but from my heart I forgive you; but, oh! Lennon, why did you not accept my apology?" Lennon, on hearing this, became nearly distracted, declaring in the most solemn manner that it was the first intimation he had of it; and, indeed, so great was the shock such intelligence occasioned, that he never recovered his spirits afterwards.'[12]

That summer, both battalions marched to the Curragh and were encamped for training until September, when they returned to their former stations. The Light Companies, being brigaded with others, marched to Dublin. In September 1805, the 1st/47th proceeded from Kilkenny to Cork, there to prepare for foreign service, and the 2nd Battalion moved to Belfast in what Harley described as 'a very fatiguing, harassing march.' After a pleasant few months in Belfast, in June 1806, the 2nd/47th marched to Aughnacloy in County Tyrone under the command of Lieutenant-Colonel William Wardrobe, who on 8th May had succeeded Skerrett in command. That winter was spent in Enniskillen where to complete the Battalion to establishment, gentlemen were offered commissions for bringing in recruits. In March 1807, the 2nd/47th were stationed at Omagh.

The 47th would at that time have learned that they had a new Colonel, for on 25th February 1807, General the Right Hon Richard Fitzpatrick assumed the appointment. He was then Secretary at War in the 'Ministry of All the Talents.' He was also a friend and admirer of the Duke of York and was later accused of defending the Duke 'in return for the foulest army job,' a suggestion that his Colonelcy of the 47th was a product of the Duke's alleged abuse of military patronage.[13]

---

[12] *The Veteran or 40 Years' Service in the British Army*, Captain John Harley, 1838, Helion reprint 2018, p. 123.

[13] Fitzpatrick (1748-1813) was an Anglo-Irish gentleman of many accomplishments: soldier, Whig politician, inveterate gambler, bon viveur, solo balloonist, noted wit, poet and political satirist. He was a life-long intimate friend of Charles James Fox and, in 1783, a founder member of the Whig Club. His first commission was in 1765, and although opposed to the war in America he fought at the battles of Brandywine and Germantown. He saw no further active service, but rose to be Major-General in 1793, Lieutenant-General in 1798 and General in 1803. His political career commenced in 1770, and he was an MP for over 40 years, holding office as Chief Secretary for Ireland in 1782, and as Secretary at War in 1783 and again in 1806-7. His few parliamentary speeches were mainly on military matters. His friend Horace Walpole described Fitzpatrick in the 1770s as 'an agreeable young man of parts', and mentioned his 'genteel irony and badinage', while another contemporary described him as 'tall, manly, and extremely distinguished; set off by his manners which, though lofty and assuming, were nevertheless elegant and prepossessing', remarking that 'no man's society was more eagerly courted among the highest orders, by persons of both sexes.' Fitzpatrick never married, but like others of his set he had numerous love affairs, and he appears to have had a taste for married ladies of the Whig persuasion. Lady Anne Foley, the subject of a scandalous

Formation of the 2ⁿᵈ/81ˢᵗ

The 81ˢᵗ Regiment had not long been in garrison on Jersey when the order came to form a second battalion. On 20ᵗʰ July 1803, Major William Plenderleath embarked for Portsmouth with six officers, ten sergeants, twenty corporals and fifty privates with orders to proceed to Wales, there to receive balloted men from the Army of Reserve. On 25ᵗʰ September, the main body of the Regiment embarked at St. Heliers for Plymouth, where at Millbay Barracks, they began to receive between eighteen and nineteen hundred men. Scant attention was given to county affiliations, and almost all these recruits for 'The Loyal Lincoln Volunteers' did indeed come from Wales.[14] By 8ᵗʰ October, these Army Reserve men had all arrived and been allocated to the two battalions, bringing them up to a strength of nearly one thousand men each.

By the 15ᵗʰ, the formation of the 2ⁿᵈ/81ˢᵗ was complete, and command was given to Lieutenant-Colonel James Kempt.[15] On 24ᵗʰ July 1804, Lieutenant Colonel John Hamilton, having been promoted to brigadier, Kempt assumed command of the 1ˢᵗ/81ˢᵗ. Small in stature and unassuming in manner, Kempt was an intelligent and popular commander.

On 30ᵗʰ January 1804 all the volunteers for unlimited and foreign service were concentrated in the 1ˢᵗ/81ˢᵗ, those for home service being enrolled in the 2ⁿᵈ Battalion. Both battalions of the Regiment were reviewed at Plymouth Dockyard on 16ᵗʰ June that year by Lieutenant-General Johnson, who expressed, in most flattering terms, his great satisfaction at their appearance.

Among those enlisted in the 81ˢᵗ Regiment in 1804 was its first known black recruit, Joseph Degenne, aged 27, born in Guadeloupe.

The 2ⁿᵈ/81ˢᵗ embarked on transports for Cork on 27ᵗʰ November and marched from there to Kinsale, where they were stationed until March 1805, when the Battalion, less its Light Infantry Company, moved to cantonments at Doneraille, Charleville and elsewhere, and then in July to Cork. On 22ⁿᵈ August, the 2ⁿᵈ/81ˢᵗ marched to Athlone, where they remained for about fourteen months.

Formation of the 2ⁿᵈ/82ⁿᵈ

A second battalion for the 82ⁿᵈ Regiment was also formed in 1804, in the barracks at Horsham in Sussex, and Lieutenant-Colonel George Smith, from half-pay of the 20ᵗʰ Foot, was appointed to command. In March 1805, the 2ⁿᵈ/82ⁿᵈ proceeded to Chichester, then in May to Littlehampton Barracks, and in November to Uxbridge, where it remained for the next twelve months, receiving and training recruits. Ensign George Wood, commissioned in August 1806, joined the Battalion there and, in his journal, painted a vivid picture of his apprenticeship and youthful indiscretions:

'I was, I must confess, much struck with the new mode of life I was about to lead, from its apparent splendour… I conceived no other could equal it in point of pleasure, idleness and grandeur; all around me seemed gaiety, freedom and ease; in fact, it was that kind of life, of all others, best agreeing with my disposition, and I

---

trial for adultery, was said to have sent him the following note after giving birth: 'Dear Richard, I give you joy. I have just made you the father of a beautiful boy. P.S. This is not a circular.' By the time Fitzpatrick became Colonel of the 47ᵗʰ in 1807 his dissolute lifestyle had taken its toll on his constitution: he suffered from gout, and in 1808 was reported to be 'more shattered by age and infirmities than ever.' He also had financial problems from years of ruinous gambling, which on one occasion saw him playing cards at the pro-Whig Brooks's Club for twenty hours at a stretch, and creditors once stopped his coach in the middle of a London street and took his horses as repayment. He was, nevertheless, much admired to the end for 'his evenness of temper and spirits, his polished manners, pure taste, sound judgement, and worldly experience.'

[14] These recruits were drawn from Anglesey, Brecon, Caernarvon, Carmarthen, Cardigan, Denbigh, Flint, Glamorgan, Hereford, Monmouth, Montgomery, Merioneth, Pembroke and Radnor.

[15] James Kempt (1764-1854), was first commissioned in 1783 into the newly raised 101ˢᵗ Foot, stationed in India. This Regiment was disbanded in 1785 and Kempt was on half-pay for nine years, during which he is said to have become a clerk at Greenwoods, the Army agents who later became Cox & Co. He rejoined the Army in 1794, and in 1799 became ADC to Sir Ralph Abercromby, serving on his staff in Holland and Egypt. By 1803 he was a major in the 66ᵗʰ Foot when, on 23ʳᵈ July, he was promoted to command the 2ⁿᵈ/81ˢᵗ.

fancied myself one of the most enviable young men in existence; but, like every thing in this mutable world, my dream of happiness was of short duration.'

'I was sent to drill every morning at six o'clock, at which exercise I remained about three hours, and to my comfort was placed in the awkward squad with strict instructions to rise gradually, till I was reported to the Adjutant fit for duty. This little difficulty was got over in about six weeks; nor did it curb my pleasures, for I used to drink in the mess as long as I could sit, and enjoyed every amusement.'[16]

In November 1806, the 2nd/82nd marched at short notice for Derby, and George Wood's journal describes the animated scenes of their early morning departure from Uxbridge:

'Every person and every thing appears, at such a time, in the utmost confusion; but the principal cause of alarm is the presence of so many creditors for the payment of their bills, and the scarcity of money to meet their demands. Next to this are the severe pangs felt at parting with sweethearts, and in this agreeable place these were experienced in an extraordinary degree; for the corps having been stationed at Uxbridge for a great length of time, there was scarcely one, from the splendid epaulette to the quivering fife, that had not charmed the heart of some sweet maid of this dear town.

'The morning soon began to dawn. The baggage already towered on the creaking waggons: the women and children scaled the massive pile, where seated, they might enjoy their short pipe and little bottle as they slowly moved along the weary way. The lively bugle, sounding the well-known "General," plainly told the sorrowful tale that "the soldiers were a-going." Then came the trying scene: the lovely lasses taking their last farewell, and clinging to their dejected lovers – crying, fainting, sighing, till another sound summoned them to tear themselves away. Poor girls! They shrieked, implored, intreated.

'Another sound! The soldiers are gone, but the dear creatures are resolved to follow. Such, however, was the concourse of despairing maidens that precaution was found necessary and sentries were placed at each end of the bridge to prevent their passing: but even this had not the desired effect; they rushed by the guard – but being unable to pass the next, one of these damsels, in despair, scaled the battlements and plunged into the water, making an effort to swim after her desponding lover; but the struggle was in vain; she was with difficulty taken out almost a corpse and restored to her hapless parents.'[17]

The 59th at Shorncliffe Camp, 1803-04

On the outbreak of war in May 1803, the 59th marched from its West Country quarters to garrison coastal forts in Sussex and Kent, with its headquarters at Dungeness. With the French concentrated at Boulogne, those counties were the most likely target for the expected invasion, and the 59th garrisoned the forts at Dover and helped to build the Martello towers which are still such a feature of that coast. A defensive line of 98 such towers on the South and East coasts of England was first proposed by Major Thomas Reynolds, 30th Regiment, in April 1798.

In July 1803, the Regiment joined Major-General Sir John Moore's Brigade[18] in camp at Shorncliffe. Preparations to repel the French continued, though by the following spring, the likelihood of an invasion had diminished. It was, nevertheless, a difficult time for the 59th, who had four commanding officers in less than a year. Promotion and the formation of new battalions accounts for some of this turbulence, but Moore, writing on 4th September 1803 to Colonel Calvert, the Adjutant General, suggests another possible reason:

'I had hopes from the pains I had taken and the mode I directed to be followed in instruction of the regiments of my brigade, to have made much progress, and if honoured with another visit by HRH [the Duke of York] to have shown him something tolerably perfect, but except for the 52nd the progress has been trifling. The other commanding officers, though many of them good enough men, have not military heads and seem incapable of acting from general instruction. I am satisfied that to have a tolerable army it will be necessary for HRH to take

---

[16] *The Subaltern Officer*, Captain George Wood, London 1825, p.p. 2 and 5-6.
[17] Wood, p.p. 7-8.
[18] Moore's Brigade consisted at first of the 4th, 52nd, 59th 70th and 95th Regiments, but his reputation as a disciplinarian was such that the 43rd Regiment, which had been in an unsatisfactory state, was later put under him as well.

some strong measures. Some commanding officers, the state of whose regiments justify it, must be told to retire from the Service, the duties of which they are not equal to. The command must not be allowed to devolve upon their majors, who may be equally incapable, but be given to officers of approved talent. One or two measures of this sort generally known would excite an exertion which at present is much wanted.'

It may be a coincidence, but within four weeks, there was a change of command in the 59th when William McLeod[19], who had commanded the Regiment since 1800 with marked distinction, handed over to his second-in-command, Bryan Philpot, who had recently transferred in as major. Philpot lasted only five months, being replaced at Sandgate on 31st March 1804 by James Dunlop, who had exchanged from the 77th. Dunlop, in turn, left within four months on promotion to brigadier.[20]

On 15th August 1804, gunfire from Boulogne could be heard at Shorncliffe, but it was only a salute to celebrate Napoleon's birthday. On the 23rd, British guns boomed out a reply over the Channel when the Duke of York arrived at Shorncliffe to review Moore's command. 'We came off with flying colours,' wrote Moore. His 'strong measures' appear to have worked.

The 1st/59th was in the famous brigade at Shorncliffe throughout the period of Moore's command, and though the green-tinted annals of that camp would have us believe that only the 43rd, 52nd and 95th were present, there can be little doubt that the 59th Regiment's subsequent remarkable performance in Spain and the East Indies owed much to its nurturing by one of the British Army's most inspirational trainers.

In September that year, Lieutenant-Colonel Dunlop was instructed to form a second battalion, and in November, a party of some twenty NCOs was sent to Chesterfield in Derbyshire to recruit volunteers for the 2nd/59th. The 1st Battalion, now commanded by Lieutenant-Colonel Samuel Gibbs[21], absorbed a draft of 348 men from the Buffs and the 12th Regiment. They marched to Dover, where, between December 1803 and May 1804, they occupied the New Barracks on the Western Heights and Archcliffe Fort.

It is a remarkable, indeed unique, circumstance that in 1803-04, all battalions of the 30th, 40th, 47th, 59th, 81st and 82nd Regiments of Foot were stationed in the United Kingdom. But with the immediate threat of cross-channel invasion receding, this was about to change.

---

[19] Born in America, William McLeod was appointed as an ensign in the 59th Foot on 29th March 1775 and was captured later that year in New York when rebels took control. Soon exchanged, he was lieutenant on the 31st October 1776, captain, on 5th December, 1781, brevet major, on 1st March 1794, major on 1st September 1795 and lieutenant-colonel of the 59th Regiment on 25th November 1799. He commanded the 59th in Antigua and saw active service with the Regiment in Holland, 1794-95, and St. Vincent, 1795-96. William McLeod retired from the Army on 1st October 1803 and settled in New York where he entered the insurance business. He was described as 'handsome, elegant in manners, rich in purse, a Highland gentleman, beloved by the women and envied by the men. He despised wealth except as it enabled him to make others happy. He was surrounded by those who flattered and plucked him. He led the fashion in everything and no affair of honour could be decided without him. He fought several duels on his own account. Very few British officers who visited New York failed to make the acquaintance of McLeod… He died at his favourite haunt, the City Hotel, March 4th, 1846.'

[20] James Wallace Dunlop of that Ilk (1759-1832), an Ayrshire gentleman, had served with the original 82nd Foot in North America 1778-83, and then with the 77th in India, where he saw much active service in the Third and Fourth Mysore Wars, in Malabar and the Carnatic. He commanded the left column at the storming of Seringapatam, 1799, and received a severe sword wound in the breach. He later served in 1810-11 as a general officer with the 5th Division in the Peninsular War, with the 30th Foot under his command, and died a lieutenant-general.

[21] Samuel Gibbs (1771-1815) was commissioned in 1783 and by the time he was appointed to command the 59th he had seen active service in the Mediterranean (1793-96), at Ostend (1798) and in the West Indies (1799-1802). He commanded the 59th Regiment 1804-11, including the capture of the Cape of Good Hope, 1806, and the island of Mauritius, 1810, the Travancore War of 1808-09, and the suppression of the 'European Mutiny' at Seringapatam in 1808. He then commanded a brigade, including the 59th, in Java 1811-12, and greatly distinguished himself at the storming of Fort Cornelis, for which he earned a Gold Medal which is in the Regimental Collection. He served in Holland in 1813 and was promoted to major-general. In 1814 Samuel Gibbs was appointed Second-in-Command to Sir Edward Packenham in the American War of 1812, and was mortally wounded at the Battle of New Orleans, aged 44. He died next day, 9th January 1815, one week after being made a KCB, and is commemorated by a monumental statue in the south transept of St Paul's Cathedral.

The Cape of Good Hope, 1806

In April 1805, the 1st/59th received orders to prepare for service in the East Indies, and on 9th July, the Battalion embarked at Gosport, over one thousand strong. At Falmouth they were joined by troops under Major-General Sir David Baird, and a further brigade joined at Cork. The 59th now found themselves part of an expedition of over six thousand men[22] with secret orders to recapture the Cape of Good Hope, which, as we have seen, had been returned to Bonaparte's Dutch allies at the Peace of Amiens. Britain could not afford to have an enemy port on the vital Cape sea route to the East. The 59th were then to resume their passage to India.

The convoy, consisting of sixty-one Indiamen and transports escorted by nine men-of-war under Commodore Sir Home Popham, sailed from Cork on 31st August, reached Funchal in Madeira on 28th September, and, sailing again on October 3rd, touched at San Salvador in Brazil, where the troops were landed, refreshed and inspected. On 26th November, the fleet set a course for the Cape, and on 4th January 1806, made a landfall near Table Bay, anchoring that evening to the east of Robben Island.

The voyage had not been entirely uneventful, for we have an account of a remarkable incident involving the 59th. It appears that a barrel of gunpowder had been opened on deck for the purpose of making cartridges. A soldier of the Regiment, unconscious of the circumstance, was attempting to light his pipe with live coal when, by a sudden lurch of the vessel, he lost both his balance and the glowing coal, which dropped into the barrel. Another soldier of the Regiment, observing the accident, boldly plunged his hands into the cask and, with great dexterity, snatched up the coal and a portion of the powder sticking to it. As he withdrew the coal, the gunpowder ignited in his hand. The name of this gallant man has sadly not been preserved, but it is probable that the lives of all on board were saved by his self-possession and daring courage.

Early on the morning of January 5th, the light companies of the several regiments, under the command of Major Alexander McLeod, 59th, attempted a landing, but the surf ran too high, and the troops were recalled. On the 6th, the seas had somewhat abated, and the leading brigade landed without much opposition[23] in Losperd's Bay (now Melkbosstrand), an inlet of Table Bay sixteen miles north of Cape Town. As the day wore on, the surf increased, and so the remainder of the army, including the 59th, did not land until the morning of the 7th.

Before dawn on the 8th, Sir David Baird began his march on Cape Town. His force was organised into two brigades, advancing in parallel columns: the 1st, commanded by Colonel Baird, comprised the 24th, 59th and 83rd Regiments; the 2nd (or Highland) Brigade, under Brigadier-General Ferguson, included the 71st, 72nd and 93rd Highlanders, with a detachment of Marines.

The route for the first four miles was little more than a sandy track, along which the guns were dragged slowly and painfully uphill towards the Blaauwberg, or Blue Mountain, an elevated ridge crossed by the road. On approaching this feature, the 59th, with two guns dragged by seamen, were ordered to occupy the pass, while the remainder of the force moved to their left, skirting round the base of the hills on the landward side.

Soon after 5 a.m., the 59th occupied the summit of the pass without serious opposition, dislodging a party of the enemy's light troops. From this vantage point they looked down and discovered on the plains below them, about two miles away, the main body of the Dutch force, drawn up in two lines and advancing to the attack. Lieutenant-General Janssens, the Dutch Governor, had some two thousand men, a remarkably polyglot mix of Dutch regulars, French sailors and marines, German and Hungarian mercenaries, mounted Boer militia, Hottentot levies and slaves from Angola and Mozambique, with sixteen guns manned by Javanese. His tactics soon became apparent: his right wing was refused, while his left, composed chiefly of mounted Burghers armed with long firelocks, moved forward to outflank the British right and sever Baird's vital communication with the fleet. The 59th soon came under artillery fire and suffered some casualties.

Sir David Baird reacted promptly, forming the Highland Brigade astride the main road and directing the 1st Brigade to take ground to its right and secure that flank. This was quickly accomplished, and the advance of the mounted Boers against the right flank was checked on the Kleinberg by the 24th Foot. The Highlanders then

---

[22] The military force consisted of the 24th, 38th, 59th, 71st, 72nd, 83rd and 93rd Regiments of Foot, two squadrons of the 20th Light Dragoons and an artillery detachment of two howitzers and six light field guns.

[23] At least one soldier of the 59th, Private (later Colour-Sergeant) Samuel Jones, was wounded by a musket ball on 7th January.

advanced under a heavy fire and, after an exchange of musketry, routed the Dutch right wing with a bayonet charge. The 59th shared in the general advance and were, for a time, the principal target of the Dutch artillery.

The enemy retreated towards Cape Town, regrouping at Rietvlei, where 347 soldiers were reported missing. British losses totalled fifteen men killed in action, 189 wounded, and eight missing. The 59th lost one private killed, Captain Alexander McPherson severely wounded, and six privates wounded, of whom one later died.[24]

Pursuit was impossible without cavalry; the infantry, out of condition after their long voyage, were exhausted with heat, thirst, and the nature of the country, which was deep sand covered with short brushwood which tore off boots and lacerated feet.

'It is utterly impossible to convey an adequate idea of the obstacles which opposed the advance,' wrote Baird in his despatch. 'A deep, heavy, and dry sand, covered with shrubs, scarcely pervious by light bodies of infantry, and above all the total privation of water under the effect of a burning sun, had nearly exhausted our gallant fellows in the moment of victory; and with the greatest difficulty were we able to reach Reit Valley, where we took up our position for the night. A considerable portion of the provisions and necessaries with which we started had been lost during the action, and we occupied the ground under the apprehension that even the great exertions of Sir Home Popham and the Navy could not relieve us from starvation.'

The Navy did manage to bring up some supplies that night, but most of the 59th marched on towards Cape Town the next morning with empty bellies. Approaching the capital, Baird halted on the bank of the Salt River so as to preserve communications with the fleet. The town looked quite formidable, protected by chains of redoubts and batteries mounting some 150 heavy guns, besides howitzers, and Baird anticipated a set-piece siege. During the day, however, a Dutch officer appeared under a flag of truce with a request from the Commandant for a 48-hour armistice with a view to negotiating a capitulation. Sir David Baird accepted on condition that the outer forts should be surrendered within six hours, and the 59th were sent that night to occupy the outworks and Fort Knocke. Next morning, the 1st Brigade marched into Cape Town and occupied the citadel.

General Janssens had retired into the interior after the battle of Blaauwberg, and on 13th January, Brigadier-General William Beresford was ordered to pursue him with the 59th and 72nd. Beresford carried a letter from Baird to Janssens, pointing out the futility of further resistance, and was authorised to negotiate terms of surrender. Beresford's force first occupied the village of Stellenbosch and then the pass of Roode Sand, threatening Janssen's flank and cutting him off from supplies. The Dutch Governor made no attempt to oppose these movements but took post with his regular troops on the summit of Hottentot's Holland Kloof, a pass leading to the district of Zwellendam, and waited to open negotiations. He was indeed ready enough to receive a flag of truce with Baird's letter but then prevaricated to such an extent that it was only when the exasperated British prepared to attack that he accepted Baird's terms and surrendered on 18th January. By the articles of capitulation the Cape and its dependencies passed under British rule, altering at a stroke the whole future of South Africa.

The 59th returned to Cape Town, where, on 7th February, the Battalion was drawn up on the General Parade Ground to receive the thanks of Sir David Baird and 'his high appreciation of its conduct whilst under his command.'

It was not until 1836 that the 59th received the Battle Honour 'CAPE OF GOOD HOPE 1806,'

Shortly afterwards, the Regiment resumed its voyage with a convoy of the East India Company, landing at Madras on 23rd April 1806.[25]

---

[24] One of the casualties on the 8th was Private William Nutt, then aged 15, who was wounded in the hand. He continued to serve with the Regiment until 1832, by which time he was Drum Major and had seen further active service in Mauritius, 1810, in Java, 1811-14, and at Bhurtpore, 1826.

[25] Not all the 59th sailed on to India, for Captain (later Colonel) Jacob Glen Cuyler was appointed Landrost (magistrate) of Uitenhage District on the Eastern Cape frontier, where he built the Drostdy (c.1809) and Cuyler Manor (c.1814), now both incorporated in Uitenhage Museum. Born at Albany, New York, Cuyler spoke the ancestral Dutch of his United Empire Loyalist parents who had left for Nova Scotia at the end of the American War of Independence.

An Expedition to the Weser, December 1805-February 1806

Before he returned to office in May 1804, William Pitt had sketched out an ambitious plan for a coalition of the European powers to take the field against Napoleon. The Neapolitans, aided by British and Russian expeditions, were to expel the French from Southern Italy while Austrian and Russian armies advanced into Northern Italy. Meanwhile, a combination of Russians, Swedes and Hanoverians, supported by a second British expedition, under Lord Cathcart, was to liberate Hanover and march on Holland from bases on the Baltic. Pitt calculated that Britain could provide fifty thousand trained soldiers to take the offensive with continental allies, but the allies were not forthcoming without considerable diplomatic effort; the Russians were suspicious, the Austrians terrified, the Prussians open to French bribery, and the Neapolitans duplicitous. Nevertheless, by September 1805, the Third Coalition against France was on the march, its wheels oiled with British gold and promises of substantial military co-operation.

At the end of October 1805, the 1st Battalion of the 30th Regiment marched from Limerick to Cork for active service. It was now once more a fine battalion, one thousand strong with 32 officers, commanded by Lieutenant-Colonel William Lockhart. The main body embarked on the 1st and 2nd November, followed on the 12th by the Light Company. The Battalion was brigaded with the 9th and 89th Regiments under Major-General Rowland Hill.

Lord Cathcart's force was to rendezvous in the Downs, but the expedition was, from the start, dogged by bad weather. Hill's brigade was caught by a gale in the Channel, and one of the transports was driven ashore near Calais, where two hundred of the 9th became prisoners of war. The remainder of the brigade landed at Yarmouth until the weather moderated. On 12th December, the transports reassembled in the Downs. They were almost immediately dispersed by another severe gale, which drove the transport *Jenny*, carrying Captain Hawker's Company of the 30th, ashore near Gravelines, to the east of Calais, where the French National Guard came to their aid. The party, four officers[26], five sergeants, 93 rank and file, twelve women, five children and a new-born baby, struggled ashore without loss and complete with baggage, but all were taken prisoner. The shipwrecked soldiers were very well treated by the French, so much so that the officers of the 30th wrote to the Mayor of Gravelines to thank the local people for their kindness. Nevertheless, they were sent to the fortress of Verdun, where they arrived on 5th January 1806. Most of the soldiers were subsequently held at Valenciennes, one of the principal depots for British internees and prisoners of war, for over eight years. At least three escaped[27], and more died, but the four officers and eighty other survivors rejoined the 30th at the peace of 1814, and the majority of these fought at Waterloo the following year.

Of the remaining nine companies of the 30th, only five reached Germany. Transports carrying four companies and the whole Battalion staff, less the field officers, were forced to seek shelter in the harbours of Kent, and a few men of the 30th were aboard the transport *Adventure,* which was driven ashore near Yarmouth, but none were lost.

On Christmas Day 1805, sixteen officers and 493 other ranks of the 30th landed at Cuxhaven on the Elbe, marching on New Year's Day for Bremen on the Weser, where they arrived on 7th January 1806.

Their stay in Germany was short, for Cathcart, arriving at Cuxhaven on 15th December, was met by the disastrous news of Allied defeat at Austerlitz and of an armistice between Austria and France. The Third Coalition at once began to unravel; the double-dealing Prussians, who wished above all to occupy Hanover, were seeking terms with Napoleon, while the defeated Russians were withdrawing eastwards and the Swedes hung back on the Elbe, leaving the British force on the Weser dangerously exposed. Cathcart remained for as long as was prudent, hoping that his presence might yet encourage the allies to stand firm, but towards the end of January, he received

---

[26] Captains Peter Ryves Hawker and Thomas Fleming Roberts, Lieutenant Robert Howard and Ensign William Sullivan.

[27] Drummer John Winterflood and Private James Waters escaped. We do not know the circumstances, but they rejoined the Regiment, and in September 1810 arrived with the 2nd/30th in Spain. We know a little more of the third escapee, Private Daniel McCarthy. As an Irishman, he was offered the alternative of enlisting in an Irish regiment in French service, which he accepted in the hope of being able to slip away when an opportunity offered. This came in 1811 when he found himself within reach of British cavalry in Estremadura, and he rejoined the Regiment in Spain that March.

orders from England to re-embark his force, now over twenty-six thousand strong, and the aborted expedition sailed with a fair wind for home.

Cathcart's expedition, which promised so much, had achieved nothing, but it had at least the rare distinction of coming back stronger than it set out, for the King's German Legion, which formed part of the force, had taken the opportunity to recruit in its native Hanover.

The five companies of the 30th who had reached Germany embarked on 28th January 1806 and landed at Margate on 8th February. There, they were joined by the companies driven back to Kent by the weather, who had been assembled at Canterbury under Captain (Brevet Major) Thomas Fleming, and the whole had marched to Faversham by early April. From there, the Battalion marched on to Portsmouth, arriving on the 17th and 18th of that same month. They were quartered at Hilsea Barracks, with four companies detached at Fort Cumberland. The 1st/30th then received orders to embark for the East Indies and were brought up to strength with a draft of seven subalterns and 352 other ranks from the 2nd Battalion at Dublin.

Maida, 4th July 1806

As we have already noted, by the early months of 1805, William Pitt felt sufficiently secure from invasion to indulge again in his weakness for frittering the British Army away in small expeditions to support unreliable allies. The goodwill of Russia, seen as essential for the formation of a grand coalition of continental powers, turned on Britain's willingness to send troops to the Mediterranean. Moreover, Admiral Villeneuve was at sea, having broken the Toulon blockade, and British ascendancy in that theatre was under threat. Accordingly, Pitt scraped together four thousand men for yet another 'secret expedition.'

On 20th March 1805, the 1st Battalion of the 81st Regiment was inspected at Plymouth by Major-General Calcroft, and on the following day, Lieutenant-Colonel Kempt was ordered to hold his battalion ready for foreign service. Embarking at Hamoaze on 1st April, the 1st/81st sailed to Portsmouth to join an expeditionary force[28] being fitted out under command of Lieutenant-General Sir James Craig[29], who was ordered to assume command in the Mediterranean. His main task was to protect Sicily from the French, with or without the consent of the Court at Naples. The size of the expedition was strongly censured in Parliament. 'The force is unnecessarily strong for the defensive,' fumed Robert Craufurd, 'and too weak to take the offensive.'

Craig sailed on 17th April with thirty-seven transports escorted by a small naval squadron under Rear-Admiral Knight. They were sailing into danger, for on 9th April, the French Admiral Villeneuve had passed the Straits of Gibraltar with eleven ships of the line and eight smaller warships, leaving Admiral Lord Nelson far behind, and had raised the blockade of the Spanish fleet in Cadiz. Admiral Knight was off Finisterre on the 30th when he learned, to his great dismay, that Villeneuve was at large and possibly at Cadiz. Fearing to encounter the French and Spanish fleets on their passage to Gibraltar, on 8th May, the convoy took refuge in the neutral port of Lisbon, where Craig made preparations to land, seize the Portuguese coastal forts and defend the transports with their guns.

This desperate and rather illegal, defensive measure was not implemented, for the *Orpheus* frigate arrived with news that Villeneuve was not, after all, at Cadiz and that Nelson had passed the Straits of Gibraltar. The convoy put to sea again on the 10th and continued towards Gibraltar. On doubling Cape St. Vincent, they passed through Nelson's fleet and learned that Villeneuve was heading for the West Indies. The little Admiral then stood away to the westward, bound for Barbados in pursuit of the enemy that he was destined to meet and conquer off nearby Cape Trafalgar some six months later.

The convoy was next detained off Gibraltar until escorts could be provided. Knight dared not anchor his transports in the bay for fear of the Spanish batteries and gunboats at Algeciras, so for six weeks, he cruised

---

[28] Craig's force consisted of the 39th, 44th, 48th, 58th and 81st Regiments of Foot and a squadron of the 20th Light Dragoons.

[29] Craig, whose early service was with the 30th and 47th Regiments, was a highly professional officer, but now in his late fifties his health was broken. 'In person he was very short, broad and muscular, a pocket Hercules, but with sharp, neat features as if chiselled in ivory. Not popular, for he was hot, peremptory and pompous:, yet extremely beloved by those whom he allowed to live in intimacy with him; clever, generous to a fault, and a warm and unflinching friend to those he liked.' (Sir Henry Bunbury, *Narratives of Some Passages in the Great War with France*, p. 182).

offshore in anxious suspense. Then, a gale caused further delay, and it was 18th June before the convoy set sail for Malta, where it arrived on 20th July. The 81st disembarked at Valletta on the 23rd and were quartered in Fort Ricasoli. On the 29th, they were inspected by Sir James Craig, who expressed his approval at their appearance.

On arrival at Malta, Sir James found despatches awaiting him, from which he learned that the Kingdom of the Two Sicilies[30] had decided to join the coalition and had invited Britain and Russia to land troops for its defence. Pitt saw the opportunity to activate the southern flank of his grand design, and so Craig was ordered to co-operate with a Russian force under General Lacy, an officer of Irish extraction, to free the Italian mainland from French domination. This took some time to arrange, partly due to the duplicity of the Court of Naples, which had also signed a treaty of neutrality with France, and partly to the difficulty of arranging the details of a campaign with an ally whose headquarters were in distant Corfu and whose national interests did not always coincide with those of Britain.

The main body of the 81st Regiment did not accompany Craig to Naples; possibly, the General judged that it had too many inexperienced soldiers to be fully effective. His report on the regiments that had accompanied him from England, dated 15th August 1805, supports this view: 'The 81st is the worst body of men of the four regiments but by far the most perfect in their movements. Any regiment in Lieut-Colonel Kempt's hands must be in good order.'[31]

However, Craig followed the custom of forming elite flank battalions, which included the Grenadier and Light Companies of the 81st Regiment. Lieutenant-Colonel James Kempt of the 81st was appointed to command the Light Battalion and set about welding it into an effective fighting unit. His enthusiastic young Adjutant, Richard Church, described this corps in October 1805:

'We are… a battalion of light companies from every British regiment in Malta: facings of every colour; men of every country: yet in my whole life I never saw such harmony as pervades the whole… Into our charge is given the first contest with the enemy, and we must endeavour to give a good account of veterans who have for ten years been conquerors. The task is arduous. The Commander-in-Chief, when he formed our battalion, made a most impressive speech… when in the most solemn manner he told us that he had formed two battalions for the purpose of making all attacks upon the enemy: and who were never intended to think of anything but going forward, without regard to numbers or situation, when ordered to commence an engagement… To die or conquer, says the General, must be the motto of the men he has chosen for that express purpose. Every soldier pants for action and pines at the delay: everyone feels the glorious idea of the first tremendous charge of 1,700 men, the flower of England: their impetuosity will be the only thing to endanger their success.'

On 15th September, the flank companies of the 81st joined their newly-formed corps, and Major William Smythe Plenderleath[32] assumed command of the line companies of the Battalion vice Kempt.

The British component of the Allied expedition sailed from Malta on 3rd November 1805 with 7,653 officers and men, joined the Russian fleet off Cape Passaro, and anchored in the Bay of Naples on the 20th. Next day, Craig's army disembarked at Castellamare, where on the 30th, with Vesuvius towering in the background, it was reviewed by the degenerate Bourbon King Ferdinand of the Two Sicilies and 'that elegant ruin' his scheming wife, Caroline. The latter, sister of the executed Queen Marie Antoinette of France, was the real ruler of Naples.

The Allies then marched north to take up positions covering the frontier of that kingdom. The British held the left, occupying Sesso and other villages on the lower Garigliano. Even as they advanced, bad news reached Naples, calling into question the practicality of the whole enterprise. Napoleon was sweeping the Third Coalition allies out of central Europe in a brilliant campaign culminating, on 2nd December, in the battle of Austerlitz. With Austria, Prussia and Russia beaten out of the field, at Pressburg on 26th December, the French Emperor denounced

---

[30] This state consisted of Southern Italy and Sicily. Its capital was Naples, whose court was a venomous source of intrigue, treachery and dissimulation.

[31] When it came to decide between the 81st and the 58th for inclusion in the expedition to Sicily, Craig reported that he 'hesitated for some time between the 58th and 81st. The latter was certainly in higher order, and in that respect more fit for service, but the 58th as a body of men, was much more likely to stand the service, and it was 100 men stronger. I therefore told them that if I saw that they exerted themselves to get into the order that is necessary, they should accompany us, but that if they did not succeed in it, I must at last turn to the 81st.'

[32] First commissioned into the 60th Foot in 1793, William Plenderleith had purchased a captaincy in the 81st in 1797 and a majority in 1803.

the Bourbons of Naples as being 'without faith, without honour, without reason,' which was pretty fair comment. 'The royal house of Naples has ceased to reign,' he proclaimed, 'its existence is incompatible with the peace of Europe and the honour of my crown. Soldiers, march, hurl into the waves, if they wait for you, the feeble battalions of the tyrants of the seas!'

Rumours of the Austerlitz disaster caused consternation in Naples on 22nd December, and on 2nd January 1806, Sir James Craig received news that over thirty thousand French troops were within ten days march. The twenty thousand Allied troops were in a difficult situation. It was generally accepted that, for lack of cavalry and transport, both defence of the Neapolitan frontier and a fighting withdrawal were equally impracticable. Recalling that his first priority was to deny Sicily to the French, Craig was anxious to re-embark his troops at once, yet he was in honour bound not to forsake the Russians, and Lacy dared not withdraw without orders. Fortunately, on 7th January orders arrived from the Tsar for Lacy to return at once to Corfu. The British began to leave their frontier positions on 10th January and started to embark at Castellamare four days later. The transports sailed on 19th January for Messina. Within three weeks King Ferdinand also took refuge in Sicily and Joseph Buonaparte was proclaimed king in Naples.

Sir James Craig's decision to withdraw without a fight was undoubtedly prudent and in accordance with his priority task to secure Sicily, but his army felt humiliated and was indignant at having been withdrawn without even having 'smelt powder.'

On January 22nd, the British expeditionary force anchored off Messina and sought leave to land, but the Neapolitan court was desperate to avoid provoking the French, and so the troops remained cooped up aboard ship until 17th February, when, with all prospects of conciliation exhausted, permission was granted, and British troops occupied the citadel.

The Light Battalion remained in Sicily under Lieutenant-Colonel Kempt, but the flank companies of the regiments which had been left in Malta returned to their parent corps: towards the end of February, those of the 81st rejoined their Battalion at Isla, where it had been stationed since 15th November. But the reunited 1st/81st were not to remain much longer in Malta, for Craig ordered the whole Battalion to Sicily. Embarking on 4th April, the 81st disembarked at Messina on the 14th and were quartered at Carraba, while the flank companies rejoined their respective Grenadier and Light Infantry battalions.

Sir James Craig's health had now broken down and he sailed for England in May, so ill that he was not expected to reach home alive.[33] Command in the Mediterranean now devolved on Major-General Sir John Stuart. One of the many American Loyalists in the British Army, Stuart was not without brains, energy and personal bravery but was also prickly, vainglorious and superficial and proved incapable of translating vaunting ambition into sustained action. He had commanded a brigade in Egypt, where its timely advance at the Battle of Alexandria had made an important contribution to victory, but Stuart felt that his role on that occasion had been undervalued and was particularly jealous of the praises showered on John Moore. His gallant naval colleague, Sir Sidney Smith, was as energetically superficial as Stuart but even more vain.

By the end of May, the British force in Sicily, reinforced to some eight thousand men, lay with its left fortified at Milazzo and with outposts on the right extending towards Taormina, confronting the French across the narrow Straits of Messina. 'King' Joseph was urged by his brother, Napoleon, to invade Sicily, but British command of the seas made this impracticable.

The 81st remained at Carraba until June 16th when, leaving their heavy baggage in Messina, they marched to Milazzo, where they encamped the next day. The massive medieval castle of Milazzo, perched on a rocky ridge, secured the port and made it a formidable base from which the Royal Navy could dominate the Tyrrhenian Sea.

The 81st were soon on active service. Following the Allied withdrawal from mainland Italy, the French had rapidly over-run the Kingdom of Naples except for the powerful fortress of Gaeta, where the Prince of Hesse held out stoutly against Marshal Masséna; but from the end of March 1806, the people of Calabria repeatedly rose in insurrection, and the French garrison of that province, some ten thousand men under General Reynier, were at once embroiled in a vicious guerrilla war. On 12th March, Sir Sidney Smith captured the island of Capri, off the Bay of Naples, which received a Corsican garrison under British command. From Messina, Stuart saw that French

---

[33] Sir James Craig recovered his health sufficiently to become Governor-General of Canada, but died in January 1812.

preoccupations at Gaeta and in the south of the Kingdom offered him an opportunity for offensive operations, and specifically for a descent on nearby Calabria with a vague intent of encouraging resistance to the French and of forcing Masséna to raise the siege of Gaeta. Accordingly, an expeditionary force of 5,531 all ranks was prepared with the greatest secrecy, and troops were assembled in the ports of Milazzo and Faro for embarkation at dawn on 25th June.

The force was made up of an Advanced Corps, under Lieutenant-Colonel Kempt, and three infantry brigades: The Advanced Corps consisted of the Light Battalion, two companies of Corsican Rangers, one of Sicilians, and two 4-pounder guns; Brigadier the Honourable Lowry Cole's Brigade had the Grenadier Battalion and the 27th Regiment; Brigadier William Acland's Brigade comprised the 78th Highland Regiment and the 81st Loyal Lincoln Volunteers, both of whom had many inexperienced young soldiers; Colonel John Oswald's Brigade consisted initially of the 58th, another 'young' battalion, and De Watteville's foreign (largely Swiss) regiment, though the 20th were to join later after making a diversion at Reggio. Three tiny but well-served 4-pounder guns moved with each infantry brigade, but Stuart had no cavalry.

The expedition sailed on the 26th June, escorted by HM Ships *Pompée* and *Apollo* and two frigates, coming to anchor in the Bay of St. Euphemia on the night of the 30th. At dawn the next day the Corsican Rangers landed unopposed on the wide beach of sand and pebbles and occupied an old tower, known as the Bastione di Malta, on the seashore below the village. They secured a thick belt of scrub bordering the beach, while the boats returned to the ships for Kempt's Light Battalion, the Grenadier Battalion and the 78th Foot.

Lieutenant-Colonel Oswald, who was in command of the advanced party, cautiously advanced through trees and scrub towards the village of St. Euphemia. Soon came a brisk rattle of musketry from the woods. The leading company of the Corsican Rangers had come into contact with two companies of French troops and five companies of a Polish battalion from the enemy post at Monteleone and was driven back on its supports. Oswald steadied his men and charged the enemy on both flanks, whereupon they fled with the loss of ten officers and over one hundred men killed, wounded and prisoners. In this affair, Sergeant O'Neal of the Grenadier Company 81st Regiment, 'a promising young man,' distinguished himself by taking several prisoners single-handed and earned additional praise for giving quarter to three Poles who had fired at him and then thrown down their arms.

St. Euphemia was then occupied, and the disembarkation proceeded rapidly, so that by the afternoon of 1st July, the entire force was ashore and holding a defensive line centred on the Bastione di Malta. On the 2nd, the Grenadier Battalion pushed on and seized Nicastro, a little town five miles inland and astride the road from Naples to Lower Calabria. Meanwhile, the expedition's stores and ammunition were landed through a heavy surf, a task which occupied the whole of the 2nd and the 3rd. During this period Sir John Stuart's force was joined by some two hundred Calabrians, described by Bunbury as 'ruffians of the lowest description.'

On hearing of Stuart's departure from Messina, the French commander in Calabria, General Reynier, marched rapidly northwards from Reggio, where most of his troops were stationed. Gathering up such of his men as were occupying outlying posts, on the night of the 2nd/3rd July, he arrived at the village of Maida, about nine and a half miles south-east of St. Euphemia. His force there consisted of some 6,440 troops, of whom 5,700 were in his nine battalions of infantry – six French, two Polish and one Swiss. He also had three hundred cavalry and four guns, while it was rumoured that another division was on the march. Despite his experiences in Egypt, where, like Stuart, he had commanded a brigade at the Battle of Alexandria, Reynier made the mistake of underestimating his enemy. His intention, as he later explained, was 'to advance swiftly on the English to throw them back into the sea.'

On the morning of 3rd July, Sir John Stuart learned that Reynier was encamped on wooded heights beyond the River Lamato, close to the village of Maida and overlooking the wide coastal plain. Accompanied by a small escort of grenadiers, Stuart went forward to examine the enemy's position, unaware that his opponent was also carrying out a reconnaissance at the same time. The two generals missed each other by a few minutes. Stuart judged that Reynier was most vulnerable on his left (inland) flank, and accordingly, he issued orders that evening for his troops to march at daybreak to attack the French before they could be reinforced. At about 4 a.m. on the misty morning of 4th July, 4,795 men marched out of the British camp, moving south along the coast in two parallel columns.

Lieutenant-Colonel James Kempt led on the inland side, his light troops making their way through marshy pastures, scrub, mainly myrtle bushes and pomegranates, and olive groves. The myrtles were in flower, and the soldiers picked sprigs of the white blooms as they passed. Behind Kempt's column tramped Lowry Cole with the Grenadier Battalion.

There was a false alarm when Kempt's baggage mules took fright as they were going through a wood, and the cooking pots with which they were loaded clanged loudly as the animals stampeded back in panic. Someone shouted, 'It's the French cavalry!' and Cole's Grenadiers scattered into the woods in confusion. Their commander, Lieutenant-Colonel O'Callaghan, was furious and thereafter remained rather sensitive to any mention of camp kettles.

The main body of the 81st trudged through the shingle on the seaward side, where Acland's Brigade led the advance, followed by Oswald's Reserve. Sir Sidney Smith cruised offshore with three frigates, ready to provide additional fire support. As the British columns made their way along the beach and through the long marsh grass and thickets bordering the shore, the sun rose and beat down upon them. The men – especially the Grenadier Battalion, which had marched all night – were already jaded when they reached the muddy estuary of the River Lamato and halted.

Stuart and his staff went forward to reconnoitre and saw, to their astonishment, that the French were abandoning their strong position on the hills and were descending to give battle on the plain. Reynier had originally intended to attack the British camp that morning and had given orders to that effect, but when he saw the British advance he decided to meet and beat them on the open plain. It was a decision which, to Stuart, showed 'more confidence than judgement.' The French columns filed down to their right and, having crossed the Lamato, swung left to march straight towards the sea and the British. Sharing the conceit of their general, they were in high spirits.

At around 8 a.m., the British force began to advance inland, keeping the shallow course of the Lamato, bordered by thickets, on their right. This three-mile march was far more fatiguing than the previous seven miles, for the Lamato spread out into marshes at its estuary; there was no road, save a track followed by Kempt, and many of the battalions were ankle-deep in black slime. As the brigades disentangled themselves in succession from the coastal marshes, they could at first see nothing of the enemy but the French cavalry and horse artillery, manoeuvring to their front and throwing up clouds of dust. This, together with a heat haze, obscured the French and it was by no means certain what they were doing. The opposing armies were, in fact, now closing on each other over a flat, open plain flanked by marshes and thickets. It was essentially a meeting engagement, and, as the regiments wheeled in turn to face their enemies, they advanced in echelon, with the columns on the British right and the French left rather in advance of the others.

On the British right, close to the Lamato, was Kempt's Light Battalion, 730 strong, with Acland's 78th and the 81st (33 officers and 570 men) to its left and slightly behind. Further back and to the left, Cole came on with the 27th and the Grenadiers. Oswald's brigade, the 58th and a wing of De Watteville's, was in second line in rear of the centre. Two light guns, carried by mules, were attached to each brigade, and three slightly heavier field guns followed Acland. As the distance between the two armies closed, the British infantry deployed from column into a two-deep line, their standard battle formation.

On the French left, opposite Kempt and Acland, Compère's brigade of veteran infantry led the French advance, two battalions each of the 1st Légère and 42nd Regiments. To their right was the two-battalion 1st Polish Regiment and a single battalion of De Watteville's Swiss[34]. The 23rd Légère formed the right of Reynier's line, flanked by four squadrons of the 9th Chasseurs à Cheval. The advancing French presented a magnificent spectacle, in particular the 1st Légère, of whom Bunbury wrote, 'never did I see a finer or more soldier-like body of men.' They were indeed reputed to be the best regiment in the French Army.

The 81st have left no first-hand account of Maida, their most notable battle, but Major David Stewart, who was with the 78th Highlanders on their immediate right, witnessed the scene as the opposing forces advanced:

'Two armies in parallel lines, in march towards each other, on a smooth and clear plain, and in dead silence, only interrupted by the report of the enemy's guns; it was more like a chosen field fixed upon by a general officer

---

[34] Their commander was a cousin of the De Watteville in the British service and, to add to the confusion, both Swiss regiments wore red jackets.

for exercise, or to exhibit a show fight, than a real battle. No two rival commanders could ever wish for a finer field for a trial of the courage and firmness of their respective combatants; and as there were some present who recollected the contempt with which General Reynier, in his account of the Egyptian expedition, had chosen to treat the British, there was as much feeling mixed up with the usual incitements, as perhaps in any modern engagement.

'In this mutual advance the opposing troops were in full view of each other, which enabled our men to make their remarks on the marching, and on the manner in which the enemy advanced. They did not always preserve a correct steady line but sometimes allowed openings and intervals by careless marching; showing, as the soldiers observed, that they did not march as steadily as they themselves did.'

The British were equally unimpressed with the French gunnery compared to their own, for whilst the British artillery made excellent practice the enemy guns fired too high.

'The lines were fast closing,' continued Stewart, 'but with perfect regularity and firmness. They were now within three hundred yards distance, and a fire having commenced between the sharpshooters on the right, it was time to prepare for an immediate shock.'

This outbreak of shooting on the right was instigated by some two hundred of Compère's *voltigeurs* who, having advanced through the scrub on the far bank of the Lamoto, routed the Corsican and Sicilian skirmishers who had been sent there to protect Kempt's right flank. These were driven back on their supports, the Light Company of the 20th, and a hotly contested firefight ensued at close range. The 20th Light Bobs were hard-pressed for some minutes, but Kempt detached the flankers of the 35th to their assistance, and the French retreated in confusion. The Corsicans rallied and pursued them, and the men of the 20th and 35th re-crossed the stream to join Kempt. The Light Battalion continued to advance, two deep and with trailed arms.

The famous clash that followed has been cited as a classic combat of the British line against the French column, but the contemporary evidence is that the French, too, had deployed into line, probably three ranks deep, with one battalion in front of the other. It follows that, while the French outnumbered Kempt's men by two to one, the British would have been able to bring marginally more muskets to bear, perhaps some six hundred and fifty as opposed to five hundred in the front two ranks of the 1st Légère; moreover, the Light Bobs were all picked men.

It was around 9 a.m., and already very hot, when the British and French light battalions closed to musketry range, and Kempt, observing that his men were encumbered by greatcoats and blankets, worn bandolier-fashion, halted them and bade them throw their burdens down. The front rank turned about to help the rear rank to obey the order, and the French apparently mistook this movement for the beginning of a retreat.

Sensing an easy victory, the 1st Légère surged forward with the 42nd in support to their right. French drums beat the *pas de charge* and, to cries of '*Vive l'Empereur!*' sixteen hundred confident veterans stepped out at 120 paces to the minute. Compère, who rode between his two regiments, counted on the shock of impact to break the thin British line and tumble his adversaries ignominiously back to the sea. '*Ne tirez pas!*' he ordered, '*Ne tirez pas! A la bayonette! A la bayonette!*'

Kempt waited until the French were within half musket range. He was outnumbered by well over two to one. 'Steady, Light Infantry,' he roared, 'Now is the time to show that you are British soldiers! – Wait for the word – Let them come close – Now, fire!'

The Light Infantry smashed a first devastating volley into the French ranks, which at once became disordered and began to lose momentum. A second crashing volley followed, and a third at very close range. Kempt ordered, 'Charge bayonets!' and with a rousing cheer, the Light Battalion pushed through the choking clouds of acrid musket smoke. Few of the 1st Légère waited to meet Kempt's charge; already faltering, with most of their officers down, they turned and ran for two miles or more, through their camp and the village of Maida, with the victorious Light Bobs hot on their heels. It was a total rout, and some three hundred French fell to the bayonet; as a British gunner put it, the Light Battalion 'ran down the heroes of Marengo like a flock of sheep,' many of the fugitives being overtaken and bayoneted at a dry water-course. Compère was badly wounded, unhorsed and taken prisoner, swearing volubly as he was led away. His men were hunted off the field, leaving nearly nine hundred men killed, wounded or prisoners, including twenty officers. Kempt's losses were barely fifty.

By this time, Acland's brigade, the 78th and 81st, were engaging the two battalions of the 42nd Regiment, which had come up on the right flank of the 1st Légère. Colonel Huard, commanding the 42nd, asked Reynier whether he should order his men to load, to which the General jocularly replied, 'Certainly, unless you are going to wait for the English to order it.' The 42nd, who had advanced rather more deliberately than the 1st Légère, were disconcerted by the sudden rout of the battalions on their left and, after exchanging fire with Acland's brigade, they retreated. Major David Stewart again, Second-in-Command of the 78th Highlanders, witnessed this phase of the battle:

'The enemy seemed to hesitate, halted, and fired a volley. Our line also halted, and instantly returned the salute, and when the men had reloaded, a second volley was thrown in. The precision with which these two volleys was fired, and their effect, were quite remarkable. When the clearing off of the smoke (there was hardly a breath of wind to dispel it) enabled us to see the French line, the breaks and vacancies caused by the men who had fallen by the fire appeared like a paling, of which parts had been thrown down or broken. On our side it was so different that, glancing along the rear of my regiment, I counted only fourteen who had fallen from the enemy's fire. As soon as the smoke had cleared our line advanced at the charge and the 42nd Ligne withdrew swiftly but not in confusion. They halted just in front of their second line, a constant running fire being maintained, until they had reached a position about a mile away. Here they could support Reynier's right wing and cover his left if Kempt's Light Brigade should turn in on them instead of chasing the remnants of Compère's brigade.'

The 78th and 81st followed the retreating 42nd for some distance, then encountered Peyri's brigade, two battalions of Poles and De Watteville's Swiss regiment, fifteen hundred fresh enemies. The 81st very rapidly routed both battalions of the 1st Polish Regiment, at least three times their own strength[35], who broke at the first shock though Reynier himself had ridden up to them and made every effort to keep them steady. Four Polish officers and nearly 250 men were captured, mostly unwounded.

The situation on the right of Acland's brigade was less fortunate. The appearance of De Watteville's is said to have caused some hesitation among the young Scots of the newly-raised 78th, who took the red-coated Swiss for friends and ceased fire, allowing them to approach. This circumstance, though doubtless true, may, however have served after the event to mask a more serious confusion, the public knowledge of which might well, in Stewart's words, have been 'injurious to the character of some brother officers, long dead.' It seems that there was, at the least, a temporary breakdown in command and control affecting both battalions of Acland's brigade. Those present remained very reticent as to the circumstances, but a later memorandum by Major Stewart throws some light, from his perspective, on what happened.

He wrote that after the enemy had been driven back by the first charge, he saw that Major Plenderleath, commanding the 81st Regiment to his left, 'did not seem to understand or to act on his instructions.' Stewart, therefore rode over to him and 'remonstrating with him, a remedy was instantly applied, and by this timely interference was prevented a serious calamity which might have affected the character of that officer and the general success of the day.' Quite what instruction the Commanding Officer of the 81st was supposed to have misunderstood, or how, is unclear, but Stewart clearly felt that it threatened to disrupt the British advance. Accepting Stewart's account at face value, the most plausible explanation is that Plenderleath had halted to gather up his mass of prisoners instead of keeping station to the left of the Highlanders. It is, however at least as likely that Stewart, in his retrospective account, was attempting to shift attention from the undoubted confusion and hesitation in the ranks of his own regiment.[36]

On returning to the 78th, Stewart learned that they had been ordered to retreat, possibly because their left flank was unprotected. Stewart hurried off to see Acland, the brigade commander, and begged him to rescind the order, 'adding that the enemy had already been forced to fly by three separate charges with the bayonet and had

---

[35] The 81st were some six hundred strong and the 1st Polish Regiment over eighteen hundred.

[36] Whilst Sir John Stuart commended Plenderleath in his report on the battle of Maida, it appears that, following a secretive but nonetheless telling smear campaign involving Major Stewart of the 78th, he was later prevailed upon not to recommend the Commanding Officer of the 81st for the Gold Medal normally awarded to commanding officers after a successful engagement. William Plenderleath would appear hard done by as the 81st had twice defeated their opponents with ease whilst the 78th had undoubtedly fallen into confusion. Despite this, Major James Macdonell, commanding the 78th, was awarded the Gold Medal for Maida and was subsequently promoted. Plenderleath, in contrast, retired in June 1808 and, still at major, died at his Ramsgate home in 1863, aged 88. He had at least the consolation of being the senior surviving officer to receive the Military General Sevice Medal with bar for Maida.

retreated upwards of two miles – that if these advantages were followed up the victory would be complete, and the enemy driven from the field, which was already so strewed with their dead and wounded that it required attention to keep clear of the bodies when riding through them, but that if the order was persevered in the enemy would resume their confidence, return to the charge, and occupy the ground vacated by the Highlanders and thus cut off the communications between the Light Infantry and the 81st Regiment, attack them in detail, and obtain that victory which the British had all but gained.'

Acland insisted that he had not ordered a retreat and that there must have been some mistake. Riding hastily back to his own regiment, Stewart found all but one company in close column, ready to march off. He ordered them to face to the right about and form a line and to open fire on companies the instant they got into line. It may have been at this dangerous time that Acland was observed to have 'behaved conspicuously well – seizing the Colours and leading his men to the charge.' The Highlanders' mistake was soon turned to advantage, for by the time they recommenced firing, the Swiss were so close that the fire of the 78th was doubly effective. 'So correct and deadly was the aim of our young soldiers,' recalled Stewart, 'that in ten minutes the field to their front was cleared of the enemy.'

Acland was unable to follow up this second success as his left flank was in the air, threatened by Reynier's chasseurs à cheval and horse artillery. The 78th and 81st were accordingly ordered to halt and form square to fend off the cavalry, which was done, albeit in some disorder, after their rapid advance and overthrow of five enemy battalions. This dense formation left them vulnerable to the French guns, and both regiments suffered some loss. The *Record of Service* of the 81st Foot states that the Regimental losses were 'principally owing to its left being for some time exposed,' presumably at this time. The Brigade remained in square until the end of the battle, when the French cavalry withdrew.

By this time, the battle had spread to the far left of the British line, where Cole's brigade (the 27th Foot and the Grenadier Battalion) had at last come up. Reynier reacted by holding them in front with the 23rd Légère, the rallied Swiss and two guns while his light infantry and cavalry made a counter-attack through close country onto Cole's open left flank. Cole threw back three companies of the 27th and brought two companies of Grenadiers across from his right to counter this threat, but still, the enemy advanced, and their skirmishers, infiltrating round his flank through the scrub and bushes, began to cause significant casualties amid the burning stubble on that part of the battlefield. The chasseurs à cheval appeared to be about to charge, and behind them came a mass of French infantry. Lieutenant-Colonel O'Callaghan of the Grenadiers rode along the line and exhorted his men, 'Grenadiers, remember the camp kettle mules, you damned rascals! Remember the camp kettle mules!'

At this critical juncture, the British left flank received an unexpected but most timely reinforcement, for the detached 20th Foot had landed and, marching in double quick time to the sound of the guns, came up on Cole's left. Lieutenant-Colonel Henry Bunbury rode to meet them and briefed their commander, Robert Ross.

'He caught the spirit of the affair in an instant, pressed onward, drove the swarm of sharpshooters before him, gave the French cavalry such a volley as sent them off in confusion to the rear, and passing beyond the left of Cole's brigade, wheeled the 20th to their right and opened a shattering fire on the enemy's battalions. The effect was decisive.'

Reynier ordered a retreat and drew off his troops skillfully, falling back on his 42nd Regiment and covering the withdrawal with his cavalry and horse artillery. The British infantry followed their beaten foe as far as the Maida-Nicastro road and then halted, utterly exhausted. Within two hours of the first shot, the veteran infantry of France were in flight, leaving nearly one in three of their number on the field of battle. 'Such a thing,' wrote a French officer with only mild exaggeration, 'has not been seen since the Revolution!' Had the British possessed cavalry, it is probable that few of Reynier's army would have escaped.

It will be noticed that throughout the above narrative of the battle of Maida, no mention has been made of the British commander. Indeed, little credit for this famous victory belongs to that officer, and Bunbury, his principal staff officer, was scorching in his sarcasm:

'But where was Sir John Stuart? And what great part did he play in this brilliant action? In truth he seemed to be rather a spectator than a person much, or *the* person *most*, interested in the result of the conflict. He formed no plan, declared no intention, and scarcely did he trouble himself to give an order. Perfectly regardless of personal danger, he was cantering about, indulging himself in little pleasantries as was his wont.'[37]

Fortunately Stuart had competent and energetic subordinates who carried the burden of the day, and Bunbury singles out Kempt and Ross for special praise. As for the soldiers, he goes on to say that, 'The behaviour of our troops was remarkably good, and excepting a momentary confusion in Acland's two young regiments, for which the soldiers were less to be blamed than the commanding officers of the two battalions, nothing went amiss. The men were cool and ready, and their fire was deadly.' As Lowry Cole justly commented after the battle[38], 'Everything is due to the steadiness and good discipline and gallantry of the troops, without which we must have been defeated as they were near twice our number – with cavalry also, of which we had none.'

French losses at Maida amounted to 490 killed, 870 wounded, 722 captured[39], and four guns taken. British losses were astonishingly light: one officer, three sergeants and 41 men killed and thirteen officers, eight sergeants, two drummers and 260 men wounded. Over half the British casualties fell on Acland's brigade: the 78th had eighty-five all ranks killed and wounded, and the 81st lost a total of eighty-four[40].

'MAIDA' was the first Battle Honour of the 81st Foot, which was the only regiment represented in all three forward brigades. This action remained one of the proudest achievements of the Loyal Lincoln Volunteers, commemorated on their regimental buttons and celebrated by their lineal successors, the 2nd Loyal North Lancashires, as a Regimental Day[41].

Except for the Light Infantry, who were away in the Maida hills, there was no pursuit after the battle. 'By mid-day our soldiers were resting on their arms,' recalled Bunbury, 'gasping with heat and thirst, and watching through the dust, with disappointed eyes, the rapid retreat of the French column. Our ammunition was nearly spent; there was no water for the men, save on the right, and every step we might make in advance led us farther away from our supplies of every sort.'[42]

Stuart ordered his troops back to the beach for rest and replenishment, and one brigade at a time was allowed to bathe in the sea. Some amusement was caused when a 'noggin' of a staff officer raised a false alarm of French cavalry, at which the Grenadiers and 27th rushed out of the water and, throwing their belts over their shoulders, grasped their muskets and drew up in line, stark naked, to repel what proved to be a herd of buffaloes.

Separated from the rest of the force that evening, the Light Infantry Battalion remained out on the hills without supplies of any kind, and James Kempt was more than thankful to make his supper off a small tortoise found by his servant. Many years later, General Sir James Kempt, as he became, had the shell mounted in silver and made into a snuff box[43], which he presented to the Officers' Mess of the 81st Regiment, of which on 12 July 1819 he became Colonel. Kempt brought his men into camp the following morning.

Next day, the column marched to Maida where, so Bunbury complains, 'during forty-eight hours our troops remained kicking their heels and eating grapes' while Sir John Stuart composed and polished his dispatch on the action and published an order to the troops under his command:

Plains of St. Euphemia, near Maida
6th July, 1806

---

[37] Bunbury, p. 248.
[38] Letter dated Monteleone, 11th July, 1806.
[39] On 6th July Captain Henry Sullivan, who had commanded the Light Company 81st at Maida, was appointed to escort the prisoners to Sicily with two companies of the 81st.
[40] The eight battalion companies of the 81st had nineteen men killed and two officers and 63 other ranks wounded. The two officers were Captain Peter Waterhouse and Lieutenant and Adjutant Joseph Ginger. The transport carrying the wounded back to Sicily was driven ashore at Scylla; those aboard were captured but almost immediately exchanged. The losses of the detached Grenadier and Light Companies are not known. Captain Waterhouse subsequently served with the 1st/81st in Eastern Spain, where he was mentioned in dispatches for Denia, 6th October 1812, and died a brevet lieutenant-colonel and major, in command of the 81st at Halifax, Nova Scotia in 1823, having served in the Regiment for twenty-two years. Lieutenant Ginger, who was commissioned into the 81st Foot on 25th September 1803, was promoted to a captaincy in the 81st, without purchase, 1st May 1811 and went on half-pay in 1826.
[41] Maida Day was celebrated by Trooping the Colour followed by Annual Sports and the Sergeants' Mess Maida Ball.
[42] Bunbury, p. 249.
[43] The Maida Tortoise remains in the possession of the Regiment, and as the original is now fragile a silver replica is placed before the Colonel of the Regiment at Mess dinners, a reminder of his forebear's more frugal supper.

'Major-General Sir John Stuart finds himself incapable of expressing to the troops the sentiments excited in him by their brave and intrepid conduct in the late action of the 4th, in which they gained so signal a triumph over a boasting and insolent enemy... The 78th and 81st Regiments, which formed the brigade of General Acland, shared the first and severest part of the action with the Light Infantry, whom they were ordered to support, and the gallantry and good conduct of the Brigadier-General in fulfilling this duty were most nobly seconded by the brave regiments under his orders...'

In his triumphant euphoria, Stuart forgot that the original purpose of his descent on the mainland, and its only justification, was to assist Gaeta. Instead, having harvested the victor's palms, he was content to complete 'the destruction of the enemy's establishments on the shores contiguous to Sicily' and then return to Messina. Consequently, on 8th July, the troops took the road south to Monteleone, where they captured a French detachment, hospital and magazine. Four days later the British column marched on to Palmi, arriving there on the 14th.

By this time, Gaeta had at last fallen to Masséna, but a British force had crossed the Straits of Messina to capture Reggio on the 10th, and Sir Sidney Smith was bombarding the seemingly impregnable fortress of Scylla. Captain Henry Sullivan of the 81st, who was returning through the Straits of Messina after escorting the French prisoners to Sicily, volunteered his services with the two companies of the 81st under his command. His offer was accepted, and the fortress was soon closely invested by Sullivan with a force which included, in addition to his own men, marines, seamen with two guns off the lower deck of HMS *Pompée*, a brigade of artillery and some two thousand Calabrese. The French had already hoisted a flag of truce when the besiegers were joined by Oswald's Brigade, which, of course, deprived Sullivan of his unusual command and the honour of taking the fortress's surrender on 23rd July. He rejoined the 81st at Reggio.

Despite this additional success, Stuart's Calabrian excursion was drawing to a close. On receipt of news that Masséna was about to descend on Calabria, he re-embarked his troops at Reggio. Garrisons were left there and at Scylla, thereby denying to the French, for a few months, their mounting bases for an invasion of Sicily.

Viewed in retrospect as a pre-emptive strike to disrupt French invasion plans and to dislodge them from the mainland side of the Straits of Messina, Stuart's descent on Calabria was a remarkable, albeit local and temporary, success, though its wider strategic objectives had not been achieved. Its moral impact, however, was rather more substantial and longer-lasting. Even more than the 1801 Egyptian campaign, it broke the legend of French invincibility and reminded Europe what marvels well-trained and disciplined British infantry could accomplish. Since Maida, some fifteen hundred prisoners had been taken in Calabria, together with heavy guns and large quantities of stores, equipment and munitions. Reynier's army was a wreck: he had lost some four thousand men, almost half his strength, and many of the exhausted and demoralised survivors were without weapons, boots or even uniforms; the 42nd Regiment had lost 690 muskets, while the men of the 1st Légère were reduced to '*une nudité presque entière.*'

Despite the fall of Gaeta, which had released Masséna's entire army for counter-insurgency operations further south, Sir Sidney Smith had not given up his earlier enthusiasm for beating up the coast of the occupied territories and supporting a largely illusory anti-French insurrection, supplying arms and money to anarchic bands that were little better than brigands. To assist in the Admiral's demonstrations off Naples and Salerno, Stuart embarked the 58th and 81st Regiments[44], still under Brigadier Acland, and sent them to cruise offshore and to establish communications with the garrison of Capri. Acland's force stood off the islands of Procida and Ischia in the Bay of Naples, but early in September, it was ordered back to Messina by Sir John Moore, for there had been a change of command in the Mediterranean; General Fox had come out as commander-in-chief, with Moore as his second-in-command, and the latter had sailed up the coast to make his own assessment of the situation. Moore soon concluded that Sir Sidney Smith's interference on the mainland was doing more harm than good, and on 24th August, he made a scathing report to Fox: 'In his imagination,' he wrote of the vainglorious admiral, 'he is directing the operation of armies, but... in reality he is only encouraging murder and rapine, and keeping up amongst that unhappy people, whom we have no intention to support, a spirit of revolt which will bring upon them the most severe vengeance of the French government. As long as Sir Sidney had money he distributed it; and now, with as little judgement, he is distributing arms, ammunition and provisions.'

---

[44] A Strength Return dated 1st August 1806 shows the 81st, then cruising off the Neapolitan coast, with 612 rank and file, exclusive of the Flank Companies.

26

On their return to Sicily, the 81st were quartered in the Citadel at Messina, where they remained in garrison for the next sixteen months. Battalion strength was considerably augmented in 1807 by two large drafts from the 2nd Battalion; one hundred and seventy-five men joined in January and a further seventy-five in November.[45] In April 1807, a Sicilian company was attached to the Battalion, remaining on its strength for six months[46].

On December 1st, the 1st/81st moved out of the Citadel into cantonments in support of the most obviously vulnerable section of the coastal defence lines, stretching from the ancient Norman monastery of San Salvatore Dei Greci, on the north side of Messina, to Faro village, with Battalion Headquarters at the hamlet of Santa Agata.

On 16th October, Major the Honourable Alexander Abercromby replaced William Plenderleath, who retired the following June; but, in consequence of James Kempt being appointed Deputy-Quartermaster-General in Canada (on the recommendation of Sir James Craig), Lieutenant-Colonel Patrick McKenzie came out from the 2nd/81st in Ireland to assume command on 19th August 1808.

In September 1807 orders arrived from the Ministry for Moore to take a force to Lisbon. This left the garrison of Sicily dangerously weak. Sir Hew Dalrymple sent what reinforcements he could from Gibraltar, including a detachment of the 82nd Regiment who, billeted in Jesso and other mountain villages above the Straits of Messina, reinforced the coast watch for some months early in 1808.

Although Nelson had swept the seas clean of French and Spanish battle fleets, and the survivors were blockaded in Toulon and elsewhere, British shipping in the Mediterranean remained vulnerable to marauding warships and privateers operating from smaller enemy ports, and so the passage from home to Sicily could be hazardous. On the morning of 13th December 1806, the 16-gun brig-sloop HMS *Halcyon*, Captain Henry Pearse, was 18 miles North North East of Cape San Martin in Valencia when three vessels, a polacre, a brig and a zebec, were seen standing out from the land. When they closed within four or five miles, they were seen to be warships, and were reinforced by five settees. When within musket shot, the strangers hoisted Spanish colours. Despite the odds, Captain Pearse closed as soon as possible and engaged the enemy. *Halcyon* was undermanned, sixteen short of her complement of 94, so her four military passengers took an active part in the action, including Captain Henry Sullivan of the 81st, who was given command of the small arms. At about noon, the enemy fire slackened and, in a calm, the brig and zebec hauled away to the southward assisted by sweeps and boats. The polacre tried to escape to the north, but *Halcyon* swept after her and, about an hour later, forced her to strike. She was the 14-gun privateer *Neptuno Dios de los Mares* from Denia, with a crew of 72 men. Aboard *Halcyon*, two officers and a seaman were wounded. Sullivan was mentioned in the Gazette.[47] Captain Richard Cole of the 81st was less fortunate: on 18th March 1807, when on passage to England, he was taken prisoner by a French warship after an action of two hours' duration.[48]

In February 1808, the French assembled a large force in Lower Calabria and invested in the fortress of Scylla, which fell on the 18th after a gallant defence. During this alarm, the Grenadier and Light Infantry Battalions of the British force in Sicily, which still included the Flank Companies of the 81st, were deployed to deal with any French attempt to cross the Straits: the former occupied positions on the coast south of Messina, while the latter was posted in mountain villages in rear of the coastal defences. The main body of the 81st remained at Faro and Santa Agata till the end of June 1808[49], when they marched to quarters in the mountain villages of Jesso, Sulica, St. Georgia and Castania, Battalion Headquarters being based at Castania. In September, the 81st marched to

---

[45] By 1st July 1807 the rank and file strength of the 81st had risen to 908.

[46] The affection of the Sicilian peasantry for the British Crown was such that a Horse Guards order of 23rd July 1806 directed a number of British regiments, including the 40th and 81st, to raise each a company of one hundred Sicilians, to serve for seven years. In the case of the 40th this order was not carried out. The Sicilian Company of the 81st did not last long, for in October it was transferred to the 61st Regiment.

[47] Colonel Henry Sullivan CB (1782-1841) purchased an ensign's commission in the 81st on 17th May 1798, aged 16, and saw active service with the Light Company in South Africa, where as an 18 year old ensign of the Light Company 81st he took part in the action against the French frigate *Preneuse* in Algoa Bay, 1799. He commanded a division of the 81st at Maida and commanded the regimental detachment at the siege of Scylla. Sullivan was promoted into the 67th Foot on 21st July 1808, serving 1811-15 in India and Java.

[48] Richard Cole was soon exchanged, subsequently serving with the 81st in the Corunna and Walcheren campaigns, and then in Eastern Spain, including the battle of Castalla, in North America, and the occupation of Paris, rising to the rank of lieutenant-colonel. He was twice wounded.

[49] A draft of 74 men from the 2nd Battalion joined at Santa Agata on 28th April.

occupy the fortified peninsula of Milazzo. Whilst stationed there, the Battalion received the welcome Horse Guards order abolishing the men's queues.

Sicily remained fairly secure in British hands, but theirs was not a comfortable situation; the British generals deeply, and rightly, distrusted the Neapolitan court at Palermo, which constantly importuned them to engage in another expedition to the mainland but was suspected of treacherous dealings with the enemy. Fox and Moore successfully resisted all temptations to engage in mainland adventures, and the latter applied himself to strengthening the island's defensive arrangements; but in July 1807, Fox was superseded, and two months later, as already mentioned, Moore was ordered to Gibraltar together with a large part of the garrison of Sicily.

The energetic Major-General Sherbrooke was a worthy successor[50], but in April 1808, Sir John Stuart returned, to the unfeigned delight of the court at Palermo, and by the summer of that year, there was a discernible decline in the garrison's morale. 'There was no longer the hearty good-will and energy of which it bore the stamp under Moore and Sherbrooke; and even the officers of high rank were anxious to leave us... There grew up grumblings and scoffs amongst our officers; duties were neglected; and the vessel floated along mainly through the former *impetus remorum*.'[51]

Stuart reacted to the growing discontent by preparing a further descent on the mainland, where the fiery and impetuous Marshal Joachim Murat had replaced the quiet and ineffective Joseph Buonaparte on the throne of Naples.

Stuart's first move was to reinforce the garrison of Capri by adding a Maltese battalion, but on 4th October, Murat mounted an audacious assault on the rock-bound island. The flower of Murat's army scaled the vast cliffs of Anacapri and routed the Maltese in a night attack, then descended the precipitous rock-cut steps, which were then the only link between Anacapri and Capri proper to invest the town. Colonel Hudson Lowe, commanding the Corsican garrison, managed to send a boat to Messina, and Sir John Stuart despatched reinforcements as soon as they could board transports. At Milazzo, the 81st and 58th Regiments, with the 4th Battalion of The King's German Legion, were embarked in three hours on the evening of the 7th and sailed that night under convoy of HMS *Fame*, 74.

That same day, the French opened their siege batteries against Capri, but they were, in turn, cut off from the mainland by the arrival offshore of British and Neapolitan warships. The three thousand besiegers were now in a dangerous situation and were only saved from a humiliating reverse by an abrupt change in the previously calm weather. As the British reinforcements neared Capri, they were struck by a tempest, and for the next ten days, they were tossed about the Tyrrhenian Sea. The transports carrying the 81st were driven back to Messina, and the convoy did not arrive off Capri until the 22nd, when they saw flags of truce flying on all the works. With his ammunition and provisions nearly spent, Lowe had capitulated under condition of withdrawing his garrison, with arms and baggage, to Sicily. Murat's rash venture had succeeded, and the British convoy could only return to Milazzo. Whilst Capri was of negligible strategic importance, its capture undermined confidence in British arms and caused panic in Sicily.

The 81st Regiment was now quartered in the Upper Town and Castle of Milazzo, which it occupied until May 1809. Early that month, Stuart embarked thirteen thousand troops at that port, including the 81st, 656 strong, for an expedition to capture the offshore island of Ischia and threaten Naples. Its ostensible purpose was to create a diversion in favour of the Austrians, who were once more at war with France, but Stuart also wished to still the widespread discontent in his army. Bunbury described the scene on 11th June, when two hundred transports set sail:

'The fleet which issued forth from the anchorage of Milazzo made a splendid show. It was a great armada. Innumerable vessels of all descriptions, convoyed by three ships of the line, and some frigates and brigs of war, covered the blue sea from the Lipari Islands to the coast of Calabria... and in outward seeming we might have

---

[50] 'From the moment Sherbrooke assumed the command of our little army, he applied himself to the improvement of our means of defence... forts and batteries were formed along the shore of the Straits; roads of communication were opened; the fortresses were improved; the discipline of our troops was confirmed by the personal attention of the General, and the activity which prevailed in every quarter revived the spirits and the confidence of our officers.' (Bunbury, pp. 328-29).
[51] Bunbury, p. 341.

vied with the proudest armament which had carried the standards of England to fields of glory. But our General had done with fields of glory.'[52]

Late on the 23rd, the convoy anchored in the Bay of Naples, between Baia and the island of Ischia. Although reconnaissance revealed that the shore batteries were more formidable than had been expected, orders were issued for a landing at daybreak on the eastern side of Ischia. The Light Infantry, 81st Regiment and Corsican Rangers were to lead the attack. Around midnight, the assault troops boarded ships' boats, which assembled under the stern of HMS *Spartiate*, 74, whose captain was to regulate the landing. British and Neapolitan warships and gunboats were to engage the French batteries at first light and provide covering fire.

The heavily-laden boats had to be towed for six miles, and as the day broke, the French batteries opened fire. Nevertheless, the three battalions made good their landing in the small bay now known as Spiaggia degli Inglesi, between Ischia town and Casamicciola. The coastal batteries were soon turned, and after a short resistance, the garrison withdrew into the castle. Some 180 prisoners were taken, mostly from the 1st Légère, while the assaulting troops had no loss. By that evening British troops controlled the whole island except for the castle, the medieval Castello Aragonese. This massive fortification, perched on the cliffs of an isolated rock, could only be approached along a two-hundred-yard causeway, but its ancient walls were no match for siege guns. Heavy artillery was brought ashore and 24-pounders dragged into place on heights commanding the castle, which surrendered on 30th June. The adjacent island of Procida also capitulated.

Sir John Stuart's thirteen thousand troops, with their transports, were now poised within sight of Naples, which was in a ferment. Throughout Italy, the French and their enemies anticipated a British landing on the mainland, but Stuart would not stir. He would not risk his spurious reputation as the victor of Maida, and it took only a report of unusual naval activity in Toulon for him to scuttle back to Messina. The 81st Foot remained quartered in the town of Ischia until 26th July when, having destroyed the coastal batteries, it was the last corps to embark.

On its return to Milazzo, the 81st was shifted into three transports, which sailed under a convoy of HMS *Delight*, a sloop of war, to make demonstrations along the Calabrian coast until the end of September.

The Regiment was then disembarked at Messina and was quartered in the Citadel until the middle of November 1809, when it moved to the convents on the north side of that town, with headquarters in the monastery of San Salvatore dei Greci. For the next two years, the 81st occupied the coastal defenses between Messina and Faro Point. The latter was frequently exposed to a distant and ineffective bombardment from French batteries across the Straits, a distance of 2,800 yards at its narrowest point.

By mid-summer 1810, Murat had concentrated an invasion force of twenty to twenty-five thousand men and nearly five hundred boats in Lower Calabria and ostentatiously set up his pavilion tent and a huge tricolour banner on the heights of Pezzo, in full view of every British post on the Straits. Along the Sicilian coast, the British army made energetic preparations for defence. A chain of Martello towers and coastal batteries connected Faro Point with Messina, and these were supported by fortified posts and barracks from where battalions could be moved to threatened points along over fifty miles of newly constructed roads, while a flotilla of near one hundred light craft was mustered at the Faro, ready to attack the flanks and rear of any French armada. The Sicilian peasantry, who showed more affection for the British than for their own corrupt monarch, came voluntarily to work on the entrenchments with cries of 'Viva King George.'

The effectiveness of these arrangements was proven on the night of 17th September when the advance detachment of an attempted French invasion was ignominiously defeated on the beach at St. Stephano, south of Messina, with the loss of at least twelve hundred men. Towards the end of that month, Murat thinned out his forces in southern Calabria and withdrew his invasion fleet from the Straits of Messina.

We have a glimpse of the 1st/81st on 22nd December 1810 when Major-General George Cockburn visited their quarters at Faro: 'We walked round to the barrack-huts, lately occupied by the 58th Regiment, and now by the 81st; but they are so badly finished, and so cold in this season at night, that in one large room, four officers have pitched their tents, by which they have good shelter.'

---

[52] Bunbury, p. 364.

The 1st/81st were still quartered at Faro on 30th June 1811, when they received a draft of four sergeants and 258 rank and file from their 2nd Battalion, and remained there until November, as the French still had a considerable force on the opposite side of the Straits. On 14th November 1811, the 81st marched in three divisions to Milazzo, where they again occupied the castle and nearby convents.

Meanwhile, the treacherous Neapolitan court at Palermo not only continued its duplicitous contact with the French but squandered their British subsidy and oppressed their own people to the extent that the exasperated Sicilians threatened revolt. This compromised the British presence, which now appeared to underpin the hated Bourbons. The British Ministry belatedly recognized the necessity of restoring proper government to the island, not least because this would permit a reduction in the garrison, and Lord William Bentinck was sent to Sicily with powers as Envoy Extraordinary and Commander-in-Chief. In December 1811, he took decisive action against King Ferdinand and his opium-raddled Queen, cutting off their subsidy, summoning British reinforcements from Malta, and demanding a change in the administration. Ferdinand abdicated on 16th January 1812, and Palermo was occupied by British troops, including the 81st Regiment.

Sailing from Milazzo at the end of the month, the expedition arrived off Palermo on 2nd February. The 81st Regiment was quartered in the Convent of San Neto, near the San Rosolia Gate. On the arrival of the Regiment in Palermo, the Fathers of the great baroque church of San Domenico gave a magnificent dinner to Lieutenant-Colonel McKenzie and his officers, whom they treated with uniform kindness during the Regiment's five-month stay at the convent.

Bentinck's action and the withdrawal of all but one French division from Italy for service in Napoleon's ill-starred invasion of Russia, made it possible to release a part of the Sicilian garrison for service elsewhere, and so on 6th June 1812, after more than six years based in Sicily, the 81st sailed for Spain.

Copenhagen, July-September 1807

We last noted the 1st/82nd in Ireland, where they served 1801-07. From 1805 onwards, they absorbed successive large drafts of militiamen and other recruits from their Depot at Littlehampton and from the 2nd Battalion.[53] In June 1804, the Battalion marched from Omagh to Mullingar and from there at the end of July to the Curragh, where they formed part of a 'camp of manoeuvre,' training under Lord Cathcart. This camp broke up in mid-September, when the 1st/82nd returned to Mullingar. In May 1805, the Battalion marched to Dublin, where they remained doing garrison duties until early August, when they again encamped for training at the Curragh. When the camp dispersed, they marched to Limerick and then to Cork. There, they were joined by another large draft of officers and men from the 2nd Battalion, including Ensign George Wood, who was delighted to find himself in the midst of his Irish friends and relations.

'Behold me now, then, stationed where I receive every indulgence and friendship; in short, I am quite at home. After adorning my person with plenty of powder and perfumes, a long queue, and all the *et cetera* of military finery, away I strut to the grand parade, admiring the belles and the *bon-ton* of this gay place and fancying myself equally admired, little dreaming how soon these fine ornaments would be tarnished, and the white powder exchanged for black on a more arduous and active kind of service.'[54]

On 5th July 1807, the 1st/82nd embarked at the Cove of Cork for the Downs under command of Lieutenant-Colonel George Smith[55]. Landing at Deal, the Prince of Wales's Volunteers went into barracks, where, in a few days, they received orders to join a secret expedition to Copenhagen. Denmark had tried to remain neutral between England and France, but it had become known to the British intelligence service that, as agreed with the Emperor

---

[53] A draft of 240 men, mostly volunteers from the English Militia, joined from the Depot in September 1805; one hundred came from the 2nd/82nd in May 1806 and a further ninety in March 1807.

[54] Wood, p. 14.

[55] George Smith, who had assumed command of the newly-raised 2nd/82nd on 14th November 1804 from the half-pay of the 20th Regiment, had earned particular distinction in command of the 20th on the 1799 Helder expedition, where he was severely wounded, and in Egypt. He assumed command of the 1st/82nd on the retirement of Colonel Roger Coghlan on 15th August 1805. Coghlan, who had held the appointment for nearly nine years, retired on half-pay 'to attend to the recovery of his health', impaired by West Indian fevers and the damp Irish climate, but subsequently rose to the rank of lieutenant-general on the staff in Ireland. His biographical note in *The Royal Military Calendar, 1820*, states that 'He left the 82nd in the highest order and best state of discipline.'

Alexander in a secret clause of the Franco-Russian Treaty of Tilsit, Napoleon intended to seize the powerful Danish fleet, thereby making good his losses at Trafalgar and securing the strategically-important entrance to the Baltic. To prevent this imminent danger, Britain demanded that the Danes send their fleet into protective custody in British ports, and the Danes, quite naturally, refused. A British fleet of seventeen ships of the line and, twenty-one other warships, and a force of eighteen thousand troops were speedily assembled[56] under the command of Admiral Gambier and Lieutenant-General Lord Cathcart,[57] and the 82nd was allocated to Major-General Brent Spencer's 3rd Brigade of Sir David Baird's 2nd Division, together with the 32nd and 50th Regiments.

When a regiment fought in close order it was particularly vital that its leaders should remain steady and composed under fire, and so before the expedition to Copenhagen, Colonel Smith called a meeting of all his officers at Deal barracks to give them some salutary advice:

'Now, gentlemen, you are about to join a grand expedition; and if I mistake not, there is not one of you that has yet had the honour of seeing a shot fired from an enemy. It is therefore necessary to acquaint you that the whizzing of the balls is apt to cause a disagreeable sensation; but this, gentlemen, arises from a mistaken idea, for the moment you hear that sound the danger is past. You will not, therefore, show a bad example to the men by ducking your heads and flinching your bodies, for that is unsoldier-like and may cause a panic in the troops; but always keep the head up, the body erect, and even in danger show a pleasing and determined aspect, which may command respect and admiration in your men, and animate them to that glory which Britons have a right to anticipate.'[58]

The 82nd marched to Ramsgate for embarkation, and on the 26th and 27th of July, the expedition set sail from Yarmouth Roads for the Baltic, where they were joined by a further seven thousand of the King's German Legion from Rügen. On the morning of 16th August, Cathcart's troops landed without resistance at Vedbæk on the Island of Zealand, about twelve miles north of Copenhagen, towards which they marched the following day. Spencer's Brigade, whose transports had been sent further up the sound as a diversion, landed on the morning of the 17th at Skovshoved, four or five miles north of the town, and occupied ground near the coast on the left of the line of investment. About noon, the Danes attempted to dislodge Spencer's picquets; but their advance, though supported by gunboats, was easily frustrated.

The defences of Copenhagen appeared strong, but the city was inadequately garrisoned and apathetically commanded. Work on siege batteries was begun on the 18th. However, on the afternoon of the 24th, the garrison made a feeble attempt at a general sortie, and the British took advantage of their repulse at all points to occupy the suburbs of the city, which the Danes had imprudently left standing, in places within four hundred yards of the ramparts. It may have been on this occasion that Ensign John Mackay of the 82nd volunteered for and led the forlorn hope. The twenty-one-year-old officer came from County Antrim, and at his special request, the party for this desperate service was composed entirely of Irishmen.[59] Following this advance, the distant batteries were abandoned, and new ones erected much closer to the place.

According to the *Regimental Record of Service*, 'The 82nd formed the left of that part of the army which besieged the city of Copenhagen; and although the junior regiment, it occupied, by special order of the Major-General, the important post of the Windmill, on the extreme left, which it maintained during the whole of the operations.'

The 82nd behaved most creditably and were singled out for praise by Lord Cathcart for their tenacity and good work at the Swan Windmill (*Svane Moelle*) Battery, where Ensign Robert Dixon of the Colour party was killed, and Captain Charles Holland Hastings lost an arm in repulsing the most serious of the Danish sorties, while the Commanding Officer subsequently received the very unusual distinction of promotion and a knighthood. The following anecdote is from an officer of the 28th Foot:[60]

---

[56] Remarkably, only nine days elapsed between political decision and embarkation.
[57] By the time the expedition was fully assembled in Danish water it consisted of 65 warships and 377 transports, convoying some 27,000 troops.
[58] Wood, p. 15.
[59] Mackay served in the 82nd for 42 years, fighting throughout the Peninsula War and in Canada, and died in command of his Regiment, aged 62, in 1847.
[60] *Narrative of the Campaigns of the 28th Regiment*, Lieutenant-Colonel Charles Cadell.

'During the siege, that excellent officer, Colonel Smith, of the 82nd Regiment (afterwards Sir George), had a fortunate escape: he commanded at the Windmill Battery, on the left of the British line. One forenoon he was sitting in a chair close to the windmill, looking on the operations, when seeing something going wrong, he arose to give directions. At that instant a cannon shot from one of the Danish gun-boats broke the chair to pieces!'

We have an account of the siege from Harry Ross-Lewin of the 32nd, also in Brent Spencer's Brigade:

'Our first work was the erection of batteries. The troops bivouacked in the fields, building wigwams of branches of trees, and thatching them with sheaf corn. The Danish gunboats and praams threw heavy shot amongst us occasionally, but they did little damage.'[61]

'About the 25th [August] we began to work day and night, erecting mortar batteries within a quarter of a mile of the city. The weather was sultry, and the dews at night were very heavy. The Danes did not seem to be inclined to venture out; and the few that showed themselves were picked off by our riflemen.

'At length they made two sorties; the first along the lower road, near the beach, on the extreme left of our line, where a heavy battery [thirteen 24-pounders] had been lately erected [at the Windmill], and two field-pieces placed behind a traverse on the road by the British. Sir George Smith, a zealous and indefatigable officer, though in very bad health, had been stationed since the investment at this post, and soon repelled the attack; it was a point of much importance, as the battery covered the landing of our stores.'

This sortie, on the 31st of August, was led in person by the garrison commander, Major-General Peymann, with a force comprising three battalions of infantry, the chasseurs of the King's Guard, riflemen of other regiments, and huntsmen from the country; in all between two and three thousand men, supported by eight field guns and by praams, gunboats and floating batteries. The Danes moved out from their right, through a garden in front of the citadel, to destroy the British batteries on the flank where the 82nd stood. The advanced British pickets gallantly opposed their progress until Sir David Baird brought up supports and immediately drove in the enemy, who retired in confusion through the gates of the citadel. The British loss on this occasion was trifling, but the Danes lost nearly one hundred killed and wounded, General Peymann being among the latter.

It was probably on this occasion that Captain William Balfour of the 40th, Aide-de-Camp to Major-General Brent Spencer, had a horse shot under him. He had already been noted for his 'marked spirit and gallantry' during the Helder campaign, and his obituary states that at Copenhagen, 'by his uniform, zealous, and gallant conduct, [he] secured the esteem of his brethren in arms.' Many years later, he would command the 40th in New South Wales and Tasmania and then the 82nd on the island of Mauritius.

By 1st September, the British siege batteries were ready, and a summons was sent into the city. Lord Cathcart, who had little heart for coercing the neutral Danes and was anxious to avoid a bombardment, offered to spare the city and withdraw his troops on the surrender of the Danish fleet. His summons was naturally rejected, and so that evening, the British guns opened fire, causing widespread conflagration and numerous civilian casualties. On the 5th, the Danes asked for an armistice, and two days later, they capitulated, delivering up their fleet and naval stores to British control. It had been a sad necessity, comparable to the sinking of the French fleet at Oran during World War II.

Having borne the brunt of the siege, when Copenhagen and the Danish fleet surrendered, Spencer's brigade took possession of the arsenal and dockyard and were sent on board the prizes as marines. They remained there until the city was evacuated by the British force on 20th September and sailed home aboard British and Danish warships. Apart from the Danish fleet[62], some three and a half thousand artillery pieces and vast quantities of naval stores were captured, but in view of the fact that Britain and Denmark were, technically, not at war, prize money was restricted.

---

[61] 'On the 22nd three Danish prames, mounting 20 guns each, and from 28 to 30 gun-vessels, placed themselves in readiness to interrupt the army in the construction of some mortar batteries in advance of the Swan-Mill battery.' *The Naval History of Great Britain*, W. M. James, Vol. 4, p. 289.

[62] Seventeen Danish ships of the line were captured, together with fifteen frigates, six brigs and twenty-five gunboats. Indeed, so many British seamen were required to man the prizes that the troops had to assist the fleet to sail home. Exclusive of the valuable stores shipped on board British and Danish warships, 92 transports brought away full cargoes of masts, yards, timber, sails, cordage and other naval stores.

The loss of the Prince of Wales's Volunteers before Copenhagen amounted to one officer (Ensign Robert Dixon[63]) and seven rank and file killed, and two officers (Captain Charles Holland Hastings and Lieutenant John Souter) and seventeen men wounded. The high proportion of officer casualties suggests that they had taken to heart Colonel Smith's robust injunction at Deal.

The high-handed pre-emptive attack on avowedly neutral Denmark was of dubious international legality and attracted much high-minded criticism at the time, but as a military operation it must be accounted a major success. It had taken just seven weeks for the Army and Navy to effect the British Cabinet's decision to secure the Danish fleet. 'There never was,' wrote Castlereagh's secretary, 'an expedition of such magnitude so quickly got up, so secretly sent off, and which was conducted from the beginning to its termination with greater ability or success.' The result was a major upset to Napoleon, who had intended to combine all the maritime powers of Continental Europe against the Royal Navy.

Returning to England, five companies of the 82nd landed at Deal on 4th November and, after two days at Babourne-Lees, marched to Portsmouth, where the other five companies had disembarked. The reunited battalion was at once added to a force, commanded by Major-General Brent Spencer, for secret service and was accordingly brought up to strength with drafts from the 2nd Battalion and the Irish militia.

During the absence of the 1st Battalion on active service, the 2nd Battalion had successively moved to Hull, Bridlington and Scarborough. Whilst at the latter place, a newspaper correspondent reported how, on 30th July 1809, 'The band of the 2nd Battalion 82nd Regiment took their station on Sunday evening in Bean's Subscription Garden and added to the pleasure of the promenade... The only drawback to the full enjoyment of this beautiful spot is the unfavourable state of the weather. We have frequent showers which compel the fashionable to a precipitate retreat.'[64]

Whilst the 1st/82nd was on the Copenhagen expedition, Lieutenant Joseph Francis Delmont, commanding a recruiting party of the 82nd at Stroud, was the victim of a particularly scandalous duel. After dinner on 14th August 1807, the handsome 22-year-old officer went for a walk with Lieutenant Benjamin Heazle, an Irish officer of the Buffs, in the course of which the latter took offence at a jocular remark by Delmont about a lady. An instant apology was demanded and refused, at which Heazle demanded satisfaction, and the two officers agreed on a duel that same evening. The whole rushed business was badly managed by the standards of such affairs, with only one second (Lieutenant Sargeaunt), no surgeon and unmatched pistols (including a horse pistol). The result was that young Delmont was left mortally wounded on the field. He died on the 18th, having accused Heazle of shooting him in the back before he could turn around. The next day, a jury gave a verdict of wilful murder against Heazle and Sargeaunt, both of whom fled the country and died in exile.[65]

---

[63] The 1807 Army List names him as Alexander Dixon.

[64] *The Morning Chronicle*, London, August 5th 1809.

[65] Duelling remained endemic despite severe penalties. In 1811 Lieutenant Dominick French of the 47th was sentenced by a General Court Martial at Guernsey to be cashiered for provoking a duel on three occasions, twice with Assistant-Surgeon Scott and once with Ensign Howard. In 1814 Lieutenant William Scott of the 47th was sentenced by a General Court Martial at Bombay to be cashiered for challenging Lieutenant James Hutchinson to a duel, as was his second, Lieutenant Henry Pierard of the same regiment. The latter was, however, re-instated by order of the Prince Regent.

Light Company 40th in the breach at Monte Video
death of Captain Rennie

Private 47th Foot, 1806

Storming of Monte Video

Chapter II:
South America 1806-07

Expedition to Buenos Aires 1806 – Maldonaldo (47th) – Storming of Montevideo 1807 (40th and 47th) – Action of San Pedro (40th) – Advance and Attack on Buenos Aires (40th and 47th) – Evacuation.

Commodore Sir Home Popham, like many naval gentlemen in an age when fortunes could be made from prize money, had a buccaneering streak. Having been informed in April 1806 that the inhabitants of Montevideo and Buenos Aires would welcome a British landing to free them from Spanish rule, as commander of the naval squadron at the Cape, he took it upon himself, with the concurrence of Major-General Sir David Baird, to plan an expedition against those places.

Leaving Table Bay with a force of twelve hundred men under Major-General Beresford, he landed near Buenos Aires on 25th June that year and, dispersing a body of Spanish troops, he summoned the city. Buenos Aires capitulated on 2nd July, and treasure to the value of over one million dollars was shipped aboard one of Home Popham's frigates; but the victors were not to enjoy quiet occupation of their conquest. The Commodore had been misinformed as to the extent of South American disaffection, and on 10th August, an insurrection led by Colonel Liniers, a French officer in Spanish service, overwhelmed Beresford's little force and obliged him to surrender.

Maldonaldo, 1806-07

Meanwhile, on 9th April 1806, the 1st Battalion of the 47th Regiment had embarked at Cork for the East Indies, 803 strong with Lieutenant-Colonel Thomas Backhouse in command.[66] At Portsmouth, the battalion transhipped into three East Indiamen and sailed again on 14th May with a convoy which also included the 1st/30th. On arriving at the Cape of Good Hope, the 47th landed and was inspected by Sir David Baird, who selected it to form part of a reinforcement for the South American venture. This force, consisting of the 38th and 47th Regiments, three dismounted squadrons of dragoons and a company of the 54th, some 2,180 men in all, including 685 of the 47th, sailed from Simon's Bay on the 29th of August under the command of Colonel Backhouse.

On 12th October, these reinforcements reached the River Plate, where Sir Home Popham awaited them with the mortifying news of Beresford's defeat. Colonel Backhouse now found himself the senior military officer, off a strange and hostile shore, with no orders and no idea of British strategic intentions. After consultation with Home Popham, he decided to establish his little force ashore. An attempt on 28th October to assault Montevideo from the sea had to be called off when the ships could not come close enough inshore to silence the batteries, and the force then sailed for Maldonado, a small coastal town with a deep-water port some seventy miles to the southeast, which was considered a suitable place to occupy and await reinforcements or further instructions.

The British squadron anchored off Maldonado on 29th October, and Backhouse landed that evening with four hundred men, mostly of the 38th Foot under Lieutenant-Colonel Vassal[67]. Advancing through sandhills, he found six hundred Spaniards, mostly mounted militia with some light artillery, drawn up in front of the town. These were soon swept aside with the loss of fifty men and their guns, and the town capitulated. The coastal batteries and the fortified island of Garrita were subsequently taken by Vassal, securing a safe anchorage for the squadron.

The troops established themselves in the town, but their situation was precarious; Maldonado was untenable against serious attack, starvation was imminent, and the force had to fight for supplies, for the

---

[66] Thomas Joseph Backhouse entered the Army in 1780 and, after early service in the West Indies, in 1788 obtained a company in the 47th Regiment and was Major in 1797. A cautious officer, sometimes characterized as weak and irresolute, Backhouse assumed command of the 1st/47th in Bermuda on 6th June 1798. He later served in India and died a lieutenant-general at 87 Wimpole Street, London, aged 65, in 1828.
[67] Lieutenant-Colonel Spencer Thomas Vassal had served 1778-1801 in the 59th Regiment, including the Great Siege of Gibraltar and the 1794-95 campaign in the Low Countries before being appointed to command the 38th.

surrounding country was infested with enemy horsemen who harassed 'bullock-hunting' foraging parties. Their tactics were troublesome rather than dangerous: 'They ride up, dismount, fire over the backs of their horses, mount and gallop off.'[68]

On November 7th, the Light Company of the 47th were present at an action near the village of San Carlos, about seven miles north of Maldonaldo, in which the enemy were repulsed in hand-to-hand fighting and retreated in disorder.

Montevideo, 1807

Meanwhile, in Britain, widespread commercial avarice at the prospect of new markets overcame any ministerial annoyance at Home Popham's rash and unauthorised intervention in the affairs of South America, and oblivious of Beresford's defeat, the Ministry reacted to early reports of success by sending reinforcements.

In August 1806, both battalions of the 40th Regiment marched from Bexhill to Hilsea Barracks, Portsmouth, which they reached on the 15th. Next day, the 1st Battalion moved to Portsea Barracks, from where, on 16th September, they embarked on eight transports for the River Plate as part of a force of some four and a half thousand men under the veteran Sir Samuel Auchmuty[69]. The 40th was the strongest battalion, with 43 officers, 54 sergeants, 22 drummers and one thousand rank and file, commanded by Lieutenant-Colonel Gore Browne, an experienced officer of 26 years' service.[70] The 2nd/40th also embarked, bound for Ireland.[71]

Private William Lawrence of the Light Company 1st/40th, a strongly built youngster of fifteen, spent his last night ashore in Portsmouth:

'I naturally felt rather timid, as all young recruits must feel on entering so soon on foreign service, as I then found myself obliged to do. But the worst and most disheartening spectacle of all was in the morning when the bugle sounded for the assembly of the regiment; for only about six women to a company of a hundred men being allowed to go with us, many who were married had to leave wives and children behind, with the thought that it might never be their lot to see them again. When the order was given to embark, the scene was quite heartrending: I could not see a dry eye in Portsmouth… Husband and wife, father and child, young man and sweetheart, all had to part, and perhaps none were more affected than the last, though with least cause: it was indeed dreadful to view. I myself was much affected, but it was at the woes of others, for I had not one to throw so much as a parting glance at myself; and thus, amid the cheers of the crowd and with the band playing the tune of *The Girl I Left Behind Me*, we embarked.'[72] Among the families who accompanied the 40th were the pregnant wife and two-year-old child of Captain Peter Redmond Jennings, a Catholic officer who had joined the Regiment in 1804 from the Army of Reserve. Officially, Roman Catholics were not permitted to hold military commissions, but the prohibition was routinely disregarded, and Jennings, a devout and open Catholic, appears to have had no difficulty in practising his faith.

---

[68] Sir Samuel Auchmuty to the Secretary of State, 7th February 1807.

[69] Auchmuty (1756-1822), an American loyalist, had seen much active service in America, India and Egypt before being appointed to command the reinforcements for South America. His later services included the capture of Java, when the 59th Regiment earned great distinction under his command. Auchmuty was deservedly respected by the men of the 40th, who considered him a most excellent commander. William Lawrence observed that 'He always delighted in a good rough-looking soldier with a long beard and greasy haversack, who he thought was the sort of man most fit to meet the enemy.'

[70] Gore Browne was commissioned in 1780 and joined the 40th as a lieutenant-colonel in 1799, serving with the Regiment in Holland, Malta and South America. At Walcheren he commanded a brigade and was severely wounded. He was afterwards GOC Western District at Plymouth and became a full general in 1837. In 1820 he became Colonel of the 44th, and the destruction of that regiment in the famous Afghanistan disaster of 1842 greatly affected him. He died at Weymouth on 18th January 1843, aged 80. He was described by contemporaries as 'an elegant soldier' and 'an accomplished gentleman.'

[71] It appears that the Depot 40th Regiment remained in the Hastings area until the early summer of 1808, when it was ordered to Dublin, a stay so long that the Regiment became jocularly known as the 'Sussex Rangers' and the 'Hastings Guards' (Hibbert papers).

[72] *The Autobiography of Sergeant William Lawrence, a Hero of the Peninsula and Waterloo Campaigns*, ed. George Nugent Bankes, 1886, p.p. 17-18.

The convoy sailed from Spithead on 20th September but, owing to contrary winds, put into Cowes Roads and Yarmouth before reaching Plymouth on the 25th. Here, they took on water and provisions before sailing on 7th October for Falmouth, where the expedition was assembled.

The transports sailed on 9th October, escorted by HMS *Ardent*, 64, two frigates and two sloops. By the evening of the 14th, they were in the Bay of Biscay where, as Captain Peter Jennings recorded, 'the weather now became boisterous, with a foul wind which increased every moment in violence and in the morning became a perfect storm threatening every instant to plunge us into a watery grave, but from which Divine Providence was pleased to rescue us, and we received no other damage from the gale than the inconvenience and personal fear it caused us. Towards morning of the 15th, the wind having moderated, allowed us to observe the scatter'd situation of the convoy, and we discover'd two sail thereof missing, which we found to be the *Daphne* frigate and *Tuscan* transport, this latter having 150 of the 40th on board including one major, three captains, four subalterns and one assistant surgeon, for whose unknown fate many fears and doubts presented themselves to our minds.'

William Lawrence, together with many of his comrades, was seasick for nearly a week, but, as he remarked, when their appetites returned, they could readily have eaten 'a donkey with a hamper of greens.' He went on to describe the voyage to South America, including on 26th November the rough nautical ceremony of Crossing the Line:

'We had good weather until we reached the tropics, when a dead calm followed for a fortnight. As we were nearly upon the Equinoctial Line, the usual ceremony of shaving took place, which was no doubt very amusing to those who escaped by treating the sailors to a bottle of rum or those who had crossed the Line before; but to us on whom the barber, who was the sailor who had crossed the Line most often, operated, it was not so pleasant... A large tub of water was placed on deck, and each one who was to be performed on sat in turn on the edge; then the barber stepped forward and lathered his face all over with the tar and grease and with a piece of iron hoop as razor scraped it off again; after which he pushed him backwards into the tub, leaving him to crawl out anyhow and sneak off to clean himself. All passed very well, however, as there was plenty of rum provided to drink from those officers and men who were more disposed to join in the pay than the play.

'During the calms, we amused ourselves fishing for dolphins, and practising for the first time with ball-cartridge, a bottle being corked and flung overboard as far as possible to serve as a target, and a dollar being offered to the first man who could break it, each firing once. No one broke it, but I got a glass of grog from the major for being the nearest; so near that I made the bottle spin round. The major remarked that if I went so close as that to a Spaniard, I should make him shake; and he likewise asked me what trade I was in before I joined the Army. As I knew I was too far from England now to be sent back, I told him that I was a builder's apprentice; and he only said, "Well done, my boy, so you prefer knocking down houses in the enemy's country to putting them up in your own?" '[73]

On 14th December the fleet anchored off Rio de Janeiro to water, take in provisions and make repairs. The 40th went ashore, where they were reviewed by the exiled Queen of Portugal, who had taken refuge in her Brazilian colony from the French occupation of her homeland. Next day, she sent a quantity of onions and pumpkins on board as a present, which was well received by the troops. 'It is dreadful hot here,' recorded Private John Kibby of the 40th, 'and very unhealthful.' Captain Peter Jennings and his wife went ashore for the christening at the Benedictine Monastery of their new baby son, born at sea the previous week.

'We experienced much attention and civility from the Viceroy and inhabitants during our short stay,' he wrote in his journal, 'which must be ever remembered by us with gratitude. Some instances of misconduct occurred on the part of our soldiers when on shore, but which had no serious consequences and only originated in intoxication, and I trust may not have left any bad impression of the British general character on the minds of our hospitable and friendly allies of this city.'

After a fortnight in Rio, Auchmuty sailed south to Maldonaldo, where on 5th January 1807, he found Backhouse's little force, isolated for three months and short of provisions, which he took under command. Backhouse may not have been among the more brilliant officers in the Service, and indeed, Popham accused him

---

[73] Ibid., p.p. 18-20. The officer mentioned in this anecdote would have been Major Donald Campbell.

of 'turpitude,' but he had at least established and maintained a base for future operations. Also at Maldonaldo, the 40th were relieved to find their missing transport, *Tuscan*, safely at anchor and all aboard her well.

Auchmuty now had some six thousand men; not enough to recapture Buenos Aires, he decided, but sufficient to make an attempt on Montevideo, where the defences were reported to be weak and the garrison irresolute. Even this was no easy matter, for the British force was ill-equipped for a siege, with no battering-train or sappers, little ammunition and powder, and few entrenching tools. Nor were his troops all of the best quality: the experienced 38th and 40th Regiments were excellent, but the 87th was full of boys, and the 47th, who had seen no campaign service since Saratoga thirty years before, were in indifferent order.[74]

Inaction, however, was not an option, and on the 13th, Auchmuty evacuated Maldonaldo and sailed up the Plate estuary. Early on the morning of the 16th, covered by a naval bombardment, the 40th Foot took part in an assault, landing in a little bay to the west of the Caretas rocks, about nine miles below Montevideo. It was William Lawrence's first action:

'Boats were ordered alongside the troopships to convey us on shore, which movement, as the enemy was on the banks about fifteen thousand strong to receive us, put rather a nasty taste into our mouths, there seeming nothing but death or glory before us. The signal was hoisted from the admiral's ship, and we started for the shore amid the fire of the enemy's artillery. They killed and wounded a few of our men and sank some of the boats, but as soon as we struck the shore, we jumped out and, forming line in the water, fired a volley and charged, soon driving them from their position on the bank. We found even as early as then that the Spaniards were not very difficult to encounter.'[75]

That night, Auchmuty posted his army under cover of a range of sandhills to cover the landing of supplies and guns, the latter being hauled forward by sailors as there were no horses. At 2 a.m. on the 19th he was ready to advance across a grassy plain towards Montevideo, with his light troops leading and the 47th bringing up the rear. The Spanish Viceroy, with over 2,500 men, disputed the ground for a couple of hours, but a brief cannonade and a charge sufficed to sweep them away, and they retreated in great disorder.

Montevideo stood on a granite peninsula, surrounded on three sides by water, and that night, Auchmuty halted his main body on heights about two miles east of the town, encamped in a line of tents and bullock-hide bivouacs stretching from sea to sea, cutting all landward communication. An outlying picket was pushed forward into the demolished eastern suburbs, almost to the walls of the town. The troops were delighted to find that in the ruined suburbs were orchards of peach, lemon, nectarine, fig and orange trees. 'The country around,' recalled Lawrence, 'abounded with ducks, geese, turkeys, fowls, and plenty of sheep and bullocks, which it may be made sure our men found oftentimes very providential.'

At 6 a.m. the following morning, the enemy made a sortie from the town with about three thousand men and four guns under the Spanish General Bernardo Lecocq, which advanced in two columns to attack the forward troops. The column on the right, consisting of 600 cavalry, threatened to turn Auchmuty's left flank and cut him off from the fleet. On the left, some 2,400 infantry, under Lecocq himself, came out along the Camino Reale through the eastern suburbs, where they were initially checked by the British picquets, four hundred strong, but these were in danger of being overwhelmed. According to Lawrence, the British troops were horrified when two wounded grenadiers of the 40th, left behind as the picquets withdrew, were 'deliberately cut to pieces' by the Spaniards.

Colonel Gore Browne, in charge of the suburbs, ordered up three companies of the 40th, under Major Donald Campbell, to support the picquets and check the Spanish advance. Campbell formed his men across the road in a marshy hollow among 20-foot-high bullrushes. When Lecocq appeared, Campbell's heavily outnumbered companies made a gallant bayonet charge into the head of the Spanish column, but they were firmly received, and great numbers fell on both sides before the enemy began to inch back. The Spanish infantry were then suddenly and unexpectedly attacked in flank by a body of Auchmuty's light troops, including the Light Companies of the 40th and 47th, who burst from a peach grove with three cheers and charged with fixed bayonets. Lecocq's column gave way, and his disordered men were pursued with great slaughter into the town. The Spanish

---

[74] At Maldonaldo the army was brigaded, with the 38th, 40th and 87th Regiments in the First Brigade under Colonel Gore Browne, the 47th and 71st under Lieutenant-Colonel Backhouse, and the light troops and cavalry under Brigadier-General Lumsden.
[75] Lawrence, p.p. 20-21.

cavalry retired without drawing swords, their departure hastened by a devastating broadside from HMS *Encounter*. It was all over by about 8.30 a.m. In the words of Private John Kibby of the 40th, 'we gave them a sweet brushing.'

At least three hundred Spaniards were killed and as many captured in this affair[76], sometimes known as the battle of El Cristo del Cardal, while the British loss amounted to 25 dead and up to one hundred wounded. The three companies of the 40th bore the brunt of the casualties, which included Lieutenant Timothy FitzPatrick and twelve men killed and Major Campbell and Captain Thomas Rogers slightly wounded. Captain Jennings reckoned the casualties of the 40th at 'between eighty and a hundred men killed and wounded.' Following this action, there were no more sorties from the town and the Spanish Viceroy, who had been approaching Montevideo with a large relief force, retired and left the garrison to its fate.

There is in the National Army Museum a Regimental Medal awarded on this occasion by Major Campbell to Sergeant H. Bowles of the 40th 'For Gallantry on the Field Jan. 20th. 1807.'

The fortifications of Montevideo consisted of a stone wall some four feet thick and fifteen feet high, with batteries mounting 160 pieces of artillery, of which 75 were on the landward side. This side was further strengthened by a bastioned citadel astride the peninsula, the town walls falling obliquely away from it for a thousand yards north and south, each side pierced by a gateway. The bedrock on the approaches was close to the surface, so Auchmuty had little prospect of conducting a regular siege even if he had possessed the resources.

The British landed a number of 24-pounder guns from the ships, and on 25th January, the first two batteries were opened, and naval vessels came close inshore to cannonade the town. Finding that the garrison was not to be intimidated into surrender, Auchmuty constructed a further battery against the citadel, which was equally ineffectual. He then decided that the only prospect of success was to erect a battery as close as possible to the town wall by the south gate, near the sea, and endeavour to breach it. Six 24-pounders were established within six hundred yards of the wall, and although they were exposed to a very heavy fire from the defenders, a breach was reported practicable on 2nd February. A summons was sent under a flag of truce to the Governor that same evening, demanding his surrender. No answer was received, so orders were given for an assault on the breach an hour before daybreak the following morning.

During the bombardment, Sergeant William Luxton of the Light Company 40th received the following mention in General Orders, dated 2nd February 1807:

'The Commander of the forces, in publishing to the Army the gallant conduct of Sergeant Luxton of the Fortieth Regiment, who took up a live shell which fell among his comrades in the advanced battery and threw it over the parapet, where it burnt without doing injury to any of them, adds his best thanks for the very spirited behaviour this brave soldier evinced upon that occasion.'

For this act of selfless bravery, Sergeant Luxton was also awarded a special Regimental Medal, depicting a burning shell on one side and Montevideo on the other.

Colonel Gore Browne was appointed to command the assault troops, which were formed in two columns of attack. The principal attack, against the breach near the South Gate, was to be made by the Light Infantry of the army, two companies of Grenadiers led by Major Donald Campbell, and two companies of Rifles, with the 40th, under Major John Dalrymple, and the 38th in support. Another column on the right, composed of the 87th and one company of Rifles, was posted near the North (San Pedro) Gate, ready to enter when it was opened from within when the storming troops had cut their way through the town. The main body of the 47th, with other troops, protected the rear.

The British troops were ordered under arms at 11 p.m., and, at about midnight, marched to their assembly positions. At about three o'clock on the morning of 3rd February, the infantry moved silently forward to the assault. It was a pitch-black night. The left column had to traverse difficult ground, and in the dark, the head of the column missed the breach. A sudden flare illuminated the attacking troops, at which the approaches were swept at close range by a murderous flanking fire of grapeshot and musketry, in particular from a demi-bastion which commanded the breach at less than two hundred yards range. When the breach was eventually discovered by Captain Charles Renny of the 40th Light Company, it was found to be barricaded with rolled hides. Renny fell

---

[76] Lecocq estimated his casualties in the sortie at 700 killed, wounded and captured, while British estimates of the Spanish loss ranged up to 1,500.

dead as he mounted the rubble, but the Light Infantry followed his lead and forced their way up and through the narrow passage, which would admit but three men abreast, jumping down 12-15 feet into the town. The Grenadiers were next to swarm up the breach. The main body of the 40th then came up; they, too, missed the breach at first and suffered severe losses, including their commander, John Dalrymple, before it was pointed out to them by Lieutenant Harry Smith, the future General Sir Harry Smith.

Over four hundred British soldiers fell in and around the breach, but once it was gained, the Spaniards gave way, and numbers of them were bayoneted, while a French detachment defending the breach was annihilated. Once in the town, the 'Light Bobs' turned to their right and made for the bastion behind the citadel, where the Governor had taken post; having refused quarter, he was mortally wounded, and there was a great slaughter of the garrison. Meanwhile, the 87th, impatient to join the fight, had scaled the northern wall to occupy the San Pedro Gate[77], and the Grenadiers under Campbell, turning left from the breach, had carried all the batteries in that direction at bayonet point.[78] The entire town was soon in British hands except the citadel, which made a show of resistance before surrendering at 5 a.m.

The following account is an extract from Sir Samuel Auchmuty's despatch:

'At the appointed hour, the troops marched to the assault; they approached near the breach before they were discovered, when a destructive fire from every gun that could be brought to bear upon it, and from the musketry of the garrison, opened upon them. Heavy as it was, our loss would have been comparatively trifling if the breach had been open; but during the night, and under our fire, the enemy had barricaded it with hides, so as to render it nearly impracticable. The night was extremely dark. The head of the column missed the breach, and when it was approached it was so shut up that it was mistaken for the untouched wall. In this situation, the troops remained under a heavy fire for a quarter of an hour, when the breach was discovered by Captain Renny of the 40th Light Infantry, who pointed it out, and gloriously fell as he mounted it. Our gallant soldiers rushed to it and difficult as it was of access, forced their way into the town. Cannon were placed at the heads of the principal streets, and the fire for a short time was destructive; but the troops advanced in all directions, clearing the streets and batteries with their bayonets and overturning their cannon. The 40th Regiment with Colonel Browne followed; they also missed the breach and twice passed through the fire of the batteries before they found it.'

Private William Lawrence of the 40th, aged only 16, was with the Light Infantry stormers, receiving a slight leg wound which kept him on light duties for a fortnight:

'The ladders were placed against the hides of earth, and we scaled them under a heavy fire from the Spaniards. We found the earth better stuff to encounter than stone, and though our poor captain fell in the breach whilst nobly leading on his men, we succeeded in forcing our way into the town, which was soon filled with the reinforcements that followed us. We drove the enemy from the batteries and massacred with sword and bayonet all whom we found carrying arms: the General's orders being not to plunder or enter any house, or injure any woman, child, or man not carrying arms, or fire a shot until daylight… When the heat of the fighting was subsided, the drums beat to assembly in the square, and orders were then given for the massacre to be stayed, but that all the prisoners were to be taken that we could lay our hands on.'[79]

Captain Peter Jennings of the 40th painted a similar picture in his journal:

'Owing to the extreme darkness of the night, the breach was with much difficulty discerned, and it was rendered less perceptible from the chasm having been filled up from within by hides and other materials so as to bring it up to its former level, but the advance party, having once scaled it by means of scaling ladders and throwing down the newly raised work, rendered the passage free for those following. The greater part of the storming force made good their entrance by it before daylight, altho' opposed by a commanding fire of great guns and musketry from the batteries and principal streets leading to it.

'The scene within was now dreadful: our troops dealt carnage wherever they moved, carrying everything before them… The 40th Regt. twice missed the road to the breach and were exposed to a most destructive fire of

---

[77] Lieutenant Dudley St. Leger Hill, formerly of the 82nd, commanded the scaling party that took possession of the San Pedro Gate. Lieutenant Tade Heatley of the Light Company 47th had volunteered for the Forlorn Hope, but his services were not accepted.
[78] Major Donald Campbell of the 40th, who distinguished himself both in the action of 20th January and the storming, later received a Patriotic Fund vase valued at £100 for his services in the campaign.
[79] Lawrence, p. 24.

grape from the Citadel and Shot Yard batteries: however, when they got into the town, they made good for the delay and in the course of an hour after their entrance the town and citadel were entirely in our possession. The slaughter on both sides was immense but not greater than might be expected from the gallant manner with which the town was defended and the no less valiant and determined manner [in which] it was attacked. Great credit was due to the conquerors for their orderly and good conduct after the assault: the moment the town was in our possession all further hostilities ceased on both sides and in the course of that same day everything appeared as quiet within the walls as in time of profound peace.'

According to Auchmuty's report, upwards of two thousand Spanish officers and men were taken prisoner, while about eight hundred were killed and five hundred were wounded. The remainder of the garrison fled in boats or hid in the town. 'Two hours after the assault,' wrote a Spanish witness, 'a profound and deathlike silence reigned throughout the city. No object was to be seen save the scattered bodies of the slain and wounded.'

British losses were not light: six officers and 110 men were killed, and 21 officers and 258 men were wounded. The composite Light Battalion suffered worst of all, with 63 killed and 84 wounded – perhaps half its effective strength. We do not have the full casualty list of the 40th Regiment, but it included three officers killed, two died of wounds, and another five seriously wounded[80], while throughout the operations at Montevideo, the 40th had a total of 18 men killed and 76 wounded. Total losses of the 47th Regiment at Montevideo were recorded as three men killed and sixteen wounded. In neither case do the regimental totals include the considerable casualties incurred by their detached Light Companies.

Furious and bloody as the assault on Montevideo had been, the British troops generally obeyed their commander's strict injunction to spare the inhabitants and their property, and Auchmuty was able to report that 'early in the morning the town was quiet, and the women were peaceably walking in the streets.' Such slight disorder as occurred, due to the inhabitants handing out liquor to the troops, was apparently of 'trifling consequence and soon checked.' This was largely due to the decisive efforts of Gore Browne and his officers, who took immediate action to prevent the terrible excesses which almost invariably took place after a storming. The Cavildo, magistrates of Montevideo, later presented Browne with an elaborate address expressing their profound gratitude:

'On the morning of the assault, you, Sir, entered this city with the general command of the troops. At this eventful period, the Cavildo, in awful suspense, were assembled at the hall of the capitol, in momentary expectation of death from enraged and victorious soldiery, who had burst open the doors and were rushing in with all the fury inspired by success. From the impending bayonet, we were rescued by the great exertions of a gallant and amiable officer, who fortunately came in at the instant and preserved us at the hazard of his own person. You, Sir, were presented to us by him and received from our hands the sword and insignia of justice. You had the generosity to return them immediately to our possession. You requested us to return to our hall, and placed a guard at the gates for our protection. You pledged your word for our safety and secured our persons from the smallest insult or affront.

'In the first moment of confusion, some trifling excess was committed; but, the same day, in the great square of the city, the perpetrators of this excess were publicly chastised with the utmost severity; and alone at the earnest entreaties of some of the Cavildo were you induced to pardon the lives of two offenders who were condemned to die.

'Every article, however small and insignificant, found in the possession of any soldier or sailor, was sent to the Cavildo that it might be restored, if possible, to its proper owner. Families were treated with the utmost

---

[80] Major John Dalrymple, Captain Charles Renny and Lieutenant Thomas Alston were killed; Lieutenants Hugh Wallace and Alexander Cameron died of wounds; Captains Thomas Rogers and John Whetham (right leg amputated), and Lieutenants James Johnston, Charles Lewis Ramus and Charles Harvey Smith were seriously wounded. Lieutenant-Colonel Vassal of the 38th (late of the 59th) also died of his wounds, and Lieutenant Thomas Backhouse of the Light Company 47th was wounded. John Whetham, despite losing a leg, continued to serve in the 40th and died a major-general in 1853. James Johnston, aged 17, who had volunteered from the 2nd Battalion to join the expedition, was so badly wounded that he was confined to bed for eight months; the following year, although still unable to march, he embarked with the 1st/40th for Portugal and Colonel Kemmis allowed him to ride, enabling him to be present at the battles of Roliça, Vimiero and Talavera. He subsequently gained great distinction in command of Portuguese troops and was wounded at Albuera. The Patriotic Fund made grants to most of the wounded officers and to six wounded men of the 40th – Richard Darte, Edmond Sorell, William Petty, Edward Wilson, John Backhouse and Joseph Guppey – in appreciation of their gallantry.

tenderness and respect. The pride of victorious troops, who had just conquered a city and entered through blood and fire, was in a moment suppressed, and their exultation reduced to quiet and tranquillity. At no time since that period have they caused the least disturbance or vexation to the inhabitants.'

Colonel Gore Browne was appointed Governor of the town, and in order to encourage the townspeoples' return to normality, William Lawrence recalled, 'our general issued a proclamation that they should open their shops and carry on their business as usual: and if any declined to open, he was kind enough to send parties to do it for them.' Within hours of the town's capture, a naval officer happened to pass a grocer's shop in which he observed a soldier of the 40th Regiment:

'Fearing that so immediately after an assault the soldier might be about to commit some exaction from the grocer, curiosity induced him to wait, unperceived, until he should ascertain the man's intentions, when to his great astonishment and satisfaction he saw the grocer deliver a quantity of sugar to the soldier, who taking out a dollar desired him to pay himself, and on receiving the change put it into his pocket with the remark only – "Well, dear enough, too!" '

Private John Kibby of the 40th confirms the good order maintained by the troops after the storming of Montevideo and their subsequent good relations with the inhabitants:

'We had strict orders not drink too much. But we could not help disobeying the orders because the ladies, even on the day we took the city, did give us to eat and drink. And indeed, for all the time that we were there, there was not one murder committed, neither by them nor us. Indeed, they are a people I dearly love.'

Captain Peter Jennings, who lodged his family in Montevideo throughout the occupation, was equally impressed by the conduct of its inhabitants:

'From the period of our entrance into the town until our departure, the general tenor of their behaviour was such as to gain the esteem of their conquerors, and in no instance during our stay there were they known to have departed from the strictest rules of conduct of citizens and loyal subjects, and at all times appeared perfectly satisfied with the government of their conquerors, and at our departure evinced the strongest marks of regret at returning to the government of their native country. From the monks of the Order of St. Francis myself and my family in particular experienced innumerable marks of kindness and beneficence.'

Fraternisation had its complications: Sergeant Henry Goodfellow of the 40th was seduced into deserting by the offer of a large bounty, but as he left the town in disguise, he was recognised by Auchmuty himself, brought back, and court-martialed the following day. Colonel Gore Browne begged for the sergeant's life, and, on account of the regiment's good conduct in the field, the capital sentence was changed to transportation for life. Such temptations were not rare, as William Lawrence recalled: 'I was myself offered a fortune by a Spanish gentleman, together with his daughter, if I would desert and remain in the country.'

In his despatch, Auchmuty commended Colonel Gore Browne for conducting the siege 'with great judgement and determined bravery' and wrote:

'The gallantry displayed by the troops during the assault and their forbearance and orderly behaviour in the town speaks so fully in their praise that it is unnecessary for me to say how highly I am pleased with their conduct. The service they have been engaged in since we landed has been uncommonly severe and laborious, but not a murmur has escaped them; everything I wished has been effected with order and cheerfulness.'

The 40th subsequently received royal authority to bear the Battle Honour 'MONTEVIDEO' on their Colours and appointments 'in commemoration of the gallantry evinced at the capture of that place on the 3rd February 1807.'

News of the storming of Montevideo reached Lieutenant William Hibbert of the 2nd/40th at Kinsale, from where, on 29th April, he wrote to his parents: 'You must have seen by the papers what a great loss our regiment has sustained. The greatest part of my brother officers who fell were very fine young men, with whom I had always been on habits of intimacy. The officers of the second battalion all wore black crepe on their arms for their loss.' Hibbert expected to be sent out to South America with the next draft, but meanwhile, was busy recruiting from the Militia, a duty he did not enjoy: 'I am so tormented by a set of vagabond soldiers, to whom I am sent to make fine speeches to induce them to volunteer into our regiment, that I can scarcely sit down to anything.'

Action of San Pedro, 7th June 1807

After the storming of Montevideo, Sir Samuel Auchmuty strengthened his position by sending out detachments to watch the enemy and obtain supplies while he waited for further reinforcement. Lieutenant-Colonel Backhouse of the 47th was despatched with two hundred men to Canalones, some twenty miles north of Montevideo, while another party commanded by Lieutenant-Colonel Dennis Pack was sent to occupy the small port of Colonia-di-Sacramento, on the north shore of the River Plate and opposite Buenos Aires. On 22nd April, the enemy made an unsuccessful attempt to surprise Pack's detachment, and early in May 1807, six companies of the 40th under Major Donald Campbell were sent by sea to reinforce Colonia, disembarking there on the 16th. The remaining four companies of the Regiment, under Captain Peter Jennings, followed on 17th May, joining Pack on the 23rd. Major Campbell commanded the 40th at Colonia as Colonel Gore Browne remained in Montevideo as Governor.

The isolated troops at Colonia were constantly threatened with attack, and on the evening of 6th June, Colonel Pack received intelligence that a Spanish force was encamped at San Pedro, some twelve miles away. An account of the ensuing action is given in Pack's despatch:

'I resolved upon moving to attack him, and commenced my march accordingly at 3 o'clock the next morning, with a force of one thousand and thirteen rank and file.[81] We arrived at St. Pedro at 7 o'clock and found the enemy strongly posted on an eminence, with his front and flanks secured by a deep and marshy river, over which there was only one pass, scarcely practicable, and that defended by four six-pounders and two howitzers. The bravery of the troops soon overcame all difficulties; they crossed the ford reduced to a front of less than sections, many up to their middles, and under a heavy fire from the artillery. After effecting the passage, the troops formed and advanced to the attack without firing a shot; the enemy's cavalry soon gave way, but the infantry, to my surprise, stood until we approached within 30 paces when they fled in disorder, throwing away their arms and ammunition, and leaving us in possession of their guns and camp, with one standard and 105 prisoners (including one lieutenant-colonel, one major, two captains and two lieutenants). Had it been possible to bring our guns and cavalry across the ford, I am confident that we should have taken or destroyed the whole force of the enemy, which consisted of upwards of one thousand men. The chief loss fell on the 40th Regiment, which corps supported most gallantly its well-established character.'

In addition to the prisoners, the Spanish lost 120 dead and seven guns. Total British casualties amounted to two privates killed, both of the 40th and ten men wounded, of whom four were from the Regiment. The men of the 40th gave ten dollars from their prize money to each of the widows.

In later years, William Lawrence recorded his own reminiscences of this engagement, which added some interesting and graphic detail to Pack's official account:

'We were called under arms at midnight and supplied with half a pound of beef for each man; the order then being given to return to our lodgings for two hours, and at the end of that time to fall in again… A little after two in the morning, we left the town with an Indian for our guide. We asked, in the best manner that we could, where we were going to, but all we could understand from him was that we were on the way to fight some Spaniards, which, of course, we had pretty well guessed before, and that we should have some four or five thousand of them to encounter. This last bit of news made us think that we were going to have hard nuts to crack, but we found them a very cowardly sort of folk to deal with, for after marching some five or six miles, we despatched skirmishing parties, who fell in with their pickets and took a few prisoners, and soon made the others retreat without doing anything further than to send up some rockets to alarm the body of the enemy.

'We marched on still further till we came nearly up to them, when we found a river in our way; fortunately, it was not very deep, so we waded through it under a fire from the Spanish cannon, which killed two of our men while in the act of crossing; and as soon as we were over we formed line and advanced towards the enemy, who lay on some fine rising ground in our front. They had some few pieces of cannon with them and opened the first fire with both cannon and musketry, but every shot seemed to rise over our heads, and I don't think that volley

---

[81] Including the 40th (481) under Major Campbell, 95th (200) and three companies of Light Infantry (247). Lieutenant Thomas Backhouse of the 47th accompanied the force as Pack's staff officer, and Lieutenant Dudley St. Leger Hill, formerly of the 82nd was also present, commanding a company of the 95th Rifles.

killed a man. We were up and at them like dragons, wounding and taking their general with about a hundred and fifty other prisoners; likewise, a stand of colours, three pieces of cannon, and their baggage. Moreover, we found a nice breakfast cooking for us in the shape of fowls, geese, turkeys, beef, rice, and *calavancos* (though the latter were rather too warm with cayenne pepper and garlic), all of which the enemy had had to leave in his hurry, and which came in very acceptably at the end of a large march.'[82]

Captain Peter Jennings of the 40th also left an account of this battle:

'About daybreak, we came in sight of the enemy camp, situate on a rising ground with a deep morass or river in their front and apparently well supported by a considerable train of field artillery. The name of the position occupied by the enemy was San Pedro, distant about five leagues from Colonia, and by the time we reached it, the troops were much fatigued but at the same time eager for action. The enemy were drawn up in order of battle and in all appearance determined to receive us in the warmest manner.

'As we approached within cannon shot of their line, we were commanded from eight field pieces and two howitzers, which however did little execution, and we passed the morass without much loss. As soon as the troops had all passed, they moved briskly up and formed line under cover of the rising ground on which the enemy's force was posted. As soon as formed, they charged up the hill with great gallantry and halted within fifty paces of the enemy, who now received them with a warm fire of musketry and a discharge of all their guns, which was returned by the British troops by a discharge of file fire from left to right, accompanied by a general huzza and, at the same time, charging up the hill. The enemy now gave way and fled in all directions, leaving us masters of all their artillery except two small 3-pounders. The whole of their ammunition, camp equipment, etc, became also ours, and we returned to Colonia at 6 o'clock that evening with four 6-pounders, two howitzers and a standard of one of their battalions, together with an immense booty made by our troops. The ammunition was destroyed for want of means of bringing it off. We made one hundred and six prisoners, including six officers. Our loss was trifling, having only 23 wounded, some few of whom afterwards died of their wounds.'

'The thanks of the Commander in Chief were in a few days after communicated to the garrison of Colonia for their spirited conduct in this affair, and the usual gratuity of Gun Money was immediately distributed to the troops employed therein.'

In the aftermath of the action, while the British were plundering the Spanish stores, a careless spark from a looted cigar caused the explosion of an ammunition wagon, injuring twenty men, mostly of the 95th, and in another incident, young William Lawrence had a narrow escape:

'I entered one of the enemy's storehouses, at one end of which a quantity of bullocks' hides were lying, at a sufficient distance from the wall to allow a man to pass or hide behind them; and there beside the heap stood a Spaniard whom I knew well, as he had sold cakes to us while we were at Colonia, and who now offered me a pot of honey to eat. I had my misgivings, however, so made a motion for him to eat first, for fear of poison; and at the same time, casting my eye to the left, I saw a Spaniard emerge from between the hides and the wall with a pistol, which he levelled at me. I became pretty active, as may be supposed under the circumstances, and managed to guard it off; but the shot whizzed very close to my head nevertheless, which made me very much enraged with the man and determined he should not escape. Unfortunately for him, one of our dismounted cavalry, an Irishman, came in, and on my telling him there was a Spaniard behind the hides, who had just fired a pistol at me, "Tare an' 'ounds," says he, "I'll fetch him out; you stand at one end to stop him with your bayonet while I drive him out." So Paddy went round with his sword, and after a little exercise behind, "Look out, comrade," he sang out, "he's coming"; and sure enough, I skewered him to the wall by driving my bayonet right through his body, while Paddy came out and finished him by splitting his head nearly in two with his heavy sword, remarking as he did it, "Bad luck to ye, I don't think ye'll ever shoot another Englishman, or Irishman either." The other man had meanwhile made off.'[83]

Meanwhile, Colonel Backhouse's little detachment at the village of Canalones was in trouble, surrounded by 1,400 Spaniards by whom, on 11th June, they were summoned to surrender. Faced with such overwhelming strength, Backhouse withdrew the following day towards Montevideo. However, on nearing the town, he met a

---

[82] Lawrence, p.p. 31-32.
[83] Ibid., p.p. 33-34.

relief force, the 9th Light Dragoons; whereupon he turned about, and the two bodies advanced and forced the enemy to retire.

Buenos Aires. 1807

A further eighteen hundred British reinforcements had now reached Montevideo, together with a new commander. Lieutenant-General John Whitelocke was not an obvious choice for this important independent command. The bastard son of Lord Aylesbury's steward, he had made a good marriage and had shown some talent in the West Indies, his only experience of active service, but his appointment owed more to powerful patrons than ability. 'His most objectionable characteristic,' wrote Fortescue, 'seems to have been arrogant but spasmodic self-confidence, with an affectation of coarse speech and manners which he conceived to be soldier-like bluntness, but which often degenerated into mere rudeness towards some of his inferiors and familiar obscenity of language towards others. He stooped to court the favour of the rank and file by affected use of their phrases, with the inevitable effect that he earned only their thorough contempt.' It soon became clear that, for all his demotic bluster, Whitelocke's modest military competence hardly extended to tactics, logistics, or, indeed, leadership. He was, in short, a sorry replacement for the capable Auchmuty. His second-in-command, Major-General Leveson Gower, was to prove an equally poor choice.

Whitelocke determined to attack Buenos Aires with the greater part of his force, leaving Colonel Gore Browne in command at Montevideo with a garrison of 1,350, including the battalion companies of the 47th (which then numbered 685 rank and file).[84] The troops selected for this enterprise sailed up the Plate estuary from Montevideo to Colonia, which was reached on 24th June. There, the 40th and the Light Battalion embarked on the 26th, at which the whole force crossed the River Plate to Ensenada de Barragon, some thirty miles below Buenos Aires.

Whitelocke had some nine thousand men, organised into four brigades under Auchmuty, Craufurd, Lumley and Mahon. The Light Companies of the 40th and 47th were in Robert Craufurd's Light Brigade, while the main body of the 40th was with the Reserve under Colonel Mahon. Whitelocke had nine infantry battalions, but his force was unbalanced by a critical shortage of horses: only 150 men out of two and a half regiments of cavalry could be mounted, only 16 out of the 28 available guns could be pulled, and there were a mere forty horses to carry provisions.

At dawn on 28th June, the Light Brigade waded ashore, unopposed, in the Bay of Ensenada to cover the disembarkation of the rest of the army and squelched forward for two miles through a waterlogged swamp of black mud to occupy a ridge about four miles from the landing place. The men had been ordered to land with three days' cooked provisions, but by the end of the first day, when the troops were at times up to their waists in muddy water, much of this had been spoiled.

On their first night ashore, a marauding corporal and private of the 40th paid dearly for their plunder when they were killed and another soldier seriously wounded by lasso-wielding Indians, who stuck the dead corporal's head on a stake as a trophy and used his firearm to harass the camp. It was an inauspicious start.

Next day, Craufurd's brigade pushed forward to find a route, for prior intelligence had been sadly lacking in all but optimism. The tracks were, in fact, bad, intersected every two to three miles by more swamps or creeks, and the heavy going soon led to the abandonment of five guns, some seventeen thousand pounds of biscuit and many casks of rum. The march was trying and fatiguing work, and many of the newly-arrived and unseasoned soldiers, out of condition after months cooped up on transports, fell by the wayside and were picked up by hovering bands of irregular horsemen or slaughtered by hostile Indians.

---

[84] The Light Company 47th, and possibly the Grenadiers, accompanied Whitelocke to Buenos Aires. The strength of one of these companies was one captain, two subalterns, four sergeants and 59 rank and file. The following officers of the 47th are known to have been at Buenos Aires: Captain Richard George Elrington and Lieutenants Thomas Backhouse, Tade Heatley, William Rutledge and George Forster Sadleir, the first two of whom were subalterns with the Light Company. The *Regimental Digest of Service* states that the Grenadier Company was at Buenos Aires, and the number of officers certainly suggests that a second company was present, but there is no trace of the Grenadiers in Whitelocke's published order of battle.

That night the main body halted on the ground previously occupied by Craufurd's men. The seasoned 40th acted as rearguard and, as Private William Lawrence recalled, they had further encounters with the Indians:

'I remember that night was very foggy, and an officer and some men having gone out in search of bullocks for the supply of the army, the officer was very nearly lassoed by an Indian who came on him suddenly in the darkness. Fortunately he had the presence of mind to ride after him, which saved his life, for so the Indian could not pull him over; and then he managed to cut the lasso with his sword.

'As we marched along on our next day's journey, about two hundred Indians kept following us, the foremost of them wearing our dead corporal's jacket and carrying his head... We went on for some distance through a great many orange-gardens, till we came to a lane thickly hedged on both sides, which was entered by a gate, and there, after the body of our army had passed through, some few men, including myself, waited in ambush for the Indians, having a reserve placed a short distance down the lane in case of combat. The Indians soon approached, but seemed to have some misgivings, though we could not exactly understand what they said. There being only a few of us, not quite twenty in all, I rather shook in my shoes on seeing their number; but we soon found there was very little occasion for this, for on our firing directly, the front party had passed the gate, killing two of them and wounding and capturing their chief, who was the one who was so proud of his head, the rest fled for their lives, not liking the smell and much less the taste of our gunpowder. We picked up the wounded man and carried him, and left him, more dead than alive, in a neighbouring village.'[85]

Four companies of the 40th had been left behind to cover the landing and conveyance of the artillery, ammunition and stores, and such were the difficulties of movement through the mud that, according to Captain Peter Jennings, they had to abandon four 6-pounders in the marsh and destroy a great quantity of stores and ammunition.

On the evening of July 1st, the straggling and hungry red-coated columns reached the village of Reduction, nine miles from Buenos Aires and two miles inland from Point de Quilmes, where the army might originally have landed and from where it was now planned to resupply the troops from the fleet. Whitelocke decided to allow his tired and famished men a day's rest, which would also permit his guns, escorted by the four companies of the 40th, to catch up. However, he sent orders to Major-General Gower, his second-in-command, to press on with the two leading brigades, those of Craufurd and Lumley, and occupy the northern suburbs of Buenos Aires. Then, early the following morning, just as the starving troops of the main body were about to be fed, Whitelocke peremptorily ordered his entire army to march at once, leaving their undistributed food, and their blankets, on the ground.

As Craufurd's Light Brigade approached Buenos Aires, they had one major obstacle to cross, the River Chuelo. Its single bridge was defended by a Spanish force of nine thousand men and fifty guns, but by a stroke of good fortune, Craufurd saw a body of enemy horsemen retire across the river by a ford some five miles upstream. It was decided to follow them, and although the water was at least waist-deep, both leading brigades were safely across by late afternoon on 2nd July. Having bypassed the main Spanish army, the British now had the initiative. Craufurd saw that the enemy to his front were wavering; ignoring Gower's orders to halt, he pressed on at speed into the western suburbs of Buenos Aires, driving in the enemy's picquets and leaving Lumley's exhausted regiments, the 36th and 88th, trailing well behind. It will be recalled that the Light Brigade, now numbering some nine hundred, included the Light Companies of the 40th and 47th Regiments.

Craufurd halted near White's House, in an open space which was, in fact, the Corral (Corrale del Miserere), or slaughter-yard, of Buenos Aires, and waited for his light guns to catch up before resuming the advance to his appointed position in the northern suburbs. The ground about the Corral was very close, covered with gardens, orchards and hedged enclosures, and the British force was completely surprised when concealed Spanish guns, supported by some three thousand infantry under General Liniers, suddenly opened fire at close range with grape and roundshot. There was a momentary confusion, but then Craufurd launched his brigade straight at the enemy batteries. The light troops rushed forward with a cheer, and an irresistible, curving surge of men chased the enemy gunners and infantry into the town, bayoneting many of the fugitives and capturing ten guns and a howitzer. This hot pursuit was halted by repeated orders from Gower, directing Craufurd to return to

---

[85] Lawrence, p.p. 37-8.

the Corral. Craufurd, seldom a compliant subordinate, later testified to his belief that, given his head, he could have captured Buenos Aires that evening.

The light troops were ordered to retire about a mile and a half, where they lay on their arms all night amid the offal of the slaughter-yard in a drenching rain. Lumley's Brigade eventually straggled in to join them at last light, but it was mid-afternoon on the following day, 3rd July, before Whitelocke's main body reached the Corral in torrential rain. Mahon's Brigade, some eighteen hundred men, including the 40th, had been ordered to remain in the village of Reduction.

That morning, Liniers rejected Gower's summons to surrender Buenos Aires. The Spaniards then advanced from the city to attack the British outposts. As they pressed on, the picquets slowly retired, and for over two hours, there was much firing amongst the hedges and gardens. At length, the enemy withdrew into the city, leaving many dead and wounded in the enclosures. There were further outpost skirmishes the following day, with some loss on both sides, and Lieutenant Thomas Backhouse of the 47th was thanked by Gower for repulsing a night attack on the 4th of July when in command of an advanced picquet.

Whitelocke's original plan had been to attack the city from the north in conjunction with the fleet, landing heavy guns to bombard the place into surrender. He now decided on an immediate assault, citing the fatigue of the troops, want of provisions, and the inclemency of the weather as imperatives for early capture of the city: the first two of these were the result of his own poor planning and neglect. On the evening of the 3rd, Whitelocke asked Gower whether, having been outside Buenos Aires for 24 hours, he had thought of a plan for the attack of the city. Gower answered that he had and expounded his scheme: Whitelocke, against his better judgement, accepted it.

The city was laid out on a regular grid, with streets sloping gently eastwards towards the River Plate and from north to south. The principal buildings were all close to the shore. In the centre, the Plaza Mayor, or main square of the city, was bounded on its eastern side by the Fort and to the north by the Cathedral, while just to the south lay the Franciscan Church, the Jesuit's College and the Convent of Santo Domingo, the largest ecclesiastical building in the city after the Cathedral. Nearly a mile to the north of the Plaza Mayor, the Plaza de Toros occupied a commanding position, while at the southeast corner of the town stood a large building called the Residencia. Many of the townhouses had flat roofs with parapets, making them particularly suitable for defence.

Gower's plan, accepted without amendment by Whitelocke, was for thirteen separate columns to advance from west to east on parallel streets to secure objectives close to the river. Whitelocke's written orders were meagre and extremely obscure. There were no plans for coordination between columns or for subsequent operations on reaching the river and virtually no reserves. Moreover, he grossly underestimated the Spaniards' determination to defend their city and the difficulties always inherent in close fighting in built-up areas. Expecting little resistance, the rest was left to chance. The attack was scheduled for 6.30 a.m. on July 5th.

Liniers had taken advantage of the two days since his rout at the Corral to prepare defences and rouse the population to patriotic resistance. Cannon were placed to sweep the main streets, which were barricaded, cut with trenches, and dominated by well-stocked fortified houses. The defenders, some nine thousand in formed units and a further six thousand irregulars, outnumbered their attackers by more than three to one.

At sunrise the following morning, a cannon shot signalled the British advance. A deadly silence hung ominously over the city as the columns entered their appointed streets. For some time, there was no resistance, and they marched on, drawn ever deeper into a trap.

The thirteen columns were divided into the Left Attack, under Auchmuty, and the Right Attack under Craufurd, with a central gap of four streets opposite the Plaza Mayor. The Left Attack consisted of, from left to right, the 38th, 87th, 5th, 36th and 88th Regiments, the last two under Brigadier Lumley; the 45th and the Light Brigade formed the Right Attack. Each regiment, apart from the 38th, was split into two wings advancing down adjacent streets. The Light Brigade was also divided into two columns: on the left were five light companies, including the Light Company 47th Regiment, and four companies of the 95th, all under Colonel Pack, while the Light Company 40th was one of four light companies and four of the 95th on the right under the personal direction of Craufurd. The troops were to push on to the far end of their designated streets without firing; indeed, Whitelocke had ordered that they should advance with fixed bayonets only, unloaded and with the flints removed from their muskets.

Both columns of the Light Brigade passed through the city to the river with little opposition, receiving only a few cannon-shot from the Plaza Mayor. Then, correctly assessing that they had bypassed the main centre of Spanish resistance around the Plaza Mayor and the Fort, they moved to their left. Craufurd determined to advance on the Fort, some five hundred yards to his north, by the beach, and called on the 45th Regiment, which had easily secured the Residencia, to support him. Pack divided his own column in two and, having given command of one half to Lieutenant-Colonel Cadogan, also advanced north along two parallel streets.

Pack had reached the Franciscan Church when a sudden fusillade from an invisible enemy struck down half his men and wounded him. Cadogan's column was similarly ambushed by the gate of the Jesuit's College, where every man of his leading company and every horse and man of his single field gun were, in an instant, shot down. Both columns retreated. Pack, who had been present at Beresford's debacle the previous year, found Craufurd at the back of the Convent of Santo Domingo and urged a withdrawal to the Residencia, but Craufurd hesitated, representing the advantage of occupying and holding the great Convent, and Pack reluctantly gave way. The door of the convent was blown open by a field gun, and the British Light troops rushed in. The defenders of Santo Domingo retired to the dome, while the Spanish outside opened a heavy fire from adjacent houses and attempted to recapture the building. The pock-marked walls of the tower still bear witness to Craufurd's stand.

At noon a Spanish officer appeared at the Convent with a flag of truce. Anticipating an offer of capitulation from Liniers, Craufurd was horrified when the messenger informed him that the 88th Regiment had surrendered and called upon him also to lay down his arms. The summons was at once dismissed, but shortly afterwards, a large body of Spanish troops approached.

The Left Attack had indeed met with mixed fortune. Auchmuty had captured the Plaza de Toros and the Retiro, together with the batteries and barracks in that area, and had taken some thousand prisoners and 32 guns, but at heavy cost to the 38th and 87th. Further south, Lumley's brigade had suffered a major disaster: both wings of the 88th were trapped in the vicinity of the Church of La Merced, and the survivors were eventually obliged to surrender; the 36th had eventually to fight their way out with heavy loss to join Auchmuty.

Realising his precarious situation, Craufurd attempted to break out and withdraw to the Residencia, but the enemy fire was too heavy and he was forced to resume the defence. Presently, all firing ceased except around the Convent, indicating that the assault on Buenos Aires had failed; and just after 3.30 p.m., outnumbered about ten to one and seeing that further resistance was hopeless, Craufurd surrendered. The prisoners were taken to the Castle, where the officers were received with courtesy by General Liniers.

Cadogan, who had occupied the house of the Viceroy's wife, a few hundred yards to the west, had already been obliged to yield. The house had been quickly surrounded, and an intense firefight went on for nearly three hours between the British troops on the roof and Spanish troops on top of the surrounding buildings. Such was the carnage that the drainpipes are said to have flowed with blood. Hard pressed, short of ammunition and isolated, the British force was relieved when a Spanish officer appeared with a flag of truce, imagining, like Craufurd, that the Spaniards wanted to surrender. This was far from being the case: the officer had come to demand Cadogan's capitulation. During the parley that followed, the Spaniards crowded in on the British positions, making it untenable, and Cadogan, having lost over two-thirds of his strength, was indeed obliged to surrender at about 11 a.m.

Whitelocke spent the entire day in the vicinity of White's House near the Corral, miles from the battle and uncomprehending of the unfolding debacle until it was too late to act. Although Mahon's reserve brigade, including the 40th, had come forward during the day to within two miles of the Residencia, they remained uncommitted. Private Lawrence summed up their indignant view of the situation:

'Buenos Aires was much more easy to take than Montevideo, as it was very slightly fortified towards the country. There were some cannons placed at the end of each street, but they proved a very small difficulty to be overcome, as there seemed nobody efficient to work them, and after passing these our soldiers were soon in possession of the city. Then they hoisted the King's flag on a convent and waited, expecting every minute that the body of our army would come up; but instead of this, General Whitelock encamped about a mile out of the town and remained there. If he had attended properly to his business, he would have followed up and relieved the [Light] Brigade; but as it was, the Spaniards rallied and overpowered it. I was with the main body and so was not

48

able to enter the city to see what was going on. We all fell under arms when we heard the muskets at work, waiting for the general's orders to advance: but there we lay the whole night, not doing a stroke.'[86]

This was not entirely correct. On the morning of the assault, the 40th, with a strength of 823 all ranks, had marched with Colonel Mahon's detachment from Reduction to the bridge over the Chuelo, crossing it at 5 p.m. to take post a short distance beyond in the village of Barracka, where they spent the night. Early the following morning Whitelocke sent Captain Samuel Whittingham to find Mahon and order him to march the Reserve to the Corral. Having delivered this order, Whittingham went on to the Residencia escorted by one hundred men of the Grenadier Company 40th under Captain John Gillies. They reached the Residencia, held by the 45th Regiment, at about one o'clock, just as the post was attacked by a body of the enemy supported by guns. The British force, including the Grenadiers of the 40th, mounted an immediate counter-attack on the Spaniards, who withdrew in panic with the loss of two guns and many prisoners, leaving the Residencia secure in British hands. Captain Gillies's detachment then rejoined the Regiment at the Corral.

It was not until the morning of the 6th, when Liniers sent proposals for a total British withdrawal from the country, that Whitelocke appreciated the full extent of his defeat. His force had suffered very nearly three thousand casualties, including 401 dead, 649 wounded and 1,924 wounded and unwounded prisoners, or more than half of those engaged, and the survivors had lost all confidence in their general. The Light Battalion had lost three sergeants and 24 men killed, four sergeants, one drummer and 57 men wounded, and 62 men missing. The component companies are not shown separately, but we know that the 40th lost at least two soldiers killed and Lieutenant Smith[87] and one man wounded, while the *Gazette* recorded a similar loss for the 47th, Lieutenant William Rutledge severely wounded, one rank and file killed and two wounded, and one missing. The total casualties of the two Light Companies were almost certainly greater than this, for we know that two more officers of the 47th were also wounded: Lieutenant Thomas Backhouse, previously wounded at the storming of Montevideo, was hit three times, while Lieutenant Tade Heatley was severely wounded by a canister shot through his body.

A cessation of hostilities was agreed upon, and terms were concluded on 7th July under which prisoners were to be exchanged, and the British force was to evacuate South America within two months. On the 8th, the 40th Regiment joined the main body of the army at the Retiro, and the troops withdrew from Buenos Aires on 12th July. The furious army had no doubt who was to blame for their humiliating reverse: 'General Whitelocke is either a traitor or a coward or both' was scrawled on street corners, and 'Success to grey hairs, but bad luck to white locks' became a favourite toast. Nothing could disguise the fact that the ill-fated expedition had ended in disaster, and Captain Whittingham summed up the mood:

'History will record, and posterity with difficulty will recall that such an army as ours surrendered to the rabble of a South American town… Would to God that the waters of Oblivion were as near at hand as are those of La Plata.'

Captain Peter Jennings of the 40th shared in the army's disgust at its senior commanders, describing their plan of attack as 'at the best the most injudicious they could possibly have devised.'

On August 1st, the 47th, having received a draft of 86 privates from the 45th, set sail for the Cape of Good Hope, from where, in October, the Regiment resumed its interrupted voyage to the East Indies. They reached Madras on 29th December 1807 to start a 22-year tour in the East.

The 40th remained at Montevideo until 9th September, when the town was evacuated. According to Private Lawrence, a detachment was first sent about one hundred miles upriver for fresh water. An unusual circumstance attended the embarkation of Colonel Gore Browne, for so much had his conduct as Governor won the respect of the people of Montevideo that the Spanish Governor and Council presented him with an address expressing their 'deep regret and heartfelt sorrow' at his departure, and accompanied him to the boat with their heads uncovered.

The homeward voyage began well enough, the men of the 40th in general keeping very healthy, but William Lawence's transport was then was delayed by calms.

---

[86] Lawrence, p.p. 38-9.

[87] Lieutenant Charles Hervey Smith of the 40th was wounded three times, twice severely. He had already received 'an alarming head wound' at the storming of Monte Video and would be wounded again the following year at Vimiero. Assistant-Surgeon Charles Boutflower, 40th, was among the prisoners.

'Our water supply ran very short,' Lawrence told his biographer, 'and had to be served out in allowances of half a pint a day. A small supply, however, fortunately, came before long. Our captain, seeing a cloud in the distance, foretold that we were going to have a thunderstorm and ordered the scupper-holes to be stopped and all except the watch to remain below. I happened to be one of the watch at the time, and well, I remember how it very shortly after began to thunder and lighten, the rain falling in torrents for two or three hours; it was the heaviest thunderstorm I had ever witnessed. We baled up some twenty or more casks of water, which was none the better, perhaps, for there being pigs, fowls, geese and turkeys all over the deck, but still was very acceptable to us in our parched state, as till then we had had to cook our food and wash ourselves in salt water only.'[88]

Captain Peter Jennings, whose company and family were aboard the brig *Jane*, kept a daily journal of the 14-week voyage, from which the following is an excerpt:

'We experienced much bad weather and constant succession of gales during the first fortnight of our departure from Rio de la Plata, and on the night of the 22nd [September], the transport brig on board of which I was embarked with my company was run foul of by another brig, which carried away our gib boom and injured the bowsprit considerably… The weather having moderated, we were enabled in the course of the two following days to repair our damage and put the vessel to rights. On the afternoon of the 24th, a soldier of my company, of the name of John Bond, who had for some few days before complained of illness but who on this morning reported himself much better, died rather suddenly after having made a hearty meal of a shark which we had caught that day.'

It was December before the Regiment reached home waters. The wind was unfavourable for England, so on the 17th, the 40th made the Cove of Cork. 'We spent the Christmas of 1807 on board,' recalled Lawrence, 'sending on shore for raisins, flour, fat and beer, and so being enabled to enjoy ourselves very comfortably.' Assuming that they would sail on to England when the wind changed, the 40th had already laid in their 'sea stock' for the voyage when orders came for them to land in Ireland on 30th December and proceed to Bandon.

On 28th January 1808, Lieutenant-General Whitelocke was tried by a court-martial and was sentenced to be cashiered 'and declared totally unfit to serve His Majesty in any military capacity whatever.' Posterity has confirmed the justice of this harsh but fair verdict. Regrettably, neither Home Popham, who had instigated the rash South American adventure, nor the ministers and speculators who had endorsed and encouraged it, shared in Whitelocke's fate.

It was to be three years before the men of the 40th received their share of the prize money for the South American adventure, but by that time, the Regiment was engaged in a much greater venture as allies of their former Spanish foes.

---

[88] Lawrence, p.p. 39-40.

Battle of Vimeira, 21ˢᵗ August 1808,
where the 40ᵗʰ & 82ⁿᵈ, in line, routed successive French columns
with musket volleys followed by a bayonet charge

Major (later Maj-Gen) James Kemmis,
an eccentric officer, commanded the
40ᵗʰ in the Peninsula including the
Battles of Roliça, Vimeira & Talavera

The 81ˢᵗ Foot advance to contact at the Battle of Corunna, 16ᵗʰ January 1809. When their ammunition was
exhausted, the 81ˢᵗ were relieved in the front line by the 59ᵗʰ Foot

Chapter III:
Rolica to Corunna 1808-09

French Invasion of Spain & Portugal, Popular Resistance & British Intervention, 1808 – Spencer's Expedition (82nd) – Diversion to Sicily – Landing at Mondego Bay (40th & 82nd) – Battles of Roliça 17th August & Vimeiro 21st August 1808 (40th & 82nd) – Convention of Cintra & Occupation of Lisbon – 40th at Elvas – Moore & Baird Advance into Spain (59th, 81st & 82nd) – Retreat to Corunna – Action at Lugo (59th) – Battle of Corunna 16th January 1809 (59th, 81st & 82nd) – Evacuation – Sir John Moore.

War in the Peninsula

The British Army has fought many memorable campaigns, but very few can match the epic quality of the war in Spain and Portugal between 1808 and 1814, and even fewer have left such a potent legacy of Regimental lore, myth and tradition. All six predecessor Regiments of the Queen's Lancashires served in the Iberian Peninsula, earning fifteen battle honours, and the old 'Fighting Fortieth' shared with the 45th and 60th Regiments the rare distinction of having fought from the beginning to end of that remarkable six-year campaign. Over those six years, Regimental predecessors were present at all but two of the actions for which medal clasps were issued, those two being exclusively cavalry actions.

It was a vital part of Napoleon Buonaparte's strategy against England to close all the ports of Continental Europe against her commerce, and at the end of 1806, he signed decrees to enforce this 'Continental System' on his satellites. The Emperor's plan was frustrated by one loophole, Portugal, which continued to trade with her oldest ally, and in November 1807, he took measures to coerce that country into his system. At the same time, he prepared to reduce Spain, his supposed accomplice in this venture, to the status of a French vassal. The corrupt and effete rulers of Spain were too stupid to fathom the Emperor's designs on their country's independence and too cowardly to resist. French troops flooded across the Pyrenees, occupied the strongholds of their ostensible ally, and swept on to capture Lisbon on 15th December and drive the Portuguese government into exile without firing a shot. Then, in May 1808, the Emperor treacherously forced the King of Spain to abdicate, replacing the Bourbon monarch with his own brother, Joseph Buonaparte.

Popular resistance to the French coup broke out almost at once. On 2nd May 1808, an insurrection in Madrid ignited the flame of revolt across the Iberian Peninsula, and provisional governments in the Spanish provinces appealed to Britain for help. In Parliament, Government and Opposition were united in their eager declarations of support for this patriotic uprising against the Corsican tyrant.

Spencer's Expedition

Whilst the 40th Foot, so recently returned from South America, were enjoying their Christmas Dinner in Cork harbour, the 1st/82nd were enduring a considerably less festive experience in the Bay of Biscay. On 18th December 1807 they had embarked at Portsmouth, in company with the 29th, 32nd and 50th Regiments, on a secret expedition under Major-General Brent Spencer. The Battalion was commanded by Major Harry Eyre[89] and, having received drafts from the 2nd Battalion and the Irish Militia, mustered 1,048 all ranks.

Spencer was ordered to take his force of nearly eight thousand men to Lisbon, where it was thought he might co-operate with Sir John Moore to cover the evacuation of the Portuguese Royal Family and the evacuation, or surrender, of the Portuguese fleet. He was then to reinforce the garrisons of Gibraltar and Sicily.

The fleet sailed for the Tagus on 20th December, but one week later, it was dispersed by a violent storm. Ensign George Wood was among some two hundred of the 82nd on one of the transports. This ship, which had

---

[89] Henry Samuel Eyre, born 1770 in London, had been Major to the 1st/82nd since 1st August 1804.

recently returned from South America, was greatly in need of a refit, and Wood later recalled the horror as it was battered by the gale:

'At length a storm stay-sail only was left standing. This was soon literally shivered to rags, and we were left to scud under bare poles. The storm now increased, and the density of the clouds became thicker and thicker, till it blew a most tremendous gale, which continued with little variation about ten days and nights. During this time, we were prevented obtaining either fire or candlelight, and those who could eat were glad to make their Christmas dinner of cold junk and biscuit… I cannot recollect half the dreadful sensations that seized me – from the noise of pumps that were continually kept going, the different parts of the masts and rigging giving way, with the bustle and confusion of the crew endeavouring to work the vessel, and the great probability that we should founder… In this plight, our situation became each moment more dreadful, distress was depicted on every countenance; to look around, all was awfully sublime – nothing to be seen but huge waves, on the tops of which we seemed like the inhabitants of the skies; then descending into the trough of the sea, we were as if entombed in the bottomless pit, never more to rise. Every swell seemed as if it would overwhelm our little bark; not a single ship was in sight, for the convoy had long since dispersed, many of them never again to meet.'[90]

When at length the storm abated, the transport was intercepted off Vigo by a French privateer. The decks were at once cleared for action and the seasick soldiers were ordered to prime and load their muskets; half the 82nd lay concealed below decks, while some helped to man the guns and others prepared for boarding. The enemy warship closed with the transport, but having noted its determined defensive preparations, the Frenchman sheered off and fled, followed by a British roundshot. No sooner had this enemy disappeared than another strange sail was sighted, and again, the ship prepared for action, but this vessel proved to be another of their own convoy, which had weathered the storm. Many of the other transports had been forced back to Falmouth or on to Gibraltar, but the survivors opened their sealed orders and, as directed, made for a rendezvous off Lisbon. By 1st January 1808, fewer than half of the transports had reached the Tagus, and it was to be a further five months before the storm-scattered parts of the 82nd were re-united.

The British ships stood off Lisbon for some days. Fresh orders now arrived, instructing them to proceed to Gibraltar, from where Sir Hew Dalrymple sent the 82nd detachment on again to reinforce the hard-pressed garrison of Sicily.

Sailing by way of Sardinia and surviving a squall as sudden as it was severe, George Wood's transport put into Palermo for repairs. The officers of the 82nd were enchanted by the seductive ambience of the Sicilian capital and enthused at such sights as the great Norman cathedral of Monreale, but after three weeks, they sailed on to Messina, where they disembarked. Marching inland, the 82nd detachment occupied a string of hill villages from which their picquets descended by precipitous paths to watch the threatened coastline of the straits. George Wood, now promoted to Lieutenant, was billeted at Jesso in 'a very large monastery, part of which was allotted to the men and the remainder occupied by a great number of jolly fat friars.' It was here that the young subaltern learned a lesson in man-management:

'Our men, after being so long at sea, now began to feel comfortable and asked for a little money to add to their happiness; when, although I gave them only the value of one sixpence each, to my great surprise, on visiting their rooms, I found them all completely intoxicated, the wine being here so exceedingly strong and cheap – about one penny per bottle. This circumstance made me more cautious in future how I distributed their pay.'[91]

After a few weeks' duty, the 82nd detachment was ordered back to Messina for embarkation and sailed down to the ancient port of Syracuse. Here, they remained at anchor for about a month. The troops landed daily to exercise, and the officers found time to explore the extensive ruins of antiquity, but at length, they received orders to sail for Cadiz, there to rejoin the main body of Spencer's expedition. The detachment's return voyage was not without incident, for one night, a large vessel ran aboard their transport, causing severe damage, even greater consternation, but also 'much mirth' at the sight of the doctor, who appeared on deck drenched with the contents of his own chamber pot.

Having re-assembled his scattered force, including those companies of the 82nd that had been driven back to Falmouth, Spencer had reached Gibraltar on 10th March 1808. He considered an attack on the Spanish North

---

[90] Wood, p.p. 17-18.
[91] Ibid., p.p. 35-36.

African port of Ceuta, but it was too well fortified. From Gibraltar he sent fresh reinforcements to Sherbrooke in Sicily, asking in return for the detachments of his regiments that had earlier been forwarded to that island by Sir Hew Dalrymple. It was not, however, till the end of May that the 82nd Regiment was reunited off Cadiz, and it was at anchor there on 14th June when a luckless French naval squadron, survivors of Trafalgar, surrendered.

Spain was then in a state of insurrection against French rule, and in June, the Portuguese, too, rose in rebellion. Provincial governments, or juntas, in the Spanish provinces, appealed to Britain for help, and the British Government decided on military intervention to support the patriot cause. Planned attacks on Spanish possessions in the Mediterranean and South America were cancelled, and the troops assembled for these operations, including the 40th, were re-directed to aid their erstwhile enemies against the French.

Also re-tasked were Major General Brent Spencer's five battalions off Cadiz, including the 82nd. Spencer had sailed from Gibraltar on 14th May with 3,107 men, leaving orders for his detachment in Sicily to join him as soon as possible. He received no orders from home until mid-July but acted on his own initiative to support the Spanish and Portuguese patriots in Seville and on the Algarve. His offer to garrison Cadiz was spurned by the Spaniards, who had a morbid fear that the British, with whom they were technically still at war, would turn that great port into another Gibraltar; and so on 12th June, he sailed north to Ayamonte, at the mouth of the River Guadiana, where the presence of his troops encouraged the insurgents in the south of Portugal and sufficed to deter the French troops in Portugal from reinforcing General Dupont's army in Andalucia. Next, on a false report that the French garrison of Lisbon had been reduced to four thousand men, Spencer showed himself at the mouth of the Tagus, but, finding that the Portuguese capital was defended by fifteen thousand Frenchmen, he sailed back to Cadiz.

He was eventually permitted to land his troops at Puerto de Santa Maria, at the head of the Bay of Cadiz, remaining there and at Jerez for some three weeks. As Lieutenant George Wood related, they were 'very comfortably situated… but the weather was so excessively hot that we were obliged to exercise in the night and sleep during the meridian heat – a heat, indeed, so intense that the Spaniards have a proverb which says that only Englishmen and dogs are to be seen in the streets at that time.'[92] From Jerez, Brent Spencer wrote on 18th July, proposing a landing in Portugal.

The Battle of Roliça, 17th August 1808

It will be recalled that on their return from South America, the 1st/40th landed at Cork on 30th December, 1807, and proceeded to Bandon. There, they received some two hundred and fifty reinforcements from their 2nd Battalion, which had been based in Ireland for some twelve months.

Among those who joined the 1st/40th at this time was Thomas Skeel, who had served for four years in the ranks of the 2nd Somerset Militia before volunteering into the Regular Line on 21st August 1807, along with three officers, four sergeants, five corporals and 290 other militiamen 'as I did wish to see some foreign parts.' His choice of regiment was determined when he heard that his old captain had volunteered into the 40th and had made a wager with the officers in the mess room that he would get more men to go with him into the 40th Regiment than would volunteer for the 9th Regiment. Thomas Skeel was attested the next day, joining the 40th Foot for seven years and receiving ten guineas bounty. His diary, which unfortunately stops short as he travelled to join the 40th in Ireland, paints a vivid picture of the riotous scenes which often attended such volunteering:

'On Sunday morning the 23rd [August 1807], we march off for Horsham, 14 miles… We had the band to play us two miles on the road, and almost all the regiment to wish us well as they were all sorry to part with us. We received one half of our bounty, the remainder we was to receive when we joined the regiment… During the time I remained in Horsham, there was some lively diversion as the men was full of mirth. Every gentleman's carriage they could find, they took [the] passenger off. Some got inside while others acted as horses to run through the street, with all kind of music, some men stark naked with their skin painted different colours. Some bought several lights and ate it for a wager, others roasted a cat alive and ate it, some roasting a goose's feathers and guts and ate it as it was. Every public house in the town was open for one week, day and night. [Despite] all the drinking, there was no fighting all the time, nothing but brotherly love.'[93]

On 1st September the Militia volunteers set out for Hilsea Barracks to await transports for Ireland, where they would join the 2nd/40th. Thomas Skeel reflected on his decision to enlist: 'Now my troubles begins to come on, for I knowed but little about soldiering at that time, for after I had been abroad for some time I counted all the time I was in the Militia nothing but pleasure to what it was to be a Regular soldier.'

On 21st March 1808, the 1st Battalion marched from Bandon to Fermoy, and from there on 12th-14th April to Limerick, before returning 19th-23rd May to Fermoy in readiness for active service. Lieutenant-Colonel James Kemmis assumed command, bringing with him one hundred more men of the 2nd Battalion, including Thomas Skeel, and the 1st/40th embarked with 958 rank and file. For every hundred men, six women were as usual permitted and it was ordered that 'they should be carefully selected as being of good character, and having the inclination and ability to render themselves useful.' The balance of women and children were to be sent to their homes.

James Kemmis, a 57-year-old Irishman from Queen's County, was an officer whose very considerable experience[94] was coupled with a remarkably pompous and grandiloquent turn of phrase. Many stories were told about him. One day, the Colonel was dissatisfied with the appearance of his Regiment on parade and, calling his officers out to the front, he upbraided them, with appropriate gesticulation, in the following singular terms:

'Field Officers, ye do nothing! Captains, ye are the worst of your kind! Avaunt, ye Subalterns, nefarious crew, delinquents of the deepest dye!'

On another occasion, when an elderly lady asked him whether she might safely cross the barrack square, the Colonel ungallantly replied, 'Madam, your age and your visage protect you.'

The 40th were part of an expeditionary force of some five thousand men being assembled at Cork under Lieutenant-General Sir Arthur Wellesley, then aged 41, a well-connected commander who had gained some reputation and considerable experience from his remarkable victories in India. He had also grasped the importance of logistics, especially in a hostile environment such as India – or the Iberian Peninsula – and he had identified this as a critical vulnerability of the French position. 'Bonaparte cannot carry on his operations in Spain excepting by means of large armies,' he mused, 'and I doubt much whether the country will afford subsistence for a large army, or if he will be able to supply his magazines from France, the roads being so bad and the communications so difficult.'

The Ministry's original intention had been to use Wellesley's force for a renewed attack on the Spanish colonies in South America, but on 4th June 1808, deputies from the Asturias reached London with news of the insurrection in Northern Spain and a plea for assistance. On hearing this news, Wellesley recommended that a large force should be sent out at once to join Spencer's detachment off the coast of Spain, in readiness to take advantage of any possible opportunity. Within days, the strength of his little army was doubled, and on 14th June, he was confirmed in his command. His orders, issued by the Secretary of State for War on the 30th, were unambiguous if somewhat ambitious, 'the entire and absolute evacuation of the Peninsula by the troops of France.'

Wellesley's troops, including the 40th Foot, embarked on 15th-17th June 1808; but contrary winds kept them in Cork harbour for nearly four weeks, by which time they had been joined by additional troops from England. Their destination remained secret.

'We are this day all ordered on board,' wrote Lieutenant William Hibbert of the 40th on 6th July from the Cove of Cork to his mother in Manchester. 'One of the staff officers informed me that the General will be in Cove tonight and that he believes we will sail tomorrow evening. I have purchased a cot and bedding, complete (for the voyage). I have also added to my stock of shirts, by procuring about nine cotton ones, which I got made for 10s each. For night watches, guards, and I suppose very often for my bed, I have a very thick, large, warm cloak, which is almost indispensable.

'Two additional regiments, the 36th and 45th, have this day embarked, and some dragoons are expected. It is rather remarkable that nearly all the regiments who were in South America are again embarked and that the

---

[93] The original spelling of Thomas Skeel's diary has been amended to improve readability.
[94] Kemmis had fought in the Saratoga campaign with the 9th Foot, and with the 40th in Holland in 1793-94 and 1799, and in San Domingo.

staff officers appointed were nearly all at Montevideo and Buenos Ayres. This looks as if we were going there again.'

On 12th July, the whole force, 10,728 men, set sail for Portugal with instructions to act 'as circumstances might point out' in support of the insurgency. Wellesley preceded his troops in a fast-sailing frigate, calling at Corunna and Oporto to gain intelligence. At the latter port, he was advised to land at the mouth of Mondego Bay, a relatively sheltered anchorage protected by the fort at Figueira da Foz, which had been captured by students from Coimbra University and occupied by British Marines. On 30th July, James Kemmis, commanding 1st/40th, wrote from HMS *Indefatigable* 'off Mondigo on the Coast of Portugal' to his brother William:

'After an unpleasant voyage, we are in this bay, and preparations are being made for landing. The difficulty will be great on account of the surf, as this coast from Corunna to Lisbon is very dangerous and difficult to approach; however, as the French are in possession of the forts, there is no alternative but marching from hence, a distance of eighty miles, over a very rough country, and with innumerable difficulties. I shall have my share of them, having unfortunately lost my horse that you so kindly sent me: the closeness and agitation threw him into a fever, he burst a blood vessel and was thrown overboard.

'It appears to me that the object of this expedition is to secure the French fleet in the Tagus and, if possible, the French troops. They are supposed to be 14 or 15,000 men, well posted and, of course, determined on resistance. Some lives must be lost in this conflict, let the result be what it may.'

Disembarkation began on August 1st, through a heavy surf which upset many boats with the loss of several lives. But the troops were in excellent spirits, for news had arrived of Dupont's surrender of seventeen and a half thousand Frenchmen on 20th July at Baylen in Andalucia. Brent Spencer, too, had received this news at Puerto de Santa Maria, and with the threat to Cadiz thus removed, he embarked his five battalions and sailed north in the expectation of meeting with Wellesley. He came into Mondego Bay on the 5th, just as the last of the troops from Cork disembarked. This timely reinforcement raised the strength of Wellesley's army to some 14,300 men, including 1,040 of the 40th and 929 of the 82nd.

The troops were ordered to land 'each with one shirt and one pair of shoes, besides those on them, combs, razor, and a brush, which are to be packed up in their greatcoats.' The soldiers' knapsacks and all baggage were to be left on the transports, and each man was to have three days' bread and two days' cooked meat, together with three good flints for his musket.

The army was divided into six small brigades of two or three battalions each. The 40th Regiment, 926 strong, was in Major-General Ronald Ferguson's 2nd Brigade with the 36th and 71st, while the 82nd Regiment, 929 strong, was with the 29th in Brigadier-General Miles Nightingall's 3rd Brigade. Wellesley was remarkably weak in cavalry, which was limited to 180 sabres of the 20th Light Dragoons. Brent Spencer became Second-in-Command to Wellesley, though Sir Arthur made it pointedly clear to him that there was to be only one commander in the army.[95]

It has been confidently repeated by some historians of the campaign that the force which landed at Mondego Bay lacked experience. In fact, the majority of Wellesley's battalions, including the 40th and the 82nd, had seen serious active service within the previous twelve months in the expeditions to South America and Copenhagen.

Once ashore, Wellesley's first priority was to collect horses, mules and bullock-carts, for the Ministry had sent no transport with the expedition, and so it was not until the 9th that he was able to advance on Lisbon, about one hundred miles to the south. The army marched by the coast road so as to maintain contact with the fleet, not least because two additional brigades were expected from England. For many of the troops, who were out of condition after weeks of shipboard confinement, the desolate, sandy shore was hard going under a scorching

---

[95] Despite Spencer's very considerable combat experience on three continents and previous successes against the French, which was considerably greater than his own, Wellesley had little time for him. Sir Arthur could be cutting in his criticism, which was not always fair, and he later reported that his Second-in-Command was 'exceedingly puzzle-headed... He would talk of the Thames for the Tagus... He has no mind, and is incapable of forming any opinion of his own. I cannot depend upon him for anything.' However, he is also reputed to have said of Spencer that 'There never was a braver man.' It was, indeed, characteristic of Wellesley that whilst his practical judgements were almost invariably cool and moderate, his otherwise repressed temper was apt to flare to extremes in private and on paper.

August sun, and they suffered severely from thirst. Lieutenant George Wood of the 82nd described the daily march routine:

'The route having been received, the drum beats… to assemble the troops – I cannot say in all cases to strike the tents, for in this campaign we had none. After the Adjutant has collected the reports, the troops move off in as large divisions as the nature of the road will permit to march commodiously… till they arrive at the ground on which they are to bivouac for the night. Here, after piling arms, parties are sent out under the superintendence of a subaltern to fetch water, others to draw rations, some to cut wood both for fuel and to build huts, while others are selected for guard, piquet, foraging and other duties. This being done, fires are lighted, and (should the utensils have arrived) cooking commences. After getting a scanty meal, a parade is formed to see that the men have cleaned themselves and their accoutrements in readiness for the next day's march and that they have their necessaries, particularly their ammunition, complete. This daily routine of duty being performed, the soldier is glad to lie down soon after on his bed of fern, straw or, if nothing else is to be had, to repose his wearied limbs on that cold bed which will eventually receive him into its bosom.'

Lieutenant William Hibbert of the 40th was entering on his first campaign: 'Our first halt was at a village, about 15 miles from the bay, where we were encamped for a few days, and then commencing our march up the country, as harassing and fatiguing as perhaps ever troops encountered. To give you some idea of campaigning, our first day's march was begun in the heat of the day and continued till after midnight. We then took a little rest and, before daylight, were again on the move; so that out of the twenty-four hours, only three were allowed for the troops to procure a little sleep. The country has been reduced to a state of the greatest wretchedness, owing to the depredations of the French. The greatest scarcity prevails, provisions are hard to be procured, and the most extravagant prices paid. The excesses these wretches have committed are too shocking to be related here. We continued our march till the 16th, the enemy retreating before us, when we were informed they intended to make a stand in a very strong position they had taken up.'[96]

By the 14th Wellesley reached Alcobaça, where he received his first intelligence of French movements. The French army in Portugal was commanded by General Junot, who had 25,000 men at his disposal. Once he was aware of the British landing, Junot sent Delaborde with some 4,350 men to observe and delay their advance while he gathered all the troops he could to form a field army. Loison, with another six and a half thousand Frenchmen, was barely a day's march behind Delaborde.

On the 15th, Wellesley's advance guard ran into Delaborde's rearguard at Obidos, and the next day, the two armies met at the village of Roliça. This village sits on the side of an isolated hill in the middle of a sandy plain, enclosed to the south, east and west by steep ridges. Delaborde had initially occupied a forward position on rising ground to the north and west of the village, blocking the road to Lisbon. Wellesley observed that both flanks of his enemy could easily be turned through the hills, and so at dawn on 16th August, he advanced in a crescent-shaped formation with his wings thrown forward to envelop the French position while his main body demonstrated in front of Roliça. On the left wing, Ferguson struck out over the hills with two brigades, including the 40th, to turn Delaborde's right flank, while a Portuguese force under Trant did the same on the right. The main body advanced across the plain on a broad front with three brigades in line and one in reserve. Nightingall's Brigade, with the 82nd, was in the centre of the front line. Seen by an officer on the French position, the British advance was a magnificent sight:

'They came on slowly but in beautiful order, dressing at intervals to correct the gaps caused by the inequalities of ground, and all converging on the hill of Roliça.'

Delaborde had no intention of fighting to hold this forward position: his purpose was merely to delay the British advance, and so with skirmishers in action to his front and the enveloping forces appearing on his flanks, he gave the order to disengage. Covered by their cavalry, the French skillfully withdrew to a very steep scrub-covered ridge one mile south of the village, where Delaborde intended to inflict further delay and maximum casualties on his opponents. This escarpment was about three hundred feet in height with a rough stone breastwork in places across its summit, and appeared too steep to climb except by way of four very narrow, boulder-choked

---

96 William Hibbert's letter dated 22nd August 1808 to his father at St Anne's Square, Manchester.

gullies. Its flanks were protected by defiles. The French occupied a short enough front (some three-quarters of a mile) to have a reasonable prospect of holding it until reinforced by Loison.

It was a strong position, and so Wellesley planned to manoeuvre the French out of it as before, sending Ferguson and Trant on further arduous flanking marches over the hills to reach the rear of Delaborde's position. His main body was reorganised into four columns, one for each gulley. On the left were the 45th, 5th/60th, and 95th, in the next gulley were the 82nd, then the 29th supported by the 9th, and finally, on the right, the Light Companies of the 9th, 29th and 82nd, supported by the 5th. Wellesley's intention was that these columns should make diversionary demonstrations against the gullies to distract and pin down the French on the ridge while Fergusson and Trant enveloped the position.

In the event, the cautious advance of Wellesley's centre was upset when, in a burst of misplaced enthusiasm, Colonel Lake of the 29th led his inexperienced regiment in a gallant but premature and unsupported assault up the largest of the rugged gullies. This impetuous attack was repulsed with heavy loss, and Lake was killed. Seeing that his plan was compromised by Lake's rash action, Wellesley ordered a general assault on the ridge. The 29th, supported by the 9th, advanced again, and the other columns scrambled up their respective gullies and the intervening slopes to join in the attack. For two hours, the British columns struggled up the narrow, rocky defiles, only to be held by a stubborn defense at the heads of the gullies, but at length, they fought their way onto the crest just as Ferguson's men, headed by the 40th, at last, appeared behind Delaborde's right rear. The French general then conceded the ridge and ordered a withdrawal.

We have some slight account of the experience of the 82nd at Roliça from the pen of Lieutenant George Wood:

'We came up with the enemy, who had taken an amazingly strong position on the heights of Rolessa [sic], from which, after marching four leagues that day, we had to attack and dislodge them. Having previously fixed bayonets, primed and loaded, &c, we drew nearer and nearer the scene of action... We now began to advance over those who had fallen: among them was my brother Sub[97], who had been out skirmishing; and we came under what I then thought a pretty hot fire, both of field pieces and musketry, not having witnessed the like before: but this I found was a mere joke to what I was hereafter to experience. However, it gave me a seasoning, as I was soon after knocked down by a musket-ball striking me on the left groin; and I only attribute escaping a severe wound to having some papers in the pocket of my pantaloons, which prevented its penetrating the flesh; but it caused a great contusion[98]: I was, however, in a few minutes able to proceed with the Regiment, and soon had the pleasure of seeing the French flying before us. We followed them till the lateness of the evening compelled us to halt.'[99]

Both sides had some reasons for satisfaction. Delaborde had fought a skillful and obstinate delaying action, but at the cost of six to seven hundred men and three guns. Wellesley had gained the field, and this relatively modest but hard-fought early victory was enough to confirm his soldiers' confidence in their superiority over their adversaries. British losses totaled 474, nearly half of whom were from the unfortunate 29th. The 82nd suffered 26 casualties that day, six rank and file killed and two officers and 18 wounded, while the 40th had one soldier killed and two wounded, presumably when their outflanking march brought them onto the French right flank at the end of the battle. The 40th appear to have traversed the scene of action, for Lieutenant William Hibbert wrote that, 'After the French had retreated, we passed over the field of battle. You can have no conception of anything more horrid.'

---

[97] Lieutenant Richard Read of the 82nd was reported 'dangerously wounded' at Roliça. He survived, and was again wounded on 1st August 1809 near Flushing during the Walcheren campaign, and then once more in Lord Blayney's attempt on Fuengirola, 17th October 1810, from which he again recovered, only to die at Cartagena on 9th November 1812 whilst DAQMG of the British garrison of that Spanish port. He had meanwhile been taken prisoner in December 1811 while carrying dispatches, remaining in captivity until March 1812.

[98] A 'contusion' was a severe bruise which did not break the skin and was often caused at that time when soldiers were hit by nearly-spent low velocity musket balls. Those who suffered contusions were sometimes listed as 'slightly wounded' but usually fought on and were seldom incapacitated for long.

[99] Wood, p.p. 51-2.

The Battle of Vimeiro, 21st August 1808

In the days following the Battle of Roliça, both sides received reinforcements. British transports with four thousand infantry of Acland's and Anstruther's brigades were off the coast, and at noon on the 18th, Wellesley moved forward to cover their disembarkation in Maceira Bay, fifteen miles to the southwest. The army reached the rendezvous that evening and took up positions on heights astride the Maceira River and around the little village of Vimeiro.

The reinforcements brought the very welcome news that by order of 20th July 1808, powdered hair and tarred queues had been abolished. The forthcoming battle would be fought by the greater part of the British soldiers with short, natural hair, though the officers of the 82nd were still wearing powder (and pomade) in their hair at Gibraltar in 1810.

Already the army's peacetime uniforms were showing the wear, tear and dirt of active service, and as early as 18th August, on outpost duty with 'no covering but my great coat, no pillow but my cocked hat,' Lieutenant George Wood noted that 'the fine ornaments that had shone so conspicuously on the parades on home service began to lose their brilliancy: the glittering epaulette was crushed into a thousand forms, and the pretty tight boot cut with many a slit to ease the blistered foot.'[100]

Later in the Peninsula campaign, the soldiers of the 4th Division, including the 40th, became known as 'the Honeysuckers' on account of their propensity for robbing beehives, and it was at Vimeiro that Private William Lawrence showed early talent in this field:

'On the first night of our encampment there, two of my comrades and myself were strolling over the hills together when we fell in with a hive of bees, weighing, I should think, at least a hundredweight, which we carried back into the camp: not without difficulty, however, for we found them very uncivil passengers to carry, and our faces and hands were fearfully stung; but our honey and grapes, for we had profited too from being encamped in some very fine vineyards, paid us for this a little.'[101]

Sir Arthur Wellesley had a more serious problem: the latest reinforcement had included Sir Harry Burrard, who would supersede Wellesley in command of the army pending the arrival of Sir Hew Dalrymple, an even more senior officer. Burrard arrived on August 20th but, having vetoed Wellesley's plans for a further advance on the 21st, he decided to spend one more night aboard ship before assuming command. Wellesley would have a few more hours in charge of the army, and these would suffice to bring him victory and to plunge him into controversy.

Meanwhile, General Androche Junot, Duc d'Abrantes, had, with some reluctance, marched out from Lisbon. Having met up with Delaborde and Loison at Torres Vedras, he led a united French force of some fifteen thousand men and 24 guns to defeat the British before they could receive further reinforcements. Marching through the night, on the morning of 21st August, he approached Vimeiro from the southeast. By seven o'clock, Junot's army had halted within four miles of the British picquets, and there he formed his columns of attack.

Wellesley received the news of the French advance at around midnight. He had, not unreasonably, expected a French advance on the direct route from Lisbon and had accordingly positioned his troops facing south on high ground around the village of Vimeiro, some two miles inland from Maceira Bay. The village lies between two steep-sided and dominating ridges divided by the gorge of the River Maceira, one ridge on its western, seaward side and the other running away to the north-east, whilst a much lower, round, flat-topped hill (Vimeiro Hill) commands the approaches to the village from the south-east. The latter ridge (usually known as the eastern ridge) rises to a small plateau and then sinks steadily down towards the east, where the hamlet of Ventosa lies some three thousand yards from the gorge. The main strength of the army was posted on the western ridge, with two brigades forward on Vimeiro Hill and just one battalion, the 40th, detached on the waterless eastern ridge to guard against a flank attack from that direction.

The British, as was their custom, had been 'stood to' for an hour before first light on the morning of Sunday 21st August; but at daybreak, as there was no further sign of the French, the army was ordered to pile arms, cook breakfast, and parade later for divine service; and so Private Lawrence and his comrades were enjoying another meal of honey and grapes when, shortly after eight o'clock, the picquets of the 40th on the left were driven

---

[100] Wood, pp. 53-4.
[101] Lawrence, p. 44.

in and the Regiment beat to arms. The French army was indistinctly seen through dense clouds of dust, advancing directly on Vimeiro astride the Torres Vedras road.

Junot shared the arrogant self-confidence of many French officers of that time, and after a cursory reconnaissance, he deployed his main body for an assault on Vimeiro Hill, the centre of Wellesley's position, also sending a strong column to turn the British left on the eastern ridge. This latter force consisted of the four battalions of Brenier's brigade, a regiment of dragoons and three guns.

Noting Junot's flanking movement against his almost unprotected left, Wellesley rapidly redeployed his own troops. When the alarm was sounded, General Ferguson led the balance of his brigade up to reinforce the 40th on the eastern ridge. Wellesley joined him there and at once ordered up three further brigades from his uncommitted right wing, those of Nightingall, Bowes and Acland, 'making his dispositions in the most cool and masterly style.' The first reinforcement to appear was Nightingall's brigade, which included the 82nd.

Seeing this extensive redeployment, Junot sent a second brigade, that of Solignac with a further three battalions and three or four guns, to support Brenier's attack on the British left. His decision divided the French army into two almost equal halves, which, separated by nearly two miles, in effect, fought separate battles. This dispersion of effort was compounded by a marked lack of coordination between the frontal and flanking attacks and between Brenier and Solignac.

Over the next three hours, Junot's repeated assaults on Vimeiro Hill and village were comprehensively defeated and driven back in confusion in a series of classic conflicts of massed French column against two-deep British line, and he had committed his last reserves against the British centre by the time his flanking attack was launched in the area of Ventosa at around 10.30 a.m. Both Brenier and Solignac had been forced to move further to the north than Junot had anticipated in order to avoid a deep re-entrant (called a ravine by participants in the battle) which runs up to Ventosa from below the eastern ridge; but whereas Solignac chose to pass this obstacle by climbing tracks close to Ventosa[102], Brenier made a much wider diversion to the north in search of an easier route.

It would be useful at this point to consider some characteristic French and British tactics for, although many exceptions can be found on both sides, the general course of the battalion and brigade-level clashes at Vimeira would be repeated again and again throughout the war.

Early in the Revolutionary War the French had discovered that a concentrated assault of solid infantry columns could overawe and break an army of Prussians, Russians or Austrians by its physical momentum and moral force. Such an attack would be preceded by clouds of skirmishers, or *tirailleurs*, found by the *voltigeur* companies of French regiments and supported by their excellent artillery. The intended effect of these was to disrupt the enemy as the columns advanced. A battalion column would normally have a one-company frontage and would be propelled forward by massed drummers in its centre beating the *pas-de-charge*, punctuated by enthusiastic shouts of '*En avant,*' '*A la baionette*' and '*Vive l'Empereur.*'

The French attack column was usually met and almost invariably defeated by the British in line. Historians have made much of the devastating effect of British musketry, delivered in well-drilled volleys by a two-deep line. There was a mathematical certainty about the superior firepower of a British line opposed to a French column, for every musket in a British regiment deployed in line could be brought to bear, whilst only the front two or three ranks of a French column could reply. There is little doubt that the musketry of the British Army in the Peninsula was particularly effective, as was its tactical employment, but the accounts of contemporary witnesses suggest that too much emphasis may have been placed by some later historians on this one element of a battle-winning formula which was rather more complex.

Firstly, the British Army too used strong bodies of skirmishers, both to prevent the *tirailleurs* from causing casualties in the British gun lines and infantry and to disrupt the French advance, often forcing the columns to deploy prematurely. Wellesley also made effective use of artillery to cause chaos and attrition, and at Vimeiro, the Royal Artillery fired shrapnel for the first time in Europe.

---

[102] There is an ancient track which emerges onto the ridge-top some 500 yards east of Ventosa which local tradition holds to be Solignac's route. However, with some four and a half thousand troops to move, including cavalry and guns, it is likely that Solignac used several routes up to the ridge.

As the French columns approached, the British skirmishers were withdrawn, and the infantry battalions, scrambling to their feet, presented a solid red line whose moral effect was heightened by their disciplined silence and steadiness, which was in marked contrast to the clamorous advance of their enemy. British battalions would normally hold their fire until the heads of the opposing columns were some 40 to 50 feet away before delivering a devastating first volley. This might be followed by one or more further volleys until the British commander considered his enemy to be wavering and unbalanced, whereupon the British line would let out a thunderous 'Huzza!' and advance with levelled bayonets, each 17 inches of cold steel. The contrast between this sudden outburst of controlled aggression and the previous disciplined restraint was usually enough to make the unsteady men of an already wounded column seek safety in flight, and it was a rare event for unbroken bodies of the opposing sides to cross bayonets. Throughout their advance, the British infantry would be kept in hand, and if the enemy succeeded in reforming, further volleys of musketry would be delivered, followed by another cheer and a renewed advance with lowered bayonets. The overall effect of these British tactics was as much moral as physical and is well described by a French officer, the future Marshal Bugeaud:

'The advance began, and as soon as we reached about one thousand metres from the English line, our men would begin to get restless and excited; the march pace begin to get more hurried and disorderly. Meanwhile, the English, silent and impassive, arms at port, looked like a great red wall – most forbidding to our young soldiers. As we get closer, shouts of '*Vive l'Empereur*,' '*En avant, á la baionette*' break from our ranks. Some men hang their shakos on the end of their muskets; our march becomes a trot; the ranks begin to intermingle; men fire their muskets into the air. Three hundred metres to the front, the scarlet line stands motionless, ever silent. It is a striking contrast. Some of us know that it will be devastating when, at last, they do fire. Their unshakable calm is unnerving. Our enthusiasm begins to wane; we try to restore our men's confidence by redoubled shouting. Then, at last, the English make a quarter turn, and their muskets come down – they are making ready. Appalled, many of our men are nailed to the spot and open a hesitant fire, which makes no impact on the rock-steady wall to our front. Then it comes, the English volley: precise, deadly, thunderous. Decimated, our column wavers, reeling under the blow, half turns, trying to regain its balance. As we try to do so, the enemy's silence is broken by three fearsome Hurrahs, and with the third, they are at us with the bayonet, chasing us in disorderly retreat.'

There was nothing particularly novel about this drill in 1808: indeed, it would have been regularly practised by every British battalion present at Vimeiro. But while Sir Arthur Wellesley's tactical success in Spain was built on the firm foundations of rigid discipline, sound battle drills and indomitable regimental spirit formed on parade grounds and battlefields over generations, he brought to the campaign his own distinctive qualities as a field commander.

Sir Arthur Wellesley's character was formed for command. Supremely self-disciplined and imbued with a high sense of duty, he had trained himself to cool and detached self-control. His aloof patrician demeanour was not calculated to make him loved, but his troops knew that he would beat the French, and his very presence in the field inspired battle-winning confidence. Sir Arthur had studied his enemy with care, respected their capabilities, and set a high priority on gaining intelligence. He had an excellent eye for ground, characteristically using the reverse slope of a ridge to achieve security, deception and surprise and minimising casualties by keeping his troops hidden from direct fire and observation until the last safe moment, when their sudden appearance would have maximum impact. Finally, Wellesley had an extraordinary knack of being present at the right place at the right time to read and personally influence the battle. This enabled him to deploy reserves when and where they were needed, often using covered approaches to move them to the point of decision.

General Ferguson, a capable and experienced officer, coordinated the British defense of the eastern ridge, effectively taking the other troops under command as they arrived. Wellesley, who rode over before the French attack developed and remained on the eastern ridge throughout the battle, probably had a hand in the deployment, though whether he personally placed the brigades or merely concurred in Ferguson's dispositions is unknown. Brent Spencer was also there, and Lawrence states that it was he who led the eventual advance on that flank.

The British force was sited on and behind a low crest-line on the ridge-top west of Ventosa, facing east astride the road to Lourinha. It consisted of seven battalions, 5,782 men in all[103], supported by about three guns.

---

[103] The strength of the 40th at Vimeiro was 923 and that of the 82nd was 904.

They were in three lines. The first line consisted of the seven light companies, including those of the 40th and 82nd, in skirmishing order on the crest-line. The second or main line, lying or sitting down in formation just behind the crest, was composed of the three regiments of Ferguson's own brigade, with the 40th in the centre flanked by the 36th (on the right) and the 71st. The third or supporting line consisted of the four battalions of Bowes' and Nightingall's brigades, with the 82nd on the right flank.

Solignac had nearly four thousand infantry[104] and five hundred dragoons. Having reached the ridge-top just east of Ventosa, he deployed, brought up his right shoulder and advanced past the hamlet along the eastern ridge under a hot August sun. An extended line of *tirailleurs* preceded his three massed battalion columns, which advanced briskly in their white summer uniforms with drums beating. To their front, all Solignac's men could see was a heavy line of red-coated British light infantry, who engaged the French skirmishers. Private William Lawrence of the Light Company 40th Foot later recalled his part in this skirmish:

'I remember this well on account of a Frenchman and myself being occupied in firing at each other for at least half an hour without doing anyone any injury; but he took a pretty straight aim at me once, and if it had not been for a tough front-rank man that I had, in the shape of a cork-tree, his shot must have proved fatal, for I happened to be straight behind the tree when the bullet embedded itself in it. I recollect saying at the time, "Well done, front-rank man, thee doesn't fall at that stroke," and unfortunately for the Frenchman, a fellow-comrade, who was left-handed, came up to me very soon afterwards and asked me how I was getting on. I said badly and told him there was a Frenchman in front, and we had been trying to knock each other over for some time without either of us having been able to succeed; on which he asked me where he was, that he might have a try at him. I pointed out the thicket behind which the Frenchman was, and he prepared his rifle so as to catch him out in his peeping manoeuvres, but not without himself, as well as I, being well covered by my old front-rank man. By-and-by, Mr Frenchman again made his peep round the bush, but it was his last, for my comrade, putting his rifle to his left shoulder, killed him at the first shot.'[105]

The outnumbered *tirailleurs* made little impression on the British light companies, and after about half an hour, Solignac had to send the French columns forward to clear the crest. Indeed, he may have mistaken the seven companies visible to his front for the main position; if so he was soon to be disabused. The British light companies were now ordered to fall back to the main position, which they appear to have done by filing to the rear. As Lieutenant William Cowper Coles of the 40th wrote:

'It became soon necessary to withdraw them in order to give scope for action and likewise ground for our army. The Light Infantry retired by degrees under a most desperate fire, and no sooner had they gained the flanks of their respective brigades than the action became general.'

Lying down behind rising ground, the British regiments were protected from direct fire, but on the right, at least, they were starting to take some casualties from the French artillery, which had been laboriously dragged up the heights. Lieutenant George Wood of the 82nd recalled:

'I was laughing and joking when one of my brother officers [Lieutenant Robert Donkin] came to me, with his visage very much cast down, being unwell at the time, and remarked that I ought to be thinking of something more serious at that critical moment. He observed that many a fine fellow would soon be laid low and sent to the next world; adding that he had a presentiment that something fatal would that day happen to himself. The poor fellow, in about ten minutes after, received a cannon-ball in his neck which almost severed his head from his body.'

Shortly afterwards, George Wood saved another subaltern of the 82nd from meeting a similar fate:

'He was very near-sighted, and the French artillery playing on us at some distance, the unevenness of the ground made the balls come hopping similar to those bowled at cricket, which caused the men to open right and left to let them pass: at one of these openings this officer stood and, addressing himself to me, asked what was the matter? I replied, "Do you not see what is coming?" at the same time, giving him a hard pull. I was the means of saving him from the sudden death the other had just experienced; however, taking his quizzing-glass to his assistance, he gladly observed the ball pass about one hundred yards to his rear.'[106]

---

[104] 3rd/12th Légère (1,253), 3rd/15th Légère (1,305) and 3rd/58th Ligne Regiment (1,428).
[105] Lawrence, p.p. 44-5.
[106] Wood, p.p. 57-8.

The fire of the French *tirailleurs* also took some toll of unwary spectators, as Lieutenant William Hibbert of the 40th described in a letter to his father in Manchester:

'The 40th was on a hill on the left, opposite a French column, which were advancing on us from an opposite hill, covered by their riflemen, who were in front in the valley engaged with some of our light troops. Before our regiment commenced firing, I had a narrow escape. The men were seated on the ground to rest themselves, and whilst I was standing watching the light troops engaged, and conversing with another officer [Lieutenant Thomas Decimus Franklyn], we were marked by the riflemen on the hill opposite and fired at by several at the same time. One bullet unluckily passed through my brother officer's thigh. I escaped without injury, though several balls struck the ground within a foot of me.'

The French columns had become somewhat disorganised in their advance, having presumably deployed at least partially into line to engage the British skirmishers, but they reformed and came on with great confidence towards the crest[107], all three columns abreast with frontages of some forty men each and intervals of about three hundred yards between them. The left of the French advance extended beyond Ferguson's right, so the 82nd came forward from the support line to occupy that flank.

As the heads of Solignac's columns breasted the crest, the leading four British battalions advanced silently in line to meet them and delivered a thunderous volley from some three thousand[108] muskets at close range, followed by a rolling succession of half-company volleys. The leading ranks of the French columns were devastated; though shaken, the gallant veterans of Friedland and Austerlitz continued to edge forward as they struggled unsuccessfully to deploy into line and returned an irregular fire. After some two minutes of murderous musketry, Ferguson gave the order to charge, at which his men gave three loud cheers and advanced with levelled bayonets. The French did not wait to cross bayonets but wavered, disintegrated and fell back in disorder. The four British battalions pressed after them, halting at intervals to pour a volley into the struggling mass, which retired fighting in a north-westerly direction carrying their wounded commander. The pursuit continued for the best part of a mile on the general line of the Lourinha road, when, having made several unsuccessful attempts to check the British advance and having lost their guns as they tried to withdraw across a saddle-backed depression, the French were driven into low ground.

A colourful contemporary report in the *Edinburgh Review* states that the French 'came up to the charge like men accustomed to victory, but no troops, however brave, however accustomed to victory, have ever withstood the charge of the British bayonet. In a moment, their foremost rank fell, like the line of grass beneath the scythes of the mowers.'

It is doubtful, however, whether many Frenchmen actually fell to the bayonet and eye-witness accounts give a rather more persuasive account of the British advance. William Hibbert of the 40th wrote that 'The Regiment… advanced, and after some smart firing, charged the enemy, who did not wait to receive it, but chose to trust rather to legs than arms.'

William Lawrence of the same regiment recalled that:

'After we had been… skirmishing for some time, a large body of French made their appearance in our front. Our artillery greeted them pretty sharply, ploughing furrows through them with ball and throwing them into a confused state, after which our columns advanced under General Spencer, our cannon still playing over our heads, until we got within a short distance of the enemy, when we fired and charged them, driving them from the position they had occupied after some very severe fighting well kept up for some time on both sides, and capturing about seven pieces of cannon[109] with ammunition wagons.'[110]

George Wood's narrative paints a similar picture from the point of view of the 82nd, who moved up into the first line on the right flank of Ferguson's advance:

---

[107] In later years, the Duke of Wellington reflected that at Vimeiro the French came on 'with more confidence, and seemed to *feel their way* less than I always found them to do *afterwards*. I received them in line, which they were not accustomed to.'

[108] The total strength of the four regiments, the 36th, 40th, 71st and 82nd, was 3,353 men, from whom some ten percent must be deducted for officers, sergeants and drummers.

[109] Although Lawrence may have counted seven captured French guns in this area at the end of the battle, only 3-4 could have been captured from Solignac's brigade at this time.

[110] Lawrence, p. 45.

'We came in for our share of the conflict of that day by being opposed to a strong French regiment, which advanced to within half pistol-shot of us, when a most tremendous point-blank fire ensued. This not proving effectual, 'Charge!' was the word now vociferated from flank to centre: but, on their seeing us come to this awful position of destruction in the art of war, they had not the courage to withstand our impetuous movement; for, just as we were in the act of crossing bayonets, to the right-about they went, in the quickest time. We followed as rapidly, driving them from their artillery, I believe about twelve field-pieces, passing it on the right flank at the same time as the 71st Regiment did on the left, and I trust we had an equal share in the honour of capturing them. The French, however, having now gained possession of the village on the heights [Ventosa], which had been strongly barricaded, remained there for the present, and we received orders to halt in the ravine. Indeed, a little breathing-time had become very necessary, as we had for the last two hours been firing, shouting, running, swearing, sweating and huzzaing.'[111]

Taking the 36th and 40th, Ferguson pushed on in pursuit of the wreck of Solignac's brigade, which he trapped in low ground, probably near the village of Pregança, leaving the 71st and 82nd resting in low ground around the captured guns. There, the two battalions were caught off guard by Brenier, who, marching to the sound of battle, appeared belatedly but unobserved on the ridge above them and descended on their flank with four fresh battalions and a regiment of dragoons. The French had every advantage of surprise, higher ground and superior numbers in their favour[112]. The 71st and 82nd withdrew to a more defensible position, and the French guns were recaptured; but any confusion was momentary, as the two battalions quickly rallied on higher ground, assisted by the 29th, which came up to attack Brenier's flank. All three British battalions opened a heavy and effective volley fire and then swept forward with a cheer to overthrow Brenier's disordered columns and retake the guns. The French broke and fled, covered by their cavalry. George Wood makes light of the temporary reversal to the 71st and 82nd, representing their withdrawal as deliberate:

'We were ordered to make a retrograde movement, as a *ruse de guerre*, which had the desired effect of enticing the enemy to rally. Having thus drawn them to a sufficient distance from their fastnesses, we came to our proper front and gave them such a reception that they again ran off and took possession of their stronghold [Ventosa], whence we soon had the pleasure of seeing the gallant Riflemen[113] completely drive them. It was near this spot that I saw, as we advanced, a Scotch piper of the 71st Regiment lying on the ground wounded. This, however, did not prevent his cheering his comrades on to glory with their national music.[114] They certainly are a brave people: but, as to their being more so than their neighbours, I never saw anything in them as men or soldiers to make me think they were.'[115]

General Brenier himself was captured. Wood recalled him being brought to the surgeon of the 82nd: 'On the ground, we found General Brenier, concealed in the rushes: he had been wounded in the leg, and was taken prisoner, and brought to our surgeon to dress. On cutting off his boot, we were surprised to see he had no stockings on; on this being observed to him, he very coolly replied, "*Le soldat Français n'a pas besoin be bas.*"[116]

The two brigades engaged on the British left had soundly beaten and routed twice their number of Frenchmen, capturing all their guns, and Ferguson, with the 36th and 40th, had the remnants of Solignac's brigade,

[111] Wood, p.p. 54-55.

[112] Brenier had over 4,500 fresh infantry, 640 dragoons and three guns: the total strength of the two British battalions before the battle had been 1,858, but following the earlier clash with Solignac this had probably been reduced to around seventeen hundred effectives. The exact positions of the opposing forces are uncertain, but assuming that the French guns were captured at the head of the re-entrant to the south-west of Ventosa, an advance by Brenier along the Eastern Ridge, keeping to the north of Ventosa, would have enabled him to appear on the ridge above and to the left of the 71st and 82nd. Equally, such a move could have left Brenier's right flank vulnerable to counter-attack by the 29th.

[113] There were in fact no British riflemen in this part of the field as the 60th and 95th were nearly two miles away with Fane's and Acland's brigades around Vimeiro Hill and, contrary to Laurence's observation, the Light Companies were armed with muskets. Amid the smoke of battle it could have been difficult to distinguish the exact nature of skirmishers and it is probable that what Wood saw was Ferguson's light companies driving a French remnant out of Ventosa.

[114] This was Piper George Clark, who when badly wounded sat down on his knapsack and continued playing his pipes, saying, according to one version, 'Deil hae me, lads, if ye shall want music.'

[115] Wood, p.p. 55-6.

[116] 'French soldiers have no need of stockings' (Wood, p. 55).

some fifteen hundred men, pinned into a position where he could have forced their surrender had he not received an unexpected order to halt.

This order to stand fast had come from Burrard, who had come ashore when the firing started but had generously declined to assume the responsibilities of command. With the battle won and with half his army still uncommitted, Wellesley galloped up to Burrard and, raising his hat, declared, 'Sir Harry, now is your time to advance. The enemy is completely beaten, and we shall be in Lisbon in three days.' Cautious to the point of inertia, Sir Harry feared that Junot might have unbroken infantry reserves and was conscious of his own lack of cavalry compared to The French. Burrard was unmoved, even when an aide-de-camp arrived from Ferguson with the news that 'a column of broken troops 1,500 to 2,000 strong had in their confusion got into a hollow[117], and could be cut off from their main body by a movement in advance of his brigade.' Wellesley did not hide his disappointment: turning to his staff in disgust and frustration, he declared, 'Gentlemen, nothing now remains to be done but to go and shoot red-legged partridges!'

As they marched back to camp in triumph behind their regimental bands, Colours flying, dragging the captured cannon and waggons[118] and herding hundreds of prisoners, the troops were equally surprised and angry at Burrard's squandering of the fruits of victory. Lieutenant George Wood of the 82nd recalled their astonishment at the lack of orders to follow the retreating enemy: 'I well recollect the observation of every individual, "What keeps us here after so complete a victory? Why do we not advance and overtake the foe?" No one could tell – all was conjecture and amazement.'

The 40th Regiment lost six rank and file killed at Vimeiro, and two officers and thirty wounded[119], while the casualties of the 82nd totaled one officer (Lieutenant Robert Donkin) and seven men killed, and 53 wounded. After the battle, those who had escaped injury exchanged congratulations. A junior officer of the 82nd, seeing his senior's cocked hat much shattered by a shell-splinter, offered commiserations, 'Oh, my dear fellow, I am very sorry to see your hat so broken!' 'Thank you,' the other replied with grim humour, 'but I suppose you would rather have seen my head, and then you would have risen a step.'

The 40th Foot received special thanks for their conduct at Vimeiro, and the 82nd were also particularly mentioned in the despatches concerning that battle, while Major Harry Eyre, who had commanded the 82nd at both Roliça and Vimeiro, was promoted on 10th September 1808 to Lieutenant-Colonel of the 19th Regiment.

For his part in the campaign, Brent Spencer was made a KCB, and Wellesley wrote of his knighthood that 'there never was a braver officer or one who deserved it better,' while Princess Augusta, who had a long-standing relationship with Spencer, received a glowing report on her hero from an ADC who stood by the General under fire: 'He says he never in his life saw anything like his coolness, good temper, intrepidity and steadiness – that he was, if possible, greater on the 21st [at Vimeiro] than on the 17th [at Roliça] and that his conduct on the first day was enough to establish his military character, if it had not been so often seen before, and each time with credit to his head and heart.'

The Battle Honours 'ROLEIA' and 'VIMIERA' (sic) were not awarded until 1824, and only 51 all ranks of the 40th and 44 of the 82nd survived to receive the Military General Service Medal with bar for "Roleia,' while 114 of the 40th and 79 of the 82nd received the bar for 'Vimiera.' Major John Rainey of the 82nd received the Army Gold Medal for his services as AQMG at Roliça and Vimeiro.

---

[117] The remains of Solignac's brigade had probably been driven into the re-entrant north-east of Ventosa, and a British advance east along the ridge from Ventosa to the Lourinhao road would have cut off their retreat.

[118] Lieutenant William Hibbert of the 40th wrote that 'After the action, it fell to my lot to command a party to drag home the waggons taken from the French. I did not reach the camp till after dark, and then quite exhausted with hunger and fatigue, not having eaten scarcely anything for twenty-four hours.'

[119] The *Regimental Record* says 13 killed and about 60 wounded, but the former may include some who died later of their wounds while the latter may include those whose wounds were slight. Lieutenant Thomas Decimus Franklyn of the 40th was seriously wounded in the thigh, as was Captain (later Brevet Lieutenant-Colonel) Charles Hervey Smith, commanding the Light Company, who had been wounded on two occasions the previous year in South America.

The Convention of Cintra

Sir Harry Burrard's command of the army lasted only until the early hours of the following morning, when Sir Hew 'Dowager' Dalrymple landed and relieved him. Dalrymple and Wellesley appear to have taken an instant dislike to each other, and the new commander-in-chief pointedly rejected all advice offered by his victorious subordinate. Within twenty hours of victory at Vimeiro, the British army had seen three commanders and its operations had ground to a halt while Dalrymple awaited further reinforcements.

It was with some surprise that on 22nd August, Sir Hew received an emissary from Junot with proposals for negotiations. A 48-hour armistice followed, and talks began, the eventual outcome of which was that in return for handing over the places remaining to them in Portugal, Junot's army of 25,747 men was to be returned to France in British ships, complete with their arms, horses, baggage (including much loot) and military chest. This agreement, the Convention of Cintra, was ratified on 31st August.

On 1st September, the British Army began a leisurely advance on Lisbon, during which the 40th passed some 150 carts laden with Junot's wounded.

On 6th September, in camp at 'St. Antonio de Tugal,' Colonel James Kemmis, Majors Henry Thornton and Richard Archdall of the 40th, and Majors Harry Eyre and Chichester McDonnel of the 82nd were among the Officers of the Army who signed an Address to Sir Arthur Wellesley on presenting him with a piece of silver plate in recognition of his victory at Vimeiro.

The main British camp was established at Queluz, northwest of Lisbon, but by about 15th September, both the 40th and the 82nd were quartered in the city, where the latter occupied the citadel, the old Moorish Castle of St. George. Soon afterwards, a virulent fever swept through the 82nd, putting thirteen officers and more than one in three of the men into hospital. This they attributed to having their bivouac ground swamped by a sudden storm during the advance on Lisbon, an event recalled by George Wood:

'We halted in a most delightful spot in the midst of vineyards, olives, and orange-groves. My comrade and myself set about constructing our little hut, and pitched upon a hollow piece of ground for that purpose. This slight shelter merely consisted of a few green branches to screen us from the scorching rays of the sun and the dews of the night. A finer evening than this there could not be; and at dusk, we stretched ourselves on our bed, made of fine soft rushes which grew here in abundance. We had enjoyed the blessings of a sound repose but little more than an hour when we were awakened by peals of thunder breaking over our heads; these became more loud and dreadful the nearer they approached, until the whole earth seemed to tremble. The thunder was accompanied by vivid flashes of lightning followed, in a few minutes, by the most impetuous torrents of rain. Our snug settlement in the ravine was very quickly covered by a rapid stream in which, by the constant light of the electric fluid, we perceived all our loose articles of dress, the only part we had taken off, such as shoes, hats, sashes, belts, &c., all floating away, and we had great difficulty in saving them. So heavy did the rain fall that it ran down the boughs of our hut like as many small water-spouts pouring upon us, and we found it more eligible to stand out in the midst of it than to remain in occupation of the hut.'[120]

By 21st September, most of the French had sailed[121] aboard the same transports that had carried the British Army to Portugal. George Wood watched them embark:

'An extraordinary sight it was; for they had their standards displayed in the square at Belem with as much *sang-froid* as if they had been the victorious army and had dictated the agreements. Indeed, they seemed to have some reason for considering themselves so, from the terms they made; for they embarked with their heavy baggage (I should rather say plunder), their arms, horses and artillery, with colours flying, drums beating, bayonets fixed, &c.'[122]

The Convention of Cintra caused an outcry against the generals held responsible. Dalrymple and Burrard were recalled to face a board of enquiry. Wellesley, having been superseded, also went home, as did Brent Spencer on medical grounds. The board of enquiry opened on 14th November, and Dalrymple, Burrard and Wellesley were cross-examined. Brent Spencer gave evidence in which he strongly supported Wellesley's view that the victory

---

[120] Wood, p.p. 60-61.

[121] The last French troops to be evacuated under the Convention did not leave the Tagus until 5th December.

[122] Wood, p. 62.

of Vimeiro could have been more fully exploited, but that, Burrard's caution having prevailed, the Convention was expedient and justifiable. The board of enquiry ended in an anti-climactic fudge, with the Convention, approved and no blame apportioned, but neither Dalrymple nor Burrard held operational command again.

The departure of Dalrymple, Burrard and Wellesley left Sir John Moore in command of the army in Portugal. Opening his sealed orders on the afternoon of 6th October 1808, Moore found that he had been tasked to take an army of not less than 30,000 infantry and 5,000 cavalry to the north of Spain 'to co-operate with Spanish armies in the expulsion of the French from that kingdom.' Following the successive defeats in July and August of Dupont in Andalusia and Junot in Portugal, the French had evacuated all of Spain except the northwest, leaving Madrid in patriot hands. With French strength in the Peninsula reduced to some 50,000 men, who had retired beyond the River Ebro, the Allies confidently planned a final clearance of these remnants by one hundred thousand Spaniards supported by a substantial British field army under Moore.

The 40th were mustered at 'Monte Santo' (Monsanto) Camp on 24th September[123] and in the Benedictine Convent in Lisbon[124] on 24th October, where they prepared for the coming campaign. Medical boards selected sick and wounded for repatriation to England or Oporto, while arrangements were made for the convalescents to remain at Lisbon with the Regimental stores and heavy baggage until they were fit to march.

The families of the 40th were sternly warned that 'unless they avail themselves of the opportunity of returning to England as directed in the orders of the 20th instant… they cannot expect to have any part of their baggage carried for them or any indulgence granted to them' since the regiments of Sir John Moore's army 'will probably have to perform a march perhaps of six hundred miles to gain the army in Spain, and it is impossible to obtain carts even for the conveyance of the sick.' Five days later, the women were further informed that 'should they fail to embark when ordered no rations will be allowed them after the transports sail.'

Billhooks and camp kettles were issued to the companies, and they were ordered to be prepared with 'good and sufficient mules or horses to carry their camp kettles on the march,' while officers commanding companies were to provide their men with such 'necessaries' as soap, pipeclay and other small articles for cleaning their arms, accoutrements and belts. Finally, on 1st November, each man was issued with new musket flints and 60 rounds of ammunition.[125]

The 40th, like the 82nd, had sickened during their stay in Lisbon and were rendered unfit for service for several weeks, but on 3rd November, the Regiment marched up to the Portuguese frontier where, for some two months from mid-November, they occupied the strategically important fortress town of Elvas. A *Regimental Order Book* entry for 15th November advises that 'it is probable that the Battalion will remain in its present quarters for some time,' but writing from Elvas to his brother on 23rd December, James Kemmis was still expecting to join Moore's army:

'It is not unlikely, but the 40th may pass the Frontiers shortly. They were sent down to accompany the first party, and would have gone, but for a violent fever that broke out in the Regiment in Camp St. Anna before Lisbon. It ran like wild-fire through officers and men – many of the latter have fallen victims and one of the former.'

Lieutenant William Hibbert was the sick officer referred to by Kemmis. Weakened by illness, he was obliged to leave the 40th on their first day's march and returned to find indifferent accommodation in Lisbon, from where, on 21st November, he wrote to his mother:

'Many officers have had billets on the inhabitants, and received much attention in their houses. From my bad state of health, I was entitled to one, which, after much trouble, I obtained, but found the house so objectionable in every respect that I could not for a moment think of residing in it. I got another afterwards in a large old house belonging to a doctor of laws, who fitted up two apartments for me in a sort of lodge belonging to the building, which had not been inhabited for some time. In this place, I remained in purgatory for two or three days, literally swarming with bugs. The bedstead and walls behind an old paper, which had apparently been on for ten years, were so thickly inhabited by these gentry that I was not only bitten till I was half mad but nearly poisoned with the smell. It is no small mortification to me to be left behind the Regiment; and, to add to my

---

[123] The 40th were returned on 26th September as 926 strong. The 82nd mustered 932 on that day.
[124] The 40th appears to have moved a short distance from their encampment at Monsanto, just west of Lisbon, to the vast 16th century Benedictine monastery of São Bento da Saúde. The site is now occupied by the Palacio de São Bento, seat of the Portuguese Parliament.
[125] Manuscript *Regimental Order Book*.

uneasiness, I am told that unless I intend to sacrifice myself, I must not again attempt to engage in any active service.'

William Hibbert sailed from Lisbon in January 1809 but died at home in Manchester the following month.[126]

Elvas[127] was the army's most advanced post at that time, and so Colonel Kemmis made contact with the Spanish garrison of Badajoz, nine miles distant, and sent Lieutenant Conyngham Ellis into Estremadura to establish contact with Cuesta's Spanish army and gather intelligence on French movements. The uncomfortably exposed situation of the 40th at Elvas is evident in a series of letters from Kemmis to Sir John Cradock, who commanded the troops left in Portugal when Moore advanced into Spain. On 17th December, he complained that Fort La Lippe, the supposedly impregnable citadel of Elvas, 'has not been supplied with provisions as I had been taught to expect.' The neighbouring Spanish fortress of Badajoz offered no security, for on the 27th, he reported that 'Badajoz cannot make resistance in any degree, either to check or stop the progress of the enemy. From the statements made to me last night by the governor, they want arms, ammunition and provisions.' Writing to his brother on the 23rd, Kemmis explained that if attacked, he would base his defence on Fort La Lippe:

'It overlooks and commands the town, is very formidable and, by my directions, is to be my residence in case the French come this way, which is by no means unlikely, having, since entering Madrid, pushed a body of troops in the direction. The affairs in Spain are wrapped in mystery. Though [we are] so close and in constant habits of hearing from the Junta in Badajoz, the information is never correct. On all sides, it is allowed the Spanish nation are decided in opposing [the French]. But let us reflect on the undiminished resources in good soldiers the French chief can command, and should he hold his resolution of imposing on the Spanish nation, the contest must be long and bloody.'

The *Order Book* of the 40th from this period at Elvas records thorough administrative preparations for the forthcoming campaign: inspection of arms, accoutrements, clothing and blankets, repair of uniform jackets and greatcoats by the Master Tailor and his assistants, and marking and conditioning of the soldiers' canteens and haversacks.

It was probably from this time that the following characteristic tale was told about Colonel Kemmis, whose forceful manner and grandiose diction could sometimes lead to ambiguity and misunderstanding:

'Observing that one of the men in the ranks had a particularly dirty face, which appeared not to have been washed for a twelvemonth, [he] was exceedingly indignant at so gross a violation of military propriety. "Take him," said he to the corporal, who was an Irishman, "take this dirty man, and lave him in the waters of the Guadiana!" After some time, the corporal returned. "What have you done with the man I sent with you?" inquired the Colonel. Up flew the corporal's right hand across the peak of his cap, "Sure an't plaise y'r honnur, an' didn't y'r honnur tell me to lave him in the river? And sure enough, I left him in the river, and there he is now according to y'r honnurs orders!" The bye-standers, and even the Colonel himself, could hardly repress a smile at the mistake of the honest corporal, who looked innocence itself and wondered what there could be to laugh at.'

Meanwhile, the 82nd Regiment had left Nightingall's brigade. Before doing so, they were paid a handsome compliment in a special order, issued at St Antonio de Fayal on 6th September:

'Brigadier-General Nightingall cannot allow the 82nd Regiment to leave the 3rd Brigade without expressing his sincere regret at losing so distinguished a corps. Their soldier-like conduct during the whole time he has had the honour to command them, entitles them to every mark of his approbation and praise; but their brilliant conduct

---

[126] This was the time when the Duke of York's mistress, Mary Ann Clark, was trafficking in commissions, and so when the dying officer attempted to resign his commission his father was advised that, 'If the Duke thought your son very dangerously ill, it would be his interest not to allow him to sell out at all, but probably occasion his refusal, on a supposition that the commission would fall into his hands for nothing, and that he could make money by it.' When the young officer died the Horse Guards had to be kept in ignorance of his demise until the value of his commission had been realised. Writing on 8th March a letter of condolence, General Gore Browne recommended William's father 'not, at present, to say anything relative to his decease, but to let the matter remain quiet until you are informed officially of the resignation having had acceptance.' Shortly afterwards the Duke of York faced accusations of complicity in his mistress's scandalous activities and, although formally acquitted, he resigned as Commander-in-Chief.
[127] On 6th January 1809 the garrison of Elvas, commanded by Colonel Kemmis, consisted of the 40th, with 712 rank and file, and a detachment of the Royal Artillery. This was the only element of the British army in Portugal deployed on the frontier at that time, for Sir John Cradock, commanding in Portugal, had concentrated his troops around Lisbon in anticipation of early evacuation.

in the glorious victory of the 21st ultimo [Vimeiro] has made impressions on his mind which can never be effaced. The Brigadier-General therefore requests that Major Eyre and the officers and soldiers of the 82nd Regiment will accept his thanks for their orderly and meritorious conduct during the above period and to rest assured that he shall ever regret their being removed from his brigade.'

The 82nd did not leave the Lisbon area immediately, for until the end of October they were providing fatigue parties at Belem and orderlies at the general hospital. However, on 2nd November, together with the 97th, the Regiment was sent by sea to garrison Oporto.

They were received in that port with generous hospitality. 'We were here shown the greatest attention possible,' wrote George Wood, 'I never heard men or officers complain of their billets, so accommodating were the inhabitants in consequence of the great intercourse between this place and England.' By December, the health of the greater part of the 82nd had so far improved that the Regiment was considered fit for active service.

The Second Battalions 59th and 81st Foot

Moore's army was to be joined by some eighteen thousand troops from home under Lieutenant-General Sir David Baird, a veteran of campaigns in India, Egypt and South Africa. These reinforcements were made ready as soon as the news of Vimeiro reached England, and they included the new and as yet untried second battalions of the 59th and 81st Regiments of Foot. Apart from bolstering home defence, the principal purpose of these second battalions had originally been to find reinforcing drafts for their first battalions, but circumstances now required their presence on the front line.

The 2nd/59th had been raised at Chesterfield in Derbyshire in 1804. Recruiting was not easy, and eighteen months later, there were still only fifty men in the battalion. Then, in June 1805, Lieutenant-Colonel Charles Fane, aged only 24, assumed command. The following July, the 2nd Battalion marched to Ashbourne, where the ranks began to fill with volunteers from the English and Irish militia regiments. In 1806, the 2nd/59th received one hundred men from the Irish Militia, and in 1807, the Battalion received another five hundred militiamen, notably from Leicestershire, Nottinghamshire and Tipperary. Lieutenant William Chadwick, one of three brothers commissioned into the 59th at that time, must have been a particularly persuasive recruiter, for he brought in two hundred men at one time from the Tipperary Militia and one hundred from the Tyrone Militia.

These part-trained soldiers were welded into an effective battalion through the 'indefatigable pains' of Lieutenant-Colonel Fane[128] and Major George McGregor, whose efforts were recognised in 1806 by Lieutenant-General Pigot, commanding their district, who complimented the Regiment on its very superior discipline. In the spring of 1807, the Battalion marched, by way of Newark and Norman Cross, to Weeley Barracks[129], where by the end of that year, some nine hundred rank and file were under training. Early in 1808, the 2nd/59th was inspected by Brigadier-General Acland, who expressed his unequivocal approval of its equipment and discipline. The quality of the former militiamen, in particular, appears to have been good, and within a year or so of enlistment, several of them were promoted to corporal or even sergeant.

Charles Fane had a reputation as a strict disciplinarian, and on 7th November 1807, he had Captain Charles Farquhar Thompson superseded for being absent without leave from his recruiting duties. Charley Thompson was brother to the notorious courtesan Mrs Mary Ann Clarke, venal and unscrupulous mistress to the Duke of York. She was selling commissions and promotions to fund her extravagant lifestyle, which may account for her brother's rapid rise from cornet in the 14th Light Dragoons to captain in the 59th in little more than two years. His services in the 59th, according to his relative, the novelist Daphne du Maurier, 'were largely confined to the narrow scope afforded within the bars of a spunging-house'[130]. The scandal broke on 27th January 1809 when a series of

---

[128] Charles Fane was born in 1781 at Fulbeck Hall in Lincolnshire. He received a military education in Germany and had seen service 'with distinguished credit' in Egypt.

[129] Weeley Barracks extended over some 50 acres of the Weeley Estate, between Colchester and Harwich, and consisted of mainly wooden structures with brick foundations. The barracks was a temporary wartime provision and was demolished in 1815, but the parade ground, hospital and hut sites were still pointed out one hundred years later. Ash Farm was used as officers' quarters, and a piece of sacking was discovered there in 1905 on which was printed '50 P Gt. Coats, 59th Ft. 2nd Batt. Weeley Barracks.'

[130] A spunging or sponging house was a bailiff's house for the initial confinement of arrested debtors,

trumped-up charges were brought against the Duke of York for corrupt employment of his patronage in the grant of military appointments, commissions and promotion. Mary Ann Clarke, who had instigated the accusations against her former lover, was called to give evidence before a committee of the whole House. On 12th February that year, Captain Thompson was arrested at the door of the House of Commons for 'a long tailor's bill.' The arrest took place in Palace Yard, where his sister's chariot had just arrived, into which, after Mrs Clarke had alighted, the captain and the sheriff's officer immediately jumped and drove away 'in the very first style.'

The 2nd/81st, raised at Plymouth on 15th October 1803, had been in Ireland since December 1804. The Battalion was stationed in Charles Fort, Kinsale, until March 1805, when all but the Light Company moved north into cantonments at Doneraile, Charleville and elsewhere. The 2nd/81st concentrated again at Cork from July to August, when they marched to Athlone. In September 1806, they went on to Galway, then in June 1807 to Dundalk, and in January 1808 to Mullingar. From there, the Battalion marched in June to the Curragh, where they encamped until they returned to Kinsale in August. At Kinsale, the 2nd/81st were warned for active service.

During nearly four years in Ireland the Battalion had undergone considerable change. It had lost many of its original Welsh recruits, for drafts totalling 319 men had been sent to the 1st Battalion in Sicily. Whilst in Dundalk, in June 1807, the men who had been raised for limited service received permission to volunteer for general service. About four hundred men volunteered and were attested to serve seven years, receiving a bounty of ten guineas each. The Battalion also received a great number of volunteers from the Dublin, King's County, South Devon and Royal Montgomery Militia Regiments. Then, on Christmas Day 1807, the establishment of the 2nd/81st was raised to 44 sergeants, 22 drummers and eight hundred rank and file.

The 2nd/59th and 2nd/81st were now ready for foreign service and were selected to accompany Sir David Baird to Spain. On 9th September 1808 the 2nd/81st marched from Kinsale for Monkstown, near Cork, where it embarked on five transports and sailed to Falmouth, the rendezvous for Baird's expedition. The 81st, 719 rank and file under the command of Major Henry Milling, was joined at Falmouth by the 59th, which had embarked at Harwich on 12th September with 640 rank and file under Lieutenant-Colonel Fane.[131]

The Advance into Spain, October-December 1808

Baird's force left Falmouth on 9th October in a convoy of upwards of two hundred ships. After a very good passage, the transports carrying the 59th and 81st reached Corunna on the 12th and 13th respectively, intending to join Moore's army at Valladolid. Their eagerness to assist their Spanish allies was immediately constrained. First they were refused permission to disembark by the Junta of Galicia. The troops remained cooped up aboard ship for another fortnight or more while emissaries were sent to the Central Junta in Madrid. Eventually, Baird received leave from Madrid to disembark his troops, albeit without any sign of appreciation or offer of help and cooperation. The Galician Junta were even more unhelpful, making it abundantly clear that they did not want British assistance and wished Baird and his army would go elsewhere. Baird had been led to expect that all necessary arrangements had been made for the reception and accommodation of his troops and, critically, for the provision of horses, mules and carts. None of this was the case, and so Baird decided to land and canton his troops in the towns and villages along the two principal roads leading out of Corunna, to Santiago de Compostella and Lugo, until such time as his commissaries could procure locally the necessary field equipment and transport.

According to their respective *Records of Service*, the 59th landed at Corunna on October 30th, and the 81st did not disembark until 7th November. On 1st November, the 59th tramped out of Corunna along the Camino Inglès, the ancient pilgrim route to Santiago, nearly 50 miles to the south, which they reached in two days. The concentration area of the 81st was rather closer, at Betanzos just 15 miles down the road to Lugo.

Before leaving Falmouth, both the 2nd/59th and the 2nd/81st had been allotted to Major-General Mackenzie's brigade, but shortly after landing, the 81st joined the 3rd/1st and 1st/26th in Major-General Coote Manningham's brigade. The 59th remained in Mackenzie's brigade with the 51st and 2nd/76th.

Having landed and at least partially equipped his troops, Baird hastened south to join Moore at Valladolid, their intended rendezvous. Captain Adam Wall of the Royal Artillery marched with Manningham's brigade from

---

[131] These were the soldier strengths on 2nd October, not counting officers, sergeants, drummers and staff, a total of up to one hundred more per battalion. The *Record of Service* of the 81st puts its total strength on leaving Ireland at 750.

Betanzos, and his diary offers some brief glimpses of the 81st on this march of nearly 190 miles, and of the conditions they encountered:

'Major General Manningham arrived on the 7th and directed me to march on the 8th [November] with the 81st Regiment; to encamp two nights, and arrive at Lugo on the 10th. I marched accordingly early in the morning (raining very heavy) and had a bad and hilly road to encounter. We ascended the mountain by a road curiously constructed, from which, when at the top, the whole road from the bottom could be discerned, although forming upwards of thirty zig-zags, apparently parallel for two miles. On the top of this mountain, a village is situated, consisting of about five or six houses, or rather stables, as the whole appeared to be built for the accommodation of mules or oxen. Here we encamped on a heath with the ground very wet; the 81st Regiment found the tents of the [1st] Royals standing, which Regiment left the ground the preceding day. On the 9th, [we] marched at 8 o'clock, and proceeded to a village named Barmonde, where we again encamped and procured good provisions for men and horses. On the 10th, struck our tents and marched to Lugo, a large straggling town, with some tolerably good houses and several convents, with which this country abounds. Here we met with a miserable reception...'

'On the 12th, I marched to the village of Constantino, the road extremely heavy and hilly... I encamped for the night and marched the following morning to Nogales, a very fine corn country, but extremely hilly; overtook several convoys of musquet ammunition and provisions going up to the head of the Army.

'On the 14th, we encountered one of the most tremendous mountains I ever marched over, its name Piedrahita. I should imagine its height at least seven miles, and great part of it so extremely steep that I was obliged to leave part of the carriages on the hill while I took the horses to get the others up, by which means, after the most distressing exertions of the horses, I arrived on the top of this tremendous ascent at 3 o'clock p.m.... From the top of this mountain the road descends into a rich valley; the descent as long and almost as steep as the ascent, but the road considerably better. At about 6 o'clock we arrived at a little kind of hamlet called Herreria. This road must have been made at an immense expense, as it is supported on the side of the mountain by a very high wall. I don't know how it is kept in the very good order we found it, but should suppose it is supported by the nation at large, as it is called the Royal Road to Madrid. We encamped near this hamlet upon very good ground, but found difficulty in getting the horses under cover as the 81st Regiment occupied every building in the neighbourhood. The inhabitants of this hamlet bear a very bad character, as a respectable person travelling told me that it is a harbour for banditti that robbed in the mountains we had passed...

'On the morning of the 16th we marched to Villafranca. The scenery in the valley into which we now descended is truly beautiful, a little river runs on the right, with very large trees hanging over it on each side, the river is very rapid, and meeting with obstacles of large pieces of rock, makes a continued murmuring through the trees, which is truly pleasing to the ear and eye. A deluge of rain fell during our encampment at Villafranca.

'Nov. 18th, I proceeded on our march to Astorga; the weather was tolerably fine, but the march was long and very hilly, so much so that we did not arrive at Bembibre until dark, and the horses much fatigued. Here we got billets for officers, men and horses; we got a comfortable room in the house of an old man, who wished to be hospitable but had nothing to give; our rations supplied our table, and we made a hearty meal of beef soup.

'On the 19th, we marched early and arrived at Manzanal, a miserable village on the top of a mountain; our approach to this village was up an immense hill, nearly nine miles in length, through a very long Pass called Sierra Sevada. This hill winds up the side of a mountain, with a steep descent, on the right, at the bottom of which runs a small river, and a mountain rises almost perpendicularly on the other side... On the morning of the 20th we descended the hill, and arrived in a flat country; the lofty spires of the City of Astorga made their appearance at about four miles distant, and at 1 o'clock, we arrived.'

The 2nd/81st remained at Astorga for the next three days, in the course of which Major William Williams joined from the 1st Battalion in Sicily and assumed command.[132]

The regiments of Mackenzie's Brigade were the last to move for lack of transport. They remained around Santiago until the 13th November, when they marched for Lugo, covering the 75 miles within four days. The 59th then marched on to reach Villafranca on the 21st and Ponferrado on the 25th.

---

[132] Williams had ten years service in the 40th Foot before transferring into the 81st as a major 26th October 1804.

Meanwhile, in mid-October, Sir John Moore's main force had set out from Portugal for Valladolid, his chosen point of concentration. Due to erroneous intelligence and inadequate route reconnaissance, Moore had been persuaded that the direct road via Ciudad Rodrigo to Salamanca was impassable to artillery and had accordingly sent his cavalry and guns, under Hope, on a very circuitous easterly detour along the Royal Road through Badajoz to Madrid before turning north to join the main army. He thereby not only split and unbalanced his force but delayed its concentration. Moore did not reach Salamanca until 13th November, by which time he had received disquieting rumours of French advances.

As the 59th and 81st marched south towards their planned juncture with Moore, confident Allied expectations of a victorious advance were already being overtaken by events, for the Emperor Napoleon had decided that Spain demanded his presence. Angered by French defeats, and in particular by Dupont's capitulation at Baylen, Napoleon Buonaparte entered Spain on 4th November at the head of six army corps and his Imperial Guard, determined to deal with his enemies with one massive stroke of overwhelming force. The robust confidence of Moore's officers and men was undaunted by the Emperor's arrival. 'I am delighted,' wrote a brigadier, 'to hear that Boney is with the army. If he beats us, we shall be like the rest of the world. If we beat him, we shall be like ourselves alone.'

As Baird, Hope and Moore advanced on their separate routes, news arrived of successive Spanish reverses and French advances, real or imagined, and Moore and Baird became increasingly aware of their exposure to attack by Buonaparte before the British army had completed its concentration. Moore cancelled his plans for forward concentration at Valladolid and redirected Hope to Salamanca in anticipation of a possible withdrawal to Portugal. As confirmation of repeated Spanish defeats reached the British columns, Moore's dreams of glory evaporated in disappointment and frustration as he contemplated the awful prospect of his fragmented army being defeated in detail before it could even unite.

On 22nd November, amid conflicting rumours of advance or withdrawal, Baird reviewed his force on the plain outside Astorga. That same day, he decided to retire to the coast, ordering Manningham's brigade to march on the 24th. Captain Wall was again with the brigade when it set off at 10 o'clock in the morning:

'This Brigade was ordered to move by the same route we had advanced. Here, a transaction occurred which was ill-judged indeed (whether orders had been issued or not, I cannot say); but prior to the moving of the troops from the town of Astorga, the stores were destroyed. This occasioned such a scene of confusion as I believe never was witnessed before; the streets flooded with rum, casks of beef and pork, and bags of biscuits strewed in every street, the troops conveying the rum in camp kettles, and drinking it to horrid excess.'

Manningham's Brigade, including the 81st, reached Bembibre, two day's march north of Astorga, on the 25th and encamped there for four days. Then, at 7 am on the 29th, a courier arrived with orders to return at once to Astorga, for Baird had decided to resume his advance. The troops were at once under arms, tents were struck, and the brigade retraced its steps, but on reaching Manzanal later that day, new orders arrived.

Having learned of the defeat of Castanos' army at Tudela, on 28th November, Moore himself was sufficiently concerned to make preparations for a withdrawal from Salamanca to Portugal, and he ordered Baird to conform. On 30th November, Baird began a withdrawal to the coast with the intention of shipping his army round to Lisbon.

It is probable that the 59th had not reached Astorga when they were ordered to about-turn, for on 2nd December, Captain Alexander Gordon of the 15th Light Dragoons passed them on the march five miles north of Villafranca, and by the 9th, the Battalion was at San Gregorio, some eight miles south of its former concentration area at Santiago.

The 81st, too, retraced its steps, and we are again indebted to Captain Gordon for glimpses of them along the way, for on 3rd December, he breakfasted at Villafranca with some officers of the Regiment. The town was then full of troops, and the camp rumour was that Baird would make a stand there until the Spanish troops could be rallied. The withdrawal, however, continued, and on December 7th, Coote Manningham's brigade reached

Lugo and halted.[133] This may have been as far as the 81st retired before the next change of plan, though some units of the brigade marched on to Guitiriz, halfway between Lugo and Corunna.

The 59th also reached Lugo on 7th December. They had by that date already marched some 380 miles since landing in Spain, and the 81st well over 300 miles.

Assured that Madrid was determined to resist Napoleon's advance, Moore had been persuaded to delay his withdrawal, and so on 5th December, he sent orders to Baird to suspend his retreat to the coast, followed on the 8th by orders for a cautious advance:

'The wishes of our country and our duty, demand this of us,' he wrote, 'with whatever risk it may be attended. I mean to proceed bridle in hand; for if the bubble bursts, and Madrid falls, we shall have to run for it.'

On December 14th, Moore received a captured French despatch which not only revealed the Emperor's ignorance of the movements of the British army, which Buonaparte thought to be in full retreat towards Portugal, but gave the dispositions of the various French corps. Moore saw his opportunity to pounce with a superior force on Soult's corps of 15-16,000 men, which was in an exposed position at Saldaña on the northern flank of the French advance, and he issued orders for Baird to cross the River Esla and join him.

The comings and goings of Baird's force along the roads between Corunna and Astorga had now been subject to four changes of plan, and the previous plan of withdrawal was now so far advanced that it was estimated that Manningham's brigade was unlikely to return the 120 miles to Astorga before 16th December, while Leith's brigade was at least three marches further away. On the morning of the 9th, the 81st received orders to march back to Astorga 'with the least possible delay,' and they did indeed reach Astorga by the 16th, for the following day, they marched out on the road to La Bañeza, where they halted. Next day, as described in the *81st Regiment History of Services*, they were hurried forward on a night march of nearly twenty miles over the Plain of Leon to the River Esla. The weather, which had been warm for the season, now turned bitterly cold, and snow began to fall:

'The Brigade marched by a sudden route on the night of the 18th and arrived early the following morning at Villa Marrana [Villamañan]. From cold, constant snowstorms and the difficulty of finding the roads on the plains owing to the darkness of the night, this was a very fatiguing march. After some hours rest, the Brigade again marched and crossed the Eslar at Valencia-de-Leon[134] (this occupied many hours, there being no bridge and but a few boats) and continued the march to Majorca [Mayorga], where it arrived late. Here, the junction of the two armies was first known.'[135]

By the time they joined Moore at Mayorga on the night of the 19th December, the 81st had covered 55 miles in three days, including a difficult crossing of the icy River Esla. Their effective strength on arrival at Mayorga was 615. The pay-rolls of the Battalion account for no more than three privates dead and six missing, so the 95 men unaccounted for on that date were probably sick in hospital at Lugo or Astorga or on command (i.e. detached) at Corunna or elsewhere.

Moore's combined army now numbered some 28,000 infantry, 2,700 cavalry and 50 guns. Despite the weather, the troops were in excellent spirits and supremely self-confident in anticipation of an early encounter with the enemy.

On the 21st, the army marched north-east towards Sahagún through deep snow, which turned to muddy slush in the afternoon as a thunderstorm lashed the red-coated columns. Manningham's brigade must have been one of the last to leave Mayorga, for the *81st Regiment History of Services* relates that on the 21st the brigade made a night march to a small village about three leagues off, and on the 22nd arrived at Sahagún. Lieutenant Andrew Leith Hay[136] marched at 10 p.m. with Manningham's brigade:

'The depth of the snow, with some intricacies of the road, rendered more serious by the darkness, occasioned frequent halts, during which the excessive cold was severely felt. It was 2 o'clock in the morning before General Manningham's brigade had accomplished a march of eight miles. At daylight it again proceeded,

---

[133] From the 2nd to the 20th December Major-General James Leith commanded this brigade whilst Coote Manningham was in temporary command of a division. On Manningham's return, Leith assumed command of Mackenzie's brigade of Hope's division, which included the 59th Foot.

[134] Valencia de Don Juan. The crossing was difficult, with immense pieces of ice floating rapidly downstream.

[135] *81st Regiment History of Services*.

[136] *A Narrative of the Peninsula War*, by Lieutenant-Colonel Leith Hay, published London 1834, Vol I, p. 96.

arriving at Sahagun early in the forenoon of the 22nd. The weather continued very inclement, but the numerous convents afforded shelter to the troops.'

At Sahagún, Manningham's brigade was allocated to Sir David Baird's division. The army was heartened by news of a spirited cavalry encounter outside the town in which Lord Paget had routed a force of enemy horse.

On December 22nd, orders were given for an advance against the enemy, Moore's intention being to force a bridge over the River Carrión to attack Soult at Saldaña. However, at 6 p.m., just two hours before British columns were due to march, Moore received a letter from the Spanish General Romana with the news that the Emperor Napoleon, now aware of the British army threatening his flank, was marching north to intercept it with the greater part of his force.

The Retreat to Corunna 24th December 1808 – 11th January 1809

On receiving Romana's letter, Moore at once countermanded his orders for an advance and began preparations for a retreat across the River Esla to Astorga. This unexpected decision on the eve of battle was received with shock and dismay by the army.

It would be no easy matter,' wrote Charles Stewart[137], 'to describe the effect which this unlooked-for event produced upon every man and officer in the army. The troops who had long panted to meet the enemy, and who but an hour ago were full of life and confidence, suddenly appeared like men whose brightest hopes were withered and their favourite expectations overthrown. Few gave vent to their feelings, either by complaint or murmur; but all retired to their quarters in a state of sullen silence, which indicated, more powerfully perhaps than any words could have done, the extent of the mortification under which they laboured. We rose next morning perfectly ignorant, and to a certain extent quite indifferent, as to the fate which awaited us.'

At midday on Christmas Eve, the retreat began. It was raining as the troops set off through the slush in low spirits. The 81st, who formed an escort for a 'disabled' artillery brigade, reached Mayorga that day and, on the 25th, marched on to a small village near Valderas.

'During the night a number of muleteers got away with their mules, by which the march of the Battalion was much delayed, and it was very late when it arrived with the convoy at Valencia-de-Leon. Early on the following day the river [Esla] was passed and [the Battalion] halted in a miserable village. From there it marched to Santa Maria and remained some days, having rejoined the Brigade. Shoes (which were much wanted) and blankets were served out.'[138] On the 26th, Andrew Leith Hay watched the passage of the Esla:

'There was but one boat, of a ponderous description, extremely ill managed, and very slow in its operations; the crossing of the soldiers alone by this conveyance would have occupied the whole day, while the rapid rise of the river rendered it important to gain the right bank with the least possible delay. It having been ascertained that a ford a little lower than the ferry was still practicable, over it [a] great part of the infantry, with the carriages of every description, were passed.

'It is difficult to conceive a more gloomy scene. The weather continued as bad as possible, and the pouring rain was rendered more galling by a piercingly cold wind. The animals of burden, the followers of the army, with the women and children accompanying a column of 8,000 men, added to the confusion. Many were seen struggling in the rapid stream that rolled past, while groups on either bank watched their progress. Nothing could be more comfortless than the appearance of all present; but notwithstanding the overturning of cars, the refractory exertions of mules, the terror of the women, and the vociferation of the Spaniards, the whole reached the right bank of the Esla without any lives being lost, or any serious accident having occurred.'[139]

After crossing the Esla at Valencia, Baird halted his division for two days during which Manningham sent off the whole of his baggage, the women and children, and the sick, to Astorga and on to Lugo.

---

[137] *Narrative of the Peninsula War*, by Lieutenant-General Charles William Vane KG GCB GCH PC, Marquess of Londonderry, published London 1828, based upon letters written by him to Lord Castlereagh (his half-brother) during the war, At the time of the Corunna campaign he was Brigadier the Honourable Charles Stewart.
[138] *81st Regiment History of Services.*
[139] Leith Hay, p.p.98-9.

Meanwhile, the main body of Moore's army made all haste to cross the Esla at Benavente and were all across the river by the 28th, when the bridge was blown in the faces of Napoleon's pursuing troops.

At Benavente, Moore received a final reinforcement from Portugal, the 82nd Foot. In early December, Cradock had tried to reinforce Moore by sending forward Brigadier-General Alan Cameron's brigade from Oporto, consisting of the 45th, 82nd and 97th Regiments, but of these, only the 82nd got through to Moore. The Prince of Wales's Volunteers crossed the Spanish border at Ciudad Rodrigo on about 12th December, halted at Zamora on the 23rd, and arrived at Benavente by forced marches on the 26th: the other regiments turned back. At Benavente, the 82nd were inspected by Lieutenant-General Mackenzie Fraser, commanding the 3rd Division, who allocated them to Brigadier-General Fane's brigade.[140] The Regiment mustered, on 19th December, an effective strength of 812 rank and file commanded by Major Chichester McDonell.[141] The 82nd had joined an army already in retreat, for they had hardly been united with their new brigade when it marched out of Benavente with Fraser's division, reaching Astorga on 29th December at the head of Moore's columns.

On 27th December, the 81st marched with Manningham's brigade from Santa Maria via Hospital de Orbigo to Astorga and, on the march fell in with Romana's defeated Spanish army. On rejoining Moore's main body at Astorga on the 29th December, the 81st found themselves amidst two armies in apparent dissolution and headlong flight. The discipline and the morale of many of the British troops, fragile ever since the retreat began, had been pushed beyond breaking point by a combination of cold, hunger, fatigue, sickness, lack of clear direction, administrative chaos and, above all, intense anger and frustration at being denied the opportunity to stand and fight their pursuers. Charles Stewart identified this intense disappointment as the principal cause of the unfortunate change which he witnessed at Astorga:

'The army had hitherto fallen back under the persuasion that it would not be required to retreat beyond its present position at Astorga; but here, or hereabouts, matters would be brought to the issue of a battle. Though their conduct, in many respects, cannot certainly be spoken of in high terms, it is probable that this prospect, and this alone, had hitherto kept the men in something like a state of subordination. They had committed various excesses, it is true; many had individually robbed and plundered and got drunk by the way, and some had thus fallen into the hands of the enemy or perished from the inclemency of the weather: yet the army, considered as a body, was still efficient and required nothing more than a few hours of rest, and a moderate supply of provisions, to restore it to the state of high order in which it was at Salamanca. From the moment when preparations began to be made for a continued retreat from Astorga, all this may be said to have been at an end. In Astorga, the blowing up of ammunition wagons, the destruction of intrenching tools, and the committal to the flames of field-equipments for a whole division[142], gave the signal, as it were, for all the bad passions of those who witnessed them to be let loose; and mortifying as it is to confess it, the fact cannot be denied that from that hour we no longer resembled a British army. There was still the same bravery in our ranks: but it was only at moments when the enemy were expected to come on that our order and regularity returned.'

'The soldiers were exasperated against the Spaniards for their indolence and supineness; they were also enraged by the conduct of some poor peasants, whose carts had been pressed to carry the sick and wounded, and who, as many of them as could, had fled with their mules during the night, because the movements of a retreating army exposed their own persons to imminent hazard, and their mules to certain destruction. Weary and disheartened, in want both of rest and food, disappointed in all their fond hopes of victory, and indignant at being compelled to turn their backs upon an enemy whom they despised and would so eagerly have met in battle; it was no doubt a relief for them to vent these their feelings, in transports of rage, upon the only objects within their reach. In this frame of mind, they commenced a scene of plunder and havoc as they went along; and the officers, many of whom already murmured loudly at the excessive rapidity of the retreat and were discontented with the

---

[140] Brigadier-General Henry Fane was the elder brother of Lieutenant-Colonel Charles Fane of the 59th Regiment.
[141] Chichester McDonell, who had been Major of the 2nd/82nd since 2nd August 1804 on promotion from the 5th West India Regiment, had served for six years in Butler's Rangers during the American War of Independence. For his part in the Corunna campaign he received a Gold Medal and was promoted to Lieutenant-Colonel on 16th February 1809. He transferred to the 34th Foot in December that year and died on service in India.
[142] This was the heavy baggage of Baird's Division, including the camp equipment of the 81st Foot.

stern silence which the commander-in-chief maintained respecting his future measures, did not exert themselves, as they ought to have done, to prevent these excesses.'

Adam Neale, an army surgeon, witnessed the suffering of the troops and shared their dismay at Moore's unexplained and precipitate retreat:

'Our troops had been assured at Benevente, that we were not falling back upon Corunna but that we were only retiring towards a more favourable position. But our soldiers, judging from all they had already seen, were incredulous on this point; and when our Commander reached Astorga and issued his orders, it was but too manifest that we were not only retreating but actually flying before the enemy. Ammunition-waggons were here burnt, and an entire depôt of intrenching tools abandoned, so that the army was thus deprived of a most valuable means of resisting the progress of the French. The position at Villa Franca, which our Commander had formerly mentioned in his despatches, was no longer thought of... General Fraser and his division were directly pushed on, with orders to proceed to Lugo. Sir John Hope and General Baird followed, and their instructions were to make forced marches to the coast. "We must all make forced marches," said General Moore in one of his despatches to Lord Castlereagh, "from the scarcity of provisions and to be before the enemy, who, by roads upon our flanks, may otherwise intercept us." Hence it appears that Sir John was as ignorant of the nature of the country through which he was passing, as he had formerly been on his setting out through Portugal.'[143]

When training troops at Shorncliffe, Sir John Moore had set great store on making his officers and men understand what they were doing and why: during the Corunna campaign, his troops were constantly kept in the dark as to their commanders' intentions, confused and wearied by conflicting orders, and blamed when they needed encouragement. Moore berated his army with a petulance that betrayed his personal disappointment and frustration. Moreover, he ordered the premature destruction of the army's depots as he withdrew, so that meat and biscuits were burned in front of hungry men, and shoes were destroyed as barefoot soldiers struggled over the wintry roads.

The 81st, in Baird's 1st Division, and the 82nd, in Fraser's 3rd Division, marched out of Astorga for Villa Franca on 30th December. The steep, uphill road to the Pass of Manzanal was covered in deep snow, and the twelve-mile incline was soon strewn with the debris of an army in retreat: dead draught animals, abandoned wagons and exhausted stragglers, many of them already dying from cold and dysentery.

By New Year's Eve they were encamped at Bembibre, whose wine cellars were too great a temptation for many of the troops, and when the divisions marched on the following morning, they left nearly one thousand intoxicated stragglers in the village. Despite the best efforts of the rearguard, many of these drunkards remained in Bembibre on the 2nd, when they fell victims to the sabres of the French dragoons.[144] Almost equally disgraceful scenes followed at Villafranca, Moore's largest depot, where he had again ordered the destruction of the stores.

On New Year's Day 1809, the Emperor Napoleon had entered Astorga at the head of 70,000 foot, 10,000 horse and 200 guns. Having received secret intelligence of intrigues against him in Paris, and news that the Austrians were preparing to take the field in the spring, he hastened back to France, leaving Marshal Nicolas Jean de Dieu Soult, Duke of Dalmatia (or 'Duke of Damnation' to the British troops) with 41,000 infantry and 6,000 cavalry to pursue Moore, who had a 36-hour start.

On January 3rd, the 81st and 82nd marched out of Villafranca, doubtless shedding a few more marauding 'hard bargains,' dead drunk on army rum amid the piles of still-blazing stores. Their route for the next fifty miles lay through the most difficult and desolate country of the whole retreat, including a six-thousand-foot pass, and their sufferings were graphically described by Adam Neale:

'After passing Villa Franca, the road is one continued ascent, up Monte del Cebrero for about fifteen miles to Castro, through one of the wildest, most beautiful, and most defensible countries in the world. It is a royal road, cut with great labour and expense along the side of the mountain and following all its windings; and for some part of the way it hangs over the river Valcarce, a rapid mountain stream... This country was now covered with deep snow. There was neither provision nor shelter from the rain, nor dried fuel for our fires, nor place where the weary and foot-sore could rest for a single hour in safety. All that had hitherto been suffered by our troops, was but as a prelude to this consummate scene of horrors.

---

[143] Adam Neale, 'Spanish Campaign of 1808.'

[144] Leith Hay reckoned that 'the really serious aspect of the retreat' began at Bembibre.

'It was still attempted to carry forward our sick and wounded; the beasts which dragged them failed, and they were of necessity left in their waggons to perish amidst the snow. As we looked round on gaining the highest point of those slippery precipices and observed the rear of the army winding along the narrow road, we could see the whole tract marked out by our own wretched people, who lay on all sides expiring from fatigue and the severity of the cold – while their uniforms reddened in spots the white surface of the ground.

'Our men had now become quite mad with despair: excessive fatigue and the consciousness of their disgrace, in thus flying before an enemy whom they despised, excited in them a spirit which was quite mutinous. A few hours' pause was all that they coveted; an opportunity of confronting the foe, the chance of a speedy and honourable release, and the certainty of making their pursuers atone in death for all the miseries they had suffered… throwing themselves down to perish by the way-side, [they] gave utterance to feelings… of shame, anger, and grief; but too frequently their dying groans were mingled with imprecations upon the Spaniards, by whom they believed themselves betrayed, and upon the General, who chose rather to let them die like beasts, than take their chance on the field of battle.

'That no degree of horror might be wanting, this unfortunate army was accompanied by many women and children – of whom some were frozen to death on the baggage-waggons, which were broken down or left upon the road for want of cattle, some died of fatigue and cold, while their infants were seen vainly sucking at their clay-cold breasts.'

As pointedly mentioned by Neale, this road passed many defensible positions where, had he chosen to do so, Moore could easily have checked the pursuing French long enough for his army to continue its march in reasonably good order. Instead, as Oman explains, 'Moore hurried his troops forward at a pace that, over such roads, could only be kept up by the strongest men. On January 5th he compelled the whole army to execute a forced march of no less than thirty-six continuous hours, which was almost as deadly as a battle… It was not merely drunkards and marauders who now began to fall to the rear, but steady old soldiers who could not face the cold, the semi-starvation, and the forced marches.'

An Attempted Reinforcement

Meanwhile, ignorant of the adversely altered situation on the plains of Leon, on 5th January Brigadier-General Cameron tried again to advance from Almeida in Portugal with the 45th and 97th Foot and with recovered sick and wounded for Moore's regiments, but news of Moore's retreat caused them to turn back on the 9th. Lieutenant George Wood led a detachment of the 82nd Regiment's convalescents into Spain:

'This being the winter season, I marched with my party a most fatiguing route, in the worst of weather, and over miserable roads, through dreary woody mountains interspersed with wretched villages inhabited by the most deplorable objects of poverty and filth I ever beheld; in fact, misery appeared to be the only visible object of the day… We had proceeded some distance beyond Almeida, and within a few days' march of the army, when we were met by an express informing us that the French had reached Astorga and had consequently cut us off from Sir John Moore, who was now in full retreat.'

George Wood reckoned that the sufferings of the troops falling back on Portugal were comparable with those taking part in Moore's better-known retreat, 'encountering the similar wet weather, equally bad roads, the same if not greater distance, and probably more privations than any other part of his army, having no commissary with us, and being obliged to retrace our steps through cork and chestnut forests which were in many places rendered impassable from swamps and quagmires. The country, too, had been so continually ransacked that poverty, wretchedness, filth and disease only were to be met with. Everything that could be got at had already been destroyed by the enemy, and Desolation had laid her withering hand on all within her grasp. In this deplorable state of affairs, I was compelled to endure such unusual hardships, immediately on getting the better of my late illness, that I was brought to a very low condition and obliged to crave assistance even from these unhappy peasants, into whose huts I was often driven from weakness, fatigue and hunger. In these dwellings of sorrow have I frequently begged the scanty meal of boiled chestnuts which these poor people cheerfully gave me.'[145]

---

145 Wood, p.p. 66-7.

Action at Lugo, 6th-9th January 1809

Napier's assertion that 'a British Army may be gleaned in a retreat but cannot be reaped' was certainly true of the Retreat to Corunna, for whenever even small parties made a determined stand, their pursuers declined to close with them, and when Moore gave his troops the opportunity to fight their military ardour and discipline almost instantly returned. Such was the case at Lugo.

Since we last saw them near Santiago on 9th December, we have rather lost sight of the 59th, but they too had toiled south again through the snow and mud in response to the Moore's orders of the 8th December. By the 19th, they were between Lugo and Villafranca, and on Christmas Day, they arrived at La Bañeza, Leon, after a march of nearly 220 miles. There, on news of the retreat, Leith's brigade had turned about once more and commenced a relatively unhurried withdrawal towards Lugo, where the 59th arrived on 4th January 1809. When Moore reached Lugo on the 6th, the brigade was a welcome addition of some 1,800 comparatively fresh men.

Lugo was fifty miles inland from Corunna, and although its defensive possibilities were no better than several positions Moore had previously abandoned, he determined to halt and face his pursuers. His main aim was to bring his army back together and give the exhausted troops time to rest after their gruelling forced march over the mountains.

For the 82nd and other regiments of Fraser's Division, this trial had been extended and compounded by tardy decision-making and poor communications. For it was not until he reached Herrerias (near Villafranca) on January 4th that Sir John Moore decided which port he was heading for. The alternatives were Vigo on the west coast, where there were transports waiting, or Corunna to the northwest. Moore opted for Corunna and despatched the necessary orders to his leading divisions, who had previously been ordered to strike south-west from Lugo towards Vigo; but the orderly dragoon entrusted with the orders to Fraser's division, got drunk on the road and lost them. This was not discovered until the following morning, when fresh orders were instantly sent off, but by the time they reached Fraser, his division, including the 82nd, was already a day's march down the road from Lugo to Vigo. The result was that this division spent two extra days fruitlessly marching and counter-marching through the mountains, and its regiments had lost some four hundred additional stragglers by the time they returned to Lugo, thoroughly worn out.

On the evening of the 6th, Hope's division, with the 59th in Leith's brigade, marched out some 3-4 miles in advance of Lugo to bivouac on the ground selected by Moore to check Marshal Soult's advance. It was, as grudgingly described by Charles Stewart, 'a tolerably advantageous position, along the summit of a range of low hills.' Its flanks were protected by the river Miño to the right and by inaccessible hills to the left, while to the front was a line of low stone walls and hedges, and then a ravine. Andrew Leith Hay, ADC to his uncle Major-General James Leith, described the frozen bivouac:

'The position occupied by the British was much elevated, and exposed to a piercing north-west wind. Rain fell without intermission; the ground, covered with underwood, was wetted to a degree; neither hut nor tent to shelter from the elements; the only heat to be procured was flitting, comfortless, and uncertain; the glimmering, pale, expiring fires of the enemy were alone seen at intervals, proving the slight chance we had of producing a brighter blaze; the wet broom emitted dense clouds of smoke that loaded the atmosphere, and almost appeared to give weight and substance to the falling rain. Such was the situation of all ranks in the bivouac at Lugo!

'Morning dawned; the rain became less violent. The men, suffering from the effects of cold and wet, were without bread, [and were] with difficulty preparing some flour and water to appease their craving appetites. Everything was dreary and comfortless, except the presence of the enemy. There was excitement in that, and not a murmur of complaint was heard.'[146]

Indeed, morale had revived, and a large number of stragglers rejoined their units when they learnt that a battle was likely. In all, the British had around 19,000 men at Lugo, with Leith's brigade and the 59th on the left flank where, according to Napier, 'Moore had posted the flower of his troops.'

---

[146] Leith Hay, p.p. 111-12.

Marshal Soult reached Lugo on 6th January, but his army had also been stretched out during the long march through the mountains, so only half of it was with him on that day. Even after the other half arrived, on 7th January, the French were probably slightly outnumbered by the British. At full strength, Soult's army would have contained 20,000 infantry and 6,000 cavalry, but by the time it reached Lugo, he is reported to have had 13,000 infantry and 4,000 cavalry, a total of 17,000 men.

At first, Soult was unsure whether he was facing Moore's entire army, or just a rearguard, so on 7th January, he made a series of probing attacks, starting with an artillery bombardment during which Leith's brigade was fired on by four guns. This was soon silenced by the fire of fifteen British guns. He then launched a feint against the British right, which was easily seen off by the Brigade of Guards. The most serious fighting came on the left, where the 2nd Légère and 36th Ligne regiments of Merle's division launched an attack which was beaten back by Leith's brigade. Andrew Leith Hay left an eye-witness account of this action:

'About noon the firing towards our left became more serious, and it was evident a reconnaissance of some importance was meditated. Five pieces of cannon opened upon General Leith's brigade; a column of infantry at the same moment passed the ravine, drove in the outposts, following them rapidly up a road leading directly to the centre of our position. The light companies were thrown out in front, and the regiments stood to their arms. The soldiers posted down the slope of the ravine in extended order were soon forced back, retiring in some confusion. That the attack was not to be repulsed by the fire of sharp-shooters alone was evident; the light companies were consequently assembled, met the enemy when near the summit, poured in one discharge, and rushing forward with the bayonet, drove all before them. Brigade-Major Roberts and [Leith Hay] accompanied the light infantry, who continued in pursuit until they reached the commencement of the ascent upon the other side.

'The road, or lane, up which the French attacked was flanked by walls and overhung with trees, being also so narrow as to occasion considerable confusion in the melee which took place. Filled with smoke from the incessant and vivid fire of the parties, it was almost impossible to distinguish friend from foe, but our people cheered and, rushing forward, occasioned great loss to the enemy… Sir John Moore was present during the latter part of this affair and expressed himself satisfied with the manner in which the attack had been repelled.'[147]

This bayonet charge into the ravine, which caused some three to four hundred French casualties, ended the fighting at Lugo. British casualties are not known, but the *Digest of Service of the 59th Regiment* states that 'the loss on our side was inconsiderable.' The 59th undoubtedly played an active part in this engagement, but the only first-hand reference to their involvement is in a letter of appreciation received from General James Leith shortly after the Battalion returned to England. Leith wrote of 'the gallantry and good conduct of the 59th Regiment in the field near Lugo, and their cool and steady execution of his orders under a heavy fire from the enemy.' According to the *Regimental Digest*, 'This letter was ordered to be read to the Battalion on parade and copied into the books of each company as an honourable testimonial on its records of the gallantry and discipline that the Battalion displayed on the first occasion on which it had an opportunity of acting against the enemy.'

As darkness fell that evening, the troops were lashed by another bitter storm, but on the morning of the 8th they formed up in the drifting snow, anxiously awaiting a renewed attack. Moore rode over early to the left, which was the most vulnerable point of his position. All was ready, but Soult had prudently decided to wait for reinforcements. There was disappointment and frustration in the British ranks, whose ardent wish was to stand and fight.

'I can never look back to the scenes in front of Lugo,' recalled Leith Hay, 'without a feeling of regret that the battle was not there fought, nor ever bring to recollection the gallant bearing of the troops, under all their miseries, without admiration of the spirit that appeared to animate them, and must have led to certain victory.'[148]

As the 8th January wore on, it became increasingly clear that the French were not going to attack. Moore dismissed any suggestion that he should launch his own attack. He believed that Soult's army was as large as his, and the French were in just as strong a defensive position as the British. A costly victory, he felt, would have been as disastrous as a defeat. Accordingly, with supplies running short, Moore made preparations to abandon the Lugo

[147] Ibid., p.p 113-14.
[148] Leith Hay, p. 115.

position. To deceive the French as to his intentions, he ordered the infantry to erect huts. Then, at 10 p.m., leaving their fires burning, the British slipped silently out of their lines and resumed the retreat to Corunna.

Sir John Moore had hoped that the pause at Lugo would restore the strength and discipline of his troops, but he was sadly mistaken, for almost immediately, a combination of poor staff work and atrocious weather once more sapped both. Andrew Leith Hay recalled the confusion and misery that ensued:

'The whole army filed off to the rear, by different routes leading to Lugo. Although a matter of necessity, this night-march became a most serious evil. It was excessively dark, the wind blew loud, and hail showers superseded the preceding rains. The track by which General Leith's brigade marched was of the roughest and worst description, as may be conjectured from the fact that untired men took five hours in travelling as many miles, namely the distance from the position to the city of Lugo. Without halting in that town, the whole moved forward; but even daylight did not materially improve the state of affairs. The storm raged with increased violence; the country, after passing Lugo, became more level, the wind, hail, and sleet swept resistless across the plains… At last, the straggling and confused column reached the villages of Guitteriz and Valmeda. These towns were perfectly inadequate to afford accommodation and shelter for the troops… The regiments were consequently marched off the road and halted in some fields to its right, without even a tree to defend them from the blast, the ground streaming with water, the rain and snow descending in torrents.[149] To men worn out with fatigue, hunger, and want of sleep, this short rest afforded slight comfort.

'When the order arrived to stand to their arms and set forward, they rose un-refreshed, foot-sore, weak, and depressed. A second night's march completed the disorganisation; the whole road presented a mass not of battalions but one continuous line of stragglers, mixed in confusion, without reference to regiment, brigade or division, pressing onwards to the best of their physical ability, but many having lost sight of their officers and their Colours.'[150]

This account conforms closely with the experience of the 59th Regiment as briefly related in their *Digest of Service*:

'On the [9th][151] the Battalion marched and after a very circuitous route reached Lugo the following morning. It marched on the same day, exposed to the most inclement weather, until the afternoon, halted till six p.m., and again marched all night, and arrived the [10th] at Betanzos, a distance of fifty-four miles. [This] was performed without food or refreshment of any kind, and many men perished on the road, and many that dropped from fatigue came up in the evening of that day and the day following.'

Other than such summaries in the Regimental Digests of Service, our only regimental glimpses of this last and most terrible stage of the Retreat to Corunna are in a biography of Private Christopher Ludlam[152] of the 59th Foot, which recalled that:

'He would often tell of the sad scenes he had witnessed during that disastrous campaign. How, the wells having been poisoned, they suffered from the want of water. How the officers had to stand with drawn swords and keep the soldiers from drinking what they knew would be the waters of death. How men of noble birth might be seen with their toes peeping through their boots and their once splendid military costume hanging in rags, glad to gnaw a hard and mouldy crust to appease the cravings of hunger. How women and children, who in disobedience to orders had followed the army, miserably perished by the roadside… Among the general mass of suffering which he witnessed, one incident seems to have made a deep impression upon his mind. The army was on its retreat to Corunna when the piteous cries of an infant, proceeding from behind a hedge, attracted the notice of some of the passing troops. On proceeding to the place, a mother was seen lying dead from fatigue and hunger, and her little one, almost starved to death, had been vainly trying to extract nourishment from its mother's breast.

---

[149] This hard lying would appear to apply to Leith's brigade. Other commanders, from mistaken kindness, allowed their troops to disperse and to seek shelter. When the time came to march, many of these men could not be got together again and some regiments, including those of Manningham's brigade, left large numbers behind.

[150] Leith Hay, p.p. 115-17.

[151] *The Digest of Service 59th Regiment* has incorrect dates for the march from Lugo to Betanzos.

[152] Christopher Ludlam, an unhappily married tailor from the village of Tetney in Lincolnshire, volunteered for the 59th on 25th August 1807 from the Derbyshire Militia. He later fought at Vitoria and was discharged on 10th January 1815 having had his right shoulder amputated following the storming of San Sebastian, 31st August 1813. A deeply religious man, despite his missing right arm he was for over 45 years the highly-regarded village schoolmaster at Kelstern in the Lincolnshire Wolds where he died, aged nearly 88, in 1870.

The incident was noticed in the public papers at the time and produced a profound sensation… A kind-hearted soldier belonging to the Horse Artillery took up the child and, remounting his gun, wrapped it up in the tails of his great-coat. The officers, afterwards hearing of the incident, had the child duly cared for. He was subsequently educated at the Duke of York's Military Asylum [now School] and became a commissioned officer in the East India Company's service.'

Colonel Fane's able conduct was particularly conspicuous, and from his attention to the comforts of his men, no regiment was in better shape at the end of the retreat than the 59th, or more effective in the battle which followed. There was a long-standing regimental tradition in the 59th that their cherished nickname, 'the Lilywhites,' arose from the strict discipline maintained by the Regiment during this famous retreat, including an insistence by Colonel Fane that his men's white facings, and no doubt their muskets, should be kept in pristine condition. Many years later, in 1940, this example of smart turn-out and discipline in adversity was recalled by an East Lancashire officer during the retreat to Dunkirk, prompting him to pause and polish his boots. Such is the power of tradition.

Sir John Moore's terrible retreat from Lugo to Betanzos drove his men beyond their failing strength. 'Flesh and blood cannot endure such a trial even in good weather,' concluded Sir Charles Oman, 'and these were nights of hurricane and downpour. Who can wonder that even well-disposed and willing men lagged behind, sank down, and died by hundreds under such stress?'

The real hardships of the retreat ended at Betanzos, where Moore called a halt to his army's headlong flight. On arrival there on the morning of January 10th, some regiments of Leith's brigade had not fifty men with their Colours, while in one regiment of Manningham's brigade (not the 81st), only nine officers, three sergeants and three privates were present, but during the course of the day numerous stragglers hobbled in to join their ranks and discipline was reasserted. When the march resumed early next day, the sun was shining, and Andrew Leith Hay noted a remarkable change, highly creditable to the soldiers, as they tramped the last fifteen miles into Corunna:

'The battalions that on the morning of the 10th entered Betanzos reduced to skeletons, marched from thence on the 11th strong and effective; the column composed of all the infantry of the army, which ascended the road towards Coruña, was orderly in appearance and perfectly unlike what could have been expected to reform from the debris of an army, which but the previous day had exhibited an alarming state of demoralization and exhaustion. On the 11th, a favourable change had taken place in the state of the weather; the sun shone upon the troops; and as the column ascended the winding road from Betanzos, it presented a very brilliant appearance, more particularly when contrasted with that of the preceding day.'[153]

Since landing at Corunna a little more than ten weeks earlier, the 59th had marched well over eight hundred miles while the 81st had covered around seven hundred miles in seven weeks. The 82nd had marched over eight hundred miles since leaving Oporto in early December.

On arrival at Corunna, the filthy, exhausted and, in many cases, disease-ridden troops appeared in so terrible a state that the people of the town made the sign of the cross as they passed. The 59th were quartered in the suburb of St. Lucia, which extended along the western side of the harbour, while the 81st and 82nd occupied the Old Town. The ranks were considerably thinned by disease, and even after four days rest, the 59th could field fewer than three hundred effective rank and file out of over five hundred present, while several of the officers were sick.

The Battle of Corunna, 16th January 1809

When Sir John Moore reached Corunna he found that the British fleet and transports had not as yet arrived from Vigo, and so he began preparations for embarkation or battle, depending on whether the fleet or Soult arrived first. On January 12th the leading French infantry had closed up to the wide and tidal river Mero, where the British rearguard faced them across the demolished bridge at El Burgo. Later that day, when the French discovered an undamaged bridge upstream, Moore withdrew his rearguard.

---

[153] Leith Hay, p. 118.

He had selected a position some two miles south of the walls of Corunna where the road from Betanzos ran over a ridge, the Monte Mero. This ridge was some 2,500 yards long, with the Rio del Burgo estuary protecting its eastern flank. The lower western flank of this ridge was more vulnerable, for beyond its end a narrow valley, skirting the Heights of Cristobal and Santa Margarita to the west, offered a direct approach to the peninsula on which stood the port of Corunna. Nestled in front of this western end of Monte Mero was the village of Elviña, while further east, astride the road from Betanzos, stood the village of Piedralonga. To the south, and within long cannon-shot of Monte Mero, the Heights of Penasquedo and Palavea overlooked the approaches to Corunna. Moore had insufficient troops to occupy this higher, but longer, feature and was despondently aware that, in his own words, 'my position in front of this place is a very bad one.'

On the evening of January 12th, Hope's division occupied Monte Mero with two brigades forward and one in reserve, Leith's, with the 59th being the right forward brigade. On the morning of the 13th, Baird's division marched from Corunna onto its battle position on the western end of the ridge, above Elviña, with its right flank bent back, or 'refused,' to cover the valley. Manningham's brigade of Baird's division, with the 81st, formed to the right of Leith's, with Bentinck's on his right, and the Guards brigade in reserve. Aware of the weakness of his right flank and anticipating that Soult might try to exploit this apparent vulnerability, Moore retained Paget's and Fraser's six thousand men in depth positions, ready if necessary for a counter-stroke. On the 16th, when Moore's deployment was complete, Paget's Reserve division stood half a mile to the rear of Monte Mero, prepared to counter any attempt to turn the right flank of that position, while Fraser's division, including the 82nd, occupied the Heights of Santa Margarita, covering the road from Vigo and the western approaches to the town and harbour.

On 13th January, there was a massive explosion when a magazine containing some four thousand barrels of gunpowder, given by Britain to the Galician Junta, was blown up to prevent it from falling into French hands. Although the magazine was three miles from Corunna, almost every window in the town was shattered and, believing that there was an earthquake, the whole population dashed out of their houses. Leith Hay was with Leith's brigade on Monte Mero, where the troops were momentarily stunned by the blast:

'The unexpected and tremendous crash seemed for the moment to have deprived every person of reason and recollection; the soldiers flew to their arms; nor was it until a tremendous column of smoke, ascending from heights in front, marked from whence the astounding shock proceeded, that reason resumed its sway. It is impossible ever to forget the sublime appearance of the dark, dense cloud of smoke that ascended, shooting up gradually like a gigantic tower into the clear blue sky.'

Leith's brigade had not been warned of the impending explosion, and three men of its picquets were killed at a distance of one mile from the magazine. It seems that some men of the 59th were among those caught by this explosion, for when Private Jeremiah Riorden was discharged to pension in 1822, he was described as 'a drunken but gallant soldier who was wounded in the left eye and the eyebrows by the explosion of the magazine at Corunna in 1809.'

On the afternoon of 14th January the long-anticipated British fleet sailed into Corunna harbour, over one hundred transports escorted by twelve warships. Moore began at once to embark his cavalry, most of his artillery, over nine hundred women and children, and about three thousand sick and wounded, leaving some fifteen thousand infantry and nine light guns to hold Soult. Some two thousand horses could not be embarked, and were destroyed, together with most of the vast quantity of stores held at Corunna. Lieutenant Basil Hall of the frigate HMS *Endymion*, who was busy all day with the ship's boats, saw the surviving army wives embark:

'In this curious assembly, I observed several women, who, strange to say, had gone through the whole campaign, unbroken in spirit and apparently not much fatigued. They even talked as if they had done no great things.'[154]

---

[154] Basil Hall, who wrote extensively about his voyages, notably led a party from HMS *Endymion* to make the first known landing on the island of Rockall, 8th September 1811.

One of these indomitable women was 25-year-old Dinah, wife of Private Joseph Kitcher of the 82nd. She had already been widowed once when her first husband, a sergeant in the 95th, was killed in action, and had since accompanied Joseph to Copenhagen and Vimeiro.[155]

It was not until the 15th that, having repaired the bridge at El Burgo and gathered his stragglers, the Duke of Dalmatia appeared on the Heights of Penasquedo and Palavea with some 15,500 infantry, 4,500 cavalry and about 36 guns [156], pushing back the British picquets. With a view to an attack the following morning, Soult established a battery of ten 12-pounder guns on the Heights of Penasquedo opposite Elviňa.

'The whole ridge was soon covered with French troops,' recalled Leith Hay, 'The weather was clear and beautiful, every movement of the enemy being discernible from the high ground. During the course of the day, the piquets were often slightly engaged.'

The 16th dawned cold and misty before the sun broke through to reveal a cloudless winter sky. All morning, the two armies watched each other as Soult completed his preparations for battle. Lieutenant Basil Hall, aged just 21 and eager to watch a land battle, obtained leave to go ashore and spent the day as a spectator with the forward troops. He has left a vivid description of the British infantry as they waited that morning, in the uncertain lull before battle, on the rocky crest of Monte Mero:

'The soldiers lay scattered about, wearied and dispirited, ragged in their dress, and many of them sickly, or rather broken down in appearance, by the fatigue of this celebrated retreat. Most of their chins had been untouched by a razor for some days, perhaps weeks, while their hands and faces being rather less familiar with soap and water than with the smoke of their muskets and the charcoal of their cooking fires, gave evidence enough of the want of comforts to which the army had been so long exposed. The muskets of the troops stood in pyramids, piled along the ridge amongst the men stretched out on the ground fast asleep – not in any very precise order, but keeping within a few yards of one another on the summit line of the position. I observed many of these hardy fellows lying on their backs, with their hands under their heads and faces half-covered by what remained of a hat, becoming still more deeply tanned in the sun. Many, however, were sitting on the grass or on the loose blocks of granite strewed over the ground and gazing, every now and then, in silence, with very wistful eyes towards the ships.'

Around noon, with no sign of movement from the French, Sir John Moore concluded that Soult did not intend to attack and ordered Paget's division to prepare for embarkation. At about 1.45 p.m. he remarked to his Military Secretary, 'Now, if there is no bungling, I hope we shall get away in a few hours.' Ten minutes later, Sir John Hope galloped up to inform him that the French were advancing in great force.

Soult's plan appears to have been very much as Moore had anticipated. Two French divisions, those of Merle and Delaborde, were to pin down Hope's division while Mermet's division was to seize the western end of Monte Mero from Baird and, turning the right of Moore's front line, advance on Corunna supported by the bulk of the French cavalry. The attack was to be preceded by an artillery bombardment.

The battle was opened at around 1.30 to 2 p.m. when the French 12-pounders on the Heights of Penasquedo opened a heavy preparatory fire on the British centre above Elviňa. Basil Hall was amazed at the almost instantaneous and miraculous transformation of the men around him:

'At the first discharge from the French battery, the whole body of the British troops, from one end of the position to the other, started on their feet, snatched up their arms, and formed in line with as much regularity and apparent coolness as if they had been exercising on the parade in Hyde Park. I really could scarcely believe my eyes when I beheld these men spring from the ground, as if touched by a magic wand, full of life and vigour, though but one minute before they had all been stretched out listlessly in the sun. I have already noticed the silence which reigned over the field; now, however, there could be heard a loud hum, and occasionally a jolly shout, and many a peal of laughter, along a distance of nearly a mile. In the midst of these sounds, the peculiar sharp "click-click-click" of fixing bayonets fell distinctly on the ear very ominously.

---

[155] Joseph Kitcher served for 17 years in the 82nd, and Dinah later followed him through campaigns in France and Canada. She fell on hard times on his death, eventually entered the Royal Cambridge Home for Soldiers' Widows, where she died in 1870, aged 86. She had previously been modelled for Madame Tussaud's Waxworks Museum – undoubtedly the only regimental wife to be so honoured.

[156] The exact numbers of the French are very uncertain, and some authorities have estimated their total strength as low as sixteen thousand and as high as twenty-four thousand.

'Many thousand stand of new arms had been issued to the troops from the stores at Corunna, and I could observe the men rapping the flints, tightening the screws, and tossing about their firelocks, with the air of veteran sportsmen eager to try their new pieces. The officers, who up to this moment had seemed so languid, might be seen everywhere, brushing along the line, speaking to the sergeants, and making arrangements which we did not pretend to understand. Aides-de-camp galloped past us, dropping their orders into the ears of the commanding officers of the various corps, as they moved swiftly along the position. Not a single face could now be seen turning towards the ships, and we found it difficult to obtain an answer to any of our questions. All had become animation and cheerfulness, over minds from which, but a short time before, it seemed as if every particle of spirit had fled. There appeared to be much conversation going on, and not a little jesting among the men, as they braced themselves up, buckled on their knapsacks, and made various other arrangements, preparatory to the hard work they foresaw they would have to perform before the night fell. Their kits, or stocks of clothes (none of them very large), being soon placed on their shoulders, the army, in a few minutes, stood perfectly ready to meet that of the enemy, whose troops, in three immense close columns, by this time were pelting rapidly down the side of the opposite heights.'

The main weight of Soult's initial attack fell as planned on Lord William Bentinck's brigade (4th King's Own, 42nd and 50th) on the right of Baird's division. Preceded by a thick crowd of their *voltigeurs*, two brigades of Mermet's division pushed through Elviña, driving out Bentinck's picquets and the Light Company of the 50th, and climbed the forward slope of Monte Mero, while a third brigade tried to turn Bentinck's right flank on the lower ground at the end of the ridge. Beyond them, the French cavalry slowly picked their way forward through enclosures and broken ground.

Seeing that Baird's position behind Elviña would be the vital ground of the battle, Sir John Moore positioned himself there and sent an officer with orders for Paget's division to counter the enemy flanking movement and for Fraser's division to march out from the town to occupy its blocking position on the Heights of Santa Margarita.

An early victim of the French artillery bombardment was the veteran Sir David Baird, who was seriously wounded, and Sir John Moore took personal command of Baird's division.

As Mermet advanced from Elviña towards the crest of Monte Mero, he was met by the 42nd and 50th, and a protracted struggle ensued during which the village changed hands several times. Meanwhile, the attempted encirclement of the British right flank was thwarted by the 4th King's Own, who were ordered by Moore to throw their right wing back at a right-angle and deliver a flanking fire on the French column while Paget's division pushed forward to extend the right flank of the British position. Soult's first attack was defeated; Elviña was retaken by the 42nd and 50th, and on the right, Paget's men were engaged with the now largely dismounted French cavalry and were slowly gaining ground. In conformity with this general movement forward on the British right flank, Fane's brigade of Fraser's division, including the 82nd, descended from the Heights of Santa Margarita to the valley, but they were not engaged.

Lieutenant Basil Hall of the Royal Navy watched the opening of the battle from among the granite boulders and gorse of the Monte Mero ridge to the east of Elviña:

'The intermixture of the combatants on this day was probably rendered greater than usual in consequence of the peculiar nature of the ground. It could hardly be called a plain, for it was crossed in all directions by roads cut into the earth like deep trenches, eight or ten feet below the surface; while on the ground above lay a complete network of walls, hedges and rows of olive trees and aloes, of such intricacy that I should imagine it nearly impossible to have formed fifty men abreast anywhere. Thus, each cornfield, or little patch of garden-ground, became the scene of a separate fight.'

'We were quite near enough to see the soldiers scrambling over the walls and meeting one another in these open spaces or amongst the trees; while the smoke and the flashes of musketry from the hollow roads showed that a subterranean sort of warfare was going on at the same time.'

By mid-afternoon, Mermet's division had regrouped, and they came forward again, supported on their right by a column from Merle's division. The 42nd and 50th were driven out of Elviña and were in urgent need of reinforcement: the 50th, after heavy losses in the village, was a spent force, while to their left, the 42nd, short of ammunition, was also faltering. Moore ordered the two battalions of the 1st Foot Guards forward to relieve the

84

50th, while the 3rd/1st Royals and the 2nd/81st of Manningham's brigade were brought down to counter Merle's column and to support the 42nd Regiment in a renewed counter-attack on Elviňa. The Royals and the 81st took post to the left of the French-occupied village, where the 81st were soon hotly engaged with the 2nd Légère and 36th Ligne[157] of Reynaud's brigade, Merle's division, whose battalions were drawn up at intervals to their front on a hillside so steep that the French columns in rear were able to fire over the heads of those in front. The 81st took the brunt of Reynaud's attack and suffered most severely, but took up a second and more advantageous position from where they fought on until their ammunition was expended and some 150 of their officers and men lay dead or wounded, including the Commanding Officer, Major, Adjutant and Sergeant-Major.

Shortly after the 81st joined the fight, Sir John Moore was struck from his horse by a cannon-ball and carried off the field, mortally wounded. Sir John Hope assumed command.

It was nearly dusk when Major-General Leith was ordered, presumably by Hope, to advance one of his battalions to relieve the battered and exhausted 81st. Leith led forward the 59th, who were the reserve battalion of his brigade and, on the spot, paid the 81st a high compliment for their gallant conduct. The 81st resumed their original place in the line near the crest of Monte Mero. Shortly after his return to England, Leith wrote to General Alexander Ross, Colonel of the 59th, with an account[158] of his Regiment's action:

'I conceive… that the interest you naturally feel in the reputation of your Regiment will induce you to receive with satisfaction this communication and that you will further do me the honour to convey to the 59th Regiment my perfect approbation of and thanks for their cool and steady execution of my orders which exposed them to a heavy fire from the enemy in the action of 16th January last. As the Battalion had not, I apprehend, been engaged in any general action before the affair at Corunna, I think it will not be uninteresting to you to know the manner in which the 59th Regiment went up to the enemy on the 16th January.

'It was directed eventually to support the 81st Regiment, who were very warmly engaged, and accordingly, when their ammunition was entirely expended in repelling the enemy (who directed his principal efforts towards that part of the British line after failing in the first instance on his left) I directed the 59th to advance from the left of companies by files to the front, which they did with as much regularity as the broken nature of the ground admitted of, and without paying the slightest attention to the enemy's fire they formed, and soon obliged him, although advantageously posted, to retire.[159] Opposite to the left of the Guards and on the right of the 59th, the enemy still continued to keep up a galling fire from behind fences and cover, from which there was no attempt to drive him, I sent my Brigade Major to inform the left of the Guards that the 59th were going to dislodge the enemy in their front, and not to fire on their friends. The Grenadier Company, and immediately afterwards the First Company, marched and, without firing a shot, mounted a strong fence by individuals, and with the bayonet destroyed or obliged to fly all of the enemy who were there opposed to them[160], and except the local attack on the village on the left [Piedralonga], which began after the general action ceased, were the last of the whole line engaged. On that occasion, Captain Wilson, a very deserving officer, was wounded.[161]

'Lieutenant Colonel Fane, who led the Battalion with great spirit and paid much attention to its comforts on all occasions, is deserving much commendation, and I hope will soon be able to return to his duty.'[162]

---

[157] These were the same two French regiments that had been engaged with Leith's brigade at Lugo.

[158] Letter dated 10 Cork Street, Burlington Gardens, London on 3rd March 1809.

[159] Of this attack, *The 59th Regiment Digest of Service* states: 'The Battalion charged a body of the enemy much its superior in number, advancing upon it and completely routing them.'

[160] It was almost certainly on this occasion, when the 59th fought their enemy at close quarters, that Private Luke Marley received a sabre wound in his neck and Private Henry Thompson a bayonet wound in his left hand.

[161] When Captain Thomas Wilson fell wounded, Lieutenant William Mandeville of the Grenadier Company continued the assault and 'highly distinguished himself.' Major-General Leith wrote a testimonial for Mandeville, dated 15th April 1809, in which he described how 'the Grenadier and 1st Companies dislodged the enemy in a very gallant manner from behind strong fences which they occupied in front of the left of the Guards, and from whence a galling fire was kept up on the British line, which was silenced by the very spirited attack of the companies with which you acted.' Mandeville, who was particularly pointed out by Colonel Fane and his brother officers as 'one of the foremost in the action', was recommended for promotion to a company. He died, still a captain, when the 59th was stationed at Berhampore, Bengal on 1st October 1819.

[162] Colonel Fane was hit in the head by a musket-ball which completely disabled him, and Major George McGregor too was severely wounded: Captain Richard Fairfield assumed command and was highly praised by Leith for his conduct.

We are fortunate to have a glimpse of the 59th Regiment just prior to this action from Lieutenant Basil Hall of the Royal Navy. Hall had been watching the battle from the exposed forward slope of Monte Mero when he came under effective enemy gunfire. Prudently withdrawing to a safer vantage point on top of the ridge to his left rear, out of range of the French artillery, he there encountered a regiment which, from its position at that time and its subsequent movement, could only have been the 59th Foot:

'Here, we enjoyed the additional advantage of making acquaintance with the colonel [Charles Fane] and the other officers of one of the regiments of the reserve. The colonel, whose name I do not recollect, held a pocket spy-glass in his hand and very kindly described to us the nature of the different movements as they took place. By this time the centre and a portion of the left of the English line, gradually became engaged in the valley; but the severest fighting of all appeared at the village of Elvina, which we could easily distinguish was sometimes in possession of one party, sometimes of the other. The uncertainty, indeed, of what was going on became greatly augmented by the broken nature of the ground, which, I suppose, prevented any manoeuvre on the grand scale; but this circumstance may probably have taken nothing from the fierceness of those mortal struggles, which we could discover, from time to time, in the open spaces, when a puff of wind blew the smoke on one side.

'The road leading into Corunna[163], and lying between us and the severest part of the action, passed at no great distance and was soon covered along its whole length with wounded men; some of whom were walking alone, some supported by their comrades less severely hurt, and a good many had been placed in carts. We observed Sir David Baird led or carried off the field; but from the smoke and dust, we could not exactly make out which, though I think he was walking. Shortly afterwards, another and a larger group passed near us, bearing along a wounded officer. It was evident, from the appearance which this second party presented, that some person of consequence was under their charge; and while we were trying to discover who it could possibly be that engaged so much attention, an officer rode up the hill. After he had delivered his message, he pointed to the party which had just gone by, and told us, that in the centre was carried along their brave commander-in-chief, Sir John Moore, who, a few minutes before, had been struck off his horse by a cannon-shot. The command now devolved upon Sir John Hope, whom we could readily distinguish, from his being surrounded not only by his staff but by the aides-de-camp of his two wounded senior officers.

'I shall not seek to describe how greatly the interest of this scene, so new to us in all its parts and so remarkable in itself, was heightened by these proofs of the serious nature of the conflict. The colonel of the regiment along with which we had taken up our station, had just said to us, "Well, gentlemen, I don't know how you get on at sea, but I certainly never saw on land a hotter fire than this," when a breathless messenger came galloping up, with orders to carry his brigade as smartly as he possibly could down to the right, to support some regiments [presumably Manningham's] which he described as being severely pressed in that quarter. In a few minutes, we found ourselves quite alone on the summit of the ridge, watching, with a painful degree of interest, the movements of our newly-made acquaintances, who trotted off, at double-quick time, right down the hill and ere long were lost sight of in the thick of the action. So completely, indeed, were they enveloped in smoke and dust, that we could only distinguish their presence by the movement in advance of the British line, which took place on the right almost immediately after their arrival.[164]

'The battle, which had commenced nearly at the foot of the English hill, had gradually, though not without several fluctuations, moved itself forward towards the French side of the valley; and the much-contested village of Elvina remained finally in our possession… The eventual advantage… remained manifestly on the side of the English; for it became easy to distinguish, towards the end of the day, that the struggle was carried on at a position removed considerably in advance of that on which the English had stood when first attacked.'

As darkness forced an end to the battle, the troops returned to their bivouacs. Leith Hay recalled a feeling of anticlimax in Leith's brigade:

---

[163] This would be the side-road leading from Elviňa to the main highway, the most direct route for casualty evacuation from the battle around the village.

[164] Leith Hay (p. 126-7) says only that 'After the left of General Manningham's brigade had been for some time engaged, General Leith was ordered to advance one of his battalions to relieve the 81st Regiment, which had not only suffered severely, but nearly exhausted its ammunition. He marched down the 59th, taking up the ground under a very heavy fire of musketry, which wounded Colonel Fane and six of his officers. A successful charge with the bayonet put a period to these volleys in our immediate front.'

'At the close of this action, there was not the same exhilarating feeling, the same excitement, as usually attends a victory. No pursuit, no trophies, nor any prisoners, at once attested to the services and the fortune of the army. The situation of the soldiers and their various occupations, were the same as on the preceding night, while darkness prevented any trace of the action from being perceptible. A stillness prevailed for hours. The repose of the camp was only interrupted by the formation of the troops at midnight, when the whole, with the exception of the piquets, marched towards the harbour.'[165]

That night, as Sir John Moore lay dying in Corunna town, his army remained masters of the field of battle, but Sir John Hope had decided to continue with the planned evacuation that had been interrupted by the afternoon's battle. It was argued by many who were present that Hope had the opportunity of turning a successful defensive battle into a decisive victory by pressing on with Paget's Reserve division, supported by Fraser's uncommitted division, to turn Soult's left, capture his battery on the Heights of Penasquedo, and roll the French back to the river Mero. This might well have been possible given a couple more hours of light, for Soult was very much on the back foot and was short of ammunition, but manoeuvring over rocky heights at night would have been hazardous in the extreme, and by the following morning the French would be rebalanced and probably reinforced.

About midnight, leaving picquets to tend their campfires, the 81st marched down to the beach, from where thirty officers, 291 other ranks, 23 women and one child were ferried out to HMS *Victory*, 100.[166] The *Regimental History of Services* records that they 'experienced from both officers and men the most kind and humane treatment.' Five officers and the balance of the men embarked on other transports and warships, including seventeen on HMS *Rodney*, 74.

Despite the best efforts of the Royal Navy, the evacuation was not completed without some difficulties. At daybreak on the 17th, the French were quick to place batteries on a headland to the east of the harbour, from where they opened a long-range bombardment of the shipping. The guns did little material damage but caused a panic among the civilian transports: some 80-90 of these cut their cables and attempted to run out to sea, many without taking troops aboard. The result was chaos, with nine vessels run aground, of which all but two were lost.

The 59th embarked soon after dawn, but the transport carrying battalion headquarters was one of those which sank, having been engaged by enemy batteries. The troops were transferred, and the Colours were saved by Sergeant-Major Perkin, who, at the risk of his life, went below when the ship was actually sinking, took them from the captain's cabin and brought them away with him. It is not known which vessels carried the 59th from Corunna, except that 25 of the sick and wounded were aboard the hospital ship *Alfred*.

Corunna was a victory of sorts, a salvation comparable to Dunkirk, but the British Army could not afford many more like it. The losses of the adversaries are uncertain as neither side preserved full casualty returns for the battle, but Hope, in his despatch, estimated that the British loss 'did not exceed in killed and wounded from seven to eight hundred,' and this is probably as close as we are likely to get. One of the problems is that many regiments did not distinguish in their returns between casualties incurred during the retreat and those suffered on 16th January. Among the British regiments, the greatest losses at the battle of Corunna appear to have been sustained by the 50th (185), 81st (151), 42nd (150) and the 59th (61). The 82nd, though present, were not engaged and suffered no casualties. French losses were certainly greater and were probably in the range of fifteen hundred to two thousand.

Nearly one in four of Moore's army, 7,035 men, did not return to England from Corunna. Of these, 589 rank and file made their way to Portugal, passed from village to village by peasants until they reached safety, and another four hundred convalescents were released from French captivity by Galician insurgents and sent back to Lisbon in the spring of 1809, while at least fifteen hundred sick were evacuated to Portugal from Salamanca before that line of communication was broken. Another 2,189 men were sent as prisoners into France, and 287 died at sea during the evacuation. It would be reasonable to assume that most of the remaining two thousand died in battle, by the road or in hospital.

---

[165] Ibid., p. 128.

[166] HMS *Victory* had recently been re-commissioned after a major refit to make good her extensive damage at Trafalgar. This was to be her last sea-going commission.

It is difficult to be certain about overall regimental losses over the full period of the Corunna campaign, but between 19th December (before the retreat) and embarkation on 17th January, the rank and file strength of the 59th fell by 60 while those of the 81st and 82nd fell by 137 and 210 respectively. For the 59th and 81st, this included a significant number of battle casualties.

This total is not, however, the full extent of the 59th and 81st casualties, for a proportion of the men who fell sick on the march before 19th November must have died, and many more must have been captured when Moore abandoned his hospitals at Astorga, Villafranca, Lugo and Corunna. Taking the strengths of these two regiments on leaving Falmouth as the start point, their losses rise to 143 for the 59th and 241 for the 81st, and this does not include the substantial number who died shortly after their return to England from wounds and sickness or who were so debilitated by their privations as to be unfit for further service.

The strength returns for 25th February 1809 show 176 of the 2nd/59th sick, 208 of the 2nd/81st and 414 of the 1st/82nd, though by June, the numbers of non-effectives still with those regiments had reduced to 32, 33 and 28 respectively.

The sickness was predominantly typhus and dysentery, which spread rapidly in the crowded transports during the voyage home to such an extent that some twenty percent required treatment for one or the other disease. It was also unfortunate that, in a misconceived effort to save money, the Army Medical Board had closed the military hospitals at Portsmouth, Gosport and Deal.

The muster rolls of the 59th list twelve men as 'died' and 109 as 'missing' on the march from the start of the retreat, of whom at least 25 were left in abandoned hospitals, and several stragglers are known to have made their way to Portugal. At the battle of Corunna seven officers[167] of the 59th and 54 other ranks fell. Among those who survived the battle almost unscathed was Private Christopher Ludlam who received a musket ball through the waistband of his trousers, a narrow escape which made a deep impression on him. 'If I had been shot then,' he lugubriously reflected, 'I should have perished in my sins.'

The losses of the 81st before and during the Retreat were Lieutenant Samuel Corbet[168] and seven privates 'died,' and Assistant Surgeon John Steele[169], two sergeants, one corporal, one drummer and 160 privates 'missing.' At Corunna, the 81st had a total of 151 casualties: two officers[170]: one sergeant, three corporals and 22 men were killed, two officers[171], the Sergeant-Major, two sergeants, two corporals and twelve privates died of their wounds, and eleven officers[172], five sergeants and 91 other ranks were wounded.

---

[167] Lieutenant-Colonel Charles Fane suffered a severe head wound, the top of his skull being carried way; Major George McGregor was reported to have died of his wounds at Plymouth (obit. in *The Gentleman's Magazine*, February 1809), but in fact survived and earned further promotion in 1812; other officers wounded were Captain Thomas Wilson (severely), Lieutenant John Fothergill, and Ensigns Nicholas Chadwick (severely wounded by grapeshot in the right thigh), John Cowper (severely) and Abraham Dent. The nature of the other rank casualties is not known.

[168] The *81st Regiment History of Services* records that 'a few hours previous to the march out of the town [on January 13th] Lieutenant Corbett of the Regiment, who died from fatigue and sickness a few days before, was buried with military honours in one of the bastions of the Old Town.' Samuel Corbet [sic] died on 11th January.

[169] Assistant Surgeon John Steele was last seen at Sahagun where, in the best tradition of his profession, he stayed behind to care for the sick and there perished. He had served with the 81st since 31st January 1805.

[170] Captain Robert Digby and Ensign Robert Hanmer. The Regimental history states that Hanmer died of his wounds and was buried at sea.

[171] Major Charles Crigan and Ensign Thomas Griffin. Major Crigan died at Plymouth on 1st February 1809, while Thomas Griffin died in the Royal Naval Hospital, Plymouth on 2nd March, leaving 'a wife and child to deplore him.'

[172] Majors William Williams and Henry Milling; Captain Adam Gifford Downing; Lieutenants & Adjutant John Lutman, Lieutenants David Fair, Josiah George Hort, George Pearson, Lawrence Macartney and Bartholemew Vigors Derenzy (wounded in both knees); Ensigns Thomas Manning and Thomas Lloyd Serjeant; Volunteer John Adrian Lutman. On 25th February 1809 Milling, Lutman (senior) and Fair were listed as 'wounded, in the Naval Hospital, Portsmouth' while Hort, who lost his right leg, Manning and Serjeant were in the Naval Hospital at Plymouth. Volunteer Lutman, aged 16 and probably the Adjutant's son, was wounded in the left thigh and was rewarded with a commission in the 81st Regiment dated 1st February 1809. His father never fully recovered, for his memorial tablet in St. John's Wood Chapel, London records that 'after painfully lingering from a severe wound' received at Corunna, he died on 20th January 1821. In consideration of his incapacitating wound, John Lutman (senior) had been promoted to a captaincy in the 4th Royal Veteran Battalion and retired in 1814 on full pay, a rare distinction. Henry Milling subsequently received a pension of £200 per annum in consideration of serious injury to his right arm, but continued to serve. Josiah Hort was promoted to captain in 1810 and became Adjutant of the Royal Hospital at Kilmainham.

Discounting the Corunna battle fatalities, percentage losses during the retreat suggest that the 59th (around 7.5%) and 81st (just over 15%) were among the most disciplined of Moore's regiments. The 82nd suffered a loss of 28%, a little above the average, but many of the soldiers had only recently been discharged from fever hospital when they set off on their 800-mile march. These losses are also proportionately reflected in the monthly sick returns after Corunna.

On their return to England, the 2nd/59th, under the temporary command of Major George McGregor, were once more stationed at Weeley Barracks, Essex, where Captain Frederick William Hoysted was presented with a sword,[173] and in June 1809 some six hundred recruits were received from the Militia.[174]

The 2nd/81st landed at Plymouth on the 5th and 6th of February in a 'dispersed state,' re-assembling on the 12th at Lewes[175] in Sussex under the command of Major Williams. On April 12th, they marched to Bletchingley barracks, where the officers of the Battalion voted swords of honour to Majors Milling and Williams for their distinguished conduct at the Battle of Corunna.[176] There, too, during the months of May and June, the Battalion received two hundred and fifty volunteers from the Militia.[177]

The 1st/82nd disembarked at Portsmouth on the 8th February and also marched to Lewes, where during April and May, they received drafts of two hundred volunteers from various Militia regiments and two hundred and fifty from their 2nd Battalion, then quartered at Scarborough.

Such is the British propensity for celebrating narrowly averted disaster that the Corunna campaign remains one of the better-known episodes of the Peninsula War, though the regiments involved had to wait until 1811 before 'CORUNNA' was awarded as a Battle Honour, and it was not until 1848 that 78 surviving members of the 2nd/59th, 98 of the 2nd/81st and 63 of the 1st/82nd received the Military General Service Medal with 'Corunna' clasp. Meanwhile, Lieutenant Colonel Charles Fane and Majors Chichester Macdonnell and William Williams received the Army Gold Medal.

Sir John Moore

Posterity has on the whole been kind to Moore's reputation[178], too kind perhaps, for despite his attractive character and personal gallantry, his well-publicised ability as a trainer, and his previous successes as a subordinate commander, he showed very serious flaws in the Peninsular as a general in independent command. From the outset of his campaign, Moore made grave strategic misjudgements, most notably his incorrect appreciation that he could, with security, advance deep into Spain on three widely separated routes. The consequence of this dispersion was that his army began the campaign structurally and logistically unbalanced, vulnerable to Napoleon's swift and unanticipated advance. Indecision and delay were the hallmarks of his subsequent actions throughout the campaign, with order succeeded by counter-order and long periods of inaction succeeded by days and nights of terrible forced marches.

---

[173] The sword was inscribed 'From Lt. Col. Fane and his Brother Officers of the 59th Regiment to Captain F. W. Hoysted in token of esteem, 1809.' A veteran of over thirty years' service, he later commanded the 2nd/59th in the Peninsula, earning a Gold Medal for Vitoria with a bar for the Nive, and served with the 59th in the Waterloo campaign.

[174] This intake of militiamen for the 2nd/59th was drawn from Westmorland, North Lincolnshire, Derbyshire, Kildare, Tipperary and South Cork.

[175] Preston Barracks, Lewes was built in the 1790s. This Regency barracks was demolished in the 1990s to make way for a hypermarket.

[176] William Williams was first commissioned into the 40th Foot on 23rd June 1794. He was wounded as a lieutenant in the 1st/40th at Oude Karspel, 1799, served in Egypt in 1801, was promoted to major in 1802 and obtained a majority in the 81st Foot on 26th October 1804. After commanding the 81st in the Walcheren campaign, he was promoted to lieutenant-colonel in the 60th Rifles on 15th November 1809 and commanded the 5th/60th in the Peninsula from January 1810 to June 1812. He earned further distinction, and another wound, in 1811 when he commanded the light troops in the village of Fuentes d'Onoro, and in 1814 he commanded the 13th Foot on the Richelieu River, Canada, during the War of 1812. He became Major-General Sir William Williams KCB, Knight of the Tower and Sword of Portugal, and died in 1832. His medals, including his Gold Cross for Corunna, Fuentes d'Onoro, Ciudad Rodrigo, Badajoz and Salamanca, are in the Royal Greenjackets Museum.

[177] The 2nd/81st received men chiefly from the South Gloucester, Dorset, Montgomery and County Dublin Regiments of Militia.

[178] Writing in 1902, Sir Charles Oman judiciously observed, 'The accepted view of the present generation… is strongly coloured by the circumstance that William Napier, whose eloquent history has superseded all other narratives of the Peninsular War, was a violent enemy of the Tory ministry and a personal admirer of Moore.' Many historians to the present day have followed Napier's uncritical lead.

Once the retreat began Moore lost all confidence in his mission and his troops, committing his army to headlong flight when a more measured and resolute withdrawal would have been both possible and less costly in lives, materiel and morale. Having repeatedly failed to deliver what he had led his officers and men to expect, he repaid their understandable loss of faith in his leadership by petulantly scolding when he might have encouraged and by acting as commander of the rearguard when he would have been better employed in sorting out the logistic chaos which prevented him from making a morale-raising stand. Even when he was obliged to offer battle, at Lugo, he apparently had little heart for the fight.

'A somewhat gloomy cast of mind,' wrote Adam Neale, 'conjoined with too much sensibility for his iron-hearted profession, accustomed him to look rather on the dark than the bright side of affairs. He had imbibed a high opinion of the French as a military people, and of the ability of their generals, and the great wisdom and skill of their Emperor: which impressions, joined to too much diffidence in his own great talents and the unrivalled valour of British soldiers, at times depressed his energies and spirit of enterprise.'

Brigadier-General Charles Stewart held a very similar view: 'The truth is that Sir John Moore, with many of the qualities requisite to constitute a general, was deficient in that upon which, more perhaps than any other, success in war must ever depend. He wanted confidence in himself – he was afraid of responsibility – he underrated the qualities of his own troops and greatly overrated those of his adversary.'

Captain Alexander Gordon of the 15th Light Dragoons was equally critical, commenting in his campaign journal that 'I am fully persuaded that the distresses the army encountered are chiefly to be attributed to the misconduct of its leader.'

Such heartfelt strictures, however, cannot negate the central strategic result of the Corunna campaign. There is general agreement that Moore's advance into Spain and subsequent northerly withdrawal, drawing after him Napoleon's main effort, saved both Portugal and the southern provinces of Spain from the imminent danger of being overrun by French armies and bought time for the defeated Spanish armies to collect themselves, reorganise, and continue resistance. Without this respite, short as it was, later Allied successes in the Peninsula would have been improbable. This was certainly the verdict of the future Duke of Wellington, while Napoleon, musing in exile on his defeat in the Peninsula, agreed that 'It was only Moore's action which stopped me taking Spain and Portugal' and recorded his admiration for the British general.

Finally, there can be little doubt that Sir John Moore was a decisive and inspirational battlefield commander who, to the very end, led from the front. His skilful conduct of the battle of Corunna and his heroic death, went a long way towards redeeming his own reputation and the honour of his army.

The siege of Flushing, August 1809, during the Walcheren campaign. The 47th & 59th were both present

The 40th charge
at the Battle of Talavera
27th-28th July 1809

The 40th & a strong detachment of the 82nd fought at Talavera

Chapter IV:
Walcheren to Talavera 1809

The Walcheren Expedition 1809 (59th, 81st & 82nd) – Landing & Advance to Middelburg & Flushing (82nd) – Siege of Flushing (59th 81st & 82nd) – Walcheren Fever – South Beveland (59th & 82nd) - 59th & 82nd ordered home – 81st in Walcheren Garrison – Reinforced by 82nd – Demolition and Evacuation – Lasting Effect of Fever – 40th in Seville – the Battalions of Detachments – Beresford's Portuguese Army – Wellesley Resumes Command – Oporto – Battle of Talavera (40th & Detachments) – Withdrawal to the Frontier – 40th at Badajoz & Olivenza.

Walcheren, July-December 1809

The Corunna regiments had hardly recovered from their ordeal in Spain or absorbed their reinforcements when they were rapidly re-equipped and warned for another expedition. Britain was once again attempting to support an alliance of European powers against Napoleon Buonaparte. Austria took the field in April, and early Habsburg success in Italy, a rising in the Tyrol and Napoleon's defeat at the battle of Aspern-Essling on 21st and 22nd May 1809 encouraged the British Government to despatch a large expeditionary force.

Its principal object was to divert Napoleon's attention from Central Europe by capturing Antwerp in a coup de main operation. It was hoped, rather than expected, that success in this quarter might encourage Prussia to declare against France and stimulate insurrection in Germany and Holland. There was an additional sound reason for the selection of this target, for the French Emperor had put much effort into establishing Antwerp as a commercial rival to London and building up naval forces in the Scheldt, which had become France's second-largest naval arsenal. The Dutch coast had, in effect, become 'a pistol presented at the breast of England.' Unfortunately, the principle strategic purpose of the expedition had become redundant before it sailed, for on 5th-6th July Napoleon had consolidated his grip on the Continent by defeating the Austrians at Wagram.

On 21st June 1809, after three months' deliberation confused by factional dispute, and despite the strongly expressed advice of the Horse Guards urging the impracticality of the intended assault, the Cabinet authorised the largest expedition that had ever left British shores. In addition to the wider strategic aims outlined above, the immediate purpose of this force was to capture or destroy enemy shipping in the Scheldt, destroy the docks and arsenals at Antwerp, Flushing and Terneuse, and reduce the island of Walcheren, leaving a garrison there.

Whilst at a strategic level, this intervention made some sense, insufficient consideration was given to the tactical, logistic, navigational and even medical difficulties of the venture, which should have been evident on a cursory examination of what little was known about the approaches to Antwerp. It was left to shrewd old King George to comment, when reluctantly agreeing to his ministers' plans, that 'His Majesty could have wished that the information upon which the practicability of the expedition has been finally decided had not been so imperfect.'

Antwerp lay some fifty miles up the estuary of the River Scheldt, its approaches protected by successive fortifications and by difficulties of navigation and safe anchorage around the low-lying, pestiferous islands and shifting shoals of the estuary. The forts and batteries whose guns dominated the seaward approaches were not strongly manned, but some, notably the fortified port of Flushing (Vlissingen) on the island of Walcheren and Fort Batz on South Beveland, would have to be reduced before a British fleet could enter the Scheldt. The Royal Navy would then be faced by a chain of forts on both sides of the river, of which Fort Frederick, Lillo was the strongest and most important, together with a boom and a powerful French flotilla. Finally, the islands of the Scheldt estuary were notorious for disease, most prevalent from mid-August until the winter frosts. Unfortunately, there was remarkably little accurate intelligence about the intended theatre of operations, its geography, climate and defences.

The only, very slight, chance of success for the expedition lay in a surprise landing on the mainland near Cadzand, followed by an immediate and rapid march to take not-too-distant Antwerp by coup de main before it could be reinforced. It was indeed planned that part of the British force should do just that while the remainder cleared a passage up the Scheldt estuary by capturing the islands of Walcheren, Schouwen and North and South Beveland, operations which must inevitably involve a regular siege of Flushing.

Surprise was unfortunately out of the question: writing from Ramsgate on 27th July before embarkation an officer of the 81st remarked:

'As to the destination of our Expedition, it is, by this time, tolerably well known to both our friends and foes. This is one of our secret Expeditions, the precise object of which is known to all the world. If anything be impossible, it is for England to have a secret Expedition.'[179]

Such a doubtful operation would clearly require, in addition to unlikely quantities of good luck, a united and determined leadership of the very highest order. Unfortunately, the prospects for a successful outcome to this hazardous amphibious venture were further compromised by the Government's choice of its leaders. Lord Chatham, the eccentric elder brother to the late Prime Minister William Pitt the Younger, was appointed as military commander. Chatham, who had risen with little trace of military achievement in the field, was reputed to have a good brain but preferred not to work it too hard. He had shown real administrative talent as Master General of the Ordnance and was capable of sound judgement, but was unapproachably aloof and notoriously lazy, nicknamed 'the late earl' because of his difficulty in rising from bed in the morning.[180] Chatham was accompanied to Walcheren by his pet turtles. A concerned officer of the 81st observed him prior to embarkation:

'I could wish the Earl would be more active in putting his talents forth… He is indolent beyond any man I have ever seen. At the present moment, he bustles about with some appearance of alacrity; but it is evidently only a fit and a start, and all of us begin to apprehend a relapse. If you pass his window in his hours of leisure, you will invariably see him yawning, or with a book, over which he is sleeping.'[181]

The impulsive naval commander, Rear-Admiral Sir Richard Strachan, known in the Service as 'Mad Dick,' was a difficult partner who soon proved to be out of his depth in the shallow waters of the Scheldt.

So it was that in July 1809, a force of some 245 naval vessels and 400 transports carrying 39,219 soldiers assembled in the Downs, off the coast of Kent, preparatory to sailing for the Scheldt estuary. The 2nd/59th, 2nd/81st and 1st/82nd, all recently returned from Corunna, were among the regiments selected for this expedition.

The 2nd/81st, still commanded by Major William Williams, received orders on the 4th of July to march from Bletchingley to Portsmouth. Hurried preparations were made: the Paymaster's accounts show that on the 11th he was authorised to write off the sum of £850 for replacement of necessaries 'lost in the last campaign,' and on the same day, it was noted that two officers (Captain John Lutman and Lieutenant Josiah Hort) must be left behind as they were 'insufficiently recovered from wounds received at Corunna.' The 81st embarked on 18th July at Portsmouth on HMS *Achille*, 74, with a strength of 39 officers, 40 sergeants, nineteen drummers and 658 rank and file. They were brigaded with the 2nd/23rd and 1st/26th under Major-General Gore Browne, late commanding officer of the 40th, and formed part of the Left Wing of the Army tasked to capture Walcheren.

Also embarked at Portsmouth on 15th July, were the 1st/82nd, with 36 officers and well over one thousand men[182], commanded by Lieutenant-Colonel William Grant, an experienced veteran of American and Indian wars.[183] The 82nd were brigaded with the 2nd/14th and 1st/51st under Brigadier-General Houston, forming a reserve for Major-General Graham's Right Wing.

---

[179] *Letters from Flushing* by an Officer of the 81st Regiment, London, October 1809, p. 6. The identity of this well-informed officer is unknown, but he appears to have been on the staff of Fraser's division.

[180] In 1774-75 Pitt had served briefly with the 47th Regiment in Canada on the staff of Sir Guy Carleton.

[181] *Letters from Flushing*, p.p. 3-4.

[182] On 31st July the 82nd had 1,035 NCOs and men.

[183] William Grant was first commissioned in 1773 and had seen extensive active service in America, the West Indies and India. He was with the 42nd Foot at the battles of Long Island, Brandywine, Paoli and Monmouth, and the capture of New York, Philadelphia and New London, and with the 55th at the capture of St. Lucia. With the 77th in India, he served in Cornwallis's successful 1791-92 campaign against Tipu Sultan (Third Mysore War), and commanded the Light Company of that Regiment at the capture of Cochin and Columbo in 1795. Promoted to brevet major on 1st January 1798, he commanded the 77th in Wellesley's 1800 campaign against the brigand Dhoondia Waugh, 'King of the Two Worlds.' In 1801 he marched against the Poligars of Mysore, storming the strong fort of Panjalamcourchy in Tinnevally at the head of his Regiment, and received the thanks of the Governor of Madras for his conduct. He returned to England in 1802 and was promoted to Lieutenant Colonel of the 82nd on 15th August 1805.

The 2nd/59th embarked at Harwich on 15th July under Lieutenant-Colonel Charles Fane, still suffering from his Corunna wound. The Battalion, which on the 31st mustered 42 officers and 863 NCOs and men, was brigaded with the 11th and 79th under Major-General Leith, their commander in the Corunna campaign, and was in Lieutenant-General Lord Grosvenor's division.

Our anonymous 81st officer witnessed the scene at Ramsgate immediately prior to departure:

'Everything is bustle, agitation, running backwards and forwards. The place is full of the wives, friends, and daughters of the officers about to embark. We hourly meet many lovely faces actually suffused in tears or with evident marks that they have just taken the last embrace of some beloved objects. How happy must those be who are thus beloved by those angelic figures!'[184]

At five o'clock on the morning of the 28th, the fleet set sail from the Downs for the mouth of the Scheldt. The initial landing, at Breezand at the north end of Walcheren Island was made by Gore Browne's brigade, including the 81st, on 30th July 1809. Already circumstances conspired to thwart the expedition, for foul weather had delayed disembarkation and diverted the landing to the corner of the island furthest from its objective, Flushing, and although the troops were ordered into boats at 11 a.m. the tide and a gale-force wind further delayed the landing until 6 p.m.

Each man was issued with sixty rounds of ammunition and had a good flint in his musket, with two spare flints in his pouch and three days' provisions in his haversack. The troops were landed from flat-bottomed craft, each carrying forty men, towed by ships' launches, and they were ordered to remain seated, in strict silence and with muskets unloaded, until they went ashore.

Breezand was, as the name implies, a sandy beach backed by dunes. As the landing craft ran in, they were supported by gunboats and mortar brigs, which silenced a Dutch battery covering the beach and forced some 1,200 defenders, French, Dutch, Irish and Prussians, to retire into woods behind the sandhills. After resisting there for about two hours, the defenders were driven back with the loss of four guns and about 150 prisoners, and the British troops moved inland to occupy a position facing Oostkapelle. Further regiments were then landed, including the 82nd, late that night, which was bitterly cold and wet.

The following morning, whilst part of his force invested the nearby fortified town of Veere, Chatham rather cautiously advanced south towards Middelburg, the largest town on Walcheren, which was abandoned without a fight by its garrison. Houston's Brigade, led by the 82nd, passed through the town at daybreak on August 1st and continued on the main road towards Flushing, driving the enemy before them in several sharp engagements.

At Groote Abeele, two miles beyond Middelburg, they found the French deployed with three guns behind a breastwork, deep ditch and abatis, with their sharp-shooters lining enclosures on each flank. The Light Infantry carried the village smartly, capturing the guns, and advanced in hot pursuit for some two miles towards the next village, East Souburg. Here again, the French offered resistance, but Houston's advance guard, including the Light Company of the 82nd, turned the position, dashed into the houses and forced the enemy to retire with the loss of two guns.

'At the entrance of the village,' wrote Private William Wheeler of the 51st (in the same brigade as the 82nd), 'they had planted two 9-pounders, equal to our 12-pounders. These were loaded with grape; in a few seconds more, their contents would have been discharged on us, but such was the impetuosity of the charge, they were driven from the ground, leaving the guns behind loaded. We punished the enemy severely from this place to the Swann Inn, distance about a quarter of a mile. The road was strewed with their dead and wounded, and a great many prisoners were made; from the buttons of the prisoners' clothes, it appeared they belonged to the 1st and 2nd Battalions of the Irish Legion and the 1st Colonial Battalion.'

The 82nd pursued their enemy closely to within half a gunshot of the walls of Flushing, and it was even suggested, by armchair commentators at home, that they could have entered the fortress with the fugitives, though this was strongly denied by those closer to the action. 'It is true that the 82nd Regiment had a very brave affair almost under the walls on the night following our landing, but they were not mad enough to have attempted entering the town. The gates were, in fact, closed long before they reached the fosse, and a number of the enemy

[184] *Letters from Flushing*, p.p. 2-3.

were killed from the caution of the garrison guard in admitting the fugitives into the town.' During this advance, Lieutenants Charles Pratt and Richard Read and a few men of the 82nd were wounded, the former seriously.

The fortified port of Flushing had now to be formally besieged, and British siege lines were established in a semi-circle from the northwest to the east of the town.[185] The 82nd took up a position a little in advance of East Souberg, while the 81st halted near West Souberg. The port of Veere capitulated on the 1st of August, and the 59th landed there next day, marching with Grosvenor's division to East Souberg that evening to reinforce the besieging army. Early on the morning of the 3rd of August, the division redeployed to West Souberg and took up a position between Graham's and Paget's divisions.[186]

The infantry at once began entrenching and bringing up stores, and the 81st were said to have been the first regiment to break ground before the west side of the town. Siege guns were landed and laboriously hauled the eight miles from Veere by teams of men, and on August 3rd, the erection of batteries began in unseasonable rainstorms.

That same day, the intended landing on Cadzand was finally abandoned due to a combination of bad weather, confusion over orders and growing enemy strength ashore. Thus, the expedition failed to take its most vital immediate objective, for without control of the Cadzand channel, the Royal Navy had to wait for the fall of Flushing before they could move up the Scheldt estuary towards Antwerp, and the reduction of Flushing was itself delayed for lack of naval gunfire support.

The reduction of Flushing was indeed no easy task. The port was strongly fortified, and despite the efforts of the Royal Navy, its original garrison of 4,638 men was reinforced in the first week of August by 3,143 men ferried over the channel from Cadzand. On the afternoon of August 7th the French mounted a sortie to the west of Flushing with some two thousand men in two columns, which was driven back with heavy loss. Our anonymous officer of the 81st described this warm action:

'They marched towards us as if on parade. The British, upon their part, allowed them to come within musket-shot, when they poured upon them such a cool and deliberate fire as immediately threw them into some confusion. Our men then leaped from the trenches and charged the enemy with bayonets. The French made many fruitless efforts to keep their ground, and after they were broken, to form again, but the English repeatedly attacked them. The battle continued… nearly two hours, at the end of which time the enemy were completely routed.'[187]

It was probably on this occasion that the 81st suffered the majority of their battle casualties, which during the siege amounted to one drummer and three rank and file killed, and four officers[188] and five rank and file wounded, mostly from gunshot. The 59th also had one soldier wounded that day, while their total loss during the siege amounted to two rank-and-file killed and one officer[189], a sergeant and three rank-and-file wounded.

Whilst wet weather made life unpleasant for troops standing knee-deep in waterlogged trenches or sheltering in sodden bivouac huts, worse was to come. As early as 2nd August, our unknown officer of the 81st confided his concern to friends in London:

'I am afraid we are about to suffer a most dreadful inconvenience… The Flushingers, as we have learned, are about to cut the dikes and to admit the sea.' On August 11th, he confirmed that 'The dikes have been cut, and the water begins to flow very fast. If Flushing do not fall in less than ten days, we must re-embark, or we shall all be drowned.'[190]

In a letter of 9th August from before Flushing, the same officer gave his impressions of conditions in the siege lines:

'Our army, as you may suppose, is very unpleasantly lodged. They have built themselves huts; but the rain penetrates them, and nothing can be more comfortless. We look to the fall of Flushing for better accommodation.

---

[185] The besieging force consisted of some 17,000 men commanded by Lieutenant-General Sir Eyre Coote.
[186] On August 7th Lieutenant-Colonel Fane was appointed to command the port of Veere and Major George MacGregor assumed temporary command of the 59th.
[187] *Letters from Flushing*, p. 62.
[188] Captain P C Taylor and Lieutenants Bartholemew Vigors Derenzy and Knox Montgomery were slightly wounded, while Assistant Surgeon Henry Chislette lost his right leg. Major-General Gore Browne, late 40th, was shot through the jaw and teeth.
[189] Lieutenant Charles Marlborough Seymour.
[190] *Letters from Flushing*, pp. 39 and 87.

There are positive orders against landing more than a certain weight of baggage. Many of the soldiers are without blankets, and there is scarcely a change of linen throughout the army.'

'The weather is dismally bad, and the enemy annoy us by their incessant fire. Whilst our men are at work, a soldier is constantly employed to watch the flashes of the town guns. As soon as he sees a flash, he gives the word, and the workmen all fall prostrate. You can scarcely imagine how effectual this method has been. It necessarily, however, delays the workmen.'[191]

By August 13th the water had risen considerably. Most of the low ground in front of Flushing was flooded, roads were nearly impassable, and the 59th Foot had to be moved to higher ground on the right when their left flank was inundated.

Worse trials than flooding were still to come. On August 12th, our correspondent of the 81st noted the rapid spread of what came to be known as Walcheren Fever:

'Our condition becomes very uncomfortable. We are already knee-deep in water; and unless the city surrenders before the end of next week, we must re-embark. The water begins to flow so fast, that there is scarcely an inch of dry ground. All the fresh water of the island, moreover, is spoiled.'

'From the flowing of the waters, above and below, for it rains incessantly, we begin to suffer very much in our health. You can almost see the exhalations as they rise, and you may most assuredly smell them. Nothing can be so insufferable as the stench of the hollows.'

'There is a kind of pestilence which is said to prevail here in the autumn. We already begin to feel its effects even in the open country. Not a regiment is to be found, but what has suffered considerably... The centinels are sometimes relieved twice instead of once, by reason of the sudden indisposition of the men. I confess that this increasing disease has alarmed me exceedingly. Men are frequently carried from parade. The attack is sudden and violent; the prevalent diseases are the dysentery and the intermittent. They of course originate in the infected air and in the unwholesome water. The climate for this past week has been variable in the extreme. In the morning, it rains heavily – at noon, there is a burning sun, which covers one with perspiration. The nights, again, become extremely cold.'

'Our men are dying hourly, and almost by the minute; and an order has just been issued, doubtless from this frequency, that all burials shall be by night, and without candles or torches... How is it possible, indeed, to avoid disease when, added to the variable nature of the climate, not an inch of dry ground is to be found in the island? We are for hours together up to our knees in water. You will confess that all this is but a very bad prospect of our future success; and I can assure you that some of our officers begin to wear very long faces.'[192]

The available sources suggest that Walcheren Fever was not a single disease but a lethal combination of several diseases prevalent in marshy areas – malaria, typhus, typhoid, and dysentery – acting together on troops in many cases already debilitated by the arduous Corunna campaign, aggravated by weeks confined on crowded transports followed by exposure to the temperamental climate and waterlogged countryside of Walcheren. The Emperor Napoleon was delighted at this development. 'I rejoice,' he wrote, 'that the English have packed themselves in the morasses of Zealand. Let them be only kept in check, and the bad air and fever peculiar to the country will soon destroy their army.'

Nevertheless, at about 2 p.m. on August 13th+, the British siege batteries opened against Flushing, together with Congreve's rather unpopular rockets:

'The island shook as if under an earthquake, and every report of the cannon was followed by a most horrible crash. Bricks, timber and splinters of wood flew about in every direction; and when the chimnies or any high point was struck, they were sometimes driven, almost whole, over the walls. The batteries were all so near that the guns had their full force; they literally appeared as if they were tearing the city up from the roots... The walls fell in large fragments, the churches took fire, the houses fell in, and every thing was shortly so involved in smoke that the guns were aimed at random.'[193]

---

[191] *Letters from Flushing*, pp. 60 and 63-4.
[192] Ibid., p.p. 117 and 119-121.
[193] Ibid., p.p. 150-151.

Next morning, the British warships added their broadsides to the bombardment, and by about 5 p.m., the guns of Flushing were entirely silent. Chatham ordered a cease-fire and summoned the garrison, but as no answer was received after three hours, the bombardment was resumed with even more terrible effect:

'Imagine yourself within four hundred yards of a walled town – this town on fire in five or six parts – the flames raging amidst the darkness of the night – the cannons still thundering, and the walls, and chimnies, and roofs falling under the stroke of the balls, and you may have some faint idea of the dreadful scene which was presented to us. The interior of almost every house was visible; and when there was an interval of the noise of the cannon, it was filled up by shrieks of the women from the city. Even the very dogs howled, and several owls and bats flew affrighted round the light.'[194]

Early on the morning of 15th August, General Monnet, the commandant of Flushing, surrendered the survivors of his garrison, 5,803 men.[195] On the morning of the 18th, the 82nd Foot formed part of the hollow square in which the French laid down their arms prior to being marched as prisoners to Veere and embarked for England. Some thousand sick and wounded Frenchmen had been evacuated to Cadzand before the surrender, and 1,816 prisoners and deserters had previously been taken, making a total French loss on Walcheren of some nine thousand men. British battle casualties amounted to 738 killed, wounded and missing.

Meanwhile, British forces had speedily occupied the other islands of the Scheldt estuary – Schouwen and North and South Beveland – and, on 2nd August, had taken Fort Batz at the southernmost point of South Beveland. Unfortunately, as we have noted, the rather more vital landing at Cadzand, which just might have enabled the capture of Antwerp, had been aborted. This left Chatham with only one option for a further advance: a crossing from South Beveland to the east side of the Scheldt, landing around Santvlied to besiege Fort Lillo and Antwerp in turn.

With Flushing in his hands, Chatham ordered the greater part of his army, including the 59th and 82nd, to concentrate around Fort Batz in South Beveland. The 59th re-embarked with Grosvenor's division at the port of Rammekens on 19th August, sailing up the Scheldt the next day to anchor on the 23rd off Fort Batz. The 82nd followed a day later with Graham's division. By the 25th, when Chatham eventually arrived, he had a force of some 23,000 infantry and 2,000 cavalry poised for further operations: but it was already much too late.

British preparations for a raid on the Dutch coast had been known to the French for some three months. They had accordingly repaired and extended the defences along the Scheldt and had made contingency plans for rapid reinforcement of their six thousand troops around Antwerp. By the time Flushing fell on 15th August, the French force had been reinforced to some twenty thousand men commanded by Marshal Bernadotte, and ten days later, the British intelligence estimate was that they faced some 36,000 enemy troops; the defences of Antwerp were in good order, and the dikes had been opened.

Whilst the French grew daily in strength, the British on South Beveland were wasting from disease, with four thousand sick by the 28th of August. On the 27th, Lord Chatham assembled a council-of-war at Fort Batz to consider whether to proceed with the siege of Antwerp or to attempt any minor operations. His commanders unanimously advised him that nothing further could now be achieved, and on the 28th Chatham began preparations to evacuate Beveland. He had decided to strengthen the garrison on Walcheren, which he was under orders to hold and to embark the remainder of the army for England.

On the 27th of August, the 59th were ordered back to Flushing, which they reached on the 30th. On 9th September the regiments ordered home, including the 59th and 82nd, sailed away. Weakened by disease, oppressed by their expedition's failure and attacked by the London press, the troops were understandably despondent:

'Who that was to see us now would recognise the gay, gallant body of men who, under the cheering salutations of their countrymen, left Ramsgate about six weeks since, promising themselves those additional laurels which should eclipse, or at least equal, the battles of Maida and Vimeira?… Our poor fellows have learned by some means that they have not equalled the expectations of their countrymen; and under this persuasion, I do really believe that they are ashamed to come back. They are as slow in their preparations for re-embarkation as they were brisk and active in their landing. But everything is now changed. They look to a cold reception at home.

---

[194] *Letters from Flushing*, p. 158.
[195] The Emperor Napoleon was unforgiving, and Monnet was tried in Paris in his absence and sentenced to death for cowardice and treason. Wisely, the General remained in England until 1814.

I should hope, however, that you will not have the injustice to impute the failure of the Expedition to any fault of the men. Believe me, in every individual action and throughout the whole business, they conducted themselves in a manner worthy of their countrymen.'[196]

Among the returning troops who had suffered least from disease were the 2nd/59th, whose exposure to the worst rigours of Walcheren was relatively short and whose sick list was correspondingly low. The Regiment lost only three men dead from the time they left Weeley Barracks until their return, though six officers and sixty men fell sick. It is tempting to surmise that, as in the Corunna campaign and later in Spain, the strict discipline imposed on his Battalion by Charles Fane may have contributed to its comparatively healthy state.

The 1st/82nd, which appears to have suffered rather more severely, returned to England with the first division of the army and was sent to its old quarters, at Lewes in Sussex, about the middle of September.

Much less fortunate was the 2nd/81st, which was one of the battalions selected to garrison Walcheren when the advance on Antwerp was abandoned. Immediately after the fall of Flushing, the 81st marched with Gore Browne's brigade to Middelburg, remaining there until early September, when it was sent to occupy St. Joost's Land, then an island to the south-east of Walcheren, from which it was separated by a narrow channel.

The 18,670 men who were detailed to remain in garrison at Walcheren, under Sir Eyre Coote, suffered the most terrible ravages of disease. Already on 7th September, there were nearly six thousand in hospital, and by the end of the month this had risen to some nine thousand, with around one thousand dead and 6,310 evacuated sick to England. The garrison of Walcheren was rapidly wasting away, and on the 29th of September, Eyre Coote wrote in great distress to Lord Chatham: 'Something must be done, or the British nation will lose the British army – far more valuable than the island of Walcheren.'

Although the 81st was one of the last regiments to be attacked by the prevalent fever, its losses over the next few weeks were dreadfully severe. The officer of the 81st reported that their healthiest men were no better than 'walking corpses.' 'In one day,' recalled Harry Ross-Lewin of the 32nd, 'the 81st buried twenty of their men.' By 7th September, the number of men fit for duty had dropped from 717 to 505, with 257 sick, but on the 29th September, the 81st had only forty men fit for duty. On St. Joost's Land, the men suffered so much from fever that it became necessary to relieve the Regiment, which was struck off duty on the 23rd and returned to Middelburg.

On the 27th of October, Eyre Coote handed over the command at Walcheren to Sir George Don, a former commanding officer of the 59th, whose first act was to request transports to move nearly six thousand more invalids to England as the only chance of saving their lives. His situation was precarious in the extreme. With a force reduced to fewer than 4,500 effectives and a rather larger number of sick, he had received intelligence of French preparations to recapture Walcheren. On 4th November, the Ministry accepted the inevitable, ordering Don to destroy the docks and fortifications of Walcheren and then to bring his surviving troops home.

The 1st/82nd was included in a brigade scraped together in England to assist the weakened garrison in this work of demolition. The Regiment had scarcely been a month at Lewes before it was ordered to re-embark every man fit for duty to Flushing; and consequently, two hundred rank and file of the 82nd, under one-legged Major Henry King, proceeded a second time to Walcheren, where they remained until that island was finally evacuated on the 11th of December.

The sad remnants of the 81st, who had been stationed in Middelburg from late September until the evacuation of the island, embarked on the *Fame* transport at Flushing with only 59 all ranks[197] and, detained in the Scheldt by adverse winds until the 23rd December, arrived at Portsmouth on the 26th and reached their old barracks at Bletchingley on the 31st.

The Walcheren disaster, for such it must be called, had a lasting impact on the regiments involved. Besides the victims who died on the spot or soon afterwards, nearly four thousand in all[198], the constitution of many survivors was forever weakened, and most of the Walcheren regiments took several years to regain their previous

---

[196] *Letters from Flushing*, p.p. 283-4, Letter of 8th September.

[197] The embarkation state of the 81st from Walcheren, exclusive of those previously evacuated sick, was just one major, two captains, four subalterns, one battalion staff, five sergeants, one drummer and 45 rank and file.

[198] The Adjutant General's return of 1st February 1810 shows that of the 39,219 all ranks of the Army who embarked for the Scheldt, forty officers and 2,041 other ranks had died there of disease, twenty officers and 1,859 other ranks had died since their return, and 217 officers and 11,296 other ranks were still reported as sick. Only seven officers and 99 other ranks had been killed in action.

vigour. It was to be four years before the 2nd/81st, who had suffered at least 297 deaths[199], were again selected for active service. As for the 1st/82nd, Lieutenant George Wood says in his memoirs that the flower of the old veteran corps of 1808 had perished from Walcheren Fever, and afterwards the regiment had to be built almost anew from raw levies before being sent back to the Peninsula in 1810. Even then, the 82nd suffered from recurrent sickness, which rather unfortunately earned them the displeasure of Wellington during the 1812 retreat from Burgos, and it was 1813 before the Regiment regained its previous fighting form.

It would be easy to pin the blame for this debacle on the naval and military commanders, and popular opinion at the time and since has done just that; but in truth, as Sir John Fortescue has more justly concluded, 'the British force was sent upon an errand in which success was at best very precarious, and practically impossible.' The odds were indeed heavily stacked against success and should have been more carefully researched and considered by the Ministry, who rejected experienced military advice. In particular, the fatal prevalence of disease in the islands of the Scheldt estuary at that time of year was entirely predictable.

An Expedition to Seville, February-April 1809

Following the evacuation of Sir John Moore's army from Corunna, just one British infantry regiment remained on the frontier with Spain. This was the 40th Foot, which had been in garrison at Elvas since November 1808. Lieutenant Conynghan Ellis of the 40th, sent out from Elvas to gather intelligence in Estremadura, had detected the disruption to Napoleon's plans occasioned by Moore's advance. Ellis, a forerunner of Wellington's 'exploring officers,' reported to Colonel Kemmis the arrival of French troops in Trujillo on 26th January, with their cavalry screen approaching Merida (only 41 miles from Badajoz and 48 from Elvas); but on the 28th Kemmis wrote to Sir John Cradock at Lisbon with news of a French withdrawal the following morning: 'The enemy marched into Trujillo on the 26th, at half-past 12 o'clock in the day; but at two on the following morning a French officer arrived there and they fell back four leagues.' That same day, Lieutenant Ellis sent word to Kemmis that the main body of the enemy, having left Trujillo in haste, had retired across the bridge of Almaraz and were heading north to Plasencia and Salamanca.

With the immediate threat to Portugal deflected by Moore's northward diversion of the French armies, in January 1809 the 40th handed over Elvas to the Portuguese. The Regiment had been ordered south from the Portuguese frontier to Seville on a 'long and tedious march' across the wintry sierras.[200] As the 40th marched down to Andalusia, they were not impressed by what they saw of Spanish military preparations; on arrival at Seville, Colonel James Kemmis reported to Sir John Cradock on 7th February that 'in passing through the Sierra Morena mountains, where nature has done much for the defence of this province, it was painful to observe the pitiful works they were about to throw up. In this whole direction, there is but one body that has anything like the appearance of a soldier, viz. dismounted cavalry.'[201]

The Spanish Central Junta had withdrawn from Madrid to Seville before Napoleon's advancing armies, and General Cradock in Lisbon, believing there to be an immediate threat to the defenceless Andalusian city, had been prevailed upon to move the 40th down to Seville as a small gesture of support and, at the instigation of Sir George Smith[202], to send a larger force by sea to Cadiz. This was in accordance with the prevalent military and ministerial opinion that Portugal was indefensible and that future British operations in the Peninsula should be in

---

[199] The loss of the 81st during its four months on Walcheren amounted to one officer (Major Edward Davies Maurice) nineteen sergeants, eight drummers and 269 rank and file, of whom only four were killed in action.

[200] Both the *Regimental Record of Service* and Lawrence's autobiography indicate that there was an intention that the 40th should join Moore's army, but any such orders were soon changed, and when the 40th marched out of Elvas they headed in the opposite direction to Corunna, from where the British army had already been evacuated.

[201] The passes of the Sierra Morena were held by six thousand local levies.

[202] We last saw Sir George Smith at Copenhagen in 1806, when he earned his knighthood in command of the 82nd Regiment. Sir George was one of several British military agents in Spain, and landed at Cadiz on 3rd June 1808, the first British soldier in what was about to become the Peninsula theatre of operations. On the basis of his firm advocacy of British occupation of Cadiz, with or without the Central Junta's permission, Oman somewhat unfairly characterised him as 'a hasty and presumptuous man, full of zeal without discretion.' Sir George Smith died of fever at Cadiz on 15th February 1809, aged 49, and a fine marble memorial was erected in the parish church at Peter Port, Guernsey.

the south with a firm base in Cadiz. The plan eventually came to nought, for Moore's advance to Sahagun had delayed French designs on both Andalusia and Portugal, while mistrustful Spanish authorities would not permit the six thousand British reinforcements to land and occupy Cadiz. Eventually, this force was recalled to Lisbon.

The 40th, who had received an enthusiastic welcome in Seville, were held there for some weeks longer by John Hookham Frere, the British ambassador to the Junta, who refused for political reasons to allow the Regiment to be withdrawn. In a letter to Sir John Cradock dated 22nd March, Frere wrote, 'The 40th remains here: under the present circumstances I could not think of their removal, unless to meet a British force from Elvas,' and in a message to Sir Arthur Wellesley, dated 21st April 1809, he stated that the 40th had not been sent from Seville as Wellesley had desired 'from motives of delicacy, the place being so immediately menaced by the French.' According to Kemmis, the Regiment received 'various orders, at times to… join the Spanish army, under General Cuesta, at others to Lisbon.'

Whilst at Seville, eighteen-year-old Private William Lawrence of the Light Company absented himself from guard for 24 hours. He was brought before a drum-head court martial and, although this was his first offence, was sentenced to 400 lashes. The sentence was carried out in the square of a convent:

'I found the Regiment assembled all ready to witness my punishment… As soon as I had been brought in by the guard, the court-martial was read over me by the Colonel [Kemmis] and then I was ordered to strip, which I did firmly and without using any of the help that was offered me, as I had by that time got hardened to my lot. I was then lashed to the halberds, and the Colonel gave the order for the drummers to commence, each one having to give me twenty-five lashes in turn. I bore it very well until I had received a hundred and seventy-five, when I became so enraged with the pain that I pushed the halberds, which did not stand at all firm on account of their being planted on stones, right across the square amid the laughter of the Regiment. The Colonel, I suppose thinking then that I had had sufficient, ordered, in the very words, "the sulky rascal down," and perhaps a more true word could not have been spoken, as indeed I was sulky, for I did not give vent to a single sound the whole time, though the blood ran down my trousers from top to bottom. I was unbound, and the corporal hove my shirt and jacket over my shoulders and conveyed me to the hospital, presenting about as miserable a picture as I possibly could.'[203]

Lawrence carried the scars of his flogging for the rest of his life; but he was, at least in retrospect, philosophical about this brutal punishment, musing that 'perhaps it was as good a thing for me as could then have occurred, as it prevented me from committing any greater crimes which might have gained me other severer punishments and at last brought me to my ruin.' After three weeks in hospital, William Lawrence, now over six foot tall, was transferred to the elite Grenadier Company.

The 40th remained encamped at Seville until Colonel Kemmis received orders from Sir Arthur Wellesley, dated from Coimbra on 2nd May:

'I beg that, as soon as it may be convenient, after you shall have received this order, you will march with the Regiment under your command from Seville to Port St. Mary, by such route as may be settled for you by the Government of Spain; and you will there embark in transports which will have been sent round for the Regiment; and will proceed to Lisbon, where you will receive further orders. As it may be inconvenient to the officers of the Regiment to part with the horses and mules which they may have, and as they would be unable to take the field immediately upon their arrival in Lisbon, if they should part with them, I have requested the Admiral to send to Port St. Mary transports to convey the horses and mules, as well as the Regiment.'

The 40th marched to Puerto Santa Maria, across the bay from Cadiz, where transports were waiting to take them to Lisbon.[204] On the evening before embarkation, they had a pleasant surprise:

'On that night,' recalled Lawrence, 'an English wine-merchant asked permission to give each man in our Regiment a pint of wine, and each woman half that quantity, with a pound of bread apiece; and accordingly, we were all drawn up in line and marched into a tremendous cellar, big enough, had they been so disposed, to have admitted the whole Regiment, with two doors, one at each end, at one of which we entered to receive our share,

---

[203] Lawrence, p.p. 48-9.
[204] The 40th embarked at Puerto Santa Maria in view of Spanish hostility to a British presence in Cadiz.

and went out by the other. He likewise invited the officers to dine with him; and so that night, after drinking the merchant's little kindness, as most of us did to pretty quick time, we slept a good deal sounder.'[205]

Private John Kibby also recalled this incident, writing as follows: 'Then we marched to the City of Sherry. The nobility and gentry did kindly entertain us, both the officers and men. The ladies solicited the pleasure of seeing the English exercise. We fell in, in the afternoon, to parade, and the gentry was highly pleased with us.'

The Battalions of Detachments

Writing from Lamego on 16th January 1809, Brigadier-General Alan Cameron informed Sir John Cradock that 'I have collected several detachments of recovered men belonging to Sir J. Moore's army, whom I found scattered in all directions, without necessaries and some of them committing every possible excess that could render the name of a British soldier odious to the nation.' It has been estimated that some 589 of the stragglers of Moore's army managed to elude or escape the French and make their way some three to five hundred miles through enemy-occupied territory to Portugal. They included soldiers from both the 59th and the 81st, such as Private John Stamp of the 59th, who was listed as 'made prisoner of the French during the retreat to Corunna, but escaped,' and Private Martin Gready who was posted as 'missing' from the same Regiment at Corunna. It was later supposed by Wellesley that many of these men acquired a taste for pillaging during their period of enforced self-sufficiency, which may well be true, but their escape was a remarkable feat of initiative and endurance.

To these, escapees and stragglers were added recovered sick, wounded and detached officers and men who had been left behind in Portugal when Moore's regiments marched. On 16th January 1809 some of these men were formed into the 1st Battalion of Detachments, and a 2nd Battalion was established by early February. The 1st Battalion was joined by soldiers from the 59th and 81st Regiments. A particularly strong company of the 82nd Foot was formed in the 2nd Battalion, ten officers and 96 NCOs and men commanded by Captain Robert Carew, and that battalion also had a few individuals from the 59th. Lieutenant George Wood, who was with the 82nd Company attached to the 2nd Battalion, reckoned the Battalions of Detachments, who numbered over two thousand all ranks, to be 'a very fine body of men.'

Wood was lucky to be among them. Returning sick to Oporto from his abortive attempt to join Moore's army, he had been billeted on a wealthy Portuguese hidalgo, in whose hospitable, enchantingly luxurious mansion his health soon improved. This sybaritic existence had lasted some three weeks when most unwelcome news arrived. Soult was within three days march of Oporto, and the small British force there was ordered to evacuate the city, the sick embarking on a transport for Lisbon. It was, however, a large vessel, and there was supposedly not enough water in the river to carry her over the bar. Eventually, seeing the French advance guard on the neighbouring heights, Wood and his companions determined to ignore the advice of their pilot and make a dash for safety.

'We cut our cables and struck with great violence on the bar; but fortunately the succeeding swell carried us clear out to sea, and on our arrival at Lisbon we learned that the French had entered immediately after we had quitted the Douro, which made us not a little pleased at our narrow escape from being made prisoners by them.'[206]

Beresford's Portuguese Army

In February 1809, the Portuguese Regency agreed to a radical plan whereby the British government would pay and supply their army, which was to be reorganised, trained, and partly led by British officers and NCOs. General Sir William Carr Beresford was appointed to command what quickly became, in effect, a British auxiliary force of high quality and spirit, fully integrated into divisions of the Peninsula army. Officers and NCOs were seconded to the Portuguese Service from throughout the British Army, with the remarkable inducement of two steps in rank, so that a captain might be promoted to a British majority and assume a lieutenant-colonel's appointment in a

---

[205] Lawrence, p. 52. It is most probable that the English wine-merchant responsible for this hospitality at Puerto Santa Maria was Thomas Osborne Mann, founder of the well-known Osborne brand whose bodega remains in the port to the present day and whose advertising boards, featuring a bull, feature on many Spanish roadsides.

[206] Wood, p. 72.

Portuguese battalion. This powerful incentive was soon reduced by the Horse Guards as too expensive, but most officers went up a rank in the Portuguese Service, and 23 British senior NCOs gained commissions. A total of 350 British officers were seconded, and at least nineteen of our regimental predecessors took advantage of this career opportunity.

Good regimental examples are: Lieutenant Bartholemew Vigors Derenzy of the 81st, who in December 1810 became a captain in the 7th Caçadores and by the age of 22 was four times recommended for a majority; Lieutenant James Johnston of the 40th, who in April 1810 was appointed to a captaincy in the 5th Portuguese Regiment, earned a majority for distinguished conduct at Vitoria, and by October 1818 was Lieutenant-Colonel of the 24th Portuguese Regiment; Captain Edmund Keynton Williams of the 81st, who rose to command the 4th Caçadores; Captain Henry Pynn of the 82nd who was given a Portuguese majority in 1809 and in 1810 was promoted to Lieutenant Colonel commanding the 18th Portuguese Regiment; and Sergeant Robert Hughes of the 3rd Buffs, who after two years very active service as Adjutant with the Portuguese was granted a commission in the 30th Foot and eventually rose to the rank of colonel. Such seconded officers, who so very rapidly transformed the Portuguese Army into an effective fighting force, deserve to be remembered and their services will be mentioned where appropriate in this history.

The British officers and NCOs at once set about drilling the Portuguese troops in Dundas's Eighteen Manoeuvres, with the immense advantage that later in the campaign, both British and Portuguese troops could be moved by the same words of command and in the same tactical formations.

Wellesley Resumes Command

Absolved of responsibility for the Convention of Cintra, Sir Arthur Wellesley returned to Lisbon on 22nd April 1809. Assuming command, he at once prepared for offensive action, for unlike Moore and Cradock, he was convinced that Portugal could be defended. Immediate threats were posed by two, widely separated, French armies. In the north, Marshal Soult had occupied Oporto, while Marshal Victor was concentrated in Spanish Estremadura, albeit preoccupied with the defeated but still numerous Spanish armies of Cuesta and Vinegas. Within two days of arrival Wellesley had mapped out a plan of campaign to deal with each of his enemies in turn:

'I should prefer an attack on Victor in concert with Cuesta, if Soult were not in possession of a fertile province of this kingdom and of the favourite town of Oporto, of which it is most desirable to deprive him. But any operation upon Victor, connected to Cuesta's movements, would require time to concert, which may as well be employed in dislodging Soult from the north of Portugal, before bringing the British army to the eastern frontier.'

His first move, then, was against Soult in Oporto, and with him went the Battalions of Detachments. George Wood was on the march with the 2nd Battalion near Coimbra when, on 2nd May, they were overtaken by Wellesley, whose reputation already instilled battle-winning faith in the ranks:

'I well remember with what enthusiastic huzzas we cheered him as he passed our line of march; the men from that moment, as if by instinct, wore a countenance of confidence, which never forsook our army even to the end of the conflict.'[207]

By the 5th, the army had completed its concentration at Coimbra, where a grand review was held. It was an imposing spectacle, and Charles Stewart was struck by the superior quality of the troops: 'The whole were, indeed, in the highest state of discipline and efficiency; and all appeared animated by one spirit – an ardent desire to meet the enemy.' Indeed, Captain George Wood looked forward to 'revenge on those fellows who had so recently broken the enchantment of my princely residence [in Oporto] and endangered my liberty on the bar of that port!'

From Coimbra, the army closed up to the River Douro, a formidable obstacle behind which Soult sat in the imagined security of Oporto, dreaming of the Portuguese throne.

As George Wood noted, the mutual savagery that was to characterise guerrilla warfare in the Peninsula was already apparent:

---

[207] Wood, p. 74. Not everyone was delighted at Wellesley's return. Lieutenant-Colonel James Kemmis of the 40th groused to his brother that 'I found more kindness unsolicited from Sir John Cradock during his short but brilliant command than I think I ever shall from his successor.' His reservations were to prove unfounded, for Wellesley at once gave him command of a brigade.

'The enemy's advanced posts had in these parts left numerous marks of their ravages and traces of their skirmishing. We now began to see the dying and the dead: some of these had been mangled in a manner too shocking to describe by the Portuguese females, out of revenge for the brutal treatment previously experienced from them. Now we passed clusters of inhabitants hanging mutilated on one tree, and on the next as many French were suspended, all hacked and gored in the same manner by way of retaliation; such was animosity subsisting between these inveterate foes.'[208]

Making a rapid final approach march, on May 12th, Wellesley made an audacious crossing of the wide and fast-flowing River Douro. Completely surprised, Soult beat a precipitate retreat over rugged mountain tracks. George Wood's euphoria at 'seeing the foe run helter-skelter away as fast as their legs would carry them' was quickly deflated when, on making a congratulatory visit to the house of his generous former host, he found the mansion reduced to bare walls with everything of value or beauty carried away or vandalised, and even the gardens despoiled. Visiting another friend in Oporto, he was even more shocked:

'He showed me into the parlour; and, pointing to an arm-chair, told me that in that seat, a French officer had, a few hours before, blown out the brains of his poor old father-in-law because he would not resign one of his daughters to gratify the abominable lust of this detestable assassin, who suspected that she was secreted in the house.'[209]

The 2nd Battalion of Detachments then joined in Wellesley's pursuit of Soult, a forced march through the mountains that continued for three days under driving rain and with little food or shelter:

'We pursued the enemy night and day, barely taking sufficient rest to support nature,' wrote Wood, 'till we came to the frontiers of Spain, taking a great many prisoners, baggage and commissariat stores. At length, finding themselves so hardly pressed, and not being able to make another stand, they were compelled to take to the mountains and disperse in all directions, which rendered it impossible for a regular army to follow them any farther.'[210]

By the time the pursuit was called off, Soult had lost nearly six thousand men, together with all his guns and baggage. British losses were some three hundred killed and wounded, but the sufferings of Moore's army had been fully avenged.

After weeks of almost incessant marching, the troops were exhausted but were at once required to retrace their steps from Chaves to Oporto and march south to deal with Victor. This was, as George Wood recalled, 'an exceedingly severe trial for troops who for the last four months had been incessantly harassed and were now in the greatest want of every article of dress, shoes in particular, and of almost every comfort of life. The very moment in which we thought we should have rest, by ending the campaign in the dispersion of the French, brought the orders to continue a march with little intermission of about five hundred miles. Yet not a murmur was heard on this critical occasion; for what will not British soldiers perform under a brave and victorious general?'[211]

The Talavera Campaign June-September 1809

It was early June 1809 before the 40th Foot reached Lisbon from Puerto Santa Maria, too late to share in Wellesley's victory at Oporto. But Wellesley was planning further offensive operations and, writing from Lisbon on the 11th, James Kemmis anticipated the forthcoming campaign:

'I have been in this city only a few days and, by order, am preparing to join the Army that are on their march from Oporto to Abrantis [Abrantes], a town not too far distant from the borders of Spain, into which country I conclude the army will march as soon as they can. At present, they are in want, I find, of shoes and other conveniences, added to a great difficulty… of obtaining provisions for so large a body.'

His preparations were timely, for that same day, Wellesley was authorised by London to cross the Spanish frontier so long as Portugal was left secure. He wrote to the British minister in Lisbon, 'The ball is now at my feet, and I hope I shall have strength enough to give it a good kick.'

---

[208] Wood, p. 76.
[209] Ibid. p. 79.
[210] Ibid., p.p. 80-81.
[211] Ibid., p. 81.

On June 15th, orders were issued for the 40th to be carried up the Tagus by boat to Santarem, from where they marched to join Brigadier-General Alan Cameron's brigade, further up-river at Tancos. Shortly afterwards, the Regiment reached Abrantes, where Wellesley's army was concentrated for the forthcoming campaign. There, they were joined by seventy Irish volunteers for the Regiment (three corporals and 67 privates) who had been attached to the 97th Foot since 12th June.

Whilst at Abrantes, the British brigades were grouped into divisions, and at Placencia on 16th July, Colonel James Kemmis was appointed to command a brigade of Brigadier-General Alexander Campbell's 4th Division, composed of the 40th and 97th Foot and the 2nd Battalion of Detachments, together with a rifle company of the 5th/60th to augment his skirmishing line. Kemmis's brigade was unique in one respect: his battalions consisted almost entirely of veterans of Vimeiro, and most of the men had been in the Peninsula ever since, whereas the great majority of Wellesley's troops were fairly recent arrivals in Portugal. As Kemmis was commanding the brigade, Major Henry Thornton commanded the 40th Regiment.[212]

After its long march south, the 2nd Battalion of Detachments had arrived at Abrantes some days before the 40th, and its veterans had made a comfortable encampment.

'We had had time,' wrote George Wood, 'to build our huts with neatness, regularity, and strength; they were thatched with boughs, had chimneys, were railed in, and formed into regular streets, which gave them the appearance of a fine green village.'[213]

Final preparations for the forthcoming campaign included the allocation of fifteen mules to each infantry battalion: one per company to carry the camp kettles, one for the surgeon's instruments, one for the paymaster's books and one for entrenching tools – five spades, five shovels, five pickaxes and five felling axes.

Wellesley had agreed to advance on Madrid in concert with General Cuesta's Spanish army, hazarding his small force in this bold offensive on receiving assurances that supplies and transport would be provided and that his flanks would be protected. In the event, none of this happened.

It was mid-summer on the parched plains and arid hills of Estremadura, and as the army crossed the frontier, George Wood noticed an abrupt climatic change:

'In Portugal, we had experienced the most distressing cold and wet weather; it was now as suddenly become as intensely hot, and we had very little except the olive trees, which we were prohibited from cutting, to screen us from the scorching rays of a sun almost vertical. This being an open corn country, we were the whole day exposed to its beams, and the ground was so exceedingly warm that it produced the greatest number of insects I ever saw. We were infested and annoyed, beyond measure, by the scorpions and centipedes crawling all over us and the mosquitoes stinging us in such a manner that I have frequently seen officers and men with their eyes so swollen that they could not see out of them for some hours.

'Our advance continued, and the weather retained its sultry heat. Many a weary step, over many a dreary league, we dragged through the dusty way; sometimes not seeing a house for days together, sometimes without a drop of water to wet the parched and swollen tongue of the way-dropped soldier – for there were many who sank under the oppression of this excessive heat.'[214]

On the same march, young Private William Lawrence of the Grenadier Company 40th Foot was more pleasantly, and profitably, impressed by the local wildlife, if not by Cuesta's Spanish army:

---

[212] Henry Thornton, aged thirty, had been a lieutenant in the Scots Greys in 1796. He obtained a captaincy in the 40th Foot on 25th November that year, and served in the West Indies and Holland, where he was wounded. He was promoted to major on 2nd August 1802. On 4th June 1811, he received the brevet rank of lieutenant-colonel, and nine days later became lieutenant-colonel in the Regiment. He was with the 1st/40th in the Peninsula from August 1808 to June 1811, and from July 1813 to April 1814, and commanded during some of the Regiment's most arduous service there, receiving the Army Gold Cross for Talavera, Nivelle, Orthez and Toulouse in addition to the Military General Service Medal with four clasps (Roleia, Vimiera, Busaco and Pyrenees), and a Companionship of the Bath, to which he was appointed on 4th January 1815. He was slightly wounded during the repulse of a sortie from Badajoz, and seriously wounded at the Nivelle. Being called as a witness at a general court martial in London on the return of the 40th from America early in 1815, he was not present at the battle of Waterloo, but rejoined the Regiment shortly afterwards in France, and commanded it from that time at home and in Australia until June 1827 when he exchanged with Colonel Valiant into the 82nd Regiment. He retired the following year, and died at Camberwell aged 77 in April 1856.
[213] Wood, p. 84.
[214] Ibid., pp. 84-6.

'We then advanced across a fine plain, which I should think was more famed for hares than anything else, for I never saw any place that swarmed so with that kind of game. They were running in all directions, and often even right into our lines, for they are stupid animals when frightened, as they then were by the noise our men made; and I managed to kill one with the muzzle of my musket and sold it to the captain of my company for a dollar.

'The bands played each before its own regiment as we crossed the plain, and Sir Arthur Wellesley took the opportunity of reviewing the Spanish troops as they passed. They looked a fine enough set of men, but they were fit for scarcely anything except to fall into disorder and confusion, as we had already found when we had taken the field against some of them at Montevideo, Colonia and Buenos Ayres, the smell of powder often seeming to cause them to be missing when wanted, either from not having been properly disciplined or else because they had not good officers to command them.'[215]

Wellesley halted his army for a few days' at Plasencia[216] while he attempted to co-ordinate plans with Cuesta, a jealous, proud and obstinate old man with an unbroken record of military incompetence. Sir Arthur's proposals for joint action were met with suspicion and obstruction, rather than cooperation; nevertheless, a compromise was reached, and by July 20th, the allied armies had reached Oropesa in Castille, within one day's march of Talavera de la Reina, near where Victor lay with some twenty-two thousand men. Outnumbered and surprised by the Allies, on the 22nd Victor slowly withdrew behind the River Alberche, east of Talavera, under no great pressure from Cuesta's cavalry. Wellesley, too, reached Talavera that day and that evening ordered one-third of each of his regiments 'to remain accoutred in their lines, and the whole to be on the alert.'

The allies agreed on a set-piece dawn attack across the fordable River Alberche the following morning, but to Wellesley's anger and disgust, the Spanish army failed to move from their bivouacs. The same happened on the morning of the 24th, and again that afternoon, as Cuesta's lame excuses for inaction led to mounting British frustration and contempt. By the morning of the 25th Victor had gone, prompting a sudden change in Cuesta from lethargy to quixotic hyperactivity and a determination to give chase to the enemy. He set off that day in hot pursuit on the road to Toledo and Madrid, only to be checked on the morning of the 26th and sent reeling back in disorder. The cause of this abrupt change of fortune was the arrival around Toledo of French reinforcements under King Joseph and General Sebastiani, doubling Victor's force to some 46,000 men and ninety guns. Cuesta retired across the Alberche next morning, covered by Sherbrooke's and Mackenzie's British divisions, and on the afternoon of July 27th, both armies took up positions some four miles to the west on ground that Wellesley had previously selected at Talavera.

The ground was well chosen for a defensive battle. On the right, the town of Talavera stood on the north bank of the River Tagus, its ancient walls hidden among olive groves, gardens and enclosures, a strong position anchoring the Allies' southern flank. The shallow, stony-bedded Portina stream, flowing south through the town to the Tagus, ran for three miles along the Allied front line from the Sierra de Segurilla, a high barrier range securing Wellesley's northern flank. Forward of the Allied position, from the Portina to the Alberche, stretched a flat plain studded with olive groves and vineyards. Two miles north of Talavera, the open slopes of the Cerro de Medellin, an east-west ridge rising to some 250 foot above the plain, dominated the left centre of the Allied line, its eastern end falling abruptly into a ravine formed there by the Portina. On the far side of that ravine was a lesser but still important height, the Cerro de Cascajal. Halfway between Talavera and the Cerro de Medellin and some two hundred yards east of the Portina, rose a low hillock, the Pajar de Vergara, on which an artillery redoubt was being constructed.

Wellesley deployed his 20,000 British troops on the more open ground from the Pajar de Vergara to the Medellin hill, key to the whole position, with his front line largely behind the Portina. Already doubtful as to the reliability and effectiveness of his allies, he allocated to Cuesta's 32,000 Spaniards the more defensible close country around the town of Talavera. The Spanish front line, screened by olive groves and enclosures, ran along an embanked lane from the eastern edge of Talavera to the Pajar de Vergara.

---

[215] Lawrence, p.p. 52-3.
[216] On 15th July the 40th were at Plasencia with 42 officers, 39 sergeants, 17 drummers and 753 rank and file present. Ten sergeants, 4 drummers and 142 rank and file were sick, while 5 sergeants and 21 rank and file were 'on command.'

Kemmis's brigade of the 4th Division, the 40th and 97th of Foot and the 2nd Battalion of Detachments, was posted among olive groves just behind the Portina bed on the extreme right wing of the British line, with Spanish troops of Portago's Division on their right and the Guards brigade of Sherbrooke's 1st Division to their left. In front of them, on the far bank of the Portina, stood Alexander Campbell's own brigade of the same 4th Division, the 2nd/7th and 2nd/53rd, with Lawson's 3-pounder battery on the Pajar de Vergara to his right. Campbell's total effective divisional strength on 25th July was 2,960, and the strongest units were the 40th and the 2nd Battalion of Detachments, with 745 and 625 men, respectively. Lieutenant-Colonel George Ridout Bingham[217] of the 53rd, who we last noticed as a captain of the 81st in South Africa in 1799, described the ground around the 4th Division in a letter home four days after the battle:

'Just on the left of [the Spanish] line was a small eminence that commanded the plain. On this, a battery was established and a work hardly more than traced out, having been interrupted by the unlooked for rapid advance of the enemy. In front of this were two small enclosures, and beyond that all the enemy's movements were obscured by olive trees. On the left of the battery, a small plain began to extend itself with olive groves on each side and with a dry watercourse running through it. As you went on to the left, the plain widened and the olive groves ceased where the ground began to rise, which it did suddenly and terminated in a high conical hill.'

According to George Wood, by 27th July, the 4th Division had been on the ground for some three days when, 'as we had just commenced cooking, the drum beat to arms, and we distinctly heard the advanced division under General M'Kenzie… severely engaged. We seized the meat, half-cooked as it was, out of the camp kettles, and, putting it into our haversacks, marched off and arrived at the position just in time to receive the enemy.'[218]

Victor had pressed forward from the Alberche, and an attack on the 4th Division indeed appeared imminent:

'About 6 p.m., the enemy, driving in our advanced picquets, debouched in large masses between the rocky heights and the vineyards in front of the English right wing. The appearance of their black columns was very imposing, and as they moved forward rapidly, we expected an immediate attack.'[219]

French manoeuvring against the Allied centre and right was, however, a diversion, for Victor had his sights set on the Cerro de Medellin. By 7 p.m., French artillery had occupied the Cascajal, from where they opened an enfilading fire along the British line. This lasted until sunset but did little damage.

More serious was a demonstration by a few squadrons of French light cavalry, who trotted forward to feel for Cuesta's front line, which was well concealed in close country. Well-disciplined troops would have held their fire in the face of this provocative but essentially unthreatening advance, but before the French chasseurs and lancers had come within range, a tremendous fusillade broke out right along the Spanish front line, followed by panic. Suddenly, four battalions of Portago's Division, on the immediate right of the British 4th Division, shouted 'treason!' and bolted to the rear in complete disorder. Wellesley, who chanced to be near Kemmis's brigade, witnessed this shameful flight:

'Two thousand of them ran off… not 100 yards from where I was standing, who were neither attacked, nor threatened with an attack, and who were only frightened by the noise of their own fire. They left their arms and accoutrements on the ground, their officers went with them, and they plundered the baggage of the British army, which had been sent to the rear.'

Fortunately, the Spanish troops to the right and rear of the fugitive battalions held firm, and the line was restored, but this incident confirmed the growing conviction in the British army, from Wellesley down, that they could not rely on their allies.

At about 9 p.m. that evening, Victor mounted an attack with nine veteran battalions on the vital Medellin hill, surprising and routing two unsuspecting King's German Legion battalions who were asleep on the hilltop. General Sir Rowland Hill, whose 2nd Division was forming in rear of the Medellin summit, rode forward in the dark with his staff to investigate the firing and was almost captured, while his Deputy Adjutant-General, Captain Alexander Fordyce of the 81st Foot, was shot dead.[220] Hill at once ordered Stewart's brigade (29th, 1st/48th and the

---

[217] Letter dated Camp near Talavera, 1 August 1809. Bingham had served 1796-1801 as a captain in the 81st, earning distinction with them in the Third Kaffir War, and then served as Major of the 82nd in 1801-05, including service in Minorca.
[218] Wood, p. 86.
[219] Sergeant John Cooper, 7th Fusiliers.
[220] Fordyce, a captain in the 81st since 1804, had accompanied Hill from Ireland in August 1808 as his Brigade Major.

1st Battalion of Detachments) to recapture the hilltop. The 1st Battalion of Detachments, which included a handful of soldiers from the 59th and 81st, was first in contact with the enemy and exchanged a furious fire with the leading French battalion. Both sides halted in some confusion, and the impetus of the British counter-attack was in danger of being lost. 'The soldiers [of the 1st Battalion of Detachments] seemed much vexed,' wrote an officer of the 29th, 'we could hear them bravely calling out "There is nobody to command us! Only tell us what to do, and we are ready to dare anything."' Fortunately, Hill then came up with the 29th and, passing through the Detachments, cleared the hilltop by a desperate charge.[221]

That night, the British troops lay on their arms, anticipating another attack, and there were sufficient alarms along the line to deny sleep.

'Towards midnight,' George Wood recalled, 'there was a general cessation of fire, as if by mutual consent, each army appearing to wish a respite from this destructive carnage. During this short pause, by the light of the bright moon, reclining on their arms, the expectant warriors stood, sanguine for the renewal of the fight.'[222]

Out in front, the French were deploying: flickering lines of flambeaux filed across the plain, and the rattling of gun-carriages, the noise of wheels, and the cracking of whips betrayed the movement of Victor's artillery. Dawn revealed the French army massed for a major assault:

'With the growing light, it was possible to make out broad black patches dotting the whole of the rolling ground in front of the British army. Every instant rendered them more visible, and soon they took shape as French regiments in battalion columns, ranged on a front of nearly two miles, from the right end of the Cerro de Cascajal to the edge of the woods facing the Pajar de Vergara… In front of them, artillery was everywhere visible… In the far distance, behind the infantry, were long lines of cavalry dressed in all the colours of the rainbow – fifteen or sixteen regiments could be counted – and far to the rear of them, more black masses were slowly rolling into view. It was easily to be seen that little or nothing lay in front of the Spaniards and that at least five-sixths of the French army was disposed for an attack on the British front. There were 40,000 men visible, ready for the advance against the 20,000 sabres and bayonets of Wellesley's long red line.'[223]

At about 5 a.m. a canon fired from the French lines was the signal for Victor's artillery to open a tremendous bombardment, which was at once followed by a renewed attack on the Medellin. It was a clash between some 4,900 French in column and 3,700 British in line, with the usual outcome. The French were first checked and then chased off the hill and across the Portina with a loss of 1,300 men. There followed an unofficial truce, while both sides recovered their wounded. As the sun rose high in the sky, the suffocating heat rose inexorably to over 100 degrees Fahrenheit. Parched British and French soldiers mingled amicably to refill their water bottles in the stagnant Portina and, as William Lawrence of the 40th recalled, 'even going so far as to shake hands with each other.' The French cooked a meal; but few of the British ate that day as the runaway Spaniards had plundered what few provisions were available. Wellesley used this lull to reinforce Lawson's 3-pounder battery on the Pajar de Vergara with four Spanish 12-pounders.

Having twice failed to take the Medellin, the French mounted a general attack right across the British front with their full infantry power, some thirty thousand men, supported by eighty guns, or 62 battalions against 25 British battalions and thirty guns. Shortly before 1 p.m., the French artillery opened an accurate and destructive bombardment at ranges of 600-800 yards, producing a storm of shot and shell to which the lighter British guns had no adequate response.

The first contact came at 2.30 p.m. on the British right, where the five regiments of Leval's Division Allemande[224] advanced in a single line of nine battalion columns through olive trees, vineyards and thickets towards the Pajar de Vergara, accompanied by three artillery batteries. Due to the thundering guns and the close country, the approach of Leval's four and a half-thousand men was undetected, but as they emerged from the trees

---

[221] The 1st Battalion of Detachments suffered 70 casualties on the 27th and a further 203 on the 28th out of 609 effectives, but we do not know how many of these were from the 59th or 81st. Lieutenant Alexander Napper of the 81st was present.

[222] Wood, p. 87.

[223] Oman, Volume II, p. 521.

[224] From north to south, Leval's division consisted of Nassau, Netherlands, Baden, Hesse-Darmstadt and Frankfurt regiments, numbering 4,537 men in nine battalions. Its exact formation is uncertain, for the columns had become disordered in their move through the woods and vineyards.

into the enclosures in front of the Pajar, they met the skirmishers of the 4th Division, including the Light Companies of the 40th Foot and 2nd Battalion of Detachments. The advancing Germans sowed confusion by calling out '*Espanholas*' and '*Viva los Inglesis.*' The light troops held their fire, and 24 of them were captured[225], but the attackers' ruse was revealed when they delivered a 'rattling volley.' The British skirmishers hastily retired on the main line of Campbell's brigade, which had been reinforced by the 40th, brought up into the first line from Kemmis's brigade. On the right of the British line, adjacent to the guns on the Pajar, were the 7th Fusiliers, and to their left in succession were the 2nd/53rd and the 40th. These battalions now sprang to their feet, making a red-coated wall of nearly eighteen hundred men, which held its fire until the enemy cleared the olive woods and crossed an enclosure bank sixty yards from the British line.

It is unfortunate that William Lawrence gives no detail of the part played by the 40th in this action, but it is possible from other accounts to reconstruct the likely sequence of events. Wellesley, from his vantage point on the Medellin hill, could see Leval's movements and, according to Bingham, sent an ADC down to warn Campbell that 'a body of the enemy was moving down for the purpose of turning the right, and on our exertions depended the fate of the day.' The main thrust of the Dutch-German attack was opposite the Pajar, where the Baden Regiment came up on the right flank of the 7th Fusiliers, drove back its raw young soldiers with a rolling fire and penetrated almost to the artillery redoubt. The Fusiliers were rallied by their commanding officer, and regular British volleys slowly prevailed. The Baden battalions, additionally lashed by canister from the guns on the Pajar, were the first to recoil and seeing their disorder, General Campbell ordered his right to charge. As the Fusiliers and the 53rd charged, the Germans ran, but before they could scale the enclosure bank, British bayonets caught up with them.

'In this charge,' wrote Bingham, 'we passed at first the outermost of the two enclosures in front of the work, and in the retreat of the enemy, they left a brigade of ten guns and some tumbrels of musket ammunition. The brigade then lined the ditches of the enclosures and thus formed a flanking fire on the column that attacked our line more to the left [the 40th], by which the Nassau Regiment suffered severely.'

It appears, then, that the Fusiliers and 53rd dealt with the Badeners and Dutch before turning to assist the 40th against the two-battalion 2nd Nassau Regiment, which must have emerged from cover slightly later. It would be reasonable to assume that, after an exchange of musketry, the veteran 40th would have seen the green-coated Nassauers off at bayonet point.[226]

With the defeat of Leval's centre and right, the Hesse-Darmstadt and Frankfurt Regiments on his left, who had been exchanging inconclusive volleys with the Spaniards, withdrew to avoid being outflanked. Campbell kept his three victorious battalions well in hand, calling off the pursuit before they could become dispersed in the thickets. The captured guns were spiked, and the 7th, 40th and 53rd were brought back to their old position, where Campbell reinforced his line by bringing forward the rest of Kemmis's brigade, the 97th and the 2nd Battalion of Detachments. Wellesley had watched the action with satisfaction: 'Sir Arthur sent down to General Alexander Campbell commanding our brigade to say we were the bravest fellows in the world, and he had no words to express how highly he was pleased with our conduct.'[227]

He had rather less cause for pleasure with the outcome of the attack on his centre, which developed whilst the 4th Division was still battling with Leval's Germans. Here, two French divisions, 24 battalions in all, advanced against the eight battalions of Sherbrooke's 1st Division. Columns were again met by line, and the first wave of nine French battalions was promptly thrown back in confusion across the Portina, with Sherbrooke's men in reckless hot pursuit. Unfortunately, unlike the 4th Division, the Guards brigade and two brigades of the King's German Legion became dispersed and out of control. Sherbrooke's scattered and disordered troops were caught in enfilade by French guns and harried back across the Portina with heavy losses by a second wave of twelve fresh enemy battalions and two regiments of dragoons. This disaster opened wide gaps in the British front line, which twenty thousand French troops were poised to exploit. The situation was restored by the gallant stand of

---

[225] Of the 24 Light Company men who were taken, an officer and 21 were from the 97th and one man each from the 40th and the 2nd Battalion of Detachments.

[226] These Nassau troops defected to the Allied cause in the Pyrenees in December 1813 and fought well under Wellington at Waterloo, where they defended Hougoumont, Papelotte and La Haie.

[227] Lieutenant John Carss, 2nd/53rd. In his Talavera Despatch, on 29th July, Wellesley stated that 'I was highly satisfied with the manner in which this part of the position was defended.'

Mackenzie's brigade (24th, 31st and 45th), which moved up from second line to fill the gap left in the centre right by the Guards and by a famous advance by the 48th onto the ground left open by the King's German Legion on the centre left. Between them, these four battalions effectively held the French advance while Sherbrooke's shattered brigades re-formed behind them. The centre was saved.

Meanwhile, Leval's Dutch-German division had rallied upon their supports and were ordered forward again to cover the flank of the attack on Wellesley's centre. Leval's second attack on Campbell's 4th Division was made at about 4 p.m. over the same ground as before but was not pressed with the same energy. The German columns again emerged from cover in front of the Pajar de Vergara, where Campbell had deployed his entire division slightly further forward than before, under cover of the enclosure banks. British musketry at a range of 40 yards was decisive, and as Leval's men fell back in disorder before Campbell's bayonets, the Spanish cavalry Regimiento del Rey charged into their flank. The Dutch and Germans had lost over one thousand men and seventeen guns in their two attacks and, as Sergeant Cooper of the 7th Fusiliers remarked, 'we were not troubled with their company any more.'

The reported casualties of the British 4th Division totalled 236, including 58 of the 40th and 21 of the 2nd Battalion of Detachments. According to the official return, the 40th suffered seven rank and file killed, Captain Archibald Colquhoun and 49 men wounded, and one man missing, but the *Regimental Record Book* shows sixteen killed and about ninety wounded and, according to his family, Captain Arthur Rowley Heyland was among the wounded, and Lieutenant Thomas Decimus Franklyn was slightly wounded.[228] This major discrepancy may possibly be explained by the official return of those killed, not taking account of those who subsequently died of wounds, while the list of wounded may exclude those whose injuries were not considered serious enough to be reported. The 2nd Battalion of Detachments lost seven men killed, thirteen wounded and one missing, of which its 82nd Company suffered five rank and file killed and wounded. Private Martin Gready of the 59th, presumably serving with the 1st Battalion of Detachments, is also known to have been wounded at Talavera.

Whilst the musketry ceased that evening in front of the 4th Division, the artillery duel continued. 'We [the 2nd Battalion of Detachments] were now under a most tremendous fire of shot and shells,' recalled Lieutenant George Wood of the 82nd, 'but luckily, our flank only was exposed to it, they fell in every direction about us without doing material mischief.' With immediate danger receding, hunger and tiredness took over:

'By this time, I became much exhausted for want of food; for the meat that we had taken half-cooked with us had, from the heat, become so full of animalculæ that I could eat but little of it; I therefore gave it to the man next me, who, not being quite so nice, gobbled it up in a moment. Bread, however, was out of the question, and water only to be procured by going into great danger. In this state, as we were resting on our arms, notwithstanding the roar of cannon, I fell asleep for an hour or two as soundly as if I had reclined on the softest couch. The dawn re-appeared, and one of the men roused me from my slumber, which indeed he had some trouble in doing.

'The cannonading had ceased, and we again stood to our arms, expecting another attack; but it appeared the enemy had got enough of it, for they, as we afterwards found, had moved off the ground, taking care to leave their advanced sentries to the very last moment. These were constantly calling out *Qui vive?* And making a great noise to make us believe that the enemy were still there; but, as they did not come on to renew the contest, our light troops were sent out to reconnoitre; when they found that the French, under cover of the night, had taken the opportunity of retreating from the scene of action, leaving us masters of this hard-fought field.'[229]

Hard-fought indeed, for in two days of fighting, the British army had suffered 5,363 casualties, more than one in four of those present, including over eight hundred dead, while the French had lost 7,268 and Leval's seventeen guns.[230] The Spanish admitted to a loss of 1,201 men, but this must include the 'missing' fugitives from

---

228 Although not listed among the casualties, it appears that Ensign Richard Burgess of the 40th was taken prisoner after Talavera and died, presumably in captivity, before 1814. A family story, retold in the South Lancashire *Chronicle*, that he was killed days before the battle having successfully stormed two French guns, lacks credibility.

229 Wood, pp. 88-9.

230 Many of the dead were left unburied on the battlefield, where their remains were seen over three years later by Captain John Harley of the 47th, who visited Talavera in the course of his escape from French captivity in Madrid: 'My guide brought me into the centre of the field. Then, indeed, I beheld a scene which even a soldier cannot contemplate without his feelings being harrowed up – the bones of horses and men lying close together; the rider and his steed, and the skeletons, in rank, just as the poor fellows fell on that memorable day. My guide being an intelligent fellow, I asked his opinion of the scene and the contest that had taken place; he said it was a drawn

Portago's division, on some of whom Cuesta exacted a terrible vengeance after the battle. George Wood was witness to 'a most shocking spectacle':

'In consequence of many of the Spanish soldiers having run away during the action, twenty-seven of these unfortunate men, who had been taken, were tried by courts-martial and sentenced to be shot. They were placed rank-entire on the battlefield, already strewed with dead bodies, and the priests having confessed and absolved them, the fatal word was given to a company of their own countrymen, drawn up for the purpose, to fire; and, in an instant, these poor wretches lay prostrate, adding to the dreadful slaughter, already too great, and affording a melancholy example to the cowardly.'[231]

There were many other horrors on that stricken field. Private William Lawrence of the 40th was appalled by 'a very dreadful occurrence' after the battle: 'The long dry grass in which many of the wounded were lying caught fire, and many were scorched to death before assistance could be brought to convey them to hospital in Talavera.'

Lieutenant George Wood of the 82nd was equally shocked at the behaviour his Spanish allies, who had started to kill the wounded French. The British intervened to protect their former adversaries:

'There was in consequence an officer and twenty men from each brigade immediately sent; and I was one on this duty. I had only gone about one hundred yards when one of my men, who were scattered for the purpose, called out for me to go to him and told me that a Spaniard, whom he pointed out, was about to shoot a Frenchman, badly wounded, who was crying most piteously "*Mon Dieu! Mon Dieu!*" I waited to see what was really the Spaniard's intentions: he deliberately loaded his piece and was going to present it at this unfortunate creature when I arrested his arm and sent him away; but on looking behind me, I observed him creeping through the vineyard to return and accomplish the diabolical and cowardly act of killing a fallen enemy in cold blood! On seeing this, I ordered my men to take the wounded man and remove him from the spot where he was to some shady olive trees, with which this plain was planted; and there I formed a kind of depot for these poor suffering wretches, with a guard to protect them till the carts came to take them away.'

'On passing the ravine where the contest had been most severe, I perceived that a quantity of high sere grass which grew there had taken fire from the wadding of the guns; and the poor fellows who had fallen there, wounded and deprived of the power of escape, were literally burned to death; which gave them all the appearance of pigs that had been roasted. A huge desperate-looking bravado of a Spaniard, passing at the time, drew his sabre and deliberately plunged it into the body of one of these dead Frenchmen, who could now be distinguished only by their ear-rings, as the English and French lay here in mixed numbers, with their clothes entirely consumed. He then, pulling it out, all reeking with gore, triumphantly made use of a common Spanish expression, not proper here to mention, looking, at the same time, ferociously at me. I certainly thought his conduct most dastardly; but on cool reflection, imagined that his motive was probably revenge.'[232]

Despite the ghastly scenes all around, pangs of hunger were a predominant concern for the British troops, who had eaten almost nothing for two days. Apart from rotting meat, George Wood's 82nd Company had received only one biscuit each.

'I in vain searched among the dying and the dead in hopes of finding some food to eat; but, if they had had any, it had already been taken by the men on duty and the Spaniards. All I could see that strewed the field, besides their apparel and accoutrements, was an immense number of *billet doux*, for which the French are so famous. For these, however, I had at this time very little relish, as they were a poor substitute for food.' For three days after the battle, Wood recalled, his men's ration consisted of a pint of wheat each, causing one soldier of the 82nd to wryly comment, 'They have given us corn today; I suppose they will give us hay tomorrow.'[233]

---

battle, both English and French claiming it. When I remarked the numerous skeletons that covered the plain, he told me the cause of their remaining there was, that, when the British and the French armies retreated, the dead bodies were left on the field; and that there being no one to inter them, the vultures, therefore, had fed on the bodies. Even then the birds were hovering over this recent scene of carnage, seeking fresh prey.'
[231] Wood, p.p. 94-5.
[232] Ibid., p.p. 89-91.
[233] Ibid., p.p. 91-4.

In addition to clearing the battlefield of casualties, as the only British formation still effective on the 29th, with under eight percent casualties, the 4th Division provided the outpost line on the Alberche until relieved by Craufurd's Light Brigade, who had arrived that morning.

Despite this addition to his strength and the withdrawal and division of French forces to his front, Wellesley was in no position to advance. 'The extreme fatigue of the troops,' he wrote on 1st August, 'the want of provisions, and the number of wounded to be taken care of, have prevented me from moving from my position.' He was, however, still intending to move on Madrid, unaware of an imminent and most dangerous threat to his lines of communication to Portugal. Marshals Soult, Ney and Mortier, with fifty thousand men, were marching south from Salamanca to fall upon his flank and rear, and Mortier was already in Plasencia, capturing Wellesley's supplies and sick in that town. Wellesley and Cuesta were aware of French movement from the north but believed its strength to be no more than twelve to fifteen thousand men. Accordingly, on August 2nd, after a long and stormy meeting, it was decided that Wellesley should march on Plasencia to deal with this new threat while Cuesta remained at Talavera, watching Victor and accepting responsibility for some five thousand British and French wounded who lay in the hospitals there, notably in the convent of St. Geronimo.

Withdrawal to the Frontier

On the morning of August 3rd Wellesley moved out from Talavera with his full strength, some eighteen thousand half-starved men, marching that day to Oropesa. There he learned that he was faced with not fifteen thousand enemy, but at least thirty thousand, whose advanced detachments were already at Almaraz on the Tagus and whose cavalry had clashed with his at Navalmoral, only one day's march away. Outnumbered and with his lines of communication cut, Wellesley had to reconsider his plans at very short notice. His difficulties were compounded when Cuesta sent notice that he was evacuating Talavera, which he did at once, marching overnight to Oropesa. His precipitate abandonment of the British wounded disgusted George Wood:

'Having taken up our ground for the night at Oropesa, a little town about a day's march from Talavera, we began to boil our kettles, and make dumplings with the flour that was this day delivered to us in lieu of bread; when we perceived the Spanish army, in whom we had placed such confidence, in full retreat, and close at our heels; and to this dastardly conduct alone is the abandonment of our unfortunate wounded to be attributed, as well as the necessity of our commencing a retreat.'[234]

Wellesley had, in fact, already given orders that all the wounded capable of being moved should be evacuated and had begged for transport, but Cuesta provided only seven ox-carts and a few mules, to which the British could only add forty assorted wagons. Few of the serious cases could be moved, and some fifteen hundred of them were taken prisoner when the French occupied Talavera on 6th August.[235] The walking wounded set off to follow their regiments: 'The road to Oropesa,' wrote one of them, 'was covered with our poor limping bloodless soldiers. On crutches or sticks, with blankets thrown over them, they hobbled woefully along. For the moment panic terror lent them a force inconsistent with their debility and their fresh wounds. Some died by the road, others, unable to get further than Oropesa, afterwards fell into the hands of the enemy.' Some two thousand of the wounded managed to keep up with the army until they reached safety; five hundred either died at the wayside or were taken by the French. It is pleasing to record that Victor treated the British wounded with kindness and humanity.

By early morning of August 4th, there remained just one practicable course open to Wellesley and Cuesta, to withdraw at once over the Tagus bridge at El Puente del Arzobispo, nine miles to the south. Setting off without delay, Wellesley had his whole army across the bridge that evening, followed on the 5th by Cuesta. Having put two days' march and the Tagus between Soult and themselves, the Allies now had some security from pursuit, if not

---

[234] Wood, p. 96. He voiced a general opinion about the Spaniards. A few days earlier, George Bingham had written, 'The Spanish Army is in so disorganise state, the under officers such poltroons, the superior such traitors, I am afraid one day or other they will lead us into a scrape from which it will be difficult to extricate ourselves.'

[235] One of the wounded taken after Talavera was Thomas Skeel of the Grenadier Company 40th Foot. He had joined the Regiment in August 1807 after four years in the Somerset Militia, and would remain in a French prison until 1814. Another was Captain Francis Milman of the Coldstream Guards who, as a Lieutenant-General, became Colonel of the 82nd Foot 1850-56. Severely wounded, Milman was saved from being burned to death on the battlefield by a private soldier of his regiment.

from lack of provisions. Kemmis's brigade provided the rearguard from Oropesa to Arzobispo, from where their road became a mountain track over which guns and wagons had to be manhandled:

'In its [Arzobispo's] neighbourhood we remained three day,' wrote George Wood, 'to get the cannon up a steep mountain. This fatiguing duty came to our turn twice a day, to enter on which we had to wade through a river waist high – a very pleasant employment truly, on not very full stomachs! However, by attaching about fifty men with ropes to each gun, besides oxen, we accomplished this work, with indefatigable labour, in the time specified.

'During our halt here, as some of our men were prowling about, seeking wild honey, goats, or any thing they could find to satisfy their wants, they by chance discovered, secreted in a cavity of a rock, about five hundred pairs of Spanish shoes, and a great many sacks of flour, which were most seasonably divided – the shoes among those who were most in need of them, many being now entirely destitute, and the flour equally among the brigade.'[236]

After Oropesa, Wellesley had of necessity to abandon his lines of communication from Abrantes and, in the almost complete absence of the expected Spanish logistical support, his troops were obliged to live off the land. Lieutenant George Wood and his servant Thomas Standfast became adept at foraging: 'Our principal employment, at this time, after the march, was to invent new modes of satisfying hunger.' George gathered wheat ears from the fields, rubbing out the corn, and milked a wild goat he had caught in the mountains, while his servant found ripe mulberries, all of which, when boiled up together, 'afforded us a most delicious repast, much resembling the furmenty which I got when at school.' Whilst not rising to those culinary heights, Private William Lawrence and his comrades of the 40th faced the same challenge of living on less than half rations:

'Our provisions rarely exceeded two pounds of meat a day, and sometimes a pint of wheat took the place of one of the pounds of meat, with occasionally, but very rarely, a little flour. Our way of cooking the wheat was to boil it like rice, or sometimes, if convenient, we would crack the kernel between two flat stones and then boil it, making a kind of thick paste out of it. This having so little bread or other vegetable substance to eat with our meat was one of the great causes of illness.'[237]

Whilst Cuesta left a rearguard to hold the bridge at Arzobispo – which they managed to do until Soult cunningly attacked at siesta-time on the 8th – Wellesley sent Craufurd in advance by forced march through the pass of Mesa de Ibor to secure the only other Tagus crossing, at Almaraz, on the main road to Trujillo, Merida and Badajoz. He followed with his main body, toiling slowly through mountain defiles by way of Valdelacasa and Deleitosa to Jaraicejo. From there and the defile of Miabete, he could support his advanced troops on the river-line at Almaraz, block any French move towards Seville, Cadiz or Badajoz, and maintain contact with the Spanish, who took up an almost impregnable position a few miles to his east at Mesa de Ibor.

Soult decided against following the Allies south into the mountains, and on 10th August he began to withdraw and disperse his concentrated forces. This would have offered Wellesley the opportunity to strike north across the Tagus, but his options were now increasingly limited by lack of provisions and the exhaustion of his troops. Despite his mounting indignation at the lack of promised supplies, Wellesley felt a political obligation to maintain cooperation with the Spanish as long as possible, and so he remained behind the Tagus for the next fortnight. Finally, on 20th August, he was compelled by starvation to withdraw, marching his exhausted troops by easy stages from Jaraicejo, through Trujillo and Miajadas to the valley of the Guadiana, where on September 3rd the army was quartered around Badajoz, Merida and Montijo.[238] Writing from Miajadas on the 22nd, Wellesley explained the urgent imperatives for this withdrawal:

'I have no provisions, no horses, no means of transport; I am overloaded with sick; the horses of the cavalry are scarcely able to march, or those of the artillery to draw their guns. The officers and soldiers alike are worn down by want of food and privations of every description.'

Kemmis's brigade marched to the fortified frontier town of Badajoz, where the 40th were hutted until November 3rd, when they moved to the smaller town of Olivenza, eleven miles to the south.

---

[236] Wood, p.p. 99-100.
[237] Lawrence, p. 56.
[238] Captain Francis Hoblyn of the 40th died on 28th August during this retirement, aged 23. He was from St. Austell, Cornwall and had served in the Regiment since 1805.

The 2nd Battalion of Detachments went into camp in the wood of Albuquerque until the 23rd of September, when they marched to Lisbon, for the necessity of forming the Battalions of Detachments had passed, and their officers and men were to be returned to their parent regiments. Whilst thanking the battalions of detachments for their exemplary services in the field[239], Wellington was characteristically forthright about the disciplinary shortcomings of 'the few, of whose conduct he cannot but complain, even upon this occasion… He will not flatter them by saying that he has not had, upon several occasions, reasons to be dissatisfied with their conduct in their quarters, their camps and on their marches.'

The Talavera campaign was over. For the British Army it had brought a stubbornly-fought victory, albeit a pyrrhic one, a narrow escape and an abiding distrust of their Spanish allies. Sir Arthur Wellesley was created Viscount Wellington,[240] and James Kemmis and Henry Thornton received Gold Medals, but it was 1824 before the 40th were authorised to add the Battle Honour 'TALAVERA' to their Colours, and 1848 before the survivors of the battle, including 135 all ranks of the 40th and 24 of the 82nd, received the Military General Service Medal with 'Talavera' bar.

The uniforms of all ranks were in tatters, recalled Lieutenant George Wood, who had lost his baggage at Talavera:

'Our coats were patched over with different coloured cloth, for which purpose we had even cut off our skirts. My own coat was mended with the breeches of a dead Frenchman, which I found on the field – the only trophy I yet had to boast of having retained from the spoils of the enemy.'

Since the Battalions of Detachments were about to be sent home, the 82nd Company would receive no exchange of clothing until they rejoined their own regiment. The wants of the 40th Foot were more immediately supplied. 'On leaving Talavera,' William Lawrence recalled, 'our clothes had been completely threadbare, and now, through having no change for so long, we were smothered in vermin. When we had been a little while in Badajoz, however, we were supplied with new clothes, linen, blankets and great coats, our old ones being burned; and more livestock was destroyed in the process than there were troops in the country at the time.'[241]

Until the 20th century, the greatest mortality during military operations was not from enemy action but from disease. Wellington's troops, weakened by months of hard campaigning and weeks of an unbalanced starvation diet, were susceptible to the typhoid fever and malaria which were endemic to the marshy Guadiana valley and were particularly prevalent in September. The terrible epidemic which devastated the army between September 1809 and January 1810 resulted in 3,798 deaths, far more than any battle. The mortality in November alone (1,269) was considerably worse than the subsequent bloodbaths of the battle of Albuera (849) or the storming of Badajoz (654), and only comparable to Waterloo (1,248 British dead). Medical resources, already fully stretched caring for the wounded of Talavera, were overwhelmed.

The 40th Foot, who suffered fewer deaths from disease than most regiments, lost 53 men between October 1809 and January 1810, exactly the same number of fatalities as their later heavy loss in the breach at Badajoz, and their sickness rate throughout this period was about one in five. Among these was Private William Lawrence:

'Whilst we were at Badajoz, numbers of us fell sick daily, and among these was unfortunately myself. We were conveyed to a Portuguese town some four leagues from Badajoz, called Elvas, which was the strongest fortified town in Portugal… We invalides occupied the convents of the town.[242] Our loss here through the sickness, which was some kind of fever, and was increased through the want of doctors and medicine, was very great, cart-loads of the dead being carried out of the town every day for interment in the ground kept for the purpose outside the fortifications. I recovered sufficiently after about six weeks to be able to get out a little on the ramparts, and there a fearful spectacle often met my gaze, for the dead were brought out of the convents completely naked, and after they had been pitched into carts like so many pieces of wood, were carried out and put into holes scarcely large enough to admit of such a number. This unpleasant office of burying the dead fell chiefly on the Portuguese convicts, and it was surprising with what readiness these men went to work. They carried one body at a time,

---

239 General Order, Badajoz 22nd September 1809.
240 He signed himself 'Wellington' for the first time on 16th September 1809.
241 Lawrence, p.p. 56-7.
242 The British used the purpose-built Portuguese military hospital in Elvas, which was in the Convent of Sao Joao de Deus (now a hotel), while convalescents were accommodated in barracks within the walls.

having the legs over their shoulders and the head dangling down behind them, and when they came to the graves, on account of the piece of ground appropriated for the burials being so small, they had to pack their burdens with the greatest nicety. This sight soon cured me, as I thought what a narrow escape I had had of being handled by these same men; and I was glad to get back to my regiment at Badajoz as soon as possible.'[243]

At Badajoz, the 40th were joined in September by Charles Boutflower[244], aged 27, who had previously served as an Assistant-Surgeon with the Regiment 1802-08, including South America, where he was taken prisoner at Buenos Aires. He was glad to return as Surgeon to 'my old friends in the 40th,' though 'the short time I had been absent from them had produced great changes, as I perceived a variety of new faces.' He was soon fully engaged in the regimental hospital and, for several weeks, was unable to keep up his journal. He resumed on 22nd October, noting that 'sickness has constantly prevailed in the Army to an alarming extent, there being seldom less than eight thousand sick on an average, of which number the deaths have been most afflicting.' At Olivenza, the 40th Foot continued at first to suffer from 'Guadiana Fever,' but on 5th December Charles Boutflower noted in his diary that: 'A continuance of fine weather has had a most happy effect on my sick. Those in hospital are getting considerably better, and those out keep well.'

Apart from this epidemic, the British Army's stay in Badajoz was not a happy one, for the locals were on the whole unfriendly and many of them were suspected of being *Afrancecados*, or pro-French. Within days of their arrival at Badajoz, the half-starved men of the 4th Division had incurred Wellington's wrath by stealing from the bakeries and plundering bee-hives, the latter robberies earning them the nickname 'the Honeysuckers.'[245]

'They are evidently getting tired of us,' wrote Charles Boutflower, 'and tho' they have no objection to us fighting for them, they would wish the troops to remain in the fields during the winter; some of them are so extremely uncivil that nothing will be sufficient but the entrance of French troops into their houses to convince them of their ingratitude.' Two and a half years later, Badajoz would pay dearly for its perceived hostility.

Nevertheless, Boutflower and his brother-officers were disappointed when the 40th were ordered to Olivenza: 'Having formed an acquaintance with several of the most pleasant families, we were enabled to pass our evenings agreeably. Olivenza, I hear, does not abound with many of these houses, and the difficulty and trouble of getting acquainted with these few is also to be surmounted. Another reason why I most prefer the place we are now is its being Head-Quarters, by which means we get the earliest intelligence of any news there may be stirring.'

There was certainly a thirst for news; for after the disappointing outcome of the Talavera campaign, with its unfortunate revelations of Spanish incompetence or worse, there was much rumour and speculation in the Army and a gloomy consensus that Portugal would be evacuated. The talk in the 40th was that, being one of the strongest and most effective regiments, they would be redeployed elsewhere and not sent home. It was not until the 28th November that they learned from recently arrived English newspapers that the Ministry had determined on defending Portugal. Even then, this remained a contentious issue. 'There are various opinions on the subject,' wrote Charles Boutflower, 'that we shall ultimately be compelled to quit, I think admits of little doubt, tho' probably the approaching season, and the difficulty of procuring supplies, may prevent the enemy from annoying us for some time.' What he could not know was that in October, when visiting Lisbon, Wellington had already conceived a secret plan for the defence of the Portuguese capital, issuing orders on the 20th for the construction of an immense series of fortifications, the Lines of Torres Vedras.

---

[243] Lawrence, p.p. 57-8.

[244] Charles Boutflower FRCS (1782-1844) – sometimes spelled Boatflower or Boat Flower – had been an Assistant-Surgeon with the Royal Navy 1800-1802 before joining the 40th on 27th April 1802 in Malta. In 1808 he became Surgeon to the 96th Foot, but on 10th August 1809 he transferred back to the 40th, with whom he served until appointed as a Staff Surgeon on 3rd September 1812. Boutflower retired on half-pay in 1816, and worked as a surgeon in Colchester for sixteen years. In 1834 he moved to Liverpool where, as a result of his duties as a member of the committee to take in hand the city's drainage, he died of typhoid fever in 1844. His *Journal of an Army Surgeon during the Peninsular War* covers his service, largely with the 40th, between August 1809 and May 1813.

[245] General Orders of 7th and 12th September 1809. Collective restriction was ordered: 'The 4th Division having again in three instances plundered bee-hives... the regiments of that division are forthwith... to be turned out and placed under arms, and they are not to quit their arms till one hour after sun-set, when they are to be sent to their huts and sentries placed around the camp to prevent all men from straggling... and so on day after day till the soldiers shall have been discovered who have been guilty of these outrages... Colonel Kemmis will report whether the orders of the 4th instant, requiring that the rolls should be called in the 4th Division every hour, have been obeyed.' The bee-hive plunderers (not, on this occasion, from the 40th) were discovered on the 14th and sentenced to between five and seven hundred lashes.

Gibraltar was held 1809-11 by the 30th, 47th & 82nd Regiments

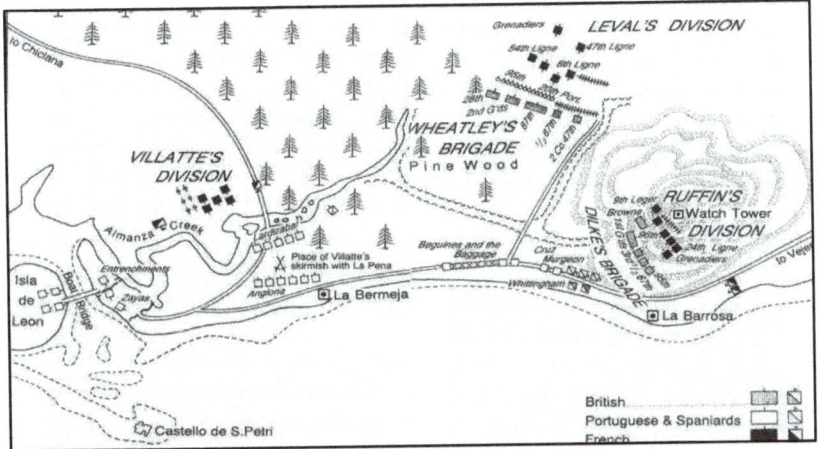

Private 30th Foot, 1806

Left & below:
Battle of Barrosa
5th March 1811

Chapter V:
The Defence of Portugal and Andalusia – 1810-11

Peninsula Strategy 1810 – Reinforcements for Portugal – 30th in Ireland 1806-9, & Lisbon – 47th in Ireland, Preston, Chelmsford & Jersey 1803-9 – Gibraltar 1809-11 (30th, 47th & 82nd) – Tarifa 1810 (detachments 30th, 47th & 82nd) – Defence of Cadiz 1810-11 (30th & 47th) – Fuengirola 1810 (82nd) - Wellington's Defence of Portuguese Frontier,1810 (40th) – Battle of Busaco (40th) – Lines of Torres Vedras (30th & 40th) – Battle of Barrosa (detachments 47th & 82nd) – Pursuit of Masséna (30th & 40th) – Combats of Redinha & Casal Nova (40th) & Sabugal (30th).

Peninsula Strategy

Early in 1810 the Secretary of State for War in London, Lord Liverpool, wrote to Wellington: 'Your chance of successful defence are considered here by all persons military as well as civil to be improbable,' and asked about his contingency plans for evacuating the British Army from Portugal. Wellington had other, more cautiously sanguine, ideas and a considerably broader strategic vision: 'If we can maintain ourselves in Portugal,' he wrote, 'the war will not cease in the Peninsula, and, if the war lasts in the Peninsula, Europe will be saved.'

Whilst the maintenance of a foothold in Portugal was Wellington's central strategic purpose, he was very aware that he had been entrusted with Britain's only major field army, the loss of which would be hard to remedy. He also felt obliged to offer what limited assistance he could spare to his Spanish allies who, despite repeated defeats and mutual mistrust, were still in the field. Cadiz in particular, the seat of the Spanish government, its main naval base, and the principal port for the riches of Spain's New World colonies, remained vital to the Allied cause.

Reinforcements for the Peninsula

Among the reinforcements received by Wellesley during 1809 was the 2nd Battalion of the 30th Foot, who we last saw in the Royal Barracks, Dublin in 1805. In April 1806 the Battalion (less its Light Company) marched to Strabane, with a small detachment stationed at Omagh to help in the suppression of illegal whisky stills there, and twelve months later they moved on to Londonderry.

The soldier strength at that time totalled 457, for the 2nd/30th had been stripped of the greater part of its effective manpower on leaving Dublin when, on 19th April 1805, a draft of seven lieutenants and four hundred other ranks was embarked for Portsmouth to join the 1st Battalion, which was under orders for India. On 25th November 234 former militiamen, who had declined to volunteer for overseas service, were transferred to the 9th Garrison Battalion.

This was a defining moment for the Battalion: no longer a mere depot for the 1st/30th, it was now required to become an operationally effective and deployable unit. William Minet[246], in command of the 2nd/30th since 25th September 1804, had to rebuild the corps and prepare it for active service at a time when the supply of recruits fell short of demand.

---

[246] William Minet (1762-1827) was of Huguenot extraction, his great-grandfather having escaped persecution in France to found a banking business in Dover. Minet received his first commission in 1778 during the American War of Independence. He served 1780-82 with the 14th Foot both on board ship, at the Relief of Gibraltar and in the West Indies, where in April 1783 he was promoted to a company of the 30th, with which he served until reduced on half-pay later that year. He had subsequently served with the 4th Foot 1785-98 in Newfoundland and Canada, and as a major with the 5th Foot in the 1799 Helder campaign. He commanded the 2nd/30th in the Peninsula until May 1809 and again from June 1810 to 4th June 1811 when he was promoted to major-general. He eventually rose to the rank of lieutenant-general.

Neither a pay rise in June 1806 nor bounties offered to men of the Irish Militia were sufficient to fill the ranks with able-bodied men; consequently, the Battalion was obliged to enlist a high proportion of boys and lads, and to re-enlist old soldiers. This led to an imbalance in the Battalion's age profile, which would remain until the youngsters matured to become the men of Badajoz, Salamanca and Waterloo.

Early in June 1808 the 2nd/30th marched from Longford to the Curragh for the drill season, at the end of which they moved to Athlone, arriving there on 3rd August. Twelve days later, the Battalion was rejoined by a detachment of 102 NCOs and men who had been on their way to embark at Cork as a draft for the 1st Battalion when they were turned back at Fermoy. This clearly meant active service for the 2nd/30th in the not-too-distant future. In January 1809 the Battalion marched from Athlone to Dublin, and after a week's rest, continued the march to Kinsale, where it arrived on 2nd March.

On 11th March 1809 the Battalion embarked at the Cove of Cork with 24 officers, 39 sergeants, 35 corporals, 17 drummers and 559 privates, leaving 53 men sick in Ireland. As usual, lots were drawn to determine which of the families would accompany their men, and the unlucky remainder, 97 women and 209 children, were sent to their home parishes with a gratuity of £1-2s-8d for each woman and 5s-5d for each child. The heavy baggage was left at Kinsale with the Depot.

The Battalion landed at Lisbon after 'many miraculous escapes' on 7th April, or later in the case of one transport. Its strength was still well short of establishment and imbalanced in composition. There were far too few company officers and still far too great a proportion of growing boys and lads in the ranks. Only the previous December had Colonel Minet promoted 26 boys to men's pay, and the 2nd/30th had embarked with 14 recruits and 34 boys, while many of the older soldiers were past their prime.

It probably came as no surprise, then, that when Sir Arthur Wellesley prepared to march north against Soult he left the 30th as garrison in the Castle of St. George, Lisbon. Over the next few weeks, large parties of the Battalion were detached from there on escort duties.[247] On May 19th, as Wellesley called off his pursuit of Soult, the 30th were ordered forward to Azambuja, on the road to the army's new concentration area, but this move was almost immediately countermanded. Wellesley had decided to exchange two of the newly arrived second battalions, those of the 29th and 30th, for the more acclimatised first battalions of the 48th and 61st from Gibraltar. Accordingly, on 27th May the 2nd/30th embarked for Gibraltar.

The 2nd/47th were also sent to the Peninsula in 1809. Formed in 1803, they had served for four years in Ireland, at Clonmel, the Curragh, Cahir, Belfast, Aughnacloy, and Enniskillen. In May 1807 the Battalion sailed from Dublin to Liverpool. They were then quartered for some months at Preston in their home county.

The Battalion was then commanded by Lieutenant-Colonel William Wardrobe[248], described by Captain John Harley, the paymaster, as 'one of the most severe and tyrannical officers that ever commanded a regiment... whose propensity for flogging his men was such that it made him detested, not only by the soldiers, but by the inhabitants of every town in which we happened to be quartered... He delighted in courts-martial, which he always ordered on the most trifling occasion. He usually read the sentence himself, a duty which is well known to belong to the adjutant, proceeding over it as quickly as possible, and then calling out, with an air of exultation, and the feelings of a hero, the awful command "strip"! He stood by until the sentence could be fulfilled to the letter, viewing the infliction of the punishment with brutal ecstasy, and never having been known in one solitary instance to remit one lash of the sentence that had been passed.'

At Preston Wardrobe was thwarted in a humiliating manner:

'He ordered one of the recruits, a mere boy, to be brought out for some very trifling offence and flogged on the race ground of Preston[249]. However, on the regiment going out to escort him and witness the ceremony, it was attacked by a large body of women belonging to the cotton manufactories, with which that town and

---

[247] In the first fortnight of May the 30th had seven sergeants, two drummers and 145 privates detached on escort duties.

[248] William Wardrobe, who was promoted to command the 2nd/47th on 8th May 1806 from the half-pay of the York Hussars, appears to have been an American Loyalist from Georgia, to where he returned following retirement in 1810. He died at St. Simon's Island, Glynn County in October 1812.

[249] The race ground was on Fulwood Moor, the future site of Fulwood Barracks.

neighbourhood abounded, and actually forced back into the town. The numbers increasing from hundreds to thousands, the magistrates were obliged to interpose their authority, and only succeeded, after much difficulty, in dispersing the mob, having been compelled to read the Riot Act, and give an assurance that the boy should not be flogged.'

'This colonel did incalculable injury to the efficiency of the men, and consequently to the service, by his propensity for this mode of punishment – greater injury, indeed, than any other officer I have known or heard of.'[250]

In November that year, the 2nd/47th marched to Chelmsford, where they completed their full strength with volunteers from the Militia regiments, including some two hundred from Lancashire. Harley recalls a scurrilous occurrence at that time relating to Major Humphrey Dalrymple Bland[251]:

'He was an extraordinary character, and so fond of the fair sex that he never went into a town in which he did not pick up some female companion. At Preston, he had one residing with him; and when the regiment left that town she remained behind under the assurance that she should be sent for as soon as he was settled in his next quarters. The regiment remained at Manchester for three weeks, during which period he had another lady residing with him, to whom he made the fairest promises: and on the regiment leaving that town, she continued in it under a similar assurance. In Derby he met another, and at Leicester a fourth, to each of whom he told the same story. And, on the very evening the regiment marched into Chelmsford, he formed an acquaintance with a female of that town, whom he took into his apartments in the barrack to reside with him.

'After a few days had elapsed, he received several letters from his quondam friends, complaining of breach of promise, and saying they would join him as soon as possible. These letters he never answered, foolishly thinking that none of them would undertake the journey. But he was mistaken. He was scarcely a fortnight in Chelmsford when the lady from Preston arrived with all her luggage, and sent a message to him from the inn, informing him of the circumstance. As he could not bring her to his quarters in the barracks, which were already occupied, he was obliged to procure a lodging for her in the town and advanced her some cash. In the course of another day or two, the Manchester dame arrived, for whom he had to provide another lodging. And lastly came the Leicester lady, who also required the like attention. Having then no less than four on his hands, he knew not how to act, and was in a state bordering on distraction. However, by sending Captain Featherstone and other friends to negotiate for him, the three ladies were, after much difficulty, prevailed upon to return to their respective homes; but not until they had been handsomely remunerated for their time, trouble, and travelling expenses.'[252]

In May 1808, the 2nd/47th moved to St Ouen's Barracks, Jersey, where they were quartered for eighteen months. Harley enthused that 'The people, from the lowest to the highest, we found uncommonly civil and obliging: and we were never more hospitably entertained. The climate, too, was delightful, and the necessaries of life were cheap and good.'

In October 1809 the 2nd/47th embarked for Gibraltar. Harley records that they stopped for a few days at Falmouth, 'where we were when the Jubilee took place on the 50th year of the reign of George the Third.'[253] Private Adam Reed recalled an eventful voyage:

'On our passage one night by a contrary wind, we were very near driven onto the French coast. In the morning we espied a French frigate coming after us in full sail, our commodore being ahead of us with the remainder of the fleet. I suppose (but am not certain) the distance to be about 3 miles. The captain that commanded my company resolved not to be taken and therefore ordered every man upon deck and to unloose their ammunition for he was determined to be sunk rather than taken. Likewise the guns to be loaded which were mounted on deck

---

[250] Harley, p.p. 130-31.

[251] Bland, who had been Major of the 47th since 28th August 1804, later assumed command of the 2nd Battalion on 3rd May 1810, and subsequently commanded the 1st Battalion in India, where he died in 1816. He was from an Anglo-Irish military family whose seat was Blandfort House near Abbeyleix, Queen's County (now County Laois).

[252] Harley, p.p. 144-45.

[253] Lieutenant Lewis Montfort wrote to his brother from on board the transport *Annie* at Falmouth on 20th October. Commissioned in 1806 into the 82nd, Montfort had recently transferred to the 2nd/47th.

(which consisted of eight 24-pounders). At that time the commodore espied the strange sail and returned back. The French frigate left us. Then we escaped being sunk, as I suppose we should have been if the commodore had not returned.

'In a day or two we entered the Bay of Biscay where the waves rolled mountain high. One day, as we were getting our grog (rum and water) served out, we were standing upon deck, the ship gave a heave over one of the swells, and threw one of our men overboard and he was drowned.'

The 47th reached Gibraltar on 20th November after a three-week voyage and were quartered in the South Barracks[254], where they were based throughout their tour on the Rock. At their next muster, in December, the Battalion numbered 784 effective other ranks and 64 sick. Like many nominally English regiments at this time, they had a strong Irish contingent.[255]

Gibraltar Garrison 1809-11

In 1809, Gibraltar was above all a naval base, capable of projecting power across the Mediterranean and the Atlantic coasts of North Africa, the Iberian Peninsula and further east. But despite its strategic importance, Gibraltar was something of a military backwater, far from the seat of war. The main battle was to maintain military efficiency in the face of boredom and cheap drink – Malaga at sixpence a bottle and gut-rotting 'black strap' for four pence. Discipline suffered, and in 1809 the 2nd/47th recorded five sergeants, seven corporals, five drummers and 148 privates brought before regimental courts martial.[256]

Apart from the cheap wine, Private Adam Reed of the 47th found Gibraltar 'very fruitful, healthy and flourishing.' He and his comrades encountered the Barbary apes: 'The way we used to trap the young ones was to tie a bottle round the neck and fill it up to the neck with peas. Then they used to come and put their hand down the neck of the bottle and take a handful of peas, and they, not having sense to let go, were caught. Often they would come into the barrack rooms and hospital by night and carry away as much as they were able.'

Paymaster John Harley, as was his wont, found Gibraltar a fertile source for his repertoire of scurrilous tales, including one about the Marquess of Sligo, a wealthy regency buck and patron of pugilists, dancers, courtesans, artists and jockeys who visited the Rock in the course of a grand tour of the Mediterranean, when he hired a ship and visited the antiquities of Greece with his friend Byron:

'He dined very frequently at our mess and made himself extremely agreeable. He was particularly generous. He gave our band ten doubloons (£36 British) on St. Patrick's Day [17th March] in order that they might enjoy themselves on the occasion. As such a sum of money enabled them to get drunk morning, noon and night, for three successive weeks after St. Patrick's Day, our Colonel was greatly annoyed, and attached all the blame to me, as he said that I countenanced the Marquis's generosity – or I should have used some endeavours to prevent it. For a full month it was impossible to tell what tunes the band played, as the men were in a state of continual inebriation.'

Another strange occurrence related by Harley was the arrival in the Regiment of Ensign Davy Stapleton, an impecunious former Irish excise officer, complete with wife and nine children for whom he proceeded to draw excessive quantities of rations.

As for the 2nd/30th, a carefully equivocal inspection report, whilst encouraging, and giving praise where it was due, made it very clear that the Battalion was not yet fit for active service:

'Colonel Minet has commanded this battalion since the last inspection. He appears a very zealous officer. The battalion exercised and manoeuvred with tolerable accuracy; the officers and non-commissioned officers appeared desirous to perform their duties to the best of their abilities, and without any deviation from His Majesty's regulations. But this battalion having lately been upon service in Portugal and having been much separated, and employed upon small detachments, I apprehend the marching and general appearance may be very

---

254 The striking Palladian South Barracks, completed in about 1730, is now St. Joseph's Elementary School.
255 When mustered at Gibraltar in 1810, the 2nd/47th numbered 541 English (57%), 388 Irish (41%) and 15 Scots.
256 Prior to 1812 regimental courts martial were empowered to try NCOs and men for all non-capital offences.

much improved before the next inspection… The men of the battalion are not in general stout, and many of them are very short… No complaints from any of the men… The hospital appeared clean, books regularly kept, and the patients very well attended… There have been twenty-eight [regimental] courts martial held in this battalion since the last inspection, the sentences of which appear to be conformable to the usages of the army. There have been few punishments during the last two months.'

On December 20th Lieutenant Richard Heaviside of the 2nd/30th, aged twenty, appeared before a General Court Martial in Gibraltar on a capital charge, in that he 'did on the morning of the 15th day of December 1809 wilfully and of malice aforethought kill and murder Lieutenant Lewis Montford of the 47th Regiment of Foot with a pistol in a duel near Fort Barbara in Spain.' There had been an altercation between the two subalterns at guard mounting at the Land Port Gate on the 12th of that month when, according to a witness: 'some words passed between them' and Lieutenant Montfort was heard to use 'very harsh expressions' to Lieutenant Heaviside, ordering him either to sit down or quit the guard room. Heaviside, who was junior in rank, answered, 'As my commanding officer, I obey you,' and was leaving the room when Montfort followed him towards the door and challenged him with the words, 'My name is Montfort.' At their meeting near the Spanish Lines, they exchanged five shots, of which the final discharge left Lewis Montfort bleeding to death. All those present at the duel, seconds and surgeons alike, affected to have seen and heard nothing, and their blatant collusion was accepted without question by an understanding court. This was, after all, a matter of a gentleman's honour. Richard Heaviside was acquitted and went on to command a company at the storming of Badajoz and at the battles of Salamanca, Villa Muriel, Quatre Bras and Waterloo.

In January 1810, the French armies under Marshals Soult and Victor turned their attention to Andalusia, chasing the Supreme Junta out of Seville. On 5th February, Victor, with nearly twenty-two thousand men, laid siege to Cadiz. Gibraltar was now on the allied front line, and Lieutenant-General Colin Campbell, the energetic Lieutenant-Governor, took steps to improve the defences of the fortress. In particular, he ordered his Chief Engineer to demolish the Spanish Lines, the substantial old Spanish siege-works that faced Gibraltar across the Neutral Ground. We know that the 47th Regiment took part in this work[257], and it is probable that the 30th were also involved. On 14th February, with the demolition charges set, an advanced guard of two to three hundred French troops reached San Roque, just beyond the Lines, and Campbell ordered the charges to be blown. The local newspaper recorded that 'every part of the Garrison facing the Spanish Lines was crowded with spectators to witness the explosion, which was truly great and picturesque… the entire front of [Forts San Felipe and Santa Barbara] being blown into the ditch, and the whole rendered a complete mass of ruins.'[258] For several days afterwards, the soldiers hauled away the debris, leaving Gibraltar unopposed across the Neutral Ground for the first time since 1704.

General Campbell did as much as he could to support the Spanish resistance in Andalusia, and Private Adam Reed of the 47th recalled an occasion when the Spanish General Ballasteros, who had been driven under the protective guns of Gibraltar, received British assistance:

'One day the garrison was alarmed by an army of Spaniards, whom the French had engaged and drove under the Rock, and they made application to the Governor (General Campbell), but he did not just then grant their request for he supposed them to be a superior number to the French. Therefore he thought they had no need to apply to him for refuge, but being as they would not engage the French anymore he ordered all the English troops on the Rock to be under arms and he gave them leave to pass through and to go on board a ship and to be landed in some other part of Spain.'

Captain John Harley of the 47th recalled how 'that celebrated heroine known as the Maid of Saragosa… resided in the town while we were there, and dined in our mess. I afterwards met her at the Governor's ball,

---

[257] Private Adam Reed of the 47th recorded that 'Just after we arrived [in Gibraltar we] were sent out on the Spanish Lines to destroy all their batteries and fortresses for fear the French would take them in possession as they lay within 1 league from us.'
[258] *Gibraltar Chronicle*, 17th February 1810.

dressed in a blue uniform, with laced hat and feathers, and a small sword to her side. She appeared to be about twenty-four years of age, and was rather handsome.'[259]

Tarifa 1810

By February 1810 the French had overrun the whole of Andalucia except for Cadiz and the small coastal town of Tarifa, some twenty miles from Gibraltar and sixty miles from Cadiz. This place was important as a base from which the Allies could mount operations against the French in western Andalusia, and in particular threaten their siege lines around Cadiz, and as a link in the supply chain to that besieged city.

Early in April 1810, Lieutenant-General Campbell sent a small force from Gibraltar to reinforce the Spanish garrison of Tarifa. His intention appears to have been to disrupt the depredations of French foraging parties in that area, thereby diverting Marshal Victor's attention from the siege of Cadiz. The precise composition and order of arrival of the troops sent to Tarifa over the next few months is a little uncertain, but they mainly consisted of companies of the 30th and 47th Regiments. The initial force was a battalion of detachments from the Gibraltar garrison commanded by Major John Frederick Browne[260] of the 28th Foot, probably consisting of the Captain John Hitchen's Grenadier Company of the 30th, the Light Companies of the 9th, 30th (under Captain Elias Malet) and 47th Regiments, and a battalion company of the 28th, together with two 6-pounder guns, a total of some 380 all ranks.

According to Sergeant Peter Facey of the 28th Foot, Browne's detachment embarked from the New Mole, Gibraltar at 5 a.m. on the morning of April 12th, but due to contrary winds the troops disembarked at Algeciras at about 2 p.m. They remained there that night and marched at 9 a.m. next morning for Tarifa, which they reached at about 4 p.m. on the 13th after a march of about 18 miles over a narrow mountain track whose precipitous passes rose to a height of some 13,000 feet. Three battalion companies of the 30th, those of Captains Thomas Bamford, Robert Blake Lynch and Samuel Fox, followed a week later, bringing the total strength of the 30th at Tarifa up to five captains, ten subalterns, thirteen sergeants, eleven corporals, three drummers and 273 privates.

As soon as Marshal Victor learned that Tarifa was occupied by British troops, he sent a reconnaissance force to ascertain its strength. All remained quiet at Tarifa until early on the morning of the 20th (or possibly 21st) when Major Browne was informed that the French were approaching in superior strength. A bugle sounded the alarm, and in ten minutes the detachment was under arms and at their posts on the walls. At about 8 a.m. the enemy attacked, their force consisting of some four hundred infantry and one hundred and fifty cavalry. The French kept up a constant fire for three and a half hours, then retired to the adjacent Convent of San Francisco, some houses and a small hill to the north-west of the town. At about 6 p.m. the garrison of Tarifa anticipated a fresh attack, but a company of the 28th sent out by Browne to clear the French positions discovered that the enemy had all withdrawn.

At half past seven the troops were dismissed to their respective quarters, but almost immediately, a false alarm circulated through the town that the French were again advancing. The soldiers were already undressed and cleaning their muskets, but when the alarm was sounded, they were on the wall in six minutes, some of them stumbling over women and children in their haste. After about ten minutes, it became clear that the enemy had moved off, leaving behind them four officers and 27 men killed. The defenders' loss was one British gunner and a Spanish soldier killed, and a few wounded.

Following this French reconnaissance in force, Major Browne sent to Gibraltar for reinforcement, and General Campbell at once ordered four companies of the 47th under Captain John O'Donoghue to embark for

---

[259] This was Agustina Zaragoza, who, on 2nd July 1808, at a critical moment during the First Siege of Saragossa, ran forward to take the place of a dying gunner, said to have been her fiancé, and single-handed fired a 24-pounder cannon at point-blank range into an oncoming French column. Young, slender and pretty, Agustina became a symbol of Spanish resistance to Bonaparte, and as such was immortalised by Goya in his 'Disasters of War' series and by Lord Byron in *Childe Harold's Pilgrimage*.

[260] Browne was known to the Spanish inhabitants of Tarifa as *Il Commandante Loco* on account of his ungallant habit of lifting the concealing mantillas of passing ladies with a hooked stick.

Tarifa. On account of contrary winds, they again landed at Algeciras and marched over the hills to Tarifa. It is probable that this detachment of the 47th relieved the 30th companies, who returned to Gibraltar at the beginning of May. The 47th companies, around three hundred strong, remained at Tarifa until September 1810, when they were relieved by the 28th Foot and returned to Gibraltar. It appears that a detachment of the 82nd Foot with seventy other ranks also served at Tarifa from June to September 1810. Captain Lewis Northern of that Regiment died at Tarifa on 11th July 1810. Northern, aged 37 and a veteran of Roliça, Vimeiro and Corunna, is buried in the Trafalgar Cemetery at Gibraltar. Over this period, the garrison, still led by Major John Browne, was engaged in frequent skirmishes with French foraging parties.

When not so engaged, the British garrison was received with great hospitality in the pleasant little town of Tarifa, whose ladies were famed throughout Spain for their beauty and where, according to Lieutenant Robert Blakeney of the 28th, 'oft we played and sang and danced the gay fandango.'[261]

The Defence of Cadiz 1810-11

We have already noted that Cadiz was besieged by the French from 5th February 1810. The city stood at the end of a long sandy spit, only two hundred yards wide at its narrowest point, leading to the triangular Isla de Leon, which was in turn separated from the mainland by a tidal creek, the river Sancti Petri, and by extensive salt marshes. The natural defences of Cadiz made it, in the words of Sir Charles Oman, 'one of the strongest places in the world.' The city had in the past proved vulnerable to assault from the sea,[262] but the Spanish defenders were supported by the Royal Navy, which barred most approaches to the sea-girt city, and Wellington, though loath to lose men from his main effort on the frontier of Portugal, was prompt to send troop reinforcements to stiffen the landward defences. Between the 12th and 15th February, some three thousand five hundred British and Portuguese soldiers arrived from Lisbon to join the Spanish garrison of some twelve thousand five hundred. Cadiz was now almost impregnable.

Direct regimental involvement in the defence of Cadiz did not commence until 12th May 1810 when the 2nd/30th, recently reunited at Gibraltar, received orders to embark for the port city, whose British and Portuguese contingent of eight thousand men was now commanded by Lieutenant-General Thomas Graham. The Battalion landed at Cadiz on 2nd June with a nominal strength of 704 non-commissioned officers and men, including thirteen boys and 34 sick. Two days later they paraded with the rest of the British troops for a *feu de joie* to mark King George's birthday.

Graham had divided his troops between the Isla de Leon, the only landward approach to Cadiz, and a garrison in the city under Major-General Daniel Hoghton. The 2nd/30th joined the 2nd/87th and two companies of the 95th Rifles in the city, where they occupied bomb-proof casemated barracks beneath the ramparts of the Puerta de Tierra, the massive Land Gate. Captain Richard Machell of the 30th became Hoghton's Brigade Major, and on 17th August, Captain Elias Malet was appointed Town Major of Cadiz and DAQMG of Graham's division. Thomas Graham, an old friend of the Regiment from Toulon, Malta, Egypt and Ireland, also applied to General Manners, Colonel of the 30th, for the services of Lieutenant Michael Sparkes, recalling his good work as an acting engineer in Ireland. Sparkes, a 1st Battalion officer who was recruiting in Lincolnshire, was released for service on Graham's staff.

On 8th July 1810 Major-General George Cockburn landed at Cadiz and, on a hot Sunday afternoon, found the band of the 30th playing on a public walk near the sea, observing that 'the crowd was very great, as much so as at Kensington on Sundays.'

A prominent feature of the rather desultory siege of Cadiz was a long-running but almost entirely ineffective artillery duel between the French batteries at Matagorda, San José and San Luis on the Trocadero

---

[261] *A Boy in the Peninsular War*, Robert Blakeney, London, 1899, p. 209.

[262] It was in Cadiz harbour that, in 1587, Sir Francis Drake 'singed the King of Spain's beard', delaying the Spanish Armada by a year, and in 1596 an English expedition took and sacked the city itself. In consequence of these devastating attacks, the fortifications of Cadiz were comprehensively rebuilt in the early seventeenth century.

peninsula, the nearest point on the mainland to the city of Cadiz, and the Allied battery at Fort Puntales, only 1,200 yards across the harbour from Matagorda. The 30th loaned a number of men to the artillery and engineers to serve as gunners, artificers and drivers[263], and on 19th June, Private William Page died from a wound received in the Puntales battery, and Private Thomas Horner was seriously wounded.

When the 2nd/30th first landed at Cadiz, Graham was very much dissatisfied with the physique of the majority of the soldiers, describing them as either too young or too old for service,[264] and Hoghton had to report to Graham that, though the men were clean and steady in the ranks, the Battalion was still deficient in field training. These were truthful appraisals of the 30th at that time, but the Battalion's condition was steadily improving as its boys and lads, and its young officers, grew to maturity and new drafts arrived from the Depot, which was now at Wakefield.

In September, Captain Thomas Walker Chambers brought out a substantial draft for the 2nd/30th, three officers and 85 other ranks, including two soldiers[265] who had escaped from captivity in Verdun. With them was Ensign Parke Percy Nevill, aged sixteen and greatly excited at the dramatic scene unfolding before him:

'Never shall I forget the striking effect this beautiful city and harbour had upon us on our approach to it, about five o'clock in the evening of a fine day. There our fleet lay, and at that hour each ship fired a signal gun, and in the air at that moment were some large shells, fired by the enemy, which were seen bursting over the city and the fleet[266]; but they appeared to do little harm and were not much heeded in the town, for around its seaboard were seen crowds of Spanish women, some splendidly dressed, who, with their cavaliers, were promenading about, intermingled with British and Spanish officers in full dress. There were also numerous monks and friars in their varied costumes, and altogether it was a novel and impressive sight.'[267]

On 23rd September 1810, Graham received an order for the immediate embarkation of the 2nd/30th and 2nd/44th to join Wellington's field army. Reporting their embarkation for Lisbon on the 25th of that month, Graham added, 'I take this opportunity of mentioning two officers of the 30th highly deserving of notice whom I have long known and served with on various occasions; Major Hamilton, who has often distinguished himself by his gallantry, and Captain Malet, a most intelligent and attentive officer.' Both these officers received preferment, for Alexander Hamilton commanded the 30th when it left Cadiz (vice Colonel Minet, who commanded the brigade consisting of the 2nd/30th and 2nd/44th for a few weeks until promoted to the rank of major-general) and, owing to Graham's recommendation, Elias Malet was attached to Mendizábal's Spanish army as DAQMG.

Very shortly after the departure of the 2nd/30th from Cadiz, on 2nd October, the 2nd/47th under Lieutenant-Colonel Humphrey Dalrymple Bland arrived there from Gibraltar with a rank and file strength of 807 (690 effectives) and was initially assigned to replace the 30th in the city garrison. Together with a detachment of the 2nd/95th Rifles, they now formed the 2nd Brigade under Colonel William Wheatley. Private Adam Reed gave some account of the 47th at this time:

'After we landed we were ordered to go and work every night to build batteries and a more strongly fortified island and we built upward of 15 batteries round the island, and one we built particularly strong in the centre of the island which was called the Friars (or Priest's) battery, for there was only one strong fort when we landed there, called Pontilla [Puntales]. It consisted of three tiers of guns, the lower tier commanded by Spanish artillery, and the second tier commanded by Portuguese, and the upper (or third) tier commanded by British. This fort was supposed to be about one mile from where the French lay and they also had a strong fort called Matagoda [Matagorda] and it lay on a point of land called Matagoda Point. They almost continually kept bombarding the

---

[263] A sergeant and nineteen privates of the 30th served as gunners at Puntales, and seven privates were artillery drivers, while a sergeant and seven privates were employed as carpenters and artificers.

[264] Carole Divall has produced some telling statistics for the 2nd/30th at this time: 'Fifty-six privates had seen more than twelve years' service, while only forty-two had served between seven and twelve years, and 662 had less than seven years' service. Similarly, 467 were under 30, including half the sergeants.' (*Redcoats Against Napoleon*, p. 43).

[265] Drummer John Winterflood and Private James Waters.

[266] From the Trocadero peninsula the French could reach the nearest parts of the city with their 12-inch mortars and with 36-pounder cannon fired at optimum elevation.

[267] *Some Recollections in the Life of Lieut.-Col. P. P. Nevill*, London, 1864, p. 3.

fort (Pontilla), and one gun in particular, called by the British 'Long Tom,' used to fire red hot shot into Cadiz (supposed to be about 2 miles and a half) and they very often used to drop on the top of our barracks.'

Graham was concerned that the defences of the Isla de Leon were vulnerable to attack across the Sancti Petri creek and marshes, and pressed the Spaniards to improve the island's defences. The response was complacent indifference, and Graham found that he could expect little help from either the Spanish military or the local population, but [he] must rely on his British troops to carry out the necessary work. Accordingly, some thousand British soldiers laboured daily to build batteries on the Isla de Leon and an entrenched camp on the Isla heights, with a further five hundred under arms. The men worked for a week at a time under engineer direction, and received a welcome allowance of six pence a day for the 'wear and tear of necessaries.' The 47th were among those tasked, as Adam Reed recalled:

'Shortly after that our Regiment and the Guards was ordered to the south part of the island [Isla de Leon] to a town called Aziar which is about seven miles from Cadiz. We were put into the barracks which were called the Upper Galleria,[268] and there we were sent to build more batteries in the night, for we was obliged to work there, for our own barracks lay in front of a large garrisoned town called Chicalana [Chiclana] which was occupied by the French.[269]

'Duty being very hard, we could scarcely get one night sleep in the course of the week, for we had some men of our regiment (and other regiments likewise) deserted to the enemy... After that, duty was harder than ever for it was an order that if any one sentry was found more than 10 or 12 paces from his post (or box) he was to be brought to a court martial. I myself declare that I have walked on sentry almost asleep upon the account of duty being so very hard.'

On arrival at Cadiz, Lieutenant Colonel Bland made the error of appointing Ensign Davy Stapleton as acting quartermaster. 'A more unfit person could not have been appointed,' recalled Harley, 'for he knew nothing of accounts or returns; and, whether by design or not, drew rations for forty men more than were in the Regiment, which surplus remained with himself. His barrack room was a curiosity at St. Rock [San Roque], in Cadiz, hung up all round with pieces of salt pork and beef, and loaves of bread piled up. He took pleasure in showing to anyone his room, telling them, in his Irish accent, "there is nothing like rations"... and blurting out that "it is the finest thing in the entire army; for I am only three months acting, and I have more money than all of yez put together, barring Harley, our paymaster."' When pressed to expand on his peculations, he explained, "Och, boys, ye'z don't understand at all; for sure, faith, it is very easy to add a few men to the return of rations for provisions, and then I have all that's left to myself; and faith, I do all this for Lucy and the children."[270]

Inevitably, some of the young officers took advantage of Stapleton's simplicity. On one occasion, Lieutenant Henry Wainwright and Assistant-Surgeon William Harper of the 47th waylaid the acting quartermaster in the dark passage of a bombproof shelter, belabouring his head with a bladder full of shot or small stones. When Stapleton cried out, 'What is this for? What can it mean?' a sepulchral voice answered, 'I am a dead soldier, and you cheated me of my rations.'

In October and November, Cadiz was attacked by a virulent fever, known as 'the black vomit,' which by 5th November had carried off two officers, the sergeant-major and thirty other ranks of the 47th.[271]

The siege offered no opportunities for infantry action, and it may well be that the 47th shared Graham's view that Cadiz was little better than 'a loathsome prison.'

---

[268] The British brigade on the Isla de Leon was quartered in the San Fernando barracks.
[269] The French siege lines, mounting some 300 guns, ran for 25 miles from the mouth of the Sancto Petri round the inner and outer harbours of Cadiz, with entrenched camps at Chiclana, Puerto Real and Santa Catalina.
[270] Harley, p.p. 155-56.
[271] According to Captain Harley, 'We lost in two days a very fine young man, Lieutenant [Samuel] Clarke, a sergeant-major, and ten of our best men.'

Fuengirola, October 1810

The final regimental arrival on Gibraltar at this time was the 1st/82nd Foot. Having returned from Walcheren to their quarters at Lewes Barracks in December 1809, the main body of that regiment were shortly afterwards joined there by the 82nd company of the 2nd Battalion of Detachments. They had recently landed at Gosport from Lisbon, and with them was Lieutenant George Wood, still wearing the stained, tattered and much-mended regimentals in which he had landed at Mondego Bay in August 1808:

'In this state, we marched for Salisbury, when we were invited to dine with the Mayor and Corporation of that town. It so happened that I sate next to a major of the local militia, whose splendid uniform and sparkling epaulettes contrasted with my thread-worn patched jacket and mud-like looking shoulder-knot, once so brilliant on these parades, afforded a fertile source of amusement for the jocose part of the company. However, the jest was rather in my favour – a circumstance which caused some mortification to my bedizened neighbour.

'In this town, our battalion was broken up; each detachment proceeding to join its respective regiment. I marched with mine to Lewes, in Sussex; and on our arrival we certainly cut a very ludicrous appearance, from our ragged state, but were received with a hearty welcome by our long-lost comrades after so long an absence. We were now, however, able to get at our heavy baggage, and undergo a thorough refit, so that I again appeared bedecked in new finery and, forgetting all my past troubles, I strutted, and dressed, and thought myself as fine a fellow as ever; but these splendid trappings, alas! were also doomed ere long to be dyed of a deeper stain than those they had replaced. We had only remained in our native land about six weeks when we were again ordered on foreign service.'[272]

In February 1810, though still 'in a state of little more than convalescence' from Walcheren fever, the 1st/82nd, The Prince of Wales's Volunteers, received orders to embark at Portsmouth for Gibraltar, where after a five-week voyage they arrived on 31st March. Lieutenant George Wood was on the whole favourably impressed with conditions at their new station:

'The Rock is rather a desirable quarter for soldiers, particularly the private men, as it is impossible they can live better in any part of the world. They have a good basin of coffee or cocoa for breakfast, good meat, soup and vegetables for dinner, and bread and cheese for supper; wine and spirits being so cheap that they commonly get too much of them.

'Here [the officers'] time passed on very agreeably. Sometimes we dined with the Governor and other families in the garrison, or went to balls, concerts and evening parties. Before dinner, we generally promenaded on the Saluting Battery or retired from the heat to the more edifying lounge of a grand library.[273] Occasionally, we explored the Rock, rode on the Neutral Ground, or bathed.'

There were, however, some disadvantages: Garrison guards and duties were much more severe than expected, the sultry autumn heat brought 'malignant' (yellow) fever in 1810 and 1811,[274] and the barracks swarmed with bugs and rats: 'We were obliged,' recalled George Wood, 'to collect all the bones and scraps that remained at dinner and, on lying down on the stretcher at night, leave them on the floor for these gentry [the rats] to devour in order to prevent their scampering over our faces as we lay asleep, and gnawing the powder and pomatum out of our hair.'[275]

In October 1810 Lieutenant-General Colin Campbell, Governor of Gibraltar, saw an opportunity to aid the Andalusian insurgents and, taking advantage of the Royal Navy's command of the sea, planned a small Anglo-Spanish amphibious operation employing a remarkably polyglot force of some 2,600 men including the 82nd (932

---

[272] Wood, p.p. 112-14.

[273] The Gibraltar Garrison Library was founded in 1793 and its present premises, completed in 1804, would have been familiar to generations of regimental officers.

[274] Captain Richard Tribe of the 82nd, a veteran of Roliça, Vimeiro and Corunna, died at Gibraltar on 25th May 1811 and was buried in the Trafalgar Cemetery, where his headstone may be seen. Aged 30, he had volunteered for the 82nd from the Devon and Cornwall Fencibles on 30th May 1795 and was commissioned on 5th December that year.

[275] Wood, p.p. 114-15. The officers of the 82nd still wore their hair in powdered queues at Gibraltar two years after this had been abolished throughout the Army.

strong), under Lieutenant-Colonel William Grant, four companies (353 men) of the 2nd/89th, the Spanish Toledo Regiment (650 men) and a 'foreign battalion' made up 509 German, Italian, French and Polish deserters from the French army.

This disparate force, commanded by Major-General Lord Blayney[276], was to land at Fuengirola, twenty miles south-west of Malaga, where a hilltop medieval castle, garrisoned by 150 Poles of the 4th Infantry Regiment of the Grand Duchy of Warsaw, and a few French dragoons[277], dominated the sandy beaches.

The intention was that Blayney should make a demonstration against Fuengirola sufficient to entice General Sebastiani, the French commander at Malaga, to march to the relief of that castle with a large part of his garrison. On Sebastiani's approach, Blayney was to re-embark his troops and, sailing along the coast, capture the lightly-defended town of Malaga with the aid of local partisans before Sebastiani could return. The expedition also carried 20,000 stand of arms for the Spanish guerrillas. The enterprise was not without risk, but was entirely consistent with the British policy of supporting widespread Spanish resistance in order to tie down large numbers of French troops, to prevent their concentration, and to interdict supplies for the besiegers of Cadiz.

Blayney planned to leave Gibraltar on October 10th, call at Ceuta to embark the Spaniards, and land at Fuengirola on the 12th. Unfortunately, when the Spanish hulk *El Vencedor* 74, which was to carry the 82nd, arrived at Gibraltar on the 5th, she was in such a state of disrepair that the dockyard were unable to make her seaworthy enough to be taken in tow by HMS *Rodney* before the 14th. In consequence, Lord Blayney departed without the greater part of his British infantry.

Early on 14th October, Blayney's expedition was off the coast south of Fuengirola, where he learned from the frigate HMS *Swiftsure* that the arms had been delivered to the guerrillas. The troops landed that morning two miles south-west of Fuengirola, and the motley force appeared in front of the castle at 2 p.m. They were supported at sea by five gunboats, for shoaling water prevented the larger warships from coming close inshore. Blayney's summons to the garrison was summarily rejected, and in the exchange of fire that followed, the officer commanding the 89th was mortally wounded, a gunboat was sunk, and the Spanish battalion refused to fight as it was a Sunday.

Blayney, who was apparently unconvinced by the plan for a *coup de main* attack on Malaga, determined to take the inconsequential Fuengirola castle instead. He had to wait till night to land his artillery, for the castle guns could sweep the beach, but by dawn on the 15th he had a battery of two 12-pounders and a howitzer in position. These, however, proved inadequate to breach the castle walls, which would have required 24-pounders.

By mid-morning, Blayney received the hardly-unexpected intelligence that 4,700 infantry, 800 cavalry, and 16 guns, commanded by General Sebastiani in person, were on the march against him from Malaga. Withdrawal would now have been prudent and in accordance with his instructions, but Blayney's fatal decision to land guns, his inability to re-embark them by daylight, and his determination not to abandon them, left him little choice but to make preparations for receiving the enemy in the best manner possible.

It was at this difficult time that the 1st/82nd enter the story. They had embarked at Gibraltar on 14th October aboard the *El Vencedor*, and sailed to join Blayney's expedition in company with HMS *Rodney*, 74. On 15th October, when about fifteen miles off Fuengirola, they were signalled from inshore by the frigate HMS *Topaze*, 38, to the effect that 'Lord Blayney had landed on the 14th and was in want of immediate assistance.' Seven boats from HMS *Rodney* were then sent to the hulk and carried ashore eighty rank and file of the flank companies of the 82nd, together with Lieutenant-Colonel Grant.[278] They landed at about noon, only to discover a disaster. Lord Blayney had been captured, together with his three guns, and the remnants of his force had retreated to the shore with the loss of over two-thirds of the 89th.

---

[276] Lord Blayney had recently been promoted after long and distinguished service in command of the 1st/89th, known as 'Blayney's Bloodhounds.' The 2nd/89th, by contrast, had like many second battalions seen no active service.
[277] Fuengirola had been reinforced by a further 60 Poles before the siege commenced.
[278] The total strength of the 82nd landed at Fuengirola, including officers, sergeants and staff, cannot have been much more than ninety-five all ranks.

What had happened? The sequence of events is somewhat clouded by Polish myth, but it appears from Lord Blayney's account that, while he was making anxious preparations to receive the 82nd as most welcome reinforcements, the besieged mounted a pre-emptive attack:

'A desperate sortie was made from the castle by about six hundred and fifty infantry and sixty cavalry[279], and entirely directed to the left, where the Spanish and other foreign troops were posted, who fled with scarce any resistance, and abandoned the artillery to the enemy. At this moment I observed the boats with the troops had pushed off from the ships, and were fast approaching the shore, which gave me hopes of being still able to retrieve the day, both from the strength of our position, and from my confidence in the 82nd Regiment; I therefore immediately formed the 89th, and, though consisting of only two hundred and eighty men, retook the guns by the bayonet. In advancing to the charge, my horse was wounded, and soon after killed by a second shot, so that I was obliged to charge on foot. After a short but very severe contest, the enemy wheeled and fled; at the same moment, a strong body came running across us in front, dressed precisely similar to the Spanish troops, and a cry of "They are Spaniards!" at the same time took place. I therefore ceased firing for a few minutes, both in order to form the troops more regularly, and to ascertain whether this body was really Spaniards or French, as well as to economize the ammunition which began to fall short... Being dismounted I could not go to the left sufficiently quick to ascertain whether the approaching body were French or Spaniards: I soon, however, observed a column close in from the left, on whose caps I perceived the number 4 with an eagle, and which proved to be the Quatrième Polonois. The troops with me, after firing a few rounds, charged this column, and a very severe conflict ensued, which unfortunately ended in my being made prisoner, having but nine men remaining of those that advanced with me.'[280]

The new enemy column was not in fact Sebastiani but a further two hundred Poles and a squadron of French dragoons, whose untimely arrival caught Blayney and his few British troops between two fires. The detachment of the 89th was effectively destroyed, losing some 240 out of 353 men, while the routed Spanish and 'foreign' battalions headed for the shore with few casualties, having relinquished, as General Campbell acidly commented, their honour and the field.

As Lord Blayney was led as a prisoner into the castle, he saw its guns still firing at the *Rodney* and at the boats with the 82nd flankers as they approached the shore. On landing, Colonel Grant attempted to rally the retiring Spanish and assorted deserters, but it was too late; so he took up a position from which his small body of flankers kept the enemy in check until about 4 p.m., covering the re-embarkation of the remnants of Blayney's force. The remainder of the 82nd, being at least twelve miles out at sea, could not be landed for lack of boats, which were soon full of the survivors of Blayney's expedition. The Regiment appears to have suffered negligible casualties in this operation, though Lieutenant Richard Read of the Light Company was wounded – for the third time. The flank companies of the 82nd were the last to leave the shore, covered by *Rodney*'s guns.

For the 82nd it had been a most frustrating and disappointing experience, and their only compensation as they sailed back to Gibraltar was to be transferred from the jury-rigged *El Vencedor* into transports where, as Lieutenant George Wood remarked, 'we were a little more comfortable, not having taken off our clothes from the time we left the Rock till now – about a fortnight; lying all this time about fifty of us together on the cabin floor, on a sail-cloth spread out for our accommodation... Those who escaped were exceedingly glad to reach their comfortable station again after their expedition to Malaga. Indeed, we might on the whole consider ourselves very fortunate, as the rotten old Spanish hulk in which we first sailed soon after went to the bottom and all hands on board perished; so that the Regiment, every man of which was in her but a few days previously, had an almost miraculous escape.'[281]

On return to Gibraltar, Colonel Grant received the following letter of appreciation from the Governor, dated 28th October 1810:

---

[279] The strength of the Polish sortie could have been no more than 150 infantry and a handful of dragoons.

[280] Lord Blayney's *Narrative of a Forced Journey through Spain and France as a Prisoner of War in the Years 1810 to 1814*, London 1814.

[281] Wood, p.p. 117-18.

'Had it not been for the steadiness of the few of the 82nd under your orders, together with the able assistance of HMS *Rodney*, who covered the retreat, the embarkation could not have been effected; for which I beg you to accept my warmest acknowledgements.'

Wellington's Defence of Portugal 1810

We last saw the 40th Foot when, following the Talavera campaign, in November 1809 they moved their quarters from Badajoz to the small fortified town of Olivenza, where the greater part of the 4th Division was concentrated under its new commander, Major-General Lowry Cole. Wellington anticipated an early French invasion of Portugal and had estimated that their main line of advance would be on the northern route through Ciudad Rodrigo and Almeida, and on to Lisbon by way of Coimbra. Accordingly, leaving General Hill with his 2nd Division in the Alemtejo to watch the southern route from Badajoz and Elvas, in December 1809, he redeployed the greater part of his army, including the 4th Division, to the north. There he would face Marshal André Masséna, Duke of Rivoli, a rough and unscrupulous old campaigner with a weakness for loot, who was accompanied on campaign by his 18-year-old mistress wearing the tight breeches and pelisse of a hussar. Praised by Buonaparte after Rivoli as '*l'Enfant Chére de la Victoire*,' Masséna was among the most capable of the imperial marshals.

The 40th received their route[282] on the 16th December and marched the following morning, in drenching rain, for Abrantes. At Estremoz, Dr Boutflower was much heartened to receive English newspapers:

'They state ten thousand men being about to embark for this country, which has been confirmed by letters received by different officers. This renders it probable that the defence of this country is certainly to be attempted.'[283]

The 40th reached Abrantes on Christmas Day, crossing the Tagus on a bridge of boats. After a two-day halt, the Regiment set out for Coimbra, which they entered on 3rd January 1810.[284] At Tomar, on 30th December, Boutflower saw Portuguese troops at drill and was greatly impressed:

'Marshal Beresford is at present there. We had an opportunity of seeing one of the regiments at parade, which have been drilled by English officers. They were well clothed and made an excellent appearance. The soldier-like manner in which they went through their evolutions astonished the English officers. I should really expect much of them if opposed to the enemy.'[285]

Leaving Coimbra in fine weather on 5th January, the Regiment's route lay east up the Mondego valley, heading for Celorico, forty miles short of the frontier with Spain. Their march took the 40th through Ponte da Mucela on the River Ava, behind which Wellington had ordered a formidable blocking position of earth redoubts to be entrenched on the Serra da Atalhada. After three days march over miserably poor roads, through inhospitable uplands and between snow-capped hills, the destination of the 40th was altered to Melo, where they halted on 8th January. Ten days later, the Regiment was at last called forward to Celorico, twelve miles further east, only to find their march extended again to Guarda, Portugal's highest town, perched on a bleak hill at 3,465 feet on the northern flank of the Serra da Estrela. Charles Boutflower commented on the 'extremely steep' ascent to Guarda with which the 40th concluded their three-hundred-mile march:

'About halfway up the hill, we found ourselves amongst snow, which, we observed, increased in depth as we advanced to the summit. Here we were enveloped in it. The cold is intense, not less severe than in the northern

---

[282] The Regiment's route from Olivenza to Abrantes was via Juromenha, Vila Viçosa, Estremoz, Cano, Avis (where the whole Regiment was quartered in the Convent) and Ponte do Sor, a distance of about one hundred miles.
[283] Boutflower, p. 28.
[284] The route from Abrantes to Coimbra lay though Punhete, Tomar, Aldea Cruz, Leiria, Pombal and Condeixa, a distance of some ninety miles.
[285] Boutflower, p.30.

parts of England; notwithstanding the inhabitants are not more provided for it within doors than if it did not exist. There is not a fireplace in any of the houses with the exception of the kitchen.'[286]

Cole's 4th Division spent the next eight months stationed in and around Guarda. Early in February, the 40th heard that three hundred reinforcements had embarked from England to join the Battalion. Rumours abounded, and on 2nd February Dr Charles Boutflower, who, like many officers, was still rather doubtful of British success in Portugal, mused on possible future postings:

'Whether affairs are soon brought to a termination or not in this country, there is no prospect of our returning to England, as we shall doubtless be employed on some other service. In the present critical and unsettled state of affairs it is impossible to conjecture where we may next be sent to serve; the Mediterranean, India, or North America, it may be, will prove our destination... The Mediterranean would certainly be the most pleasant, and India the most profitable. With respect to America, I should have no other satisfaction in going there than in the hopes of witnessing the chastisement they so richly deserve for their perfidious treatment of Great Britain, and their unnatural connexion with France.'[287]

On 17th March Charles Boutflower recorded in his diary that the three hundred men from England, 'a very fine detachment,' had recently arrived, and he declared with pride that:

'The 40th may with truth be considered at present the very finest Regiment in the Army. Our strength, including sergeants and drummers is near thirteen hundred men. I feel the responsibility attached to the care of so large a body. The weather is very bad; the rains are incessant and come down in torrents. Notwithstanding, the Army generally is in as good, if not better, health than a force of the same magnitude would be in England.

'This being St. Patrick's Day, I much fear lest the intemperance that will certainly prevail should be the cause of disease to many. The Regimental Bands played through the streets, as is usual on this occasion, commencing at midnight. On hearing it, the inhabitants were with hope, conceiving it could be from no other reason than the arrival of some great news.'[288]

The role of the 4th Division during the long months at Guarda was, together with Picton's 3rd Division further north, to support the outpost line of Craufurd's Light Division, which was soon in contact with the French between the Rivers Agueda and Coa on the frontier with Spain.

Wellington knew that the borders of Portugal could not be defended with the limited forces at his disposal. 'The whole country is frontier,' he wrote, 'and it would be difficult to prevent the enemy from penetrating by some point or other.' He therefore aimed at 'preserving what is most important – the capital,' but he needed to buy as much time as possible for the defences of Lisbon to be prepared. He had pinned his hopes of a protracted forward defence on the resistance of the border fortresses of Ciudad Rodrigo, with its Spanish garrison, and Almeida, which was held by Portuguese troops with a British commander; however, Wellington also appreciated that once these fortresses were besieged by the French he had insufficient strength to relieve them without offering battle at unacceptable odds.

Colonel James Kemmis was still commanding the brigade[289], and in May 1810, Lieutenant-Colonel Charles Amédée Harcourt arrived in Portugal from a staff appointment at the Cape of Good Hope to assume command of the 1st/40th. Harcourt was a Norman, or rather Anglo-Norman, aristocrat who had joined the British Army as a volunteer in 1793 and, having fought with distinction in Flanders in 1793-94 and Holland in 1799, had obtained a half-pay majority in the 40th in 1802 and had been promoted to lieutenant-colonel on the staff in 1804.[290]

---

[286] Ibid, p.35.
[287] Ibid., p.37.
[288] Boutflower, pp. 42-43.
[289] Confirmed by General Orders dated 22nd February 1810.
[290] Charles Amédée Harcourt CB (1771-1831), otherwise known as André Marie Charles François d'Harcourt-Olonde, came from a noble Norman family which had been allied to England during the Hundred Years War and had produced many soldiers including five Marshals of France. In 1793 he joined the British Army in Flanders, and after a year's service as a volunteer he raised a troop in the Prince of Salm's Hussars, a French émigré regiment in British service. In 1794 he was at the battle of Le Cateau, 26th April, and on 10th May he took several cannon from the enemy before Tournai, for which service the Duke of York presented him with a sword. He was

Guarda was known as 'the Siberia of the army.' As late as May, the weather there remained cold and almost constantly wet, with snow still threatened. The rivers down below, swollen with rainwater, remained obstacles to military movement; but already the French were on the move and, as Boutflower recorded in his diary for 2nd June, Wellington prepared for a delaying battle:

'Everything indicates an immediate movement. An order has been issued for each Regiment to be prepared to march at half an hour's notice; every man not entirely fit for service has been sent away, and one day's provisions are kept constantly cooked beforehand. Whether this movement will be forward or backward, to the right or left, we are in profound ignorance. The weather has become fine, and it does not appear probable that an engagement between the two armies can be many days delayed.'[291]

Ciudad Rodrigo capitulated on July 10th after a spirited resistance which, in Boutflower's words, 'excited universal admiration.' Craufurd's light troops were pushed back over the Coa on the 24th, and on August 25th a catastrophic magazine explosion led to the unexpectedly early surrender of the devastated fortress of Almeida three days later. The frontier breached, Marshal Masséna with 65,000 men stood poised to invade Portugal.

Among Wellington's covering troops at this time were the 13th Light Dragoons, and on 22nd August at Laduera, near Fraxedas, a fifty-strong troop of that Regiment, commanded by Captain William White, encountered a patrol of French dragoons, taking two officers and sixty prisoners. Major Charles Albert Vigoureux of the 38th Foot, who would serve with distinction in the 30th from 1813 to 1826, including the Waterloo campaign, took a leading part in this dashing action:

'Major Vigoureux, who was employed in the reconnoitring service, gave Captain White information of the presence of the enemy, and concerted with him the plan of attack. He requested Captain White to mount him, which he did, on one of the largest horses of his troop, and being a very tall and powerful man, his appearance was most formidable. He charged with Captain White at the head of the Thirteenth, and rode with uplifted sabre straight at the French commanding officer who was leading: on their meeting, that officer, instead of defending himself, dropped his sword to the salute, and turning it, presented the hilt to Major Vigoureux.'

Meanwhile, the 40th remained at Guarda, now largely deserted by its inhabitants, and had time for sporting diversions:

'We amuse ourselves in this place chiefly at cricket,' wrote Boutflower on August 9th, 'and from the ground where we play can distinctly see the fire from the garrison of Almeida. From the spirit with which the officers in general enter into this game one would hardly suppose there was an enemy within an hundred leagues of us.'[292]

Following the fall of Almeida, Wellington ordered the 4th Division back from Guarda to São Martinho, to the north of the Serra da Estrela, as part of a general retirement down the valley of the Montego. On 30th August, the 40th Foot marched down from Guarda and were quartered in the village of Faia, from where on 2nd September they made a short march to nearby 'Villa de Porco' [Vila Pouca], but as Boutflower relates, their stay in that village was very short:

'We had just begun to make ourselves comfortable in this latter place when we were directed to proceed as quick as possible to Lenhares [Linhares], intelligence having been received that the enemy had forced our

---

engaged in several more actions and served as ADC to his English relative, Lieutenant-General (later Field Marshal, 3rd Earl) Harcourt prior to the evacuation of Holland, when he remained for two years in Bremen with a board investigating claims against the Army on its march through Allied countries. Meanwhile, on 11th December 1794 he had purchased a British commission and, after serving as ADC to Major-General Don in the Isle of Wight, he was sent with that officer on a secret mission to gain Dutch support prior to the Helder campaign, in which he then took part. On 3rd October 1799, at the head of a party of dragoons, he took possession of Alkmaar and captured a strong picket covering the enemy's retreat, holding the town until relieved. He then accompanied Sir Home Popham on a mission to Russia, served in Malta as ADC to General Fox, in Ireland as Assistant-Quartermaster-General, and, as a half-pay major of the 40th Foot, at the Cape as Deputy-Quartermaster-General before joining the 40th in the Peninsula and assuming command. He was present at Busaco and the first siege of Badajoz, when he was slightly wounded, and at Ciudad Rodrigo and the storming of Badajoz, when he was severely wounded and earned a Gold Medal and CB. Harcourt was promoted to Colonel in 1813 and Major-General in 1819. He obtained British denization in 1816, but on the death of his father in 1820 he became Marquis d'Harcourt and a peer of France. On 14th September 1831 he was thrown from his horse near his home at St. Leonard's Dale, Windsor, and died on the spot.
[291] Boutflower, p.48.
[292] Ibid., p. 53.

dragoons at Alverca, and that they were only two leagues and a half [about seven and a half miles] from us on our flank. It was nearly dark when we marched. Our road lay across the mountains through a road nearly impassable. The night being dark rendered the march a most fatiguing one. It was nearly four in the morning when we reached Lenhares, pretty well tired. On our arrival there, we found an order to proceed again at five to Santa Marinha [near to São Martinho]. The day being very hot, the men were generally quite knocked up by the time they reached their quarters.'[293]

The Battle of Busaco, 27th September 1810

It was not until the evening of the 15th, the day that Masséna began his advance from Almeida and entered Guarda, that the 40th received orders to resume their march the following morning at daybreak. Wellington had ordered his army to withdraw to his prepared position behind the Alva, at Ponte da Mucela, where he proposed to fight a delaying action on the main road to Coimbra, south of the River Mondego. To his surprise, though, Masséna chose to advance by a longer and more difficult route, to the north of the Mondego, through Viseu and Busaco (Bucaço). 'There are certainly many bad roads in Portugal,' wrote Wellington, 'but the enemy has taken decidedly the worst in the whole kingdom.' On the 17th, Masséna's intentions became clear to Wellington, who redeployed his army across the Mondego to occupy another strong natural position which he had previously surveyed. This was on the ten-mile-long Busaço ridge, about eight miles north-east of Coimbra.

For his troops, including the 40th, this change of plan brought some confusion and more long marches over poor roads to the new concentration area. The 40th were on the move at daybreak on September 16th, marching till dark to Galizes, on the road to Ponte da Mucela; but next morning new march routes were issued and, 'after a great deal of order, counter order and disorder,' the Regiment reached Villa Cova about noon. 'Whatever are the present movements of the enemy,' wrote Charles Boutflower that day, 'the Army is kept in entire ignorance of them; but from the short time we are now allowed to halt we conclude they are advancing upon us.'

At dawn on the 18th the 40th started on a long day's march to Paradela, and on the 19th they crossed the Alva at Ponte da Mucela, 'where our grand stand was to have been made,' and halted for the night at the village of San Miguel, about a mile out of the highroad to Coimbra. Speculation was rife as to where Wellington might seek battle, but there was general surprise on the 20th September when the 4th Division marched north and the 40th forded the Mondego at Barca de Conselto. As Dr Boutflower noted:

'The crossing of the River excited a good deal of astonishment throughout the Army, as it was generally supposed that our position would be immediately in the vicinity of Coimbra. Our halt that night was at Penna Cova [Penacova], where we found very good accommodation, and from the circumstance of our advancing towards the enemy the inhabitants were more civil than we had experienced from them while we were retrograding.

'Yesterday morning [21st September] we again commenced our route and marched several leagues thro' crossroads till we reached the high road leading from Coimbra to Vizeu. We halted at a most miserable village called Sula, where we could with difficulty procure covering even for the officers, the men being obliged to go into huts. Here we still remain, and are likely to do so till the enemy come on us, our positions being all round this neighbourhood. Nothing in appearance can be stronger than the country about here… Lord Wellington's Head Quarters are near this place, at a celebrated Convent called Busaco… Lord W. is constantly on horseback reconnoitring, and if we may judge from his countenance and spirits he anticipates a complete triumph over the enemy.'[294]

Having concentrated his divisions to cover the Vizeu-Coimbra road, Wellington was certainly in a buoyant mood and wrote from Busaço Convent on the 22nd, 'We have an excellent position here, in which I am strongly tempted to give battle.' On the 24th, Boutflower resumed his narrative:

---

[293] Boutflower, p.p. 55-6.
[294] Ibid., p.p. 57-59.

'We still remain at Sula, but are in constant expectation of an order to change our ground a little more to the left. There was smart skirmishing yesterday, a few miles to our front. The firing was very loud and distinct. Last night, the whole of the cavalry retired to our rear. The Light Division continue in advance. If hardly pressed, they will fall back upon us, and the action is then likely to become general. All has been quiet hitherto this day, and it is now past noon.'[295]

Next day, the 25th, the whole army, 26,843 British[296] and 25,429 Portuguese, took up its position on the famed Busaco ridge. The 4th Division was on the extreme left (north) of Wellington's line, with Kemmis' brigade on the left of the division, but with the exception of the partial engagement of some of its light companies the division was not actively engaged when Masséna attacked on 27th September, and indeed suffered no loss. From their vantage point on the high ridge-top, though, the 40th had a very extensive grandstand view of the French encampment and the battle, as described by Charles Boutflower:

'On the morning of the 26th there was a thick fog, which at length cleared up, and displayed to each other the rival armies drawn up on opposite hills. A valley between of considerable breadth separated them: their numbers appeared most formidable, but the eagerness evinced by our troops to receive their attack may have been equalled but can never have been surpassed. The morning passed with only now and then a random shot. They were evidently unprepared. In the afternoon, the skirmishing between the light troops became brisk; it ceased at dusk without much loss on either side. General officers were observed busily reconnoitring our position, and the expectation of an attack the following morning was universal.

'Our ideas were well founded; at dawn of day, the enemy made a most furious assault upon our right and centre. All remained quiet on the left, in which was our Division. We were consequently spectators, and a most gratifying view we had of the whole affair. Lord W[ellington] had directed the troops to suffer the enemy to come within a short distance of the top of the hill, when they were to give them a deliberate volley and charge. This we distinctly observed. They were almost instantly thrown into the greatest confusion, and fled precipitately. This action lasted but a short time, and skirmishes concluded the day. It was a subject of universal regret that they did not make a general attack upon us. From the nature of our position, and the valour of our troops, there is little doubt but their army would have been nearly annihilated.'

'Having failed in their attempts on our right and centre, we were in hopes they would the next morning (28th) endeavour to force our left. In this however, we were deceived. All remained tranquil, with the exception of skirmishing between the sharp shooters. They did not appear so numerous this day as before, and in the afternoon we observed their cavalry in motion & moving to the rear.'[297]

Wellington's losses at Busaco amounted to 200 killed, 1,001 wounded and 51 missing, of which the totals of British and Portuguese casualties were, remarkably, identical at 626 each. French losses totalled some 4,479 killed, wounded and missing.

Although the 40th received no 'Busaco' Battle Honour, a distinction which was only awarded to the regiments on whom the main French attack fell, 101 officers and men lived to receive a 'Busaco' clasp to their Military General Service Medals. The only regimental casualty was Captain George Preston, who was slightly wounded whilst serving as ADC to Sir Brent Spencer.[298]

Lieutenant-Colonel William Williams, late 40th and 81st, who commanded the 5th/60th, was slightly wounded, as was Captain Edmund Keynton Williams of the 81st Foot, who was 'Noticed in General Orders' as Major of the 4th Caçadores in Pack's 1st Independent Portuguese Brigade.[299] This brigade was posted on the left

---

[295] Ibid., p. 59.

[296] The 40th, with 42 officers and 1,007 men, was easily the strongest of Wellington's British Regiments at Busaco.

[297] Boutflower, p.p. 60-61.

[298] Captain Robert Francis Melville Browne of the 40th was another of Spencer's ADCs June 1810-July 1811.

[299] Major-General Sir Edmund Keynton Williams KCB KTS (1781-1850) served 1803-22 in the 81st Foot including the battle of Maida, the occupation of Sicily and capture of Ischia. His first commission in 1799, aged 17, was in the 4th King's Own, with whom he saw service in Holland under the Duke of York (wounded). Captain Williams served with the Portuguese 4th Caçadores 1810-14 as Major and Lieutenant-Colonel, and distinguishing himself on several more occasions. He was present at Badajoz in 1811, Salamanca (twice wounded) and Burgos in 1812, Vitoria, Tolosa, San Sebastian (wounded), Bidassoa, Nivelle and Bayonne (wounded) in 1813. For his

centre of Wellington's line between Spencer's 1st Division and Cole's 4th Division, and was highly praised for their defeat of Maucune's brigade of Marchand's division, an action in which the whole of the 4th Caçadores were sent forward as skirmishers. It was probably this engagement, which occurred on a hillside in full view of the 4th Division, that prompted Charles Boutflower's enthusiastic encomium:

'Gratifying as was the result of this battle, it was more particularly so from the great gallantry evinced by our Allies the Portuguese. It was true much had been expected from them by many, but there was a possibility of their failing in the hour of trial. Such however, was their conduct during the action (and they were very much engaged) that they gained the entire admiration of the whole British Army.'[300]

Private William Lawrence of the Grenadier Company, 40th Foot had another reason for recalling Busaço Ridge with pleasure:

'Whilst strolling one day on these heights I caught a fine cock, which I tamed by tying him to my knapsack by the leg and carrying him about with me, much to the amusement of my comrades; for after I had had him about a fortnight he became so tame that he would sit on my knapsack quite quietly, without even the string to his leg. We named him Tom, and I took to carrying him about everywhere, even on the battlefield.'[301]

The Lines of Torres Vedras, October 1810-March 1811

Having failed with heavy loss to force Busaço Ridge, Masséna at length discovered a track by which he could outflank the ridge to the north, and in the early hours of the 29th Wellington ordered a withdrawal towards his prepared positions in front of Lisbon. That night, the 40th halted short of Coimbra, which they passed through on the 30th. Next day saw a cavalry skirmish in front of Coimbra, which was then abandoned and, as Boutflower recorded, 'a large part of our Army commenced its march this day towards Lisbon, and it became pretty generally known that no further opposition would be made to the progress of the enemy till we should reach our lines in the neighbourhood of the capital.'

In addition to the Lines of Torres Vedras, the other key aspect of Wellington's strategy became very apparent to his withdrawing troops – scorched earth. The Portuguese government had reluctantly acquiesced in the devastation of great tracts of their country in order to deny food and shelter to Masséna's advancing soldiers, and this policy was ruthlessly enforced, including civilian evacuation of areas on the French line of march, which were stripped almost bare of provisions. Charles Boutflower described the march of the 40th Foot on 1st October:

'At noon, we received a sudden order to march two leagues on the high road leading to Lisbon. The enemy evinced every disposition to press our rear, and we expected to be engaged in the course of the afternoon. To describe the confusion of this day is utterly impossible. The road was so thronged with fugitives that it was with the utmost difficulty we reached our destination before sunset. On passing through Condixe [Condeixa], a considerable town, I observed Lord W[ellington] at a window evidently affected at the scenes of distress which were passing. It had never been apprehended that the enemy would advance so rapidly, and therefore a great proportion of the inhabitants had not left their houses. In one mixed scene of confusion and misery were seen the old, the lame, and the blind, all hastening away as fast as their infirmities would allow, and all alike insensible to the blessings of French protection which so immediately they might have enjoyed. We passed the night in an olive grove near the roadside, and could distinctly hear through the whole of it the noise occasioned by the fugitives.'[302]

Private William Lawrence, too, witnessed scenes of panic as thousands of the civilian population fled with the French close on their heels:

services in the Peninsula he was awarded the Gold Cross and one Clasp, made Commander of the Bath and, by the Portuguese, Knight of the Tower and Sword. He became a Brevet Lieutenant-Colonel 21st June 1813 and Regimental Major 4th King's Own in 1822. In 1827 he became Lieutenant-Colonel of the 41st Foot, and it was at his request that in 1831 the King approved the re-titling of that Regiment as 'The 41st or The Welch Regiment.' He became a Major-General in 1841 and Colonel of the 80th Foot in 1848.

[300] Boutflower, p.p. 60-61.
[301] Lawrence, p. 65.
[302] Boutflower, p. 62.

'I never before or since saw such a wholesale move as this was, for every one seemed anxious to carry as many of his effects as he could find room for. The further we proceeded the more confused our retreat appeared, for multitudes were obliged to rest weary and exhausted by the roadside, and often, though made eager in their endeavours, as they heard of the enemy's approach, to renew their tedious journey, were found dying or even dead from their hard exertions, and the road was everywhere strewn with pieces of all kinds of furniture, which the fugitives had vainly attempted to get forward.'

'On the march we passed a nunnery, where we halted for about a quarter of an hour. A great many of the nuns were crowding the balconies to watch us, and as the French were following us up pretty close, the Colonel [Harcourt] ordered the doors to be broken open by a party of grenadiers, which was soon done, myself being among the number told off for the purpose. This was not carried out, however, without an accident, for one of the women fell from a balcony, owing to the crowded state in which they were packed on it. The poor women seemed very glad to get their liberty, for they came out as thick as a flock of sheep, and a great many of them soon passed us bound for Lisbon, being fearful of consequences if they took any other direction, as the French were after us so near as to skirmish with our rear-guard.' [303]

On 2nd October the 40th marched 25 miles to Pombal in an oppressive heat, accompanied by swarms of refugees, and on the 3rd they passed through the deserted town of Leiria. They marched again on the 5th, and over the next four days halted successively near Cavalho, near Rio Major, at Abrigada and some three miles short of Sobral de Monte Agraço. Cavalry skirmishes continued between the British rearguard and Masséna's vanguard, which by the 5th had some knowledge of the existence, if not the formidable nature and extent, of the Lines to their front. Charles Boutflower spoke that day to some of the French prisoners:

'They were perfectly aware of our retiring to a strong position, but remarked, whatever might be the strength of it Massena had no alternative but must of necessity attack us. They allowed the possibility of his failure, and accompanied it with a shrug more significant than could have been expressed in any language. They admitted that since entering Portugal, they had scarcely seen an inhabitant, which was of course productive of much distress to their army. It is said that Massena wrote to Lord Wellington remonstrating on the order he had given to the people to quit their homes on the approach of the enemy; to which his Lordship merely replied that "He regretted extremely his Excellency suffered any personal inconvenience from it."' [304]

On 8th October, as Wellington's divisions approached the Lines of Torres Vedras, the weather broke:

'Yesterday,' wrote Boutflower next morning, 'I consider as the most uncomfortable day of my life without any exception. We commenced our march [from Abrigada] at daybreak, having to go to Sobral, a distance of about three leagues. It blew and rained with the most dreadful violence, and in a very short time rendered the roads nearly impassable. Unfortunately we had a brigade of Portuguese in our front, who, unused to march in such fearful weather, could with difficulty be persuaded to face the pitiless pelting of the storm. Such was our delay in consequence that at the end of thirteen hours we found ourselves still a league from our destination. Most fortunately an order arrived for us to take up our abode for the night in villages near us, where by means of large fires, we succeeded in making ourselves tolerably comfortable.' [305]

On the morning of 10th October, the 40th passed through the small town of Sobral, held by outlying detachments of Sir Brent Spencer's 1st Division, and occupied a village some two miles from that place. The Regiment now formed part of the outpost line of the Lines of Torres Vedras.

It had been nearly a year since Wellington had ordered the construction of the Lines, blocking the approaches to Lisbon, and although incomplete, they were now a formidable defensive complex and an almost impenetrable refuge for Wellington's field army. The term 'Lines' is misleading, for the fortification was far from linear and the Duke's concept of operations, far from passive, was of manoeuvre by the mass of his field force divisions around a strong defensive framework designed by by his Chief Engineer, Lieutenant-Colonel Richard Fletcher.

---

[303] Lawrence, p.p. 68-69.
[304] Boutflower, p. 63.
[305] Ibid., p. 64.

Taking advantage of the steep hills, ridges and valleys across the peninsula on which Lisbon stands, the Lines comprised two chains of mutually supporting redoubts some 15-25 miles north of the capital, stretching from the Atlantic to the Tagus along the commanding heights of two ranges of hills. There was also, as an insurance against disaster, a smaller final line west of Lisbon to cover embarkation. Most of the 126 redoubts completed by October 1810 were small closed earthworks, faced with stone, holding 3-6 guns and 200-300 men, but a few, notably Fort São Vicente at Torres Vedras and the Great Redoubt on Monte Agraça, were in effect fortified camps. The redoubts were sited on high ground to cover obstacles which spanned a wide range of engineering artifice. Rivers and streams were dammed to inundate the valleys, sections of hillside were dug or blasted away to make steep scarps, while ravines and gullies were blocked by entanglements. The approaches to the redoubts, each defended by a dry ditch and counterscarp, were obstructed with abbatis, *cheveaux de frise* and *trous de loup*, while their fields of fire were comprehensively cleared of cover and converted into glacis. Remarkably, all this was accomplished by Portuguese militiamen and labourers, under the direction of Wellington's engineers, without word of it reaching the French.

The redoubts and other fixed defences were largely garrisoned by Portuguese Militia, Ordenança and gunners, some 29,750 men manning 247 artillery pieces, leaving Wellington's field army of 35,000 British, 24,500 Portuguese and 8,000 Spanish troops free to manoeuvre and counter any threatened French incursions. The field army also provided an outpost line, and indeed, the only fighting involved the outlying troops around Sobral. The seaward and estuarine flanks of the Lines were protected by the Royal Navy, who additionally provided rapid communication of orders and intelligence across the frontage of 29 miles through semaphore stations sited on the highest ground.

Wellington had originally intended the First, or outer Line, as a delaying position, but by the time he fell back into the Lines in October, work there was sufficiently far advanced for him to make it his main line of defence, massing his field force divisions on the most likely lines of approach. Of these, the most vulnerable was from Sobral south through the Zibreira valley to Pero Negro, where Wellington's headquarters lay, and on to the centre of the Second Line at Montachique. The defences in this sector were not fully completed.

On October 11th Montbrun's cavalry approached Sobral, which was occupied by outposts of Spencer's 1st Division. Spencer prematurely evacuated his advanced positions in the town and was ordered to reoccupy them, which he did with Cole's 4th Division, including the 40th, in support:

'On the evening of the 11th,' wrote Boutflower, 'it was intended that General Spencer's Division should attack the enemy who had possession of Sobral, and our Division was in consequence ordered out on the road leading to that place to support them in case of necessity. The night was dreadful. After remaining upwards of an hour we were directed to return to our cantonments, the French having retired from Sobral.'

By the following afternoon, the French force in front of Sobral had grown and was conducting widespread reconnaissance. On the afternoon of the 12th Junot's 8th Corps appeared at Sobral, pushing Spencer's piquets back some three hundred yards. Having identified this as the main threat, Wellington concentrated four British divisions, the 1st, 3rd, 4th and 6th, in that sector, with the 5th and a Portuguese division in reserve. On the 13th Junot extended his troops to his right, west of Sobral, where they encountered the piquets of Cole's 4th Division. Several hours of sharp skirmishing ensued near Dois Portos before Cole drew back his outpost line towards the higher ground on which stood the Portella (No. 150) and Patameira (No. 151) field artillery redoubts. Writing next day, Charles Boutflower gave some account of his Regiment's part in this affair:

'Yesterday morning broke upon us in thunder and clouds and storms; notwithstanding, we were ordered to remain under arms. Fortunately, about eight, when we received our orders to march, the weather had cleared considerably. We ascended some hills behind the village we had occupied, where we remained till the afternoon, when we were again put under cover... The skirmishing between the picquets was considerable, and the first Fortieth blood was drawn in the afternoon, one man on picquet being severely wounded.'[306]

---

[306] Boutflower, p.p. 65-66.

The only attempt by Masséna to feel the strength of the Lines was made on the 14th when a limited probe by Junot's corps was easily countered. Masséna, who witnessed the action, and the frowning redoubts on Monte Agraça and the Portella heights, was forced with dismay to conclude that a successful assault on the Lines was unlikely without reinforcement, and reported to his Emperor that 'The Marshal Prince of Essling has come to the conclusion that he would compromise the army of His Majesty if he were to attack in force lines so formidable defended by 30,000 English and 30,000 Portuguese, aided by 50,000 armed peasants.' There was no further attempt by the French to break into the Lines, but Masséna was proud and obstinate, and he shrank from withdrawal and acceptance of defeat. Bereft of ideas, he sat his increasingly starving and sickly army down in front of the Lines and sent to Napoleon for advice and reinforcements. Insignificant in themselves, the skirmishes around Sobral had proved to be a turning point of the campaign, and of the Peninsula War.[307]

The 40th settled into the village of Patameira, from where they took their turn in the outpost line of the 4th Division. Private William Lawrence of the Grenadier Company contrasted their comfort with the privations of Masséna's men:

'Our Regiment was situated in a village called Patamara, in the front of our works, where we lay as comfortably as if we had been living in peaceful times; though we were so near the enemy that we very often wandered into the same vineyards, and exchanged compliments by shaking hands.'[308]

Writing up his journal on the 21st, Charles Boutflower confirmed the easygoing relationship between the adversaries:

'Scarcely a single shot has been fired since the last date [18th October]. Our advanced posts and those of the enemy are within three hundred yards of each other. It was for several days the practice of the men of both armies to meet in the same vineyards in the valleys, and even to talk and shake hands with each other. This has, however, very properly been put a stop to, it being very justly considered that the simplicity of our fellows was no match for the cunning of a Frenchman.'[309]

There was at this time a bizarre incident on the 4th Division front, occasioning much amusement. It happened that a bullock, destined for slaughter, escaped from the French lines to the British, where it was at once shot and skinned. That evening, a French bugle sounded and, under a flag of truce, an exchange of animal prisoners was proposed. A French sergeant led forward General Cole's dog, Dash, who had been lost during the withdrawal from Guarda. In response, Cole had to admit that the bullock had been killed and divided, but as a gesture of thanks, he sent a portion to the French general.

William Lawrence and his comrades were up to their usual tricks. The Grenadiers were quartered in a large cellar where they discovered and expropriated, the Portuguese owner's hidden hoard of money. The outraged owner complained to Lieutenant-Colonel Harcourt, but since Lawrence, who had by then a fair grasp of Portuguese, acted as interpreter, much was lost in translation, and neither a search nor Major Archdall's financial inducements to supposedly susceptible soldiers succeeded in parting the wily Grenadiers from their ill-gotten gains, which they had concealed in a pile of pumpkins.

Wellington's army had by then been reinforced, and among the arrivals were the 2nd/30th and their old friends the 2nd/44th, who disembarked at Belem from Cadiz on the afternoon of the 6th October. The previous day, they had taken aboard a pilot, who brought news of Wellington's victory at Busaço. The 30th marched to the Castle of St. George in Lisbon, familiar from their stay in 1809.

On October 10th they set out in very wet weather to join the field army, halting for two days and nights at Montachique, where the men occupied a flooded barn while the officers slept on the floor of a large house wrapped in their boat cloaks. On the 12th the 30th joined Lieutenant-General James Leith's newly-formed 5th Division at Enxara dos Cavaleiros. The 30th and 44th were allocated to the second brigade, which was completed on 8th

---

[307] Sir Charles Oman went even further, stating that 'The high-water mark of French conquest in Europe was reached on the knoll by Sobral on the wet and gusty 14th of October, 1810.'

[308] Lawrence, p.p. 70-71. Charles Boutflower was less satisfied with the accommodation at Patameira, complaining that: 'The place we are in is most wretched, and furnishes no one species of comfort. Scarcely a house in the whole village is weatherproof.'

[309] Boutflower, p. 67.

November by the arrival of the 1st/4th King's Own. Major-General James Dunlop, formerly lieutenant-colonel of the 59th, had been appointed to command this brigade, but he did not arrive and assume command until 11th November, and meanwhile, Lieutenant-Colonel Minet of the 30th was in charge. The 5th Division further comprised Hay's first brigade (3rd/1st, 1st/9th and 2nd/38th Regiments) and Spry's Portuguese brigade (3rd and 15th Portuguese Line).

Soon after the 30th joined the field army, they had 25 officers and 611 rank and file present and effective, with 31 sick left in Cadiz and three officers and 52 rank and file sick in Lisbon. Ensign Robert Daniel, the former battalion quartermaster-sergeant, had remained in Cadiz with the heavy baggage, while Minet had also left two drummers and eleven boys in Lisbon.

With Masséna probing the Lines of Torres Vedras, on 13th October Lieutenant and Adjutant William Stewart of the 30th was warned for an early move forward from the regimental quarters at Enxara do Bispo in anticipation of an attack:

'A sudden route [was received] in the night to send our baggage to the rear, & we marched at daylight for Enxaro dos Cavalieros, the other brigades of our division having previously moved forward from thence. This day it rained heavier than I had witnessed in Portugal, yet as an attack was expected to take place, we were kept under arms most part of the forenoon & at length quartered in the deserted houses & allowed to cook our rations. My ass having turned sulky, I had no mode of conveying my luggage, [and] I was therefore obliged to leave a mattress, [bolster] & many other articles at Enxara do Bispo as fair plunder for the first lucky visitor. Being completely worn for want of rest & with fatigue to which I was more exposed as an Adj[utant] than any other officer in the Regt, I lay down in a miserable wash house amongst some dirty straw at my horse's head & in my wet clothes enjoyed two hours of the sweetest sleep I had ever experienced. No sumptuous bed had ever afforded me such comfort.'

By 16th October the 30th were encamped behind the Great Redoubt of Monte Agraça, 'on the reverse of the heights directly in rear of that work.'

Living conditions under canvas were wet and miserable. According to Ensign Nevill of the 30th, they were occupied in 'strengthening those lines and the usual exercise and drill of regiments.' Andrew Leith Hay, Aide-de-Camp to his uncle General Leith, has left an account of daily routine in the Lines at that time:

'During the period of the French army continuing in the immediate front of the lines, the Allies were invariably under arms every morning long before daybreak. Frequently in the course of the first ten days, dense fogs prevailed, rendering objects at any distance imperceptible until the mist dispelled, which it usually did, gradually, after sunrise. On these occasions Lord Wellington remained in the redoubt of Monte Agraça, receiving the reports of the night, by sound alone able to judge whether the enemy was moving in advance. The few musketry shots sometimes heard early in the morning, proceeding from the French picquets feeling their way in the mist, occasioned some degree of anxiety to ascertain whether the firing continued, or assumed a more serious noise. This never was the case; nor was there the slightest attempt made to assail any of the works, or an endeavour to penetrate the line... Deserters arrived daily from the enemy's alignment, reporting the distress and scarcity which therein prevailed; and it being evident that the Prince of Essling would not attack the allies, the period of his departure became the only matter of speculation.'[310]

On the night of 4th November, Sergeant Charles Watson, a long-serving NCO of the 30th, was murdered while drinking with some Portuguese in the Great Redoubt. As a result of this crime, a sergeant's party was sent out every day to send British soldiers home from the drinking booths by sunset.

On 10th November, Masséna accepted the inevitable and issued orders for a retirement towards Santarem on the Tagus. There, entrenched in a strong defensive position. He hoped to feed his army and maintain his forward posture in Portugal until reinforced. Having suffered great hardships through hunger, cold and rain, the French abandoned their hutted encampments in front of the Lines and successfully broke contact on the foggy night of the 14th/15th November. Indications of their imminent departure were noted by the picquets of the 40th Foot:

[310] Leith Hay, Volume 1, p.p. 265-6.

'On the evening of the 14th we observed that the enemy made larger fires than usual, which gave reason to believe they were about retreating. Our ideas were well founded, as on the morning of the 15th when day broke not one of them was to be seen.'[311]

Captain Bamford and Lieutenant Stewart of the 30th rode out on the evening of the 14th towards the front of the British lines and saw the Enemy retire their videttes and advanced sentries 'in high style and at full gallop.'

Wellington followed the retiring French with three divisions, leaving the remaining four, including those of Cole and Leith, to guard the Lines until he was sure of Masséna's ultimate intention. On the 18th, however, mistakenly concluding that the French were making a further withdrawal, leaving only a rearguard at Santarem, Wellington called up the 4th and 5th Divisions.

The 5th Division had already moved forward to the deserted town of Sobral on the 16th, marching at such short notice that the 30th left their tents standing. Leith Hay remarked on the weather, which had become 'more than usually boisterous and inclement; the rain fell incessantly, rendering the roads, already injured by the passage of the enemy's army, rough, deep, and all but impracticable.' Around the billets of the 30th that night, William Stewart saw ample evidence of the terrible fate of so many of Masséna's men:

'The doors and windows were surrounded with dead bodies, not buried more than a few inches under the ground. The enemy must have lost great numbers in this place, as every garden contained heaps of their dead and even amongst the rubbish in the houses many unfortunate wretches were found by our soldiers in the same state.'

On 17th November the 30th marched the short distance to a small, pleasantly situated village called Eiras, and on the morning of the 18th they continued in heavy rain over bad roads to Alenquer, Masséna's former headquarters, which had been vandalised by his retreating soldiers.[312] William Stewart was disgusted at the 'horrid sights' on their line of march:

'Bodies of men, horses, asses, mules, bullocks, etc lay so thickly strewed along the road as really even this cold day to contaminate in a high degree the air we breathed.'

Next day, the 5th Division marched on through the ruined town of Azambuja to reach Cartaxo that evening, passing hundreds of French prisoners in a state of exhaustion. Cartaxo too was covered with the muddy debris of Masséna's army: 'The dirty streets were everywhere up nearly to your knee,' wrote William Stewart, 'and, here and there, stacked up with dead horses as well as several houses with dead and dying soldiers left by the enemy.'

Wellington was still intent on turning Masséna out of his position, some nine miles to the north. As Adjutant of the 30th, Stewart was preparing orders until the early hours, and at daybreak on 20th November the 5th Division marched out towards Santarem. Leith Hay described the situation:

'The town of Santarem is encircled by plains, through which the River Mayor, and other minor streams, flow into the Tagus. To the south, the town is elevated on ground rising precipitously from the Tagus; in all other directions it is alone approached through morasses, rendered additionally difficult by the overflowing of the rivulets intersecting them.

'The route from Cartaxo crosses the River Mayor near to Santarem, the bridge being approached in either direction by a walled causeway leading through the swampy ground upon its banks, elevated several feet above the level of the plain, and 400 toises' [a French *toise* equalled 6.39 feet or 1.95 metres] 'in length. Behind a strong abattis, formed of large trees placed across the road, was stationed the advanced post of [Reynier's] Second Corps; a rising ground, close to the extremity of the causeway on the Santarem side, was armed with artillery, commanding its whole extent; the approach to the position was further defended by intrenchments, and trees cut down, rendering it extremely difficult of access.'[313]

Wellington's plan was for Hay's brigade of the 5th Division, with Pack's Portuguese brigade, to ford the River Mayor above the town and turn the enemy's right while Craufurd's Light Division attempted to cross the

---

[311] Boutflower, p. 70.

[312] Beneath a French notice announcing that this was the headquarters of Masséna, a British officer could not resist immediately adding *'Qui a fait plus de bruit au battant la caisse qu'en battant les Anglais'*, a reference to the Marshal's supposed military debut as a drummer. Boutflower p.p. 71-72.

[313] Leith Hay, Volume 1, p. 272.

swamp near the Tagus. Spencer's 1st Division and Dunlop's and Spry's brigades of the 5th Division were to advance in column along the causeway and charge the centre of the French once it was clear that these flank attacks were making good progress.

'Before daybreak,' wrote Leith Hay, 'we marched to carry into execution these movements. It had rained constantly during the night; the roads were deep to a degree. As the divisions approached the high ground on the right bank of the River Mayor, the weather improved, the rain ceased to be violent. The troops halted on the eminence domineering the western extremity of the causeway, from whence every preparation for defence made by the enemy was clearly discernible.'[314]

There they remained in anxious suspense, expecting at any moment to hear the brigades on their left engaged. Reynier was alarmed as the Allied threat to his flanks became apparent, but he had no need for concern: the rain had improved the water obstacles to his front and his attackers had neither pontoons nor bridging materials. Wellington was obliged to call off his attack. The 30th returned to Cartaxo with the rest of the 5th Division.

After his aborted attack of 20th November, Wellington decided to take no further offensive action, but to let famine continue to weaken the French until Masséna was forced into a further disastrous retreat. Accordingly, he ordered most of his army back into winter quarters.

The 5th Division marched south-west from Cartaxo on the morning of the 23rd, halting that night at Aveiras de Baixa before moving on to Alcoentre, where they remained for the next three weeks. Then on 18th December the Division was ordered back to Torres Vedras, according to William Stewart, 'in consequence of sickness so prevalent in the Division.' They marched in the usual downpour, and on 20th December reached the town of Torres Vedras, where they found 'tolerably comfortable quarters.'

The largely inexperienced officers and men of the 2nd/30th clearly still had campaigning skills to master, for twice during the recent manoeuvring their brigade commander, Dunlop, had occasion to lecture them, on timely preparation of rations and on correct conduct when in contact with the enemy. This is hardly surprising, for only three of the officers with the Battalion in November 2010, Majors Hamilton and Grey and Captain Lynch, had seen serious campaign service, and but for a few veterans of Egypt, the NCOs and rank and file were equally ignorant of practical field soldiering.

The 30th was also suffering from exposure to the winter weather, a further indication of inexperience, not helped perhaps by Colonel Minet's decision not to draw sufficient blankets for an individual issue to his men on the grounds that it would overburden them. The sick returns peaked in December at nine officers and 160 other ranks sick in Lisbon and one officer and 31 other ranks sick present with the Battalion.

The 4th Division had followed the 5th Division on 18th November. According to Boutflower, the 40th marched from Patameira on the morning of the 19th, reaching Alenquer that evening and halting on the 20th at Azambuja and nearby villages, where the 40th were quartered for the next three and a half months.

Whilst there the 40th were paid their prize money for South America, and Private William Lawrence, who received eight dollars, appreciated the irony that this was 'money taken from the very people we were now allied with, so that a great part of it was spent amongst them again,' remarking that 'the Lisbon traders must have got scent of this, for a quantity of boats laden with little requisites ascended the river from Lisbon to trade amongst the soldiers, and so we were soon enabled to rid ourselves of our little spare cash. Our Colonel was very considerate to these people, and being determined as far as possible to prevent all plunder, had their boats or stalls guarded by sentries.'[315]

The 30th, meanwhile, passed the winter months around Torres Vedras, where the 5th Division occupied Fort São Vicente.[316] William Stewart tells of how, apart from training, the officers passed the winter in country walks, game shooting and entertaining, with occasional leave visits to Lisbon. There were even athletic contests,

---

[314] Ibid., p. 273-4.
[315] Lawrence, p. 76.
[316] The fort of São Vicente de Torres Vedras crowns the highest hill in the area and was a major fortification of the Lines, mounting 39 guns and able to hold up to four thousand troops.

and a considerable sum was won by Captain Richard Machell in a leaping match with Lieutenant Boyd of the 4th Regiment. The social round sometimes led to hard drinking, and Stewart records how, after a dinner on 4th January, Major Hamilton 'had a bad fall down his own stairs in consequence of inebriation,' and a visiting colonel was almost lost down a drain on his way home. He also tells of a day's sporting and sightseeing jaunt on 27th February:

'Captains B[amford] & H[itchen] & myself went out fowling & kill'd a couple of cocks. We visited the Queen's palace & gardens to the north of Torres Vedras. This palace is much inferior to Runa, but the gardens and fountains are well worth seeing.'

'My companions noted me conductor for the remainder of the day's excursion, & on this occasion I assumed to myself a thorough knowledge of the country! Having conducted them thro' roads, over mountains, & across villages until I began to tire, I was at length obliged to confess that my topographical abilities were not quite so perfect as I had supposed them to have been!! In some degree, however, Captain B[amford] & I were excused by the reflection that Captain H[itchen] was on this occasion amply repaid for having taken us a much more unpleasant walk on a former occasion by way of showing us game. It was evident he made a 'game' of us. Captain H[itchen] dined with us, & having by the assistance of a little wine & a glass of grogg nearly got the better of his fatigues, he amused us with many pleasant & laughable stories relative to his scenes with excise officers when he was a wine merchant, as also of a new mode of duck shooting struck out by himself thro' the means of a cannon!!!'

As the months passed, Masséna's half-starved army grew progressively weaker and began to lose heart while Wellington's amply-provisioned men received reinforcements. The Anglo-Portuguese army was, however, depleted by sickness, with over five thousand men in hospital and almost another thousand sick with their units.[317] On March 1st, Surgeon Charles Boutflower opined to his journal that:

'It appears impossible that the enemy can remain long in their present position: there are the most unquestionable proofs of them at present undergoing the severest privations, and two French officers who passed through this place prisoners a few days since unequivocally stated that the French Army was too weak to hazard the attempt of forcing the Lines. Indeed, they avowed their opinion that Portugal would not be conquered, now or at any other time.'[318]

Wellington, ever conscious of his need to avoid unnecessary casualties, was more than content for his adversary's force to decline as his own grew:

'It is wonderful that they have been able to remain in the country so long, and it is scarcely possible that they can remain much longer. If they go, and when they go, their losses will be very great, and mine nothing. If they stay, they must continue to lose men daily, as they do now.'[319]

The Battle of Barrosa, 5th March 1811

In January 1811, Marshal Soult reduced the French army besieging, or rather blockading, Cadiz to some nineteen thousand men, leaving Victor with the difficult task of maintaining the siege and securing his rear with a force inferior to the Allied garrison of twenty thousand Spanish and nearly six thousand British troops. This weakening of the French position was not lost on the defenders of Cadiz, who planned a major sortie to raise the siege.

The Allied plan was to mount a sea-borne descent in strength, sailing from Cadiz to Tarifa, from where an Anglo-Spanish army would advance north to attack the rear of Victor's army while a smaller force of Spaniards under Major-General Zayas was to cross from the Isla de Leon. The intent was to draw Victor out from his lines and bring him to battle, enabling the Cadiz garrison to make a grand sortie to destroy the French siege works.

---

[317] On 15th February the 30th had 30 officers, 33 sergeants, 19 drummers and 553 rank and file present and fit for duty, with five sergeants, two drummers and 134 rank and file sick. The 40th had 28 officer, 34 sergeants, 18 drummers and 582 rank and file present and fit for duty, with four sergeants, two drummers and 112 rank and file sick.
[318] Boutflower, p. 76.
[319] Wellington's Supplementary Dispatches, Volume VII, p. 1.

6,800 Spanish troops were found for this expedition, commanded by General Manuel La Peña, the senior Spanish officer on the Isla de Leon. Lieutenant-General Thomas Graham provided some four thousand men, all the British troops in Cadiz except the battalion companies of the 47th, and Lieutenant-General Colin Campbell willingly agreed to add another thousand men from Gibraltar and Tarifa. Generous to a fault, Graham agreed to serve under La Peña, a plausible, selfish and disloyal officer who was known to his Spanish subordinates as 'Dona Manuella' on account of his indecision and avoidance of responsibility.

The British contingent, including the Grenadier and Light Companies of the 47th,[320] sailed from Cadiz on 21st February 1811. The allied rendezvous was Tarifa, but Graham's force was blown past it and into the Bay of Gibraltar, where they landed on the 23rd at Algeciras. There they were joined by six flank companies from Gibraltar, including the Grenadier and Light Companies of the 1st/82nd Foot[321] and those of the 1st/9th and 1st/28th, making an elite Flank Battalion of 536 bayonets.

On the 24th, the troops marched over the mountain road to Tarifa, where the battalion companies of the 28th Foot were added to Graham's force, bringing his total British strength up to 5,196 men. While waiting there for La Peña, Graham allocated his force to two brigades. The first, under General Dilkes, consisted of two battalions of Guards[322], the Flank Battalion from Gibraltar under Lieutenant-Colonel John Browne, and two companies of the 95th Rifles. The second brigade, under Colonel Wheatley, was composed of the 1st/28th, 2nd/67th and 2nd/87th, together with a second Flank Battalion, under Colonel Andrew Barnard[323], consisting of the flank companies of the 2nd/47th and 20th Portuguese, with four more companies of the 95th Rifles. In addition, Graham had two squadrons of cavalry, from the 2nd Hussars of the King's German Legion, and ten guns under Major Duncan – three 9-pounders, four 6-pounders and three 5.5-inch howitzers.

Whilst at Tarifa, the officers of the 47th and 82nd were among the many who enjoyed the hospitality of the mess of the 28th Foot, as Lieutenant Robert Blakeney of that regiment describes:

'During the few days which the British troops spent at Tarifa, our time was passed in that joyful conviviality always to be observed among British soldiers on the opening of a campaign... Our mess-room was very spacious, and at either end was a room which entered into it; and not only these three, but in fact every room in the house, had tables put down; and many there were who felt glad to procure a dinner even in the kitchen. The draught on our cellar was deep, and profiting by the experience of the first day of the jubilee, on the second day, the 24th, we passed a restriction act limiting each officer to a pint of port and half a bottle of claret; but notwithstanding this precaution, we ran a pipe of port dry in less than four days... It was calculated that, including port, claret, brandy and porter, two thousand bottles were emptied in our mess-house within the week.

'Even the sergeants contrived to procure a room, where they enjoyed themselves as much as the officers in the mess-room; and their jokes, if not equally refined, were not the less entertaining.'[324]

The weather having improved, La Peña's Spaniards landed on the morning of February 27th, and orders were given for a march the following morning. Robert Blakeney paints an exuberantly nostalgic picture of the final evening at Tarifa:

'The night of the 27th being the last jovial one the army were to pass at Tarifa, one hundred and ninety-one officers dined at the mess. The exhilarating juice of the grape was freely quaffed from out the crystal cup, and the inspiring songs of love and war went joyfully round, and the conclusion of each animating strophe was loudly hailed with choral cheers; for such is the composition of a soldier that the object of his love and his county's foe alike call forth the strongest and most indomitable effusions of his heart, so closely allied is love to battle. Hilarity and mirth reigned throughout. Lively sallies of wit, cheerfully received as guilelessly shot forth, added

---

[320] A total of eight officers and 209 men deployed with the Flank Companies 47th Foot. The Grenadier and Light Companies were commanded by Lieutenant Henry Maxwell Wainwright and Captain Francis Featherstone respectively. The Cadiz strength return of the 47th for 25th February 1811 shows 513 effective rank and file of the 47th remaining in Cadiz out of a total 781.
[321] The 1st/82nd Flank Companies were commanded by Captains Henry Adolphus Proctor and James Stewart and had 202 other ranks.
[322] 2nd/1st Guards, two companies Coldstream Guards and three companies 2nd/3rd Guards, a total of 1,144 men.
[323] Andrew Barnard's first active service was as a captain of the 81st on St. Domingo in 1795.
[324] Blakeney, p.p. 170-72.

brilliancy to the festive board. Officers having entered their profession young, mutual attachment was firmly cemented, genuine and disinterested. Each man felt sure that he sat between two friends.'

'Our revels continued until the morning; and in the morning, while many a Spanish fair with waving hands and glistening eyes was seen in the balcony, we marched out of Tarifa with aching heads but glowing hearts.'[325]

Marching north, from Puente de Facinas, the combined army had a choice of two routes. There was an inland road through Casas Viejas to Medina Sidonia, and a track that ran nearer the coast through Vejer de la Frontera, Conil and Chiclana. Of these, the inland route was by far the better course, posing a direct threat to the left rear of Victor's besieging army, and it was initially selected. These two routes were separated by the long lagoon of La Janda, which, after a wet winter, was both deep and extensive.

La Peña had a misplaced belief in night marches, which Graham did not share. The British general's laconic diary entry recorded the outcome of the first night's march, stumbling along country roads from Puente de Facinas in the face of a strong, cold wind:

'Marched in the evening, very tedious from filing across water (the stream which fills the head of the lagoon of La Janda) and other difficulties. Misled by the guides on quitting the Cortigo de la Janda (farm at the head of the lagoon), the counter-march made a most fatiguing night… It was twelve noon before the troops halted, having been nineteen hours under arms.'

In this time, Graham's division had advanced only thirteen miles. Led by Lardizbal's Spanish division, the army was passing Casas Viejas on the morning of the 2nd March when the small French garrison in the convent there attempted belatedly to withdraw. They were charged and cut down by the hussars of the King's German Legion, and the mutilated survivors were carried into the convent yard for treatment by Assistant Surgeon Henry Goodsir of the 82nd Regiment, who was attached to Browne's Flank Battalion.

A result of this minor action was that La Peña learned from prisoners that Medina Sidonia was held by some three thousand French, who were preparing to defend its walls. This intelligence sufficed to weaken La Peña's resolution, and instead of embracing the golden opportunity to draw Victor away from his siege lines and, as always intended, bring him to battle, the Spanish general baulked at the prospect of action. To general astonishment, he ordered the army to turn away from Medina Sidonia and make a night march across country to Vejer de la Frontera and the coast road to Cadiz. Graham protested against a second night march, and when it was discovered that the proposed route was under water, La Peña consented to wait until the next morning.

The army marched at 8 a.m. on the 3rd, led again by Lardizbal's Spaniards. Their eventual route involved a five-hundred-yard causeway crossing around the north end of the lagoon of La Janda. When Graham reached the crossing site, he found the narrow causeway submerged in a flood, and the Spaniards halted irresolutely on the near side. The gallant old veteran at once set an example by riding into the flood with his staff, finding the submerged track and placing guides along it at intervals. He then sat on his horse in the middle of the ford, encouraging the troops as they struggled past up to their waists in water. The passage took three hours, and it was midnight before the cold, wet and exhausted, troops reached Vejer, having taken fifteen hours to cover just ten miles.

There is a revealing account of the uncomfortable relationship between the British and Spaniards at this stage of the campaign by Captain James Stanhope, extra aide-de-camp to General Graham, who described the unfortunate course of events on 3rd March:

'The Spaniards issued the order to march at 11 that night [2nd March], but General Graham, finding they knew nothing of the road, persuaded them to postpone their march till the morning; we were ordered to follow the march of their corps at 6 a.m. At midday they were just moving off & then marched back above a league on the road towards Facinas, though Vejer lay before us on a hill about 10 miles off and the road to it over the plain was perfectly evident. General Graham was so convinced that they were taking the wrong road that he galloped to the head of their column and pointed out the straight one to General La Pena, & was answered that that road

[325] Ibid, p.p. 175, 177.

was impracticable for artillery & that we must move round a lake in our front, which would make the march 20 miles.

'Having continued some time, they found some peasants & it turned out that the circuitous route was impracticable, but that the short & straight road which General Graham had pointed out was a very good one. It became necessary to counter-march the whole column. After marching in our new direction some time, we found the Spaniards halted. Again General Graham galloped to the front and found the delay to arise from a natural canal over which was a causeway knee deep in water with some stepping stones, & over these (each man taking off his shoes & stockings) did the Spanish army begin to file, the officers being carried over on the shoulders of the men; four and twenty hours would not have passed them. It was already late, & General Graham represented the necessity of getting our guns across before dark. They were brought up, & Barnard with the 95th as their guard, who marched through locked up as if on parade. A gun stuck in a deep part, the general threw himself into the water & putting his shoulder to the wheel, with the assistance of his staff got it out. The Spaniards gradually became ashamed of themselves, the Prince of Anglona went up to his ankles at first, and little by little they set a good example, & the Spanish troops marched through very well. We arrived at the end of our twelve mile march at midnight & bivouacked in an olive wood near Vejer.'[326]

Meanwhile, preparations for the planned sortie from Cadiz had taken place on the night of the 2nd-3rd March when Zayas, according to the pre-planned schedule, threw a bridge of boats across the Sancti Petri creek and established a bridgehead. This foothold on the mainland was successfully stormed by the French the following night, but as they failed to capture the pontoons, the threat of a sortie from the Isla de Leon remained.

Victor now made a plan to contain, or at least delay, any move by the Cadiz garrison while he dealt with the Allied field army, the main body of which he knew was moving towards him from Vejer. Leaving Villatte's division to block the approaches from the Sancti Petri creek and the Isla de Leon, he marched Ruffin's and Leval's divisions south to the woods around Chiclana. Victor's concept of operations was for Villatte with nearly 3,000 men to fight a delaying battle in his blocking position on the low, wooded Torre Bermeja ridge for long enough for Ruffin and Leval with 7,170 all ranks, under his personal command, to emerge from the woods and pounce on the extended Allied line of march. Just three battalions were left to defend the Cadiz siege lines.

La Peña obliged by marching straight into Victor's trap, compounding his previous errors by insisting on another exhausting sixteen-hour night march, which at first light on the 5th found the head of his column on the road to Chiclana instead of the intended seaside track to the Sancti Petri creek and Cadiz. Graham expressed his exasperation in his journal:

'Soon after it being reported that our columns were misled and were marching on Chiclana instead of keeping nearer the coast, I halted them and galloped on. Found they had followed the Spaniards, and coming up to the head saw the whole staff in the greatest confusion from the contradictions of the guides. I could not help exclaiming, somewhat improperly, "*Voilà ce que c'est que les marches de nuit*" [Look what happens with night marches]. After some further rather ludicrous scenes of distress, several people of the country agreeing that a path to the left led through the heath towards Santa Petri, and that, the country being dry, the guns could move in all directions over the plain, it was agreed that the march should be continued as I had originally recommended, by a flank march left in front, forming lines of columns, the cavalry and rearguard on the right in first line, and so on. Our columns closed up, and the army proceeded in this way across the extensive heathy plain of Chiclana, making a remarkably pretty field day.'

La Peña's vanguard reached the coastal track shortly after daybreak near the Torre de la Barossa, a fifteenth-century lookout tower. The track passed below an isolated low ridge known locally as the Cerro de Puerco (Boar's Neck)[327], according to Robert Blakeney, 'from its curving shape bristling with pine trees.' On the highest point of the 160-foot feature, immortalised as Barrosa Hill, stood an old watch post, the Vigia de la Barrosa. The ridge was surrounded by scrub and by cork and pine woods, with shallow valleys ('ravines' in early

---

[326] *Eyewitness to the Peninsular War & Waterloo, Letters & Journals of Lieutenant-Colonel James Stanhope*, ed. Gareth Glover, Pen & Sword, 2010, p.p. 46-7.
[327] The hill is now known as Loma de Sancti-Petri.

nineteenth-century parlance) and broken ground to the north, between the hill and the tree-line of a denser wood. To the north-east, a long, gentle slope descended to the heath-covered plain of Chiclana, while on the north-western side, beyond the woods, the Sancti Petri creek and the Isla de Leon were just four miles away.

Barrosa Hill was at once recognised by Graham as vital ground dominating the coastal route to the Sancti Petri creek and Cadiz, and he urged La Peña to occupy it in strength. It was, he explained to the Spanish general, 'the key both to offensive and defensive movements.' The Spaniard characteristically spurned this advice, but Graham occupied the eastern slope of the Barrosa height with his own division.

Having located Villatte's blocking force on the low, wooded Bermeja ridge to his front, La Peña ordered Lardizbal's vanguard division to attack it at once, clearing the way to Cadiz. The attack went in at about 9 a.m. and was repulsed with some loss, but when La Peña committed the leading brigade of his second division, and Zayas advanced across the Sancti Petri to take the French in the rear, Villatte abandoned the Bermeja ridge and withdrew as planned north over the marshy Almanza Creek. La Peña had taken the bait, splitting his force, which was now left vulnerable to Victor's proposed attack.

Ignoring the whole purpose of the Allied operation, La Peña now appeared only intent on reaching Cadiz unscathed. He halted Lardizbal's pursuit of Villatte, and about noon ordered Graham to abandon his strong and secure position on Barrosa Hill and move down to Bermeja. Graham's patience was now exhausted: the concentration of the whole Allied army on the enemy side of the Sancti Petri in the face of a French force of unknown strength, location and intention was clearly dangerous. He refused to move from the hill until suitably relieved. La Peña relented and sent five Spanish battalions, four guns and all the Allied cavalry, the whole commanded by General Cruz-Murgeon, to hold Barrosa Hill as a rearguard until Graham's division should have safely reached the main body. To this force Graham prudently added Browne's Flank Battalion, including the Grenadier and Light Companies of the 82nd Foot, ordering Lieutenant Colonel Browne to occupy the western point of the hill around the small watch house.

The rest of Graham's division descended from Barrosa Hill and, rather than taking the coastal track to Bermeja, marched on a more direct path through thick woods of pine and scrub, lost to sight of friend and foe. Wheatley's brigade led, followed by Dilkes,' then Duncan's guns and Barnard's battalion, with the flank companies of the 47th, and two companies of the 95th as rearguard.

As they departed, at about 12.30 p.m., Victor advanced at speed from the shelter of the Chiclana woods with the intention of seizing Barrosa Hill, which his cavalry had reported to be unoccupied. His intention was to roll up the rear division of the Allies as they defiled through the woods across his front before striking at La Peña's main body before they could cross the one pontoon bridge to the safety of the Isla de Leon.

Ruffin's division, 2,553 men supported by six guns, headed for Barrosa Hill while Leval's division, 4,050 men with another six guns, directed their advance in four columns towards the woods through which Graham's troops were marching across his front. The French advance was not at first noticed by the Spanish troops occupying the nearest end of Barrosa Hill, but at length Colonel Browne saw 'a confused and hasty movement' among the Spaniards and sent Lieutenant Robert Blakeney to find out the cause:

'I was told by General Cruz-Murgeon that they merely wished to take ground to our left,' recalled Blakeney, 'but seeing the hurry of the Spaniards increase, I instantly galloped beyond their extreme flank, and now discovered the French cavalry moving towards the coast road and rather inclining towards our position. Retiring quickly, I reported the circumstance to Colonel Browne. By this time, the greater part of the Spanish troops had passed between us and the coast road and were soon in rapid march towards the beach leading to Bermeja. Colonel Browne strongly and rather indignantly remonstrated against their conduct. At this period Colonel Whittingham [an English officer in the Spanish service] rode up, and addressing Colonel Browne said, "Colonel Browne, what do you intend to do?" The pugnacious reply was, "What do I intend to do, sir? I intend to fight the French." Whittingham then remarked, "You may do as you please, Colonel Browne, but we are decided on a retreat." Very well, sir," replied Browne; I shall stop where I am, for it shall never be said that John Frederick Browne ran away from the post which his general ordered him to defend'[328]

The Flank Battalion was soon alone, 'four hundred and seventy bayonets bristling on the neck of the boar,' and made preparations to hold their position:

'The Spaniards being now out of the way and soon out of sight, Colonel Browne directed Lieutenant [Michael] Sparkes, 30th Regiment, who acted as engineer, to loophole a chapel [the watch house] which stood on the summit of the hill. Some men were loosely thrown in, and the remainder of our little battalion formed three sides of an oblong square, the low tower or chapel supplying the fourth face.'[329]

It soon became clear, even to the fire-eating Browne, that Barrosa Hill could not be held by so small a force. We can do no better than continue Robert Blakeney's narrative:

'By this time, the French cavalry [1st Dragoons] had gained the coast road, probably either to cut off the retreat of the allies by that route or to prevent any troops coming by way of Vejer. Be that as it may, they now turned directly towards us. On approaching nearly within musket range, they opened right and left, apparently to gain both our flanks; and now for the first time their artillery were discovered not far behind, and at the same moment their infantry were seen moving forward, darkening the distant part of the plain which skirts the town of Chiclana. Hesitation would now be madness. Our men were instantly withdrawn from the chapel, and forming column of quarter distance we proceeded quickly down the hill towards the pine forest which shut out Bermeja from our view. The enemy's horsemen were soon on every side of our little column and kept gradually closing in; but dreading that, before we could get away to a sufficient distance from the hill, the artillery, which we had seen whipping over the plain, would open their fire upon us, we durst not halt to form square; our situation was rather perplexing, but we were determined. In this order we moved rapidly down the hill, which being uneven and woody favoured our retreat; but on crossing a ravine, we became more exposed, having entered on comparatively level ground, scarce of wood. Colonel Browne now threw out a few loose files, but not far from each angle of the column, to warn the cavalry off, some few of whom were hurt by their fire. To say the truth, the cavalry showed rather a wavering inclination than a firm determination to charge us. Having passed over the level ground, we touched the skirts of the forest, and on our forming line the cavalry drew off.'[330]

Meanwhile, the main body of the British division was pressing along a sandy path through the pine woods when, according to Private Adam Reed of the 47th, 'a Spanish mountaineer brought tidings to Sir Thomas Graham and told him that the French was on our rear.' Then the General dispatched an aide de camp to the Spanish general to engage the French, and he returned and told him that the Spaniards could nowhere be found. The General's reply, according to Reed, was, "My lads, we shall have to bear the burden and heat of the day, by Spaniards led astray." Whatever Graham's actual words, and whoever brought news of Victor's advance, those were certainly his sentiments, for he at once saw that only immediate and resolute action by his division could avoid disaster to the whole Allied army. Above all, he needed to reoccupy Barrosa Hill in strength, and he was turning his columns about for that purpose when, much to his surprise, the red coats of Browne's Flank Battalion were glimpsed approaching through the pine woods. Lieutenant Robert Blakeney left a graphic account of what followed:

'General Graham came forth instantly to meet us, saying, "Browne, did I not give you orders to defend Barossa Hill?"

"Yes, sir," said Browne, "but you would not have me fight the whole French army with four hundred and seventy men?"

"Had you not," replied the General, "five Spanish battalions, together with artillery and cavalry?"

"Oh!" said Browne; "they all ran away long before the enemy came within cannon-shot."

The General coolly replied, "It is a bad business, Browne; you must instantly turn round and attack."

"Very well," said the Colonel; "am I to attack in extended order as flankers, or as a close battalion?"

---

[328] Blakeney, p. 184.
[329] Ibid., p. 185.
[330] Ibid., p.p. 185-86.

145

"In open order," was the reply, and the General returned to the troops in the wood. The flank battalion were instantly extended into skirmishing order, which had scarcely been done when the General again rode back to Colonel Browne, saying, "I must show something more seriously than skirmishing; close the men into compact battalion."

"That I will, with pleasure," cried the Colonel, "for it is more in my way than light bobbing." The order to close on the centre was instantly bugled out, during which movement the Colonel sent to know from the General, who had again retired, if he was to advance as soon as formed, and whether he was to attack immediately in his front or more towards his right. The answer was, "Attack in your front, and immediately."

'All being now ready, Colonel Browne rode to the front of the battalion and taking off his hat said in a voice to be heard by all:

"Gentlemen, I am happy to be the bearer of good news: General Graham has done you the honour of being the first to attack those fellows. Now follow me, you rascals!" He pointed to the enemy, and giving the order to advance broke into his favourite air, *Hearts of Oak*: "Now cheer up, my brave lads! 'Tis to glory we steer, to add something new to this wonderful year!"'[331]

While Browne prepared to buy time with a desperate attack, back in the wood, Graham was struggling to reverse his march and patch together a hasty but coherent counter-attack. His plan was simple: on the right, Dilke's brigade of Guards was to attack Ruffin's division on the summit of Barrosa Hill, while on the left, Wheatley's brigade was to deal with Leval's division, which was advancing across the plain from Chiclana. Major Alexander Duncan's ten guns were to be pushed forward in the centre between the two brigades. While Browne bought time for this deployment on the right, Graham sent four companies of the 95th, from Andrew Barnard's Flank Battalion, and two companies of the 20th Portuguese to do likewise on the left, checking Leval's advance. Barnard's other two companies were the Grenadier and Light Companies of the 47th, and these were tasked by Graham to protect Duncan's guns.

First contact was on the right, where Browne's flankers at once began their sacrificial attack on Barrosa Hill: 'Thus we moved forward,' recalled Blakeney, 'with four hundred and sixty-eight men and twenty-one officers to attack the position, upon which but three-quarters of an hour previously we had stood in proud defiance of the advancing foe, but which was now defended by two thousand five hundred infantry and eight pieces of artillery, together with some cavalry. To this force were added two battalions of chosen grenadiers, commanded by General Rousseau, the whole under the orders of the General of Division, Ruffin.'[332]

Leaving the pine woods, the Flank Battalion had first to cross a broad but shallow valley, and then to climb the gentle slope of the Cerro. The outcome was, as anticipated, disastrous for the battalion.

'The enemy, seeing so small a force, detached from any apparent support, advancing against them, allowed us to approach close; and the orders given by Colonel Browne were that not a shot should be fired, but to proceed to work as soon as possible with the bayonet.'

Legend has it that when they got close to the French, Colonel Browne, who was riding on a large Spanish horse, spurred his troops on with a fiery speech: 'There they are, you rascals, if you don't kill them, they will kill you; so fire away!' He was supposedly in between the two opposing lines when he gave the order to fire, but escaped without injury. Many of his men were not so lucky, for the first French volley and cannonade was devastating:

'Nearly two hundred of our men and more than half the officers went down by this first volley, thus opening the battle propitiously for them. We now literally stood in extended order; the battalion was checked. In closing on the centre and endeavouring to form a second efficient line, upwards of fifty more men and some officers were levelled with the earth; and all the exertions of Colonel Browne could not form a third line. We had by this time lost upwards of two hundred and fifty men and fourteen officers, between killed and wounded. The

[331] Ibid, p. 187-88.
[332] Ibid., p. 188.

remainder of the battalion was now scattered. The men commenced firing from behind trees, mounds or any cover which presented, and could not be got together.'[333]

Meanwhile, the rest of Graham's force was struggling out of the wood to face Leval's division. Among the first to emerge were Duncan's guns, who found an escort of 47th flankers waiting for them at the edge of the trees. With the 47th was Private Adam Reed:

'At that present time we was in a grove (or wood) so that we could not see our enemy, and [Graham] ordered us to face to the right about, and commence our march back out of the grove and there we espied our enemy ready for action and it was a very surprising thing to see them formed on the same ground we had marched upon... As soon as we saw our enemy, we being rear in front (by going to the right about) we was ordered to change our front by the counter march of companies, and then we brought our right in front. Our General (Sir Thomas Graham) then said to us "My lads, prepare for action. Let's give them three cheers for Old England."

Major Duncan's despatch, written on the day after the battle, paints a similar picture of a hurriedly improvised but determined redeployment:

'No sooner had the British entered the wood, which was of considerable extent, than the main body of the French troops, who must have been well concealed, marched rapidly to possess themselves of the ground we had left... The whole of our [artillery] brigades, amounting to ten pieces, were marching together in column near the front of the troops; they immediately counter-marched with the rest and got out of the wood with all speed. As soon as we cleared it, the enemy were seen to be within 1100 yards, and deploying into line on an advantageous position, whilst ours could scarcely have been worse, being much confined, low, and in the midst of high furze.'

Protected from the advancing French *voltigeurs* by the Flank Companies of the 47th, Major Duncan's ten guns unlimbered at the edge of the wood and came into action in the centre of the British front line, with Barnard's thin line of British and Portuguese skirmishers to their immediate left and Browne's shattered battalion on the hill-slope to their right front. Graham's line formed a shallow obtuse angle with the guns and their escort at the point.

The sudden appearance of Duncan's battery animals, some two hundred horses and mules, appears to have convinced the French of Leval's division that they were about to be attacked by cavalry, and three of the leading battalions formed square. Duncan at once opened a devastating fire on their packed formations, firing spherical case shot, as shrapnel was then termed, to 'conspicuous effect,' raking them from the front and side.

'Such was [Graham's] anxiety for the artillery to get into action,' reported Duncan, 'that we did so before our troops were up, so that for more than 20 minutes while our light corps engaged the enemies on their right flank the ten guns (formed together in line) carried on a most destructive fire against their centre and left flank. The ground admitted of no manœuvering, so that the action very quickly became general, and I believe a warmer one never took place. Our guns were much exposed to the enemy's light troops and were, besides, enfiladed from the beginning by their artillery [six guns] on our right flank.'

'The whole of the enemy's fire [was] for a considerable time from the commencement of the action directed against the battery formed by our guns; indeed their whole force seemed to be directed towards us, and occasioned General Graham to make his formation in rear of the guns, so that much of the fire intended for us reached them and caused dreadful destruction.'

Meanwhile, the survivors of Browne's Flank Battalion had not retreated, but were continuing the fight from what cover they could find, firing independently at the French battalions on the crest of the Cerro above them.

Dilkes' brigade, some 1,400 men in total of the 1st and 3rd Guards, half the 67th and two companies of the 95th, had emerged from the wood during the flankers' sacrificial attack, 'in little order indeed, but in a fierce mood.' Inclining to their right, and without waiting to form, they climbed the hill on Browne's right where the ground afforded greater cover. Protected from serious casualties by dead ground and scrub, the British line had almost reached the hilltop when it was attacked head-on by two battalions of Ruffin's infantry, the 24th Ligne,

---

[333] Ibid., p.p. 189-90.

with the 96th in support, charging downhill in column with drums beating and bayonets fixed. British musketry tore into the French ranks, bringing the attack to a halt. Marshal Victor took personal charge and renewed the attack, adding two battalions of grenadiers, but after a bloody exchange of musketry, the French again faltered and recoiled.

As Dilkes' men closed with Ruffin's left wing, Lieutenant Blakeney gathered a few of Browne's flankers and charged forward, capturing a howitzer at bayonet point:

'Scarcely had the gun been taken than we were joined, as if through magic effect, by upwards of a hundred men of the flank battalion – a proof that they were not far distant. They darted forth from behind trees, briars, brakes and out of hollows… It was a magic effect. We now confidently advanced up the hill, and unlike most advances against a heavy fire, our numbers increased as we proceeded, soldiers of the flank battalion joining at every step.'[334]

With his left wing in trouble from the resolute British counter-attack, Victor tried to restore the situation on the hill by bringing forward Ruffin's right, some thirteen hundred men of the 9th Légère and 96th Ligne, but in Blakeney's words, these were furiously attacked and driven backwards by the remnant of Browne's Flank Battalion, now amounting to nearly two hundred men and one wounded officer [himself].

'And now the battle for a moment hovered in the zenith of its glory; the contending foes were not above ten yards asunder, and scarcely were the enemy seen to move. Tenaciously maintaining their hold of the hill, they fought with desperation, defending every inch of ground; for the precipice was near. Their hardiest veterans stood firm; their bravest officers came forth displaying the banners of their nation; the heroic example of Marshal Victor was imitated by all. Conspicuous in the front, the Marshal was recognised by both armies waving his plume in circling motion high above his head, to fasten his troops to the hill; but his gallant deeds and surprising valour were vain against his more than equal foe.

'General Graham at this critical moment darted to the front, and by one short word, loud and inspiring, made nought of all the Marshal's bravery and combinations. The word was "Charge!" Like electric fluid it shot from the centre of the British line to the extremities of its flanks, instantaneously followed by the well-known thundering British cheer, sure precursor of the rush of British bayonets. The Guards and flankers now rushed forward, when with loud and murmuring sounds Ruffin's whole division, together with Rousseau's chosen grenadiers, were instantly in whirling motion rolled down into the valley below, leaving their two brave generals mortally wounded on the hill, which was now in possession of their bloodstained conquerors. The battle was won; and the gallant Graham triumphantly stood on the bristling crest of Barossa's blood-drenched hill.'[335]

As the French fell back in confusion from Barrosa Hill, those of Browne's flankers who were still on their feet collected on the summit and, as a parting gesture, gave them three hearty cheers. Graham's later dispatch was genuinely effusive in its praise for this gallant band:

'No expressions of mine could do justice to the conduct of the troops throughout. Nothing less than the almost unparalleled exertions of every officer, the invincible bravery of every soldier, and the most determined devotion to the honour of His Majesty's arms in all, could have achieved this brilliant success, against such a formidable enemy so posted.'

On Graham's left, the main body of Wheatley's Brigade, the 28th, 87th, half the 67th and two companies of the 2nd Guards, at length struggled through the pine woods to relieve Barnard's skirmishers, who were being pushed back at the wood's edge by sheer weight of numbers. Despite the havoc inflicted by Duncan's guns, and further losses from Barnard's outnumbered riflemen, Leval's division continued to move slowly forward over the plain in imposing masses, their drums beating the *pas de charge* and the leading battalions firing their muskets. The French advance was led by four battalion columns, from their left, the 1st/8th and 2nd/8th Ligne and the 2nd/54th and 1st/54th Ligne, each with a frontage of some seventy men, supported at some distance by the 1st/45th Ligne on the left and a composite grenadier battalion on the right. 'Never did a finer sight present itself,' wrote a British rifleman, 'The grenadiers had long waving red plumes in their caps, at least a foot in length; while the light

---

[334] Blakeney, p. 192.
[335] Ibid, p.p. 195-196.

infantry had feathers of the same length and make, but green with yellow tops. The whole of the French army had on their best or holiday suits of clothing, with their arms as bright as silver, and glancing in the sun as they moved in column, gave them really a noble and martial appearance.'

Forming in haste as they emerged from the wood, Wheatley's brigade numbered only 2,600 men against Leval's 4,050, but this disparity in numbers was hidden by the wood, by the wide extent of the British line, and by the confidence with which it moved forward. The 28th were on the left of Wheatley's line, then the 2nd Guards, the 87th and, nearest to the guns, half of the 67th. Once the infantry line was formed, reported Sir Thomas Graham, 'the guns advanced to a more favourable position, and kept up a most destructive fire.'

As soon as the light troops had cleared from their front, the British infantry advanced, and the first clash was in the centre between the Irish 2nd/87th in line and the French 2nd/8th in column. A single volley was exchanged at under sixty yards, with the usual result, then Major Hugh Gough's 87th charged with a 'most unearthly howl,' driving furiously through the broken ranks of the 2nd/8th Ligne. Trapped by the weight of numbers in their column, the French were unable to escape and were cut down by the score. The 1st/8th, its left flank swept by the fire of the British guns and by the 67th, fell back towards its disordered second battalion and the whole mass was forced back in panic and confusion by the 87th, who famously captured the regimental Eagle. The 45th Ligne, standing in reserve behind the 8th, put up little resistance before fleeing from the field. On the right of Leval's division, the 1st/54th and 2nd/54th Ligne stood for some time, and the latter even attempted to turn Wheatley's left flank, but finally they gave way on being charged, for the third time, by the 28th and the 2nd Guards.

It appears that the 47th Flank Companies took part in the general advance of Wheatley's brigade, for Private Adam Reed recalled that 'our ammunition being nearly spent, and a great number of our men killed and wounded, we had only one remedy, that was to show them our bayonet, which accordingly our General ordered us to fire and come to the port. We was then ordered to advance some distance and to double quick time. Our General then said "Charge my lads, and stick close to each other." The French stood firm till we approached: they then went to the right about face and retreated…'

This was not quite the end of the battle, for Victor managed to rally his wrecked divisions on the plain to the east, where he attempted to make a stand. However, when Graham's united force approached, his guns began to play upon the disorganised masses, and the hussars of the King's German Legion charged, whereupon the French fell back in a rush towards Chiclana. 'A new and more advanced position of our artillery quickly dispersed them,' reported Graham, 'The exhausted state of the troops made pursuit impossible.' The battle was over in rather less than two hours.

Had La Peña's Spaniards appeared, even at this latest moment, there is little doubt that Victor's rout could have been completed and the siege of Cadiz raised, thereby achieving the strategic object of the Allied expedition. The Spanish general had over ten thousand men in hand only three miles from Barrosa Hill, but, convinced that the British would be defeated, he refused to move a man to support Graham.

'Had the whole body of the Spanish cavalry,' wrote Graham, 'with the horse artillery, been rapidly sent by the sea-beach to form on the plain, and to envelop the enemy's left; had the greatest part of the infantry been marched through the pine wood to the rear of the British force, to turn his right, he must either have retired instantly, or he would have exposed himself to absolute destruction; his cavalry greatly encumbered, his artillery lost, his columns mixed and in confusion; and a general dispersion would have been the inevitable consequence of a close pursuit. But the movement was lost.'

The result of La Peña's shameful timidity and selfishness was that Victor retired unmolested to continue the siege, albeit with the loss of 2,062 men and six guns, two generals and an Imperial Eagle. Acrimonious public recriminations followed between the Allies, as a result of which Graham challenged La Peña to 'an early morning meeting' which the Spaniard, characteristically, declined.

'After the battle was over,' recalled Adam Reed, 'the General said "Providence is on our side, the field is ours," and after we had watched our enemy a considerable distance, and night approaching very fast, we was ordered to gather in our dead and wounded and to form a hollow square. The dreadful shrieks and cries of the wounded and dying during the night was most painful.

149

'The 6th March came, being a beautiful day, and we were ordered to bury the dead. That day passed on but no enemy appeared anymore. We then marched towards the Island of Lyons [Isla de Leon] and they formed a pontoon bridge across the channel at St Peter's Point, and glad enough was the soldiers that they arrived on the island once more.[336] Our General then ordered us to have liberty for three days.'

Graham's little force suffered almost one in four casualties at Barrosa, 201 killed and 1,037 wounded. Browne's Flank Battalion had the most severe losses, a total of 236 out of 536. The 82nd flankers took more than their share of these casualties, ninety in all, including five rank and file killed, and three officers[337] including both company commanders, two sergeants and eighty men wounded. The flank companies of the 47th had a slightly lower total of casualties at 71, but these included one officer, a drummer and twenty men killed, as well as one officer and 49 wounded.[338] Despite these proportionately very heavy casualties, neither the 47th nor the 82nd received the Battle Honour for Barrosa as their headquarters were not present, but 51 of the 47th and 43 of the 82nd survived to receive a 'Barrosa' clasp to their Military General Service Medals, as did one soldier of the 30th Foot.[339]

Shortly after Barrosa, in May 1811, the 2nd/47th Foot, still at Cadiz, were brigaded with the 87th, 95th Rifles and 20th Portuguese under Colonel Skerrett.[340]

The 1st/82nd continued to garrison Gibraltar[341], where in September 1811 a draft of 250 men was received from the 2nd Battalion[342], taking its strength to a remarkable 41 officers, 59 sergeants, 21 drummers and 1,150 rank and file. The Battalion appears to have enjoyed reasonably good health at that time, with an average over the next nine months of 56 in hospital and one or two deaths.

Pursuit of Masséna March-April 1811

March 5th, 1811 was marked by two British victories, for on the same day that Graham beat Victor at Barrosa, three hundred miles to the north, Masséna reluctantly accepted defeat in Portugal and began a costly withdrawal. Hoping to maintain his army in Portugal until reinforced, he initially fell back to the north, towards Coimbra.

Wellington had early intelligence of Masséna's retreat, and on the evening of 4th March the 4th Division, including the 40th Foot, received orders to move forward the following morning from Azambuja to Cartaxo. They spent the night of the 6th in Santarem.

'It is a town of very considerable size,' wrote Charles Boutflower, 'but exhibits a melancholy instance of French barbarism; the churches in particular have suffered the most unheard of devastation; one only was spared, and that had been converted into a regular theatre, where, so late as Sunday evening last, the triumphal entry of the French Army into Lisbon was represented.'[343]

Uncertain as to enemy intentions and lines of retreat, Wellington set out rather tentatively in pursuit, marching in two columns towards Torres Novas and Tomar. The 40th were on the latter route, reaching Golagã on

---

[336] It was in fact on the morning of the 6th that Graham withdrew his division to the Isla de Leon.
[337] Captains James Stewart and Henry Adolphus Proctor were both slightly wounded, the latter suffering a 'contusion on the body', while Lieutenant John Mackay was severely wounded, for which he was recompensed with one year's pay.
[338] Ensign Nicholas Delacherois of the 47th, aged 22, from Donaghadee, County Down was killed, and Captain Francis Featherstone was slightly wounded. The day was warm, and it is said that Delacherois had opened his jacket and was stooping to drink at a little stream when he was observed and shot by a French *tirailleur*.
[339] Private John Hill of the 30th was present at the battle as servant to Sir Thomas Graham. Hill must have given good service, for later in the campaign he became servant to Sir George Murray, Wellington's trusted and efficient principal staff officer, and in 1848 he received the General Service Medal with clasps for Barossa, Ciudad Rodrigo, Vittoria, San Sebastian, Nive, Orthez and Toulouse.
[340] Captain Ponsonby Matthews, 47th, was captured on 26th May 1811 on his way to join the Regiment at Cadiz and was sent to Verdun.
[341] The Jewish inhabitants of Gibraltar raised the sum of 738 Spanish dollars by voluntary subscription for the relief of the widows and orphans of the soldiers from that garrison, including the 82nd, who had fallen at Barrosa.
[342] The 2nd/82nd was then stationed on Guernsey, having embarked for that island at Tynemouth in early June 1811. They had previously marched from Scarborough to Hull in December 1809, and had been moved on from there to Tynemouth in April 1811.
[343] Boutflower, p. 77.

the afternoon of the 7th and Tomar on the 8th, always a few hours behind the French. By this time, Wellington had learned that Masséna's columns were moving towards the lower valley of the Mondego, and he issued orders to concentrate his army on the *Estrada Real*, the paved main road from Leiria through Pombal to Coimbra. The 4th Division were accordingly ordered to march on Pombal[344], and after two days' forced marches by way of Caxarias, the 40th joined Wellington's main force north of that place late on the 11th March.

The 5th Division, commanded in Leith's absence by Major-General James Dunlop[345], was the last to leave the Lines of Torres Vedras, and it was 6th March before Lieutenant William Stewart, Adjutant of the 2nd/30th, was warned to be ready to march at short notice.[346] Next day, the Battalion marched to Cadaval, and on the 8th to Rio Maior. The 5th Division then moved up to join Wellington, marching north to reach Alcanede on the 9th and Porto de Mos on the 10th, arriving above Pombal on the 11th March in time to see the French rearguard driven back into that town. 'From this place,' wrote William Stewart, 'we saw the advance of most of the divisions of our army in every direction – It was one of the grandest military spectacles I had ever witnessed.' Wellington had now achieved his concentration and was ready to press his pursuit of Masséna's main body.

Masséna's rearguard, ably led by Marshal Ney, had clashed repeatedly with Wellington's advance guard, found mainly from the 3rd and Light Divisions. The rear divisions, including the 4th and 5th, played a relatively small part in these engagements, but both the 30th and the 40th saw some action over the next few days.

On the evening of the 11th, the 40th came up with the French north of Pombal, where Ney had taken up a delaying position at Venda da Cruz. At 5 a.m. the following morning, Wellington advanced in three columns, with the 4th Division in support on the highroad, but Ney had slipped away to Redinha, where he occupied a plateau flanked by woods with two divisions, Mermet's and Marchand's. Wellington closed his leading divisions up to this position, and at 2 p.m. he launched the 3rd and Light Divisions at both flanks. The 4th Division and Pack's Portuguese brigade were halted beyond musket-range in the centre, where they suffered some casualties from artillery fire while they waited for the flanking attacks to develop. The 40th had eight men wounded. After some twenty minutes of skirmishing, Ney's flanks were turned, and he pulled back over a stream to a second position. The British divisions advanced and repeated their flanking attacks, at which the French fell back five miles upon Condeixa. Ney had delayed Wellington's advance for a day, marked by skilful manoeuvring on both sides. Writing up his journal on the evening of the 12th, Surgeon Charles Boutflower gave an account of these operations, known as the Combat of Redinha:

'In the evening [of 11th March] the enemy took up a position on some heights on the right hand of the great road leading to Coimbra. Lord W[ellington] took up his position immediately opposite to them. Between the two armies was a flat about half a mile in breadth and a river waist high running in the centre of it. The crossing of this, it was generally conceived, would occasion much loss in our Army, it being so completely commanded by the enemy's artillery. This loss however we had not to sustain, as at daybreak we found that the foe had disappeared. We consequently lost no time in pursuing them. We came up with them about a league and a half from Pombal, when the Army was formed for a regular attack, which they again evaded by a precipitate flight. There was however a most beautiful affair of posts, in which the enemy lost several hundred in killed, wounded

---

[344] On the 8th Wellington had directed Beresford to march to the relief of Badajoz with the 2nd and 4th Divisions, but these orders were countermanded the following day when the 4th Division marched to join Wellington's main body. 'We halted on the 9th [at Tomar]', wrote Boutflower, 'on which day it was generally understood, & indeed certainly intended, that our Division with the Second & a brigade of cavalry, should proceed into the Alemtejo, and attack Mortier at present besieging Badajoz. This arrangement was however altered, an order arriving in the night for our marching the next morning in the direction of Pombal.'

[345] Leith had gone home sick with malaria in February 1811, but returned to command the 5th Division at the end of November. On Leith's departure, command of the Division passed briefly to Major-General Sir William Erskine who was succeeded on 7th March 1811 by Dunlop.

[346] The 30th took the field with twenty-three officers and 611 other ranks, commanded by Major Alexander Hamilton.

& prisoners; our loss was about a hundred.[347] Lord W[ellington]'s dispositions for the attack today excited the greatest admiration throughout the Army, & proved him to be a consummate General.'[348]

On the afternoon of the 12th the 30th Foot marched through Pombal, where William Stewart saw the sad debris of the French retreat:

'The enemy left in & near the town of Pombal a great number of their killed & wounded, & it was distressing to see in the streets of this dirty town the mangled remains of our fellow creatures bruised & blended with the mud by the trampling of horses & mules as well as the passage of guns, waggons &c over them, until those once valiant heroes could no longer be distinguished from the filth of the road.'

The 40th halted that night at Redinha. Next day, the 13th, was marked by the most critical decision of the French retreat. Masséna had to decide whether to stand and fight at Condeixa, a strategically most important point where the highway to Coimbra was joined by the last road which meets it south of the Mondego, that which ran through Ponte de Murcella to the Spanish frontier. Masséna's original intention had been to cross the Mondego at Coimbra, now only eight miles away, and maintain his army between there and Oporto. The alternatives were to retreat eastwards over the Ponte da Mucela to Spain or to seize the bridge at Coimbra, but on the 12th, the French cavalry had been unexpectedly checked at Coimbra by Trant's Portuguese. With his road to the north blocked, and Wellington at his heels, Masséna decided against offering battle at Condeixa and committed his army to an eastward withdrawal by way of Miranda de Corvo to the highway through Ponte da Mucela, Celorico and Almeida to the frontier.

Ney remained at Condeixa to detain Wellington for as long as possible while Masséna toiled along the bad and mountainous road towards Miranda de Corvo, but the Marshal was rapidly manoeuvred out of the town by Wellington on 13th March. While the 3rd and 6th Divisions turned Ney's flanks, the 4th and Light Divisions stood on the heights above Arrifana, ready to advance as the encircling attacks developed.

'We halted above a league from Condexa [Condeixa] & could distinctly see the town burning the whole day. In the afternoon [the French] retired, taking the direction of the Ponte de Murcella. The Light Division took up a position on the enemy's side of the town; it was feared the French would make a forced march in the night and pass the Ponte de Murcella without further opposition. At daylight this morning [14th March] we commenced our march & passed through Condexa; not a solitary house remained that was not burned to the ground. It was a beautiful town when we were last here.'[349]

Private William Lawrence, too, was saddened at the destruction: 'Their object in burning such a little town [was] probably to prevent our cavalry, cannon and ammunition from following them up too closely. We were, however, delayed but a short time, for we marched through the burning town, certainly not letting the grass grow under our feet, as the ground was much too hot. It appeared once to have been a beautiful town but after this it was one sad mass of ruin.'[350]

The 40th were less than a mile beyond Condeixa when they heard sharp firing to their front, where the French rearguard, Marchand's division supported by Mermet, were holding the village of Casal Novo, a strong position on rising ground surrounded by stone walls and enclosures. The Light Division launched a mismanaged attack in the misty dawn only to find themselves, as the sun rose, faced by a battery and eleven battalions. Casualties mounted until the 3rd Division came up and mounted a right flanking attack, which forced Marchand to withdraw. The French were then manoeuvred out of two further positions in the course of a twelve-hour running fight over fourteen miles. The 4th Division moved forward in support, and Lawrence saw something of the action:

'Next day we came up with the enemy, posted in a strong position at Casal Nova... Part of our division was in this engagement, and I never saw cannon play with better or more deadly effect on any body of men than ours did on the enemy, situated as they were on the heights of Casal Nova.

---

[347] Casualties of the two sides were in fact almost equal, 133 British (including eight men of the 40th wounded, and 73 Portuguese to 217 French.
[348] Boutflower, p.p. 78-79.
[349] Ibid., p. 79.
[350] Lawrence, p.p. 78-79.

'The thing I noticed most particularly in this fight was the singular death of a man in our regiment, who was named William Halfhead, but considering the size of his head… he was the sport of the whole regiment, who named him Bushelhead. His head was indeed so large that he had to have two caps to make him one. This poor fellow was standing within five yards of me when a shot from the enemy's cannon took this same head clean off. I heard one of the men exclaim, "Hullo, there goes poor Bushelhead," and that was all the sympathy he got.'[351]

That afternoon, Cole's 4th Division was ordered to march by Penela to Espinhal. This movement not only threatened Masséna's left, or southern, flank but also put the Division on the right road for a projected redeployment. It will be recalled that when in December 1809 Wellington marched north with the greater part of his army he left General Hill with his 2nd Division in the Alemtejo to watch the southern route into Portugal from Badajoz and Elvas, and when he marched north again in pursuit of Masséna, the 2nd Division, now commanded by Sir William Beresford in Hill's absence, continued to observe this southern approach. The situation on that front changed in the New Year of 1811 when Marshal Soult advanced from Seville into Estremadura. He took Olivenza after a short siege on 22nd January, besieged Badajoz on the 26th, destroyed Mendizabal's Army of Estremadura outside Badajoz on 19th February at the battle of the Gebora,[352] and took the surrender of Badajoz on 10th March.

The news of the fall of Badajoz reached Wellington by the 14th March, and he decided to detach Cole's 4th Division to assist Beresford in Estremadura. On the afternoon of the 15th the 40th Foot received orders to march south towards Tomar the following day.

The 30th, meanwhile, were still moving up behind the army, endeavouring to keep within supporting distance, but were never quite near enough to come into action before the pursuit continued. On the 12th, they marched on to camp at Redinha after the engagement at that place, and on the night of the 13th they halted near Condeixa. On the 14th, while the combat of Casal Nova raged, the 30th marched through Condeixa and halted some distance from the action. Resuming their march at 11 a.m. on the 15th, the Regiment passed through the blazing village of Podentes, strewn with dead French soldiers and murdered Portuguese. Next day they marched with difficulty through Miranda do Corvo, which had been fired by the French and where some five hundred hamstrung horses, mules and asses floundered in the mud amid the debris of Masséna's abandoned baggage train.

Navigation was often difficult in the Peninsula due to poor maps and unreliable guides, and on the march beyond Miranda do Corvo, William Stewart bemoaned the consequences when the 5th Division strayed from the road:

'Thro' an error in the usual manner, our Division was conducted through a vineyard instead of continuing to pursue the road, which tho' not very good, was nevertheless passable. This gross want of knowledge of the country was the means of retarding our march at least two hours during which time Col. Offley of the Lusitanian Legion and myself waited in the road and saw the troops pass in true Indian file, for they could not be made to march otherwise.

'Such [of] the mounted officers who were with the column had very narrow escapes from breaking their necks over its walls and stumps of vines etc. Our march now lay considerably to the right of the Ponte de Maracalla [Murcella] road, and over mountains and by rocks. This circumstance, joined with the unpleasantness of a long and most tedious night march, rendered our sufferings by no means trifling, indeed, many of the officers and men actually were sleeping at intervals as they walked, and for my own part, I nearly fell off my horse seven or eight times.'

Two days later, having crossed the river Ceira and passed through Povoa and Ceira dos Albas, the Regiment was near Foz de Arouce, scene of another rearguard action the previous day. The French had marched before dawn for Ponte da Murcella, where Ney took up a delaying position on the river Alva, a formidable obstacle. Rather than attempt to force the river line, Wellington decided to turn the French out of it by a flanking march to threaten Ney's line of retreat. Ordering two divisions to follow Ney's withdrawing troops, he sent his

---

[351] Lawrence, p.p. 79-80.
[352] Captain Elias Malet of the 30th, DAQMG with the Spaniards, reported to Wellington that Mendizabal's Army had lost all an army had to lose, and that what remained of it was huddled under the walls of Badajoz.

other four divisions, including the 5th, eastwards by a steep road along the watershed through the Serra da Alcaria, fording the river Alva at Pombeiro to reach the main Coimbra-Celorico road on 18th March.

Outflanked and in imminent danger of being cut off, Ney fell back from Ponte da Mucela in great haste and confusion, and Masséna's whole army made a long and fatiguing forced march over the mountain road to Celorico, shedding some six hundred stragglers to be picked up by the British cavalry.

Provisions were now very scarce for the Anglo-Portuguese army, which had out-run its supplies. St. Patrick's Day passed for the 30th without the customary libations, and by the end of the flank march, William Stewart and a brother officer were reduced to sharing half a carton of chocolate and some stale biscuit from the bottom of his haversack. On March 20th Wellington diverted what little food remained to the 3rd, 6th and Light Divisions, who continued the pursuit, while the 1st and 5th Divisions, and two Portuguese brigades, were grounded at Moita and neighbouring villages on the main road to await the arrival of a provision train from Coimbra.

The 5th Division crossed to the north bank of the Alva on the 19th, and two days later the 30th Foot were bivouacked in woods near Moita at a place called Venda do Valle in regimental returns. They remained there for four days, long enough to build huts. It was a welcome respite, for two weeks of constant marching, bad weather, and short rations had increased the number of sick among the rank and file by forty-four.

On 25th March, the first convoy of provisions reached the camps on the Alva from Wellington's new logistic base at Coimbra, and the 5th Division, with the 2nd/30th, resumed its eastward advance along the Celorico road. That night they bivouacked near Galizes, on the 27th they were quartered in Vinho, and on the 28th they halted at Vila Cortés da Serra. Next day, the 30th Foot left the Celorico road and followed a mountain track over the Estrela foothills through Linhares, Prados and Mizarela to reach the village of Vila Pouca, near Celorico on the river Mondego, where they bivouacked for another three days.

It must have been about this time that the 30th received news of an unexpected addition to its strength. Private Daniel McCarthy was one of the men shipwrecked at Gravelines in December 1805 and imprisoned in the fortress of Verdun. As an Irishman, he had been offered the alternative of enlisting in an Irish regiment in French service, which he had accepted in the hope of being able to slip away when an opportunity offered, much as so many British captives had done in the War of American Independence. His chance came in March 1811 when he found himself within reach of British cavalry in Estremadura. His sworn statement that he had never raised a weapon against British soldiers was accepted, he rejoined the Regiment, and went on to serve with the 2nd/30th until 1817, including the Waterloo campaign.

The Combat of Sabugal, 3rd April 1811

Meanwhile, much to the surprise and consternation of his exhausted, starving and demoralised army, Masséna's pride overcame his better judgement and the protests of his generals, and he resolved on a last desperate effort to salvage his military reputation. Abandoning his retreat to the security of Almeida, Ciudad Rodrigo and the plains of Leon, where his army could finally find supplies, on 22nd March he issued orders for a movement from Celorico to Guarda. His intention was to march through the mountains to the Tagus valley with a view to a joint offensive with Soult, which, by threatening Lisbon, would force Wellington to retire for the protection of the capital.

On 29th March, after several days of hard marching in the mountains, Masséna was forced to abandon this impossibly over-ambitious plan, and by the 31st all his corps had reached the Coa valley. Then, rather than complete his withdrawal into Spain, Masséna decided to let his men rest for a few days. This left his corps widely dispersed on a twenty-mile front, with Reynier's 2nd Corps at Sabugal, on the far left of the French line, looking rather isolated and vulnerable.

Wellington saw an opportunity to inflict a crushing defeat on Reynier before he could be reinforced, forcing the French back beyond the Coa, and so on the 29th he manoeuvred Loison's Corps out of Guarda and moved south against Reynier at Sabugal with five divisions, leaving one division to contain Loison. The 2nd/30th made a long march from Vila Pouca on 2nd April in heavy rain. Crossing the Mondego by the stone bridge at Porto da Carne and climbing the steep ascent to Guarda, they reached Vila do Touro that night. Early next morning, they marched south again to take up their ground for the forthcoming attack. Having posted their picquets close to those of the French, the 30th lay down to rest near the west bank of the Coa, opposite and just above the little walled town of Sabugal.

Wellington's concept of operations was for Major-General Sir William Erskine[353] with the Light Division and two cavalry brigades to move around the French left flank and ford the Coa at least two miles above Sabugal. His role was to get behind Reynier and prevent him from retreating eastwards. Once Erskine was underway, the 5th Division was to mount a frontal assault over the Coa to the south of Sabugal town, with the 3rd Division on their right, followed by the 1st and 7th Divisions. It was a promising plan, but went badly wrong from the start, derailed by a combination of poor visibility and the incompetence of General Erskine.

The morning of 3rd April was foggy. Unable to see their objectives across the river, Picton and Dunlop, commanding the 3rd and 5th Divisions respectively, halted and sent to Wellington for new orders. Not so Erskine, who, having rashly ordered the Light Division across the Coa by the wrong ford, nearly a mile north of the intended crossing point, promptly got himself lost in the fog with the cavalry, few of whom came into action. The consequence was that Beckwith's leading brigade of the Light Division, instead of enveloping the French left flank, blundered unsupported into the midst of Reynier's position on the heights behind the Coa. In a very confused fight, Beckwith's men, and notably the 1st/43rd, engaged a succession of enemies with such skill and gallantry that Wellington later referred to their action as 'one of the most glorious that British troops were ever engaged in.' Nevertheless, even when Drummond's brigade arrived on the scene, the leaderless Light Division remained in real danger.

Then suddenly, at about eleven o'clock, the fog lifted, revealing the battlefield to the rival commanders. Wellington could see the outnumbered Light Division fighting desperately on the crest to his right front, but he was at last able to launch his main assault across the Coa. Whilst Dunlop's 5th Division took Sabugal town without loss, Picton's 3rd Division forded the river to attack the right flank of the French forces facing the Light Division. Having stripped his right and centre to counter the Light Division, Reynier found himself unbalanced and quite unable to contain the British divisions now pouring across the Coa. He ordered an immediate retreat towards Alfaiates and the Spanish frontier. Fog and torrential rain precluded a full pursuit, but the combat of Sabugal was a welcome minor success for the Anglo-Portuguese army. Reynier had suffered at least 760 casualties, while Wellington had lost 162 men, nearly half of whom were from the 43rd Foot.

Whilst historians of this action have rightly lauded the invincible gallantry of Beckwith's men, the issue of the day remained in doubt until the 3rd and 5th Divisions crossed the Coa. Bannatyne, in his *History of the XXX Regiment*, gives some detail of how the 5th Division occupied Sabugal without losing a man:

'The manner of it was thus: The French brigade in Sabugal, ignorant of the fact that the head of Dunlop's column was on the other side of the river and only prevented by the fog from crossing, had spent a peaceful morning in cooking their dinners, which had not been a thing of everyday occurrence lately: their interest in this occupation seems to have interfered with their watchfulness, and when the fog lifted the Light Company of the 44th ran across the bridge at Sabugal, the 30th and the other light companies splashed across the river where they could, and at the same time the order came from Reynier for the French to fall in and double to the rear. There was no help for it; they had to be off and leave their dinners to be eaten by the light companies.'[354]

Masséna's campaign of 1810-11 had proved an unmitigated disaster. His casualties in Portugal approached 25,000 men, three times Sir John Moore's loss during the Corunna campaign, together with nearly half his horses

---

[353] Sir William Erskine was in temporary command of both the Cavalry and Light Divisions. Wellington had objected to Erskine's appointment to the Peninsula army, complaining to the Horse Guards that he 'generally understood him to be a madman.' The Military Secretary, Colonel Henry Torrens, complacently responded that, 'No doubt he is sometimes a little mad, but in his lucid intervals he is an uncommonly clever fellow; and I trust he will have no fit during the campaign, though he looked a little wild as he embarked.' Terribly short sighted and dangerously incompetent, Erskine had already cost the Light Division needless casualties at Pombal and Redinha.

[354] Bannatyne, p.p. 252-53.

and almost all of his transport and munitions. Strategically, Lisbon was no longer threatened, and Wellington stood poised on the frontiers of Spain. Allied losses during the pursuit amounted to just 594 men.

Sortie from Tarifa, besieged 1811-12

Tower & Castle of the Guzmans, Tarifa

Major Henry King, 82nd (later General Sir Henry), Commandant of Tarifa Commanded the 82nd at Walcheren & on several occasions in the Peninsula including the Battle of Vitoria

Convent of San Francisco, Tarifa, held by the 47th

Repulse of French assault on Tarifa 31st December 1811

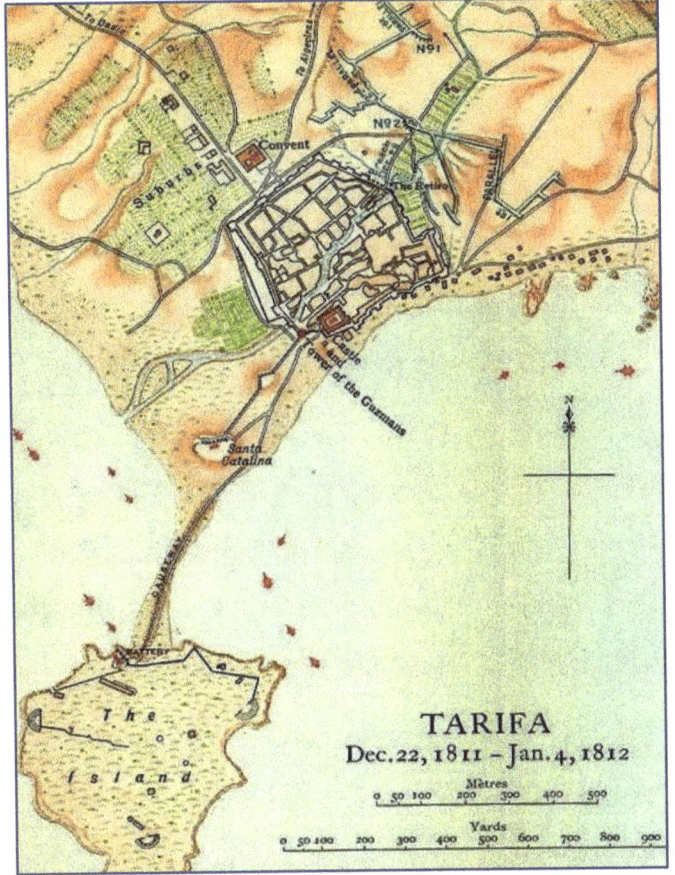

First Siege of Badajoz, 1811 showing ground held by 40th

Convent of San Francisco, Ciudad Rodrigo, captured by the 40th on 14th January 1812

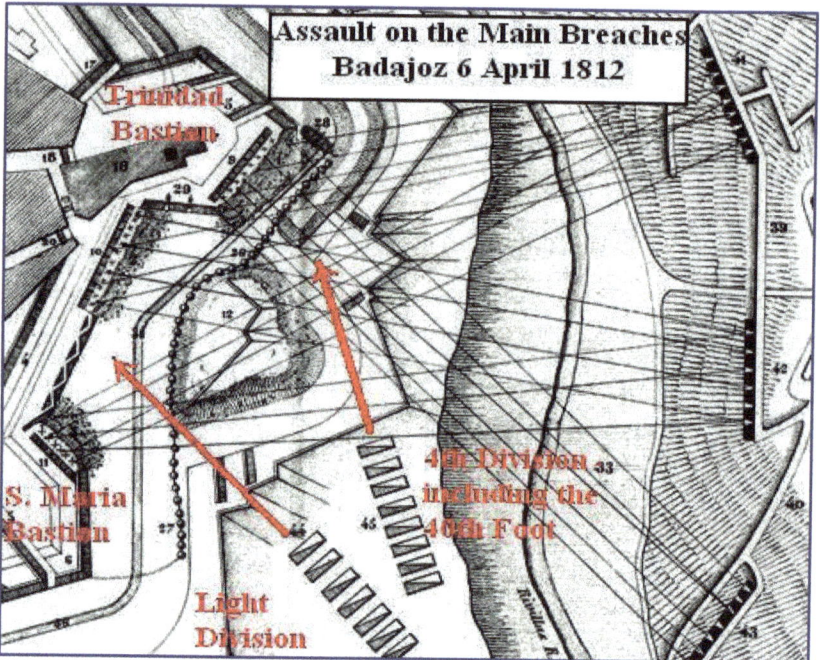

Lt-Colonel George Grey, commanding 30th mortally wounded at storming of Badajoz

Lt-Colonel Charles Amedee Harcourt 40th, wounded at sieges of Badajoz on 10 May 1811 & 6 April 1812

30th escalade the San Vicente Bastion, Badajoz, 6 April 1812

Chapter VI:
The Border Fortresses 1811-12

Battle of Fuentes d'Onoro & Affair of Barba del Puerco (30th) – the 40th march south – Siege of Olivenza & First Siege of Badajoz 1811 (40th) – Battle of Albuera (detachment 40th) – Stalemate on the Caya (30th & 40th) – Attempted Relief of Tarragona (47th) – Defence of Tarifa (47th & detachment 82nd) – 82nd in Gibraltar & Ceuta 1812 – 30th & 40th on the Portuguese Frontier 1811-12 – Siege & Storming of Ciudad Rodrigo 1812 (40th & detachment 30th) – Siege & Storming of Badajoz 1812 (30th & 40th) – Assault on the Breaches (40th) & Escalade of San Vicente (30th).

The Battle of Fuentes d'Onoro, 3-5 May 1811

After the combat of Sabugal, 3rd April 1811, the 30th Foot moved up to the Spanish frontier where the Army of Portugal under Marshal Masséna, rapidly reorganising after their devastating withdrawal from the Lines of Torres Vedras, still held the fortified border towns of Almeida and Ciudad Rodrigo. These fortresses together commanded the northern corridor between Portugal and Spain. Wellington's first objective was to take Almeida, the last French stronghold in Portugal. Almeida was a perfect example of a Vauban-style fortress and, lacking the battering-train for a regular siege, Wellington could only impose a blockade and prevent its relief by Masséna until starvation forced the garrison's surrender. Stores in Almeida were known to be low, and the British commander assessed that some four weeks of blockade would reduce the place.

The 30th Foot, in Dunlop's brigade of the 5th Division, were part of the blockading force. On 9th April, the division occupied the ruined Fort Concepcion and the nearby village of Aldea do Obispo, on the main road from Almeida to Ciudad Rodrigo. After a long wait in heavy snow while billets were allocated, the 30th were quartered in the village, comfortable enough after over a month on the march. Reveille on the 14th was at 3 a.m., and by sunrise the 30th were supporting the blockading picquets in front of Almeida, where they remained all day.

The 5th Division were also tasked with support to the Light Division, who provided a covering force in the direction of Ciudad Rodrigo, and on the 16th, the 30th were roused at 2 a.m. when Masséna passed a heavily-escorted convoy into that town. The Regiment marched to Gallegos that day, but due to the careless incompetence of Erskine, commanding the Light Division, the convoy reached Ciudad Rodrigo without interference, and the 30th returned to their quarters. On 1st May, the Regiment mustered 20 officers, 32 sergeants, 14 drummers and 414 rank and file commanded by Major Alexander Hamilton.

By early May, the French were ready to attempt the relief of Almeida. Masséna, making a last desperate attempt to retrieve his military reputation, advanced with 42,000 infantry, 4,500 cavalry and 38 guns. His chosen line of attack was not on the direct road through Aldea do Obispo, where the 30th lay, but along a secondary route through the village of Fuentes d'Onoro.

Wellington was perfectly well prepared to meet this movement, though the ground was far from ideal. His army of 34,397 infantry, 1,854 cavalry and 48 guns was extended on a 12-mile front behind the Dos Casos stream, from Aldea del Obispo in the north to Nave de Haver, with his main strength in and behind the village of Fuentes d'Onoro. The village, a jumble of alleys rising from the stream to the church, was barricaded and held by 2,200 men of the light companies of the 1st and 3rd Divisions under Lieutenant Colonel William Williams[355]. They were supported on the high ground above the village by the 1st and 3rd Divisions, with the 7th and Light Divisions in depth. Wellington's vulnerable right flank was not held in strength but watched by cavalry, with Julian Sanchez's Spanish forward at Nave de Haver, five miles away across an open, rolling plain. On the left flank, the 5th and 6th Divisions were thinly extended for some five miles along the west side of the Dos Casos stream, which flows through an increasingly deep ravine as it nears the direct route from Ciudad Rodrigo to Almeida through Aldea del Obispo.

---

[355] Promoted to command the 5th/60th from Major of the 81st after his good work at the battle of Corunna.

At 2 p.m. on May 3rd, Masséna launched two brigades (ten battalions) in a frontal assault across the Dos Casos stream into Fuentes d'Onoro. The first brigade entered the forward edge of the village but was driven out by Williams' light companies. The second brigade then attacked, and its 2,300 men pushed the depleted light bobs back to the church at the top of the village. Williams was wounded. Wellington then ordered a counter-attack by the 24th, 71st and 79th, who recaptured the village at bayonet point and even crossed the Dos Casos in pursuit until recalled. A final French attack by four fresh battalions met with no success. The 30th, like the rest of the 5th Division, were not engaged on this first day of the battle.

On the next day, 4th May, an informal ceasefire was observed by both armies. Casualties were collected under flags of truce, and there was fraternisation, with bands playing, parades, football matches and dancing. But appearances were deceptive, for both sides were redeploying for renewed hostilities. In the course of that day, Wellington covered his open right flank by deploying the 7th Division towards Nave de Haver, while that night, Masséna redeployed a considerably more powerful force to the south. The French plan for the 5th was to mount a coordinated attack on both Wellington's right and the village of Fuentes d'Onoro while keeping the British left flank in place with a demonstration.

At dawn on the 5th Masséna made what was intended to be his decisive move, an attempt to turn Wellington's right flank through Nave de Haver and Poco Velho with three infantry divisions and most of his cavalry (17,000 infantry and 3,500 horse). Outnumbered, the British made a fighting withdrawal, but the 7th Division was in danger of being cut off despite excellent work by Sir Stapleton Cotton's cavalry. It was a desperate, potentially disastrous situation. Wellington realised that Masséna was trying to force him to retreat by threatening his lines of communication, but instead of withdrawing, he took a calculated risk. He sent 'Black Bob' Craufurd's Light Division to aid the extraction of the 7th Division while he swung back the 1st and 3rd Divisions to face south. The Light Division covered the infantry withdrawal in fine style, moving in seven battalion squares over three miles of open ground, ably supported by Cotton, with the loss of just 43 men. On completion of this manoeuvre, the British line was rebalanced and Masséna's plan was thwarted.

In the centre, meanwhile, there was a renewed French attempt to capture Fuentes d'Onoro, and savage hand-to-hand fighting ensued in the maze-like alleyways and houses of the village. Ferey's Division attacked first, just after dawn, driving the 71st and 79th to the top of the village, from where the French were counter-attacked and driven back to the lower houses. Masséna then committed eighteen elite grenadier and carabinier companies under D'Erlon, who drove the defenders back again to the top of the village. Wellington fed in supports, first the 24th, then British light companies and Portuguese caçadores. In an effort to break the stalemate, D'Erlon committed 8-10 fresh battalions for a final blow, capturing the church. The situation in Fuentes d'Onoro was critical, but a final counter-attack by two battalions of Mackinnon's brigade (the 74th and 88th) recovered the village. By 2 p.m., the battle in the centre had subsided. The two days of fighting in the village had cost the defenders 800 casualties out of the 4,000 engaged, while the attackers had lost 1,300 out of 7,000.

On the French right flank, Reynier's 2nd Corps was ordered to support the main attack on 5th May by making a 'general demonstration' in the direction of Fort Concepcion, fixing the British divisions there to prevent their redeployment. To that end, Reynier sent forward the 31st Légère, supported by two guns, who skirmished with the light companies of the 5th Division across the Los Casas ravine. The light bobs of the 5th Division had the best of this exchange, inflicting 52 casualties on the French for the loss of 21 wounded, including a sergeant and three men of the Light Company 30th. It appears that Major Alexander Hamilton was also hit, but the wound must have been slight, as he did not report it. It is likely that, as a very experienced field officer, he was commanding the light companies of the division on this occasion. John Hennen, Surgeon to the 30th since 1807, was publicly thanked by Major-General Dunlop on the field of battle for his exertions.[356]

---

[356] John Hennen (1779-1828) was one of the foremost military surgeons of his day. He had previously served as Assistant Surgeon to the 40th in the Mediterranean 1800-1802. His skill was soon recognised by Dr (later Sir James) McGrigor, head of the Medical Department in the Peninsula. On the retreat of the French from Portugal in 1811, being the Senior Surgeon of the 5th Division, he performed the duties of Acting Staff Surgeon, and after the action of Fuentes d'Onoro he continued to serve as Acting Principal Medical Officer with the Division until October, 1811, when he was promoted to the rank of Surgeon to the Forces. As such he was in charge of some of the most important surgical hospitals in the Peninsula. After the battle of Waterloo Hennen was Principal Medical Officer at the Jesuits Hospital in Brussels, where in addition to treating the wounded of all nations he had sole charge of the wounded General Staff officers and performed many operations on notable persons (including the amputation of the Marquess of Anglesey's leg). Hennen was

Total casualties over the two days of battle were 2,844 French and 1,800 Allies. Despite their part in the action on 5th May, the 30th did not receive the Battle Honour of 'Fuentes d'Onor,' though eight officers and 31 men survived to receive the battle bar when the General Service Medal was issued.

The Affair of Barba del Puerco, 10-11 May 1811

Following his defeat at Fuentes d'Onoro, Massena made no further attempt to relieve Almeida, but ordered the garrison to abandon the fortress. On May 10th the 30th returned to their former quarters in Aldea del Obispo, but that same night, as Captain William Stewart recorded in his journal, there was a sudden alarm:

'About 11 o'clock this night the enemy in Almeida blew up the works and strange to say escaped through the piquets to the bridge of Barba del Parco, which post had been ordered to be occupied by the 4th Regt from our Brigade, but unfortunately that Corps lost its way and instead of being at the spot to prevent the enemy passing, it was only enabled to come up with them in conjunction with the 36th and some [light] companies of our Division whilst they were in the act of crossing the bridge. The result was, however, better than might have been expected under the circumstances of this truly unfortunate affair.'

We have more detail in another regimental account of this incident from Ensign Nevill of the Light Company 30th, who was present:

'Lord Wellington… had ordered a strong regiment of our brigade [4th King's Own]… to occupy the bridge in question, supported by the light companies of the brigade. Unfortunately through the darkness of the night, the advancing regiment missed its way. The light companies, who marched later, reached the bridge about daylight, just as the rear of the garrison was passing, which they instantly attacked, capturing about two hundred and fifty men and some baggage: the rest escaped to the French army, who retreated, and immediately after appeared the missing regiment. The light company I belonged to, with the others engaged, lost no time opening French knapsacks and securing their valuable contents, and the officers had some trouble to get them into order, and secure the prisoners.'[357]

The circumstances of the escape of the French garrison of Almeida were certainly controversial. Wellington blamed Lieutenant-Colonel Charles Bevan of the 4th King's Own, but many in the army subsequently felt that this was unjust. The full truth will never be known for certain, but the most probable sequence of events was as follows.

On 7th May, Masséna managed to get a message through to General Brenier, commanding the fortress of Almeida, instructing him to evacuate that place and make for the bridge over the River Agueda at Barba del Puerco, beyond which Reynier's corps would be placed to assist the crossing. Having received an acknowledging signal from Almeida, Masséna made a planned withdrawal on 8th May, while Brenier made preparations to blow up the fortress's defences and to spike its guns. By the evening of the 10th the garrison of Almeida was ready to break out.

Meanwhile, Wellington had entrusted the blockade of Almeida to Major-General Alexander Campbell's 6th Division and, having made a personal reconnaissance on the morning of the 10th, had concluded that the Roman bridge at Barba del Puerco must be defended to prevent Brenier's escape by that route.[358] At about 1 p.m. that afternoon he despatched written orders to Sir William Erskine, then commanding the 5th Division and responsible for defending the line of the Agueda nearest to that point, ordering him to send the 4th King's Own to guard the vital bridge. Erskine was at army headquarters in Vila Formoso, dining with Sir Brent Spencer, when the orders reached him at about 4 p.m. He later told Wellington that he had immediately sent on the orders to the 4th, but this

---

promoted in 1815 to Deputy Inspector of Military Hospitals. In 1817 he published an important work based on his extensive experience, *The Principles of Military Surgery*. He died of yellow fever in Gibraltar when in charge of the Medical Department there during an epidemic, and there is a memorial to him in King's Chapel, Gibraltar.

[357] Nevill, p. 6.

[358] Wellington had his own personal reason for preventing Brenier's escape. The Frenchman, captured at Vimeiro, had the temerity whilst on parole in London to ask Sir Arthur Wellesley for a loan of £500 to cover his debts. The loan was made, but Brenier was then exchanged and the substantial loan had never been repaid.

was untrue. It appears that he stuffed them in his pocket and, convivially irresponsible, neglected to forward them until it was near midnight.

At 11.30 p.m. on that bright moonlit night, the French garrison of Almeida, some 1,400 men, left by the north gate of the fortress in two columns, followed by the demolition teams once their charges were set. Advancing in close formation, Brenier's men brushed through the complacently ill-supported picquets of the 6th Division at around midnight, just as their demolitions exploded, and made their way by a circuitous 13-mile cross-country route towards the bridge at Barba del Puerco.

It was about that time when Charles Bevan received orders for the 4th King's Own to guard that bridge. His battalion was at that time stationed at a bridge over the Dos Casos stream, some 7-8 miles south of Barba del Puerco. Unfamiliar with the ground, and apparently assuming a degree of discretion that Wellington had not intended, Bevan delayed for three hours before marching. He then, according to both our 30th diarists, lost his way.

Meanwhile, other troops were converging on the bridge at Barba del Puerco: Campbell was chasing after Brenier with the 36th Foot, as were detachments of British and Portuguese dragoons. As for the light companies of the 5th Division, according to Erskine, they were despatched by him to Barba del Puerco after he heard explosions at Almeida. The Light Bobs of Dunlop's brigade, including the 30th, arrived first, followed by those of Hay's brigade.

Brenier narrowly won the close-run race to the stone-arched bridge, which his columns reached shortly before 6 a.m. Spanning the deep, boulder-strewn gorge of the River Agueda, the narrow bridge was 350 feet long and approached from each side by a steep zig-zag track. The first column passed the bridge, on the far side of which French troops could be seen. Then, as Brenier reported, their pursuers ran up:

'The enemy was arriving from all sides and had reached the rear of our column. Then it was with sorrow that I saw some of our brave comrades perish. Finally, General Reynier, commanding the 2nd Corps, sent troops down towards the bridge and covered our passage. He gathered all the wounded and had them taken to San Felices, where we were reunited with about 1,000 men. In the whole of the operation, I lost 360 men, of which about 150 were killed, mostly in the gorge, and 200 prisoners, who became separated, not being able to keep up with the rapid march of the column.'

The scene around the bridge and gorge was one of complete confusion on both sides as the French struggled to escape and the British, throwing off their knapsacks, recklessly plunged after them into the ravine. The light companies, including the 30th, appear to have been the first to arrive, but it was the 36th Foot, with some of the 4th King's Own, who crossed the bridge and climbed the far slope until repulsed with loss by three battalions of the 31st Légère.

Wellington was understandably very angry at the incompetence and disobedience of his subordinates, complaining that the escape of the garrison of Almeida was 'the most disgraceful military event' of the Peninsula campaign. A number of officers should have shared the blame, most notably Erskine and Campbell, and though it appears that Charles Bevan was also at fault, it was unfortunate that Wellington was persuaded to uniquely scapegoat the Commanding Officer of the 4th King's Own. Mortified by the appearance of Wellington's critical despatch in the London papers and by His Lordship's refusal to hold an inquiry, Bevan subsequently shot himself.

Brenier's escape was of little consolation to Masséna, who on 10th May learned that he was replaced by Marshal Marmont. Napoleon Buonaparte, too, wanted a scapegoat.

The Fortieth Foot Marches South

It was the 16th March 1811 when Lowry Cole's 4th Division, including the 40th Foot, was sent south to join Marshal Beresford's Army of Estremadura in countering French successes in the south, where Marshal Soult had destroyed Mendizabal's Spanish Army of Estremadura on 19th February at the battle of the Gebora and taken the frontier fortress town of Badajoz on 11th March. The 40th had the mortification to hear when they reached Tomar early on the 17th that the governor of Badajoz had disgracefully capitulated, while on the 22nd at Portalegre, they learned that the Portuguese frontier fortress of Campo Maior had also fallen to the enemy after a resolute defence. The 4th Division had done well to march 110 miles over mountain roads in six days, crossing the Tagus at Tancos by a bridge of boats. On their arrival, Beresford had 18,000 men concentrated around Portalegre, within forty miles of Badajoz.

Rations on this long march were inadequate, and the light-fingered grenadiers of the 40th Foot were up to their usual tricks. On one occasion, confessed by William Lawrence with a degree of contrition, they stole and skewered a farmer's pig on a sergeant's halberd and, to avoid retribution, hid it beneath the long robe of a statue of the Virgin Mary in the chapel where they were billeted. In another incident, Lawrence and four or five accomplices retained the attention of a baker for an hour with soldiers' tales while their comrades used their bayonets to dig a hole in the oven at the rear of her shop and removed the half-baked loaves, which to the soldiers were at that time a greater luxury than meat.

Lawrence himself was the culprit of another theft. He had stolen a cock from a farmyard, and having, as he thought, killed it by wringing its neck, he put it away out of sight in his shako. 'On my return to camp,' he recalled, 'the company had just fallen in on parade, and no sooner had the captain passed close to me than my cap-tenant crew, or made a terrible noise of some sort, much to the astonishment of myself and the captain, who said, "Hullo, Lawrence, what have you got there?" I told him a cock, which I had bought when out foraging. "Yes," he said, "you offered four and took it with five," meaning, I suppose, my fingers. He was perfectly right, but I did not think it would have passed off quite so smoothly, as many in the Peninsula were hanged for plunder.' It seems that Lawrence's company commander was sympathetic to his soldiers' undoubted privations.[359]

Beresford's orders were to attack the French at Campo Maior, and so on the 22nd, he moved out towards that recently captured fortress, leaving the 4th Division at Portalegre for two days' rest after their fatiguing march. The 40th marched to Arronches on the 24th, and arrived before Campo Maior at about 2 p.m. on the 26th.

Having learned of Victor's bloody defeat at Barrosa, Marshal Soult had departed for Andalucia on 14th March, leaving Mortier and Latour-Maubourg with some 11,000 men in Estremadura. The French held the fortresses of Badajoz, Olivenza, Albuquerque and Campo Maior. Beresford's arrival before the last place was a complete surprise to Latour-Maubourg, who withdrew in haste towards Badajoz.

'We found the enemy had quitted it at noon,' wrote Charles Boutflower, 'and that they were closely pursued by our dragoons. It is impossible to describe the joy of the inhabitants as we passed the town; they hailed us with the loudest acclamations. We had not proceeded more than two miles further before a very different scene presented itself; the road was strewn with the dead and dying.'[360]

This was the controversial action in which the 13th Light Dragoons and 7th Portuguese Cavalry caught up with the retiring garrison of Campo Maior. The 13th gallantly overthrew the French 26th Dragoons and then, with the Portuguese, impetuously galloped in pursuit for seven miles to the very gates of Badajoz, where they were checked and suffered heavy losses. Recriminations followed, and both the cavalry and their commanders were blamed for a disappointing outcome to a promising action.

The 40th remained at Campo Maior until 1st April, when they marched to Elvas, the Portuguese garrison town familiar to the Regiment from their stay there in 1808. Elvas was crowded with troops and refugees, large-scale preparations for future operations were underway, and despite strict security, it was obvious that Badajoz was shortly to be besieged.

The Siege of Olivenza

Three days later, the 40th moved painfully on from Elvas, still without the new boots ordered up from Lisbon to replace those worn out on their long marches. That night, the 4th April, they were encamped with the rest of the 4th Division in woods near Juremenha, waiting for a floating bridge to be completed across the nearby River Guadiana. Construction had been delayed first by lack of pontoons and then by high water, and it was not until one o'clock in the morning of the 7th that the 40th crossed in file on an improvised bridge of mixed pontoons, wine casks and trestles. They camped near the village of Villarreal on the road to Olivenza, six miles away, which remained in French hands.

---

[359] Lawrence, p.p. 81-86.
[360] Boutflower, p. 82,

'Our entrance into Spain was marked by an event sufficiently calamitous, when it is considered it might have been avoided by common prudence. We had just laid down on reaching our halting ground on the morning of the 7th when we were alarmed by a sharp firing in the midst of the camp; the confusion was general, most of the men being in a sound sleep. The cause of the alarm was a party of French dragoons who had forced our picquets and had the audacity to come to the very confines of our camp; fortunately, they were not aware of our confusion, and they retired. We had however the mortification to learn very soon that they surprised two squadrons of the 13th Dragoons, & that they had taken them off in triumph to Olivenza.'[361]

The 40th were then halted for a further two days while artillery, stores and munitions crossed the bridge, and on the 9th they marched up the road to Olivenza, halting about a mile from that minor fortress town. That afternoon, Marshal Beresford sent in a flag of truce offering terms, which were rejected by the French even though their garrison numbered fewer than four hundred men and the three miles of walls mounted few serviceable guns. Rather than swamp the place by escalade, Beresford ordered the 4th Division to besiege the town in textbook style with 24-pounder brass cannon from Elvas. There was a delay while the modest siege-train of six ancient guns was brought up from Elvas and ferried across the Guadiana on flying bridges, and the breaching battery was not ready to open until dawn on 15th April. At 5.30 a.m. that day, the garrison was again offered the honours of war, which they again refused, upon which the guns immediately opened fire. Before noon, a breach was nearly practicable, and the governor was obliged to surrender at discretion.

The British gunners had taken care to avoid damage to the town, and when the 4th Division marched in, they were received with cheers by the inhabitants. The besiegers had suffered few casualties, but after three weeks of mishaps and delays, there was a growing awareness in the army that Beresford was not in the same league as Wellington:

'There does appear… that there is a fatality attending the operations of this army,' mused Charles Boutflower, 'which forms a striking contrast with the energy and foresight displayed in every movement by the troops under Lord W[ellington].'[362]

It was during the siege of Olivenza that Private William Lawrence was tricked by Colonel Harcourt's servant into selling his pet cock, Tom: 'He told me he wanted to take him to England, and gave me a dollar for him, but I afterwards found out that he had killed him for his master's dinner. I think I felt as sorry for that as I ever did for anything, for I dearly liked Tom.'[363]

The First Siege of Badajoz, May 1811

It was certainly no fault of Beresford that he was unable to move on at once to besiege Badajoz, for Wellington's army had no siege-train. Assuming that the war in the Peninsula would be essentially defensive in character, Whitehall had made no provision for capturing fortified places, and the British Army in Portugal had only field artillery: 3, 6 and 9-pounder guns. Consequently, the Allies had to rely on what could be found in Portuguese fortresses and arsenals, including some brass museum pieces over two hundred years old, and it would clearly take some weeks to organise even these into a make-shift siege-train. Whilst the artillery and munitions were being assembled, Beresford not unreasonably occupied his army in clearing the French field army, now commanded by Latour-Maubourg, from southern Estremadura.

On 16th April, the 40th, who were expecting to march on Badajoz, were surprised to be ordered to Santa Marta, on the high road to Seville, in pursuit of Latour-Maubourg. Fortunately, a convoy of new boots had at last arrived from Lisbon, and the Regiment covered the thirty miles through Almendral to Santa Marta by the next morning. Latour-Maubourg retired south into the Sierra Morena, and on the 20th, the 4th Division marched back to Almendral, where the 40th were pleased to learn that Wellington was at Elvas. On the 22nd the Regiment was at Valverde, 25 miles due south of Badajoz, from where at noon the following day Kemmis's brigade was ordered back across the Guadiana at Juremenha. The 40th halted that night in a small village short of the river, but were unable to follow the rest of the brigade next morning as heavy rain had swollen the river and carried away the

---

[361] Ibid., p. 84. The 40th had one soldier wounded in the confusion of this raid, and another taken prisoner.
[362] Boutflower, p. 85.
[363] Lawrence, p. 92.

bridge. The Regiment was redirected back on a circuitous route through Olivenza to Valverde, and on through Talavera Real and Lobon to cross the Guadiana bridge at Merida and rejoin the brigade at Montijo on 2nd May. The 40th were then quartered nearby in the village of Puebla. 'We are so comfortable here,' wrote Boutflower, 'that all, officers and men, are anxious to stay,' and there was speculation that they might remain as part of a covering force during the forthcoming siege. It was not to be, for the brigade marched early on the morning of 7th May and bivouacked in woods near Badajoz.

The fortress town of Badajoz, lying on the left bank of the broad river Guadiana, was a first-class stronghold, protected on its north-west side by the river, nowhere less than three hundred yards wide, and for the remainder of its perimeter by eight 18th-century bastions with ditch, counter-scarp and ravelins. The road from Elvas entered Badajoz across the Guadiana by way of a thirty-two arch bridge with a fortified bridgehead. A medieval Moorish castle at the highest (north-west) point in the town formed a citadel. The fortress was further covered by four outworks: three of these, Pardeleras, Picurina and San Roque were on the south bank, while the strongest, the almost impregnable Fort San Cristoval, crowned a bluff on the right bank of the Guadiana and overlooked the castle, effectively dominating the northern part of the city.

Wellington made a detailed personal reconnaissance of Badajoz, and on the advice of his Chief Engineer, Rchard Fletcher, he directed that the main attack should be against San Cristoval, with diversionary attacks against the Pardeleras and Picurina redoubts. The reasoning behind this decision was that once San Cristoval was taken, it would be very possible to breach and storm the castle, which must inevitably lead to the fall of the town. This approach also appeared to offer the best prospect of a quick result before Soult could march north from Seville to relieve the fortress. On 25th April, Wellington returned to his main army, leaving Beresford to conduct the siege of Badajoz.

It was 5th May before the British gunners and engineers could report to Beresford that they had gathered sufficient resources to commence the siege, and over the next three days the investment of Badajoz on both sides of the Guadiana was completed. Kemmis's brigade was allocated to the main attack on San Cristoval, and appeared opposite that formidable fort at 10 a.m. on 8th May, breaking ground that same night some 450 yards from the walls, where a crest provided cover for work to start.

The difficulties on this approach were immense. There was little topsoil on the stony slopes around San Cristoval, with solid rock within inches of the surface. The results of the first night's digging were consequently disappointing, with only enough cover produced for ten men to continue working next day. It was at once clear that the parallels and batteries would have to be built of gabions, with earth carried from a distance. Progress was slow under a furious fire from both San Cristoval and the Castle, and the 400-strong working party from Kemmis's brigade suffered many killed and wounded. Casualties of the 40th included Captains Arthur Rowley Heyland and Robert Henry Wood, severely wounded, Lieutenant James Butler wounded, and an unknown number of the rank and file.[364]

Nevertheless, a breaching battery was begun at the eastern end of the parallel, provoking a vigorous response. At 7 a.m. on the morning of the 10th, a 700-strong French battalion crossed the river to launch a strong and determined sortie from San Cristoval and the fortified bridgehead, entering the British trenches to destroy the works. The infantry covering force, some 800 men including the 40th, at once counter-attacked from behind the crest. This was the Regiment's first real opportunity to engage the French at close quarters since Talavera, nearly two years earlier, and they flew at the enemy without restraint. The French were driven out of the trenches within five minutes after a sharp struggle, but were then rashly pursued in what Wellington in his dispatch called 'a gallant but imprudent advance to the glacis of San Cristobal.' The result was disastrous for Kemmis's brigade, with the heaviest loss falling on the 40th Foot:

'Unfortunately, our troops pursued them with their usual ardour to the very walls, where they were exposed to a most destructive fire of shell, shot and musquetry; notwithstanding with a very inferior force they completely routed their enemy. Tho' the affair was but of short duration, the brigade lost four hundred men, of which two hundred were of the 40th; the loss of officers was also very great; we had eight wounded, amongst whom my two messmates, the Lieut.-Col. & Major, were severely handled: it was one of the most painful days of my life.'[365]

---

[364] The *London Gazette* records that Captain Arthur Rowley Heyland was wounded in the trenches before Badajoz 8-15 May 1811.
[365] Boutflower, p. 90.

One sergeant, one drummer and 56 rank and file were killed on 10th May, while Lieutenant-Colonel Charles Harcourt, Major Henry Thornton, and Lieutenants the Honourable Thomas Browne, William Waldron Kelly, George van Strawbenzie, Alfred Street and John Thoreau were wounded, together with about two hundred and fifty rank and file.[366] Lieutenant van Strawbenzie died of his wounds on 8th June. Next to the storming of Badajoz in 1812, this was the heaviest casualty list suffered by the 40th during their seven years in the Peninsula.

Writing on the 15th, Wellington was forthright in his criticism of 'the frequent instances which have occurred lately of severe loss… by officers leading the troops beyond the point to which they are ordered and beyond all bounds,' citing as an example 'the severe loss incurred by the troops in the siege of Badajoz on the right of the Guadiana on the 10th instant' and threatening to 'bring before a general court-martial, for disobedience of orders, any officer who shall, in future, be guilty of this conduct.'

Private William Lawrence, a seasoned grenadier at twenty and over six feet tall, showed conspicuous gallantry and determination in this affair:

'I succeeded in capturing a straggler here, but was not able to get him into our lines by myself on account of his lying down and refusing to come; so I broke his musket, but not feeling inclined even then to leave him, I knelt down to protect myself a little from the enemy's shot, and waited for some assistance. This was not long in coming, for the Colonel, seeing my position, allowed a man, Towser by name, who had volunteered, to come and lend me a hand, and thus we were enabled to get my captive safe at last to the lines: not, however, without some risk to our own lives, as the enemy were firing at us all the time from a fort situated a short distance from the river. The man was not at all willing at first to walk, so we dragged him by the leg along the ground for some way; but owing to the roughness of the road, he soon found that he preferred walking. We searched him and found a doubloon and a half on his person, which Towser and I divided equally between us. The Colonel reprimanded me for running such a risk for one prisoner, but he was satisfied with my answer, which was that perhaps the man had been on the alert to fire at some of us, which might have terminated in the Colonel's own death, or maybe in mine.'[367]

Lieutenant-Colonel Harcourt had earlier been slightly wounded in the leg and was subsequently evacuated to the hospital at Elvas, from where he sent a quantity of rum, amounting to one pint each, to be divided among the men who had taken part in the counter-attack.

Among the many other wounded was Private James Dilley, aged 18, who later wrote to his parents at Southill, Bedfordshire:

'I suppose that you wonder at my long silence in not sending to you before, but I received a very severe wound at the siege of Badajoz. A shot went in at my belly & it was cut out of my side, but by the blessing of God I am quite recovered… I was wounded on the 5th [actually 10th] of May after a severe action which took place on that day. The French sallied out of the Town in order to take our batteries, but was repulsed by our picquets, which I was on. The shots flid (sic) like hail on every side, which every man that was on the same duty with me was ether killed or wounded… I lay in Hospital four months & had no opportunity of sending [a letter]… I hope to God that my brother will never think of going for a soldier, for I cannot express the sufferings in the compass of a letter that we undergo in this distressed country.' [368]

That night, William Lawrence was posted as an outlying sentry in a wheat field before San Cristobal. After an hour in this exposed position he was disturbed by the enemy taking pot shots at him, attracted by the gleam of his large brass shako badge: 'I took the loading-rod from my musket, and stuck it fast into the ground, and placing my cap upon it, I proceeded about ten yards to the right and sat down; and it was fortunate that I did so, for during the night they put two shots through my cap, and that would have been awkward if my head had been inside.'[369]

Despite the French sortie, a breaching battery was completed that same night and, armed with three venerable 24-pounders and two 8-inch howitzers from Elvas, opened fire at 4 a.m. on 11th May. Effective counter-

---

[366] Casualties as listed in the *Regimental Record of Service*. Oman puts the loss of the 40th at a much lower total of 207 out of a total of 400 for the brigade. Doubtless the *Regimental Record* included lightly wounded patched up by the regimental surgeons.
[367] Lawrence, p. 88.
[368] Letter dated Gallegos, 5th November 1811, spelling and punctuation amended. James Dilley survived the war and was buried at Southill, near Biggleswade, in 1838, aged 46. He was of course mistaken as to the date of the French sortie.
[369] Lawrence, p.p. 89-91.

battery fire from San Cristoval and the Castle silenced the Allies' ancient guns before nightfall. On the 12th, when replacement guns were also overwhelmed, it was apparent that the main attack had ground to a halt with the loss of 726 casualties in the trenches and the sortie.

On 13th May, the siege was raised: Marshal Soult was reported to be hastening north from Seville with 19,000 infantry, 4,000 cavalry and 48 guns, intent on the relief of Badajoz, and was but three marches away.

Marshal Soult, Duke of Dalmatia, was a skilful strategist, but Wellington was correct in his assessment that 'he never seems to me to know how to handle troops after the battle has begun' He was also a world-class plunderer who had looted 1.5 million francs worth of art in Andalucia. His adversary, Marshal William Carr Beresford, had successfully reorganised and trained the Portuguese Army, and was very brave, but was known to be an indecisive tactician, a reputation that was soon to be confirmed.

The Battle of Albuera, 16 May 1811

In his detailed orders to Beresford, Wellington had advised him that if Soult should attempt to raise the siege of Badajoz, and provided that relative strengths were reasonably favourable, the Allied troops should concentrate to give battle at the village of Albuera. Accordingly, on 14th May Beresford marched to that place, taking the Spanish armies of Blake and Castaños under command. He commanded an Allied force of 35,284 (including 3,850 cavalry and 36 guns), of whom 10,449 were British or King's German Legion, and 10,201 were Portuguese.

Cole's 4th Division was left to the last in front of Badajoz, where until the 15th it covered the withdrawal of the improvised siege train to Elvas, the destruction by burning of a mass of gabions and fascines, and the removal of a floating bridge across the Guadiana. This bridge, five miles below Badajoz, was the main communication between the Allied troops north and south of the river. The 4th Division, less Kemmis' brigade, were all on the south bank, and it was intended that Kemmis should join Cole by using a ford below Badajoz before the Division left for the rendezvous at Albuera. Unfortunately, on the night of the 15th-16th the water rose and Kemmis was obliged to make a thirty-mile detour through Elvas to cross the river by the bridge of boats at Jerumenha, reaching Olivenza after dark on the 16th. Thus it was that when the Cole marched at 2 a.m. on the 16th he was accompanied by only the three light companies of Kemmis's brigade, those of the 2nd/27th, 1st/40th and 97th, a total of eight officers and 157 men who had apparently been acting as sharpshooters on the south bank.[370] The 4th Division reached the field of Albuera at 6.30 a.m. and was placed in reserve, covering the road to Badajoz.

Indeed, Beresford's main concern was to block the road to Badajoz, and so he took up a position on low hills astride that road behind the river and village of Albuera. Alten's King's German Legion held the village, supported by William Stewart's 2nd Division and, on arrival, the Fusilier and Portuguese brigades of Cole's 4th Division. Hamilton's and Collins' Portuguese were on Beresford's left, while the Spanish armies of Blake and Castaños extended the Allied line to the right, which was not securely anchored. 'Five hundred paces from the right of the Spanish line was a hill which dominated our position, the possession of which was essential to our safety, which should have been fortified or at any rate held very strongly.'[371]

Soult's plan was to make a relatively weak diversionary attack against Albuera bridge and village, then to advance in strength against Beresford's uncovered right wing to outflank and roll up the Allied position. The French diversion went in at about 8 a.m., fixing Beresford's centre throughout the day. Meanwhile, over half of Soult's army[372] moved to their left under cover of woods, and, crossing the Nogales and Chicapiena streams, appeared on the Allied right flank and advanced on the 'fatal hill.'

Beresford ordered Blake's Spanish army to change front to its right and meet this threat while the British 2nd Division moved up to form a second line, but Blake refused, choosing to believe that the French flank march was a deception and that the real attack would be frontal. Fortunately, his subordinate, Zayas, realised the true situation and deployed his four battalions on the hill, a prominent north-south ridge, to confront the French advance. Girard and Gazan attacked with nineteen battalions in 'order mixte' (column and line), with Girard's

---

[370] The Light Company 40th was commanded by Captain Fielding Browne.
[371] Major Roverea, ADC to Sir Lowry Cole.
[372] Soult's outflanking force comprised the infantry divisions of Girard and Gazan (8,437) supported by the greater part of Latour-Maubourg's strong cavalry division (3,289). Werlé's strong brigade (5,621) followed in reserve.

division leading on a frontage of about 500 yards, described as the most massive single attack of the Peninsula War. Zayas's battalions, some of the best in the Spanish service, held firm though outnumbered two to one, and suffered 30 percent casualties.

Meanwhile, at about 10 a.m. Stewart brought forward his 2nd Division, led by Colborne's brigade (3rd Buffs, 2nd/48th, 2nd/66th and 2nd/31st) to support Zayas. Colborne formed on the ridge to the right of Zayas and, as his battalions came up, advanced in line against Girard's left flank. There was an exchange of fire, then Colborne's men cheered and charged down with the bayonet. The French started to give way.

Just then, visibility was suddenly obscured by a torrential storm of rain and hail, under cover of which eight hundred Polish lancers and French hussars approached in dead ground and smashed into Colborne's open right flank, rolling it up. The Buffs on the right were virtually annihilated, with 85 percent casualties, while the 48th and the 66th suffered 75 and 61 percent casualties respectively, losing their Colours. British muskets were soaked and useless, and only the 31st had time to form square. Colborne's brigade was effectively destroyed. The lancers rode on behind Zayas, where they were counter-attacked by English and Spanish cavalry. There followed a confused close-quarter melee, in which Beresford became involved, which was only resolved when Hoghton's brigade came up and, firing indiscriminately at French and Spanish, forced the French cavalry to retire.

There was then a lull in the battle while Gazan's battalions passed through Girard's battered ranks and, just below the ridge, the 2nd Division brigades of Daniel Hoghton and Alexander Abercromby relieved Zayas. The 31st were on the far right of the new line, Hoghton's brigade took up the centre ground with the 29th, 57th and 1st/48th, while Abercromby's 28th, 34th and 39th moved up on the left. At about 11 a.m., Stewart called for three cheers and led his men forward to the crest, his light companies driving back the French *voltigeurs*. The two-deep British line advanced silently to within 60 yards of the French mass, outflanking it on both sides. Then began an intense hour-long musketry and artillery duel: 3,600 British and four guns against 8,000 French and 24 guns. It was a killing match at ranges of 20-60 yards, with neither side giving way. Directly opposite Gazan's massed ranks, Hoghton[373] was killed, two-thirds of his brigade were down[374], and ammunition was failing, but the survivors did not yield an inch. Some two thousand Frenchmen had fallen to their musketry, but Gazan's men were also unwilling to yield.

On the left flank, Abercromby's battalions, who had suffered less severely in the firefight, edged forward and inwards, but otherwise the situation looked desperate. Hoghton's heroic brigade was reduced to barely battalion strength, but, despite Beresford's strenuous personal efforts, the Spaniards would not move forward to support the rapidly diminishing British line. The Marshal belatedly ordered Alten's Germans and Hamilton's Portuguese to march south to strengthen the sad relics of the 2nd Division; but, obsessed by the perceived need to keep his line of retreat open, he was unwilling to engage his final British Infantry reserve, Myers' Fusilier Brigade of the 4th Division. Instead, he began to make preparations for a withdrawal.

The French still had large reserves: Werlé's Division (5,600) was moving forward behind the left flank of Gazan and Girard, while Latour-Maubourg's powerful cavalry was still largely intact. Soult remained optimistic, though final victory eluded him: 'The day was mine,' he ruefully remarked, 'but they did not know it and would not run.'

Sir Lowry Cole, commanding the 4th Division, had observed the distant battle on the 'fatal hill' with mounting anxiety. When the French cavalry overthrew Colborne's brigade, he had been ordered to move south by about a mile from his original position astride the Albuera-Badajoz road and change front in the direction of the main threat. Cole's new position, on the Valverde road, was still over a mile from where he could see Hoghton's men fighting for their lives, and he sent his ADC, Major Roverea, to seek authority to advance in support of the embattled 2nd Division. No such order came from Beresford.

'General Cole was impatient with being compelled to withhold support under an evident demand for succour – and such at length appeared to be the critical state of the conflict that he took on himself the

---

[373] Major-General Daniel Hoghton, of Hoghton Tower, Lancashire is buried in the British Cemetery at Elvas. His earliest service was with the 82nd Foot.

[374] Of a total strength of 31 officers and 476 other ranks the 29th lost 17 officers and 363 other ranks killed, wounded or missing at Albuera, while the 57th, reduced to barely two hundred commanded by a subaltern, fully earned their 'Diehard' nickname.

responsibility of moving his division to reinforce the battle, without receiving any order from his superior to do so.'[375]

Sir Lowry Cole then formed his division for a counter-stroke from the Valverde road onto the 'fatal hill' one mile away. They moved off at 12.15 p.m. in battalion columns, marching obliquely across the open plain to mount the hill on the right flank of the 2nd Division.

Soult's response was to order Werlé's brigade to move round the left flank of Gazan's battalions and meet the Fusiliers head-on, while Latour-Maubourg was to charge the Portuguese. The advancing dark mass of Werlé's nine battalions in three regimental columns, supported on their left by 26 squadrons of Latour-Maubourg's cavalry, would decide the battle.

As the 4th Division approached the hill Cole deployed his two brigades into line, with Myers' Fusiliers – 1st/7th, 2nd/7th and 23rd (2,015 men) – slightly ahead on the left, and Harvey's Portuguese – two battalions each of the 11th and 23rd Line (2,355 men) – on the right. The seven battalions marched rapidly forward in line, taking ground to their left as they advanced. Each flank of the mile-long line was protected by an open column, ready to form square if attacked by cavalry: a battalion of the Loyal Lusitanian Legion moved forward on the left, and Cole's six British light companies, including those of the 40th, were on the exposed extreme right, where the divisional artillery and Allied cavalry also moved. Cole had this to say about his plan:

'The movement itself was hazardous and difficult to execute without exposing the right flank of the Fusiliers to an acknowledged great superiority of [French] cavalry, ready to take advantage of any error that might occur. In moving forward to the attack, the Fusiliers advanced in echelon of battalions from the left – a manoeuvre always difficult to perform correctly even on a common field day; and as the Portuguese brigade in advancing had two objects to effect, namely to show front to the enemy's cavalry, and at the same time to preserve its distance from, and cover, the right flank of the Fusilier brigade, its movement was even more difficult to effect than the former. Thinking it desirable (with all due confidence in the Portuguese brigade) to have some British troops on the extreme right of the division, I directed the light companies of the Fusilier brigade (including the three light companies of Kemmis's brigade) to form a column on the right of the Portuguese, where I also placed the brigade of guns, and sent the Lusitanian Legion (in column) to the left of the Fusiliers.'

The French cavalry were first to attack, supported by artillery and sharpshooters. Six regiments of dragoons, some 1,800 strong, charged Cole's right flank, confidently expecting to break the Portuguese line as they had so often done against Spanish troops. Harvey's four battalions, untried in battle but well trained, remained steady and delivered a series of volleys which twice repulsed the French squadrons. The British light companies, including the 40th, formed a hollow square to meet this attack, providing a solid right shoulder for Harvey's brigade, and it is likely that they were the first to engage the French horse, setting a confident example to the Portuguese. Some 250 saddles were emptied, then the green-clad dragoons went to the right-about and galloped off. The Allied loss in this engagement was slight, including 32 of the Portuguese and twenty of Kemmis' light bobs. The latter, according to the official return, included three men of the 40th wounded.[376]

With their right flank secure, Myers' Fusiliers pressed on up the hill in the teeth of a murderous fire of musketry and cannister, and closed with Werlé's brigade. Although outnumbered by two to one, after some twenty minutes' close engagement the Fusiliers prevailed and, from their position on the right the light companies at length saw red coats crown the ridge as their enemy broke. This advance, one of the most heroic episodes of the war in Spain, is famously immortalised in William Napier's most vivid prose:

'Such a gallant line, issuing from the midst of the smoke and rapidly separating itself from the confused and broken multitude, startled the enemy's heavy masses, which were increasing and pressing onwards to assured victory: they wavered, hesitated, and then vomiting forth a storm of fire, hastily endeavoured to enlarge their front, while a fearful discharge of grape from all their artillery whistled through the British ranks... The fuzileer

---

[375] *Marches, Movements and Operations of the 4th Division*, by Sir Charles Broke Vere, AQMG 4th Division, p. 12. Sir Lowry Cole was probably influenced in his decision to advance by the urging of Beresford's staff officers, in particular Major Henry Hardinge, but the responsibility was his alone.

[376] The *Regimental Record Book* states that three of the Light Company 40th were killed at Albuera and several wounded. One of the latter was Private Joshua Smith who, though severely wounded, survived to fight at Waterloo. 35 of the 40th Light Bobs survived to receive the 'Albuhera' bar to the Military General Service Medal.

battalions, struck by the iron tempest, reeled and staggered like sinking ships. Suddenly and sternly recovering, they closed on their terrible enemies, and then was seen with what strength and majesty the British soldier fights. In vain did Soult, by voice and gesture, animate his Frenchmen; in vain did the hardiest veterans, extricating themselves from the crowded columns, sacrifice their lives to gain time for the mass to open out on such a fair field; in vain did the mass itself bear up, and fiercely striving, fire indiscriminately upon friend and foe, while the horsemen hovering on the flank threatened to charge the advancing line. Nothing could stop that astonishing infantry. No sudden burst of undisciplined valour, no nervous enthusiasm, weakened the stability of their orders; their flashing eyes were bent on the dark columns in their front; their measured tread shook the ground; their dreadful volleys swept away the head of every formation; their deafening shouts overpowered the dissonant cries that broke from all parts of the tumultuous crowd, as foot by foot and with horrid carnage it was driven by the incessant vigour of the attack to the farthest edge of the hill. In vain did the French reserves, joining with the struggling multitude, endeavour to sustain the fight; their efforts only increased the irremediable confusion, and the mighty mass giving way like a loosened cliff, went headlong down the ascent. The rain flowed in streams discoloured with blood, and fifteen hundred unwounded men, the remnant of six thousand unconquerable British soldiers, stood triumphant on the fatal hill.'[377]

As Cole pushed back and then routed the French left flank, so Abercromby's battalions assailed their right, and even the valiant survivors of Hoghton's brigade joined in the general advance. The French infantry broke at about 2 p.m. and streamed away across the Chicapierna brook, their retreat covered by Latour-Maubourg's cavalry. Cole's light companies, including the 40th, followed them on the right as far as the stream.

As the afternoon and evening wore on, it became apparent that neither of the opposing commanders had any intention of renewing the battle. The French encamped in the woods on the east bank of the Chicapierna while Beresford, apparently convinced that Soult would attack again the next day, made plans for a withdrawal.

The balance was altered on the morning after the battle when Kemmis's brigade reached the field of battle, having marched at 1 a.m. from Olivenza by way of Valverde. Kemmis turned his late arrival to advantage, for to deceive the enemy as to his strength, he ordered an extended line of march within view of the French. So successful was this ruse that Soult was led to believe that Beresford was being substantially reinforced, and in his despatch, he reported that a reinforcement of four thousand men had joined the British Army on the morning of the 17th. This supposed accession of a large number of fresh British troops sufficed to persuade the French Marshal to withdraw that night, leaving the Allies in possession of the stricken field.

The number and density of casualties on and about the 'fatal hill' was indeed horrific. Allied losses totalled 5,916, including 4,159 British[378], 389 Portuguese and 1,368 Spanish (mostly of Zayas's Division) – while French casualties were near 8,000. Surgeon Boutflower of the 40th described how 'on our arrival on the field of combat a scene the most horrible that the imagination can conceive presented itself. The ground was covered with the dead & the dying… It is to be hoped that we shall see but few more such battles as that of the 16th, as they would in a very short time render the British Army a mere name.'

On the 19th, Kemmis's brigade was employed in evacuating the wounded to the field hospital at Valverde, nine miles distant, where the 40th camped overnight. Next day, they marched back to Albuera and spent two nights in the woods occupied by the French after the battle.

At daybreak on the 22nd the 40th marched with Beresford, who advanced cautiously south-east with the battered remnant of the 2nd and 4th divisions in pursuit of Soult, who had retired on Llerena. On the 23rd the Regiment was quartered in the village of Aceuchal, a 'miserable place' which the French had quit the previous morning, and there they remained until 11th June as part of the covering force during the renewed siege of Badajoz. This second attempt to take the fortress, again with insufficient means, was once more unsuccessful and, following failed attempts to storm Fort San Cristoval on 6th and 9th June, Wellington decided to abandon the siege.

---

[377] *History of the War in the Peninsula*, Colonel W. F. P. Napier, CB, Vol.II, p.p. 193-94.

[378] Apart from the Light Company casualties, the 40th wounded included Captain James Johnston, serving with the 5th Portuguese Infantry in Collins' Brigade which took part in the final Allied advance. Johnston had served with the 40th at Monte Video, where he was wounded, and at Roliça, Vimeira and Talavera, before being seconded to the Portuguese Service in May 1810. He served with that Army for the remainder of the Peninsula War, and afterwards until 1826, attaining the rank of lieutenant-colonel and receiving the Order of the Tower and Sword. He subsequently returned to British Army, in the 99th Foot, and retired on 17th October 1839.

Stalemate on the Caya June-July 1811

The armies of Marshals Soult and Marmont were fast approaching, and whilst his siege train and stores were removed to Elvas, Wellington pulled his covering force back to Albuera, where the 40th arrived in the early hours of the 14th June, and encamped again in the woods. The British headquarters were in the village and, writing the following day, Surgeon Boutflower surmised that another battle would take place there in a day or two. It was not to be, for Wellington had been receiving intelligence that the enemy was about to concentrate in greatly superior strength, some 60,000 men, and had decided to withdraw to a more defensible position over the Portuguese frontier. One of his exploring officers at that time was Lieutenant John Ayling of the 40th Foot:

'On the 14th, in the night, Lieutenant Ayling, of the 40th Regiment, who had been employed at Truxillo to observe the movements of the enemy, arrived at Albuera with the account that the advanced guard of the enemy's Army of Portugal, from Castille, had entered Truxillo at noon on the 13th... and as from Truxillo they might have been at Merida on the 15th, and in communication with the Army of the South, I determined to raise the blockade of Badajoz, and that all the Allied troops should cross the Guadiana on the 17th.'[379]

Writing up his journal on the 16th, Boutflower summed up what was known of the situation:

'Of the intentions of his Lordship we are ignorant, but it is generally conceived we are going to the other side of the Guadiana for the purpose of taking up some strong position till we can be joined by Genl. Spencer, who is said to be advancing with our Northern Army. This necessity is to be lamented as it compels us to uncover Badajoz, and thus defeats at once what we have spilt so much valuable blood in endeavouring to attain.'[380]

The 40th marched from Albuera at 3 a.m. on the morning of the 16th, halted that night in a wood near Badajoz, and on the 17th forded the Guadiana to camp in an olive grove near Elvas. 'The day turned out most severe,' recorded Charles Boutflower, 'and during the night the thunder and lightning were truly awful, no person in the camp having experienced anything so dreadfully terrific; the rain came down in such torrents that in a very short time we were almost completely under water. In consequence, yesterday morning we were ordered into Elvas, which place we quitted again this day; we are at present halted about two leagues on the road leading to Portalegre, and, as we suppose, in the neighbourhood of our position, provided the French choose to attack us in it. They have an immense force, Marmont having certainly united with Soult. To counteract this General Spencer with the principal part of our Northern Army has made a parallel movement, and can join us in a few hours.'[381]

Boutflower's information was correct, for Spencer's 'Northern Army' was indeed on the march, and with them came the 2nd/30th Foot. After the affair of Barba del Puerco that Regiment had moved from Aldea del Obispo to Nave de Haver. In Wellington's absence in Estremadura, Sir Brent Spencer was in charge of the four divisions in the north with very specific instructions to cover all eventualities. Consequently, when on 5th June Marshal Marmont, made a demonstration across the Agueda, Spencer withdrew to Alfayates, and when it was revealed that the French move was a feint, and that Marmont was, as Wellington had anticipated, marching south to join Soult in Estremadura, Spencer too turned south. Marching parallel to the French, Spencer's divisions headed through Castello Branco for the Vila Velha boat-bridge over the Tagus, then on through Nisa to Portalegre. The 5th Division, with Slade's cavalry brigade, halted at Castello Branco to cover the other divisions while they crossed the Tagus, crossing themselves on the 18th and 19th June. After eighteen days of hard marching over bad roads in the heat of summer, the 30th hutted themselves near the town of Arronches, on the road between Portalegre and Campo Maior, on the 23rd.

Wellington's whole army of 54,000 British and Portuguese was now united on the Caya, sufficient to hold its own against the combined armies of Soult and Marmont. He took up a strong position on a twelve-mile front between the fortress of Elvas and the walled town of Ouguela, near the Gebora river. The 4th Division were stationed between Campo Maior and Elvas, while the 5th Division, with the 30th, remained in reserve on the Portalegre road. Battle was offered to the French marshals, but they did not intend to attack and risk a general action in a position deliberately chosen by Wellington. Indeed, Marmont and Soult, having made plans to contain

---

379 Wellington's Despatch dated Quinta de St. Jao, 20th June 1811.
380 Boutflower, p.p. 99-100.
381 Ibid., p. 100.

Wellington, were about to go their separate ways. On the 24th the latter had learned of trouble in Andalucia requiring his presence, and on the 29th his divisions began to march south. On the 15th Marmont retired to Merida. This refusal of battle on the part of the French was significant, marking a shift of the moral and strategic balance in favour of Wellington.[382]

As soon as Wellington became aware of Soult's departure, he began to move his troops out of the malarial river valley of the Caya, though he was obliged to keep his army concentrated until Marmont too moved off. The 4th Division marched to Estremoz on the 24th, though the 40th Foot remained in their encampment near Elvas until 21st July, with dire consequences for their health.

The 2nd/30th, with the rest of the 5th Division, were ordered back to Portalegre on 18th July. They were initially quartered in the town, and then hutted outside around Quinta de Almeria, a wooded area called 'Vauxhall' by the officers from its fancied resemblance to the glades of the celebrated London place of outdoor amusement, an illusion furthered by the music of the regimental bands. Hamilton signed the monthly return there on the 25th, and it is evident from this return that the 30th too were suffering from the prevalent Guadiana fever, with eleven sergeants, six drummers and 190 rank and file either in hospital or convalescent, leaving only 28 sergeants, 14 drummers and 394 rank and file fit for duty.

At Portalegre, there had been a melancholy sequel to the escape of the garrison of Almeida. On 8th July Colonel Bevan of the 4th, overcome by the burden of blame after the Barba del Puerco affair, took his own life. Every officer of the division made a point of attending his funeral in the castle yard.

Scandal also touched the 40th at that time. At Campo Maior on 15th July Lieutenant Waldron Kelly was court martialed for disgraceful and infamous conduct after 'associating' with the wife of Private Noah Cooper in defiance of the repeated orders of his commanding officer and for assaulting the soldier on 14th June when the latter demanded his wife, who was in a hut with Lieutenant Kelly. The court found Kelly guilty and sentenced him to be cashiered, but in consequence of an extraordinary act of clemency by the Duke of York, he escaped with a severe reprimand 'upon the grounds of his high military character.' What Noah Cooper thought of this is not recorded.

Two days earlier, also at Campo Maior, Quartermaster John Forster Kingsley[383] of the 2nd/30th faced a general court-martial. He had been passing through Moita on 1st June with a convoy of eight ox carts carrying urgently required regimental stores from Lisbon, escorted by a party of soldiers. Two more of his carts had broken down outside the town, so he applied to Assistant Commissary Dankaerts for help as 'the regiment was in great distress for the want of trousers and shoes,' which he had with him. The Commissary refused all assistance, apparently telling Kingsley that he must 'shift for himself.' It is not unknown for quartermasters to bend the rules when the welfare of their regiment is at stake, and it was unfortunate for Kingsley that Sergeant Gunning and two privates of his party were intercepted whilst making off with two of the Commissary's carts. An altercation ensued, in the course of which Gunning refused to give up the carts without an order from his Quartermaster, or to halt, whereupon it was claimed that the sergeant was hit and had his cap knocked off by Lieutenant Rae of the Royals, who arrested both him and Private Ward. In the confrontation that followed, Rae tried to pull rank on Kingsley, which the Quartermaster rejected, intemperate words were apparently exchanged, and Kingsley offered to meet Dankaerts with pistols, which the Commissary scorned, saying that he was an officer and gentleman while his opponent was a quartermaster and a blackguard. About one hour later, an armed party of the 30th was again discovered leaving Moita with two 'borrowed' carts: the determined Quartermaster had done his duty by his regiment, but at the subsequent court-martial, he was reprimanded and lost three years' pay and seniority. It is, however, clear that the court was sympathetic.

General Brent Spencer went home in August 1811, having been superseded as nominal second-in-command of the army by Sir Thomas Graham, with whom Wellington was to enjoy a much closer relationship. Spencer's services in the Peninsula have been rather marginalised by historians, who have followed Wellington

---

[382] Oman, the great historian of the Peninsula campaigns, commented that from this time 'the French armies in Spain found themselves thrown upon the defensive; and so things were to remain for the rest of the Peninsular War. The offensive, though it was hardly realised as yet, had passed to Wellington.'

[383] Kingsley had been Quartermaster of the 2nd/30th since its formation in 1803 and served in the Regiment until 1824 when he died at sea on his voyage home from India.

in dismissing him as unreliable and defeatist. But he had a long record of success in battle, and in the Peninsula he made a sound, albeit subordinate, contribution to the victories of Roliça, Vimeiro, Busaço and Fuentes d'Onoro. His obituarist, in the 1829 *United Service Magazine*, had no doubt of his quality and pointed in particular to his advocacy of the bayonet: 'The military character of Sir Brent Spencer has been marked by an ardent zeal, an inflexible firmness, and a devotion to the performance of the trusts reposed in him, almost unparalleled. The charge and the use of the bayonet have been his constant mode of warfare. In the numerous actions in which he was engaged, he on all occasions possible adopted it with the most powerful effect, and he must be considered to have been particularly instrumental in establishing a practice which has in all our late military movements given a decided superiority to our arms, and in restoring to the British soldier that mode of fighting the most consonant to the national character.'

Attempted Relief of Tarragona June 1811

Meanwhile, at Cadiz, the Spanish Regency had implored Graham to send assistance to the garrison of Tarragona, the main base of Spanish resistance in Catalonia, which since 8th May had been besieged by General Suchet's Army of Aragon. The Spaniards urged that 'a few hundred British troops now would be of more importance than thousands at a later period.' Graham was understandably wary of close co-operation with Spanish forces after his recent experience at Barrosa, but agreed to send Colonel Skerrett with his own 2nd/47th, a detachment of the 3rd/95th and half a company of Royal Artillery.

On 14th June, Graham ordered Colonel Skerrett to embark his troops that evening on the armed troopship HMS *Regulus* and other transports, and to put in to Gibraltar, the Governor of which was asked to make a small contribution to his force. Graham limited the risk, and the expedition's freedom of action, by his specific instruction to Skerrett that, 'You will before landing your detachment [at Tarragona] state to the Governor that you must have at all times free and open communication with His Majesty's ships-of-war; and in the event of the place being under the necessity of surrendering, that you are at liberty to withdraw the troops on board of the said ships previous to the capitulation.' These instructions would have constrained the most impetuous of commanders, but John Byrne Skerrett, though personally brave, was apt to take counsel of his fears and only too happy to conform with such precautionary orders.

Picking up some light companies at Gibraltar, thus making up his little force to a total of 1,147 men, Skerrett's transports arrived off Tarragona early on 26th June in very rough weather. Admiral Sir Edward Codrington was offshore with a squadron which had for some weeks been doing all in its power to aid the defenders, running Spanish reinforcements into the besieged city and repeatedly bombarding the ever-advancing French siege works. Despite these naval efforts, and those of a relief force under the Marquis of Campoverde, Captain-General of Catalonia, Suchet had pressed the siege with skill and energy, and it was clearly only a matter of days before the beleaguered city fell. The lower town had been stormed by the French on the 21st, effectually closing the harbour to Codrington's ships, so that Allied landings and embarkations had to be made over the open Milagro beach. The admiral assessed the situation on the 26th:

'The surf was so high on that day that we had no other communication in the forenoon than by a man swimming ashore with a letter. And upon Colonel Skerrett putting questions to General Doyle and myself upon the conduct he should pursue according to his orders, we agreed in our opinion that although the arrival of the troops before the Puerto was taken would probably have saved the garrison, it was now too late; and that their being landed, if practicable, would only serve to prolong the fate of the place for a very short time, at the certain sacrifice of the whole eventually.'

Despite this negative assessment, Skerrett, Codrington and other officers went ashore that evening, with great difficulty through a heavy surf. They toured the weakened defences and conferred with Contreras, the Spanish governor, and unanimously agreed that the town was untenable. Contreras doubted that the weak inner walls could hold and told them that he intended, when the French opened their breaching batteries, to sally out and try to cut his way through the French lines to reach Campoverde. He invited Skerrett to land his troops and join him in this desperate sortie, and then offered him the alternative of defending the walls against the imminent storm. The despairing governor was clearly undecided as to the best, or rather least worst, course of action, but participation in either of these options would have invited the total destruction of the small British force. Skerrett and Codrington were confirmed in their view that a landing would invite disaster by their own perilous embarkation, and they therefore declined both of Contreras's alternative offers.

An emissary then arrived from Campoverde, with an appeal to Skerrett to land his troops at Sitges and join the relief force. This course of action appeared better than nothing, and so, with Codrington's approval, early on the morning of the 28th the British transports sailed north.[384]

Meanwhile, Contreras had resolved to fight his way out of Tarragona that evening and had made his plans accordingly. These were unfortunately pre-empted when Suchet launched an overwhelming assault at 5 p.m., which carried the breaches and, after desperate street-fighting, took the city. Some two thousand Spanish soldiers were killed, and eight thousand were taken prisoner. In the sack that followed, over two thousand civilians were slain, including 450 women and children. The French attack was so rapid that there was little that Codrington's squadron could do but send in their boats to pick up some of the hundreds who stripped and endeavoured to swim out to the ships. Suchet's success was a stunning blow to Spanish resistance in Catalonia.

Indeed, when Campoverde learned that a French column was on its way from Tarragona to attack him, he abandoned his headquarters at El Vendrell and fled inland as his army melted away. His departure exposed his coastal depot at Sitges, which the French took on the 20th, capturing ships, stores and wounded in the hospital. Skerrett's British were lying off the place in their transports, preparing to land and join Campoverde, as the latter had asked. Finding that disembarkation was now impossible, and that the Catalan army had disappeared, Skerrett sailed for Minorca. After a short stay there, the expedition returned by late July to Cadiz after a most humiliating experience.

Colonel Skerrett was subsequently blamed by some for not landing his troops at Tarragona, but Sir Edward Codrington had no doubt that this was the correct decision:

'It was very well we did not land the regiments, for the place was taken the next day; and without being able to save it they would have been obliged to capitulate. The only thing Graham said to me when he trusted them to me was, "Do not put them in a situation to be taken or to capitulate."'

As for the 47th, Captain John Harley probably spoke for them all when he wrote, 'We returned to Cadiz quite disappointed and out of temper with our fruitless expedition, and because we had no opportunity of assisting our friends and foiling the atrocious Suchet.'

Shortly after their return to Cadiz from Tarragona, the 47th moved to the Isle of Leon, some eight miles from the city, where they were brigaded with the 87th Foot and 20th Portuguese under Colonel Skerrett. Major Richard Broad commanded the Regiment.

Defence of Tarifa, November 1811-January 1812

The 2nd/47th Foot remained at Cadiz until October 1811 when Colonel Skerrett was sent to Tarifa with a brigade of 1,358 all ranks, comprising eight companies each of the 2nd/47th and 2nd/87th and a company of the 2nd/95th Rifles, seventy hussars of the King's German Legion and six field guns. The 47th sailed with 616 all ranks[385], leaving two companies on the Isle of Leon.

Skerrett's orders from Major-General Cooke (who had relieved Graham) were to threaten and molest the rear of Marshal Victor's force besieging Cadiz and to co-operate with the Spanish General Ballasteros. Tarifa had for years been a thorn in the side of French troops in Andalucia, both as a base for Spanish resistance and 'the great point of assembly for supplies of every nature for Cadiz.' In addition to removing a threat, the French wished to secure Tarifa for themselves as a port through which their troops in Andalucia could import supplies and horses from the Barbary coast of North Africa.

Skerrett landed his brigade at Tarifa on 14th October. On arrival, he took under command the existing British garrison, consisting of two companies of the 2nd/11th and four companies (287 other ranks) of the 1st/82nd on detachment from Gibraltar under Major Henry King, a one-legged officer of great energy and resolution who

[384] Private Adam Reed of the 47th, in his Memoirs, stated that the troops were in boats ready for landing when the French stormed Tarragona, at which they rejoined the ships. This is almost certainly incorrect, though it may subsequently have been the case at Sitges.
[385] The 2nd/47th comprised 27 officers, 38 sergeants, 17 drummers and 534 rank and file.

was British commandant of the town. King was better known to the Spaniards as *Il Commandante Cojo* (lame), his predecessor Major Browne having been *Il Commandante Loco* (mad). The total strength of the British garrison was now 1,774 all ranks.

On October 17th Skerrett marched his brigade out three miles from Tarifa and made a demonstration as far as the Sanctuary of the Virgen de la Luz, returning that evening. On the 19th he moved north along the coast road to the defile of La Peňa, withdrawing again that night to Tarifa. There he found a Spanish brigade of 1,350 all ranks[386] under General Don Francisco de Copons y Navia, which had landed that day from Cadiz. On the 23rd the British brigade marched out again, taking up a position on the wooded heights of the Sierra del Retin, 24 miles north-west of Tarifa, for two days. On the 26th, they formed in column on the coast road leading to La Peňa and marched in quick time past Copons.

On 4th November the British and Spanish brigades, carrying three days' supplies, made a combined move against the French rear, reaching Facinas that day and taking up a strong position. No enemy appeared, and so on the 12th the Allies advanced on Vejer de la Frontera. This town, on a conical hill halfway to Cadiz, was held by a French outpost of three hundred men, who withdrew. The light companies, including the 47th, entered the town that evening, but were obliged to withdraw the following day on the approach of a large force of the enemy, which almost captured Skerrett and his staff.

On the 27th the Anglo-Spanish force marched east across the hills to Algeciras, intending to join Ballasteros in an attack on French troops retiring from San Roque towards Ronda. Throughout this period, there was considerable activity by 'observation parties,' British officers riding with escorts of Spanish guerrillas, troopers of the King's German Legion, and, on one occasion, riflemen uncomfortably mounted on artillery horses. One of these observing officers was Lieutenant Richard Read of the 82nd Regiment.

By mid-November it was apparent that the French were assembling a force to attack Tarifa, Marshal Soult had delegated the task of reducing Tarifa to Marshal Victor, who by December 8th had put together a siege train of sixteen guns from the lines around Cadiz and had moved two thousand men forward to Vejer de la Frontera. Tactical command of the force was entrusted to the veteran General Jean-Francois Leval.[387] This concentration was reported to General Campbell at Gibraltar, who ordered Skerrett's brigade to return on 2nd December for Tarifa, and Copon's Spanish brigade soon followed. The combined Anglo-Spanish garrison of Tarifa now numbered some three thousand men with 26 guns. The Spanish General Copons was nominally in command of the garrison, though Skerrett, prompted by Major King, retained the keys of the town.

Tarifa was a small decayed town lying behind its ancient Moorish walls on a promontory some seventeen miles south-west of Gibraltar. The place was overlooked by a range of low heights within two to three hundred yards of its north-east front, which was the obvious main point of attack. The walls, and the square towers set in them at intervals, were no defence against siege artillery, and the largely thirteenth-century citadel, the Castle of the Guzmans, was little better. On the seaward side of the town, half a mile beyond it to the south-west, lay a bare, rocky island, the Isla de las Palomas, connected to the mainland by a sandy causeway. This had been fortified and would have made a strong, if temporary, final refuge for the garrison.

As a siege appeared imminent, the garrison laboured to improve the defences under the expert direction of Captain Charles Smith, Royal Engineers. It was recognised that the weakest point of the walls was in the north eastern front, where the steep-banked ravine of the Retiro, a seasonal torrent, entered the town. The entry point of this stream was barred by a medieval tower with an iron portcullis, known as the Retiro Tower, in front of which palisades were planted in the ravine, which provided a perfect covered approach to the town.

The ancient curtain walls, as found, were too weak and narrow to mount guns, and they were entirely exposed to both artillery bombardment and musketry from the nearby heights. They had no glacis and practically no ditch. Accepting that siege-guns could breach the vulnerable outer defences with ease, the defenders made a great effort to create an inner line of defences behind the walls, where there was a fourteen-foot drop into the town. The narrow streets were blocked with defensive traverses and entanglements improvised from iron window

---

[386] Copon's force consisted of the Regiments of Irlanda (469 all ranks) and Cantabria (609 all ranks), a detachment of the Seville Regiment (183 all ranks), 120 cavalry and ten gunners.

[387] Leval (1762-1834) was a veteran of Fleurus, Jemappes, Neerwinden, Jena, Eylau, Talavera, Ocaňa, Barossa, and many other actions, and had commanded a division since 1799. His previous encounters with British troops had met with defeat.

grilles torn from buildings, while strongly built houses behind the wall and flanking the Retiro were barricaded, loopholed, and stocked with grenades. In the south-western corner of the town, the stream-bed passed two fortifications, the tower and castle of the Guzmans, which formed part of the walls.

Some of the wall towers on the north-east front were strengthened to bear artillery, four light 6-pounder guns, two 12-pounders and four coehorn mortars. A naval 18-pounder was mounted on the tower of the Guzmans, and two 6-pounders were allocated to the Jesus Tower, which flanked the eastern wall. The town was held by some eleven hundred British and four hundred Spanish troops.

Outside the town, houses in the northern suburbs were demolished and large working parties entrenched and loopholed the Convent of San Francisco, seventy yards from the north (Cadiz) gate, to serve as a redoubt. This work, connected to the gate by a parapet and covered-way, was held by one hundred of the 47th under Captain Archibald Campbell and an equal number of Spaniards.

Another fortified post, Santa Catalina, with a 12-pounder gun, was erected around an old chapel on an isolated rock outcrop west of the town to block approaches to the island causeway and enfilade the southern and western beaches. The Isla de las Palomas itself was fortified and mounted twelve artillery pieces, including four 24-pounders, while a series of caves there were converted into casemates and store-rooms. Major King was in command on the island, with three hundred British and two hundred Spanish troops, and detached fifty of each nation under Captain Robert Wren, 11th, to the adjacent Santa Catalina fieldwork.

The defence of Tarifa was additionally supported by the naval gunnery of HMS *Stately*, 64, the *Druid* frigate and several mortar and gun-boats which lay in-shore and were able to bombard the flanks of any French attack.

Leval began to move towards Tarifa on 8th December, but persistent heavy rain and interdiction of the coastal road past the Torre de la Peña by the Royal Navy slowed progress of the French siege-train, and the first of the 10,000 men allocated to the siege itself did not reach Tarifa until 19th December. This slow journey over poor roads played a major part in the failure of the French plans, for the country around Tarifa was sparsely populated, and they had to carry all their food with them, using up a significant amount of their supplies during the march.

Captain Thomas Bunbury recalled an occasion at this time when an 'observation party' of mounted riflemen and guerrillas, with Lieutenant Richard Read, 82nd, and himself, were sent to ascertain the strength of the enemy assembling near the defile of La Peña:

'It was about noon, and the enemy were cooking (the French are always cooking), and so engaged that they did not notice us until we were amongst them. Trumpets sounded and drums beat "to arms" in all directions; they must have imagined that a British army was at our heels. In the meantime we placed our men in a single rank of skirmishers to make as great a display as possible, and an officer of the name of Reed, who had accompanied me, rode back to look out, as if impatient for the arrival of reinforcements.

'Having satisfied our curiosity, we put about and retraced our steps, but a little faster than we came, for the French, perceiving they had been hoaxed, sent a party of dragoons in pursuit, and every moment I expected we should be overtaken. Our artillery horses were clumsy and could not go the pace, and the riflemen could not ride… Altogether it would have been a most ludicrous scene if we had not been at the same time in imminent danger, for the enemy were gaining upon us very fast. I kept with my friend Reed in the rear, calling out to the men to hold on like grim death, as we had not much further to go before we should meet with our own troops prepared to protect us.

'In the midst of this confusion, Reed called out to me that one of our guerrillas, in whom I had hitherto placed great confidence, had gone over to the enemy. He had in fact joined them, and was in close communication with the officer leading the party. Suddenly the Spaniard drew his pistol and shot the officer dead, then putting spurs to his horse at the same instant, he was again at our side. There was evidently a great commotion in the ranks of the enemy's cavalry, and they ceased to pursue us.'[388]

Skerrett marched out from Tarifa on December 18th for a reconnaissance in strength, with 250 men, hussars and light infantry, including the Light Company 47th. Having taken up a position on high ground covering

---

[388] *Reminiscences of a Veteran*, Major Thomas Bunbury, London, 1861, p.p. 113-4.

the pass near the sanctuary of the Virgen de la Luz, he pushed on towards Facinas, feeling for the head of the approaching French column, but after a cavalry skirmish lasting some hours he sent Captain Captain John O'Donaghue, 47th, his acting ADC, to order a retirement, and returned to Tarifa towards evening.

Next day, the French appeared on the hills above Tarifa, driving in the advanced posts. The garrison's outlying pickets were doubled that night, and half the men were ordered to sleep fully dressed and accoutred. At the Convent, Captain Campbell was placed particularly on the alert, and seventy marines, landed from HMS *Stately*, were added to the island garrison under the command of Major King.

At daybreak on the 20th the French advanced in two columns, two and three thousand men strong, and were met by Major Richard Broad, 47th, with the Light Companies of the 47th and 87th, and the 95th company, supported by two 6-pounder field-guns, the pickets and a company of Spanish cazadores. The enemy were held in check for about an hour, suffering much loss from the defenders' artillery. Eventually, as the French pressed on with superior numbers, the Light Companies retired within the walls. The French dragoons then advanced with great boldness until they were suddenly put to flight by a volley from the pickets of the 47th and pursued by mortar-shells from the island.[389] Nevertheless, by four in the afternoon Tarifa was invested.

At daybreak on the 21st the Light Companies of the 47th and 87th and the 95th company sallied out from the north-east front, advanced three hundred paces to drive in the enemy's advanced picquets, and then retired without loss. Captain Charles Edward Livesay of the Light Company 47th was mentioned in despatches. The guns on the island played the whole day on the enemy's lines, and did great execution.

On the 21st the guards and alarm posts within the town were allocated to regiments, and the 47th was made responsible for the Castle, the west wall and Sea Gate, together with a picket for the artillery reserve, a total of six officers, eight sergeants, four drummers and 170 rank and file on duty at any one time, in addition to those stationed at the Convent. The 87th held the north-east front, while there was a Spanish battalion on the west front and another within the town.

Private Adam Reed, 47th, complained that 'duty was never more harder to a British soldier, for I myself have mounted a guard one day and come off the next and when I went into the barrack yard our Adjutant has pressed me to go on another guard the same day, being 48 hours on guard without having any rest.' Meanwhile, troops were busily employed in throwing up more traverses in the town and in making, on the east side of the island, beds for two 10-inch mortars which had arrived from Gibraltar.

That night the French pushed a picket incautiously close to the north-west front of the town, and on the morning of the 22nd, before daybreak, Major King ordered the Light Company 11th under Captain Wren to fall on this party from Santa Catalina, which they did, dislodging the picket from a small house on the western beach, killing eleven of them and taking a sergeant prisoner for the cost of two men slightly wounded. The regiment to which the picket belonged, 16th Légère, then turned out and obliged Wren to retire, at which the British flank companies made a sortie, drove the French regiment from a strong position in front of the Convent of San Francisco and threatened to take possession of the west hill, near the town. In the course of this daring attack Lieutenant Benjamin Welstead of the 82nd actually entered one of the French camps and captured a field-gun there, and, although he was unable to carry it off in the face of the French reserves, the latter were drawn by the skirmish to expose themselves to the fire of the town, island and ships, and suffered severely before they recovered their captured field-piece from under the guns of the north-east tower. In this affair, the British loss was one man killed, and five wounded, while the besiegers had three men killed and four officers and 19 men wounded, mostly from the 16th Légère.[390]

---

[389] The British loss on the 20th was one man killed and 22 wounded, including two of the 47th, while the Spanish cazadores, who behaved very well, suffered fourteen casualties. Leval acknowledged only one officer and three men killed, and 27 wounded, though a Spanish officer estimated their loss at three hundred.

[390] Captain John William O'Donaghue, 47th Foot, Acting ADC to Colonel Skerrett, was slightly wounded that day. He had previous service in the 4th, 9th and 63rd Regiments before joining the 47th in 1803. He then served with the Regiment in South America. After the siege of Tarifa he was selected by General Cooke to carry home the victory despatch, in which he was honourably mentioned, receiving a brevet majority. He later served with the 47th in the Pindari War and in Burma, retiring in 1831 with a CB and the rank of lieutenant-colonel.

When Skerrett asked the French sergeant if he thought that his countrymen would take Tarifa, the prisoner coolly replied, 'It is a positive order from Napoleon, our Emperor, that we should do so, and he generally provides means adequate to the end.'

That night, the French siege-train arrived, for a gale had driven the British ships offshore and French engineers had been able to repair the coastal road at La Peña. On the 23rd Leval's engineers surveyed the approaches to the town and, as had been anticipated, recommended an attack against the central portion of the north-east front. Work on the first parallel, some three hundred yards from the walls, began that evening. The investment had become a regular siege. The following day, a second parallel was started, a section of which came within 180 yards of the town. The Allied artillery and ships attempted to disrupt the work, the latter directed by signallers on Guzman's Tower, but to little effect.

It is clear that the responsibilities of his command weighed heavily on Skerrett. Although physically fearless, as a commander, he was excessively cautious, fidgety and rather prone to take counsel of his worst fears. Captain Thomas Bunbury, who was his reluctant brigade major at Tarifa, said that 'Skerrett, as an individual, was brave to rashness; but I should have doubted it had I not so frequently witnessed proofs of his cool intrepidity and contempt of danger. At the head of troops he was the most undecided, timid and vacillating creature I have ever met.'[391] According to an anonymous diary of the siege, he was already, on the 23rd, making preparations to secure his retreat to the island prior to embarkation:

'This night, at 10 o'clock, Colonel Skerrett, having informed Major King that the enemy intended storming the island and town, made the following disposition. Captain Wren, 11th [Regiment], was placed on the alert, at Santa Catalina, and reinforced with 50 men; a piquet of one captain and fifty men was placed on the causeway, to communicate with Santa Catalina; Captain [Robert] Carew, 82nd Regiment, was placed on the left flank of the island, it being considered the most vulnerable point; and Captain Vavasour [Royal Engineers] constructed a temporary work on the pier, and placed two loaded carronades at the entrance. The island, too, was reinforced by 86 men of the 47th Regiment, who lined the parapet. The whole lay on their arms till broad daylight, when the enemy not appearing, they were dismissed.'[392]

On the morning of the 24th Colonel Skerrett received orders from Major-General Cooke: he was to embark his brigade and return to Cadiz. This faced him with a dilemma, not least because it exposed the Tarifa garrison's divided command responsibilities and loyalties. Whilst his own brigade was detached from the Cadiz garrison, which was itself subordinate to Wellington's headquarters, Major King's battalion received its orders from Lieutenant-General Colin Campbell, Lieutenant-Governor of Gibraltar, who regarded Tarifa as being within his own command and had appointed King as Commandant; and General Copons, Spanish Commandant of Tarifa, had his own Spanish chain of command. Furthermore, it was already becoming apparent that there were divergent views among the officers as to whether Tarifa should and could be held. Skerrett, ever prone to indecision, called a council of war that night.

Colonel Skerrett had always had doubts about the practicality of defending Tarifa: indeed, he had already made preparations to leave, sending his cavalry and staff horses to the island on the 21st for early embarkation, and on the 24th ordering that his stores and provisions should be moved there from the town. That day he also made a personal reconnaissance 'to look out a place of security on the west of it, for the purpose of embarking.'

At the council of war, Skerrett argued in favour of early abandonment of Tarifa, withdrawing the garrison into the island, and in support produced the orders which General Cooke had sent, at his behest, giving him discretion to withdraw.[393] Charles Smith, the senior engineer officer, was firmly of the opinion that the town could be defended for some time even if the wall was breached. Henry King of the 82nd stated that he had been ordered

---

[391] Bunbury, p. 116. According to Bunbury, Skerrett's second-in-command, Lord Proby, was a laid-back hypochondriac who spent most of his time in a darkened room.

[392] *Journal of the Siege of Tarifa*, an anonymous account in T*he Royal Military Chronicle*, Volume IV, May 1812.

[393] In fairness to Skerrett, it should be noted that he was only following the direction given by Wellington to Cooke, which suggested to him 'the expediency of drawing back Colonel Skerrett's detachment' for fear that it would become embroiled in another Spanish disaster. 'I know the Spaniards well', he wrote on 15th November to his brother Henry in Cadiz, 'and particularly Ballasteros. They will never stop till they shall have lost that detachment. It may well have been very proper to send it to secure Tarifa, or for any special object, taking care that its communications should be always secure with the sea coast. But it will not answer to allow our troops to remain in search of adventures under the guidance of such as Ballasteros.'

by General Campbell to hold Tarifa to the last extremity. They were supported by Lieutenant-Colonel Hugh Gough[394] of the 2nd/87th, who urged that evacuation would be wholly premature. Skerrett dismissed the council of war without coming to a decision, requesting the officers who had voted for further defence of the town to put their opinions in writing.

This they did in the most resolute terms, Henry King's note reading, 'I am decidedly of opinion that the defence of Tarifa will afford the British garrison an opportunity of gaining eternal honour, and it ought to be defended to the last extremity.' That same night, Major King took the additional precaution of sending a messenger by boat to Gibraltar, warning General Campbell of Skerrett's faint-hearted intentions and stating that, with a few reinforcement companies, he would, with his own flank battalion and the Spaniards, try to hold Tarifa even if Skerrett withdrew. Campbell acted promptly and decisively to thwart Skerrett's despondent preparations for an ignominious abandonment of his post. He ordered the officers commanding the transports off Tarifa to bring their ships back at once to Gibraltar. Retreat was now impossible.

In the days that followed, as the French sapped forward through the sandy soil, the two sides exchanged heavy cannon and musket fire. There were casualties on both sides, and the defenders would have suffered more severely behind the town's medieval battlements but for a copious supply of sandbags sent from Gibraltar. Private Adam Reed of the 47th was more concerned about the theft of his greatcoat:

'The French used continually to be firing shot and shell (night and day) and red hot shot likewise, to try to blow up our magazines but they failed. One night I was on guard and the French fired a shell close by where I was sitting, and I having off my great coat started up when the shell fell with the remainder of the guard before the shell bursted. The officer that we had on guard drew his sword and said with an oath that if he had that Frenchman before him who fired that shell he would sever his head from his body. When I started up, leaving my great coat behind me after the shell has bursted, I returned to look for it but it was gone. When the captain of my company missed it he asked me where it was and I told him that when I was on guard the other night close by where I was sitting a shell fell, and being in haste to get away I left it behind me and when I returned I could not find it. He said it could not be lost but must be in the garrison and to look among the Spaniards for it. The next day as I was passing by a Spanish guard I saw my coat on the sentry's back, and I knew it to be my own it having a particular button on it. I returned back to the barracks and told the captain that I had saw my coat, and he asked me where, and I said on a Spanish soldier, and he said I will go with you and quickly make him pull it off. We went to the Spanish officer of the guard and told him that one of his men had a great coat belonging to a soldier of his company. Therefore, he came to demand it, and he asked me whether I knew it, and I told him yes, by a particular button upon it. He was then quickly ordered to pull it off, and I then regained my coat again.'

On the 26th the weather broke, and for the next few days both sides laboured in heavy rain, while a violent south-easterly gale forced the British gunboats to leave their station off the south shore, to avoid being driven aground, and take shelter in the lee of the island, very considerably reducing the defenders' firepower. Meanwhile, Skerrett remained obsessed by the need to secure his retreat, diverting troops from the town to work on the defences of the island. The following orders[395] were issued on the 27th:

'In the event of a retreat, the 47th Regiment were ordered into the castle, to defend it. The Spanish troops were to form at the sea-gate, and the 87th and 95th on the ground near their own quarter. The Spanish troops were to retire through the gate first, instantly followed by the 87th Regiment; those corps were to form between the sea and Santa Catalina, there to wait for the 47th Regiment, and to be particularly careful not to fire on the troops retiring by the streets. The Convent troops, should they not have been retired before, were to join the 87th; or, should they meet with difficulty, were to follow up the troops retiring through the gates. The artillery, after destroying the guns, were to fall in with the 47th, which corps was to protect their retreat. All the guards were to retreat, on their own corps, when ordered to do so. Major Broad was to have a strong guard, to shut and secure the gate.'

A steady downpour continued on the 27th and 28th, but the French worked night and day to advance their trenches and construct breaching batteries. In the early hours of the 29th the garrison made another sortie:

---

[394] Later Field Marshal Viscount Gough (1779-1869). The 40th fought under his command in 1843 at the battle of Maharajpore, India.
[395] *Journal of the Siege of Tarifa.*

'At three o'clock Captain Wren was directed by Major King to surprise a piquet of the enemy which lay on a rising ground near the western shore. He was to march an hour before daylight. Captain Wren, with his light company, accordingly sallied out, on the morning of the 29th, but it being bright moonlight, a French sentinel saw him, and, having fired, gave the alarm, which turned out their whole line. The sentinel was immediately killed, and several of the enemy shared his fate. Captain Wren being well supported by Lieutenant [Edmund] Davenport, 82nd Regiment, who volunteered on that occasion, and Lieutenant Welstead, with fifty of the 82nd Regiment. The enemy, advancing under the range of the guns, suffered severely from a well-directed fire from the east tower… which covered the retreat of Captain Wren, to Santa Catalina.' [396]

Such sorties appear to have been ordered by Major King on his own initiative, causing Captain Thomas Bunbury, Skerrett's Brigade Major, some annoyance. 'A great deal of divided authority existed in the garrison, occasioning no little confusion and some mischief. Sorties were made by the troops doing duty with us from Gibraltar, without the knowledge of the staff or the authority of the officer holding the supreme command.' [397]

At ten o'clock on the 29th the enemy opened fire from two batteries. A breaching battery of four 16-pounders and two 12-pounders was sited nearly opposite the Retiro Tower at a distance of only two hundred yards from the wall. The first shot passed right through the Moorish wall and lodged in Bunbury's quarter to its rear, and each successive shot battered the masonry so that in a few hours a small breach, some five feet wide, was made in the curtain wall to the right of the Retiro Tower. The second battery, consisting of two 8-inch howitzers and one 12-pounder, sited one hundred yards in rear of the first, engaged the boats at anchor in the eastern bay (the wind then blowing westerly), so that they were soon obliged to cut their cables and put to sea. It then threw shot and shells to almost every part of the island, but as the troops were at work in the traverses, little damage was done.

Indeed, it appeared to many of the garrison that the most substantial injury to the defence was self-inflicted: 'The sixteen pounder, on Guzman's Tower, and a thirty-two pound carronade, were spiked by Captain Hughes, of the Royal Artillery; a circumstance which, being whispered among our troops, they were filled with indignation, and expressed much apprehension and discontent, lest they should be ordered to abandon the town, without having a fair set-to with the enemy. Whence the order proceeded, is unknown, but General Copens appeared highly enraged when he was informed of it.' [398]

The spiking of the 16-pounder, the only large-calibre gun in the town, was ordered by Colonel Skerrett, who was still clearly preparing for withdrawal.

When night fell, the bombardment ceased, and working parties of the garrison cleared the debris from the front of the breach, despite the area being swept by discharges of grape. At daylight on the 30th, the French batteries opened again, and by ten o'clock the breach was 23 yards wide with an easy ascent. At about half past twelve, a flag of truce was seen approaching, through a thick fog, from the French lines with a summons from General Leval to the Governor of Tarifa:

Sir, The defence made by the fortress under your command has sufficiently established that fair name, which is the basis of military honour. I do not doubt, but that, convinced of the uselessness of a longer resistance, you will endeavour to avert the fatal consequences with which your obstinacy may be attended to the city and inhabitants of Tarifa. A breach has been opened since yesterday, and within a few hours it will be practicable; make then your choice, between an honourable capitulation and the horrors of an impending assault. I flatter myself that you will admit my first proposition, if you reflect, that the same honour which prompts you to resistance, at the same time imposes it as a duty upon you to spare the lives of a whole population, whose fate is in your hands, rather than see them buried amidst the ruins of their town. Be pleased, Sir, to accept the assurances of my highest consideration. (Signed – Leval)

P.S. I beg leave to inform you, that I can give you but two hours, to send your answer.

As Commandant of Tarifa, a quarter past two in the afternoon General Copons sent a terse and quixotic reply:

---

[396] Ibid.
[397] Bunbury, p.p. 121-22.
[398] *Journal of the Siege of Tarifa.*

Sir, When you propose to the governor of this fortress, to admit a capitulation, because the breach will shortly be practicable, you certainly do not know *that I am here*. When the breach shall be absolutely practicable, you will find me upon it, at the head of my troops, to defend it – Then we will negotiate.

I am yours, Francisco de Copons

P.S. Be pleased not to send any more flags of truce.

Copon's response was greeted with some scepticism by at least some of his British allies. Lieutenant William Raynes of the Royal Artillery commented that it was 'decidedly *very Spanish* indeed. It was likewise *very Spanish* to forget the engagement, which Copons certainly did; for he was neither in the breach, nor near, when the time came for him to redeem his pledge.'

The truce lasted till three o'clock, when the French reopened their bombardment of the breach, which by the evening measured nearly sixty feet wide between the Retiro Tower and the next tower to its right. At dark, working parties of the garrison again went out and, though again harassed by discharges of grapeshot, cleared the foot of the breach. The French prepared for a dawn assault.[399]

Early in the night, all work by both sides was halted by a terrific downpour, which filled the trenches and drove the gunners from their batteries. Torrents of water poured down the hillsides, scouring out the French trenches, and filled the Retiro ravine with planks, gabions, fascines and even dead bodies. The mass of debris swirled against the town walls, smashing the palisades in the stream bed and bending back the portcullis to make an opening into the town through which the flood surged to sweep away some of the internal defences of the town. Captain John Harley of the 47th wrote:

'On the 30th and 31st of December, the rain poured down in such torrents, day and night, that the enemy's trenches were filled with water, the men in them being actually up to their hips; besides this misfortune, their convoy, with ammunition and provisions, was swept away in crossing the river by the heavy rain that poured down the sides of the mountains, and had given the river an unusual depth and rapidity. Muleteers, mules, and all, were carried off and lost in the current.'[400]

Once the storm had abated a little, the garrison worked with an urgent energy to repair the damage, which they completed soon after daylight. Early on the morning of 31st December, great activity was observed in the French lines, and it was clear that an assault was imminent. The garrison made their final dispositions.

In accordance with Copons' express wish, a Spanish battalion was ordered to defend the breach, flanked by Gough's 87th, the 'Aiglers' of Barossa fame, who also defended the Retiro Tower and Gate and held two companies in reserve to bayonet any enemy who might leap down the fourteen-foot drop behind the breach. To the right of the breach, two or three companies of the 47th under Captain Charles Livesay were stationed on the south-east, or Jesus, tower and the adjacent wall, from where they could pour a flanking fire into any column advancing against that front of the town. Such was the plan. However, according to Gough, 'The Spaniards were nowhere to be seen, except behind a palisade in the street, a considerable way from the breach.' The truth appears to be, as Charles Napier put it, that 'The Spaniards were *ordered* to defend half the breach, but in *fact* did not appear there.' This unequivocal conclusion is supported by three further eyewitness accounts.

Artillery officer William Raynes wrote that 'If the defence of the place had been left to Copons and his people, it would have been evacuated upon the first appearance of the enemy before it; and it was well for us that the French did not attempt an escalade at the same time as the attack of the breach, for the Spaniards abandoned their part of the walls, having upset the two Spanish guns which flanked the breach. This, fortunately, was seen by Captain Livesay, 47th Regiment, who at once took over their ground, with his fine Light Company, and made great havoc among the Frenchmen. Some of the Spanish officers were well thrashed by Livesay and his officers with the flats of their swords; and one wretched creature, said to be a lieut.-colonel, begged them *not to beat him before his men*. This is a positive fact.'[401]

According to Private Adam Reed of the 47th, 'As soon as the action began the Spaniards all fled into a small isle in the Straight [sic] of Gibraltar called Drake's Isle about half a mile off, for they left the English to fight as they didn't like it.'

---

[399] Lieutenant John Henry de Burgh, 47th Foot, was slightly wounded that day.
[400] Harley, p. 178.
[401] *The Siege of Tarifa – Rough Notes taken from an Old Journal in 1811-12*, Lieutenant William Raynes.

Skerrett stationed himself, with his brigade major, in the church tower of San Mateo, close behind the breach, from where he could see the entire front under attack. When the Spanish were seen to abandon their posts on the wall, Bunbury was sent down to rally them.

'I found that they had not absolutely fled on the first approach of the enemy as reported, but they were huddled together in one or two towers, leaving the curtain wall from which their fire might have been effective without troops. Fortunately, the French did not perceive it, for with ladders they might have walked into the town without difficulty, or had they brought a gun to bear upon the tower in question, the Spaniards would have paid dearly for their cowardice. I was intimately acquainted with one of their officers, and I prevailed upon him to extend a few of his men to where they had been before: but the others assailed me with obscene gestures and language.'[402]

However, next day, songs were sung through the streets of Tarifa praising the bravery of the Spaniards and in honour of the Virgen de la Luz, patron saint of Tarifa, whom many had apparently witnessed standing in the breach to repulse the French assault.

It is reasonably clear, then, that the Spaniards abandoned their positions around the breach, which were filled by the 47th and 87th moving to their left and right, respectively. 'Thus they stood, and cool determination sat upon their countenances.'

Uncomfortable though the night had been for the defenders of Tarifa, the French had fared much worse. The tempest had swept away or waterlogged their trenches and batteries, and they had spent a miserable few hours in sodden bivouacs on the bare hillside, unable to dry themselves or cook their rations. Leval had intended to launch his assault at dawn, but had been obliged to delay for some hours in order for his gunners to reoccupy their batteries and for the infantry to return from their camps. He determined to attack the town as soon as his troops could be assembled. His storming force consisted of some 2,200 grenadiers and voltigeurs, the chosen men of his army, and two companies of sappers, while demonstrations in brigade strength were made to be made to the right and left of the assault.

The French plan was to approach in dead ground along the tortuous bed of the Retiro to within a few yards of the wall. The grenadiers were then to move off to their left to storm the breach while the voltigeurs were to attempt an entry into the town under the Retiro Tower or, if that was not possible, open fire to divert attention from the main attack.

The morning mist had not yet cleared when, at about 8 o'clock, the grenadiers at the head of the French column emerged from trenches near their advanced breaching battery and made their way silently down the muddy Retiro ravine. The leading grenadiers then pushed forward across the space before the breach. The British infantry, silent behind their parapets, had watched and waited for this moment. We have two contemporary eyewitness accounts of the attack, both written in 1812:

'When Colonel Gough saw them advancing, he drew his sword, and throwing away the scabbard, ordered his band, which was stationed in the rear, to strike up the favourite Irish air of *Garryowen.* The men immediately cheered and poured a most galling and tremendous fire on the advancing column. They were well seconded by the 47th, who lined a wall descending from the south-east tower, and completely flanked the column. The enemy halted for a moment, as if stunned by the fall of those around; then advanced with desperation, as if to escape the fire they were then receiving. They ran to the edge of the breach, but, finding it impracticable, they hurried off under the wall to the right, and made a dash at the portcullis. [This] being well barricaded, the enemy were again deceived; and observing the dreadful fate of hundreds of their companions, they faced about, and fled with precipitation. Seeing them fly, Colonel Gough (though slightly wounded) called out to his band, to play *Patrick's Day,* and this national air so inspirited his men, that it was scarcely possible to restrain them from following the routed French up to their very trenches.'[403]

'All around was still, when just about eight o'clock a.m. twenty companies of French grenadiers and voltigeurs, and two companies of sappers, presented themselves before the breach. These troops were close up before they could be discerned through the haze, but all was ready for them in the town, as our men always "slept

---

[402] Bunbury, p. 129.

[403] *Journal of the Siege of Tarifa.* According to Raynes, the Irish band played 'most lustily', but their performance was apparently 'most alarming' to the more musical ears of the many Italians among the besiegers.

upon their arms" from the commencement of the siege. At the head of the French column there was one solitary drummer beating the "pas de charge," which was generally known in the British army by the name of "old trowsers" – I cannot say why – something in the sound, I suppose; but so it was, and our soldiers shouted out, "Here they come," "Here comes old trowsers," and then the work began! The result is [a] matter of history. A rolling volley was delivered with such terrible effect that the head of the column was annihilated, and all that composed it perished, from the officer that led to the poor boy whose "old trowsers" were to awake our merriment no more. The river bed was choked with corpses – that approach was effectively barricaded by the dead. The French grenadiers made desperate efforts to retrieve the honour of their country, but the day was irretrievably lost.' [404]

Somewhat later, in the 1840s, Bunbury set down his own recollections of the attack: 'A ploughed field of deep alluvial soil lay between us and their lines, and it was almost impassable from continued rains. Their storming party plunged up to the knees at each step, whilst some proceeded down the bed of the stream, following its course towards the portcullis. At length they began to hesitate. The fire of our people was galling in the extreme, and did great execution. The French officers advanced in front and cheered their men on to imitate their example, but at length the men put about and fled. The officers, thus abandoned, were obliged to run up to the wall for shelter from our fire, and were thus taken prisoners.' [405]

It appears that the bulk of the French grenadiers, instead of turning to their left as planned, to storm the breach, continued along the hollow way and reached the town wall at the portcullis, where they were halted by a crashing volley of musketry and by a short-range blast of case-shot from a field gun in the north-east tower. The leading officer, covered with wounds, fell against the portcullis and gave up his sword through the bars to Colonel Gough; his drummer, who was beating the charge, dropped lifeless by his officer's side, and the dead and wounded soon filled the hollow way. The survivors, confined on their right by a high bank, spread out in small groups along the foot of the scarp wall to their left, searching for the breach, or opened an irregular fire of musketry. Pinned down and exposed, they were picked off from the ramparts or swept away by enfilading cannon fire. The voltigeurs also opened fire, having advanced from their trenches and jumped into pits, but to no avail.

Those French grenadiers who reached the breach were equally devastated, hit from both flanks by the musketry of the 47th and 87th. On arriving at the foot of the breach in great disorder, the French column hesitated, and many men began to fire instead of pressing on. A few brave men climbed the breach, only to fall at its crest. The attack had lost momentum, and when the shattered stormers could endure no more, they plunged once more into the relative shelter of the stream bed and retired to their own lines, leaving behind the officers who had led the column. As related by Captain John Harley of the 47th, these were saved by Colonel Skerrett:

'I cannot pass over the generous feelings of the brave Colonel Skerrett on the last attack of the enemy from their trenches. The two leading officers of the French were encouraging their men to follow them, who were driven back or fell in the attempt; they stood alone, and would have been instantly killed had not the General [Skerrett] prevented the men firing, and held his hand to them as they leaped in, extolling their bravery and treating them as friends until their exchange took place.' [406]

The account of Lieutenant William Raynes provides more circumstantial detail: 'Ten French officers, eight of whom were wounded, some very badly who afterwards died, were taken at the portcullis, which they had attempted to force, after failing at the breach. They handed their swords through the bars of the gate to Skerrett, who stood up to the middle in water to receive them. I can vouch for this fact, as I was standing by him. He had an armful of swords.'

The French dead covered all the slopes and filled the bed of the torrent. Two hundred wounded crawled under the breach, and thirty of these, with nine wounded officers (presumably those mentioned by Raynes), were carried into the town. Leval asked for a truce to remove the rest of his wounded and bury his dead, which Skerrett granted. Adam Reed of the 47th witnessed the civilities which followed:

'The French general made application for association of arms for three hours to bury their dead, and accordingly it was granted, and our officer and trumpeter and the French officer and trumpeter met and a flag of

---

[404] Raynes, *The Siege of Tarifa.*
[405] Bunbury, p.p. 128-9.
[406] Harley, p. 178.

truce was stuck down. Our soldiers and the French then met together and discoursed and drank with each other during the three hours. About 1/4 hour before the time was expired each party returned to their post. When the three hours was up the flag of truce was pulled down and we commenced firing again.'

The French admitted a loss in this assault of only 48 killed and 159 wounded, which is not credible: Copons and Skerrett both estimated the loss of their enemy at nearly five hundred, and the evidence suggests that this is closer to the mark.[407] The British lost two officers and seven men killed, and three officers, two sergeants and 22 men wounded, while the Spaniards had a total of eleven men wounded. The 2nd/47th had Lieutenant Richard Hall and one man killed, and Lieutenant John Hill and two men wounded.

After this failed assault, continued tempestuous weather effectively brought siege operations to a halt. On New Year's Day the roads from the main French armies around Cadiz were impassable, and Leval's muddy encampments were even cut off from each other, while the besiegers' waterlogged trenches and batteries were quite untenable. The dispirited French soldiers, who had already been on reduced rations for three days, received none that day, and many men wandered miles to the rear in search of food and shelter. Nearly one-third of their horses had died from cold and starvation. All the powder in the siege batteries was soaked, as were the greater part of the musket cartridges. Word reached the Allied lines from deserters that two regiments had refused to storm again, and that there were a thousand sick in the sanctuary of the Virgen de la Luz. General Leval was convinced of the need to raise the siege and retreat, but Marshal Victor obstinately refused to endorse such a confession of failure.

When the storm died down on the night of the 2nd January, the Marshal, who had come forward to the sanctuary of the Virgen de la Luz, ordered the bombardment to be resumed, with an attempt to sap forward towards the Jesus Tower.

The defenders too were adversely affected by the weather: 'The new year commenced with a dreadful storm, the wind blowing strong from the eastward; two Spanish gun-boats were wrecked, under the guns of the island, being full of male and female fugitives from the town, of whom 42 unhappily perished! Fifteen men were taken off a rock, where the waves impetuously dashed over them, by the exertions of the officers and men stationed on the island… On this occasion, John Layton, a private in the 82nd Regiment, sprang off a rock and saved the lives of two Spaniards, who were just perishing, at the risk of his own.'[408]

On the night of January 2nd, a company of the 47th, commanded by Captain Archibald Campbell, made a sortie from the Convent of San Francisco into the enemy's trenches, near the north-east tower, which they found flooded and abandoned, and took away some entrenching tools. The same company carried out another raid the following night, and again found the French trenches unoccupied.

The reinforcements requested by Major King now began to arrive from Gibraltar. The Light Company of the 9th disembarked on the afternoon of January 3rd, and that of the 82nd, commanded by Captain William Vincent[409], landed at 4 o'clock the following morning from Spanish gunboats, also laden with ammunition. The 82nd company immediately marched into Tarifa town, where they were attached to the 47th Regiment. The 82nd Light Bobs were very lucky, for about an hour after they landed, a terrific hurricane drove ashore three of the gunboats on which they had so recently been carried. One of those boats was cast away on shore a mile from the enemy's advanced picket to the west, and Major King, apprehensive that the ammunition it carried might fall into enemy hands, ordered the Light Company 11th and fifty of the 82nd, who were at that time at Santa Catalina, to march to the beach and secure the wreck. This was done, and the men of the 82nd carried off or destroyed the stores and ammunition, and spiked the boat's four carronades, all amidst torrential rain.

This same storm finally forced Marshal Victor to concede that continuation of the siege was hopeless. An hour after nightfall on January 4th, the French advanced close to the north-eastern wall of Tarifa, pouring musketry at the town. This fire was warmly received by the guards on the wall, and the whole garrison stood to and marched

---

[407] It is recorded that 18 French officers were killed or wounded that day, while the sapper detachment which led the storming column lost 43 men out of 50 and the 51st Ligne, which found just four of the 23 storming companies, lost seven officers and 81 men. Lastly, two officers rescued by Skerrett apparently declared that they saw at least 500 men fall in the attack, and Raynes gave the same number.
[408] *Journal of the Siege of Tarifa.*
[409] William Vincent, who had recently graduated from the Senior Division of The Royal Military College, had volunteered to take the Light Company to Tarifa as its captain was on leave in England.

to their posts. The enemy then retired, and the defenders returned to their quarters, but at midnight the French made another demonstration, firing on all sides of the town, and the troops were again called out. Suddenly, the firing ceased, and all was quiet.

As dawn was breaking on January 5th, the reason for this deceptive nocturnal activity became evident. The French had retreated at midnight, spiking nine of their twelve heavy guns, which they were unable to move, and abandoning most of their transport and stores. An attempt was made to fire the mass of wagons, but was foiled by the rain. The abandoned French lines were full of carts, limbers, tools and stores, some spoilt but others fit for use, while ghastly corpses lay around or floated in the water-filled entrenchments.

Major Richard Broad of the 47th was at once ordered to advance on the French position with the light companies, the 95th company and a party of Spanish guerrillas. Leval had made a clean break, and only his rearguard was in sight. Broad pursued the enemy as far as the Rio De La Jara, the banks of which were strewn with dead bodies, but had to be content with bringing in a few prisoners and deserters, who complained bitterly of their suffering from exposure and want of food. Private Adam Reed of the Light Company 47th took part in the pursuit:

'[On the evening of 4th January] we was alarmed by the French, who kept continually firing, and we thought that they were engaged with an army of Spaniards. Therefore when the dawn of day appeared our General was determined to see. Therefore, he dispatched a small party to ascertain what was going on in the French lines, and the party soon returned and brought word that they had abandoned their earlier trenches and batteries and were retreating (on a plain about 2 miles and a half from Tarefa) towards Bohea [Vejer?]. Our general then ordered all the soldiers (except 200 who were left in the town) to go and visit the French entrenchments and when we reached these we found that the birds had flown from their nest. The firing that we heard was the French firing one gun into another to damage them, and also they were spiked. We then followed after them as far as we dare, for they were about four to one, and we then returned back to Tarefa.'

Next day, a *Te Deum* was celebrated in Tarifa, to which all the British officers were invited, and after this ceremony, the troops fired a *feu de joie* of three volleys and the artillery three rounds. The 47th paraded at the Castle, while the 82nd lined the fortifications of the island.

On the 7th all the troops were employed in levelling the French siege-works. With any threat to Tarifa removed for the foreseeable future, full responsibility for defence of the town was handed to the Spaniards, and on 21st January, Skerrett's brigade embarked for Cadiz. Colonel Skerrett may be forgiven the triumphant tone of his despatch:

'We have seen the greatest effort the French are capable of making frustrated by eighteen hundred British and Spanish troops, with only the defence of a paltry wall; and an army of ten thousand men, commanded by a marshal of France, retreating from them silently in the night, after having been repulsed and defeated, leaving behind all their artillery and stores, collected at great expense and by immense exertions.'

Bunbury, whilst acknowledging the merits of the defenders, was of the opinion that 'without detracting from the merit of the troops engaged in the expedition, or the skill of those engaged in the defences, which were unquestionably great, our ultimate success was mainly attributable to the unceasing rains. For these not only deluged the open country, and destroyed the materiel of the besieging army, but dispirited the men by spreading disease and death through their ranks.'[410]

Despite its victorious outcome, the siege of Tarifa remained controversial. Major-General Cooke and Colonel Skerrett, were understandably irritated at the manner in which the Lieutenant-Governor of Gibraltar, supported by junior officers, had forced their hand, and they relayed their dissatisfaction to both Wellington and Whitehall. The official line in response was that Lieutenant-General Campbell, in inspiring and sustaining the defence, and in particular in compromising the security of Skerrett's brigade and frustrating the legitimate orders to that brigade from Major-General Cooke, had exceeded his authority, and Campbell was accordingly mildly rebuked by Lord Liverpool. Wellington, while supporting Skerrett and Cooke, chose his words carefully to defuse ill-will between the commanders:

---

[410] Bunbury, p.p. 131-2.

'We have a right,' he wrote to Cooke on 1st February 1812, 'to expect that His Majesty's officers and troops will do their duty upon every occasion; but we have no right to expect that comparatively a small number would be able to hold the town of Tarifa, commanded as it is at short distance, and enfiladed in every direction, and unprovided with artillery, and with walls scarcely cannon-proof. The enemy, however, retired with disgrace, infinitely to the honour of the brave troops who defended Tarifa, and it is useless to renew the discussion. It is necessary, however, that you should now come to an understanding with General Campbell regarding the troops which have been detached from Cadiz and this army under Colonel Skerrett.'

Even the utility of holding Tarifa was questioned, but the French never had any doubt as to its strategic importance. Three months after the siege, Marshal Soult advocated another attempt at the place. 'The taking of Tarifa,' he wrote, 'will be more hurtful to the English and to the defenders of Cadiz than the taking of Alicante or even Badajoz, where I cannot go without first securing my left and taking Tarifa.'

Tarifa would not have been held without the resolution and leadership of Smith, Gough and King, strongly supported by Campbell. Skerrett earned official approval for his caution, but both informed contemporaries and posterity have been less impressed. In April 1812, Major-General Sir Robert Wilson called at Cadiz, where he heard the story of the siege from Hugh Gough. Having then viewed the town, he wrote in his diary that, 'had Skerrett abandoned it, he ought to have been hung.'

In 1816, the 47th Regiment was awarded the Battle Honour 'TARIFA.' Strangely, no medals or clasps were ever issued for the successful defence, but it is pleasing to note that Major Henry King, whose determination was largely responsible for that outcome, was promoted to brevet lieutenant-colonel. For the 47th the defence of Tarifa was long remembered as a notable achievement, and for many years the Sergeants' Mess of 1st Battalion The Loyal North Lancashire Regiment, successors of the 47th Foot, celebrated Tarifa Day with a ball, and a *Tarifa March* was composed.

The 82nd in Gibraltar and Ceuta 1812

Major King's detachment was relieved at Tarifa and returned to Gibraltar in May 1812. In that same month, the 82nd sent a detachment to that other Pillar of Hercules, the Spanish North African port of Ceuta, to relieve the 2nd/4th in garrison. Lieutenant George Wood was impressed by the strength of the fortifications, and with his brother-officers of the 82nd, 'found this a healthy, plentiful and agreeable quarter, in which we partook of every pleasure and amusement; frequenting their tertullias, conversations, bull-fights, &c. We were also highly entertained by their fandangos, boleros, concertos and serenatas.' All good things come to an end, and about six weeks later, the detachment was relieved by part of the 26th Regiment and returned to Gibraltar. All was bustle on the Rock, for the 1st/82nd had been ordered to join Wellington's field army.

On 9th June 1812, the Battalion embarked for Lisbon. To mark their departure, Lieutenant-General Colin Campbell issued a complimentary order:

'The first battalion of the 82nd Regiment will embark this day and proceed on its voyage to Lisbon. The Lieut.-General feels great regret at parting with a corps which has on all occasions distinguished itself, as well in the field as in garrison. The memorable battle of Barrosa and the gallant defence of Tarifa bear ample testimony to the bravery and spirit possessed by this fine corps, and which is equally distinguished for its discipline. His Excellency will not fail to mark his approbation in the strongest manner to General the Earl of Wellington, under whose command the first battalion of the 82nd Regiment is destined to serve.'

The 30th and 40th on the Frontier, 1811-12

The dispersal of the French armies by mid-July 1811 from their confrontation on the Caya left Wellington with the strategic initiative. A resumption of the siege of Badajoz would require the army to remain in the unhealthy valleys of the Guadiana and Caya over the summer months, which was unacceptable; and so, leaving Hill with two divisions to watch the Estremadura frontier, the Duke marched his main army north. His next objective was to take Ciudad Rodrigo, but he realistically accepted that this might be beyond his present capabilities. On 18th July, before he began his northward march, he wrote cautiously to Lord Liverpool:

'I am tempted to try this enterprise, but I beg your Lordship to observe that I may be obliged to abandon it. When the relative forces of the two armies will be so nearly balanced… it is impossible for me to foresee all the events which may lead to this result. But the arrival of reinforcements to the enemy, or further information, which may show them to be stronger than I now imagine, or a falling off in the strength of our army owing to sickness, would necessarily oblige me to abandon the enterprise.'

The 30th left their hutted camp at Sierra d'Arronches with the 5th Division on 29th July, marching on rocky mountain roads through Castelo de Vide and Nisa. After bivouacking in a wood on the 31st, on 1st August the division descended the steep hill to the Tagus crossing at Vila Velha; the road wound through rocks and precipices, and was often cut out of the hillside, and the march afforded a most picturesque sight. After crossing the bridge of boats at Vila Velha, the division bivouacked on the riverbank.

On the following day, in intense heat, the 5th Division began to ascend the mountains of Beira, bivouacking that night at Larnades. Castelo Branco was reached on the 3rd, seen on its hilltop many hours before the wearied troops arrived there. A short march was made next day to Atalaya, passing through woods of oak, cork and chestnut; the broom and heather were in flower. Quantities of game, including partridge, quail and hares, were seen. Many officers had their guns and pointers with them, some even a brace of greyhounds, and in such a good game country, there was an opportunity of a change of diet from the eternal over-driven ration bullock. Mail from England, only seven weeks old, put everyone in additional good humour.

On the 7th there was a very hard march of about fifteen miles, and many horses, mules and asses died of fatigue. The mountain road was lined with the rotting carcasses of the transport animals of a division in front. Expectations of imminent action were raised by the number of refugees fleeing from the French. On the 8th, the 5th Division marched into Sabugal and bivouacked. The town had been completely wrecked by the enemy.

The 40th moved off from Estremoz on 31st July, marching by way of Fronteira, Crato, Alpalhão and Nisa to cross the Tagus at Vila Velha and reach Castelo Branco on 7th August. At Crato on August 1st, they were joined from the 2nd Battalion by a draft of four hundred men, with a proportion of officers, commanded by Captain William Porter.

There was speculation as to the Army's destination. Surgeon Boutflower, concerned at the deteriorating health of the Regiment, hoped that they were heading for cantonments in the north, as 'there is no doubt that a vast number of lives will be saved by such a change of quarters… The excessive heat of the weather renders it impossible to go long marches without infinite injury to the troops; a great deal of sickness at present prevails, to which a number of officers are victims; indeed I consider the climate of this country during the hot months in autumn as little less unhealthy than the West Indies.'[411]

He was thankful that they were given four days to complete the next leg of their march route, to Penamacor, a distance of some 32 miles. On August 11th, the 4th Division went into cantonments around Pedrogao, just short of Penamacor, and the 40th Foot were quartered in two 'wretched villages, merely affording covering' including Aldea de João Perez, where they were mustered on 24th August. The northward march resumed on the 28th, by way of Meimaõ and Vila do Touro, and on 2nd September, the 40th reached the village of Sao Pedro de Rio Seco, some six miles from Almeida and just two miles from the Spanish border. Boutflower described this place as nearly a heap of ruins whose misery beggared description, having frequently been visited by the enemy.

As they neared the border with Spain, even the battle-hardened grenadiers of the 40th were appalled at evidence of the visceral hatred of the Portuguese peasantry for the French invaders:

'I myself was witness to one of their barbarous acts,' recalled William Lawrence. 'They had laid a ring of straw round a wounded Frenchman and set fire to it, and when the poor man tried to crawl out, he was only received with a pitchfork which sent him again into the centre. We soon made the Portuguese fly by firing in amongst them; but when we came up to the poor man, his hair, fingers, and face were fearfully burnt already. He implored us not to leave him, but we were obliged to, and no doubt either the Portuguese returned and killed him, or else he died of the injuries he had sustained at their hands, or from the wounds that had before disabled him.'[412]

On August 10th the 30th Foot passed Alfayates, from where they marched south-east over the Spanish border to Navasfrias (appropriately meaning 'cold snows'), a small but clean mountain town at the source of the

411 Boutflower, p. 104.
412 Lawrence, p.p. 97-8.

Agueda. The 5th Division was tasked with guarding the passes over the Sierra de Gata on Wellington's right flank. Headquarters 30th were in the mountain village of Peñaparda. For the next few weeks the light companies of the division took turns to provide the forward pickets on the freezing, wind-swept heights in front of El Payo, seven miles to the east, and Valverde, a dozen miles to the south of Navasfrias, supported in rotation by one or two of the battalions, hutted against the bitterly cold nights. The light companies took pride in the speed with which they could make the changeover, running twelve miles over mountain tracks with full equipment in two hours. There was only one serious alarm, on 16th August, when a King's German Legion outpost was surprised at the village of San Martin de Trevejo. The light companies hurried up in support, but the French had escaped.

Major (Brevet Lieutenant-Colonel) George Grey[413] was now in command of the 2nd/30th as Alexander Hamilton had been granted four months' leave in England on promotion.[414]

By then, the army was wracked with 'Guadiana fever.' 'Sickness unhappily prevails to a melancholy extent in our Army,' wrote Surgeon Boutflower on 11th September. 'In my Regiment alone, the present returns of sick are fifteen officers and six hundred men. As the weather however is beginning to get cool, we are in hopes that the troops will be more healthy; the total amount of ineffectives at present is, I believe, not less than twenty thousand men.' This was not far from the truth, for the strength return on the 15th of that month shows the army as a whole had 12,517 sick in hospitals and a further 1,720 sick with their units, while the 40th Foot had 791 of all ranks effective and 513 sick. Mortality in the 40th that year was particularly high, with 196 deaths of whom only 59 are known to have fallen in battle.

The 30th, who had not spent time in the pestilent valleys of the Guadiana and Caya, suffered less severely, but even so they had 245 sick on 31st August, with only 388 all ranks present on 15th September, and by the end 1811 the Battalion had lost three officers, five sergeants, two drummers and 91 rank and file dead, all from disease, and a further 258 men had been invalided home.

Despite this major setback, which reduced the fighting strength of his seven divisions on the northern front to 46,000 British and Portuguese, Wellington pushed the 3rd and Light Divisions across the frontier to blockade Ciudad Rodrigo, and on September 23rd the 4th Division marched to Fuenteguinaldo, where they entrenched to support the forward troops. The 40th, who had moved south by the 18th to Forcalhos, 'the most wretched of all wretched villages,' advanced with the rest of the division to bivouac on the banks of the River Agueda, two miles in front of Fuenteguinaldo, where Wellington had his headquarters.

William Lawrence's comrades of the Grenadier Company 40th, quartered in a house at Fuenteguinaldo, were up to their usual mischief. The principal culprit on this occasion was an Irishman called 'Pig' Harding, who located with his bayonet thirty pounds of the household's garlic sausages hidden at the bottom of an olive oil jar. The sausages were at once removed, and the incriminating evidence eaten long before the woman of the house rushed in shouting, 'Ladrone, ladrone, the French are bad enough, but you are worse!' She reported the theft to Major John Gillies, who had no doubt who was to blame and immediately came to the grenadiers' room, saying, 'Then you are up to your prigging tricks again.' He asked the woman how much the sausages were worth and at once gave her sixteen dollars, saying he would deduct it from the miscreants' pay, which he never did.

'On another occasion,' Lawrence recalled, 'whilst we were at the same place, some Spaniards came into our camp with wine for sale, contained in pigskins carried across mules' backs, one on each side, and whilst the Spaniard was measuring it out of one skin, a hole had been made in the other with a penknife, which lightened both burdens at once considerably, much to the discontent of the Spaniard on finding it out.'

In September 1811, Wellington had sufficient resources to blockade Ciudad Rodrigo, but insufficient to prevent its resupply or relief, or to undertake a formal siege. He had at last received from England a heavy

---

[413] George Grey had transferred into the 30th from the 6th Dragoons in March 1799. He served at the capture of Malta and the campaign in Egypt, earning a mention in despatches for gallantry at the siege of Alexandria. Promoted to major in 1804, he served with the 30th in the Peninsula until he assumed command.

[414] Major (Brevet Lieutenant-Colonel) Hamilton was promoted without purchase into the Royal West India Rangers vice Lieutenant-Colonel Charles Turner, who was appointed to command the 2nd/30th vice Colonel William Minet with effect 25th July. However, Turner had been seriously wounded at Badajoz on 11th July, in command of a Portuguese regiment, and remained incapacitated. Consequently, both appointments were cancelled and Hamilton was given command of the 2nd/30th. Hamilton's appointment was backdated to 25th July 1811, but as he was on leave in England, and getting married, he did not rejoin and assume command until 3rd June 1812.

battering-train of siege artillery, which had landed at Oporto in August, but it would take some two months to bring this up from the coast.

It was no secret that Marmont would not let Ciudad Rodrigo fall and was preparing a large escorted convoy to resupply the blockaded garrison, but for once, Wellington underestimated the scale and scope of the French operation. On 23rd September, Marmont appeared on the plain beyond Ciudad Rodrigo with some 58,000 men, leaving Foy's division at Plasencia to threaten an advance against the 5th Division through the passes of the Sierra de Gata. Wellington concluded that the French had come merely to resupply the garrison, not to take the offensive over the Agueda. Accordingly, he did not concentrate his army, and when on the 25th Marmont made a great cavalry reconnaissance in force, the blockading 3rd Division, and Alten's and Anson's screening cavalry brigades, were widely dispersed, with only the 4th Division at Fuenteguinaldo close enough to support them. Fortunately, the situation was saved, at El Bodon, by the discipline and tenacity of the outnumbered British infantry and cavalry, who fought their way back to the half-completed entrenched camp at Fuenteguinaldo. The French drew off short of the 4th Division, who were not engaged that day.

There followed an anxious 24 hours for Wellington, who, as night fell on the 25th, had only two infantry divisions, the 3rd and 4th, at Fuenteguinaldo. That evening, and throughout the 26th, Marmont enjoyed a growing superiority in numbers. As Charles Boutflower of the 40th recorded:

'In the evening [of the 25th] both divisions took up a position in front of Fuente Guinaldo, having the enemy three miles from us in great force. We fully expected to be attacked the next morning at daylight, & Lord [Wellington] ordered every species of baggage to be out of the village an hour before daybreak; they did not however come on. We remained the whole day in the same position, and from the height in our possession had a distinct view of the French Army, which was vastly superior to what we had supposed, amounting to about six thousand cavalry and thirty thousand infantry; whereas our force opposed to them was not more than fifteen hundred of the former and about twelve thousand of the latter. In the course of the day, further reinforcements were observed to come up to them, as also a large force of artillery of the largest calibre.'[415]

Despite his considerable advantage in numbers, Marmont shrank from attacking, apparently convinced that Wellington would only offer battle in advantageous circumstances, and that his partially entrenched position was impregnable. The British commander's reputation for prudence had saved him and cost Marmont his best chance of a victorious battle. The French marshal gave orders for a withdrawal that night.

Unaware of Marmont's intentions, after dusk that same evening, Wellington slipped away in good order on the road to Sabugal, where he had previously selected a strong defensive position between Aldea da Ponte and Alfaietes. Here, he was able to concentrate his army of 45,000 men on a seven-mile front, which he was confident of holding. The 4th Division halted on the morning of the 27th in the right-centre of the intended line of battle, near the Convent of Sacaparte above Aldea da Ponte.

The 5th Division, in their outposts on the Sierra de Gata, could hear the sounds of battle at El Bodon on 25th September, and at 4 a.m. the following morning, they were under arms in anticipation of a call to action. They marched to join Wellington on the 27th and occupied the right flank of the British position, holding the village of Aldea Velha. There they halted to cook, but camp kettles were hardly over the fires when the alarm was given, and soup and beef were thrown in every direction as the regiments stood to arms.

At about 9 or 10 a.m., the French vanguard attacked the 4th Division outposts in Aldea da Ponte, provided by the light companies of the Fusilier brigade, and drove them back. The village, which lay outside Wellington's main line of defence, was recaptured when he committed the whole Fusilier brigade, and lost again to the French at dusk.

Seeing the French advance towards the 4th Division on his left, General Dunlop moved the 5th Division to a better position on a steep hill by the source of the Coa, where they formed in close column to support the division in action. The men were tired and hungry, lacking even wine and spirits, but eager for a fight, hammering their flints and making their usual preparations for battle. The leading French cavalry looked at the 5th Division's position at about noon, but considered it too strong to attack.

---

[415] Boutflower, p. 109-10.

Indeed, neither the 30th nor the 40th saw action that day, for Marmont did not press his attack. There was some redeployment that night, and at 2 a.m. the 40th moved to Souto, and at dawn occupied high ground above the village. Wellington was ready to give battle again on the 28th, but Marmont, after a survey of the position, again declined the offer and ordered a retreat.

By the morning of the 29th the crisis was over, and Wellington ordered his troops into cantonments. The 30th marched through Souto and Sabugal, and on via Vila do Touro to the mountain-top city of Guarda, 'as bad a march as ever was undertaken,' recalled Corporal Douglas of the Royals, 'extremely dark and the road broken, craggy and rocky, a perfect valley of stones. The inhabitants on our retreat flying in every direction to the woods and mountains, carrying their miserable shreds – a very heavy rain, during which we halted three hours and afterwards slept in a wood. Our baggage had gone to the rear on the 25th, so there were no greatcoats or blankets… At Sabugal, there were two other divisions, and we heard our baggage had gone on to Guarda. We had not washed or shaved since the 24th and looked like Portuguese.' They arrived at Guarda on the 30th and were thankful to be reunited with their greatcoats and other baggage.

The 40th Foot remained encamped above Souto until the 30th September, when they marched north to Bismula, and from there moved forward to the frontier village of Nave de Haver. Surgeon Boutflower was unimpressed with these winter quarters: 'This place is not less miserable than those we have lately occupied; in wet weather, the very best houses are absolutely incapable of affording protection.'

On October 17th the 40th moved forward again, to Gallegos, under eight miles from Ciudad Rodrigo. There was little expectation of early conflict with the two thousand-strong French garrison of that place, though on the 26th there was a false alarm of a foraging raid, causing the troops to sleep that night fully accoutred.

Wellington continued to blockade Ciudad Rodrigo and anticipated another attempt to resupply the town, but when it came on 2nd November, a well-executed French deception plan enabled them to send in a victualling convoy with a small escort. The 40th moved forward to El Bodon that morning to join the Light Division in an attack on the enemy convoy, but on arrival, they found that the French had been and gone. On the 3rd, the Regiment returned to its cantonments, where they remained inactive until the 23rd, making themselves as comfortable as possible. Chimneys were built on the bivouacs, and Wellington rode to hounds twice a week, but due to adverse winds, there had been no mail from England for some two months.

The 30th Regiment remained at Guarda for two months, during which, despite the cold, 'there was an equal share of duty and merriment.' There were officers' guards at each of the five gates of the city, and divisional field days were held twice a week. The weather became more severe as winter closed in, and by 22nd November, the surrounding hills were white with snow.

Throughout the autumn, Wellington was making his preparations to take Ciudad Rodrigo. His battering train and siege stores were on their way from Lisbon, a major logistic effort involving the movement of heavy artillery, ammunition and equipment by sea to Oporto and then up the Douro in barges to Lamego, from where they were carried by road to the restored fortress of Almeida. The siege stores and the first of the guns reached Almeida on 22nd November, and their arrival was accompanied by a general move forward of the several divisions of the army to cantonments between the Agueda and the Coa.

The 40th Foot marched up to El Bodon again on the 23rd-24th, then retired to Fuenteguinaldo, where they remained until ordered back to Gallegos on the 29th. The 30th Foot were also on the move on the 23rd, being suddenly ordered forward from Guarda at five in the morning, leaving at ten. They marched south-west to Vila do Touro that day, and then on through Aldea da Ponte to Alfaiates.

However, as there was insufficient forage and food to maintain the whole army in forward positions, the 5th Division was then sent to winter quarters in the valley of the Mondego. The 30th returned through Vila de Touro to Guarda, which they left on 2nd December on the road to Oliveira do Hospital. Their progress is described in the diary of Ensign John Carter:

'Shortly after leaving Guarda we passed the beautiful vale of the Mondego over the Ponte at Murcella. The vale was cultivated in the highest degree, but showing melancholy proofs of the ravages of war. Leaving this and passing through the village of Murcella [Mizarela], we began to ascend the Estrella, a most shocking road, during which we were obliged repeatedly to halt the troops. At length we arrived at the summit & proceeded to Linhares, where my servant lost his firelock & in looking for it in the dark fell down a wall, cut his head & hurt his back. This confused him so much that he was nearly senseless. One of the Light Company met a peasant walking off with his firelock & took it away from him.'[416]

The 30th Foot reached Bobadela, just outside Oliveira do Hospital, on December 4th, but were moved on the 6th two miles further to Vila Nova de Oliveirinha, and then on the 7th to their final quarters, where six companies were housed in the village of Coito and four in the neighbouring village of Midões. They remained there for almost a month, practising battalion drills, with the occasional brigade field day. The weather was cold but clear. Officers and men alike were perennially short of money, and cheese, bacon and imported butter to supplement their issue rations were very expensive, but oranges, olives and chestnuts were cheap and plentiful, and there was game in the valleys running down from the Sierra Estrella. As Ensign Carter recorded, they somehow managed to scrape together food and drink for seasonal celebrations:

'Christmas Day: We had a parade at 3 o'clock in the morning. At 10 the brigade assembled for divine service. The parson being taken ill, instead of praying we formed line, saluted General Walker[417], [and] marched past in slow & quick time. In marching past in quick time he abused us very much indeed. When we wheeled into line again he found fault with the movement, the men not sloping their arms properly, called the officers 10 paces in front & told them to examine the men & put them to rights. He found fault with the supernumerary officers, in particular after advancing & retiring in line. We marched home. In consequence of all this palaver he ordered the whole regiment to drill at 8 o'clock every morning. In the evening, we dined with the Adjutant, Lieutenant [John] Garland, & Ensign [William] Campbell. We had a famous, jolly time of it, sung several songs. At 9 o'clock, we adjourned to Colonel Grey's, where we had an eloquent supper [and] a great deal of jolly rum, with which I play my part pretty well.[418]

'26th December: Doctor [Staff Surgeon Henry Gresley] Emery [attached 5th Division] breakfasted with us & caught us in bed. The doctor [Assistant Surgeon John Evans] and I were so merry the night before that we asked a whole lot of fellows to dine with us. Neither had much money, but the doctor raised 2 dollars, which enabled us to buy a [k]eg of wine; this, together with the ration rum we got the day before, wined us pretty well. The Adjutant also was so good as to send up three pints of whisky. We were very much puzzled as to how to get a table & table-cloth: however, I proposed to the doctor that we should bring up some planks, which were in the yard, & rest them on a chest & make a table. Now we did not know how it was possible to procure a cloth. Coming up from the kitch[en], to my great astonishment I saw the doctor very busy spreading a cloth & bestowing great pains to brush some dirty yellow spots off it. When I asked him where he had raised that, he told me that it was one of the sheets which he had taken from the bed & that it would do very well after he had brushed the lice & fleas off. Dinner was served up [and] everyone seemed to enjoy himself very much. After sitting some time & making rather merry, the company retired. I forgot to mention that I had employed myself all the morning in making apple dumplings, which would have been very good had they not been boiled too much.'[419]

The festive season, such as it was, ended abruptly for John Carter when, on the 28th, Sergeant-Major James Woods warned him for subalterns' drill at 7 o'clock the following morning, followed by drilling the Battalion by divisions.

The Siege and Storming of Ciudad Rodrigo 8th-19th January 1812

In the closing months of 1811, Wellington had been making detailed preparations to capture the strategic border fortress of Ciudad Rodrigo. By the end of December, he had his siege artillery, less mortar ammunition, ready to move up from Almeida, where artificers had secretly constructed a trestle bridge required to move stores and

---

[416] The Peninsular Diary of Ensign John V. Carter, 30th Foot, Ed. Gareth Glover, Pub. Ken Trotman 2006, p. 5.
[417] Major-General George Townsend Walker had assumed command of the 2nd Brigade of the 5th Division on 3rd October 1811.
[418] Carter, p. 8. Major (Brevet Lieutenant-Colonel) George Grey, in command of the 2nd/30th, was accompanied on campaign by his wife Elizabeth, who was herself a soldier's daughter. On Christmas Eve Ensign Carter and Assistant Surgeon Evans had gathered oranges for Mrs Grey.
[419] Carter, p.p. 8-9. Assistant Surgeon John Evans, with whom Ensign Carter shared a house at Coito, served with the 30th in the Peninsula, Holland, Waterloo campaign and India until 1821, when he died at Secunderabad.

heavy guns across the Agueda[420], and his troops had prepared thousands of fascines, gabions and pickets for the siege-works. His Lordship had also kept a careful watch on French movements, and by the last week in December he was satisfied that Marshal Marmont had dispersed his forces and would be unable for some weeks to re-unite them in sufficient strength to relieve Ciudad Rodrigo. Marmont had been aware of Wellington's preparations, but could not bring himself to accept that his adversary would attack in winter, preferring to believe that it was all a bluff designed to make the French concentrate at a time when the roads were bad and food and fodder short. This was just the window of opportunity Wellington needed, and accordingly, on 1st January 1812, he issued orders for his army to move forward and commence siege operations in the depth of winter. It was a well-prepared and carefully calculated risk, and a surprise.

On New Year's Day 1812, the 30th Foot, with the rest of the 5th Division, were still enjoying the relative comfort and society of winter quarters in the Mondego valley:

'The division met about two miles from [Coito],' wrote John Carter. 'Here we received orders from General Hay not to move from Midoes till further orders. After we were dismissed, the doctor [Evans] and I took a long walk [and] met with two ladies who greeted us with preserved fruits. They detained us for some time. We went into a garden hard by, filled our pockets & hands with oranges, & came home. We then took a walk to Midoes to call on Lieutenant Garland, but he was not at home so the lady of the house entertained us by singing. We dined with Ensign [Robert] Smith & Lieutenant [Richard] Mayne, who gave us a pretty good set out. They gave us plenty of good brandy which made us rather merry. In going home my foot slipped by a hole full of dirty water, I fell down & the doctor, who was behind me, tumbled over me into the middle of the water and he got a pretty good soaking.'[421]

That night, there was a heavy fall of snow around Ciudad Rodrigo, and adverse weather conditions continued until the 5th, with deep snow and violent gales slowing the movement of siege guns and stores so that the investment had to be delayed until the 8th.

On 6th January, Wellington and his staff crossed the Agueda without escort to make a close personal reconnaissance of Ciudad Rodrigo. It was certainly not a first-rate fortress in the same league as Badajoz, Elvas or Almeida, but the fortified town was formidable enough for an army with minimal engineer and artillery resources. There were no bastions on its ancient thirty-foot walls, which were surrounded by a ditch and protected from artillery by a more modern, low-profile fausse-braie and by occasional ravelins, though since the top of the surrounding, steeply-sloping glacis was nine feet lower than the fausse-braie the latter was not fully protected from bombardment and the ancient walls behind were even more exposed. Outworks covered the most practicable, northern approaches, and these would have to be taken as the siegeworks advanced. The Redoubt Renaud stood on the Great Teson, a low ridge 600-700 yards from the town and thirteen feet higher than its ramparts, an obvious siege battery position, while the outlying fortified Convents of Santa Cruz and San Francisco, and entrenched suburbs near the latter, would also have to be secured before the town could be stormed. Below the Great Teson, the Lower Teson offered an ideal breaching battery position only 180 yards from the fortifications, but this could not be occupied until the two convents on its flanks had been taken.

Wellington decided to make his attack from the north, and his first move was to capture the Redoubt Renaud by escalade at 8 o'clock on the evening of the 8th, securing the Great Teson ridge. Ground was at once broken, and by dawn, the ridge-top trenches of the first parallel were three feet deep, and sites for three batteries had been marked out. At the same time, a large convoy of engineer stores left Gallegos, crossed the Agueda by the trestle bridge erected at Marialva, and established an engineer park.

The weather continued excessively cold, and since the army had few tents, and there was no cover to the rear of the siege-works, Wellington ordered that siege operations should be rotated between the 1st, 3rd, 4th and Light Divisions, each in turn providing working parties and trench guards for 24 hours from noon to noon, then returning to their quarters in surrounding villages, so that the men had three days in shelter for every day of exposure in the trenches. The relieving battalions were to march from their cantonments before dawn, carrying their entrenching tools, a day's cooked rations, two days' spirits, and no other baggage, leaving sufficient men to

---

[420] The only bridge and main ford crossing the Agueda near Ciudad Rodrigo were within musketry range of the town walls, and none of the other fords could be depended on in winter when the river would often rise five to ten feet in a single day.
[421] Carter, p. 10.

cook a hot meal when the battalion was relieved. In addition, each division was to provide a permanent detachment of twenty miners and thirty artificers to assist the engineers, and they were encamped at the engineer park.

Wellington's careful arrangements for reliefs was his response to very real concerns about undertaking a siege in winter, articulated on January 4th by Surgeon Charles Boutflower of the 40th:

'The consequences to the health of the army I shudder to think of. It is scarcely too much to expect that everyone who has suffered from disease during the last six months will not relapse. Should this be the case, the troops will be absolutely inefficient to any active operations in the Spring. Everyone appears astonished, and all contemplate the preparations with a horror equal to their wonder.'[422]

We last saw the 40th Foot at Gallegos, but by early January, when Wellington's headquarters and the engineers moved in, the place became, in Surgeon Boutflower's words, 'a scene of the utmost hurry and bustle; nothing to be seen but engineers & all the implements requisite for a siege.' On 7th January, the 40th, with an effective strength of 734, marched to the small village of Villa de Porco, twelve miles from Ciudad Rodrigo, from where they took their turn in the trenches.

The 4th Division was now under the command of Major-General Charles Colville. Their first tour of duty in the trenches was on the 10th/11th January, by which time the first parallel was nearly completed, and work on the batteries was well advanced. This provoked a very fierce fire from thirty French wall-guns, which caused considerable damage and a number of casualties. Most of the work had to be done after dark, and over the night 10th/11th there was a working party of 1,200 men in the batteries, parallels and trenches of communication and support, while the garrison shelled them and threw up light-balls. In the morning, a thousand men toiled to complete the batteries and excavate magazines; but the French gunners found the range and dropped two-thirds of their shells into the siege-works, while their round shot caused many casualties and salvoes of shells with long fuses blew away the work of hours. So many men were hit in the more exposed trenches that Wellington ordered work there to be discontinued. By the time the 4th Division was relieved at noon, the 40th had suffered three men killed and twelve or fourteen wounded, more than half the divisional loss.

On the night of the 13th/14th, siege guns were moved into the three batteries on the Great Teson, the fortified Convent of Santa Cruz was stormed, and a flying sap was pushed in zig-zag trenches down the slope towards the Lower Teson, where the second parallel would be dug.

On the 14th, when the 4th Division arrived at the appointed hour to relieve the 1st Division, they found a scene of confusion. Determined not to allow the second parallel to be established so close to their walls, the French had mounted a well-timed sortie with five hundred men. They had noted that the 1st Division had withdrawn their workmen and guards at about 10 a.m. as soon as they saw their relieving division approach, leaving the trenches and works unmanned. The French recaptured the convent of Santa Cruz, swept along the second parallel and made a dash at the first parallel where they could have caused significant damage to the batteries and spiked the precious siege guns if the duty engineer had not rallied a few belated workmen to make a stand until the 4th Division came running up from the rear. The French then retired into the town, but the convent and the Lower Teson were not reoccupied by the besiegers until nightfall.

Meanwhile, at about 4.30 p.m., the three batteries on the Great Teson opened with 27 guns. Two 18-pounders and twenty-three 24-pounders began to breach the northern wall and fausse-braie. Two 18-pounders on the left opened against the garden and other walls of the Convent of San Francisco, from where the French were able to enfilade the second parallel with two guns and a howitzer mounted on the flat roof.

The bombardment of the Convent walls proved ineffectual due to an intervening low rise in the ground, and so at dusk it was stormed by three companies of the 40th, who escaladed the walls to surprise the garrison. 'Considerable resistance was expected,' according to Boutflower, 'but, on the men appearing on the walls of the Convent, the enemy fired a volley and fled to the town with precipitation; only three men were wounded in this affair.'[423] Private William Lawrence of the Grenadier Company 40th gave a more detailed account of this operation:

'We had to commence throwing up our batteries and breastworks under a particular annoyance from three guns situated on a fortified convent a little distance from the town, near where our brigade's operations were in

[422] Boutflower, p. 120.
[423] Ibid., p. 121.

progress, so our Colonel for one, volunteered to storm the convent, which offer was accepted. Several companies, therefore, including my own, advanced under him unobserved by the enemy in the darkness of the night, and succeeded in effecting an entrance into the convent, the garrison being taken by surprise, but managing to decamp. I then volunteered with a few men to march on up the tower where the guns were situated, a priest being made to show us the way, as the path which we had to tread was so winding. When we arrived at the top, which must have taken us at least ten minutes, we found no French there, but the three shattered cannon still remained, which we were ordered to pitch down, not much improving their condition thereby, and so we gained the object for which we had come. All the French that were left in the convent, or at least all I saw there, were two of their wounded, but they were good enough to leave us a room full of cabbages, which came in very handy.'[424]

The 40th went on to occupy the entrenched suburbs to the south of the Convent, from which the enemy had also retired, and instead of returning to their quarters at Villa de Porco, they held both Convent and adjacent suburbs for the remainder of the siege. They were within 400 yards of the walls, so as Lawrence relates, their residence at San Francisco was not without incident:

'After this affair we took our quarters in the convent, but still continued our groundwork. Once the enemy sallied out of the town and attacked us during these operations, and a smart brush ensued, but they were soon obliged to retire again. Now and then the garrison would greet us with a cannon-ball, which often did some little mischief; a sergeant was killed by one, which at the same time took another's arm off, and I myself had a narrow escape one day whilst in the breastworks from a six-pounder, which, having struck the convent, rebounded and caught me in the chest. Luckily, it was nearly spent, but as it was, it knocked me down, and it was some time before I could recover my breath, and then not until my comrades had poured some rum and water down my throat. My chest was much discoloured and swollen, through which I was ill for nearly a week.'[425]

Occupation of the outlying convents enabled a further breaching battery of seven 24-pounders to be established on the Lower Teson, and by January 19th two steep but practicable breaches had been blasted in the walls. Wellington ordered that the assault should be launched at seven o'clock that same night, allowing the defenders no time to repair the breaches. Picton's 3rd Division was to storm the Main Breach in the north wall while the Light Division, led by 'Black Bob' Craufurd, assaulted the Lesser Breach, directly opposite the Convent of San Francisco. Meanwhile, Pack's Portuguese Brigade was to make a false attack to the south on the Santiago Gate and the 2nd Cacadores were to cross the Agueda by the Roman bridge and escalade a small Castle outwork to capture two guns enfilading the ditch, enabling Campbell's Brigade of the 3rd Division to advance on the Main Breach from the Convent of Santa Cruz.

Picton's direct attack, advancing from the 2nd Parallel on the Little Tesson, was made by Major General Henry Mackinnon's Brigade, the 45th, 74th and 88th, supported by a Portuguese Brigade. The irascible Picton addressed the 88th Connaught Rangers (known as 'the Devil's Own'): 'Rangers of Connaught! It is not my intention to expend any powder this evening. We'll do this business with the cold iron.' Led by the Forlorn Hope, the stormers raced up the glacis, dropped into the first ditch, bounded over the rubble of the *fausse-braie* and jumped into the main ditch, then scrambled to the top of the breach. There they were met by *cheveaux de frises*, a 16-foot drop into the town in front, and retrenchments with ten-foot ditches on either side. The breach was swept by 24-pounder guns mounted on both flanks, and then a large mine detonated beneath it, killing Mackinnon and many others. Undaunted, men of the 88th and 74th crossed the chasms to take the guns, at which the stormers of Henry Campbell's Brigade broke into the town, which had already been entered by the Light Division, some three hundred yards to their left.

'The first conflict was terrible,' wrote Charles Boutflower. 'No description, however, can do justice to the grandeur of the scenery; the rapid fire of the musketry, the infinite number of hand grenades, and the explosion of two mines, presented a coup d'oeil beautifully awful. We soon had the satisfaction of hearing our brave fellows give the cheer of victory.'[426]

William Lawrence watched the Light Division form up behind the Convent of San Francisco, where Wellington pointed out the Lesser Breach to the commanders of the storming party:

---

[424] Lawrence, p. 101-2.
[425] Ibid., p. 102.
[426] Boutflower, p. 122.

'The forlorn hope assembled between seven and eight o'clock under the walls of the convent we were then occupying, which protected them a little from the enemy's shot. All was deathly silent amongst those men, who perhaps could not help thinking it might be their last undertaking: in fact, this is much the worst business a soldier can enter upon, as scarcely anything but death looks him in the face. There they were, watching with intense anxiety for the, to many, fatal signal; and at length the order to advance was given.'[427]

The 40th would then have heard Craufurd's final exhortation: 'Soldiers, the eyes of your country are upon you. Be steady, be cool, be firm in the assault. The town must be yours this night. Once masters of the breach, let your first duty be to clear the ramparts, and in doing this, keep together. Now lads, for the breach!'

Breaking cover from the right of the Convent, the leading troops crossed the 400 yards to the *fausse braie*, then down into the ditch. The French opened fire on the mass, and in the confusion, some of the stormers made for a damaged ravelin and suffered heavily. Craufurd was mortally wounded on the glacis, and Colborne and Vandeleur were also hit. But the breach was soon gained, and storming parties turned to their right, clearing towards the Main Breach.

Pack's Brigade, on the far side of the town, stormed the redan in front of the Santiago gate, capturing its garrison. Captain William Queade of the 40th, who had been serving with the 1st Portuguese Line since May 1810, was wounded.

With both breaches forced, the fate of Ciudad Rodrigo was sealed. There was a little street fighting before the majority of the garrison laid down their arms in the Plaza Mayor. The town was then sacked for twelve hours by thousands of over-excited, and increasingly drunken, soldiers. This was the first time that the Peninsula Army had taken a place by assault, and there was an understanding among many of the troops that in recompense for their extreme labour, danger and losses during the siege and storming, a period of plunder would be licensed. Private Lawrence of the 40th, who was not usually averse to a little pilfering, on this occasion assumed the moral high ground:

'This successful achievement was attended with all the horrors of the soldiery, excesses, riot, and drunkenness taking place on every side. Houses were plundered of their contents, cellars broken open and emptied, and many houses were even set on fire amid the yells of the dissipated soldiers and the screams of the wounded. Thus the night passed, but in the morning order was a little restored, and those men who were sensible enough returned to their own regiments.'[428]

The capture of Ciudad Rodrigo cost the besiegers rather over one thousand casualties (the exact figures are uncertain), split almost equally between siege operations and storming.[429] The bill, high as it was, was modest by the standard of similar operations. Indeed, this first of Wellington's sieges had gone almost entirely as planned and was concluded in only half the anticipated time, lasting only twelve days from breaking ground to storming. The French defenders suffered 1,890 casualties including 1,360 prisoners, and lost 153 guns including the whole siege-train of the French Army of Portugal. Marmont had been thoroughly out-manoeuvred and caught off-balance, losing both his base for future operations in Portugal and the northern key to an Allied offensive into Spain. Stunned and rebuked by his Emperor, he could not help but remark that 'Never was such an operation pushed forward with the like activity.'

The main body of the 30th Regiment was not involved in the siege. They had received their annual issue of new clothing on the 12th and marched from Midões at daybreak next morning, following the well-worn, icy mountain route to Guarda and Vila de Touro. It is likely that they were preceded by a detachment of officers and men who had responded to Wellington's call for volunteers to take part in the siege of Ciudad Rodrigo. With the exception of two skirmishes in May 1811, the 30th had hardly fired a shot since joining Wellington's army in October 1810. But the unseasoned battalion of Lisbon and Cadiz days, having served two campaigns and marched many hundreds of miles, was now more than ready and understandably impatient for action. There was a critical shortage of sapper officers to supervise the siege-work, and so eleven officers of the 30th volunteered for

---

427 Lawrence, p. 103.
428 Ibid., p. 104.
429 The losses of the 40th at the siege of Ciudad Rodrigo are not known, but 33 of the Regiment died in January and 43 in February, a large proportion of whom must have been killed in action or died of wounds, or as a result of accidents and privation in the trenches.

engineering duties, while an unknown number of men also stepped forward to join the working parties in the trenches.[430]

On 17ᵗʰ January, the 30ᵗʰ marched from Vila de Touro through Aldeia de Ponte to billets in the village of Casillas de Flores:

'Soon after we left Aldeia de Ponte, we met an orderly dragoon. He told us that Ciudad Rodrigo had fallen, but when we proceeded a little farther, we heard the report of cannon in that direction very plainly, which convinced us to the contrary.

'18ᵗʰ – We heard very clearly firing the whole of the day, & hourly expected to receive orders to match. The doctor received orders to get his medicine all ready, which he did accordingly, & as we daily expected to be engaged, he gave me a tor[niquet] & directions how to use it.

'19ᵗʰ – The firing was still heard until about half past seven in the evening, when it ceased. We were within 5 leagues of Ciudad & could not hear the least news.

'20ᵗʰ – At daybreak we got the route to march to Ciudad, we supposed to take our turn of duty in the trenches, but when we reached [Fuente]guinaldo we heard from one of the artillery that the town was stormed the night before at half past seven o'clock & had surrendered. This was soon confirmed by the Light Division, which we met returning from the town loaded with plunder of every description. When we got within two miles of the town we met 1600 French prisoners of war. Our Regiment was quartered in the suburbs. I took a walk into the town & there beheld a most melancholy sight, the streets covered with dead bodies, broken firelocks, bayonets, balls, caps, &c.'[431]

According to Costello of the Light Division, 'as we marched over the bridge dressed in all varieties imaginable, some with jack-boots on, others with white French trousers, others in frock-coats with epaulettes, some even with monkeys on their shoulders, we met the 5ᵗʰ Division on their way to repair the breaches. They immediately formed on the left of the road, presented arms, and cheered us.'

The 5ᵗʰ Division, who marched in at about noon on the 20ᵗʰ, was indeed set to work that afternoon clearing and repairing the breaches and making the place defensible in view of reports that a French army was approaching from Salamanca. The division, including the 30ᵗʰ, provided working parties at Ciudad Rodrigo for the next month, clearing away debris, repairing the walls, filling in the trenches and other siege-works, improving the defences on the Greater Teson and strengthening the fortified convents. It rained for much of this time, but the 30ᵗʰ were billeted in the town and received extra pay, 8d a day for a six-hour shift.

Work was interrupted on 25ᵗʰ January for the burial of General Craufurd, who had died of his wounds. 'The procession was grand,' wrote John Carter, 'Our division opened file & rest[ed] on their arms whilst the funeral past betwixt us. The 52ⁿᵈ, 95ᵗʰ Regiments & Cacadores marched in front, in the rear came the corpse, followed by Lord W[ellington], Marshal Beresford & several other great men, their staff followed. He was buried at the foot of the lesser breach, which he himself wanted. Something moved the Colonel [Grey] & he ordered the ensigns to the Colours on the march.'

The younger officers of the 30ᵗʰ, many still in their teens, took advantage of their extended stay in the town for some excessively high-spirited riot. On 8ᵗʰ February, revealed Ensign Carter, 'Several of the officers who had been drinking at Ensign Lockwood's sallied forth about 2 o'clock in the morning into the street & began to throw stones at Lieutenant [Richard] Maynes's & Ensign [Robert] Smith's quarters. It enraged Smith so much that he fired a fowling piece out of the window & hit Lieutenant [and Adjutant] Garland. Ensign Smith reported this to the Colonel [and] Ensign Lockwood was put under arrest.' Colonel Grey appears to have viewed the shooting of his Adjutant as a relatively trivial offence, for two days later Lockwood was released from arrest with a severe reprimand.

On February 11ᵗʰ Carter was himself involved in a fracas with the locals. 'About 12 o'clock at night, the doctor returned from a dance, & also the people of the house, but when the doctor got into bed we were disturbed

---

[430] Lieutenants Andrew Baillie, Parke Percy Nevill and John Lorraine White, Ensign Robert Smith and Privates John Bonsor, Edward Braesland, Athony Cullinan, Moses Dyer, John Hill, John McAndrew, Thomas Murray and Thomas Slavin lived to receive the medal clasp for Ciudad Rodrigo granted in 1844. As for their duties during the siege, we only know that Lieutenant Nevill, on the first of his three tours as assistant engineer, 'was set to work in making gabions and fascines for the batteries.'

[431] Carter, p. 18.

by the people singing below stairs. We asked them to be silent & go to bed for we wished to sleep. They made reply that it was their intention to dance & sing all night. This enraged us so that when they were in the midst of their glory, we employed the contents of the chamber pot in the midst of them. They with the greatest fury laid siege to our room. The girl of the house, whom I had told that I was the son of a parson, called me the son of a farther' [sic] '& a bastard. After soaking them pretty well with water, & turning them out of doors, they were quiet.'[432]

Meanwhile, the 40th had returned to their former quarters at Vila de Porco, where they remained until 10th February. They were no doubt please to be mentioned by Wellington on 20th January:

'In my despatch of the 15th I reported to your lordship the attack on the convent of Santa Cruz by the troops of the first division, under the direction of Lieutenant-General Graham; and that of the convent of St. Francisco, on the 14th instant, under the direction of Major-General the Honble. Charles Colville; the last mentioned enterprise was performed by Lieutenant-Colonel Harcourt with the 40th Regiment. This regiment remained from that time in St. Francisco, and materially assisted our attack on that side of the place.'

Despite this acknowledgement of the Regiment's significant part in the capture of Ciudad Rodrigo, the 40th were denied the battle honour, which was restricted to those regiments who took part in the final assault.[433] However, 126 surviving Peninsula veterans of the 40th, together with twelve of the 30th, received the 'Ciudad Rodrigo' bar when it was granted in 1844.

The Siege and Storming of Badajoz, 17th March – 6th April 1812

In less than one week after his capture of Ciudad Rodrigo, Wellington was issuing orders for the siege of Badajoz. His first priority was to assemble a proper siege-train at Elvas. There was less urgency for the divisions to march, for the movement of artillery and stores would take some weeks, and meanwhile, the Commander-in-Chief wished to deceive the French as to his intentions by retaining his infantry divisions in the north for as long as possible. The general strategic situation in Spain favoured an attempt on Badajoz, for Marmont was held in the north by nonsensical orders from Paris, Soult had his hands full in Andalusia with his siege of Cadiz and the activities of Spanish forces, and Napoleon had withdrawn troops from the Peninsula for his ill-starred march on Moscow.

The 40th marched south at dawn on 10th February, but at Aldea de Ponte that night they were ordered back to Vilar Formoso to await the arrival of their much-needed annual clothing issue, which was on its way. On the 12th, the Regiment marched to Vila de Ciervo, which they finally left on the 27th en route to Castello Branco, which they reached on 5th March. On the 8th the 40th reached Nisa, 'a most fatiguing march,' wrote Surgeon Boutflower, 'of five leagues and a half over the worst roads in Portugal, added to which we had the dragging of the nine-pounders up two most tremendous hills. The men came in so exhausted in the evening that we have had much accession to our sick list.' They reached Portalegre on the 10th, and on the 14th they were ordered forward to Elvas, their third visit to that place. Arriving there on the 15th, they found that the 4th Division, together with the 3rd and Light Divisions, were to form the besieging force at Badajoz, while the 1st, 2nd, 6th and 7th Divisions, the cavalry and horse artillery were to form the covering force under Sir Thomas Graham. Also at Elvas, a pontoon bridge was ready to cross the river Guadiana, and 52 guns and howitzers had been assembled.

On March 16th the whole army moved on Badajoz. In anticipation of St. Patrick's Day, the 17th, there was a grand parade at which the troops were inspected in review order:

'The parade was magnificent and imposing. The Colours of each regiment proudly, though scantily, floated in the breeze; they displayed but little embroidery. Scarcely could the well-earned badges of the regiments be

---

[432] Carter, p. 21.

[433] In 1824 Colonel Thornton, who had himself commanded the 40th in the Peninsula, tried to have 'Ciudad Rodrigo' added to the Regiment's battle honours, but this was refused by the Duke of Wellington. His reason, conveyed in a letter 0f 6th April 1824 from Fitzroy Somerset (the future Lord Raglan), being that 'as it was thought proper at the time [only] to confer the grant of a medal [i.e. the CB] to the commanding officers of the corps engaged in the assault of the place, and as, in recommending regiments for honorary distinction, the Duke has been guided by the fact of the commanding officers having received medals, he cannot comply with your request that the 40th Regiment should be recommended for the badge of Ciudad Rodrigo.'

discerned; yet their lacerated condition, caused by the numberless wounds which they received in battle, gave martial dignity to their appearance and animated every British breast with national pride. The review being terminated, a signal was given for each corps to proceed to that spot of ground which they were destined to open. He whole moved off. All the bands by one accord played the same tune, which was cheered with shouts that bore ominous import and appeared to shake Badajoz to its foundations. The music played was the animating Irish air, *St. Patrick's Day*... Never was St. Patrick's Day more loudly cheered, or by stouter hearts, and never was the music more nobly accompanied, nor with more warlike bass; for all the troops echoed the inspiring national air as proudly they marched to their ground.'[434]

Badajoz was invested on the evening of the 17th March. The fortifications had been expertly renovated and improved since the sieges of the previous May-June. Taking Badajoz was always going to be considerably more challenging than Ciudad Rodrigo. Modernised in the mid-eighteenth century, the fortress had eight bastions some thirty feet high, deep ditches, and counter-scarps averaging twenty-five feet in height. The curtain walls between the bastions were protected by ravelins, unfinished but still effective, while in the north-east corner, at the highest point and 130 feet above the Guadiana, stood an ancient Moorish castle, the garrison's final refuge. Four strong outworks commanded approaches: the Picurina and Pardeleras redoubts, the San Roque lunette and, on the far bank of the Guadiana, the repaired Fort San Christoval. The south-eastern approaches were additionally strengthened by damming the boggy river Rivillas, creating an inundation stretching about one thousand yards upstream from the San Roque lunette, near where the stream was dammed. The garrison of 172 officers and 4,742 men under Baron Armand Phillipon, included seven infantry battalions, and their morale was high after defeating two previous sieges in 1811.

Instead of selecting the Castle and Fort San Christoval for his attack, as had been the case in 1811, Wellington decided to breach the Trinidad and Santa Maria Bastions in the south-east corner of the fortress. To that end, ground was broken to the east of Badajoz on the night of 17th March by 1,800 workmen protected by a 2,000-strong guard. This first parallel was only two hundred yards from the Picurina redoubt, which would have to be taken before breaching batteries could be established. By dawn, the trenches were already three feet deep, and despite a heavy French fire of cannon and musketry during the day, the working parties continued to improve both the parallel and the zig-zag communication trenches behind it, and that night they began the first two batteries.

Deeply concerned at the imminent threat to the Picurina, Phillipon decided to mount a spoiling sortie. About noon on the 19th, one thousand infantry, forty cavalry, and one hundred engineers left the Trinidad Gate and formed unobserved behind the Picurina. Moving out rapidly upon the parallel, they wheeled to their right to enfilade the besieger's works before the surprised workmen could stand to their arms or the guard form to receive them. Both guard and working party were driven out of the parallel in disorder, but were rallied by their officers within fifty yards and charged their assailants. The French were dislodged and withdrew in good order, having caused some damage to the parallel and carried off some 545 entrenching tools. The sortie cost the besiegers nearly 150 casualties, while the French lost twenty men killed and 13 officers, and 147 men wounded. Private William Lawrence of the 40th took part in the hand-to-hand fighting:

'I killed a French sergeant myself with my bayonet in this action. I was at the time in the trenches when he came on the top and made a dart at me with his bayonet, having, like myself, exhausted his fire; and while in the act of thrusting, he overbalanced himself and fell. I very soon pinioned him to the ground with my bayonet, and the poor fellow soon expired. I was sorry afterwards that I had not tried to take him prisoner instead of killing him, but at the time we were all busily engaged in the thickest of the fight, and there was not much time to think about things. And besides that, he was a powerful-looking man, being tall and stout, with a beard and moustache completely covering his face, as fine a soldier as I have seen in the French army, and if I had allowed him to gain his feet, I might have suffered for it: so perhaps in such times my plan was the best – kill or be killed.'[435]

Lawrence was fully engaged, with the rest of the 40th, in the arduous, dangerous and generally unpopular work of sapping forward and building batteries, often in pouring rain:

[434] *A Boy in the Peninsular War*, Robert Blakeney, p.p. 259-60.
[435] Lawrence, p.p. 108-9.

'About eight hundred of us were every night busily engaged in the trenches, whilst a large number, who were called the covering party, were on the lookout in case of an attack from the enemy. The rain poured down so fast that balers were obliged to be employed in places, and at times, the trenches were in such a state of mud that it was over our shoes. We were chiefly employed during the day in finishing off what we had done in the night, as very little else could be done then, owing to the enemy's fire. We had not been to work many days before we got within musket shot of a fine fort, situated a little distance from the town, and garrisoned with four or five hundred of the enemy, who annoyed us rather during our operations.

'One night, as I was working in the trenches near this place, and just as the guard was about to be relieved, a shell from the town fell amongst them and exploded, killing and wounding about thirty. I never saw a worse sight of its kind, for some had their arms and legs – and some even their heads, which was worse – completely severed from their bodies. I remember my comrade, Pig Harding, who was working near me at the time, and had, like myself, become hardened to the worst of sights during our sojourn in the Peninsula, saying as a joke, "Lawrence, if anyone is in want of an arm or leg he can have a good choice there"; little knowing, poor fellow, that soon he would himself be carried out, numbered with the slain. On the morning after this explosion, a terrific scene of our mangled comrades presented itself, for their remains strewed the ground in all directions.'[436]

Lieutenant Parke Percy Nevill of the 30th, who was again acting as an assistant engineer, commented that the troops worked under 'torrents of rain, which deluged the trenches, the camp, and everything about us. This weather continued several days, and we were often above our knees in water; but our men worked with an ardour beyond all praise – the Royal Engineer officers and their assistants had only to tell them what to do, and it was done.'[437]

The 5th Division, meanwhile, was the last to march south from Ciudad Rodrigo, and the 30th do not appear to have left until about 9th March, having first made brief excursions north to Salices el Chico on 27th February and Ituro de Azaba on the 29th. Ensign Carter was probably correct in his conjecture that the motive for these moves, in the opposite direction from Badajoz, was to deceive the enemy. We have no details of their route, but on 22nd March, their Division was called forward from Campo Maior to complete the investment of Badajoz by watching Fort San Christoval. They remained there until the night of the 5th/6th April when they were relieved by Portuguese troops and crossed the Guadiana to bivouac about a mile and a quarter to the south-west of the town behind the Cerro del Viento.

At 10 a.m. on the 25th, two British batteries opened against the Picurina redoubt, which was stormed that evening by detachments under Major-General Kempt, who we last saw in 1806 as Commanding Officer of the 81st Foot at Maida. This capture enabled breaching batteries to be established on the Picurina ridge, from where they could bombard the Santa Maria and Trinidad bastions at a range of some five hundred yards. These batteries, mounting twenty 18 and 24-pounders, opened on the morning of the 30th, and by April 4th practicable breaches had been opened in the southern face of the Trinidad bastion and the eastern flank of Santa Maria. The time was fast approaching for what the besiegers knew would be a bloody assault:

'A very desperate resistance is apprehended at the storming,' wrote Surgeon Boutflower on 2nd April. 'It is impossible to anticipate the carnage that must ensue without feelings of the utmost horror; no idea is entertained of a capitulation, indeed it is one of the fundamental rules of the Code Napoleon that any governor giving up a fortress without standing a siege shall be shot.'[438]

The garrison was indeed putting up a skilful and determined resistance. Every night, despite harassing fire from the British batteries, French working parties cleared the rubble under the breaches, keeping the slopes as steep and difficult as possible, while others retrenched and repaired the ramparts, and prepared some unpleasant and ingenious surprises in the surrounding ditch, which they deepened.

There was now an even greater sense of urgency to the siege, for Marshal Soult had scraped an army together and by 4th April was only seventy miles, or 4-5 marches, away. Wellington needed to strike as soon as possible, and at noon he ordered the assault on the Santa Maria and Trinidad bastions for that evening; but at 4 p.m., persuaded that the defenders were preparing all manner of obstacles in and behind the breaches, he

---

[436] Ibid., p.p. 109-10.
[437] Nevill, p. 12.
[438] Boutflower, p. 128.

postponed the assault for a day while a third breach was battered in the badly-built curtain wall between the two bastions. On the morning of the 6th, all three breaches were reported to be practicable, so Wellington ordered that Badajoz should be stormed that night.

It should be noted here that, for lack of time and engineer resources, there was a serious flaw in the preparations for the attack on the breaches. An established rule of siege-craft was that, in addition to breaching the walls, the counter-scarp should be blown into the ditch, usually by mining. This enabled a strong body of stormers to descend into the ditch by one ramp of rubble and climb into the breaches by another without losing formation and control. At Badajoz, Wellington lacked the trained sappers to undertake a mining operation, and in consequence, his storming parties would have to jump or climb down into the ditch, then re-form under fire before assaulting the breaches, risking loss of mass. impetus and cohesion.

The main attack on the three breaches was to be made by the 4th and Light Divisions. Two subsidiary assaults were to be made: the 4th Division trench guard was to take the San Roque lunette and cut away the Rivillas dam, while at the particular request of Picton, the 3rd Division would attempt an escalade of the Castle. Finally, two diversionary attacks were planned: one by Power's Portuguese brigade on the bridgehead beyond the Guadiana, and the other by the Portuguese brigade of the 5th Division against the Pardeleras. At the last moment, Lieutenant-General Leith, commanding the 5th Division, was told that he might use one of his two British brigades to escalade the bastion of San Vicente, on the north-west corner of the town next to the river, if a favourable opportunity arose, and should be prepared to support this brigade with the remainder of his division.

Facing the breaches, the Light Division was to assault the flank of the Santa Maria bastion, on the left, while the 4th Division, formed on their right, was tasked to storm the face of the Trinidad bastion and the curtain between the two bastions. Attempts to break the Rivillas dam had failed, and the inundation, swollen by heavy rain, restricted approaches to the breaches and flooded much of the ditch below the Trinidad. In consequence, the two divisions had to advance to the attack side by side on a very narrow front with the inundation to their right and large quarries, some three hundred yards from the breaches, on their left. A small stream marked the inter-divisional boundary. On descending the counter-scarp into the ditch, the Light Division was to keep to the left of an unfinished ravelin which stood in front of the curtain wall, and the 4th Division was to keep to its right.

Each division was to be headed by a forlorn hope and by an advance guard of five hundred volunteers, split between a storming party, carrying ladders and hay-bags and accompanied by carpenters and miners with axes and crowbars, and sharpshooters who were to line the crest of the glacis and keep down the enemy fire. The main bodies of the battalions were not to expose themselves until they could see the heads of the storming parties ascend the breaches, when they were to 'move forward to the storm in double quick time.' Each division was to leave a reserve of one thousand men at the quarries.

The time of attack was originally to be 7.30 p.m. so as to prevent repair or retrenchment of the breaches after dark, but it had to be delayed until 10 p.m. to allow more time for deployment.

This delay was fatal, for it gave the French time to improve their defences. They blocked the breaches with *chevaux de frise* – immense baulks of timber studded with sharpened cavalry swords and immovably chained down – and retrenched behind the breaches with breastworks of fascines, wool packs, and sandbags. Twelve hundred men, principally French 3rd/103rd Ligne and Germans of the Hesse-Darmstadt Regiment, were ready to defend the breaches, armed with three muskets each and hand grenades, while explosives, gunpowder barrels, logs, and large stones were ready to be rolled down on the stormers. The slopes of the breaches were strewn with crowsfeet and hung with beams, planks, and doors set with nails and spikes. The ditch had also been thoroughly prepared: it had been filled with all manner of combustible obstacles – upended carts, boats, and broken gabions – and sixty 14-inch shells had been readied, planted as mines at the foot of the breaches. Finally, a cunette (a 6-foot deep ditch within the ditch) had been dug below the intact counter-scarp, increasing its drop to 16 foot, and it was flooded for much of its length, making it a lethal obstacle and, for the 4th Division, a very considerable restriction on their ability to form before storming the Trinidad bastion. The preparations in the ditch, designed to restrict the formation of storming columns and then to destroy them, were invisible to the besiegers.

As dark fell on 6th April, the guns fell silent. It was obvious to the French that Badajoz would be stormed that night, and they made their final preparations.

By 8 p.m., the assault battalions were silently gathering, without stocks or knapsacks, their collars unbuttoned and trousers tucked up, their faces a mix of mortal foreboding, self-confidence, and grim determination. Private William Lawrence of the Grenadier Company 40th, joined the forlorn hope of the 4th Division:

'We were supplied with ladders and grass bags,' he recalled, 'and having received and eaten our rations, and each man carrying his canteen of water, we fell in at half-past eight or thereabouts to wait for the requisite signal for all to advance. During the interval our men were particularly silent.'[439]

After three weeks of losses and hard toil in flooded trenches, and with bitter memories of previous failures in front of Badajoz, the troops were desperate to close with their enemy. Many were also convinced that the Spanish inhabitants of the town, who had treated them unkindly after Talavera, were pro-French and had been seen firing from the walls. Hardened rogues, who had taken part in the looting of Ciudad Rodrigo – or wished that they had enjoyed that freedom from military discipline, and had noted that the perpetrators were unpunished – saw a rare opportunity to make themselves rich, or at least memorably drunk, and there were many who, in Napier's words, had grown incredibly savage. William Lawrence and his comrades had made their own nefarious preparations:

'I will relate an engagement that myself, Pig Harding, and another of my comrades, George Bowden by name, entered into before we even started on our way, of which the result showed what a blind one it was. Through being quartered in Badajoz after the battle of Talavera, all three of us knew the town perfectly well, and so understood the position of most of the valuable shops; and hearing a report likewise that if we succeeded in taking the place there was to be three hours' plunder, we had planned to meet at a silversmith's shop that we knew about, poor Pig even providing himself with a piece of wax candle to light us if needed. But all this was doomed to disappointment.'[440]

At 9.30 p.m., the storming columns moved forward to their assault positions. It was a very dark, misty night, silent except for the croaking of frogs in the Rivillas inundation and the calls of French sentries on the ramparts. Occasionally, the gloom was brightly illuminated as carcasses and fire-balls were thrown from the town, then dark once more descended.

The various attacks were supposed to be launched at the same time, but this did not happen. At 9.40 p.m. there was a rattle of musketry as Major Wilson and three hundred of his 48th took the San Roque lunette, and some five minutes later the defenders opened fire on the 3rd Division, who they had seen lining up for their escalade of the Castle. Kempt ordered his men to advance. All remained quiet in front of the breaches, and at 10 p.m. the 4th and Light Divisions stepped off at the agreed time.

The forlorn hopes and advanced guards stole forward in silence, and had reached the glacis when they heard firing from the direction of the Castle. Some two minutes later, they were followed by the main bodies of the divisions. A single warning shot was discharged by a French sentry in the covered way, but the ramparts remained silent as the stormers placed their ladders, threw down their hay-bags, and descended the counter-scarp into the ditch. The assault began with disaster for the 4th Division, for many men, not waiting for the ladders, leapt down the counter-scarp into the flooded cunette, where scores were drowned. The remainder of the division moved to their left to avoid the flood, and either scrambled down the ladders or plunged some fourteen feet onto the hay-bags. The French waited till the forlorn hope approached the Trinidad breach and the storming parties were mostly in the ditch, with the Light Division slightly in front. An officer of the 4th Division described what happened next:

'Suddenly, an explosion took place at the foot of the breaches, and a burst of light disclosed the whole scene: the earth seemed to rock under us – what a sight! The ramparts crowded with the enemy – the French soldiers standing on the parapets – the 4th Division advancing rapidly in column of companies on a quarter circle to our right, while the short-lived glare from the barrels of powder and combustibles flying into the air, gave to friends and foes a look as if both bodies of troops were laughing at each other.

---

[439] Lawrence, p. 111.
[440] Ibid.

'A tremendous firing now opened on us, and for an instant we were stationary; but the troops were in no way daunted… The soldiers flew down the ladders, and the cheering from both sides was loud and full of confidence.' [441]

The French had blown their mines, the explosion of which ignited the obstacles below the breaches, turning the ditch into an inferno into which the defenders poured musketry and threw grenades. The explosion nearly annihilated the forlorn hopes and the heads of the storming parties.

Among the early casualties were the engineer directing officers whose task was to guide the stormers to the breaches, and their loss caused serious confusion and disorientation. The 4th Division, forced to their left by the inundation, could only approach the breaches in the Trinidad and curtain wall by passing through a very restricted gap between the flood and the unfinished ravelin. Many of them, including the party detailed to storm the breach in the curtain wall, reached the foot of the ravelin, mistook its rubble for a breach, and clambered up. There they were joined by many of the Light Division, who had swerved to the right away from their Santa Maria objective and, faced by an apparent breach, climbed it, only to discover that they were exposed on top of an earthen bank and separated from the breaches by a fiery gulf. From this unfortunate point both divisions became inextricably intermixed, and all regular formation was lost. Some men opened fire from the ravelin while others slid and scrambled down and, in a disorganised mass, headed for the breaches.

Again and again over the next two hours, officers gathered groups of men together and led them up one of the breaches with desperate valour, only to be hurled back with the loss of their bravest soldiers. British bugles constantly sounded the advance, and some forty such gallant but uncoordinated attempts were made, all in vain. The survivors took what cover they could among the burning obstacles in the ditch, then dashed once more with redoubled fury towards almost certain death or wounds. Most of these attacks were against the Trinidad bastion, rather fewer against the Santa Maria, and probably none against the curtain wall, which, because the French had insufficient time to retrench it, would undoubtedly have been the easiest to assault.

'Gallant foes laughing at death met, fought, bled, and rolled upon earth; and from the very earth destruction burst, for the exploding mines cast up friends and foes together, who in burning torture clashed and shrieked in the air. Partly burned, they fell back into the inundating water, continually lighted by the incessant bursting of shells. Thus assailed by opposing elements, they made the horrid scene yet more horrid by shrieks uttered in wild despair, vainly struggling against a watery grave with limbs convulsed and quivering from the consuming fire. The roaring of cannon, the bursting of shells, the rattle of musketry, the awful explosion of mines and the flaring sickly blaze of fireballs seemed not of human invention, but rather as if all the elements of nature had greedily combined in the general havoc, and heaven, earth and hell had united for the destruction alike of devoted Badajoz and of its furious assailants.' [442]

Surgeon Charles Boutflower of the 40th watched in awe from his medical post near the quarries:

'A scene of horror at once dreadful and sublime presented itself. There was no moon, but the stars afforded just sufficient light to enable the men to find their respective destinations. On their being discovered by the enemy, a fire so tremendous opened on them that the oldest military men present declare that they never witnessed anything that could be at all compared to it. The explosions from the several mines the enemy had prepared were indescribably awful, but certainly furnished a coup d'oeil such as I never expect, or indeed wish, again to witness.' [443]

Private William Lawrence of the 40th, who had volunteered for the forlorn hope of the 4th Division, made it to the top of the Trinidad breach, but no further:

'I was one of the ladder party, for we did not feel inclined to trust to the Portuguese, as we did at Ciudad Rodrigo. On our arriving at the breach, the French sentry on the wall cried out, "Who comes there?" three times, or words to that effect in his own language, but no answer being given, a shower of shot, canister, and grape, together with fire-balls, was hurled at random amongst us. Poor Pig received his death wound immediately, and my other accomplice, Bowden, became missing, while I myself received two small slug-shots in my left knee and a musket shot in my side, which must have been mortal had it not been for my canteen, for the ball penetrated

[441] Peninsular Sketches, W. H. Maxwell, London, 1844, Vol. I, p. 277.
[442] Blakeney, p. 264. The writer took part in the storming of Badajoz on the staff of Major-General Bowes of the 4th Division.
[443] Boutflower, p. 130.

that and passed out, making two holes in it, and then entered my side slightly. Still I stuck to my ladder and got into the entrenchment. Numbers had by this time fallen; but the cry from our commanders being "Come on, my lads!" we hastened to the breach, but there, to our great surprise and discouragement, we found a *chevaux de frise* had been fixed, and a deep entrenchment made from behind which the garrison opened a deadly fire on us. Vain attempts were made to remove this fearful obstacle, during which my left hand was dreadfully cut by one of the blades of the *chevaux de frise*, but finding no success in that quarter, we were forced to retire for a time. We remained, however, in the breach until we were quite weary with our efforts to pass it.'[444]

The 40th were taking the heaviest losses in the 4th Division: around half of the Regiment were down, including Colonel Harcourt and three-quarters of his officers. Private William Lawrence was eventually forced to retire wounded:

'My wounds were still bleeding, and I began to feel very weak; my comrades persuaded me to go to the rear; but this proved a task of great difficulty, for on arriving at the ladders I found them filled with the dead and wounded, hanging some by their feet just as they had fallen and got fixed in the rounds. I hove down three lots of them, hearing the implorings of the wounded all the time; but on coming to the fourth, I found it completely smothered with dead bodies, so I had to draw myself up over them as best I could. When I arrived at the top I almost wished myself back again, for there of the two I think was the worse sight, nothing but the dead and wounded lying around, and the cries of the latter, mingled with the incessant firing from the enemy, being quite deafening.

'I was so weak myself that I could scarcely walk, so I crawled on my hands and knees till I got out of reach of the enemy's musketry. After proceeding for some way, I fell in with Lord Wellington and his staff, who, seeing me wounded, asked me what regiment I belonged to. I told him the Fortieth, and that I had been one of the Forlorn Hope. He inquired as to the extent of my wounds, and if any of our troops had got into the town, and I said "No," and I did not think they ever would, as there was a *chevaux de frise*, a deep entrenchment, and in the rear of them a constant and murderous fire kept up by the enemy. One of his staff then bound up my leg with a silk handkerchief, and told me to go behind a hill which he pointed out, where I would find a doctor to dress my wounds; so I proceeded on, and found it was the doctor [Boutflower] of my own regiment.

'Next after me, Lieutenant Elland [Ayling] was brought in by a man of the name of Charles Filer, who had seen him lying wounded at the breach with a ball in the thigh, and on his asking him to convey him from the breach, had raised him on his shoulders for that object. But during his march, a cannon ball had taken the officer's head clean off without Filer finding it out on account of the darkness of the night and the clamour of cannon and musketry, mingled with the cries of the wounded. Much it was to Filer's astonishment, then, when the surgeon asked him what he had brought in a headless trunk for. He declared that the lieutenant had a head on when he took him up, for he had himself asked him to take him from the breach; and that he did not know when the head was severed, which must have been done by one of the bullets of which there were so many whizzing about in all directions. Some may doubt the correctness of this story, but I, myself, being both a hearer and an eye-witness to the scene at the surgeon's, can vouch for the accuracy of it. Certainly Filer's appearance was not altogether that of composure, for he was not only rather frightened at the fearful exposure of his own body at the breach and across the plain, but he was evidently knocked up, or rather bowed down, by the weight of his lifeless burden, which he must, if he came from the breach, have carried for upwards of half a mile, so that under these disadvantages the mistake might easily have been made even by anyone of harder temperament than his. But the tale did not fail to spread through the camp, and caused great laughter over Filer, sentences being thrown at him such as "Who carried the man without a head to the doctor?"[445]

There is only one other casualty of the 40th for whom anecdotal information has survived. Lieutenant James Anthony was among those wounded in the breach. A contemporary newspaper reported that, 'On marching to the assault of Badajoz this heroic youth was shot through the wrist; but instead of retiring he coolly wrapped his sash round the wound and proceeded with undaunted courage to the breach. He there received a second ball, which, entering his breast, went quite through his body and brought him to the ground, where, on a momentary repulse of his party, he was wounded in the thigh by one of the enemy with a bayonet.'

---

[444] Lawrence, p. 112.
[445] Ibid., p.p. 112-5.

Towards midnight, the fruitless assaults on the breaches ceased. The largely leaderless survivors, sullenly impotent and bewildered, crouched among piles of their scorched and mutilated dead and wounded in the debris-strewn ditch, and fired ineffectively at the ramparts from which incessant musketry continued and French and German voices taunted them with, 'All is well in Badajoz' and 'Why do you not come into Badajoz?.' Unable to get forward, the men of the 4th and Light Divisions were stubbornly unwilling to fall back.

Captain John Jones, Brigade Major of Engineers at Badajoz, examined the breaches after the siege. His opinion was that the breaches could have been carried if they had been 'properly assaulted by strong columns, closely formed up.' In the event, a disastrous combination of failure to blow in the counter-scarp, loss of so many of the storming parties drowned, killed or maimed in the explosions, and of the engineer directing officers, and the mistaken ascent of the unfinished ravelin, made such formed assaults impossible.

Charles Broke Vere, Assistant Quarter-Master General of the 4th Division, voiced the opinion of many when he listed some of the causes of failure:

'The inundation in the ditch opposite the bastion of Trinidad; the depth of the ditch at the inundation; the contiguity of the columns of attack, and their collision in their approach; the steep and difficult nature of the breaches, and the collected force and formidable defences on and flanking them; occasioned the failure of the attack on the side of the place into which a way seemed to be opened by the batteries.'[446]

Just after midnight, Wellington, who had received a succession of bad and worse reports from the breaches at his post near the quarries, accepted the inevitable and ordered the 4th and Light Divisions to retire and re-form for a renewed assault. The bugles rang out repeatedly before the troops unwillingly withdrew, climbing the few remaining ladders with difficulty, and formed up again near the glacis in much reduced numbers. Their losses had been truly terrible but, though they did not yet know it, the fate of Badajoz had already been decided elsewhere.

Hardly had the order to withdraw from the breaches been issued when Wellington learned that the 3rd Division had successfully escaladed the Castle, many of whose Hessian defenders had been withdrawn to reinforce the breaches. Picton's men had secured the Castle by about midnight, but they were unable to break out into the town through the single unblocked postern gate – though the threat of such an incursion had the effect of drawing in the French reserves.

'The blow, however, that actually finished the business, and caused the French to fail at the breaches, was delivered by quite another force.'[447]

On the opposite side of the town, Leith's 5th Division escalade of the San Vicente bastion had been delayed. It was, in any case, a high-risk operation, requiring the assault troops to overcome layers of obstacles to enter the town.

Besides, it had not been included in the original plan of attack because a French warrant officer of engineers had deserted to the British with detailed plans showing that the glacis there had been mined. The bastion was at the northwestern extremity of Badajoz, where the river Guadiana ran close to its right flank. Having crossed the glacis, the storming parties would have to force their way through a palisade into the covered way, then descend the sheer 12-foot counter-scarp into the ditch, cross a water-filled cunette (6½ feet wide and 5½ feet deep) before scaling the 31½ foot rampart of the bastion.

The San Vicente bastion, and the adjoining San Jose Bastion, were held by the 3rd/9th Légère, 580 strong, but by the time of Leith's attack, two of its companies had fortuitously been redeployed to join an unsuccessful French counter-attack on the Castle. Some two hundred yards east from San Vicente, at the Las Palmas Gate on the river front, a reserve of some three hundred men was posted, armed Frenchmen of the civil departments, called the Battalion of Administration, and Spaniards in the service of King Joseph, whilst along the walls to the south the Santiago, San Juan and San Roque bastions, which would also have to be cleared, were held by the 1st/28th Légère (597 men) and 1st/58th Ligne (450 men). Furthermore, in the course of the struggle in the bastions, the defenders were reinforced by all or part of a Hessian battalion, while the small detachment of French cavalry was encountered in the town.

[446] *Marches, Movements and Operations of the 4th Division of the Allied Army in Spain and Portugal*, Charles Broke Vere, Assistant Quarter-Master-General of the Division, p. 25.
[447] *A History of the Peninsular War*, Volume V, page 253, Sir Charles Oman. Fortescue, in his History of the British Army, Volume VIII, page 408, agrees.

The attack was to be made by Walker's brigade of the 5th Division – 1st/4th, 2nd/30th, and 2nd/44th, supported by the 2nd/38th of Hay's brigade and the 15th Portuguese Line. The storming party comprised the Light Companies of that brigade[448], plus that of the 2nd/38th, the whole commanded by Lieutenant-Colonel Francis Brooke of the 4th, and was supported by the remainder of his battalion, with the 30th, commanded by George Grey, and the 44th in reserve. Walker's fourteen to fifteen hundred British and up to eight hundred Portuguese[449] would have to overcome a succession of at least two thousand strongly-posted defenders.

The 5th Division's attack was delayed because the officer conducting the scaling ladders lost his way between the engineer park and the divisional bivouac area, so that Leith was unable to leave his bivouac area until after 11 p.m. There has been speculation as to what effect the prompt arrival of the ladders might have had. On the one hand, had San Vicente been stormed at 10 p.m., the complete garrison would still have been in place, together with the garrison reserve battalion in the cathedral square, which would have stacked the odds more heavily against the escalade. On the other hand, an earlier 5th Division attack, if successful, might have saved many hundreds of lives in the breaches and at the Castle.

The 30th Foot have left no eye-witness narrative of their part in the storming of the San Vicente bastion, but it can be pieced together from other first-hand accounts, notably those of Captain Leith Hay, ADC to the divisional commander, and of Lieutenant Ellers Hopkins of the 4th Foot, who described the approach up the glacis to the palisades:

'The column halted a few yards from a breast-work surmounted by a stockade, and a *chevaux de frise* concealing a guard-house on the covered way, and at this moment, a most awful explosion took place, followed by the most tremendous peals of musketry. "That is at the breaches," was the whisper among our soldiers, and their anxiety to be led forward was intense, but their firmness and obedience was equally conspicuous. The moon now appeared. We could hear the French soldiers talking in the guard-house, and their officers were visiting the sentries. The engineer officer who preceded the column said, "Now is the time." The column instantly moved to the face of the gateway. It was only at this moment that the sentry observed us, and fired his alarm-shot, which was followed by musketry. The two companies of Portuguese carrying the scaling-ladders threw them down, and deaf to the voices of their officers, made off. This occurrence did not in the least shake the zeal and steadiness of our men, who occupied the space left, and shouldering the ladders, moved on. We could not force the gate open, but the breast-work was instantly crowded, and the impediments cut away sufficiently to allow two men entering abreast… The engineer officer was by this time killed. We had no other assistance from that corps, and the loss was most severely felt at this early period of the attack.'

This last statement was not quite accurate, for Lieutenant Nevill of the 30th, was present, acting initially as an assistant engineer.

Descending the counter-scarp and crossing the flooded cunette, the leading men raised their ladders against the bastion, when it was found that, at 24-foot, they were far too short.

'The troops were now fast filling the ditch,' recalled Ellers Hopkins. 'They had several ladders, and I shall never forget the momentary disappointment amongst the men when they found that the ladders were too short… The enemy took advantage of this to annoy us in every way, rolling down beams of wood, fire-balls, etc, together with an enfilading fire.'

'This did not appear the description of [a] situation where defence could be difficult, or entry practicable to ordinary men,' wrote Leith Hay with some understatement. 'At first few of the ladders could be placed, some of them, after being reared, were thrown from the walls back into the ditch. Others, constructed of green wood, opened and separated, or were not of sufficient length.'[450]

Thwarted in their attempt on the front of the bastion, Lieutenant-Colonel Francis Brooke and some of the 'Light Bobs' moved round the base of the bastion onto the river front. Here they discovered a point where the

---

[448] The Light Company 30th was commanded by Captain Thomas Chambers, with Ensign John Pratt. Lieutenant Parke Percy Nevill of the Light Company was detached, again acting as an assistant engineer.

[449] The exact number of men taking part in the assault cannot be known, and the best we can do is to take the other rank strengths from the March returns, add officers and subtract an estimate for those 'left out of battle.' In the case of the 30th, with a strength of seventeen officers and 382 other ranks, the attack strength must have been rather under four hundred.

[450] Leith Hay, Vol. I, p. 295.

scarp was only vertical for twenty-one feet, due to unfinished work, above which was a rough earthen shelf which sloped steeply for about six feet to just below an embrasure. Ladders were planted, and the Light Companies were able to scramble up the slope and force their way onto the ramparts.

Meanwhile, under the covering fire of two companies of the 44th, ranged along the crest of the glacis, Major Piper made a renewed attempt on the front of the bastion with the main body of the 4th:

'We observed near us an embrasure unfurnished of artillery,' recalled Lieutenant Hopkins, 'its place being occupied by a gabion filled with earth. A ladder was instantly placed under its mouth, and also one at each side. This allowed three persons to ascend at once, but only one at a time could enter in at the embrasure. The first several attempts were met with instant death. The ladders were even now too short, and it was necessary for one person to assist the other by hoisting him up the embrasure.'

The defenders gathered to resist this attack, but they were taken in the flank and driven back when the Light Companies swarmed up the ladders on the river face of the bastion.

As the stormers entered the San Vicente bastion, they were fired on from a building behind the ramparts, and the greater part of the 4th Regiment moved into the town to deal with this threat. Major-General Walker formed the rest of his brigade and, as ordered, advanced to his right along the ramparts towards the breaches. The San Jose Bastion was taken, but French resistance stiffened at the Santiago bastion where the 1st/28th Légère and 1st/58th Ligne stood a thousand strong[451] with artillery support. There was a close engagement, in which Walker was seriously wounded, as was Lieutenant-Colonel Grey of the 30th, and as Leith Hay explained, by unhappy chance, a check became a potentially serious reverse:

'The flame of a [French gunner's] port-fire struck a momentary terror into the minds of men that artillery, musketry, walls, and the bayonets of French infantry had failed to daunt. Part of General Walker's brigade, mistaking this appearance for the forerunner to the explosion of a mine, broke, and were bayoneted back to the spot where they had previously surmounted difficulties which there could have been no discredit in failing to overcome. Fortunately, General Leith had advanced part of the right brigade of his division in support of that already in the town. The second battalion of the 38th Regiment, under Colonel Nugent, had ascended and were formed on the ramparts. When the circumstances above detailed occurred, that corps, being prepared, received the pursuing enemy with a volley and bayonet charge that speedily terminated all contest.'[452]

It is probable that Captain Richard Machell of the 30th, Walker's brigade major, also fell severely wounded at about this time, for Captain Charles Barnard of the 38th, in a letter home, described how Machell was rescued:

'I was the first [of the 38th] to mount the ladders. We supported Gen[era]l Walker's Brigade, the 4th, 30th & 44th. The remainder of our Brigade, the 1st & the 9th, had nothing at all to do, indeed never fired a shot. An [officer] & two or three men of my company came up just in time to save Machell. Three men had got hold of him & were going to bayonet him altho' he was shot thro' the neck. It was the most bloody thing ever known.'

Having rallied at the San Vicente bastion, the reinforced 5th Division resumed its advance, both along the ramparts and through the town. Following the defeat of the French counter-attack, resistance on the walls crumbled, though it is probable that by this time a part of the Hesse-Darmstadt Regiment had been called up from the breaches, for one of its standards was captured by the Light Company of the 4th.

The situation in the town was more complex and confused. A party of Walker's men had initially penetrated to the Cathedral square through deserted, illuminated streets, and then pushed on towards the rear of the breaches. There is some evidence that as they advanced, they were fired on from within the houses, possibly by pro-French Spaniards who were said to have also held out lights to guide their allies. As the British party approached the breaches, the garrison there turned about and threw them back to the square. Lieutenant Ellers Hopkins remarked on the strange atmosphere in the town:

'All the houses in the streets and squares were brilliantly illuminated, from the top to the first floor, with numerous lamps. This illumination scene was truly remarkable – not a living creature was to be seen, but a continual low buzz and whisper around us, and we now and then perceived a small lattice gently open and re-shut, as if more closely to observe the singular scene of a small English party perambulating the town in good

---

[451] Colonel Lamare, the French garrison engineer, claimed that the total strength of the 1st/28th Légère and 1st/58th Ligne 'did not exceed 400 men', but did not account for the apparent disappearance of the majority of these two battalions, nor the known reinforcements.
[452] Leith Hay, Vol. I, p. 296.

order, the bugleman at the head blowing his instrument. Some of our men and officers now fell wounded; at first we did not know where the shots came from, but soon observed it was from the sills of the doors.

'We soon arrived at a large church facing some grand houses in a sort of square. The party here drew up, and it was at first proposed to take possession of this church, but that idea was abandoned. We made several prisoners, leading some mules laden with loose ball-cartridges in large wicker baskets, which they stated they were conveying from the magazines to the breaches. After securing the prisoners, ammunition, etc., we moved from the square with the intention of forcing our way upon the ramparts. We went up a small street towards them, but met with such opposition as obliged us to retire with loss. We again found ourselves in the square.'

Meanwhile, other elements of the 5th Division, possibly including part of the 30th, headed for the Las Palmas Gate, where they appear to have engaged the French cavalry and other reserves. A final push, with bugles blowing, brought Leith's men into the rear of the breaches, whose bewildered and dispirited defenders abandoned their posts and, by about 2 a.m., most of them surrendered to the 5th Division. Isolated groups of the defenders held out for some time longer, and an officer of the 43rd asserted that the 5th Division 'continued to be hotly engaged in the streets during the whole night.' It has also been claimed that, in the pre-dawn confusion, Leith's troops exchanged fire with the 3rd Division, who had still to break out of the Castle. Leith's ADC described this last phase of the 5th Division assault:

'Having succeeded in penetrating, and dispersing his opponents, [Leith] next sent an officer to report to Lord Wellington that the 5th Division was in the town. His bugles sounded the advance in all directions, distracting the enemy's attention, and inducing him to believe he was to be assailed from all quarters. Whether it proceeded from a knowledge that the castle was in possession of the Allies, or an impression that further resistance was in vain, the efforts of the garrison relaxed, the 5th Division drove everything before it, and having opened the communication with the bastions of La Trinidad and Santa Maria, the 4th and Light Divisions, which had previously been withdrawn, again advanced, and marched into the town by the breaches.'[453]

In any event, when the 4th and Light Divisions advanced once more into the breaches, they found them abandoned and, forcing their way through the obstacles, entered the town. An experienced officer who examined the breaches by day stated, 'I was fully satisfied that they were impregnable to men, and I do declare, most positively, that I could not have surmounted the *chevaux-de-frise*, even unopposed, in the day-time.'

Governor Phillipon, with a few hundred followers, escaped across the Guadiana bridge to Fort San Cristobal, where he surrendered at dawn.

Badajoz was then completely given over to plunder. The storming troops, maddened with wounds, loss of comrades, revenge, avarice, and drink, were joined by their women, camp followers, Spanish and Portuguese in an orgy of unrestrained looting and violence which lasted for three days.

Ensign Parke Percy Nevill of the 30th, aged seventeen, was caught up in the mayhem and later wrote an account of his experiences in the captured town:

'No tongue could tell the atrocities committed on that terrible night. I witnessed one on entering the town. I intended to join the 30th, my duty of engineer being over, when I met my servant coming from the arsenal, where he and others had conveyed our commanding officer, poor Lieut.-Col. Grey, who was mortally wounded. He had his haversack seemingly well filled with plunder. I asked him where the regiment was; he answered that he did not know, but that he would conduct me to the camp, as I appeared to him to be wounded, having some clotted blood on my face. I certainly was hit in the head, but in the excitement of the escalade did not mind it, neither did I feel a slight wound in my leg; but as I began to be rather weak, I took his advice and he assisted me to the bastion we had escaladed.

'In passing what appeared to be a religious house, I saw two soldiers dragging out an unfortunate nun, her clothes torn to pieces: in her agony, she knelt and held up a cross. Remorse seized one of the soldiers, who appeared more sober than the other, and he swore she should not be further outraged; the other soldier drew back and shot his comrade dead.

'Immediately after, some Portuguese soldiers appeared; they ordered us to halt, and presented their muskets. I said to my servant, "Throw them some of your plunder"; he instantly took off his haversack and threw

_____
[453] Leith Hay, p. 297.

it amongst them, when several dollars and other silver rolled out, and they let us pass. Had he not done this, I am sure those ruffians would have shot us, for the Portuguese troops, I heard, murdered every one they met.

'We got safe to the bastion, and with much difficulty I got down a ladder more than half-way to the ditch, when I could hold on no longer and tumbled down the rest of the way into some mud and water, which seemed to revive me. My servant helped me out and carried me on his back to the camp, where I got a draught of water, and I shall ever recollect how delicious it was. I was then wrapped up in a blanket, placed on some straw, and fell asleep instantly.

'I did not waken on the 7th until nearly mid-day, when I saw Assistant Surgeon Evans at my side. He had some tea ready, but I felt so stiff I could not move. He washed my head, which a ball had grazed, and extracted a pellet or very small ball which had entered over the left ankle joint, but was not in so far that he could not see it.'[454]

Whilst there is no doubt that many of the troops were completely out of hand, and some even offered violence to anyone seeking to restore order, there were officers and men who tried to protect the inhabitants from outrage. One such was Ensign Purefoy Lockwood, aged nineteen, who carried one of the Colours of the 30th at the storming of Badajoz. The story goes that when the city was taken, a young nun implored Lockwood to protect her, and he gallantly restored the lady safely to her parents.[455] Lockwood apparently had his reward three years later: shot in the head at the battle of Quatre Bras, it was the intercession of a nun that saved his life.

Much less fortunate was Lieutenant-Colonel George Grey, whose wound proved fatal. He had been accompanied on campaign by his wife, who had implored him always to take a tourniquet into action. This day was the first he had neglected her advice, and he died on the 7th from nine hours' loss of blood, having lain unattended for much of this time among the dead and wounded. His death, aged 33, nearly involved that of his pregnant wife, Elizabeth, who was then living in Lisbon. When the news of the capture of Badajoz reached the capital, she was sitting in an upstairs balcony of her hotel, chatting with other officers' wives, when her attention was attracted by shouting in the street below. Hearing her husband's name mentioned, she at once anticipated the worst and fainted, and when her fears were confirmed, she went into premature labour. She gave birth to a boy, who became Sir George Grey, soldier, explorer, colonial governor and statesman.[456] George Grey had for some years been a close friend of Sir John Moore, and he had apparently expressed a wish that should he meet his death on the field of battle, it should be from a similar wound to Moore's, and the story goes that this was precisely what happened.[457]

We last saw Private William Lawrence when he dragged himself wounded from the breach, but next day, determined not to miss out on the much-anticipated plunder, he made his way into Badajoz:

'Our troops found the city illuminated to welcome them, but nevertheless then began all the horrors that generally attend a capture by assault – plunder, waste, destruction of property, drunkenness and debauchery. I was myself exempt from all this, owing to my wounds, which kept me in camp at the time the town was taken; but although I was at least a mile off, I could distinctly hear the clamour of the rabble, as the guns and musketry had ceased; and next morning I hobbled as well as I could into the town with the help of the handle of a sergeant's pike chopped up so as to form a stick, and there sure enough I found a pretty state of affairs.

'Pipes of wine had been rolled into the streets and tapped by driving the heads in, for anyone to drink of them who liked, and when the officers tried to keep order by throwing all of these over that they could, the men that were in a state of drunkenness lay down to drink out of the gutters, which were thus running with all sorts of liquors; doors were blown open all through the city, both upstairs and down, by placing muskets at the keyhole and thus removing the locks. I myself saw that morning a naked priest launched into the street and flogged down

---

[454] *Some Recollections in the Life of Lieutenant-Colonel P. P. Nevill*, London, 1864, p.p. 15-16.

[455] There was a rumour, that Corporal Douglas of the Royals picked up, that amidst the drunken chaos of that night 'an officer of the 30th lost his life in attempting to save a young woman from violation.' No officer of the 30th died in the town that night, so this can only have been a half-understood version of Lockwood's good deed.

[456] Sir George Grey KCB (14th April 1812 – 1898) led two expeditions to explore Western Australia before becoming Governor of South Australia, 1841-45, twice Governor of New Zealand, 1845-53 and 1861-68, Governor of Cape Colony 1854-61 and Premier (Prime Minister) of New Zealand 1877-79.

[457] His widow placed a memorial to George Grey in Christ Church, Newton-Fertullagh, County Westmeath.

it by some of our men who had a grudge against him for the treatment they had met at a convent when staying in the town before.

'I happened to meet one of my company, and asked him how he was getting on, to which he replied that he was wounded in the arm, but that he had got hold of something that compensated for that a little, showing me a bag of about a hundred dollars that he had succeeded in obtaining, and saying that I should not want whilst he had got it.

'But whilst all this debauchery was going on amongst some of our soldiers, I will give a word of credit to a great many of the more respectable, who were trying as much as lay in their power to stop the ferociousness of the rest. That morning, I met many about who said they were sorry to think that the soldiers could not carry it on without going to such excesses as they did, respectable houses being ransacked from top to bottom, with no regard to the entreaties of the few inhabitants who remained within the walls. Things that could not be taken were often destroyed, and men were threatened if they did not produce their money, and the women sometimes the same. Comparatively few murders were, I believe, committed, but some no doubt occurred.[458]

'It was not till the drunken rabble had dropped into a sound slumber or had died in consequence of their excesses, that the unhappy city became at all composed; but in the morning some fresh troops were placed on guard, and a few gallows erected, but not much used. Two or three officers had been killed in the act of keeping order, and I have been given to understand that some of the Fifth Division, having arrived after most places had been ransacked, plundered their drunken fellow-comrades, and it was likewise reported that a few were even murdered. Lord Wellington punished all offenders by stopping their grog for some time; but in these times such scenes as these were generally found to occur after a place had had to be so hardly fought for.

'All being now over, thoughts of Pig Harding, George Bowden, and our engagement, ran in my head, and how it had all failed, poor Pig having received seven shots in his body, and George Bowden having had both thighs blown off. Both must have met with instant death, and I myself had four wounds and was disabled for some time from getting about. I resolved then that I would never make any more engagements under the same fearful circumstances. We missed poor Pig more than any man of the regiment, for he passed many an hour away pleasantly with his jokes, being a thoroughbred Irishman, and not only that, but he supplied us with many an extra piece of tommy by his roguish tricks.'[459]

As soon as it was light next morning, Robert Blakeney made his way from the Castle along the ramparts to the Trinidad bastion:

'When I arrived at the great breach the inundation presented an awful contrast to the silvery Guadiana; it was fairly stained with gore, which through the vivid reflection of the brilliant sun, whose glowing heat already drew the watery vapours from its surface, gave it the appearance of a fiery lake of smoking blood, in which were seen the bodies of many a gallant British soldier. The ditches were strewn with killed and wounded; but the approach to the bottom of the main [Trinidad] breach was fairly choked with dead.

'A row of *chevaux-de-frise*, armed with sword blades, barred the entrance to the top of the breach, and so firmly fixed that when the 4th and Light Divisions marched through, the greatest exertion was required to make a sufficient opening for their admittance. Boards fastened with ropes to plugs driven into the ground within the ramparts were let down, and covered nearly the whole surface of the breach; these boards were so thickly studded with sharp pointed spikes that one could not introduce a hand between them; they did not stick out at right angles to the board, but were all slanting upwards.

'In rear of the *chevaux-de-frise* the ramparts had deep cuts in all directions, like a tanyard, so that it required light to enable one to move safely through them, even were there no opposing enemy. From the number of muskets found close behind the breach, all the men who could possibly be brought together in so small a place must have had at least twenty firelocks each, no doubt kept continually loaded by persons in the rear. Two British soldier only entered the main breach during the assault; I saw both their bodies.'[460]

[458] Some modern accounts have claimed that 4,000 of the inhabitants were killed. There were undoubtedly some murders and many more people were ill-treated, but the French Colonel Lamarre, chief engineer of the garrison, states that the majority of the inhabitants had left before the siege, leaving only 4-5,000, and there are remarkably few first-hand accounts of killings.

[459] Lawrence, p.p. 116-119.

[460] Blakeney, p.p. 272-3.

There has always been some rather invidious controversy over which division was principally responsible for the fall of Badajoz. Greater prominence in the histories of the siege has tended to be given to the gallant escalade of the Castle by Picton's 3rd Division, but, as fairly and succinctly summarised by Leith Hay, the equally daring storming of the San Vicente bastion was more decisive:

'Had [Leith] not escaladed at all, Badajoz must have fallen in consequence of the castle being carried by the 3rd Division, but not till the following day, when the enemy might have given further trouble. Had the attack by General Picton failed, still the success of the 5th Division ensured the fall of the place. It was consequently the escalade of the bastion of San Vicente that occasioned the immediate reduction of the fortress.'[461]

The engineer John Jones agreed, writing that 'Badajoz may be said to have been twice carried by escalade this night. First by General Picton with the Third Division in getting possession of the Castle, from which moment further resistance was useless, as from the Castle the besiegers could have poured their whole army into the town, and secondly by General Leith and the Fifth Division, which was the more immediate cause of the fall of the place; for although General Picton's successful escalade of the Castle placed the garrison at the mercy of the besiegers, still the Third Division remaining formed in the Castle without further movement, their success produced no instant effect upon the defence and the Fifth Division met with the same opposition as if the Castle had not been escaladed.'

British and Portuguese casualties at the storming of Badajoz totalled 3,713 (added to the 957 incurred earlier in the siege). In the 4th Division, the 925 British casualties included all the general officers and all but one of the field officers, while the 5th Division's escalade cost 536 British casualties, a few more than the 3rd Division, and both the divisional and the brigade commanders, Leith and Walker.

The 40th suffered at least 236 casualties at the storming of Badajoz. According to the 'official' casualty returns, two officers and 51 men were killed, and 13 officers and 170 men were wounded. This is rather short of the totals for officers given by Surgeon Boutflower, who wrote, 'In my Regiment twenty-four officers marched off from the camp ground, of which number only six escaped.' Boutflower's total accords closely with the *Regimental Record Book*, which also states that five sergeants and eighty rank and file were killed or died of their wounds, and about two hundred were wounded. The monthly strength returns show that 82 other ranks of the 40th died in April and a further 34 died in May, while the number of sick and wounded other ranks rose in April to an extraordinary 718, nearly 65 percent of the total battalion strength, leaving only 360 fit for duty. Discrepancies are probably accounted for by some of the more minor wounds, dealt with by the regimental surgeons, not being reported to higher authority, and by many of the wounded dying later.[462]

Also in the 4th Division, Captain Francis James of the 81st Foot, Assistant Adjutant-General of Colville's Brigade, died of wounds[463], while Captain Walter O'Hara of the 47th was seriously wounded serving with the 7th Portuguese Caçadores.

---

[461] Leith Hay, Vol. I, p. 298.

[462] According to the Regimental Record Book the officer casualties of the 40th were: Lieutenants John Ayling and James Greenshields, and Volunteer O'Brien killed; Lieutenant Alfred Street and Ensign Edward Johnstone died of their wounds on the 9th and 11th April respectively; Lieutenant-Colonel Charles Amédée Harcourt, Major John Gillies, Lieutenants James Anthony, James Butler, John F. Gray, Henry Miller, Robert Moore, Oliver Sandwith, William Toole and William Turton were severely wounded; and Captain Robert Phillips, Lieutenants John Richardson and Constantine Gormon, and Volunteer Joseph A. Widenham were slightly wounded. There is a memorial to John Ayling, aged 23, in All Hallows Church, Tillington, Sussex. Alfred Street, an Old Etonian who had served with the 40th at Roliça, Vimeiro, Talavera, Busaço, Redinha, the first siege of Badajoz (wounded) and Ciudad Rodrigo, has a chest tomb in St Andrew's Lower Churchyard, Clifton, Bristol.

[463] Memorial at St. Mary's Church, Hampstead Norreys, Berkshire: 'To the memory of Francis James Esqr. eldest son of Sir Walter James Bart and Lady Jane James of Langley Hall in this parish, Captain in the 81st Regiment and Assistant Adjutant General in Major General Colville's Brigade of His Majesty's Forces in Portugal serving under the command of the Marquess of Wellington. This promising young officer died on the 11th of April 1812 of the wounds he received in the Assault at the breach of the walls of Badajos. Although born to affluence he chose the Military profession and although not more than 24 years of age had seen service in the West Indies in Denmark in Egypt at the Battle of Maida and in Spain and Portugal. The remains of this gallant officer were interred by the leave of the Governor of Badajos in the Bastion close to the breach which he had been one of the first to ascend. His afflicted parents have caused this record to be placed in this church as a lasting memorial of their irreparable loss and of the distinguished worth and gallantry of their son.'

The 30th suffered a total of 134 casualties, of whom two sergeants, three corporals and 23 privates were killed, Colonel Grey, a corporal and four privates died of wounds, and a further five officers and 93 other ranks were wounded.[464]

All the Light Company officers were wounded, and eight of their men were among those who died. Fifteen of the Regiment's fatalities were Irish.

Badajoz was the most costly day's action in the long history of the 'Fighting Fortieth,' while the losses of the 30th were only surpassed at Waterloo, in the Crimea, and during World War I, most notably on the Somme.

Wellington was visibly affected and moved to tears by the losses, writing, 'The capture of Badajoz affords as strong an instance of the gallantry of our troops as has ever been displayed. But I greatly hope that I shall never again be the instrument of putting them to such a test as they were put to last night.'

It was customary for officers in command of battalions in such actions, and their successors if they became casualties, to be honoured with the Army Gold Medal, but after Badajoz, only the family of Colonel Grey received that award for the 30th Regiment. This suggests that Grey's second-in-command, Captain Thomas Bradgate Bamford, did not take part in the assault, and that the next two senior officers, Captains John Hitchen of the Grenadiers and Tom Chambers of the Light Company, fell early in the action and before their commanding officer. In the 40th, the Gold Medal was awarded to Colonel Harcourt and his second-in-command, Major John Gillies, both of whom were seriously wounded, and to Captain Fielding Browne, who brought the battalion out of action, as he would do three years later at Waterloo. It was 1848, though, before most of the officers and men achieved any recognition for their action, when 102 survivors of the 30th and 116 of the 40th received a 'Badajoz' clasp to the General Service Medal. The Battle Honour 'BADAJOZ' was awarded to the 40th in 1824 and the 30th in 1825.

The long history of the British Army holds many examples of truly heroic persistence against all odds, not least in the Peninsula, but the breaches of Badajoz remain unsurpassed for sheer gallantry and tenacity in the face of almost certain death or wounds. By midnight on 6th April, the narrow confines of the ditch below the breaches were choked with some two thousand two hundred bloodied, scorched, and mangled bodies, including over five hundred dead or dying, while scores of drowned soldiers floated in the inundation. In one of the best-known passages of his *History of the War in the Peninsular*, William Napier painted the horrific scene:

'Let any man picture to himself this frightful carnage taking place in a space of less than a hundred square yards. Let him consider that the slain died not all suddenly, nor by one manner of death; that some perished by steel, some by shot, some by water, that some were crushed and mangled by heavy weights, others trampled upon, some dashed to atoms by the fiery explosions; that for hours this destruction was endured without shrinking, and that the town was won at last, let any man consider this and he must admit that a British army bears with it an awful power. And false would it be to say that the French were feeble men, for the garrison stood and fought manfully and with good discipline, behaving worthily. Shame there was none on any side. Yet who shall do justice to the bravery of the soldiers? The noble emulation of the officers?… Many and signal were the other examples of unbounded devotion, some known, some that will never be known; for in such a tumult much passed unobserved, and often the observers fell themselves ere they could bear testimony to what they saw; but no age, no nation ever sent forth braver troops than those who stormed Badajoz.'[465]

---

[464] Those killed in action were Sergeants Thomas Aitchinson and John Tully, Corporals Robert Langford, William Throstle and James McDoole, and Privates John Chamberlain, John Clarke, John Collins, William Cook, John Doonican, Valentine Flanagan, Elijah Fletcher, William Gunn, John Hodge, Richard Kelly, Pat Macken, Samuel McBeth, Henry McCann, Eugene McDonagh, Thomas Mobbs, Francis Owen, Robert Paul, John Rizen, James Rouston, Michael Rowe, Thomas Thackery, Joseph Tidds and James White. Of the 98 wounded, Corporal James Wadworth and Privates James Buckingham, James Cherry, Matthew Devens and Richard Rosengrove are recorded as died of wounds, and Sergeants W. Brassish and George Metcalfe, who died on the 10th and 20th April, were probably also among the wounded. The officers wounded were: Captain Thomas Walker Chambers (severely) and John Hitchen (slightly), commanding the Light and Grenadier Companies respectively, Lieutenants Andrew Baillie (slightly) and Parke Percy Neville (severely), and Ensign John Pratt (slightly), together with Captain Richard Machell (severely), Brigade Major. The next monthly strength return shows a total of 33 other ranks dead from all causes.

[465] *History of the War in the Peninsula*, W. F. P. Napier, Book IX, Chapter V, p.p. 362-63.

Advance of Leith's 5th Division, including the 30th, and Le Marchant's Heavy Cavalry (right)
Battle of Salamanca, 22nd July 1812

View of the battlefield of Salamanca from the Greater Arapil showing the ground over which the 4th & 5th Divisions advanced right to left

Capture of a French Eagle at Salamanca

Eagle of the French 22nd Infantry

Puente Larga, defended by the 47th

Chapter VII:
Salamanca Summer 1812

The 30th & 40th move north, April 1812 – Advance to Salamanca & the Douro, June-July 2012 (30th & 40th) – Marmont advances – Affair of Canizal (40th) – Battle of Salamanca (30th & 40th) – the 82nd join Wellington – Advance to & Occupation of Madrid (30th, 40th & 82nd) – Cadiz & Seville 1812 (47th) – Siege of Burgos (30th in Covering Force) – Eastern Spain (81st) – Denia (81st) – Rearguard Actions of Villamuriel (30th) & Puente Larga (47th) – Withdrawal to Salamanca (30th, 40th, 47th & 82nd) – Manoeuvres at Salamanca – Withdrawal to Portugal – Suffering of the Army – Winter Quarters 1812-13

The Army Moves North, April 1812

In April 1812, following the storming of the border fortresses of Ciudad Rodrigo and Badajoz, Lord Wellington had the keys to Spain in his pocket, leaving his surprised and disunited opponents strategically outmanoeuvred and unbalanced. Marshal Soult, who had marched to the relief of Badajoz with 25,000 men, turned back from Villafranca towards Andalusia as soon as he heard that the fortress had fallen, a prudent move since Wellington was ready to meet him on the old battleground of Albuera with an army of some 40,000. Marmont, instead of combining with Soult to relieve Badajoz, as promised, had been ordered by Napoleon to advance with the Army of Portugal into the Beira. This he did, though well aware that, with his siege-train captured, he was impotent against Ciudad Rodrigo and Almeida and that there was nothing else at which he could effectively strike. Marching with 25,000 men, he blockaded Ciudad Rodrigo on 30th March and pushed on across the frontier against ineffectual opposition from German cavalry and Portuguese militia to temporarily occupy Sabugal, Guarda, and Castelo Branco to no strategic advantage. This was the situation when, on 15th April, Marmont learned that Wellington had taken Badajoz and was already marching north against him with seven divisions. By the 22nd, Marmont had withdrawn to Fuenteguinaldo as the leading British troops closed on Sabugal and the 4th and 5th Divisions were a full march north of Castelo Branco.

The 2nd/30th Foot, under temporary command of their senior (and only) captain, Thomas Bamford, had marched from Badajoz with their division on the familiar route by way of Campo Maior, Portalegre, Nisa, Vila Velha and Castelo Branco, to Sortelha, a few miles west of Sabugal, which they reached on the 25th with only 256 men in the ranks. A further 281 had been left behind, sick and wounded.

The 1st/40th marched from their encampment at Badajoz on 12th April, following the same well-worn route as the 30th, reaching Quintas de Sao Bartolemeu, just north of Sabugal, on the 24th.[466] The troops were not impressed by yet another long march.

'Everyone is horrified at the idea of again going to the North,' wrote Charles Boutflower on the 15th, 'but it is rendered necessary by the enemy taking advantage of our absence at the siege of Badajoz, and making incursions into Portugal in considerable force… It is to be feared that we shall be kept continually in hot water between the two Fortresses of Badajoz & Rodrigo: so much marching is disheartening in the extreme.'

Dr Boutflower was even more concerned that 'the Army is far from healthy, or rather that part of it employed in the late siege. The dreadful weather, aided by the horrid intemperance that took place after the assault, is making a melancholy ravage amongst the men.'

He was right to be concerned, for on April 25th, the 40th mustered only 360 effective other ranks, while nearly double that number (718) were sick or wounded. Amongst the latter was Private William Lawrence, who left an amusing anecdote of his time in hospital:

---

[466] The 40th reached Campo Maior on the 12th, Arronches on the 13th, Portalegre on the 14th and Castelo de Vide on the 15th, where they halted next day before marching on to Povoa de Meadas on the 17th and, after another day's halt, they crossed the Tagus to Vila Velha on the 19th and reached Castelo Branco on the 20th. On the 21st the 40th reached Escalos de Cima, Aldeia de Santa Margarida on the 22nd, Val de Lobo on the 23rd and Quintas de Sao Bartolemeu on the 24th.

'The wounded were all conveyed to hospital, some to Elvas and some to Estremoz. I was amongst the latter, as was likewise my comrade whom I mentioned as meeting me in the streets of Badajoz, as we were considered better able to stand the longer journey, the distance on from Elvas to Estremoz being about six leagues the other side from Badajoz.

'On our arrival at hospital, we were allowed to take in no spirits or wine, which, as we had lately had so much of them, seemed to be more of a hardship to us than our wounds: but we were not long in working a system by which we were enabled to procure something to drink. The window of our ward looked out into one of the streets, on the opposite side of which was a wine shop, which for some time tormented us horribly: it was something like the fable of the fox and the grapes, sour because it was out of reach. The man of the house was often at his door on the look-out, the natives there seeming to suffer from that general complaint as much as in our own country villages, where if there is anything fresh in the streets, perhaps only a strange man, or even one of the inhabitants in a new coat or hat, the whole place works itself into an uproar.

'We soon devised a plan to gain our desired end. There was in the ward a tin kettle, holding nearly two gallons, and having procured a long string we put our money into this, and lowered it to the Portuguese, who soon getting used to our plan would put the money's value in the shape of wine into the kettle and again tie it to the string, so that we could hoist it up to the window again. After that we arranged for our ward to be pretty well supplied with grog too in the same way. Some suspicions being entertained by the doctor on the inflamed appearance of our wounds, he told us two or three times that he knew we had been drinking something we ought not, and blew the sergeant of the guard up for not being more strict in his search at the door, little dreaming how we had contrived another way to get this aggravator of our wounds in. But the appearance of our wounds did not stop us from lowering the kettle, which soon went down twice and sometimes three times a day, for the neighbouring wards got scent of the affair, and sent money to be lowered as well.'[467]

The 30th and 40th were both in the Sabugal area when, to their surprise, instead of moving on across the Coa in pursuit of Marmont, they were ordered away to the north. The reason for this abrupt change of direction was that the French Army of Portugal had left that country for the last time, fording the Agueda on the 22nd and 23rd of April, and retiring rapidly on its depots at Salamanca. On the 24th Wellington halted his pursuit, directing the 4th and 5th Divisions up into the valley of the Douro, where they could be supplied by river. It was obvious that after Badajoz, the army needed a period of rest.

The 30th were quartered in a village (Taliora?) near Lamego, where they remained until early June. The 25th May return reveals that its other rank strength, 269, had barely improved since Badajoz. On 3rd June, Lieutenant-Colonel Alexander Hamilton returned to the Battalion and assumed command. He had reached Lisbon in mid-April, newly-married, and, with no early prospect of action, he had remained in the capital for some weeks. The 30th were still in the same brigade of the 5th Division, but with Walker still recovering from his Badajoz wound, the brigade was commanded by Major-General William Pringle.[468]

The 40th were billeted at Sao Joao da Pesqueira, a small town which did not impress Surgeon Boutflower:

'We are much disappointed in this place, having heard it was an excellent cantonment, and furnishing everything in abundance; whereas it barely affords accommodation for two weak regiments, and there is scarcely any single thing to be procured with the exception of wine.'

Whilst there, the 40th were inspected in May by Major-General William Anson, who had assumed command of their brigade.[469] Captain Fielding Browne was still in command of the Battalion, of which the effective other rank strength had risen to 406 by the 25th of that month. Anson reported favourably on all ranks, commenting that 'the officers mess together when the circumstances of the service admit of it,' and that 'officers commanding companies settle personally with their men.'

---

[467] Lawrence, pp. 120-22.
[468] Pringle's brigade of Leith's 5th Division consisted of the 1st/4th, 2nd/4th, 2nd/30th, 2nd/44th and a company of Brunswick Oels (known to their British comrades as 'Owls').
[469] Anson's brigade of Cole's 4th Division consisted of the 3rd/27th, 1st/40th and, to supplement their skirmishing line, a company of riflemen of the 5th/60th. On 25th March 1835 General Sir William Anson, Bt., became Colonel of the 47th Regiment, an appointment that he held until his death in 1847.

Sir Lowry Cole had recovered from his wound and was back in command of the 4th Division, but on arrival in Lisbon he was despondent at the extent of casualties, writing on 5th June that 'I have lost almost every friend and every good officer, with at least a third of the Division at the siege of Badajoz.'[470]

Wellington Advances into Spain June-July 2012

The French still had 230,000 men in Spain in five armies, of which the most immediate threats to Wellington were Soult's army in Andalusia and Marmont's Army of Portugal in central Spain, while Suchet's army in Valencia had also to be taken into account. To prevent Soult and Marmont from concentrating against him, Wellington despatched Hill to destroy the bridge at Almaraz on the Tagus, the only practicable route between the two French armies. This was achieved brilliantly on 12th May, and Hill then guarded the approaches to Estremadura with 18,000 men based at Elvas and Badajoz. Wellington then felt able to tackle Marmont, and, to prevent the other French armies from sending assistance to his selected adversary, the Spanish provincial armies and guerrillas were stirred into heightened levels of activity, British naval diversions were also arranged, and an Anglo-Sicilian expedition was to land in Catalonia.

By early June, Wellington was ready to advance on Salamanca, and both the 30th and 40th marched on the 5th for the army concentration area around Ciudad Rodrigo.[471] The troops were in a buoyant and confident mood, as Lieutenant Andrew Leith Hay commented:

'On no occasion had the allied army taken the field in a more efficient state; every description of force composing it was serviceable and well appointed. The cavalry had recovered their condition. Experience taught the practical minutiae of active warfare. The weather was beautiful. Confidence in their leader and themselves occupied the minds of the troops; while presages of success and anticipated variety of scene imparted gaiety and buoyancy of spirit.'[472]

There was one abiding problem: sheer want of money. The military chest was almost empty, the troops' pay was five months in arrears, the muleteers had not been paid since June 1811, and there was little cash for local procurement of supplies during the forthcoming campaign.

From Ciudad Rodrigo, the Anglo-Portuguese army of 48,000 men and 48 guns advanced in three columns on Salamanca. The 4th, 5th and Light Divisions were in the centre column under the immediate command of Wellington. They crossed the Agueda by the Roman bridge at Ciudad Rodrigo on the 13th and bivouacked that night between Sancti Spiritus and Tenebron. 'The weather is so intensely hot,' wrote Boutflower, 'that it is scarcely supportable.' On the 14th they reached Munoz, encamped near Robliza de Cojos on the 15th, and on the 16th they were within sight of Salamanca, which was evacuated by Marmont that day.

The French had been caught widely dispersed, for although Marmont was expecting an Allied advance, he lacked the supplies to keep his army concentrated. Being temporarily inferior to Wellington in strength, the Marshal decided to gather his full force some twenty miles north of Salamanca on the Toro road, and meanwhile, he left garrisons in three fortified convents in the city.

The 6th Division was tasked to reduce these convents, the 'Salamanca Forts,' while the main body of the Army crossed the river Tormes on the 17th and took up a classic reverse slope position facing north and east behind the San Cristobal ridge, inviting attack. Cole's 4th Division bivouacked that night in a wood near the fords of El Canto below the city; Leith's 5th Division crossed the Tormes on the 20th and were quartered that night in the village of Aldeaseca on the left of the line.

Marmont approached, intent on relieving the forts, and for the next few days he probed, skirmished, and manoeuvred ineffectually without committing his numerically inferior army to a full-scale engagement. On the 21st it looked as if Marmont might force an action, and Wellington deployed for battle, with the 4th Division in

---

[470] Memoirs of Sir Lowry Cole, London, 1934, p. 80.

[471] The 30th march route was through Trancosa, Freixidas, Castelo Mendo, Poco Velha and Espeja to the Agueda at Carpio. The 40th followed a parallel route slightly further north. They marched to Ranhados on the 5th, the village of Cotimos on the 7th, Pinhel on the 8th and Aldea del Obispo on the 10th. Next day they continued on their original route to Espeja, but on reaching Alamada they were ordered to bivouac there.

[472] Leith Hay, 'A Narrative of the Peninsular War', Volume II, p. 4.

the centre of the Allied line and the 5th Division in reserve; but the Marshal hesitated and declined to attack, and neither the 30th nor the 40th was engaged.[473]

Wellington would have welcomed a French attack, and was indeed very tempted to leave his chosen position and to launch an attack himself, but caution prevailed and the opportunity was missed. The forts surrendered on 27th June, and early next day Marmont started a well-executed withdrawal.

The 40th had been joined on their march to Salamanca by Major Richard Archdall, aged 28, who assumed command. Archdall had been commissioned into the 40th in 1800, aged 16, and had passed all his service in the Regiment. He was an experienced field commander, having served as Major with the 1st/40th at Roliça, Vimeira, Talavera, Busaço, Redinha, and the first siege of Badajoz, but it appears that there were high-handed and arbitrary traits in his character, and these would eventually prove to be his undoing.

Marmont withdrew north-east towards Valladolid and to a strong defensive position behind the River Duero,[474] where he would complete the concentration of his army. Wellington followed early on the 29th through a wasted countryside, but found all but one of the bridges demolished, the fords guarded, and the river-line too strongly defended to force. The army went into cantonments between Medina del Campo, Rueda, and Nava del Rey. The 30th had marched by way of Fuentelapena and Alaejos to reach Torrecilla de la Abadesa on 2nd July, hot on the heels of the French, and camped on the right bank of the River Zapardiel, near the intact Duero bridge at Tordesillas. The 40th had reached Medina del Campo on the 2nd, remaining near there until the 10th.

From Medina del Campo on 2nd July Major Archdall wrote to Wellington drawing attention to the acute shortage of officers, and in particular captains, in the 1st/40th, observing that out of ten of the latter 'I have but one actually present and belonging to the Battalion doing duty, and I have only one of the Second Battalion also doing duty.' Wellington took prompt action, writing personally on the 7th to the Adjutant-General of Ireland, where the 2nd/40th were quartered, and four more captains were ordered out to Portugal at the earliest opportunity.

'The weather is most oppressively hot,' wrote Boutflower on the 9th, 'and such is the nature of this part of the country that it is altogether impossible to procure wood or any other substance for the purpose of sheltering the troops from the excessive power of the sun.'

That same day, the 5th Division, with the 30th, moved south-west to Nava del Rey, where the heat was so intense that the men found what shelter they could from the sun by day and slept in the fields by night, despite the heavy dew which soaked their blankets. One victim of the excessive heat around this time was Ensign John Carter, diarist of the 30th, who died of sunstroke on the 23rd at Ciudad Rodrigo.

The 40th moved up from Medina del Campo to occupy ground vacated by the French. 'In point of shelter,' Boutflower commented, 'we are not a bit better off than we were before.' Access to water became important, and on the 16th he mentioned an instance of the fraternisation between British and French troops which so often occurred in the Peninsula:

'It is not uncommon to see five hundred of the enemy, and as many of our men, bathing together in the Douro in the most perfect good humour possible, at the same time that the cavalry of the two rival armies come down on their respective sides of the river to water, it being perfectly understood that neither party shall ever approach the river armed.'[475]

The Affair of Canizal, 18th July 1812

This martial fraternity was about to end, for by 7th July Marmont was fully reinforced and the opposing armies were about evenly matched.[476] The French Marshal had devised an ingenious plan to unbalance his opponent before launching an offensive. He attracted Wellington's attention to the bridge at Toro, at the western end of his

---

[473] The strength of both regiments, though still weak, had continued to improve, and on 25th June the 30th mustered 301 effective other ranks and the 40th had increased to 463, but 229 and 500 men respectively were still sick and wounded.
[474] The Spanish River Duero is the same as the Portuguese Douro.
[475] Boutflower, p. 145.
[476] Marmont's 15th July strength returns show a total of 49,646 all ranks including 41,525 infantry, 3,379 cavalry and 78 guns. Wellington's total strength on the same day was 51,139 (29,762 British and King's German Legion, 18,017 Portuguese and 3,360 Spanish) including 45,558 infantry (24,777 British and King's German Legion), 4,035 cavalry (3,553 British and King's German Legion), and 54 guns.

line, by very openly repairing the bridge there and, on 16th July, pushing two divisions across the Duero. This feint caused Wellington to draw the obvious conclusion, that the French were about to turn his left flank and to strike directly at Salamanca, and to react by adjusting his own deployment in that direction to protect the roads from Toro to Salamanca.

The 40th were under arms an hour before daylight on the 16th, and that evening received a sudden order to march south to Villaverde de Medina, between Medina del Campo and Nava del Rey, and from there were directed on, south-west, to Castrejon. On the 17th the 5th Division, including the 30th, marched further south-west to Canizal on the Toro-Salamanca road.

Having achieved his well-planned deception, Marmont withdrew his divisions from Toro and counter-marched east to cross the river at Tordesillas, over twenty miles upstream. Wellington had for once been outwitted. By the evening of the 17th, the bulk of the French army had advanced to Nava del Rey, posing an imminent threat to the nearest British troops, the 4th and Light Divisions, and Anson's cavalry brigade, which had in effect become his rearguard. Wellington's immediate task was now to extract this rearguard and pull it back to join his main body, which was posted in the area Canizal-Catrillo-Fuentelapeña. At daylight on the 18th he went himself to undertake this withdrawal, and with him marched two more cavalry brigades. He ordered the 5th Division to take up a position at Torrecilla de la Orden, about four miles south-west of Castrejon, where it could support the 4th and Light Divisions if their retirement was closely pressed. The division marched at 3 a.m.

Early on the morning of the 18th, the French advanced in force on Castrejon and attacked the British cavalry outposts at about 6 a.m. When Wellington reached Castrejon at 7 a.m. he discovered George Anson's cavalry in some trouble, and he was lucky to escape the confused melee that ensued.[477] Andrew Leith Hay, riding ahead of the 5th Division, witnessed the action:

'I rode to the infantry encampment near Castrejon, and there found General Cole dismounted, surveying the warm affair in progress between our cavalry and that of the enemy, supported by infantry and artillery; the plain was filled with smoke, while the hostile parties appeared engaged in a very unequal conflict. The British cavalry were outnumbered, and losing ground… When Lord Wellington arrived on the spot, much anxiety prevailed to learn what movement he would direct; the enemy was pressing forward on both flanks, thereby rendering an immediate change of position necessary. The whole French army was in movement.'[478]

Marmont's entire army was now in sight, moving in two long columns, one of which pressed after the British rearguard. The other, further west but within sight, headed for Castrillo on the River Guareña to turn the Allied left. Wellington ordered the 4th and Light Divisions to retire over the Guareña to the heights of Canizal, covered by Anson's cavalry and horse artillery. The withdrawal, over some eight miles of open downs, was carried out in perfect order and with few casualties, the battalions marching in company columns at quarter distance [around 20 yards between companies], ready to form square to receive cavalry.

'The ground upon which the Light and 4th Divisions stood was neither sufficiently extensive, nor otherwise well calculated to afford a good defensive position for the Allied army,' explained Leith Hay, 'the strong heights of Canizal were in its rear, and to these the British general determined to retire.'

As the 4th and Light Divisions retired past Torrecilla de la Orden, they were joined by the 5th Division, which then marched on the southern flank down to the Guareña. As they reached the river, the French artillery crowned the heights behind them and opened fire into the mass of troops in the valley:

'The 5th Division, unaware of the near approach of the enemy's cannon, had halted to obtain water from the river. This was rendered more desirable by an atmosphere of excessive heat occasioning parching thirst, superinduced by quantities of dust, with which the soldiers were absolutely covered. The first discharges from the enemy's cannon convinced General Leith that retiring in column under this fire would be attended with

---

[477] In the course of the cavalry skirmishes on 18th July, Cornet William Williams of the 11th Light Dragoons was mortally wounded and died in the arms of his son, also William, aged twelve, who had accompanied him on campaign. According to Captain John Harley of the 47th, who knew the family, 'the dear child clung to his dying father, endeavouring to raise his spirits by the most affectionate endearments; and, after his decease, was with the utmost difficulty removed from his corpse.' Young William was within weeks awarded a commission in his father's regiment, but being too young for active service he was sent home on half-pay. He transferred to the 40th as an ensign in 1822, serving with them in Australia and India until his death at Bombay, aged 34.

[478] Leith Hay, Vol. II, p.p. 32-3.

considerable loss: he, therefore, directed the brigades to deploy as quickly as possible; which being accomplished, the shot plunged over the lines, occasioning but few casualties, and the division took up its ground on the heights of Canizal.'[479]

As the 4th Division descended into the valley of the Guareña, they found themselves racing parallel to the western French column, which opened fire on their right flank with artillery. What happened next is recounted by Lieutenant-Colonel Charles Broke Vere, Assistant Quarter-Master-General to the 4th Division:

'This attack was met with great promptitude by General Cole, who posted his artillery, supported by light infantry, so as to effectually answer and silence the enemy's guns.

'The column crossed the river, and by order of Lord Wellington, halted and formed into line along the margin of the stream – the 5th Division was in line on the right of the 4th Division. This halt near the water, short as it was, gave refreshment and rest to the troops after a rapid march over an arid country in extremely hot weather.

'The enemy soon appeared in force on the heights above the river, and several batteries opened successively on the lines of the allies. The line marched with a steady pace up the slopes on the left bank of the valley, under the fire of the enemy's cannon, with little loss, and took position on the heights.

'The enemy's cavalry [Carrié's brigade of dragoons] pushed around the left of the allies, but were met and delayed in their progress by Major-General Alten's brigade of light cavalry. The enemy's cavalry was however the more numerous, and it continued to move on, followed closely by a division of infantry (General T[au]pin's),[480] which advanced with great boldness and celerity on the left of the position, and up the lower slopes of the heights occupied by the 4th Division.

'Lord Wellington, who was on the spot, ordered General Cole to attack the French infantry with his division. The General moved down with the 27th and 40th Regiments[481] in line, leading them upon the enemy's columns, which had gained the lower falls of the heights; and he directed the 11th and 23rd Portuguese Regiments to support the line in columns at quarter distance.[482]

'The enemy's columns halted, and allowed the line to close, and to envelope their flanks; when they gave way in the greatest disorder. The loss on the part of the enemy was very considerable, and an opportunity was offered to a regiment of cavalry on the left of the infantry, of acting with great effect.'[483]

Lieutenant Andrew Leith Hay viewed this last action from the nearby 5th Division: 'The cavalry encounters had been to a certain extent successful on the part of the allies; but when General Cole proceeded to charge the enemy's infantry with the 27th and 40th Regiments, the French stood with unusual firmness, as if determined to await the encounter at close quarters: the British regiments, however, pressed forward with alacrity, resolution and discipline, overthrew the enemy, who fled, closely pursued by General Alten's [cavalry] brigade, and two hundred and forty prisoners were secured; about four hundred of the French being left dead or wounded on the plain.'[484]

Other accounts from staff officers tell a similar story: Lieutenant-Colonel Charles Cathcart said that the French 'came on in very gallant style and stood the charge of the 40th Regt. until they came within about five yards of them when they were completely routed and 200 prisoners taken,' and Colonel Colin Campbell wrote that 'Genl. Cole immediately advanced upon them and charged them with the bayonet, put them to the rout and took upwards of 200 prisoners, but his men were so much exhausted that they could not follow them far.'

---

[479] Ibid., p.p. 34-5.

[480] Taupin's 6th Division was composed of the 17th Légère (2 battalions), 22nd Ligne (3 battalions) and 65th Ligne (3 battalions), a total of 4,558 all ranks.

[481] According to the 15th July strength return, the 3rd/27th fielded 19 officers and 633 men and the 1st/40th had 24 officers and 558 men, a brigade total of 1,215 all ranks.

[482] A French officer's memoirs, of doubtful reliability, attributes Taupin's rout to 'three or four battalions of Portuguese', who apparently rushed down the hill and hurled themselves on the French division with a 'rolling fire', but this can be discounted. The two Portuguese regiments were in support, and the sudden collapse of Taupin's division before the bayonets of the 27th and 40th would have precluded any requirement for supporting troops to be committed, even if there had been time. Besides, being in column the Portuguese would have been unable to deliver an effective 'rolling fire', which would in any case have been masked by the British line which had enveloped the flanks of the French column.

[483] Broke Vere, p.p. 28-9.

[484] Leith Hay, Vol. II, p.p. 35-6.

An officer on Wellington's staff, Lieutenant Thomas Browne, recorded that 'Wellington ordered General Cole to attack with a brigade of the 4th Division (the 27th & 40th) in line, supported by a Portuguese regiment in column on each flank. The enemy stood & fired little. They were very firm until within fifty or sixty paces, when our fellows gave them the bayonet with cheers, routed the column, & left of the French about 80 dead & 100 prisoners besides wounded. Our men charged at too great a distance, their ranks were in confusion, & they were so breathless and exhausted when they came up with the French that they could scarcely use the bayonet.[485] It was ascertained from the prisoners that these two battalions of ours had charged six of the enemy, about 3,000 men, & that their force across the stream, & at hand to support, consisted of two divisions which had concealed themselves in the inequalities of the ground. General Cole hastened back to his division after this creditable affair, & before the enemy's superiority could annoy him. Our cavalry, probably owing to the roughness of the ground, did not make much of the enemy's broken column.'[486]

Finally, the journal of Surgeon Charles Boutflower gives an account of the day's events from the perspective of the 40th Foot:

'Early on the 18th skirmishing commenced, & about six o'clock the French appeared in great force. As our army was not concentrated we fell back upon the divisions in our rear, and as was understood into the neighbourhood of a position Lord Wellington meant to meet them in. During the day there were several severe skirmishes, and amongst others, some most furious charges of cavalry. The enemy had two opportunities of cannonading, which they availed themselves of most vigorously, but happily our loss was but little. I was myself very nearly being one of the victims, a cannon shot passing within a few inches of my head.

'The enemy pressed us in a manner, and with a spirit, we were never before accustomed to. At length, a favourable opportunity occurring, Lord W[ellington] directed the 4th Division to attack their advanced guard; as the attack was made by the Division left in front, it fell to the 27th & 40th Regts composing the left brigade to bear the brunt of the affair. These two regiments, on approaching the enemy, advanced to the charge in the most undaunted manner, notwithstanding the force opposed to them was near three times their number. The French presented a firm front till our people arrived within about twenty paces of them, when they fired a volley and flew in the utmost confusion. Unfortunately, the assailants were so much exhausted from a long previous march and the great heat of the weather (which was so excessive that several men and officers actually died on the march), that they were unable to follow them up as could have been wished. The business was soon over with a loss to the Division of 5 officers killed and wounded, and about two hundred men, of which one officer and seventy [men] belonged to my Regiment. The loss of the enemy was estimated at upwards of six hundred men.'[487]

Surgeon Boutflower's contemporary estimate accords closely with The Regimental Record Book statement that 'In this affair, one sergeant and twelve rank and file were killed, and about sixty rank and file wounded.' However, the official return for 18th July has eight men of the 40th killed in action, one officer[488] and 59 men wounded, and one man missing out of a divisional total of 170 casualties. Although the 5th Division came under artillery fire, they suffered few casualties, five in all, of which none were from the 30th.

French casualties are more difficult to assess. Whilst an arithmetical extrapolation from known officer casualties on 18th July might suggest a loss to Taupin's Division of some 475,[489] Leith Hay's 640 and Boutflower's 600-plus eye-witness observations carry more weight.

This was in some respects a classic column versus line engagement, with the usual result, even though the odds were more than three to one. It appears that the French division advanced uphill from the Guareña in regimental columns, each with only a two-company frontage, making them very vulnerable to the concentrated and enveloping musketry of a two-deep British line. There is no indication in the various accounts that the French were preceded by skirmishers or that they, even belatedly, attempted to deploy into line, so it is possible that

---

[485] This statement appears an improbable exaggeration after a short downhill charge starting, by his own estimation, within 50-60 paces of the enemy, and within 20 paces according to Boutflower of the 40th. It is, however, clear enough that the troops were too exhausted after their close-quarter combat to do more than gather up their prisoners, leaving exploitation of their victory to the cavalry.

[486] *Napoleonic War Journal*, Lieutenant T. H. Browne, Army Records Society, 1987, p. 163.

[487] Boutflower, p.p. 146-7.

[488] Lieutenant William Waldron Kelly of the Grenadier Company 40th was slightly wounded but was back in action on the 22nd at Salamanca.

[489] *Salamanca 1812*, Rory Muir, Yale, 2001, Appendix I.

Cole's counter-attack caught Taupin by surprise. There must, however, be some doubt as to whether Anson's brigade fired even one volley before they raised a cheer and charged with the bayonet. Only one contemporary mentions a volley, and he was not present, whilst seven witnesses attribute the French rout to a physical advance or charge by the 27th and 40th, and several specify a bayonet charge. The 40th were probably influenced in their tactics by their former commander, that enthusiastic advocate of the bayonet, Sir Brent Spencer, and used that weapon, or the threat of it, with great success on a number of occasions. Even their surgeon was thoroughly imbued with the spirit of the bayonet, writing in his journal, after the battle of the 22nd, that 'the whole business was performed by the Bayonet, & the most sceptical must now be surely convinced how superior in the use of it is the British Soldier to every other in the world.'

The 40th gained a very fine trophy in what the Regiment called 'the Vale of Canizal,' the silver-mounted Drum-Major's staff of the 65th Ligne. This handsome staff was carried on parade by the 40th Foot and its lineal successor, 1st Battalion The South Lancashire Regiment, for well over a century, and it is now displayed in the Regimental Museum. It replaced another French staff, captured in Holland in 1799, which had seen hard service and was much knocked about. Major Richard Archdall, commanding the 40th, was mentioned in Wellington's dispatch.

By late afternoon on the 18th Wellington had succeeded in extricating his rearguard and concentrating his army in a very tenable position, disappointing Marmont's well-laid plans, and the two armies faced each other across the Guareña in what appeared to be, if not a stalemate, at least a pause for breath after two days of forced marching. It had been a remarkable day, demonstrating the rare abilities of the opposing commanders.

'The skill with which both generals had handled their troops and the ease with which these troops executed complicated manoeuvres must excite admiration. Both generals had large bodies of men under their command; it is true they operated in close order and the generals could frequently see most of the battlefield, but they had no signallers to convey their orders, no proper intelligence staff to mark their maps; their command posts were no more than the saddle of a horse, or a map thrown over a bush. Yet in the past two days, Marmont, by a brilliant manoeuvre, had crossed the Duero by a bridge which the day before had been guarded by four British divisions. He had restored his communication with Madrid and very nearly caught Wellington with his army divided. The British army which, under another commander, might well have suffered a disaster, was now poised ready for battle on a strong position covering the main route to Salamanca. Two very accomplished armies confronted each other across the Guarena.'[490]

The 40th, with the 4th Division, were on the left (northern) flank of the Allied position, near Castrillo, while the 30th were nearer to Canizal with the 5th Division.

'The night passed in perfect tranquillity,' recalled Leith Hay, 'the whole country blazed with the fires of the bivouacs, while in its stillness voices were heard from one encampment to the other. Daybreak displayed no movement or preparation for battle in the enemy's lines: a pause appeared to have taken place, and the bustle and turbulence that had distinguished the early part of the preceding day seemed to have been succeeded by an unexpected cessation of hostilities. As day advanced, we anxiously inspected all parts of the French encampment to observe if any signs of renewed activity were visible… The often resorted to glasses were closed, with the disappointing declaration that all appeared quiet and immovable.

'At length, towards evening, it became evident that this stillness was to be interrupted. Marshal Marmont, having in vain assailed the left, now manoeuvred against the other flank of the allies, and marched his whole army by its left towards the plain of Vallesa. In consequence of this movement, the Light and 5th Divisions got under arms and marched in a parallel direction to that adopted by the French army.'[491]

This parallel march continued through the night and the next day, the 20th July, providing one of the most extraordinary scenes of the whole Peninsula War. Some hundred thousand men of the two armies marched at best speed in parallel columns in clear sight of each other, often within cannon range and sometimes within musket-shot. Each army marched in a formation that could readily be ordered into battle line by facing its units left or right. Wellington's men marched in three long columns, the one nearest the French being composed of the 1st, 4th, 5th and Light Divisions. In his memoirs, Marshal Marmont stated that in his long military service, he never, before

---

[490] *Wellington's Masterpiece*, Lawford and Young, 1972, p.p. 190-191.
[491] Leith Hay, Vol. II, p.p. 36-7.

or after, saw such a magnificent spectacle. The two armies moved at the same speed with parade ground precision, so close that, as Napier recalled, 'their officers, like gallant gentlemen who bore no malice and knew no fear,' exchanged salutations.'

'When the two armies were thus put in motion,' recalled Leith Hay, 'they were within cannon-shot of each other; the French occupying higher ground than the Allies: but the space between them was lower than either of the routes, and nothing intervened to obstruct a view of the columns of enemies, that thus continued to pursue their course without the least obstacle to prevent their coming into instantaneous contact; for the slightest divergement from either line of march towards each other would have brought them within musketry distance... No spectator would have imagined the two immense moving columns that filled the whole country, and seemed interminable, being lost to the eye in dust and distance, comprised two armies actuated with earnest desires for the destruction of each other, but who... were persevering on their way, as if by mutual consent refraining from serious hostility until arrived at the arena destined for the great trial. To which either was now advancing with confidence, and without interruption.'[492]

The two armies almost clashed when their columns converged on the village of Cantalpino, where the French artillery shelled approaching battalions of the 4th Division; but Wellington was not inclined to risk an engagement and ordered Cole to avoid both action and the village by moving away to the west. This shift in the Allied direction of march from south to west enabled the French to head for the Tormes river fords of Huerta, giving him a tactical advantage. Sir Charles Oman succinctly summarised the situation:

'The net result of the long parallel march of July 20th was that Marmont had practically turned Wellington's extreme right, and was in a position to cross the Upper Tormes, if he should choose, in prolongation of his previous movement. The Allied army was still covering Salamanca, and could do so for one day more, if the marching continued: but after that limit of time it would be forced either to fight or to abandon Salamanca, the main trophy of its earlier campaign.'[493]

The 30th and 40th Regiments halted that night with their respective divisions at Pitiegua. At dawn next day, Wellington withdrew his whole army onto the San Cristobal position, where he waited for Marmont to reveal his next move. The French began to defile across the Tormes fords near Huerta, and from late that afternoon into the evening, most of the Allies also crossed the river, at the Santa Marta ford and elsewhere, and occupied low wooded heights to its south, facing east. On the right flank of the army, the 4th Division camped in a wood just west of the chapel of Nuestra Señora de la Peña, while the 5th Division bivouac was a little further north, 'in rear of an extensive wood and on the summit of a plateau.'

As the troops settled into their bivouacs, wrote Leith Hay, 'the appearance of the air bespoke an approaching storm. The rain soon fell in torrents, accompanied by vivid flashes of lightning, and succeeded by instantaneous peals of thunder. A more violent crash of the elements has seldom been witnessed; its effects were soon apparent. General Le Marchant's brigade of cavalry had halted to our left; the men, dismounted, were either seated or lying on the ground, holding their horses, who, alarmed by the thunder, started with violence, and many of them, breaking loose, galloped across the country in all directions. This dispersion, and the frightened horses passing without riders in a state of wildness, added to the awful effect of the tempest.'[494]

The Battle of Salamanca, 22nd July 1812

Before midnight, the storm had passed, and next morning, 22nd July, a brilliant sun soon dried the ground and revealed the battlefield of Salamanca. The future field of battle, centred some five miles south of the city, was dominated by the Greater and Lesser Arapiles, isolated hill features which rose steep and rocky above the gently rolling, open countryside. The Lesser Arapile, which early that morning lay just beyond the right (western) flank of the 4th Division, would prove to be a vital pivot for the Allied manoeuvres: to the left of this feature, the low wooded hills, occupied the previous night, ran north-south, while to its right a more prominent ridge, the Teso de San Miguel, ran at a right-angle away to the west, offering excellent concealment. These two ridges formed an

[492] Ibid., p.p. 38-40.
[493] Oman, Vol. V, p. 414.
[494] Leith Hay, Vol. II, p.p. 45-46.

L-shape, with the Lesser Arapile in its south-eastern angle. The Greater Arapile rose some 900 yards to the south of its smaller brother and was both more extensive and even more dominant. From the rear of this feature, a low ridge, the Monte de Azan, ran away for three miles to the west, where it culminated in the Pico de Miranda knoll, beyond and below which lay the village of Miranda de Azan. To the south of this ridge were extensive, scrubby woods. The ridges of San Miguel and Monte de Azan were around one mile apart, and in the shallow, largely treeless, valley between them, about a mile west of the Arapiles, lay the little village of Los Arapiles. One final feature of note was a long, low, wooded ridge, El Sierro, running south-west behind the Greater Arapile and on the edge of the rough country, covered in scrub and woods, which lay between the battlefield and the town and river bridge of Alba de Tormes, eight miles to the south-east.

An hour before dawn, both armies stood to their arms. In terms of numbers, they were fairly matched. Marmont had eight infantry divisions and four cavalry brigades, with a total strength of around 49,000 men and 78 guns. Wellington's army comprised seven Anglo-Portuguese infantry divisions, two independent Portuguese infantry brigades, a small Spanish division, and five cavalry brigades, totalling some 51,400 men (of whom 30,000 were British and King's German Legion), and 62 guns. Marmont had the advantage in guns; Wellington, unusually, had more cavalry and slightly more infantry, though the 3,360 Spanish were of less value and took almost no part in the subsequent battle. Moreover, Marmont was expecting a substantial reinforcement within days.

The 2nd/30th entered the battle with twenty officers and 329 other ranks[495]; the 1st/40th, taking their losses on the 18th into account, mustered some 24 officers and perhaps 490 other ranks. The Light Company 30th was detached, reducing the main body strength by two officers (Lieutenants Nevill and Pratt) and up to fifty other ranks.

Unfortunately, neither regiment left first-hand accounts of their actions on the 22nd: even Surgeon Boutflower of the 40th gave no detail of the part played by that battalion when he wrote up his journal on the 26th, confining himself to generalities and to effusive praise of the victorious troops and their commander. We can only attempt to reconstruct their actions from other sources.

Marmont had undoubtedly enjoyed the best of the previous week's manoeuvres and was in a confident, if not complacent, mood. He was convinced, not unreasonably, that Wellington was a cautious general who would not, on past form, take the risk of attacking him, and he was looking for an opportunity to cut up the Allied rearguard whilst edging them out of Salamanca.

'My object,' he wrote after the battle, 'was to prolong my movement to the left, in order to dislodge the enemy from the neighbourhood of Salamanca, and to fight him at a greater advantage. I calculated on taking up a good defensive position, against which the enemy could make no offensive move, and intended to press near enough to him to be able to profit from the first fault that he might make, and to attack him with vigour.' He added that 'I considered that our respective positions would bring on not a battle but an advantageous rearguard action, in which... I should probably score a point.'

Wellington was indeed rather more cautious, conscious as ever that he commanded Britain's only substantial field army. Writing on the evening of 21st July, he summed up his intentions:

'I have determined... to cover Salamanca as long as I can: and above all not to give up our communications with Ciudad Rodrigo: and not to fight an action unless under very advantageous circumstances, or if it should become absolutely necessary.'

As dawn broke, commanders rode forward to check their own dispositions and to try to make sense of any discernible enemy movement.

'On the morning of the 22nd of July, before daybreak, General Cole went to visit his outposts, and those of his troops camped in the wood; and at dawn, the enemy's outposts were discovered on the high ground near Calvarossa de Arriba and Nossa Senora de la Pena.

'The heights on which the allied outposts were placed, terminated towards the valley in their front, in a singularly rocky knoll – it was the lowest of two similarly isolated heights called "the two Aripiles" [Arapiles],

---

[495] The 30th strength on 25th June comprised 22 sergeants, 14 drummers and 287 rank and file.

from being near a village of that name… General Cole immediately saw the necessity for occupying the lowest Aripiles and ordered a detachment to take possession of it.

'It was nearly daylight when Lord Wellington rode up to the General. By the indistinctness of objects, as seen by the early morning light, the greatest Arapiles appeared to be more distant than it really was – but by the time full daylight allowed its true distance to be seen, Lord Wellington ordered it also to be occupied; but before the order could be executed, it was in possession of the enemy.'[496]

William Anson's brigade, the 3rd/27th and 1st/40th, was ordered at first light to occupy the vital Lesser Arapile, while the 7th Caçadores from the same division were just too late to secure the Greater Arapile. The 27th held the sugar-loaf summit of the former feature, with the 40th in support in rear and to the right.[497] The remainder of the 4th Division moved south from their camping ground to the heights of the Teso de San Miguel, above and to the left of the village of Los Arapiles. The village itself was occupied by the Light Companies of the Fusilier Brigade of the 4th Division, together with the Guards Light Companies of the 1st Division under Lieutenant-Colonel Woodford.[498]

At much the same time, skirmishing broke out around Nuestra Señora de la Peña as the *voltigeurs* of Foy's division bickered with the light troops of the 7th Division and with Alten's cavalry brigade, probing the Allied left.

Timings throughout this battle are more than usually uncertain, and often contradictory, but it is apparent that in the course of the morning, Marmont considered an attack on the Allied left, or rearguard, and that slightly later Wellington planned a limited advance to take the Greater Arapile, and that neither move was executed. Marmont then began to mass his divisions behind the Greater Arapile, which he occupied with the 120th Ligne of Bonnet's division as a strong advanced post.

Noting this concentration, at about noon Wellington started to redeploy the bulk of his army to the right, on or behind the Teso de San Miguel, well poised either to retire on Ciudad Rodrigo or to fight a defensive battle. The former still appeared the most likely option, and his Adjutant-General, De Lancey, prepared plans for the withdrawal, while the baggage train was already on the road. Packenham's 3rd Division and D'Urban's Portuguese cavalry brigade, which had remained north of the Tormes overnight, were also on the march, by the Salamanca bridge and fords, to Aldea Tejada, where they could form the advance guard in case of a retreat on Ciudad Rodrigo, or the right flank of an attack.

Leaving the 1st and Light Divisions in his original position left of the Lesser Arapile, Wellington moved four infantry divisions to the right of that feature, facing south: the 5th Division came up to the right of the 4th Division and Dennis Pack's Portuguese brigade to the left, while the 6th and 7th Divisions were in second line behind the 4th and 5th Divisions respectively, some 25,000 massed infantry. Bradford's Portuguese, Espana's Spanish, and the bulk of the Allied cavalry were further back, in reserve near the village of Las Torres. Most of these troops remained concealed from sight and fire behind the San Miguel ridge, but the 5th Division moved to a position on the crest, to the right rear of Los Arapiles, where they were exposed to the French guns on the opposite ridge.

Marmont, from his vantage point on the Greater Arapile, had a partial view of this Allied movement, much of which was masked by the heights. Wellington's left was clearly thinning out, and clouds of dust marked the movement of the Allied baggage and the 3rd Division in the direction of Ciudad Rodrigo. Marmont interpreted what he thought he saw as the early stages of an evacuation of the Allied position. With his preconception confirmed, at around 1 or 2 p.m. he gave orders for a continuation of his hitherto successful tactic of marching round Wellington's right flank, forcing his adversary to retire from Salamanca. His own left wing was to extend along the Monte de Azan, led by Maucune's division and Curto's cavalry brigade, supported by Thomières' division and a powerful battery of at least twenty guns. Clausel's division, when it arrived, was to follow in reserve nearer to the Greater Arapile, behind and on top of which stood Bonnet's division. French columns started

---

[496] Broke Vere, p. 31.
[497] Around noon a company of the 40th hauled two 6-pounder guns of 'E' Troop Royal Horse Artillery, tasked to defend the Lesser Arapile, to the top of that vital hill.
[498] Alexander Woodford would command 2nd Coldstream Guards at Hougoumont during the battle of Waterloo and was Colonel of the 40th Regiment 1842-61. He became Field Marshal Sir Alexander Woodford GCB KCMG.

to emerge from behind the Greater Arapile and from the sheltering woods, and the grand battery on the Monte de Azan began to bombard the Allied line, and in particular the 5th Division.

'The French army was evidently pressing forward to gain the Ciudad Rodrigo road,' wrote Andrew Leith Hay, 'and the greater proportion of his force had now assembled either to the southward, or to the left of the Arapiles; the 5th Division soon after received orders to march in that direction; in executing which we passed close to the rear of the 4th Division, taking up ground to its right, and on the same line.'

'About three o'clock, a force of not less than twenty pieces of artillery were assembled by the enemy on the heights directly opposite to the 5th Division. The ground upon which the division stood was flat, and the troops without any means of shelter. It became consequently advisable to make the regiments recline on the field, and by so doing avoid in some measure the effects of what was evidently to become a very heavy cannonade. For at least an hour did these brave soldiers immovably support the efforts made to annihilate them by the showers of shot and howitzer shells that were either passing over or ricocheting through the ranks. General Leith, on horseback, passed repeatedly along the front of his division, speaking to and animating the men, who earnestly expressed an anxious desire for permission to attack the enemy.'[499]

Maucune, possibly disregarding or mistaking Marmont's orders, marched his division some two-thirds the length of the Monte de Azan before halting, putting him beyond the support of Clausel's division. To compound this dispersion of the French left wing, Thomières did not take up a position to support Maucune but marched straight past him to take the lead. 'Maucune and Thomières, who were already dangerously isolated from the rest of the army, ceased to be able to support each other and were strung out over a wide front, lacking depth and solidity.'[500]

This did not go unnoticed by watchers on the opposite ridge. It was mid-afternoon (probably after 3 p.m.), and Wellington was snatching a cold meal, when the news came that Marmont's army was extending and spread out. 'The devil they are! Give me the glass quickly!' he cried, throwing a chicken bone over his shoulder, and then, 'By God! That will do!' adding to his Spanish liaison officer, '*Mon cher Alava, Marmont est perdu!*'

At much the same time, Marmont, who was having a more leisurely luncheon on the Grand Arapile, realised his faulty disposition and scrambled down the hill to take charge of his left wing. Before he could mount his horse, he was hit by a British shell and seriously wounded. His successors, Clausel and Bonnet, were in turn also hit. Clausel was not seriously hurt and was able to assume command, but for some critical time the French army had no effective overall commander.

Wellington rode at once to Pakenham at Aldea Tejada, ordering him in the most succinct terms to launch an immediate attack on Thomières: 'Edward, move on with the 3rd Division and take those heights in your front, and drive everything before you.'

At about 3.30 p.m. the 3rd Division came obliquely up with Thomières' eight battalions, who were strung out near Pico de Miranda. Packenham's well-drilled veterans moved from column into line without halting and attacked at once. A threat to their right by Curto's cavalry was easily brushed off, and the leading regiments of Thomières' division, surprised and confused, crumbled, dissolved, and fled in panic with the loss of their general, many hundreds of men, and all the divisional artillery. Packenham's men then drove the survivors eastward along the ridge, where they attempted to rally on their as yet uncommitted third regiment, the 1st Ligne.

Wellington, meanwhile, rode over to give orders to Major-General Gaspard Le Marchant's heavy cavalry division, telling him to take advantage of the first favourable opportunity to charge the French infantry. 'You must then charge,' he ordered, 'at all hazards.'

He then rode on to Leith's 5th Division, and then to Cole's 4th Division, behind Los Arapiles and the Teso de San Miguel, and gave them similar orders to attack the enemy to their front.

At about 4.15 p.m., it was the turn of the 5th Division to advance against Maucune. Leith had the strongest division in the army, 4,386 British and 2,305 Portuguese, all ranks; Maucune's division numbered 5,244. Lieutenant Andrew Leith Hay, his uncle's ADC, wrote a graphic account of the divisional advance:

'At length the welcome intelligence was imparted that we were no longer to be cannonaded with impunity. Lord Wellington arrived from the right, and communicated to General Leith his intention of immediately attacking

---

[499] Leith Hay, Vol. II, p.p. 50-52.
[500] *Salamanca 1812*, Rory Muir, p. 65.

the enemy. It is impossible to describe the energetic exultation with which the soldiers sprang to their feet; if ever primary impulse gained a battle, that of Salamanca was won before the troops moved forward!'

'General Leith was directed to form his division in two lines [each two ranks deep], the first of which was composed of the Royals, 9th and 38th Regiments of Greville's brigade, with part of the 4th Regiment from General Pringle's brigade, necessarily brought forward for the purpose of equalising the lines, of which the second was formed by the remainder of Pringle's brigade [on the right, including the 30th] and the whole of General Spry's Portuguese infantry. When General Bradford's [Portuguese] brigade came up, the division was to appui itself on to his left, march directly up the heights, and attack the enemy's columns.

'Lord Wellington, on this, as on all occasions, gave his orders in a clear, concise and spirited manner; there was no appearance of contemplating a doubtful result; all he directed was as to time and formation, and his instructions concluded with commands that the enemy should be overthrown and driven from the field. He then proceeded towards the 4th Division.

'The 5th, formed as he had directed, with its General in front of the centre of the first line, impatiently awaited the arrival of General Bradford; the moment he was in line, General Leith gave the signal, and the whole advanced in the most perfect order.[501] Previously to this movement, he had dispatched his aides-de-camp… to different points in the line in order to restrain any effort at getting more rapidly forward than was consistent with the important object of its arriving in perfect order close to the enemy, and at all points making a simultaneous attack.'

'In ascending the height on which the French army was placed, the division continued to be annoyed by the artillery fire from its summit. The ground between the advancing force and that to be assailed was also crowded with light troops in extended order, carrying on a very incessant tiraillade. The General desired me to ride forward, make the light infantry press up the heights to clear his line of march, and if practicable make a rush at the enemy's cannon… the light troops soon drove back those opposed; the cannon were removed to the rear; every obstruction to the regular advance of the line had vanished.

'In front of the centre of that beautiful line rode General Leith, directing its movements and regulating its advance. Occasionally every soldier was visible, the sun shining bright upon their arms, while at intervals all were enveloped in a dense cloud of dust, from whence at times issued the animating cheer of British infantry.'

'[Maucune's] columns, retired from the crest of the height, were formed in squares, about fifty yards removed from the ground on which, when arrived, the British regiments would become visible. The French artillery, although placed more to the rear, still poured its fire on the advancing troops.'

'The second line of the division' [including the 30th] 'was about a hundred yards in rear of the first; and between these, during the march towards the enemy, Lord Wellington at one time was, observing the progress of the attack.

'We were now near the summit of the ridge. The men marched with the same orderly steadiness as at first; no advance in line at a review was ever more correctly executed: the dressing was admirable, and spaces were no sooner formed by casualties than closed up with the most perfect regularity, and without the slightest deviation from the order of march. General Leith and the officers of his staff, being on horseback, first perceived the enemy, previous to the infantry line becoming so visible as to induce him to commence firing. He was drawn up in contiguous squares, the front rank kneeling, and prepared to fire when the drum beat for its commencement. All was still and quiet in these squares – not a musket was discharged until the whole opened.

'Nearly at the same moment General Leith ordered the line to fire, and charge. The roll of musketry was succeeded by that proud cheer that has become habitual to British soldiers on similar occasions – that to an enemy tremendous sound, which may without exaggeration be termed the note of victory…

'In an instant every individual present was enveloped in smoke and obscurity. No struggle for ascendency took place: the French squares were penetrated, broken, and discomfited. The victorious division pressed forward, not against troops opposed, but a mass of disorganised men, flying in all directions.'[502]

The nine battalions of Maucune's division had been in square on the reverse slope of the ridge, with guns in the intervals, not the most effective formation to meet infantry advancing in line; but Maucune must have seen

---

[501] Leith did not in fact wait for Bradford's brigade to draw level before launching his attack.
[502] Leith Hay, Vol. II, p.p. 52-7.

a new threat. Le Marchant's heavy cavalry, over one thousand mounted 'heavies' of the 5th Dragoon Guards and the 3rd and 4th Dragoons, were trotting up the slope towards his left front. The 3rd Division opened files to let the horsemen through, and the heavy dragoons fell on the disordered mass of Thomières' and Maucune's divisions, some broken and others attempting to rally, sabreing the terrified fugitives and shouting to Leith's men as they passed, 'Now boys, lather them and we'll shave them!' It was a scene of utter confusion, with some French units, notably the 1st Ligne, withdrawing in relatively good order, others scattered, and many Frenchmen seeking protection from the dragoons' swords under British infantry bayonets.

General Leith was wounded as the 5th Division closed with their enemy, as was his nephew, Andrew Leith Hay, and so for the later stages of the battle we lose the latter's valuable narrative. Indeed, the lack of good primary sources makes any attempt to reconstruct a narrative of the latter stages of the 5th Division battle rather speculative. It appears, however, that Maucune's second line regiments, deployed behind a deep gully or trench, checked Greville's brigade with their musketry. But the British battalions raised a cheer and bounded forward over the gap, at which their enemy gave way in confusion.

As the two leading French divisions collapsed, Taupin's division, the recent opponents of the 27th and 40th, emerged from the woods behind Maucune's position. Taupin's leading regiment, the 22nd Ligne (two battalions strong, with 1,547 all ranks), formed in *colonne serrée* (tight column of companies), coolly reserved their fire until Le Marchant's 3rd and 4th Dragoons were within some twenty yards, then poured it in with deadly effect, bringing nearly one third of the horsemen to the ground and killing Le Marchant. The remaining cavalry pressed on, and broke the French formation. The 22nd Ligne was scattered and destroyed. Among that regiment's thousand or so casualties was Lieutenant Joseph Meullenacre, the *porte-aigle* (eagle-bearer), who was wounded.[503] The Eagle, which the 22nd had received in 1804 from the hands of Napoleon on the Champs de Mars in Paris, was captured, together with *porte-aigle* spontoons and pennants, and the wounded commanding officer, Colonel Joseph Delom.[504]

At Salamanca, the light companies of the 4th, 30th, and 44th were detached to form a light battalion commanded by Lieutenant-Colonel Alured Faunce[505]. When Leith advanced, this light battalion was extended on his right flank to connect with Packenham's left and was soon in the thick of the fight. Two Eagles and a battalion Colour, or fannion, were captured by this battalion. The 62nd Ligne, part of Thomières' shattered division, was charged in thick cover and its Eagle taken by Lieutenant Pearse of the Light Company 44th, and at some point a Colour was captured by Lieutenant Francis Maguire of the 4th King's Own. Whilst there is no certain knowledge of how the Eagle of the 22nd was captured, it is more than probable that Pringle's light companies, including that of the 30th under Lieutenant Nevill, would have been following up close behind Le Marchant's dragoons and would accordingly have been well placed to exploit his gallant charge and deal with whatever remnants of the 22nd Ligne remained in the field, and to secure trophies. It was then that, according to John Garland, Adjutant of the 30th at Salamanca, 'another eagle came into possession of an officer of the 30th Regiment in the same brigade who accompanied the officer of the 44th Regiment to the Headquarters of the British Army where they deposited the two eagles.' That officer was Ensign John Pratt.[506]

---

[503] French Eagle-bearers were appointed by the Emperor. Each one had to have ten year's service including four major campaigns. He was to be a lieutenant, receiving captain's pay, and he was to be illiterate so that he would know that the position of Eagle-bearer was the highest to which he could aspire. He was to guard the regimental Eagle with his life, and had two assistants, also illiterate veterans, armed with swords and halberds.

[504] The Eagle of the 22nd, carried by that regiment on campaigns in Germany, Spain and Portugal, was taken to London where, on 30th September, the captured Eagles and Colours were paraded through the streets, made obeisance before the Prince Regent and the Royal Family, to the cheers of thousands of spectators, and were then deposited in Whitehall Chapel. *The Times* wrote of that occasion that 'It was impossible to view, without feelings of exultation, those trophies which bore witness to the prowess of British soldiers, and which were won from no despicable enemy, but from troops whose military reputation stands so high in Europe.' The Eagle of the 22nd was subsequently lodged at the Royal Hospital, Chelsea for many years before being presented back to the East Lancashire Regiment at a ceremonial parade in 1947. It is now displayed in the Regimental Museum at Preston, one of only five such Napoleonic Eagles taken in battle by the British Army.

[505] Alured Faunce of the 4th King's Own was the son of Thomas Faunce, a Quebec veteran of the 47th Regiment.

[506] There has been some confusion as to who captured, or otherwise acquired, Eagles at Salamanca. It has even been claimed that Lieutenant Pratt was serving with Portuguese Caçadores, but this is incorrect: he was always a Light Company 30th officer.

We have very little evidence of the activities of the 30th, or other units of the 5th Division, in the inevitably chaotic aftermath of their victorious advance. It may, however, be reasonably supposed that, with the 3rd and 5th Divisions attacking on converging lines, they would both have been halted and re-formed, in the case of the 5th by Major-General Pringle, who assumed command when Leith was wounded. Since Pringle's brigade was in second line during the divisional advance, the main body of the 30th were not directly engaged in the overthrow of Maucune's division, the brunt of that action falling on Greville's brigade, and casualties were light. There were still formed bodies of French, including three unbroken infantry regiments, on the fringes of the wood to their front, and Pringle may well have moved his own brigade into first line to confront them, for the leading battalions of both divisions would have been encumbered with several thousand prisoners and their depleted ranks would have been further thinned as soldiers took the opportunity to search their stricken enemies for valuables.

Indeed, it was probably at this time that a watch was given to Sergeant John Ward of the 30th Foot by a wounded French prisoner for 'an act of kindness.' The Frenchman died shortly afterwards. John Ward became Quartermaster of the 30th in 1824 and retired in 1847, the last serving member of the Regiment to have fought in the Peninsula.[507]

To the left of Leith, Cole's 4th Division advanced at about 4.30 p.m. (15-20 minutes later than the 5th Division). With Anson's brigade committed to defend the Lesser Arapile, he had two brigades in hand, Ellis's Fusilier brigade and Stubbs' Portuguese, both under strength after Badajoz. With some 3,900 men, including 1,359 of the Fusilier brigade, Cole advanced to attack the 6,562 as yet unseen men of Clausel's Division. Unlike Leith, Cole had insufficient men to form two lines. The Division filed through Los Arapiles, formed two ranks deep, and advanced 'in great order and regularity.'

The further they advanced, the more exposed they became to French guns and troops on and behind the Greater Arapile. Cole became concerned and detached the 7th Caçadores from Stubbs' brigade to protect his open and increasingly vulnerable left flank.

Leaving the Greater Arapile behind his left flank, Cole's line crested a rise to discover the leading troops of Clausel's division, which had recently arrived to his front. A fierce fire-fight followed, with five battalions on either side, until the French were driven back 200 yards to where their second line was drawn up. Cole was wounded by now, and his attack lost impetus.

At about this time, Dennis Pack was ordered by Wellington to capture the Greater Arapile with his Independent Portuguese brigade, presumably to take some pressure off Cole. Pack made a gallant but futile direct assault on the north face of the hill, but was decisively halted at a rocky natural scarp and was thrown back with heavy loss by the three-battalion 120th Ligne.

At around the time of Pack's attack, or possibly a little earlier, the 40th Foot were led forward from their initial position on the right rear slope of the Lesser Arapile, 'for the purpose of supporting the left of the 4th Division.'

Pack's Portuguese had hardly fallen back when the French right wing mounted a perfectly-timed counter-attack against the 4th Division, which was attacked in front by the five battalions of Clausel's second line, over three thousand men, and in flank by elements of Bonnet's division, supported by Boyer's three dragoon regiments, four and a half thousand infantry and eleven hundred cavalry. The Fusilier brigade, on the right, was hit by a disciplined advance in column before they had formed after their previous fire-fight, and after some wild firing, they wavered and gave way. At much the same time, or a little earlier, Stubbs' Portuguese on the left were attacked in their left flank and also gave way. It appears that the 4th Division fell back in confusion to a hollow in the rear, probably towards Los Arapiles, where they rallied, and at least some formed square to receive Boyer's rather ineffective dragoons.

What then of the 40th, who appear to have advanced by this time to the left rear of the 4th Division? The manuscript *Record of Service of the 40th Regiment*, which was ordered to be 'prepared forthwith' in accordance with a Horse Guards circular of 6th November 1822, and was completed by the following summer, has persuasive

---

[507] John Ward's medals are in the Officers' Mess 1st Battalion The Duke of Lancaster's Regiment. 'The Frenchman's Watch', as it is called, with an illustration of a French soldier on its face, is in the Regimental Museum. The watch is marked 'Breguet à Paris', but it is in fact a contemporary fake of the work of that famous master watchmaker.

detail about Salamanca which could have been verified by officers and men still serving in the Regiment at that time. It reads as follows:

'When the British attack had been determined on, the 40th Regiment descended from the hill it had occupied in the morning, for the purpose of supporting the left of the 4th Division, which was ordered to attack the centre of the enemy's line. In its advance, having inclined somewhat to the right, a considerable space was left between it and the Arapiles. The enemy at once attempted to take advantage of this by moving two columns forward on the left of the division.[508] To check the advance, Major Archdall, commanding the 40th, was ordered to bring up the right of his regiment and deploy into line. This he did, and, attacking both columns with the bayonet, forced them to retire in confusion. In the heat of the pursuit, however, some of those who had surrendered as prisoners were not sufficiently guarded, and these, resuming their arms, fired on the regiment, thereby wounding Lieutenant Hudson and several of the rank and file.'

This account is corroborated by Major John Scott Lillie of the 7th Caçadores, who was nearby with a wing of his regiment:

'I happened to be at the time with some companies of the Caçadores and the 40th Regiment… This was one of the few occasions on which I saw the bayonet used; the 40th under the late Colonel Archdall, having come into close contact with Bonnet's French brigade in consequence of this movement, which was directed by General William Anson in person; he was moving on with the 40th, leaving the [Greater Arapiles] on his left and in his rear, on which a corps moved from behind the hill in rear of the 40th for the purpose of attacking it, the regiment being at the time engaged in front. I happened to be between the 40th and the enemy, and rode after the former to tell Colonel Archdall of his situation, on which he wheeled round and charged the enemy's column with the bayonet and this terminated the contest at that point.'[509]

In a testimonial of 27th January 1847 Sir John Scott Lillie, as he had become, elaborated on this statement when he wrote that 'towards the close of the day the 40th Regiment advanced in close column, on the enemy's position, passing by one of the Arapiles which was still occupied by the enemy, and from which a close column was moved out in an oblique direction on the rear of the 40th, unperceived by them until I rode up to Sir W. Anson, who was with that regiment, and appraised him of the fact, the enemy being at this time close upon their rear, when he immediately ordered the 40th to wheel round and, with the aid of the left wing of the 7th Caçadores, which was on the right of the 40th, charged them with the bayonette and threw them back. [William Waldron] Kelly was at that time senior lieutenant of the 40th, in command of the Grenadier Company, which led the column during the charge, and this was the only occasion during the war on which I observed two corps come into actual contact,' adding that 'It was on this occasion that the Standard borne by the French Regiment fell into my hands, which I presented next day to headquarters.'

Major Charles Broke Vere adds the information that Anson moved forward with the 40th by order of Wellington to cover the gap between Cole and Pack when the latter made his unsuccessful assault on the Greater Arapile.

This battalion action does not fit neatly into historians' best attempts at a coherent narrative of the rather confusing sequence of events around the 4th Division's encounters with Clausel and Bonnet, so it is worth examining the evidence with some care to establish when and where this action may have occurred, and what happened. The accounts indicate that the 40th were well forward in a position where they could cover and support Cole's left flank, with the Greater Arapile to their left rear. It is clear that the Regiment was advancing in a formation that permitted speedy deployment into line, and that when Bonnet's column or columns suddenly appeared to their rear they were already 'engaged in front,' though the facility with which Archdall was able to disengage and wheel his companies round to the left suggests that this may have been no more than a light infantry skirmish. The presence of the 7th Caçadores puts the timing of this action before the repulse of the 4th Division.

---

[508] This was part of the counter-attack by Bonnet's division.

[509] Rory Muir interprets Major Lillie's account as a claim that the 40th single-handedly drove back Bonnet's advance, which he opines is 'manifestly absurd.' In fact Lillie only speaks of the 40th defeating one regimental column, though the *Record of Service* says two, most probably battalion columns of the same regiment. It may, however, here be noted that at Sorauren in 1813 the 40th Regiment did indeed single-handedly defeat this same division.

As major, Lillie commanded the left wing of the Portuguese regiment, at least three hundred strong, who would have been a useful support to the 40th.

As to the nature of the fighting, it is clear that the 40th had once again indulged their predilection for charging home with the bayonet. But who were their opponents? It appears that three of Bonnet's regiments, the 118th, 119th, and 122nd Ligne, took part in the French counter-attack with a combined strength of some 4,500 men. One of these, the 122nd Ligne, had already fallen back before the 7th Caçadores, while a second regiment, with some dragoons, appear to have attacked the left flank of Stubbs' Portuguese brigade. This leaves just one regiment, the 118th or 119th, respectively 1,637 and 1,329 all ranks, to meet the 40th.[510]

Broke Vere is understandably rather coy about the detail of the set-back to the 4th Division, of which he was a staff officer, but states that both the 7th Caçadores and the 40th were 'overpowered,' presumably in consequence of Bonnet's advance, and that General Anson, with the latter, was 'compelled to fall back to his ground in the original position.' Broke Vere was almost certainly not in a position to see exactly what was happening on the division's left, but despite their success against Bonnet, the 40th would certainly have been obliged to conform with the general retirement, and Anson would doubtless have wished to re-establish his whole brigade on and about the Lesser Arapile. In any event, it is clear enough that what the historian Napier termed a 'rough charge' by the 40th against Bonnet would have assisted the 4th Division's disengagement, and it is strange that a regiment supposedly 'overpowered' should lose no prisoners. A more or less orderly withdrawal appears more likely.

It should also be noted that it was Boyer's dragoons, and not Bonnet's infantry division, who initially exploited the collapse of the 4th Division, suggesting that the latter had previously suffered a fairly severe check. Meanwhile, Clausel's division made only a limited advance in pursuit of the Fusilier brigade, probably because their left flank was increasingly exposed to the 5th Division.

The immediate crisis on this front was soon resolved, for Wellington had already ordered forward the 6th Division, while Marshal Beresford had gathered up Spry's Portuguese brigade from the left rear of the 5th Division and swung it to the left to threaten Clausel's flank. According to secondary accounts, the situation was restored by the 6th Division, who threw back Boyer's dragoons and then went forward to sweep away Bonnet's division.[511] The rallied 4th Division again advanced and regained from Clausel's division the ground they had lost, while the 3rd and 5th Divisions eventually drove slowly east along the Monte de Azan, driving Sarrut's and Taupin's divisions before them.

The French made a final stand on the wooded El Sierro ridge south of the Greater Arapile. Ferey's division, with seven battalions in line and a square at either end, fought a determined musketry duel with the 6th Division for nearly an hour, with severe losses on both sides. Wellington ordered the 1st and 4th Divisions to turn Ferey's right flank, while the 5th Division moved up to fall upon his left. The French rearguard broke and, as dark fell, Clausel's rearguard was in full retreat towards Alba de Tormes.

At this last stage of the battle there is another glimpse of the 40th Foot. It appears that when the 4th Division fell back, the 40th may have retired towards the left of the Lesser Arapile, for their *Record of Service* goes on to state that 'The 40th joined in the pursuit, and for three days was attached to the German brigade of the First Division.' During the final Allied advance, the 1st Division, with Anson's brigade, advanced to the left of the Greater Arapile, which was occupied by Lowe's King's German Legion brigade. It was presumably at this time that the latter brigade suffered 75 casualties, half the divisional total.

The French retreated towards Alba de Tormes, which should have been held by Carlos de Espana, who had withdrawn without informing Wellington. The growing dark and broken wooded country precluded further pursuit that night, and the 40th bivouacked near Calvarrasa de Abajo at about one o'clock in the morning. It appears that Anson's brigade, together with the 1st and Light Divisions and some squadrons of cavalry, continued the pursuit next morning.

---

[510] The 118th suffered the loss of 14 officers and 393 men at Salamanca, while the respective losses of the 119th were 20 and 314.

[511] Lieutenant Edward Stephen Marlay of the 82nd, serving with the 8th Portuguese Line, was severely wounded as Brigade Major of Rezende's Portuguese Brigade of the 6th Division. He had previously served with the 82nd at Roliça and Vimeira and, with the 2nd Battalion of Detachments, at Talavera.

Wellington's army suffered 5,220 casualties at Salamanca, including nearly seven hundred killed in action. Marmont's casualties totalled around 12,500, together with twenty guns, two Eagles and six Colours.

The 30th Foot had remarkably few casualties: two killed, Lieutenant John Garvey and nineteen rank and file wounded, of whom four died later of their wounds, and one man taken prisoner.[512]

The 40th, by contrast, had some 132 casualties, including two officers, one sergeant, and twenty-five rank and file killed in action or died of wounds, over one in four of its strength and rather above the average for the 4th Division. Whilst the official casualty return for the 40th shows twelve men killed, and no officers, and five officers and 115 men wounded, the *Regimental Record* shows the eventual outcome, with the number of fatalities increased by those who subsequently died of wounds. The *Regimental Record* also indicates only 'about eighty wounded,' presumably not counting those lightly wounded men who had returned to duty.[513]

Gold Medals for Salamanca were awarded to Lieutenant-Colonel Hamilton of the 30th and Major Archdall of the 40th, while in 1848 the surviving officers and men, 77 of the 30th and 137 of the 40th, received the silver Army General Service Medal with a 'Salamanca' clasp.[514] In addition, Major Archdall was mentioned in dispatches and rewarded with a brevet lieutenant-colonelcy. Both the 30th and the 40th Regiments earned the Battle Honour 'SALAMANCA.'

Salamanca was, by any standards, a major victory with a moral and material impact well beyond the Peninsula. Within the army, the grumblers were effectively silenced. Dr Boutflower, his finger as usual on the pulse, enthused on 26th July that Wellington had 'placed himself almost beyond the reach of rivalry,' adding that 'splendid as are his military talents, he must consider himself in great measure indebted to his success from his good fortune in commanding the bravest troops in the world; men who when well led on will hesitate at nothing.' The French general Foy, whose division survived Salamanca almost intact, was even more effusive, writing in his diary six days later:

'The battle of Salamanca is the most masterly in its management, the most considerable in the number of troops involved, and the most important in results of all the victories that the English have gained in these latter days. It raises Lord Wellington almost to the level of Marlborough. Hitherto we had been aware of his prudence, his eye for choosing a position, and his skill in utilising it. At Salamanca, he has shown himself a great and able master of manoeuvres. He kept his dispositions concealed for almost the whole day: he waited till we were committed to our movement before he developed his own: he played a safe game: he fought in the oblique order – it was a battle in the style of Frederick the Great.'

Advance to and Occupation of Madrid

After Marmont's defeat at Salamanca, the disorganised remnants of his army fell back on Burgos, while King Joseph retreated towards Madrid, and then on to join Suchet, and eventually Soult, in Valencia. Wellington pursued the erstwhile Army of Portugal as far as Valladolid, then chose to leave a small containing force watching the line of the Duero while he marched on Madrid with his main army, including the 4th and 5th Divisions. This course of action was based on his assessment that whilst Marmont's defeated army was not an immediate threat, he could shortly face a more potent combination of enemies to the south, where the armies of Soult, Suchet, and King Joseph could concentrate a formidable force.

---

[512] The official casualty return shows three men killed and 22 wounded. Those of the 30th killed in action were Privates Thomas Livesay, from Northampton and Timothy Meara, from Tipperary, while Sergeant Joseph Matthews of the Light Company, from Hereford, and Privates Edward Flanagan, from Dungannon, and Francis Pibble and James Woollen, both from Lincoln, died of their wounds.

[513] Five officers of the 40th were wounded, of whom Lieutenant and Adjutant J. Bethell and Lieutenant John Gray, severely wounded, died of their wounds on 21st and 27th October respectively, and Lieutenant Richard Hudson was severely wounded. Bethell, commissioned on 11th September 1806, had been Adjutant of the 1st/40th since February 1812, while Gray had previously been seriously wounded at the storming of Badajoz. Lieutenant the Honourable Thomas Browne and Lieutenant William Turton were slightly wounded. Bethell's widow, Martha, received an allowance from Parliament of £30 p.a. 'in consideration of his meritorious service, and the destitute situation in which she is left.'

[514] In addition, the medal was awarded to Lieutenant Marlborough Seymour of the 59th, who was at Salamanca attached to the Commissariat Department.

On 25th July Wellington's infantry assembled between Nava de Sotrobal and Peñaranda de Bracamonte, some 15 miles east of Alba de Tormes, from where they advanced next day in two columns, preceded by the cavalry.[515] By the 28th the columns reached San Vicente del Palacio on the Zapardiel River, and on the 29th both the 30th and 40th crossed the Adaja with the left column. Next day they marched on, fording the Eresma and crossing the Cega by bridge to halt near the village of Boecillo, within sight of the spires of Valladolid, which the French evacuated that day. The 30th and 40th did not enter the liberated city, which received Wellington with great enthusiasm, but remained for the next week near the Cega, moving up towards Cuellar. Clausel's shattered army had meanwhile retreated towards Burgos.

The 1st/82nd reached Salamanca a few days after the battle. Their strength shortly after landing at Lisbon had included 1,063 men but, as Lieutenant George Wood described, a forced march up country soon reduced the effective strength of a battalion still suffering the effects of Walcheren fever, which had in consequence left over one hundred dead at Gibraltar, and whose ranks were full of unseasoned young soldiers.

'We ascended the Tagus some distance in boats and landed at Villa Franca, whence we proceeded, by forced marches, to overtake our army previous to its being engaged. Expresses continually met us on the road to hasten our movement, as an action was every moment expected to take place; and we had barely time to give nature sufficient repose, as we continued marching nearly night and day towards Salamanca. We found this excessively harassing, as the weather was in its height of summer heat. We at length reached Ciudad Rodrigo, where we were obliged to halt one day, leaving two officers and some men sick from fever brought on by extreme exertion.

'Having nearly reached Salamanca, we heard the sound of cannon-shot all through the day; and on arriving at that town we learned that an action had taken place, which rendered all our forced marches useless. The enemy were, as usual after a battle, flying; and we still continued, if not increased, our exertions to come up with the army, which was now on the high-road to Madrid, leaving behind us in this place more officers and men that had fallen sick.

'We passed over the distressing yet glorious field of Salamanca, about the third day after the battle – a scene, if possible, more horrid to us than if we had been in the battle itself and gone on with the conquering army. The ground was now becoming disgusting from the number of dead that lined the roads; and these, from their putrescent state, caused by the heat, were so obnoxious that we were obliged to stop our noses with our pocket-handkerchiefs; which, in spite of all precautions, proved as fatal to us as if we had actually been in the action.'[516]

Also making his way up to Salamanca at that time was Private William Lawrence of the 40th, still carrying a slug shot from Badajoz in his knee. After six weeks in hospital at Estremoz, and another fortnight's convalescence with a local family, he was determined to rejoin his Regiment.

'I received intelligence that a hundred and fifty others were well enough to rejoin the army, so I asked the doctor if I might accompany them. He told me that my wounds were not yet sufficiently set for me to undertake the journey; but I was by this time sick of hospitals, physics, Estremoz, and the lot of it, and was mad to get back to my regiment, so I went to the captain [John Hitchen], who was still lying wounded in the hospital, and asked him to speak to the doctor to let me go. The result was that next morning I again saw the doctor, who said I could go, but I must abide by the consequences myself, as he would not be answerable for my safety; so about three days after that our little group started on the way to the army, which had meanwhile moved northward from Badajoz to Salamanca, about two hundred miles distant, which we found rather a tedious march in our then condition.

'I had not been many days at Salamanca before a fever broke out, which I caught very badly, and so was ordered back into hospital at Ciudad Rodrigo, along with a number of fellow troops who were troubled with a like malady with myself. On my arrival at the hospital, my hair was cut off by order of the doctor, and my head

[515] Whilst on the march, the 30th were joined at Flores de Avila by a draft of 27 men which had been brought out from the Depot at Hull. Ensign Harry Beere, an enormous Irishman from Tipperary, arrived to the news that his brother Hercules, a lieutenant in the 61st, had died of wounds received at Salamanca.

[516] Wood, p.p. 127-29. Writing on 7th August from Salamanca, Lieutenant-Colonel George Bingham, formerly of the 82nd, reported, 'The 82nd have been here since I last wrote. Of course the regiment has changed since I left them eight years since. I met however some old acquaintance, that made the two days they remained here pass pleasantly enough.'

blistered; and I had not been there many hours before I became quite insensible, in which state I remained more or less for three months, which brought on great weakness. I received kind treatment, however, from the doctor and our attendants, and was allowed to eat anything my fancy craved, and amongst other things, without having to resort to any contrivance as at Estremoz, I could get wine.'[517]

The 82nd were also attacked by a 'malignant fever' at this time, and Lieutenant George Wood was one of those who fell sick on the march. He was carried back to Salamanca on a bullock-cart in a wretched condition. There was no doctor to be found, and the penniless subaltern had to sell his shirts to buy food. His life was saved, quite fortuitously, by a surgeon he had known in Gibraltar, who gave him both medicine and, equally important, money to buy comforts. Two of his brother-officers, Lieutenants Thomas Lambert and Patrick Tully, were not so fortunate and died on 6th and 18th August respectively.

The 82nd moved on to join the army on 5th August at Cuellar, where, after a march of some five hundred miles, they were halted. The Battalion was allocated to Cole's 4th Division, but in consideration of their sickly condition, they were left behind, attached to the 6th Division, when the division marched.

Having beaten the Army of Portugal, which was, for the present, harmless, Wellington was now ready to turn his attention to King Joseph, who on 1st August had evacuated Segovia, heading over the Guadarrama pass to Madrid. Leaving a small containing force to watch Clausel, he marched the main body of his army, including the 4th and 5th Divisions, south towards Madrid.

The 40th had been in bivouac on the banks of the river Cega, about two miles from Cuellar, since 2nd August, but on the morning of the 6th, they joined the advance on Madrid. The 4th and 5th Divisions halted near Mudrian on the river Piron that night, at Yanguas de Eresma on the 7th, at the Palacio Real de Riofrio, near Segovia on the 8th and 9th, and El Espinar on the 10th before crossing the famous Puerto de Guadarrama on the 11th and camping that night in the park of the Escorial Palace.[518] Charles Boutflower found the mountain scenery and its cooler climate 'a pleasing contrast to the insipid flats we have so long been marching through,' and 'as we pass thro' the several towns and villages, the acclamations of the people are unbounded.'

King Joseph had abandoned his capital on the 10th, leaving two thousand troops to defend the Retiro citadel and arsenal.[519] On the 12th, when Wellington made his unopposed entry into Madrid, the 30th and 40th, with their respective divisions, bivouacked at the Puente de Ratamar on the river Guadarrama, three leagues outside the city, which they entered early next day and camped in the Royal Park near the Puente de Segovia. Lieutenant Nevill of the 30th experienced the ecstatic welcome on the 13th when the 5th Division marched through the city with drums beating, fixed bayonets, and Colours flying:

'Our appearance was hailed with joy and triumph by all ranks; thousands of the inhabitants, bearing flowers and laurel, came forth to welcome us. As my regiment was passing the principal street, in succession with others, some ladies, handsomely dressed, laid hold of our Colours, to which they affixed laurel, and actually embraced the bearers of them with the greatest enthusiasm.'[520]

'It was with difficulty we could get into the town,' wrote Charles Boutflower of the 40th, 'so excessive was the joy of the people.' That evening, he witnessed the proclamation of the new Constitution:

'The sight was truly affecting. The houses of the streets through which the procession passed were ornamented with silks of various colours, & the windows filled with remarkably fine women; everything bore the appearance of the most unsophisticated joy. At length the Constitution was proclaimed amid the acclamations of thousands, who once more respired the air of liberty after having for more than four years endured the galling chains of the most odious slavery. The rejoicings continued for three days, and for the same number of nights the town was most beautifully illuminated.'[521]

---

[517] Lawrence, p. 123.

[518] On this march, Surgeon Charles Boutflower and others of the 40th took opportunities for some sightseeing. He found Segovia 'a very ancient town, and very worthy of observation', but he was greatly disappointed at the Escorial: 'The Palace itself is as far destroyed as it well could be, the enemy having entirely stripped the regal apartments of everything that decorated them.'

[519] The Retiro citadel and arsenal surrendered on the 14th, when Boutlower watched the French garrison march out: 'They were nearly all in a state of intoxication, and their gestures and language was very violent; they exclaimed that they were sold, and that their officers ought every one to be burnt alive.'

[520] Nevill, p. 20.

[521] Boutflower, p.p. 155-56.

He was less impressed by a bull fight which he attended on 5th October, leaving the 'barbarous amusement' in disgust after the first bull was despatched: 'It is to the credit of the English character,' he fulminated, 'that scarcely a British officer has gone to witness it a second time.'

In general, though, for the 30th and 40th, their brief occupation of Madrid was a delightful respite from the rigours of campaigning, their only complaints being the summer heat and sore feet from the hard city pavements. And so it was with great regret that, on 18th August, the 4th Division marched out of Madrid. The 5th Division had preceded them at dawn on the 15th, re-tracing their march from the Guadarrama foothills to escape the worst of the heat.[522]

By the 19th, the 4th, 5th and 7th Divisions were all quartered in the Escorial, where Anson's brigade of the 4th Division was joined in early September by the 82nd Regiment.[523] George Wood, who rejoined his Regiment there, found it 'an uncommon place, rendered famous not for its beautiful palace but for its enormous pile of buildings… This palace was now converted into our barracks; indeed I believe there is room enough to accommodate twenty thousand men here, so large is this astonishing fabric.'

The sickness at this time was very great. The 30th, when quartered at the Escorial, had twenty sergeants, four drummers, and 340 rank and file sick and wounded, leaving only 21 sergeants, 13 drummers and 186 rank and file fit for duty. The effective rank and file strength of the 40th was only 298, with 639 sick and wounded. Captain Archibald Colquhoun died on the 19th. The 82nd, who had yet to see action, were already reduced to 706 in the ranks and 377 sick. The weekly strength returns show a mounting toll of deaths in the 82nd Regiment, a lasting legacy of Walcheren.[524]

Cadiz and Seville, August 1812

One of the results of Wellington's victory at Salamanca was that Marshal Soult was reluctantly obliged to withdraw from his Viceroyalty of Andalusia, drawing down and evacuating his garrisons, and loot, and raising his siege of Cadiz. Soult prepared for his withdrawal from Cadiz by unleashing a final two days of furious bombardment on the city and Puntales fort. Under cover of this barrage, many of his heavy guns were disabled, and the work of destruction was continued on 24th August by blowing up the remaining powder, burning his stores and huts, and sinking thirty gunboats.

In anticipation of this French withdrawal from their Cadiz lines, Wellington had written on 16th August to General Cooke, commanding at Cadiz, bidding him make a general sortie to cut up the enemy before they could retire. This letter came too late, for Cooke had already committed the greater part of his troops, some 1,625 men, under Colonel Skerrett of the 47th, to a joint expedition with the Spanish General Cruz Murgeon. Skerrett's force consisted of detachments of the Guards, 2nd/87th, 2nd/95th, 20th Portuguese, and 2nd Hussars King's German Legion, but not the 2nd/47th, who remained as the only British battalion at Cadiz.

Skerrett landed at Huelva, some sixty miles north of Cadiz, on 13th-15th August, and advanced with Cruz Murgeon on the 16th towards Seville. At Niebla, the British troops found the castle abandoned and blown up, and at Sanlucar la Mayor on the 24th they drove out a French outpost. Then, hearing that Soult was evacuating Seville on the 26th, leaving behind a small rearguard, they decided to attack the city next day. Having surprised the French outworks in the western suburb of Triana, they stormed the barricaded and defended bridge between there and the city, driving out the garrison in a running fight and capturing a rich convoy of plunder.

---

[522] It was on about the 17th, during the march from Madrid to the Escorial, that Private John Riley of the 30th, a prisoner under escort, fell out from the rear guard due to a 'violent flux' and was struck off strength as a deserter. He returned to the Battalion at Tralee, Ireland in October 1815, claiming arrears of pay and other allowances as a prisoner of war. A General Regimental Court Martial was held, at which Riley stated that he had been picked up by Spanish brigands who handed him over to the French at Saragossa. In attempting to escape over the castle wall there he hurt himself and was recaptured. On recovery, he was imprisoned in succession at Perpignon, Besancon, Montpellier, Lyons and Selines until the peace, when he was given a pass to proceed to Hanover. He eventually obtained a passage from Cuxhaven to Harwich, where he reported himself to the commandant. The court accepted his extraordinary story.

[523] By a General Order dated 17th August the 82nd were transferred to the 4th Division.

[524] Five men of the 82nd died in the week ending 8th September, eleven in the week ending 15th September, twelve in the week ending 1st October and sixteen in the week ending 8th October.

Meanwhile, on the 25th, the morning after the French raised their siege of Cadiz, the British and Spanish troops took possession of the enemy lines. Large quantities of ammunition and stores were recovered, together with some five hundred intact guns.[525] Soult withdrew to Granada, from where he retired on 17th September to join Suchet in Valencia.

On 9th September Wellington sent orders to Cooke directing that Colonel Skerrett was to lead 4,500 men north to Trujillo, adding that: 'Whenever the 2nd Battalion 59th Regiment shall arrive after you have carried these orders into execution, you will send to Lisbon whichever of that battalion or the 2nd Battalion 47th Regiment is most fit for service, retaining at Cadiz one British battalion.' His orders again came just too late, for Cooke had anticipated the commander-in-chief's wishes, and when the 59th reached Cadiz on 7th September,[526] the 2nd/47th were already marching north from Jerez to Utrera on their way to join Skerrett at Seville.

Unsurprisingly, Lieutenant David Stapleton of the 47th managed to make an exhibition of himself and his family:

'Davy's appearance, on leaving Cadiz, was the most extraordinary; the wagon that moved his baggage, one of the largest size, drawn by eight mules, was loaded with monkeys, birds, dogs, and everything he could meet with, for he indulged his children to excess, and gave them everything they fancied.'[527]

Private Adam Reed of the 47th described the first day's 27-mile march from Cadiz:

'[Utrera] is about 7 leagues from Xerxes [Jerez] and we had to march that in one day in the burning sun (it is very hot in the south of Spain), and we marched till we almost died of thirst it being a very bad place for water. The first halt we made was close by a well, but it contained a very small quantity. Some of us waited a small space of time before we drank and some drank almost immediately. One man I saw, and soon after he drank he turned pale and died almost immediately. When the troops arrived at the town there was scarcely half the number that had set out in the morning, they were obliged to stop on the road, being famished with thirst, but they however arrived there before it was dark. One or two of each regiment died through drink that day.'

On arrival in Seville on 8th September, the 47th joined a brigade under Colonel Skerrett, preparing for the long northwards march to join Lord Hill in Castille. The brigade[528] left Seville on the 30th of that month, proceeding by way of Los Santos, Villafranca, and Medellin to Trujillo in Extremadura, which was reached on 12th October.

'On reaching Trujillo,' recalled John Harley, 'Major Broad, of our Regiment, fell ill of a violent fever, and died in the very house in which, it is said, Pizarro had lived and died. There was an extraordinary circumstance attending his death. On his first entering this house, having tripped against a board which caused him to stumble, he exclaimed, though by no means superstitious, "I hope that board may not make my coffin." His loss was a very severe one for the Regiment of which he was a very valuable officer... In the course of my experience, it has been my lot to meet with few persons whom I had so much reason to respect, on various accounts, as my friend the major.'[529]

The long, hot march resumed on the 14th, through Talavera and Toledo to Aranjuez, which was reached on 26th October, a distance of over four hundred miles from Cadiz.

---

[525] Among the trophies was a huge mortar, cast in Seville in 1811, which could fire a shell over three miles into Cadiz. 'The morning after the French raised the siege of Cadiz', wrote Harley (p. 173), 'we crossed the Isla de Leon and took the large mortar which now stands in the park, opposite the Horse Guards. It was taken near Santa Maria, opposite Cadiz, and had been spiked by the enemy previously to their retreat.' This mortar was put on display in 1816 at the Horse Guards, London, where it remains.

[526] Since their return from the Walcheren campaign in 1809, the 'Lilywhites' had spent over two years on duty in Ireland, Jersey and England, and it was not until August 1812 that they were again ordered on active service. On the 26th of that month they marched from Chichester to Portsmouth, where they embarked for Cadiz on the transports *Briton*, *Duchess of Richmond*, *Orlando* and *Colus*.

[527] Harley, p. 159.

[528] The brigade consisted of a detachment of the 3rd/1st Guards, the 2nd/47th and 2nd/87th, two companies of the 2nd/95th, the 20th Portuguese, a squadron of 2nd Hussars King's German Legion and two companies of artillery. The strength of the force at Seville was 5,122, while the effective rank and file strength of the 2nd/47th on 24th September was 641.

[529] Before he died on 31st October, Richard Broad told his story to Harley. He had received a good education, but was left destitute on his father's early death. He enlisted in the 6th Foot, and as a gentleman ranker who paid strict attention to his duties, he was soon noticed by his officers and earned early promotion to sergeant. In 1799 he was appointed ensign and adjutant to the newly raised Royal Cornwall and Devon Miners, a Militia regiment, from where he was promoted into the 85th Foot. After service in the 43rd and the 1st Royals, he transferred into the 47th as major in February 1811.

The Siege of Burgos

French activity in the north had claimed Wellington's attention since August, when Clausel had advanced to recover Valladolid and Zamora. Major-General Henry Clinton, who had been left to watch Clausel, had let this offensive go unchallenged; but the Commander-in-Chief determined to deal with the French in the north before returning to meet the greater threat of Marshal Soult coming up from the south. On 23rd August the 5th Division, with the 30th Foot, left the Escorial to join Clinton at Arévalo, where Wellington, who had left Madrid on 1st September, joined them in what was meant to be a brief excursion. Some 28,000 men were available to him, the 1st, 5th, 6th and 7th Divisions, with cavalry in proportion. He outlined his intentions on the 2nd in a letter to the Spanish General Castaños:

'I believe that Soult has the intention of leaving the south of Spain, but whether or not he has this intention, it is absolutely necessary to hunt down Marmont's [i.e. Clausel's] troops without waste of time, to leave me at liberty to oppose Soult with all my forces. I shall take advantage of the moment that the King's departure has given me to come to this side, and I shall push matters as far as I can... I have some large guns, and I have the idea of undertaking the siege of Burgos.'

Wellington was about to make the greatest error of his career, for Burgos Castle was a stronger fortress than he anticipated, expertly defended, his 'large guns' comprised just three 18-pounder guns and five howitzers, inadequate for a serious siege, whilst his engineer resources were equally wanting.

On 4th September, the army moved north against Clausel, reaching Olmedo on the Valladolid road. The undefended line of the Duero was forded on the 6th, and the cavalry bumped into a strong French position on the heights of Cisterniga, outside Valladolid. It took all that afternoon for the British infantry, led by the 5th Division, to file across the Duero and deploy, and Wellington declined to attack that evening. Clausel, who had no intention of fighting, slipped away that night towards Burgos. He was followed, very cautiously, and it was not until the 18th that the French evacuated Burgos, leaving a two-thousand-strong garrison, commanded by General Thouvenot, in the Castle.

Instead of dealing decisively with Clausel, which would have allowed him to take his main army south to face Soult, Wellington inexplicably and unhappily decided to besiege the Castle of Burgos, despite his lack of an adequate battering-train. The 30th were not involved in this unfortunate siege, for the 5th Division was allocated to the covering force. However, as usual, the army's deficiency in engineers was supplied by volunteers from the infantry, amongst whom was once more numbered Lieutenant Parke Percy Nevill of the 30th.

Nevill is noticed twice in accounts of the siege. On 1st October, according to the sapper John Jones, he was wounded in a musketry duel while trying to suppress the destructive fire of the French guns:

'The best marksmen were selected from the guard of the trenches, and posted in different situations, from 30 to 100 yards distant, to fire in at the [gun] embrasures. Some officers, good shots, who had frequently shown their skill in picking off individuals, attempted to play the same game on this occasion; but the French marksmen speedily drove them out of the field – Lieutenant N[evill], assistant engineer, lost part of an ear in this personal contention.'[530]

Then, on the evening of October 4th he was attached to the 24th Regiment when they successfully stormed breaches in the first, or outer, defence line of the Castle. Nevill gave his own account of what followed, when, at 5 p.m. the following day, three hundred French *voltigeurs* made a determined sortie:

'During the night we formed our lodgement, notwithstanding the heavy fire kept up on us, and the live shells incessantly rolled down from the glacis of the upper line. Then the enemy made a most determined sortie, upsetting our gabions and in part driving us back; but we speedily rallied, and had a regular stand-up fight, in some cases hand to hand. I felt suddenly paralyzed and became unconscious, until a hand pulled me out of some rubbish: it was a sergeant of the 79th. A ball had struck me on the left shoulder, passing out through the blade-bone.

---

[530] *Journals of Sieges in Spain and Portugal*, Major-General Sir John Jones, London, 1846, Vol. I, p.p. 300-301 (drafted early in 1813).

'The kind sergeant carried me to my quarters, refusing to take my watch as a present. On making enquiries, I learned he was killed, together with his gallant commanding officer, the Honourable Major Cox. Thus ended my humble part in this siege.'[531]

Bannatyne's *History of the Thirtieth* adds that 'In the struggle which followed [the sortie] Neville (sic) was conspicuous, being seen engaged with two French soldiers, before he fell. He narrowly escaped being completely covered with earth, but managed to grasp the foot of Lieutenant Pitts of the engineers, and make himself known.' Nevill watched the rest of the siege from a large house, 'rather too close to the castle,' which, he recalled, the French did not fire at unless they saw anyone looking out on them from the back windows. Nevill was rewarded with one year's extra pay, while the following year he was honoured for his efforts at Badajoz and Burgos with the Freedom of the City of Dublin, a remarkable accolade for a young man of only eighteen.

Throughout the siege, the 30th was encamped with the covering force, under Sir Edward Paget, on hills some ten miles north-east of Burgos.[532] For the next month, they had a fairly quiet time, although uncomfortable due to lack of tents and wet weather. Hale of the 9th Regiment described the daily routine:

'About one hour before break of day we stood to our arms till it was quite broad daylight, and as soon as our general officers were fully satisfied that the enemy were making no movement, we were dismissed, and parties immediately sent out for wood and water for the purpose of cooking, while our butchers were killing and dressing our meat.'

This routine changed towards the end of October, when the French made a move. Souham, who had taken over the Army of Portugal from Clausel, had been substantially reinforced, and, having concentrated his whole force, some 40,000 men, around Monasterio on the 18th, he was prepared for a general advance on the 20th. His intentions were frustrated by a despatch from King Joseph informing him of the intended French advance on Madrid from Valencia, which would force Wellington to fall back from Burgos, and ordering him to not to risk a general action. Nevertheless, on the 20th Souham pushed forward a reconnaissance in strength against the Allied centre, intent on occupying a wood in front of Paget's line. Wellington deployed the 1st and 5th Divisions against the flank of the French force, which withdrew in haste. Captain James Stanhope witnessed the action:

'In the afternoon the French made their appearance on the road to Monasterio, and at 3 o'clock two divisions of infantry & some cavalry advanced rapidly, driving in our pickets, and soon began a sharp firing at the Spaniards in the valley, the whole line of whom began firing volleys at ½ a mile from the top of their hill. In the skirmish at the bottom of the hill, the Spaniards behaved well against some conscripts and took a few prisoners. By the movement of the enemy they presented their flank to us & Lord Wellington galloped up to General Paget, saying "By God, I never saw so impudent [a] thing in my life, do move down and attack them." The 1st Division immediately descended the hill in three lines, supported in echelon by the 5th Division & artillery on the left, & some cavalry on our right flank. Though the ground was not favourable, it was a beautiful advance & our people seemed to have recovered their spirits. The enemy would not stand, Gardiner pounded them with his guns, but the dark prevented pursuit.'[533]

Despite the gallant efforts of Nevill and others, the siege of Burgos Castle ended in failure on 18th October when an assault on the second line was repulsed with considerable loss. On the 21st Wellington gave orders to raise the siege the following day and to withdraw.

Recriminations, accusations, and counter-accusations followed, but the engineer John Jones, who had been intimately involved in the siege, was probably right in his professional judgement that the failure at Burgos was almost entirely due to lack of resources:

'Considering… how much was effected with scarcely any engineers' means, it may fairly be concluded that, had there been a siege establishment with the army, even moderately efficient, so as to have admitted of the successful performance of the rudiments of the art, the proposed attack, even with the inadequate support of artillery it received, would have been carried through, and Burgos have fallen under it in ten days.'[534]

---

[531] Nevill, p.p. 23-4.
[532] Captain James Stanhope, who was on Paget's staff, states that 'The 5th Division is hutted below the covering position beyond Hurones.' The British covering position extended from there to Rubena, with Spanish troops on both flanks.
[533] Stanhope, p.p. 92-4.
[534] Jones, Vol I, p.p. 337-38.

An important, albeit diversionary, contribution to Wellington's overall strategy for 1812 was to be made by an expedition mounted from Sicily, where there had been a strong British garrison since 1806. The almost complete withdrawal of French troops from Italy for Napoleon's invasion of Russia had made this force available for operations elsewhere, and it was eventually agreed by both the Ministry and Wellington that its destination should be the east coast of Spain. The latter wished to see these troops used for a descent on Catalonia, aimed at Barcelona or Tarragona, which would oblige Marshal Suchet to march north from Valencia and prevent him from interfering in western and central Spain during the forthcoming campaign.

Lord William Bentinck, commanding the British forces in Sicily, would have preferred a landing in Italy and was reluctant to fully commit his strength to Catalonia. Instead of the anticipated ten thousand troops, in the end he made available only three British and two German Legion battalions, with elements of three foreign battalions, a total of 6,890 men under Lieutenant-General Frederick Maitland.[535] The 1st/81st Foot, 44 officers and 1,230 men commanded by Lieutenant-Colonel Patrick McKenzie, was the strongest battalion of this small expeditionary force.

After being inspected at Palermo by Bentinck, the 81st boarded transports on 6th June 1812, together with the 10th Foot and Calabrian troops, and sailed for Minorca, escorted by HMS *Redwing* brig of war. The convoy anchored in the harbour of Port Mahon on the 16th and remained there until 6th July, waiting for troops from Messina. As these did not arrive as soon as expected, the convoy put to sea to find them. Two days later, the convoy anchored in Palma Bay, Sardinia, where the Messina convoy appeared next day. The united force then made sail for Port Mahon, where they arrived on the 15th. Picking up Major-General Whittingham's Spanish brigade at Majorca, Maitland headed for the coast of Catalonia, where the expedition finally anchored in the bay of Palamos on 31st July. As a result of Bentinck's perversity and hesitation, the Allied force had arrived much later than originally intended and was far weaker. Moreover, it was not equipped for operations away from the coast.

The only possible option appeared to be to lay siege to Tarragona, but Maitland became aware that the Spanish Army of Catalonia was weak and had divided counsels, that local transport and provisions would be scarce to non-existent, that there was no sign of the anticipated popular rising, and that it would take some ten days to reduce Tarragona. In addition, he would probably have to fight General Decaen, who could concentrate at least 15,000 French troops, and the Navy could not guarantee to re-embark the army in case of defeat. Maitland's resolution wavered. He called a council of war, which advised him not to land, and accordingly the fleet sailed south.

The expedition reached Alicante on 9th August. It was a critical time, for O'Donnell's Spanish Army of Murcia had been humiliatingly defeated on 21st July at the (first) battle of Castalla, and Alicante itself had been in danger.

The troops disembarked on August 11th, when the 81st were brigaded with De Rolls' and Dillon's Regiments as the second brigade of the Division of Reserve. Lieutenant-Colonel McKenzie, 81st, commanded the brigade, so Major James Farrer[536] stepped up to command the Regiment, which was probably quartered amid the celebrated date palm groves around Elche, some twelve miles south-west of Alicante. Maitland was joined by Roche's Spanish division, by the 2nd/67th from Cartagena, and by a siege train sent by Wellington from Lisbon, giving a total of some 14,000 men, all paid for and supplied by Britain, plus the remnants of O'Donnell's army. To meet this threat, Suchet abandoned his advanced positions in front of Alicante and concentrated his army behind the River Xuquer, covering Valencia.

Maitland marched out on August 16th, intending to drive the French from their posts at Castalla and Ibi, only to find that they had already retired. He advanced through Monforte to Elda, but could go no further for want

---

[535] 1st/10th, 1st/58th and 1st/81st Regiments, 4th and 6th Line Battalions of the King's German Legion, three companies of De Roll's, five companies of Dillon's, and a battalion equivalent of the Calabrian Free Corps, plus small detachments of cavalry and gunners.
[536] Commissioned in 1794 into the 61st, James Farrer was promoted to major in the 81st on 2nd July 1807 and was awarded a brevet lieutenant-colonelcy on 4th June 1813. He went on half-pay in 1820 and became a major-general in 1841.

of transport and provisions, and had to be content with feeling out the French outpost line with his cavalry. He then heard that King Joseph, pushed out of Madrid, was advancing on Valencia with 15,000 men, and there was a rumour that Soult was about to evacuate Andalusia in that direction. The immediate reality was bad enough, and Maitland drew back to his cantonments around Alicante, expecting that he might be besieged there. King Joseph's army reached Suchet's outpost at Almanza on 25th August. Wellington wrote to Maitland, bidding him to hold out for as long as possible but to keep his transports close at hand in case an evacuation became necessary. The 81st returned to their previous quarters. It had been a disappointing start to the operations of the Anglo-Sicilian army, though its intervention had at least ensured that Suchet could not send troops into central Spain.

Forced idleness bred discontent, and relations between the British and Spanish were not always cordial. On 11th September, Captain Thomas Scott of the Royal Artillery recorded in his diary that 'a row took place between some Spanish officers and those of the 81st in consequence of some insult, or fancied one, at the billiard table… A cadet was well served by being kicked down the stairs, and the maitre d'hotel confined by the governor in the jail – his house shut up in consequence.'

Denia 5th October 1812

The Allied force remained inactive around Alicante for the next few weeks, and Suchet began to raid its outposts. To check this activity, on the evening of 4th October the left wing of the 81st, five companies under Major Peter Waterhouse[537], embarked at Alicante on HMS *Fame*, 74, and the *Cephalus* brig of war. They were accompanied by the Grenadier Company of De Rolls Regiment, a company of Marines, and some light guns, and the whole force of about six hundred men was commanded by Major-General Rufane Shaw Donkin. It was bound on a secret expedition, so secret that the naval commander was not informed that its destination was the small port and castle of Denia, some fifty miles north from Alicante and the southernmost coastal outpost occupied by the French. This was unfortunate as the naval officer could have informed the planners that a previous attempt had been made on Denia, when the place was found to be too strong. Donkin had been ordered to seize Denia by coup de main on the erroneous assumption that the castle was lightly held.

Early on the morning of 5th October, the troops were landed near a hermitage south of Denia. The Light Company 81st, which was thrown out to cover the advance, drove in the French outposts, and pressed them so closely that they nearly entered the castle with the fugitives, several men of the company being wounded in the ditch.

General Donkin then made a reconnaissance, concluding that the castle was too strong to be carried without heavy artillery. He also heard that French reinforcements were on their way. The Light Company was accordingly ordered back to the main body and retired with evident reluctance. Sergeant James Patterson of the 81st was highly commended by the General on this occasion for volunteering to carry the 'recall' order under heavy fire to the Light Company, who appear to have ignored previous bugle calls.

The main body was posted in a ravine, from which they now retired to the heights of San Nicolas, above the hermitage, and from there down to the beach. As they withdrew, they were attacked by a strong force of the enemy with two guns. These were repeatedly driven back, but continued to annoy the troops during their retreat to the beach. Re-embarkation was then completed in good order, covered by the guns of HMS *Cephalus*.

Some further detail is contained in the Detachment Orders issued by Major-General Donkin on 6th October aboard HMS *Fame*:

'Major-General Donkin begs leave to express his approbation of the conduct of the troops during the operations on shore yesterday. The light infantry of the Eighty-first Regiment, under the command of Captain [George] Pearson, distinguished itself throughout, and particularly by its advance in pursuit of the enemy; but those gallant soldiers must learn to obey the sounds of the bugle, for, by advancing close under the walls of Denia – although the halt was repeatedly sounded to keep them under cover in the wood – they exposed themselves to be destroyed by the fire of troops whom they could not, with all their bravery, get at, as they were behind high walls.

---

[537] Peter Waterhouse had served in the 81st since 1799, and was with the Regiment in South Africa, Southern Italy, where he was wounded at the battle of Maida, 1806, and in Sicily, where in November 1811 he was promoted to major.

'Captain Ryh[i]ner's support of that advance with the Grenadiers of De Roll's was very handsome; and the sharp-shooters of the Eighty-first, under Lieutenant [William] Fenton, when sent to sustain the left, behaved very well.

'Major General Donkin feels much indebted to Major Waterhouse of the Eighty-first Regiment for his assistance during the whole day, but particularly at the moment of embarkation, which he covered in a manner that did him the highest credit. The good conduct of Lieutenants [Edward Percival] Kingsbury, [William] Fenton, [David] Fair, [Alexander] Gordon, and Ensign Norlock [James Imlack] of the Eighty-first Regiment was conspicuous on that occasion, as was the steadiness of the troops.'[538]

'The re-embarkation of the detachment, it is to be recollected, was not a measure of necessity, but of choice. With such gallant troops it is more than probable that the castle of Denia might have been taken by assault, but defended as it was by at least four times the number of men expected to be there, the height of the walls became too serious an obstacle to encounter under the fire of so much musketry; and too many valuable soldiers whose services will be required for more important occasions, would have been lost in the attack.

'What the troops have done, they have done with credit to themselves; what they have left unaccomplished was from choice and in conformity with the plain intentions with which they were embarked at Alicant: they were landed at Denia with a determination not to attempt the assault of the castle unless it could be carried with ease.'

The British account may interestingly be compared with Marshal Suchet's self-congratulatory dispatch from the Army of Aragon to the Minister of War in Paris, dated Valencia, 17th October 1812:

'In the night between the 4th and 5th instant the English General Donkin, Quarter Master General of the Anglo-Spanish Army, disembarked near the heights of St. Nicholas, before Denia, with the 81st Regiment of the line, some gunners and other troops, to the amount of from 1,000 to 1,200 men, and two pieces of cannon; two 74-gun ships, a brig of war, and several gun boats and smaller vessels protected the disembarkation without gun-shot to the fort.

'These troops formed behind a ravine, established a battery, and towards morning marched in columns upon Denia, driving in the advanced posts, who slowly retired, disputing the ground. The Chief of the Artillery Battalion, Bonafoux, Superior Commandant of Denia, had from break of day discovered the enemy and made with his garrison dispositions of defence, composed of the 117th Regiment. The English General summoned [Denia]. The Commandant Bonafoux coolly replied that he awaited the effect of his threats.

'At the same time, with his handful of brave men, he resolved to march upon the enemy, profiting by the arrival of the Captain of the 117th Voltigeurs, Faubert, who on the report of the fire ran with his company; he marched it on the left of the enemy to turn it, and with the remainder attacked them in front. This double movement made the enemy recede, who precipitately embarked their cannon, and approached the shore, ordering their boats to approach the land. We pursued them with so much vigour that [we] overthrew them [so]that they left 4 killed and 18 wounded upon the heights of St. Nicholas, and ran in crowds into the water in order to escape more quickly under the protection of the fire of their vessels and of the Grenadiers of the 81st, who formed upon the beach in order to arrest us; but the French precipitated themselves upon them with so much vigour that they overthrew them, and caused them a considerable loss before they could re-embark. The enemy had in all 30 killed and nearly 80 wounded. On our side, we had one killed and 15 wounded.'

Rearguard Action of Villamuriel, 25th October 1812

We now return to the situation around Burgos, where on 21st October Wellington had ordered a withdrawal. There was an almost clean break as the forward divisions marched off that night in two columns, leaving their campfires burning. The 5th Division, leading the northern column, retired from Hurones through Villatoro, on the north side of Burgos, and moved on Tardajos, from where, on the 22nd, they marched along what is now the pilgrims' *Camino de Santiago* to Hornillas. The 30th reported two casualties on the 21st, one dead and one missing, and a further two missing on the following day. On the 23rd, they made a gruelling 26-mile march to Cordovilla on the River Pisuerga, shedding another two men en route. The southern column had meanwhile

---

[538] George Pearson and David Fair had both been wounded with the 2nd/81st at the battle of Corunna, 1809, and together with Alexander Gordon and James Imlach, had also served with that Battalion in the Walcheren campaign.

reached Torquemada, where thousands of exhausted soldiers succumbed to temptation and broke into the wine-vaults. The scenes of drunkenness and disorder that followed were apparently not replicated at nearby Cordovilla, for the 30th left not a man behind there.

Lieutenant Nevill, now just able to mount his horse, had meanwhile left Burgos on the 16th, painfully making his own way back to Salamanca and Portugal:

'My baggage, not much, was carried on a mule, with a piece of boiled pork, some biscuit, and a bottle of sour wine; this was all I and my servant had to subsist on for many a weary day. By the time I reached Valladolid, I was quite done up, and with my poor servant, horse, and mule, nearly starved. Three days of complete rest somewhat restored me, and having laid in a supply of grain for my horse and mule, and of bread, eggs, and chocolate for myself and servant, proceeded on my way, as the English army in miserable plight, pursued by the French, were approaching.'[539]

On the 24th the 30th Regiment moved on through the town of Palencia on the River Carrion, behind which, and on the Pisuerga to the south, Wellington intended to check the French advance for some days. Due to poor staff-work, the 5th Division marched for two leagues beyond its intended position, and had to retrace its steps, reaching its bivouac area after dark and without rations.

The Anglo-Portuguese line then extended from Duenas on the right to Villamuriel de Cerrata, where the 5th Division was posted, with two Spanish divisions, both from Galicia, on its northern flank, of which one occupied Palencia. Engineers set to work, preparing the bridges along the Carrion river-line for demolition, including those at Villamuriel and Palencia, and one over the Pisuerga at Tariego.

The Carrion, swollen by rain, was a reasonably effective obstacle, albeit with some fords. The village of Villamuriel, four miles south of Palencia, lies on the west bank of the river, which is crossed there by a stone bridge. This had been mined and was ready for demolition. Behind the village, the dry bed of the Canal of Castille, running parallel to the river, offered concealment and protection, and the ground then rose, gently at first and then more steeply, to a dominating plateau some half a mile to the west.

Whilst the general outline of the subsequent action at Villamuriel is clear enough, there can be few actions in the Peninsula about which so little detail is known, including the initial deployment of the 5th Division on the foggy early morning of 25th October. The 9th Foot, of Barnes' brigade, provided the bridge guard and, together with the 38th and the 8th Cacadores, extended along the riverbank. The 2nd/4th were formed in column, in the village close behind the bridge, with the 1st/4th in support, ready to counter-attack if the mine should fail.[540] Other troops, including at least part of the Portuguese of Spry's brigade, formed a second line in the dry canal bed.

We do not know the position of the 30th, but it is probable that, with the remainder of Pringle's brigade, they too were in the canal bed, in which case they were most likely to have stood on the left of the brigade, with the 44th to their right and Losada's Galicians to their left. It is also possible, but unproven, that part of the 30th, perhaps the Light Company, was forward on the river-line[541], while a few men were with a divisional working party on the bridge at Tariego. At least one battery of British artillery, Lawson's, was posted on the rising ground behind the 5th Division.

The 5th Division had been deployed by Major-General Pringle, but before the French attack developed, Major-General Oswald arrived and assumed command. He described the position that morning as follows:

'Major-General Pringle had already posted the troops, and the greater part of the division were admirably disposed of about the village, as also in the dry bed of a canal running in its rear, and in some places parallel to the Carion. Certain of the corps were formed in column of attack, supported by reserves, ready to fall upon the enemy if, in consequence of the mine failing, he should venture to push a column along the narrow bridge. The river had at some points been reported fordable, but these were said to be at all times difficult and in the then rise of water, as they proved, hardly practicable.'

[539] Nevill, p.p. 25-6.

[540] It appears that the village was held by elements of all three brigades of the 5th Division, but Lieutenant Ellers Hopkins of the 4th Regiment stated that 'Villa Muriel was occupied by the brigadier Pringle with a *small* detachment of infantry, but at the time we considered that it required a larger force, as its maintenance appeared of the utmost importance to the army.'

[541] It is difficult to account otherwise for the nine wounded men of the 30th, and one unwounded, who were taken prisoner in Villamuriel when the French crossed the Carrion.

At about 8 or 9 a.m. Maucune's division advanced against the bridge at Villamuriel. 'As the enemy closed towards the bridge,' wrote General Oswald, 'he opened a heavy fire of artillery upon the village. At that moment, Lord Wellington entered it and passed the formed columns well sheltered both from fire and observation. His Lordship approved of the manner the post was occupied and of the advantage taken of the canal and village to mask the troops.'

The French brought eighteen guns into action, neutralising the British artillery on the high ground and engaging the troops in the canal, inflicting some loss. Then, in Oswald's words, 'The French, supported by a heavy and superior fire, rushed gallantly on the bridge, the mine not exploding and destroying the arch till the leading section had almost reached the spot. Shortly afterwards, the main body retired, leaving apparently only a few light troops.' For the next four hours or so, these *voltigeurs* engaged in a 'sharp skirmish' with the Allied troops across the river.

The 3rd Royals, of Barnes' brigade, had been detached to Palencia to stiffen the Galician Division there, which had been tasked to defend the most important of the Carrion bridges, and it was here that Wellington's plan unravelled. Immediately before the repulse of the enemy in front of Villamuriel, an orderly officer arrived to inform Wellington that the Spaniards and the Royals had been tumbled rapidly out of Palencia, where the bridges had been captured intact by General Foy before they could be blown. The routed Galicians had fallen back towards the heights above Villamuriel, pursued by French cavalry and covered by Ponsonby's dragoons.

Wellington reacted swiftly to this sudden setback: 'This rendered it necessary to change our front, and I directed Major-General Oswald to throw back our left, and the Spanish troops upon the heights, and to maintain the Carrion with the right of the 5th Division.' It appears that the majority of the British brigades of Barnes and Pringle were immediately pulled out of Villamuriel and ordered to ascend the heights to their rear, and then moved north along the plateau to check any French advance from Palencia, leaving Spry's Portuguese brigade and a detachment of the 9th to hold the river-line, supported on the slopes behind by Losada's Spaniards. This manoeuvre stabilised the Allied left flank and enabled Cabrera's Galicians to re-form. Indeed, Foy made surprisingly little immediate effort to exploit his success at Palencia.

However, Wellington's prompt redeployment was resented by at least some of the 5th Division who, ignorant of his Lordship's intention, blamed their newly-arrived divisional commander, Oswald, for the order to disengage from the river-line, apparently imagining it to be the start of a withdrawal.

Wellington had no sooner redeployed the greater part of the 5th Division from the Villamuriel river-line when French cavalry crossed the Carrion by a ford, pushing back its Portuguese defenders and rolling up a surprised company of the 9th Regiment on the riverbank. The French moved quickly to reinforce this bridgehead, first with eight companies of *voltigeurs*, then passing more infantry across a second ford and on ladders over the demolished bridge arch. Spry's Portuguese were forced out of the village and the dry canal, which the French occupied in force, skirmishing with the Spaniards whose position on the heights was now directly above Villamuriel.

Another French success came further south, where their cavalry seized by *coup de main* the partially-destroyed Pisuerga bridge between Baños and Tariego, capturing some forty of the 5th Division working party, drawn from the 4th, 30th and 44th.

Normally imperturbable in action, on this occasion even Wellington showed the pressure of command: 'I do not think I ever saw Lord Wellington so visibly annoyed at anything,' wrote Captain Stanhope of the staff, 'fatigue and anxiety had moreover told considerably and he looked very haggard.'

The main concern at this point remained Foy's success at Palencia. According to Oswald, 'No serious attack from [Villamuriel] was to be apprehended until an advance from Palencia. It was on that point, therefore, that attention was fixed. Day was closing when Lord Wellington came upon the heights and said that all was quiet at Palencia, and that the enemy must now be driven from the right bank.'

The 5th Division had not proceeded far towards Palencia when, according to Oswald, 'an order came directing it to retire and form on the right of the Spaniards, and when collected to remain on the heights till further orders.'

With both flanks turned, an Allied withdrawal from the river-line had now become imperative, but first Wellington had to buy time for his army to disengage and march south by throwing back the enemy incursion at

Villamuriel. The 5th Division was then to occupy the village in force and hold it until ordered to withdraw, which Oswald was told would probably be very early the next morning.

Wellington expected Maucune to make a further advance from Villamuriel, and intended to charge him with the whole of the 5th Division as he breasted the slopes to the west of the canal, but the French general, understandably wary after his Salamanca experience, was content to hold his bridgehead. An hour-long stalemate followed, broken when Wellington, having made a personal reconnaissance, ordered a counter-attack to drive Maucune's division back across the Carrion.[542] Lieutenant Ellers Hopkins of the 4th Regiment witnessed what followed:

'Lord Wellington immediately ordered some artillery to be opened on the enemy. I happened to be close to the head-quarter staff, and heard Lord Wellington say to an aide-de-camp, "Tell Oswald I want him." On Sir John Oswald arriving he said, "Oswald, you will get the division under arms and drive the enemy from the village and retain possession of it." He replied, "My Lord, if the village should be taken I do not consider it as tenable." Wellington then said, "It is my orders, General." Oswald replied, "My Lord, as it is your orders, they shall be obeyed." Wellington then gave orders to him "that he should take the second brigade [Pringle's] of the division and attack in line, that the first brigade [Barnes'] should in column first descend the heights on the right of the second, enter the canal and assist in clearing it of the enemy," and saying 'I will tell you what I will do, Oswald. I will give you the Spaniards and Alava into the bargain, headed by a company of the 9th Regiment, upon your left."'

Accordingly, at about 4 p.m. a brigade of Losada's Spaniards was sent against Maucune's right wing. They advanced shouting *Vamos adelante, carajo, carajo, carajo!*, but their courage soon evaporated, and they fled in confusion. Alava, Wellington's Spanish liaison officer, was severely wounded in an attempt to rally them.[543]

Oswald launched his two British brigades, with two battalions each leading[544], against the canal and village. According to his account, Wellington 'directed the first brigade to attack the enemy's left flank; the second to advance in support, extending to the left to succour the Spaniards who were unsuccessfully contending with the enemy in their front. The rapid advance of the first brigade cut off the enemy from the bridge and forced them into the river, where many were drowned. The casualties were not heavy considering the fire to which our men were exposed. The enemy suffered more severely.'

During the attack, Hopkins recorded, 'Lord Wellington sent the Prince of Orange under a heavy fire for the purpose of preventing the troops exposing themselves at the canal,' while Douglas of the Royals, who was clearly aware of Wellington's intent, was critical of his brigade's advance from the canal to the river-bank.[545]

Desultory musketry and cannon-fire continued well after night, but Maucune made no further attempt to cross the river. It had been a long, hard day's fight, and the men's ammunition pouches had to be replenished more than once.

We have no first-hand account of the part played by the 30th in this rearguard action, but in 1839, Alexander Hamilton's obituarist summarised the Colonel's part at Villamuriel in the following words:

'An important and dashing affair was performed by the companies of the 30th and 44th Regiments, under the command of [Lieutenant-Colonel] Hamilton, which has hitherto been unnoticed in the services of the corps:

---

[542] Wellington's own account in his dispatch is characteristically laconic: 'I made Major-General Pringle and Brig.-General Barnes attack these troops, under the orders of Major-General Oswald, in which attack the Spanish troops co-operated, and they were driven across the river with considerable loss. The fire upon the left had been very severe throughout the day, from which we suffered a good deal.'
[543] Wellington's adverse comment on the Spanish performance at Villamuriel further confirmed his reservations about their effectiveness: 'I was sorry to observe,' he wrote, 'that in the affair of the 25th October, although the Spanish soldiers showed no want of spirit or of disposition to engage the enemy, they were totally unable to move with the regularity and order of a disciplined body – by which alone success can be hoped for in any contest with the French.' This strongly suggests that, despite Alava's best efforts and the example of Pringle's brigade, the Spaniards failed to make much headway and the main burden of the counter-attack fell on the two British brigades.
[544] The Royals and 38th led the attack of Barnes's brigade, while the 30th and 44th led Pringle's attack.
[545] 'Our first fire and advancing with the bayonet cleared the canal and here, if Wellington's orders had been obeyed, our loss would have been trifling as we were to halt and keep possession of it, and then it would have been impossible for those dispossessed of their lodgings to have escaped… But, instead of occupying this post, we were ordered to follow the fugitives to the river's brink, exposed to a front and flanking fire of round and grape shot with occasional shells.'

while in the Peninsula, on the 25th of October, 1812, they advanced in line against seventeen pieces of cannon, and carried the adjacent village, taking more prisoners than their own force was composed of: by some unaccountable accident this was not mentioned in the despatches.'

The successful outcome of this advance is supported by a statement in a biographical note on Major John Guthrie[546], who succeeded in this affair to the command of the 2nd/44th, that the 30th and 44th 'drove the enemy from the village, and forced him to re-cross the fords and bridge.'

Although no battle honour or medal bar was granted for the action at Villamuriel, the 2nd/30th counted it as one of their finest achievements. Their casualties, over one in five of some 230 all ranks present, indicate a hard-fought engagement. Seven out of seventeen combatant officers were wounded[547], Volunteer John Hughes was reported as missing, and two sergeants and two privates were killed[548], while 25 other ranks were carried off the field wounded, of whom Private Tanzy is known to have died. A further nine wounded men were taken by the French during their temporary occupation of Villamuriel, together with one unwounded prisoner. Seven of the 30th were among forty of the working party at the Tariego bridge, taken prisoner when the demolition charge there failed to fully demolish the arch and French cavalry were able to charge across.

The passage of the river at Palencia ruined Wellington's plan for defending the line of the Carrion; but having stabilised the situation around Villamuriel, he deftly wrong-footed his adversary by withdrawing that night, covered by the 5th Division, and re-crossing the Pisuerga at Cabezan to take up a new and stronger position on the left bank. The 5th Division followed in the early hours the 24th and, after an unmolested march of fifteen miles to the Cabezan bridge, took up its place on the right wing.

On 27th October, still standing on the line of the Pisuerga and the Duero, Wellington sent a dispatch to Hill ordering him to withdraw forthwith so as to combine both wings of the army:

'The enemy are infinitely superior to us in cavalry, and from what I saw today, very superior in infantry. We must retire, therefore, and the Duero is no barrier for us. If we go, and we cannot hold our ground beyond the Duero, your situation will become delicate. We certainly cannot stand against the numbers at present opposed to us in any situation, and it appears to me, therefore, to be necessary that you, as well as we, should retire.'

Rearguard Action of Puente Larga, 30th October 1812

The 4th Division had remained at the Escorial until October 6th, when they marched south, bypassing Madrid by way of Las Rozas and Mostoles, to reach Valdemoro and Pinto in La Mancha on the 8th. There they came under the command of Sir Rowland Hill, who was preparing to defend the southern approaches to Madrid against the combined armies of Marshal Soult and King Joseph, amounting to over 60,000 men and 84 guns.

It appears that the 40th and the 82nd were both initially quartered in the large village of Pinto amidst a country rich with fruit and wine.

'Although still destitute of money,' recalled George Wood of the 82nd, 'yet in this abundant country we managed to procure many comforts besides our rations. As for the fruit, the inhabitants had no objection to our eating what we chose, frequently giving us wine and other presents. But as it often happened that where we found ourselves the most comfortable we remained the shortest time, so it proved here; for [on 20th October] we had to continue our advance till we came to the pretty village of Ciempucellas [Cempozuelos], situated on a river, on the opposite side of which was the fine town of Aranjuez, where the enemy were in great force.'[549]

Charles Boutflower, promoted to Staff Surgeon, had applied for appointment to the 4th Division, and meanwhile visited his old friends at Cempozuelos, close to the banks of the Tagus:

---

[546] *The Royal Military Calendar*, 1820, Volume V, p. 357.

[547] Captain John Hitchen, Lieutenants Matthias Andrews, John Rumley, and George William Augustus Brisac, and Ensigns Henry Beere, George Madden and Francis Tincombe were wounded. Rumley was seriously wounded, the others slightly.

[548] Sergeants James Keith of Paisley and John Nightingale of London, and Privates Patrick Shearin of Longford and Morgan Blakeney of Athy were killed in action.

[549] Wood, p. 144.

'On the 23rd I bade adieu to the 40th Regiment after having been with them nearly eleven years. They are unquestionably one of the finest Regiments in the Army, and will always have my warmest wishes for their welfare.'[550]

Skerrett's brigade from Cadiz, including the 2nd/47th, marched into Aranjuez from Toledo on 26th October and were attached to Cole's 4th Division. Hill now had 36,000 men, of whom about 8,000 were Spaniards. Heavily outnumbered by Soult, he appreciated that it would be difficult to defend the line of the Tagus on account of the number of fordable crossings, and decided to pull his divisions back a short distance to a new line from Anõver to Alcala de Henares. Lieutenant George Wood of the 82nd was preparing defences on the Tagus bridge at Aranjuez when Hill ordered its destruction:

'I was sent with a party of men to the river that divided us, to throw up breast-works at the bridge, in order to obstruct the enemy should they attempt to cross; but, after being at work the whole day, I had the mortification of seeing all our labour blown into the air, according to orders received for that purpose, the more effectually to prevent their crossing.'[551]

On the 28th Skerrett's brigade evacuated Aranjuez and fell back two miles to Puente Larga, where the plane-lined road to Madrid crossed the River Jarama. Hill was fully intending to fight on his new chosen ground when, on the morning of the 29th, he received a dispatch from Wellington ordering him to retire without delay, abandoning Madrid. Sir Rowland's response was to set most of his army in motion at dawn on the 30th, except for Skerrett's brigade, which was ordered to stand fast as rearguard at Puente Larga, and to hold the bridge there at all costs for some 24 hours to give the main body time to retire. The 4th Division, defending the Tagus river line in front of Anõver, had the longest march of all, having to make a lateral march behind Skerrett's force to reach the highway to Madrid; accordingly, they were the first to move on the night of the 29th. George Wood was holding one of the Tagus fords until the 82nd joined the retirement:

'The night that preceded this movement I was on piquet, with about seventy men, having strict orders to guard a ford by which the enemy cavalry were expected every moment to cross, and to make every resistance in my power, but on no account to give way; and that, as soon as they heard me engaged, I should receive support. This of course kept me on the alert the whole night, expecting every moment to see their dragoons plunge into the river to ford it, as they were in great numbers on the other side, and ready accoutred: fortunately for me they did not attempt it, although they kept up a great noise and bustle the whole night, which was merely a *ruse de guerre*, as they crossed a few miles higher up.'

'We moved off our ground about mid-day; and about five in the evening it began to rain, which seemed to increase as we moved through the dark and dismal night. As the day began to dawn, the weather became clearer; and we now made greater progress, halting only a few minutes at a time, when necessity compelled us; and late in the evening lay down on some ploughed land by the road-side, after a march of about ten leagues across a fine country; but the finest country is, from the depth of the soil, in general, the most difficult to get over in bad weather. Such was the case here. On the swampy bed, after eating a melon, the only thing I had left, I was so overcome with fatigue and hard marching that I fell fast asleep; and in all probability I should have remained there till this time had I not been roused by the men.'[552]

The 4th Division reached the main road to Madrid at Valdemoro before dawn, very fatigued. Unfortunately, the soldiers discovered the wine cellars for which the region was famous, and when the Division marched on at noon, they left some hundreds of stupefied drunkards behind, notably from the 82nd, as hinted at by George Wood:

'It was with the greatest difficulty, and even severity, that we could restrain [the troops] from taking too much of the strong wine, which was now let flow into the vaults, to prevent it from falling into the hands of the French.'[553]

The 47th, meanwhile, prepared for action at Puente Larga. The broad river Jarama was spanned there by a 25-arch stone bridge,[554] dominated on the southern side by rising ground. On the northern side, a causeway ran

---

[550] Boutflower, p. 162.
[551] Wood, p. 144.
[552] Ibid., p.p. 145-46.
[553] Wood., p. 147.
[554] The Puente Larga, completed in 1761, still stands.

away across flat ground. The bridge was mined, but an attempt to blow a centre arch failed on the morning of the 30th; one parapet and part of the roadway remaining intact. There was insufficient time to complete the demolition, so an abattis and breastwork were erected at the northern end of the bridge, where it met the causeway on a terrace with stone seats and balustrades. The demolition work was initially covered by the 3rd Guards, but on the 29th they were relieved as rearguard by the 47th and 87th.

Marshal Soult had occupied Aranjuez in strength on the 29th and repaired the River Tagus bridge there, while his cavalry explored the Jarama river line for practicable fords, but he made no attempt to take the Puente Larga until the 30th. He then ordered Raymond's division to force the partially-demolished bridge. Charles Broke Vere summarised the action which followed:'

'Colonel Skerret with the [47th] and 87th Regiments kept the bridge against a brisk attack of a brigade of French infantry, supported by the fire of six guns from the heights above the bridge. The bridge being at the end of a long causeway, the guns of the rear guard could not give any effective support to the troops disputing the passage of the bridge. At the close of the day, General Cole ordered Colonel Skerret to draw off the troops from the bridge; and the column moved towards Madrid, covered by the cavalry.'[555]

We can add some detail to this bare account. The misty dawn of October 30th 1812 was followed at 9 a.m. by rain, which persisted all day. Soult's cavalry could not discern the strength of opposition across the river, and whether it was a light covering force or a determined defence. The bridge was, in fact, strongly held. The breastwork at the north end of the bridge was defended by a party of the 47th (most probably a wing) and two companies of the 2nd/95th Rifles, while their supports, the rest of the 47th and the 87th, were drawn up in close column in the shelter of the near end of the causeway. Three Portuguese 9-pounder guns were sited to the right of the bridge. Half a mile to the rear, at the north end of the causeway, was Skerrett's reserve, the 3rd/1st Guards and 20th Portuguese, with another three guns. In addition to Lowry Cole, Sir Rowland Hill was present.

The action began with a protracted firefight across the river. A French battery on the rising ground shelled the breastwork and the Portuguese guns, while the *voltigeur* companies of the 12th Légère lined the river bank and engaged Skerrett's men in a long-range duel. After some hours, the Portuguese guns fell silent for lack of ammunition, and Soult seized what appeared to be a favourable opportunity to assault the bridge with a column of the 12th Légère. The head of the column was beaten back by British musketry before reaching the broken arch and retired in disorder. A second infantry assault was attempted a few minutes later, and may briefly have taken the breastwork, but the 47th counter-attacked 'strongly and furiously' to recapture the barricade. It appears that Soult then brought up twelve more guns and shelled the defenders out of their breastwork, but his attempts to exploit this withdrawal with cavalry charges failed. At this, Soult called off the attack and withdrew both troops and guns, leaving Skerrett in possession of the bridge.

A little later, a French officer appeared with a flag of truce and was given leave to remove the many wounded lying at the south end of the bridge. Each side then remained watching the other until it was dark, when Skerrett quietly withdrew. Dummy sentries were left in the British position, and it was not until dawn the following day that they were seen to be greatcoats stuffed with straw. The brigade, therefore, made a clean break and made an undisturbed march through the night to Madrid.

Private Adam Reed of the Light Company 47th left an account of this action from his own slightly different perspective, albeit with the same outcome:

'After we heard where the French was, there was sent out strong advance picquets, which consisted of both foot and horse. Early one morning, I asked the major of the picquet to give me liberty to fall to the rear as my comrade had got one something to eat. He said that I might, as he did not see any danger at present. I had not got many paces before a gun was fired and the officer called out for that man to whom he gave liberty. I answered "I am here, sir," and he ordered the picquet to stand to their arms, for the enemy was advancing. At that moment the advanced picquet was engaged and retiring, and we was ordered to advance. We were soon obliged to retire as the enemy was many more in number.

'At the bridge we was joined by the other parts of the 47th and 87th Foot and by 2 companies of Rifles which in all consisted of about 1,500. The French still kept advancing (being about 16,000) till they came in front

555 Broke Vere, p. 41.

of the bridge, and there they formed up for action… [Sir Lowry Cole] came down to us about 10 o'clock in the morning, and we asked him to send some troops down to our assistance, for we found ourselves growing weak for want of some refreshment. We was told that relief should be sent down in the middle of the day, but no relief came when the appointed time arrived. During that time the enemy had gained possession of the bridge, and with a handful of men we again charged them and retook it.

'Sir Lowry then came down again about 2 in the afternoon and he was told that no relief came at the time promised. He said, "Now my lads, you began the day, you will have to go through with it, for I should lose more men in bringing them down tha[n] you will the whole of the day, the enemy having a great many guns." We then kept on till the dusk of the evening, and then left a horse picquet to keep the bridge. They soon found out, however, that we was gone. The horse picquet retired and left the bridge about an hour afterwards. When we arrived at the top of the hill where Sir Lowry Cole's division lay, we took the front and they took the rear, so that if the French advanced during the night they would be the first for action, but they did not.'

Whatever the detail of this successful rearguard action, the 47th were complimented by Sir Rowland Hill, who was present, who remarked in his dispatch to Wellington on the 'handsome manner' in which the Regiment repulsed the vigorous French attempts on the bridge, while a French witness recorded his admiration of the steadiness of the defence.

Allied losses at Puente Larga totalled three officers and sixty men killed and wounded, of whom all three officers and thirty-five to forty men belonged to the 47th, who bore the brunt of the action. Regimental casualties included Ensign Andrew Lindsay killed, and Lieutenant Edward Vaughan and Ensign Robert George Mountain wounded. French casualties are, as usual, more difficult to determine, but appear to have been five officers and around one hundred men.

Retreat to Salamanca

The southern wing of Wellington's army was now in full and precipitate retreat, as recalled by George Wood of the 82nd: 'At last we reached the stately avenues leading to the capital, which now looked gloomy enough, where we halted, and the troops got as much biscuit as they could carry, with other provisions, and an allowance of rum. The rest of the stores were destroyed, and the remaining casks of wine and spirits stove in and let run into the street in the greatest profusion to prevent it becoming a booty to the enemy, who were close at our heels. We remained here barely sufficient time to receive our rations, and then continued our retrograde movements.'[556]

Adam Reed was not far behind with the 47th: 'After the battle, which was in October 1812, we had to march to Madrid, the capital of Spain, which was about 6 leagues, in the night. After we had fought that battle we had nothing to eat until we entered Madrid. There was then 6 men out of each company sent to fetch food, and they got 2 pounds of biscuit for each man. My brother, being one of the 6 he had gotten more than his allowance and had it tied up in a blanket and had got his head through where the blanket was tied, and he found that it was almost too heavy for him. He then rested it upon a brick wall. It being narrower than the blanket and biscuits, [his load] got on the other side. He would have been hanged had not a Spanish woman been present and lifted the burden over from the other side and relieved him. When he came to me and told me what a dangerous peril he had been in I told him to beware of putting his head in a blanket for the future. We rested in Madrid that day and night and the next morning went on our march to Salamanca.'

It was at Las Rozas, near Madrid, that Captain John Harley of the 47th, with two other officers, unexpectedly fell in with a French cavalry reconnaissance party and all three were made prisoners. Soult had recently entered that capital, and as the British prisoners were escorted to the city, strongly guarded, they met the Marshal, accompanied by his entire staff and the main body of his army, passing over the great plain near Madrid. Harley recalled the grand display with pensive wonder:

'I never beheld a more magnificent sight. It consisted of 14,000 cavalry, well mounted and clothed, with 44,000 infantry, all in the highest spirits and order, and about seventy pieces of cannon. It was then the 4th of November, and the morning was extremely fine; and, as we were approaching Madrid, they passed us on the

---

[556] Wood, p. 147.

beautiful and level plain, as if they were marching in review upon some favourite gala day. At any other time, or upon any other occasion, I must have enjoyed the grand and imposing spectacle which their splendid appearance presented to the eye; but when I recollected that they were about to engage in hostile combat with our army, composed of my own countrymen, and in which I had a son and two nephews, I felt a sudden pang that made my spirits sink within me. It was not that I doubted that the issue of the contest would be favourable to our side, if the numbers were nearly equal, but feelings, in which a soldier can seldom indulge, possessed me for the moment, on seeing Marshal Soult's fine army going out to battle; and I involuntarily shuddered, when I reflected on the thousands who were doomed to fall so soon on the field of blood – who were now buoyant with life and hope, anxious to take part in the dreadful struggle, and yet utterly unconscious of the awful fate that awaited them.'[557]

As the prisoners entered the city they were, according to Harley, respectfully saluted by King Joseph and his suite. Less respectfully, they were soon locked up.

'We had neither bed nor bedclothes, nothing in fact, but a small bench upon which we could scarcely sit. We continued in this state until about six o'clock in the evening, when a female came to the door and demanded admittance. The little turnkey, instantly obeying her, opened the door, and ushered her in. The moment she saw us huddled up in one corner of the room, she exclaimed, in Spanish, "Poor English! I pity you!" and then adding, "Have patience for a little, and I will return." She left us, and returned in less than half an hour, accompanied by three other women, two of whom brought us mattresses, blankets, and pillows; and the third, a comfortable supper of soup, rice, and boiled mutton, with one pint of wine for each; and also a supply of chocolate and bread for our breakfast the next morning, telling us, on taking her departure, that she would visit us again the next day. On inquiring of the turnkey, after she had gone, we learned that this excellent creature whom we justly named our guardian angel, was the *Madrio Prisonero*, that is, the mother of prisoners, and a Sister of Charity, from a neighbouring convent.

'The following day, however, we were more cheerful and reconciled to our fate – our worthy friend again visited us; and, while she was making preparations for our dinner, what was my astonishment, when, in the person of another prisoner, who was put into our small room with us, I recognised a Lieutenant Colonel of the Spanish army, a young man about twenty-seven years of age, with whom I had been for some time living, near Cadiz, on the most intimate terms, each of us having conceived a more than common regard for the other. His filial affection having induced him to risk everything, he came to Madrid in disguise to see his family, and had scarcely entered it when he was unfortunately captured. He had not been more than one hour with us, when a lovely and interesting young lady, his sister, called on him, to whom he introduced me as an old friend and companion of his in Spain. On hearing this, the poor creature paid me nearly as much attention as her brother, making room for me to sit near her at dinner, helping me equally with him, and promising that we should want for nothing. As the Sister of Charity abated nothing in her attentions, notwithstanding the assistance we had from our new friend and ally, we had a profusion of everything we could require.'

Having been a week in close confinement, a French officer called on them and informed them, 'in the most gentlemanly manner,' that they were to prepare, with all the other prisoners in Madrid, to march. After about half-an-hour's delay, on descending from the place of confinement, 'We met our friend the Sister of Charity at the foot of the staircase, who, seeing the attention of the two French grenadiers, who were with us, withdrawn for a moment, seized the favourable opportunity, and, pulling me suddenly by the arm, shoved me into a small dark apartment, but faintly lighted by a loop-hole facing the street, where I concealed myself without detection, as the new guard knew neither the persons nor the number of their prisoners at the time. And, what is really singular, she succeeded in securing the escape of my servant, Pat Dolan, also, whom she contrived to secrete in the neighbourhood of the convent until we were both enabled to venture out, when the remainder of the French had evacuated the city.

'I remained in concealment during the day, keeping, according to her directions, from the light which the narrow casement but very partially admitted, that there might be no possibility of my being seen. She informed me that I might consider myself safe, as the governor and turnkey were her friends, whom she had persuaded to favour my escape, seeing the miserable state of my mind, and hearing that I had a family. At nine o'clock, she

[557] Harley, p.p. 187-88.

brought me refreshment, and during the night my ears were assailed by the noise of cannon and military stores, passing by the prison on their way to join the French army. She appeared again in the morning, brought me breakfast, and cheerfully told me that she hoped she would set me at liberty in the evening, as the French were evacuating Madrid.[558] "I must be well satisfied," said she, "that they are all really gone before I can allow you to appear in the streets during the day." She then visited every public place, and, amongst others, the *naverios*, or coffee-houses, to ascertain if any of the French army yet remained in the city; and, on her being fully satisfied that they were all gone, she returned to me at four o'clock, accompanied by two Spanish gentlemen, whom I understood to be merchants. The head turnkey immediately opened the door, the governor took off his hat and shook hands with me, the little turnkey himself bowed most graciously, and I was quickly released from confinement, and ushered into the street with this truly worthy person and her friends.'[559]

After several more narrow escapes, Captain Harley rejoined the British army and the 47th Regiment.[560] He was perhaps fortunate to have enjoyed the resourceful services of his servant, Pat Dolan, an inveterate forager who had a pragmatic approach to living off the land:

'One day, on my remonstrating with Pat, and telling him, if Lord Wellington knew how he obtained the fowls, pigs, &c., I feared he would punish him severely; his reply was:

"Sir, neither you nor Lord Wellington understand it right; for," said he, "sure *our* king, sir, is fighting for *their* king, and to put Ferdinand back on his throne; and sure, sir, all that can be done is to charge what I take to our king."

"Why Pat," said I, "you seem to think there is an account between the two monarchs, and that your plundering can be settled in that way."

"Certainly, sir," replied Pat; "it is the only plan, in my opinion."[561]

The 40th, 47th and 82nd had meanwhile marched from Madrid to Galapagar, and on 2nd November made their way with the rearguard over the Guadarrama Pass to Villacastin, and on through Fontiveros to reach Alba de Tormes on 7th November. Some regimental wives remained with the battalions, and Harley relates the hardships of one of them at that time:

'An excellent woman, our mess cook, and wife of one of our sergeants, Cowell, followed the regiment from Cadiz, and although repeatedly advised to remain behind, in consequence of the situation she was in, being near her confinement. Notwithstanding every remonstrance, she persevered in going, and joining the regiment, which was then encamped near Madrid, she was, on the night of her arrival, delivered of twins. As the regiment had no tents, this poor creature was obliged to lie under a tree; the soldiers, indeed, like men, taking off their coats to cover her. Two days after the entire army moved; and this poor woman, with her twins, unaccountable as it may appear, traveled with her infants in her arms, or on her back, during the retreat from day to day, under incessant rain and hail. Though she frequently had to pass over two or three rivers in the day, up to her knees in water, the enemy pressing us in the rear, and the shot and shells constantly falling about her, yet she escaped and arrived safe at Ciudad Rodrigo.'[562]

The indomitable Mrs Cowell and her twins returned safely to England, but Sergeant Cowell was one of the many men of the 47th who died next year at the storming of San Sebastian.

The 82nd Regiment, still debilitated from their Walcheren sickness, were already suffering severely. Writing from Cuellar on 4th November, Wellington expressed his continuing unease about the condition of the five recently-joined Walcheren battalions, including the 82nd: 'The truth is, neither officers nor soldiers are accustomed to march. The men are very irregular, and owing to their irregularities not able to bear the labour of marching in the heat of the sun.' By the end of October, 85 men of the 82nd were dead and 363 were in hospital, leaving only 646 in the ranks. George Wood was among those who fell sick during the passage of the Guadarrama:

---

[558] The last of King Joseph's army evacuated Madrid on 8th November 1812.
[559] Harley, p.p. 155-92.
[560] By the time Captain Harley reached Elvas his party included seven British soldiers, wounded at Puente Larga and concealed in Madrid, and eight French deserters.
[561] Harley, p. 198.
[562] Ibid., p. 200.

'I proceeded in the greatest torture till I descended these mountains; when I found myself in such a state from rheumatism that I was obliged to be taken off the horse and carried into a cow-house near the road. Here I lay in great agony; but, by a fortunate circumstance, the surgeon of the regiment coming to this place with some sick men, bathed my feet in spirits, which gave me great relief, and the next morning I found myself much better; but still I could neither walk nor ride on horseback, from the pain I suffered. I was, therefore, put into a spring-waggon, in which I rode for the greatest part of the day… On arriving at a cross-road, where the army turned off and proceeded by a different route, I was taken out of the waggon and again placed on my horse… and was desired to proceed to Arviola [Arevalo], where I was informed there was a depot; but on arriving at that place I did not meet with a single British soldier.'

He soon learned that the French were approaching, and together with another sick officer, he barely escaped from the town as the enemy entered.

'We instantly mounted our horses, and joined the cavalcade that were flying on the road… We were now thrown out of the route of the British army, and pursued by a part of the French; and it was only by the greatest perseverance and diligence that we got out of their reach. Being now out of the main track, many were the difficulties, in addition to preventing ourselves from being taken prisoners, which we had to surmount; but after many days' distressing traveling, and concealing ourselves in the woods by night, existing on what their shades afforded, we reached Salamanca; but in a most filthy and impoverished state, not having taken off our clothes or changed our linen since the retreat commenced.'

'In a few days I joined my regiment, previous to which I had the misfortune to see my servant, Thomas Standfast, lodged in the hospital. He in his turn, had now become ill; for there were few in these campaigns that had not their portion of illness. I heard soon after I left the town that he had ended his earthly career. Poor fellow! A better soldier or more honest man did not exist.'[563]

Notwithstanding such individual privations, and Wellington's later strictures on the discipline of his whole army, Hill's withdrawal from the Tagus was most effectively executed. Leith Hay, who was on his staff, opined that:

'Never was a retreat conducted with less confusion, or more trifling annoyance from a pursuing enemy, than that of the Allies from Madrid to the Tormes. The marches were not of excessive length, nor did the French troops come up with or harass the infantry; the rear-guards of cavalry only were engaged, and that very slightly.'[564]

Having held the lines of the Pisuerga and Duero until 5th November, Wellington decided that the two wings of the Allied army should concentrate at Salamanca. On the morning of the 8th, in a storm of wind and rain, Hill's corps, including the 40th, 47th and 82nd, defiled across the Tormes by the bridge at Alba de Tormes, and encamped around Calvarrasa de Arriba and in the woods to its south opposite Alba. On the same day, Wellington's army from Burgos, with the 30th, arrived on the old San Cristobal position in front of Salamanca.

Back to Portugal

Wellington had resolved to stand on his old battlefield outside Salamanca and invite attack. With 52,000 British and Portuguese, plus 18,000 Spaniards, he was outnumbered by the combined French armies, who numbered at least 95,000 men.

George Wood recalled some of the 82nd Regiment's experiences on the right flank of the army, facing Alba de Tormes, near where on 14th November his battalion encountered a probing reconnaissance by the French cavalry:

'Here we remained in camp several days, when the enemy threatened to cross the river, the bridge [at Alba de Tormes], which was, in consequence, blown up; but that did not prevent them from effecting their purpose. They forded it in spite of us, and made their appearance directly in our front; our brigade being in line, with two field-pieces of German artillery in the centre, which were well directed and did much execution, the first shot

[563] Wood, p.p. 148-152.
[564] Leith Hay, Vol. II, p. 94.

scattered them in all directions, and they drew off their forces from this quarter, taking with them one of the captains of my regiment prisoner, who was a little in advance on reconnaissance.'[565]

Early on the morning of the 15th, the French crossed the Tormes well to the south of Alba, too far indeed from the Allied lines for Wellington to hit them on the move, as he had done on 22nd July. In response, the whole Allied army was drawn up facing south and south-east on the old battlefield, confidently and expectantly inviting attack. The 4th Division were on the extreme left of the line, while the 5th Division, having crossed the river from their San Cristobal position, were in second line further to the right.

'The whole army being now collected,' wrote George Wood, 'took up a new and more advantageous position on the Aripales [Arapiles], a name then rendered famous by the late most glorious victory; it being the very ground on which the battle of Salamanca was fought. The relics of bones and other fragments that still strewed these memorable hills, struck such terror into the French army, by reminding them of a spot so fatal to them, that they dared not attack us in this position, but endeavoured to outflank us.'[566]

The French did not oblige by launching an attack on the Allied position, but instead circled cautiously to the west against Wellington's supply lines. The Allied commander had either to attack the much stronger French army or retire on Ciudad Rodrigo.

At 2 p.m. on the 15th November, Wellington accepted the inevitable and ordered an immediate withdrawal to the west.[567] His disappointed troops, who had been eager for action, turned to their right and moved off in battle array. As they did so, the morning drizzle turned to a torrential and persistent downpour which soaked the dispirited marching columns. Darkness fell before 4 p.m. as they struggled slowly back over muddy country tracks and saturated fields to ford the flooded River Zurgain. They spent a miserable night in cold, wet bivouacs, with meagre rations, in patches of wood on the far side of the Valmusa River, some ten miles from Salamanca. Thwarted of the anticipated battle, the troops were miserable and sullen.

Even before the army withdrew from the Salamanca position, the commissariat arrangements were breaking down, as illustrated by Lieutenant George Wood of the 82nd:

'At the time of our receiving orders to recede from this place, we were dividing the only provisions that had been served out to us for the last two days, which were some starved bullocks; but, from the hurry of the moment, we were obliged to leave the greater part behind us. I saw those men who were fortunate enough to get some tearing the raw flesh from the bones on the march, like so many hungry hounds gnawing carrion… Indeed, had we halted, cooking was out of the question: it would have given the men more fatigue in dressing their meat than the nutriment of it would have afforded them strength; the wood being far too wet for the purpose of lighting fires.[568]

Private Adam Reed of the 47th made a similar point: 'A great many of the troops started out of Salamanca with empty haversacks. We marched on the first day till night, and then no provision, and during the night it began to rain and continued for 3 or 4 successive days.'

The wet weather was an unpredictable misfortune, but the lack of provisions was the result of an extraordinary error by Colonel James Willoughby Gordon, the Quartermaster-General, who sent the army's supply train on a divergent route some twenty miles to the north of the famished troops. The Commissariat claimed to have issued three days' bread at Salamanca, but there is no evidence that any unit received it.

At dawn next day the army marched in three columns on roughly parallel routes, some 2-5 miles apart. The 4th Division, with the 40th, 47th and 82nd, formed the rearguard of Hill's southern column, marching on the 16th to the woods behind the Matilla stream. The 5th Division, including the 30th, was with the central column on the main road to Ciudad Rodrigo. A third, Spanish, column followed the northern route. Again, no provisions were issued, and on the southern route in particular, hungry and exhausted soldiers began to fall out of the ranks. The 30th, in contrast, had only one man missing that day.

---

[565] Wood, p. 152.

[566] Wood, p.p. 153-54.

[567] The 4th Division Weekly State records that on 15th November the 40th numbered 19 officers, 41 sergeants, 16 drummers and 445 rank and file, while the 82nd mustered 29 officers, 36 sergeants, 14 drummers and 568 rank and file. Neither regiment declared any sick present, so they had presumably been evacuated prior to the army's withdrawal.

[568] Wood, p. 154 and 159.

In his history of the war, William Napier records that on the 16th, 'Stragglers were numerous for the soldiers meeting with vast herds of swine quitted their colours by hundreds to shoot them, and such a rolling musketry echoed through the forest it was as though the French were attacking. It was in vain that staff officers endeavoured to stop this disgraceful practice… the hungry soldiers still broke from the columns, the property of whole districts was swept away in a few hours, and the army was in some degree placed at the mercy of the enemy.'[569]

Private Reed of the 47th made no mention of the swine, but was reduced to foraging for acorns: 'The second day's march [16th November] it continued to rain, and that night we halted in a wood, and no provision that day except the acorns, which being sweeter than those in England we boiled. We used to get up trees, cut boughs, and put them upon the ground to lay upon. A few of us together used to lay 3 or 4 blankets on the boughs, and had them that remained to cover us. We had to lay with our firelocks (not loaded) in our arms, and knapsacks on. Then in the morning we had to fold up our blankets and carry them as they were all day.'

Lieutenant George Wood of the 82nd also mentioned the acorns, 'as sweet as chestnuts' when boiled or roasted. 'Besides these,' he recalled, 'the men sometimes got meat from the bullocks and horses that were dead on the road. The soldiers would run out of the ranks, and with their knives and bill-hooks, cut them up with as much dexterity as butchers in Leadenhall market; then, sticking the flesh on the end of their bayonets, they would march on with this chance supply.' Wood also confessed that: 'With respect to the report of numbers of our men having strayed from their battalions, and carried on a kind of plunder by shooting wild pigs, with which these woods are stocked, I am sorry to say it is too correct… Nor can it be wondered at: the men conceived that they might escape punishment for plundering, but they did not think it possible to escape starvation without acting as they did.'[570]

Wellington was increasingly angry at the stragglers and their depredations, and that same day, the 16th, he focused his wrath on Lieutenant Colonel Grant of the 82nd:

'The Commander of the Forces considers the Commanding Officer of any regiment, from which there are men absent on a march, to be responsible; and he now desires the Hon. Lieutenant General Cole will put in arrest the Commanding Officer of the 82nd Regiment for having allowed soldiers to straggle from the ranks of the 82nd Regiment on the marches of yesterday and today.'[571]

On the 17th the central column, with the 30th, was without its protective cavalry screen, the result of another blunder by the Quartermaster-General. In consequence, French cavalry were able to infiltrate gaps between the marching troops, plundering baggage and even capturing Sir Edward Paget, Second-in-Command of the army, as he rode between the 5th and 7th Divisions; but the 30th lost only one man.

The southern column, meanwhile, trudged on to the Huebra, where their camp was cannonaded till dark. The troops were moving across the grain of the country, their path obstructed by numerous flooded water-courses. George Wood of the 82nd wrote:

'The rainy season had now completely set in, and our retreat at this time was almost as incessant as the rain… To increase the misery of our situation, this wet and gloomy weather was rendered still more insufferable by the tempestuous gusts of wind, which now prevailed like the equinoctial gales in this country, but with greater force; and meeting us in the avenues and defiles through which we passed, drove the rain in our faces with such violence that many were blown down, and others could scarcely make head against it: and during the short rest we got, in the darkness of the night, we had no other shelter but the thick forest, nor any covering but the cloudy sky, as we frequently did not see our baggage for days together… Our route was on no high road; but through woods, deserts, heaths, mountains and flats, covered with sheets of water, like the meadows of our own country when over-flown by the rivers… Several of the poor men at length became so exhausted that they stuck in the mud, and had not strength to extricate themselves; we were therefore obliged to leave them to their fate.'

'The moment we attempted to bivouac, that moment they commenced cannonading us; and under this destructive fire, without covering or food, having everything to apprehend, have we sat shivering on the cold ground the whole night, praying for daylight to see our way forward.

[569] Napier, Book XIX, Chapter V, p. 120.
[570] Wood, p.p. 161-62 and 177-78.
[571] General Order dated 16th November 1812.

Rising one morning from one of these swampy resting-places, our regiment was ordered to fall in and form square, when the General of Division made his appearance, and severely reprimanded us for the loss of so many men, whom we were obliged to leave on the road to the mercy of the enemy.'[572]

'The third day's march [17th November] it still continued to be wet,' recalled Private Adam Reed of the 47th, 'and during that day we heard that the enemy was following us, which in the course of the day we found out to be true, for they appeared in sight. The men, being weak for want of food and exhausted through hard marching, told the General that they would rather fight and die than to march without provision for so long a time. They begged of him to form up for action, for they would rather die than live to be harassed in that way. His reply was, "I know, my brave men, that you are exhausted with hunger and hardship, and I deeply feel for you, but I cannot afford you any relief." That afternoon we formed up for action, the French pursuing us very close, and when we formed they halted and would not engage us. The Duke then said we must retire again, and [as] we did so the enemy advanced. The evening came and it still remained raining, and no provision came that day. We had to do as we did the night before. That was to cut boughs to sleep upon and partake of more acorns.'

The 47th had over thirty men taken prisoner on the 17th. Private Oliver Jackson, a weaver from Oldham who had enlisted in 1809 on his 14th birthday, was one of those who fell out from the ranks that day. In 1831 he petitioned for an increase to his meagre pension, which took no account of service before the age of eighteen. His 'memorial' tells the story that, after service in Gibraltar, Cadiz and Tarifa, and at Puente Larga, 'On the morning of the 17th of November 1812 I unfortunately fell into the hands of the enemy, but as fortunately made my escape by myself, while marching through an unknown country without seeing a British officer or any resident I could apply to with safety for either support or instructions, travelling not less than 40 miles per day, passing St Indara [Santander] and onwards to Corunna, and from there procured a passage to Lisbon and finally rejoined my Regiment at Lourago [Lamego] on the 14th May 1813, having experienced and encountering in the space of six months hardships, dangers and difficulties seldom successfully overcome by the inexperienced young soldier. At this time I attained my eighteenth year of age.'

Lieutenant Henry Whalley of the 47th wrote a certificate saying that Jackson's account of his adventures was correct: 'I was present with the late 2nd Battalion and recollect every circumstance he mentions perfectly well.' Oliver Jackson subsequently fought at the battle of Vitoria, the storming of San Sebastian, the crossing of the Bidassoa, the battle of the Nive and the siege of Bayonne, then served in India and took part in the Burmese war of 1825-26, but his petition did not succeed. Perhaps the circumstances surrounding his capture may have led to a less than sympathetic consideration of his claim, for Jackson was one of the many hundreds of stragglers rounded up by the French cavalry on the 17th, a circumstance unlikely to have endeared him to senior commanders.

On the 18th the exhausted columns plodded across muddy plains and floundered through flooded gulleys by San Christo de la Laguna and Tenebron. It was for many the worst day of the retreat, even though the weather cleared in the afternoon and the bivouacs that evening were on drier ground. Woods of the 82nd, weak with dysentery, was sent on with the baggage guard:

'With the rest of the troops that passed this route,[I] had to ford upwards of twenty rivers – a circumstance which every poor fellow on this march will well remember. It was literally nothing less than wading through water, sometimes breast-high, at others knee-deep… On this occasion, as I was about to cross the most deep and rapid of these streams, being very weak and tired, I got on my horse, now become as weak as myself, and whose life I only preserved by leading him by my side. However, in order to lessen my difficulty, and imagining that he might be strong enough for this little exertion, I mounted him: but, unfortunately, when about the middle, the poor animal fell down and plunged me over head and ears into the water; so that, in order to avoid a little wet, I found myself in no small danger of being drowned, for my foot had got entangled in the stirrup, and I had great trouble in extricating it.'[573]

Even Adam Reed, a veteran Light Company soldier of the 47th, was now near the end of his physical powers. He recalled his experience of the final two days of the retreat:

'When the morning which was the fourth day [18th November] appeared, we began to retreat again, and when the bugle sounded a great many called out that they were not able to fall in, being exhausted for want of

---

572 Wood, p.p. 159-62.
573 Wood, p.p. 162-63.

food and rest. We however commenced marching as before, without any breakfast, and about 9 or 10 o'clock we observed that the enemy was not so close to our rear as they were the day before. About 12 o'clock that day, a great many men began to fall out of different regiments, being unable to march any further, and I am sorry to say a great many sat down to arise no more. During that day we halted a great many times to rest, the General knowing that we was very much exhausted. As I marched along I saw just before we halted something white lying in among the bushes, and after we halted I returned back to look for it, and it was a paunch [stomach] of some animal, but what animal I cannot say. I took out my knife and cut off a large piece and rinsed it in some water, and when I return[ed] they had kindled a fire, and I stuck it on my ramrod and held it over. I thought I should not keep it myself from the devouring soldiers, and so ate it before it was half done. They then asked me where I got it, and after I told them, they also returned and fetched the remainder and did likewise.

'We then commenced our march again, and during that afternoon there was a Spaniard who went up the lines and offered a cooked goat for sale. While the soldiers were bargaining for part of it, my brother took the opportunity of slyly seizing one of the legs and got away with it. He gave me a piece, and I felt worse after I ate it than I did before.

'We then was on our march again, and I could not keep up with the regiment, and I was left in the rear, me and many more besides. That day passed, and no provisions.

'The fifth morning [19th November] appeared, and the rain had abated. Passing on as fast as I could to keep out of the enemy's way, I saw a great many more men who had fallen out and were sitting on the wayside, and I am sorry to say I still also saw a great many dead. One man lay close by me as I passed, and I knew him to be one of my own regiment, and I went to him and turned him over to be certain who it was, and his name was Hopkins. I kept on a small distance farther, and they still kept lying on in different places on the wayside, and kept on until I came to a place where cabbages had been grown, and I saw some of the leaves scattered about in the dirt. Me and some others that were with me gathered them up, washed and ate them so as to satisfy our hunger for a little time. We still kept on till we came to a place where some animals had been slain, and we gathered up the blood off the ground and kindled a fire, boiled and ate it without any salt. No provision that day except what mentioned above.

'By this time, our army had arrived at Ciudad Rodrigo, and there they got provision. We kept on 3 days before we reached Ciudad Rodrigo, being 8 days in all. And not having any more than one quarter of a pound of bread since we left Salamanca, except what was mentioned before. My readers may think it impossible for any mortal man to undergo such hardships as these, but [they] are well founded upon facts of brick, for I saw it with my own eyes, and many more besides, for it is unknown to the public the hardships that the British Army endured in the Peninsular War.

'What few lived till they reached Ciudad Rodrigo had a small quantity of provisions served out to them. There was an officer of each regiment left there to receive their own soldiers who had fallen out and to conduct them to their different divisions. We halted there the next day, and then marched on to join our regiments.

'When we arrived there, my brother said they had reported that I was seen dead on the way, and he said, "Here is a dead man come to life again." He being cook, I asked whether he had got anything to eat. He said, "I have got no bread, but there is something in the kettle." He asked me to wait there till he returned, as he wanted to go after some fuel for the fire. While he was gone, I peeped into the kettle and took out some of the meat and ate it, though half done. When he came back, he said, "Adam, you have been at the meal." I said, "Yes, I took a little piece just to satisfy my appetite, for I was very hungry."'

Stragglers like Adam Reed continued to come in for several days. Julian Sanchez went out to search the woods with his irregular Spanish lancers and, together with the Allied cavalry, brought in some thousand weary men. There appear to have been five of the 30th among those recovered. Even so, Soult claimed to have swept up some 1,700 to 1,900 Allied prisoners between the 16th and the 18th, and for once this may not have been much of an exaggeration. Of course, some of the captured stragglers, like Oliver Jackson of the 47th, subsequently escaped, and Soult's total bag included men from the 'foreign' regiments (Chasseurs Britanniques and Brunswick Oels) who took the opportunity to desert.

Apart from captured stragglers, the 30th, 47th and 82nd appear to have suffered few casualties due to enemy action during this last phase of the retreat, though Henry McNally of the 47th is recorded as having been wounded in the head on 19th November: it may be surmised that he was one of those who fell to a French cavalry sabre.[574]

When the 40th reached Ciudad Rodrigo, Private William Lawrence, who had been recuperating there from his Badajoz wounds, was thankful to rejoin his regiment:

'After being in hospital nearly two months longer, my strength had come back enough to allow me to be removed out of the town to a convent, the very one before mentioned[575] which I had helped to storm when we were throwing up batteries for the assault of the town. There I found a number like myself who had lately recovered, and amongst them some of my own comrades of my own regiment, which made the time pass more lively than if we had been all strangers. By the time my strength was sufficiently recruited to again permit me to go on active service, November had again come round, so that from the time of receiving my wound at Badajoz, at least seven months had passed away before I was free from sickness and in a proper condition to again join my regiment.'

Keen as he was to return to his regiment, Lawrence was still not fully fit: 'Soon after I rejoined, we crossed the Agueda into Portugal again, to take up our winter quarters in that country. Although it was not many leagues from Ciudad Rodrigo to where our cantonments were to be, yet that small march seemed to be almost going to knock me up, for my leg did not seem altogether strong enough to bear much marching, both of the slug shots having entered the sinew under the knee, and while we were engaged in this march it was kept constantly on the move. However, after we had settled down for about three weeks, I began to feel more like myself, and was therefore enabled to take my regular amount of duty.' He was shortly afterwards promoted to corporal.[576]

On the 20th, the 4th Division encamped near Gallegos, and next day they were quartered around Aldea del Obispo and Villar de Ciervo. The 40th occupied the last place, while the 82nd were in the nearby village of Villar de la Yegua, and the 5th Division too was billeted in the vicinity of Ciudad Rodrigo. Wellington kept his army together behind the Agueda until it was clear that the French were withdrawing, when on November 28th he ordered the army into winter quarters.

On that same day, back in his old headquarters at Freineda, and in a 'very bad humour,' Wellington issued his most controversial and badly-received order: while meant as a circular to his generals and senior staff officers, it soon became public and caused deep resentment.

'The discipline of every army, after a long and active campaign, becomes in some degree relaxed, and requires the utmost attention on the part of the general and other officers to bring it back to the state in which it ought to be for service; but I am concerned to have to observe that the army under my command has fallen in this respect in the late campaign to a greater degree than any army with which I have ever served, or of which I have ever read. Yet this army has met with no disaster; it has suffered no privations which but trifling attention on the part of the officers could not have prevented, and for which there existed no reason whatever in the nature of the service; nor has it suffered any hardships, excepting those resulting from the necessity of being exposed to the inclemencies of the weather at a moment when they were most severe.

'It must be obvious to every officer that from the moment the troops commenced their retreat from the neighbourhood of Burgos on the one hand, and from Madrid on the other, the officers lost all command over their men. Irregularities and outrages of all descriptions were committed with impunity, and losses have been sustained which ought never to have occurred. Yet, the necessity for retreat existing, none was ever made on which the troops had such short marches, none on which they made such long and repeated halts, and none on which the retreating armies were so little pressed on their rear by the enemy.

'I have no hesitation in attributing these evils to the habitual inattention of the officers of the regiments to their duty… I am far from questioning the zeal, still less the gallantry and spirit, of the officers of the army; and I am quite certain that if their minds can be convinced of the necessity of minute and constant attention to understand, recollect, and carry into execution the orders which have been issued… they will in future give their attention to these points.

---

[574] Henry McNally, a veteran of Barrosa (where he was wounded), Tarifa and Puente Larga, later fought at Vitoria, San Sebastian, the Nive and Bayonne. He was promoted to ensign in the 47th in January 1825, and was still serving, as a lieutenant, in 1841, having seen further active service in India 1817-18 and in Burma 1825-26, where he was again wounded.

[575] The Convent of San Francisco.

[576] Lawrence, p.p. 123-25.

'Generals and field officers must get the captains and subalterns of their regiments to understand and perform the duties required of them, as the only mode by which the discipline and efficiency of the army can be restored and maintained during the next campaign.'

Wellington's intemperate and uncompromising blanket condemnation of his army and its officers, most probably born of exhaustion and frustration, was emphatically not shared by most of his subordinates. Writing to a friend on 13th December, Lowry Cole stated that the retreat from the Tormes was 'by far the severest lesson I ever experienced in my military career,' and went on to say that 'The weather was uncommonly severe, some of us ill off for bread, among these the 4th Division, and the troops suffered much. I really never saw so much misery as in the few days between the 15th and the 19th November.'[577]

As for the straggling, much of which was a direct reaction to staff incompetence and mortal hunger, it did not apply equally to all units and formations. Over the whole period of the retreat, from 21st October to 19th November, setting aside losses in the Villamuriel action, only eight soldiers of the 30th Regiment fell out and were taken prisoner, of whom just three starving and exhausted men were taken during the march from Salamanca to Ciudad Rodrigo.

As already noted, Wellington's displeasure had focused on the 82nd, whose losses of both dead (154) and stragglers were outstanding among the British regiments. In consequence of their perceived indiscipline and disgrace on the march from Salamanca, the 82nd were 'turned out' of the 4th Division and transferred on 28th November to the 7th Division.

'We were placed in the division that was considered the refuse of the army,' complained George Wood, 'but the sequel will show whether this very regiment, brigade and division were not to rank among the first for the bravery and gallantry of their conduct. Indeed, as soon as the sufferings which brought this supposed disgrace on our regiment were made known to the Commander-in-Chief, he immediately ordered our Colonel out of arrest, and gave us every facility in his power to free ourselves from these distressing calamities.'

George Wood was in no doubt as to the true reasons for the disastrous losses of the young soldiers of his Regiment:

'They were for the most part mere boys, who had never before gone a long march, for the flower of our Regiment had been lost on other services, particularly at Flushing; and these were not to be compared to the veteran troops who had become inured to change of climate, to hardship, and fatigue. When these young men began to feel the dampness of the wet ground, the want of their accustomed good fare and warm covering, and to continue an incessant march, each loaded with sixty rounds of ball cartridge, his knapsack, haversack, musket, blanket, canteen, accoutrements, and provisions (when these could be obtained), how could it be matter of surprise that we should be compelled to leave three times as many as any other corps did on the road, seeing that we were nearly treble the strength, and destitute of the advantages possessed by those regiments who had been familiarized with the arduous duties of a campaign?'

As for the regimental officers of the 82nd, Wood was equally convinced that they had done their very best under particularly trying circumstances:

'I have seen these very officers do their duty on these urgent occasions in an exemplary manner: I have known them exert the greatest severity towards these unfortunate men, and even threaten them with punishment; but all to no purpose. I have also seen them employ the kindest methods, encourage them, take their muskets, knapsacks, &c, and carry them for these poor fellows; but without avail. Entirely exhausted, the unfortunate creatures lay down on the roadside and were overtaken by the enemy in such numbers that in the course of twenty-four hours our regiment had lost from sixty to seventy men; but what was to be done in this deplorable case, more than entreaty and persuasion could effect? It was impossible to carry them on our backs; the spring-waggons and all other modes of conveyance were either too far in our front, or loaded to such a degree that they could not receive more.'[578]

The retreat had indeed taken its toll on all ranks, and on 2nd December Ensign Francis Kelly of the 30th died of fatigue in a hospital wagon near Celorico.

---

[577] Lowry Cole Memoirs, p.p. 88-9.
[578] Wood, p.p. 175-77.

The campaign of 1812 had ended on a note of disappointment and discontent, but even at the time, it could be seen by well-informed commentators that the strategic balance in the Peninsula had tipped in favour of the Allies. As the perceptive French General Foy put it, 'Wellington goes off unbeaten, with the glory of the Arapiles untarnished, after having restored to the Spaniards all the lands south of the Tagus, after having forced us to destroy our own magazines and fortifications, and deprived us of all the resources that resulted from our former conquests and ought to have secured their retention.' He might have added that the French now lacked the resources and bases for a renewed invasion of Portugal, that their lines of communication were now under increasing pressure from Spanish forces, regular and irregular, that large tracts of Spain, including the whole of Andalusia, Asturias and Extremadura, had been liberated, and that the French armies in Spain, even after reinforcement, were 30,000 men weaker than at the start of the 1812 campaign. Wellington himself reported:

'We have sent to England little less than 20,000 prisoners, have taken and destroyed, or have now ourselves the use of, the enemy's arsenals in Ciudad Rodrigo, Badajoz, Salamanca, Valladolid, Madrid, Astorga, Seville, and the lines before Cadiz, and upon the whole have taken or destroyed, or now possess, little short of 3,000 of their cannon.'

Winter Quarters 1812-13

The Peninsula Army spent some six months, from December 1812 to May 1813, in winter quarters. The men were exhausted after a full year of marching and fighting, which had left one in three of them in hospital. It was time to rest, re-equip, re-train, and reorganise; time too for sick and wounded to recover and rejoin, and for drafts from home to swell the ranks.

Over the early months of 1813, there was a remarkably effective drive to restore discipline and to make the army ready for a sustained campaign. This extended from training to administrative support. There was live firing practice, and battalions were drilled rigorously so that, for instance, they could move from column to line or line to square in thirty seconds, even in rough country. The status and training of non-commissioned officers was enhanced: the new rank of colour sergeant was introduced, and schools were set up in every unit to educate promising men for promotion.

The men were in rags by the time they reached winter quarters, and Private Reed of the 47th was among the many who were marching barefoot, but new uniforms were on the way from Lisbon, and Wellington authorised the free issue of a pair of shoes. Another very welcome improvement to the personal circumstances of all ranks was that it became possible to issue pay for the first time since 25th April, and the troops were paid up to 24th August, enabling them to purchase comforts and supplement the issue ration.

Measures were also taken to support the soldiers' health and welfare. The heavy cast-iron camp kettles, which on the march often arrived too late to be of service, were replaced by light tin cooking pots, one to every six men, which the soldiers could carry, similar to those used by the French. The mules which had carried the ponderous old kettles were instead to be used to transport 25-man bell tents; in the event, these rarely arrived in time at the end of a day's march, but they were invaluable during longer halts and reduced the number of men falling sick from exposure in damp bivouacs. Billhooks were issued, one between every six men, for cutting wood for campfires. Another well-meant change was less successful: greatcoats were replaced by blankets, an advantage during the summer campaign but less than adequate during the subsequent winter in the Pyrenees.

Medical support was, as ever, critical to improving and maintaining the strength of the army, and its provision, from regimental to central hospitals, was also overhauled. When the 1st/40th were mustered at Villar de Ciervo on Christmas Day 1812 their effective soldier strength was only 433, barely more than the 384 men of that battalion who had died as a result of enemy action or disease in the course of the year, which was the second highest mortality in the whole army. By 25th May 1813 the rank and file effective strength had risen to 694 (76% of establishment), though there were still 207 men sick. This recovery in strength was general across the army: the effective strength of the 47th rose from 387 to 421 over the same period, having dipped in February to as low as 313, and the unfortunate 82nd recovered from 425 to 477, having dropped to 340 in February, when they counted 422 sick. Nevertheless, when the 47th and 82nd marched in May 1813 to begin another hard-fought and strenuous campaign, their 'start states' still amounted to only 71.6% and 66.62% respectively of established rank and file strength.

Over the winter months there was considerable re-organisation across the Army, with the 2nd Brigade of the 5th Division particularly affected, losing the 2nd/4th (which merged with its 1st Battalion in the same brigade) and the 2nd/30th, which two battalions were respectively replaced by the 2nd/47th and 2nd/59th. The 1st/40th remained in the 4th Division, but as previously noted, the 1st/82nd was transferred to the 7th Division.

The 5th Division was quartered in the familiar neighbourhood of Lamego, where they had been stationed before the Salamanca campaign, and on arrival there, the 2nd/30th occupied the small town of Vila Nova de Souto d'El Rey[579], which they reached on about 4th December.

After four years in the Peninsula, the 2nd/30th was one of twelve battle-hardened battalions of the Peninsula Army whose diminished strength led the Duke of York, Commander-in-Chief of the Army, to call for them to be sent home at once to recruit. Wellington had other plans, and fully intended to keep fit and seasoned veterans in preference to raw reinforcements. On 6th December, on his own responsibility, he issued orders to form three 'Provisional Battalions' by pairing six of the most depleted units:

'The Commander of the Forces desires that all effective privates of the second battalions of the 24th, 30th, 44th, 53rd, and 58th shall be transferred into four companies of those battalions… The four companies of the second 30th and four companies of the second 44th are to be the 4th Provisional Battalion under Lieut.-Colonel Hamilton of the 30th… The staff of the second 30th are to perform the duties of the provisional battalion to which they are attached… The 4th to be in Major-General Walker's[580] brigade, Fifth Division.'

On Christmas Day 1812, the 2nd/30th mustered for the last time before the implementation of Wellington's order, and on that day, 22 officers, 28 sergeants, ten drummers, and only 206 rank and file were present and effective. A further six officers, four sergeants and 22 rank and file were detached or 'on command' in theatre, while eight officers, ten sergeants, five drummers and 317 rank and file were sick or wounded. On 13th February, the six skeleton companies embarked at Lisbon on the transport *Sovrig* with six sergeants, four drummers and sixty privates, commanded by Captain Bamford.

Lieutenant-Colonel Hamilton, his battalion staff, and the remaining four companies of the 30th, with sixteen officers, twenty sergeants, nine drummers, and 189 effective rank and file, remained at Vila Nova de Souto d'El Rey as the nucleus of the 4th Provisional Battalion.[581]

The temporary merger with the 2nd/44th was probably easy, for the two battalions were old friends, but it was not to last. The Duke of York remained insistent that under-strength battalions should be sent home, and Wellington was obliged to compromise by offering up the weakest of his Provisional Battalions. The choice fell on the 4th Battalion, whose April musters showed a total of only 401 effective rank and file, of whom 246 were in the 30th companies. Accordingly, the following order was issued, dated Freinada, 10th May 1813:

'1. The 4th Provisional Battalion is to march to Lisbon, and the detachments which form it are to proceed to England by the first opportunity.

'2. The Commander of the Forces returns his thanks to the commanding and other officers and soldiers of second Battalion 30th and 2nd Battalion 44th for their services during the time they have belonged to this army.'

This order, coming as it did when the army was on the point of marching, was most unwelcome to many of the 30th, including Lieutenant Nevill, who had recently rejoined on recovery from his Burgos wounds. He gave an account of their march down to Lisbon:

'We were by no means hurried, and were glad to see that the inhabitants had for the most part returned to their homes, and many were busy rebuilding their towns, which had been so recently ravaged and destroyed. The terrible scenes of horror we had passed in our advance were no longer visible, and the people cheered us as we passed them, and blessed the "*Grande Lorde*," as they usually called the Marquis of Wellington.

---

[579] Shown as 'Villa Nova del Rey' in the musters of the 30th, this place, now a village, is some 5 miles south of Lamego.

[580] The 2nd brigade of the 5th Division was still commanded by Major-General Pringle as Walker had not recovered from his Badajoz wound.

[581] A total of 25 officers, 31 sergeants, 10 drummers and 438 rank and file of the 30th remained in the Peninsula, including officers on the staff and men sick, absent or detached 'on command.'

'On our arrival in Lisbon we heard of the decisive victory at Vittoria, and we noticed some of our men grumbling, not without some reason, at not having shared in that battle, as they then might have come in for a share of the enormous quantity of property they had heard was found in and about Vittoria and the battle-ground.'[582]

Lieutenant-Colonel Hamilton embarked with his four companies on the transports *Ajax* and *Mary* on 18th June, and landed at Cowes on the 29th. He had with him 377 other ranks, including sick and wounded, while a further 60-70 men who were detached or were too sick to be moved remained in Portugal under Lieutenant Daniel. Ten officers and over 250 men of the 30th had died in Spain or Portugal. Hamilton at once asked permission to give leave to his veterans, which was granted.

The 2nd/47th had joined Pringle's 2nd Brigade of the 5th Division on 1st December[583], and occupied some villages, including Portela, in a valley to the north of Lamego. Colonel Skerrett was appointed to a brigade of the Light Division, so Captain Charles Livesay was in temporary command until the arrival of Major Robert Kelly.

The Battalion was at first in poor health, but Assistant Surgeon Thomas Fiddes of the 9th Regiment 'received the thanks of Major General Hay, Commanding the 5th Division, and the Inspector General of Hospitals, also the Officer in Command of the 2nd Battn. 47th Regiment for re-establishing the health of that Corps while in winter quarters after the retreat from Burgos.'[584]

On 12th April, the 2nd/59th, who had disembarked at Lisbon on the 6th, were posted to the 2nd Brigade as replacement for the 4th Provisional Battalion. The Lilywhites had spent six months quartered on the Isle de Leon, the only British battalion remaining in the Cadiz garrison, and had sailed for Lisbon on 31st March. The 59th were highly motivated at the prospect of active service, with spirits further buoyed by the news from Russia, as evidenced by a letter of 23rd March from Private William Windsor of that Regiment to his wife in England, telling her that they were about to join the Grand Army under Lord Wellington's immediate command:

'My dear, I hope these few lines will not trouble you, for I long to see the day when I fire 60 rounds of ball cartridge in defence of my King & Country, religion & laws, against our most inveterate enemy, who wants to bring all nations under his feet. Now, my dear, only look to the Russians & see what they have done, & to the British forces now in Spain. The children unborn will bless the day that the British landed on the Spanish coast, for the French will bury their honour in the ground, & the British will glory in the fall of so great a monarch.'

The 59th marched out of Lisbon on 21st April, and reached Lamego on 14th May. Charles Fane was still in command of the Battalion, which arrived fit and effective: only three men fell out on the long march up-country, and Fane received a letter conveying Wellington's thanks for his exertions. Brigadier-General Frederick Robinson, who had recently assumed command of the 2nd Brigade, was delighted with the addition to his strength, writing home on 27th April that 'His Lordship has flattered me exceedingly lately by adding the 59th Regt (a thousand fine fellows[585]) to [the brigade].'

Robinson, whose brigade also included the still sickly 2nd/47th, was convinced that improvement to the men's diet was the most effective means of checking the still prevalent sickness, and as soon as he took over command, he set about changing it for the better:

'I ventured my opinion on it to Lord W[ellington] and I think clearly proved to him that kitchin physick was what the men wanted to restore their constitution, that the ration was not enough with men who required every possible means to recruit their strength, & who had not money to purchase little comforts… The first thing I did on joining my brigade was to examine the state of the men's messes and the hospitals, and obliged the reluctant Commissary to issue good wine, instead of bad rum, bread instead of biscuit, and two ounces of rice per man each day to put in their soup – which makes it as smooth as mollys. I tasted one kettleful so often the other

---

[582] Nevill, p.p. 29-30.

[583] The order allocating the 2nd/47th to Major-General Pringle's brigade of the 5th Division was issued on 17th October but could not be arranged before the end of the 1812 campaign.

[584] Numbers of the 47th in hospital and deaths per month were 230 and 46 in January 1813, 247 and 46 in February, 226 and 21 in March, 169 and 11 in April, and 142 and 2 in May.

[585] Robinson's 'thousand fine fellows' is a slight and pardonable exaggeration: the 'state' of 25th April 1813 shows 782 rank and file, to which should be added about 10% for officers, sergeants and drummers.

day that the men began to look d–sh sulky, but my putting down a twelve sous piece to buy some salt restored their smiles.

'I have been reaping the benefit of these regulations for ten days at least – 150 men have been restored to the ranks, and no more new cases have occurred than would have happened in any other country. This will prove to you that good feeding has been all along wanting. The Commissary of my brigade made many objections, all of which were easily overruled… Wine is so plentiful that you can get the very best for 50 dollars a pipe, and bread is so plentiful, and excellent, that the whole country for twenty miles round is supplied from hence – and yet our men have been eating hard ship biscuit with jaws scarcely able to crack the livestock in them.'

We have already noted how the 1st/82nd was ignominiously transferred on 28th November to the 7th Division. Accordingly, the battalion marched to winter quarters at Moimenta da Serra, a 'little dirty village' at the foot of the Estrella mountains, from where they subsequently moved to better billets at the neighbouring village of Santa Marinha.

'The men were in snug quarters,' wrote George Wood, 'and had good provisions, good fires, warm beds, and fine chocolate for breakfast, with every necessary comfort, and, above all, rest after their fatigue. But this sudden and welcome change, from the greatest sufferings to a state of comfortable repose, was the very cause of our consequent calamities. No sooner were we settled in our cantonments than we experienced the fatal effects of the almost unparalleled sufferings we had undergone; and the sudden transition… to comparative plenty brought on the most malignant complaints, especially fever, dysentery and rheumatism. The entire regiment was on the sick list; for a considerable time we had not a man on parade, not even convalescent men enough to attend the sick; it was therefore necessary to call in the assistance of the inhabitants; indeed, we were now in such a deplorable state that a staff-surgeon and four assistants were sent us, in addition to our own, so much did we stand in need of medical aid. With respect to hospitals, nearly half the houses in the village were converted to that purpose. It was truly depressing to see the situation of this fine regiment… now reduced to a number insufficient to form a parade, and that too without firing a shot. The church-yard was now a more common resort for them; for we buried from seventy to eighty men in this town in little more than a month[586] – a proof how many more are killed by privations and hardships of a long campaign than by the violence of the sword.'[587]

The 40th remained in the 4th Division.[588] Early in December 1812, they marched north-west from Villar de Ciervo to Cedovim, a small and isolated hamlet in the Alto Douro.

Following Wellington's controversial memorandum of 28th November, all officers were under considerable pressure to restore discipline, and it appears that Lieutenant-Colonel Richard Archdall exceeded both the letter and the spirit of the Articles of War in his determination to punish disorder in the ranks. In February he was brought before a General Court Martial at Lamego and found guilty on five charges: 'violent conduct'; 'having on the march from Villa de Ciervo to Cedovem, and at the latter village, inflicted corporal punishment on several non-commissioned officers and private men of the 40th Regiment without any trial'; 'acting contrary to the spirit of a circular confidential letter to commanding officers from the Duke of York, limiting the sentences of Regimental Courts Martial to 300 lashes, by inflicting at one time the sentences of two distinct Regimental Courts Martial held for different offences'; using 'intemperate and improper language' to officers of the Regiment, the same being in breach of good discipline and unbecoming the character of an Officer and a Gentleman; and 'having released soldiers of the Regiment, sentenced by courts martial to receive corporal punishment, and having

---

[586] The 82nd Regiment lost 37 men dead in November 1812, 44 in December, 68 in January 1813, 49 in February, 24 in March, 21 in April and 24 in May, a total of 267, all from privation and disease. In comparison, the 30th, 40th and 47th lost 83, 79 and 162 men dead respectively over that same period, which in the case of the 30th and 47th included battle casualties. Medical officers were not immune, and Surgeon Dennis Hughes of the 30th died on 23rd January.

[587] Wood, p.p. 167-69.

[588] The adjutancy of the 40th, vacant since Salamanca, was filled on 10th December by Lieutenant Isaac Chetham on promotion from the 79th Foot. Chetham, was had enlisted in the 29th in 1797, aged 16, had risen through the ranks to sergeant-major, and was commissioned in August 1811 on Wellington's personal recommendation. He had served in Holland in 1799, and at Roliça, Vimeira, Opporto, Talavera, Busaco, Albuera and Salamanca. Isaac Chetham remained with the 40th until the conclusion of the Peninsula War, serving at Vitoria, the Pyrenees, Nivelle, Orthes and Toulouse, but missed Waterloo, being then at the Depot. He went on half-pay in 1817 and died at Nottingham, aged 73, in 1854. His memorial inscription there records that he was actively engaged in nineteen battles and sieges, and was three times dangerously wounded.

permitted those soldiers to do duty in the presence of the enemy, and at other times, the punishment still impending and afterwards put in execution.'

Richard Archdall was sentenced to be dismissed from the Service; however, the Court was sympathetic and its President, Major-General Hay, forwarded the proceedings to the Duke of York with the following recommendation: 'I am requested by the members of the Court Martial to recommend to your Excellency's favourable consideration the prisoner, Lieutenant-Colonel Archdall, as after having performed the painful part of its duty, in consequence of his having transgressed against the Articles of War, yet it most humbly begs leave to submit that there is a conviction on their minds that he has been actuated by what appeared to him a most zealous discharge of his duty. The Court also begs leave to submit to your Excellency's consideration the testimonials of Lieutenant-General Cole and Major-General Anson as to the prisoner's character as an Officer and a Gentleman, as also that of Staff-Surgeon Boatflower to the same effect, and that of Assistant-Surgeon [Thomas] Cartan, which latter evidence has also borne testimony to his humane attention towards the sick of the 40th Regiment.'

In consideration of this recommendation, Archdall was permitted to retire by sale of his substantive majority in August 1813. More remarkably, on 3rd March 1814 he was granted a commission without purchase as cornet in the 3rd Dragoon Guards, and on 24th April that year was promoted to a lieutenancy in the 60th Regiment. He subsequently served in India with the 11th Light Dragoons, went on half-pay on 25th December 1822, and died, aged 45 and still a half-pay subaltern, in 1829.

A further scandal in the 40th started during their time at Cedovim. Lieutenant William Waldron Kelly of the Grenadier Company, whose amorous misadventures had already, in 1811, earned him a severe reprimand for 'scandalous conduct unbecoming an officer and a gentleman,' began a liaison with Anna Ludovina, the eighteen-year-old daughter of a Portuguese nobleman,[589] which once more landed him in serious trouble. Corporal William Lawrence wrote a lively account of this affair:

'He was an Irishman, and being likewise a Catholic, had been in the habit… of visiting a Catholic chapel [at Cedovim]; and there he had seen and fallen in love with a Portuguese general's daughter. Correspondence and meetings had followed, unbeknown to the girl's parents, but owing to the shifting of our cantonments [to Mata de Lobos], some difficulty had arisen in the way of their engagements, and so I suppose they thought it best to arrange one final one, or at any rate one of which the memory was to last some time. One night, therefore, he proceeded with two of our company to the lady's house, where all arrangements had previously been made for conveying her from her private window into her lover's arms, ready to elope with him. These arrangements consisted of a ladder to be placed at a window, and the goods that she intended taking to be ready on the back of a horse, and were all carried out by two of the domestic men-servants who had been bribed, and who also undertook to keep a good look-out until the eloping party had got quite clear.

'But, as it proved, a worse set of people could not have been entrusted with the matter, for no sooner had they received their money, and the little company had set out from the house on their way to the officer's quarters, than the two foolish Portuguese servants immediately raised an alarm, and a party of six, including these very servants, was sent in pursuit. They soon overtook the travelling party, which was obliged to walk slowly owing to the horse laden with the goods; and the pursuers being armed with sticks, an altercation consequently took place, in which the Portuguese succeeded in capturing the horse and baggage; but the officer fought bravely for his spouse and was well backed up by his men, so that he succeeded in carrying her off at any rate. One of the Portuguese, however, lost two fingers in the affray, which was an unfortunate circumstance, and after things had come to this crisis, they left off their pursuit and went home contented in having captured the horse and baggage. The lieutenant then succeeded in getting the lady to the cantonments without any further molesting, and on the following morning he took her to a neighbouring chapel and married her.'[590]

Matters had been brought to a head when, on 28th February, the 40th had suddenly left Cedovim, re-crossing the Coa and marching some 25 miles to Mata de Lobos, near the Agueda and the frontier with Spain. This last place was described by Lawrence as 'a village which had been for the most part deserted, and there we were cantoned chiefly in empty houses.'

---

[589] Anna Ludovina was the daughter of Marechal de Campo, Fidalgo e Cavaleiro da Casa Real Dom Francisco Teixeira de Aguilar and his wife Dona Maria Ludovina.
[590] Lawrence, p.p. 128-29.

The lovers knew that family approval to a marriage between Anna and a penniless Irish officer would not be forthcoming, and with separation looming, they decided that their only recourse was elopement. A suitable opportunity arose when, on Saturday 13th March, Wellington gave a dinner and ball at Ciudad Rodrigo to celebrate the investment of Lowry Cole with the Order of the Bath, leaving the cantonments bereft of senior officers. Events then unfolded much as described by Lawrence, but the repercussions were potentially disastrous for the young couple. Wellington received an immediate letter from Dona Maria demanding the return of her daughter and severe punishment of the culprit. His Lordship replied on the 19th, agreeing to her demands subject to written assurance that Anna would not be punished, and on the same day, he wrote to Lowry Cole:

'Sir, The mother of the lady carried off by Lieutenant Kelly of the 40th Regiment, having complained to me of his conduct and having desired my assistance to remove her daughter from the disgraceful situation in which she is now placed, I have consented to grant it on the condition of a promise on her part that the daughter should not be confined to a convent, and I beg you to call upon Lieutenant Kelly to restore the young lady to her family. If he should decline to do so upon your order, I beg you to put him in close arrest and then to take measures to remove the young lady from his power into that of her family's at Cedovim; as I cannot allow any officer of this army to be guilty of such a breach of the laws of Portugal as to carry away a young lady and retain her in the cantonments of the army… If you should find it necessary to place Lt Kelly in close arrest, you will release him as soon as the young lady shall be with her relations at Cedovim, but you will inform Lt Kelly that he has my positive orders not to cross the Coa.'

Kelly was summoned by Cole and severely reprimanded, but refused to hand over the girl, maintaining that his intentions were honourable and they intended to marry as soon as this could be arranged. Cole then interviewed Anna, and reported to Wellington that 'she appears to me fully determined to go to any extremity rather than return to Cedovim.' On the 22nd Dona Maria stormed into Cole's headquarters demanding to collect her daughter. A difficult confrontation followed, as a result of which the General wrote to Wellington, sympathetically explaining the developing situation and concluding, 'I have been induced to delay the execution of Your Lordship's orders until I hear further from Your Lordship.' That same day, through the good offices of Major John Scott Lillie of the 7th Cacadores, who had witnessed Kelly's gallantry at Salamanca, the marriage was celebrated by the Portuguese chaplain of that regiment. The newlyweds returned to Mata de Lobos, where Lieutenant Kelly treated the whole of the Grenadier Company to a pint of wine each, which they drank in toasts to the happy couple.

That was not quite the end of the matter, for an increasingly angry Dona Maria made further visits to both Cole and Wellington, demanding her daughter; but her ravings received a curt retort 'No' from his Lordship. Larpent, the Judge Advocate General, who was present at this last interview, recorded that 'Before leaving Freneda, she swore that she would get Kelly and the priest transported for life and would kill her daughter should she ever see her again.'[591]

As winter turned to spring, the Army's morale and self-confidence, never far from the surface even on the worst days of the retreat, were fully recovered, and had probably never been higher. 'The former lack of success seems to make no impression on our people,' wrote Frederick Robinson of his brigade on 27th April, 'they place such confidence in their Hero that no one questions his conduct. He is their idol, for whom they will offer their lives as freely as they will drink his health.'

Even the unfortunate 82nd felt renewed strength and confidence: 'The Regiment now began to make a respectable appearance on parade,' recalled George Wood, 'mustering about four hundred men, besides convalescents; for this long continuance in quarters gave time for those who were left at depots to come up, the sick to recover, the men who had been overtaken on the retreat and made prisoners to escape and join the Regiment; as well as for fresh detachments from England to arrive.'

---

[591] Sadly, the Kelly's marriage did not end well. Despite his gallantry in a dozen general actions, in the course of which he was wounded three times, it appears that Waldron Kelly continued to have a roving eye and libidinous nature when it came to the ladies. Having given Anna five children, in 1831 Captain Kelly bigamously 'married' in Liverpool a Jane Owen, by whom he had a further two children. Following the birth of a further child by another woman in Wales, in 1834 he prudently went abroad, becoming Barrack Master at Lucea and Mondego Bay in Jamaica, where he died in a duel on 12th November 1836 from a sword thrust to his throat. Still disowned by her family, Anna was left in penury.

'We had by this time in great measure repaired our past misfortunes; the baggage we lost had been replaced, and the cattle we left drowned in the rivers and broken down on the ground had been supplied by others. We began to assume an air of gaiety, amusing ourselves with horse-racing, shooting-parties, riding about the country, &c. The ladies of the place claimed our attention, which indeed had never been altogether dormant; but we had been unable to display our gallantry before in so jovial and entertaining a style as we now had it in our power to do, from a more free circulation of money, which enabled us to decorate the ball-room, the theatres and the festive board.'[592]

As the army recovered in health and numbers, there was a renewed emphasis on training. The 4th Division made weekly route marches in 'heavy marching order' and held field days twice a week. Lieutenant James Mill of the 40th, aged 26, who had rejoined the battalion the previous month, wrote home in March from Mata de Lobos in excited anticipation of an imminent campaign:

'The army is on the point of making a decided advance towards the enemy. You may expect to hear soon something of importance from the scene of hostilities. "Once more into the breach, my friends! Once more!"'

Writing again from the same place on 10th May, he reported on an inspection of the 4th Division near Castel Rodrigo which, despite heavy rain and sodden ground, passed off well:

'The whole number of brigades were formed in one line, which extended nearly one mile and a half. I never had an opportunity of seeing his lordship close before. His usual dress is very plain, consisting of a blue great-coat and blue cloth trousers, with white neckcloth; but on this occasion he was in full uniform, wore the various insignia of the different orders to which he belongs, and decorated with gold and stars. He appeared very much pleased with the appearance of the troops, and I never saw a countenance that I liked better. He looked all complacency and good nature.

'The same day we received orders to hold ourselves in readiness to march at any notice. Some of the army have already crossed the Douro. The *matériel* of the army has been greatly added to, in the way of an extensive pontoon train, newly-constructed carts for the commissariat, and a number of Government mules provided. Captain Downs [Charles Downes] and myself have been busy preparing for the ensuing campaign. We have got a tent for ourselves, which we are obliged to carry on our own animals. The men's tents (three only allowed to each company) are conveyed on Government mules. Our regiment is in a particularly healthy condition at present.'[593]

In short, by May 1813 the Peninsula Army was in a good state for whatever the forthcoming campaign would bring. Above all, despite the most recent setback, the army had nurtured an almost invincible self-confidence. The irascible rogues who made up much of Wellington's army may have indulged in drunken behaviour when opportunity offered, while looting was an eagerly anticipated sequel to any engagement, but their commanders knew that they could count on stubborn gallantry in action. These men never doubted their innate superiority over their enemies, or their nation's superiority over all foreign powers. The French general Maximilien Foy, ruefully reflected on the character of the English soldier:

'His soul is vigorous, because his father has told him, and his officers never cease repeating to him, that the sons of Old England, plentifully replenished with porter, and with roast beef, are each of them equal to at least any three individuals of the pygmy races which vegetate on the continent of Europe.'

---

[592] Wood, p.p. 173-74.
[593] Letters of Major James Mill, quoted in *Historical Records of the 40th Regiment*, p.p. 138-39.

**Battle of Vitoria
21st June 1813**

Assault on the village of Gamarra Mayor by Robinson's Brigade, the 4th, 47th & 59th

The village was taken and held in the hardest fighting of the day, effectively denying French withdrawal to the north-east

The 40th advanced due east from the bridge at Nanclares, passing to the south of Vitoria to reach the Pampeluna road

The 82nd, meanwhile, crossed the Zadorra to attack the French right, taking part in the capture of the villages of Margarita and Hermandad

**Battle of Sorauren
in the Pyrenees
28th July 1813,**
The 40th held an outlying position (Spanish Hill) on the far right of Wellington's line against four times their number, and on the 30th July they took part in a general counter-attack, capturing a French regiment.
On the left of the line, the 82nd also attacked that day with great success.

263

Major-General Sir Frederick Robinson
Colonel 59th 1827-40, whose brigade led the
final assault on San Sebastian, suffering 880
casualties out of some 1,500 present

Model of San Sebastian in 1813

The Forlorn Hope reach the foot of the breach
at the final assault on San Sebastion

The Storming of San Sebastian, 31st August 1813
when the 47th & 59th suffered 250 & 368 casualties
respectively, while 10 out of 13 volunteers from the 40th
also fell

Lieutenant Thomas Power, 47th, though
badly wounded, rallied his Regiment in
the breach when his seniors fell

Battle of the Nivelle, 10th November 1813, the grand offensive to breach the French frontier
The 40th, 47th, 59th & 82nd were all present, and the 40th & 82nd were particularly heavily engaged

R-L: Officer, Private & Sergeant
40th Regiment of Foot

At the Nivelle, the 40th had a tough fight to take the Louis XIV Redoubt (centre, middle distance), a key part of the fortified ridge on which the French made a resolute stand

The Battle of the Nive
9th-12th December 1813
when the 47th & 59th Regiments
fought tenaciously for three days
on the Barouillet plateau to halt
Soult's counter-offensive from
Bayonne

Chapter VIII:
Over the Hills and Far Away

Situation in the Peninsula, Spring 1813 – Wellington's offensive strategy – Diversion on the East Coast (81ˢᵗ) – Battle of Castalla 13ᵗʰ April (81ˢᵗ) – Siege of Tarragona – the Great Flank March (40ᵗʰ, 47ᵗʰ, 59ᵗʰ & 82ⁿᵈ) – Battle of Vitoria 21ˢᵗ June 1813 (40ᵗʰ, 47ᵗʰ, 59ᵗʰ & 82ⁿᵈ) – Advance to the Pyrenees – Blockade of Pamplona (40ᵗʰ) – Combat of Maya 25ᵗʰ July 1813 (82ⁿᵈ) – Combats of Roncesvalles & Lintzoain 25ᵗʰ & 26ᵗʰ July 1813 (40ᵗʰ) – First Battle of of Sorauren 28ᵗʰ July 1813 (40ᵗʰ) – Second Battle of of Sorauren 30ᵗʰ July (40ᵗʰ and 82ⁿᵈ) – Pursuit of Soult (40ᵗʰ) – Siege & Storming of San Sebastian 31ˢᵗ August 1813 (47ᵗʰ, 59ᵗʰ & detachment 40ᵗʰ) – Battle of San Marcial 31ˢᵗ August 1813 (detachments 40ᵗʰ & 82ⁿᵈ) – Catalonia (81ˢᵗ) – The Bidassoa Crossing 7ᵗʰ October 1813 (47ᵗʰ & 59ᵗʰ) – Battle of the Nivelle 10ᵗʰ November 1813 (40ᵗʰ, 47ᵗʰ, 59ᵗʰ & 82ⁿᵈ) – Battle of the Nive 9ᵗʰ-13ᵗʰ December 1813 (47ᵗʰ & 59ᵗʰ).

Farewell Portugal

By the spring of 2013, the time was ripe for a decisive Allied offensive. Wellington's Anglo-Portuguese army was stronger, more experienced, better organised and equipped, and more self-confident than ever before, and the Spanish regular and irregular forces were taking control of increasingly large tracts of their country. Furthermore, Royal Navy command of the seas around the Peninsula gave the Allies a very considerable strategic advantage. It was also most helpful that Napoleon and his advisers in Paris continued to underestimate the capabilities of their opponents and planned no reinforcements for Spain in 1813.

The French still had over 200,000 troops in Spain under the nominal command of King Joseph Bonaparte, though his army commanders jealously retained considerable independence. The French effort was also dispersed: Suchet, with 60-70,000 men was kept in Valencia and Catalonia by a multi-national diversionary force of 18,000 under Sir John Murray, and Clausel's Army of the North, 30,000 strong, was trying to contain insurgency in Navarre, where Mina, Longa and other guerrilla leaders were encouraged by Wellington and supplied by the Royal Navy. This left three French armies[594] under Joseph and Marshal Jourdan in Central Spain, where over 100,000 troops could be concentrated within six days. After Napoleon's 1812 debacle in Russia[595], the French were obliged to adopt a defensive posture in Spain. They expected Wellington to attack up the Royal Road from Salamanca to Burgos, as in 1812, and Joseph prepared to hold Wellington on the line of the River Duero. To achieve the necessary troop concentration, Madrid was evacuated by the French on 27ᵗʰ May, and convoys of treasure, loot, officials and collaborators left the capital.

Wellington started the 1813 campaign with a marching strength (25ᵗʰ May) of 81,276 men, consisting of 52,484 British and King's German Legion, and 28,792 Portuguese, organised in eight infantry divisions and nine cavalry brigades, with 102 guns. He had 69,260 infantry in 50 British, 32 Portuguese, one Brunswick and five King's German Legion battalions, and 8,317 cavalry in 15 British, four Portuguese and three King's German Legion regiments. He was now also Commander-in-Chief of the Spanish Army and had Giron's 4ᵗʰ Army, 25,425 men, under command.

As early as February 1813, Wellington started planning a bold strategic offensive into northern Spain based on excellent intelligence from his exploring officers and network of 'correspondents.' His plan involved thorough logistical preparation, strategic surprises, deception, strict security and diversions.

Wellington's intention was to outmanoeuvre the French armies in central Spain by turning their northern flank, forcing them to abandon successive positions behind the Duero, at Burgos and behind the Ebro. Joseph Bonaparte would either have to fight to preserve his right flank or fall back to France, abandoning his Kingdom. To achieve this, Wellington divided his army into two wings. Sir Rowland Hill, with two British, one Portuguese

---

[594] Gazan's Army of the South, D'Erlon's Army of the Centre, and Reille's Army of Portugal.
[595] An officer of the 30ᵗʰ, Lieutenant James N. Charles, was present with the Russian army during Napoleon's famous retreat from Moscow, October to December 1812, as ADC to General Sir Robert Wilson.

and two Spanish divisions, was directed to take Salamanca, making it appear that the main British advance would be via that place on the expected route, the Royal Road from Valladolid via Burgos and Vitoria to Bayonne. A strong cavalry screen prevented the French from discovering that this was not the main force, and Wellington made himself conspicuously present.

Meanwhile, the main force of six British divisions under Sir Thomas Graham, with a pontoon train, was quietly concentrated in a remote corner of northern Portugal between Braganza and Miranda de Douro, where the terrain was considered impassable for an army with artillery and pontoon trains. Graham's force included the 40th, 47th, 59th and 82nd Regiments.[596]

Wellington had prepared another strategic surprise: taking advantage of British command of the sea, he was ready to move his logistic base from Lisbon to the Biscay Coast. The supporting supply fleet on that coast, carrying food, ammunition and heavy guns, was concentrated at Corunna, ready to move forward to Santander as soon as the French could be forced to evacuate that port.

The Battle of Castalla, 13th April 1813

The first British troops engaged in Spain in 1813 were not with Wellington but on the east coast, where they had impatiently passed the winter around Alicante. This force, including the 1st/81st Foot, was part of a remarkably cosmopolitan army which, from 25th February 1813, was commanded by Lieutenant-General Sir John Murray. In addition to 5,840 British, he had 2,000 Germans, 2,000 Italians, 9,882 Spanish in British pay, and 5,494 other foreign troops. Elio's Spanish army added another 15,000 effective troops to the Allied total. Whittingham's Spanish division held a forward line at Biar, Castalla and Jijona, while the remainder of Murray's force lay in and around Alicante. From the start of his command, Murray was unenthusiastic about his polyglot force and was concerned to manage expectations:

'Of the nature of its composition your Lordship is well informed, and as, with the exception of the British and German details, nothing from every account can be worse, I anxiously hope that the expectations of His Majesty's Government will not be too sanguine.'

Murray was confronted by Marshal Suchet, who, on paper, commanded some 75,000 men, but after providing garrisons for his extensive operational area, his Army of Aragon could only muster a field army of 15,000. His three divisions were deployed at Moxente, Xativa (with a forward brigade at Alcoy) and Denia.

Murray began a limited offensive on 3rd March, aiming to encircle and destroy an isolated French brigade at Alcoy. The 1st/81st, brigaded with De Roll's regiment, advanced to occupy Monforte del Cid, north of Elche. The Allied plan miscarried, as Murray would not commit his main force until Whittingham's flanking division arrived, and the French slipped away. In a private letter to Wellington, Murray laid part of the blame for his failure on a detachment of the 81st, but for whose drunkenness a French picket of two hundred men would allegedly have been surprised and captured. Alcoy was for a time occupied, and some skirmishing took place between outposts.

On the 20th, Murray's Anglo-Sicilian force was concentrated at Castalla, from where he could, if necessary, move forward to support the Spanish divisions under Whittingham, Elio and Roche. Unfortunately, just as Murray contemplated further offensive action, Lord William Bentinck recalled two thousand of his best troops to Sicily. With his force about to be weakened, the Allied commander decided to fall back again on Alicante and stand strictly on the defensive; but he did not move at once, and was still at Castalla when Suchet advanced.

At this time, the 81st was in Major-General William Clinton's division, together with the 1st/10th, 1st/58th, a composite 'Foreign' battalion of De Roll's and Dillon's regiments, and the 2nd Italian Levy. It is unfortunate that there are no first-hand accounts of the Battalion's services in Eastern Spain: indeed, there are remarkably few

---

[596] The effective soldier strengths of these battalions on 25th May 1813 were: 40th – 694, 47th – 421, 59th – 746, and 82nd – 477. The 1st/40th, commanded by Captain Arthur Heyland, was in Sir William Anson's brigade of Major-General Cole's 4th Division, together with the 3rd/27th, 1st/48th and 2nd Provisional Battalion. The 2nd/47th and 2nd/59th, commanded by Major Robert Kelly and Lieutenant-Colonel Charles Fane respectively, were in Robinson's brigade of Major-General Oswald's 5th Division, together with the 1st/4th. The 1st/82nd were in Sir William Inglis's brigade of Lieutenant-General Lord Dalhousie's 7th Division, together with the 51st, 68th and Chasseurs Britanniques. During Sir William's initial absence, Colonel Grant of the 82nd commanded the brigade, so Major Henry King commanded the Battalion.

surviving personal journals or letters from any of the participants in that theatre, so we must largely rely on Murray's despatch for the events which followed.

Having concentrated by the night of 11th April at La Font de la Figuera, Suchet made short work of Spanish detachments at Yecla and Vilena, and at about noon on the 12th he advanced with five thousand men on the pass of Biar, some four miles north-west of Castalla, held by Colonel Adam's advance brigade. After a gallant and well-executed rearguard action, in which he disputed every foot of the pass for nearly five hours, Adam retired in good order to the plain in front of Castalla. His final withdrawal from the pass was covered by the 81st, De Roll's/Dillon's and a Spanish battalion, of whom the latter two suffered some fifty casualties. Meanwhile, Murray's army occupied its battle positions.

The ground occupied by the Allies at Castalla was strong and had been additionally strengthened with fieldworks. The right of this position was dominated by the conical hill of Castalla, crowned by a Moorish castle, behind which lay the small town of that name. From that point, an extensive ridge, the heights of Guerra, ran away to the left (south-west) for nearly two miles, while the right was protected by a depression and a dammed stream. To defend this excellent position, Murray had some 18,716 men of variable training and reliability, comprising the British-led cosmopolitan divisions of Clinton and Mackenzie, Adam's light brigade, and the Spanish divisions of Roche and Whittingham, funded by Britain and commanded by seconded British officers. There were under one thousand cavalry and just four batteries of guns, nearly all 6-pounders.

The reverse slopes of the rocky heights of Guerra were held, in succession from the left, by Whittingham, Adam and Mackenzie. Clinton, whose division included the 81st, occupied a refused position on the right flank at Castalla, forward of which was a Spanish and Sicilian cavalry screen, supported by two of Roche's battalions. The remaining three of Roche's battalions, with the 20th Light Dragoons, were in reserve behind the town of Castalla.

It was late afternoon before Suchet emerged from the pass of Biar, having been delayed by Adam. He considered Murray's position, disliked what he could see, and was uncharacteristically slow to decide his next move, deferring his orders until the following morning. Meanwhile, he waited for his full strength to come up, and ordered a full reconnaissance.

On the morning of the 13th, urged on by subordinates who assured him that the Spanish and Italians would not stand, Suchet advanced with 13,568 men. He enjoyed a superiority in cavalry – of little advantage as the terrain did not suit the mounted arm – but his army was otherwise considerably inferior in quantity, if not quality. His plan was to first extend his cavalry to the left, where it could observe Murray's right wing and reserve, then to contain Mackenzie's centre-right division with a demonstration while the main attack, by six battalions of Robert's division, was directed at Whittingham's Spaniards on the far left of the Allied line. His subsequent intention, having driven off the Spanish division, was to move along the heights to roll up the Allied line.

Robert's attack caught Whittingham unbalanced, for he had apparently just been ordered to send troops to outflank Suchet's extreme right; fortunately, he was able to recover the situation. The Spaniards were pressed back, but quickly rallied and counter-attacked with the bayonet, driving their opponents back down the hill at every point. To Whittingham's right, the 2nd/27th defeated Robert's left-hand column in traditional style with musketry and a bayonet charge. At about 4 p.m., Suchet ordered a general withdrawal, falling back on the plain where his reserve division and cavalry were still intact. Murray, whose expectations had never been high and had even contemplated retreat, had reason to be satisfied:

'Having united his shattered battalions with those which he kept in reserve, Marshal Suchet took up a position in the valley, but which it would not have been creditable to allow him to retain. I therefore decided on quitting mine; still, however, retaining the heights, and formed the Allied army in his front, covering my right front with the cavalry, while the left rested on the hills. The army advanced in two lines to attack him, a considerable distance, but unfortunately Marshal Suchet did not choose to risk a second action with the defile in his rear. The line of the Allies was scarcely formed, when he began his retreat, and we could effect nothing more than driving the French into the pass with defeat, which they had exultantly passed in the morning. The action terminated at dusk, with a distant but heavy cannonade.'

Murray's interpretation of the latter stages of the battle put the best gloss on what many felt was a weak climax to a victory: the French had been repulsed all along the line, but were far from routed; Murray's caution hobbled the Allied advance and permitted Suchet to escape almost unmolested. There was a long hesitation before Murray defiled his right wing, including the 81st, through the streets of Castalla, and he refused to move until it had deployed in the plain as his reserve. Indeed, the only contact with the retreating French was made by Mackenzie, who pushed forward with four battalions, which may have included the 81st, until peremptorily ordered to withdraw. By the time that the whole Allied army was deployed, the French had retired through the pass of Biar, the mouth of which was blocked by a line of guns protected by infantry. Murray halted for the night of the 13th/14th, over which the French marched away to La Font de la Figuera.

In the two days' action at Biar and Castalla, the Allied loss was some 670 officers and men killed and wounded, and that of the French was nearly double. The 1st/81st was fortunate enough to have no casualties. There was neither battle honour nor medal clasp for the modest victory of Castalla.

Murray's inflated account of the battle, sent on without comment by Wellington, was carried home by Captain Charles George D'Aguilar of the 81st, Assistant Adjutant-General and Military Secretary, of whom the General wrote that 'he eminently possesses every quality which we prize in the character of a soldier.'[597]

After his setback at Castalla, Suchet re-established his line on the River Xuquer. Murray, having got in all his wounded on the 14th, advanced with the expectation of reaching the Xuquer before the French; but finding, after his first day's march, that he was too late, he halted at Alcoy for a few days, and then marched back to his strong position at Castalla, within easy reach of Alicante, while awaiting further instructions from the Commander-in-Chief.

These instructions, sent by Wellington from Freneda on 14th April, gave Murray a number of objectives: 'The objects for the operations of the troops on the eastern coast of Spain are first to obtain possession of the open part of the kingdom of Valencia; secondly, to obtain an establishment on the sea coast north of the Ebro, so as to open a communication with the [Spanish] army of Catalonia; and eventually, thirdly, to oblige the enemy to retire from the Lower Ebro.'

It was further proposed that Murray should embark a minimum of ten thousand men to make a 'brisk attack' on Tarragona, the success of which would attain the first two objects and lay a foundation for the attainment of the third object. The detailed instruction went on to warn against taking risks in such strong terms that they must have limited the operational choices of generals with considerably more self-confidence and firmness of purpose than Sir John Murray: 'It must be understood,' wrote Wellington,… 'that I shall forgive any thing excepting that one of the corps should be beaten or dispersed.'

Tarragona June 1813

There are certain episodes in the Peninsular War,' wrote Sir Charles Oman, 'which the British historian has to relate with a feeling of some humiliation, but which have to be set forth in full detail, if only for the purpose of illustrating the manifold difficulties with which Wellington had to cope. Of these, by far the most distressing is the story of General Sir John Murray at Tarragona.'

Diversionary operations on the East Coast were an essential part of Wellington's master plan to expel the French from Spain, and he had taken great pains to explain in detail what Murray and his Spanish allies were to do. By the end of May, in obedience to Wellington's instruction, Murray had handed over his forward positions to the Spanish armies of Elio and Del Parque, 43,000 strong, and concentrated his Anglo-Sicilian army and Whittingham's Spanish division around Alicante. He sailed on the 31st for Tarragona with 17,126 men, including 800 cavalry, with 24 guns and a siege train brought round from Lisbon. There had been some reorganisation of divisions, and the 1st/81st were now in General John Mackenzie's division with the 1st/10th, 1st/27th, De Roll's-Dillon's and the 2nd Italian Levy. The 81st was commanded by Major James Farrer, a veteran of Maida who on 4th

---

[597] D'Aguilar (1784-1855), born in Liverpool of a military family of Austrian-Jewish extraction, had been Assistant Adjutant-General to Sir William Bentinck in Sicily, from where in April 1812 he had been sent on a diplomatic mission to Ali Pasha in Constantinople with a present of 100 barrels of gunpowder. He eventually became Major-General Sir George D'Aguilar KCB, Lieutenant-Governor of Hong Kong and Commander of British troops in China 1843-48.

June was promoted to Brevet Lieutenant-Colonel when Colonel McKenzie was advanced to command of a brigade.

The expedition, escorted by Rear Admiral Hallowell, anchored at dusk on 2nd June off Cape Salou, eight miles south-west of their objective. Murray at once detached Colonel Prevost with two battalions to occupy the coastal defile of Balaguer, some twenty miles to the south-west, and to capture the small fort of San Filipe, blocking Suchet's movement of reinforcements from Tortosa and Valencia. The remaining troops disembarked the following morning, and the investment of Tarragona was complete that night. General Copons of Tarifa note, now Captain-General of Catalonia, rode down from his headquarters at nearby Reus and undertook to provide a covering force to the north and east against General Decaen advancing from Barcelona. The auspices looked favourable for a successful siege.

Since the storming of Tarragona by Marshal Suchet two years previously, little had been done to repair the damage caused by his siege. No attempt had been made to restore the defences of the lower town other than to patch up two isolated strongpoints on the west front: Fort Royal and the Bastion of San Carlos were cut off from the surrounding ruins and closed in at the rear; each was manned by just one company. The rest of the 1,600-strong garrison, half of whom were Italians, occupied the upper city on its high cliff, whose breaches had been repaired. It was an inadequate force to man a fortress of that size, and the sight of a large, well-equipped force of besiegers did not improve its morale.

The weakness of the place and its garrison was not appreciated by Murray, and six days were wasted in establishing batteries and bombarding the outworks. Mackenzie's division, with the 81st, held positions along the Francoli river to the west of the city, facing the French outworks. Many of the British, and in particular the infantry officers, felt that these should have been stormed at once, and began to voice their discontent at the slow progress of operations; but Murray was determined on a formal siege, and his chief engineer, Major Thackeray, advised that it would take about two weeks to breach the upper city walls. Indeed, Murray had never believed that his expedition would take Tarragona, and had convinced himself that Suchet and Decaen, commanding the Armies of Aragon and Catalonia, were about to descend on him with 25,000 men. As early as 7th June, he confessed to his fears in a doom-laden and prematurely exculpatory letter to Wellington:

'I am afraid we have undertaken more than we are able to perform, but to execute your Lordship's orders, I will persevere as long as prudence will permit. I have as yet no certain information about Suchet's movements, nor of [Decaen] to the eastward, but there are reports of both, and if they prove true in five or six days I may be attacked by a force ultimately superior, without the hopes or chance of retreat.'

Nevertheless, the siege proceeded, additional guns were landed, and on 8th June, Major Thackeray reported a practicable breach in Fort Royal, only to advise against an assault. On the morning of the 11th Murray rode out to reconnoitre the river Gaya, where he had agreed to support Copons against an expected attack from Barcelona, leaving Clinton with a warning to be ready to march in that direction with his division, and discretion to order the storming of Fort Royal. In Murray's absence, Clinton gave orders for an assault at 10 p.m. that evening by the 1st/10th, supported by the 1st/81st. Morale rose as the troops anticipated action at last. Murray returned that evening and, having been briefed by Clinton, cancelled the attack at the last moment, to the disappointed anger of all ranks:

'Ten was the hour fixed, and every one in anxious expectation of seeing it, when at ½ past 9 an order arrived to postpone it till 11. This was far from being relished, but how dreadfully disappointed and vexed was every one in half an hour after to find it was not to take place. A murmur passed along the troops, and every one expressed themselves in strong language against the horrid indecision of Sir John, and no one more so than Gen Mackenzie.'[598]

It was about to get worse. Shaken by a pessimistic intelligence estimate that Suchet and Decaen could combine their forces close to Tarragona on 12th June, Murray completely lost his nerve and ordered the immediate embarkation of his army, spiking his siege guns and, equally disgracefully, abandoning his ally Copons. In fact, the two French columns were still some 35 miles apart, and both would shortly withdraw. Suchet had only eight thousand men, and Mathieu was coming down from Barcelona with just six thousand, offering Murray and

---

[598] Diary of Major Thomas Scott, Royal Artillery, entry for 11th June 1813.

Copons, with their combined 23,000 men, an excellent opportunity of defeating them both in turn from a central position. The next few hours were marked by vacillation and confusion, with order followed by counter-order – Clinton received seven different and often contradictory orders between dawn and 1.30 p.m. on the 12th. Mackenzie and Adam tried to persuade Murray to march out and attack the French approaching from Barcelona, but he dismissed their proposal, referring to Wellington's injunction that he was not to risk a defeat. He also refused to allow the gunners another night to withdraw and embark their ordnance, and 21 guns, mortars and howitzers were left in the batteries. All ranks of the expedition were shamed and mortified as, from their ships, they cursed Murray and watched as the incredulous French garrison picked over the abandoned spoils. The British troops were furious:

'Alas! Our sun has set and nothing but a gloomy cloud of despair hangs over us. Whither we go I care not, but the more solitary the place, the more adapted to our luckless situation; for we cannot but be reviled wherever we go – 22,000 flying before an army of 8,000!! Was Britain ever so disgraced before? Never were her soldiers so debased. Plainly could we perceive the enemy dismantling our batteries, and carts innumerable employed in removing our numerous stores left behind. How shameful; plenty of time had we to prevent all this, but the stigma, thank God, rests upon the shoulders of him, whom I hope will be for ever disgraced, if not hung or shot, which he undoubtedly merits.'[599]

The morning after embarkation, Hallowell carried the army down the coast to the Col de Balaguer where, late on the evening of the 13th, three battalions of Mackenzie's division were landed to cover the evacuation of Prevost's force, together with the Allied cavalry and field artillery who had marched there from Tarragona. Next day Suchet came up from the south to reconnoitre the pass and, seeing it still held by a considerable British force, ordered General Pannetier, who with a brigade of three thousand men had been sent to by-pass the defile by mountain tracks, to withdraw. Murray, who possibly saw an opportunity to redeem himself, ordered a large-scale landing on the 15th to strike at Pannetier's isolated brigade, which had drawn back to Valdellos. Mackenzie's division made a forced march, but arrived only just in time to see the French rearguard disappear.

On the 16th Suchet marched back towards Valencia, leaving only Pannetier's three thousand facing Murray; but that same day Mathieu made another advance with his six thousand and relieved Tarragona. He then moved on along the coast road to Cambrils. This prompted Murray, who was still convinced that Suchet was about to assail him with 24,000 men while eight thousand French came against his rear, to order another re-embarkation, leaving Copons once more in the lurch.

Murray's evacuation orders had no sooner been drawn up on the 18th when Sir Edward Pellew's Toulon blockading squadron, twelve ships of the line, appeared offshore, carrying with them Lord William Bentinck, who had come from Sicily to assume command of the Anglo-Sicilian army. Admiral Hallowell surely spoke for the whole expedition when he indiscreetly ran up the signal, 'We are all delighted.'

Bentinck promptly landed to the cheers of soldiers and sailors. Having been briefed, he relieved Murray of command and ordered the force back to Alicante, in accordance with Wellington's directions in the event of failure at Tarragona. The fleet sailed on the 19th June but, because of unfavourable winds which drove a number of transports ashore, the expedition reached Alicante between the 22nd and 26th of that month. The 81st arrived on the 24th and was temporarily quartered at Palamos.

Sir John Murray was brought before a court-martial in January 1815. The prosecution was not well made, and Murray was found guilty of only one of the three charges, namely, 'For neglect of duty in hastily re-embarking the forces under his command without any previous preparations or arrangements, and thus precipitately and unnecessarily abandoning a considerable quantity of artillery, stores, and ammunition… when he was so far from being compelled to this degrading measure by the immediate approach of any superior force, or by any other sufficient cause, that by due zeal, firmness, and exertion, the greater part, if not the whole, might have been embarked in safety.' However, the court considered that Murray's conduct had proceeded from 'a mere error in judgement,' and he escaped with an admonishment.

---

[599] Scott, diary entry for 13th June 1813.

The Great Flank March

Wellington had intended to march into Spain on 1st May, but was delayed by a late spring and by his slow-moving pontoon train. Consequently, it was not until 18th May that he issued final orders for Graham's advance, and the 22nd before he left his old headquarters at Freineda. As he crossed the frontier, he is said to have turned in his saddle, raised his hat, and exclaimed, 'Farewell Portugal, I shall not see thee again!'

Further north, the 40th, 47th, 59th and 82nd had crossed the Douro well inside northern Portugal and pressed on over the wild borderlands of Tras os Montes. The 40th had received their march route on 12th May, on which day Lieutenant James Mill wrote, 'Since I commenced this letter the order has arrived to march on Tuesday. We have received the route as far as Miranda… where we shall get a fresh route.' Anson's brigade crossed the Douro at Barca de Alva on 19th May, as described by Lieutenant Charles Crowe of the 27th:

'Here about 300 yards below the junction with the Agueda we found boats, such as convey the skins of wine to Oporto, ready to carry us across to the road on the north bank of the Douro. Two strong cables secured on each shore rendered the passage direct in defiance of the rapid current. The baggage was reloaded, and we commenced at 8 o'clock our march up the steep ascent of the rocky roads of Tras os Montes, which were so narrow that we could only march in file.'[600]

Four large wine barges were indeed used for the crossing, each holding 150 men. Further downstream, at Pocinho on the high road, a flying bridge carried more troops. Anson's brigade assembled later that day at Ligares, where they were well received by the people in a place previously unvisited by the warring armies. On the 21st they marched to Mos, where the whole division assembled, and on the 22nd to Lagoaca. Next day they encamped near Vila de Ala, from where they followed the high road parallel to the right (north) bank of the Douro, via Sendim to Miranda do Douro, where they halted while the pontoon train was brought up.

The 5th Division, with the 47th and 59th, left their winter quarters on 14th May and were ferried across the Douro at Peso da Regoa, north of Lamego. They then marched by Villa Real, Mirandela and Bragança to Outeiro. Writing to a family friend from Outeiro on May 25th, Frederick Robinson, whose brigade included the 2nd/47th and 2nd/59th, could barely conceal his excitement:

'Look at your map, and you will find we are close to the frontiers of Spain. We are to march tomorrow, and on the second day shall enter that country not far from Zamora, which place we are to take, for so His Lordship wills, and what he wills must be done.

'We have had a most fatiguing march of over a fortnight, over mountains and rocky roads hitherto deemed impassable for artillery. In many instances the horses were taken off and the guns were dragged up by five or six hundred men. It is the first time any army was ever seen in this part of the country.

'No pen can describe the ignorance of these wretched people, and so dreadfully alarmed are they at our approach that nothing is to be seen but empty houses, or only the old people. Everything else is taken to the mountains, until they find through our scouts that we are not their enemies, and are ready to pay for everything… One of the officers enquired why they had put away the children: the answer was, because they understood the English would eat them!!

'The inhabitants soon flocked in, and had a most excellent ready money market for their wine, of which one Regt (59th) drank four pipes[601] during one day's stay. The wine all through this country is very pleasant, but weak, and generally upon our first coming is sold at about threepence a bottle.'

If the Lilywhites' thirst impressed their brigade commander, so too did the competitive alacrity with which they pitched camp: 'The baggage uniformly followed the division when on the advance,' he wrote, 'and was generally up in a few minutes after the troops had halted; consequently the tents were pitched and the encampment completed in less than a quarter of an hour. The 59th Regiment allowed 11 minutes! The shoemakers were put to work, a party paraded for wood and water, and the cooks had their fires and kettles ready by the time the bullocks were slaughtered.'

---

[600] *An Eloquent Soldier*, The Peninsular War Journals of Lieutenant Charles Crowe of the Inniskillings, p. 72.
[601] This may be a slight exaggeration, since four pipes would be well over 400 gallons!

The 7th Division, with the 82nd, had preceded the 4th Divisions over the crossings at Pocinho and Barca de Alva, and then took the same eastward route on the north bank of the Douro.

On the 26th, Wellington pushed the French out of Salamanca, making a strong display of force in that direction. Graham's wing of the army passed the frontier that day and was preparing to cross the River Esla. On the 29th, having shown himself at Salamanca, Wellington rode secretly for fifty miles to the north, crossed the flooded Duero in a suspended basket, and rode on a further twenty miles to the headquarters of his main force. On 31st May, he supervised the unopposed crossing of the Esla at Almendra, causing the French to evacuate Zamora. The 5th Division crossed that afternoon by a bridge of thirteen pontoons established across a narrow part of the river. The 82nd, with the 7th Division, had crossed the river earlier, as described by George Wood:

'Part of the troops forded it, but most of the battalion-men were obliged to wait for the pontoons, as many of the soldiers who attempted to ford, not being tall enough, were swept away by the rapidity of the current. We expected the French on the other side would oppose our crossing… We crossed, however, without opposition, in sight of our noble Commander, who was seated on a rock in company with General Lord Lynedoch [Graham]. We defiled with music playing, Colours flying, and bayonets glittering, which had a very imposing effect.

'On winding up the opposite hills, we halted on the top; and had no sooner got our meat on the fire, anxious to appease our appetites, after a long and sultry march, when we observed one of the Duke's staff running down a hill in the advance, and waving his hat to us. We understood him; and in less than ten minutes the troops were fully accoutered, and in march to the place which this officer had pointed out, leaving the fires, kettles and dinners to cook themselves; but the enemy finding us so much on the alert, and so quickly in position, withdrew their forces, and we betook ourselves to our old ground, where we found our rations extremely well boiled, and we were not long in demolishing them.'

Having completed his successful deception at Salamanca, Hill moved north to join Graham. By 3rd June both wings of the Allied army were concentrated around Toro on the north bank of the Duero, from where they advanced to the north-east, close together on three routes, with Giron's Galicians moving on a fourth route to their north. The 47th and 59th were on the next northern route, led by Graham, while the 40th and 82nd marched with Wellington's central, or headquarters column. Their further advance was at first across the flat, open cornfields of Castille and Leon, keeping to the north of the Pisuerga as far as Palencia.[602] Outflanked, King Joseph abandoned Valladolid and the lower crossings of the Pisuerga, falling back along the Royal Road to Burgos. Then, instead of following Joseph's withdrawal up the highway to Torquemada and Burgos, Wellington sent his columns north to cross the Pisuerga at Melgar and Zarosa respectively by June 12th, turning French positions behind that river.

The marches were long, but the weather was good, the army remained healthy, and as observed by George Wood of the 82nd, troop morale was high:

'Our march for the first two or three hundred miles was like a party of pleasure in comparison to others we had encountered: we passed through a most delightful level country, abounding in all the verdant beauties of nature, and affording the greatest plenty of forage for cattle, which is the principal support to an army *en grande route*. Everything and every countenance now wore the aspect of joy – the men singing and telling their jocose stories as they passed along hill and dale; till, leaving many fine towns and an open country in our rear, we came in sight of the enemy's *videttes*.'

With their positions on the Pisuerga outflanked to the north, the French left Burgos on 13th June, blowing up the Castle and falling back to take up a new defensive line on the Ebro. Wellington was by then near enough to hear the explosion, and it appears to have confirmed his resolution to cross the upper reaches of the Ebro and drive the French completely out of Spain. He at once ordered another bold turning movement, directing his entire army north into mountains deemed impassable for artillery and wheeled transport, and consequently undefended by the French. By noon on the 14th Graham's column was across the Ebro at San Martin, while on the 15th Wellington's headquarters column crossed fifteen miles downstream at Puente-Arenas.

---

[602] Wellington's column marched from Toro through La Mota, Castromonte, Ampudia and Palencia. Graham's column, further north, advanced by way of Medina de Rio Seco and Grijota (5 miles north of Palencia).

The army had to travel light, and as the baggage of the 5th Division passed, Wellington noticed two carts, one loaded with private baggage of the 59th Foot, and another with tents for the 4th. A reasoned rebuke was instantly forthcoming 'His Lordship,' wrote the Adjutant-General, 'has directed me to point out to you how very inconvenient these carts are to the operations of the army, and how very desirable it would be to get rid of them entirely, particularly in a mountainous country; that to carry private baggage upon carts is positively contrary to orders, and that to carry tents upon carts is quite ridiculous, as they cannot by any possible chance arrive upon the ground to be occupied by the troops before they will march from it.'

By this time the army's lines of communication were overstretched and, although Wellington had on 10th June presciently ordered supply ships forward from Corunna to Santander, the new base was not yet established. Cattle 'on the hoof' accompanied the army, but a lack of other provisions was affecting health. On 13th June, an officer of the 4th Division wrote in his diary:

'We have been three days without bread or biscuit, our advance has been so rapid that the commissariat stores from the rear cannot overtake us. Consequently, an extra half pound of meat per man has been supplied. This was highly expedient, but salt, wherewith to flavour this pound and [a] half of beef, reeking from the fresh slain bullock, was not to be procured for nine days… and the sodden flesh lacking salt made many of us painfully sensible of its great value. The effect of the want of this important article was that all of us suffered dreadfully from diarrhoea. Our eyes and our noses told us how woefully some of our men were afflicted, and their pale hollow cheeks and their nether garments confirmed the fact, for the flux ran from them as they marched.'

Fortunately, next day a magazine of French provisions was captured, and 'an abundant store of salt was freely given to each regiment as they passed. We received 3 or 4 haversacks full per company. The soldiers ate it with the greatest avidity, and it seemed to impart a vigour to them instantly.'[603]

Despite the irregularity of their rations, the troops were impressed by the striking beauty and grandeur of their mountainous surroundings, and everyone from the general to the drummer boy seemed at a loss for words to express their delight. After crossing the Esla, the columns converged on the towns of Medina de Pomar and Villar Cayo, from where they all took the south-easterly road to Berberana.

For several days, the French had no knowledge of the Allied flank march, but on 18th June, Reille and Maucune, marching north towards Bilbao with three divisions, unexpectedly bumped into the British columns, leading to simultaneous combats at San Millan and nearby Osma. In the latter fight, the light companies of the 4th and 5th Divisions were engaged in a smart skirmish before Reille withdrew. Lieutenant Colin Campbell of the 9th, afterwards Lord Clyde, described this affair as it affected the 5th Division:

'This being our first encounter of the campaign, the men were ardent and eager, and pressed the French most wickedly. When the enemy began their movement to the rear, they were constrained to hurry the pace of their columns, notwithstanding the cloud of skirmishers which covered their retreat. Lord Wellington came up about half-past three. We continued the pursuit until dusk, when we were relieved by the light troops of the fourth division. The ground on which we skirmished was so thickly wooded and so rugged and uneven that when we were relieved by the fourth division and the light companies were ordered to return to their respective regiments, I found myself incapable of further exertion, occasioned by six hours of almost continuous skirmishing.'

By 19th June Joseph, still astride the Royal Road, was behind the River Zadorra in front of the town of Vitoria, towards which Wellington's columns were now directed.

'Neither the winter gullies, nor the ravines, nor the precipitate passes among the rocks, retarded even the march of the artillery; where horses could not draw, men hauled; when the wheels would not roll, the guns were let dawn or lifted up with ropes; and strongly did the rough veteran infantry work their way through those wild but beautiful regions; six days they toiled unceasingly; on the seventh… they burst like raging streams from every defile and went foaming into the basin of Vitoria.'[604]

On 20th June, Wellington's columns were on the River Bayas, some five miles from the Zadorra, and, anticipating battle at Vitoria, were already moving into position. The 40th bivouacked near Subijana-Morillas, the

---

[603] Crowe, p. 90.
[604] Sir William Napier, *History of the Peninsular War*, Book XX, Chapter VII, p. 197.

82nd further upstream near Zuazo, and the 47th and 59th, after a flanking cross-country march, had reached Murgia. There was still a shortage of food, as described by Lieutenant James Mill of the 40th:

'One pound and a half of bread was the whole that was issued in seven days previous to the battle [i.e. 14th-20th June]. Bread was not to be purchased. Had it not been for a supply of horse-beans, which we gathered in the fields, we could not have gone through the protracted fatigue. My constitution has borne me well through the hardships; at least as well as can be expected.'[605]

Corporal Lawrence of the same regiment was also among those who, on the evening of the 20th, had to forage for something to eat:

'The only thing I with several comrades could find was some broad beans, and those we had to gather for ourselves: we got a good many, but we were certainly not out for them more than an hour altogether, as nearly the whole of my party had to go on duty that night, and as it happened at the general's own quarters, which were in a house which had been deserted by its inhabitants. We occupied a kind of outhouse, adjoining, and having lit a fire in the centre and found a kettle belonging to the house, we set to work and cooked a quantity of wheat that we found stowed away there, and on that made a very good night's meal. I likewise preserved a quantity and put it into my knapsack for a favourite comrade who had been left in camp in charge of our beans; but when I returned I found I need not have done that, for he had had just as good a meal off the greater part of the beans as we had off the wheat.'[606]

The Battle of Vitoria, 21st June 1813

The town of Vitoria stands on a rise towards the east end of a rolling plain 12 miles long by 6-8 miles wide, dotted with small villages and enclosed by hills. To the south lie the Puebla Heights, while the hills to the north are more distant. The River Zadorra enters this plain through the Defile of Salinas to the north-east, winding south-west and then south to flow out through the Defile of Puebla to the south-west. The river line is an obstacle, but, with eleven bridges and many fords on its winding course, it was not wholly defensible. To the west, the steep Hill of Arinez dominates approaches to the plain from across the Zadorra. The Royal Road from Burgos to the French frontier entered the plain by the Defile of Puebla, then ran through the village of Arinez, and Vitoria itself, before running on to the north-east, along the Zadorra and through the Defile of Salinas. Five minor roads and many country tracks converged on the plain, including the road through Salvatierra to Pamplona, the only alternative line of retreat for the French.

Manoeuvred out of successive positions across central Spain, King Joseph and his chief of staff, Marshal Jourdan, had resolved to stand and fight in front of Vitoria. They had good reasons to do so, for the alternative was to be ignominiously hustled out of Spain without a fight, abandoning the vast convoy of baggage, non-combatants, refugees and loot which had assembled under their protection. With 69,737 men and 153 guns, the combined French armies were weaker in infantry than Wellington, but stronger in cavalry and guns. Moreover, they expected reinforcement: the 30,000 men of Clausel's Army of the North were expected on 22nd June, while Foy, was collecting garrisons from the Biscay coast. Meanwhile, part of the convoy set off on the 20th and 21st escorted by Maucune's Division.

The French had convinced themselves that Wellington would attack from the west between the Defile of Puebla and the bridge of Villodas, and that any troops seen moving to the north were Spanish irregulars making a diversion. Consequently, their initial deployment on 20th June faced west in three lines. The front line was found by Gazan's Army of the South, 34,636 men (half the total French force) and 54 guns, deployed between the Puebla Heights and the Hill of Arinez above Villodas. D'Erlon's Army of the Centre, with 17,691 men and 17 guns, stood one mile back, astride the Royal Road between the villages of Margarita and Gomecha, while the 17,440 men and 46 guns of Reille's Army of Portugal lined up in front of Vitoria.

Following mounting evidence of Allied movement north of the Zadorra, there was an adjustment on the afternoon of 20th June when one of Reille's two divisions, plus Spanish troops, moved to cover this approach.

[605] Quoted in *Historical Records of the 40th Regiment*, p. 140.
[606] Lawrence, p.p. 132-33.

Marshal Jourdan was sick on the 20th June, so his confirmatory reconnaissance was not made until 6 a.m. on the 21st. He was troubled by the wide dispersion of his army, and considered moving back to a shorter, tighter line around Zuazo, but it was too late: battle had commenced.

The total Allied strength was 78,000 men, including 9,000 Spaniards and 26,000 Portuguese, with 96 guns.[607] Wellington had a good idea of the French deployment and intentions from his 'correspondents,' and had made a personal reconnaissance of all approach routes. He also appreciated that he needed to attack before the reinforcement of the French by Clausel, which was imminent.

His plan was to turn both flanks of Gazan's army, to which he added a deep envelopment on the left to cut the main French escape route. Four separate formations had to converge over a front of some twenty miles.

On the right flank, Sir Rowland Hill was to capture the Defile of Puebla, then drive east along the Puebla Heights and capture the village of Subijana de Alava. To do this he had the British 2nd Division, the Spanish and Portuguese divisions of Morillo and Silveira, and three brigades of cavalry, a total of some 20,000 men.

Next, centre right, were Cole's 4th Division (including the 40th) and Alten's Light Division, followed by four cavalry brigades and the artillery reserve, another 20,000 men. Their task, once Hill was established on the Heights of Puebla and in Subijana, was to cross the bridges at Nanclares and Villodas to make frontal attack on the French centre. Until then, they were kept concealed in hollow ways and folds in the ground.

In the centre left was Lord Dalhousie with his own 7th Division, including the 82nd, together with Sir Thomas Picton's 3rd Division, a total of 15,000 men. Their task was to cross the Zadorra around Mendoza to attack the right rear of the French front line.

Finally, on the far left was Sir Thomas Graham with the 1st and 5th Divisions (the latter including the 47th and 59th), Longa's Spanish Division, two Portuguese brigades and two cavalry brigades, a total of 21,000 men. Their main task was to cut the Royal Road, the main French line of retreat. Graham also had discretion to drive into the French rear if it did not prejudice achievement of his main objective.

Co-ordination of the widely dispersed columns, and synchronisation of their converging attacks, was always going to be difficult. Wellington sought to mitigate the problems of time and space by delegating responsibility for the critical right and far left attacks to his most trusted generals, Hill and Graham, and by co-ordinating the operations of the centre-right columns himself. He also ordered that the columns on the left should look to their right to regulate their rate of advance.

The early morning of the 21st had been misty, but by about 8 a.m. the weather cleared and there was excellent visibility; so much so that, despite the smoke, diarists commented on remarkable battle panoramas. It also became very hot, and the troops suffered much from thirst.

The attack started late because Hill had to cross the Zadorra at La Puebla, while Dalhousie and Graham had to thread their way over mountain tracks, which was not possible in the dark, before completing their approach march to the river.

Hill began his attack on the Puebla Defile and Heights at about 8 a.m.,[608] and within two hours his troops were driving along the Heights and were fighting to secure Subijana, which changed hands several times and was not finally secured until about 1.30 p.m. By 11 a.m. their advance had forced Gazan to send the equivalent of three divisions up the Heights and to recapture Subijana, but to no avail. In consequence the French centre and right were seriously, indeed fatally, weakened.

Meanwhile, Graham's columns, having marched at about 5 a.m., were approaching from the north along the Bilbao road from Murgia. At about 10 a.m. they were in contact with Sarrut's division of the Army of Portugal at Aranguiz, some two miles short of the Zadorra. Graham halted to await developments on his right. Seeing the strength of the Allied columns, Reille withdrew across the river, and Graham advanced to seize crossings. Oswald's 5th Division, with Robinson's brigade in the lead, was eventually sent to take the bridge of Gamarra Mayor. What followed was the hardest-fought, longest and bloodiest action of the battle of Vitoria.

---

[607] Including 55,664 Anglo-Portuguese infantry, 7,681 Spanish infantry and 9,607 cavalry.

[608] As is the case with all battles of this period, timings are uncertain, with the recollections, or watches, of witnesses differing by as much as two hours.

The village of Gamarra Mayor was on the north bank of the Zadorra, which at that point was not fordable and could only be crossed by a long stone bridge, approached from the village centre by a very narrow street. The compact village, centred on its church, had been barricaded and was held by Gauthier's brigade of Lamartinière's 6th division – the 118th and 119th Ligne.[609] Behind a hedge at the bottom of the lane leading into the village were three field guns, while the surrounding barricades and hedges were lined by French infantry and 'a cloud of skirmishers' deployed among the cornfields in front. A further six to eight cannons covered the bridge from higher ground on the far side of the river, where Lamartinière's other brigade was posted.

It was towards noon when Robinson's brigade advanced astride the village lane in open column of companies, supported by two guns. 'Well knowing that our Great Chief likes prompt measures,' their commander wrote, 'I ordered the Brigade to charge at once, and in a quarter of an hour we drove them over a bridge on the opposite side with dreadful havoc.' His diary gives a more detailed account:

'Having reached the furthest height we had a full view of Vittoria & the battle already commenced on the right. A large body of the enemy was in the plain before us, & the firing gradually reached the division immediately on our right. The village of Gamarra Mayor was just below us, a place of the highest importance to both armies, & likely to be warmly contended. The Spaniards under Longa were ordered to attack it, supported by my brigade, but after waiting a considerable time it was evident that they had no idea of leading the attack. I therefore marched through them, the 47th at the head of the column, followed by the 4th. The right wing of the 59th entered the cornfield on the right of the road, & the left wing that on the left. One company of the 4th acted as sharpshooters, the light companies having been detached some distance were not in the attack.

'The moment the brigade advanced the enemy commenced a heavy fire from field pieces and small howitzers behind hedges at the bottom of the lane which we were to pass to the village; the hedges were lined with sharpshooters. When the head of the column had arrived at a convenient distance for a charge, a shout was given & the brigade advanced in double quick & never halted until the enemy was driven entirely out of the village over a narrow stone bridge, where a most dreadful slaughter took place. Our loss also was very great. I thought at one moment the 47th Regt would have been cut to pieces, but fortunately the road was wide enough to admit of the 4th coming abreast of them, when they carried all before them.'

'A severe fire from 8 field pieces & a large body of sharpshooters was opened upon us from the opposite side of the river, & was returned by the brigade from the windows of all the stone houses commanding the bridge. At this critical time the rest of the 5th Division & 2 field pieces under Bt Major Lawson joined us, which secured the village although the enemy made three attempts to retake it & had a column of 15,000 men within 500 yards of us. The attacks were each time repulsed with great slaughter.

'Sir Thomas Graham with a large party of staff officers saw the whole affair from the top of an adjacent hill & expressed the warmest satisfaction at the gallant manner in which the brigade had carried the village. Colonel De Lancey, the DQMG, exclaimed that he would not sleep until he had acquainted Lord Wellington with the conduct of our people.'

The brigade took the village at bayonet point, without loading, after a 'grand charge' and fierce close-quarter fighting in which the three regiments became intermixed. In a few minutes the three guns at the head of the village were captured, and some hundred prisoners were taken.[610] Three desperate attempts were then made to cross the bridge, but the French had the narrow passage well covered and blew away the head of each column before it could make a lodgement. The village too was under continuous fire from shot and shell, and among the casualties was Lieutenant-Colonel Charles Fane of the 59th, who was mortally wounded.

'Poor Charles, finding that garden walls, & such impediments as are usual about a village, prevented his leading his regiment as he wished while on horseback, dismounted, & in this situation, after the enemy had been driven through the village & two of their guns taken, he was struck down in front of his men. His example ceasing to have effect, his regiment was repulsed a short distance, so that for more than half an hour he lay between the

---

[609] The strength of Gauthier's brigade at Vitoria was 71 officers and 2,496 men, some 500 less than they fielded at Salamanca.
[610] The statement in Cowper's *History of The King's Own*, Vol. I, p. 413, that the 4th passed the other two battalions and 'carried the place, taking 2,000 prisoners and three guns', is fanciful: Lamartinière's division had a total of 117 captured that day, whilst the 4th suffered significantly fewer casualties that day than the 47th and 59th.

opposing corps, with the heaviest possible fire from both parties passing over him, without the possibility of being rescued. Fortunately, as he poor fellow thought at the time, though the result has not proved it to be so, he was able to crawl to where the ground was rather hollow, & thus escaped immediate annihilation which otherwise would have awaited him. General Robinson told me that the brigade owed much of its success to his noble example & distinguished conduct.'[611]

Bringing up their reserves, the French made three attempts to retake Gamarra Mayor, but without success. The only approach to the bridge from the British side was by pushing straight down the narrow village street, while the French had to cross open fields. The opposing forces were equally balanced, and equally obstinate; and the murderous conflict continued until the bridge was so heaped with dead and wounded that they were rolled over the parapet into the river. Both sides fought with obstinate bravery, but neither could make headway on such a narrow front.

The riverbanks were lined with opposing light infantry, among whom was Sergeant James Hale of the Light Company 9th, whose diary entry acknowledged the gallantry of Lamartinière's men: 'It plainly appeared this day that the enemy had formed a sort of determination not to be beat: we never saw them stand so vigorous before.'

Nevertheless, when eventually the tide of battle flowed eastward along the Zadorra, Reille was obliged to fall back from the river-line with the loss in Lamartinière's division of 586 all ranks.

The battered 5th Division followed for some three miles and halted near Zurbano. They had suffered almost as severely, with 496 casualties, of whom 352 were in Robinson's brigade. Of these, the 47th had 112 casualties, of whom two officers, two sergeants and sixteen rank and file were killed[612], and four officers and 88 men were wounded,[613] while the 59th lost a total of 160, of whom a corporal and twelve men were killed[614] and nine officers and 138 men were wounded, including Lieutenant-Colonels Fane and Weir, Lieutenants Langley and Walker and 31 privates who died later of their wounds.[615] 'I have lost some officers of great value,' wrote Robinson, 'but they died in the execution of their duty, and I hope will be rewarded elsewhere.'

Colonel Charles Fane, one of the most promising officers in the Service, was much regretted. According to his obituaries, 'he had his leg and part of his thigh carried off [by cannon shot], but survived the wound some days. He wrote to some of his relations after he had received his wounds. His last moments were quiet and easy.' 'An officer more zealous in the service of his country, of a more amiable disposition, or more beloved by all who knew him well, perhaps never existed.' He died of tetanus and was buried in the garden of a convent in Vitoria, where his major, John Weir, was shortly afterwards laid at his side.[616]

Paymaster John Harley of the 47th suffered a particularly tragic loss: 'I followed the Army, having been detained by business, and on approaching Vittoria met General Andrew Hay, who had a son, a captain in the Royals. We both felt much anxiety about our sons, his being 21, and mine, a lieutenant in the 47th Regiment, only 19 years of age. I had also my nephew, Lieutenant Hill, a fine lad of 17, in the same regiment. At that time I little knew the wretchedness that awaited me, my only son having been killed, together with my nephew Hill, on that fatal day. The General also lost his son on the same day.'

---

[611] Letter from Major-General Sir Henry Fane (brother of Charles) dated Laragueta near Pampeluna 8th August 1813.

[612] The 47th Regiment strength return for 25th June 1813 shows that 22 rank and file died in the previous month.

[613] Officer casualties of the 47th were: Lieutenants John Harley and George Hill killed in action; Captains William Arthur Hodges, Henry Parsons and William Wingfield Yates, and Lieutenant Thomas Spunner Shortt wounded. Yates was seriously wounded, the remainder slightly. George Hill's mother was awarded an annual allowance of £40 from the Royal Bounty, 'she being very poor and having nine children.' Parsons died at Prome in 1825 during the First Burma War. Away from the Regiment, Lieutenant William Hay, 47th, was wounded with Picton's 3rd Division when ADC to Major-General Brisbane.

[614] The 59th Regiment strength return for 25th June 1813 shows that 14 rank and file died in the previous month.

[615] Officer casualties of the 59th were: Lieutenant-Colonel Charles Fane, died of wounds 27th June; Brevet Lieutenant-Colonel John Laing Weir, died of wounds 4th July; Lieutenant George Henry Walker, died of wounds; Lieutenant Roger Langley, died of wounds 1st August; Lieutenants Alexander McPherson, James MacGregor and William F. Mayne seriously wounded; Lieutenant Patterson O'Hara and Ensign James Pyne slightly wounded. Alexander McPherson, one of the four officer survivors of the 1816 *Sea Horse* shipwreck, died off Bombay in 1819, attributing his illness to his Vitoria chest-wound.

[616] There is a memorial to Charles Fane in St. Nicholas Church, Fulbeck, Lincolnshire close to his family home at Fulbeck Hall where his portrait still hangs.

We are fortunate to have a first-hand soldier's account of the fighting at Gamarra Mayor from Private Adam Reed of the 47th Foot:

'There lay in front of us a village called Gomarah Mayo, and we saw the enemy come into it. The way going down to this village was through a narrow lane… By this time the enemy began to fire cannon at us, and then our men called out, "Let's be at them!" The General said, "So you shall, my lads, prime and load." We then advanced to the lane which led to the village, and the enemy continued a very heavy fire upon us as we did so. The lane was very narrow so that we were obliged to go up by sections. The fields which were on the side contained very high wheat, and in it the French rifles were stationed. As we advanced I saw a gap in the hedge, and I must need go up and look over, and they fired several shots at me, but all missed. I thought to myself I would not peep at them again.

'By this time we drew nigh the village and the lane grew wider. The French having a great many guns in the village, as soon as they saw us they fired them at us. The first round they fired made great havoc in our regiment, for to hear the deadly groans of some of the men that were hit was horrible. Immediately we were ordered to fire a volley, come to port, and commence double quick time and charge. By that village runs a river, and over it a bridge which led us from the village to the town [Vitoria]. The enemy having their guns in the village, and we pushing upon them with our charge so rapidly, caused them to leave 5 behind.

'We charged at them four successive times, but was beat back by superior numbers. The last time we charged we drove them so rapidly that some were forced to jump in the river up to their necks, and we kept the village. There we stood for four hours and could not get a foot of ground on the other side as they brought up a fresh brigade every time we charged. We were very doubtful on which side the victory would end as we both kept up the very heavy fire, but they were more numerous. The killed and wounded lay very thick, and about 1 o'clock our first brigade was ordered down and then the whole of us made a desperate charge. The French would not stand against the charge, and they retired leaving a great many guns behind. We commenced firing [again] and my front rank man fell, and about [3?] o'clock I myself received a musket ball through my right arm near my shoulder. Thus ended the battle of Vittoria for me.

'I then returned to the village from whence I came, and there remained during the afternoon with the rest of the wounded in a Catholic chapel [the Parish Church of Nuestra Señora de la Asunción]. About half past three o'clock an officer came in bringing with him a wounded man. He said he thought we should be obliged to retire, and some of the wounded told him if that was the best news he had got to tell he had better take himself off and look for better. Now about half past 4 o'clock or a quarter to 5 we heard a terrible shouting in the lines, but could not tell whether it was the French or English retiring. We knew it was one of them. Another officer came in among the wounded and told us to keep up our spirits as well as we could, for the British had gained a victory and that the Dragoons were pursuing Joseph Bonaparte.'

As planned, Graham had effectively cut the main French line of retreat, leaving them only the single narrow road through Salvatierra to Pamplona.

Wellington had meanwhile been watching the developing battle from above Nanclares, and in particular, waiting with mounting concern for Dalhousie's left flank attack to begin. Picton's 3rd Division was indeed poised near Mendoza, ready to attack, at about noon, but the head of Dalhousie's own 7th Division was only emerging from the mountains, in which two of his brigades had lost their way. Only Grant's brigade, with the 82nd and the divisional artillery, were present, and Dalhousie hesitated to attack without further orders. Second Captain Robert Macpherson Cairnes, commanding the divisional artillery, gave his impression of what had happened:

'The 3rd and 7th Divisions… had made a very fatiguing march of 3 leagues over the steepest mountain we have yet crossed, when Lord D[alhousie] who was out to the front sent back for us to move on with all speed. Unluckily the Portuguese & 2nd British Brigade of our Division had mistaken their road (if it could be so dignified, for it was no road at all) by passing over (instead of skirting as ordered) a hill [Monte Arrato] on our right, so that they did not arrive till very late in the action. Our first brigade however were in their place & so… were we.'[617]

It was in fact the 3rd Division that attacked first, for Picton, resentful of his subordination to Dalhousie, had lost patience. Shooting ahead of Dalhousie, Picton rushed the undefended Mendoza bridge with Brisbane's

---

[617] Letter dated Camp near Mendival, 30th June 1813, in *The Dickson Manuscripts*, Woolwich, 1908, Vol. V, p. 926.

brigade, followed by Power's Portuguese brigade.[618] Then, together with Kempt's brigade of the Light Division, which had crossed the Tres Puentes bridge, he advanced obliquely across Gazan's ground to the hill and village of Arinez, the key to the Army of the South's position. This sudden attack forced the French to pull back and attempt, with mixed success, to form a new line of battle.

Picton's other British brigade, Colville's, crossed the Zadora by a ford some 300 yards upstream of the bridge and turned to attack the nearby village of Margarita. This village was defended by Chassé's brigade of Darmagnac's division, which had come up from D'Erlon's Army of the Centre to hold the right flank of the new French position, reaching it just as Colville deployed. Darmagnac's German brigade occupied the village of Hermandad (Lermanda on modern maps), half a mile in rear.

There was a fierce fight in Margarita, with very heavy casualties on both sides[619], and it was not until Grant's brigade came up in support that the village was taken. Corporal William Wheeler of the 51st saw Grant's brigade cross the stone Mendoza bridge and caught up with them on the far side of the village of Margarita, where his regiment had been in action: 'In passing through a village we found many wounded men, several belonging to our corps. From these men we learned the Regiment had been engaged and had taken fourteen guns. After this we soon joined.'

Wellington's account of this action, in his despatch after the battle, was succinct: 'Major General the Hon. C. Colville's brigade of the third division was seriously attacked in its advance by a very superior force well formed, which it drove in, supported by General Inglis's brigade of the 7th division, commanded by Colonel Grant of the 82nd. These officers and the troops under their command distinguished themselves.'

D'Erlon pulled back Chassé's shattered brigade to Hermandad, a better defensive position on higher ground, held by Neuenstein' five battalions, 2,678 Germans from Baden, Frankfurt and Nassau, supported by at least two batteries. Behind Darmagnac, Cassagne's division, over five thousand strong, was now drawn up in second line.

Grant's brigade, some 2,500 strong, supported by six guns, now led the attack, advancing on Hermandad under very heavy artillery fire. As they closed on the village, casualties mounted, and Colonel William Grant was seriously wounded. The brigade took cover in a deep, broad ditch only two hundred yards from the enemy, while Dalhousie came up to take direct command of the final assault. It was at this point that the bumptious young brigade major of Vandeleur's brigade of the Light Division rode up. Since Captain Harry Smith told a good story, it has been repeated without question by historians of Vitoria, so an account of the action at Hermandad would be incomplete without it:

'My Brigade, in the middle of the action, was sent to support the 7th Division, which was very hotly engaged. I was sent forward to report myself to Lord Dalhousie, who commanded. I found his lordship and his Q.M.G., Drake, an old Rifle comrade, in deep conversation. I reported pretty quick, and asked for orders (the head of my Brigade was just getting under fire). I repeated the question, "What orders, my Lord?" Drake became somewhat animated, and I heard His Lordship say, "Better to take the village," which the French held with twelve guns (I had counted by their fire), and seemed to be inclined to keep it. I roared out, "Certainly, my Lord," and off I galloped, both calling to me to come back, but, as none are so deaf as those who won't hear, I told General Vandeleur we were immediately to take the village. There was no time to lose, and the 52nd Regiment deployed into line as if at Shorncliffe, while our Riflemen were sent out in every direction, five or six deep, keeping up a fire nothing could resist. I galloped to the officer commanding a Battalion in the 7th Division (the 82nd, I think). "Lord Dalhousie desires you closely to follow this Brigade of the Light Division." "Who are you, sir?" "Never mind that; disobey my Lord's order at your peril." My Brigade, the 52nd in line and the swarms of Riflemen, rushed at the village, and although the ground was intersected in its front by gardens and ditches, nothing ever checked us until we reached the rear of the village, where we halted to reform – the twelve guns, tumbrils, horses, etc., standing in our possession. There never was a more impetuous onset – nothing could withstand such a burst of determination.'

---

[618] Lieutenant Robert Hughes of the 30th, serving with the 9th Portuguese Line in Powers' brigade, was wounded at Vitoria.
[619] Chassé's brigade, 1,794 strong, had some 800 casualties, and Colville lost 548 out of 2,276, nearly all at this point, while Grant's brigade clearly suffered some loss when they came up in support.

Against this must be set the accounts of Grant's brigade, none of whom so much as notice the presence of Vandeleur's men. Corporal William Wheeler had rejoined the ranks of the 51st as they advanced on Hermandad:

'The Brigade were in column in front of a strong position occupied by the enemy. After sustaining their fire some time we dashed forward [and] drove them from their position in such a hurry that they left ten guns behind. This charge was executed so sudden that although they sent us a shower of balls and bullets very few done any harm.'

Lieutenant George Wood of the 82nd gives some more detail:

'We advanced through the tumultuous scene, with a battery in our front dealing out dire destruction; and halting here, as if to defy its greatest efforts, we waited the signal to attack: men and officers fell in every direction; and their wounds were most dreadful, being all inflicted with cannon-balls or shells, except that of our Colonel, who received a musket-shot in his stomach. Our front was exposed to the full range of this redoubt, and had to contend with a French regiment to the right of the battery; but after politely receiving us with a few sharp volleys, which we as politely returned, they retreated firing, and bent their course into a thicket. Towards this we advanced firing, and drove them furiously before us till they were completely routed, and we had the satisfaction of passing over numbers who we had laid prostrate.' [620]

Major Henry King commanded the 82nd in this action, and his biographical entry in *The Royal Military Calendar* is unequivocal as to who took Hermandad:

'During that action he [Major King] received an order from the Duke of Wellington to carry with the 82nd Reg[iment] a village from whence the enemy, with fifteen pieces of artillery, greatly annoyed the advance of the British army. This manoeuvre he executed with promptitude, forcing the enemy, after giving his Regiment six rounds, to abandon it.'[621]

Oman, while quoting Harry Smith in full, observes that it is 'curious' that whilst Grant's brigade suffered 334 casualties, Vandeleur lost only 38 all day: hardly the likely outcome of storming a village defended by more than twice his brigade strength. The balance of evidence indicates that Grant's brigade took Hermandad, with Vandeleur in support, though the timely arrival of the Light Division men could no doubt have added weight and impetus to the assault.

The main loss at Margarita and Hermandad fell on the 68th and Chasseurs Britanniques, whose 125 and 140 casualties respectively suggests that they may have been in first line. The 82nd had Lieutenant Alexander Carroll and five men killed[622], and Colonel Grant, three other officers and eighteen men wounded.[623] The musters for June and July suggest that four men may later have died of their wounds.

Addressing the 82nd in 1875, when presenting new Colours, Field Marshal the Marquess of Tweeddale, who was a major on the staff at Vitoria, recalled an incident of hand-to-hand combat in which a corporal of the 82nd Regiment was bayoneted by a French grenadier. 'Though he had received a mortal wound, he retained his coolness, grappled with his enemy and threw him. His own bayonet not being available, he seized a firelock near at hand, unfixed the bayonet, and plunged it into his adversary. Thus they struggled on until death put an end to their sufferings.

---

[620] Wood, p.p. 183-84.

[621] *The Royal Military Calendar, 1820*, Vol IV, p. 375.

[622] The 82nd Regiment strength return for 25th June 1813 shows that 8 rank and file died in the previous month, which would include some who died subsequently of their wounds.

[623] Lieutenant-Colonel William Grant was severely wounded, with a musket ball in the stomach, but was back in action within a month; Lieutenant Thomas Ramsden Agnew lost a leg, but survived to become a major in the 82nd; Lieutenant Edward Phineas Davies 'received a severe contusion on the left shoulder from a nine pound cannon shot', but was back in action the following month; Lieutenant George Webb Derenzy lost his right arm but he too continued to serve and became a captain in the 82nd. He also invented and publicised a range of ingenious attachments for prosthetic arms. In 1822 he wrote a pamphlet, *Enchiridion: or A Hand for the One-Handed*, stating that, 'I have been induced to devote a considerable portion of my time and thoughts to the contriving and perfecting of a set of instruments which shall enable the possessor of them to dispense with the attendance of a servant, or that attention from a friend, which would otherwise be absolutely necessary, to supply to him those minute arrangements of neatness and economy, which the modes and refinements of social life render indispensable to personal comfort and happiness.' His range of instruments included a one-handed washing tray, a shaving box, a syringe, and devices for cutting quills and shuffling playing cards. Lieutenant Charles John Fitzgerald, also of the 82nd, was slightly wounded while serving as brigade major on the Portuguese staff.

On that same occasion in 1875, the Marquess of Tweeddale mentioned his old friend Lord Dalhousie's opinion of the 82nd: 'Often have I heard him speak with pride and praise of their high state of discipline, their coolness in action, and the many good qualities which they used to exhibit, both on the field of battle and throughout the campaign.'[624]

After taking the village of Hermandad, Grant's brigade (now commanded by Major King) continued its advance on the far left of Wellington's line, close to the Zadorra. It is probable that they paused while the Allied artillery was brought up, for around that time, Captain Cairnes' divisional battery engaged the French guns. He stated that his guns were exposed to their cannonade from the right for a long time and that, as there were then no enemy troops on which to direct his fire, he engaged, silenced and dislodged nine French 12-pounders, drawing their fire away from Grant's Brigade, including the 82nd, for which he was thanked by Lord Dalhousie. This circumstance strongly suggests that Grant's Brigade still led on that flank.

When the general advance recommenced at around 5.30 p.m. the immediate objective of the troops on the left was the village of Crispijana, held by the 16th Légère of Cassagne's division. Resistance cannot have been very serious, for the 16th Légère suffered the loss of just one officer and 26 men that day. There is little detail of the final stages of the advance on the left, coordinated by Dalhousie, but it appears that his columns swept through and past the village of Ali to break into Reille's final position, forcing him to retreat from the Zadorra covered by previously untouched French cavalry formations, notably Digeon's Dragoons whose commander recalled several desperate charges. It was at this time that two squadrons of the 15th Hussars, having cut through the suburbs of Vitoria, came up on Dalhousie's right and were repulsed by the French dragoons.

'When the Hussars were sent back by the French cavalry,' wrote Cairnes, 'our Division & my guns (in column unluckily) were within 100 yards of them, & seeing them running on us I rode up to Lord D[alhousie] & said, "What the devil are these fellows about?" He answered, "The damned cavalry are running back. Let the infantry form square & advance." However, the Hussars formed at the instant & the enemy retired. Some people say that the French stood their ground well. I cannot think so, for after the first two hours it was a *running* fight, at which Monsieur Crapaud must always beat us!'[625]

Digeon's dragoons went on to attack an unidentified British square, but were beaten off without difficulty.

George Wood's impressions of the final stage of the advance on this flank reflect its chaotic confusion, ending amid the French baggage train:

'It was now that the hurry, bustle and confusion of a great battle were experienced: such smoke, such noise, such helter-skelter! – the cries of the wounded – the groans of the dying – the shouts of the victors – the dragoons and artillery flying – dust in clouds – caps, muskets, knapsacks strewing the ground – baggage carriages, waggons and carts broken down… This scene continued till night put an end to the bloody fray and equally bloody pursuit, when we halted leaving Vittoria some miles in our rear.'

The 4th Division, meanwhile, cleared up the centre of the French position against Gazan's unbalanced and withdrawing troops. Having waited all morning while the enemy lines to their front were outflanked, the division advanced to the Zadorra at Nanclares. Thereafter, their pace of advance was regulated by the success of the divisions on their flanks, and in consequence there were pauses. Apart from the well-served French artillery, which inflicted some casualties, there appears to have been little in the way of formed, coordinated and determined resistance, for Gazan's infantry had been ordered to withdraw and such stands as they made were confined to short delaying actions.

The Division crossed the Zadorra at about 2 p.m.[626] Some battalions, including the 40th, crossed the Nanclares bridge, while others forded the river. We can piece together an outline of their subsequent actions from the accounts of Lieutenant James Mill and Corporal William Lawrence of the 40th, and those of other 4th Division witnesses.

---

[624] 82nd *Regimental Record of Service*, p. 104.

[625] Captain Robert Macpherson Cairnes letter dated 30 June 1813 in *The Dickson Manuscripts*, Vol. V, p. 926.

[626] Lieutenant-Colonel George Bingham, commanding the 2nd Provisional Battalion, had watched Hill's attack develop to his right, and the action around Subijana; but then his attention was drawn to 'heavy and incessant firing away to our left [which] kept us no longer in doubt where the real strife was. It was not till due impression was made in that quarter that we moved forward at nearly two o'clock.'

'Before we could get at the enemy,' wrote Lawrence, 'we had to cross a narrow bridge, which gave us some trouble owing to the enemy's cannon, which played pretty sharply on us: and a shell pitching into one of our ammunition waggons, it immediately blew up, carrying with it two horses and the unfortunate driver. But once on the other side of the river and formed into line we were up and at them in spite of a murderous fire which they kept up from their cannon.'[627]

'Having passed this obstacle,' recalled Charles Crowe of the 27th, 'we again halted in a field of standing corn, where we attracted the notice of some French artillery on our left. They systematically ascertained the range of our positions and then rattled at us most furiously with shots and shells. Our own artillery soon came to our assistance and in some degree diverted the fire. We were glad to move from this dangerous spot and form line under cover of the rising ground our artillery occupied, but here the rebounding shots were very troublesome.'[628]

'The moment we showed ourselves,' wrote James Mill, 'we were saluted by a burst of artillery, which was answered by a shout from our brigade. We were not exposed longer than about ten minutes to this cannonade; for, having got under cover of some rising ground, we continued advancing along a hollow, which obliged their guns to fall back until we came within about four hundred yards of their lines, which were formed upon a hill about as high as Primrose Hill, Chalk Farm, extending about half a mile in length. We then deployed into two lines, one about fifty yards in front of the other, under fire of their line. When done, the front line, consisting of the 27th and 53rd [i.e. 2nd Provisional Battalion[629]] gave the enemy a volley, uncased their colours, and advanced to charge the hill.[630]

'The 40th and 48th regiments formed the second line, and (situated on the right rear of the first line) were appointed to force the left of the hill in this form. We then moved on to the enemy, but under a heavy fall of shells; few of them, however, fortunately fell upon our lines. Mr. Fox, the ensign of our company, was shot through the neck at the time. The French thought proper to retire without a charge, or evincing any desire to court from our side a closer contact. By the time that both lines had ascended and crowned the position, we again found them drawn up on another hill in rear of it, from which they kept up a continuous fire of musketry, but with little execution. We again advanced precisely as before; and they in their turn also retired, and again formed on every rising ground they came to. This gave them the opportunity to select the most suitable ground on which to place their guns.'[631]

Lieutenant-Colonel George Bingham, 2nd Provisional Battalion, described the same forward movement:

'We followed three brigades of artillery across a bridge in our front, which the enemy complaisantly left to us. The batteries moved forward to a height beyond the river, and we formed in rear of them. A cannonade from the eighteen guns immediately opened and was as instantly returned. We had hardly formed in rear of the hill when up went one of our tumbrils of ammunition. We formed in two lines, covered by our light infantry, following the French and marching in line as well as I ever saw men move on a field day. The Second Division were close on our right, and a brigade of heavy cavalry in our rear. No stand of any consequence was made by the enemy in our part of the line till towards evening.'[632]

Corporal Lawrence described the part played by the 40th in capturing the hill mentioned by Lieutenant Mill: 'We soon neared them, fired, and then charged, and succeeded in driving the centre over the hill. A column of their body still appeared on our right, and we immediately received orders to wheel in that direction; but the sight of us, together with the play of our artillery on them, was quite sufficient to make them follow their centre over the hill, whither we pursued them, but were unable to come up with them.'

---

[627] Lawrence, p. 133-34.

[628] Crowe, p. 101.

[629] The 2nd Provisional Battalion consisted of four companies each of the 2nd and the 2nd/53rd, but it was the latter which provided the commanding officer (Bingham, late 81st and 82nd) and battalion staff.

[630] Captain John Cooke of the 43rd was probably referring to this attack when he wrote, 'The Fourth Division, on our right, shot forward against a sugar-loaf hill, and broke a French division, who retired up it in a confused mass, firing over each other's heads without danger to themselves, owing to the steepness of its ascent'. (*Memoirs of the Late War*, London, 1831).

[631] Quoted in *Historical Records of the 40th Regiment*, p. 141.

[632] *Wellington's Lieutenant, Napoleon's Gaoler – Letters of Sir George Ridout Bingham*, ed. Gareth Glover, Pen & Sword, 2005, p. 196.

With his usual candour, Lawrence admitted to his part in scavenging the battlefield for food and loot: 'I came across a poor wounded Frenchman crying to us English not to leave him, as he was afraid of the bloodthirsty Spaniards: the poor fellow could not at most live more than two hours, as a cannon-ball had completely carried off both thighs. He entreated me to stay with him, but I only did so as long as I found it convenient: I saw, too, that he could not last long, and very little sympathy could be expected from me then; so I ransacked his pockets and knapsack, and found a piece of pork ready cooked and three or four pounds of bread, which I thought would be very acceptable. The poor fellow asked me to leave him a portion, so I cut off a piece of bread and meat and emptied the beans out of my haversack, which with the bread and meat I left by his side. I then asked him if he had any money, to which he replied no, but not feeling quite satisfied at that, I again went through his pockets. I found ten rounds of ball cartridge which I threw away, and likewise a clothes-brush and a roll of gold and silver lace, but those I would not give carriage to. However, I found his purse at last, which contained seven Spanish dollars and seven shillings, all of which I put into my pocket except one shilling, which I returned to the poor dying man, and continued on my way up the hill.

'There I saw a French officer come out of a low copse close by, and instantly fired at him, but without doing him any mischief. He made his way up the hill as quickly as possible, using his sword as a walking-stick, but a German [Brunswick Oels] rifleman who had been on the look-out cut off his communication and succeeded in taking him prisoner. I did not take any further notice of him, therefore, but proceeded along with my company still in pursuit of the French, who were retreating in all directions in a very disorderly state.'[633]

'In our next advance,' wrote Charles Crowe, 'we took a direction to our left, but the enemy leaving the opposite hill, followed by some of our cavalry, we crossed the *Carmino* on our right in echelon of battalions. We were then ordered to advance through brush wood five feet high studded with pollard oaks and some fine timber trees… Our Portuguese kept on our left, outside the wood to clear the road. The enemy retired behind a ravine which afforded them a good opportunity to pepper us as we emerged from the wood. The Portuguese, being in compact order, fired a well-directed volley, gave a hearty shout, and advanced to the charge. Seeing us out of the wood, the French… scampered off along their ridge of ground like goats.'[634]

By late afternoon, the enemy left was in headlong retreat, and large parties of them had been bypassed by the advancing British. As Corporal Lawrence described, this additional element of confusion had most unfortunate consequence for the 40th:

'We might have taken hundreds of them prisoners had it not been for our officers, who in their flurry had mistaken them for Spaniards; for Lord Wellington had previously ordered the Spaniards to wear a piece of white substance round their left arm to make some distinction between the French dress and theirs, which was very similar; but the French had got knowledge of this, and a great number of them, who were obliged in their hurried retreat and on account of the difficulties of the road to pass near our lines, had adopted the Spanish white band. Still we fired at them both with muskets and artillery; but when the officers perceived the white on their arms, without bestowing any more consideration as to whether they were the enemy or the Spaniards, they immediately stopped us from doing so. As soon as the French in passing observed this, they sunk into the valley and piled arms as if they were allies; and directly an opportunity afforded itself, they again took up their muskets and fired right into our lines, doing terrible mischief. I never in all the days of the campaign saw men in such a rage as ours were with the officers. I really thought that some serious consequences would ensue, but as it was, all fortunately passed off as well as could be expected after such a mistake. For if this trick had before been observed, we might have taken the whole body prisoners by a direct movement of our right flank, as no other way lay open to their retreat without their encountering great difficulties; but the chance was now thrown away, and repairs could not be made of the damage done; many in our line having lost their irrecoverable lives, and others being more or less injured. We had only to make what consolation we could from beholding the almost express pace of the party as it retreated from where lay our comrades, either as groaning, wounded, or shattered corpses.'[635]

---

[633] Lawrence, p. 134-35.
[634] Crowe, p.p. 101-02.
[635] Lawrence, p.p. 135-36.

Captain Friederich Wackholz, whose company of Brunswick Oels was attached to the 4th Division, recorded the background to this incident in his diary:

'Our rapid advance almost cut off four or five French battalions – they made some resistance at first, but soon dissolved and ran pell-mell, like a swarm of bees, up the steep hill from which they began to fire down upon us. We disregarded their fire, and kept on advancing – in order to carry out our main object: broken troops are easy game.'

Despite such costly and annoying setbacks, the advance eventually became a pursuit, with few checks. George Bingham explained how the French to his front withdrew, passing to the south of Vitoria:

'They were now seen in great confusion getting towards the Pamplona road; the ground here was intersected with steep ravines that did not appear till you were close to them. Frequently towards sunset we saw the enemy apparently in the greatest confusion, regiments intermixed, and all huddled together. You expected to be up with them in a moment, the ravine passed they were gone; you saw no more of them till they had passed another of these obstacles. There was one period of the day that was to me was particularly interesting. I wished I had been a painter to have availed myself of it; it was near sunset, and we were on high ground interspersed with forest trees.

'We overlooked the whole plain and the bright evening light was streaming on the towers of Vitoria, the battle still raged in our front, and on our left towards the city, but it was all confusion and smoke. At this moment Lord Wellington rode up with all his staff; as he passed the battalion, which was halted, he desired us to move on. I asked, "In column or line?" Never shall I forget the animation of his countenance. "Anyhow, but get on" was the reply.'[636]

Charles Crowe described the same late period of the battle as it affected Anson's brigade:

'Our rifles and light companies pursued the fugitives until, protected by a strong body of skirmishers, they reformed and then retreated in close column. Our line was halted on a high ground in an oblique direction: on our right were the flying French, in our front some close columns made a show of standing their ground, but it was only a cover for those in their rear, whom we could perceive were rapidly retreating. On our left was the city of Vitoria, with the battle still raging in its front.'

'Some of the French artillery halted in their retreat, hoping to rake our oblique line. They fired many rounds at us, but finding that they were beyond range and could not disturb us, they again limbered their guns and pursued their retreat. This was fortunate, for as we had no support in our rear, we did not wish to be obliged to change our position and betray our weakness.

'General Anson, our brigadier, was authorised to advance at his own discretion, without hazarding an attack [as] we were quite as forward as our strength would justify. We next moved on a village to our right, and found it quite deserted. This brought us in advance of Vitoria, and we saw a long tract of the *Carmino Real* [Royal Road], crowded by the retreating foe, apparently in great confusion.'

'We were again advancing, but were brought to [a] check by three close columns with two guns. To make as much show as we could, we formed close columns of regiments, apart. The enemy made a feint of taking up their ground for the night by posting picquets, etc. Thus we found ourselves in an awkward predicament, for as a single brigade and without support we could not attempt to force their position and guns, which opened on us, but without effect, for we availed ourselves of the high hedge in our front to conceal as much as possible our exact locality and the smallness of our force.

'Thus circumstanced, we paid Jack Frenchman in his own coin: three companies from each regiment were sent forward, and under cover of the hedges opened a brisk fire on flanks and centre. This ruse answered well, for the French fearing a general attack, sent their guns off at full gallop and followed as quickly as they could. We pursued as long as daylight lasted, but saw no more of them.'[637]

By about 6.30 p.m. the battle was effectively over, with the French armies in full retreat abandoning all their material, all but two of their guns, and vast quantities of public and private treasure. French losses totaled at least eight thousand, including 2,824 prisoners.

---

[636] Bingham, p. p. 196-97.
[637] Crowe, p.p. 102 & 104.

Allied casualties amounted to 5,158, including 3,675 British. Against relatively light opposition, the losses of the 4th Division were less severe than some others, a total of 371, of whom 113 were from Anson's brigade. The 40th suffered ten rank and file killed in action, and four officers[638] and about 36 men wounded.

The 40th halted that night some 2-3 miles east of Vitoria, having marched over the debris of the French convoy, inextricably jammed on the Salvatierra road and in the surrounding fields and tracks. 'In the evening,' wrote Lieutenant James Mill, 'we came up with about twenty wagons full of baggage and provisions in a narrow lane, from one of which I snatched a loaf and a piece of bacon and went on with my regiment; some stayed behind and got much money. The different roads behind Vittoria were blocked with waggons and carriages of every kind, which conveyed not only equipments and necessaries for the French soldiers, but all the worldly possessions of private individuals, of fugitives from Joseph Bonaparte's Court, and of alien Spaniards. These were all taken, together with nearly all the cannon, though at first the ground was so bad that the cavalry could not act.'[639]

Some two thousand coaches, wagons and other vehicles, loaded with military stores, the personal baggage of King Joseph and his court, the military chest (including 5.5 million francs recently arrived from France) and the accumulated plunder of five years, lay blocked and abandoned, together with 151 guns, the artillery park, the government ministries, pro-French civilians, families and camp followers. Amid the tumult, soldiers and civilians of many nations were soon engaged in plundering this almost unprecedented accumulation of treasure and more mundane supplies of every description. Corporal William Lawrence of the 40th was among them:

'Numberless quantities of warlike instruments were captured, such as cannons, muskets, cartridges, and all kinds of ammunition, besides supplies for the army, food, clothing, and the like, which were, considering our need at the time, of great benefit to the Allies. I myself had my feet new rigged after this affair, and it was certainly not before I wanted a covering for them; there was certainly a part of the upper leathers of my old pair of boots left, but the chief part of the sole was my own natural one belonging to my foot. I had some little difficulty in procuring them, however; I happened to see a shoe-wagon that had been captured from the enemy and was being fast emptied by a number of our men, so I asked the captain to let me fall out, as my shoes wanted replenishing. He only answered, "No, not until the enemy is fairly away, and then you may do as you please"; so I had to disobey orders again, and on the next halt step off to the wagon to see what I could find. There were, however, such a number on the same errand that I began to despair of getting any boots, but at length I succeeded in getting into the wagon, and I hove out a hundred pairs or so to the mob, while I took up six or seven pairs for myself, or rather some likewise for some of my comrades, in hopes of making off with them quietly. My hopes, however, were far from being fulfilled, for no sooner was I off the wagon, than I was completely smothered with parties that wanted and craved for boots equally with myself; so I had to let all my lot go, finding that I could not get clear, and got back into the wagon. Then I threw out another stock to the barefooted mob, and replenished my own lot, this time, however, only getting five pairs, and of these I did not succeed in getting off with more than three after all.

'I made back to my company thinking to be unobserved, but in that I was again mistaken, for the captain himself seeing me called out, "You will disobey orders then, will you? and what are you going to do with all those shoes?" I told him I was going to put on a pair as soon as possible, to which he replied, "Very well, sir, mind you give the rest to your comrades"; which I did, as that had been my intention from the first; if not, I should not have troubled to get more than one pair, as on such marches as ours it was not likely that any man would care to carry a change in boots, or of anything else but food, which, though seldom denied to us, was more seldom obtained.'[640]

For Lawrence and his comrades, food was a high priority:

'Happily thousands of sheep were found, that the enemy had been obliged to abandon on their retreat. I had been fortunate enough to get one and bring it into camp, and was proceeding to kill it by putting my bayonet through the neck, when Lieutenant Kelly of our company happening to pass, "Hullo, Lawrence," he said, "you seem a capital butcher." I said, "Would you like a piece of it?" "I certainly should very much," he answered, "for

---

[638] Ensign J. Fox died of his wounds on 10th July; Captains John Henry Barnett and Conyngham Ellis, and Lieutenant Constantine Gorman were severely wounded.

[639] Letter dated Camp, near Pampeluna, June 30th 1813, quoted in *Historical Records of the 40th Regiment*, p.p. 141-42. Captain Sempronius Stretton of the 40th acquired King Joseph's green velvet forage cap.

[640] Lawrence, p.p. 137–38.

I am devilish hungry"; so I took out my knife and cut off one of the quarters just as it was, without even skinning it, and gave it to him, saying, "There, sir, you must skin it yourself." He thanked me and said, "Never mind the skin, I will manage that."

'Not only myself, but several of my comrades had likewise managed to get a share of these sheep, so that night a general cooking ceremony commenced: our first movement being to go round and gather all the odd sticks we could lay our hands upon, including gates, doors, chairs, tables, even some of the window-frames being knocked out of the many deserted houses and gathered together in one heap for this great purpose; and in a very short time both roast and boiled mutton were seen cutting about in all directions. Nor had we altogether forgotten our former experience of the beans which were growing plentifully at that time and place, and we found that night's meal as good a one as we had tasted for some weeks past. After it was over we lay down for the night, a body picket having previously been sent out to guard against any surprise from the enemy; but we lay very comfortable without being disturbed the whole night, and as our fires did not cease burning we kept very warm as well.'[641]

Nearby, at the end of a long day of marching and fighting, the soldiers of the 82nd took the opportunity to fill their stomachs and pockets, as recalled by Lieutenant George Wood:

'We had now taken up our ground, and piled our arms, when some of the men went to the rear under various pretences, but soon returned: some with bread, brandy, fowls and other kinds of eatables; others with dollars, doubloons, plate, and every article that could be procured from the French baggage, which we had passed, but dared not fall out of our ranks at the time, having a more serious duty to perform than attending to plunder – that of first beating the enemy away from it. I certainly must confess I regarded these waggons loaded and broken down with specie, over which we were obliged to drive the foe, with a wishful eye; but honour being with a soldier preferable to riches, I relinquished the latter for the former.

'We were, however, amply supplied with everything that was good by those who had the good fortune to share in the spoil. Indeed, for my own part, I could not complain, having contrived to get a very fine young horse belonging to the Polish Lancers, which came running in my way without a rider, completely accoutred; and a handsome quilt, which I found very useful at night. Such plenty now prevailed, that I do not suppose there was a man in the field who had not a good meal that night from the stores of the enemy, which were copiously supplied with every comfort, and now came to us so very seasonably; for, although every man had not an opportunity of partaking in the plunder, yet there was so great an abundance of every necessary brought into camp, that they were enabled to share the provision with each other.'

George Wood painted the scene as the 82nd Regiment gathered in their bivouac on the evening after the battle:

'Some were carousing over their spoils, others swearing at their ill-luck at not obtaining more; some dancing mad with *eau-de-vie*, others sharing doubloons, dollars, watches, gold trinkets, and other valuable articles. The more rational and feeling were talking of their suffering comrades, somewhat in the following strain:

"This was a devil of a fight surely! That was a woundy crack poor Barney got, wor'n't it, Joe?" "Ah! but poor Bill Flint got a worse: he be laid low, poor fellow!"

"But what do you think of that fine young lieutenant of the Grenadiers [Lieutenant Agnew]?"

"Why, dang it, his limbs be shivered to splinters: but I hope as how I shall see the brave fellow on a timber toe some of these odd days, for he be a damn'd good officer."

"Aye! that he be; and bad luck to the French frogs, if they don't hop away too fast for us, we will pay them off for it yet. But we can't help trifles, so come along Joe! here's to ye, and let's have the old song, *Our Lodgings be on the Cold Ground*."

'Amidst this extraordinary and novel scene, with a bottle of French brandy in one hand, some biscuit in the other, the fine large quilt thrown over me, and two fat fowls under my head, I sunk on my pillow to sleep.'[642]

There were other rewards for the victory, albeit mostly deferred. In 1818, the 47th and 59th were authorised to emblazon the Colours with the Battle Honour 'VITTORIA,' as were the 40th and 82nd in 1824. It was not until

[641] Lawrence, p.p. 139-40.
[642] Wood, p.p. 187-88.

1847, when the General Service Medal was issued, that 210 survivors of the 40th, 90 of the 47th, 120 of the 59th and 114 of the 82nd received the 'Vittoria' bar. Meanwhile, Captain Arthur Heyland, who commanded the 40th at Vitoria, was awarded with a brevet majority, and Captain James Johnston of the 40th, serving on the staff of Power's Portuguese brigade of the 3rd Division, was promoted by Beresford for good conduct. Army Gold Medals were awarded to the commanders: Arthur Heyland of the 40th, Robert Kelly and Charles Livesay of the 47th, Charles Fane and Captain Francis Scott of the 59th, and William Grant and Henry King of the 82nd.

Advance to the Pyrenees

There was no pursuit on the night of the 21st: the Allied infantry had been marching and fighting since before dawn, covering an average of some twenty miles, and were exhausted; the cavalry, few of whom had been seriously engaged, might have moved early the following morning but were impeded by congestion, heavy rain and the prospect of immense plunder. It was towards midday when the army, less stragglers, moved off in pursuit of the French; but their enemy, unencumbered by guns or transport, had continued their flight overnight. Contact had been lost, and few prisoners were gleaned.

There was also a stricken battlefield to be cleared. Private Adam Reed of the 47th, who was 'walking wounded,' went to see the captured French guns, 'which was a very fine sight for me to see.' Less happily, he witnessed the burial of the dead: 'They were carried to a ditch and as many could be thrown into it. The bank was limed and pushed over… By this time the women were come up from the rear to the regiment and enquired concerning their husbands. It would grieve the hardest heart to hear their shrieks and cries after they heard their husbands were dead. I am not able to state how many were killed or wounded, but there was a great number where I was.'

Meanwhile, Clausel with some 14,000 men, still unaware of the French defeat, was hurrying north towards Vitoria. In consequence, the 5th Division was halted at Salvatierra, and on the 26th marched back to Vitoria. Hearing belatedly, on the 23rd, of King Joseph's rout, Clausel reversed his march, taking the road to Logrono and intending to retire to France by way of Tafalla.

By the 25th Wellington had concentrated the greater part of his army around the city of Pamplona, into which the French had thrown a garrison. Next day he marched south towards Tafalla with the 4th and Light divisions, followed by the 3rd and 7th, in an attempt to intercept Clausel. Learning of this move, the latter diverted his route to Zaragosa, and Wellington made a corresponding march to Caseda on the 28th, with a view to cutting Clausel off from the road by Jaca into France. On the 29th, however, he gave up what had become a wild-goose chase, fearing that if he pressed Clausel further the latter would withdraw further south to join Suchet's Army of Aragon, which was not desirable.

Once the threat of a raid by Clausel receded from Vitoria, the 5th Division marched north-east to undertake the siege of San Sebastian under the overall command of Sir Thomas Graham. On 9th July, they took over the investment of that place from Spanish troops. Morale was high, despite a continuing shortage of money and supplies. On 31st July, Major-General Frederick Robinson wrote to his sister from his camp before San Sebastian:

'Many of my poor fellows have traversed the Pyrenees without either shoes or stockings to their feet; yet no complaint is heard. We do not care a straw for money, as a proof of which I tell you that neither officer or soldier has received a penny since the 24th of December last. All we want is food and clothing; of the former we now have abundance, and could never be in want if the Commissariat was but supplied with occasional sums to pay their arrears to the farmers and our muleteers.'

Having returned to Pamplona, the 4th Division was engaged in the blockade of that place, a fortress town too strong to be taken by assault. The 40th took part in the construction of artillery redoubts, armed with French guns taken at Vitoria, at long cannon shot from the ramparts, and provided picquets south of the city. Writing home on the 10th, Lieutenant-Colonel George Bingham of the 2nd Provisional Battalion cast a revealing light on the motivation of at least some of the troops: 'I was much amused the other day, whilst standing in one of the redoubts, at a private soldier of the 40th Regiment who, laying his spade coolly down, exclaimed, "My fortune is in that there town."' The soldier's hope of riches within Pamplona was in vain, for on the 16th July the Spanish took over the blockade, and at 7 a.m. the following morning the 4th Division took the road to the famous pass of Roncesvalles.

The 7th Division meanwhile, had marched north from Pamplona to Lizaso on 4th July, and then to the little town of Elizondo in the Baztan valley, which they reached on the 6th, from where on the 7th and 8th July they supported Sir Rowland Hill's capture of the Puerto de Otxondo (Maya Pass). With the exception of their garrisons at Pamplona and San Sebastian, the demoralised French armies in the Basque country had now been hustled back behind their own frontiers. The 7th Division occupied the Etxalar Pass, keeping contact with the 2nd Division on the Maya Pass some seven miles to their east. The 82nd Foot, however, was detached from Inglis's brigade and, camped on Mount Achiola, was tasked to maintain communication with the 2nd Division, whose camps were visible to their right.

After nearly two months of marching and fighting, and despite the endemic mountain mists, the 82nd found their encampment on the heights surprisingly congenial. 'We were supplied by French smugglers with brandy and wine,' recalled George Wood, 'as well as bread, fruit and other necessaries. Another thing, still more unexpected, was that among these mountains we found great quantities of wild cherries, plums and apples; and the men even discovered green tobacco, probably cultivated by the mountaineers, which they made very palatable by drying it in the sun… Here we remained some weeks, looking down on the enemy, who were in huts at a little distance in their native land.'

By 8th July Wellington held the Pyrenean passes on a sixty-mile front measured along the watershed. He did not press forward into France after his disorganised enemy for wider geopolitical reasons. A truce had been forced on Austria, Prussia and Russia following their defeats at Lutzen and Bautzen, giving Napoleon the option of reinforcing the Peninsula, and it took until 12th August for news of the British victory at Vitoria to embolden the Allies to resume hostilities. While awaiting the political outcome of his success, Wellington's immediate objectives were to consolidate his position by reducing San Sebastian and Pamplona while holding the line of the Pyrenees against any counter-attack. Allied resources were stretched to cover these three requirements, and the initiative passed to the French.

There were numerous passes over the Pyrenees (Wellington counted at least 70), but most of them were mere mountain tracks and only three were suitable for large forces: the Bidassoa crossing near the coast, on the main road from France to Spain; the route from Bayonne to Pamplona by way of the Puerto de Otxondo (Maya Pass), the Baztan valley and Puerto de Velate; and finally, the road from St. Jean Pied de Port to Pamplona over the pass of Roncesvalles.

Wellington was now opposed by an old adversary. Marshal Nicolas Soult, Duke of Dalmatia, arrived at Bayonne on 11th July with orders to supersede King Joseph and if necessary arrest him. He had four years previous experience in Spain, including Corunna, Oporto, Albuera and Orcana, and was rated by Napoleon as 'the only military brain in the Peninsula.' Wellington acknowledged that he was a good logistician and strategist, but deemed him 'very defective and irresolute in actual collision.' His assessment was that 'Soult knew very well how to bring his troops up to the field, but not so well how to use them when he had brought them up.'

Soult made an excellent start. In less than two weeks he reorganised and re-equipped the French armies, restored their morale, and launched a credible counter-offensive which nearly succeeded. He decided that Wellington's right wing was his most vulnerable point, and planned to force the passes there, relieve Pamplona and threaten the Allied rear, forcing his opponent to abandon the siege of San Sebastian and withdraw.

Soult reorganised the former armies into the Army of Spain, 84,000 men and 140 guns, split between three main groups: Soult himself was at St. Jean Pied de Port with 34,000 infantry in two columns, commanded by Clausel and Reille, followed by two cavalry divisions. His was to be the main thrust, aimed through the pass of Roncesvalles to raise the blockade of Pamplona. At Ainhoa and Urdax, D'Erlon with 21,000 infantry was tasked to capture the Puerto de Otxondo (Maya), and then advance through the Baztan and over the Puerto de Velate to Pamplona, protecting the right flank of Soult's main thrust. Finally, Villatte with 17,000 men was at Bayonne, close to the frontier at Hendaye, from where, as a diversion to the main effort, he could threaten the siege of San Sebastian. Simultaneous advances on Roncesvalles and Maya were planned to commence at 4 a.m. on 25th July.

The Combat of Maya, 25th July 1813

From the crest of the Maya Pass, the outposts of the 2nd Division could clearly see the French bivouacs around Urdax, only four miles away, and at Ainhoa. But while the British position on the heights commanded an extensive panorama, it was nearly three miles long and, at least to its right, could be approached unobserved. On the left, the high road from Urdax climbs to the head of the pass, some 2,000 feet above sea level, where there was an open grassy saddle, and then, after running along the flank of the 3,100-foot Mount Alcorrunz, it drops past the village of Maya (Maia on modern maps) to Elizondo and the Baztan. The relatively flat summit of the pass is dominated to the south-west by the Alcorrunz height and by rocky outcrops at its base, while a long, grassy-topped, steep-sided ridge, with patches of heather and gorse, broken by many dips and gulleys, runs away to its east for a mile and a half to where the isolated Gorospil (or Aretesque) peak stands as forward sentinel where the crest-line changed direction to the north. A lateral track, the Chemin des Anglais, runs from Espelette on the French side and skirts the western foot of the Gorospil; then, running behind the ridge to the head of the pass, it continues to the north of Mount Alcorrunz towards Etxalar. Immediately to the south of the point at which the Chemin des Anglais branches off the main road for Etxalar, and commanding that junction, is a rocky ridge, an outlying under feature of Mount Alcorrunz. The village of Maya lies in the valley 2½ miles, or an hour's climb, below the crest-line.

Lieutenant-General William Stewart held the Maya Pass with two British brigades of his 2nd Division (his third British brigade, Byng's, was at Roncesvalles), while his Portuguese brigade (Ashworth's) watched the Izpegui Pass. Cameron's brigade (the 50th, 71st and 92nd) were encamped just behind the crest of the main pass, supported by four Portuguese guns. Pringle's brigade (the 28th, 34th and 39th) were responsible for the secondary approach from Espelette along the Chemin des Anglais. Pringle, who had only arrived the previous day, inherited a poor deployment: there was a company picket on the Gorospil peak, supported by four light companies encamped in rear of the east-west ridge; the 34th were in camp well below, half-way to Maya, while the remaining two battalions – 28th and 39th – were near Maya village, where headquarters 2nd Division was based. However, neither Stewart nor his staff were present, for the French had made a minor diversionary attack by the French National Guard up the Aldudes valley to the south; Hill, in command of that sector, heard the firing and went to see what was happening, followed by Stewart with his entire staff. Pringle, as senior brigadier, was left in command at Maya.

D'Erlon's plan was first to attack the inadequately guarded right flank of the 2nd Division position, advancing in dead ground along the Chemin des Anglais from Espelette to take the Gorospil and, then swinging right to clear along the east-west ridge with Darmagnac's Division, followed by Abbé. Maransan's division was then to make a frontal attack on the pass up the main road from Urdax.

Although some French troop movement had been noticed early on the morning of 25th July, it was mostly hidden in dead ground, and by 10.30 a.m. D'Erlon's two divisions were able to approach unobserved to within half a mile of the Gorospil. Almost complete surprise was achieved, and although the Gorospil picket had been reinforced by the supporting light infantry companies, the odds were some twenty to one and after 40 minutes the picket was overwhelmed. The rest of Pringle's brigade arrived piecemeal from the valley below between about 11.30 and 12 a.m., and were able for a short while to check the French advance in confused and desperate clashes before being driven back in some disorder by superior numbers. As they engaged in a long, scrambling, delaying fight along the ridge, moving slowly back towards the main pass, they were joined in succession by over half of Cameron's brigade; first the 50th and then wings of the 92nd and 71st. The right wing of the 92nd, extended two-deep across the ridge-top, put up a particularly gallant defence, holding back an entire division for twenty minutes until, with 60% casualties, the survivors were ordered to retire, probably through the 71st. At about this time heavy French columns were directed at the 28th and 34th, who were forced back down into the valley.

At some time between 1 and 2 p.m. Stewart at last arrived to take command. With his right wing pushed right back, eastwards along the ridge, he decided to hold the French on the saddle behind the head of the pass, including the rocky ridge at the junction of the main road with the Chemin des Anglais. Darmagnac's Division had now been fought to a disordered halt, but at about 3 p.m. Maransin's division, supported by Abbé, moved against Stewart's second position. The French were met by the left wings of the 71st and 92nd deployed across the main road, supported by the right wing 71st and the 50th. These retired slowly, firing, through their campsites which were overrun and pillaged.

It was then that, around 4.30 p.m., the 82nd arrived, coming in from the left on the Chemin des Anglais. Lieutenant George Wood outlined what happened from a regimental perspective:

'Being one day on piquet, I heard a brisk fire of musketry on my right, and on getting on higher ground (fearing a surprise) I observed the advanced brigade desperately engaged; and, to my great regret, I perceived those gallant regiments, the 50th and 71st, overpowered by numbers, falling back for support, and had the mortification of seeing the French take possession of their camp and strike their tents. However, the support they needed was most promptly afforded by my regiment, which after a hot contest was also compelled to move to the rear by alternate wings: a part, however, still kept possession of a commanding height, which the French wished to gain; and in the defence of it our men, having expended all their ammunition, resorted to the novel expedient of throwing stones at the enemy, and in this manner preserved it till the remainder of the division arrived… The evening drawing to a close, the firing gradually ceased, and both parties kept their ground… With the cloudy night came on a thick fog, accompanied with misty rain; and it was very dark.'

William Stewart, in his rather crestfallen report to Hill, gave some more details of events from when he arrived on the field:

'When I arrived at the heights… I found both the Aretesque and Lessessa passes retired from by our troops; and the enemy's columns on the ridge advancing in such superior force, with apparently a fresh division [Maransin's] pushing up the Maya, and the ravines to the left as far as the front of the 92nd camp, [and] that there appeared no other alternative but ceding that pass and retiring upon the rocky ridge, which could bring us in communication with the 7th Division.

'I sent instructions to the 82nd Regiment to advance to our support, leaving its picquets, &c, for Colonel Grant to dispatch a report to Major General Inglis, and to Lord Dalhousie, all which was done by him with great alertness; I detached some companies of the 71st to the highest rock, and afterwards placed that important ridge to the position under Major [William] Fitzgerald 82nd Regiment, with an additional company of that corps. I cannot too warmly praise the conduct of Major Fitzgerald, and that of his brave detachment. They maintained the position to the last, and were compelled from the want of ammunition to impede the enemy's occupation of the rock by hurling stones at them!'

'Having made those dispositions, it only remained to withstand the advance of the enemy, whose numbers much exceeded the force of the five regiments, including the 82nd Regiment, under my command… These gallant corps executed their duty in a manner that did them honor, and effectually prevented the enemy from gaining ground on us in any degree commensurate with his numbers. When the retreat on the slope of the ridge became necessary it was effected by wings of regiments, in the best order, about six o'clock. The expected support from the 7th Division not being arrived, our supply of ammunition not to the amount desirable, and the enemy pushing up parts of troops to our left and rear, it became expedient for my main force to retire by the ridge which is in rear of the high rock. I had even made arrangements for a further retreat if indispensible, to the heights of the 82nd camp, when the opportune arrival of Major General Barnes's brigade enabled us not only to retain, but even to recover, by a general charge upon the enemy, the whole of the ground which is in line on the left of the high rock, and which commands the late encampment of the first [Cameron's] brigade and also that of the Maya Pass. A very spirited charge by the 6th Regiment, led on by Major General Barnes in the most animated style upon the enemy's corps which had gained our left, preceded this success. It enabled us to close an inauspicious day in a manner that imposed upon our enemy, and left us in an eligible situation, from which, had such been your orders, and had succor arrived, we might this day have regained that ground, the loss of which I have been detailing with much pain to my feelings.'

'I feel it my duty to recommend to your attention and favourable report to the Commander of the forces, the conduct and spirit of Colonel Grant and of his brave corps, the 82nd Regiment; also the whole of the first brigade (composed of the 50th, 71st, and 92nd), than which his Majesty's army possesses not men of more approved discipline and courage.[643] The wounds of him and every commanding officer in that brigade were attended with circumstances of peculiar honour to each of them, and to those under their orders.'

In summary, by late afternoon Cameron's brigade and the main body of the 82nd had been pushed back, step by step, down the road, leaving Fitzgerald's detachment dangerously isolated and without ammunition. Stewart sent word for them to withdraw over the hills, but before this could be effected there was a dramatic change in the situation. Barnes, with the 6th Regiment and a company of Brunswick Oels, had arrived at about 6 p.m., marching at speed along the Chemin des Anglais and put in a successful flank attack below Fitzgerald's position; whereupon the remaining British troops gave three cheers and joined in the counter-attack, rolling Maransin's Division back one mile to the head of the Maya Pass. Stewart's men held ground close to the vital summit at dusk; but as they were still outnumbered three to one he did not press his advantage, and firing died down.

British losses in this combat of Maya totaled 1,488, and D'Erlon reported 2,100 casualties. The loss of the 82nd was one sergeant and seven rank and file killed; Captain Brook Firman severely wounded (twice), Colonel William Grant, Captain George Marshall and Ensign Samuel Walker Lacy slightly wounded[644], and seven sergeants and sixty rank and file wounded. Captain William Stewart of the 30th, Brigade Major, was twice severely wounded, received a contusion and had his horse killed under him, but would not quit the field.

The battle was over when General Hill arrived, bearing unwelcome news: Cole had abandoned Roncesvalles, and in consequence, he felt obliged to order Stewart back to the Baztan valley. The weary troops were to withdraw after midnight that same night. There was a clean break, but, as George Wood recalled, that did little to diminish the horrors of the ensuing retreat:

'Previous to quitting this gory spot, we were employed in collecting our wounded, by the sound of their piteous groans, as the foggy darkness prevented our finding them by any other means. These poor fellows were brought and laid by the fires made for that purpose. Now an order came to light more fires, to make the enemy imagine we were cooking, and meant to keep our ground; but this was mere *finesse*, for as soon as this order was executed the word, or rather whisper, was circulated through the field to stand to our arms, and we moved off by sections to commence this perilous retreat, leaving the wounded by the dwindling fires to the mercy of the foe: many were scattered about the bleak mountains far out of the main track, where perhaps they had a shorter period put to their existence by the hungry wolves, as several were at their last gasp when we left them; but there was no alternative. We could scarcely make our way over these unfrequented craggy wilds, and it was therefore impossible to render our comrades more assistance; and as to spring-waggons, carts, or any mode of conveyance, these were now out of the question – nothing of that kind being able to come among these mountains.

'On quitting this position, the most dismal sensations took possession of our breasts. Not a voice, not a sound was heard, save the slow step and casual murmur of the dejected soldiers, intermingled with the moans and groans of the wounded. To add to these horrors, I once or twice trod, in the dark, directly upon, and fell over, a dead body, cold and naked as the clay it was stretched on.

'In this state we kept moving on the whole of this sad and sorrowful night, amidst the mountains, the woods and the rain; the ways being so deluged with mire, owing to the great number of cattle and baggage passing before us, that it was with difficulty we could wade through it.'

The 82nd passed through Elizondo at dawn on the 26th and briefly halted on the heights beyond that town. Then, with the French advanced guard close at hand, they marched on:

'We were obliged to leave this bivouac, and march till we were benighted, and completely obscured in darkness and rain. So entangled were we among carts, horses, vicious mules, baggage, and artillery broken down, together with ammunition and other stores, which lined the roads, that we could not extricate ourselves from these impediments. Some lighted sticks and candles which the muleteers had with them, only added to the confusion;

---

[643] Wellington's despatch to Earl Bathurst, dated San Esteban August 1st 1813, echoed this praise, stating that 'all the regiments charged with the bayonet; the conduct of the 82nd Regiment… is particularly reported. It is impossible that I can extol too highly the conduct of Major-General Barnes and these brave troops, which was the admiration of all who were witnesses of it.'

[644] Captains Brook Firman and George Marshal were regimental veterans, having both joined the 82nd in 1799, and were promoted to captain in 1805 and 1808 respectively. Both had served at Minorca, Copenhagen, Gibraltar and Vitoria, and Marshal was also with the 82nd at Roliça, Vimeira and Corunna.

for we were not able to see one yard beyond the light, owing to the thick haze, which seemed to render even darkness still more dark.

'Here the Colonel asked me where my men were, for I had only three with me out of forty, the strength of the company of which I had the command: I told him I did not know as I could not see in the dark: however, he did not put me under an arrest for it, and a short time after daylight the lost sheep in question rejoined their battalion.

'In this bewildered spot, many who could not stand were obliged from fatigue to sit down in the mire: to attempt going on was impossible, except by climbing over the different vehicles that lined the road. In this miserable plight, I seated myself against a tree, where weariness caused me, even amidst this bustle, mud and riot, to fall fast asleep. My servant coming up, disturbed my repose by presenting me with his cap full of tea, having trod in a box of it on the way: but he might as well have given me some of the mire that we were in to eat, as, at this time, there were no fires to make it, or, if there had, there was no utensil to have boiled it in, or anything to have eaten with it; but still I felt grateful for his attention.'

Moving on a few miles further, to a more congenial spot, where some fires were lighted, near one of them I could not but observe our brave and hardy Colonel… He was stretched on his back and sound asleep, and seemed to be in a pleasant dream, although the rain, which was mizzling fast, trickled down his weather-beaten furrowed cheeks: this, added to the appearance of his venerable snowy locks, and his projecting bristly eye-brows, and his manly Caledonian countenance, presented one of the most martial and dignified pictures that a poet could describe, or a painter depict.[645]

The Combat of Roncesvalles, 25th July 1813

The cause of Hill's decision to withdraw from the Maya pass lay at Roncesvalles. This pass was held by Byng's brigade of the 2nd Division (3rd Buffs, 57th and 1st Provisional Battalion) and eight battalions of Morillo's Spaniards (2,000 British and 3,800 Spanish troops), supported by Sir Lowry Cole's 4th Division, , including the 40th, which lay about five miles in the rear, around Espinal, Viscarret and Lintzoain on the road to Pamplona.

The Pass of Roncesvalles, or Puerto de Ibañeta, was the main route from St. Jean Pied de Port to Pamplona, and rose to a height of 3,600 feet at its summit, which was the central and lowest point of a three-mile saddle-back ridge stretching from the Altobiscar (5,000 feet) on the east side to the Linduz (4,000 feet) to the west. From the French side three possible approaches led to the crest: immediately below (where the modern road runs through Val Carlos) a mule track ran up a deep wooded gorge in 1813, with a steep final climb; however, the preferred route to the head of pass at that time was to the east, where an ancient (Roman) highroad[646] climbed from St. Jean Pied de Port to the watershed via the Altobiscar; a third, less obvious, route was by a narrow track which climbed the steep western slope from the village of Val Carlos to the Airola crestline, then snaked through beechwoods for 5-6 miles to the Linduz plateau, some 1½ miles west from the col of Ibañeta. The Altobiscar track alone was practicable for guns and cavalry, but there were good defensive positions to block that approach at Chateau Pignon, the Leizar Atheka peak and Altobiscar. It should also be noted that a track from Altobiscar to Orbaitzeta outflanked the main pass to the east, while from the Linduz several paths descended into Spain.

Byng's light companies held a strong position at Leizar Atheka, with outposts pushed forward to Chateau Pignon. The Buffs and the Provisional Battalion were on the Altobiscar, while the 57th and two Spanish battalions watched the Val Carlos gorge. There was a Spanish battalion on the track to Orbaitzeta, and a Spanish picket in an old redoubt on the Linduz plateau.

Soult's main thrust to Pamplona, with 34,000 infantry followed by two cavalry divisions, called for an advance on two parallel approaches: Clausel with three divisions (17,000 men) was to march up the Roman road and take the Altobiscar and the Ibañeta col, followed by the guns and cavalry, while Reille with another three

---

[645] Wood, p.p. 199-204.

[646] There were those in the army who knew well that they stood on one of the most famous mountain passes in Europe: Charlemagne's paladin Roland, immortalised in the *Chanson de Roland*, was ambushed and killed in the pass by the Basques in 778, the Black Prince passed that way with his men at arms and archers in 1367 en route to the battle of Navarrete, and it was, and remains, on the famous pilgrimage route to St. James of Compostella.

divisions (also 17,000 men) was to climb the western ridge and move along the narrow crestline path to the Linduz plateau.

Cole had overall command of this sector. His orders from Wellington, given to him on the 23rd, were to support Byng's troops as effectually as possible, and in the event of being compelled to give up the passes he was to make arrangements further back for stopping the enemy's progress towards Pamplona. This gave him discretion to withdraw if he considered it necessary. Final, much less equivocal, orders from Quartermaster-General Murray were delivered at 9 a.m. on the 25th: 'Lord Wellington has desired I should express still more strongly how essential he considers it that the passes in front of Roncesvalles should be maintained to the utmost and every arrangement made for repelling effectually every direct attack that the enemy may make in that quarter.' He was also urged to disregard any wide turning movement by Soult to his east. By the time this last message was received, Byng's light companies were already engaged.

During the night, 24th/25th Byng had informed Cole that he expected to be attacked in the morning. Cole ordered Robert Ross's Fusilier brigade of his division (the 7th, 20th & 23rd) to march at dawn to the Linduz plateau, and moved Anson's brigade, with the 40th, up to Espinal.

Both French columns advanced on time at 4 a.m. An attempt by Clausel's advance guard to surprise the picket at Chateau Pignon was unsuccessful, meeting with strong resistance, and his column did not approach Leizar Atheka till 6 a.m. For the next four hours all French attacks were beaten off with heavy loss by Byng from an excellent defensive position. The French advance stalled and there was no further attack until noon. At noon Soult ordered a renewed attack on the Altobiscar by Clausel's leading Division, but three further assaults failed. By about 3 p.m. Byng was running out of ammunition and fell back to the Altobiscar position, followed slowly by Clausel, who did not renew his attack.

Unfortunately, Byng's tactical withdrawal to the Altobiscar position uncovered the track to Orbaitzeta, and, although the Spanish there repulsed the first attack, Cole became nervous. He ordered Anson's brigade to reinforce the Spanish at Orbaitzeta, and Stubbs' Portuguese to the Ibañeta; then, learning of Reille's move towards the Linduz, he countermanded his order to Anson, directing him to move up immediately to support Ross. However, the evidence indicates that only part of Anson's brigade had made the detour towards Orbaitzeta.

George Bingham's Provisional Battalion certainly marched in that direction until, half-way there, they were overtaken by an aide-de-camp who informed them of attacks on both Byng and Ross. 'We hastened to their assistance, but we had many miles to traverse and it was late in the day before we arrived. The firing had by this time ceased; we found the remainder of the division on the crest of the mountain.'[647]

Charles Crowe of the 27th makes no mention of a march towards Orbaitzeta, but rather gives a very detailed account of a move by his battalion by way of Roncesvalles Abbey to the Ibañeta col by early afternoon at the latest.

The accounts of that day from our 40th diarists are disappointingly thin in circumstantial detail. Indeed, William Lawrence's principal recollection was of a drumhead divine service bizarrely interrupted[648] by the call to arms, but what little there is from James Mill appears to support Crowe's narrative:

'Our brigade advanced in support beyond Roncesvalles, on the French side. There lay extended before us the beautiful plains and diversified country of France. The prospect was, I doubt not, a tempting and inviting one to the Spanish marauder, when it was felt as such by many of our own hungry soldiery. Our envy and admiration of it, however, was not of any long duration. The French, under Soult, were advancing in force. It was futile to attempt to arrest their progress long, though our people in front continued to be masters of their ground during the day.'[649]

---

[647] George Bingham, letter dated Camp near Etxaler, 3rd August 1813. This shows that his battalion could not have reached the Ibañeta until after about 5 p.m.

[648] 'A square had been formed into which a parson entered to read prayers and preach, and a drum being placed for his books and a knapsack for him to kneel on, he had proceeded with the service for some little time when all of a sudden up he jumped with his traps and made a bolt, before anyone had hardly time to see the cause, amid the applause and laughter of the whole of the troops at his running, which was as fast as his legs could carry him… never after that did we have a service in the field.'

[649] Lieutenant James Mill, letter dated Camp near Lezaca, 5th August 1813, quoted in *Historical Records of the 40th Regiment*, p. 143.

At around 1.30 or 2 p.m. a new front had opened at Roncesvalles: the head of Reille's column was spotted filing along the crest-line two miles short of the Linduz plateau. Ross led the 20th forward, and on the narrow track was able to bring the advance of Reille's three divisions to a halt with deadly volleys and bayonet charges. When the 20th ran out of ammunition they were replaced by the 7th and 23rd Regiments. The 27th, and most probably the 40th, watched this conflict from the Ibañeta until about 3 p.m. when the French hauled up some 9-pounders. As they were brought to bear, Anson's men were moved to their left, behind the Fusilier brigade on the Linduz plateau.

Thick fog rolled up from the valley at about 5 p.m., obscuring the battlefield and halting hostilities. Reille's divisions, blocked by a very much smaller force, were ordered to halt and bivouac where they stood. The victorious defenders now had 11,000 men deployed across the saddle between the Altobiscar and Linduz positions, both of which were securely held, and they were cheerfully confident.[650] But their commander was uneasy and took nervous counsel of his fears: Cole was outnumbered three to one and felt his right rear threatened by way of Orbaitzeta. Prompted by Byng, who was already pulling back on his own initiative, he ordered a withdrawal from Roncesvalles that night.

Cole has been widely criticised for his decision to disobey the order to maintain the passes 'to the utmost,' not least by Wellington, who wrote: 'All the beatings we have given the French have not given our generals confidence in themselves and in the exertions of their troops. They are really heroes when I am on the spot to direct them, but when I am obliged to quit them they are children.' There is considerable truth in this criticism, and Cole, in a private letter of 4th September, admitted as much: 'The two days previous [25th and 26th July] I had a good deal of mental as well as physical fagg, and if you knew what difficulties we generals of division occasionally have when separated, you would not think our situation enviable. All's well that ends well, and so has this been.'

The withdrawal from Roncesvalles started as soon as it was dark enough to screen movement. Two routes were used: the main track from the Ibañeta past Roncesvalles Abbey, and a footpath, the Mendichuri, which descended from the Linduz plateau and met the Pamplona road at Espinal. Anson's and Ross's brigades, having left men to keep up their campfires, were sent on the latter route. It was a particularly black night, increased by the dense beech canopy.

'We had to get through a very thick wood of quite three or four miles in extent,' recalled Corporal Lawrence, 'which took us the whole night to accomplish; and in the morning when we were finally through we lay down like so many loaded donkeys; still obliged, however, to remain in readiness, as we expected to be pursued.'[651]

Contemporary brigade accounts agree, Colonel Bingham remarking that they had 'nothing but a shepherd's path to follow, intersected frequently by trees felled across it,' while Crowe of the 27th said that 'We could not see our own hand[s] when we held them up. The Colonel placed the drummers along the line of march to direct us by a single tap. Our route was very dreary, and right glad were we to emerge from this utter darkness and again to observe the obscure outlines of objects, for the night was very cloudy and dark.'[652]

The Combat of Lintzoain, 26th July 1813

As Cole fell back towards Pamplona, Anson's brigade provided the rearguard. There was no immediate pursuit, and it was early afternoon when Clausel's cavalry patrols, probing cautiously forward to Espinal, made contact with Anson's light companies between there and Viscarret. There followed a scrambling rearguard fight which went on all day, costing the 4th Division 163 casualties, almost all in Anson's brigade, including 93 in the 40th Regiment. Lieutenant James Mill's laconic account summarised the day:

'On the 26th our brigade took up a position on a favourable point to hold the French in check – a spirited action with them – ordered to continue our retreat towards Pampeluna – skirmished with the French retreating.

---

[650] British losses at Roncesvalles totaled 350, while those of the French were at least 500.
[651] Lawrence, p.p. 146-47.
[652] Bingham, p. 206 and Crowe, p. 124.

Some brisk combats took place here and there. At one place the enemy's cavalry got round in the rear of those who were engaged skirmishing with the enemy, in order to cut them off. Our brigade drew up a second time in the afternoon, and made preparation for a pitched fight, but the French did not feel disposed to accept it.'[653]

Having discovered the British rearguard, Clausel ordered up his nearest infantry, but they were some distance away and it was about 3 p.m. before Taupin's division, with some guns, came up just as the light companies were falling back on their brigade. The 31st Légère, leading the French column, engaged briskly, and at one point a squadron of chasseurs attempted to charge the flank of Anson's 'light bobs.' The latter retired on the main body of the 4th Division, which had taken up a strong position beyond the River Erro and the village of Lintzoain. Soult halted, and did not resume his attack until he had brought up and deployed two divisions. He did not press the Allied front with any vigour, but instead manoeuvred to occupy high ground on Cole's left flank which the latter had insufficient troops to hold. The 4th Division then fell back about a mile towards the village of Erro, and again offered battle in a strong position on the lower slopes of the Puerto de Erro, on the steep Zubiri ridge separating the valleys of the Erro and Arga. Soult did not attack, for he could see British reinforcements coming over the pass.

That afternoon, Sir Thomas Picton rode up and joined Cole at Lintzoain, leaving his 3rd Division just three miles back at Zubiri. The two generals now had nineteen thousand men available. The troops anticipated action, but the normally bellicose Picton agreed with Cole to continue the withdrawal back towards Pamplona that night, giving Soult a free run over defensible heights, on the grounds that their flanks could be turned. Picton justified his decision to Wellington in the following terms:

'The affair terminated with the day, and the country offering no post between this place [Zubiri] and Pamplona where it would be safe to hazard anything like an effectual stand against such superior force, I agreed with Lieut.-General Sir Lowry Cole in opinion that it was advisable to retire, and we have in consequence ordered the baggage, &c., on the Vitoria road, where we shall take up a position at as short a distance as practicable from Pamplona.'

He was effectively giving Soult a day's march, and making Wellington's response that much more difficult. Lieutenant James Mill of the 40th was sent to clear the way for this further retreat:

'After the last action, I was ordered to carry despatches to Count de la Bispal, the general commanding the Spanish army, and also to the stations in the rear of Pampeluna. These orders were, first: to clear the whole of the valley of Zubiri of cavalry and baggage, to enable the troops in the pass to effect their retreat to the main body of the army. Second: to demand assistance from the Spanish general in support of the retreating division… Third: to break up the hospitals and depots in the rear of Pampeluna, preparatory to retreating.'

We have no first-hand witness of the part played by the 40th in the combat of Lintzoain, but their high casualties indicate that they bore the brunt of the action, while Captain (Brevet Major) Arthur Heyland, in command, was mentioned in despatches as having distinguished himself. According to Captain Sempronius Stretton, who assumed command when Heyland was wounded, the 40th lost six officers and near one hundred men, which is very close to the official account, which has one officer (Lieutenant Malone) and three other ranks of the Regiment killed, and five officers[654] and 84 men wounded. That evening, Charles Crowe noticed a glimmering fire:

'Approaching, we found a party of the 40th Regiment strenuously exerting themselves to make a grave in the rocky ground to bury the body of poor Lieutenant Malone[655], who had for a short time held a Staff appointment and only rejoined his regiment in the morning. [Lieutenant Thomas] Radcliffe [27th] had known him, and feelingly expressed his sorrow as we stood beside the fine, manly, lifeless corpse, in his trousers and shirt, describing him as having been a spirited, generous-hearted fellow, beloved by all who knew him. The gloomy, solemn, melancholy scene can never be effaced from my memory; it was worthy of the skill of the best artist, although he could not possibly delineate the feelings and circumstances attending the impenetrable darkness of the night. The

---

[653] Quoted in *Historical Records of the 40th Regiment*, p. 143.

[654] Captain (Brevet Major) Arthur Heyland, in command, Captain Edward Cole Bowen, and Lieutenants William Waldron Kelly and John Thoreau, were all seriously wounded, and possibly Lieutenant Hugh Boyd Wray slightly wounded.

[655] Lieutenant Anthony Malone, commissioned into the 40th on 15th April 1807, served with the Regiment at Roliça, Vimeira, Talavera, Busaço, Redinha, 1st Siege of Badajoz and Vitoria. He was ADC to Major-General Kemmis June 1811 to July 1812.

conviction of the proximity of the enemy, the difficulty of digging, the occasional firing of our skirmishers, which as half-minute guns sounded the knell of the departed, could not be depicted, but added greatly to the solemnity.

'The rubble defied the exertions of the pioneers, whose dark visages [were] gilt with a bright outline from a small fire above them, besides which a sergeant on his knees endeavoured to make the green fuel burn to enlighten and accelerate the work. Ever and anon it glared up with a fitful blaze, showing the wax-fraught countenances of officers and men around. On the other side stood Lieutenant [James] Anthony [40th], the particular friend and chief mourner of the deceased, absorbed in grief. The grave was little more than two feet deep when the order resounded on all sides, "Stand to your arms and form ranks!" on which one of the pioneers dropped his shovel in utter despair. The sergeant indignantly sprang from the fire, bundled the fellow out in an agony of desperation, and levelled the bottom of the grave; then mournfully received and deposited therein the corpse of his beloved officer, and everyone around assisted with hands and feet to close the grave of the highly reputed subaltern.'[656]

As James Mill rode west, he was concerned at the doubt and confusion engendered by the retreat: 'It would not be superfluous to mention that the incidents of the last few days and the general appearance of matters had given birth to much doubt and perplexity, and to some misgiving that things were going wrong. I found all along the route, when conveying the despatches, that the most unfavourable rumours were current. The retreat of our troops, and the total ignorance relative to the distribution and distance of the main army, combined with the general haste and confusion, were altogether in no degree calculated to allay this mistrust.'[657]

The First Battle of Sorauren, 28th July

After another night march, early on the morning of 27th July the retreating British columns reached the village of Zabaldica in the Arga valley. Picton had originally intended to offer battle on the final defensible line before Pamplona, the contiguous Heights of San Cristobal and Huarte; but the former were clearly too close to the guns of the fortress town, which could have interdicted lateral communications, so Cole selected a position two miles further forward, on the Heights of Oricain, while Picton sat his 3rd Div to the right rear of the 4th Division on the Heights of Huarte, with four cavalry brigades protecting his right flank. The campaign-defining battles of Sorauren took place on the Heights of Oricain and the adjacent valleys of the Arga and Ulzama over four days.

The Heights of Oricain lie between the river valleys of the Arga, to the east, and the Ulzama. Between these valleys, two steep ridges, divided by a deep valley, or ravine, run east to west for 1½ miles between the villages of Sorauren, on the east bank of the Ulzama, and Zabaldica, perched on the valley-side at the eastern end of the ravine. Historians have termed the southern feature 'Cole's Ridge,' with 'Clausel's Ridge' to its north. Some 500 yards above Zabaldica a narrow saddle or land bridge links the two ridges, while above that village a detached feature known as Spanish Hill overlooks the Arga valley. Finally, at the west end of Cole's Ridge, above Sorauren, stood the Chapel of San Salvador. The rocky ridges had a covering of scrub and small fir trees. James Mill put together his impressions of the ground:

'By an early period of the day our entire division was drawn up for action to dispute the further progress of the French upon the summit of a broad and precipitous mountain, the form of which was uniform, except being highest in the middle; and from its side, lower down on the right, a second hill protruded towards the enemy; but the general surface of all was broken and rocky, and here and there pinnacled; the whole difficult of access… It was, in fact, an elevated ridge of country that lay exactly in a line of route between the French and the fortress they endeavoured to succour, and commanded, at that point, all the approaches to it.'[658]

To defend this position, Cole had his own 4th Division plus Byng's brigade, Campbell's Portuguese brigade, and two Spanish battalions. Ross's brigade was on the left of Cole's Ridge, then Campbell's Portuguese brigade, with Stubbs's Portuguese brigade behind (less the 7th Caçadores, who held the Chapel), and Anson's

[656] Crowe, p. 128.
[657] Mill, letter dated 5th August 1813, quoted in *Historical Records of the 40th Regiment*, p. 144.
[658] Mill, quoted in *Historical Records of the 40th Regiment*, p. 145.

brigade on the right, covering the land bridge. The Spanish battalions of Principe and Pravia, detached from the force blockading Pamplona, were on Spanish Hill, behind which, on a lower spur, the divisional artillery battery (Sympher's) covered the Arga valley. Finally, Byng's brigade was in reserve, some 500 yards to the rear on the Oricain summit. In accordance with usual British practice in the Peninsula, Cole's light troops were deployed forward as skirmishers while his battalions were over the skyline, concealed and protected.

Clausel reached Zabaldica at about 9 a.m. and, halting Conroux's division there, he deployed his other two divisions, those of Taupin and Vandermaesen, onto the ridge to his right. Cole's troops were still moving into position and, sensing an opportunity, one of Conroux's regiments made a dash at Spanish Hill:

'In the first instance, as preparatory to their struggle to carry our heights, the enemy expeditiously possessed themselves of the two hamlets at the foot of them, installed therein their columns of attack, and then opened fire from some cannon against the shelving hill [Spanish Hill] already referred to that jutted out on our right front. This latter was defended by a Spanish corps and – under cover of skirmishers and the fire of the cannon above referred to – a compact but inconsiderable party of French moved up in order to possess themselves of it; but they were gallantly met and repelled by its occupants.'[659]

Marshal Soult arrived on Clausel's Ridge by about 11 a.m., just in time to hear, and perhaps wonder at, the rousing cheers that greeted his adversary's appearance on the opposite ridge. Starting early on the 27th, Wellington had ridden down at speed from his headquarters at Almandoz, shedding all his staff but Fitzroy Somerset and leaving his able and trusted Quartermaster-General, George Murray, to pass on orders. He reached Sorauren at 11 a.m. just as French cavalry patrols moved down to the village from Clausel's Ridge, saw the situation at a glance, and coolly dismounted at the bridge to write quick orders (just thirteen lines)[660] to Murray on the parapet. Somerset spurred north with the despatch, evading the approaching chasseurs. This dramatic moment was captured by Wellington:

'At one time it was fairly alarming, certainly, and a close run thing. When I came to the bridge at Sorauren I saw French on the hills on one side, and it was clear that we could make a stand on the other hill… but I found that we could not keep Sorauren as it was exposed to their fire, and not ours. I was obliged to write my orders accordingly at Sorauren, to be sent back instantly. For if they had not been dispatched back directly, by the way I had come, I must have sent them four leagues round, a quarter of an hour later. I stopped therefore to write accordingly, people saying to me all the time, "The French are coming! The French are coming!" I looked pretty sharp after them every now and then, till I had completed my orders, and then set off. I saw them just near the one end of the village as I went out of it at the other end. And then we took up our ground.'

Wellington rode his thoroughbred alone up the steep track to the Chapel, where he was instantly recognised by the Portuguese Caçadores, who broke into cries of 'Douro, Douro,' which were followed by British cheers as he passed along the line.

'It was about this time that the near approach of Wellington was announced. On all occasions, in the field or on the line of march, his lordship was invariably greeted with a burst of welcome and enthusiastic cheers – a just and sincere tribute from the humbler ranks to the hero of so many victories. But today these acclamations were still more marked and hearty as he showed himself near the brigades; and I cannot adequately express the sense of confidence and assurance that was revived by his mere presence in the midst of a single division of his army. Cheers upon cheers were vehemently raised along the whole line, which were only lulled to quiet by the joyous conviction that all would yet go well.'[661]

Wellington halted on the central rise of Cole's Ridge, facing Soult and his staff, who could clearly be seen. The British commander needed to play for time: he had sent for the 6th Division, followed by the 7th, but even the 6th could not arrive until the 28th. He apparently observed that the applause marking his appearance in the field might cause Soult to hesitate: 'Yonder is a great commander,' he mused, telescope in hand, 'but he is a cautious

---

[659] Mill, quoted in *Historical Records of the 40th Regiment*, p. 146.
[660] These orders, sent via Murray, were for the 6th and 7th Divisions to concentrate at Lezaso then move through Marcelain to join and prolong the left of Wellington's line.
[661] Mill, quoted in *Historical Records of the 40th Regiment*, p.p. 145-46.

one and will delay his attack to ascertain the cause of these cheers: that will give time for the 6th Division to come up, and we shall beat him.'

Clausel urged action, but Soult was waiting for Reille's corps and, having eaten lunch, went to sleep. Clausel beat his forehead and exclaimed, 'Who could go to sleep at such a moment?' Reille eventually arrived that afternoon, but apart from a probing demonstration by Foy on the left towards the Heights of Huarte, there was no further offensive move that day, though according to James Mill 'vast hordes of skirmishers continued to be flung out by the French, and were scattered along the base of the heights for some distance up the ascent, keeping up a concentrated fire on our general line.'

Wellington approved of Cole's deployment and made just one adjustment, which critically concerned the 40th:

'So far our brigade had been kept together and disposed along the high land at about the right centre of the mountain, at a spot which was adjacent to, but retired from, the hill of the Spaniards; but now our regiment was directed personally by Lord Wellington to proceed to its position in support, and here we remained with the Spaniards, detached from our own brigade, during that and the succeeding days.

'This day, however, the endeavours of the French to take possession of any part of our ground were not repeated; but the fusillade proceeded briskly, and was sustained by us in the same order of formation and spirit. The fire from their guns at the hamlet just below us did slight execution, thanks to our loose order and skilful disposition.'[662]

As the afternoon wore on, lowering clouds gathered, and at about 7 p.m. the weather broke, putting an end to the firing. A terrific thunderstorm with heavy rain drenched both armies, and, as on the eve of Salamanca and Waterloo, the tired, wet and hungry troops took what rest they could on the open hillsides. Soult had let his best opportunity of success slip from his grasp, for in the morning Wellington would be reinforced.

The 28th of July dawned fine and bright. Soult planned an attack at 1 p.m. with five divisions, leaving Foy to face Picton in the Arga valley: all three of Clausel's divisions were to attack from ridge to ridge across the steep-sided valley, of which Maucune's division was to assault across the land bridge. Lamartinière (replacing Conroux at Zabaldica) was to take Spanish Hill, supported by four howitzers. It took all morning to move the French divisions into position.

Meanwhile, Pack's 6th Division was approaching from the west, Madden's Portuguese brigade appearing over the hills west of the Ulzama towards noon, followed by two British brigades on the main road south of Sorauren. This prompted Soult, at about 12.30 p.m., to change his plan, sending Conroux with 7,000 bayonets through Sorauren to confront Pack. They advanced too far and fell into a trap, attacked on three sides by Madden, Pack and Ross, and fell back into Sorauren.

The main frontal attack, 20,000 French infantry, was launched early, with Taupin, Vandermaesen and Maucune attacking in echelon from the right, crossing the ravine in brigade columns preceded by clouds of tirailleurs. Lamartinière's attack probably started last, at about 1 p.m.

Taupin reached the Chapel, but was then flung back by Ross's Fusilier brigade at bayonet point. Maucune was heavily defeated by Anson's brigade (27th, 48th and 2nd Provisional Battalion) at the land bridge and was driven back in ten minutes with 6-700 casualties. But Vandermaesen's brigades pushed back Campbell and Ross (the latter short of ammunition), gaining a foothold on the ridge, and for a time, the situation was most critical; but the French were blown and becoming disorganised. One of Vandermaesen's brigades, having broken through on Campbell's left, continued to gain ground; but then Wellington brought down Byng's brigade to support Ross, and launched the 27th and 48th in a diagonal downhill bayonet charge against Vandermaesen's flank, and by about 3.30 p.m. the Anglo-Portuguese line on Cole's Ridge had been restored.

Meanwhile, the five battalions of Gauthier's brigade of Lamartinière's division, directed by Reille in person, made four assaults from the village of Zabaldica onto Spanish Hill. Captain Sempronius Stretton described what happened:

'The 40th Regiment, at this time under my command, which, from previous losses, was reduced to one captain, nine subalterns, and less than four hundred men, was directed by the Duke of Wellington in person to

---

[662] Mill, quoted in *Historical Records of the 40th Regiment*, p. 146.

occupy the summit of a rocky hill, which was considered to be the key of the British position. Two Spanish regiments [Pravia and Principe] and the 40th composed the entire force placed there, with which I was directed to keep the hill to the last.

'We passed the night [of the 27th] under the continued fire of four small guns, without sustaining any material loss.[663] On the morning of the 28th, about ten o'clock, the enemy made their attack with a powerful force, as I was subsequently informed, consisting of several thousand men. Our line was formed across the hill, with a space of about eighty yards in our front, the two Spanish regiments being posted upon our flanks. No sooner did the enemy's fire reach us, than the Spaniards retired in the utmost confusion, and scattering themselves over the face of the mountain in our rear (on the summit of which the Duke and his staff were stationed), were seen no more, leaving the 40th totally unsupported.

'As soon as the head of the attacking French column reached the brow of the hill and formed, a volley was fired by the 40th, and a charge of bayonets made, which drove them down again in the utmost confusion. Four times the enemy renewed the attack, and each time they were driven back at the point of the bayonet, leaving the 40th in final possession of the hill which they had so resolutely defended; not, however, without their having sustained considerable loss.'

'His Serene Highness the Prince of Orange, who conveyed to the regiment after the second charge the thanks of the Duke of Wellington, narrowly escaped, and the brigade-majors of Sir Lowry Cole and Sir William Anson, Roverea and Avemen, who came down shortly afterwards, were both killed near me in the struggle which took place.[664]

'The following day a French officer of rank came to me with a request that he might have his wounded carried off, and after speaking in the highest terms of the gallantry displayed on the 28th in defence of the hill, he assured me that several hundred of his men were placed *hors de combat* on that occasion. Severe as this loss appears, I cannot, when I consider the position of the enemy, crowded as they were on the brow of the hill, without the power of immediately retiring, when the several charges were made, for a moment suppose that this statement, from such an authority, was an exaggerated one, more particularly as I was witness of the severe loss sustained by the enemy on that occasion from the bayonet alone, to which we considered ourselves solely indebted, placed as they were in the hands of brave men, for the successful defence of the position entrusted to us.'[665]

Lieutenant James Mill gave a more detailed account of this epic regimental action:

'The 40th, with about four hundred Spaniards, were in occupation of the hill already described in front of our position, and within musket-shot of the French. Early in the day the whole of the French army were observed in motion, and there were seen compact bodies of them ascending on the left of our ridge of defence, and the battle soon after commenced in earnest.

'About 12 o'clock a considerable force, numbering about five thousand in the integral, but which consisted of two separate columns of attack, some distance apart, so as to co-operate in support, were observed marching straight towards us from diverse points. The first column[666], about two thousand five hundred strong, was somewhat in advance of the other; it moved up with the utmost gallantry, and, undeterred by the well-directed missiles from the hill, still preserved its steady form and solidity. The Spaniards, at the moment the French got half way up the ascent, coolly ran away, leaving us, the 40th, about four hundred and twenty strong, to our fate. All attempts to rally them were ineffectual. They were gone in a moment.

'We were drawn up, eight companies in a line, a little retired from the brow of the hill, and were prepared for the worst. When the French had gained the brow of the hill the order to charge was given, and with a threatening shout, vehement and prolonged, our battalion singly fell upon them with the bayonet, shivering their compact order and sweeping them some distance down the descent Our men were hardly restrained from

---

[663] In fact, the 40th had eight men wounded (out of total 17 casualties at Sorauren that day).

[664] Captain Alexandre de Roverea, a Swiss officer, was ADC to Sir Lowry Cole, and a close friend, while Captain Charles Avemann of the King's German Legion was indeed Anson's brigade major.

[665] Letter to the Editor of *Colburn's United Service Journal* by Colonel Sempronius Stretton CB, dated Athlone, West Meath, 8th February 1840, quoted in *Historical Records of the 40th Regiment*, Appendix VII, p.p. 566-67.

[666] Three battalions of the 120th Ligne.

following too far, and reluctantly obeyed the orders of their officers to return to the hill; but a halt was made in time, and as expeditiously as possible the companies again formed up, and quietly awaited a renewal of the attack.

'The second column of the French[667], two thousand five hundred strong, soon appeared, and ascending in precisely the same formation as the first, advanced with great steadiness and spirit. It was, however, also driven from the ridge and hurled down the hill. As in the former case, our men pursued the enemy too far, and the lapse of time enabled the enemy to re-form their first column, which they did, and advanced a second time, but when it reached half-way up the hill, and within twenty-five yards of us, we again charged through fire and smoke and bayoneted all who stood in our way.

'After these rencounters, which assumed for the time the proportions of a desperate and prolonged struggle, we could see that our fire was very destructive to the French, and they fell into utter confusion. One more effort was, however, made to rally, but without effect, and we could descry the French officers at the head of their divisions trying to animate the soldiers, by gesture and example, to renew the assault. The standards were even carried to the front, and the drums beat the "advance," but all to no purpose; there was no obedience to the summons, and our small cohort remained victorious on the heights.

'Lord Wellington was close at hand, a witness of the whole, and sent the Prince of Orange to thank the regiment, and we were immediately afterwards reinforced with two regiments.'[668]

Corporal William Lawrence recalled his experience of the day:

'The French soon made their appearance and attacked the Spanish corps, who fired at them long before they came within bounds of shot, not having proper officers to guide them; those that ought to have been leading them on having instead placed themselves out of the way, leaving their men to do the dirty work; and of course these latter soon decamped too. Our Regiment, however, was soon on the scene; and hastening in that direction, we managed to get there before the enemy had gained the summit of this important ridge.

'Orders had been issued by our officers not to fire till we could do good work; but this soon came to pass, for the French quickly sallied up and fired first, and we returned it in less than a minute. I never saw a single volley do so much execution in all my campaigning days, almost every man of their two front ranks falling; and then we instantly charged and chased them down the mountain, doing still further and more fearful havoc. When we had done we returned to our old summit again, where the captain cheered and praised us for our gallantry, saying that he had never seen a braver set of men, and that he hoped we would always succeed in holding our ground equally well.

'Our likewise brave enemy tried again two hours later to shift us and take possession of our ground; but they were again received as before, and again sent down the hill. We were again praised by our commander, who said, "I think they have got enough of it by this time, and won't make a third attack in a hurry"; but we were mistaken, for four hours had not passed before they were up again with fresh reinforcements. Some of our men then seemed to despair, for I heard them even say to the officers, who were so bravely leading us on, "We shall have to be off this time." "Never mind," said the officers, "keep your ground if possible and don't let yourselves be beaten"; which we did like bricks, for on their arrival and trying to outflank us, so that we were obliged to wheel round to the left, the right flank opened fire as they were close upon us, and instantly charged right into them with the bayonet, forcing them to retreat.

'They again fell up to support their other companies, who were attacking our other flank; but we reloaded and were then ready to meet them, again pouring another of our deadly volleys into their ranks and then going at them again with our bayonets like enraged bulldogs. The fight that ensued was sanguinary, but we succeeded again in driving them down the mountain at last. I should think they must have numbered five to our one.

'We encamped that night on the same ground that we had so well defended. Our captain, who was as nice a man as ever commanded in the Peninsula, always seeming to share everything with the men and bear the blunt as well as the smooth, and the losses as well as the profits, now said, "Come, my brave men; turn to and cook

---

[667] Two battalions of the 122nd Ligne.
[668] Mill, quoted in *Historical Records of the 40th Regiment*, p.p. 147-48. The reference to 'two regiments' is understandable, for the men of the 2nd Provisional Battalion, who were moved up in support of the 40th, wore the uniforms of their parent 3rd and 53rd Regiments. This battalion was in reserve all day, losing just one man killed and nineteen wounded.

yourselves something to eat, for you have earned it well"; an order which we soon set about to obey. A quantity of rum had been sent up for us, so we were able to sit down, tired as we were, and enjoy ourselves as if nothing extraordinary had occurred that day. We then sent out a picket and prepared to take our rest for the night, the French not seeming inclined to sally up any more to engage us on those heights.

'When the returns were called off the list, we found our killed and wounded amounted to seventy-four, but one more of our number was soon to be added to the sum total. A comrade of my own company went in search of sticks to liven up our fire: I told him to be careful and not get in sight of the enemy's picket, or they might have a pop at him, and he replied never fear, he would be careful; but the foolish fellow had been gone but a few minutes when he was shot through the neck. Instead of keeping his own side of the hill, he had diverged onto the other, close enough to be observed by one of the enemy's riflemen, who shot him as I have described. I happened to hear the shot, and found that it had been at him, so I went and dragged him back pretty quickly, for I was fearful lest I should be shot likewise myself. The poor fellow was not dead, but exclaimed, "Oh Corporal, I am a dead man!" When I had got him out of the enemy's reach and near our own lines, I took his stock from his neck and he expired directly; so I had to leave him and rejoin our company with the news that another of us was gone, making seventy-five in all.'[669]

The French lost at least 600 men that day on the slopes of Spanish Hill.[670] The official return shows that the 40th had 129 casualties on the 28th, rather more than stated by Lawrence and Mill, though those present may have included men who were wounded but still in the ranks to answer their names. Lieutenant Galway and nineteen rank and file were killed,[671] and four officers[672] and 105 men were wounded. Captain Stretton recounted some lucky escapes, including an incident when he himself had an epaulette shot away:

'Whilst I was giving some directions to a serjeant of the regiment during the time we were under a smart fire from the enemy's guns on the 28th, he was suddenly wheeled about by the effect of a round-shot which struck the end of his knapsack, and, tearing it from his back, scattered the contents of it in the air without doing him the smallest injury. At the same moment I received a musket-ball, which struck the front of my cravat, which it tore, and, passing under the collar of my coat, grazing the skin of my shoulder, escaped through an aperture of its own making.

'Not so fortunate was Lieutenant Galway[673], who during our first charge, received two musket-balls in his body, from the effect of which I found him, on returning to our ground, lying upon a heap of stones, and bleeding rapidly to death. Whilst we were rendering him every assistance (no medical man being with us), we were called away from our exertions by the return of the enemy, and when they were again driven back, and we regained our former ground, Lieutenant Galway was found lying upon his back where we had left him: his pulse had ceased to beat, and life to all appearance had passed away. "Is he beyond all hope, and can nothing be done for him?" inquired one of the party. The reply was, "Nothing – he is dead!" At this moment, to our astonishment, he rose upon his seat, and, staring wildly about him, said, "Dead!" It was the last effort of nature: he had no sooner uttered this, than, falling upon his back, he died without a struggle.'[674]

The French made no further attempts on Wellington's position. At around 4 to 5 p.m., Soult ordered his troops back to their original positions, and firing had ceased by 7 p.m. The day had been fought with desperate gallantry on both sides. Allied casualties totaled 2,652, of whom 1,358 were British, while the French lost around

---

[669] Lawrence, p.p. 147-51.

[670] The 120th Ligne lost six officers killed and five wounded that day, and the 122nd Ligne had five officers wounded, two mortally. Applying the rule of thumb that there would be around twenty other rank casualties for every officer, we arrive at a total casualty estimate of 884, but in the assault on Spanish Hill a higher proportion of officer casualties may well have been sustained, making a total loss closer to 600 quite possible.

[671] The 4th Division Weekly State as at 1st August shows 26 rank and file dead in the previous week, which equates to those killed in action on 26th and 28th July, 22 in all and four subsequently died of wounds. The number of 'sick' rank and file, which included wounded, rose by 190 that week. 199 men are known to have been wounded over that period.

[672] Lieutenant Michael Smith was seriously wounded, and Lieutenants Nathan Truman Carter, Andrew Eugene Glynn, and Theobald O'Doherty were slightly wounded.

[673] Commissioned into the 40th on 27th August 1809, Lieutenant Anthony Galway had served in the Peninsula since January 1810, seeing action at Busaço, Redinha, the 1st siege of Badajoz, Castrejon, Salamanca and Vitoria.

[674] Sempronius Stretton, quoted in *Peninsular Sketches*, W. H. Maxwell, London, 1845, Vol. II, p.p. 346-47.

4,000. 'I never saw such fighting as we have had,' reported Wellington, 'The battle of the 28th was fair bludgeon work.' He later asserted that the stand made by the 40th Regiment at Sorauren was the finest individual feat of arms he had witnessed in Spain.[675]

The Second Battle of Sorauren, 30th July 1813

On July 29th, there was a tacit truce, with hardly a shot fired all day as both sides adjusted their dispositions, buried their dead and tended their casualties, as described by Lieutenant James Mill of the 40th:

'This was a day of perfect rest, but of melancholy duties; for it was occupied in burying the dead, The loss of the enemy on and about the hill we defended was six hundred; our loss, in killed and wounded of the 40th, only one hundred. The company I commanded lost more men than its due proportion of these numbers – probably from being near the centre. I had sufficient leisure to walk over part of the position. Not a shot was fired from either side, and the armies occupied precisely the same stations they did before the battle of yesterday.'[676]

Corporal William Lawrence described a local truce for casualty evacuation:

'A French officer was seen coming up the mountain, having laid down his sword, so our captain sent a lieutenant who could talk good French to meet him and see what he wanted. He found that he wished to know if we would allow him to send for their wounded, so an agreement was entered into that we should take all their killed and wounded halfway down the mountain, and that they should meet us there with ours in return. This plan was soon carried out; and when we had buried our dead, the wounded were conveyed to hospitals.'[677]

But Lawrence had, as he candidly admitted, spotted an opportunity:

'I happened to observe an officer of the French army moving at some distance in front of our lines, having hanging from his pocket a fine watch-guard, which particularly took my attention and which I thought at the time would look very well on me; and being more daring than wise, I crawled towards him with my musket loaded, and when near enough as I thought to him, I fired; but it did him no mischief and only made him take himself off at once. I nearly got into a scrape through it, however, for I was fired at myself in return, the bullet fortunately only taking the butt end off my musket. I turned to run off, and another shot hit the knapsack on my back, but I soon got out of reach of their shot again, luckily, as it happened, without any injury; but it must have been a near thing, for when I next opened my knapsack, I found the ball had gone through the leather and my thickly-folded blanket and had at last been stopped by the sole of a shoe, and was lying there as flat as a halfpenny and about the same size.'[678]

Both Soult and Wellington took advantage of the pause in operations to adjust their plans and deployment. Soult's new plan on the 29th was to disengage that night and move off to the north, with the greater part of his army marching up the Ulzama valley. This required a complicated initial manoeuvre as he had first to move divisions, in the dark, from east to west across Clausel's Ridge, then hold Sorauren with a rearguard through the 30th while his army moved up the road to Ostiz. To complicate matters, Maucune's division was to take over the defence of Sorauren village from Conroux. This was in effect a retreat, but to save face he claimed a mere alteration of strategic direction: he would march north to cut the road between Pamplona and San Sebastian. His real intent is shown by the withdrawal on the night 28th/29th of the greater part of his guns, wounded and baggage on the road to Roncesvalles.

For his part, Wellington adjusted his deployment in preparation for offensive action on the 30th. His most hard-hit brigades, those of Ross and Campbell, were replaced in the front line by Byng and Stubbs; he had already sent the 2nd Provisional Battalion to support the thinned ranks of the 40th; guns were hauled up onto the heights by the 4th and 6th Divisions; and finally, anticipating Soult's intentions, he ordered Hill with the 2nd Division to take up a position at Lizaso and Beunza.

---

[675] *Ellesmere Personal Reminiscences*, p.129.
[676] Mill, quoted in *Historical Records of the 40th Regiment*, p. 150.
[677] Lawrence, p. 152.
[678] Lawrence, p.p. 150-51.

With regard to the reinforcement of Spanish Hill, which probably happened late on the 28th, Corporal Lawrence says that Colonel Bingham of the 2nd Provisional Battalion 'offered to occupy our heights, so that we might fall back to the rear, but our captain would not consent to that, "For," as he said, "my men have fought well to defend their position, and I think they will be strong enough to keep it." He proposed, however, that they should keep out an outlying picket, so that we could take our rest, which was the best way of relieving us, and their commander readily agreed to do so.'

Meanwhile, as ordered, the 7th Division had arrived after a particularly arduous four-day march over the mountains. Lieutenant George Wood of the 82nd described the marches of the 28th and 29th, which brought them over the mountainous Puerto de Velate to Lizaso by noon on the 28th, and on through Marcalain to reach what amounted to an ambush position, behind high hills above the right bank of the Ulzama, deep on the French right flank.

'We now continued, I may say, flying the whole of the day, without any food being issued, except half an allowance of rum, which recruited our sinking spirits. After refreshing ourselves with this and a little rest, we proceeded on the whole of the next night, descending the most rugged and dangerous precipices, and surmounting the highest hills with indescribable fatigue.

'The next day, which was the fourth of this disastrous march, and during which we had scarcely tasted food, Division Orders were issued whilst we halted a few hours. I well remember reading them: they were the most distressing, at the same time most feeling orders, that I ever heard, commencing somewhat in this manner: "The General is aware of the many privations and hardships the troops have suffered during the last few days; but he assures them that if they will bear them with patience and fortitude for another day, their wants shall be supplied."… After halting a few hours we went forward, and, before night came on, reached a strong position on the heights of Pampeluna: here we found these orders fulfilled according to promise, a full portion of rations being delivered to us – the most seasonable supply that troops so famished and harassed could possibly obtain. We now commenced boiling our kettles, and got some tea, our allowance of rum, meat and biscuit – the first since our retreat commenced, and which, indeed, we had hardly the patience to await the cooking of, having been four days without a morsel to eat except the withered leaves of the trees, which we chewed as we passed along to assuage the cravings of hunger… We were literally wallowing in luxury, which gave us such spirits that woe to the enemy who should dare to oppose us!

'We had taken up our ground on a very elevated spot, which commanded an extensive view[679]; and I was here highly amused, just before dark, by observing many of our soldiers run into a field between the hostile piquets, and dig with their bayonets. Soon I saw many of the enemy do the same thing: they did not molest each other, but appeared even familiar, laughing and joking promiscuously. How strange, thought I, that these men, who tomorrow would be slaying each other, should now be so good-humouredly employed together! They were digging potatoes: and this ground, I believe, is generally, in point of honour, allowed to be neutral.

'We now laid ourselves down to repose: our arms piled, and every man wrappd up in his blanket, close to the butt-end of his firelock; the enemy immediately to our front, and our piquets within half pistol-shot.'[680]

According to the *Record of Service* of the 82nd Regiment, a detachment of ten sergeants and two hundred rank and file joined from the 2nd/82nd on the 30th and showed 'uncommon spirit' in action the following day.

At midnight the French attempted the major night move of their divisions across the Anglo-Portuguese front, from east to west across Clausel's Ridge and down into Sorauren and the Ulzama valley: the result was chaos, for at dawn the divisions of Maucune and Foy were still straggling across the heights, and the relief of Conroux in Sorauren had not been effected.

The Allies were under arms an hour before dawn on 30th July, and at about 9 a.m. Wellington's guns opened fire and he assumed the offensive. His outline plan of attack, as stated in his subsequent dispatch, was to turn both of Soult's flanks before assaulting Clausel's Ridge, which he described as 'one of the strongest and

---

[679] Wellington's orders to Lord Dalhousie at Lizaso, sent on the evening of the 29th, were that: 'Lord Dalhousie will be so good as to close his division towards its right that it may be in a situation whence it can with facility move to the ground on the wooded ridge, where Major-General Pack's left now is; and he will ascertain whether one of his brigades could be moved up to a high ridge which lies between the wooded ridge above mentioned and the great hill in its front'.
[680] Wood, p.p. 204-06.

most difficult of access that I have seen occupied by troops'… 'I, however, determined to attack their position, and ordered Lieut.-General the Earl of Dalhousie to possess himself of the top of the mountain in his front, by which the enemy's right would be turned; and Lieut.-General Sir T. Picton to cross the heights on which the enemy's left had stood and to turn their left by the road to Roncesvalles. All the arrangements were made to attack the front of the enemy's position as the effect of those movements on their flanks begin to appear.'

As ordered, Picton pushed up Arga valley, through Zabaldica and onto the east end of Clausel's Ridge, and Dalhousie attacked the French columns retiring north up the Ulzama valley, where Clausel had halted Taupin's and Vandermaesen's divisions at a defile near the village of Olabe, with Vandermaesen to the rear.

Inglis's brigade of the 7th Division, led by the 82nd, first defeated a two-battalion flank guard sent by Vandermaesen up the heights to the west of the Ulzama, then descended to the road to attack Taupin's and Vandermaesen's divisions, who withdrew north after a close and bloody fight, leaving some three hundred prisoners. The part played by the 82nd that day is told by George Wood:

'Before the day dawned, we were awakened by the fire of musketry close upon us, with an alarm that the enemy had surprised us in our camp; and half asleep, "Fall in, fall in! Stand to your arms! Quick, quick!" was the word, and instantly we were wheeled into line. The piquets only were engaged; but they were so near that their balls came whistling among us. Ours were directly called in, and the dazzling rays of this day's sun, peeping over the tops of the hills, displayed to our view the unfurled banners and glittering arms of the Gallic lines, which were drawn up in order of battle.'

'The fight was already begun, and it was our turn to come in contact with the formidable foe. They were posted on a great height, and to that spot we hastened to dislodge them: here we saw the enemy in such force that we were obliged to show a front of six hundred men, when in reality we had not four; but we boldly advanced, till the shot flew as thick as a shower of hail about us, with a noise like the buzzing of bees. This was severe fighting; as we were compelled to drive the enemy from mountain to mountain at the point of the bayonet, without the assistance of either the dragoons or the artillery.

'I am informed by a gentleman on the staff, who was immediately near his Grace at this moment, that the Duke, seeing the corps advance so gallantly, asked what regiment it was; and when informed, replied, "Oh! let them alone; they will do the business well, I am sure!" or words to that effect.

'In less than ten minutes one half of my company were killed or wounded; my brother subaltern and the sergeant gone to support the Colours, the ensign [Mason] being shot; my corporal was knocked down, and myself severely wounded by a musket-ball. My men were now, therefore, left without even a non-commissioned officer to command them; but the brave fellows went on in line with the Regiment, and in about five minutes more I had the satisfaction of seeing them carry the hill.'

'After lying some time, I was taken to the rear and dressed; and horses and mules being sent for, as no other conveyance can pass in these mountains, I soon joined my Colonel and half-a-dozen other officers of the Regiment in the same predicament, who were waiting a conveyance, and proceeded with them towards Vittoria, the depot of the wounded. It was here that I heard this brave man, who, as I before observed, was placed under arrest in winter-quarters by the General of the Division, and who was subsequently shot in his stomach at the battle of Vittoria, then slightly wounded at the pass of Maya, and now covered with similar bleeding honours, after having his horse shot under him in this great action, exclaim, "You see, by Gad! – You see we can fight as well as the General and his division – You see, though he did turn us out of it – by Gad! You see…," or some such words as these.'[681]

A letter from Corporal William Wheeler of the 51st Regiment, in the same brigade, adds some more detail, and also covers the latter part of the action, after Lieutenant Wood was wounded:

'In our front was a lofty mountain on which was posted the enemy's right. This was the key to their position, it being almost impregnable and commanded their whole line. It fell to our lot to drive them from it… The attack was made as follows. The brigade marched to its left some distance, when the 51st turned to the right and under the cover of brush wood and trees began to ascend the steep front of the mountain. The 82nd and C[hasseurs] B[rittaniques] Regiments ascended on the enemy's right. The 68th advanced farther round the hill

[681] Wood, p.p. 206-09.

before they began to ascend, so that we were marching to the attack in their front, on their right, and in their rear... The wood completely covered us and helped us in climbing. Some places were so difficult that we were obliged to assist each other. I understand the 68th met with the same difficulties on their side. The 82nd and C[hasseurs] B[rittaniques] met with less difficulty and advanced in good order in two lines. It was in their direction the enemy expected the attack, and were formed ready to receive them. Fortunately we all arrived at our different points of attack at the same time.

'The enemy allowed the 82nd and C[hasseurs] B[rittaniques] to come nearer them in their usual custom before they opened their fire. At length the enemy fired a volley, which was instantly returned by the 82nd. We then slapped a volley into them that seemed to say "Well done 82nd." Before the noise was well subsided bang goes the 68th, which spoke as plain as possible "Well done the whole." Now fifty buglers were sounding the charge, and the drums of the 82nd and C[hasseurs] B[rittaniques] were beating time to the music. A general rush was made by the whole brigade, accompanied by three tremendous British cheers. The concert was to[o] powerful for the nerves of monsieur, who without ceremony changed the concert into a ball, and off they danced, the devil take the hindmost, down the hill to our right, the only way they had to escape.

'We followed them close to their heels, and soon got them on a small level. Here they soon got huddled together like a flock of sheep. This place was well studded with thick bushes of underwood, and here and there a cork tree. As we were galling them with a sharp fire, they summed up resolution to turn on us, and threatened us with a taste of their steel. As soon as their intention was perceived our bugles sounded the charge, and in a moment we were on the level with them. Now the tug of war began. As they could only get away by a few at a time, not only were the bayonets used but many were the fractured skulls by the butts of firelocks. Every bush was soon turned into a citadel, and in many instances the same bush was occupied by each party... The enemy was soon thinned by some getting away and by their loss in killed and wounded; the remainder we made prisoners.

'We then returned back to the top of the hill, and received a lecture from Genl. Inglis for following the enemy down the hill, contrary to the sound of the field bugle. He informed us that had we remained on the hill and fired, the end would have been gained with less loss to us, for the remainder of the division were posted to gall them by cross fire. He said he could not but admire our ardour, but hoped we should be more attentive in future... The General is a good old soul, and although he endeavoured to look mighty angry we could see he was not so much displeased as he pretended.

'We now had a view of both armies. They were hot at it, but from the nature of the ground nothing extraordinary was done... In the afternoon we perceived a movement in the enemy's line. In a short time after their whole army retreated. We descended into the valley and by a cross fire annoyed them for some time. Here I found my comrade: he had with a few more followed the enemy from the level.'[682]

After a close and bloody fight in the valley between Inglis's brigade and Vandermaesen's division, Clausel withdrew his men and retreated up the road, followed by the 7th Division, with Inglis pressing along the road and the other two brigades outflanking the enemy on the hills west of the river.

The loss of the 82nd on 30th July was nine rank and file killed, seven officers, ten sergeants and 69 rank and file wounded,[683] including Colonel Grant, who was wounded another three times.[684]

Meanwhile, Cole's 4th Division made a frontal attack across the ravine onto Clausel's Ridge, which was then being traversed by Foy's division. The assault was led by the Portuguese of Stubbs' brigade and by the 40th and 2nd Provisional Battalion of Anson's brigade, followed in second line by Ross with the 27th and 48th. Foy put up little resistance, but retired north across the hills, pressed by the main body of the 4th Division. The 40th took a

---

[682] Letter of Corporal Wheeler, 51st Foot, dated Camp near Eschellar 17th August 1813.
[683] Colonel William Grant, Major William Edward FitzGerald, Lieutenants John Boyd, John Mackay and George Wood, and Ensign Edward Ussher Mason were severely wounded: Lieutenant and Adjutant Samuel Holdsworth was slightly wounded (a contusion and a musket ball in the wrist). In addition, Lieutenant-Colonel Henry Pynn of the 82nd, commanding the 18th Line of Ashworth's Portuguese brigade, 2nd Division, was dangerously wounded. Mackay, who had served with the 82nd at Copenhagen, Roliça, Vimeira, Corunna, Flushing, Barrosa, Vittoria and Maya, had previously been seriously wounded at Barrosa. Mason was wounded carrying one of the Colours. Holdsworth, born near Bradford, had joined the 82nd as a sergeant from the East Yorkshire Militia. He was promoted from Sergeant-Major in 1807, aged 29, and continued to serve in Spain, France, Canada, New South Wales, the East Indies and Mauritius.
[684] William Grant did not serve again with the 82nd, and on 4th June 1814 he was promoted to major-general.

different direction, advancing to their left along the ridge for a mile to a point above the road north from Sorauren, where the battle still raged.

Sorauren had been bombarded and assaulted from three sides: the 6th Division attacked frontally up the village street, Byng's brigade descended from Cole's Ridge, and Madden's Portuguese brigade attacked to the west of the Ulzama. Conroux's and Maucune's divisions, almost surrounded, attempted to withdraw. It was too late, for at about 10.30 a.m., the 40th Foot came down from the heights just north of the village to cut the French line of retreat, charging a mass of some two thousand of Maucune's Division. Captain Sempronius Stretton described the regimental action:

'On the morning of the 30th we were again ready for any service that might be required of us. We were not long without occupation: about 10 a.m. an order arrived for the troops to cross the ravine at the foot of our position, and attack the enemy on the summit of a range of high and steep mountains in our front. The day was broiling hot, and it required great exertion to ascend these rocky heights: it was, however, effected; and after much gallantry on both sides the enemy were driven at all points to defend as ineffectually every subsequent position which they took up to their rear.

'At this moment, the 40th Regiment was ordered by, by Lieutenant-General Sir Lowry Cole, commanding our division, to proceed down the mountain to our left, and arrest the progress of a column of the enemy who were retiring in the valley. The road, if so it can be called, by which it was necessary to descend, which in winter was evidently a water-course, was obstructed by masses of rock and deep gulleys.

'Under a smart fire from the retiring force, we at length reached the bottom of the mountain, and a rush being made with the bayonet, we succeeded in taking prisoners the whole of the 32nd French light battalion[685], consisting of twenty-four officers and nearly 700 men – more than double the numerical strength of the 40th Regiment at that time. The Commanding Officer, *chef-de-bataillon*, a very gentlemanly man, who had been wounded in the arm that morning, presented me his sword, which is still in my possession… Shortly after this piece of good fortune, and [when] the prisoners were collected together, the Duke of Wellington arrived in the valley, and, in person, I reported to his Grace the fruits of our exertions, requesting to be informed how I was to dispose of them; when his Grace, smiling, said, "What! the 40th again?" and desired that they should be sent to the rear, under an escort of the Regiment, on their way to Vittoria.'

'It was a curious circumstance that, upon inspecting the prisoners' knapsacks, a quantity of drinking cups were found, which the Quartermaster of the 7th Fusileers, in our division, had sent for to England for the officers, and which it is supposed had been landed at Passages, but on their way through the mountains to the Fourth Division, had been taken by the enemy. As I heard no more of them, I presume they at length reached their original destination, the Quartermaster of the 7th having been informed of the circumstances.

'Amongst the officers taken prisoners by us was one of almost gigantic size. A short time previous, he had been the tambour-major of his battalion, and had been recently promoted to the rank of sous-lieutenant. I found him extremely troublesome, making several attempts to escape; and it was not until severely rebuked for it by his commanding officer that he desisted from his attempts. On the return of the escort from conducting the prisoners to the rear, I learned that our troublesome friend had, during the morning of the action, been the bearer of an Eagle, which, upon our approach, he had thrown into a rapid stream, along the left bank of which the corps to which he belonged was retiring. It is needless for me to say how greatly annoyed I was, that all hope of discovering so valuable a trophy was thus irretrievably lost. This piece of information explained to me Sir Lowry Cole's motive for inquiring of me, during our pursuit of the enemy that day, whether the 40th Regiment had not taken an Eagle with the prisoners.'[686]

Lieutenant James Mill took part in this remarkable action:

---

[685] This is a mistake: it was the 34th Légère of Montfort's brigade, Maucune's division. They reported the loss of 13 officers and 531 men taken prisoners on the 30th out of a strength of 773; the higher total quoted by the 40th may well include men from other regiments of the disintegrated and routed division, which lost some eleven hundred men captured that day.
[686] Sempronius Stretton, quoted in *Peninsular Sketches*, W. H. Maxwell, London, 1845, Vol. II, p.p. 343-46. Assuming that the Eagle of the 34th Légère was carried at Sorauren, it would appear that the obstreperous Porte-Aigle threw the treasured trophy into the Ulzama. There is no reason to believe it was ever recovered.

'This day we attacked the enemy's position in our front, and carried everything before us. The position it occupied was said to be stronger, also more difficult and rugged of ascent, than our own, and the one we had lately left. The 40th Regiment, with the light company of the 53rd Regiment [i.e. 2nd Provisional Battalion], alone, after carrying the heights in our front, charged a body of two thousand French, and took seven hundred of them prisoners. I took a French officer under my protection, who implored me not to deliver him into the hands of the Spaniards.'[687]

The account of Corporal William Lawrence agrees in every particular with those of the two officers, and adds his own accolade:

'We followed up the retreating French to a village situated in a valley of the Pyrenees, where they were delayed owing to having to cross a river. General Cole immediately ordered our regiment to stop them if possible; so off we went in quick time to the river, and on their seeing they were so quickly pursued, and that there was no hope of escaping, they threw down their arms and gave themselves up prisoners to the number of about seven hundred. We took a gold-mounted sword from their commander, and a gold plate out of his cap with an eagle engraved on it, which were given to our captain by the regiment as a present, as he was a universal favourite for his behaviour to the men in general.'[688]

The casualties of the 40th on 30th July were remarkably light: just one officer[689] and six men wounded.

The divisions of Conroux and Maucune were effectively destroyed in two hours with the loss of some 1,700 prisoners. Foy, Lamartinière, and the lost and wrecked remnants of Conroux's and Maucune's divisions escaped across country in rear of Clausel's Ridge to Lantz, pursued by the 3rd and 4th Divisions, while the 6th and 7th Divisions followed Vandermaeson's and Taupin's divisions up the road to Olague.

Sir Lowry Cole was jubilant at 'our late hard-fought and brilliant victory,' writing on 9th August to a friend: 'I do not know what John Bull will say to it, but the Army here ranks it first among those in the Peninsula. I have a strong interest to think so, as almost the whole of it fell on the 4th Division. Nothing could be finer than their conduct throughout, and Lord Wellington speaks of nothing else.'

Indeed, it was the victory at Sorauren that prompted Wellington to declare 'That he felt that he could have gone anywhere and done anything with those men who fought with him on the Pyrenees.'

The combats of Maya, Roncesvalles and Lintzoain, the battles of Sorauren and associated affairs are commemorated with the single Battle Honour 'PYRENEES,' which was awarded to the 40th and 82nd Regiments in 1824, while 146 survivors of the 40th and 99 of the 82nd received a Military General Service Medal clasp. Gold Medals were awarded to Colonel William Grant of the 82nd, Lieutenant-Colonel Henry Pynn, 82nd attached 18th Portuguese, and Captain Sempronius Stretton of the 40th.

The Pursuit of Soult, 31st July – 2nd August 1813

By the evening of 30th July, Soult was unequivocally in full retreat north, and the victorious Anglo-Portuguese divisions were in pursuit. Wellington quite reasonably assumed that Clausel's and Reille's battered corps would take the shortest way home to France, which was by the Puerto de Velate, Elizondo and Maya, and accordingly, he directed his main pursuit, including the 4th Division, on that route. Soult, however, had opted to withdraw by way of Lizaso and the more westerly Puerto de Arraiz (the principal route of the Donamaria passes). Clausel and Reille were to march west to Lizaso and then north through the pass to Santesteban, covered by D'Erlon.

Only Dalhousie's 7th Division had been directed to take the Puerto de Arraiz route, where on the 31st they came up with D'Erlon's rearguard. In a tough, scrambling fight over steep hillsides, known as the Combat of Venta de Urroz, the division took 117 casualties, but the 82nd had only three men wounded that day. Thick fog at 5 p.m. brought an end to the action, and the French continued their withdrawal to Santesteban.

---

[687] Mill, letter dated 5th August 1813, quoted in *Historical Records of the 40th Regiment*, p.p. 150-51,
[688] Lawrence, p.p. 152-53.
[689] Lieutenant John Foulkes was slightly wounded while commanding a company.

By that evening, Wellington had much clearer information as to Soult's line of retreat, which could now only be north down a twelve-mile gorge of the Bidassoa River. Very early the following morning, he sent the 4th Division across from Irurita to Santesteban to join in the pursuit, with orders to push the French on the east bank of the Bidassoa while the 7th Division came up on the west bank. The 4th Division started early on 1st August, and by 7 a.m. they were attacking the French rearguard, found by Vandermaesen. Long lines of British skirmishers moved out to take the high ground above the defile, and outflanked the French left; whereupon Vandermaesen's battalions broke. After further confused fighting above the village of Sumbilla, and on the road below, all three of Clausel's divisions made off across the hills. They cannot have made a serious stand at any point, for the 4th Division suffered just 48 casualties in the Combat of Sumbilla, including two of the 40th wounded. We have an account of his part in this advance from Corporal William Lawrence of the Grenadier Company 40th:

'At one time we came on about two hundred of their stragglers, and we fortunately numbering very strongly, were able to engage them and drive them back. Soon after this I had another very narrow escape. One of the enemy had lain in ambush in a thicket at the top of a mountain where I myself was straggling. I had no one near me at the time, and this fellow in the bush fired at me. The shot took the ground and then bounded up against my brass breastplate, which was fixed on my cross-belt, and probably served on this occasion to save my life. The Frenchman, as soon as he had spent his shot, bolted; I had my own musket loaded at the time, but I did not think of firing, but proceeded after him with all my speed till I came up with him. I did not think I could run so fast. I have made Frenchmen run before, but it was generally after me. When he saw he was outdone he showed very poor pluck, for he immediately threw down his arms and gave himself up to me… I then began to strip him of his accoutrements and ransacked his knapsack, but I was sadly disappointed in finding nothing about him; so I took his musket and broke the stock, and left him, not feeling inclined to be troubled with a prisoner, or to hurt a man in unfair play.'

'I then went on in search of my comrades, who had by this time left the mountain for the neighbouring valley, and after running down the slope, I found them posted in a house situated at the bottom. They had been in search of provisions, but all they found was a cask of sweet cyder, the French having evidently been there before us and the place having been ransacked of everything but this. We drank as much as we wanted and put the rest into our canteens, but we were greatly disappointed in not finding anything to eat, for we were dreadfully hungry and very short of provisions.

'However, after we had refreshed ourselves with the cyder, at which our officer helped us, he ordered us to be getting on, or rather led us on himself to a small village about half a mile off, which we knew was occupied by some French. We found that a river intervened between us and this village, with a bridge over it guarded by about two hundred of the enemy; and a long lane had likewise to be traversed before we got up to them, in passing through which several of our men were wounded, either by some of the enemy lying in ambush or by stragglers. Still we did not take long altogether in arriving at the bridge, and when there, having our firelocks all ready, we opened fire and then charged; but our attack was in vain, for we were met and overpowered and obliged to retreat behind a large hill at a short distance from the bridge… We rested a short time behind this hill, and came to a determination to make another attack on the bridge. This time we met with more success, for though we only effected it after a long and severe brush, we made them retreat, leaving the hard fought but really insignificant bridge in our possession. We found nearly thirty of the enemy lying there killed and wounded, while we only lost about fifteen in all. But we did not delay over our captured bridge, for the blood of victory once in our veins, we pressed on for more and traced them down, continually firing as we passed through the village.'[690]

While the 4th Division hounded the French rearguard, Soult's vanguard was engaged at the bridge of Yanzi, opposite which a minor road turned east from the Bidassoa gorge towards Etxalar and the frontier. At Yanzi the French, jammed between river and mountain, were first harassed by a Spanish regiment and then had to run the gauntlet of leading elements of the British Light Division. Many of the bolder spirits escaped on the road to Etxalar or fled over the hills, but some thousand of the wounded, and exhausted, demoralised stragglers, surrendered to the leading troops of the 4th Division.

---

[690] Lawrence, p.p. 159-62.

The Duke of Wellington was with the 4th Division that day, and it may have been then that William Lawrence had an opportunity for distinction in his presence:

'The enemy by some means got three pieces of cannon on to the top of a steep mountain, probably by men dragging them up with ropes, as it was impossible for horses to have done it; and on our entering the valley, Lord Wellington happening to be with us, a shot from one of these carried his cocked hat completely off. Our colonel remarked to him, "That was a near miss, my Lord," to which he replied, "Yes, and I wish you would try to stop them, for they seem determined to annoy us." Our colonel immediately said he would send some of the grenadiers up for that purpose, so I, being a corporal and right-hand man of the company, volunteered with a section to undertake the job. Six men were accordingly chosen besides myself; rather a small storming-party for the object in hand, as they numbered twenty-one artillerymen and an officer, according to my own counting.

'I led my little band up the valley and approached the mountain whence they were tormenting us. The artillerymen kept up a fire on us from the cannon, which consisted of light six-pounders, but owing to our movement they could not get the elevation. We slowly scaled the hill zigzag fashion to baffle their aim, until we got so close that the cannon could not possibly touch us, owing to a slight mound on the hill. We were then within a hundred yards of them, and I took their number, and found at the same time that they had no firearms with them but the cannon, which were of not much use at close quarters for such a few men. I should say we lay there on the ground for at least ten minutes, contemplating which would be the best mode of attack, while they were anxiously watching for our reappearance.

'At last when ready I said, "Now, my men, examine your flints and priming, so that all things may go right." They did so, saying, "All right, Corporal, we will follow you"; so I too sang out, "Now for a gold chain or a wooden leg!" and having told them what to do and to act together, we jumped up, and giving them a volley, we charged them before they had any time to take an aim at us, and succeeded in gaining the cannon and driving the men down the mountain to a body of their infantry that was stationed at the foot. I immediately made a signal with my cap for our brigade to come up, for they were all ready and on the watch, but we found that the enemy's infantry was likewise on the move for our height. Fortunately, our brigade was the first to arrive, and reinforced us on the mountain, and on seeing this the enemy decamped. By great luck not one of my men was injured, whilst our volley killed or badly wounded five of the artillerymen.

'After the enemy's retreat, the Colonel came up to me and said, "Well done, Lawrence; I did not think you were half so brave, but no man could have managed it better." He likewise praised my six fellow-stormers, and a short time afterwards Lord Wellington himself came up and asked me my name, and on my telling him, said, "I shall think of you another day."[691]

Some weeks later William Lawrence had his reward: 'Our captain, who was my best friend in the whole regiment, rejoined us, having been left behind owing to a slight wound which he had received whilst on the march three or four weeks previously, but of which he was now quite recovered. Our company was at that time very short of sergeants… so he recommended my promotion to fill one of the vacancies to the Colonel, who gave him a written order for the purpose… I was of course very proud of my new title, and not only that, but I received one shilling and elevenpence pay per day, being an additional sixpence on what I had formerly.'[692]

The 7th Division never caught up with the French on 1st August, but played a major part next day. Soult had gathered some 25,000 disheartened men and deployed on the slopes of a mountain pass behind Etxalar. Wellington had some 12,000 tired, hungry, but supremely confident men immediately to hand. He planned to attack this formidable position frontally, with the 4th, on the right, and 7th Divisions, while the Light Division was to turn Soult's right flank.

Cole's 4th Division, however, was delayed by a shortage of ammunition and by the immense blockage of debris in the Bidassoa gorge between Sumbilla and the bridge of Yanzi:

---

[691] The chronology of Lawrence's recollections around this period does not match known events. The supposed presence at this incident of 'the Colonel', Lieutenant-Colonel Henry Thornton, who resumed command of the 40th on 31st August on recovery from his Badajoz wound, does not fit the operational circumstances of this anecdote, which rather suggest the fighting on 1st August, when Captain Sempronius Stretton was still in command.

[692] Lawence, p. 166.

'For two miles there were scattered along the road papers, old rugs, blankets, pack-saddles, old bridles and girths, private letters, hundreds of empty and broken boxes, quantities of entrenching tools, French clothes, dead mules, dead soldiers, dead peasants, farrier's tools, boots and linen, the boxes of [French] officers, the field hospital of the 2nd Division, and all sort of things worth picking up – which caused stoppage and confusion.'[693]

The 7th Division, on the other hand, marched up the heights from Sumbilla with Barnes's brigade leading, and was in position early. Taking advantage of a screen of fog, Dalhousie launched Barnes's brigade unsupported in an uphill charge against Conroux's unsteady division, which was swept away without making a stand.

'We have been licking and kicking the fellows along every day since we saw you,' reported Dalhousie, 'Yesterday… we caught them cooking above and plundering below in the village. I thought it best to be at them instantly, and I really believe Barnes was among them before their packs were well on.'[694]

Barnes's surprise attack was enough to disrupt Soult's defence. By the time Inglis's brigade and Anson's brigade of the 4th Division arrived, the action was almost over, the pass was won, and Soult's demoralised troops were streaming over the frontier towards Sare and Ainhoa. Neither the 40th nor the 82nd suffered any casualties that day, which for them was probably most memorable for fog and confusion, as described by Wheeler of the 51st:

'The next morning we ascended the mountains. Our left brigade [Barnes] was sharply engaged this afternoon, and but for a dense fog that came on we should have assisted them, but so dense was this fog that we could not identify the man next to us. The whole brigade was soon intermixed. As we proceeded the fog became so thick we could not see the ground, the confusion was beyond everything, men calling to each other, in every direction. The C[hasseurs] B[rittaniques] Regt. were bawling in the French language, so that we were not certain if we were not intermixed with the enemy.'[695]

Soult crossed into France on 2nd August in disarray, having lost some 13,163 men in the course of his counter-offensive. Allied casualties in the Pyrenees over the same period totaled about 7,048, including 4,708 British. The Allies were now back on the ground they occupied on 25th July before Soult's advance. It was tempting to pursue the broken and demoralised French army over the frontier, for it was in no state to resist, but Wellington, with an eye to the greater strategic picture, was still resolved to await the outcome of events in central Europe. Meanwhile, the 40th and 82nd were both initially stationed at Etxalar, from where the former were redeployed within days to Lesaca.

The Storming of San Sebastian, 31st August 1813

The 47th and 59th Regiments had, meanwhile, been in front of San Sebastian since 9th July, encamped in apple orchards between that place and Hernani. Once Soult's incursion of 25th July to 2nd August had been dealt with, the reduction of this border fortress town was Wellington's prime operational objective.

It was the end of a very long march from Portugal. Private William Windsor of the 59th, writing to his wife on 9th July from 'Saint Savasted Ann,' reckoned that he had marched 1,500 miles and concluded, 'My dear, 'tis time for you to look out for another husband, for I am on my last legs.'

The strongly fortified old town lay on a peninsula, with a land frontage of some 400 yards rising steeply on its seaward, northern, side to Mount Orgull, a 400-foot sandstone hill surmounted by the Castle of La Mota. To the west was a wide bay, with the harbour, and the island of Santa Clara, while the east side of the town was washed by the tidal estuary of the River Urumea.

The town fortifications consisted of a massive hornwork, with counter-scarp, covered way and glacis, covering the landward approach, backed by a high curtain wall with a central bastion and two flanking demi-bastions. Curtain walls continued round the sea-girt sides of the town, overlooking the river and the bay, until they joined the Castle defences. The eastern rampart, its foot washed by the Urumea at high tide to a depth of four

---

[693] Larpent's diary, p. 214.
[694] Letter of Lord Dalhousie to Captain Cairnes, dated Echalar 3rd August 1813. (*Dickson Manuscripts*, p. 1030).
[695] Letter of Corporal Wheeler, 51st Regiment, dated Camp near Eschellar 17th August 1813.

feet, was a plain curtain wall with a small bastion, St. Elmo, and two ancient round towers, Amezqueta and Los Hornos.

Beyond the hornwork, the partially demolished suburb of Santa Catalina, and the hilltop Convent of San Bartolemeo, held by the French as an outwork, lay on the sandy isthmus. To the east, beyond the Urumea, the rolling Chofre dunes rose some 7-800 yards from the sea wall, and Mount Olia rose steeply some thousand yards from the town.

San Sebastian was defended by General Emanuel Rey, a coarse old Jacobin but a skilled and resolute veteran, with a garrison of 3,185 men, including an infantry brigade of four battalions. Guns were mounted on the ramparts and bastions, and there were three powerful batteries on Mount Orgull.

The task of taking the place was given to Sir Thomas Graham with the 5th Division, the self-styled 'Storming Division,' and Bradford's Portuguese brigade. Captain Sir George Collier was offshore with a small naval flotilla, but this was insufficient to interdict reinforcement, resupply and casualty evacuation along the coast to and from St. Jean de Luz.

Sir Richard Fletcher, the army's senior engineer, saw that the weakest point of the town was on the eastern waterfront, where it had been successfully attacked in 1719 by the Duke of Berwick. He decided to breach the south end of the eastern curtain wall between the Amezqueta tower and the demi-bastion of San Juan at the east end of the high curtain. The high curtain was at a right angle to the curtain wall, and between the two lay the demi-bastion of San Juan, which before bombardment was 10-12 feet lower than the east end of the high curtain.

The approach to the proposed breach in the eastern curtain was only possible at low tide, for the breach would be distant from the nearest trenches on dry ground, but it appeared to offer the earliest chance of success.[696]

On 7th July the first siege guns were landed from Santander at the nearby land-locked harbour of Passages, and on the 17th the French outwork at the Convent of San Bartolemeo was taken, allowing siege lines to be dug and batteries established on the isthmus. Working parties of the 47th had the unpleasant task of constructing a battery in the convent burial ground.

'Here was presented a melancholy spectacle as the soldiers proceeded in their work,' recalled their Paymaster, Captain John Harley. 'Coffins and bodies appeared in every stage of decay; some recently interred, and becoming decomposed, others already mouldering into clay. From the miners being under the level of the burying ground, I myself saw two coffins tumble down, and the bodies roll out... During these scenes, every heart became callous, even the coffins were broken up and made fuel of.'[697]

By the 20th, there were forty guns in position on the Chofre sand-hills and the isthmus; and on the night of the 23rd/24th, a parallel was completed across the isthmus, from which the assault on the breaches would be launched. By 23rd July, two practicable breaches, the Main and Lesser, had been opened, and Major-General Frederick Robinson wrote that day to his sister:

'We have been besieging this place ten days, and this night it will be stormed. I have just received notice that my brigade is in the trenches tonight, but whether I am to be honoured with the advance or not I cannot tell, but be that as it may I hope I shall do my duty. I have a brave set of fellows under me, that will follow wherever I will lead. I do not feel any of the Falstaff symptoms, and place my trust in him who protected me at Gamarra.

'We are in hopes of having some rest if we succeed like Good Boys in taking the place. Our noble Lord is arrived, and if he places himself within view of the men they will fight like Heroes. It is not easy to describe the enthusiasm of the Army about him, although he appears to harass them more than any army suffered before. Our whole division are nearly bare footed, and the clothing torn to pieces, besides which they are constantly covered with mud from head to foot owing to their working in the trenches night and day in the most dreadful weather I ever remember. Still no complaint is heard and their only hope is that the town may not be allowed to capitulate *after all the trouble they have had*. They little care for the poor inhabitants, but you may form an idea of their situation when I tell you we fire about 400 cannon shot & shells every hour.'

---

[696] The estuary, with its 16-foot tidal rise, is now embanked, and is much deeper and narrower than it was in 1813. Due to land reclamation, the site of the main breach is now one street back from the waterfront, where Breach Market stands.
[697] Harley, p. 208.

Robinson's diary relates how his 2nd Brigade was indeed ordered to lead the assault, and was ready in the trenches at 8 p.m. on the 23rd when it was decided not to attack that night as fire had broken out in the town:

'The Division was ordered back to camp, leaving seven hundred men of the 2nd Brigade as a covering party in the trenches. On the 24th similar orders were issued except that the 1st Brigade [Hay's] were to take the lead. The 1st Brigade moved off at 1 o'clock, followed by the Portuguese, & the 2nd Brigade marched off at 2, but owing to difficulties it was nearly daybreak before the Division was properly stationed in the trenches.

'Between 4 & 5 [actually 5 a.m.] a mine was sprung (this was the signal to advance) & as the 1st Brigade issued from the trenches along the beach a most tremendous fire of guns, mortars & small arms commenced against them. They had gained the top of the breach when firing suddenly ceased, which those remaining in the trenches supposed was from our success. In a few minutes I received the mortifying intelligence that the cessation was occasioned by a flag of truce on our part requesting permission to carry away the wounded. The great cause of the failure was the men leaping from the breach instead of turning to the right & left along the curtain.'

The attack was a badly managed failure, costing 571 casualties and resulting in recriminations. Despite not taking part in the assault, the 59th had some thirty casualties in the trenches, including Ensign and Adjutant Thomas Crawley.[698]

Captain Henry Oglander[699] of the 47th laid the blame on the leading assault regiment, the Royal Scots: 'The principal breach was to my eyes the most practicable I ever saw, being wide and of easy ascent… I cannot but think, had they been well supported, the breach would have been carried. It is whispered that the men of the Royal [Scots], even by the confession of their officers, would not, excepting the Grenadiers and the 1st Company, follow them to the attack.'

Others blamed the commanders and, with greater justice, the engineers for a poor plan. After this failure it was resolved not to hurry, but to wait for more and better guns and ammunition: these did not arrive until the 23rd August. The plan then was to repeat the previous attack but with more guns, a bigger breach and more supports. The original difficulties remained: an attack was only possible at low tide, when the Urumea shrank to between 40-50 yards wide, and it involved a narrow 180-yard approach across slippery rocks and a tidal flat, exposed at short range to flanking fire from the east side of the hornwork.

Rey's elaborate defensive preparations added to the difficulty of the operation. The breaches were mined, and their inner faces were scarped to make a sheer drop of between 17 and 30 feet to street level, while the steps and ramps behind the ramparts had been cut away. The defenders had built a thick loop-holed stone wall, 15 feet high, using debris and the ruined houses of the street immediately behind the breaches. Successive stone traverses were constructed on the ramparts on either side of the breaches, and on the high curtain above the demi-bastion: these mounted masked cannon and were held by elite companies with three muskets each, while bombs and live shells were ready to be thrown down on the stormers. Finally, the city streets were defended by mutually supporting chicane-like barricades, some of them mined, and by loop-holed houses.

There was also the ever-present chance of a sortie by the energetic French garrison, such as the trench raid at midnight on the 24th August recalled by Private Adam Reed of the 47th:

'About a week before the town was taken the French sallied out upon the entrenchments which quite alarmed us when we heard the firing of the picquet and the bugle sounding "turn out the whole," for most of us were asleep in the camp. We however were not long dressing, some were in their red jackets, others in their white ones and some in their shirt sleeves. We soon flew to our guns and were not long before we were down to their assistance. In less than half an hour they were all dispersed and we again returned to the camp.'

On the night of the 26th/27th there was a seaborne assault in which a large contingent of the 47th joined a force of two hundred men, which, in the boats of HMS *Surveillante*, captured the small rocky island of Santa Clara in the bay. Private Reed, who had recently rejoined the Regiment on recovery from his Vitoria wound, was in support:

---

[698] Thomas Crawley had enlisted in the 59th in October 1807 and was commissioned from Sergeant Major on 24th September 1814. He suffered a severe gunshot wound which lamed him for life, and went on half pay in 1816 as a Lieutenant.

[699] Henry Oglander had lost an arm at Badajoz, serving with the 43rd, before being promoted to a captaincy in the 47th.

'In about 9 or 10 days before we stormed the town there was a party (which consisted of about 100 men) sent to Passarches [Passages], a small seaport town not far from St Sebastian. Between us and St Sebastian there was a small island in the harbour in the occupation of the enemy, and those men had to come from Passarches in boats and storm it by night. There was another party on the beach (amongst whom I was) ready if the others were not successful. Betwixt 12 and 1 o'clock I heard the French sentry challenge "Who comes there?" And as soon as he had challenged I heard the men in the boats shout and begin to fire, and in less than an hour it was taken. In taking that we lost one man belonging to my company, as there were 6 out of each company sent. The party who were on the beach then returned to camp.'

On the 27th Robinson's brigade had a short but welcome respite from siege duties at San Sebastian when they marched to the lower Bidassoa (probably to the heights of Salain) to counter a demonstration being made by Villatte's division as a diversion in support of Soult's ill-starred offensive:

'We (that is my brigade) had been ordered from hence at two o'clock on the morning of the 27th in consequence of the French having shewn themselves in front of the Spaniards to the amount of 5 or 6,000, and although our valiant allies were at least 20,000 strong they did not think they could maintain the rocky precipices of those stupendous mountains against such a handful without the assistance of a few British troops.

'I was delighted at the event, because it not only took us from the detestable siege, but gave us an opportunity of seeing France as far as the eye could reach from the Pyrenees… As we had our Commissary with us, I was in hopes of remaining some days in this healthful spot, that my poor worn out men might recover from the fatigue of watching whole nights in the trenches amidst the unceasing roar of cannon. I had just ordered my suite to prepare for a visit to the Spanish guerrilla general Longa, about two leagues along the mountains, when a vile dragoon put a slip of paper in my hand that reversed all my plan in an instant, by an order to retrace my steps to this abode of demons without delay – a place that has already cost the lives of many of our bravest officers and soldiers, and will set us at defiance for a month longer unless the plan of operations is totally changed.'[700]

The reinforced siege batteries opened on 26th August against the sea front, widening the main breach to 300 yards, bringing down both faces of the demi-bastion of San Juan, and improving the lesser breach to 80 yards, while the guns on the walls, except three that were concealed, were disabled.

The 47th and 59th continued to take their turn in the trenches, with casualties including four of the 59th died of wounds and Lieutenant John Nason of the 47th wounded on 10th August. We have first-hand accounts of this arduous and dangerous work from the 47th. The first is from Private Adam Reed:

'As we were going to the parapet [i.e. the parallel in front of the hornwork] for picquet we halted in some old building waiting for the other picquet to come out before we entered, and the enemy saw us and fired a shell and killed and wounded 13. When the other picquet arrived up we went down and took our post for the 24 hours. The enemy were continually firing grape and canister. In the entrenchments we had one particular post called the advance post and the sentry that occupied that post was called the advance sentry as it was nearest the town, from which it was about 50 yards. His orders were to keep close, and not to lift his head above the surface of the earth for if he did it would very soon be off if they saw him. There was a man put on there one day for 2 hours, and he was ordered by the sentry whom he relieved to be very careful with himself and he had not been there more than half an hour before he was killed. That however was no new thing, for there was seldom a day passed that there was some killed or wounded.'

Captain Henry Oglander's diary entry for the 28th of July tells of his experience in the trenches:

'I was not relieved from working party until midday, making the time during which the men were working no less than 18 hours, much too long a period for men to work with effect. I divided mine into two parties, and relieved every hour. The French got some guns to bear upon us, and threw shots into the battery, but fortunately without doing any injury.'

Unhappy with the 5th Division's performance on 25th July, Wellington called for volunteers from other divisions to make the assault 'men who could show other troops how to mount a breach.' All ranks of the 5th Division strongly objected to what they saw as an unjust slur on their military honour, and Graham supported them, so it was agreed that, under Leith's command, Robinson's brigade (the 4th, 47th and 59th) should lead the

---

[700] Letter to his sister dated Camp before San Sebastian 31st July 1813.

assault on the main breach. They were to be supported by 750 volunteers from the 1st, 4th and Light Divisions, amongst whom were Lieutenant William Turton[701], a sergeant and eleven men of the 40th. Meanwhile, 300 volunteers from Bradford's Portuguese brigade were to ford the Urumea and assault the lesser breach. Spry's Portuguese brigade and Hay's brigade were to be in reserve, while a detachment of the 85th in boats were to feint at landing behind Mount Orgull.

The assault was to be launched on 31st August, and the time was determined by the tide. Low tide was at noon, so the time was fixed at 11 a.m. At 2 a.m. three small mines were blown under a sea wall obstructing the approach to the beach, gapping it for seventy yards – and incidentally alerting the garrison; though there was so little possibility of surprise that crowds of spectators, military and civilian, assembled on nearby Mount Olia and at the Convent of San Bartolemeo to watch the assault.

It was a sultry morning, threatening thunder, oppressively hot and with visibility down to a hundred yards. At 10 a.m. the assault troops filed into the trenches on the isthmus, packing into the east end of the parallel and communication trenches, where the men had a glass of wine each, which they drank to their officers' health and success. Major Robert Kelly, who commanded the 47th, met with Captain John Harley at about seven o'clock when he was going down to the trenches, and asked the Paymaster to dine with him at half-past four, remarking with soldierly black humour, 'provided I live as long.'

'There were a number of candidates for leading on the forlorn hope'[702], recalled Harley, 'but Lieutenant McGuire of the 4th Foot was chosen, and fifty picked men from the different regiments.' It was Francis McGuire's 21st birthday, and he was prominent in his best uniform and an old-fashioned cocked hat with a large feather. Well aware that his chance of survival was slim, when asked why he was so well turned out he simply replied, "When we are going to meet all our old friends whom we have not seen for many years it is very natural to look as well as possible"'

It was 8 a.m. before the early haze had cleared sufficiently for the artillery to open, and under a stormy sky an intensive final bombardment began, and went on until 10.55. As Robinson's brigade prepared to advance they could hear the French drums beat to arms, and every man of the stormers was well aware of the imminent probability of either death or wounds:

'At ten o'clock in the morning I had a thousand men[703] in the trenches,' wrote their commander, 'ready to rush towards the breach the moment I should give the signal. They were to gain the top and maintain themselves there until supported by the rest of the division and a reinforcement which had arrived the evening before from the other divisions in front.

'We were all aware of the strength of the place, although according to the technical term there was a breach, but that breach was as high and as steep as your house, and the descent on the other side was thirty feet perpendicular, and at a little distance enclosed with high walls behind which were stationed sharp shooters, and bombs were placed before them to be thrown down upon my people as soon as they should descend.

'Never did hearts beat so high in dreadful expectation as those of the lookers on, at the head of whom were Sir Thos Graham, Sir Jas Leith, Gen[erals] Oswald and Hay. We had to pass from the mouth of the trenches over the sea shore for about a hundred yards, which was covered with large slippery stones or deep mud. Our First Brigade had failed in this attempt, with cruel slaughter, about a month before, and the natural emulation of soldiers made my gallant fellows the more determined to conquer or die.

'At eleven o'clock I gave the word to advance, which was instantly obeyed with a shout that gave promise of success.'

Captain Harley watched the stormers leave the trenches, headed by the Forlorn Hope under Francis Maguire:

---

[701] There was no shortage of volunteers from the 40th. According to William Turton's obituary in *The Gentleman's Magazine*, 1813 Supplement, Part II, p. 699, 'To his honour, and as a proof of the respect borne him by his comrades in arms, sixty men sprang from the ranks to share the glory and danger of their young hero.' These volunteers arrived at Oyarzun in front of San Sebastian on 30th August.
[702] Volunteers to lead the Forlorn Hope included Lieutenant Lewis Carmichael of the 59th.
[703] As the effective rank and file strengths (i.e. less officers, sergeants and drummers) of the 4th, 47th and 59th on 25th August 1813 were 539, 378 and 626 respectively, at least one third of the brigade may have been 'left out of battle' or held in reserve.

'I saw poor Maguire, a handsome, fine young fellow, lead on his men to the breach under a fire that actually mowed them down, and observed him turning about and waving his hat to the remaining five or six, and encouraging them on. The poor fellows dropped one by one until the whole party were killed, including poor Maguire himself, who fell at the very breach in sight of the whole army.'

Next out of the trenches were the three light companies of the brigade, followed by the main body of the stormers, who rushed forward cheering. They were in two columns, one aimed at the main breach, the other at the demi-bastion of San Juan where the eastern curtain met the high curtain. Observers saw the previously unoccupied walls suddenly black with defenders, who emerged from shelter and opened a devastating fire of musketry and grapeshot. In Robinson's words, 'the strand and bottom of the breach was in five minutes covered in dead and wounded.'

As they ran the gauntlet between the hornwork and the river shallows a mine exploded under the salient angle of the covered way of the hornwork, killing an heroic sergeant and twelve volunteers, who were trying to find and cut its train. This explosion appears also to have caught some scores of the 59th, including three officers[704] and some of the Grenadier Company. It was probably the incident described by Private Reed of the 47th:

'From the entrenchments a wall was built a yard or more thick to keep the tide from flowing farther and under this wall a great many of our wounded got to shelter from the enemy's shot thinking they were safe. When the enemy sprung their mine under the breach it shook the wall and it fell, and buried alive most of the soldiers who were under it. In springing their mine, a great many of their own men likewise perished for I saw them lying on the wall and they looked as if they had been roasted.'

The main breach was difficult to ascend, being steep and consisting of large stone blocks and lumps of concrete, but the head of Robinson's brigade climbed to its crest in good order. There they came to a halt, confronted by a sheer drop, lashed by concentrated musketry from the retrenchment in front, from flanking traverses, and from the left branch of the hornwork, and swept by close-range canister from three unmasked guns and by more distant fire from the Castle batteries. The foremost ranks of Robinson's brigade were nearly annihilated, but the survivors lay down close to the top of the breach, from where they could fire and throw large stones at the defenders.

Bugles sounded 'Advance,' and party after party was led forward, only to be cut down. Repeated gallant charges at the strongly manned traverses, the only exits from the breach, were met with devastating musketry and canister. The most promising point of attack was across the ruined demi-bastion of San Juan against the east end of the high curtain; but this approach proved equally impregnable, for the curtain was considerably higher than the demi-bastion, and the only entry was so narrow that only one man at a time could pass the traverse:

'Many desperate efforts were made to rush up, the officers showing a noble example of intrepidity and devotion in leading the assailants; but the defensive traverse not being more than fifteen yards distant from the crest of the breach, and being strongly occupied by grenadiers who fired with rapidity and steadiness, every one that gained the rampart was immediately killed or wounded; whilst the dense mass of men at the foot of the breach were fast falling under the close musketry fire directed on them from the left branch of the hornwork.'[705]

'Again and again,' says Napier, 'the crowded masses of stormers swarmed up the face of the ruins, but on reaching the crest line they came down like a falling wall; crowd after crowd was seen to mount, to totter, and to sink; the deadly French fire was unabated, the smoke drifted away and the crest of the breach bore no living man.'[706]

As casualties mounted in the breach, Sir James Leith stood on the strand feeding reinforcements forward from the trenches: first the reserve companies of Robinson's brigade, and then the volunteers, until he fell wounded. At 11.45 the volunteers of Bradford's Portuguese brigade made a gallant advance of 700 yards over tidal rocks and pools, then waded waist-deep for 200 yards across the mouth of the Urumea to assault the lesser

---

[704] The officers of the 59th killed by this mine were Ensign James Pyne of the Grenadiers and Ensigns Lawrence Watson and Marcus O'Hara.
[705] Jones, *Journal of Sieges in Spain*, Vol. II, pages 75-6.
[706] Napier, Book XXII, Chapter II, p. 284.

breach. This new attack caught the defenders by surprise, but although there was no retrenchment behind this breach it was still traversed, and the Portuguese were equally unable to break out into the town.

'For two hours had the troops, with the utmost perseverance, continued to struggle for entrance into the town, not one minute of which elapsed without the fall of many of the bravest men, and at the termination of that period the capture of that place appeared as distant as ever; while the whole extent from the mouth of the trench to the crest of the breaches was thickly strewn with dead bodies, or persons writhing under severe and dangerous wounds.[707] In the centre of this scene of destruction, in which not a soldier had receded or shown an inclination to give way, Sir James Leith continued, animating the men by his presence and example, addressing words of encouragement as they passed. The soldiers, with increased energy, stepping over the bodies of their fallen comrades, rushed to the murderous ascent.'[708]

Most of the regimental officers had now fallen, and command within battalions had passed to young captains or subalterns. When Major Kelly of the 47th fell dead before the breach, Captain Charles Livesay, a hero of Tarifa, succeeded to the command until he was mortally wounded. 'He was an officer of long standing,' wrote John Harley, 'having served since he had been a very young man in the 47th Regiment. He possessed every good quality which could endear him to his brother officers, who all regretted him deeply. He fell bravely leading the Light Company through the breaches, being shot from the top of a wall by a French rifleman.'

One-armed Captain Henry Oglander then took command until he was wounded in five places, shot through his body, thigh and surviving arm, and losing a finger. The senior surviving officer was then Lieutenant Thomas Power, but he was lying with a severe head wound when a non-commissioned officer stumbled against him and urged him to take command. 'Take off my sash,' said Power, 'and tie up my head'; and he then led the Regiment on into the breach.

Captain Francis Scott, commanding the 59th, was killed as he took them, cheering, up into the breach. Captain Francis Fuller, aged 25, then took command, though Major Frederick Hoystead came up and assumed command in the afternoon, after the place was taken.

By noon the situation was desperate. Unable to break out from the breaches, the stormers sought shelter in the rubble away from the crest of the breaches; but there was no shelter there as they were still fired at from both flanks at short range. The impetus of the attack had slackened, and success seemed most doubtful.

It was then that Sir Thomas Graham, standing in the batteries on the Chofre sandhills, made a bold decision. At 12.15 p.m. he ordered all 47 of the breaching guns, howitzers and carronades on the dunes to fire very close over the heads of the stormers at the defenders massed at the east end of the high curtain above the demi-bastion. The range was known from long practice, and their accurate enfilade fire proved very effective as the ramparts were packed with French troops. Remarkably, there appear to have been no casualties among the assailants, who flattened themselves among the fallen masonry as cannon-balls and shells passed close above their heads. Later inspection of the defences revealed that:

'The tremendous enfilade fire on the high curtain, though only maintained for twenty minutes, had dismounted every gun but two. Many of these pieces had their muzzles shot away, and the artillerymen lay mutilated at their stations. Further, the stone parapets were much damaged, the cheeks of the embrasures knocked off, and the *terre-plein* cut up and thickly strewed with headless bodies; in short, the whole land-front had, from the effects of the cannonade, been rendered a scene of destruction, desolation and ruin.'[709]

At 12.35 the British guns ceased fire, the stormers surged forward again, and the balance began to swing in their favour. At 12.40 British troops were seen descending from the main breach into the town and waving their hats from the *terre-plein* of the high curtain. A final blow for the defence was an explosion, probably accidental, on the central bastion of the high curtain, where a number of fire-barrels, grenades and shells had been heaped. This killed or scorched some 60-70 defenders of that vital point just as Leith's final reserve, Hay's brigade, reached the crest of the breach. After a desperate fight in the bastion, the 5th Division and volunteers bayoneted

---

[707] Casualties might well have been even more devastating, for a mine beneath the main breach, charged with twelve hundredweight of gunpowder, failed to explode when the saucisson leading from its chamber to the retrenchment was accidentally broken and discovered.
[708] Leith Hay, *A Narrative of the Peninsular War*, Volume II, pages 246-7.
[709] Jones, Vol. II, p. 80.

their way down wide steps into the town or scrambled through imperfectly-demolished buildings to reach street-level. At 1.15 p.m. the French flag on the high curtain was lowered to the cheers of spectators.

There is a graphic description of the assault by an unknown private of the 47th, recounted many years later when he was a Chelsea Pensioner 'of frosty head but upright carriage of body':

'Well, I was in the Forty-Seventh; and what I am going to tell you happened at the time we took San Sebastian, a terribly strong place that cost us a power of men, as I heard old Nosey himself say the day after we took it. We had to wade across a river, holding our muskets and cartridge boxes above our heads, and many was the poor fellow the enemy picked off while we were in the water. But "Forward men!" said the Colonel, and our blood being up, we did not much mind losing a comrade or two. "Hip, hip, hurrah!" and on we went until we gained dry land; and then, my stars! there was fighting!

'A hundred thunderstorms are nothing to the roar which stunned us, as we marched up to the breach like good English soldiers and tight Lancashire boys. The shot rattled like hail on every side of me, and many glanced off the barrel of my musket. You may say as you like about us old soldiers stretching, but as true as I stand here, my right and left hand men were knocked over before we had gone ten steps. It was worse than fighting – it was murder; for as the hole in the wall was too small for us to get through, and too high for us to reach, we were obliged to stand and pepper away at fellows we could not see, and be knocked over like nine-pins by them,

'It was awful, and our friends on the other side of the river saw how the thing was, and fired bang over our heads. We did not at first quite understand it, and thought it hard to be between two fires; but when we did see the rights of the thing, we lay down quietly, and waited for the word to move. By-and-by the stones came flying about our ears; and what with the cannon-balls of our friends behind us, and the musket ones of the enemy before us, we were in a rather peculiarly dangerous position. But it was necessary; a soldier must take every chance; and when the word was given to advance, we sprang up like bees, and with a shout that drowned the cannon's roar we dashed at the wall. Three times we were driven back, and half our men were sprawling on the ground, or choking in the ditch that surrounded the town. But "at 'em again" was the word; and at the fourth or fifth grand rush the gallant 47th scaled the wall, drove the enemy before them like flies brushed from a table, and we were in the town.'

The assault was far from over, for General Rey had ordered the main square of the town and every street to be blocked with a succession of barricades and entrenchments:

'This had been carried into effect in the most substantial manner. Material from the ruined houses assisted in constructing traverses of a formidable description. These stone barriers were defended by cannon, forming part of their line across the streets. They were also loopholed, and behind them were posted reserves of French infantry. From each and all of these, after repeated contests, the enemy was driven.'[710] The street defences were cleared in about one hour of fierce fighting, possibly because there were now too few defenders left to hold them.

At 1.20 p.m. Lieutenant-Colonel Alexander Frazer on the Chofre sandhills noted 'very heavy fire inside the town,' at 1.35 he recorded that 'many prisoners are being brought out of the town into the trenches,' and at 1.45 he heard 'heavy musketry fire in the town, our bugles sound the advance in all parts of it.' At 2 p.m., the town was on fire near the lesser breach, and by 2.15, the tide of battle had extended to the Castle outworks, and firing in the town decreased. Rey escaped into the Castle with about one thousand of the garrison, leaving behind 750 prisoners, of whom 350 were wounded.

At about the same time a whirlwind picked up the sand of the beach and fanned the conflagration[711], which soon spread across San Sebastian, and then the lowering thunderous clouds broke, drenching the combatants with rain and adding to the chaos in the town. At 3.30 p.m., Frazer noted 'Great fire in the town; as dark as it is generally at half-past six. Nothing of the town to be seen from excessive smoke.'

As was the case at Ciudad Rodrigo and Badajoz, there was a widespread expectation among the troops that their hard toil in the trenches and the extreme hazards of the storming would be rewarded with a period of

---

[710] Leith Hay, Vol. II, p.p. 252-53.

[711] At least some of the fires were almost certainly, though unintentionally, caused by the Allied bombardment, and others by the explosion of French mines and combustible material.

license in the captured town. Indeed, some appeared convinced that plundering had been explicitly condoned by Sir Thomas Graham. Private Adam Reed described the final assault:

'About 3 o'clock our troops again mounted the breach and drove the enemy off. The enemy also fought valiantly for when we took one gun they flew to another. When we entered the town we found that every street was barricaded; but there was a small space left enough to admit one soldier at a time. The enemy fought desperately when we were in the street and it was likewise seen that some of the Spanish inhabitants were fighting against us. Before we could get rid of them out of the town we were obliged to charge them 3 or 4 times. After much fighting we at last drove them to their last place of refuge which was the castle. The castle lay on a hill above the town about a quarter of a mile, and was very strong. As the enemy ascended the hill our batteries fired grape and canister at them as fast as they could which cut them up desperately. On the castle wall was engraved in large letters VIVE NAPOLEON BONAPARTE[712] but the shot from our batteries knocked a great many of them down. The General (Thomas Graham) seeing that the Spanish inhabitants fought against us gave us liberty to plunder the town.'

The surviving stormers were largely leaderless, for Leith, Oswald and Robinson had all been wounded, and Hay was the only senior officer of the 5th Division still on his feet. Battalions were all mixed up, with few officers: only five in the 47th had survived death or wounds, and four in the 59th. Looting broke out, and, like Badajoz, there is evidence of violence against civilians. A soldier of the 47th candidly recalled his motivation and actions that night, and their terrible consequence:

'Slaughter was the word, and with a vengeance at our hearts, and many dreadful thoughts in our heads, we broke off into parties of tens or twenties. I was with one of about a dozen, and the first thing we did was to tap a wine cask, and drink about a quart of it out of our hats, without drawing breath. What with the excitement of the wine, and our hatred of the enemy, we were fit for anything, and as all order was at an end, every man did as he thought proper.

'I had often heard the place contained the beautifulest ladies in all Spain, so I was determined to see some of them. I loaded my piece, and leaving my drunken comrades, went down a street that looked quieter than the rest. Every house was closed and barricaded, and alone I could not force an entrance into any one of them. Getting very savage, I was resolved to go inside one of them, and selected the most respectable looking. Two or three of our men came up at the same time, and we held a council of war as to what we should do. One of them, Corporal Worthington, a little fellow from Stockport, proposed that we should blow the door in with our guns, but as none of us had more than a round or two left, which might be wanted, it was voted a no go, and as the door was too strong for us to burst open, we went round to the back to see what could be done. There we smashed a window, and entered pell mell.

'The furniture was of the most costly description, and everything betokened the proprietor to be a rich man; but we could not find what we wanted – the women. Don't be offended, sir, at my saying that; a soldier who has fought for three or four hours, and is bespattered with the blood of his comrades, does not reason very Christian-like.

'Well, we came to a room, and there we saw a sight which made us, bold and ferocious as we were, turn pale and fall back. On a bed lay three grown-up girls, dead; they must have been angels when alive, for they smiled beautifully as they lay in their blood; for that they had been killed was too evident, for the red liquid bubbled from each of their breasts. Standing by the bed-side was a tall grey-headed man, with a bloody knife in his hand. His eyes flashed fire, and he pointed to the bed with a proud and noble, but rather mad look, as much as to say, "I did it."

"He is a murderer!" shouted the corporal, levelling his gun to bring him down on the spot.

"He is a man!" roared Ned Jackson, the strongest man in the regiment, as with one blow of his enormous fist he sent the corporal flying to the other end of the room. "Noble, by Heaven!" said Ned, laying down his gun and going up kindly to the old man, he added: "Can we do anything for you?" The wretched father, for such we guessed him to be, looked at us for a few minutes, and seeing that we pitied him, uttered a groan that made us all

---

[712] As a gesture of defiance, the garrison had marked Napoleon's birthday on 15th August with a display of six-foot high illuminated letters, 'Vive Napoleon Le Grand', on Mount Orgull.

tremble, and then fell down on his face. When we raised him he was dead – his heart had broken. We looked at each other a moment, and then left the house in silence.

'I thought I should ha' cried, but as Ned held up like a man, I felt bound to do the same; and none of us spoke until we had got into the front street again. I believe all of us would rather have taken San Sebastian twice over than have seen such a sight. However, we were soldiers, and accustomed to scenes of blood and horror; and if we said not much about the affair, I am sure we all felt the more. It did us good; for the remainder of that dreadful day and following night we stuck together, and instead of committing any outrage, did all we could to restrain the men.

'But, as perhaps I tire you, I will just tell another adventure I had that night, and then hie me away, and drink your good health. It was about midnight, and the uproar was at its height, when Ned and me, being restless and uneasy, had a ramble; and during it, we saw a young girl in the hands of some dozen very drunken fellows. They said they had just found her stowed away in one of the cellars of a house near at hand, and were about to cast lots as to who should have her, when Ned, whose blood was never long in getting up, shouted at the top of his voice, "Hurrah for the 47th, and death to the men who would injure a woman!" With that he made no more ado, but sprang into the midst of them, and, clubbing his musket, laid about him right and left. I followed his example, and both of us being sober, and strong Lancashire fellows to boot, soon cleared the course. In less than five minutes not a man of them was to be seen on the ground. The poor girl, finding in us protectors, clung to us, and we swore to ourselves that we would shoot the first man that put a hand on her.

'We soon had the pleasure of placing her in the arms of her parents, and, for our share in the matter, had the prayers of every member of the family, and something weighty in our pockets besides. Some weeks afterwards, we were publicly thanked by our Colonel; and Ned, I do think – nay, I am sure – was the most petted and looked-up-to man in the whole British Army.'

Captain John Harley, also of the 47th, witnessed unedifying scenes in the town and heard stories of worse:

'I went, in the evening, through the breach, which was filled with dead bodies, so that I could scarcely get over them. The scene that presented itself to me was horrifying – the dead lying in heaps in the streets – the French and British lying side by side; and not infrequently a drunken soldier of ours was seen amongst them fast asleep; plundering parties, too, women as well as men, were very active in every direction, breaking not only into private houses, but into the churches and theatres. It was laughable, notwithstanding the melancholy scenes around us, to see those thoughtless fellows coming out of the theatre dressed in the costume of the players, and others leaving the churches in the robes of the clergyman, and singing through the streets.

'During the time of plundering the soldiers' wives were some of the most active. I have gone into a church and found three or four of them seated together, dividing watches and jewellery, and, on my speaking to them, they asked me did I want to interfere with them, and desired me to go off about my business… I saw, in the course of a few days after, ladies purchasing their own silk stockings, and other articles, from the soldiers' wives on the roads.'[713]

Portuguese soldiers robbed drunken English and Irish of their loot. Among the latter was Harley's servant Pat Dolan, who, having provided himself with a corn sack, had slipped into the town on the second day of plundering and, whistling merrily at the prospect of 'golden treasure,' made his way to a previously unlooted house, near the citadel, where he eventually uncovered the family silver in abundance. "Accordingly," reported Pat, "I filled the corn sack with coffee-pots, tea-pots, spoons, forks, and everything of plate I could carry, and proceeded by a private way to get to the gate which led to my way home." He was, however, intercepted by a group of Portuguese who relieved him of his loot and gave him a good drubbing. 'He returned home that night,' recalled Harley, 'with his face all cut and bruised, vowing vengeance against the entire Portuguese nation.'

Harley also heard, from Lieutenant Thomas Power, 47th, who, though wounded, had taken the lead during the assault, of a dreadful rape that could not be prevented:

'He was passing along the streets, when he was addressed by an old servant woman from a window, who cried out in Spanish, "*Aqui tiene toda que quieres guards vos nosotros*," which is, in English, "Here is everything you want – protect us." Lieutenant Power went upstairs, and on entering a splendid room, beheld a lovely young

---
[713] Harley, p.p. 212 and 215.

Spanish lady. Her father and mother had gone away during the siege, through dread of the English, and left her and the old lady in charge of the house. They pulled out various drawers, showing Power a quantity of money, plate and jewellery, proposing him to take all, but entreating that he would remain and protect them. No officer in the army would be more willing to do so than Power, but his time was not his own.

'Whilst he was in the room, and considering how he could serve this interesting female, a drunken soldier of the plundering party proceeded upstairs, and unceremoniously entered the drawing room. Power remonstrated with him. And advised him to go away, but the man refused, and was inclined to be sulky… This fellow had a firelock in his hand, and Power, finding all argument unavailing, and that he was determined on violence, seized the firelock from him, and pitched him down the stairs to the bottom. As he had thus gained possession of the firelock, the fellow had no redress, and skulked away.

'Power was, however, unfortunately called off to the trenches, and put on duty for the night, which prevented him from remaining and protecting these unfortunate females. His first object in the morning, as soon as he got off duty, was to fly to the house, to see how they had got on during the night. On entering it, he was horror struck on witnessing the scene before him – the poor woman lying on the floor, not able to speak or move – the young lady reclining on a sofa, with her hair hanging loosely over her neck, and her garments torn to pieces. She covered he face, on seeing him, and, when she could be understood for her cries, she begged that Power would have compassion on her, and shoot her… She told Power, when she got a little quieted, that after he had left her the day before, the soldier whom he had thrown down the stairs returned, with many others, and took everything they possessed, committing all the violence they could, and remained there during the night. Power felt as a man for this lovely and interesting female, but he, unfortunately, could give her no redress. He left her with regret, quite miserable at her wretched fate.'[714]

There were, however, other soldiers whose behaviour was exemplary. One such was Private John Russell of the Light Company 59th Foot, a volunteer for the Forlorn Hope. When his company commander fell dead on the breach, a soldier of another regiment took a watch from the officer's pocket. Russell who was loading his musket nearby, immediately put the muzzle of his piece to the thief's breast, declaring that if he did not instantly restore the watch he would send the contents through his body. The watch was at once given up and handed by Russell to the Sergeant Major with directions to give it to Lieutenant Carmichael, the only surviving officer of the Light Company. In consequence of Russell's coolness and integrity, Carmichael requested the Commanding Officer to promote him, which was agreed. Russell, however, declined the appointment, stating that 'he could not write, and if he allowed other people to do his duty he would lose all conceit of himself, that in his present position he considered no private in the Army his superior, and that he would at any time cheerfully volunteer a Forlorn Hope and endeavour to protect the property of officers of the regiment, more especially the captain of his company, without desiring or expecting any reward for it.'

Next morning, Lieutenant Andrew Leith Hay walked into the town through the breach:

'The whole ascent of the breach was covered with dead bodies. During the intervening day, circumstances had not permitted their being interred; stripped and naked, they now lay on the ground where they had individually fallen, but in such numbers, that on a similar space was never witnessed a more dreadful scene of slaughter.'

'Having walked up the face of the breach, I proceeded along the curtain, which presented a scene of indescribable havoc and destruction. The heat from the blazing houses was excessive; and from the midst of this mass of fire was at intervals to be heard the noise of soldiers still busied in adding to the miseries that had overtaken the devoted town…

'The buildings all having communication, and being very closely arranged, ensured the conflagration becoming general; roofs falling, and the crashing of ruined walls that rolled down, and, in some cases, blocked up the passage in the streets, it was rendered more impressive from the obscurity occasioned even at midday by the dense cloud of smoke that shrouded this scene of ruin and desolation.

'After descending the great flight of steps leading from the curtain, in the centre of this chaos, I found General Hay, blackened with smoke and dust, not having had a moment's rest, and still busily employed in

---

[714] Harley, p.p. 216-17.

restoring order to the troops, or in vainly endeavouring to obstruct the unquenchable flames that surrounded him in every direction.'[715]

He was assisted by the few surviving officers of the 5th Division, such as Major Frederick Hoystead of the 59th, who reported: 'As to plundering being permitted, I can assure you that every exertion was made by me and the officers to prevent anything of the kind, and that I sent frequent patrols, by your order, to arrest any man found in the town, and to afford assistance to any inhabitant who might ask for it.'

Halberds were set up in the square for punishment, and soldiers leaving the town were searched, but there is no doubt that the place was thoroughly plundered by combatants and camp followers alike. We can draw our own conclusions from a subsequent letter to his wife from Private William Windsor of the 59th:

'I have got the earrings for you & the children, the best that can be bought for money, & a gold locket for yourself, & if it pleases God to spare my life I have money to put us in a comfortable situation at my return. I beg you will not mention what I say, but await God's appointed time, & that will be a happy day to us both.'

The Castle had yet to be reduced, and according to Adam Reed, at least some of the 47th had already, on the night of the 31st, been engaged in this operation:

'That night we were ordered to go and work to turn the enemy's guns that were on the town wall towards the castle, and to make fresh portholes with bags full of sand of a great thickness, and it was completed by daylight. We then began to fire upon them with their own guns as well as ours.'

The Castle eventually capitulated on 8th September after bombardment by 61 guns. The 59th Regiment, who had suffered one man killed and one wounded during the siege of the Castle, had the satisfaction of taking possession, though not before John Harley had introduced himself to the governor:

'After the surrender of the citadel, about nine o'clock next morning, accompanied by an engineer officer, I walked up with an intention of going to the citadel, but meeting General Rey and his staff, at a small guard-house, we stopped. The general politely asked us in, and, as they were at breakfast, pressed us to take some refreshment. It appeared that they were waiting until the hour should arrive when they were to go into the town... At twelve o'clock, the ceremony of surrendering the citadel took place. The brave General Rey and his garrison, having marched down, I witnessed his handing his sword to General Oswald, and the French soldiers grounding their arms.'[716]

The siege of San Sebastian cost the Allies 3,800 men, of whom 2,391 fell in the final assault, with an unusually high proportion of killed (870) to wounded because of short-range cannister repeatedly scouring the breaches. Robinson's brigade suffered 880 casualties on 31st August, including twenty officers and 322 other ranks killed, out of some 1500 present.

The 47th and 59th suffered 250[717] and 368[718] casualties respectively. The 47th lost seven officers, nine sergeants, one drummer and 98 rank and file killed in the assault, while nine officers, eight sergeants, one drummer

---

[715] Leith Hay, Vol. II, p.p. 29-61.

[716] Harley, p.p. 213-15.

[717] The officers of the 47th who died were Major Robert Kelly, Captain William Arthur Hodges, Lieutenants Thomas Spunner Short (or Shortt) and George Norris, and Ensigns [Blakewell?], John Campbell and Thomas Bennett. Captain Charles Edward Livesay was severely wounded and died on 15th September. Captain Henry Oglander, Lieutenants Thomas Power, John Robert Nason and William McKenzie Johnson, and Ensigns Stephen Burke and Alexander Hall were all severely wounded, and Hall died of wounds on 4th September. Lieutenants William Kendall and Edward Agar were slightly wounded. A total of 216 rank and file fell out of an effective strength of 378. Lieutenant Short, 'a brave fellow and generally beloved', had not fully recovered from his Vitoria wound when John Harley encountered him hastening to rejoin the 47th before San Sebastian: 'Never was I so astonished as at meeting him not cured of his wound, and limping along into Hernani. I asked him for God's sake what brought him out of hospital, and begged he would return. He told me he was resolved to join his regiment, then in front of San Sebastian and preparing to storm next morning. He congratulated himself that he had been up in time.' Serjeant-Major Thomas Carmichael of the 47th, who was among those wounded at San Sebastian was promoted to ensign on 23rd October 1813.

[718] Officers of the 59th who died were Captain (Brevet Major) Francis Scott, Lieutenants George Fane, Robert Parke, the Hon William Cecil Pery (son of the Earl of Limerick), James Pyne, Charles Nicholas Vevers, and Ensigns Marcus O'Hara and Lawrence Watson. Captain John Fothergill was severely wounded and died next day, while Lieutenant George Fraser Freeze, who lost an arm, died on the 5th. Captain Abraham Pilkington, and Lieutenants Archibald Campbell, Lewis Carmichael (injured three times), Edward Duncan, Henry Hartford, Nicholas Hovenden, Aeneus McIntosh McPherson, Patterson O'Hara (injured twice), and Ensign Wright Edwards were all

and 118 rank and file were wounded. The 2nd/59th lost eight officers, four sergeants, five corporals, one drummer and 110 privates killed in action, and fourteen officers, eight sergeants, one drummer and 229 other ranks wounded, of whom two officers, one corporal, one drummer and 28 privates later died of their wounds. The loss of the 59th was the highest of any regiment that day, and greater than on any other occasion in the 'Lilywhite's' history. Ten of the thirteen 40th volunteers became casualties.[719]

Major-General Frederick Robinson, who was himself wounded, wrote on 2nd September to his sister:

'Out of the 1,000 brave fellows who accomplished this extraordinary feat, with the addition of 200 more that came up some time after, seven hundred & forty, together with fifty officers, were killed & wounded on the breach & in advancing to it – among the rest, My Excellency was laid sprawling in the mud by a ball through my beautiful face, which occasions my sitting as unnaturally upright as any Boarding School Miss.'

'My people are the constant theme of admiration, not only of our own Army, but of the French prisoners, 300 of whom are now under my window confined in a garden, and whenever I happen to stand at the window they pay me every compliment in their power. Sir Thos. Graham could not express his approbation without tears, and for a moment could not proceed. Sir James Leith said it appeared to him as if every individual of the brigade had determined to conquer or die in the breach. I have no doubt that our Great Chief will think we have done our duty.'

Robinson also wrote, on 5th September, to General Alexander Ross, Colonel of the 59th Regiment:

'I should feel myself unworthy having such a Regiment as the 59th under my command, if I were to omit mentioning to you as its Colonel its conspicuous conduct on the 31st of August in the assault of the breach of this place. The 59th formed part of 1,000 men destined to attack the breach, and to form a lodgement on the top, with positive orders not to advance beyond it; which was effected under a fire from the front, and double cross-fire, after three hours hard fighting, almost muzzle to muzzle; and the troops destined to support them came forward and carried the town.

'The loss of the brigade has been dreadful, that of the 59th twenty officers, twelve serjeants, two drummers and three hundred and thirty-eight rank and file killed and wounded. Three officers have died this morning, and, I fear, more in danger.

'Nothing could exceed the intrepidity of the Regiment – it rushed forward cheering, and gained the top of the breach, under a fire that threatened the destruction of the whole party. Sir Thomas Graham, Sir James Leith, General Oswald, and other officers of distinction were witness of this display of British valour, which they acknowledged, at the time, with acclamations, and have since spoken of in terms of their highest approbation.

'Of the surviving officers, those who merit the most particular mention, after their seniors had been wounded, are Captain Fuller of the Grenadiers, who commanded the Regiment for a considerable time, in the heat of the action; and Lieutenant Carmichael of the Light Infantry, who continued in the most active discharge of his duty after receiving three wounds, and never quitted the field. These officers are of the most promising merit.

'I cannot do justice to the subject I have attempted, owing to excessive pain: but hope I have said enough to convince you that the 59th Regiment is an ornament to the British Army.'

Captain Francis Fuller, commanding the Grenadier Company of the 59th, wrote the following day to his mother:

'I have great pleasure in acquainting you with my safety after the murderous storm of this town… Our Regiment is literally cut to pieces. Nineteen officers killed and wounded. I know not how I escaped, but thank God I have come off well: a shot-hole through my cap, and my breeches torn by scrambling up the breach, being the only damage done to my agreeable person… I trust no more storming; I am sick of it. I believe we have not 250 men left.'

The following note appeared in *The Star*, 25th April 1825: 'The surviving officers of the Second Battalion 59th Regiment, who were present at the storming of San Sebastian, have lately presented Captain Fuller, of that

_____

severely wounded, and Lieutenants Henry Brown and Samuel Stuart (or Stewart), and Ensign Peter Robertson were slightly wounded. 341 rank and file fell out of an effective strength of 626.

[719] Lieutenant William Turton was so severely wounded that he died the following day. Three rank and file were killed, and the sergeant and five rank and file were wounded, most of them severely.

Regiment, a valuable sword in testimony of the high opinion they entertain of his gallant conduct on that occasion, when he succeeded to the command of the Regiment almost immediately on their quitting the trenches, and maintained it in the most distinguished manner during the whole of the assault, and until the next morning, when he was relieved by Major (now Lieut.-Colonel) Hoysted, who had just arrived from England. Captain Fuller, although commanding the Regiment and setting a most brilliant example to those under him, escaped unhurt… Captain Fuller has since been twice wounded but is sufficiently recovered to accompany his (the Grenadier) Company on service, for which they are now under orders.'

Ironically, in 1826 Francis Fuller would lead the 59th at the storming of Bhurtpore.

Lieutenant Lewis Carmichael, who commanded the Light Company 59th, was the only officer out of thirteen in Robinson's advance who entered the town at the end of the day, despite three wounds and two contusions. Like Francis Fuller, he would earn future distinction at Bhurtpore.

The Battle Honour 'ST SEBASTIAN' was awarded to the 47th and 59th in 1818. Military General Service Medals with the 'St Sebastian' bar were given in 1848 to 90 survivors of the 47th and 115 of the 59th. Eight were also issued to men of the 40th, and twenty to the 82nd. Those to the latter regiment may have been earned in the defensive actions on the heights of Salain that same day.

Meanwhile, Army Gold Medals for San Sebastian were awarded to Majors Robert Kelly and Henry Oglander, Captain Charles Livesay and Lieutenant Thomas Power of the 47th, and to Major Francis Scott and Captains Francis Fuller and George Halford of the 59th, though it appears that Halford did not take part in the actual assault, being on duty in the trenches. Charles Livesay was additionally, and most unusually, awarded with a posthumous brevet majority.

In his diary entry for 4th September, Alexander Frazer wrote, 'As the really brave always fall in a day of open assault, our late loss is in truth a severe one. It was impossible to look at the dead on the breach without admiration for the brave men who had fallen, their wounds all in front, & filling, when dead, the places they filled whilst living.'

The Battle of San Marcial, 31st August 1813

Having reorganised his shattered army yet again, on 31st August, Soult made a final attempt at the relief of San Sebastian. Wellington anticipated this attack, and moved the 1st and 4th Divisions into positions from where they could, if required, support the Spanish troops on the lower Bidassoa. The two British brigades of the 4th Division, including the 40th in Anson's brigade, were moved north from Lesaca on 30th August and placed on a high north-eastern spur of the Pena de la Aya, behind and to the right of the Spanish deployment. Further south, Inglis's and Miller's (former Stubbs') brigades of the 7th Division were redeployed on the same day from Etxalar to Lesaca, covering a group of Bidassoa fords below the Heights of Salain.

At dawn that day French troops forded the Bidassoa at two points, around Hendaye and near Vera. The northern attack by three divisions under Reille was blocked and repulsed on the steep San Marcial ridge by three Spanish divisions under Freire with the loss of some 2,500 men. Captain Elias Malet of the 30th, attached to the Spanish army as DAQMG since 1810, was killed in this action.

Further south, Clausel advanced cautiously with four divisions, of which only three forded the Bidassoa. His attack was intended as a turning movement to assist Reille's assault, The divisions of Taupin and Darmagnac climbed the heights of Salain beyond the river, while Vandermaesen's division turned south to protect the left flank of Clausel's attack from the Light Division, massed on the heights of Santa Barbara.

Between 7 and 8 a.m., as the morning haze thinned, the French clashed with Miller's Portuguese brigade and pushed it slowly uphill. At about 11 a.m. the Portuguese fell back through Inglis's brigade, including the 82nd, which had been brought up from Lesaca to take up the fight.

The two brigades now held a strong position and there was a severe struggle, with attack and counter-attack, until Darmagnac's division came up through woods on Inglis's right, forcing a withdrawal to another ridge a mile to the rear. Clausel followed slowly, increasingly aware that the further he advanced the more he exposed his flanks. By noon Clausel had lost momentum and halted the advance of his main columns in front of Inglis's position, considering it was 'not possible or prudent' to continue until Reille had taken the heights of San Marcial.

At about 2 p.m. Taupin's division, on the right, was engaged with skirmishers of Anson's brigade of the 4th Division, which Wellington had moved south to a spur above the Convent of San Antonio. This action involved a picquet of the 40th commanded by Lieutenant William Waldron Kelly.

Between 3 and 4 p.m. the battlefield was suddenly drenched by the same blinding and torrential thunderstorm which had deluged San Sebastian that afternoon. This effectively put an end to fighting. At 5 p.m. Clausel received orders from Soult to withdraw across the Bidassoa. The French divisions retired with difficulty, only to discover that the cloudburst had caused a six-foot rise in the Bidassoa fords by dusk, cutting off the retreat of the whole of Vandermaesen's division and the rear brigades of Taupin and Darmagnac.

The only possible crossing was now by the bridge at Vera, barricaded and held by Captain Daniel Cadoux with eighty men of the 2nd/95th. Cadoux held off repeated French attacks for two hours, inflicting 231 casualties including Vandermaesen. He appealed for reinforcement to John Skerret, whose brigade of the Light Division lay only half a mile south of Vera, but Skerret, true to his Tarifa and Tarragona form, refused help. Cadoux was eventually overwhelmed, and the chance was missed to force the surrender of four French brigades the following morning. Nevertheless, Soult's final incursion into Spain had ended in a humiliating reverse and the loss of a further 3,800 men.

The fighting on the heights of Salain cost Clausel's divisions 822 casualties, the Portuguese 128, and Inglis's and Anson's brigades 304 and 42 respectively. The 82nd suffered 65 casualties: Lieutenant Benjamin Welstead and four rank and file were killed, Lieutenant Hugh Donnellan was slightly wounded,[720] and five sergeants and 54 rank and file wounded. The casualties of the 40th amounted to one man killed, three wounded and one missing.

Catalonia July-September 1813

One consequence of the Allied victory at Vitoria was that, early in July, Marshal Suchet prudently withdrew his field army from Valencia, though with rather less foresight he left nearly ten thousand men in garrisons holding towns and fortresses, in expectation that he would return to recover them at a future date. The French fell back to the line of the River Ebro, and then to the River Llobregat, covering Barcelona.

Lord William Bentinck, who had previously planned an offensive in Valencia, followed the retiring French into Catalonia, leaving his Spanish allies to blockade the isolated garrisons. Bentinck occupied the city of Valencia on 9th July, passed the Ebro at Amposta by ferry and fishing boats from the 26th, and on the 30th marched his army of sixteen thousand men from the Col de Balaguer to Tarragona, which was invested on 31st July.

The 81st and De Rolls/Dillon advanced in line at dawn from the Francoli river, and found cover under some banks, three hundred yards nearer the place than the most advanced point occupied during the previous siege. The battering train was not landed, for Bentinck was waiting for Spanish forces to come up in support, and meanwhile the 81st were employed in making fascines and gabions. The Spanish troops joined on 3rd August, and preparations for breaking ground were almost completed when the movements of Marshal Suchet caused them to be abandoned.

On 14th August Suchet launched a concentric forced march from the Llobregat with 28,000 men in three columns, the right-hand of which circled through the mountains to Reus in Bentinck's rear. Accordingly, on the night of the 15th Bentinck made a timely retreat along the coast road through Cambrils to the Col de Balaguer and escaped. Contact appears to have been largely limited to cavalry skirmishes, though *The Historical Record of The 81st Regiment* states that 'during this movement the Eighty-First, with the Reserve Division, was engaged with the enemy.'

On the 17th Suchet approached the Col de Balaguer and, having observed the strength of Bentinck's position on and about the defile, supported offshore by warships, he fell back on Tarragona. He destroyed that place's outer defences, and retired once more behind the Llobregat. The Allies then occupied the undefended city, which became their point of contact with the fleet for the remainder of the campaign. The 81st, with the Reserve, were posted at Altufalla, on the coast road some eight miles east of Tarragona.

---

[720] Oman (Volume VII, p. 531) shows four officers of the 82nd wounded on this occasion, but this is incorrect.

The hostile armies then remained inactive until early September, when the Allies understood that the French were steadily withdrawing troops from Catalonia. Bentinck moved twelve thousand of his Anglo-Sicilians forward on the 5th to Vilafranca del Pinedes, fifteen miles up the inland road to Barcelona, and from there on the 12th he pushed an advance guard under Colonel Adam forward to occupy the defile of Ordal, just ten miles from the French lines on the Llobregat. Adam's force of 1,600 men included the 2nd/27th, Calabrians, Italian Levies, and detachments of the King's German Legion and De Rolls/Dillon. It was personally positioned by Bentinck, and was reinforced that afternoon by a Spanish brigade, but Adam neglected to occupy, or even observe, the bridge over a ravine to his front.

That night Suchet advanced up the road to Ordal with eleven and a half thousand men, while Decaen with a further seven thousand men moved inland on a converging route. Adam's post was attacked before midnight and, after a confused but hard-fought night combat the defenders were driven back with very heavy loss.

At dawn Suchet sent his cavalry on towards Vilafranca, in front of which they found the Allies drawn up in two lines with a reserve, with their left on the village of San Cugat. The French marshal held back at first, waiting for Decaen's column to approach, then made a move to turn the Allied left.

Bentinck, appreciating that he would be outnumbered once all the French came up, drew off towards Tarragona. Accounts of this movement are few and patchy, and Bentinck's laconic despatch sheds little light on what was clearly a well-executed operation not unlike the withdrawal of the 7th Division at Fuentes d'Onoro. He pulled back some eight miles to Arbos (l'Arboc), with an intermediate position behind a ravine near the isolated inn of Venta de Monjos.

It appears that Bentinck's two infantry divisions passed in turn through each other, under artillery fire, covered by his cavalry. Suchet had left all but one battalion of his infantry behind, but attempted with his two brigades of cavalry (1,500 sabres) and his horse artillery to break the Allied formation. They were met most effectively by Bentinck's heterogenous collection of cavalry[721], though at times the infantry, including the 81st, had to retreat in square and fire volleys to hold off the hovering French horsemen. The retreat was a fine display of steadiness, control and discipline, and Suchet repeatedly expressed his admiration at the manner in which it was conducted.

The ground behind Vilafranca offered no good defensive position until Arbos, where a ravine and bridge about a mile beyond the town offered a break clean line. Bentinck filed his army over the ravine and drew up on the far side while preparations were made to demolish the bridge. The 81st formed on the left of the road to cover the final retreat to the bridge of the 10th, 27th and two Portuguese 6-pounders with their cavalry escort.

Enemy cavalry, the 13th Cuirassiers and 4th Hussars, pressed close, and it became necessary to repel them to give time for the rearguard to pass the ravine. The 20th Light Dragoons and Brunswick Hussars made a gallant charge which, in fierce fighting, drove the superior French cavalry back on their infantry. The bridge, roughly mended with fascines, caught fire before the rearguard was over, but held until all the troops had passed, the 81st Regiment being the last to withdraw. Suchet's pursuit was halted by the bridge of Arbos at about 3 p.m., and he withdrew and dispersed his army.

Losses on both sides were largely among the cavalry – 106 of the Allies and 107 French – and the 21 casualties to the Anglo-Sicilian infantry were all from the French horse artillery. The 81st had two men killed and five wounded by cannon shot and shell splinters.

On 23rd September Lord William Bentinck was called away to Sicily, handing over command to his senior divisional commander, Lieutenant-General Clinton. At the end of September the troops went into cantonments, and the 81st, with the Reserve, occupied Valls, ten miles north of Tarragona.

The Bidassoa Crossing, 7th October 1813

Wellington was still waiting for political news before invading France; then on 3rd September, he heard that Austria had declared war on Napoleon. The time was now ripe for his army to advance. The frontier was

---

[721] 20th Light Dragoons, Brunswick Hussars, Sicilians and 'Foreign Hussars' commanded by Lord Frederick Bentinck, the general's brother.

fortified with redoubts, entrenchments and obstacles, particularly around the dominating La Rhune feature and on a low ridge 1-2 miles east of the Bidassoa estuary. Wellington observed that the French deployment near the coast was weaker than further inland. He had also discovered from Spanish shrimpers that the wide Bidassoa estuary opposite Fuenterrabia was fordable, to mid-thigh, at low tide. A particularly low tide at dawn was required, and the next would be on 7th October.

Wellington's plan was to attack on two main fronts: the 1st and 5th Divisions were to cross the Bidassoa estuary, while the Light Division, Spanish and Portuguese were to assault the high east-west ridge which rose at its eastern end towards La Rhune. As a distraction, Colville's 6th Div was to demonstrate on Soult's left against Urdax.

At 3 a.m. on 7th October, the 5th Division left their tents standing[722] and crept forward to their assault positions behind the village of Fuenterrabia and houses to its south. The men wore their caps reversed so that the brass plates would not show. At 7.15, they emerged from the cover of Fuenterrabia and, preceded by the light companies of each brigade, waded across the sandy estuary to Hendaye in column on three routes, guided by Spanish shrimpers. Almost complete surprise was achieved, and the French did not open fire until the heads of the columns were nearly halfway across. Captain Leith Hay summarised the historic crossing:

'It fell to the lot of the 5th Division to be the first British troops whose colours waved over the 'sacred territory' of Napoleon. The regiments crossed the Bidassoa with the utmost regularity and firmness, regardless of the depth of water, or of a fire poured by the enemy from the opposite bank. General Robinson passed the river on foot at the head of his brigade, and, in the midst of a shower of musketry, supported by artillery, up to the middle in water, pressed forward; and in the exhilaration of the occasion, increased by enthusiastic cheering, and the bands of the regiments playing the National Anthem, established his brave soldiers on the soil hitherto unvisited, during the reign of Napoleon, by the horrors of war.'[723]

Robinson himself, in a letter of October 9th, added more details of his brigade's crossing:

'At two o'clock on the morning of the 7th we received orders to move from our encampment in front of Oyazun towards the Bidassoa, which separates Spain from France. My brigade to Fonterabia, there to wait for instructions. An hour before day break, my people being hid behind the walls, I was desired to procure three guides from the Alcalde for fording the river, viz one for ourselves, a second for the 3rd, or Portuguese Brigade, and a third for the 1st Brigade, who were to cross about a mile & a half higher up, and on their right the First Division and a large body of Spaniards were to cross at the same moment. The signal to advance was to be the waving of one of our Colours from the high steeple of Fonterabia.[724]

'At half past seven, it being low water, the signal was made; when to my surprise my guide, who was full as tall as myself, told me the water would be up to our chins at least. However, the Peer (i.e. Wellington) had ordered us to cross and therefore there could be no impediments. To prevent the chance of drowning, or being exposed to a severe fire from the enemy, I dismounted, and placing myself with the guide a little in front of the brigade, gave the word to advance. The men [held] their arms and ammunition over their heads, sacrificing cheerfully three days provisions which they had in their haversacks rather than injure the ammunition, and with hearty cheering we greeted the French shore. The event justified the judgement of our sagacious Chief, for the French were taken so completely by surprise that we were safely landed and formed before a single shot was fired, & those that did oppose us were soon dispersed by the Light Infantry.'

Robinson's brigade (the 4th, 47th and 59th), on the extreme left, skirted Hendaye and advanced to the coast, where they captured a battery at Pointe Ste. Anne. The brigade continued along the coastal heights, then changed direction half-right, crossed a stream in the valley below, and unexpectedly approached the unoccupied Sans Culottes Redoubt in the French right rear.[725] The brigade had most effectively turned the flank of the main French position on the Croix des Bouquets ridge, which was under frontal attack. The 2nd/105th Ligne was sent by Reille

---

[722] Before the Bidassoa crossing, Robinson's brigade was encamped between Guadelupe and Oyarzun.

[723] Leith Hay, Vol. II, p. 271.

[724] Captain Batty (*Campaign of the Western Pyrenees*) says that the signal to advance was a rocket from the church steeple, but it may have been a case of 'belt and braces'.

[725] The Sans Culottes Redoubt, an old entrenchment of the Revolutionary War, lay on a long spur running north-east from the Croix des Bouquets ridge.

to counter this critical threat to the French position, but was routed. The brigade was then ordered to halt and hold its ground. Major-General Hay, commanding the 5th Division since Leith was wounded at San Sebastian, was with Robinson's brigade and reported:

'I cannot express how obliged I feel to Maj-Gen Robinson for his able assistance in turning the enemy's right flank several times, in one of which movements a detachment of the 47th and a Grenadier Company of the 3rd Portuguese charged the enemy posted in and behind a battery on our left near the sea, and took it with four 24-pounders and a considerable quantity of ammunition... The column still continued turning and driving the enemy until we got to the flank and nearly to the top of their position, where they were strongly posted behind some field works and strong hedges, which were carried by a charge of the 47th supported by the 59th and a part of the 3rd Portuguese. At this time my left flank was attacked and the flankers driven in by a very superior body of the enemy, who were most gallantly repulsed – whilst I was with the 47th – by Maj-Gen Robinson and the 4th Regiment, and driven, till I had ordered to halt, to the ground where our advanced picquets now stand.'

'Immediately after passing the sand hills,' wrote General Robinson, 'the country became exceedingly rugged and steep, and more undulating than any I have ever seen. The enemy continued collecting from all parts, but they did not impede our progress, nor did any but the light infantry deign to fire a shot. A battery of four 24 pounders was taken, and then I saw the necessity of halting a few minutes to collect the men and give them time to breathe, which we did under cover of very high bushes. The enemy fancied we were afraid to advance further, & came on boldly to the attack. We let them come very near, and then, with the Gamarra War Whoop, rushed forward to the charge, which had the effect of proving that Frenchmen can run faster than the English when they have a mind to try.

'From the hill we could see the rest of the army advancing with equal success. The enemy made another stand from a hill a very short distance from us, from whence they were quickly driven, and at that moment an aide de camp rode up with orders for me not to advance any farther, as our part in the day's work was done, and that we were to maintain our position, in case of attack, to the last. We had now time to view what was going on, and in about twenty minutes more every hill that the Peer was desirous of occupying was in his possession, and he declared it was the best executed and most brilliant advance he had ever seen. From a height he saw all the brigades of the 5th Division distinctly, & in the fullness of a manly heart he exclaimed before all his staff, "Admirably done Fifth Division, by Heavens they are gallant fellows, I never saw anything so bravely or so well performed!" Just at that moment a regiment in our First Brigade (the 9th Foot) charged two French regiments and drove them like sheep, and as the Peer came past they gave him three cheers, and continued the pursuit until they had reached the hill intended for their position.[726] And thus ended this brilliant and fortunate invasion of France by the Nation of Shop Keepers.'

Robinson had every reason for euphoria: the Croix des Bouquets ridge was carried by 9 a.m., and by 11.30 all was over. His brigade had achieved their vital part in this victory at a cost of only one officer and thirteen rank and file wounded, of whom five were of the 47th and three of the 59th.

Wellington halted the advance on the left short of Urrogne and the Chapel of Socorri to its north. 'My brigade is entrusted with the advanced post on the left of the whole Army,' wrote Robinson on the 9th of October. 'There are only two or three fields between us and the enemy, and our sentries are quite hand in glove with theirs, but so polite, that we never fire at each other. The pickets of both parties sit over their comfortable fires, as quietly as if peace had been proclaimed.'

Ten days after the Bidassoa crossing, on 17th October, there was a reorganisation of the 5th Division whereby the 2nd/47th was transferred to Major-General Hay's 1st Brigade.

---

[726] This account accords with a letter of 8th October by Lieutenant-Colonel Alexander Frazer, RA, who was with Wellington and wrote, 'On ascending the hill we found our troops formed somewhat in advance of it. An instantaneous hurrah burst from the line on seeing Lord Wellington, who rode a little to the left, where the enemy showed a feeble line disputing (with Robinson's brigade) some wooded ground. He thanked the 9th Regiment on the field for their gallant conduct.'

Battle of the Nivelle, 10th November 1813

The crossing of the Bidassoa and capture of the dominating heights of the Rhune were necessary preliminaries to Wellington's invasion of southern France. His next step was to break through Soult's last line of fixed defences in the Pyrenees on a twenty-mile front from the coast to beyond Maya. To do this, he had the equivalent of ten Anglo-Portuguese and six Spanish divisions, including 82,000 infantry – 38,000 British, and 22,000 each Portuguese and Spanish. Neither side was able to use cavalry, which were held back, and the movement of guns over the rugged mountain tracks was very challenging.

Soult had 62,000 men, of whom 23,000 were on the coastal plain from the sea to Ascain, which was the most heavily fortified part of his line, with fifteen redoubts and six closed works on the heights south of the River Nivelle and, further east, the fortified camp of Serres. The remaining two thirds of his front, rugged mountainous country, was more thinly held by five divisions, but again was fortified in depth. Indeed, Soult was over-reliant on fixed defences rather than manoeuvre and in consequence had too few reserves. He was, moreover, complacent: 'When he had conceived and written down a scheme,' observed a critical contemporary, 'he seemed to regard it as an inevitable decree from heaven.'

From 9th October onwards, Wellington was able to ascend La Rhune, from which dominating vantage point he could make what amounted to an air reconnaissance, considering almost every redoubt and trench in Soult's position. It was there that with Sir George Murray, his trusted Quartermaster-General, he made his plans and issued orders for the forthcoming offensive. The attack was scheduled for 7th November, but was delayed by bad weather until the 10th.

The plan was to make a feint attack on the coastal plain to pin down 23,000 French with an equal number Allied troops, while the main effort was made in the centre, where Wellington would achieve local superiority in numbers for a break-through on both sides of the Nivelle, where that river ran south to north through a gap in the surrounding heights. He would assault the centre and right, held by Clausel and D'Erlon with 40,000 men, with 60,000 Allied troops, but concentrate an even greater superiority in the centre, where he would oppose Clausel's 16,000 men with 33,000 between the Lesser Rhune and the Bridge of Amotz.

The attack frontage was so long that Wellington in effect appointed 'corps commanders': On the left, Sir John Hope had the 1st and 5th Divisions, Aylmer's brigade, Campbell's Portuguese and Freire's two Spanish divisions with which to demonstrate against strong entrenched camps in front of St.-Jean-de-Luz, which he did to perfection. On the right was Hill with the 2nd and 6th Divisions, Hamilton's Portuguese and Morillo's Spaniards, of whom the 6th and Hamilton's were to co-operate with the main thrust, advancing to the east of the Nivelle, and the remainder were to contain D'Erlon's troops further south-east. The main and most powerful thrust was to be in the centre, where Beresford had the 3rd, 4th, 7th and Light divisions, together with Bradford's Portuguese, and Giron's and Longa's Spaniards. This concentrated force, with the 6th Division and Hamilton's Portuguese on its right, was to punch through Clausel's left and D'Erlon's right on a narrow front, seizing crossings over the Nivelle at St. Pée and the Bridge of Amotz. This would force the withdrawal of both wings of Soult's army.

The battle on the critical centre ground was opened at 4 a.m. on 10th November by attacks on Soult's forward positions. On the left, the Light Division advanced at dawn to capture fortifications on the Lesser Rhune, the Mouiz Star Fort and three redoubts on a jagged rocky ridge. On the right, the 4th and 7th Divisions had first to assault the Ste. Barbe and Grenada redoubts, outworks of the fortified village of Sare, each strongpoint held by a battalion of Rey's brigade of Conroux's division.

The troops destined for the attack paraded just after 3 a.m. and moved silently forward from their camps to the picket line in bright moonlight. Arriving about an hour before dawn, they lay down to await the order to advance.

The 4th Division, led by Anson's brigade, was tasked to storm the Ste. Barbe redoubt. The parapets of this enclosed fieldwork were engaged with shrapnel by two 9-pounder batteries and a horse artillery troop, eighteen guns pushed up close, while the redoubt was approached in cover by Anson's light companies and the 2nd Provisional Battalion. The French garrison evacuated the work without making a stand. Lieutenant-Colonel George Bingham, commanding the 2nd Provisional Battalion, gives an interesting account of the capture of the Ste. Barbe redoubt, though he, characteristically, gives all the credit to his own unit:

'As soon as the fire of the artillery had made an adequate impression, the battalion which I commanded was to carry it by storm. Accordingly, leaving our packs behind and carrying bags filled with leaves to facilitate our descent into the ditch, we moved off, and suffering but little from the fire of the work, established ourselves under cover of the hill within thirty paces of it. There was another redoubt [Grenada] to our right within four-pounder range which part of the 7th Division were to carry, and before their attack began we had the fire on us; to save our people from this teasing, before the artillery had made any impression on the redoubt, we jumped up and dashed at the gorge of it, but found the French had been too quick for us. We were only in time to secure a few prisoners who were making their escape. Thus this work which had appeared so formidable was taken with a very trifling loss within half an hour after the commencement of the action.'[727]

The British guns then switched their fire to the Grenada redoubt, which was again captured with little resistance by Inglis's brigade of the 7th Division. The French fell back on Sare, a fortified camp held by seven of Conroux's battalions.

A further bombardment followed; then, headed again by the brigades of Anson and Inglis, the 4th and 7th Divisions attacked the village on converging lines with the church as their direction point. With their right flank exposed to the almost unopposed advance of Giron's Spaniards on the lower slopes of the Rhune, Rey's brigade was pushed out of Sare by 9 a.m. and retired in considerable disorder through their hutted camp on the 'brown bank' ridge beyond the village, which was also taken.

The way was now open for a general advance between the Rhune and the Nivelle to take the French second line. This consisted of a mile-long abattis north of Sare, then a line of fieldworks on the high ground from the St. Ignace pass to the Nivelle, notably the Signals, Louis XIV and Madelaine redoubts. The 3rd Division, moving to the right of the 7th, was the first to force its way through the abattis, and its leading brigade then rushed the Amotz bridge by about 10 a.m., cutting communications between Clausel and D'Erlon, and took the Madelaine redoubt after sharp struggle in which Conroux was killed. On the far side of Nivelle, the 6th Division and Hamilton's Portuguese took the Harismendia redoubt to link up with 3rd Division.

At 10 a.m., the 4th and 7th Divisions, having regrouped after their capture of Sare, advanced again, covered by a skirmishing line of light companies and caçadores. Anson's and Inglis's brigades still led, to save time, with the other two brigades of each division in support. They had first to force the abattis, manned by Baurot's brigade. According to George Bingham, it was the 27th who carried this work on Anson's front 'in fine style,' while Corporal Wheeler of the 51st described the action by Inglis's brigade:

'As soon as our stragglers had formed we advanced, drove the enemy from behind a hedge, and was soon over after them, and they, by being reinforced, tried to drive us back again. In this they were deceived: we allowed them to come within a very short distance of us, then we poured a volley into their faces, and before they had well got over their surprise we were upon them with our bayonets. Here was a fearful slaughter on the part of the enemy, nearly every shot told and their dead and wounded covered the place. All that could, scampered back, and we after them.'[728]

The 4th and 7th Divisions then climbed the heights, the crests of which were crowned by the Louis XIV redoubt and by flanking entrenchments and breastworks, covering the Col de Mendionde, the only route across the hills to the Nivelle bridge at St. Pée. This vital ground was initially held in strength by Clausel with the wrecks of Conroux's division and two brigades of Maransin's division, supported on the right flank by at least nine guns. Two regiments of reinforcements were subsequently called forward.

The action that ensued in and around the Louis XIV redoubt, and then back towards the Col de Mendionde, was the heaviest and most protracted of the whole battle, and the most decisive. 'The enemy was driven out and the redoubt carried by the 40th and 48th Regiments,' wrote General Cole, 'the former commanded by Lt. Col. Thornton.'[729]

---

[727] Letter dated Ascain 20th November 1813.
[728] Letter dated General Hospital, St. Jean de Luz, 20th November 1813.
[729] Cole's report to Marshal Beresford dated 10th November 1813.

It is abundantly clear that the fight was stoutly maintained by both sides, with attack and counter-attack[730], and that the casualties were very heavy, but there is no coherent overall narrative of the course of that desperate hill-top struggle. The outcome, though, was the capture of the key to Soult's position. The Light Division advanced slightly later to take the St. Ignace and Signals redoubts, completing the clearance of the heights.

We have an account of the battle from Lieutenant James Mill, who gives a succinct summary of the 4th Division's actions but disappointingly little detail of the part played by the 40th Regiment:

'The point of difficulty between us and the river, which had to be encountered by our brigade, was a strongly fortified redoubt [Ste. Barbe], surrounded with a deep ditch, hedged in by palisades, which was situated far in advance of, and protected the approaches to, the village of Sarré [Sare]. The houses of the last were well defended, being occupied in force by the enemy, and again in rear of this was a high ridge, strongly fortified by a cordon of field works, the ascent of which was difficult and steep, and covered with abattis and entrenchments.

'These lines of defence were silently approached before daylight, and in the attacks upon them nothing could withstand for any length of time the impetuous onset of our men. The French, finding themselves enveloped and beset by an enemy who were resolved on winning their object or dying in the attempt, evacuated first the large redoubt rather precipitately, and then fled before us.

'Our brigade, not long after this occurred, and against a moderate resistance, carried the village of Sarré [Sare], and then the contest was maintained on the fortified ridges behind, where the French made a resolute and protracted stand – indeed, so pertinacious were they, that it is not too much to aver that British soldiers only would have been adequate to effect a dislodgement of them. This, nevertheless, by hard fighting, was effectively accomplished.'[731]

When the Louis XIV redoubt fell, Clausel made an effort to rally his troops on the Col de Mendionde, and then at the Arostegui redoubt half a mile above the Nivelle, but to no avail. By mid-afternoon, the French centre was comprehensively penetrated to St. Pée, and Clausel's shattered divisions had struggled back over the Nivelle. The 3rd and 7th Divisions crossed the bridge at St. Pée, and Inglis's brigade pushed on to take high ground to the north-west of the village, where Clausel made a final stand with the wrecks of Maransin's and Taupin's divisions to check the Allied advance. The 82nd played a major part in this last action of the day, but as the *Regimental Record of Service* indignantly noted, they received scant recognition:

'During the operations of this day the 82nd Regiment in conjunction with other regiments of the brigade drove the enemy in very superior force from the heights St Pée, for which service the 51st and 68th Regts were particularly mentioned in the published dispatches, it would appear thro' a mistake in the report of the Assistant Adjutant-General attached to the Division… in answer to a question from the Marquis of Wellington to the following purport, viz: "What corps is that which is carrying those heights in such a gallant style?" mentioned the above named regiments when it was in reality the 82nd which bore the brunt of the affair after the other two regiments, being very weak, had been checked.'

Clausel's desperate and costly rearguard actions, by delaying the Allied breakout, saved Soult from complete disaster. The November evening was now drawing in, and although Wellington had wished to complete the day's victory by enveloping Soult's right wing, he had run out of daylight. The 4th Division, together with the Light Division and two Spanish divisions, ended the day close to the fortified camp of Serres, but it was too late for further offensive action that day. 'Soult had a very narrow escape,' wrote Wellington. 'If I had an hour or two more of daylight, or two fresh divisions in reserve, I could have caught his right before they could have got back into the entrenched camp at Bayonne.'

Soult had done almost nothing to influence the battle, organising neither concentration nor counter-attacks; but that evening he was obliged to order an immediate withdrawal to the shelter of Bayonne.

Whilst the main attack developed further east, the 47th and 59th had taken part in Sir John Hope's false attack against Reille's elaborate fortifications on the coastal plain. Hope's orders were to make a noisy demonstration against the strong entrenched camps in front of St.-Jean-de-Luz, but not to commit himself to a general action, and this he did. The 5th Division was, as before, on the far left next to the sea.

---

[730] Corporal Wheeler of the 51st, who was lying wounded, counted seven times that the hilltop was taken and retaken.
[731] Letter dated Usteritz January 1814.

Early on the morning of the 10th, Robinson's brigade drove in the French pickets from the Sans Culottes Redoubt; then, once the fortified village of Urogne was captured by Aylmer's brigade, the 5th Division pushed forward to the inundations which covered the fort of Socoa and the fortified village of Ciboure, across the Nivelle estuary from St.-Jean-de-Luz. Just after last light the troops were recalled. Casualties in the 59th were light, including two privates killed in action and Volunteer John Blood[732], a drummer and six rank and file wounded, of whom just two privates were seriously enough injured to feature in the returns.

The situation changed dramatically that night, for Reille had withdrawn in haste, abandoning his redoubts, spiking the guns in his batteries, demolishing the bridges over the Nivelle, and falling back overnight to a new forward line beyond Bidart, guarding the highroad to Bayonne. Next morning some twenty thousand British, Spanish and Portuguese converged on the Nivelle crossing between Ciboure and St.-Jean-de-Luz, but the tide was in, so it was afternoon before the 5th Division was able to ford the estuary.

'It rained torrents the whole forenoon, but the spectacle of the allied columns descending from the fortified position in files to the banks of the river, and then forming columns in the most perfect order; with the grand style in which the troops forded the river and ascended the opposite bank, was remarkably striking. The ford was broad enough to cross by platoons, and though the water was deep, and the right bank exceedingly muddy, all passed in high spirits. Many of the soldiers' wives were seen wading through the river and dragging themselves through the muddy banks and swampy ground of the opposite shore by the sides of the companies to which their husbands belonged.'[733]

The town of St.-Jean-de-Luz, with its magazine, harbour and shipping, was then occupied without fighting, and the 5th Division pressed on up the highroad to the village of Bidart. Tents and camp stores arrived the following day, but the bad weather continued without a break until the 18th, precluding further offensive action.

The French loss on the Nivelle was some 4,500 men, including 1,200 prisoners, and 59 guns. The total Allied loss was 2,700, of whom 2,526 were British. The 40th suffered the heaviest casualties in the 4th Division, a total of at least 106: one officer, a sergeant and sixteen rank and file were killed in action; seven officers and eighty men were wounded (the *Regimental Record Book* puts the latter figure at 'about one hundred'). [734] In addition, Captain Bartholemew Vigors Derenzy of the 81st, serving with the 7th Caçadores of Stubbs' Portuguese brigade in the 4th Division, was dangerously wounded (reported killed).

The 82nd suffered 89 casualties: nine rank and file were killed in action, and six officers, six sergeants and 68 rank and file were wounded.[735] Major William Vincent resigned from the staff of the 6th Division to assume command of the Battalion.

Just 83 of the 40th survived to receive a 'Nivelle' clasp to their Military General Service Medal, and 67 of the 82nd, together with only 29 of the 47th and 17 of the 59th. Gold Medals were awarded to Lieutenant-Colonel Thornton and Major William Balfour of the 40th and to Major John Walmsley of the 82nd. Both the 40th and 82nd were awarded the Battle Honour 'NIVELLE' in 1824, but neither the 47th nor the 59th received this honour.

The Battle of the Nive, 9th-12th December 1813

After the Battle of the Nivelle, Soult fell back to an entrenched camp in front of the fortress city of Bayonne and held a line of observation on the River Nive as far as Cambo. The rain continued, and there was a pause of some four weeks for suitable weather, during which Wellington ordered his army into cantonments. The 40th occupied part of the village of Ascain and remained there until early in December. The 82nd, with the 7th Division,

---

[732] John Blood, aged 16, had joined the 59th as a Volunteer just one week before the Battle of the Nivelle, where he received a leg wound. He was commissioned on 3rd March 1814.

[733] Batty, p. 57.

[734] Ensign Alexander Dobbyn was killed in action. Lieutenant-Colonel Henry Thornton, Captains John Henry Barnett (Burnett in the Army List) and Peter Bishop, Lieutenant John Richardson and Volunteer George Booth were severely wounded, and Lieutenant and Adjutant Isaac Chetham, and Lieutenants Nathan Truman Carter and Charles Wallace were slightly wounded. Barnett, Bishop and Richardson were with the 40th at Waterloo.

[735] Captain George Marshall, Lieutenants Kingston Cuthbert, William Mason, Charles Mortimer, and Ensigns John Buchan Sydserff and Richard Whittaker were seriously wounded.

remained around St. Pée. The 5th Division, based in and around Bidart, held the outpost line astride the Bayonne road, first on a ridge of hills at Guéthary and then further north on the plateau of Barrouillet, ten miles from St.-Jean-de-Luz. This period was relatively quiet, though minor skirmishes cost the 47th two men taken prisoners on 17th November, one killed on the 20th and a further two captured on the 22nd. On the 26th the heavy rain resumed, swelling the rivers and making many roads and tracks impassable.

Wellington took particular pains during this enforced pause to build and maintain good relations with the civilian population, and to that end, having hanged a few marauders, he sent his Spanish troops home with a stiff letter: 'I am not invading France to plunder; thousands of officers and men have not been killed and wounded in order that the survivors might rob the French.' He thereby sacrificed his numerical superiority, as his strength, less cavalry, was reduced to 63,500 against Soult's 63,800.

He quite rightly made the establishment and maintenance of good relations with the French population a very high priority: his army were to be liberators, not invaders. In this he was successful, and the local peasantry soon returned to their homes and traded freely with the British camps. There were of course a few inveterate rogues who ignored Wellington's admonitions. One of these was Captain John Harley's servant, who was probably one of the 47th men lost on 22nd November near Bayonne:

'Here, my good servant, Pat Dolan, again proved his propensity for "making his fortune," as he termed it. Being one of the foremost, on our approach to Bayonne, he entered a mansion in search of valuable articles; and, as he delayed too long examining the splendid house, his party retreated without him. Immediately after, a party of French dragoons surrounded the house, and Pat was found counting over the plate and other valuables, no doubt thinking his long-wished fortune was made. He was not a little surprised when he was taken prisoner and conveyed through France, from south to north, until he at last rested at Valenciennes. Here he remained till the peace was declared, when he joined us at Chichester in Sussex.'[736]

It was probably at this time that replacement shoes and shirts arrived for the 2nd/47th, ordered by their paymaster, John Harley, from an old and trusted acquaintance in Limerick. Harley had used the same source with satisfaction when the Battalion was stationed in Cadiz, but on this occasion it appears, by his own account, that he was scammed by the supplier:

'On the regiment marching to the Pyrenees in 1813, the men had destroyed nearly all their shoes and linen; and, as I was so well and punctually attended to in my former order, I sent another to a much larger amount, and anxiously looked for its arrival. I had particularly stated in my letters, to let every article be of the best quality, and full-sized, for which I was willing to pay a fair price. The firm was not long in executing the order, and, to the joy of the whole regiment, I received early one morning the invoices and bills of lading; and, not having the least idea but that the goods would turn out as good as the former order, I wrote back without delay, acknowledging the receipt of them, and enclosing an order on my bankers.

'The goods accordingly arrived, and the poor soldiers entreated me not to delay distributing them, some jocularly saying that they might as well be killed with a good shirt on their back as a bad one; and a poor Irishman, who was killed in the next action, remarked, "If we have dirty shirts on, the Frenchmen will think us very poor, and as badly off as themselves; and bad luck to them!" I therefore lost no time; and had the different bales arranged out according to the invoice; but, just before we had opened them, the Duke of Wellington rode up, and inquired what they were, and, on being informed, was much pleased, and said I deserved great credit in running the risk I had done, for it really was a hazardous undertaking.

'On opening the bales one after the other, judge my astonishment on finding the shirts scarcely run together, and the shoes made of sheep-skin, untanned and pasted together, and then blackened! The shirts were so small, they would not fit the drum-boys, and of course were entirely useless; as for the shoes, they were no better, for as soon as they were wet the soles came from the uppers, and, until I explained to the Army the imposition that had been practised on me, and the loss I consequently sustained, I firmly believe that they privately thought I had intended to defraud the poor privates, and enrich myself by the transaction. But quite the contrary were my intentions; for I was always a friend to the soldier; and, to the present day, I am often respectfully and

---

736 Harley, p. 220

affectionately accosted by men who had entirely escaped my recollection, and who are anxious to show that they have not forgotten the different kindnesses which I might occasionally have shown them.'[737]

The 82nd were now on the left bank of the Nive. We have already had occasion to mention the civil relations that were customary between French and British pickets, who had a mutual 'live and let live' understanding. Lieutenant George Wood experienced a variant of this convention on the Nive:

'A strong French [picket] was posted on the other side, with a breastwork thrown up to protect them, my advanced sentry being within twenty yards of them, posted in a meadow without any covering. About break of day, my attention was attracted by a great noise from the French piquet; on going to find the cause of it, I found them halooing, and making signs to my sentry to fall back, at the same time presenting their pieces at him, and threatening to shoot him. On observing these proceedings, I advanced and demanded of the French officer what were his wishes. He informed me that my sentry was too far in the advance: this caused me to consider what was to be done, as I dared not take him from his post without orders; but on looking about me I perceived, from the beaten path he had made on his daily walk, that the serjeant had not withdrawn him the usual number of paces at daybreak: I rectified this omission, and wished the officer of the French piquet good morning, who politely returned the compliment... I could not help admiring the coolness of my sentry, for, although they threatened, and presented their muskets at him, still he walked backwards and forwards on his post, with as much unconcern as if nothing had been the matter.'[738]

On December 8th the weather cleared, and Wellington ordered his troops out of cantonments and made arrangements to cross the Nive the next day. He had at last received really good news from northern Europe: Napoleon had been defeated at Leipzig and Hanau, Hanover had been restored to the British Crown, and Holland had risen in revolt against the French. The time was now right for a full-scale invasion of south-west France.

The Nive was the last natural obstacle to Wellington's advance into the plains of southern France, and would have to be crossed. If he occupied the ground between the Nive and Adour, Soult would be obliged to leave Bayonne in order to feed his field army. For his part, having at last relented of his faith in fixed defences, Soult intended to attack once Wellington's army was divided by the Nive. He had the advantage of operating on interior lines as he held the bridges of Bayonne, while British, their army divided by the Nive, would depend on pontoons. For Wellington it was undoubtedly a risk, but one he knew he must take to give scope for future manoeuvre.

The overall plan for 9th December was that Hill and Beresford with five Allied divisions should cross the Nive by fords at Ustaritz and Cambo and construct pontoon bridges, while Hope demonstrated in force towards the French entrenched camp in front of Bayonne, and the 4th and 7th Divisions came forward from their cantonments to take over positions at Arrauntz and Urdains respectively. The operation was successful at every point.

Sir John Hope's wing of the army advanced at 3 a.m. on a wet December morning astride the high road to Bayonne, running atop a minor watershed between the Nive and the sea. His objectives were to distract Soult's attention from the Nive crossing operation and to make an armed reconnaissance of the outworks of Bayonne and of the Adour estuary.

Dawn broke, and the rain ceased as the column reached the plateau of Barouillet. Then, the 1st Division moved slowly up the main road towards the village of Anglet, beyond which lay the entrenched camp of Beyris, while the 5th Division swept along the coast to their left towards the seaside village of Biarritz, both divisions covered by lines of skirmishers. Robinson's brigade, which led the 5th Division column, was headed by the 59th under Major Hoystead. After their terrible losses at Vitoria and San Sebastian, the 59th entered the field just 290 strong.

'At eight o'clock the first shot was fired; and immediately the whole line of light troops commenced a most spirited fire on those of the enemy, who tenaciously contested every hedge and bank that afforded shelter from our fire, and from whence they could take deliberate aim at our men. The artillery posted themselves on the eminences along the whole line, and by a fire of shells greatly aided in dislodging the French tirailleurs from behind the hedges and banks. The whole line made gradual progress in advance, the enemy not venturing to risk

---

[737] Harley, p.p. 286-87.
[738] Wood, p.p. 220-21.

the approach of the allied columns, but retreating before them to Anglet. At one o'clock in the afternoon, the First Division gained the heights on the right of the Bayonne road, opposite to Anglet, the light infantry driving the enemy down the slopes to the intrenched camp. The Fifth Division had made equal progress on the left, sweeping the whole country between Anglet and the sea, as far as the banks of the Adour, and occupying with its light infantry the Bois de Bayonne, a large pine-wood which covers the whole space on the left of the Adour between the intrenched camp and the sea.'[739]

French resistance in the village of Anglet called for something more than skirmishers. The 59th came forward in column, cheered, and charged, driving the enemy from the village and pursuing them right up to their batteries and the fortified camp of Beyris.

By 3 or 4 p.m., the left wing, having attained all its objectives, was halted on rising ground some three miles from the walls of Bayonne. The rain fell again, very heavily. Wellington rode up to make a personal reconnaissance, while the troops piled arms and, with difficulty, lit fires for a well-earned brew. At 6 p.m., as planned, Hope pulled his troops back to their cantonments, the 5th Division providing the rearguard. The 59th had suffered six rank and file killed that day, with seven officers[740], a sergeant, two drummers and 27 rank and file wounded, and two men missing.

The march back, in the dark and under torrential rain, was an exhausting trial at the end of a long day: 'On again entering the main road, it was found that the passage of the artillery, and the advance of so many troops along it, had so completely broken it up, and it was besides so deluged with rain that, in some of the hollow-ways, it was knee deep in mud.'[741] The 5th Division returned after midnight to Bidart, leaving only a line of pickets, considerably advanced, supported by Campbell's Portuguese brigade on the plateau at Barrouillet.

That night, Soult seized the anticipated opportunity and, concentrating eight divisions on the west bank of the Nive, launched a two-pronged attack with almost his entire strength against the Allied left wing between the river and the coast. His main initial thrust was by Clausel with three divisions, through Bassussarry towards Arcangues, which was to be followed by D'Erlon with a further four divisions. This attack was launched at 9 a.m., and half an hour later Reille made a subsidiary attack with the divisions of Boyer and Daricau, some twelve thousand men, up the main road to Barrouillet. This second attack caught the pickets by surprise and showed more promise, so two more divisions, those of Foy and Villatte, were added in the course of the day. The pickets lost some two hundred prisoners and were forced back on Campbell's Portuguese, drawn up astride the highroad. These in turn suffered at the hands of French dragoons and fell back to Barrouillet, where they defended themselves around the chateau (better known as the Mayor's House[742]) until reinforced.

Since this area became the centre of two days' desperate fighting, it is as well to describe it now. The Mayor's House stood to the right of the highroad at the eastern end of the Barouillet plateau, at a point where the long straight road from Bayonne, some five miles away, bent half-right towards Bidart and St.-Jean-de-Luz. Looking down the road from there towards Bayonne, there was a thick coppice-wood on the right, separated from the Mayor's House by a large field and an orchard. Beyond this, the ground was very close and broken, with woods, cottages and orchards offering covered approaches to right of the British line. To the left of the road manoeuvre was limited by Lake Moriscot and extensive marshes. Further east, the Barouillet plateau was more open.

Hope was undoubtedly badly deployed to meet a major sortie, with the 1st Division some ten miles away at St.-Jean-de-Luz, and he was slow to bring reinforcements forward, but the 5th Division, still under-strength after its terrible losses at San Sebastian, was nearer, with its 1st Brigade, now under Colonel Greville, at Guéthary, and the 2nd Brigade at Bidart. These rushed up, and the first to arrive was Robinson's 2nd Brigade, as described in its commander's diary:

[739] Batty, p.p. 84-5.
[740] Lieutenants John Boyle Brohier, Archibald Campbell (Acting Adjutant), Lewis Carmichael, Patterson O'Hara and Samuel Stuart (or Stewart), and Ensign William Henry Hill were severely wounded, and Captain Francis Fuller was slightly wounded.
[741] Batty, p. 86.
[742] This was the country house of the Mayor of Biarritz. It still exists, hidden behind high walls and hedges next to the A-63 Motorway Junction 4 toll station.

'Lieutenant Harry Jones of the Engineers came into my room, and informed me that there was a good deal of firing in front. I immediately ordered my horse and gave orders for the Horse Artillery and the Brigade to be in readiness to move at a moment's notice. I found that Williams'[743] Caçadores and the pickets of the Light Division were warmly engaged. The 16th Portuguese were sent to reinforce the former, the 2nd Brigade was ordered to the front with the Horse Artillery.

'In a few moments several strong columns of the enemy were perceived on the line of hills opposite. Their sharpshooters having driven in Williams' corps, occupied their ground. A heavy column formed in the high road and about 2,000 sharpshooters attacked the picquets of the 2nd Brigade, which consisted of just as many hundreds. The two Portuguese regiments actually ran away, nor could the Brigadier General or myself stop a man of them. My brigade, consisting of the 4th, 59th and 84th Regiments (the 47th, being a skeleton, were removed from the brigade), took their place.

'Sir John Hope put me in command of all the troops then arrived, while he went to the right. The sharpshooters advanced very near to our pickets and kept up an incessant fire for about 3 hours. Some cavalry got among our people and made a few prisoners. The enemy made frequent attempts to break through the brigade, but were each time repulsed with the bayonet and with great slaughter. In the afternoon the 2nd Brigade was relieved by the First, with the credit of having maintained their post to the last. Their conduct justly drew forth the praises of Lord Wellington and all his staff.'

Confused fighting continued all day around the Mayor's House, much of it at close quarters with frequent use of the bayonet. The attacks came in mostly astride the Bayonne road and from the close country on the right. General Robinson was seriously wounded, as was Major Frederick Hoystead of the 59th, and Captain William Wilkinson, his successor in command. At about 2 p.m. the 59th, having suffered severely, was relieved by the 38th, and by the time the whole 2nd Brigade was relieved it had suffered 225 casualties, including 74 of the 59th, of whom six rank and file were killed, two officers, four sergeants and 52 rank and file were wounded, and ten rank and file were missing. Private William Creighton was noted for his distinguished conduct when he rescued his officer from capture, killing the French dragoon who was taking him away.

The 1st Brigade (3rd/1st, 1st/9th, 1st/38th and 2nd/47th) bore the brunt of the fight in the early afternoon. The 47th appear to have been very roughly handled at some point, for Lieutenant Randolph Macdonnell, a sergeant and 49 men, were captured, and Sir John Hope entered the thick of the fight to rally them:

'Seeing the 47th Regiment yield to the pressure of a considerable body of the enemy near the Mayor's House, he flew into the hottest of the fire, & with his hat in his hand cheered the men, led them back to the front, & by his own personal courage & efforts at this important moment, preserved to the British the town of Bidart.'[744]

It was easy for men to become cut off and surrounded in the close country, and Private Adam Reed mentions an incident which accounts for some of the regimental loss: 'About the middle of the day the light companies were sent out as skirmishing parties, and the enemy advanced and took a great many of them prisoners, and among them my brother [Daniel] was.' On another occasion, though, the 47th are mentioned in General Hay's report as having assisted the 3rd Portuguese in a 'fine charge' on the Bayonne road. The losses of this under-strength battalion were heavy, for in addition to the 51 captured they suffered twelve men killed that afternoon, while Lieutenant Anthony Mahon, Ensign James Ewing, five sergeants and 45 rank and file were wounded.

The 5th Division was greatly outnumbered, short of ammunition, and almost surrounded. Around the Mayor's House, the 2nd Brigade was in particular danger as the line to the right of it had given way under a flanking attack by Foy's division from Bassussary. Indeed, Boyer's division at one point surged right up to the loopholed walls of the mansion and took some of the outbuildings, prompting a French officer to later compare the situation to that at Hougoumont. The Mayor's House was never captured, but its defenders were hard-pressed when relieved towards 3 p.m. by the tardy arrival of Aylmer's brigade, followed by the 1st Division from St.-Jean-de-Luz. We are fortunate that Lieutenant George Gleig of the 85th Light Infantry, in Aylmer's brigade, left a vivid account of the later stages of the day's action at Barrouillet, starting with his approach to the battle:

---

[743] Brevet Lieutenant-Colonel Edmund Keynton Williams, 81st Regiment, commanding the 4th Caçadores.
[744] *The Napoleonic War Journal of Captain Thomas Henry Browne*, p. 254 (Army Records Society).

'We had not proceeded above a mile, when indications of what was going on in front began to present themselves, in the form of baggage, mules, and horses, pouring in all haste and confusion to the rear; whilst a wounded man or two, from time to time, dragged himself in the same direction, and gave, as the wounded invariably do, the most alarming account of the state of affairs. "Push on, push on, for God's sake," said one poor fellow, who had been shot in the head, and was lying, rather than sitting, across a horse; "push on, or it will all be over. Forty thousand of the enemy are coming on, and there are not two thousand men up to oppose them." Of course, we quickened our pace with infinite good will. A group of perhaps twenty wounded privates and officers had passed, when the next body which met us was a detachment of ten sound men and a sergeant, who were conducting to the rear about an hundred French prisoners. These were saluted with a cheer, but even these urged us forward, with the intelligence that the Fifth Division must soon be overpowered.

'And now the scene of action began to open upon us. We had passed through Bidart, and were descending the little eminence on which it is built, when the combatants became distinguishable; and a very magnificent and gratifying spectacle they presented. The merest handful of British troops were opposing themselves, in the most determined manner, to a mass of men so dense and so extended as to cover the whole of the main road as far as the eye could reach. Our people were, it is true, giving way. They had already maintained an unequal contest for upwards of two [four] hours; and their numbers, originally small, were fast diminishing. But no sooner had the head of our column shown itself, than their confidence returned, and they renewed the struggle with increased alacrity.'[745]

The French responded to the arrival of British reinforcements by bringing forward artillery. Close combat then continued, in particular in the wood on the right, but by 3 p.m. the enemy efforts slackened, and Soult's exhausted divisions rolled back a mile down the road. The pause did not last: suddenly a mass of French infantry erupted from a hollow way to the left and dashed rapidly forward to surround the Mayor's House. Sir John Hope had to fight his way out, and the attackers penetrated to the reserve position held by the 59th. A general charge drove them back, with the loss of many prisoners, but the fight continued in the wood and on the road with renewed desperation until darkness compelled the fighters to separate.

'So vigorous had been the last attack, and so determined our resistance, that when daylight disappeared, the French and allied troops found themselves completely mixed together. Instead of the roar of musketry, my ears were accordingly saluted by shouts and exclamations delivered in almost every European tongue: French, English, Germans, Dutch, Spaniards, Portuguese – the natives, in short, of almost every kingdom – were here; and as each called out in his own language, as loud as he could bawl, for the purpose of discovering his comrades, and giving evidence of his own situation… So complete, indeed, was the confusion that neither the one party nor the other made the slightest attempt to avail themselves of it for military purposes; on the contrary, we were each of us heartily glad to get rid of our troublesome neighbours, and not a little pleased when order became so far restored as to permit our taking up a definite position for the night.'[746]

That night three complete battalions of Kruse's German brigade came over from the French, to be greeted in the British lines with cheers. These were men who had fought the 40th at Talavera and the 82nd at Vitoria, and their defection from Napoleon's army was a result of Leipzig. Eighteen months later, Kruse and many of his men fought for the Allies at Waterloo.

The two armies parted but remained in close proximity. George Gleig was struck by the scene:

'I do not recollect to have witnessed, during the whole course of my military career, a warlike spectacle more striking than that which was now before me. Besides my own corps, three battalions of infantry lay stretched in a single green field round their watch-fires, amounting, in all, to about a hundred. Immediately behind them stood their arms, piled up in regular order, and glancing in the flames, which threw a dark red light across the common, and upon the bare branches beyond. About twenty yards in rear, two regiments of cavalry were similarly disposed of, their horses being picqueted in line, and the men seated or lying on the ground. Looking further back again, and towards the opposite side of the road, the fires of the whole of the Fifth and First Divisions met the eye, darkened, ever and anon, as the soldiers passed between them, or a heap of wood was cast on to feed their

---

[745] *The Subaltern*, George R. Gleig, p.p. 127-28.
[746] Ibid., p.p. 130-31.

brightness. By the light of these fires, I could further perceive that the road itself was thronged with artillery and tumbrils; whilst the glaring atmosphere above the wood showed that it, too, was fully tenanted, and that its occupants were, like ourselves, reposing in an attitude of watchfulness.

'To complete the picture, the night chanced to be uncommonly dark. Neither moon nor stars were out; and though no rain fell, a considerable fog was in the air, which hindered the flames from rising beyond a certain height, and caused them to shed a stronger colouring upon the surrounding objects.'[747]

It was still perfectly dark in the freezing early hours of 11th December when the troops stood silently to their arms, ready to renew the battle.

'On the morning of the 11th, at dawn, the light troops of the Fifth Division drove in the enemy's picquets, and the most advanced sentries were again pushed forward to their old line, The rain had fallen the greater part of the preceding day, and the troops began to experience the harassing effects of being constantly on the alert, upon ground which was soon trampled into mud. Nothing material happened during the forenoon; the men receiving their rations, and parties were sent out unarmed to cut wood for cooking. The weather brightened, and all was tranquil on the outposts.

'About two o'clock, however, some stir was visible in the enemy's line, and in some places the French were seen cutting gaps in the fences for the passage of their artillery; a few moments after, they commenced a furious attack along the great Bayonne road, driving in the picquets upon their supports. The hill in front of Barouillet again became the scene of a hard contest. There was a general shout of "to arms" the moment this attack commenced; and the soldiers who had gone in front of Barouillet to cut wood ran back in all haste to get themselves armed and accoutred. The French, seeing a number of men running to the rear, imagined that the Allies had taken a panic, and set up loud cheers of "*En avant, en avant!*" In a few moments, however, the whole left wing was formed in perfect order.'[748]

Reille now attacked with five divisions, over twenty-five thousand men. The fighting was again most severe. That afternoon, the 59th, a much-diminished little band, were again to the fore, drawn up with their right on the Bayonne road and their left a little advanced so as to throw its fire onto the road. Shortly afterwards, the enemy discontinued their attack, but only to launch a final assault on the depleted ranks of the 5th Division:

'This corps was not only weak in point of numbers, but was absolutely worn out with hard fighting and want of food. It gave way almost immediately. Again the French were upon us; again we were hotly engaged, and, as it appeared to me, with a still denser and more numerous division than any which had yet attacked us. The wood and the Mayor's House were now both of them carried – the French came on with loud shouts and great courage – our Portuguese allies fairly fled the field – one or two British regiments were overwhelmed – and even we, whose ranks had hitherto been preserved, began to waver, when Lord Wellington himself rode up. The effect was electrical. "You must keep your ground, my lads," cried he, "there is nothing behind you. Charge! Charge!"

'Instantly a shout was raised. Many fugitives, who had lost their own corps, threw themselves into line upon our flank. We poured in but one volley, and then rushed on with the bayonet. The enemy would not stand it; their ranks were broken, and they fled in utter confusion. We followed, without giving them a moment to recover from their panic; and having suffered hardly any loss in killed or wounded, we once more took possession of the chateau and the thicket. This was the last effort on either side.'[749]

That evening, as soon as it was dark enough to cover movement, the 1st Division relieved the battered 5th, which went into reserve. In three day's fighting at Anglet and around the Mayor's House, Robinson's brigade had suffered 592 casualties, including 54 killed in action. On that third day of intensive fighting, the 59th suffered a further 61 casualties: seven rank and file were killed, two officers[750], three sergeants and 47 rank and file were wounded, and three rank and file were missing. The 47th had only three men wounded that day.

Meanwhile, on the morning of the 10th Clausel had pushed back the Light Division outpost line at Bassussary, but then made a feeble infantry attack on Arcangues, where the Allies were strongly posted in the

---

[747] Gleig, p. 131-32.
[748] Batty, p.p. 90-91.
[749] Gleig, p.p. 139-40.
[750] Captain Francis Fuller was again wounded, this time severely, and Lieutenant Aeneus McIntosh Macpherson was also severely wounded. His tunic, with a bullet hole in the left breast, is displayed in the Lancashire Infantry Museum.

church and chateau with both flanks anchored on ravines. By 1 p.m., when the 4th Division came up in support, 600 yards behind Arcangues, Hope's right wing was secure. Clausel did not press his attack and, having seen the British 3rd and 6th Divisions re-crossing the Nive, he called off his advance at 3 p.m., content to fortify his position at Bassussary.

After a final flurry of fire on 12th November, which prompted Wellington to move the 7th Division forward from Ste. Barbe Hill, near Arrauntz, to Arbonne, ready to support either Arcangues or Barouillet, the French drew back to Bayonne, and the fighting at Barrouillet ceased. The four days of combat had cost each side about 2,500 casualties, but the highest honours were earned by the 5th Division for their tenacious defence against great odds. On 13th December, Frederick Robinson wrote again to General Ross, Colonel of the 59th:

'You will find some difficulty in giving credit to my assertion that the 59th have outdone their exploits of Vittoria and St. Sebastian, yet nothing can be more true, not merely in my opinion but in that of Lord Wellington as well as Sir John Hope, who were spectators of the conduct of the Brigade during three days' hard fighting.

'Early on the morning of the 9th his Lordship made a grand movement on his right by crossing the Nive with Sir Rowland Hill's corps and the 3rd and 6th Divisions. The left column was ordered to advance for a grand reconnaissance near to the enemy's works in front of Bayonne, and probably to favour the movement of the right.

'As the column advanced, left in front, the 2nd Brigade led, and drove the enemy from every position for about 4 miles, till they made a stand in front of the village of Anglet, which was the principal object of the day. The 59th led the brigade, in column, and with a shout drove them not [only] entirely through the village but even to the batteries that protected the front lines of Bayonne. In doing this the 59th lost what you will see in the returns.

'Early on the 10th, Soult returned our visit with his whole disposable force on this side of the Nive; and as our column had returned the night before to its original cantonments, there was nothing to oppose him but a Portuguese brigade with two 6-pounders and a squadron of the 16th Light Dragoons. The Portuguese, most unfortunately, gave way almost immediately, and the 2nd Brigade took their places, which they maintained for 4 hours under the heaviest fire of grape and musketry almost ever heard, with repeated charges to break us. The latter were always repulsed with the bayonet. At length (without yielding a foot of ground, although not less than 10,000 men were in our front and a swarm of sharpshooters were within 20 yards) we resigned our post when regularly relieved by the 1st Brigade, and, the rest of the column coming up late in the day, after excessive hard fighting the enemy were driven back. I can say little of what passed after we were relieved, in consequence of having received a wound in my side which compelled me to leave the field.

'On the 12th [11th] the action was renewed; but I can relate no more than that the enemy was repulsed by the 5th Division and the Portuguese. The Guards were not called into action, but last night they were in the front line.

'You will see by the return herewith enclosed how severe the loss of the 59th has been in officers; I wish I could do justice to their merits, but their praise is in better hands. Lord Wellington and Sir John Hope witnessed their conduct from the first, and were lavish in their encomiums upon their obstinate valour; it certainly never was surpassed, for as they could not get at the enemy except when they attempted to force through us, the whole action was against artillery and sharpshooters until every round was expended of a first, and almost a second supply, and the men nearly exhausted with fatigue and want of food.

'This conduct gives me the opportunity of recommending to your notice, in the most particular manner, Major Hoystead, who, after showing an example of activity as well as bravery equal to any performance of his younger days,[751] received a wound which has deprived me and his Regiment of his able assistance.

'Lieutenant Archibald Campbell of the Grenadiers, for whom I have long been most keenly interested, is also among the wounded, and is but lately recovered from a wound he received on the breach of St Sebastian, where he remained cheering his men until the town was fairly in our possession. He has been Acting Adjutant for some time, and has exhibited abilities in that situation equal to his spirit in the field, which is in the true style of

---

[751] Major Frederick William Hoystead was aged 54 at the Nive, and as a young subaltern he had served with the 64th Foot in the American war, a circumstance which would have recommended him to Robinson, whose family were leading Virginian Loyalists.

a British Grenadier. I think this young man so deserving of promotion that I wish to exert all the interest I am master of to that end.'[752]

'The Regiment had only 290 men in action, out of which 159 were killed or wounded. The Brigade, and indeed the whole Division, remained on the field the night of the 11th, and are at the moment facing the enemy.'

Whilst the 47th and 59th fought with such desperation at Barouillet, the 40th and 82nd were moved up with their respective divisions in support of the Light Division, where their very visible presence thwarted Soult's plans. Although not engaged, they were much harassed and frustrated with arduous marches and constant alerts.

'We were ordered to deploy on our right,' recalled George Wood, 'in order to counteract a movement of the French troops which threatened this point: this manoeuvre was quickly performed, and the enemy seeing their designs frustrated, did not come on to the attack; but, as the evening was now wearing to a close, they drew off their forces, leaving us, as usual, masters of the field.

'After being on the alert the whole night and day, we piled our arms, and lighted fires on the ground where we stood; this was most dreadful campaigning – lying out in the open fields in this cold and wintry weather, without any covering but our blankets or cloaks. In this bleak situation we remained, wishing most heartily for morning, preferring a contest with the enemy to perishing in the cold and damp of the night. Daylight at length came, and we waited the whole of the day, expecting the French every moment to attack us again; but they thought better of it, so we lighted our fires, and set ourselves to work, broiling our rations on the wood-ashes, having no baggage or cooking utensils with us. At night we again cringed together round the fires: some fell asleep, some were telling stories to drown care, but most were grumbling and swearing, till a thick and drenching misty rain coming on, pretty well quieted us, and made us huddle more closely together, waiting in silent and sullen expectation the approach of light.'

'I fell fast asleep, with my feet close to the fire for warmth. I was awakened by the heat, and to my sorrow, on examination, I found I had scorched the soles of my shoes in such a manner that one of them literally fell from the upper leather. In this situation we stood to our arms.[753]

Having failed in his concentrated attack on Wellington's left wing, Soult deftly moved his divisions across the Nive bridges in Bayonne to attack Hill on the east bank of that river. Despite again having a marked numerical superiority, the ensuing Battle of St. Pierre, on 13th December, was another defeat for the French marshal. The 40th, with the 4th Division, crossed the Nive to support Hill, but again saw no action.

For their part in the Battle of the Nive, 41 survivors of the 47th and 37 of the 59th received a clasp to their Military General Service Medals; oddly, so did 27 of the 40th, though the regiment remained in reserve throughout the five-day combat. Gold Medals were presented to Major Richard Chetham of the 47th, to Major Frederick Hoystead and Captain William Wilkinson of the 59th, and to Lieutenant-Colonel Edmund Keynton Williams of the 81st Regiment, commanding the Portuguese 4th Caçadores. The 59th received the Battle Honour 'NIVE' in 1818, but it was not until 1910 that The Loyal North Lancashire Regiment, successor to the 47th, received the same honour.

Soult's bold strategic moves had again failed at the tactical level, and Wellington knew why: 'I will tell you the difference between Soult and me,' he said, 'when he gets into difficulty, his troops don't get him out of it; mine always do.' The British commander had, indeed, ample justification for his confident statement in November 1813 that his veteran army was 'the most complete machine of its numbers now existing in Europe.'

---

[752] Sadly, General Robinson's interest was insufficient to gain promotion for Archibald Campbell, who was Adjutant of the 2nd/59th in the Waterloo campaign and died while serving with the Regiment in India, still a lieutenant, in 1824.
[753] Wood, p.p. 222-23.

The 40th & 82nd
fought in the
Battle of Orthez
27th February 1814

Battle of Toulouse
10th April 1814
The 4th Division, including the
40th, assault the Calvinet Ridge

The 47th defended St. Etienne
against the French sortie from
besieged Bayonne, 14th April
1814, the last engagement of
the Peninsula War

341

The 82nd counter-attack at Fort Erie, Canada, 17th September 1814, during the War of 1812

Major Henry Adolphus Proctor, 82nd, led a 'fine charge' which drove back an American sortie from Fort Erie

Centre of the 82nd Regimental Colour carried 1816-32 showing the 'Niagara' Battle Honour

Fort Mackinac, between Lakes Michigan & Huron, relieved by a party of the 81st Foot,

Officer & Private 82nd Foot

Chapter IX:
1814

Winter Quarters before Bayonne – Crossing the Gaves – Battle of Orthez 27ᵗʰ February 1814 (40ᵗʰ & 82ⁿᵈ) – Liberation of Bordeaux (82ⁿᵈ) – Battle of Toulouse 10ᵗʰ April 1814 (40ᵗʰ) – Sortie from & Capitulation of Bayonne (47ᵗʰ & 59ᵗʰ) – the End in Eastern Spain (81ˢᵗ) – Last Days of the Peninsula Army – Campaign Statistical Summary – the War of 1812 – Siege of Fort Erie 1814 (82ⁿᵈ) – Defence of Canada (81ˢᵗ & 82ⁿᵈ) – 40ᵗʰ in Ireland – Wreck of the Baring & Voyage to America (40ᵗʰ) – Mississippi Excursion & Siege of Fort Bowyer (40ᵗʰ) – 2ⁿᵈ/81ˢᵗ Home Service 1809-14 – 2ⁿᵈ/30ᵗʰ Home Service 1813-14 – Holland 1814 & Investment of Antwerp 1814 (30ᵗʰ & 81ˢᵗ) – 2ⁿᵈ/47ᵗʰ Home Service and Disbandment – Occupation of the Low Countries (30ᵗʰ & 81ˢᵗ)

Winter Quarters

The winter of 1813-14 in south-west France was particularly severe, and for two months after the Battle of the Nive, the poor state of the roads, even for the mules which were the staple of army transport, precluded active military operations. Writing to his wife on 12ᵗʰ February, Private William Windsor of the 59ᵗʰ remarked that 'the weather is so bad we cannot make a movement, but I hope it will clear up, & then we shall be at the French again. The British army is in good spirits.' More reflectively, he added that his battalion, one thousand strong when they left Cadiz, was reduced to 'about 150' despite two drafts from home, and that his own 1ˢᵗ Company had lost 79 men killed and wounded, and many officers. But, he concluded with some pride, 'we are the first for action, as we belong to the Storming Division.'

The 5ᵗʰ Division, including the much depleted 47ᵗʰ and 59ᵗʰ,[754] remained in and about Barrouillet. In addition to taking their turn on outpost duty, they strengthened the fieldworks, constructing a redoubt in front of the Mayor's House, named Fort Charlotte after that worthy's daughter, which occasioned some punning ribaldry. They were relieved on 3ʳᵈ January by the 1ˢᵗ Division and moved to Arcanges, taking over from the Light Division on the Bassussary plateau.

After the Battle of the Nive, the 40ᵗʰ were quartered in the village of Arrauntz near the left bank of that river. From there on 3ʳᵈ January 1814, with less than 450 men fit for duty, they marched down to St.-Jean-de-Luz to receive a most welcome issue of new clothing. 'High time it was too,' thought Sergeant William Lawrence, 'for our old ones were scarcely worth owning as rags and fearfully dirty, the red of them having turned almost to black. I ought to have received a sergeant's suit, but owing probably to the quartermaster's obstinacy I only got a private's, the same sort as I had had before. Here we likewise received a good supply of bread and rum, which seemed to us like a new and even luxurious diet.' The 40ᵗʰ then returned to Arrauntz, but moved almost immediately to nearby Ustaritz, where the Regiment was mustered on the 24ᵗʰ of that month.

The 82ⁿᵈ passed Christmas and the New Year around Cambo, on the left bank of the Nive, from where they supported the forward divisions on the right flank of the army. Inevitably, this reserve role occasioned an inconvenient alarm:

'On Christmas day, just as we were about to make ourselves as jovial as circumstances would permit, and drink a good health to our good friends in Old England, the drum beat to arms. We immediately fell in, and left our roast beef and plum pudding (for we had exerted ourselves much on this occasion to procure so grand a dinner), and again marched to bivouac in the open fields, which we kept for several days, observing the motions of the enemy.'[755]

Lieutenant George Wood was sickening, and in his journal he describes the sad state of his clothing and equipment, last renewed at Lewes some four years earlier:

---

[754] On Christmas Day 1813 the 2ⁿᵈ/47ᵗʰ had only 240 men in the ranks, with 216 in hospital, and the respective numbers for the 2ⁿᵈ/59ᵗʰ were 275 and 355. By 25ᵗʰ February the number of effectives had only risen to 270 for the 47ᵗʰ and 319 for the 59ᵗʰ.

[755] Wood, p. 225.

'It would require the pencil of Hogarth to paint the figure I have cut… My cap, which had served me both for pillow and nightcap, crushed into different forms, my beard somewhat grown, my eyes sunk in, my cheeks quite hollow, my frame diseased and filthy, my countenance woeful, my shoes without a sole, my sword, from having been drawn all day and sheathed in a wet scabbard at night, covered with rust, my belt of a deep brown, my epaulette very blue, my shirt very black, and my coat any colour but red, and in the most wet and miry condition.'[756]

On 3rd January, the 7th Division, with the 82nd, was ordered to Urcuray, on the right bank of the Nive, and by early February they were at nearby Jatxou and Halsou.

The Battle of Orthez, 27th February 1814

In early February, the weather improved and the roads dried, enabling Wellington to resume his offensive, breaking out on a broad front between the Pyrenees and the River Adour. The country was difficult, intersected by a succession of deep and swift streams, known as gaves, which flowed north from the Pyrenees into the Adour. The plan was to force Soult away from Bayonne and back from each river line in succession by turning his left flank. To achieve this, the Allied army was formed into two groups of divisions. Hill commanded the right wing, and Beresford the left, which included the 4th and 7th Divisions with the 40th and 82nd Regiments respectively.

On 12th February the 7th Division advanced to the south bank of the Adour, which they occupied from Lahonce to Urt, covering the left flank of the army as it approached the gaves. On the 14th the 7th Division marched to Briscous, and the 4th Division, with the 40th, crossed the Nive and moved up to the heights of Mouguerre, where two months earlier the final advance of the battle of St. Pierre had taken place. On the 17th the 4th Division advanced some 15 miles east towards Bidache, from where Foy's division had retired on the approach of Cotton's cavalry brigade. Soult pulled his divisions back behind the Gave d'Oloron. On the 20th, the 7th Division moved forward to La Bastide-Clairence on the Joyeuse. There was then a short pause while Wellington attended to the crossing of the Adour below Bayonne (see below).

Early in this campaign, on 24th February 1814, a 'gentleman ranker' was commissioned into the 40th from the 14th Light Dragoons. Charles Robert Cureton had been an officer in the Shropshire Militia, but got into financial difficulties, faked suicide by leaving his clothes on a beach, and enlisted in 1808 as Private Charles Roberts, taking part with the Light Dragoons in the battles of Talavera, Fuentes d'Onoro, Badajoz, Salamanca, Vitoria, Pyrenees, Nivelle and Nive, and was twice severely wounded, before joining the 40th for Orthez and Toulouse. He became a brigadier-general and, having served at Bhurtpore, in Afghanistan, at Maharajpore, and in the Sikh Wars, was regarded as the finest cavalry officer in India when he was killed at Ramnagar in 1848, attempting to halt a fatal charge by his old regiment, the 14th Light Dragoons.

When the advance resumed, the 4th and 7th Divisions moved up to demonstrate against Soult's right wing while Hill passed the Gave d'Oloron to outflank his left. Late on the 23rd Inglis's brigade, with the 82nd, dislodged the enemy from the fortified posts of Œyregave and Hastingues, bridgeheads on the left bank of the Gave de Pau opposite Soult's headquarters at Peyrehorade. Captain Robert Carew, who in 1809 had commanded the 82nd Company at Talavera, was wounded on this occasion, together with two rank and file. Meanwhile, the 4th Division pushed forward to the Gave, a little further upstream, to find crossing places around Sorde-l'Abbaye and Léren.

On the 25th the 40th and 82nd forded both branches of the Gave d'Oleron unopposed. According to Lieutenant James Mill, 'The Regiment passed the one soon after dawn, and the other at half past 6 o'clock, when the entire ground was white with frost, and the water was so intensely cold as almost to deprive me of breath. The stream was up to my hips and up to the middle of the short men, and the breadth of water such that it occupied ten minutes for one man to pass over as quickly as possible.'[757]

On finding that the river lines had been turned, Soult ordered all his divisions to concentrate at Orthez, where he offered battle with some 33,000 infantry, 3,000 cavalry, 1,500 gunners and sappers, and 48 guns. He intended to fight a rearguard action and then, whatever the result, to continue his retirement.

---

[756] Wood, p.p. 223-24.
[757] Letter dated Grenada, near Toulouse, March 1814.

The small town of Orthez lies on the north bank of the Gave de Pau. Soult drew up his army to the north of the river on high ground, which rose to approximately 500 feet, along which ran the road to Dax. This road ascended north by easy gradients from the town of Orthez for one and a half miles to the main ridge, then turned west for another one and a half miles to Point 575, from where a track on the left dipped steeply across a long narrow neck and through the hamlet of St. Boes to its church, which stood on a rounded plateau some eight hundred yards away. The main road turned north again from Point 575 towards Dax. From the main ridge, centred on what Sir John Fortescue described as 'a great round heathery hill,' a number of narrow spurs, separated by deep re-entrants, ran down towards the river over open, rolling country to cultivated or marshy bottoms. On one of these spurs, some six hundred yards from the round hill, stood an ancient entrenchment known as the Roman Camp. Between the high ground and the river, the main road from Orthez, to Peyrehorade and Bayonne ran through Baigts, from where a minor road climbed to just west of St. Boes. From Orthez a third major route departed north-east through Sallespisse for St. Sever and Mont de Marsan.

On the morning of the 27th the French were in position. Reille held the right flank, on the ridge opposite St. Boes, where the church and adjacent houses were defended as a forward position by two battalions of the 12th Légère and by the 15th Chasseurs. Behind them, astride the Dax road, stood Taupin's division, with Paris's brigade in support to its right rear and Rouget's division to its left on the round hill, facing the Roman Camp. D'Erlon's corps prolonged the line to the left, and Clausel held Orthez and the ground to its north-east towards Sallespisse. Along the main ridge three higher knolls, at the Lafaurie, Luc and Plassotte farms, were crowned with artillery.

Beresford, with the 4th and 7th Divisions, had crossed on the 26th to the north bank of the Gave de Pau, near the village of Cauneille and about a mile above its junction with the Gave d'Oleron. He then marched east on the riverside road as far as Baigts, where he halted that night. His advance had enabled the head of Picton's 3rd Division to ford the river before dark, when a pontoon bridge was laid, whereupon the balance of the 3rd Division, followed by the 6th and Light Divisions, also crossed. Hill's corps, meanwhile, moved directly on Orthez.

Early on the morning of the 27th Wellington made a careful reconnaissance of the French line from the Roman Camp. He had available 38,000 infantry, 3,300 cavalry, 1,500 gunners and sappers, and 54 guns. He could see that Soult's position was strong: his left was protected by the town of Orthez, and the approaches to his centre were over difficult ground. The British commander therefore decided to launch his attack on Soult's extreme right to gain the heights around Point 575, above St. Boes, which he regarded as the key to the French position, and turn Soult's flank. Beresford was directed to achieve this with Cole's 4th Division, Walker's 7th Division, Vivian's cavalry brigade and a battery of guns. The 3rd and 6th Divisions were to follow along the great road to Orthez before wheeling north-east to demonstrate against D'Erlon's corps on the heights, not pressing their attack until Beresford had made decided progress at St. Boes. The Light Division (which was without two of its British battalions) was to remain in reserve at the Roman Camp. Meanwhile, Hill's corps was to close on the Gave de Pau at Orthez, cross the river above the town and envelop the French left wing.

Cole led what was intended to be the main and decisive attack with his 4th Division, marching north across a marshy valley from Baigts to climb the spur west of St. Boes, where his advanced guard began to appear between 8 and 9 a.m. Some half an hour later, Robert Ross's Fusilier brigade opened the assault. They drove the 12th Légère and the Chasseurs from around the church with relative ease, and swept on to clear the hamlet of St. Boes,

At about 11 a.m., by which time Walker's 7th Division had come up and taken over the church and the eastern edge of the plateau, Cole advanced to attack Taupin's main position on the Dax road about Point 575. Ross again led, but was checked beyond the hamlet where the open ground narrowed to a neck. Ross's column was swept by Taupin's musketry and by twelve guns on the Plassotte knoll to its front, and by sixteen guns from the Luc knoll on its right flank; then Taupin counter-attacked, covered by skirmishers in the lower ground on either side of the neck, and pushed the Fusiliers back into St. Boes. Vasconcellos's Portuguese brigade of the 4th Division was brought up on the right in support and was in turn supported on its right flank by the 1st Caçadores of the Light Division, sent forward by Wellington, but to no avail. The 4th Division was unable to take the heights, and Taupin could not drive the Allies from St. Boes, which changed hands between three and five times. After some two hours of close fighting, during which Ross fell wounded and 4th Division casualties approached six hundred, the combat on the left came to an impasse, with further action limited to skirmishing.

345

Anson's brigade, with the 40th, had meanwhile moved up at the rear of the 4th Division column and remained there in reserve all morning, hidden in a hollow[758] to the left rear of the St. Boes plateau with strict orders not to show themselves but to maintain this post until relieved by the 7th Division. Only the light companies of the brigade were thrown forward and, according to Charles Crowe of the 27th, 'experienced much sharp skirmishing,' for the French voltigeurs 'made many resolute attempts to force their way along the by-road which crossed the left opening of our hollow position: but our light bobs valiantly kept them back.' This activity was to the left of Ross's action.

Wellington, thwarted in his initial intention of forcing the French line beyond St. Boes, rapidly changed his plan. In his despatch of 1st March, he stated that:

'Marshal Beresford carried the village of St. Boes with the 4th Division under the command of Lieutenant-General L. Cole after an obstinate resistance by the enemy, but the ground was so narrow that the troops could not deploy to attack the heights. Notwithstanding the repeated attempts of Major-General Ross's and Brigadier-General Vasconcellos's Portuguese brigades, it was impossible to turn them by the enemy's right without an excessive extension of our line. I therefore so far altered the plan of the action as to order the immediate advance of the 3rd and 6th Divisions to attack the left of the heights on which the enemy's right stood.'

The new attack appears to have begun at about 11.30 against the French centre, where the holding attack of the 3rd and 6th Divisions was converted into a head-on assault with all available troops. Somewhat later, and further to the left, Wellington saw an opportunity for Colborne's 52nd to advance into a gap between Taupin's and Rouget's divisions. At much the same time the brigades of Ross and Vasconcellos were withdrawn from St. Boes[759] and replaced by fresh troops, Walker's 7th Division and Anson's still uncommitted brigade of the 4th Division, supported by Vivian's cavalry.

Walker's subsequent attack on Taupin was strong and well prepared. As flanking fire of artillery and infantry had been largely responsible for Cole's earlier repulse, the French guns were engaged by two British batteries near the church, while the slopes on both sides of the much-disputed neck were covered by Allied infantry: Doyle's Portuguese brigade on the right and the 3rd Provisional Battalion and Brunswick Oels on the left. The 6th Foot, deployed across the narrow neck beyond St. Boes, led the advance in extended order, followed in succession by the 68th, 82nd and Chasseurs Britanniques of Inglis's brigade in column. These four battalions charged down the road from the village, strewn with dead and wounded Fusiliers and Portuguese, and up the steep slope to make a frontal attack on Taupin's regiments, while Walker's flanking battalions, and the 52nd to their right, turned the French position. Taupin's men, weakened and exhausted from their earlier combat with the 4th Division, fell back behind the Plassotte knoll, where for a time they rallied. The advancing British battalions, having crossed the narrow neck, now had the space to deploy into line and, supported by their guns, closed with the French around Point 575.

Sergeant John Cooper of the 7th Fusiliers paused from his skirmishing around St. Boes to witness this advance: 'Presently on came a long line of red jackets at quick step, a little to our right, and when within eighty or a hundred yards of the enemy, poured a terrible and prolonged fire upon them. This was answered by the French until the combatants were completely enshrouded in smoke. The scattering of the powder cloud showed the British closing on the foe; but they [the French] avoided the shock by going to the right about in great haste.'

From the contemporary account of Lieutenant James Mill of the 40th, it appears that Anson's brigade advanced at this time to the left of the 7th Division, but that his Regiment at least did not have occasion to close with the enemy:

'We only showed ourselves in line, at a critical juncture, and stood a few rounds for some moments to prevent their detaching reinforcements from their station in front of us to a more central one, which had been (twice) attacked by our left brigade unsuccessfully. On the third assault by that brigade [actually Inglis's brigade, 7th Division] the centre was forced and carried. Our Regiment then pressed forward conjointly; and soon

---

[758] This hollow, which Lieutenant Charles Crowe of the 27th described as 'a little ravine between two inequalities of ground', appears to be the prominent re-entrant west of the modern D315 Route de Baigts and some 400 yards from St. Boes church.
[759] According to Colborne, 'We met, at the ridge, Sir Lowry Cole coming back with his division. He was much excited, and said, "Well, Colborne, what's to be done? Here we [4th Division] are coming back as fast as we can." I was rather provoked, and said, "Only have patience and we shall see what's to be done".'

346

afterwards the French were to be espied withdrawing in every direction. Their overthrow for a time was sustained with marked steadiness and resolution; and it is said, the retreat was effected with no material loss and with consummate skill and address. Our Regiment, indeed, did not fire a single shot, and it was only struck by two cannon shots, one of which wounded one man only, and the other killed one man and wounded four.'[760]

Sergeant William Lawrence's account of Orthez is disappointing, giving only a general account of the battle from the perspective of the 4th Division as a whole:

'On nearing Orthes, we found the French had taken up a very strong position on a range of fine heights stretching from Orthes to St. Boes, and we were ordered, in conjunction with the Seventh Division to cross a river and attack the latter place, which had one of the heights occupied by the enemy at the back of it, giving them a commanding view of the place. Some delay was occasioned at the river, for there being no bridge, a pontoon was obliged to be thrown across; but this being accomplished, our divisions were soon over it, and being joined by a brigade of cavalry and artillery, we formed line and marched on St. Boes. The village was stoutly defended by the enemy, who on our nearing them fired briskly at us, for a long time standing their ground and trying hard to retain their charge; but they soon found that they had sharp taskmasters to deal with, for our troops of the Fourth Division under General Cole poured in on them like lions, and forced them after a violent resistance to start out of the place and take refuge on their strong heights.

'We followed them up, but found that there they were for a long time more than a match for us, as they had such an advantage in the ground. We rushed up the formidable heights, but were again and again driven back by the fearful play of the enemy's artillery, the position being only accessible in a few places, and those so narrow that only a small body could move on them at once. But even with these disadvantages and the enemy's cannon playing on them our men, after receiving fresh and strong reinforcements, carried the heights; and not only this, but the whole of the army having been similarly engaged on the right, had meanwhile succeeded in driving the enemy from their lines there, capturing a great number of prisoners in their retreat, the cavalry pursued them closely; and some field-pieces were likewise taken.'[761]

Charles Crowe put the retreat of the French right wing at about 4 p.m. and described the confusion there as Soult attempted to rally his troops and Anson's brigade moved forward:

'The additional fire of our brigade threw consternation into Soult's raw conscripts: they were on the grand road from Orthez opposite our position, and which there passed along a ridge about level of that from which we were watching them. They were wholly terrified, broke from their ranks, but knew not whither to go, then huddled together in an incongruous mass, elevated their muskets and fired a volley at the clouds!! We saw Marshal Soult ride up to them, drop the reins on the neck of his white charger, sword in hand and hat in his left hand, he vehemently exhorted them, for we could plainly see his gestures, although we were too far off to hear his words. He could not prevail; they listened for a short time, but turned tail and bolted off for Peyrehorade on the road to Dax.'

'We were ordered to emerge from our ravine and rapidly follow the retiring foe: which we continued to do, until daylight barely allowed us to take our ground for encampment, beside the road. Our baggage reached us between 8 and 9 in the evening.'[762]

Captain Lapène, commanding Taupin's artillery, recorded the final action on the French right, stating that D'Erlon's corps and Rouget's division had already retired when Taupin, deeply engaged with Walker to his front, found British troops behind him on the Dax road. 'The cry, "We are cut off, the enemy is across the road," began to be heard in our ranks. The regiments, their flank turned, without any hope of safety if they held on to their position and prolonged a useless defence, ended by abandoning the ground they had so gloriously defended for nearly eight hours, and plunged to their right down a deep ravine, the only line of exit still left open.' According to the historian Oman, who walked the ground, this was the hollow way which led down to the farm of La Porte, about one mile to the north-east of the main road on the heights. From there the division went off in disorder across country and joined in the general French rout towards the bridge of Sault de Navailles. Oman supposes that the British troops on the Dax road must have been the 52nd, but in view of the relative positions of the

[760] Mill, letter dated Grenada [Grenade], near Toulouse, March 1814, quoted in *Historical Records of the 40th Regiment*, p. 157.
[761] Lawrence, p.p. 177-78.
[762] Crowe, p. 234.

advancing troops it is rather more likely that the troops between Taupin's division and their preferred line of retreat were Anson's brigade.

Taupin's was the last French division to quit the field. The 7th Division, with Vivian's cavalry on its left flank, followed the routing enemy down the northern slopes of the main ridge so as to turn the final position of Villatte's division on the Biega spur, while at least part of the 4th Division moved after the 3rd along the Dax-Orthez road against Darmagnac's final position astride the Sallespisse road.

French losses at Orthez amounted to slightly over four thousand men and six guns, of whom over six hundred men and two guns were lost around St. Boes. In the days that followed there were many deserters. The Allies sustained losses of 2,174 killed, wounded and missing, including 1,645 British.

The 82nd suffered the loss of their veteran commander, Lieutenant Colonel Charles Edward Conyers, and Lieutenant John McGregor Drummond, both severely wounded,[763] two men killed and 34 rank and file wounded. Anson's brigade, as we have noted, was barely engaged, and of their 25 casualties the 40th suffered just one man killed[764] and four wounded.

The victorious Allied army bivouacked on the heights above Sallespisse, too tired to pitch their tents when they arrived, despite a frost. Early on the 28th the 40th marched with the centre column on the great road to St. Sever, and the 82nd moved with the left column by Amou and St. Cricq, from where next day they moved on Mont-de-Marsan to seize the French magazines at that place.

Having beaten Soult again in the combat of Aire, 2nd March, Wellington halted for twelve days to rest his troops, to send Beresford on the expedition described below, and to bring up reinforcements from Spain. The 4th Division established its headquarters at Aire for several days, during which time the 40th found quarters in the surrounding farmhouses.

In 1824 both the 40th and the 82nd received the Battle Honour 'ORTHES,' while 83 survivors of the 40th and 87 of the 82nd received an 'Orthes' clasp to their Military General Service Medals. Lieutenant-Colonels Thornton and Conyers, and Major Vincent, who had again assumed command of the 82nd when Conyers was wounded early in the action, received clasps to their Gold Medals.

The Liberation of Bordeaux

On withdrawal from Orthez, Marshal Soult had to choose between defending Bordeaux or Toulouse. He selected the latter, hoping for support from Marshal Suchet in Catalonia, leaving Bordeaux uncovered. On 7th March, Wellington ordered Marshal Beresford to march on Bordeaux from Mont-de-Marsan with the 7th Division, having received assurances that the city was ready to raise the white royalist banner. He was to be followed by the 4th Division from St. Sever, one march behind. As he neared the city, Beresford learned that there would be no opposition, and so he halted the 4th Division at Langon and went on with the 7th Division alone. The 40th, having marched to Monte Marson on the 8th, Roquefort on the 9th and Captieux on the 10th, were quartered at Bazas until 13th March, when the 4th Division was ordered to march to Tarbes and rejoin the main army.

Reaching Bordeaux on March 12th, Beresford was met by Mayor Jean-Baptiste Lynch, a gentleman of Irish extraction who was the main instigator of the royalist insurrection, and a crowd of thousands welcomed the British, casting off Imperial insignia and donning the Royalist white cockade.

The men of the 7th Division at once enjoyed and reciprocated the liberated city's welcome: 'Their excellent conduct,' Dalhousie reported to Wellington, 'astonishes the city and even myself. I assure your Lordship that I am not merely paying them compliments when I say so.' These first impressions were the start of truly excellent relations, marked on the French side by great hospitality, which lasted until the troops embarked.

George Wood, now a captain and convalescent after falling ill before Bayonne, rejoined the 82nd at Langon, from where they marched to Bordeaux and went into quarters:

---

[763] Both officers recovered to serve again. Conyers commanded the 82nd 1815-23, while Lieutenant Drummond retired as a captain in 1823.

[764] This is confirmed by the Weekly State of the 4th Division dated St. Maurice 1st March 1814, which shows one of the 40th Regiment rank and file dead in the previous week.

'We remained some time in this gay town, which was indeed a different scene to what we had been accustomed. Here were amusements of every kind to be met with: elegant theatres, operas, assemblies, fine public walks, and parks adorned with beautiful females of exquisite symmetry, promenading with the most graceful deportment. To an agreeable and fascinating air, they joined great vivacity, piercing sparkling eyes, and much animation of countenance; in fact, most of them are charming pretty women.'[765]

The Battle of Toulouse, 10th April 2014

After a forced march from Bazas in appalling weather, the 40th rejoined Wellington's force at Plaisance, on the road to Tarbes, on 19th March. There had been little action in their absence; for following Orthez, the main army was much reduced in numbers, with divisions detached to Bayonne and Bordeaux. Wellington had called for his heavy cavalry, who had been left to winter in Navarre, and additional Spanish troops, and by the time the 40th arrived the Allies were reinforced and resuming their advance.

The 4th Division was now with a force under Marshal Beresford which was to make a turning movement against Soult's right flank, cutting off his withdrawal from Tarbes to Toulouse. However, after an inconclusive combat with Hill at Tarbes, on the 20th, Soult slipped away at night and made an impressive forced march to reach Toulouse well ahead of the Allies on the 24th. The 4th Division led Wellington's column in pursuit, marching over poor, water-logged roads by way of Castelnau, Lombes and l'Isle-Jourdain to regain contact with the French outposts near Toulouse on the 26th.

Standing on the right, or eastern, bank of the Garonne, the capital city of Languedoc could not practicably be attacked from the west. The western approaches to the city were protected by two lines of fortifications and by the wide river, which was crossed from the transpontine suburb of St. Cyprien by just one bridge, the Pont Neuf. The northern and eastern approaches, on the far side of the Garonne, were encircled by 12th century brick walls, with a more impressive outer line of defence provided by the Canal du Midi, some hundred yards wide and crossed by six bridges. The weakest point of the defences lay to the east of that canal, where the Calvinet Ridge, three miles long, otherwise known as Mont Rave, rose to a dominating 250 to 300 feet before falling away to the swampy valley of the River Hers.

It was very apparent that once Allied artillery was placed on the Calvinet Ridge, Toulouse was indefensible. Accordingly, Soult fortified the heights with five redoubts, from the Great Redoubt in the north to La Sypière towards the southern end of the ridge, all linked by earthworks, with fortified houses and further entrenchments on the reverse slope, behind which the canal bridges were strongly fortified and backed by guns on the bastions of the old city wall.

This presented a difficult tactical problem, for to approach Toulouse from the north, south or east, Wellington had first to cross the Garonne using his train of tin pontoons, which had been carried up from the coast with great labour. On 27th March, the 4th, 6th and Light Divisions made a demonstration in front of the western St. Cyprien bridgehead while an attempt to span the Garonne was made upstream at Portet, five miles south of Toulouse. The crossing failed as there were insufficient pontoons to span the rain-swollen river, and another attempt, at Pinsaguel, was thwarted on the 30th when Hill, having got 13,000 men across the Garonne, discovered that they had to cross another river, the Arriège, but had no more pontoons. The 4th Division was warned on the 31st for another feint attack on the works in front of St. Cyprien, but the anticipated 'broken head fair' was cancelled when Hill's crossing failed.

Anson's brigade of the 4th Division was encamped at this time near the village of Colomiers on the l'Isle-Jourdain road[766], with a clear view of St. Cyprien and the adjacent Garonne bridge. The advanced pickets facing the French lines were found from the light companies of the brigade and then the regiments in daily rotation.

The pontoon bridge was again taken up and, on the night of April 3rd, escorted by the 4th Division, was moved laboriously along byways west of Toulouse to make a crossing some eleven miles north of the city. The

---

[765] Wood, p.p. 234-35.

[766] When mustered at Colomiers on 1st April 1814 the 40th numbered 34 officers, 41 sergeants, 15 drummers and 487 rank and file, with one sergeant, one drummer and eleven rank and file present sick. A further 262 sick and wounded, including twelve sergeants and five drummers, were absent sick, most of whom would be in general hospitals.

pontoons were laid in four hours, and at about 9 a.m. next day Anson's brigade of the 4th Division led the way across the Garonne, their fifes and drums playing *The Grenadiers' March*, followed by the 3rd and 6th Divisions. By dusk some 19,000 men, commanded by Beresford, were across the river.

That afternoon, it poured with rain, the river swelled, and soon after dark, the pontoon moorings gave way. Most of the pontoons were drawn back with difficulty to the west bank, though one was swept away downstream. The state of the river was such that it proved impossible to re-lay the bridge until the morning of the 7th, and meanwhile, the Allied army remained divided, and those on the far side of the Garonne were without their tents and baggage. Anson's brigade was crammed into some 'miserable hovels.' The three isolated divisions occupied a strong position, supported by artillery on the far bank of the river, and confidently hoped to be attacked; but Soult did not oblige, remaining within his fortified lines. Lieutenant James Mill was with the 40th:

'We crossed the Garonne at two leagues below Toulouse on the 4th, continuing for several days inactive in the vicinity of the town on account of the heavy rains and swollen rivers, which made it incumbent, after a part of the army had crossed, to take up the bridges.'

The Allies advanced south around midday on the 8th, closing up to the outer defences of Toulouse. Soult's chasseurs à cheval fell back before them, breaking the bridges over the River Ers as they passed, until they reached the Pont de Croix Daurade. This too had been prepared for demolition, but the defending 5th and 22nd Chasseurs à Cheval were surprised at about 6 p.m. by Brigadier-General Vivian with the 18th Light Dragoons, who charged and broke the 22nd with the loss of 120 prisoners, and chased them across the bridge despite flanking fire from dismounted men of the 5th Chasseurs across the river. The Grenadier Company of the 40th also took part in this combat, as described by James Mill:

'On 8th April (Good Friday) [actually 9th April] I was present with the Grenadier Company in supporting the attack on the bridge of Croix d'Orade. [Captain John] Barnett commands the grenadiers, [Lieutenant James] Butler and myself are his subalterns. We were despatched down to the water-side, and lined the banks of the stream, from which position we maintained a sharp fusillade and check on the enemy, which consisted both of mixed infantry and cavalry. Indeed, the combat of the bridge commenced by, and was principally an affair of, cavalry; they fought for a time as skirmishers, mounted and otherwise; but when they were relieved by the infantry of this duty, several charges took place upon and beyond the bridge and among the scattered houses of the hamlet, all resulting in complete success to our people and the troopers, who captured many prisoners, and ultimately the object of contest became indisputably our own.'[767]

Sergeant William Lawrence was also with Barnett's Grenadier Company and told his own story of the fight at the bridge of Croix Daurade, suggesting a carefully laid plan to entice the French cavalry:

'We annoyed [the French cavalry] very considerably by our fire as we approached them, having in case of their making an attack on us a fine artificial ditch to fall back into, where it was next to impossible that they could get at us; our fire was made more daring by our knowing there was a body of hussars waiting out of their sight, ready to fall on them if they moved on us. We soon enticed out a body of about three hundred, who crossed the bridge under our retreating and destructive fire, and on their near approach we fell into our ditch, while at the same time our cavalry came up, and some close shaving ensued, a large quantity of spare heads, arms, legs, as well as many horses being soon strewn about the ground.'[768]

That night the light companies of Anson's brigade held the captured bridge, which they barricaded with carts and hurdles. Easter Sunday, 10th April, dawned fine but windy, and at about 8 a.m., or possibly a little earlier, the rest of the 4th Division moved up to the Croix Daurade bridge.[769] The light companies then rushed forward and drove a French picket from a walled country house (probably the Chateau de Nicol) at the foot of the heights on which stood the Great Redoubt.

Having seized a crossing over the Ers, Wellington issued his battle orders. Hill was to make a demonstration on the west bank in front of St. Cyprien, and Picton's 3rd and Alten's Light Divisions were similarly to make feint attacks along the northern front of the Canal du Midi. These diversions were to detain the maximum

---

[767] Mill's letter quoted in *Historical Records of the 40th Regiment*, p.p. 157-59.
[768] Lawrence, p. 179.
[769] The 40th Regiment entered the Battle of Toulouse with an effective strength of 34 officers, 41 sergeants, 15 drummers and 487 rank and file (Weekly State of the 4th Division dated Saint-Jory, April 8th 1814).

number of French troops while the real attack was made on the Calvinet Ridge by four divisions. General Freire, with two Spanish divisions, was to take the northern end of the heights, including the Great Redoubt. Beresford, with the 4th and 6th Divisions, was to march south from the village of Croix Daurade along the low ground of the Ers valley with the Calvinet Ridge to their right and the river to their left. They were then to turn to their right in two lines and assault the right of the French position on the heights. Their left was to be covered by Somerset's Hussar brigade. Beresford was given considerable discretion as to his point of attack, and Freire was to commence his assault when he saw Beresford turn to ascend the south-eastern slopes.

The northern end of the Calvinet Ridge was held by Villatte's division, and the rest of the long range by Harispe's division, while Taupin's division provided a mobile reserve, waiting in column behind the ridge, with a strong body of cavalry to the south.

Beresford's column set off on its long flank march, with the 4th Division in the lead, its three brigades moving abreast in open column. Anson's brigade was on the right, nearest to the enemy-held ridge. When the column had passed to the rear of Anson's light companies, the latter broke off the skirmishing in which they were engaged and hurried after their regiments.

The advance was very slow as there was no road across the rain-sodden ploughed fields beside the Ers, for the only tracks led down from the Calvinet Ridge to demolished bridges. The morass was so boggy that the horses of mounted officers had to be led, and the divisional artillery batteries found the going particularly heavy. After the first mile or so the column was engaged at long range by Harispe's guns on the ridge. Exploding shells caused some casualties, but little damage was done by the round-shot, which sank into the soft ground, though Sergeant Lawrence said that one of General Cole's orderlies had his horse shot under him. This flank march was described by Lieutenant James Mill in a letter from Toulouse after the battle:

'The remainder of the army that had not crossed [the Garonne] did so on the following morning, and we advanced to the attack on 10th April. After crossing the Croix d'Orade, we marched within range of thirty pieces of cannon which were planted by the French on our right. The way was long, and narrow for the numbers, and the difficulties of the defiles were greatly enhanced by reason of the deep, miry nature of the ground. You can easily conceive how we suffered, and in what manner their shot devastated our ranks. To this fire there was no reply, no rejoinder of a similar kind from our side, excepting in the way of a shout of menace and defiance from the Regiment when one or more men together were stricken down by this severe fire.'

Seeing that his guns could not keep up with the march, Beresford ordered them to turn off onto higher ground near Mont Blanc and open fire, which they did at about 9.30 a.m. Unfortunately, Freire took this movement as a signal that Beresford's attack had commenced and launched his own assault on the Grand Redoubt. The Spanish attack was flung back with heavy loss, causing Wellington to observe that he had never before seen ten thousand men running a race.

When the Spaniards were repulsed, Wellington sent an aide de camp to Beresford, advising him to attack the Calvinet Ridge from where he stood, but Beresford kept to his original plan and pushed on to a point below and to the south-east of the square Sypière redoubt, where the road from Caraman climbed the ridge. Both divisions then wheeled into three lines facing uphill, covered by their light companies, with Cole's 4th Division on the left. Anson's brigade, with the 40th, was in the first line of that division, with the brigades of Vasconcellos and Ross behind it and Lambert's brigade of Clinton's 6th Division to its right.

When Soult saw the attack forming, he ordered Taupin's division to move south from its reserve position behind the ridge to counter Beresford. Taupin came over the skyline to the south of the Sypière redoubt and, without waiting for reinforcement, charged impetuously downhill, his brigades massed in columns of battalions with Vial's and Berton's cavalry on both flanks[770], only to meet the leading British brigades some way up the long steep slope. It was a classic meeting of French column and British line, with the usual result. Captain Lapène gives a French account of the action:

'By one of those deplorable errors of which our late campaigns gave too many examples, Taupin, carried away by his ardour and the hope of a brilliant success, instead of deploying his brigade on the crest near the

---

[770] Taupin's division consisted of Rey's brigade, 3,039 men in six battalions of the 32nd and 43rd Ligne and 12th Légère, and Gasquet's brigade, 2,416 men in four battalions of the 47th, 55th and 58th Ligne. Rey's brigade was on the right, opposite Anson's brigade. On his right flank were six squadrons of Berton's brigade, and on his left a regiment of Vial's chasseurs à cheval.

Sypière redoubt, advanced with his whole force still in column, the 12th Légère leading, and pushed in that order across the front of the redoubt, whose fire he thus masked. The English, instead of giving the French time to deploy, took up a brusque offensive, and commenced a vigorous fire. Among our massed ranks no ball could fail to find a mark, and we opposed to his front of fire only the insufficient reply of the 1st/12th Légère. The men in the rear ranks, seeing comrades fall on every side without being able to retaliate, fell into discouragement. General Taupin, trying to keep up his soldiers' confidence, and to animate them by his personal example, was seen in the forefront of his leading battalion; soon – expiatory victim of his own error – he fell mortally wounded. Rey's brigade wavered – the English continued to advance, and the troops broke and poured back into the Sypière redoubt. Its garrison, (9th Légère), seized with an inexplicable panic, abandoned the redoubt the moment that Taupin's troops came pouring past it. The enemy hastened to seize it, and crowned this important position after making but a very small sacrifice of men.'

This engagement was described shortly afterwards, from a 40th Regiment perspective, by Lieutenant James Mill:

'At length we attained the point which was to be taken, and ascended the height to the right in the face of the redoubts and in the teeth of our enemies, who, on their side, were engaged in the preliminaries for making a descent in immense numbers to arrest our onward course. The several regiments of our brigade, as far as I can now judge, had hitherto advanced through the difficulties and manifold obstructions in mass – at times having no broader front than that of sub-divisions, and at others even section distance, which was imposed by the narrowness of the passage and other circumstances; but now this order was promptly converted into lines of columns facing the town walls. In this formation, protected by a cloud of skirmishers, we moved forward to encounter the advancing French, against whom we pressed forward up the acclivity, and – crowning it with loud cries – bore down every show of opposition in our course. It almost seemed that the mere sight of the bayonet and a few volleys sufficed to inspire a salutary awe and dread; for the enemy wavered, became mixed, and then turned, thus surrendering the most advanced redoubts and taking flight to the stronger works in rear, close by the town walls. We then formed in three lines (each brigade comprising a line) and in this form remained exposed to their cannonade for the rest of the day.'

Many years later, Sergeant William Lawrence recorded his impressions of this clash:

'We formed line and dashed up the hill, which was defended by some thousands of the French, nearly half of whom were cavalry. We soon returned their fire, which at that time was a perfect storm of grape and canister, and directly we got near we charged them, but in vain, as owing to the sudden appearance of some of their cavalry we had to halt and form square[771]: and indeed we must have been routed altogether by their combined infantry and cavalry, had not our Rocket Brigade stepped forward and played fearful havoc among their cavalry, driving them back. I had never before seen this rocket charge and have never either since; by all appearance it was most successful on this case, for it soon turned them to the right-about, and made them retreat.'[772]

In his journal entry for that day, Lieutenant Charles Crowe of the 27th gives a more detailed and colourful account of the effective 'artillery' support of these hand rockets:

'Immediately to our left was a strong muster of French cavalry, threatening our position, and watching our light companies skirmishing in our front, very deliberately, well knowing that our artillery could not join us. To remedy this deficiency General Cole despatched an aide de camp, who very shortly returned accompanied by two artillerymen with hand rockets. General Cole welcomed their arrival by saying "Come lads, drive away those cavalry!" The reply was, "Leave them to us general, and we will punish them!!" The shaft of the first rocket slightly touched the mound, which caused it to pass in front of the squadron under the noses of the horses, and drove them off helter-skelter! After a while they reformed on the same ground. "Now then," said the artilleryman, "I will have you!!" And he was as good as his promise! The second rocket passed through the bodies of the first horse, the second man, and the head of the third, and drove it from the shoulders. The precision of this aim was admirable! And had the desired effect, for our unwelcome visitors did not again make their appearance.

---

[771] The 79th, on the right of the 6th Division, also formed square at this time, while the 27th was ordered into close column, a formation from which square could quickly be formed.
[772] Lawrence, p. 180.

'One drunken trooper reappeared in the lower ground immediately in front of our skirmishers, evidently a good horseman, although he could not sit steadily in his saddle. He kept his steed well in hand, and with his flourishing sword appeared to offer single combat to anyone. Our skirmishers heard his vociferations, and replied by their muskets. A multitude of shots were fired at this drunken charlatan, but as he kept in constant motion not one was immediately fatal, although we could see that his clothes and face were bloody. Our sympathy was for the sober horse!'[773]

Among those who distinguished themselves in the 4th Division's actions that day was Lieutenant Bartholemew Vigors Derenzy of the 81st, attached as a captain to the 7th Caçadores of Vasconcellos's brigade. Despite a musket ball in the left arm and a shell splinter in his chest, he took command of the battalion and refused to quit the field. He earned a field promotion to the rank of major, 'he having been previously recommended for that rank by the Lieutenant General Commanding the Division on three former occasions, viz: Pampeluna [Sorauren], Nivelle & Orthes, but objected to in consequence of his then extreme youth! he being then in his twenty-second year of age.'[774]

Having taken the southern half of the Calvinet Ridge as far as the hollow Lavaur road, which cut across the ridge some three hundred yards short of the Mas des Augustins and Columbette redoubts, Beresford paused, waiting for his guns to come up and for the Spaniards to organise a second attack on the Great Redoubt. Meanwhile he deployed his troops on the ridge-top. The 4th Division faced west towards the Canal du Midi, with Somerset's Hussars on their left flank. Soult expected the division to descend from the crest to attack his entrenchments on the reverse slope, which were completely dominated from above, but this was not Beresford's intention. The 6th Division deployed at a right-angle to the 4th, facing north along the ridge, ready to drive along the crest in conjunction with a renewed assault by Freire. The task of the 4th Division, meanwhile, was to protect the left flank of the 6th Division from any counter-attack from the entrenchments along the canal.

Accordingly, the light companies of the division, with other companies in support, descended the back slope of Calvinet Ridge towards the Canal du Midi, in front of which Menne's and Rouget's brigades, with a remnant of Taupin's division, held the Bataille, Cambon and Saccarin entrenchments. The headquarters of this skirmishing line, as described by Charles Crowe of the 27th, was 'a small two-floored house south-west of our left [probably the Corriege Farm], westward of which was a garden, enclosed by a clay wall about seven feet high, through which they cut loop holes to fire at the enemy.'

The light companies had to hold this house and two by-roads, and were under fire from enemy skirmishers and raked by a cannon on a canal bridge [possibly from the Pont des Demoiselles]. The French made an unsuccessful attempt to retake the house, and some commotion was caused by a cannonball which passed through an upper room in which all the light company officers were assembled, watching the enemy. One officer jumped out of the window, while Lieutenant the Honourable Michael Browne of the Light Company 40th ran down the stairs, his face and jacket covered in white dust. 'Why sir, you are in a forlorn plight, and you seem frightened!' joked a wounded major. Browne was not amused, retorting, 'Sir, your remarks are very inappropriate; had you been in the room above, you would not have thought it an occasion for joking, and I consider your laughing as excessively unfeeling!!'[775]

It took two hours to bring up the 4th and 6th divisional guns, required to support the advance of the 6th Division, but at about 2.30 p.m. Pack's brigade, supported by Douglas's Portuguese, with Lambert's brigade in reserve, left the shelter of the Lavaur road cutting to assault the Mas des Augustins and Columbette redoubts. The combat which followed was close and bloody, with terrible losses, but at length the 6th Division prevailed, albeit at a cost of some fifteen hundred casualties. The Spanish attack on the Great Redoubt was pressed with great gallantry, but was again thrown back with heavy loss, but by about 4 or 5 p.m., as British skirmishers advanced

---

[773] Crowe, p.p. 28-59.

[774] Derenzy, who was commissioned into the 81st in 1806, aged 14, had fought with that Regiment at Corunna and Flushing, being wounded in both actions, before secondment to the Portuguese service. He survived to earn nine bars to his Military General Service Medal, together with Portuguese, Spanish and Hanoverian decorations, and retired as a major-general in 1855.

[775] Michael Browne, aged 20, was 4th son of the Earl of Kenmare. He had served with the 40th through the campaigns of 1813 and 1814, and was with the Regiment at Waterloo. His elder brother Thomas, who became 3rd Earl Kenmare in 1853, served in the Peninsula with the 40th from Roliça to Salamanca, was present at thirteen engagements and was wounded twice.

along the ridge to engage the rear of this final French strongpoint, Soult ordered a withdrawal from the Calvinet Ridge to behind the Canal du Midi. This was completed within an hour or so, and though sporadic firing continued until about 9 p.m. no further movements of importance took place.

Throughout this struggle, the 4th Division continued to hold its exposed position on the ridge facing the ramparts of Toulouse, and it was at this time that the 40th suffered the greater part of its casualties from artillery fire, as observed by James Mill:

'The oldest man in the 40th – either as officer or private – declares never on any former occasion was he exposed to such tremendous cannonading, which was maintained without any intermission for the space of four hours, and playing on our brigade chiefly. The bravery of the British was never exceeded; one regiment, the 61st, of the Sixth Division, which acted with ours, had only two officers left uninjured after the action, a lieutenant and an ensign: the lieutenant commanded the regiment. The loss of the 40th was comparatively small, if it be considered that we were engaged from 9 o'clock until dark, during most part of which time we were exposed to either cannon or small arms. The loss with us, nevertheless, was nine officers and one hundred men killed and wounded.'[776]

The total Allied casualties at Toulouse amounted to 4,558 (655 dead, 3,887 wounded and sixteen missing), of whom 2,103 were British, 1,922 Spaniards and 533 Portuguese. Apart from Freire's Spaniards, by far the heaviest loss fell on the British and Portuguese of the 6th Division, who suffered 1,520 casualties out of 5,693 present. The 4th Division lost 81 dead, 321 wounded, and three missing out of 5,363.

'I remember well the loss of a man in my company in this action,' recalled Sergeant Lawrence. '[He] had entered the army during the war for a period of seven years at first, and this period having expired for some time, he was mad to be out of the constant scenes of bloodshed and conflicts, but owing to the continuation of the war he had not been allowed to depart… His name was William Marsh, and he was a native of Bath in Somerset. He was by trade a tailor, and earned many a shilling at his trade in the army from various of his comrades who employed him. As I said, the poor man was sick of war, and before entering this very action had been wishing he could have both his legs shot off, so that he might be out of the affair altogether; little expecting that it might really be the case, or nearly as bad, for he had not been in action long before his wish was accomplished, as he was shot through the calves of both his legs by a musket-ball which took him sideways and pierced right through. Poor Marsh did begin to sing out most heartily, and I couldn't help saying, "Hullo there, Marsh, you are satisfied now your wish is fulfilled, I hope." He begged and prayed me to move him out of the thick of the fight, so I dragged him under a bank and there left him, and from that time till now I never saw or heard anything more of him.

'Another of our comrades in the front of our line had his foot completely smashed by a cannon-ball pitching right on to it, yet he managed to hobble to the rear in that state on his heel. I felt quite hurt for this poor fellow, who was a brave soldier and seemed to be enduring great agonies.'[777]

French casualties are, as usual, less easy to determine, but were certainly fewer. The official report listed a total of 3,236 casualties, of whom, extrapolating from known officer casualties, Taupin's division probably lost some 450. Sergeant Lawrence went to the assistance of a badly wounded French soldier:

'I went up him and asked him if I could do anything for him. He had been shot in the stomach, and when he asked for water and I gave him some out of my canteen, which was nearly full, out of which he drank heartily,

---

[776] Oman shows seven men of the 40th killed in action at Toulouse, and eight officers and 71 men wounded, while the parade state of the 4th Division for the week ending 15th April shows thirteen of the 40th dead, and the *Regimental Record Book* lists fifteen men killed (presumably including some who died of their wounds) and six officers and 75 men wounded. The wounded officers were Lieutenants James Anthony, Theobald O'Doherty, Thomas Decimus Franklyn and Michael Smith, and Ensign James Glynn (severely), and Captains Richard Turton and John Henry Barnett, and Ensign Donald McDonald (slightly). Theobald O'Doherty (or O'Dogherty) was one of only nine officers in the whole army who fought throughout the Peninsula War from Roliça to Toulouse, during which time he took part in twelve battles and was wounded twice, but remained a lieutenant throughout, as did Lieutenant John Thoreau of the 40th, who fought in thirteen battles and, like O'Doherty, was twice wounded. Thoreau later served in the 37th and died a Brevet Major on St. Helena in 1843(M.I. in St. James's Church, Jamestown. Donald McDonald was gazetted as ensign in the 40th on 22nd October 1812, from Sergeant-Major in the 1st Foot; he subsequently served as a lieutenant at Waterloo, and survived to receive the Military General Service Medal with clasps for Corunna, Fuentes d'Onoro, Badajoz, Salamanca, Vittoria, Pyrenees, Nivelle, Nive, Orthes and Toulouse.
[777] Lawrence, p.p. 181-82.

354

in a short time it only fell out again through his wound. But the most astonishing thing was that he pointed out his father's house, which was as far as I could judge about half a mile off, and said that he had not seen his parents for six years, for since he had come back to this place he had not been able to fall out to go and see them. He begged me to take him so that he might die there in the presence of his parents, but I told him I could not do that, as there were a quantity of French there. However, I got an old blanket and wrapped it round him, making him as comfortable as I could under the circumstances.'[778]

That evening, Soult held a council of war and decided to evacuate Toulouse the following night rather than stand a siege, which with the Allies on the Calvinet heights could have only one outcome. In a letter to Suchet that night, the despondent Marshal outlined his situation: 'The fighting has been most bloody: Wellington has suffered great loss, but has won the position on the right side of Toulouse. If attacked again the army will defend itself, but it is impossible to hang on for long.' The French accordingly spent the 11th making preparations for departure, and marched out after dark on the Carcassonne road, which, flanked as it was by the Garonne and the Canal du Midi, was still open.

Wellington took no offensive action that day, for Beresford's and Freire's battered and exhausted divisions on the blood-stained heights needed relief, and the artillery on the dominating Calvinet Ridge had expended its ammunition. Resupply was required from the far side of the Garonne, a logistic effort which was not completed until after noon. There was, in any case, no imperative to bombard a city of largely Royalist sympathy.

'On the following day there was nothing additional attempted,' wrote James Mill, 'and it was occupied in most part in burying the dead. Every arrangement was set on foot for taking the town on the third day, but we were saved this undertaking, as the French evacuated it during the previous night, and accordingly we took possession.'

In 1824, the 40th Regiment of Foot were granted the right to emblazon their Colours with the Battle Honour 'TOULOUSE,' and 176 officers and men of the 40th survived to receive a 'Toulouse' bar to their Military General Service Medal in 1847. Rather earlier, Lieutenant-Colonel Henry Thornton, who commanded the 40th, received the Gold Cross, Major William Balfour was promoted to brevet lieutenant-colonel, and as we have noted, Lieutenant Derenzy of the 81st was promoted to major in the Portuguese Service – an appointment he held until the Portuguese revolution of 1820. Major Arthur Rowley Heyland, recovered from his Lintzoain wound, was appointed Commandant of Toulouse.

Early on the 12th it became apparent that Soult had evacuated Toulouse overnight, and Wellington rode in amid scenes of relief and jubilation to be offered the keys of the city by civic leaders and citizens wearing white cockades. News of Napoleon Bonaparte's abdication was received by Wellington at 5 p.m. that day and sent on at once to Soult; but it was not until the Marshal received confirmation from Berthier, the Chief of General Staff, that he reluctantly entered into a convention for the suspension of hostilities, the terms of which were finally agreed on 18th April.

The Siege of Bayonne

When Wellington took his main force north-east across the Gaves, the 1st and 5th Divisions, together with the brigades of Aylmer, Bradford and Campbell, were left with Sir John Hope to blockade Bayonne. The fortress town was held by General Thouvenot, the officer who had so skillfully defended Burgos, with 14,000 men, mostly of high quality. The 5th Division held their old ground between the Nive and the sea until 19th February,[779] when Wellington and Hope made their dispositions for a crossing of the Adour below Bayonne. This involved running a flotilla of small local vessels, under naval control, over the bar into the estuary to form a bridge of boats below Le Boucau, while the 1st Division secured both banks. The 5th Division, with the 47th and 59th, played a supporting role, taking over on the 22nd fortified positions at Mouguerre, facing the Mousserolles entrenched camp between the Nive and Adour rivers, and creating diversions on the 23rd by firing on the entrenched camp and making demonstrations of crossing the Adour above Bayonne. The difficult passage of the

---

[778] Lawrence, p.p. 182-83.
[779] The pay lists of the 47th were signed on 19th February at Urdains.

Adour was successfully completed between the 23rd and 26th February, and with the capture of the village of St. Etienne, the encirclement of Bayonne was complete.

The 5th Division returned to the left bank of the Nive, and on 19th March the pay lists of the 47th were signed at St.-Jean-de-Luz, Major Richard Chetham being then in command. He had served in the 47th since 1796.

The blockade of Bayonne continued in a fairly leisurely fashion, for Hope was convinced that the town would be reduced by starvation and that a formal siege was unnecessary. Then, on 10th April Hope received the dramatic news that the Allies had occupied Paris and Napoleon had been deposed. This information was passed under flag of truce to Thouvenot, whose ambiguous reply was that the besiegers 'would hear from him on the subject before long.' Hope anticipated that the French would cease active hostilities, and although he maintained the blockade it seems that his troops may have slightly relaxed their guard.

On the night of 14th/15th April the 5th Division, less Hay's brigade, provided pickets south of the Adour at Anglet and Bellevue. Hay's 1st Brigade, with the 47th, had by chance been ordered across the river that day as a temporary measure to bolster the defences of the bridge of boats. Most of the brigade remained at Le Boucau, but a detachment, including some of the 47th, relieved the pickets in St. Etienne.

The hilltop village of St. Etienne, the most critical and exposed point of the siege lines north of the Adour, stood close under the Citadel of Bayonne. Through the village ran the main road north, and from its crossroads hollow lanes went east and west. The village church, with its churchyard, dominated the centre, while the surrounding cottages had been loopholed and, together with their well-stocked gardens and a walled Jewish cemetery, formed the picket line. We have a good description of this place and its situation from George Gleig of the 85th, who had commanded the pickets there from 4th to 8th April:

'The post of which I was put in charge was the village of St. Etienne, and the church formed the headquarters of the guard. It was a small building, but, fortunately for us, constructed with great solidity, inasmuch as it stood under the very muzzles of half a dozen field-pieces, which the enemy had placed in a redoubt about a short stone's throw distant. To add to its strength, and to render it more tenable in case of an attack, an embankment of earth… was raised inside, to the height of perhaps four feet; above which ran a line of loopholes, cut out for the purpose of giving to its garrison an opportunity of firing with effect. When I say that the church formed the headquarters of the guard, I mean that the guard took up its station there during the night. So long as daylight lasted, the men kept as much as possible concealed behind a few houses in the rear of the building, and left only a single sentry there to watch the movements of the enemy.

'A little to the right of my post were a couple of barricades; the one cutting off the main road, the other blocking up the entrance to a cross street in the village. Besides these respectively stood a six-pounder gun. They were, I should conceive, about pistol-shot from the walls of the castle, and formed our most advanced stations. Our line of sentinels again ran through the churchyard and streets, winding away by the right and left, as the shape of the place required; and they were planted as close to one another as the occurrence of trees or other species of cover would permit.

'At night… the utmost vigilance was necessary. The enemy were so close to us that the slightest carelessness on our part would have given them free and secure access through our chain – a circumstance which rendered it impracticable for the videttes to give sufficient warning to men who should not be at every moment in a state of preparation. No man slept, or so much as lay down. The privates stood round the embankment within the church, as if they had been all on watch; the officers crept about from place to place in front of it, or listened with deep anxiety to every sound. In these wanderings, the conversation of the French soldiers could be distinctly overheard, so near were the troops of the two nations to each other; and so perilous, or rather so momentous, was the duty which we were called upon to perform.'[780]

This, then, was the post held by men of the 47th and others of Hay's brigade on the night of 14th/15th April. To their right the picket line was manned by Stopford's and Maitland's brigades of Guards, while Hinüber's brigade of the King's German Legion lay in reserve behind St. Etienne.

Early that night a French deserter presented himself to General Hay, who as General Officer of the Day had taken post at St. Etienne, warning him that the garrison of Bayonne was under arms and about to mount a

---

[780] Gleig, p.p. 250-52.

major sortie. Unfortunately, Hay could not understand French and sent him on to Hinüber. By the time the warning was taken seriously, and reinforcements were stood to, it was too late.

The sortie opened with a feint attack to the south-west, towards Anglet. The 59th, who were stationed in that area, were probably not actively involved in countering this move and suffered no recorded casualties.[781]

The main attack, however, was launched north of the Adour, against St. Etienne village and cross-roads, and the Guards pickets to their west. It was a pitch dark, moonless night when almost six thousand French troops in three columns suddenly erupted from below the Citadel and, without firing a shot, rushed upon the British pickets, bayoneting surprised sentries before they could raise the alarm. The eastern column, coming up from the bridge and village of St. Esprit, quickly overwhelmed Hay's pickets, capturing all but two of their posts, while the central column penetrated up the Bordeaux road for some three hundred yards beyond the crossroads, and the western column overran the Guards pickets in close and confused fighting, taking 160 prisoners.

Hay threw himself into St. Etienne church, but was killed by a musket shot through a loophole, and Sir John Hope, riding down the hollow road towards St. Etienne, was wounded and captured.

The surviving pickets from St. Etienne rallied on the German brigade in their rear, from where, joined by Bradford's Portuguese, the whole retook the village.

It took longer to mount counter-attacks further west, but by around 7 a.m. the French had been driven back across their whole attack front. According to Adam Reed, the main body of the 47th took part in the counter-attack from Le Boucau, which is probable, though unconfirmed from other sources.[782]

The struggle was close, confused and ferocious, particularly in St. Etienne, where bayonets, swords and musket butts were in full play at close quarters. George Gleig reckoned that the village changed hands nine times, and the slaughter in a small space was terrible:

'The street of St. Etienne, in particular, was covered with killed and wounded; and round the six-pounder they lay in heaps. A French artilleryman had fallen across it, with a fuze in his hand; there he lay, his head cloven asunder, and the remains of the handle of the fuze in his grasp. The muzzle and breech of the gun were smeared with blood and brains; and beside them were several soldiers of both nations, whose heads had evidently been dashed to pieces by the butts of muskets. Arms of all sorts, broken and entire, were strewed about… The wounded, too, were far more than ordinarily numerous: in a word, it was one of the most hard fought and unsatisfactory affairs that had occurred since the commencement of the war. Brave men fell, when their fall was no longer beneficial to their country; and much blood was wantonly shed during a period of national peace.'[783]

This unjustifiable and purposeless sortie by General Thouvenot cost the French 905 casualties and the Allies 838. The 47th suffered one drummer and two men killed, two officers[784] and eleven rank and file wounded, and ten rank and file missing.

Early on the morning of 28th April, the 47th and 59th, with the whole of the Allied troops, paraded to witness the raising of the white flag of the French monarchy over the Citadel of Bayonne:

'We had stood in our ranks about an hour,' wrote Gleig, 'dressed in our best attire, and having our muskets loaded with powder only, when a signal gun was fired from one of the batteries of the town, and a magnificent tricoloured flag, which had hitherto waved proudly in the breeze, was gradually lowered. For perhaps half a minute the flagstaff stood bare; and then a small white standard, dirty, and, if my eyes deceived me not, a little

---

[781] Among those present with the 59th at Bayonne was Ensign James Gammell, who died at Bath on 23rd September 1893, the last surviving officer of the Peninsula Army. James Gammell retired as a captain in 1825. One day in December 1888, while visiting his bank, he struck up a casual conversation with a Colonel Balguy in the course of which the venerable officer happened to mention that it was just 75 years ago that he had first donned the red coat. Further discussion revealed that Captain Gammell had been in the Peninsula but had never applied for the Military General Service Medal to which he was entitled, and Balguy undertook to apply for the medal on his behalf. The belated application was at first refused, but Colonel Balguy approached the Duke of Cambridge, Commander-in-Chief, who informed Queen Victoria. The happy outcome was that the medal was sanctioned, and the Queen, taking a personal interest in Captain Gammell's case, with a characteristic touch added her Golden Jubilee Medal, which the old soldier, a fervent monarchist, cherished even more than the campaign medal.

[782] According to Private Adam Reed, 'We hearing the firing in the camp, which was about a mile from them [the pickets], the drum beat and we were quickly down to their assistance. It was a sharpish skirmish, but we forced them to retire.'

[783] Gleig, p. 261.

[784] Lieutenants John Henry de Burgh and William Kendall were slightly wounded.

torn, was run up. Immediately the guns from every quarter of the city fired a salute. By such of our people as kept guard at the outposts that day, it was asserted that each gun was crammed with sand and mud, as if this turbulent garrison had been resolved to insult, as far as they could insult, an authority to which they submitted only because they were compelled to submit. On our parts, the salute was answered with a feu-de-joie from all the infantry, artillery, and gun-boats; and then a hearty shout being raised, we filed back to our respective stations, and dismissed the parade.'[785]

The six-year Peninsula War was effectively over.

The End in Eastern Spain

At the end of October 1813, the 1st/81st moved forward from Valls to cantonments at Vendrell; but the three-month lull in operations in Catalonia was about to be broken, for on 25th November Buonaparte ordered Marshal Suchet to evacuate Lerida, Tortosa and other places, adding their large garrisons to his much-diminished field army. Suchet judged it necessary that, before carrying off these isolated garrisons, he should defeat Clinton's Anglo-Sicilian army. Accordingly, on 2nd December he advanced in force from the river Llobregat in a reprise of his September attack on Bentinck, with the intention of surprising the British at Vilafranca del Penedes. Timely intelligence of this movement having been obtained, the Advance fell back on Arbos (l'Arboc), and the Reserve Division moved forward from Vendrell in support. Suchet looked at the Allied position, decided it was too strong, and withdrew to the Llobregat.

At the end of January, having sent another ten thousand of his best troops to aid Buonaparte's final desperate campaign in front of Paris, Suchet fell back to Gerona, leaving isolated garrisons in Barcelona, Lerida, Tudela and elsewhere. Anticipating this withdrawal, the Anglo-Sicilian-Spanish force moved up to the line of the Llobregat, which was forced by Spanish troops on 16th January. By 7th February the 81st, with the Reserve, were quartered at Esplugues, within four miles of Barcelona, which became strictly blockaded.

On 17th February the 81st marched, with its brigade and a squadron of cavalry, through Molins de Rei to the pass of Martorell. They had a part to play in an elaborate ruse, excoriated by the historian Oman but highly effective, by which the outlying French garrisons of Lerida, Mequienza and Monzon were duped into abandoning their posts. The plot depended on a defector from Suchet's staff, Van Halen, who used forged documents and cipher messages to convince the French commanders of those places that an imaginary 'Convention of Tarrasa' had been concluded between the Spanish General Copons and Marshal Suchet, including an armistice of twelve days during which all the outlying French garrisons might fall back unmolested to Barcelona. The deception worked, and the garrisons, over two thousand men led by General Lamarque, marched out with their baggage. On the 18th they ran into a British outpost near Martorell, whose captain denied all knowledge of the spurious 'Convention' and refused passage to Barcelona, a statement that was backed up by his superiors who drew up the 2nd Brigade across the road. Catalan troops then crowned the hills on both sides and in rear of the French column, whereupon Copons appeared to inform the French general that he and his troops were prisoners.

It was now considered by Wellington that Spanish troops might reasonably be expected to deal with the residual French presence on the east coast, and as early as 4th March he wrote to Clinton asking that the bulk of the British troops there should march to join him 'as soon as you shall hear of the removal of Marshal Suchet from Catalonia.' On 7th March another ten thousand of Suchet's troops marched off to join the Emperor, and the Marshal had perforce to evacuate all his Catalan strongholds except Figueras and the isolated city of Barcelona. However, the Spaniards could not provide sufficient troops to blockade Barcelona and match Suchet's field army, so Clinton felt obliged to remain. It was not until 6th April that he received news, false as it turned out, that Suchet had retired into France.

A division of six battalions, including the 81st, was accordingly concentrated at Tarragona, and on 14th April they departed under Clinton from the neighbourhood of Barcelona to join Wellington. The division marched by way of Lerida, Saragossa, Pamplona and Tolosa, crossed the Bidassoa at Irun, and reached Biarritz on 14th

---

[785] Gleig, p.p. 264-65.

May. On route, they probably received Wellington's valedictory message to them, dated Toulouse, 19th April 1814:

'Upon the breaking up of this army I perform a most satisfactory duty in reporting to your Lordship my sense of the conduct and merit of Lieut.-General Clinton, and of the troops under his command, since they have been employed in the Peninsula. Circumstances have not enabled these troops to have so brilliant a share in the operations of the war as their brother officers and soldiers on this side of the Peninsula; but they have not been less usefully employed; their conduct when engaged with the enemy has always been meritorious; and I have every reason to be satisfied with the General Officer and with them.'

After the war, Wellington was prompted to remark that Clinton 'did nothing in particular – and did it pretty well.' This was an accurate assessment, for whilst Clinton was severely constrained by the nature of his cosmopolitan force and by his commander-in-chief's injunction to avoid the risk of defeat, his very presence on the east coast in the final months of the war gave Marshal Suchet all the excuse he needed to avoid sending assistance to his rival Soult.

The Last Days of the Peninsula Army

Meanwhile, in Bordeaux, the 82nd were revelling in the fruits of victory, and George Wood noted how quickly the war-worn soldiers recovered their health and well-being:

'Their countenances were now beaming with health and content, for this was a most excellent quarter: the finest fat beef, fed on the luxuriant pastures of the fertile meadows which border the lively Garonne, was here to be had for about twopence per pound; bread, wine, fruit, and every article of life in proportion, except tea and sugar, which were imported in a great measure from England. Our troops, living on this kind of fare, the sick and wounded now recovering, and fresh detachments arriving, increased our Regiment so much that it again became one of the strongest in this country; it was consequently one of the first ordered to embark for America – an unlucky order, for it deprived us of sharing in the honour of the battle of Waterloo.'

'For this service we were allowed a considerable time to prepare; which interval we passed very pleasantly, living in the most sumptuous style. For about half-a-guinea a day we got, at the first inns in the town, a sumptuous dinner, with champagne, claret, and all kinds of rich wines, as well as an excellent dessert; after which we generally went to the play, the opera, a ball, or some private party; for the gentry of the town took great pleasure in paying the most marked respect to the English officers, and showed them all imaginable civility.

'The ladies in particular were exceedingly attentive and affable; so much so that they made a strong impression upon the hearts of our young sparks, and one of our officers was fortunate enough to make a lovely damsel of this neighbourhood the partner of his life… So very engaging and agreeable are the charming young ladies of this town that, I may with truth assert, nearly the whole of the officers had in great measure lost their hearts: even the married ones, it required the greatest constancy and resolution to retain their attachment for their affectionate wives at home.'[786]

The 40th also passed through Bordeaux and experienced its hospitality. After the Battle of Toulouse, they had joined in the pursuit of Soult's army towards Carcassonne until halted at St. Félix-Lauragais. Whilst encamped there following the cessation of hostilities, they belatedly took on strength a draft of four officers, six sergeants and one hundred rank and file, under Captain John Amos, from their 2nd Battalion.[787]

From St. Félix, the Battalion marched by easy stages to cantonments at Valence d'Agen, where they were mustered on 24th April with an effective soldier strength of 490. With a return to peacetime soldiering, it was time to smarten up, and on the 27th Colonel Thornton issued the following Battalion Order:

'The Battn will parade tomorrow morning in complete marching order, under a subaltern per company & the Captain of the Day, every man, field officers excepted, to be present. They are to pile their arms in open column & to proceed to wash themselves & every part of their linen, & to return to their quarters with every thing clean upon them & in their packs. Commanding officers of companies will be expected to supply their men with soap for this purpose. This parade is to take place every Monday & Thursday at eight o'clock in the morning &

---

[786] Wood, p.p. 235–37.
[787] Among the arrivals was Ensign George Hibbert, who would command the 40th in the First Afghan War.

the Captain of the Day is to report to the Comdg Officer when the parade is dismissed. In future the Batt^n is to parade at 10 o'clock every morning & 3 every evening excepting washing days.'[788]

Early in May, the 40th marched from Valence to Montréal de Gers and nearby Sos. On their march, the troops were delighted at the general good will of the French population towards the British Army, as illustrated by the experience of Sergeant William Lawrence at Montréal:

'The inhabitants could not have behaved better to us if they had been our own countrymen; and I well remember how at the last stage where we put up before coming to Bordeaux two of us, myself and a private of the same company, were billeted at quite a gentleman's house, the owners of which were unusually kind to us. We found we had completely jumped into clover, and fortunately it happened to be Saturday night, so that our halt was till Monday morning.'

'As soon as we arrived at our house we were shown into our room, which was a very nice one and beautifully furnished; and when we had taken off our accoutrements, we went downstairs to a sort of bath-room, where we had a good wash in tubs of water that were placed in readiness for us. Then the gentleman had some clean stockings brought up to us, and when we had made ourselves comfortable he sent up to our room a loaf of bread and a large bottle of wine holding about three pints, which we found very acceptable; and it not being long before the family's dinner was ready, our hostess would insist on our dining with them. For my part, not being used to such pomp, and never having before seen it… I would sooner have crept out of the invitation; but being pressed we consented, and having been shown into the dining-room, we sat down to an excellent repast with nobody else but the lady and gentleman.

'The table was laid out most gorgeously with glittering silver, which came very awkward to our clumsy hands, as we had been more accustomed to using our fingers for some years; to set off which gorgeousness our waiter, who was evidently the family footman, wore an out-of-the-way fine and ugly dress, with his hair powdered up with white powder, of which I had such an aversion during the first part of my stay in the army. A most palatable dinner was served, of which I freely partook, though I had very little idea of what it consisted, and some good wine was likewise often handed round, with which our glasses were constantly being filled.

'After dinner was over, the white-headed gentleman entered with coffee, a fashion which then surprised us very much; but nevertheless, more out of compliment than because we needed it, we took a cup each with some sugar-candy which was also handed round to sweeten it. When that was finished, just to keep us still going, the gentleman asked us if we smoked, and on us saying we both did, the bell was rung, and the footman entering with tobacco, we took a pipe with the gentleman, the lady having previously retired into the drawing-room. Then getting more used to the distinguished style, and the wine no doubt having made us more chatty, we for a time thoroughly enjoyed ourselves with our pipes, and began to feel new men with all our grandeur. We were next invited to partake of tea in the drawing-room, but being very tired, we begged to be excused; and this being granted, the bed-candle being rung for, and having wished him good-night, we went to our room, and there had a hearty laugh over the evening's business; though we had not been able to understand half what the gentleman had said, not being used to the French so well as to the Spanish language.

'We retired to rest in a fine feather bed, which being a luxury we had not seen for years, was consequently too soft for our hard bones, and we found we could not sleep owing to the change. My comrade soon jumped out of bed, saying, "I'll be bothered, sergeant, I can't sleep here!" "No," said I, "no more can I"; so we prepared our usual bed by wrapping ourselves in a blanket, and then with a knapsack as a pillow we lay on the floor and soon sank into a profound slumber.'

Next morning Lawrence had to explain to his hostess, with the aid of a French-English dictionary, why they had not slept in bed: 'I told her we had not slept on a feather bed for six years, and answered her other questions, giving her a slight description of the trials of a soldier in time of war. She was very much touched, and could not forbear from crying, more especially when I added that two privates were to be whipped that very morning for having got drunk over-night and making a disturbance in the town, to serve as an example to the Regiment.

---

[788] Battalion Order 1st/40th, written up by Sergeant Lanty Toohey in the Orderly Book of Major Stretton's Company.

'They had been tried by court-martial and sentenced to a hundred lashes, to be administered in the town and witnessed by the inhabitants. Although it was Sunday, the drums beat for the Regiment to assemble, and the men were brought into our square; and their sentence having been read in the presence of all, the first man was led to the halberds, and the drummers got ready to begin. But five or six gentlemen of the town made their way into our square and begged the Colonel so hard to let them off, as that was the general wish of the inhabitants, that at last he dismissed the victims with a reprimand. The two then thanked the Colonel, but he told them not to do so, for had it not been for the timely interference of the gentlemen, he would have given them every lash.'

This demonstration of British Army discipline had, as Wellington intended, a lasting impact on the attitude of the French population, as was seen a few days later when the 3rd/27th passed the same way:

'None but the 40th Regiment had pursued this line of march and had left such a strong impression of the good discipline of British soldiers, and of [the] suavity of their officers, that we were welcomed with the greatest cordiality; and I trust did not prove unworthy of our precursors! All our officers were invited to a ball in the evening at a large private mansion, between 7 and 8 o'clock. Our old friends of the 40th had attended, en masse, at a similar fete and we followed their good example.'[789]

When, at seven o'clock in the morning, the 40th paraded to march from Montréal, Sergeant Lawrence bade farewell to his kind hosts, who sent him off with a canteen full of their best wine and a parcel of sandwiches. After a long march through the sandy tracks of the Landes, the 40th reached Bordeaux that night and camped at Blanquefort, two miles north of the city on the banks of the Garonne. This was a large transit camp in which the 40th, 81st, 82nd, and eight or more other regiments awaited embarkation. Here, the 40th stayed for some five weeks to the evident enjoyment of all ranks. Lawrence relates that:

'The inhabitants made many excursions from the city, especially on Sundays, to inspect our army; swarms of costermongers likewise visiting us every day with wine, spirits, bread, meat, fish, and fruit of every description for sale. Every Sunday afternoon the bands of all the regiments played, while the French amused themselves with dancing, many of them, both male and female, on stilts, which entertained us more than anything, and besides this there were all kinds of other jollities, in which our soldiers freely joined.'[790]

After their long march north from Tarragona, the 1st/81st had remained at Biarritz until 18th May, when their brigade marched through Bayonne to Bordeaux, arriving there on the 26th. On the 30th they were ordered to march to Blanquefort camp, to join a brigade being assembled there under Major-General James Kempt, their former commanding officer. Kempt inspected the brigade, consisting of the 9th, 37th and 81st Regiments, on 1st June, and three days later the Battalion embarked at Pauillac.

It appears that the press picked up some stories of disturbances in Bordeaux, but Lieutenant James Mill, writing from the camp on 4th June, dismissed them as untrue and ridiculous:

'The truth is everything here is quite quiet, and the people particularly civil to the English. One sees frequently French and English soldiers walking arm in arm together, drinking in each other's company, and united in all goodwill and fellowship. The two days I was billeted in the town, I lived entirely with my landlady's family. They would not allow me to provide my own meals separately or apart from them.'

All good things come to an end, and the 40th embarked at Pauillac, down the Gironde estuary from Bordeaux, on 12th June, sailing two days later. The 82nd had already departed, embarking at Pauillac on 3rd May and sailing for Quebec on the 5th. The 81st was the last to leave the Gironde, sailing for Quebec on 16th June 1814.

Not all the regiments departed from Bordeaux. The 47th and 59th had remained around Bayonne after the surrender of that place. 'We being the Storming Division were left to the last,' wrote Corporal William Windsor, 'to see all the guns put on board, & that kept us two months longer than we expected.' The 2nd/59th embarked at Passages for Cork on 25th June, with 426 effective other ranks under command of Lieutenant-Colonel Henry Austen. The 2nd/47th, who were one of the very last British units to leave Spain, having lain for three days at the village of Renteria, sailed for Portsmouth on 27th August under Major Richard Chetham.

When the regiments sailed away they left a number of sick and wounded still in hospital. Among them was Corporal Wheeler of the 51st, seriously wounded at the Nivelle, who spent some time in the 'incurable' ward of the General Hospital in Fuenterrabia, where a sergeant of the 82nd lay dying: 'His wife was nurse to the ward.

[789] Crowe, p.227.
[790] Lawrence, p.p. 191-92.

She pricked her finger with a pin left in one of the bandages [and] caught the infection. Her finger was first amputated, then her hand; the sluff appeared again on the stump. She refused to undergo another operation, the consequence was that she soon died.'[791]

Casualties during the intensive final year of the Peninsula War had been severe. Between June 1813 and May 1814 they included five officer and 147 other rank deaths in the 1st/40th, thirteen and 185 in the 2nd/47th, fourteen and 268 in the 2nd/59th, and three and 136 in the 1st/82nd, together with one officer of the 30th, and over the course of the six-year Peninsular War a total of 71 officers and nearly three thousand soldier forebears of The Queen's Lancashire Regiment lost their lives.

The *Record of Service* of the 40th notes that over that period the Regiment lost thirteen officers, 22 sergeants and 280 rank and file killed in action, while an additional 1,359 other ranks died or otherwise became non-effective due to wounds and illness. Of the non-combat casualties, at least 659 other ranks are known to have died, and the record is not quite complete.

The Fighting Fortieth was one of only three regiments present throughout the Peninsula campaign (the others being the 45th and the 5th/60th), and despite such heavy casualties there were a number of men, including William Lawrence, who served with the Regiment continuously. Indeed, out of forty men who earned thirteen clasps to their Military General Service Medals, four were from the 40th: Sergeant John Tanner, Corporals James Coates and John Davis, and Private James Wolfe. Many others, such as William Lawrence, only missed this distinction on account of wounds and sickness.

Overall, the 30th, 40th, 47th, 59th, 81st and 82nd took part in some fifty battles, sieges and lesser affairs in Spain, Portugal and the South of France, earning sixteen Battle Honours, including 'PENINSULA.'

The War of 1812

The United States Congress declared war on Britain on 18th June 1812, but the defeat of Napoleon Buonaparte had first claim on British resources, and until the Emperor's abdication in 1814 hostilities in America had been largely confined to defending Canada against opportunist American attacks and blockading their ports. The end of the Peninsula War made veteran British troops and commanders available for employment in America, and the 1st/40th, 1st/81st and 1st/82nd were all in due course committed to that theatre.

The 82nd and the Siege of Fort Erie

On 5th May 1814, the 1st/82nd embarked for North America at Pauillac under Major William Vincent, and after a fine passage, reached Quebec on 25th June. Despite repeated failures, the United States had persisted in attempts to invade Canada, and on 3rd July a large American force under General Brown crossed the Niagara River and captured Fort Erie.

The 82nd, who had immediately proceeded up country, reached Kingston on 20th July, relieving troops who five days later fought at the hard-contested victory of Lundy's Lane. Following his defeat of the Americans at Lundy's Lane, Lieutenant-General Gordon Drummond had invested Fort Erie on 3rd August, but an attempted storming of the fort on the night of the 15th, in the face of a garrison whose numbers exceeded those of the assailants, had failed with heavy loss when a powder magazine exploded under a captured bastion.

Next day, the 82nd joined the force in front of Fort Erie. They were soon in action, for on the 27th of August Drummond reported that, 'On the evening of the 25th the enemy, hearing us at work in the wood, moved out in considerable force and made an effort to drive back our picquets to discover what we were doing at that point. The gallantry of part of the 82nd Regt. (which happened to be on duty) defeated his plan, and he was repulsed by our picquets after a sharp contest of ten minutes. The enemy must have suffered very considerably. Our loss was two killed and thirteen wounded of the 82nd Regt.'[792] The names of several men hit by buckshot were not included in the casualty returns.

---

[791] Letter of Corporal William Wheeler dated Fuenterrabia 14th May 1814.
[792] Lieutenant-General Drummond to Sir George Prevost, Camp before Fort Erie, 27th August 1814. This incident was mentioned by Field Marshal The Marquess of Tweeddale, formerly George Hay, when addressing the 82nd in 1875: 'During the siege of Fort Erie an

Conditions in the siege lines rapidly deteriorated under incessant rain: there were no tents, the roads were almost impassable, and the camp had the appearance of 'a lake in the midst of a thick wood.' Rations were short, and the troops suffered from sickness and exposure. Moreover, American strength within Fort Erie had risen by 31st August to 5,528, outnumbering the dwindling force of besiegers by two to one. On 16th September Drummond decided to raise the siege, but before he could do so Brown mounted a major sortie to destroy the British batteries.

At noon on 17th September, under cover of torrential rain, a heavy bombardment and the thick woods, two strong American columns advanced from the fort. Despite obstinate resistance, they surprised and overran the pickets and their supports, found by the 8th Kings and De Watteville's Regiments, gaining possession of No. 2 and No. 3 Batteries. As soon as the alarm was raised, reinforcements marched from the main British camp, one and a half miles in the rear, to recapture the batteries and check the further progress of the sortie.

'The 82nd and three companies of the 6th were detached to the left to support Nos. 1 and 2 Batteries, the enemy having at that time possession of No. 2 Battery and still pushing forward. Seven companies of the 82nd, under Major [Henry Adol[phus] Proctor, and three companies of the 6th, under Major Taylor, immediately charged him with the most intrepid bravery, driving him back across our intrenchments and also from No. 2 Battery.'[793]

There was severe close-quarter fighting against the 9th, 11th and 19th U.S. Infantry under Brigadier-General Miller, as exemplified by an incident, witnessed by British surgeon William Dunlop, when Captain Robert Pattison of the 6th led two companies of the 82nd into Battery No. 2:

'They poured a volley into the mass of the enemy, who were huddled together into so small a space that they could not return it. Pattison immediately sprung forward, and called out to the American officer in command to surrender, as resistance would only cause loss of life and could do no good. He did give an order to ground arms, and some of his men were in the act of doing so, when an American soldier raised his rifle and shot Pattison through the heart. In one moment a charge was made by the 82nd into the battery, and every soul in it was put to the bayonet.'

General Drummond expressed his admiration for 'the brilliant style in which Battery No. 2 was recovered' which, in his words, 'very much decided the precipitate retrograde movement made by the enemy from the different points of our position of which he had gained short possession.' Major Proctor was awarded with promotion to brevet lieutenant-colonel, effective from the date of this action.

The action was over within two hours, when Brown ordered a withdrawal to the fort. The Americans had destroyed three guns in Battery No. 3, but had failed to take Battery No. 1 and had been expelled from Battery No. 2 before they could do any damage.

There were heavy casualties on both sides. The American loss was around 125 killed, 216 wounded and 170 captured, while British casualties amounted to 49 killed, 178 wounded and 382 captured, most of these last from the pickets. Two sergeants, three corporals and seven rank and file of the 82nd were killed in action, while seven officers[794], five sergeants and 33 rank and file were wounded and eight rank and file were missing.

On the night of 21st September, Drummond's force, reduced to some two thousand effectives, withdrew to the Chippewa River. The 82nd moved to Lundy's Lane, and by the 24th they were in comfortable cantonments behind French Creek.

It was not until 13th October that General Izard, now in command of an American force of 6,300 men, began a cautious advance, only to find that the British, some 2,500 strong, had strongly fortified the line of the Chippewa Creek. Finding Drummond's position impregnable, he withdrew to Fort Erie.

On 19th October the 82nd were with a force of 750 men under Colonel Myers which 'felt' and out-manoeuvred a 1,400-strong American column at Cook's Mills, near Lyon's Creek, in a sharp little action, one of

---

officer of the Engineers was sent out with some sappers to reconnoitre the Fort, a company of the 82nd forming a covering party. A sortie was made by the garrison which drove in the advanced party and charged the 82nd. There was a hand-to-hand fight for some time, but the enemy were finally driven back... The Regiment was then composed of old soldiers, very tough, with their hearts in the right place.'
[793] Major-General Watteville, despatch dated Camp before Fort Erie, 19th September 1814.
[794] Captain John Mercer Wright, Lieutenants Robert Latham, William Mason and Henry Pigott, and Ensign Cooper Langford were severely wounded, and Captain George Marshall and Lieutenant George Harman were slightly wounded. Captain Wright and Ensign Langford later died. All the officer casualties were Peninsula veterans. Captain Marshall, who had served at Roliça, Vimeira, Corunna, Walcheren, Vitoria, the Pyrenees, San Marcial, the Nivelle and Orthez, had previously been wounded at Sorauren and the Nivelle, and Lieutenant Mason, a veteran of Tarifa, the Nivelle and Orthez, had been wounded at the Nivelle.

the last engagements of the war on the Canadian frontier. On 5th November Izard blew up Fort Erie and withdrew altogether from British territory. In 1815 the 82nd were awarded the Battle Honour 'NIAGARA.'

The Battalion remained on the Niagara frontier for a further eight months, during which news arrived that a treaty of peace between Britain and the United States had been signed at Ghent on 24th December and ratified by the Senate on 16th February. In January 1815 the 1st/82nd received a draft of five sergeants and 120 rank and file from the 2nd Battalion. On 16th June the Battalion left the frontier on their way to Quebec, where on the 28th they embarked for Portsmouth.

The 81st in Canada

The 1st/81st were also sent to reinforce Canada, boarding transports at Pauillac on 4th May 1814 as part of a brigade commanded by Major-General James Kempt. The expedition dropped down the Gironde, and sailed on 16th June under the convoy of HMS *Plantagenet*, arriving at Quebec on 8th August. The 81st at once proceeded in divisions up the St. Lawrence to Montreal, where they remained for about a month and were inspected by Kempt. Lieutenant-Colonel James Farrer was left sick at Quebec, so Captain Adam Gifford Downing commanded.

Early in the war a British force had captured Fort Mackinac, which controlled access to Lake Michigan from Lake Huron. An American attempt to retake the island fort was defeated on 4th August 1814, but the blockade of Mackinac by two gunboats threatened the garrison with starvation until these boats were captured in a daring surprise attack. Even so, it remained vital to resupply the garrison before Lake Huron froze at the start of winter; if Mackinac fell, the British stood to lose the support of their Indian allies in that area and the valuable fur trade would be strangled. On 8th September Captain John Murdoch Wardrop's company of the 81st, with a subaltern's detachment of twenty gunners, paddled up the Ottawa river with sixteen large bateaux laden with gunpowder, rum and other necessary stores for the relief of the Fort. Travelling on a traditional fur-trading route, they reached the mouth of the Nottawasaga River, where they met with the two captured gunboats with sufficient provisions to keep the garrison supplied until the end of the war.

The main body of the Battalion marched by divisions on 10th September to Cotean-de-Lai and Matilda, where they remained quartered until 17th October, when they marched to Kingston in three divisions to rejoin their brigade. At Kingston the 81st worked on the defences of the place, which had become the arsenal for Lake Ontario.

Desertion was always prevalent in Canada and the 1st/81st lost 68 men, tempted by the prospect of settlement in America. In January 1815, for instance, it was reported that 'a sergeant and ten men of the 81st Regiment deserted last night with arms, clothing, appointments and 60 rounds of ball cartridge.' A party was sent in pursuit, but they were not caught.

On 1st March it was announced that peace had been concluded with the United States, but that same day Napoleon Buonaparte landed in Provence and war returned to Europe. The 81st was in consequence withdrawn from Canada, leaving Kingston in mid-May for Montreal and Trois Rivières, from where on 15th June they embarked in bateaux for Quebec. Transferred to transports, the Battalion dropped down-river to Brandy Pots, from where on 4th July they sailed for Portsmouth under convoy of HMS *Bulwark*.

The 40th Expedition to Louisiana, October 1814 to May 1815

The 40th were initially selected for the American campaign, but in consideration of their long service in the Peninsula, this was deferred, and on leaving Bordeaux they were instead bound for Ireland. On 9th June 1814 they were ordered from their camp at Blanquefort for Pauillac, which was reached on the 11th. From there, they were taken downriver in transports to the anchorage of HMS *Sultan*, 74, on which they embarked on the 12th and sailed on the 14th for the Cove of Cork.

Arriving on the 30th, they disembarked on 2nd July at Monkstown and proceeded to Cork. From there, they marched on the 4th to Fermoy, and on the 12th to Athlone, which was reached on the 20th. The 2nd/40th arrived there on the same day from Dublin, and on the 25th they transferred 72 rank and file to the 1st Battalion. Whilst at Athlone, as Sergeant William Lawrence recalled, the Peninsula veterans received their arrears of pay:

'The Regiment had never been settled with during the whole of our Peninsular trip for six years, though money had been advanced to us at various places, so now while we were waiting at this place the accounts were made up, and some of our sergeants found they had as much as [£]50 or [£]60. to receive. My own lot amounted to [£]40, I being one of the younger sergeants. When our pay had been given us, a week's furlough was granted to the whole Regiment, and no doubt most of the money melted away in that period – at least, I know mine did, for not having been in the British Isles for so long, we were all resolved to have a spree. I never went away from Athlone, however, the whole time, but slept in barracks every night, though there was no duty to be done as the militia were ordered out for that. I knew that it would be useless to cross the Channel in that short time to see my parents, though I should have liked to have done so, but I did not altogether forget them, and wrote to them to ease their minds about my whereabouts, as I had written to them during my stay in the Peninsula.'[795]

The stay of the Regiment at Athlone was curtailed, for shortly after its arrival Colonel Thornton received orders to prepare the 1st/40th for immediate service. Both battalions left in August for Mallow, where they were inspected on the 15th by Lieutenant-General Lord Forbes who complimented the 1st Battalion on its 'steady, soldierlike, and generally healthy appearance.' A further two sergeants and eighty rank and file were transferred on the 18th to the 1st Battalion from the 2nd, which was by that time reduced to a cadre.

The Regiment remained at Mallow for another six weeks; then the 1st Battalion marched to Monkstown. On 7th and 8th October the 1st/40th embarked on the *Lord Wellington*, *Ajax* and *Baring* transports, and these, with four others, were placed under convoy of HMS *Sultan*, which also had a company of the 40th on board. Their destination was at that time unknown, but it later transpired that they were to reinforce an expedition against New Orleans.

The intended operation had no plausible military purpose, but was more in the nature of a buccaneering enterprise instigated by certain Royal Navy officers motivated chiefly by their desire for prize money. The river port of New Orleans appeared to be an easy target offering rich spoils.

The convoy sailed on the 9th, but no sooner had they cleared the harbour than the wind changed. It blew so hard that Captain West ordered his charges to put into Bantry Bay, and himself led the way in *Sultan*. Unfortunately, it was night-time, and the master of the *Baring*, which had nearly five companies of the 40th on board, was unfamiliar with the entrance to this bay. He lost sight of the *Sultan*, and when he tried to bring his vessel up in the hope of obtaining a pilot, she ran onto the rocks. The rudder was lost, and the *Baring* drifted helplessly across the channel, with a large hole in her bottom through which the sea rushed freely. Catastrophe seemed inevitable, but by great good fortune, instead of being blown onto more rocks, the wind grounded her on a sandy bank on the opposite shore, from where most of those aboard were able to make their way to land. But for this fortuitous chance, there is little doubt that all on board would have drowned. As it was, only four or five men lost their lives, but all the regimental arms, accoutrements and baggage went to the bottom. Lieutenant Hugh Boyd Wray of the 40th, who was on board the *Baring*, made the following entry for the 10th in his journal:

'We, thank God! have just been saved a watery grave. At 2 o'clock this morning, on entering Barehaven [Bear Haven] (which is extremely narrow at the entrance), our captain wished to heave-to for a pilot; but, unfortunately, he attempted it too close to the mouth of the channel, had a press of sail on, and was going at the rate of eight knots, consequently the ship would not 'wear,' and went smack upon the rocks, which were tremendous. Kind Providence would befriend us, for – had we remained where the ship first struck – not a soul could have been saved, as the surf would have dashed a swimmer to atoms. The vessel here lost her helm, and broke a large hole in her bottom. In about seven minutes we felt a great shock: this was the ship being absolutely heaved off the rock, and she went right across the channel (which was narrow) and put into the only spot we could have been saved in, as if steered by the best helmsman in the navy… Indeed, at one time I thought we had but a chance of escaping, as the water was up to the main deck, and the capstan was on fire from the velocity with which it was worked. We have lost all our baggage, it being ordered into the hold to clear the ship. Yesterday it

---

[795] Lawrence, p. 195. This statement, and others, such as his consultation of a French-English dictionary, contradict the assertions of successive editors of his autobiography that the sergeant was illiterate.

was all put down by [Major Sempronius] Stretton's order. I was the last officer on board, along with my servant, to look for my baggage, but in vain. I saved my little canteen and portfolio, which this [his journal] was in.'

On the 11th he wrote, 'We had a rough night last night, being obliged to remain out on the mountains, as there were only two or three small houses, which we gave to the married ladies, who were three in number and in a miserable state, nearly without clothes to cover them, being all in bed when the scene took place yesterday. We have been put on board another transport this morning, called the *Cyrus*, not near so large as the wreck, comfortable only for a few, and we have sixteen officers and three hundred men on board her. All the men are nearly naked, as they came ashore without their kits.'[796]

While Major Stretton went to Cork to report the wreck, the unfortunate half-battalion remained for over a week at Bearhaven, with few clothes and nothing to eat but junk (hard salt meat) and potatoes. It was not until the 19th that the vessels were ordered back to Cork. Luckily the weather had improved, and the transports reached Cove harbour on the 20th. At daybreak next day the shipwrecked men disembarked and marched to Cork to be re-clothed and equipped. New kits were unavailable, time was precious, and Colonel Thornton had to accept old militia packs and other accoutrements for his men. By the 26th the wrecked companies were re-embarked on HMS *Sultan* and the *Plantagenet* transport; but there was then another week's delay for orders, and it not until 2nd November that the convoy sailed, accompanied by no fewer than two hundred merchantmen, with the *Crescent* frigate and *Shamrock* gun-brig.

The voyage was not without incident. For the first few days out, the weather was foul, but afterwards it cleared. 'Enemy in sight' was signaled on the 8th, but he sheered off. Another storm broke on the 11th, and Lieutenant Wray, who was now aboard the *Plantagenet*, made the following entry in his journal:

'Last night we experienced a complete gale of wind, and we had a narrow escape of being run down by the frigate [*Crescent*], which passed close under our stern. It was owing to the wind shifting, and carelessness of the helmsman, who was a young sailor. The ship was taken aback (which is the most dangerous thing can be when blowing hard), and by that we could scarcely clear the frigate. We could only see each other when the lightning would flash. It was really the most terrific sight I, or many others, ever witnessed. It was my watch from 12 to 4, and this happened about half-past 2.'

The fleet sighted Madeira on the 13th, and soon after the expedition's sealed orders were opened. On the 16th, Hugh Wray made the following journal entry:

'Another enemy in sight, but a very long way from us; there is a frigate sent in chase, and I hope may come up with her. Two more ships of war came up with us last night. The Colonel came aboard us this morning. He told us our orders were opened, and that we were to proceed to New Orleans, in America, to join General Ross's army of the south. This is welcome news to us all, as nothing can give us more pleasure than seeing that country.'[797]

Barbados was sighted on the morning of 14th December, but after a brief stay in Carlisle Bay, the fleet continued on its way, passing St. Vincent on the 16th, Puerto Rico on the 18th, and then St. Domingo, before coming to anchor at Port Royal, Jamaica on the 22nd. Here on Christmas Day, they received bad news, as recorded by Lieutenant Wray:

'We were ordered to proceed to sea the following morning. It is reported the reason for hurrying so much is that the expedition against New Orleans has failed, with much loss on our side, and that they want us to renew the attack. We are to go up the Mississippi to New Orleans, where we may expect some hard fighting.'[798]

Ironically, Britain and the United States were already at peace, the Treaty of Ghent having been signed on 24th December.

The fleet remained becalmed for some days off Port Royal, which was fortunate for those of the officers, including Colonel Thornton, who had gone ashore to make purchases, for in the evening, when they wished to get on board again, they found that no boats could be obtained. Lieutenant William Neilley of the 40th was one of those left behind, as explained in his diary entry for 26th December:

---

[796] Lieutenant Hugh Wray's Journal, quoted in *Historical Records of the 40th Regiment*, p.p. 169-70. Wray's Peninsula journal was unfortunately lost in the wreck of the *Baring*.

[797] Wray, quoted in *Historical Records of the 40th Regiment*, p. 171.

[798] This could not have been bad news from New Orleans, which the British expedition did not reach until 23rd December.

'We continued [shopping] until after 6 o'clock, when – to our mortification – we were told we could not get a boat if we were to give any sum of money for it. What added to our misery [was] we knew the fleet was to sail before daylight next morning. On our way to the wharf we met Colonel Thornton, Colonel [Brevet Lieutenant-Colonel] Gillies, and a number of the officers placed in the same predicament. This, of course, made us easy, knowing that means would be taken to put the Colonel on board, so we accordingly made ourselves comfortable for the night.

'27th: Got out of bed before daylight to look for a boat. We could plainly perceive the fleet had sailed, and were lying to outside the harbour. Captain and Mrs Durand, [Ensign Donald] McDonald and I, got a canoe and proceeded to Port Royal, where we found it was impossible to reach the ships by that means. Colonel Thornton and the remainder of the officers shortly after arrived, and were told by a captain of the Navy that, unless we could procure a large vessel to take us out to the fleet, we should remain behind, as no boat could overtake them. Colonel Thornton wrote to Captain West, and an armed schooner, named '*The Edward,*' was immediately ordered to put to sea, and proceeded to the fleet for the purpose of putting us on board. The boats of the *Sultan* attended and put us on board the schooner; she immediately got under weigh, and it was difficult she would overtake the sternmost ship of the fleet. This happened to be the *Sultan*, and by 6 o'clock in the evening we were all on board. The officers behaved remarkably attentive, and appeared desirous of making us comfortable.'[799]

On New Year's Day 1815 the fleet was off Cuba, and on the evening of 9th January the transports anchored at the mouth of the Mississippi.[800] The 40th were ordered to be ready to proceed eighty miles up-river the following day to join the main body of the army. This was no easy matter, for their way lay across a swampy river delta, through creeks and a lagoon, navigable only by boats with a shallow draught. Squalls often occurred, and the prospect of several days and nights in open boats was not agreeable.

However, three days' rations were cooked, and on the morning of the 10th, the 40th Regiment was ready to move. Unfortunately, there were insufficient boats to take them all in one lift, and consequently, some did not start until the following day. The troops embarked on towed boats and barges, holding about one hundred men each. Lieutenant Wray was in one of the boats which started on the 10th, and made the following journal entry the next day:

'Last night it came to blow so hard we were obliged to make for a vessel that we saw a light from, not knowing whether English or American; but we were in the greatest danger possible of being swamped. Captain [William] Fisher commanded the boats. I did not think in any part of the world the climate was so changeable as here – one day it is as cold as charity, and the next as hot as love.'[801]

Lieutenant William Neilley was in another boat that day:

'This morning the weather was excessively rough, and the prospect of going eighty miles in an open boat was by no means pleasant. A captain of the navy came on board to further the disembarkation, and informed us the officers might go in a schooner and the men in transport launches. We got on board the schooner 'L,' and weighed anchor immediately. We had not proceeded fifteen miles up the river when the schooner grounded.'[802]

The 40th were in any case too late, for on 8th January the British assault on New Orleans had been disastrously defeated with heavy casualties. Its commander, General Sir Edward Packenham, had been killed, as had his second-in-command, Major-General Gibbs[803], The 40th had nearly reached the army when they were ordered to turn around and return to the ships, which was done, though according to Sergeant Lawrence at least

---

[799] Lieutenant William Neilley's Diary, quoted in *Historical Records of the 40th Regiment*, p.p. 172-73.

[800] On 9th January Lieutenant Neilley recorded a sad event in his diary: 'The *Ajax* closed, and hailed us to enquire if we were all well, and informed us of the death of Captain [George] Crompton by fever. The loss of this young man is universally regretted from his amiable and interesting character. What adds to increase regret, particularly to his friends, was his having exchanged with a captain of the 2nd Battalion (Downes), and given up a considerable difference, for the purpose of remaining on the full pay establishment.'

[801] Wray, quoted in *Historical Records of the 40th Regiment*, p. 174.

[802] Neilley, quoted in *Historical Records of the 40th Regiment*, p. 174.

[803] Samuel Gibbs was mortally wounded at the Battle of New Orleans, aged 44, and died next day, 9 January 1815. After service in the Mediterranean (1793-96), at Ostend (1798) and in the West Indies (1799-1802), he commanded the 1st/59th Regiment 1804-11 in South Africa, India, Mauritius and Java (see Chapter 10). By proclamation of the Prince Regent, he was posthumously knighted, an exceptional honour, and he is commemorated by a monumental statue in the south transept of St Paul's Cathedral. His Army Gold Medal for Java, and a gold mourning ring, are displayed in the Regimental Museum.

some of the Regiment were 'put on shore near that place' with a force consisting of 'five English and two black regiments and a battalion of marines.'

'We marched on the same day and encamped about two miles from the city. Skirmishing was kept up with this our new enemy during the night, but without any great casualties happening. On the following morning, however, we advanced in a body to attack a battery that had been constructed near the city, chiefly out of barrels of brown sugar. We were at first warmly received with the cannon and musketry planted there, but they soon got tired of our Peninsular medecines: I suppose the pills disagreed with them, for they were very quickly obliged to retire into the city and no more fighting ensued; and some terms having been hinted at. When the black regiments had eaten a quantity of the fortifications, which they seemed to be very fond of, and we had put some into our haversacks as likely to be useful to sweeten our cocoa, we returned to our boats.'[804]

Major-General Sir John Lambert, the senior surviving British officer in front of New Orleans, decided against a renewal of the attack, and on the 18th began a difficult down-river withdrawal.

Writing up his journal on 19th January, Hugh Wray explained the hardships of their Mississippi excursion:

'We are now, thank God, on board our old ships, and it is almost time; we have been the last six days, and only two regular days rations for that time. Two days out of the six we had nothing at all; we were obliged to keep some to the last, fearing we should be out any longer; but the moment I came in sight of the fleet I ate away all I could catch.'

Re-embarkation did not mark the end of the campaign, for the fleet sailed to the mouth of Mobile Bay, which was protected by Fort Bowyer, a wooden fort of some strength, which would have to be reduced in order to open the passage of the bay. Lieutenant Wray's journal entries between 7th and 16th February describe the movements of the 40th during that period:

'*7th February*: We have just received orders to weigh and proceed, in two divisions, to attack (it is supposed) Fort Mobile, which is reported amazingly strong – we are now off. We are to go as far as possible in these ships, and then proceed in small boats. I trust we may succeed, and, indeed, I have no doubt. One division, consisting of the 95th, 7th, and the old 40th, are to make the first attack, and the other, under command of the senior officer of the Second Brigade, to support us.

'*12th February*: We are now as far as the large ships can go, and the small boats are all ready – some off. We are to be commanded by General Lambert, and expect to be close under the fort by morning. We this moment arrived – 10.6 a.m. – on our island (called Dauphine), within two small miles of the fort we are to *take* in the morning.

'*13th February*: Last night, about 12 o'clock, one of our corvettes, with two hundred Indians, attempted to storm the fort, but, unfortunately, in the dark, the vessel grounded, and our sailors were obliged to blow her up. The explosion illumined the whole bay. The Indians were made prisoners and, of course, all failed. We, as yet, have received no orders to move.

'*14th February*: Last night we received orders to be under arms before daylight, and I am now before the fort, in our bivouac, out of range of shot. The fellows are pelting away shot and shell like mischief. This morning I came off a working party, when we were close enough. We have not lost many men.[805]

'*16th February*: Our people have been hard at work these two days back, forming some batteries and getting the guns mounted. We were to have commenced cannonading at 10 o'clock this morning, and to have stormed where they would breach for us; when – much to our surprise – they (the enemy) sent an officer and flag of truce, at half-past nine, with terms of capitulation. The prisoners of war, consisting of one full colonel, some officers, and about six hundred rank and file, some women and children,[806] are all embarking on board some flats, and are going on board the line-of-battle ships. Their fort was a square of embrasures, mounting altogether twenty-two guns, all eighteen and twenty-four pounders; and our position was two small sand hills on each flank of the enemy, with a small sand-bag battery in their front, on which were mounted four howitzers. It is said we are to

---

[804] Lawrence, p.p. 198-99.

[805] British casualties at the siege of Fort Bowyer, 8th-12th February, totaled thirteen killed and eighteen wounded, including one rank and file of the 40th killed and one wounded.

[806] Sixteen American officers, sixteen sergeants, sixteen drummers and 327 rank and file were captured, together with 23 guns, howitzers and mortars.

return tomorrow to the [Dauphin] island, which is about two miles across the channel, and that we will get tents soon, which is a comfort not yet enjoyed by us. We always bivouac, though the rains are very heavy.'[807]

The tents did arrive in due course, which was fortunate, for torrential rain continued day after day. The army remained until 18th March on uninhabited Dauphin Island, suffering at first from a shortage of provisions, a difficulty which ceased once notification of peace was received. The troops appear to have made themselves fairly comfortable, and their ingenuity seems to have satisfied needs most effectively. Sergeant Lawrence described how he and his comrades improvised baking ovens and gathered oysters:

'We soon set to work, however, to construct [an oven] by burning a quantity of oyster-shells for lime, and having mixed that with sand and water we made some very good cement; after which we got a lot of iron hoops from the vessels, with which we formed the arch, and so we put one oven together; and I much doubt if it did not bake as well as any English one, considering the style of dough that we had. After it had been found to answer so well, at least twenty more were constructed on the once desolate but now busy little isle.

'We were constantly on the coast in search of oysters, of which there was an abundance; and some of the more industrious of us even collected them for sale among the troops who either preferred buying them to taking the trouble of collecting them for themselves, or else were unable to go on the sands on account of being on duty.'[808]

With hostilities at an end, the 40th kept themselves busy with, as Lawrence put it, 'various games and freaks,' and in particular with a playhouse in which 'some of the more clever among the officers and men amused the troops.' Writing on 3rd March, Hugh Wray described the theatre:

'Last night our private theatre opened. The house is made of the boughs of trees, and covered in with large sails belonging to the ships of war. The boxes are only one on each side of the stage for the admirals and generals, and then there are seats made of some planks, which form the pit. The scenery was almost all painted by a young man of the name of Haymes, 1st Lieutenant of the *Royal Oak*, and his chief colours were pipeclay, verdigris, and oker. The dresses were mostly made up here, and some were got from the *Royal Oak*. The stage is regularly erected and boarded, and a good green room. The performance was '*The Mayor of Garrett and the Lying Valet*,' which was uncommonly well done. Altogether, a person would not believe it was near so well got up if they did not see it.'[809]

Performances were given in this impromptu theatre no less than three times a week, and, after peace was declared, the American officers joined with the English in enjoying the fun. Ensign George Hibbert's retrospective comments on Dauphin Island were rather less appreciative:

'I never wish to go again to the part of America we left; we were most miserably off. The country is one complete swamp. When we first landed we had nothing but what we could carry on our backs, and neither tents or horses. We, however, secured ourselves against the weather by building little huts with the branches of trees, or rearing up a blanket and sleeping under, like so many gipsies. The latter part of the time our provisions fell very short, being entirely supplied by the ships, and we were put on half allowance of rations. Fortunately I brought out a quantity of tea and sugar from Ireland. There were no inhabitants except a few Indians in that part, therefore there was nothing to be bought. What the island chiefly abounded in were enormous large alligators; a great number of them were caught. One I saw shot measured seven feet in length.'

On 18th March, the 40th embarked for home on the *Ajax*, *Lady Banks*, *Plantagenet* and *Wellington* transports, and sailed on the 21st under convoy of the *Alceste* and *Bellepoule* frigates. The ships sailed first to Havana to take on provisions, but encountered a severe storm in the Gulf of Mexico. On the 25th there was a terrific thunderstorm, and the mainmast of the *Ajax* was struck by lightning, which ran down the mast and exploded in the hold, injuring several men and causing the death of one soldier as he sat at mess. 'His mess tin was burned black,' recalled William Lawrence, 'his shirt was singed, and the top of his bayonet – which had been standing close to him – melted like lead,' and 'when the main hatchway was opened, the smell of sulphur was suffocating.' On the 28th, Hugh Wray, on board the *Lady Banks*, recorded another curious incident:

---

[807] Wray, quoted in *Historical Records of the 40th Regiment*, p.p. 174-76.
[808] Lawrence, p.p. 199-200.
[809] Wray, quoted in *Historical Records of the 40th Regiment*, p. 177. The play was a farce by Garrick, first performed in 1741.

'The master of the ship dined with us today, and whilst he was below, the mate happened by chance to head the commodore, when the commodore fired five or six muskets at us, none of which told.'

The convoy did not reach Havana until 3rd April, and having watered and victualled, set sail for England on the 12th. After a fast passage, the 40th reached Spithead on 15th May. One week later, the first shots of the Waterloo campaign were fired near Mons.

Home Service – 2nd/81st Regiment December 1809 to January 1814

After the disastrous Walcheren expedition, in December 1809, the disease-ridden remnant of the 2nd/81st returned to Bletchingley in Surrey, where they remained until 12th June 1810. They then marched to Bexhill, on the coast of East Sussex, from where on 12th November they moved to nearby Eastbourne and were quartered in temporary huts erected on the sandy beach near the town. An officer of another regiment remarked of the 81st at that time that 'their officers being a jovial, pleasant set of fellows, our rooms presented many a display of merriment and glee during the brief space of our companionship.'

During the summer of 1811, the 2nd/81st received some 150 militia volunteers from Dorset, Gloucestershire and Warwickshire, and in turn, on 5th July, sent a draft of six sergeants and 126 rank and file to their 1st Battalion in Sicily. Despite this influx of English militiamen, 36% of the soldiers were Irish.

On 3rd October 1811, the Battalion marched to Portsmouth and embarked for Jersey on board the transport *Sir Joseph Banks*, reaching that island on 22nd November. Due to their proximity to France, large garrisons were maintained on the Channel Islands, and Jersey was a fortified camp; but despite being on an active service footing the 2nd/81st continued to act as a home battalion, receiving recruits and sending drafts overseas. On 11th January 1813 six subalterns, three sergeants and seventy rank and file were sent from Jersey to the 1st Battalion, then quartered at Alicante, and on 1st April the 2nd Battalion received 103 volunteers from the militia of Devon, Dorset, Montgomery and Warwickshire. This feeder role, stripping the Battalion of effective soldiers and replacing them with recruits, was reflected in an inspection report of 18th November that year when Major-General John Hatton noted that 'the privates, with the exception of a hundred and fifty much too young for service, are a good body of men,' and that there was a good cadre of experienced non-commissioned officers. The Battalion was relatively weak in numbers, with just 376 rank and file. Lieutenant-Colonel Henry Milling remained in command throughout this period.

Home Service – 2nd/30th Regiment February 1813 - January 1814

It will be recalled that when in December 1812 the staff and four companies of the 2nd/30th became part of the 4th Provisional Battalion, the remaining six companies, deprived of their effective other ranks, were sent home to recruit. These skeleton companies, mustering just six sergeants, four drummers and sixty privates under command of Captain Bamford, reached Portsmouth on 24th February 1813 and joined the Depot at Hull in early March. On 14th April, the combined companies, now mustering 245 non-commissioned officers and men, marched to Berwick under the command of Major Morris William Bailey[810] and were quartered in the 'old but substantial barracks.' There they were joined on 13th May by Dr James Goodall Elkington, newly promoted to Surgeon of the 30th for his outstanding services in the Peninsula.[811]

Elkington's diary records that, having been warned in June to prepare to leave for Jersey, the Depot companies marched to Holy Island on 25th June and embarked there, anchoring at Spithead on the 28th. They were detained there until 13th July due to the court martial of a naval lieutenant, who was dismissed the Service for

---

[810] Morris William Bailey CB (1780-1845), who transferred into the 30th as major in 1811, was from a military family. Commissioned in 1795, he served in India with the 10th Foot and as aide-de-camp to the Governor-General, Lord Wellesley. In 1801 he accompanied the 10th to Egypt, marching across the desert under Sir David Baird. He subsequently served in Malta and Gibraltar as aide-de-camp to Generals Fox and Drummond. In 1809 he raised men in Spain for De Meuron's Regiment and obtained a majority in that corps.

[811] Elkington (1784-1853) was appointed Assistant-Surgeon in the 24th Foot on 12th July 1808. In the Peninsula he was twice taken prisoner, tending the wounded after the battle of Talavera and the siege of Burgos. On the first occasion he was sent to France and in due course exchanged, and on the second occasion he escaped. Dr Elkington had been present at Fuentes d'Onoro, Ciudad Rodrigo, Badajoz, Salamanca and the capture of Madrid.

being drunk and abusive when visiting the guardroom of the 30th. The half battalion reached its destination on the 16th, landing at St. Aubin with 17 officers, 29 sergeants and 353 rank and file.

'Landed at Jersey and marched to Grouville Barracks – wooden barracks built some years before for the Russians. The 6th Regiment quartered near us in Grouville [Mont Orgueille] Castle. We were within a few minutes walk of the sea. General Don commanded; he had made most excellent roads round the Island, and numerous Martello towers to defend any bays where the enemy could land. The Castle, on a rock off the town of Saint Pierre, is very strong, and a fortification commanding the town was erecting, with bomb proofs and the ditch excavated in the solid rock.'[812]

On September 23rd, the 2nd/30th were reunited when Hamilton disembarked with his four service companies. They had landed at Cowes from Lisbon on 29th June and marched to Sandown with a strength of 377 non-commissioned officers and men. After leave, Hamilton's Peninsula veterans sailed for Jersey, albeit taking ten days to cross from the Isle of Wight to St. Aubin.

The 30th remained quartered at Grouville Barracks on the east coast of the island throughout their short tour on Jersey, and in December 1813 they had detachments deployed along the coast at Bouley Bay, Rozel Barracks and Mont Orgueille Castle, this last being a medieval stronghold crowning a headland above Gorey harbour. They also manned two signal stations, on Mont Mado above Bouley Bay and at Verclut Point, near Rozel, part of a chain of ten such posts established on commanding heights around the island to give early warning of French invasion.[813]

In November, the Battalion was inspected at Grouville by Major-General Hatton. There were present under arms 37 sergeants, 30 corporals, 13 drummers and 537 privates. Hatton said of the non-commissioned officers that 'the greater part are very young. They perform their duties with promptitude and energy, and attend to the best of their abilities the discipline of the Regiment. The privates with the exception of about 100 much too young for any service, are a good body of men with the appearance of health and cleanliness, who were well drilled, attentive and well behaved.' He went on to observe that the interior economy was well-regulated, that the interior arrangements of companies were duly attended to, and that the conduct of the men was soldier-like on duty and in quarters. 'One hundred and ten have joined since the last inspection. Every attention appears to have been paid in perfecting them in their duty. From the general appearance they are an acquisition to the Corps, with the exception of ten, who from slight make, and indifferent health, do not promise to improve.' Field exercises and movements 'were performed with precision, and the formations made with correctness, and a proper degree of celerity,' and he noted with satisfaction that 'the Regiment is in the habit of practising with ball ammunition.'

Commenting on this favourable report, Lieutenant-General Don, former commanding officer of the 59th and Lieutenant-Governor of Jersey since 1806, observed that 'This Battalion is commanded by Lieut Colonel Hamilton, who pays particular attention to it. 372 men of the Battalion now present are fit for duty in the field, besides which number there are 75 rank & file recruiting, and 58 rank & file on furlough considered fit for duty in the field.' The 2nd/30th were clearly ready for further active service.

Holland 1814

As the tide of history turned against Napoleon Buonaparte, and his client states in northern Europe fell away, the British Army became engaged on a new front in Holland, where in November 1813 an insurrection had broken out against French occupation. Securing the Low Countries from French expansion had long been a central object of British foreign policy, hence the campaigns of 1793-5 and 1799, and so a force under Sir Thomas Graham was sent to assist the Dutch, in conjunction with Prussian and Russian troops. Graham's force, initially some six thousand men, was deficient in both quantity and quality, being made up of London-based Guards, depot units, and relatively inexperienced battalions brought back from the Stralsund garrison by Major-General Samuel Gibbs, late of the 59th. As the Duke of York would later admit, this force was composed of 'everything which we could scrape together on the spur of the moment with the idea of them being placed in garrison, and not to be

---

[812] Elkington's Diary, in the *XXX* Journal, April 1911, p. 12.
[813] The 2nd/82nd were at that time stationed on nearby Alderney, where they were joined by Captain George Wood.

employed in the field.' A second wave of two brigades, mostly composed of home-based second or third battalions of their regiments, together with cavalry, artillery and engineers, would take longer to assemble.

On 19th December 1813, the 2nd Battalions of the 30th and 81st were ordered to Holland as reinforcements, part of the above-mentioned second wave. They embarked from Jersey at St. Aubin's pier on 2nd January 1814, the horses of both battalions being shipped in a separate transport, and sailed in convoy next day. The 30th were allocated three transports: Lieutenant-Colonel Hamilton sailed with the headquarters wing in the *Union*, Lieutenant-Colonel Charles Vigoureux[814] with the other wing in the *Saragossa*, and Lieutenant Benjamin Nicholson went aboard the *Earl of Cathcart* with officers and men to form a depot at Winchester. It was a slow and hazardous voyage in foul weather, and after three and a half weeks they were still at Spithead, where they had first anchored on the 16th.

The bad weather, which so delayed the transports from Jersey, was disastrous for a detachment of the 30th, which had sailed from Lisbon just after Christmas 1813 aboard the 340-ton *Queen*, transport no. 332, and joined a convoy of eight other transports bound for Portsmouth. The *Queen* had a crew of 25 under Captain Carr and carried 325 soldiers, ten French prisoners, 63 women and 68 children, including 32 men of the 30th commanded by Lieutenant Robert Daniell, whose wife and five children were also aboard. The men were mostly recovered, sick, and wounded.

After a rough passage, on 10th January, the *Queen* reached Falmouth and anchored in Carrick Roads within the supposed safety of the great natural harbour. There was a strong easterly wind and a forecast of more unsettled weather, but despite lying about three hundred fathoms off the treacherous rocks of Trefusis Point, the Captain only put out his port anchor with a much reduced length of cable. Even so, the ship lay happily there for three days until the night of the 13th when a violent south-easterly gale swept in and she began to drag her anchor. The watch on deck failed to notice what was happening at first, and by the time they alerted the Captain, it was too late to prepare the starboard anchor.

It was an exceptionally wild moonless night, with snow gusting across the harbour and only lightning flashes to illuminate the scene when disaster struck. The port anchor cable parted and, as the crew struggled desperately to get the starboard anchor ready, the *Queen* was blown uncontrollably towards Trefusis Point. By this time most of the troops were on deck but the women and children were still below. There followed, according to *The West Briton* newspaper, 'a scene of indescribable confuson and horror... the sea breaking in an awful manner over the ship, whilst the endeavours of those who were below to get on deck, and the alarming shrieks of the women and children, whom neither force nor entreaty could render quiet, augmented the distress.'

As the *Queen* crashed onto the Point, at a time variously estimated between 4.30 and 6 a.m., she broached-to, and huge waves smashed over her and poured down the hatches, flooding the vessel from stem to stern. Attempts were made to fire a cannon as a distress signal, but the guns were swamped and heavy snow made it almost impossible for anyone to see the wreck from the shore. The Captain ordered all the masts to be cut away, and as they fell they crushed or knocked overboard many people. The ship then gave a sickening lurch which caused guns to break free and bulkheads to give way, and as the hull collapsed all below were either crushed to death or drowned. In less than twenty minutes of striking Trefusis Point the *Queen* had been reduced to matchwood.

Some of the troops, including most of the 30th detachment, managed to scramble ashore and ran to the village of Flushing to raise the alarm. Other survivors escaped in boats or by clinging to wreckage, and valiant attempts at rescue were made by local men; but daylight revealed scores of bodies washing about in the shallows, many entangled in the ships rigging, and others strewn around the rocks.

It was the greatest ever loss of life on the coast of Cornwall. Only 89 soldiers, nine women, one child, and four prisoners survived, while Captain Carr and his entire crew, except for the bosun and a cabin boy, perished in the disaster. Only five (or perhaps four) of the 30th detachment died[815], but Lieutenant Daniell lost his wife and all five children. Some two hundred and fifty bodies were eventually recovered, and 136 of them were laid to rest

---

[814] Vigoureux had transferred from the 38th into the 30th as Major (Brevet Lieutenant-Colonel) on 4th June 1813.
[815] Died in the wreck of the *Queen*: Privates Philip Garrett, Philip Grant, Josh Hunt, George Rawden and James Waters, though there is some doubt about Rawden since a man with his name claimed a Military General Service Medal with 'Badajoz' clasp in 1848. Waters had previously been wrecked on the *Jenny* in 1805, but had escaped from captivity and rejoined the 30th.

in a mass grave in Mylor Churchyard. A memorial, with a dramatic naive carving of the foundering ship, was erected there by villagers, and reads, 'To the memory of the warriors, women and children who, returning from the coast of Spain unhappily perished in the wreck of the Queen, transport, on Trefusis Point, January 14th, 1814. This stone is erected as a testimony of regret by the inhabitants of this parish.' Lieutenant Daniell erected his own memorial[816] to his family, and 'though much bruised' in the disaster he continued to serve and was wounded the following year at Waterloo.

We must now revert to the story of the expedition to Holland. The fleet of transports with the 30th and 81st on board, escorted by HMS *Rinaldo*, eventually sailed again from the Solent on the 27th, but, as related by Surgeon James Elkington, the situation of the wing on the *Union* transport soon worsened:

'*Jan 27th*. Sailed from St. Helen's, and in the morning found ourselves alone, having lost the fleet in the night. Under easy sail all day; brought up at 4 p.m. at Dover, near the South Foreland. Wind light, off shore. The fleet passed us and anchored in the Downs. What could possess our Master of the transport not to follow them, I could never learn.

'*Jan 29th*. During the night a heavy gale from the S.W. came on, right on shore. Feeling the vessel pitching heavily, I looked out of the cabin windows and saw the South Foreland light every now and again as we were tossed up by the swell. I well knew our danger, [and] we all got up. The whole day the gale continued, we had two anchors down. The Master drunk and many of the crew. Having some deserters from the Navy among our men, they were useful in lashing old jackets around the cables to prevent the chafing. No pilot could leave Dover to our aid. A regiment from the Garrison was sent to the beach, waiting with assistance in case we should part from our anchors, that was expected at any moment. It was a Sunday, and we afterwards heard that the prayers of the Church were offered up for a transport full of troops in distress. Towards sunset, the wind came more off shore and we did not ride so heavily.

'*Jan 30th*. Weather more moderate. A pilot came on board us, who prepared to unmoor, in attempting which he sprung the windlass and capstan. One anchor was raised, the ring of which was opened; he cut from the others, and we made for Ramsgate Pier, where we arrived at sunset.

'*Jan 31st*: Embarked on board another transport [the *Sophia*], the one we arrived in being found too strained to proceed. Sailed from the pier and anchored in the Downs. The horse transport, being also damaged, was obliged to put in, and joined us the day after.'[817]

Lieutenant Park Percy Nevill of the 30th recalled 'a frost of a most severe kind' and tempestuous weather from the north:

'We were obliged to anchor in the Downs for several days, and had not our anchors held we must have gone on shore. During this time the frost was so intense that we were always obliged to remain below, and the sailors suffered so much that they could hardly manage to guide the ships.'[818]

The fleet sailed again on 2nd February, heading for the fortified naval base of Hellevoetsluis, which had been occupied by the Royal Marines on 6th December as the British point of entry. They were without the *Saragossa*, which had parted from the convoy, and on the 6th the *Sophia* struck on a sandbank, having to be bumped off by all aboard moving aft. Passing the Schouwen Light that evening, a great expanse of floating ice was encountered in the Haringvliet, and although by the 8th the *Sophia* was within hailing distance of Hellevoetsluis pier, she was driven from her anchor by the weight of ice. There were fears for her safety, and it was not until the 10th that she could be worked into the basin, hauled in by pier-mounted capstans.

The *Saragossa*, with Lieutenant-Colonel Vigoureux and his wing of the 30th, was obliged to put back to the Downs and did not arrive until the 14th, by which time the men had been aboard for 42 days. The 81st disembarked two days later. The horse transport was wrecked off the Helder, where the horses were thrown

---

[816] Headstone in Mylor Churchyard, Cornwall: 'In memory of Catherine, wife of Lieut. Robert Daniell, 30th Regiment; also their children, viz. Margaret, Eleanor, William, Robert and Edward Alexander, who unhappily perished in the wreck of the *Queen*, Transport, on the awful morning of the 14th Jan 1814. Leaving an unfortunate husband and father to lament their loss to the end of his existence.' There are two other memorials in adjacent parishes to those lost in the disaster.
[817] Elkington's Diary, in the *XXX Journal*, April 1911, p.p. 12-13.
[818] Nevill, p. 31.

overboard to swim ashore, with some loss, including Colonel Hamilton's charger. Altogether, the voyage was not an auspicious start to the campaign:

'The cold was terrible,' recalled Lieutenant Nevill, 'and the ice-boats that brought us on shore had to be dragged by Dutch sailors over nearly five miles of frozen sea, and we greatly felt the severe chill and cold, so different from the fine climate of the Peninsula.'

As detachments of the 30th disembarked, they marched to the fortress of Willemstad, where their forebears had landed for the Regiment's first campaign in 1690, and were quartered in the small village of Fineart. There they remained about a week. All ranks were issued with winter necessaries, two pairs of woollen stockings each and a warm blanket. The 30th then continued south to join Graham's army at Loenhout on 2nd March, while the 81st marched to Brasschaat.

By the time the 30th and 81st disembarked, the French had withdrawn their field army from the Netherlands, leaving garrisons in Antwerp, Bergen-op-Zoom and a few lesser places, and the Prussians too had departed, summoned to join their main army in its final struggle against Napoleon in France. Graham was left to continue the campaign almost alone and, having insufficient resources to besiege Antwerp, he resolved to storm Bergen-op-Zoom before his troops were re-allocated for service in America or elsewhere.

He had also to blockade the port of Antwerp, third city of the Napoleonic Empire and a naval base of strategic importance, and in particular to neutralise the French warships in the Scheldt. On joining the army, the 30th and 81st were assigned to the 2nd Division, then under the temporary command of Samuel Gibbs, which was employed on this task. Lieutenant-Colonel James Carmichael Smyth, Graham's Chief Engineer, described the British lines facing Antwerp.

The right of the 2nd Division 'was placed at Fort Frederick close to Lillo upon the Scheldt and its left at the village of Braschaet [Brasschaat]. At Fort Frederick a battery secured by strong palisades, *trous de loup*, &c has been constructed to cut off all communication by water from Antwerp to Bergen op Zoom and Batz; and the village of Braschaet upon our left has been strengthened by field works.'

The main position at Brasschaat was based on a large square former distillery, which was converted into a loopholed barracks for three hundred men, surrounded by extensive entrenchments and palisades. There was no accommodation at the ruined Fort Frederick, so regiments took it in turn to hold the post and put it in a state of defence, and were relieved daily. On 5th March the 30th marched to the works at Brasschaat for a 24-hour duty, which was repeated on the 8th.

It was at this time that 16-year-old Edward Nevil Macready[819] joined the 30th as a Volunteer, hoping to earn a commission. Highly opinionated, proud, touchy and quarrelsome, Macready was nonetheless a carefully honest and credible witness and diarist. From a family of actors, he was also an acute observer of people, places and atmosphere, making his journal a rich and lively account of his regiment's life and times.

Macready had intended to join the 69th Regiment, as he was related to Brevet Major Lewis Watson of that corps, but Sir Thomas Graham, who interviewed the young soldier, advised otherwise. 'No,' he said, shaking his head, 'I had rather you joined the 30th. I know Colonel Hamilton well, and I am certain he will take care of you.' Next morning Macready received a letter of introduction to the 30th and set off for Loenhout.

'I hired a guide,' wrote Macready, 'and after a walk of six miles through the snow, with trembling steps I entered the house, or rather hovel, of my future commander. He was a veteran officer who had served under Abercrombie and Nelson in his younger days, and had shared in the late campaigns in Portugal and Spain. He welcomed me most kindly, asked me to dinner, assigned me a quarter in a windowless room already occupied by a dozen officers, and on this day, February 28th, 1814[820], put me on the strength of the Light Company.'

'The Army in which I now had the honor to serve had been hurried over from England on the first appearance of the insurrection which broke out in Holland soon after the glorious battle of Leipsig and was composed of very indifferent materials. Most of the battalions had never seen a shot fired[821], but Graham was at their head, and under his orders all were anxious to initiate themselves. The sum total of our force might amount

---

[819] He spelt his name 'McCready' at this time, but for the sake of consistency we will use the later spelling.
[820] The date Macready was taken on strength does not quite fit regimental movements, but may have been back-dated.
[821] Of Graham's sixteen line infantry battalions, only the 2nd Battalions of the 30th, 44th and 81st had served in Spain, and only the 2nd/30th and their old friends the 2nd/44th had recent service there. Many others had seen little or no active service before Holland.

to 10,000 men.[822] It was cantoned in the villages between Bergen op Zoom, Batz, Antwerp, Breda, and Williamstadt, the three first of which were occupied in force by the enemy.

'Our Allies, the Saxons and Prussian Landwehr, under Thielmann and Duke Bernard of Saxe Weimar, were on the left bank of the Scheldt, opposed by Count Maison, who commanded a less numerous but better-organized body of troops who more than once, particularly near Courtray, handled our friends rather roughly. Bulow's corps (which had co-operated with our force in two reconnaissances made towards Antwerp) had ere this marched to France to reinforce Blucher, who had suffered severely at the different affairs of La Fere, Montmirail and Champaubert.

'Carnot[823], of republican notoriety, commanded the force opposed to us and distributed them as follows: He garrisoned Antwerp with about 7000 men, composed of Marines, the *Corps d'Etrangers*, in which was incorporated the late Irish Brigade, and the conscription of 1815. Bergen op Zoom was occupied by near 2000 men, of whom one third might be old Marines and the rest mere boys. Batz contained about 500, and Lillo with Loefenshock as many more, while Flushing and the other forts on the river might contain about 4000.

'This force, if united, might have given us a repetition of the campaign of '93; but they were so divided, and we so snugly between them, as effectively to prevent co-operation or even communication. Little else could be expected from us. Indeed, the weakness of our army, the season of the year, and the ultimately trifling result of operations in this quarter were such as seemed to preclude every idea of very active hostilities commencing. Posts were established and works thrown up on the principal roads, and our advanced sentries were pushed close up to the fortresses we were blockading. I could not for some time believe that war could be reduced to such a mere sparring sort of contest, and notwithstanding my hourly acquired experience I never, for the first month after I joined, went up to a hedge or house without half expecting to see a Frenchman, or received my rations without a blush as I hadn't the honor of taking them from the enemy.

'The morning after I arrived at Loenhout, the Regiment marched to relieve the 35th, who were erecting a battery near the village of Braschaet [Brasschaat] to command the high road from Breda to Antwerp. Our men appeared fine young fellows, and I soon discovered from their swarthy cheeks and frequent exclamations of '*Jesu Maria*' and '*Malvito carrhaco*' that many of them had shared in the Spanish campaigns. I particularly remarked their uncommon cleanliness. The Colonel introduced me to most of the officers, who appeared affable and gentlemanly fellows. We arrived at our destination about six o'clock, and half the men were set at work with pickaxes and spades on ground which turned the iron at every stroke.

'Our post was composed of two or three barns, well loop-holed and connected by stockades; at the angle nearest the road we were throwing up a small redoubt, to contain two guns for sweeping the chaussée, which was defended for some distance by abattis and felled timber. Every approach was obstructed in the same manner, and it was altogether a very pretty field-work, but required a much larger body of men than our Corps to defend it. Our videttes were about a mile in advance. In twenty-four hours we were relieved, and returned to our hovels at Leonhout.

'The snow was at this time deep on the ground, and continued so till late in April. This, with the thick fogs, frequent sleet showers and chilling breezes, rendered our working duty rather harassing. The villages we occupied had been abandoned by their inhabitants and destroyed by the Prussians. Not an article of furniture or a pane of glass was to be found in them. They were mere sheds, and when we awoke in the morning we were petrified with cold and frequently covered over with snow. Indeed, but for the accomplishments of smoking and gin-drinking, which I speedily acquired and most strongly recommend to all campaigners in Holland, I think this unusual freezing would have proved as injurious as it was unpleasant.

'After one day of rest, we marched again to our battery, and I was sent on outlying piquet with Lieutenant [John] Rumley and a subdivision of the Light Company. The nights we passed on this duty – for from this day we were invariably detached – were I think the most tedious in my life. The cold was intense. Our shed was open on

---

[822] The monthly return on 25th February 1813, shortly after the arrival of the 30th and 81st, shows that Graham's force then included 11,812 rank and file, of whom 8,597 were effective. The total strength of the 2nd/30th on that date was 29 officers, 46 sergeants, a drum major and ten drummers, and 745 rank and file. Of these last, 208 were on command or furlough, reducing the number in the ranks to 537.

[823] Lazare Carnot, the 'Organiser of Victory' in the early Revolutionary years, came out of retirement to defend Antwerp.

two sides, and the enemy was not near enough to make the duty interesting. Rumley and I walked round and round the sentries, examined every loiterer we could catch, and even sent off some who were particularly unintelligible, as spies, to headquarters. We talked of everything, did everything that could divert us, but could not kill the time. We have often awoke shivering with cold and, expecting it to be morning, called to the sentry for the hour, and he has answered, 'Past ten.' Our first sleep being over, our boiled eggs and potatoes all eaten, and our patience exhausted, there we would sit over our expiring fire, and damn the climate until day-break. This sort of business soon rubbed off my boyish timidity and I rapidly acquired the quantum of bronze requisite for outpost duty. In a few days I could cross-question a peasant as saucily and curse his stupidity as conscientiously as the oldest campaigner. After our twenty-four hours' work we returned to Loenhout, and next day marched back to Braschaet.'[824]

Lieutenant Nevill of the 30th had again volunteered his services to the engineer department, and as an assistant engineer he was employed in front of Fort Frederick, constructing a howitzer breastwork. Whilst there he saw something of the 81st Regiment.

'About seven in the morning, our attention was drawn by the firing of the front picket of the 81st, that regiment being on duty in the fort at the time. It was caused by some French skirmishers, who had advanced on ours, from a body of French troops marching towards us along the dyke. We all instantly turned out, and the 81st formed a column facing them, when the enemy halted and gave us a couple of rounds from a light gun; we returned the compliment by an 18-pounder, and they speedily retired. We had no casualties, and it appeared to be only a reconnoitring party of the enemy.'[825]

In his *Recollections*, Nevill stated that this incident occurred on the 8th of March, but he must have been mistaken, for that same night he took part in the disastrous attempt to storm Bergen-op-Zoom, of which he left an account:

'We took possession of seven bastions out of thirteen, and the water port gate; but no effort appeared to be made to establish a body of troops in the town, which had been done on all former occasions of our sieges in Spain. With the exception of small parties of the enemy appearing and firing upon us, we remained in possession of what we had got, and expected the garrison would surrender in the morning. But we found it quite the contrary. In many parts about the works, close to us, were houses of the town; and as daylight appeared, the enemy opened such a storm of fire upon us, from loopholes and from the windows, that half our officers, and a great number of our men, fell in the course of a quarter of an hour. Major-Generals Gore and Skerrett[826] were killed, and nearly all the commanding officers of regiments; and then great was the confusion, for there appeared nobody to give orders as to what was to be done. At this crisis no one thought of turning the guns upon the houses of the town. There they were, all loaded, and their slow-matches in readiness.

'In a short time large bodies of French troops opened fire upon us, calling upon us to surrender, which many of our men did, throwing down their arms. All was lost; and some of us sprang over the parapets, or through the embrasures, into the ditches, now with several feet of water on the ice. Some escaped this way; others were shot down in the attempt; but I was fortunate, and got over with only a few bruises.'[827]

Neither the 30th nor the 81st, who had joined the army less than a week earlier, were directly involved in this disaster, though Macready tells how the 30th marched in preparation for the intended next phase of the operation, an attack on Fort Frederick at Lillo:

'On the following morning, as we were entering Wustwesel [Wuustwezel], to which we were now directed to change our cantonments, a staff officer galloped up to the head of the column, and ordered us to march to Calmpthout [Kalmthout], as Bergen op Zoom had been stormed on the preceding evening, and we, with some other corps, were on the following night to attack Lillo. Anxiety of some kind beamed in every face, and we

---

[824] *The Journal and Opinions of Edward Nevil Macready*, National Army Museum 6807-209. This Journal, in two volumes, was held by 1st Battalion The East Lancashire Regiment, direct lineal successor of the 30th, in the 1880s, when extracts were published in the *XXX Journal* and they were used as a source for regimental history instruction.

[825] Nevill, p.p. 34-3.

[826] Gallant and indecisive to the end, John Byne Skerrett, former commanding officer of the 2nd/47th, contributed to the disaster by leading his men in the wrong direction in an attempt to take the Antwerp Gate. There are memorials to him in St. Paul's Cathedral, St. Nicholas's Cathedral, Newcastle, and St. Mary's Church, Ponteland, Northumberland.

[827] Nevill, p.p. 35-7.

stepped out famously. The spire of Calmpthout was already in sight when our Brigade Major met us with a horribly long phiz, and told us to counter-march; for that Bergen was lost, and with it 2,000 men of Cooke's division. The road which seemed to fly from under us on our advance, appeared to lengthen as we returned, and it was night before we entered the ruins of Wustwesel. Our men had gone thirty miles after twenty-four hours' work, preceded by a march, and were growling like bears. 'Why weren't we sent there?' was indignantly murmured from the ranks. For my part I felt, like all young fellows on these occasions, an apprehensive sort of anxiety as we pushed on, and abused Cooke's people as roundly as the rest of them, when we retired.'

'From what I have been able to learn of this disastrous assault, it appears to have been admirably planned, as Sir Thomas lodged the troops within the walls and occupied the greater portion of the works with little or no loss. But it seems that the officer in command of the division had no named *point de rendez-vous* and that our people were attacked in detail by the united force of the enemy, who were at first so much alarmed as to send a flag of truce. The officer who carried it was shot by Mr Ryan, 69th, since dismissed the Service. I believe the 44th, 55th and 69th Regiments behaved gallantly, but the reputation of other corps suffered dreadfully on this occasion. Sir T. Graham, in his despatch, accuses the Royals and 33rd of leaving their post, and I have heard most people agree in the unqualified censure of the Guards and General Cooke. But a privileged Corps is often the object of unmerited obloquy and it is by no means unusual for young and indignant soldiers to soothe their own wounded vanity by attributing their disgrace to the incapacity of their General. However, I have been assured by an officer[828] who served in the column to which General Cooke attached himself that he never allowed them to quit the neighbourhood of the rampart except to repulse advancing bodies of the enemy, which they repeatedly [did], and as often as they pursued them towards the centre of the town they were recalled by him. For some hours they did not fire a shot or see an enemy and, as the irritated relater declares, it seemed as if they were brought into the town merely to lay down their arms.

'There must certainly have been gross misconduct somewhere. Had the troops merely defended the gorges of the bastions till daylight had shewn them their relative situation, a combined attack must have succeeded. Generals Skerrett and Gore, truly gallant officers, "led their ragamuffins where they got finely peppered," and were themselves killed with about 150 men. Perhaps three times as many were wounded, and about 1400 made prisoners.[829] Among these last was General Cooke. The garrison was considerably inferior in number to their prisoners. This was the shameful and unparalleled result of an affair which, had it been executed with half the zeal and ability with which it had been plan'd, would have ranked as high in the annals of British achievement as the glorious assaults of Rodrigo and Badajoz.'

After the Bergen-op-Zoom debacle, Graham's remaining troops continued their observation and containment of Antwerp.

'Our Regiment continued to take the Braschaet duty as usual,' wrote Macready, 'and the outposts were ordered to be doubly vigilant. Our situation was rather critical, as the garrison of Antwerp were equal to us in number, and Maison could have thrown a few thousand men over the river whenever he pleased. He attacked some Saxons a few miles to our left one day, and completely routed them, we remaining under arms during the firing, which was very brisk.

'About 13th March, the regiment changed its quarters to Putte, a neat village in tolerable repair, between Bergen op Zoom and Antwerp, and as we marched thence to Braschaet, our stupid guide led us close up to the French videttes. They sat on their horses like statues, and we did not molest them.

'On the 17th, St. Patrick's Day, I was initiated in drunkenness, and since my entrance in the Service I cannot tap myself with having once neglected the due observance of this important holiday.

'We now ceased our Braschaet duty, and in exchange were to go twice a week to occupy a battery erected on the Scheldt, to prevent any communication by the river between Antwerp and Bergen op Zoom. It was erected near an old fort called Frederick Hendrick, and was about ten miles from our cantonment. We started for it the first time at 12 o'clock on the night of the 19th. It was dark as pitch. Our men were incessantly slipping over the icy roughness of the road, and occasionally some unfortunate fellow would plump through the thin ice of some running stream. The only guide we had to keep the path were the curses of those who were falling off it, and just

---

[828] This officer was probably his friend Lieutenant Nevill, who appears to have been with that column.
[829] Casualties at Bergen-op-Zoom amounted to 381 killed, 536 wounded and 2,058 all ranks taken prisoner.

as light dawned, and we were congratulating each other on the conclusion of our annoyance, we found ourselves checked by a branch of the inundation which crossed the road. It was about up to our middles, and through it we dashed; the very recollection of it chills me! We reached our post in a dense fog, and I was told we had relieved the 78th Highlanders.

'About eight o'clock a breeze sprang up, and carrying off the [fog], showed us a six-pounder pointed down the dyke, and an howitzer in battery towards the river. The remains of the old fort and two or three houses were close to us, and about a mile lower down the dyke was our battery of six long twenty-four pounders, with its furnace for heating shot. In the contrary direction, and at about double the distance, was Lillo, and Liefenshoeck immediately opposite. Between them were a French line of battle ship and some craft at anchor. The river was here at least a mile in breadth, and the enemy having opened the sluices, the whole country was under water. The forts and houses looked like islands which the roads and dykes connected with each other. Our advance, composed of riflemen, were on the bank towards Lillo at near a mile from us and about 300 yards from the French sentinels.

'Just before the fog had cleared up, we were alarmed by a heavy fire from our lower battery, which was thundering hot shot at an enormous lump of ice, which sustained the cannonade with exemplary *sang froid*; the officer of artillery had mistaken it for a boat. This gave rise to some military discussion, and our gallant Colonel was describing how he intended to decoy the enemy into "the *fleur de luces* in front of the palisades." The Engineers called them '*trous de loup*,' but as the Colonel says, "the French language has altered damnably since he was at Toulon."

'The day passed quietly enough, with the exception of a few shots exchanged at the advanced posts. I was down with the Riflemen, and admired them very much. They hit every time I saw them fire. We were on the alert all night, and twice got under arms, anticipating a sally from Lillo and conjecturing, from the noise on board the ships, that they were moving down to co-operate with the garrison. Morning broke, and exhibited *L'Anversois*, 74, laid broadside opposite our howitzer, with her stern chasers pointed at our heavy battery. She was about half a mile from us, and behind her were the small craft. 'This looked rebellion.' However, she did not open, so we went to breakfast, and I was just discussing an egg, when off went a broadside, down came the chimney in a shower of brick bats, and our poor egg-woman was cut in two by a round shot.

'We hurried under the dyke, and formed regularly in companies, while they kept up their infernal din, and splashed mud and ice about our ears by bushels full. Our howitzer and a traversing 24-pounder answered them. Parker, of the Artillery, behaved most gallantly. When the first shot was fired, he jumped upon the bank and, tho' exposed to their whole fire, continued there throughout. A man was knocked down between him and the wheel of the howitzer, and the ground ploughed up all around him.'

'The Regiment had nothing to do but to sit down and wait for a sally. Just as we had formed, a flank fire opened on us from Lillo, and dislodged our company, but as soon as we turned an angle of the old fort we were under cover. The cannonade was kept up till near eleven o'clock, when some Congreve rockets arrived, and tho' badly thrown, alarmed the enemy so much that they cut their cables and stood off in confusion. Their loss could not be ascertained, but fourteen shot and shell were seen to strike the line-of-battle ship. The 73rd Regiment relieved us about ten o'clock. Our Drum Major and another man were killed, and four wounded, by the flank fire which dislodged our company. The Artillery had one man killed, and another wounded, and the egg-woman, with an orderly hussar's horse, made up our list of casualties. Our colour-staff was broken, and the houses knocked to pieces.

'Thus ended the first of my fields, in which I was probably as much funked as Frederick the Great, but not being so well mounted, couldn't run as far; so luckily I saved my character and was hailed as a lad of pluck. But joking apart, a two hours' exposure to a thundering cannonade, without the excitement of active exertion, is a very serious initiation for a *debutant* in our profession; and if posterity will believe that it was possible for a McCready to know fear, I candidly confess I never was so near an intimate acquaintance with the gentleman as on this occasion. We had a number of tyros besides myself, and I saw enough to convince me that a young man must not be judged harshly of for a little timidity on his first essay in arms. My Captain, Chambers, made this remark, and pointed out a young fellow who seemed somewhat alarmed, and who has since behaved with distinguished gallantry. When we returned to Putte, we buried our dead with military honours.'

Private Joseph Gabett was killed in this action and Drum Major Thomas Vipond was mortally wounded, two men had each a leg carried off and two more were wounded. Vipond, a Manchester cotton spinner before he enlisted, died the same day. He had served with the 2nd/30th since its formation. The Battalion raised funds to support his widow Eliza, who soon received this and the Drum Major's back pay at the Regimental Depot.

One of the Colour pikes was cut in two and Colonel Hamilton, who was eating his breakfast nearby, had a narrow escape. He was sitting on a bank with his legs drawn up to support his plate when a round shot struck the ground beneath them, throwing the plate into his face and covering him with mud, blood and fragments of flesh.

In his diary, Surgeon James Elkington puts the date of this action at 21st March, and has slightly different casualty figures, but his narrative is substantially the same:

'About 8 a.m., as we were at breakfast, a line of battle ship and some brigs dropped down within musket shot of the Fort and commenced a heavy fire of round shot, 32-pounders; many rattled through the house we were in. The guns were fired with a small charge of powder so as to fall in the Fort; many fell in the inundation, the ice of which had not disappeared. We had one howitzer only in the Fort... and it replied most vigorously, and having the stern of the line of battle ship in a proper direction, every shot told. A little after noon the Rocket Corps came down and launched a few at the ships, but with no effect more than frightening them, for they soon after went up towards Antwerp again.

'We lost in this affair two men killed and one man wounded, the Drum Major one of the former; by one shot only, five legs of the three soldiers were shattered; the man who lost one leg only, suffered amputation and recovered, the others died in a few hours.'[830]

After the affair of 20th March, according to Macready, 'the force at Fort Frederick was decreased to a Wing, and afterwards to a captain, two subalterns, and 100 men. I went there successively with Majors Bailey and Vigoureux, and Captains Machell and Chambers. The inundation had entirely flooded the road, and we were obliged to march on the dyke round by Santvliet, about sixteen miles. Our bivouacs were now shockingly cold and tiresome. Sitting with our shins to a fire which half roasted them, while our backs were assailed by the piercing sleet, we seldom exchanged a word, or heard a sound except the abrupt 'Who goes there?' of the sentinel, and the clank of his firelock as he brought it to 'the port,' or the more thrilling report of a shot, which roused us up and often kept us under arms for half the night.

'The day Chambers commanded our detachment, a small party of the enemy advanced to annoy our riflemen, and I went with Chambers and ten men to drive them in. They retired immediately that one of them was wounded. This inglorious and fatiguing warfare was detestably annoying, and I was delighted when I could stretch myself in the straw on our floor at Putte. It was the most comfortable quarter we had been in as it was partially inhabited, and we were only four in a room. We had a fine brick floor to lie on, a good roof over our heads, and a rousing fire all night.

'Our vanity was, however, repeatedly shocked by references to the infernal business at Bergen op Zoom, and whenever we felt inclined to be agreeable to the 'yanny frows,' and were twisting our bad French into complimentary addresses, they intimated that we should find plenty of pretty girls at Bergen, and would end off laughing, and repeating 'Bien jolies, bien jolies, monsieur – ma parole.' The ugly French sentries too, after this repulse (tho' seldom inclined to come near enough to favor us with their sweet voices), would exhibit their manual wit by turning up their jackets and applying their hands to the broadest part of their hind quarters. This joke generally provoked a retort from the Riflemen, and their insinuations a posteriori were very soon discontinued.[831]

'The weather became milder in April, but hardly more pleasant; as the thaws rendered the roads (which were principally on the tops of the dykes) deep in mud, and so slippery as to be difficult to walk on, and as a Volunteer I was out with every party that marched.'

---

[830] Elkington's Diary, in the XXX Journal, May 1911, p.
[831] A similar tale was told by Private (later Sergeant) Tom Morris of the 73rd: A French sentry had fired at a British captain, but missed; whereupon, 'turning himself round, [he] placed his right-hand on a certain part of his person.' A rifleman engaged him, 'and no sooner had the Frenchman placed his hand in the manner I have stated, when both the hand and the part of the person on which it was placed, were perforated by the rifleman's bullet. The fellow bounded about a yard in the air, fell heavily to the ground, and was carried away.'

The 30th and 81st shortly left Putte for Brasschaat, where they shared the limited accommodation with the 52nd and 73rd Regiments. A dozen officers were stowed into every room, and the soldiers lodged in barns or stables.

On 4th April, Graham learned that Paris had fallen, and news of the peace reached him on the 9th. In consequence, Carnot proposed an armistice on the 12th, but it was 1st May before the 30th and 81st occupied the villages of Kontich and Edegem in the suburbs of Antwerp. Meanwhile, Edward Macready had an adventure:

'We were now all idlers, and each one followed his business or desires… Some of our moneyed men took trips to Brussels and other towns in possession of the Allies, and as my inclination was as strong, tho' my purse was weaker than theirs, I resolved to have a look at the good city of Antwerp and its French garrison.

'I borrowed a broad-brimmed Dutch hat and a white handkerchief, and thinking my grey great-coat, waistcoat and trowsers sufficiently bourgeois, mounted the diligence as it passed through Braschaet, and in less than two hours rattled over the drawbridge of the Porte de Bergerout. Here we were stopped, and a French corporal, stepping up, demanded our passports. "Je n'en ai pas," said I. "Eh bien, Monsieur," said the rascal with a smile, for he knew I was an Englishman, "descendez s'il vous plait, vous y trouverez des camarades je crois." I looked about the hole into which the ruffian was so politely ushering me, and discovered [Lieutenant John] Gowan of ours in similar durance. He did not understand French, so I was spokesman; and hearing that our appearance before Monsieur Fauconnet, the Lieutenant-Governor, was indispensable, I requested as early a presentation as possible.

'We were accordingly paraded between the bayonets of the party, and marched up to our destination… Fauconnet was a gentleman; and learning that curiosity alone was the motive of our trip, after chiding us for our indiscretion, and reprimanding the corporal for marching us as prisoners, gave us leave to remain in the town till seven o'clock, after which hour, if found, we should be detained.

'We amused ourselves till near six, looking at the dockyards and other public buildings. The garrison were a set of ragged, slovenly-looking fellows, but I've no doubt were effective enough on the working day. A great number of them were our countrymen, and were inclined to be very civil; but I avoided them; there is something loathsome in the very idea of these belly-traitors[832]. On our return from Antwerp… we found an order had arrived for our march towards Brussels.'

It had been a generally unsatisfactory campaign, and young Macready was surely not alone in welcoming a peace that would 'conduct us from the swamps of Holland to a more congenial scene. I was positively sick of the dull uniformity of the Dutch prospects and the boorish, phlegmatic disposition of the people. Adieu, thou land of snipes and agues! May I never revisit thy inhospitable shores. Hard work, little credit and good gin are all I have to thank thee for.'

The 2nd/47th – Home Service and Disbandment

After five years' service in Spain, the 2nd/47th landed at Portsmouth on 18th August 1814. 'We unfurled our Colours,' recalled Private Adam Reed, 'and the drums and fifes played as we marched through the town, and thus we landed in happy England, the harbour of all peace and safety. While we were marching through the town, some of the inhabitants said, "Look at those dirty Colours, full of holes and all rags, more like dishcloths than colours." The officers who were carrying them said, "Yes, and if you had been where they have, you perhaps might have been full of holes and all rags, but we count those Colours, or dishcloths as you call them, an honour to our regiment."[833]

The Battalion marched that day to Chichester, where they went into barracks for a short time, and their prisoners of war rejoined from France. From there, according to Adam Reed:

---

[832] The French 3rd Régiment Etranger, which was part of the Antwerp garrison, was raised in 1803 as the Légion Irlandais and disbanded on 12th May 1814.

[833] The Peninsula Colours of the 2nd/47th are in the Regimental Museum. They bear only one Battle Honour, 'TARIFA', which was not granted until 1816, while 'PENINSULA', 'VITTORIA' and 'ST SEBASTIAN' were not granted until 1815 and 1818, and the Regiment had to wait until 1910 to receive the Honour for 'NIVE'. Although complete, these so-called 'Tarifa Colours' are indeed 'full of holes and all rags', and will require extensive conservation before they can be displayed.

'We had orders to proceed on to Sandhurst to work at what is called King's Work. That is we had to make roads and level small hills at the Royal Military College Sandhurst, which is near Blackwater, as the head Colonel of our Regiment, Sir Alexander Hope[834], was governor there. Just before we arrived there we unfurled our Colours again and when our Colonel saw them his words were quite different to those of the inhabitants of Portsmouth, for he pulled off his hat and said, "Well done my brave lads. I have heard of your fame in the Peninsula, although I had not the honour to be with you. But now I witness it with my own eyes, by your Colours, what you have been through. We had an order from him as soon as we landed not to change our arms or belts, caps, etc, till he saw us. When he came to inspect us, he saw through some of our belts and pouches shot holes, and likewise through our caps. He said:

"Now your bravery will prove itself, for though I myself was not with you I have heard of your valour at Vittoria, Tarefa, Saint Sebastian, the Pyrenees, Barrosa, Nive, Nivelle, Haranquez [Aranjuez, i.e. Puente Largo] and the skirmish at Bayonne. Now, for what I have heard and witnessed, I shall give you a good treat and 3 days liberty." The treat was 5 shillings to each man and 3 days liberty to spend it in. After the 3 days were over we went to work as usual at Sandhurst and we remained there after that about one month.'

Early in October 1814, the 2nd/47th marched to Liverpool, where it arrived on the 10th; and there on the 24th the Battalion was disbanded. Most of the effective officers and men were sent out to India to join the 1st Battalion at Bombay.[835]

Occupation of the Netherlands 1814-15

In retrospect, the most fortuitously significant result of the 1813-14 intervention in Holland was that it placed the nucleus of a British army in the Low Countries well before the campaign of 1815, for at the end of hostilities a sizeable contingent of British troops, including the 2nd/30th and 2nd/81st remained there with the Allied army of occupation. The situation was difficult on two counts. Firstly, the British Government was committed to uniting the Low Countries under the Dutch Prince of Orange, a political outcome which was widely unpopular in the Belgian provinces. There was also a problem with the Prussians, whose aggressive attitude to the population in Brussels and elsewhere was provoking disorder. Not for the first or last time, British bayonets were obliged to guarantee the peace settlement.

On 2nd May, the 2nd/30th marched south from Antwerp to Malines, where Macready, billeted with a doctor, enjoyed his host's excellent wine and 'inimitable' cook, revelled in his white sheets and lusted after his wife. Indeed, the susceptible young soldier thought himself in paradise, and was particularly smitten by the 'delightful' *Flamandes* who 'seem to hit the happy mean between the French frivolity and the English *mauvaise honte*. There is a mélange of archness and *naiveté* in their manner, which is irresistibly fascinating. It proceeds from a total absence of affectation and that desire to please, both in word and look, which nature has bestowed on the sex as their strongest talisman upon the heart of man... They were "the starlight of my boyhood" and are still a treasure in my memory.'

He was far less impressed with what he heard of the Prussians, who had occupied Brussels, but noted that 'thanks to their brutality "la politesse et la douceur des Anglais" became proverbial.' After a few days at Malines, the 30th on marched to Vilvorde, north-west of Brussels, where they remained about a fortnight. His unfavourable impression of the Allies was soon confirmed and reinforced by observation:

'Of all the troops that assembled to teach France "the great moral lesson," none were so unexceptionably detested as the Prussians. Their conduct was wantonly cruel. I can make every allowance for the burning hatred which the injuries and insults of years must have excited, but nothing could palliate their brutality. Their officers frequently drew their swords on women, and even struck them. They robbed the houses in which they were quartered, and often, when called upon to meet the men they had injured, pitifully declared they fought solely in the service of their country. I saw one of them disgraced for horse-stealing, and it was no unusual occurrence to

---

[834] Lieutenant-General Sir Alexander Hope GCB MP, Colonel of the 47th Regiment 26th April 1813 to 25th March 1835, was Governor of the Royal Military College 1811-19.
[835] On the renewal of hostilities in 1815, the 2nd/47th was re-formed at Chelmsford, only to be disbanded there in January 1816. This brief resurrection may account for the addition of 'TARIFA' to the Colours before they were laid up.

witness an overgrown, drunken beast exposing his person at the door of a coffee house. In short, their conduct was such as to implant a feeling of deep hatred in the minds of the Belgians and to make the name of Prussian a byword for bestiality and cowardice.'

'On the 19th May[836], our brigade assembled at Malines, and next day marched into Brussels to the mutual delight of ourselves and the inhabitants. We looked forward to pleasure and society, and they calculated on civil treatment. Our billets were excellent. People of the first rank welcomed us to their houses, and entertained us most hospitably – in a few days we became '*enfans de la famille.*' Our days were passed in the pleasures of good society, and our evenings were devoted to public amusements, a little drinking, and some intrigue.'

'The public mind at Brussels was in great agitation, as it was not understood to what Royal Legitimate they owed their allegiance. However, the Congress at Vienna were sharing out the European livestock, and report said that the Belgians were to be allotted to the King of Holland.'

Elkington has much the same story about the attitudes of the people of Brussels to the Prussians and the House of Orange:

'The entrance of the British appeared to give great pleasure to the inhabitants, who had suffered much from the Prussians who proceeded us, and who treated the whole of the *Pays Bas* as a conquered country. Billetted on a Madam Goffin, a rich banking house, I lived much with the Family. The idea of their country being separated from France and attached to Holland did not please the younger members of the Family. They styled the King of Holland "*Le Roi de Fromage*." [837]

'In the middle of June,' wrote Macready, 'it was whispered that our Regiment was to move towards the frontier, and tho' I was anxious to traverse a country in which every field is hallowed by some gallant action, yet I dreaded the confirmation of the rumour. I was young in pleasure, and Brussels was the scene of my initiation… I had latterly, too, become more independent, as Colonel Vigoureux (during a temporary command) excused me from all parades except that for muster. I was infinitely obliged to him, for hitherto I had attended them daily with my arms and accoutrements.'

On 27th June the 30th marched for Tournai by way of Halle, Enghien and Ath. 'On our march to Ath,' wrote Macready, 'we fell in with the 33rd French Regiment of Infantry, returning from the north of Germany, where they had formed part of Davoust's Corps d'Armée[838]. Several of our fellows conversed with them in Spanish, and we had some difficulty in preventing a little conversation à la Belcher[839] between the parties; swords and bayonets were unsheathed more than once. The soldiers all retained the eagle and N on their shakos, and some, who had lost these insignia, had imprinted their resemblance in chalk. We heard a few days later that on their inspection at Lisle [Lille] they concluded the parade with an unanimous shout of *Vive L'Empereur*.'

'The Duchess of Oldenburg was at Ath when we arrived, and our flank companies remained behind the Regiment as her Guard of Honour. After her departure, we followed the Corps, and, as we marched left in front, the Grenadiers swore they'd run over us. The challenge was no sooner given than the Lights shouted "Double quick," and away we went – a musket on my shoulder and sixty rounds in my cartouch box. We stop'd at Leuze, about seven miles from Ath, when only three 'bacon bolters' (and these were overgrown light bobs) were visible. I was in high favor with the greasy rogues for keeping up, and received three or four pats on the shoulders which nearly shook out what little wind I had left, accompanied with the assurance that "By J---s, I was o' the right stuff." A Roman general, on being hailed Imperator, could not have felt more grateful for his exaltation.'

The 30th clearly enjoyed their few weeks at Tournai. 'Dissipation was the order of the day here,' wrote Edward Macready. 'Wine was cheap and the flesh was frail. The dancers of the ci-devant court of Westphalia occupied the Theatre, at which we were constant attendants. Their style was the most lascivious I have seen, and their conduct consistently demoralised. On the 22nd July we celebrated the Anniversary of Salamanca. General

---

[836] Elkington states that the whole of Mackenzie's division was ordered into Brussels on 12th May, arriving at 1 p.m.
[837] Elkington's Diary, in the *XXX* Journal, April 1911, p. 9.
[838] The 33rd Regiment d'Infanterie de Ligne had participated in many of Napoleon's most famous engagements, including Rivoli, Austerlitz, Jena, Eylau, Wagram and Borodino. They had suffered severely during the 1812 Retreat from Moscow, and most recently had fought at Dresden, Kulm and Leipzig. They were in Spain in 1808, and again in 1813. The Regiment was disbanded on 12th May 1814, but re-raised at once and fought at Namur during the Hundred Days.
[839] A reference to Jem Belcher, a redoubtable English pugilist of that period and former Champion of England.

Gibbs honoured us with his company, but not even his presence (and I never knew man more generally or deservedly respected) could check the libations which were poured down the living in honour of the dead, till the former were as motionless as their departed friends.'

'We were much surprised and chagrined to receive an order to make forced marches to Antwerp, in consequence of the turbulent behaviour of the French marine. In one instance the garrison were obliged to turn out with guns loaded and matches lit. Our friends were determined to give us some mark of their esteem, and, on the evening before we marched the officers, and I among the rest, were invited to a ball at the Stadthouse. Our efforts at gaiety were useless. We lingered out the hours in the expression of fruitless regret and of constant recollection, and when the bugle sounded we left the ball-room. I took an affectionate farewell of my friends, and, shouldering Brown Bess, trudged away to Avelghem [on] August 21st. Our second march was to Oudenarde, the scene of Marlborough's defeat of Vendome, and Ghent, or Gand, was our next halting place. We halted one day and made a long march to St. Nicholas.

'As we were moving on the following morning towards Locheren, a sergeant of the 44th Regiment, which had served with ours in Egypt and Spain[840], happened to be passing in a cart. As soon as his button was recognised, a scream of congratulation was heard through the column, and every canteen was unstrapped in an instant. He was dragged from his seat and shoved from rank to rank, every fellow stopping his mouth with his canteen and shouting "Good luck to the old boys, and how are they?" till the worthy non-commissioned officer was replaced in his seat, speechless and motionless. This is certainly an instance of killing kindness, but as an affectionate remembrance of auld lang syne even the most starched disciplinarians must forgive it. For my part I felt a thrill of joy and pride at this rough exhibition of feeling in our fellows.'

The 30th crossed the Scheldt on a flying bridge, and on the 27th August entered Antwerp, which was garrisoned by eleven British battalions, including the 81st, and was commanded by Major-General Halkett.[841] Soon after their arrival, the warships and naval stores were divided as decided at the Congress of Vienna, and the French sailed away with their share. In consequence, the British garrison was reduced, and only the 25th, 30th, 37th, and 81st remained, though they were soon reinforced by a force of Hanoverians.

'As I was parading for muster on the 24th September,' wrote Edward Macready, 'I learned that on the 8th of the month I had been appointed an ensign in the 30th Regiment.' The news was most welcome, for whilst serving in the ranks, he had found it difficult to control his passionate temper. 'By not curbing my own sufficiently, in calling an ignorant fellow to account, I lost the friendship and support of my captain [Captain Thomas Chambers] the whole time I was a volunteer. He did not use me very well, but still, had my conduct been guarded we never should have differed.' Macready soon learned that it was Sir Thomas Graham who had personally recommended him to the Military Secretary and Colonel of the Regiment. 'I now bade adieu to the greasy rogues of the Light Company, who roared out my health till the *genièvre* had silenced them, and was appointed to No. 6 Company.'

'On my return to Antwerp, I found that Major Ryan had arrived with a detachment of two hundred men and a proportion of officers.[842] This made us above six hundred bayonets.'

'My lodgings (for we had no billets here) were immediately under the Cathedral, and as Daniel Asher, my faithful squire, happened to come home blind drunk one evening and find his master in a very similar predicament,

---

[840] The close friendship between the 2nd Battalions of the 30th and 44th dates from 1809-1810, when they served together in Cadiz. Both battalions then joined the same brigade of Wellington's field army in October 1810, fighting side by side at the storming of Badajoz, the Battle of Salamanca and the action at Villa Muriel. From December 1812 until May 1813 the surviving effectives of both battalions were combined in the 4th Provisional Battalion, commanded by Hamilton of the 30th. Additionally, many years earlier the 1st Battalions of the 30th and 44th had served together in Doyle's brigade in Egypt, including the Battle of Alexandria, 1801.

[841] Major-General Sir Colin Halkett KCB had served in the Peninsula with the King's German Legion, commanding a brigade at the battles of Albuhera, Salamanca and Vitoria, and earning particular distinction and Wellington's thanks for a brilliant rearguard action during the retreat from Burgos, 1812. He would command the 5th British Brigade, including the 30th, at Quatre Bras and Waterloo. He was succeeded in Antwerp by Major-General Kenneth Mackenzie.

[842] Brevet-Major Matthew Ryan had exchanged from the half-pay of the 85th Regiment. His draft, which left the Regimental Depot for embarkation at Harwich in early October 1814, consisted of Captain Donald Sinclair, Lieutenants Robert Daniell and Benjamin Nicholson, Ensigns Edward Drake and Robert Rogers, Quartermaster John Williamson, five sergeants and 210 rank and file, accompanied by twenty-two women and twelve children.

he very sagaciously commenced pulling off my boots; and before he had relieved me of one he had contrived to set fire to my curtains, and in an instant the bed was in flames. The first thing I did was to kick Daniel arsy-versy. The next was to drag away the bedclothes, and in a short time the fire was extinguished… And now comes what some people will call a judgement. Being *Bacchi plenus*, and not much cooled by the above-mentioned conflagration, I sallied forth and joined in converse chaste with a damsel, who led me, nothing loath, to her bower of bliss.' This intoxicated youthful escapade did not end well, for in a week's time, 'that *preux chevalier* Edward Nevil McCready was confined to his house for two months, and lost all the gaiety of the Carnival.'

Surgeon Elkington, more mature or less susceptible than young Macready, was among those of the 30th who thoroughly enjoyed the Antwerp season:

'The balls and concerts, with plays, dinner parties and excursions, served to make the winter pass rapidly. My Regiment remained extremely healthy, having buried only three or four men since our landing.'

'Soon after my recovery,' wrote Macready, 'General Halkett, who was much beloved, was ordered to give up the command to General McKenzie in consequence of his disagreement with the civil authorities. They would not keep the town clean, and I believe he sent fatigue parties, who collected the filth and deposited it at their doors. Whatever was the real cause, he was ordered away, and the officers of the garrison resolved to give him a dinner. Forty cards of invitation were sent to him, and he asked the Municipality, General Kunily – a sort of nonentity sent by Congress – and all public characters. We sat down three hundred red jackets, English and German, neither nation remarkable for temperance. In an hour we were all drunk, and, our feelings getting the better of our manners, we attacked the head of the Mayor – his weakest point, I believe – with champagne corks. Never was the *caput* of the Antwerp magistrate in such danger since the days of Alva and Parma. Poor man, he underwent the operation like a philosopher: "He stir'd not, he spoke not, he looked not around." The concussive corks started the powder from his jazey, which, settling on the perspiration that poured down his cheeks, gave to his physiognomy an expression "horrible, most horrible." To describe the finale of this party would be impossible. It may be fancied when I mention that seven hundred bottles of champagne alone were consumed.'

'Our soldiers and the Hanoverians had unfortunately some cause of disagreement, and numerous heads were broken before they could comprehend the necessity of a better understanding. However, amity was restored and they were seen beastly drunk together as often as ever.'

'I had now been long enough in the Regiment to have friends. I sincerely esteemed Rumley and Pratt, the Light Infantry officers, both of them fellows with good and kind hearts. Rumley was much indebted to nature; he was handsome, brave and sincere, but his information was limited and he wanted that perfect ease which is only gained in the best society. Pratt had every gift of providence as liberally bestowed on him as his comrade. His education had been liberal, his manners were open and gentlemanly, and his address engaging. Our friendship was reciprocal and most sincere. My companions in folly were Warren, Moneypenny and Rogers. I liked them all, but their places would be easily supplied. I was a favourite with the Colonel and most of the officers, and there was not a man in the Corps that I could call my enemy.'

The uneasy peace of 1814 was a deceptive calm before a renewed storm in which young Macready and his friends would meet their most severe test.

Fort George, Madras, where the 30th were stationed
1807-09, 1815-17, 1825-26 & 1829, & the 59th in 1806

Trichinopoly Hill Fort, where the 30th were
based 1809-11 & 1826-28

Fort St. Angelo, Cannanore, where the 30th were stationed
1811-15

Sergeant
Light Company
30th
East Indies
1806-15

Below: The 47th took part in the destruction of Pirate lairs in the
Persian Gulf, 1809

The 47th took part in the storming of pirate lairs at Ras-al-Khyma (pictured) and elsewhere in the Persian Gulf
November 1809

Major-General Sir Samuel Gibbs commanded the 59th 1804-11 in South Africa, India, Mauritius & Java

The 59th disembark from the transport Upton Castle to take Mauritius from the French, 29th September 1810

Batavia (now Jakarta), Dutch East Indies, captured in 1811 by a British expeditionary force including the 59th

Light Company Officer 59th 1815

Fort Cornelis, the main Dutch stronghold in Java, stormed on 26th August 1811

The Sultan's Palace (Kraton) of Palembang, Sumatra, captured by a small force including the 59th in a daring advance in 1812, & again in 1813

Chapter X:
The East Indies 1806-15

30ᵗʰ, 47ᵗʰ & 59ᵗʰ to India – Vellore Mutiny 1806 (59ᵗʰ) – Marine Service in Dutch East Indies 1806-7 (30ᵗʰ) – Travancore 1808-9 (30ᵗʰ) – Occupation of Portuguese Colonies of Macau, Diu & Daman (30ᵗʰ & 47ᵗʰ) – Persian Gulf 1809 (47ᵗʰ) – the White Mutiny 1809 (30ᵗʰ & 59ᵗʰ) – Capture of Mauritius 1810 (59ᵗʰ) – 47ᵗʰ in India 1811-15 – Expeditions to Navanagar, the Peishwa's territory & Baroda – 30ᵗʰ in India 1810-15 – Wynad rising – Capture of Batavia & Storming of the Lines of Cornelis, Java 1811 (59ᵗʰ) – Expeditions to Palembang, Sumatra, 1812, Yogyakarta 1812, Bali 1814 & Macassar, Celebes 1814 (59ᵗʰ)

Passages to India

We now turn east to follow the fortunes of the 1ˢᵗ Battalions of the 30ᵗʰ, 47ᵗʰ and 59ᵗʰ in the theatre known as the East Indies, in the course of which they not only took part in the global conflict with the Napoleonic Empire and its satellites, but undertook campaigns against turbulent local princes and their lawless mercenary adherents, dealt with dangerous mutinies and bloodthirsty Arab pirates, and generally upheld British interests from the Persian Gulf to the East Indian islands of Java, Sumatra, Bali and Celebes. These are the 'forgotten wars' of the Napoleonic period, attracting little attention today compared to the concurrent conflicts in Europe; but they include episodes of remarkable skill, unsurpassed gallantry and bold leadership, usually in the face of extraordinary odds and great physical difficulties, while the achievements of the few thousand British and Indian troops who took part undoubtedly helped shape the future of South Asia.

It is worth considering how it was that a mere handful of men were able to exert an effect out of all proportion to their number: the answer was not superior technology, for their enemies usually had similar arms, and often more of them; but, as we have noted in the Peninsula and elsewhere, British soldiers had an exceptional self-belief and determination. They brought with them to the East Indies that same deeply ingrained conviction of their own distinct superiority which marked their relations with foreigners of all nations, and all ranks took great pride in maintaining this exalted notion of themselves in action whenever the opportunity arose and whatever the odds.

In April 1805, the 1ˢᵗ/59ᵗʰ, commanded by Lieutenant-Colonel Samuel Gibbs, was ordered to prepare to embark for India. In May, the Battalion marched from the New Barracks on the Western Heights of Dover to Redding Street Barracks, and on 21ˢᵗ June moved from there to reach Gosport on the 29ᵗʰ. On 9ᵗʰ July, the 59ᵗʰ embarked at Gosport with 39 officers, 54 sergeants, 50 corporals, 22 drummers and 848 privates.

They sailed a few days later with a convoy which put in at Falmouth and Cork to embark more troops under Sir David Baird, destined for the capture of the Cape of Good Hope. Leaving Cork about the end of August in a 63-ship convoy, they reached Madeira on 20ᵗʰ September, and sailed from there on 6ᵗʰ October for San Salvador, Brazil, where they remained a month before proceeding to the Cape of Good Hope. Their part in the capture of Cape Town is related in Chapter I of this volume, and we pick up their story on 7ᵗʰ February 1806 when they sailed again on their interrupted voyage to India.

The Battalion reached Madras on 23ʳᵈ April with 34 officers, 54 sergeants, 50 corporals, 22 drummers and 814 privates. Immediately after landing, the 59ᵗʰ marched out about fifteen miles from Fort St. George to Poonamallee[843], a cantonment used for units and individuals arriving or departing Madras Presidency. From there, on 20ᵗʰ June, a detachment of three hundred men under Major Alexander McLeod moved on to Walahjabad, another established cantonment.

On 6ᵗʰ May 1806, the 1ˢᵗ/30ᵗʰ marched behind their band from Hilsea Barracks to Portsmouth Hard, there to embark on East Indiamen. Commanded by Lieutenant-Colonel William Lockhart, they were a remarkably strong battalion, numbering 29 officers and 1,157 other ranks, excluding the four officers and 105 other ranks who, having been shipwrecked on the coast of France, remained prisoners of war. Included in the rank and file

---
[843] At Poonamallee there was a barracks for 500 men and an old Mughal fort, used as a hospital.

were two volunteers, Arthur and Samuel Poyntz, aged fourteen and twelve: sons of the quartermaster, both of whom would live to become lieutenant-colonels, as would their younger brother James, who joined the 2nd Battalion. Four-fifths of the men were English, and the proportion from their prescribed Cambridgeshire recruiting area was higher than at any other time. Two-thirds of the Battalion were over 5 feet 6 inches tall.

It was a bustling time at Portsmouth, with regiments and drafts being embarked for the Mediterranean and the Cape of Good Hope, together with the 1st/30th and 1st/47th for the East Indies. Although both these battalions were destined for service in India, in the event, neither would proceed there directly.

On 13th May, the fleet of 29 ships, including Indiamen, having gathered at St. Helens, off the Isle of Wight, set sail under convoy of HMS *Lion*, 64, Captain Rolles, and two frigates. As was customary, the *Lion* carried such sail as would enable the Indiamen to keep with her, and the latter were allowed a certain freedom, but all had to be within signalling distance and ready to close and follow in her wake on the least sign of danger. The frigates scouted ahead and on the flanks. On the first day out, six strange sail were seen, and the signal was made for the convoy to close. The *Columbine* transport was not smart enough to please Captain Rolles, and the *Lion* fired a disciplinary shot at her. This was no doubt done to put things on a proper footing at once, and it had such a beneficial effect that it had to be repeated on only one other occasion during the voyage.

On the 19th of May, five British line of battle ships were met with, three of them with jury masts, under the flag of the Earl of Northesk. They were some of the ships which had fought at Trafalgar the previous October on their way home from Gibraltar after partial repairs.

The convoy headed for the Cape of Good Hope, where on 6th August the ships anchored in St. Simon's Bay. The 47th were then diverted for the campaign in South America (see Chapter II above). On the 15th, the fleet continued, with the 30th, across the Indian Ocean. The Regiment's immediate destination, however, was not India but the island of Penang on the Malacca Straits, which was reached on 13th October. As for the 47th, after their 1807 expedition to South America they returned to the Cape, from where they sailed for India in October, reaching Madras on 29th December.

The 30th, 47th and 59th arrived in India at a time of historic change in the government and military affairs of the sub-continent. The fragmentation of the waning Mughal Empire was almost complete, and the resulting semi-anarchic power vacuum was filled by a multitude of more or less formidable princes, several of whom possessed effective armies trained and equipped on European lines, while all could call on large bands of mercenary horsemen, the Pindaris, who, when not engaged in princely mayhem, lived by pillage. After the British defeat in 1799 of Tipu Sahib of Mysore, the most powerful of these princes were loosely grouped, when not at war with each other, in the Mahratta Confederacy, whose forces and strongholds had been severely reduced by Lord Lake and Sir Arthur Wellesley in 1803-5 but remained a threat to the peace of Central India.

By 1806, the most potent single power in India had by default become the Honourable East India Company (HEIC), a commercial venture. Whilst the Directors of the Honourable Company in Leadenhall Street attempted to remain true to their origins as traders, and were generally opposed to their agents in India taking on more of the responsibilities, and costs, of governance and security, the logic of their increasingly dominant position in the sub-continent had its own inexorable momentum, leading to confrontation with rival rulers, and to other local potentates more or less willingly seeking British protection against their neighbours. To complicate matters on the ground, each of the three HEIC Presidencies, Bengal, Bombay and Madras, had its own government, army and navy; but the Company also enjoyed the support of armed forces of the British Crown, the whole being directed by a governor-general appointed by the British Government who had to take account of wider national interests, most notably including the world war with Napoleon's Empire.

Major military operations in the East Indies were invariably undertaken, under integrated command, by mixed forces of Company troops, who on 25th May 1809 numbered 4,051 European and 128,418 Indian soldiers, and 'King's' regiments of the British Army, who at that time totalled just 19,843, or thirteen percent of the total 'British' strength in India.

Mutiny at Vellore 1806

The 59th had been in India for rather less than three months when they were called on to assist in suppressing a dangerous mutiny of the Indian troops in the Company's fort at Vellore, some eighty miles inland from Madras. The pretext for this rebellion was an ill-advised and pedantic attempt to assimilate the appearance of sepoys of the Madras Army, on parade and in the field, to that of British soldiers. A new pattern turban was introduced, earrings and caste marks were banned, and the shape and fashion of whiskers were regulated. These obnoxious innovations were widely condemned by Indian troops, who saw them as an assault on their culture and religion, and they sparked a secret conspiracy. The flames of grievance and discontent were fanned at Vellore by the sons of Tipu Sahib, the erstwhile ruler of Mysore, who resided in the fort as comfortable pensionaries of the Company but were unreconciled to their family's loss of power and status.

Before dawn on 10th July 1806 over eighteen hundred sepoys at Vellore made a surprise attack on their British officers and on four hundred men the 69th Foot, with whom they shared the fort. The tiger flag of Mysore was hoisted, and one of Tipu's sons was proclaimed as sultan. Scores of the British troops died in their barrack rooms, but parties of them broke out onto the ramparts, where they maintained themselves with difficulty, while a messenger galloped to Arcot for assistance.

It happened that Colonel Rollo Gillespie, commanding the 19th Light Dragoons at Arcot, was out for a morning ride when the news arrived. Gillespie, an officer of outstanding resolution and reckless daring, gathered up a squadron of his regiment and a troop of native cavalry, and set off for Vellore within fifteen minutes, leaving the rest of both regiments, with galloper guns, to follow. He found the surviving 69th still resisting, without ammunition, over the gateway, climbed up to join them on the ramparts, and led them in a bayonet charge to capture the mutineers' cannon. The remainder of the cavalry, with guns, then arrived, blew in the gate, and charged in to sabre three to four hundred of the mutinous sepoys.

Hot on the heels of the dragoons, three hundred of the 59th under Major Alexander McLeod arrived the same day after a forced march from Walahjabad. The rest of the Battalion marched from Poonamallee on 13th July, reaching Vellore on the 19th, and the Battalion provided the garrison of that fort for the next six months. As for Tipu's family, who were suspected of complicity in the mutiny, on 18th January 1807, the 59th provided a guard of one hundred men to escort them by sea to faraway Calcutta. The main body of the 59th remained at Vellore until 8th February 1807, when they marched for Bangalore in the Mysore country, where they were joined towards the end of the year by the detachment sent with Tipu's sons.

The 1st/59th received a valuable accession of strength and Indian campaign experience on 25th September 1807 when 151 volunteers were transferred to the Battalion from the 94th (Scotch Brigade), which had been ordered home.[844] This draft included many veterans of the storming of Seringapatam, 1799, and the Second Maratha War, 1803-5.

Marine Service 1806-7

Although the 30th were destined for service in Madras, before reaching India the Regiment was placed at the disposal of Rear-Admiral Sir Thomas Troubridge, British naval commander to the east of Point de Galle in Ceylon. Sir Thomas intended to use the 30th to help him reduce the threat to British shipping posed by the Dutch East Indies since the Kingdom of Holland had become a French satellite, ruled by Louis Buonaparte, and its colonial ports were actual or potential bases for French privateers.

On 13th October, the 30th reached the rendezvous at Penang, where Sir Thomas was waiting with HM Ships *Blenheim*, *Macassar* and *Greyhound*, only to discover that Captain Rolles of the *Lion* carried Admiralty despatches appointing Troubridge to command at the Cape, while Rear-Admiral Sir Edward Pellew was to assume

---

[844] In December 1807 the 2nd/59th was about to send 360 men to their 1st Battalion in India when they learned of the volunteering from the 94th, and in consequence two hundred of the intended draft were recalled. The 1st/59th, which on 24th June 1807 mustered 782 rank and file, had 942 on 24th December. This included 51 men received from their 2nd Battalion, and took account of 46 deaths and 26 discharged in the year.

command of all British naval ships in the East Indies. Troubridge sailed for the Cape on HMS *Blenheim*, but the unseaworthy old ship foundered with all hands in a cyclone off Madagascar.

Sir Edward Pellew lost no time in destroying a Dutch naval squadron in the Road of Batavia, (now Jakarta) off the island of Java, on 27th November, but decided to postpone operations against their ports pending further reconnaissance. In consequence the 30th, who had landed at Penang on 16th October, were not now required, so were re-embarked on November 12th and landed at Madras on 14th January 1807.

The 30th marched to Walahjabad Cantonment, forty miles south-west of Madras, from where in February Major Philip Vaumorel was detached with four companies (eight officers and 374 other ranks) to relieve the 59th at Vellore Fort.

Unfortunately, sickness at once cut a swathe through the unseasoned ranks of the 30th, and in their first nine months in India there were 163 deaths, mostly from dysentery.

Sir Edward Pellew was unable to return to Java early in 1807, as his ships were dispersed on separate operations across the Indian Ocean; however, during the summer responsibility for blockading the French island bases in that ocean passed from Pellew to Rear-Admiral Bertie at the Cape, and Pellew was once again free to concentrate against the remainder of the Dutch East Indies squadron. In May 1807, Sir Edward asked for men of the 30th to strengthen his ships' companies. Initially, a sergeant and fourteen men were embarked as marines, and then in June, Lieutenant C. S. Watson with 54 other ranks joined the HMS *Psyche*, a 36-gun frigate[845] commanded by Captain Fleetwood Pellew, the Admiral's son – who would prove himself as enterprising a frigate captain as his father.

The *Psyche* was on the point of sailing from Madras, in company with the frigate HMS *Caroline*, 36, Captain Rainier, under orders to reconnoitre the coast of Java and to locate a number of Dutch warships which had escaped Admiral Pellew's raid of the previous November. These vessels had been sent eastward along the coast of Java under an American-born Dutch officer named Cowell, and they eventually sheltered in a protected anchorage at the port of Griessie (now Gresik) on the river Sourabaya. This natural harbour, near the eastern extremity of Java and some 540 miles east of Batavia, was the largest naval base in the Dutch East Indies.

On 29th August the two British frigates looked into the Sourabaya estuary, and next day, off Point Panka to the east of Java, they ascertained from a Dutch prize that the ships they sought were lying at Griessie in a poor state. Having successfully completed the primary object of their mission, the two frigates stood to the west to carry their intelligence back to Madras. As they cruised along the coast, the frigate captains were, as ever, in search of more lucrative prizes, and they parted company when the *Caroline* gave chase (eventually taking seven more ships).

At midnight on the 30th the *Psyche* anchored off the port of Samarang, some two hundred miles west of Sourabaya. At daylight on the 31st, the *Psyche* weighed and stood into the road; and as the water was too shallow for the frigate, Pellew sent in his boats to cut out the Dutch vessels at anchor there. They took and towed out, under a heavy but ineffectual fire from shore batteries, an armed schooner of eight guns and a large merchant brig.

Three further vessels were observed at anchor outside the harbour, one of which was seen to be a warship. Determined to take advantage of the earliest sea breeze, Pellew collected his boats, destroyed the two prizes, and before noon was clear of the harbour in chase of his new enemies. The Dutch vessels weighed and stood out to sea, endeavouring to escape.

At 3.30 p.m., seeing that the frigate was closing with them, the enemy vessels ran themselves on shore about nine miles to the west of Samarang, and opened a well-directed fire on the *Psyche*. The British vessel anchored in three fathoms and returned fire, but with little apparent effect as the range was too long for Pellew's 12-pounders. In a few minutes, however, one of the ships struck her colours. She proved to be the *Resolutie*, an armed merchant ship of 700 tons, richly laden and carrying the headquarters staff and colours of the 23rd European Battalion in the Dutch service. At 4.30 p.m., just as the *Psyche* was hoisting out her boats to attempt boarding a second ship, she too struck, and was discovered to be the Dutch naval corvette *Scipio*, 24 guns, with a crew of 150 men. This vessel, according to Pellew's despatch, 'sustained very considerable damage, many shot having

---

[845] *Psyche* mounted twenty-four 12-pounders on her gun deck, eight 18-pounder carronades on her quarterdeck, and two 6-pounders and another two 18-pounder carronades on her forecastle. She was originally a French vessel, captured off the Malabar coast in 1805.

passed through the hull; her rigging was much cut, and her commander mortally wounded.' Shortly afterwards the third ship fired a final broadside and hauled down her colours. She was the 12-gun brig *Ceres*, with a crew of seventy, in the service of the Dutch East India Company. Pellew had too few men to be able to hold so many prisoners, so he put them ashore, paroling the officers. All three captured ships were refloated that night, and the triumphant *Psyche* sailed off with her prizes. We do not know what part Lieutenant Watson's detachment of the 30th played in this fight, but they suffered no casualties and would share in the prize money.

On 16th September a further body of fifty other ranks of the 30th were embarked as marines under recently commissioned Ensign Arthur Poyntz, and then from November under Ensign Washington Carden.

By the beginning of October Sir Edward Pellew was ready for a final operation against Dutch naval forces in the East Indies, and on the 17th he embarked Colonel Lockhart's wing of the 30th, twenty-two officers and 534 other ranks, on the transport *Worcester* at Madras. The Headquarters Wing of the 30th had been in garrison at Fort George, Madras, and Major Vaumorel brought his wing down from Vellore to hold the fort in Lockhart's absence.

Admiral Pellew sailed for Malacca, from where, having received the reports of his son and Captain Rainier, on 20th November he headed for Java with HM Ships *Culloden* and *Powerful*, 74s, the frigates *Caroline* and *Fox*, sloops *Victoria*, *Samarang* (the former *Scipio*), *Seaflower* and *Jaseur*, and the 30th aboard *Worcester*. The squadron arrived off Point Panka on 5th December.

Sir Edward sent a boat into Griessie under a flag of truce with his son, his secretary and Major Sir Charles Burdett[846] of the 30th, demanding that the Dutch commander surrender his ships. In return, Pellew undertook not to attack the settlement. Captain Cowell not only refused, but ordered the boat party to be arrested, sending an officer to inform Pellew of his action and preparing his defences.

In response, Pellew determined to attack the port and ordered that *Culloden* and *Powerful* be lightened by the removal of unnecessary stores to enable them to sail into the shallow waters of Madura Strait. On the morning of 6th December the whole British squadron moved steadily towards Griessie, coming under the fire of heated cannonballs from a battery of twelve 9 and 18-pounders at Sambelangan on the island of Madura. The shot hulled several of Pellew's ships, but without loss or significant damage, and the return fire rapidly silenced the battery. A battery at Griessie also fired a few shots, but also without effect.

On the approach of the British squadron, Cowell had sent the arrested officers to Sourabaya, 15 miles up-river, where they met with the civil governor and council of the settlement, representing to them the high-handed conduct of the Dutch commodore. Concerned that retribution was about to fall on Sourabaya, the governor sent a delegation to Pellew, disclaiming responsibility for Cowell's actions, releasing the captured boat party and surrendering the ships in the harbour.

On 7th December, Pellew agreed formal terms for the surrender of *Revolutie* and *Pluto*, each of 70 guns, fine ships but, as Sir Edward reported, 'by great neglect were considerably wanting in repair,' together with the sheer-hulk *Kortenaar*, 64 guns, the Dutch East Indiaman *Rustloff*, one thousand tons and pierced for 40 guns, and a large transport.

These vessels were at anchor in Griessie, but when British boats entered the harbour it was discovered that Cowell had ordered all his ships to be scuttled. Their wrecks, protruding from the shallow water, were burned by Pellew's seamen that evening.

The Grenadier Company of the 30th then took possession of Griessie and, with a party of gunners, destroyed the cannon and military stores, while a division of seamen destroyed the naval stores, and the remains of the battery at Sambelangan were demolished. British operations were complete by 11th December, and Pellew ordered the squadron to withdraw and return to India.

Four days later he wrote to the Madras Government that, 'This service has completed the entire destruction of the naval force of Holland in the East Indies, the previous successes of H.M. Ships having deprived them of every other man of war on this station.' In his despatch, Sir Edward spoke in high terms of the wing of the 30th under Colonel Lockhart, and thanked the Madras Government for having given him 'that valuable officer' as a colleague.

---

[846] Sir Charles Wyndham Burdett, Bart., had resigned his appointment of brigade major at Fort St. George to accompany the expedition, but resumed his staff duty on return from sea.

Lockhart and his wing landed at Madras on 14th February 1808 and re-occupied quarters at Fort St. George. Major Vaumorel's wing of the 30th had returned in January 1808 to Vellore, where they remained until December that year.[847] This was not quite the end of marine service for the 30th, as Lieutenant Watson, Ensign Carden and 63 men remained at sea.

In August the annual fleet arrived from home with, in addition to two officers, a draft of 68 volunteers for the 30th from the Cambridgeshire Militia and two men from the 2nd Battalion. It also brought Lieutenant-Colonel William Wilkinson, who assumed command on 4th August. He had been commanding a brigade in Ireland, but being unable to obtain a command on active service had applied to rejoin the Regiment.[848] In January 1809 Lieutenant-Colonel Lockhart was appointed to command the Pondicherry District, and the following year he was promoted to major-general.

Travancore 1808-9

The concentration of the 30th at Fort St. George was in consequence of a revolt of the rajahs of Travancore and Cochin. At the end of 1808, the Dewan (premier) of Travancore, a princely state on the Malabar coast under British protection, had instigated a rebellion with the assistance of the Dewan of the Rajah of Cochin. Travancore, which had previously owed allegiance to Tipu Sultan of Mysore, was obliged under a treaty of 1805 to pay for the upkeep of four sepoy battalions. This payment soon fell into arrears, the Rajah abrogated the treaty, and by January 1809, the Dewan, Velu Tampi, was in the field at the head of thirty thousand men and eighteen guns. All available troops were rushed south to crush this rebellion: four British regiments and twelve sepoy battalions, including some brought from Ceylon, were eventually deployed, and all resistance was overcome by the end of February 1809.

The 30th were initially retained at Madras to protect the capital of the Presidency, but the arrival of reinforcements from Ceylon at the end of January 1809 released the Battalion, which sailed 170 miles south to Negapatam (Nagapattinam), where they disembarked at the beginning of February.

Colonel Wilkinson was appointed to command the southern division of the Madras Army, with headquarters at Trichinopoly (Tiruchirappalli), and the 30th formed part of a field force under him. It saw no fighting, but had incessant marching until April 16th, when the field force was broken up and the Battalion went into garrison at Trichinopoly, about seventy miles north-west of Negapatam.

The spectacular hill-top Rock Fort of Trichinopoly, perched on a massive outcrop which rose abruptly from the plain, towered over the walled old city and the River Cauvery, beyond which lay the great temple complex of Srirangam. This historic citadel had always been a place of strategic importance, often fought over, and in 1809 it was one of the main British fortresses in South India.

In June 1809, Wilkinson made the half-yearly inspection of the 1st/30th. Battalion strength included 1,045 privates, of whom 182 were Irish or Scottish, and four were foreign, the remainder were English. It was noted that the sergeants carried pikes, except the five in the Light Company, who carried light muskets, and that there was a fife and drum band, with two buglers in the Light Company. Wilkinson reported that the Battalion's performance of field exercises required improvement, but he attributed this to long service at sea and little subsequent opportunity for training:

'Two hundred of the men with a proportion of officers and non-commissioned officers were upwards of nine months at sea, and thirty above one year and a half serving as Marines, and the whole of them only joined a short time before the Review; in addition to which the Battn itself was near three months in the field, most of the time on the march, and only arrived in quarters a little more than three weeks before the Review.'

---

[847] Lieutenant Denis Wood of the 30th died, aged 26, on 15th June 1808 at Vellore, where his memorial inscription survives in the Church of South India Cemetery.

[848] William Wilkinson had previously seen active service with the 30th in the American War, at Toulon and Corsica, with the Mediterranean Fleet, in Malta and in Egypt.

Occupation of Portuguese Colonies 1808

The invasion and occupation of Portugal by Napoleon Buonaparte in 1808 also had repercussions on the far side of the world, where British expeditions were sent to take Portuguese territories under their protection, by force if necessary, but preferably by persuasion, to prevent their harbours from being used by the French as bases for commerce raiding. First, the 30th and then the 47th took part in these operations.

In June 1808 a detachment of six officers, six sergeants, three drummers and two hundred rank and file of the 30th under Captain John Perceval Beaumont joined an expedition under Rear-Admiral William Drury (who had assumed command from Pellew) to take possession of the old Portuguese trading settlement at Macau, on the opposite side of the Pearl River delta from what would become the colony of Hong Kong. There were also, from the Bengal Army, two companies of the European Regiment and 650 volunteer sepoys. This expedition is of note as the first direct British military involvement in China.

Amongst the officers who accompanied this expedition was Assistant-Surgeon Sam Piper of the 30th, who later served for many years with the Depot at Chatham. He is believed to have been the original of the 'Doctor Slammer' of Charles Dickens' *Pickwick Papers*, a small, bald, fat army surgeon who was very popular in his own circle, where he 'took snuff with everybody, chatted with everybody, laughed, danced, made jokes, played whist, did everything, and was everywhere.'

After the expedition had sailed, an order came from the Governor-General in Calcutta to send in command of the troops an officer of tact and judgement who would be likely to induce the Portuguese to yield up Macao without a fight. He was to explain to them that Britain bore them no ill will and had no desire to deprive them of their possessions, but that there was a fear that Napoleon would turn their harbours into nests of privateers, as he had done with the Dutch. Major William Wright of the 30th, who had just been gazetted brevet lieutenant-colonel, was selected for this delicate mission by the Governor of Madras, and departed for the expedition rendezvous at Penang. Sadly, he died at Penang on 16th August, and the two companies went on to Macau under Captain Beaumont.

Admiral Drury anchored off Macau on 21st September and, with the forced consent of the Portuguese governor, landed three hundred troops from Madras, including the 30th companies, on the 27th. The Bengal contingent arrived on 20th October, when they too landed without delay and joined the 30th in occupying the defences of the settlement. The Chinese, who quite rightly considered the leased trading post of Macau to be an integral part of their empire, sent Drury an indignant message:

'Knowing, as you ought to know, that the Portuguese inhabit a territory belonging to the Celestial Empire, how could you suppose that the French would ever venture to molest them? If they dared, our warlike troops should attack, defeat, and chase them from the face of the country.'

The Chinese ordered the British to depart, and when Drury did not comply with their demands they took decisive action: they stopped all the profitable trade of the East India Company through Canton, embargoed provisions for British ships, and blocked the Canton River with a line of war junks, while Chinese troops moved towards Macau. Drury's attempts at negotiations were rebuffed, and when he moved up-river to break the blockade of Canton, with his troops in ships' boats, he found the junks fully manned with Chinese soldiers. An attempted parley failed and, lacking the authority or resolution to force his way through, he withdrew to avoid a potentially bloody conflict.

Throughout their three-month occupation of Macau, the British garrison was in an uncomfortable and potentially dangerous situation. The Portuguese were resentfully unwelcoming, the Chinese inhabitants overtly hostile, particularly to the Indian soldiers, so that the troops had to be confined to their quarters for their own protection. There was also an increasing threat of Chinese military intervention, so the small British force prepared to defend as much of the settlement as was practicable.

Under pressure from all sides, for the Company had lost some three months of valuable trade, Drury then accepted the inevitable and re-embarked his troops on 23rd December. The expedition returned to India in February 1809, but it was not until April that the 30th companies, under Lieutenant T. G. Richardson, rejoined the main body of their Battalion at Trichinopoly.

Shortly after disembarkation at Madras, the 47th received orders to proceed to Bombay, where they arrived on 3rd March 1808, and in April moved on to Surat, a princely state and British protectorate on the Gulf of Cambay, where they would have occupied the castle on the banks of the Tapti River. Lieutenant-Colonel John Byne Skerrett was in command by June as Thomas Backhouse had been awarded a brevet colonelcy and appointed Garrison Commander of Bombay.

In October the Right Wing of the 47th occupied the massive 16th century fort at Diu and the Left Wing, commanded by Lieutenant-Colonel James Cuming[849], was quartered at the fortified port of Daman, both Portuguese colonies on the Arabian Sea coast of India. In the spring of 1809, the Battalion returned to Bombay in a sickly condition and was quarantined for some time on Butcher Island.

The Pirate Coast 1809

In the autumn of 1809, the Flank Companies of the 47th were ordered to prepare for an expedition to the Persian Gulf, from where the Al Qasimi, or Joasmi, pirates terrorised merchant ships in the Gulf and Arabian Sea, including the profitable trade of the HEIC, and placed British relations with Oman and Persia in jeopardy. Furthermore, by 1807, the French had established consulates in Tehran and Muscat to further Napoleon's eastern ambitions and counter the growing East India Company hegemony in India, and they encouraged attacks on British shipping.

Moreover, the traditional piratical depredations of the Al Qasimi had of late been infused with additional ferocity by the fanatical Wahhabi sect, which by the end of the 18th century had burst out of the Arabian desert to dominate the Pirate Coast.[850] As effective overlords, they encouraged ruthless attacks on the ships of all unbelievers and took one-fifth of the proceeds of piracy. The pirates' atrocities were now sanctioned by a narrow and perverted interpretation of Islam, as explained by a horrified co-religionary:

'They are of the sect of the Wahabees, and are called Jouassimee; but God preserve us from them, for they are monsters. Their occupation is piracy, and their delight murder; and to make it worse, they give you the most pious reasons for every villainy they commit. They abide by the letter of the sacred volume, rejecting all commentaries and traditions. If you are their captive, and offer all you possess to save your life, they say, "No! It is written in the Koran that it is unlawful to plunder the living, but we are not prohibited in that sacred work from stripping the dead." So saying, they knock you on the head.'

Among the pirates' targets were Indian 'country ships,' smaller and weaker than the large East Indiamen, which in any case usually traveled in convoy. In 1805, the Al Qasimi captured two large ships, *Shannon* and *Trimmer*, when their dhows swarmed over the larger merchant ships and massacred the crews. *Trimmer* was converted into a formidable pirate ship, and when the Bombay Marine (HEIC) warship *Mornington*, 24 guns, attempted to recapture the ship a few months later, nearly forty Al Qasimi vessels attacked the Company warship, which only just managed to escape. In April 1808 a fleet of some seventy pirate vessels appeared off Gujarat, raiding shipping at Surat before they were driven off by ships of the Bombay Marine. Later in the same year, a fleet of 50 raiders attacked merchant shipping off Scinde, where they seized a large country ship, the *Minerva*, cut the throats of her crew one by one, and made her their flagship.

By early 1809 it was estimated that the Al Qasimi forces in the Persian Gulf and Arabian Sea numbered over eight hundred dhows and 63 large baghlahs, crewed by 19,000 men. They were opposed by just two HEIC ships, *Mornington* and *Teignmouth*, for the over-stretched Royal Navy, diverted to dealing with French and Dutch raiders based in Mauritius, Java and their dependencies, had little presence in the Arabian Sea. The Directors of

---

[849] James Cuming (1768-1839) had served in the 47th since 1784 in the West Indies, South Africa, South America and the East Indies, and was praised for his just administration in Daman. At the end of that tour the officers of the Left Wing presented a piece of plate to him with 'the grateful acknowledgement for the happiness we have enjoyed while under your command', and noted the 'constant regularity and meritorious conduct of the men, so justly appreciated by His Excellency the Governor in his public despatches to the Presidency.' James Cuming died a lieutenant-general.

[850] In 1744 Abd al Wahhab, founder of the strict Wahhabi sect, had forged a pact with the regional emir, Mohammad bin Saud, and when in 1932 the House of Saud was elevated to kingship Wahhabism, or Salafism, became the state religion. The 'Pirate Coast', as defined on 18th and 19th century maps, was centred on what became the Trucial States, which since 1972 has been known as the United Arab Emirates.

the East India Company were determined, at all costs, to avoid the risk of involvement in Arab affairs and to avert conflict with the Wahhabis. The pirates were well aware that the officers of the Bombay Marine were under strict orders from the Company not to react to hostile action unless actually fired upon, which suited the Al Qasimi perfectly since their usual tactic was to close with their victim without firing and board in overwhelming numbers. The inevitable result was that in 1808 the HEIC sloop *Sylph*, on a diplomatic mission, was overwhelmed in the Straits of Hormuz and most of her crew massacred. Appeasement never pays, and the ruler of Ras al-Khaimah, whose harbour was the principal pirate lair, showed his contempt for the Bombay Government by demanding a tribute in return for permitting their merchant ships to pass the Straits unmolested.

Provoked at length by the increasingly brazen activities of the pirates, in the autumn of 1809 the Bombay Government undertook a punitive expedition to the Persian Gulf, its purposes being to reduce the strength of the marauders by destroying their ships and bases, to release British subjects and others held in captivity, to restore the power and prestige of their ally the ruler of Muscat, against the Wahhabi fanatics, and to counter French influence in the Gulf. The coast around the pirates' harbours had not been properly charted, but it was known that the approaches were too shallow for the larger naval ships to come close enough inshore to use their guns. Landings would be needed to destroy the pirates' ships and strongholds.

The force comprised a naval squadron under Commodore John Wainwright, consisting of two Royal Navy frigates, *Caroline* and *La Chiffone*, and nine smaller HEIC ships[851], with troops embarked in four large transports. The military element comprised the 65th Regiment, the Flank Companies of the 47th, detachments of Bombay artillery and Bombay Marines, and sepoys of the 2nd Bombay Native Infantry, the whole under the command of Colonel Lionel Smith of the 65th.[852]

Wainwright and Smith were given joint command of the expedition. They were instructed that land operations were to be limited to whatever was necessary for destruction of the pirate ports, and that on no account were troops to engage in a land war against the Wahhabis.

The expedition sailed from Bombay on 17th September, after the monsoon season, but it was October before they reached their rendezvous at Muscat, where Wainwright and Smith were warned that over twenty thousand Bedouin warriors had descended on the coast to join the Al Qasimi. Despite this, they determined to make a series of raids against the principal pirate bases around the Straits of Hormuz, beginning with Ras al-Khaimah on the Arabian coast.

On the afternoon of 11th November, the British fleet arrived off the town of Ras al-Khaimah. The pirates sailed out with the 20-gun *Minerva* and a fleet of dhows, but put about and ran for safety once they saw the strength of the British squadron. *Minerva* ran aground and was abandoned on a sandbank under a small fort, where after a fierce exchange of fire she was burned by boat parties from the Company gunboats.

Ras al-Khaimah was situated on a long, low, sandy peninsula, about one quarter of a mile wide, which ran parallel to the coast and sheltered the harbour. The sea front was defended by trenches and batteries, and a high wall flanked by four towers stretched across the peninsula well south of the town. The place had a garrison of about five thousand of the Al Qasimi and their Bedouin allies.

The town was protected from offshore bombardment by sandbanks which blocked the approach of heavier warships. On 12th November, Wainwright deployed his smaller ships close inshore and bombarded the town for three hours, but made little impression on its defences. Meanwhile, preparations were made for an assault landing at dawn the following day. It was decided to land the main body of troops on the peninsula south of the wall, with a feint attack against the harbour entrance to the north of the town.

At 2 a.m. on the morning of 13th November the boats were ready. Two gunboats, with some of the ships' boats, rowed towards the harbour mouth, and opened fire at first light, drawing the enemy's attention in that direction. Meanwhile, a landing force consisting of the 65th, Flank Companies of the 47th, and detachments of Bombay Infantry and Marines, under Colonel Smith, had gathered in boats alongside one of the cruisers. Then, taking advantage of the diversion, they advanced rapidly ashore. The Arab defenders, seeing that their fire from

---

[851] The HEIC warships were *Mornington, Aurora, Ternate, Mercury, Nautilus, Prince of Wales, Ariel* and *Fury,* and the bomb ketch *Stromboli.*

[852] As Lieutenant-General Sir Lionel Smith, Bart, GCB, GCH, this officer was Colonel of the 40th Regiment from 9th February 1837 to 25th April 1842.

the towers and walls did not check the oncoming boats, came down to dispute the landing sword in hand. A desperate attack threatened the flank of the first company that reached the shore, but, when the pirates had nearly closed, the gunboats which flanked the landing opened with case shot and broke the rush. This gave time for the troops to form, after which they fixed bayonets and drove the enemy back with a fine charge, and succeeded in expanding the beachhead up to the land wall and towers.

The troops were keen to push on into the town, but were held back until proper arrangements were made, for the town was full of Arabs firing from the narrow embrasures and flat roofs of the houses. Field pieces and scaling ladders were landed and brought up, and the attack commenced.

The advance was slow, as fighting was house to house and the Arabs defended many buildings obstinately. Anxious to speed up his advance and secure the town before nightfall, Smith had his men set fire to small huts in their path, creating a pall of smoke under cover of which they were able to storm and capture the Sheik's palace by early afternoon. The Arab forces retreated to the north end of the town, which they defended until the inhabitants escaped across the harbour. They then taunted the British from the surrounding hills but did not attempt any counter-attacks.

With the town secure, Wainwright ordered his squadron into the bay and the seamen set fire to over fifty Al Qasimi craft, including thirty large bhagalas. Meanwhile, in the town Smith's troops burned the warehouses, containing valuable goods (presumably plunder), and destroyed the fortifications and ammunition stores.

By the morning of 14th November, the British force returned to their ships, having suffered light casualties of five killed and 34 wounded, none of whom were from the 47th companies. Arab losses are unknown, but were probably significant, while the damage done to the Al Qasimi fleet was severe: over half of their largest and most dangerous vessels were destroyed at Ras al-Khaimah.

The embarkation was rather hasty, as information was received that a large body of Arabs was approaching the coast. Mindful of his instruction to avoid conflict with the Wahhabis, Smith began re-embarkation at dawn, and by noon it was complete. This hurried departure, carried out amid the defiant jeers of the returning pirates, who crowded down just out of range, rather spoiled the moral effect of what was otherwise a most successful operation.

The expedition next appeared on 17th November off the town of Lingeh (Bandar Lengeh) on the Persian coast. The place was occupied without resistance or casualties, and was burned together with twenty more dhows. A further cruise down the Persian coast revealed that most of the other harbours were empty.

Commodore Wainwright now proceeded against Laft, a principal pirate stronghold situated in the Straits of Hormuz on the north side of Qishm Island. The place was defended by a strong castle and by numerous batteries. Sending ships to block the passages to the Qishm Channel, Wainwright hired local pilots and approached the town on 26th November.

The ruler, Sheik Hussain was defiant, and about 2 p.m. on the 27th Colonel Smith landed with about three hundred men, consisting of the Light Company 47th, half a company of the 65th, a detachment of the 2nd Bombay Native Infantry and some seamen and marines.

The landing was unopposed, and the troops soon took possession of the town, but the Sheik retired to the castle and prepared to defend its fourteen-foot-thick walls. Seamen bought up a 5½-inch brass howitzer to blow in the only entrance, but as Smith's troops approached the castle they were suddenly swept by a heavy and unexpectedly accurate fire of musketry from the loopholed walls, which felled so many of the attackers that the survivors were compelled to retreat, abandoning the howitzer in the open. The troops took cover behind hillocks and sand ridges, where they were pinned down until darkness fell. An Irish subaltern of the 47th, Lieutenant Standish Weld, made a gallant attempt to recover the howitzer, but was shot dead as soon as he left cover.

Meanwhile, a heavy bombardment was maintained all afternoon by the sloop *Fury*, 8 guns, and some gunboats, and by sunset the castle was, according to Wainwright, 'seriously shattered.' The place was abandoned during the night and at dawn was occupied by a detachment of the 47th. Eleven more pirate dhows were burned, and much plunder recovered. The town was turned over to a local ruler who professed support for the British, and Wainwright sailed back to Muscat.

The casualties at Laft amounted to ten killed and 55 wounded, including Lieutenant Weld and three men of the 47th killed, and one sergeant and nine men wounded. Arab losses were estimated at more than fifty killed in the castle alone.

Wainwright's squadron remained in the Gulf until January, but the Flank Companies 47th left on 9th December for Bombay, where they rejoined battalion headquarters.

The expedition had achieved most of its objectives, reducing French influence and inflicting significant damage on the Al Qasimi, but the latter rebuilt their strength and resumed their piratical activities with renewed ferocity from around 1815, so that in 1819 a further British intervention was required. On that occasion the whole of the 47th Regiment would be involved.

In April 1812, in furtherance of a mutual defence pact between Britain and the Shah of Persia to counter Russian expansion, Lieutenant George Forster Sadleir of the 47th, aged 23, (with the local rank of major) was sent from Bombay to Tabriz in Persia with four sergeants of the Regiment to train and discipline the Shah's infantry, remaining there until June 1815. For his services Sadleir was presented by Fath Ali Shah with a sword and firman, and received the thanks of Lord Hastings, Governor-General and Commander-in-Chief in India.[853]

The 'White Mutiny' 1809

On 21st October 1807 the Governor of Madras wrote to the Court of Directors in London, the governing body of the East India Company, that 'a spirit of insubordination and cabal has lately shown itself among several of your officers... which, after the events that have agitated the native army of this Presidency, might lead to consequences of the most fatal nature.'

Many of the Company's officers at that time were indeed increasingly seditious, clinging jealously to the privileges and corporate perquisites, such as 'bazaar duties' and 'tentage,' which they regarded as but just compensation for the hardships and dangers of service in India. Dissatisfaction centred on the Madras Army, whose officers received lower pay and allowances than their peers in the Bengal and Madras Presidencies. Discontented, indebted, conscious of their lower status than King's officers, and all too aware of their critical importance to the Company, they felt no strong loyalty to the commercial enterprise which employed them. Accustomed to send collective 'addresses' to each other to signify approval, they felt they had an equal right to censure; and from there it was but a short step to combination and conspiracy to maintain their perceived rights, speaking the libertarian language of the Foxite Whigs.

It was most unfortunate for the increasingly fragile relations between the Company and its officers that in December 1807 Sir George Barlow was appointed as Governor of Madras. Barlow pursued reduction of expenditure with more zeal than sense, and he hated soldiers.

The last straw for many restive Company officers came on 1st May 1809 when Barlow provocatively removed or suspended without legal process a dozen colonels and majors, and issued, as a test of loyalty, a declaration[854] to be signed by every officer of the Madras Army. This test was felt by many otherwise loyal Company officers to impugn their honour, and out of thirteen hundred officers of the Madras Army only one hundred and fifty could be induced to sign the declaration. Committees of correspondence were set up in the military stations to co-ordinate resistance to what they saw as the tyrannical and oppressive conduct of Sir George Barlow and his advisers, and as the hot season approached tempers rose, reason fled, and righteous indignation merged into hysteria and defiance. It became evident that many officers were prepared to push their dispute with the Government to the point of armed rebellion, and as the contagion spread only the King's troops stood between British India and anarchy.

---

[853] Sadleir, commissioned into the 47th in April 1805, had served with the Regiment in South America, 1807, and in the Persian Gulf, 1809.

[854] This Declaration, issued by the Madras Government in May 1809, was bluntly uncompromising, requiring all their officers to sign the following: 'We, the undersigned officers of the Honourable Company's service, do, in the most solemn manner, declare upon our word and honour, as British officers, that we will obey the orders, and support the authority of the Honourable the Governor in Council of Fort St. George, agreeably to the tenor of the commissions which we hold from that Government.'

The first outbreak of open mutiny was at Masulipatam (now also known as Machilipatnam), on the coast some four hundred miles north of Madras, where the Madras European Regiment and the 1st/19th Madras Native Infantry were in garrison. The immediate pretext was an order, issued on 1st June through the unpopular new senior officer of the station, Lieutenant-Colonel Innes, for three companies of the European Regiment to embark as marines, replacing the 30th, who by that time had only a sergeant and nineteen privates at sea. The Company officers refused to accept the order, and when Innes repeated it on 25th June they arrested him. At the same time urgent messages were sent to Secunderabad, Jalna, Seringapatam and other military stations, telling them what had happened and asking for support.

A draft of some hundred men of the 59th Foot now found themselves in the eye of the storm. They had embarked at Portsmouth on the *Streatham* Indiaman on 3rd April 1808, but, after an eventful voyage which took them to Madeira and Brazil,[855] they arrived too late in the season to land over the open beach at Madras, so were diverted to Calcutta. The detachment remained there, at Fort William, for nearly three months, then embarked again for Madras. Coasting south, they called at Masulipatam, where they landed by order of General Macdowall, the Commander-in-Chief, who at the end of January 1809 left India after making an inflammatory speech to the Madras European Regiment. The diary of Ensign James Chadwick of the 59th takes up the story:

'At Masulipatam we remained nearly six months, during the time that the mutiny in that fort was at its highest pitch; an awkward situation, indeed, for inexperienced officers as we were; none of the Company's officers would speak to us after they found that the King's troops would not join in the mutiny; though for two months we were as intimate with them as brothers, and members of their mess. A young man of the Company's service, and a townsman of mine who I was very intimate with, durst not be seen to enter my house, and when the Company's troops, consisting of one regiment of Europeans and one regiment of natives, were drawn out to oppose the hundred of the 59th Regiment, this young friend ran to the house where I was living with Lieutenant [John] Lloyd and cautioned us of the danger which we would incur by either appearing out of doors ourselves, or allowing any of the 59th to do so for a short time. We benefited by the caution, and I must do the officers and men credit to say that I'm convinced they had no hostile intentions against us, and that they only got under arms with an idea of preventing that mischief which must inevitably have incurred had they not taken the precaution of putting Colonel Innes under arrest, as the Colonel threatened them that he would have the one hundred loyal men of the 59th and four officers to attack 1,400 men, which must have ended by our being cut to pieces.'

Fortunately for the 59th detachment, the frigate HMS *Piedmontaise*, which was to have received the troops ordered to embark as marines, arrived off Masulipatam, took the detachment aboard, and carried them to Madras. There, after marching to Poonamallee, they joined a large field force of King's troops and loyal sepoys gathered at St. Thomas's Mount, about seven miles from Fort St. George, being attached in succession to the 69th Regiment, the Royals, and the 86th Regiment. This force marched north for some four hundred miles towards Hyderabad, and James Chadwick reached Gooty, where he was in charge of a field hospital, before the 59th detachment was ordered back to join its headquarters at Bangalore.

At Trichinopoly, Colonel Wilkinson took firm and decisive action to prevent any outbreak of mutiny at that station where, in addition to the 30th, there were the 6th Madras Native Cavalry and the 2nd Battalions of the 13th and 24th Madras Native Infantry, together with small bodies of artillery and engineers. On 30th July Wilkinson assembled the European officers of the Madras Army and tendered the declaration to them. Twenty of those present signed at once, but sixteen declined. Wilkinson then offered a compromise, asking the insubordinate officers to pledge themselves to have no contact with their sepoys, which under the circumstances was the very least he could safely require. Again the Company officers refused, at which Wilkinson handed them over to a guard of two hundred of the 30th, with muskets loaded and bayonets fixed, who were to escort the dissidents down to the coast at Negapatam. The officers of the escort had orders to slay their prisoners if there was the least

---

[855] Among the 59th detachment was Ensign James Chadwick, a young Irish officer with an eye for the ladies. At Madeira he 'visited all the chapels, nunneries, etc., but could only get a peep at the girls through the iron bars', and at Sao Sebastiao, Brazil, where the *Streatham* docked with a broken mast, he did no better. At the opera house one night, he supposedly mistook the door to the actresses' dressing room for that of his box, walked in and sat down to help a young lady get ready. When it was the lady's turn to go on stage, young Chadwick stayed in the room to wait for her return, only to be seized by three local soldiers on suspicion of theft. Luckily for him, the captain of the guard was a fellow-Irishman who released him with a warning never to visit the town again.

appearance of a rescue attempt on the part of their sepoys, but were also given discretion, on reaching Tanjore, to release any prisoner who would give his parole to complete the journey to Madras peaceably and without further offence.

Wilkinson replaced the commanding officer of the 6th Madras Native Cavalry with Major Christopher Maxwell of the 30th, assisted by Lieutenants William Cave and James Lewin, and sent Captain Sam Bircham and Lieutenant John Napper to the 16th Madras Native Infantry. Then, leaving Major Vaumorel in command at Trichinopoly, and accompanied by a strong detachment, in August he toured every garrison in the Southern District and sent to Madras every Company officer who refused to sign the declaration. In consequence of Wilkinson's resolute actions, his district was the only one in the Presidency to avoid open mutiny.

The most serious incident of the mutiny, and the only bloodshed, was at the fortress of Seringapatam, where by 29th July a detachment of the King's troops was expelled, the walls were manned, the drawbridge raised, and Lieutenant-Colonel Bell, commanding the fortress, ordered that fire was to be opened on any armed body approaching from Mysore or Bangalore. Next day the treasury was seized. The mutinous officers formed a committee of safety, sent out a detachment which captured a large amount of money, and summoned to their assistance the garrison at the hill fort of Chittledroog (now Chitraldrug).

The sepoys of the 1st Battalions of the 8th and 15th Madras Native Infantry, stationed at Chittledroog, were deceived into marching on Seringapatam by their European officers, who gave the false impression that the Rajah of Mysore had risen and attacked the garrison of that place. The Chittledroog mutineers, having seized the public treasury, marched on 6th August for Seringapatam, 1,120 strong led by a Captain Mackintosh, plundering villages along the way.

At Bangalore, the principal garrison in the dominions of the Rajah of Mysore, the 59th were stationed as part of a brigade of the Madras Army.[856] Lieutenant-Colonel Samuel Gibbs, as the senior officer on station, was instructed on 26th July to call on all Company officers in that garrison to sign the declaration. Those who did not were to be suspended from duty and sent to the coast. Gibbs was one of the many experienced officers who urged the Madras government to modify its hardline approach, and he thereby incurred the wrath of his superiors, but he was eventually ordered to enforce the test.

The result was that all the Company officers at Bangalore, while professing their loyalty, refused to sign what was regarded as a demeaning declaration. They offered no resistance to their suspension and were sent to the coast. King's officers filled key appointments in their place. Among these, Captain John Campbell of the 59th became Brigade Major, and Lieutenant George Darby became Fort Adjutant. Gibbs then had to explain to the Indian officers and sepoys that some of their European officers were acting out of self-interest, and called on them to remain faithful to the Company. He was initially persuaded that they would remain loyal, but subsequently had good reason to doubt their intentions if faced with fellow-sepoys.

Nevertheless, on 8th August Gibbs marched as ordered for Seringapatam with six companies of the 59th, two squadrons of the 25th Light Dragoons, the 5th Madras Native Cavalry and the 1st/3rd Madras Native Infantry. Whilst on the march, he was ordered to detach Major Alexander McLeod with three companies of the 59th, three hundred men, to secure Mysore against any attack by the mutineers. McLeod's detachment arrived at Mysore on the morning of the 11th and, with a company of the 80th Foot and a squadron of 25th Light Dragoons, together with the Rajah's forces, prepared to defend the city.

On August 10th, Gibbs encamped his force at Raghaviah's Choultry, 2½ miles north-east of Seringapatam. The following morning, the mutinous battalions from Chittledroog approached, having marched 180 miles in five days. They had been intercepted 35 miles from Seringapatam by a Mysore state force including three thousand irregular, or sillidar, cavalry commanded by Ram Row, an able officer of the Mysore government. This force had been sent at the behest of the British Resident in Mysore to impede the mutineers' progress, but the appearance of these Mysore horsemen appears to have confirmed the sepoys in their belief that the Rajah of that state was in revolt. Having warned Captain Mackintosh of the consequences of continued defiance, Ram Row harassed the Chittledroog battalions for the last twenty to thirty miles of their march, with frequent skirmishes; but when, early on the morning of the 11th, the rebel battalions were a few hours short of their destination, Mackintosh received

---

[856] The gravestone of Sergeant-Major Kelly of the 59th, dated 1808, is the oldest in Agaram Cemetery, Bangalore.

an urgent message from Seringapatam to 'push on.' They were about four miles from the rebel fortress and crossing a nullah, or stream bed, when the Madras cavalry pressed their attack on the rear of the column, capturing its baggage. The action which followed was described later that day in Lieutenant-Colonel Gibbs' report:

'I have the honour to inform you that at about eleven o'clock this morning I heard some firing towards the Chittledroog road, and instantly dispatched a patrol of dragoons to learn the cause; having received information from the Resident [at Mysore] that the sillidar horse would give timely information, I was easy, although ready to turn out almost immediately. Three of His Highness the Rajah's sillidar horse came to report that a force from Chittledroog was advancing. I ordered the line to turn out, which was done with the utmost expedition, the Sepoys joining the Europeans with the greatest alacrity. I formed the advance, consisting of a squadron of Light Dragoons, the Light Infantry Company of the 59th Regiment, and one galloper gun, under the command of Major Cardin. I left Lieutenant Col. Adams [25th Light Dragoons] to bring up the remainder, which he did as soon as it was possible, considering the nature of the ground. The difficulties the troops had to encounter through paddy-fields and morasses made this a very difficult task, but the troops surpassed every obstacle and joined in the pursuit.

'Seeing these unfortunately infatuated people flying in confusion, hard pressed by the sillidar horse, I desired Major Cardin, if possible, to overtake them by a circuitous route, for we could not cross the nullar [nullah] in our front, and to spare the effusion of blood. I wished a white flag to be sent to them by an officer, which Lieutenant Jefferies of the 25th Dragoons most handsomely volunteered taking, as my Brigade Major, Captain [John] Campbell 59th, had been dispatched with orders to another part of the field. As Major Cardin with two squadrons of the 25th Dragoons and one gun approached the rear of the column, Lieutenant Jefferies advanced with a white flag; the sepoys salamed, but a European officer ordered them to fire; the sillidar horse gallantly rushed to his rescue. Having made the necessary arrangements to prevent any interruption from Seringapatam, I advanced with the Flank Companies of the 59th towards Webb's monument, but could not, with our utmost exertions, head or even come up with these battalions; but from the hard pressure put on them by the Light Dragoons and the sillidar horse (which latter took from them two guns, and both colours from one battalion) I have every reason to think that very few reached the fort.

'During these transactions the troops from the Fort had marched to attack our camp, for the protection of which I had left the picquets, quarter-guards, and the 5th Native Cavalry with one gun, under the command of Captain Bean. The force from the Fort… immediately retired when fired upon by Captain Bean, who then detached the 5th Cavalry to the support of the infantry, posted in front of the [Cauvery River] bridge, with a village on their right, on which point this [Chittledroog] force was immediately marching.

'The prisoners taken report that their loss in killed and wounded was considerable; as far as I could judge I estimate the killed at one hundred and fifty. On our side, I am happy to say, not a man was hurt, with the exception of Lieutenant Jefferies slightly wounded; one horse of the 25th killed, and one wounded. The casualties of the sillidar horse have not yet been reported to me, but I believe they are trifling.'

Other sources amplify and correct this account. It appears that the greater part of the Chittledroog force had crossed the nullah and, under pressure from the Mysore sillidars, were hoping to find safety in the marshes beyond, when the 25th Dragoons came up with their rear. The exhausted sepoys, regarding the dragoons as friends who would protect them from the Rajah's horsemen, greeted them with salaams, and may in some cases have put down their muskets. This confusing situation was compounded when fire was opened on the white flag, for the immediate response by both the sillidars and the dragoons was to sabre several hundred of the bewildered sepoys who had not succeeded in crossing the nullah. Some 290 of these tragically misled men died or were listed as missing, 153 were wounded, and fewer than seven hundred escaped into Seringapatam. Captain Mackintosh was wounded and captured.

Soon after midnight that night the guns of Seringapatam bombarded Gibbs' camp, but to little effect. A further sortie was attempted on the 13th, but the fortress was now blockaded, and on the morning of the14th negotiations began between Lieutenant-Colonels Gibbs and Adams and representatives of the garrison. On 10th September Sir George Barlow was able to report that:

'When the officers [at Seringapatam] received information that the force at Hyderabad had submitted unconditionally, and that there was no prospect of their obtaining support or assistance, the whole of the troops which composed that garrison surrendered at discretion and marched out in the morning of the 23rd of August, leaving their arms upon the parade.'

The 59th Regiment marched in to occupy the fortress, of which Samuel Gibbs was appointed Commandant. On 20th October the 59th marched back to Bangalore, where on 5th November they were at last joined by the roving detachment which had, in Ensign James Chadwick's words, been 'twelve months knocking about India.'

Capture of Mauritius 1810

The island of Mauritius (known pre-1810 as Isle de France) and its dependencies, the islands of Rodriguez and Réunion (or Bourbon), harboured French warships and privateers, which from the renewal of war in 1803, and especially from 1808, had ravaged British commerce in the Indian Ocean. Although the East India Company suffered severely from these depredations, it was reluctant to incur the expense of dealing with the threat until losses became so serious that action became imperative, and the British and Indian Governments determined to mount a joint expedition from Bombay, Madras and the Cape of Good Hope.

As a preliminary measure, the islands of Rodriguez and Bourbon were captured by a small force from Bombay under Lieutenant-Colonel Keating of the 56th; but this success was followed in August 1810 by a disastrously rash naval adventure off Grand Port, Mauritius, resulting in the loss of four British frigates. Two more frigates were subsequently taken, though both were shortly recaptured, and the arrival in October of Vice-Admiral Sir Albemarle Bertie with five frigates from the Cape restored the naval balance in Britain's favour.

In August 1810 the 1st/59th were still stationed at Bangalore when they were ordered to prepare for foreign service. Marching on the 11th, the Battalion reached Fort St. George, Madras on the 31st of that month, where they joined a brigade which also comprised the 89th Regiment, a company of the 87th, and one wing of a volunteer battalion of Madras sepoys. On 16th September this brigade embarked, with Lieutenant-Colonel Samuel Gibbs of the 59th in command and Captain Charles Douglas of the Regiment as his Brigade Major. Lieutenant-Colonel Alexander McLeod commanded the 59th Regiment.

The Madras force sailed on 22nd September, and on 6th November it reached the appointed rendezvous for the fleet and army, the island of Rodriguez, about one hundred miles from Mauritius. The Bombay military contingent had already arrived, and when the troops from Bengal came in the combined expedition of eighteen warships and fifty East Indiamen and transports[857] sailed for Mauritius on 22nd November. The military force numbered about ten thousand men, of whom some three-fifths were British and the remainder Indian, and was commanded by Lieutenant-General Sir John Abercromby, son of old Sir Ralph of Egypt fame.

The French garrison of Mauritius comprised some thirteen hundred regular troops commanded by General Charles Decaen, who could also field ten thousand National Guards of doubtful value and was supported by a naval squadron of six frigates based at Port Louis, the island's capital, which was then known as Port Napoléon.

The island of Mauritius had previously been considered impregnable on account of coral reefs surrounding the coast, but careful reconnaissance and soundings had discovered a practicable anchorage and landing place at Grande Baie, a little to the west of Cape Malheureuse, the most northerly point of the island, and twelve miles from Port Louis. It was found that a fleet might anchor in a narrow strait between the islet of Coin de Mire and the mainland, from where there was an opening through the reef wide enough to admit three or four boats abreast. Due to light winds, the fleet did not sight Mauritius until the 28th, and it was the morning of the following day before any of the ships came to anchor.

The first troops ashore were the Reserve, under Lieutenant-Colonel Keating, and the Grenadier Company of the 59th, under Captain John Campbell, with two 6-pounders and two howitzers. Landing without opposition in Mapou Bay, to the east of Cape Malheureuse, their arrival prompted the French to retire from Fort Malartic at the head of Grande Baie. Meanwhile, two brigs of shallow draught anchored within a hundred yards of the beach to cover the main landing, which began shortly after 1 p.m. In just three hours ten thousand men, with their guns, ammunition and stores, and three days' provisions, were put ashore without loss or accident.

---

[857] Part of the 59th were aboard the *Upton Castle*, a country boat (i.e. a vessel built and based in India) converted to troop transport. The landing of the Regiment from this ship features in a picture of 1813 by R. Temple.

As soon as sufficient troops were landed, about 4 p.m., the column marched on Port Louis, for Abercromby was concerned that any delay might give the French time to occupy a very thick wood through which the road ran for the first five miles before reaching more open country. Major Henry Austen, 59th, led with the light companies and easily brushed aside a small party of National Guard. The troops were, however, soon fatigued after long confinement on transports, and suffered from a suffocating heat and no water. Emerging from the woods, the column followed the coast for another mile before halting at about midnight. Ensign James Chadwick of the 59th described this taxing march in his diary:

'We moved on directly, and had a march of 20 miles [a considerable exaggeration] through a confined jungle which rendered the air so extremely suffocating that many people died of fatigue. Amongst the number was a captain of the *City of London*, who came as a volunteer, an officer of the 12th & one of the 65th Regt. It was indeed a melancholy sight to see ten thousand men suffering from a drought which there was no possible means of quenching. As soon as we got clear of the jungle we halted for the night, & lay in bivouack in that miserable state until daylight, when we again marched forward, & after going eleven miles without being able to procure water enough to moisten our lips, we arrived at the Powder Mills [Moulin à Poudre] where, gratifying sight, we beheld a river, the waters of which then appeared to us dearer than the most precious diamonds of Golconda. The men, poor fellows, could hardly contain their joy, & directly the Regiment was dismissed they rushed into the stream, regardless of having their clothes on.'

The Moulin à Poudre was on a defensible headland some four to five miles north of Port Louis, and Abercromby decided to give his exhausted men a day's rest. That afternoon General Decaen came out to make an armed reconnaissance with a party of horse and foot. He surprised a small advanced picket and rode within a hundred yards of the British line before, as James Chadwick described, he was driven back:

'While many of the men and officers were enjoying themselves in the river our picquets were attacked. Some of them (not the 59th) gave way; however, by the steadiness of those that stood their ground, & the activity of the 59th Rifle Company, which dashed amongst the enemy, General Vandermaesen[858] was driven back with great loss, & we did not see any more of the French troops for the day.'

The 59th Rifle Company mentioned by Chadwick had but recently been formed at Rodriguez by order of Sir John Abercromby, and was commanded by Captain George Darby. The Company had no casualties in this skirmish, but apparently put a ball through Decaen's cocked hat and mortally wounded his aide-de-camp.

Before daylight next morning a brigade was sent to attack some French shore batteries and, as planned, re-establish contact with the fleet. At 5 a.m., the refreshed main body resumed its march on Port Louis. Almost immediately the light troops became engaged in wooded country, pressing their adversaries closely and pushing them back from a river crossing.

As the British Flank Battalion, forming the advance guard, pressed on along a narrow road between impenetrable undergrowth, they were engaged by a French force of some 3,500 men with several field guns sited to command the exit from this defile, about three miles from Port Louis. The British force was greeted with grapeshot and musketry, mostly too high to be effective, but despite losing their commander, Lieutenant-Colonel Campbell, the advance was hardly checked. In the words of Abercromby's despatch, they 'formed with as much regularity as the bad & broken ground would admit of, charged the enemy with the greatest spirit, & compelled him to retire with the loss of his guns, & many killed & wounded.' The detail of this action is not entirely clear, but it appears that the Grenadier Company of the 59th was prominent: forming up with deliberation, and supported by the fire of troops on their flanks, they made a charge which caused the French to break and stream away to the main defensive lines of Port Louis, half a mile in the rear. They were thanked later that day, in General Orders, for their 'steadiness and gallantry' and their 'exemplary good conduct.'

Some rising ground in front, but out of range of the French lines, was then carried, and a general deployment before Port Louis commenced, during which the 59th were exposed to a 'galling fire' from a battery on an eminence to the right of the town. It was, in any case, too late in the day to organise a general assault, and the troops were exhausted by their exertions in oppressive heat, so the leading units were ordered to retire some distance. The 59th, deployed to the left of the road, were still within range of enemy guns, and were in consequence

---

[858] It was in fact General Decaen himself who led this attack, and was slightly wounded.

ordered to retire for a further half-mile. The whole army then took up a position about a mile and a half from the town. That night James Chadwick recorded an unfortunate 'blue on blue' incident:

'A false alarm crept into the second, or rear line. They opened fire on the front line, which they kept up for some time before it could be stopped, & during which time the 59th had more mischief done to them than they had suffered during the day from the enemy.'

What had happened was that a landing party of Indian Marines, wearing their customary blue and white uniform, had been mistaken in the dark for French troops.

Next day, as preparations were made for the intended assault on Port Louis, Decaen sent out a flag of truce. With a British army investing his landward side, and a powerful fleet blockading the port and standing in to bombard its defences, he was persuaded that his position was hopeless and agreed to surrender on rather favourable terms. These were concluded on 3rd December, and that same day the 59th and 89th marched in and occupied the town while the Royal Navy took possession of the port.

A major strategic threat had been eliminated at the cost of 167 casualties, of which the 59th lost one rank and file killed and four wounded. Some two thousand British seamen and other prisoners were liberated, and the spoils included ten warships and 27 merchant ships, including three East Indiamen and other prizes made by the French, and 209 guns.

In a General Order dated 'Camp before Port Louis, 5th December 1810,' Sir John Abercromby was effusive in its praise for his troops, but there was a hint of disappointment in his assertion that 'the conduct of the enemy has deprived the Army of an opportunity of performing any brilliant service, and of acquiring any fame which could not have failed to attend them in whatever they might have been ordered to undertake.' This was reflected in his official dispatch:

'During the course of this short service the enemy has not offered an opportunity to the Army in general for displaying the ardent zeal and animated courage with which every individual is inspired; but it is nevertheless my duty to represent to your lordship, in the strongest terms, the merits of every corps under my command. The officers and men (European as well as Native) have cheerfully and patiently submitted to the greatest fatigues and privations. During the advance of the Army the troops were unable, for the space of twenty-four hours, to procure a sufficient supply of water; but this trying circumstance did not produce a single murmur, or the smallest mark of discontent or disapprobation.'

The 59th Regiment was ordered to do duty in Port Louis, of which Colonel Gibbs was appointed Commandant, while young James Chadwick delighted in the company of the French planters' daughters:

'We had the satisfaction of the society of nice, lively little girls, animals entirely foreign to the part of the world we came from. I regretted much that we were obliged to leave them so soon, as those of my acquaintance were such as a man cannot part without a regret. Alas Josephine, on the 19th of December I bid you adieu with a heavy heart…'

Chadwick's bliss was indeed short-lived, for on 22nd December the 59th embarked for Madras. Abercromby marked their departure by a General Order expressing 'his high admiration of the steadiness, gallantry, and exemplary good conduct of the Battalion during the time it was under his command.'

This was, however, far from the end of the involvement with Mauritius for Queen's Lancashire forebears: the 82nd had a long tour on the island in 1819-33, the 81st recovered there from a near-shipwreck in 1865, and their successors 2nd Battalion The Loyal North Lancashire Regiment were in garrison 1907-9.

The 1st/47th in India 1811-15

The 47th remained in Bombay throughout 1810[859] and 1811. In the cold weather of the latter year the flank companies were sent, again in company with the 65th and under the command of Colonel Smith, to act against the turbulent and refractory Jam Saheb of Navanagar, who had defied his overlord, the Gaikwar of Baroda, and his British Resident. The princely state of Navanagar was in Kathiawar, on the south coast of the Gulf of Kutch.

---

[859] There is a memento of this tour in the Kanheri Caves, a complex of ancient rock-cut Budhist shrines outside Bombay, where the following graffiti has been found: 'N. Christian 47th Regt 1810". The inscription was made by Lieutenant Nicholas Christian, a Manxman, who died in India in 1814.

The expedition sailed on 21st December 1811 and landed at Porbandar. The British force advanced slowly, giving the Jam every opportunity to come to terms, but the prince prevaricated, and matters were only brought to a head when Captain William Phelan of the 47th was killed, whilst out hunting, by the Jam's men. Navanagar (now known as Jamnagar) was reached on 21st February 1812, and as batteries were opened the Jam submitted and his territory became a British protectorate. The flank companies were back with their headquarters by the last week in April.[860]

On 6th August 1812 the 1st/47th marched from Bombay for Poona (Pune), arriving there on the 23rd of that month. On 23rd September, under command Lieutenant-Colonel Humphrey Bland, the Battalion proceeded to join, on 1st October a force under Colonel Thomas Montresor in the territory of Baji Rao, Peishwa and nominal head of the Mahratta princes. The purpose of the British intervention was to restore the authority of the Peishwa in his disordered and depressed state on a more equitable and less oppressive basis. During October the 47th were encamped at Esapoor (Isapur), and on 22nd December they returned to Bombay. Forty men had died in the course of 1812.

The 1st/47th remained in Bombay throughout 1813 and most of the following year. Lack of active employment over this long period in garrison led to boredom, fractiousness and festering resentments, as exemplified in 1814 by a string of general courts martial involving officers of the 47th. In March that year Lieutenant Henry Pierard of the 47th accused Lieutenant Michael Hanley of the 65th for having brought charges against him of 'a frivolous, vexatious, and malicious nature, highly reflecting upon my honour and character, both as an officer and a gentleman,' for having returned a sword-cane broken in two and with the blade inscribed with the words 'A Poltroon and Coward,' and with drawing a caricature of Pierard captioned 'Rascality and Cowardice.' Hanley was found guilty and dismissed the Service.

On 16th June 1814, there was a fatal duel between two officers of the 47th, Captain Archibald Campbell, a veteran of Tarifa, and Lieutenant Russell, in which Russell, who had insisted on satisfaction, was shot through the head. Campbell, who was wounded, faced a court-martial but found not guilty, but, possibly in consequence, he sailed home a few months later, only to drown in a shipwreck.

Lieutenant William Scott of the 47th was brought before a court martial in July 1814 for 'insidious, scandalous, and infamous conduct, such as is unbecoming the character of an officer and a gentleman… for having, on, or about, the 14th of June, solicited Lieutenant James Hutchinson, to forget all past differences, and by prevailing upon Lieutenant Hutchinson to agree to live on terms of intimacy and friendship with him for the future, and after some days affable and familiar intercourse, entering the quarters of Lieutenant Hutchinson, on the 4th instant (July, 1814), and then abruptly dissolving the good understanding he had so lately courted, and requiring Lieutenant Hutchinson to fight him.' William Scott was dismissed from the Service.

On 1st November 1814 the battalion companies of the 47th sailed to Surat, where they had previously been stationed in 1808-9. The Flank Companies were detained at Bombay, being required for an expedition to Gujerat, attached to their old comrades of the 65th. Embarking on 23rd November 1814, the companies landed at Broach (Bharuch) and marched to Baroda, where a strong brigade was forming under Colonel George Holmes, a veteran of 34 years' service in India.

This body of troops marched from Baroda on 12th January 1815 to act as an army of observation, keeping an eye on Scindia's borders during the war in Nepal to guard against Pindari depredations into areas under British protection. The force took up a position at Soonapore on the west bank of the River Mahi, where they remained until May, when they were recalled to Baroda, and the 47th Flank Companies rejoined headquarters at Surat on 14th June 1815.

They arrived at a particularly unfortunate time, for the Battalion was about to be devastated by one of the terrible epidemics which, throughout the nineteenth century, cut down British troops in India by the hundreds. An assistant surgeon, who had recently dealt with an outbreak of fever in the 56th Foot on their return to Bombay from Surat, later recalled[861] that:

---

[860] An Army List entry for Major John Hutchinson of the 47th states that 'he was present at the storm of Chiak in 1811, and was the first individual who entered the fort by a breach made in the gate by a six-pounder. In this service he received five wounds'. I have been unable to trace this fort, or indeed any likely action around that time involving the 47th.

[861] Richard Hartley Kennedy MD, Surgeon Bombay Army, 'Notes on the Epidemic Cholera', p.82, 1827.

'In July and August 1815, I saw His Majesty's 47th Regiment nearly destroyed in Surat by the same ['bilious remittent'] fever. The corps was below 500 strong, but was in every respect healthy and effective in the middle of June; but when the fever broke out, scarcely any escaped – of officers and men, I believe, only about 20. The casualties were at least 40 per cent; for Col. Bland, who then commanded, and who died himself of the fever a few weeks after the conversation I allude to, told me the regiment had buried more than one third of its strength.'

The epidemic was not confined to Surat, for the Bombay burial registers for that period record the deaths of nineteen of the 47th, including women and children, amongst whom were the wife and infant son of Quartermaster-Sergeant Underwood. In one year the 47th lost 359 men dead, all from disease.

Unsurprisingly, their annual inspection report by Sir John Abercromby recorded that 'discipline had materially suffered' as a result of this terrible mortality, and there were frequent courts-martial. However, not one soldier deserted throughout the battalion's ordeal.

The 1st/30th in India 1810-15

After the collapse of the 1809 'White Mutiny,' the 1st/30th remained based at Trichinopoly for a further two years. In 1810, there was renewed trouble with the rulers of Travancore, and Captain Robert Murray was sent there with seven officers and 343 other ranks. The detachment returned within a month.

In October 1810 William Wilkinson was promoted to the rank of major-general and though he remained senior lieutenant-colonel of the 30th his long service with the Regiment was at an end. His obituary in 1840 records that 'Although strict in discipline, he was much beloved by his men, and received from them the honourable title of the Soldier's Friend. He considered merit as the only passport to promotion; and when in India, whatever fell under his patronage was given to those who could produce the best testimonials of service.' [862]

Wilkinson's comments on that year's inspection of the 1st/30th, which he had so often commanded, were understandably complimentary. Having noted that all movements and manoeuvres were performed appropriately and that all arms, accoutrements and clothing were in good condition, he added:

'The Battalion is improved both in discipline and field exercises since the last review in May 1809. Major Vaumorel has been in command of the Battalion the last eight months. He is an old officer, has seen a variety of service, and is very zealous.' He also recommended that the battalion was 'fit for immediate service.'

William Lockhart returned from Pondicherry to resume command. He had already commanded the 1st Battalion, but for a short break, since 1804, and before that in 1801 he had led the 30th in their action at the Green Hill in front of Alexandria, Egypt. An officer of the Company's service described him at this time as 'of the most mild and unassuming manners, with a piety which nothing earthly could impair, he was esteemed and respected by all whose esteem and respect were worth the having.'

On August 20th, 1811, Lockhart inspected the 30th, and his description of their field firing exercises is of interest. He tells us that they practised ball firing before him and that the mark, a canvas five feet by two, with a six-inch bull's-eye, was hit at one hundred paces once in every twenty-five shots. The Battalion would go out early in the week with an ample supply of blank cartridges, perhaps thirty rounds per man, and practice such

---

[862] Wilkinson was promoted to Lieutenant-General on 4th June 1814 and remained in India until January 1815 as Commander-in-Chief of the Army of the Bombay Presidency. On return to England he was unable to obtain further military employment on account of the end of hostilities in Europe, and so retired into the country, where his family owned property in Durham and Northumberland. Although not actively employed, he received a further step of promotion, to General, and was made a Knight Grand Cross of the Maltese Order of St. Michael and St. George (KCMG). Sir William Wilkinson's health and strength was broken from 1837 by severe illnesses which led to his death at Durham City in 1840. His last advice, to a young relative just entering the 30th was, 'Be always respectful and obedient to your commanding officer, and never enter into cabals, either with or against any of your brother officers'. Wilkinson's end, as recounted in his obituary, was very sad: 'In the beginning of the year 1840, in addition to his other maladies, he was attacked by the dropsy: the few remaining weeks of his life were spent in much pain and restlessness . . . His strong mind, and extreme fortitude, bore up with his maladies for some time; but, after a few days of more than usual restlessness, on the night of the 17th of March, he awoke at eleven o'clock from a short sleep, rang his bell, and spoke in such a wild and incoherent manner that the servant, much frightened, left the room. Immediately afterwards the report of a pistol was heard, and upon again entering the room, he was found lying by his bed-side dead.'

deployments as forming line. Each company in succession, as soon as formed, would fire one or two volleys, followed perhaps by sub-division volleys from flanks to centre, or file firing from right or left. A few days later the Battalion would parade with fifteen rounds each of ball and would practice with live ammunition the movement and firing drills previously rehearsed.

In November 1811, the 30th marched to Cannanore, an ancient seaport on the Malabar Coast, and occupied St. Angelo Fort, built of local soapstone by the Portuguese in 1505 on a promontory north-west of the town, and temporary barracks in the adjacent large cantonment.[863] These were described in 1812 by Major James Welsh of the Bombay Army:

'The fort is small, irregular, and ill-constructed, although the site is well chosen; and to remedy original defects, a number of out-works have been since constructed… The old Governor's house in the fort is an excellent edifice, and has been converted into an arsenal; there are also some good store and guard rooms in it, but it is not now inhabited, and only the daily guards reside there. The cantonment, though situated in a very airy, healthy spot, is most irregularly laid out, and has an exceedingly uncouth appearance. The houses, being very slightly built, and covered with cocoa-nut mats, with roofs reaching down nearly to the ground, look more like a parcel of rude huts scattered over a plain, than the habitations of gentlemen; yet some of them are very comfortable within; and those situated on the sea face, are cool all the year round. No one who has not been stationed on this coast in the south-west monsoon, can conceive the necessity for spoiling the appearance of the houses, and depriving them of a considerable share of light; but the rains, when driven by the winds, are frequently almost horizontal, and the damp, even with this unseemly precaution, penetrates every thing. There are no regular lines for the officers of separate corps; but all are promiscuously huddled together in one part, and thinly scattered in others, covering a surface of nearly four miles in circumference.'

On New Year's Day 1812, Colonel Lockhart was appointed to command the Malabar and Kannara District[864], and Lieutenant-Colonel Philip Vaumorel again assumed command of the 1st/30th. The Regiment was indeed most fortunate in its commanders for, like Wilkinson and Lockhart with whom he had so often served, Vaumorel was a seasoned veteran. After service in the American War, he had earned early laurels with the 30th by his resolute defence of Fort Mulgrave at Toulon, 1793, and then served with the Regiment in Ireland, Sicily, Malta, Egypt and Hanover before sailing with the 1st Battalion to India.

On 25th March 1812 a short-lived rebellion of Kurichiya and Kurumba tribesmen broke out in the Wynad (Wayanad) district in response to an injudicious policy of collecting taxes in cash instead of kind. Police posts were overrun and Native Infantry garrisons at Manantoddy (Mananthawady) and Sultans Battery were surrounded and in danger of capture by the insurgents, who had few firearms but were skilled archers. Two columns were dispatched to their relief, from Cannanore and Seringapatam. The Cannanore column, commanded by Major Webber of the 3rd Madras Native Infantry, consisted of the 2nd Battalion of that Regiment, a detachment of the 5th Native Infantry, and fifty of the 30th under Lieutenant Washington Carden and Ensign John Perry.

Major Webber marched to relieve Manantoddy, where two companies of his own regiment were besieged. The passes giving access to the Wynad country were blocked, and whilst ascending the Cotiaddy (Kuttiyadi) Pass he was attacked by rebels on 9th April. The pass was forced and the Manantoddy garrison relieved at the cost of one private of the 30th killed and two wounded, and two officers and eighteen men of the 3rd Madras Native Infantry wounded. This was the only significant engagement of the rising, for a few more days of combing the jungle sufficed for the rebels to surrender or disperse. On the 23rd, Lieutenant Carden's detachment began its march back to Cannanore, and peace was restored by early May.

On 18th January 1813, the 1st/30th was inspected by Major-General Wetherall,[865] and it is worth dwelling on his report since it was the first truly independent review of the Battalion since their arrival in India, the reports for 1809 to 1812 having been made by Wilkinson and Lockhart, in effect commenting on their own time in

---

[863] Also stationed at Cannanore were the 2nd/3rd, 2nd/9th and 1st/15th Madras Native Infantry.

[864] William Lockhart, who was promoted to Major-General, saw no further service with the 30th. He died in Edinburgh on 3rd March 1817, his life probably shortened by an attack of cholera in India.

[865] Frederick Augustus Wetherall had commanded the 82nd Regiment in 1796. At the time of his inspection the 1st/30th numbered 55 sergeants, 47 corporals, 22 drummers and 972 privates, 54 men having died in the course of 1812.

command. As such, the 1813 report is an objective assessment of the sixteen years during which those two officers had alternated in command.

After praising the zeal and ability of the officers, and touching on the excellence of the mess and the band (he had obviously been most hospitably entertained), the General's report commends the steadfastness and fidelity of the non-commissioned officers in the discharge of their duty and the esprit de corps of the rank and file. He goes on to say:

'INTERIOR ECONOMY: Every branch under this head is in a most perfect state, and the result of an old and well regulated system which has been strictly attended to by successive officers on whom the command of the regiment has devolved. Such exact uniformity has been established that any individual, either officer, non-commissioned officer or soldier, armed and appointed, stamps the character and appearance of the whole corps.

'GENERAL OBSERVATIONS: I have great pleasure in reporting the high state of order and discipline which distinguishes this corps. The most perfect subordination exists in the several ranks and the system of responsibility throughout each is completely established. I have the satisfaction of stating that this corps is equal to the most active field service.'

The next inspection of the 1st/30th was carried out on 4th May 1814 by Lieutenant-Colonel Vaumorel, its commanding officer, who was in temporary command of Malabar District. If we discount any partiality that may have crept into his report, we must also allow that, as commanding officer, he was in the best position to evaluate the condition of his battalion.

Vaumorel could not have too obviously favoured the 1st/30th, for the second inspection that year, again by Major-General Wetherall, endorsed many of his judgements, commenting on 'the high state of discipline, order, and interior economy which distinguishes this Corps':

'The present Commanding Officer, Lieutenant-Colonel Vaumorel, with Lieutenant-Colonel Maxwell and Major Bircham, are officers of talent and experience. I am also gratified in stating the attention shewn by the captains and subalterns in the discharge of their duty is highly creditable to them, and is attended with the most beneficial effects to the service. The non-commissioned officers are intelligent and conduct themselves with strictest propriety. The privates… are an efficient body of men, perfectly drilled and full equal to field service.'

Wetherall did, however, make some critical comment. He was one of the growing number of officers who advocated imprisonment as an alternative punishment to flogging, and in his January 1813 report he had made an appropriate recommendation: 'As solitary confinement would lessen corporal punishment I beg leave to suggest that a certain number of cells for this purpose be erected which in Cannanore might be done with little expense.'

Although inclined to be a martinet, Vaumorel seems to have acted on this recommendation, for in May 1814 he reported that 'The necessity of frequent punishment has been much superseded by the adoption of solitary confinement.' He was, it appears, rather overstating or anticipating change, for later that same year Wetherall commented that 'eighty-two men have been tried by Regimental and General Courts Martial, on a large proportion of whom I am concerned to observe corporal punishment has been inflicted, but which I hope and trust will hereafter be superseded by a more lenient and less disgraceful measure, that of solitary confinement.' He also observed that the men were somewhat addicted to drink.

Despite this, Wetherall concluded his 1814 inspection report favourably: 'In summing up the character of this battalion, I have no hesitation in saying that I consider the general state of it calculated for the most active and enterprising service.'

The ready availability and excessive consumption of cheap local spirits, or arrack, was indeed a challenge to the health and discipline in all British regiments in the East Indies at that time and later, and the otherwise well-ordered 30th was no exception. Colonel Vaumorel later forbade the sale of arrack in the regimental canteen, allowing only British-brewed beer to be sold, but he could not prevent the sale of native spirits outside.[866] The number of regimental courts martial rose alarmingly, and nearly half were drink-related, but there was a remarkable absence of serious crime and the soldiers appear to have kept their drunken escapades within bounds. 'Whatever the men may do amiss they keep it to themselves,' writes an inspecting officer, 'for to see a man of the 30th drunk or improperly dressed is a very rare occurrence.'

---

866 In South India the arrack was generally made from fermented palm sap.

As was the case with British troops in the East until the 20th century, an enervating climate and prevalent diseases exacted an annual toll of all ranks. In 1813 alone four officers of the 1st/30th died (Majors John Curry and Thomas Leach, Captain Benjamin Nunn and Lieutenant John Napper). Many of all ranks were invalided, and the voyage home could be perilous.

In October 1814 Captain (Brevet Major) Thomas Jackson and his family, Lieutenant John Wade, also of the 30th and Aide-de-Camp to General Wilkinson, Captain Archibald Campbell, 47th, and Lieutenant Joshua Deverell, also 47th, with his family, embarked at Bombay for London on the *Alexander* Indiaman. The vessel was almost home when, at 2 a.m. on the morning of Easter Monday, 27th March 1815, she was driven by a violent south-easterly gale onto Chesil Beach, near Wyke Regis. Major Jackson, Captain Campbell, and Lieutenants Deverell and Wade were all drowned, together with Jackson's wife and three children and Deverell's wife and three children. The circumstances of the wreck were never known, for there were no witnesses ashore and the only survivors, Lascar seamen, could speak no English. Next morning the wreckage of the ship and the bodies of most of her crew and passengers were found scattered along Chesil Beach from Wyke Regis to Abbotsbury. Jackson and Wade were buried, with two each of Jackson's and Deverell's children, in a mass grave of 140 of the victims in the churchyard of Wyke Regis, where a memorial tablet was erected.[867]

In February 1815 the 1st/30th left Cannanore for Madras, under command Colonel Vaumorel, but first marched north-east for three hundred miles to take part in a troop concentration at Gooty, caused by a disputed succession to the throne of the Nawab of Kurnool. The 30th reached Gooty at the end of March and joined the army under Lieutenant-General Sir Thomas Hislop. The General was a good friend of the Regiment, having known them since Toulon in 1793, and he appointed Philip Vaumorel to command the 1st Brigade of this force. When the camp broke up in June, Vaumorel was ordered to Vellore with the 30th and the 2nd/14th Madras Native Infantry. After a halt of about six weeks at Vellore, the Battalion marched into Fort St. George, Madras on 12th August 1815.

Expedition to Java 1811

The 1st/59th returned to Madras from Mauritius on 8th February 1811, and immediately on landing marched to an encampment at St. Thomas's Mount. Lieutenant-Colonel Gibbs was appointed to command the troops in camp, the 14th, 59th and 69th Regiments. As conquerors of Mauritius, the officers were fêted by Madras society with balls and masquerades, but their time for relaxation was short, for on arrival they received orders to prepare for further active service.

The Battalion embarked at Madras between the 13th and 15th April with a strength of 41 officers, 45 sergeants, 19 drummers and 922 rank and file, of whom half sailed from Madras roads on the 18th with the 1st Madras Division of the army, and the remainder on the 29th with the 2nd Division. The *Regimental Record of Service* states that the 59th were aboard the line-of-battle ship *Illustrious*, 74, the frigates *Akbar*, *Modeste* and *Phaeton*, and four transports, and transferred at Malacca to the *Preston* East Indiaman. *Illustrious* was the flagship of Commodore Broughton, who commanded the fleet, while *Akbar* also carried the Army commander, the veteran Lieutenant-General Sir Samuel Auchmuty, victor of Monte Video. Their prompt departure was fortunate, for as recorded in the diary of Lieutenant James Chadwick, 'the night after we sailed from Madras every ship in the roads was driven ashore, and very few lives saved.' Both Madras divisions reached Penang, the first point of rendezvous, between the 18th and 21st May, and sailed from there for Malacca, their second rendezvous, on the 24th. The ships dropped anchor on 1st June off Malacca, where they joined troops from Bengal, bringing the combined total to 12,280 men, of whom 5,344 were Europeans. A few days after the arrival of the 59th, the Governor-General, Lord Minto, was present when the King's Birthday was celebrated in style:

'The fourth of June, being the anniversary of His Majesty's birthday, was celebrated as splendidly as circumstances in this remote part of the world would permit. Royal salutes from the men of war of the expedition,

---

[867] The body of Mrs Jackson, 'a very beautiful lady', was washed up near Lyme, and Anna Maria Pinney, friend of the famous fossil-hunter Mary Anning, recorded in her journal that her friend, who was only sixteen at the time, 'untangled the seaweed which had attached itself to her long hair and performed all the other offices due from the living to the dead, and the unknown corpse being deposited in the Church until some friend appeared to claim it, she daily went to strew fresh flowers over it.'

and from the batteries on shore, announced the happy day, and at noon the discharge of cannon proclaimed the number of years our venerable and beloved sovereign had attained. Lord Minto held a levee in the morning, and at four o'clock he gave a dinner to a great part of the naval and military officers, when many loyal toasts were drank with enthusiasm, and afterwards the noble lord himself was drank to, as a volunteer on the present service, with three times three. In the evening a ball closed the fete.'[868]

At Malacca the expedition was divided into four brigades, the whole under the command of Sir Samuel Auchmuty. The 1st, or Advance Brigade was made up of a British Light Battalion, included the elite Light and Rifle Companies of the 59th, a Light Battalion of Bengal Native Infantry and detachments of the 89th, Marines and Pioneers, with the Governor-General's Bodyguard, a detachment of 22nd Light Dragoons and two troops of horse artillery, and was led by Colonel Rollo Gillespie. The Right Brigade of Major-General Frederick Wetherall's (Line) Division was commanded by Colonel Samuel Gibbs of the 59th and consisted of the Grenadier and Line Companies of his own Regiment[869], together with the 14th Regiment and a battalion of Indian volunteers from the Bengal Army. Adams' Left Brigade of that division consisting of the 69th, 78th and 6th Bengal Native Infantry. The Reserve Brigade comprised four battalions of Bengal Native Infantry together with British and Bengal field artillery.

Their destination was the island of Java which, like all the Dutch colonies, had been incorporated in the Napoleonic Empire and flew the French tricolour. In 1795 the Dutch Stadtholder, William V, had fled to Britain to escape French republican advances. There he issued the 'Kew Letters,' giving Britain temporary authority over Dutch possessions overseas in an attempt to keep them out of French hands. It was not, however, until 1810 that Lord Minto received instructions from London to 'proceed to the conquest of Java at the earliest possible opportunity,' and in October that year the Governor-General had sent Thomas Stamford Raffles to Malacca as his Agent to the Malay States, with the confidential mission of preparing for an invasion of Java.

The island of Java, measuring some 630 miles long by 150 miles at its widest point, is part of the Sunda island archipelago, which includes Sumatra to the north-west and Bali to the east. In 1811 its population numbered some five million, predominantly Javanese and Malayans, with Dutch and Chinese settlers. The north coast of the island was most populous; there the country is flat, and the forest had largely been cleared, giving place to open marshland, intersected by numerous streams and canals, and to fields of rice and other crops. Near to the north-west corner of the island lay Batavia (now called Jakarta), capital of the island and of all the dependencies of the Dutch East Indies.

The Dutch-Napoleonic army in Java amounted to a mixed force of some 18,000 Javanese, Dutch and French of varied quality and reliability. At their head was the recently-arrived Governor-General, Jan Willem Janssens, a committed Dutch republican who had already suffered one notable defeat at the hands of the British, including the 59th, at Blaauwberg in South Africa in 1806. Napoleon Buonaparte was said to have dispatched him to Java with an ominous warning: 'Know, sir, that a French General is not offered a second chance.' His able predecessor, Daendels, had reorganised the defences of the island, and had in particular built a strongly entrenched and supposedly impregnable fortified stronghold at Meester Cornelis, inland from Batavia.

The British fleet of 81 warships and transports sailed from Malacca in three divisions from 11th June, leaving ashore some twelve hundred men too sick to proceed. In a few days the convoys passed the Straits of Singapore and stood direct for Borneo, passing the island of Tambelan. Then, having watered at the High Islands, where they rode out some very rough weather, the ships coasted down to reach Cape Sambar, the south-west point of Borneo, on 20th July. From there they headed south across the Java Sea and made the coast of that island on the 30th.

---

[868] Captain (later Lieutenant-Colonel Sir William) Thorn, *Memoir of the Conquest of Java, with the Subsequent Operations of the British Forces in the Oriental Archipelago*, p. 7.
[869] With Gibbs commanding a brigade, the 1st/ 59th was commanded by Brevet Lieutenant-Colonel Alexander McLeod, who was promoted to Lieutenant-Colonel without purchase on 18th June 1811. He had served with the Regiment since his commission as an ensign in 1793.

Capture of Batavia, August 1811

E arly on the afternoon of 4th August 1811, the invasion fleet anchored off the fishing village of Cilincing on the north coast of Java and some eight miles east of Batavia. The landing site was well chosen, for it was protected from landward attack by a canal, and good roads ran from it to Batavia and to the main Dutch stronghold at Cornelis, giving Auchmuty a choice of point of attack.

Gillespie's Division was rowed ashore in half an hour without opposition, and the Colonel at once seized a bridge over the canal, occupied Cilincing, secured another bridge beyond it over the Cilincing River, and pushed his advanced parties, including the Light Company 59th, up the Cornelis road. Wetherall's division, with the main body of the 59th, then landed and occupied a line further west, astride the Batavia road, with its right on the muddy seashore and its left on the canal.

'The corps of the army had ground allotted to them as they landed, on which they were to form, and as soon as the principal part of each battalion was on shore it was marched off to gain the position where it was intended the whole should halt during the night. Though the country is low, and intersected with swamps, salt-pits, and canals, yet before night the whole of the infantry, with their guns, were on shore; the advanced posts were pushed on, two miles from the landing-place, and the troops were formed in two lines, one fronting Batavia and the other on the road to Cornelis... The reserve remained at the landing-place, to support each point.'[870]

That night the army had its first contact with the enemy, when a Dutch cavalry patrol galloped into the advanced posts on the Batavia road, where they received the fire of two six-pounders and that of a picket of infantry and retired with loss.

Next day the horse artillery and cavalry were landed, and the position of the army was advanced towards Batavia. Information was received that an enemy column was within four miles of Cilincing, and accordingly the Advance was pushed forward about six miles on the road to Cornelis for the purpose of attacking it; but on hearing of this movement the enemy retired. The heat during this march was so excessive that several men, so newly landed after nearly four months at sea, and with nothing to eat or drink all day, died from sunstroke.

The Dutch settlement of Batavia formed a linear development, running inland from the mouth of the Ciliwung River. Nearest the sea was the walled city of Old Batavia, built in the early 17th century; three miles inland, the military cantonment of Weltevreden had been built on more healthy ground; and a further three miles towards the mountains stood the entrenched stronghold of Meester Cornelis.

On August 6th Gillespie and his staff reconnoitered the Batavia road as far as Anjole point, just two miles from the town, and discovered that the bridge over the River Anjole had been burned. Auchmuty ordered the Advance to counter-march from the Cornelis road to Cilincing that evening, and out on the Batavia road as far as Tanjong Priok, some distance in front of Wetherall's division and six miles from the town. The Reserve took up the ground which had been quitted by the Advance beyond Cilincing.

'It was [Auchmuty's] determination,' wrote Captain William Thorn, 'to feel the enemy on the side of Batavia, and when he had engaged their attention in that quarter, then to fall back rapidly, and advance on the road to Cornelis,' but finding his demonstration towards Batavia unopposed he converted his feint into the main advance. Thorn, who was Gillespie's Brigade Major, then took part in the occupation of Batavia:

'The inactivity of the enemy, the little appearance of force on the Batavia side of the river, and a very serious conflagration in that city, fixed the resolution of the Commander in Chief to attempt a passage the next night. Accordingly, on the seventh of August, the infantry attached to the Advance' [including Light and Rifle Companies of the 59th] 'pushed forward and crossed the Anjole River at ten o'clock at night, over a bridge of boats which had been rowed in after dark for that purpose... The troops could only pass over in single file, having to step from one boat to another, which delayed the passage considerably. A part of the horse artillery and the Bengal Light Infantry battalion, were drawn up behind the banks of the river, which concealed them, and served as a parapet to protect the passage, and to act as a reserve, according to circumstances. It was, indeed, natural to have expected that the passage of the Anjole river would have been warmly contested by the enemy, as they could not fail to be apprised of our intention by observing the boats that had been rowed up the river.'

---

[870] Thorn, p.p. 21-22.

'By midnight the whole party had crossed over, and at the dawn of day the Advance was posted near the suburbs, about one mile from the town… amongst the numerous canals and rivulets, the bridges over which had all been broken down and carried away or burnt by the enemy in the view of impeding our approach by every difficulty they could throw in the way, without hazarding the consequences of actual engagements. While the advanced troops were thus gaining ground, [Wetherall's division, with the main body of the 59th] was moved forward to the river, ready to support them; the Reserve, reinforced by a battalion of marines and a troop of cavalry remaining at Chillingching [Cilincing].'[871]

Next morning, Batavia was summoned, and, since the Dutch military had apparently abandoned the town, the Mayor surrendered the place at discretion. No certain information could be obtained as to the enemy, though it was evident that their main force was nearby and they might even occupy part of the suburbs or wait concealed in the town, large quarters of which appeared empty:

'The houses all along our present position were deserted,' recalled Thorn, 'as all the respectable inhabitants had been compelled to retire into the interior by positive orders from General Janssens, to prevent the possibility of their giving to the British any assistance or intelligence. By a general proclamation no more than one jar of water was permitted to be kept in any house or family for their own consumption; and lastly, as we advanced, the conduits by which the water used for drinking was conveyed from the inland parts of the city, were destroyed, in order to distress the army by cutting off that indispensable article.

'Thus situated, surrounded by every thing inimical, it became necessary to proceed with great caution. A small party only was directed to enter the town, to feel their way and make a report. This consisted of the rifle and light company of the Fifty-Ninth Regiment under Captain [Thomas] Watts, accompanied by Captain Thorn, Brigade Major of the advance. Several of the enemy's scouts shewed themselves as the party marched through the suburbs; but they instantly galloped off in the direction of Weltevreden. The detachment repaired immediately to the town-house, which they occupied, and by their presence put a stop to the plundering which had been carried on by the Malays since our landing, and thus several large stores of colonial goods were timely saved from plunder or the flames.'[872]

There was indeed considerable disquiet among the British and Company troops when it appeared that much of their anticipated prize-money was going up in flames, which was expressed in a letter from an officer of the Company's Service:

'The enemy… retreated to the city, which to our great mortification we beheld shortly afterwards in flames; this we knew well contained the companies' spice stores, of immense value, and appeared a perfect death-blow to our expectations of prize-money. It was not however so bad. A deputation of Dutch burghers came from the city… to give it to us, saying that General Janssens had first fired the public godowns [warehouses] and retreated, leaving no protection whatever to the numerous inhabitants, and that the slaves would plunder and murder them… We pushed on and took possession of the city, and succeeded in extinguishing the flames and saving much of the prize property, though I regret to say a million pounds of coffee was burned, besides a quantity of pepper, whereby the army lost 100,000 rupees of prize-money.'

The 59th detachment hoisted the British colours at the Crane Wharf, whereupon a royal salute was fired from the shipping in the Roads. That evening Colonel Gillespie, with the greater part of the Advance, entered the town. The troops paraded in the main square, in front of the town-house, to take formal possession of the place, and were then dismissed to their quarters.

There were only eight hundred British troops in the town that night, and no guns, and rumours circulated in the course of the evening of an intended enemy attack from Weltervreeden, not more than three miles distant. Accordingly, vigilance was increased, and every precaution was taken to prevent a surprise. Then, at about 10 p.m. Captain Robison, Aid-de-Camp to Lord Minto, who had carried a summons to General Janssens to surrender the island, returned with his answer, which was as might be expected that as a French General he would defend his charge to the last extremity. Captain Robison had been conducted blindfolded through the Dutch lines, but as he went along he heard a great bustle of men and horses, and artillery on the move, which confirmed suspicions of an imminent attack.

---

[871] Thorn, p.p. 24-25.
[872] Ibid., p.p. 25-26.

'About eleven o'clock at night, the troops were silently called out, and ordered to lie on their arms in the grand square in front of the town-house. Scarcely had they reached the square when the head of the enemy's column appeared, and opened a fire of musquetry upon our picquet that was stationed at the bridge leading from Weltervreeden to the town, under the orders of Captain Trench of the eighty-ninth regiment, who had just time to raise the drawbridge. The firing was now heard in all directions round the town, when Colonel Gillespie sallied out at the head of a party, at a gateway on the west side of the city, with the intention of suddenly falling upon the enemy's advance by surprize and charging them in flank. This movement had the desired effect. The firing soon afterwards ceased, and the enemy were no more heard or seen during the remainder of the night. Several of the assailants were killed by our videttes posted on the outside of the drawbridge, who fired into their column to give the alarm; but not one casualty happened on our side. The darkness of the night, and the positive orders given to our troops not to fire unnecessarily, but to trust to their bayonets, prevented the enemy from discovering our several posts; and consequently this want of direction for his fire, rendered it ineffectual.' [873]

The enemy had imagined that the two companies of the 59th which had marched into Batavia in the morning would fall an easy prey, and were not aware of the reinforcement which had joined them in the evening. When informed of the reinforcement, and knowing that the rest of the British army was still on the far side of the Anjole, they increased the strength of their attack, so that the rear of their column was still at Weltervreden when its head reached the suburbs. They had also relied on the effects of the great quantity of alcohol they had stashed in every house, which the Chinese and other inhabitants pressed on the soldiers in lieu of the water they wanted. This ruse was thwarted by the strict discipline imposed by Colonel Gillespie.

The troops continued under arms the whole night, and the next day, 9th August, the little garrison was reinforced by a troop of dragoons and some horse artillery. A more substantial bridge of boats was thrown across the Anjole that day, and early on the morning of the 10th Wetherall's division crossed the river to occupy the town, while Gillespie moved south on the road to Weltevreden.

Before they left Batavia, the Advance had to deal with two incidents of what we would now call terrorism.

'In the following night the town had nearly been destroyed with every soul in it, by a Malay, who most fortunately was discovered in time, with a fire-brand in his hand, in the act of firing wooden magazines, which contained a great quantity of gun-powder. It was at two o'clock in the morning of the tenth of August, when relieving the guards, preparatory to an attack on the enemy's positions near Welterveeden, that this circumstance happened, and its providential discovery saved the town and thousands of people. The incendiary was hanged the next day.' [874]

Then, in the early hours of the morning, just as Gillespie and his officers prepared to mount their horses they were served poisoned coffee by a Frenchman, who kept the quarters allotted to Colonel Gillespie and had previously been a servant to General Daendels. All who tasted the coffee at once suffered violent pains and vomiting, but fortunately nothing worse, and before departing they poured a cup of the brew down the miscreant's own throat to an even more powerful effect.

The Affair of Weltevreden

Despite these intended disruptions, at four o'clock in the morning the Advance marched out of Batavia on the road to Weltevreden, moving in profound silence past the deserted houses of Dutch burghers. At daybreak, Gillespie's column, followed closely by Gibbs' Brigade, arrived at the cantonment and found it abandoned except for an outlying picket, the enemy having withdrawn to a strong position just beyond Weltevreden, astride the road to Cornelis. The manuscript *Record of Service of the 59th Foot* [875] has the following short account of the action which followed:

'The Advance under Colonel Gillespie came in contact with the enemy about six o'clock. The attack was rapid on its part and was resisted by the enemy who was strongly supported by his artillery. The Light Battalion

---

[873] Thorn, p.p. 27-8
[874] Thorn, p. 28.
[875] The *Record of Service* for this period appears to have been compiled some fourteen year later, at Cawnpore in 1825, when Lieutenant-Colonel George McGregor made enquiries to obtain 'some authentic account' of the Regiment's earlier services.

of the Advance, in which were the Light and Rifle Companies of the 59th Regt., commanded by Captain Watts and Lieut. Evan McPherson, charged the artillery and took the guns. The Brigade under Colonel Gibbs coming up at the same time on the enemy's left flank, he retreated with the utmost rapidity and was pursued by the 22nd Dragoons to within a few yards of Cornelis.

'By this action the valuable Cantonment of Weltervreeden fell into our hands, which not only afforded cover for the troops, that had been exposed day and night to the weather, but also an immense quantity of guns and military stores of all descriptions. There were upwards of three hundred pieces of ordnance in the Arsenal.'

More detail is given in the accounts of Captain William Thorn, Gillespie's principal staff officer: 'We advanced to the attack in two columns. The enemy's right was protected by the Slokan;[876] their left by the Great [Batavia] River, over which there was a bridge, at that time in flames. Pepper plantations covered and concealed their line, and an abbatis had been felled to block up the road leading to Cornelis, which was a continuation of the one on which Colonel Gillespie's left was advancing, and behind this the enemy had placed four horse artillery guns, which opened their fire as soon as our troops composing the left column arrived within range of their grape. The infantry of the enemy occupied two villages which ran through the wood on both sides of this road, and from which they kept up a very brisk fire of musquetry.

'The enemy's guns were answered with great effect from one twelve and two six pounders, horse artillery attached to the British Advance, whilst our sharp-shooters made sure of their aim along the whole front. Dispositions had already been made for turning the enemy's flanks; which object was carried, after surmounting very great obstacles from the nature of the country. The villages occupied by the enemy were set in flames, and the British troops, rushing forward, charged their guns at the point of the bayonet. About this time our Commander in Chief, having preceded his army, arrived at the scene of action, where he had the satisfaction of beholding a handful of heroes defeat five times their own number.

'The action lasted full two hours, owing to the abbatis and other impediments which had been thrown in our way, and which the troops were obliged to remove before they could close with the enemy, who during all this time maintained a very severe fire. They were however completely defeated, with the loss of their guns, a number of killed, wounded and prisoners, both Europeans and Natives, amongst whom were several officers of distinction.'

'The army had now come up and supported the troops in the pursuit, and Colonel Gillespie at the head of a squadron of the twenty-second dragoons pressed hard upon the fugitives, who were followed close under the works of Cornelis, when a shower of grape and round shot opened upon them from their batteries, but without any injury as their guns were too highly elevated, and before they could be depressed our cavalry were sufficiently withdrawn to be covered from their sight. The infantry now occupied the advanced posts within eight hundred yards of the French redoubts, covered by the jungle from the view of the enemy.'[877]

It had been a tough fight, with every advantage to the defenders, who made good use of the close country. There is an eye-witness regimental account of this action from Lieutenant James Chadwick of the Light Company 59th:

'An hour or two before daylight we drove their advanced picquets before us. On reaching the main body of the army, they made a stand. We charged & they took to the jungle, from which they were able to annoy us for some short time in consequence of their local knowledge; but we came up with them & obliged the whole to seek shelter at a very advantageous post, where they had four field pieces planted behind immense trees, which they had placed across the road leading from Weltevreden to Cornelis. There they made us check the pace for a short time. We soon showed them it was in vain; they could not attempt to stop our progress. Their guns were charged and taken. The troops that were with them, not daring to oppose on open ground, took to the jungle, & we had an hour's tight work of it to drive them into their stronghold at Cornelis. The fellows frequently hid in the trees and hedges, and when we fancied we were driving all before us they gave a volley in our rear, which generally did great havoc, as they took a steady aim. It was generally supposed that, had the Line been up in time, we would have chased the French & Dutch troops into Cornelis this day.'

---

[876] The Slokan was a canalised rivulet which ran immediately to the east of the Weltevreden-Cornelis road.

[877] Thorn, p.p. 31-32.

413

British casualties in this action totaled 16 killed and 81 wounded, the latter including three rank and file of the 59th; enemy losses were around five hundred of their best troops, including General Alberti, Janssen's Chief of Staff, who had arrived recently from France after three campaigns in Spain, and was very severely wounded. Four guns were taken. Gillespie was rightly effusive in praising his men: [878]

'Colonel Gillespie, in appreciating the gallantry of the troops he had the honor to command in the action yesterday, cannot find words adequately to express his thanks and admiration which their behaviour excited. He will take the earliest opportunity of particularising to His Excellency the Commander-in-Chief the meritorious conduct of the officers and men during the whole of that brisk affair and trusts that the victory gained will be considered worthy of the glory of adding a sprig to the laurels already won by the distinguished troops composing the Advance.'

In his official report to the Adjutant-General that same day, Gillespie added. 'I must also express my acknowledgments to Major Miller commanding the right column, to Captain Stanus of the 14th Light Infantry Company, Captain Watts of the 59th Regiment, Lieutenant Coghlan commanding the Rifle Company of the 14th Regiment, and Lieutenant [Evan] M'Pherson commanding the Rifle Company of the 59th Regiment, and the officers and men of their different corps, as that column contributed much to the success of the day, by turning the enemy's left flank.'

This 'brisk affair' against an enemy which outnumbered them by at least two to one was an important early victory, for apart from its moral effect on both sides it gave the British force a well-sited modern cantonment and well-stocked arsenal, close to Cornelis but with good rearward communications by road and water to the fleet, from which to mount their operation to reduce the Dutch stronghold. Conversely, it also completely upset Janssen's cunning strategy, inherited from Daendels, which was to let the invaders occupy the pestilential town of Batavia, where their army would waste away from sickness while the Dutch sat in health and comfort at Weltevreden.

Storming of The Lines of Cornelis

The entrenched camp at Meester Cornelis[879] was a formidable fortification covering an area of one and a half miles north to south and half a mile east to west, bounded to the west by the wide, meandering Great Batavia (or Ciliwung) River and to the east by the Slokan Canal, both unfordable, the two being connected at each end of the works by deep ditches backed by strong palisades and regular entrenchments. Within these lines, six redoubts and many batteries, mounted with heavy cannon, occupied the most commanding ground; a further redoubt (No. 3) lay to the east of the Slokan and was connected to the main position by a narrow bamboo bridge over that stream. The fort of Cornelis was in the centre of the lines, and the fortifications were defended by at least ten thousand men and 280 artillery pieces.

Auchmuty decided on a regular siege, and began to land and bring forward his heavy guns. Ground was broken on the 14th, when a ditch facing the north end of the lines was converted into a parallel, but it was not until the 20th that construction of three batteries commenced on a rise 600 yards north of the enemy works. The Dutch did not notice the working parties until the 21st, but then took resolute action.

The batteries had been completed, and, assisted by five hundred seamen, the guns were being brought up and mounted when, just before dawn on the 22nd the defenders made a sortie. The gunners and seamen, engrossed in their work, were surprised, suffering some hundred casualties, and a twelve-gun battery was for a short time in enemy hands. Fortunately, the Grenadiers of the 59th, led by Captain William Olpherts, recaptured the battery before the guns could be spiked, and the hostile columns retired with considerable loss. 'The enemy would only acknowledge to 180 killed this day,' wrote James Chadwick, 'although I saw two wells filled with big Dutchmen myself.' [880]

---

[878] Brigade Orders by Colonel Gillespie, dated Weltevreden 11th August 1811.
[879] Now called Jatinagara, this area is now a suburb of Jakarta.
[880] This action was recalled nearly two hundred years later when 137 (Java) Battery, Royal Artillery, which had rather more recently been in direct support of 1st Battalion The Queen's Lancashire Regiment in Germany, presented the Regimental Museum with a print depicting the recapture of their guns.

The artillery duel grew in intensity until the 25th, by which time the enemy redoubts were much damaged and many of their guns were dismounted. There was, however, no practicable breach in the defences, and it became evident to Auchmuty that a frontal assault would not succeed. There could be no question of a prolonged siege, for the sickly season and fatigue under the tropical sun were already taking their toll of his army, and so Sir Samuel decided on a less direct but more immediate approach.

His bold plan was for the main assault force, led inevitably by Rollo Gillespie, to make a circuitous flanking march to the east by night, guided by a deserter. They were to take Redoubt No. 3 by surprise and break into the main fortifications over the adjacent Slokan bridge, while simultaneous diversionary attacks were to be made north and south of the Cornelis lines. The main attack was to be made by the Advance, including the Light and Rifle Companies 59th, commanded respectively by Captain William Bowen and Lieutenant Evan McPherson, closely supported by Samuel Gibbs' brigade, which included the Grenadier and Line Companies of the 59th under Captain William Olpherts and Lieutenant-Colonel Alexander McLeod. Captain Thorn was with Gillespie at the head of the attacking column:

'These troops moved off soon after midnight on the morning of the 26th of August, and took the route by which the deserter, who now acted as our guide, had escaped. We had to make a detour of many miles, through a very difficult country, intersected with ravines, enclosures, and betel plantations, resembling hop-grounds, many parts of which could only be passed in single file, and though the head of the column moved at a snail's pace, the great darkness of the night caused the troops in the rear to separate from them and miss their way.

'On arriving at a place where several roads met, our guide was perplexed which to pursue; but Captain Dickson, of the Madras Cavalry, aide-de-camp to Sir Samuel Auchmuty, having been reconnoitering in this direction some days before, very fortunately recollected the right one, which was pursued accordingly, and our guide soon confirmed the choice, by recognizing objects which he had marked in his escape, and being now convinced that it was the right road, he went forward with full confidence at the head of the column, accompanied by Serjeant Smith of the 22nd Dragoons, and both behaved with great intrepidity and cool steady courage.

'The head of the column had arrived very near the enemy's works when a report was brought to Colonel Gillespie of the rear not being up. He halted. It was an awful moment! One of those pauses of distressful anxiety, which can be better conceived than described; and can be felt only in all its force by a soul engaged in a great undertaking, on the success or failure of which depend the lives of thousands, and the honor and credit of a whole army. Too near to the enemy's works to escape being descried by their scouts and patrolling parties, it became necessary to make a retrograde movement, and after taking a few paces to the rear, we again faced towards the enemy, waiting in anxious expectation for the return of the messengers who had been sent to the rear to close up the column. The day was now fast approaching; to delay longer, therefore, for the rear would have exposed us to a discovery; while a retreat would have been pregnant with incalculable mischief, for as all the secondary attacks were to be guided by ours, these must of necessity have miscarried if the main column had retired.

'These considerations determined Colonel Gillespie to venture on the attack with what troops were already up; trusting for timely support to Colonel Gibbs, whose gallantry and military ardour he knew would bring him to the scene of action the instant the report of the firing should serve to point out the direction of the route. With full confidence then, our leader placed himself at the head of his little band, and we moved on in silent expectation.

'A deep cut across the road close to the enemy's lines, obliged us to advance slowly, to afford time for the men to form up after they had passed over. The morning dawn now shewed us the videttes of the enemy, who were posted outside, on the left of the road. They challenged us twice, and were answered "Patrole". We passed on. An officer's picquet, stationed close to one of their principal redoubts (Number Three), situated without the river Slokan, challenged us next, when Colonel Gillespie gave the Word "Forward", and so rapidly was the advance conducted that the enemy's picquet had not time to effect their retreat, but every man was either killed or taken. A general blaze now suddenly arose; blue lights and rockets being sent forth by the enemy to discover our approach, whilst the artillery on the redoubts, (Numbers Three and Four) discharged their grape and round shot, which, however, passed chiefly over our heads. The foe in the nearest redoubt (Number Three) had not time to reload, for our soldiers instantly assailed it at the point of the bayonet, and carried it with such celerity that not a man escaped.

'Colonel Gillespie continued to press forward in order to secure the passage over the Slokan, leading into the enemy's lines; and which was defended by four guns, horse artillery, directly facing the bridge, and flanked, by all their batteries. This therefore was a severe struggle, but the passage being secured, the Colonel next turned to the left, and attacked a second redoubt (Number Four) within the body of their works. Here a sharp conflict ensued. The handful of soldiers by which this post was attacked were opposed by such great numbers of the enemy as to call forth the most extraordinary efforts of gallantry on the part of the assailants. It was however carried at the point of the bayonet in the same determined manner, notwithstanding the tremendous fire kept up by the enemy both of grape and musquetry. Several officers here lost their valuable lives in the very bosom of victory, and many gallant soldiers were killed and wounded. These two captured redoubts mounted each twenty 18-pounders and several 24 and 32-pounders, while the ditches were filled with musqueteers.

'Another large redoubt (Number Two) on the right of our entrance was now to be assailed, and Colonel Gibbs just arriving at this time at the head of the Grenadiers of the Fourteenth, Fifty-Ninth, and Sixty-Ninth Regiments, Colonel Gillespie directed him to carry it, which was done in the same gallant and successful manner as the preceding had been, and under a severe fire of grape and musquetry.

'A dreadful explosion took place in this redoubt by the blowing up of the powder magazine, which occasioned the loss of many lives' [including Captain Olpherts[881] and Ensign Wolfe of the Grenadier Company 59th]. 'A great number of shells and rockets were fired by this means, and a sulphureous blast of mingled ashes, smoke, and fragments of every kind, broke upon us like a volcano, stunning all around, both friends and foes This catastrophe was followed for a minute by an awful silence. The Captains of each of the grenadier companies of the above regiments, and many others, all found a death, but few a grave! Numbers of the enemy also were destroyed, and the ground was strewed with the mangled bodies and scattered limbs of friends and foes, blended together in a horrible state of fraternity. Colonel Gibbs, and several other officers were thrown by the shock to a considerable distance, but fortunately without sustaining any material injury.'

'The enemy now renewed their fire upon our troops with increased fury from their park guns and batteries in the rear, and upon the little bridge across the Slokan, over which they had to pass. While Colonel Gibbs proceeded on to the right, Colonel Gillespie continued his operations on the left, and towards the enemy's rear. All the batteries in succession were stormed and taken; and being now joined by part of the Fifty-Ninth Regiment under Lieutenant Colonel Alexander M'Leod, Colonel Gillespie directed the attack of the enemy's artillery and reserve.

'The enemy's cavalry, formed upon the left of the line, threatened to charge, but were repulsed by the well directed fire of a party of the Fifty-Ninth, which were sent against them. The same gallant corps then moved on in column along the face of the redoubt, Number Four, and gained the saliant angle of the enemy's line of reserve, drawn up in the rear of their park guns and horse artillery, with a double front nearly at right angles, their rear and flanks being covered by the barracks and the small fort of Cornelis. The attack was carried into effect with the greatest promptitude, and though the assailants were saluted with a shower of grape, the enemy was driven from all his guns.

'An attempt was then made to effect a stand in front of Fort Cornelis, sheltered by the barracks from whence a sharp fire of musquetry was maintained; but being soon driven from this last ground, and the small fort itself at Cornelis having been carried by our troops, the enemy broke and dispersed in all directions.'[882]

Gillespie's official report, dated 27th August, echoes Thorn's narrative but adds some further detail of the part played by the 59th in the final phase of the engagement:

'Whilst Colonel Gibbs continued pushing forward to the right and driving the enemy from their works in that quarter, I attacked and carried the remaining redoubts on my left and towards the enemy's rear, and being now joined by part of the 59th Regt. under Lieut. Col. A. M'Leod, proceeded to the attack of the enemy's park of artillery, which was effected by Lieut. Col. M'Leod in the most masterly manner. A body of the enemy's cavalry, who had been drawn up the moment before, were put to flight by a few sections of the 59th Regiment. A long and sharp fire of musquetry was now kept up by a strong body of the enemy, who had taken post in the lines in front

---

[881] William Olpherts could not have known that he was in fact a major at the time of his death, having been promoted on 18th June 1811.
[882] Thorn, p.p. 56-60.

of the fort of Cornelis, but being at last driven from this also, the fort was taken possession of, and the enemy dispersed in all directions.'

The *Regimental Record of Service of the 59th Regiment* is largely consistent with Gillespie's and Thorn's accounts, but corrects their assertions with regard to responsibility for some orders and actions:

'Colonel Gillespie, in his report of the action to the Commander of the Forces, says… he proceeded to the attack of the enemy's park with the 59th Regiment. That is a mistake. He was not with the 59th Regt. at the time, nor did he give its Commanding Officer any order or instruction to that effect. Colonel Gillespie was engaged on the right, and so completely exhausted by his noble, heroic previous exertions that he was unable to move during the times the Regiment charged the batteries and park, and the enemies' column of infantry. He came up at the moment the infantry was routed by the Regiment, and he pursued them on the retreat with part of the Corps.'

The *Record of Service* also adds some colour to the attack of the 59th on the Dutch guns subsequent to the explosion in Redoubt No. 2, when their Grenadier Company 'suffered severely':

'Immediately after this the 59th rushed to charge a battery of field pieces, which were posted in front of the enemies' park of artillery and was causing much loss to our troops.[883] The Regiment gallantly advanced in the face of a very destructive fire (the men being exposed to their very feet the whole time in advancing) and drove the enemy from their guns. The cool and judicious manner in which Lieut. Coll. A McLeod led the Regt. against these guns was deservedly noticed in the Genl. Orders and Report of the Battle. At the moment this was effected, a column of the enemy's infantry was discovered to be approaching the right flank of the Regiment; the column was immediately attacked with the bayonet, repulsed, and dispersed, but not before it had thrown a destructive fire upon the Regt. On this occasion Lieut. & Adjt. [Henry Eyre] Pitman[884] by his steady and gallant conduct was of essential service to the Commanding Officer and to the Regiment.

'The enemy's [artillery] park having thus fallen into our hands, and also the Redoubt [Fort] called Cornelis, from which the whole position had its name, and which was in the centre of their position, the remaining redoubts were successively taken possession of and the enemy retreated in the utmost confusion and was pursued by the Dragoons and some infantry under the command of Colonel Gibbs. The enemy rallied in their retreat several times, but being instantly attacked were compelled as often to retreat with dreadful loss, until at last all order among them being lost, they dispersed in all directions, throwing away their arms, accoutrements, caps, &c.'

Sir Samuel Auchmuty, in giving an account of enemy losses to Lord Minto, reported that 'About one thousand have been buried in the works; multitudes were cut down in the retreat; the rivers are choked up with dead; and the huts and woods were filled with the wounded, who have since expired. We have taken near five thousand prisoners; among whom are three general officers, thirty-four field officers, seventy captains, and one hundred and fifty subaltern officers. General Janssens made his escape with difficulty during the action, and reached Buitenzorg, a distance of thirty miles, with a few cavalry, the sole remains of an army of ten thousand men. This place he has since evacuated, and fled to the eastward.'

Lord Minto visited the battlefield the following day and was horrified: 'The number of dead and the shocking variety of deaths had better not be imagined.' But in truth, the British had achieved complete victory at remarkably low cost. A total of 76 British soldiers and 20 Indian sepoys had died in the storming of the Lines of Cornelis. The heaviest loss had fallen on the 59th Regiment, whose casualties included five officers, two sergeants, one corporal and fourteen privates killed in action[885], and eleven officers[886], three sergeants, two drummers and

---

[883] An officer of the Company's Service who was present described this artillery as 'a masked battery of flying artillery, from 16 to 20 guns, in a parallel line in front of Fort Cornelis'.

[884] Henry Pitman was one of three brothers who served in the 59th, all three of whom became casualties at the storming of Bhurtpore in 1826, when Major Henry Pitman was mortally wounded, his brother Lieutenant Maurice Charles Pitman was killed, and Lieutenant William Pitman was severely wounded.

[885] Killed in action: Major William Olpherts, Lieutenants Richard Litton, John Lloyd and William Waring, and Ensign Robert F Wolfe, Sergeants Thomas Haddow and Benjamin Roberts, Corporal Samuel Rockcliffe, and Privates Joseph Aston, Thomas Bigland, Samuel Bradshaw, William Crann, Martin Freeburger, Thomas Knowland, John McCarty, Michael Millady, John Moody, Joseph Ransom, George Roberts, James Stanley, Robert Vice and George White.

[886] Officers wounded: Lieutenant-Colonel Alexander McLeod (flesh wound), Captain John Campbell (severely), Lieutenants John Butler (thigh crushed and several other wounds: lamed for life), John Dillon (head wound), Duncan Gordon (severely in foot) and John Pyne

109 rank and file wounded. Two officers, two corporals, one drummer and 27 privates of the 59th subsequently died of their wounds[887]. Lieutenant James Chadwick was aghast at the scene:

'The action was nothing to the sight we were obliged to witness after all was over – our brother officers and brave men lying in all directions dead and dying, as well as whole regiments of the enemy that lay on the ground in the same position they had taken up for defence. One of their batteries blew up during the action just as our troops had entered it. Heads, legs and mangled bodies presented themselves to the view of us that were fortunate enough to be at a short distance from the explosion; and still more horrible was it to see some that were not killed by the explosion drop, as from the sky, with their arms and legs all smashed to pieces and their bodies all covered with wounds.'

Lieutenant Thomas Sampson, who died from a gunshot wound, managed to write a last letter:

'I am now writing from my bed, to which I was brought by a musket ball I received on 26th ult. A most brilliant action we have had. The enemy was entrenched at regular intervals, & had redoubts mounting from fifteen to nineteen field pieces. We stormed them at daybreak without firing a single gun, & carried every battery by the bayonet. I never was under so tremendous a fire. In the midst of the action the enemy blew up a magazine, by which we lost a captain & several men. Our Regiment suffered severely, losing six officers killed & wounded. After the battle the scene was dreadful to behold, men horses, whites, blacks all lying in heaps together. I cannot get the ball extracted… I believe I am senior lieutenant.'[888]

For their gallant leadership at the storming of the Lines of Cornelis, Colonel Samuel Gibbs and Lieutenant-Colonel Alexander McLeod received the Army Gold Medal [889], while 104 members of the 59th survived to receive the Military General Service Medal with 'Java' bar. In 1818 the 59th, still serving in India, were authorised to emblazon their Colours with the Battle Honour 'JAVA.'

After the rout of Janssens' army at Cornelis, the 59th marched to Weltevreden and were quartered in the cantonment. Samuel Gibbs, meanwhile, commanded the force which, on the 27th, occupied the fortification of Buitenzorg without opposition, capturing a further 43 guns. James Chadwick recorded that the Light and Rifle Companies of the 59th, with the Light Company 69th, were sent to Buitenzorg, where they remained for nearly a month.

Gibbs, however, continued in the pursuit of Janssens, who had fled in an easterly direction, and he was in tactical command under Auchmuty when the Dutch Governor-General made his final stand at Jattoo on 16th September. Gibbs was thanked by Auchmuty for 'the very able and gallant manner' in which he forced the enemy position on the heights and for his energetic pursuit. Two days later Janssens capitulated, and the island of Java and all its dependencies across the East Indies were surrendered to Britain.

This short and entirely successful campaign was indeed a most remarkable achievement, summarised by Sir Samuel Auchmuty with just pride in a General Order dated Samarang 20th September 1811:

'The utter defeat, dispersion, and final surrender, of the remains of an army, which on the landing of the British force on the 4th of August last consisted of above 17,000 regularly organised troops, commanded by an officer of known ability, provided with numerous artillery and strong fortified positions, aided by firm alliances with native chiefs, and all the other resources of a long established power, requires no language but a simple statement of the facts to speak the merits of the troops. Their conduct has enabled the Commander-in-Chief, in the short space of six weeks, after pursuing to, and defeating the enemy at a distance of 360 miles from the scene of their first discomfiture, to dictate terms of capitulation which transfer to Great Britain an island, long the

---

Pennefather (slight foot wound), and Ensign William Hamilton Waters (severely), together with Lieutenants John Lowe (severely) and Jourdan (slightly) of the Madras Army, attached.

[887] 59th died of wounds: Captain Evan McPherson and Lieutenant Thomas Sampson, Corporals Henry Smith and Henry Kelly, Drummer William Reilly, and Privates John Barrett, William Burton, John Callow, William Calvert, Benjamin Cheney, Thomas Croft, Edward Doolan, Thomas Green, Thomas Hayton, Thomas Heath, John Heywood, Thomas Hughes, John Hurst, William James, John Jarvis, Samuel Johnson, Thomas Lockwood, George Massey, Denis McGuire, Hugh McKay, Francis Parkinson, John Ross, Joseph Ryan, William Simms, John Swann, John West and Thomas Worthall.

[888] On account of Thomas Sampson's death, his younger brother, aged 15 years and 8 months, was granted a special commission in the 59th. He subsequently served with the Regiment 1813-39, campaigning in Java, in the Mahratta War, and in the Candian Insurrection in Ceylon.

[889] The Army Gold Medals of Gibbs and McLeod earned at Cornelis are displayed in the Lancashire Infantry Museum.

greatest boast of the ancient government of Holland, which France has viewed as one of the most precious of the usurpations wrested from her injured allies, and which now leaves her without a spot of land to the eastward of the Cape of Good Hope on which to place that banner whose baneful influence she has long vainly endeavoured to extend to poison the prosperity of Britain in the East.'

Sir John Fortescue, in his magisterial *History of The British Army*, was in no doubt as to the extent of the accomplishment of Auchmuty and his army:

'The storming of the lines of Cornelis, though utterly forgotten both by the army and the nation, is none the less one of the great exploits of the Napoleonic war. The odds were against the British in point of numbers, while the strength of the enemy's position was enough to daunt the boldest general.'

'It must be noted that Auchmuty laid his plans for the assault in such sort as not only to drive the enemy from their stronghold, but to annihilate the hostile army and practically to close the war. Many generals would have been content with a victory against such odds; Auchmuty boldly attempted and actually achieved a conquest. Such commanders are not common in any country; and it may safely be asserted that, if Napoleon had conducted the campaign of Java exactly as did Auchmuty, whole libraries would have been written in laudation of it. Yet this brilliant and sterling soldier has been forgotten, and his greatest exploit survives as a mere name upon certain Colours.' [890]

As for Colonel Samuel Gibbs, like so many soldiers his health was eventually broken by long service in the tropics, and he obtained leave to go home. His services in Java were publicly recognised by Stamford Raffles:[891]

'The Honourable the Lieut. Governor in Council cannot omit the public expressions of his regret that the distressing state of health under which Colonel Gibbs labours, and which renders an immediate change of climate necessary, should deprive this colony of the service of this meritorious officer. To the share which Colonel Gibbs bore in the achievements which rendered the British Power paramount in Java it is unnecessary that the Lieut. Governor should bear testimony; those gallant deeds are already before the world from higher Authority, but the Lieut. Governor would be wanting in a just sense of the merits and services of Colonel Gibbs did not he embrace this opportunity of offering his grateful acknowledgements for the uniform assistance and zealous co-operation which he has received from that officer during the period which he has held and executed with so much ability, judgement and discretion the chief Civil and Military Authority in the Eastern Division of the Island.'

Samuel Gibbs' exceptional record in South Africa, India, Mauritius and Java was such that, after brief commands in Stralsund and Holland, he was promoted to the rank of major-general and appointed second-in-command to Sir Edward Packenham's ill-fated expedition to New Orleans. There, sadly, he was mortally wounded at the age of 44. Samuel Gibbs' great services to his country were, however, recognised: he was posthumously knighted and he is commemorated with a monumental statue in St. Paul's Cathedral.

Defeat of Bagus Rangin

Lord Minto's instructions from the Government had required him to organise only 'the expulsion of the Dutch power, the destruction of their fortifications, the distribution of their arms and stores to the natives, and the evacuation of the Island by our own troops.' However, Minto shared Stamford Raffles' romantic notions of Java as 'the land of promise', and was concerned for the fate of the Dutch and Chinese colonists; so, he unilaterally decided to retain the territory. He and Auchmuty returned to India in October 1811, taking with them many of the British and Indian troops, leaving Raffles as Lieutenant-Governor, with Gillespie as his military counterpart.

One of the many dissident elements in Java under Dutch rule had been a faction headed by Bagus Rangin, venerated by his followers as a prophet and variously characterised by others as a fanatical mullah or, more recently, a resistance hero. Since about 1806 his adherents had been in revolt against the Sultan of Cerebon and the Dutch, and at the end of 1811 he raised the standard of rebellion again in Indramayu, on the north coast of Java and some 110 miles east of Batavia.

---

[890] Fortescue's *History of The British Army*, Vol. VII. p.p. 624 & 629.
[891] General Order dated Batavia 19th March 1812.

Bagu Rangin had assembled in the hills of Indramayu a large and growing force of insurgents, many of whom were deserters and fugitives from the defeated Franco-Dutch army. For the past six years he had eluded every attempt by the Dutch to capture him, finding a sure retreat in the mountains whenever hard pressed. At this time, he had taken advantage of the disturbed state of Java to seize control of a number of villages, compelling the inhabitants to join his revolt, and flushed with success he went on to threaten the town and fort of Indramayu.

A detachment of Bengal sepoys was immediately sent from Batavia to strengthen the garrison, followed soon after by Captain John Ralph, 59th, with a detachment of the 59th and more Indian troops. Ralph, a veteran of the 59th Regiment's 1790s campaign in the West Indies, had orders to attack and destroy the rebels. His detachment came by surprise upon a large body of the insurgents, including over two thousand musketeers, which they immediately attacked, wading through rice fields to close with the enemy. The rebels, regularly drawn up in line behind a bank, opened a fire of musketry, but when the 59th came within reach a bayonet charge soon broke through the whole multitude, of whom considerable numbers were killed and wounded, and the rest dispersed. The British loss in this affair was slight, consisting of one rank and file of the 59th killed and several wounded. Though Bagus Rangin himself escaped for a time, the sharp check which his followers had received was decisive; for as their notion of his invincibility was destroyed, they abandoned his standard in great numbers. Captain John Ralph and his men were thanked[892] by Raffles and Gillespie for their 'ardour and zeal' when sent against 'the predatory chief Baggoor Rangin.'

In the course of 1811 the 59th had suffered the loss of nine officers[893] and 137 other ranks killed in action and died of wounds or sickness. Captain John Ralph died the following June.

Expedition to Palembang, Sumatra 1812

Java and its dependencies had latterly, under Dutch rule, been in a somewhat turbulent state, and several of the native princes had taken advantage of the conflict between Europeans to renounce their allegiance to the Dutch colonial power and its British successor. Among these was Sultan Mahmud Badaruddin II of Palembang, in Sumatra, a potentate now regarded as a national hero, who had treacherously massacred the European and native inhabitants of the Dutch factory and fort there. On receipt of the news of this atrocity, perpetrated on the inhabitants of a settlement latterly under British protection, a punitive expedition was fitted out at Batavia and dispatched on 20th March 1812.

This force consisted of the Grenadier, Light and Rifle Companies of the 59th Regiment under Captain John Campbell, five companies of the 89th Regiment, and detachments of Bengal and Madras infantry and artillery, conveyed in four transports and escorted by seven warships. The troops were commanded by Colonel Rollo Gillespie, and Lieutenant-Colonel Alexander McLeod, 59th, was second-in-command.

The city of Palembang lay some sixty miles from the sea on the flat, marshy banks of the Musi River, and the river approach was protected by strong artillery batteries at Borang, twenty miles downstream from the capital.

It was the monsoon season, and contrary winds and currents slowed the expedition's progress, but on 3rd April the fleet anchored off the remote tropical island of Nangka, in the Bangka, or Banca, Strait between Borneo and Sumatra, a frequent haunt of pirates. Tents were pitched on shore, and preparations were made for the passage up-river to Palembang. Boats were fitted with awnings to shelter the troops, as much as possible, from the burning heat of the day (averaging 90° F in April) and the humid night air, and with platforms to carry field guns, and the fleet took on water. Unfortunately, several of these boats were lost in a severe gale on the night of 9th April and many others were damaged.

The fleet sailed again on 10th April, and anchored at noon on the 15th opposite the west channel of the Musi River. Two days were then spent in getting some of the smaller warships over the bar at the river's mouth, and on the evening of the 17th the troops boarded the boats and small vessels. That night, however, another very violent storm, with heavy rain, considerably damaged the boats and destroyed the coverings which had been made

---

[892] General Orders dated Weltevreden 29th January 1812.

[893] In addition to the officers who were killed at the storming of Cornelis or died of the wounds, Captain Thomas Watts died of fatigue a few days later and Captain James Hill died in October 1811.

at Nangka with so much labour and difficulty, and priority on the few serviceable flat-boats had to be allocated to the field artillery.

A number of armed prows were seen that day at the river-mouth, and a party of seamen and thirty riflemen of the 59th were sent against them in boats. One prow, whose alarmed crew leaped overboard and fled into the jungle, was captured, but the others escaped.

On the evening of the 18th the flotilla started up-river, coming to anchor towards midnight having made about ten miles. The river, which was six to seven hundred yards wide as it crossed the delta, was little known to Europeans, and so the boats proceeded with the utmost care and vigilance.

The Sultan had received plenty of notice of the British expedition, giving him ample time to prepare for flight or fight. With a view to the former course of action, he had at a very early period removed his treasure and harem into the interior. At the same time, he had readied formidable defences on the river, centred on three well-sited batteries at Borang, forty miles from the river mouth, supplemented by numerous armed prows, floating batteries and fire-rafts. At the same time, as William Thorn put it, 'the guilty Sultan… and his ministers, putting on the air of duplicity, sent message after message to the British Commander, filled with expressions of respect, and framed with apparent candour; but hypocritical in their language, and treacherous in their object.'

An ebb tide on the 19th stalled progress until 4 p.m. when a gentle sea breeze enabled the flotilla to move, though it was only for a short distance, as the wind soon failed, and a slack flood tide caused some of the vessels to become entangled among branches of the riverside trees and bushes, which had to be cut away. The flotilla dropped anchor at about six the following morning.

That day the first of Sultan Badaruddin's emissaries arrived, wanting to know the intention of the British Commander in advancing with such a force: to which Colonel Gillespie replied that he must acquaint the Sultan in person with the propositions of the British Government.

At five in the evening the flotilla resumed its passage; but the tide became slacker every day in proportion to the distance from the sea, and as the wind was against them only six more miles were gained before the ebb tide, at six the next morning, 21st April, obliged the vessels to anchor. Two more ambassadors from the Sultan arrived that day.

At sunrise on 22nd April the batteries at Borang were sighted; but as the tide was falling the flotilla had to anchor about five miles short of the fortifications. Reconnaissance revealed that the shore batteries and armed prows had been reinforced by a large Arab ship, and that the vessels, with the floating batteries, were moored across the river in echelon so that their guns could rake the whole length of the passage, and that numerous fire-rafts had been placed to the front and flanks of the batteries, ready to be set adrift to fire the British shipping. Piles of wood, driven into the river, defended the approach to the batteries from landing parties, whilst strong palisades protected their rear and flanks. A great deal of bustle and activity was observed aboard the shipping and within the fortifications, all of which appeared to be fully manned and prepared for resistance.

Violent rain fell all that afternoon and through the night, adding to the discomfort of the soldiers and sailors in open boats. During the day they had been exposed, while rowing, to the burning tropical sun, while at night they were unable to sleep. Despite these hardships, 'nothing could shake their resolution or abate their ardour in the performance of their duty.'

That evening yet another messenger arrived, with a letter from the Sultan, saying that he should be happy to see his friend, the Commander of the Expedition, at Palembang; but requesting that he would dispense with so large an armed force, and visit the capital unattended, being fearful, as he pretended, that the appearance of so many troops would occasion serious disturbances. Needless to say, Gillespie declined this invitation, and instead demanded an unmolested passage up the river, and also a hostage; to which the Sultan's emissary instantly assented, offering at the same time to hand over the Borang batteries and the large Arab ship. Consequently, on the afternoon of the 23rd several boats of the Advance approached Borang, only to be met by boats from the batteries, and advised not to go any farther, while the armed prows made a show of resistance, attended with great shouting from the batteries, and other demonstrations of hostility, at which the British boats withdrew.

That night, arrangements were made to carry the batteries in case of resistance, and an officer fluent in Malay was sent to Borang to demand a decisive answer as to whether or not they would let the batteries be taken possession of amicably, or whether they would contest the passage of the flotilla. No time was allowed for equivocation, for Colonel Gillespie followed close after at the head of the small but formidable force of the British Advance, composed of detachments of the 59th and 89th Regiments in light boats, supported by the gun-launches and by field artillery on flat-boats. On their arrival at dawn, within half gun shot of the batteries, the Sultan's emissary came off and offered to deliver up the batteries, whose garrisons, terrified at Gillespie's sudden approach, fled in prows. The batteries and other defences were immediately occupied by the British troops, who found all 102 guns ready charged and primed. The large ship then afforded welcome shelter for a great portion of the soldiers, while the remainder were quartered in huts and covered floating batteries.

That evening, the troops re-embarked, and the flotilla moved onwards a short distance. Fires now appeared in all directions, and several of the fire-rafts were set in flames by the enemy, with the aim of destroying those vessels which had not as yet passed the batteries. Fortunately, the crews of the light boats were successful in cutting out the rafts before they were thoroughly in flames. Several shots were fired at Malays seen setting fire to the rafts, who instantly dispersed.

Early in the morning of the 25th Gillespie received news that the Sultan had fled from Palembang, followed by further intelligence that general disorder prevailed throughout the capital, from where it was reported that a massacre of the wealthy Chinese and other inhabitants was intended that very night. In view of these reports, the Colonel at once determined to hasten up-river to the capital in light boats. He led with two canoes, with an escort of seven grenadiers of the 59th, and these were followed by the gig and barge of HMS *Phoenix* with a small group of naval and staff officers and Lieutenant George Forrest of the 59th with ten more grenadiers of that regiment. The remaining troops, under Lieutenant-Colonel McLeod, 59th, were ordered to follow with all speed. Captain William Thorn, who was present in the gig, wrote the following graphic 'heart of darkness' description of Gillespie's resolute advance on Palembang:

'The distance was twenty miles, so that it was quite dark when the party reached Old Palimbang. The canoes, with the Colonel, having gained considerably on the other boats, were now completely out of sight, when the report of a signal gun, fired by the enemy, excited great alarm and anxiety among those who were in the rear. A horrible yell and shrieking was next heard, and conflagrations were perceived, extending along the banks of the river for the space of above seven miles.'

'Undismayed in the face of numerous bodies of armed men, Colonel Gillespie stepped boldly on shore, at eight o'clock at night; and with those who had accompanied him in the canoe, and the seven grenadiers, marched through a multitude of Arabs and Malays, whose formidable weapons, steeped in poison, reflected the light of the torches. Tremendous battlements, with immense gates, leading from one vast area to another, received the small party, and presented to them the frightful spectacle of human blood, still reeking and flowing on the pavement. The massy gates closed upon them, and the ensanguined court-yards through which they passed appeared like the passage to a slaughterhouse.

'While they were in this dreadful situation, a Malay, who had passed through the crowd, approached the Colonel, and was walking close by his side, when a large double-edged knife was secretly put into his hands by one of his countrymen. It was a dark, stormy night, and a ray of lightning, at the very instant when the fellow was pushing the knife up his loose sleeve for concealment, discovered the weapon to the keen eye of the Colonel, who, turning round, had the man seized, and thus happily frustrated the murderous intent. The weapon was found, but the Malay contrived, by mingling with the crowd, to effect his escape.

'The palace exhibited a melancholy mixture of cruelty and devastation, surpassing that which had already met the eye. Murder had here been succeeded by rapine; and while the place was completely ransacked, the floors were literally clotted with gore. On every side the most woeful spectacles were to be seen, and they were rendered still more awful by the glare of the surrounding conflagration, and vivid gleams of lightning which flashed amidst rolling peals of thunder.

'The devouring flames, which continued to spread destruction, in spite of the rain that poured down in torrents, had now reached the outer buildings of the palace, and threatened the quarter where the English party had taken their station. The crackling of bamboos, resembling the discharge of musketry, the tumbling in of burning roofs, with a tremendous crash, and the near approach of the fire, added to the surrounding danger of a hostile multitude, altogether, gave a fearful aspect to the condition of our little band, which consisted only of seventeen grenadiers, the officers already mentioned, and a few seamen. Having carefully reconnoitered by torch-light the interior of the palace-court, and ordered all the avenues, except one, to be barricaded, Colonel Gillespie placed the grenadiers at the principal entrance, and the strictest guard was preserved.

'Soon after midnight, Major Trench, with about sixty men of the Eighty-Ninth Regiment, arrived; and the remaining part of the Advance, under Lieutenant-Colonel M'Leod, joined the little garrison early in the morning. Thus, an unprecedented act of daring enterprize, judiciously conceived, and rapidly executed, gained the possession of the fort and batteries, defended by two hundred and forty-two pieces of cannon, without the loss of a man. The sudden arrival of a few British, at a late hour in the evening, struck a panic into the adherents of the Sultan, who, believing that the numbers were more formidable, immediately dispersed, and thereby relieved the town from the misery with which it had been threatened by the barbarity of its chief.

'The characteristic humanity of the British appeared on this occasion, in the measures that were adopted to secure tranquillity; and these were carried into effect so promptly, that the inhabitants, recovering their spirits, assumed confidence, and many who had fled into the woods returned to their houses. To the mass of the people, this revolution was peculiarly grateful, as it relieved them from a tyranny which was become insupportable.'[894]

Writing to Raffles on 28th April, from Palembang, Gillespie was unstinting in his praise of his second-in-command:

'The military reputation and gallantry of Lieut. Col. McLeod of H.M.'s 59th Regiment are already so well established that any panegyric of mine would add little to the fame he has so justly earned. I shall therefore content myself on the present occasion with returning my very best thanks for the activity, anxiety and attention he has manifested during the progress of the service.'

Having secured the city, on 14th May Gillespie installed the former Sultan's more co-operative younger brother on the throne. The expeditionary force then withdrew to the river mouth, where they formally took possession of the island of Bangka, ceded to Britain by the new Sultan, which was re-named Duke of York's Island. Having left small garrisons there and at Palembang, the expedition returned to Java, arriving at Batavia on 1st June.

Sir Samuel Auchmuty received Gillespie's reports in India, and on 30th September sent a congratulatory message from Cawnpore, of which the following is an extract:

'Although the feeble use the enemy made of his extensive means of defence and annoyance at Palambang deprived the expedition against its barbarous prince of that character of brilliancy which peculiarly belongs to active operations in the field, the Commander in Chief considers the troops employed in that difficult service as highly deserving of his approbation and thanks for their exact discipline, patient endurance of fatigue and privation, and forwardness on every occasion which seemed likely to require their active exertions.'

This was not to be the last visit to Sumatra by the 59th, for the British Resident at Palembang was persuaded, in consideration of a large sum of money paid to the Government, to restore the deposed Sultan. This arrangement was not approved by Lieutenant-Governor Raffles, and so a further expedition was mounted from Batavia under the command of Lieutenant-Colonel George McGregor of the 59th, who had joined the 1st Battalion in Java on 1st October 1812 and assumed command the following month.[895]

He embarked on 6th August 1813 on board the frigates *Hussar* and *Volage*, and four transports, with the Flank and Rifle Companies 59th, under Captain John Campbell, one hundred men from the Company's Bengal European Regiment, and a detachment of Bengal Artillery with two howitzers. Certain officers, including George McGregor, were appointed as Commissioners to deal with the affairs of Palembang.

---

[894] Captain (later Sir William) Thorn, 'A Memoir of Major-General Sir R. R. Gillespie', p.p. 157-62.
[895] George McGregor joined the 59th from the 78th as a captain in 1797, having previously served at the Cape of Good Hope and in India. He was with the 2nd/59th as Major at Corunna, where he was wounded (and received a premature obituary in *The Gentleman's Magazine*), and at Walcheren. He had twice assumed temporary command of the 2nd/59th in England, and was promoted to Brevet Lieutenant-Colonel on 1st January 1812. He joined the 1st Battalion in Java on 1st October 1812 and assumed command the following month in consequence of Lieutenant-Colonel McLeod being nominated to command the Western Division of the Army. He was promoted to the substantive rank of lieutenant-colonel on 4th June 1813.

The account that follows is taken from *The Regimental Record of Service*, compiled in India whilst George McGregor was still in command of the 59th.

'The wind being fair, the ships anchored at the mouth of the Palambang River on the evening of the 10th, and having communicated with Captain Court, [Resident] at Banca [Bangka], the troops were all in their boats and moved from the ships at 1 p.m. on the 12th. The howitzers were placed in flats brought from Batavia for the purpose, and ten boats from the frigates, manned by 150 sailors and armed, attended the troops up the river... The detachment of the Bengal European Regiment proceeded in a brig, as there were not boats sufficient. The Grenadiers of the 59th were in a heavy sloop, which moved very badly.

'The boats anchored at midnight in consequence of the ebb tide, which continued running down until 11 a.m. when they moved again, and the whole, excepting the Grenadiers of the 59th Regiment and the Bengal detachment, arrived at Palambang at midnight on the 13th; thus accomplishing in the space of thirty-five hours what... the troops under Genl. Gillespie took twenty-three days to get over in the former expedition.'

'There was a garrison of 160 native troops at Palambang, partly Bengal sepoys and partly Amboynese. These joined the troops under Lieut. Col. McGregor, and the howitzers being placed in the middle of the river opposite the Sultan's palace, and the armed sailors in their boats, [and] the Grenadiers of the 59th arriving at the moment, the whole proceeded with the Commissioners to the Hall of Audience, outside the walls of the fort, at 4 p.m. on the 14th August, when the orders of the Java Government were carried into effect without a shot being fired; and the unfortunate Sultan again relinquished his throne to his younger brother.

'Lieut. Col. McGregor then proceeded up the river two hundred miles, in a south-westerly direction to Muara-Rawas [Muara Enim?], the place where the Sultan fled to last year, of the strength of which a very exaggerated report had been made to Government, and which was found incorrect. The troops then returned to Batavia, where they landed on the 28th September.'

McGregor received the following message of thanks[896] from Rollo Gillespie, who was about to embark for India:

'In taking leave of the Army it is peculiarly gratifying to the Major General to have another opportunity of expressing his approbation of the conduct of a Detachment on its return to this Island: he is therefore desirous of expressing to Lieut. Col. McGregor his best thanks for his judicious and able arrangements, particularly evinced in the rapidity with which the troops moved up the river of Palambang. He begs the Lieut. Col. to communicate to the Detachment his highest approbation of their discipline; and he is happy to observe from the uniform good conduct of these troops that had circumstances been such as to call for active operations in the field another wreath would have been added to the laurels of the Army on Java.'

Expedition to Yogyakarta June 1812

Although the European enemy in the Dutch East Indies had been roundly beaten in 1811, there were other powers in Java who threatened British supremacy in the archipelago, the most important of which were the great historic sultanates of the hinterland, Yogyakarta (then spelt Djocjocarta) and Surakarta. These princely courts, though much diminished under Dutch hegemony, retained considerable military potential and residual prestige. They had noted the reduction of British troops in Java by the end of 1811 and saw the opportunity for a rebellion against European rule. In April 1813, correspondence between the royal courts of Java was uncovered in which the ruler of Surakarta had attempted to incite the Yogyakarta Sultan to rise against the foreigners.

Raffles decided that he needed to organise a crushing military defeat of one or other of the sultanates as 'decisive proof to the native inhabitants of Java of the strength and determination of the British Government.' His choice fell on the Sultanate of Yogyakarta as the most significant potential adversary, writing that 'the Sultan [of Yogyakarta] decidedly looks upon us as a less powerful people than the [Napoleonic] Government which proceeded us, and it becomes absolutely necessary for the tranquility of the Country that he should be taught to think otherwise.'

---

[896] General Orders from Headquarters, Weltevreden dated 7th October 1813.

Yogyakarta had inherited the mantle and prestige of past kingdoms of Java, such as Mataram and Majapahit. It was a place of high protocol and of a complex Muslim-Javanese courtly culture. During the previous two centuries, conflicts between the Dutch and Javanese princes had been typified by formalized posturing and brinkmanship, and had then usually been resolved through face-saving diplomacy, and so the Sultan of Yogyakarta, Hamengkubuwono II, never believed that the British would take decisive military action.

An expedition was hastily organised, to be led once more by Rollo Gillespie, who on 1st June 1812 had returned to Batavia from Palembang, seconded again by Alexander McLeod of the 59th. Gillespie sailed at once for Samarang, at a mid-point on the north coast, to lead the new expedition, closely followed by the Grenadiers of the 59th.

On 17th June Lieutenant-Governor Raffles and Colonel Gillespie, with a small force, reached the old Dutch fort on the outskirts of Yogyakarta, the fortified capital of that sultanate, and attempted to reach an amicable settlement with the Sultan. The latter, however, would not negotiate, but sent strong bodies of horse to obstruct any British reinforcements by destroying bridges and laying waste the country, and towards evening advanced a large body of troops to demand the surrender of the British. That night Gillespie's outposts were attacked, as were his pickets posted on the road by which reinforcements were expected. The situation looked dangerous.

Next day, despite having little ammunition, Gillespie ordered his gunners to open fire from the Dutch fort. As he said, 'I am always an advocate of promptness and decision, and I am aware that any measure of a contrary nature would not only weaken the confidence of the troops but increase the insolence of the enemy.' That night the Sultan's troops attacked four times, but were steadily repulsed.

Meanwhile, Lieutenant-Colonel McLeod with the Grenadier Company 59th had marched to Salatiga[897], from where he was ordered to proceed to Yogyakarta with the main body of the expedition, consisting of the Grenadiers of the 59th, the Flank and Rifle Companies of the 78th, a small party of Hussars and detachments of artillery. By mid-afternoon on the 18th, having had no reports of McLeod's progress, Gillespie became so anxious that he dispatched a party of dragoons, who cut their way through to meet the reinforcements.

McLeod arrived on the morning of the 19th. While the troops rested after their long march under a burning tropical sun, Gillespie prepared for offensive action against the Sultan's fortified capital and palace enclosure, or Kraton, which he described in his report to Raffles:

'The palace and Kratton of the Sultan is surrounded by regular works about 3 miles in circumference; at each corner there is a formidable bastion enfilading the curtain, and the principal entrance in front is strongly defended by cannon. The whole fortification is surrounded by a wet ditch, and the gateways are all provided with drawbridges to prevent the passage across.'

Gillespie had barely 1,200 men at his disposal, including fewer than one thousand British and Indian infantry, while the Sultan's regular army was believed to be upwards of 17,000 strong, supported by an armed population of more than one hundred thousand; but despite the odds the British commander resolved to assault the Kraton before daylight the following morning. As Captain Thorn noted, 'To assault a place of such magnitude with so small a force, and the knowledge that we had to contend with a vast superiority of numbers, could not fail to give a very serious and appalling aspect to our enterprise. But the stake at issue was nothing less than our very existence; and the fate of the whole Colony depended on the event.' Only a supremely bold commander with absolute confidence in his troops could have contemplated such a perilous assault.

That evening, the British troops were assembled in the Dutch fort, and during the early hours of June 20th, they ceased fire to lull the defenders into a false sense of security. Then, at 3 a.m., two hours before dawn, they launched their attack, heading for the north-east corner of the Kraton. Their *Regimental Record of Service* has a short and remarkably understated account of the part played by the 59th:

'The attack was made in three columns, one of which was commanded by Lieut. Col. McLeod and one by Col. Watson of the 14th Regiment. The ladders were placed against the curtain [wall] before day broke, but before half of our column had ascended the ladders broke and became useless. The column under Col. McLeod then

---

[897] Captains William Bowen and John Campbell were left sick at Salatiga, where both died.

proceeded to the principal [Princes] gate, which was blown open by means of the guns, and the column immediately entered; the ramparts were shortly cleared of the enemy, and the place was taken possession of.'

It was in fact not easy to force the Princes Gate, which was strongly barricaded, but having crossed the drawbridge the soldiers climbed on each other's shoulders to enter embrasures on the walls, which were then rapidly cleared at bayonet point. One Javanese prince observed that, 'In battle [the British] were irresistible… they were as though protected by the very angels and they struck terror into men's hearts.'

By mid-morning, the Kraton had fallen, hundreds of its defenders had been killed, 92 guns captured, and the Sultan and his heir had been taken prisoner at the cost of just 23 soldiers dead and 76, including Gillespie, wounded. Remarkably, the 59th suffered no casualties. This long-forgotten exploit of a small British force against great odds was truly outstanding, and the Commander-in-Chief of India was fully justified in ranking it 'amongst the foremost of those achievements which adorn the military annals of our country and have increased its power and reputation in Asia.' As was his style, Gillespie paid a fulsome tribute to his men[898]:

'The Commander of the Forces congratulates the troops he had the honour personally to command upon the late glorious result of their arduous and honourable enterprise. It confirms him in the opinion he has so justly entertained of their discipline, firmness and gallantry, and it affords memorable proof to the enemies of the British Government that British soldiers, when united by those valuable qualities, must not only conquer but be irresistible. It was a conviction of their super-eminence that determined him in a measure, when nothing but bravery could succeed, and it was the assurance of their intrepidity that urged him to an assault, where multitudes of men were prepared for resistance. The event has proved that his confidence was by no means mis-placed; the enemy has been routed from a regular fortified position, and 17,000 armed men have been conquered and dispersed; the person of the Sultan has been safely secured, and the circumstances attending his seizure reflect so much credit on the troops in general that the Commander of the Forces cannot sufficiently express his admiration and applause. In the heat of the storm his person was respected, his family was placed in security and protection, and no part of the property was either pillaged or molested.'

Gillespie's euphoria in his day of victory is understandable, but other accounts suggest that the victors fell to enthusiastic looting of the city and that their commander took away personal booty valued at £15,000 (half a million, in modern terms). Back in Weltevreden cantonment, James Chadwick ruefully contemplated a missed opportunity of making his fortune:

'At Djocjocarta [Yogyakarta] the officers, had they been prudent, might have made a fortune: a subaltern's share of prize money alone amounted to £800, and the plunder was beyond calculation. As I was appointed Adjutant of the Regiment on the 3rd Jan. 1812, I was deprived of the opportunities which offered themselves to the bucks employed on those services.'

Sultan Hamengkubuwono II was exiled, and the following afternoon the Crown Prince, who had been hunted down in the alleyways of the Kraton, was placed on the throne as a British puppet, signing a hastily penned treaty which acknowledged 'the supremacy of the British Government over the whole Island of Java.' Writing to Lord Minto to inform him of the victory, Raffles declared that the native princes of Java 'now for the first time know their relative situation and importance… The European power is now for the first time paramount in Java.'

Once again, as at the storming of the Lines of Cornelis and the audacious but bloodless seizure of Palembang, the brunt of the work had fallen on the 14th, 59th and 78th, characterised by Sir John Fortescue as 'three noble battalions which no hardship of a tropical campaign could discourage, no sickness of a pestilent climate could dismay, and no wiles nor numbers of a teeming and treacherous enemy could daunt for one moment.'

Expedition to Bali 1814

Immediately after the capture of Yogyakarta, the Flank Companies 1st/59th returned to Weltevreden, where the Battalion was united by August 1812. It appears that none of the 59th were killed in action or died of wounds

---

[898] General Orders dated Djocjocarta 21st June 1812.

in 1812, but even so, four officers and 135 other ranks died in the course of that year, and six men were invalided to England. On Christmas Day 1812, the Battalion numbered 51 sergeants, 22 drummers and 881 rank and file. The 1st/59th received 150 men from their 2nd Battalion that year, together with 29 volunteers from the 33rd Regiment, who were leaving Madras for England.

Apart from the further expedition to Palembang already mentioned, the Battalion remained at Weltevreden throughout 1813. On 4th June 1813 Colonel Gibbs, now in Europe, was promoted to the rank of major-general, occasioning a chain of regimental promotions. As noted above, Lieutenant-Colonel McGregor assumed command, and in his absence with the second expedition to Palembang the Battalion was commanded for two months by Captain Joseph Creighton. The strength of the 1st/59th as at 24th December 1813 was 43 sergeants, 22 drummers and 760 rank and file. One officer (Lieutenant James Butler) and 68 other ranks had died during the year, while 54 men were invalided to England.

On 10th October 1813 Rollo Gillespie, now a major-general, embarked for Bengal, and so it was his successor, Major-General Miles Nightingall, who commanded the next major expedition from Java. This was to the north coast of the island of Bali, where the Rajah of Buleleng, then called Baliling, had defied British supremacy. The port of Buleleng was at the centre of a trade in slaves and opium, and of piracy, and Raffles' attempt to abolish slavery triggered the hostility of the raja, who had attacked ports on the east coast of Java and captured an armed British boat.

On 25th March 1814 the headquarters and four companies of the 59th Regiment embarked at Batavia on board the transport *Fleetwood*. They sailed the same day for Sourabaya, the easternmost station of Java, which had been appointed as the rendezvous for the expedition. They arrived and landed on 8th April, and marched to a cantonment at De Noyo, some four miles inland, where they were quartered.

On the 13th, Major-General Nightingall and Lieutenant-Colonel McLeod landed at Sourabaya, together with the Light and Rifle Companies of the 59th and a detachment of artillery. The 78th arrived on the 17th, and on the 30th, both regiments re-embarked and sailed eastward for Panarookan, a safe harbour nearly opposite to that part of Bali which was the expedition's objective. The voyage of 59th on the *Fleetwood*, as described in the diary of Lieutenant and Adjutant James Chadwick, was a chain of mishaps from the start due to an ignorant captain and a bad crew:

'The *Fleetwood* went aground coming out of Sourabaya, and when we got to within a few miles of Panarookan she ran in between two rocks, and we had to send 400 men on shore to try if she would refloat. It was all in vain. Towards evening it appeared that the ship was left high and dry. I remained on board with Col McGregor until the captain said he was sure she could not be made to float again. Baggage was taken out of her and we went off with the Grenadier Company in small Madeira boats, and continued knocking about at the mercy of the waves until towards morning, when the *Drummond* picked us up.

'Curse on the old ship *Fleetwood* – On the 5th May, 1814, she was pushed off from the berth she had taken upon the 12th. We were again sent on board her and sailed for Bali, as if it were done purposely to try our nerves. We ran aground again on the 13th while at sea, and had to send all the men off to different ships of the fleet, where they remained until the bewitched old ship thought it proper to float again.'[899]

Whilst at Panarookan the British troops were joined by two Bengal battalions and a Javanese corps, and were brigaded, the Advance under Lieutenant-Colonel McLeod of the 59th and the Reserve commanded by Colonel Alexander Adams of the 78th. The expedition sailed on the 12th and anchored off Buleleng on the 14th May.

'The troops landed on the morning of the 15th without any opposition. Colonel Adams' brigade marched up two miles from the beach, and took post at the Cratan, or fortified residence of the Raja: an oblong measuring 180 yards by 140, the walls being of sun dried bricks, 30 feet high, and from 8 to 10 feet thick, with no flank defences nor ditch.[900] Lieut.-Colonel McLeod's brigade occupied the village on the beach: its chief defence was in a shoal, which runs out nearly two hundred and sixty yards from its western extremity.

---

[899] According to the *Regimental Record*, Captain Green of the *Fleetwood* contrived to strike a ledge of rocks at midnight on 12th May, putting the ship in 'extreme danger'.
[900] The Raja's palace was in the town of Singaraja, the capital of Buleleng.

'When the troops marched into this village, they found the Raja, Wayang Carang Assang,' [Gusti Gede Karang] 'sitting in the street with the General, attended by several hundred followers, armed with match and firelocks in excellent order manufactured by themselves at the Cratan; the remaining and most numerous part of the Raja's people were armed with spears from 12 to 20 feet long, many of the shafts of which were hollowed, for the purpose of blowing the small poisoned arrows so much used by the natives of all these islands in killing game for food as well as in war… The number of the Raja's attendants might be from 2,000 to 2,500.

'He solemnly disclaimed all intention of hostility, laying the blame of the capture of the small British vessel which was the immediate cause of this visit, upon his younger brother, the Raja Moodah, who fled at our approach, and offering to make any and every atonement required of him.

'Mean time, a report from Colonel Adams stated that several thousand natives had been employed during the whole night of the 16th removing boxes and other property from the Cratan. The boxes were, of course, said by the soldiers to contain treasure; and much discontent consequently arose among them in thus being deprived of the prize money they already considered their own. Irritation was likewise created by the extreme boldness, not to say insolence, of the Raja's followers in the village.'[901]

Lieutenant James Chadwick shared in the men's irritation, feeling that they had landed 'not to add fresh laurels to British glory, but literally to be played upon by a set of rascals who were allowed to come round us in great numbers, very well armed, with Tower firelocks and blunderbusses, and using all possible means to make us sensible of the very great contempt they had for us. I saw one pitiful looking rascal ask a lieutenant-colonel of ours to light his cheroot for him, and another ragamuffin went to where this field officer had got in from the sun and ordered him to get up directly and walk out, saying that the house belonged to the Rajah, meaning the scoundrel we had come to punish.'

It was very obvious that the smallest incident could result in open conflict, but despite provocation the troops maintained 'admirable conduct and discipline,' and every precaution was taken against surprise attack. From the 15th to the 20th, Lieutenant-Colonel McLeod's brigade bivouacked in the village street and on the beach, remaining every night on extreme alert, half the men standing with arms in their hands while the other half rested. Information was received on the 17th that there would certainly be an attack that night, but although crowds of armed men congregated around the Raja's palace, in the event nothing serious occurred: it was understood that the local brahmins had decided that the time was not propitious.

As the timely submission of the Raja had averted military action, on 19th May the British force began to re-embark. 'God knows what good we did at Bali,' complained Chadwick, but Major-General Nightingall was satisfied that, had it been necessary to resort to hostilities, his soldiers would have performed well. He thanked the troops for their 'admirable conduct and discipline,' noting that 'not a single complaint of any kind has been made to him from any quarter' throughout the operation.

Most of the troops then returned to Java, but there was further work for Nightingall, who sailed on the 20th for Macassar on the island of Celebes, and with him went Alexander McLeod and the 59th.

Expedition to Macassar, Celebes 1814

The Raja of Boni, on the island of Celebes, had refused reparations to Britain for frequent acts of hostility, including piracy and slaving. On 2nd June 1814, Major-General Nightingall reached Macassar, where the Raja had a palace, with just two transports, carrying part of the 59th, the Light and Rifle Companies of the 78th and a few sepoys, the rest of the convoy having been dispersed by bad weather. He then occupied Fort Rotterdam, a 17th-century Dutch stronghold built close to the beach.

The account of the subsequent action in the *Regimental Record* is clearly written by a participant, quite possibly by George McGregor himself. Having described the fort in some detail, the regimental narrative describes the adjacent settlements and routes:

'The Dutch town is on the north side of the Fort, and the Malay town on the south side, each being about 150 yards from it. The Dutch town has a wall round it. Beyond the Dutch town, and nearly a continuation of it

---

[901] Manuscript *Regimental Record of Service, 59th Foot*.

along the beach to the north, is the Booghis [Bugis, or Buginese] town and the palace of their chief, the Raja of Boni, distant from the Fort about a mile and a half. They are stockaded with a strong palisade all round, but have no other defence. One road to the palace, or Cratan as it was termed, leads through a narrow lane between the sea and the town and along the beach; the other takes a circuit to the eastward, passing close to the Redoubt [an outwork about 800 yards east of Fort Rotterdam] and round the wall of the Dutch town, turning to the left and having an open country on the right flank all the way to the palace. Lieutenant-Colonel McGregor and Adjutant Chadwick examined this road on the morning of the 6th of June, having ridden that way up to the palace gate unmolested, and returned to the town by the seaside; but it was not known to the Resident and Commandant of Macassar that any such road existed.'

That night Captain Joseph Creighton arrived on the *Minerva* transport with a missing eighty-strong detachment of the 59th. This was a most welcome reinforcement, for bad weather had dispersed the expedition's ships, and 172 of the Bengal European Regiment and 220 Bengal sepoys had not reached Macassar, reducing the British force, including the fort garrison, to under six hundred men. There was also a force of local auxiliaries, but these, according to the regimental account, 'did infinite mischief... as the enemy had discovered and adopted their distinguishing badge, viz. a piece of white cloth round the arm.'

The Raja, Aroug Polacca, refused the terms offered to him, and having assembled some three thousand men, he daily menaced the fort. As all attempts at substantive negotiation had failed, and the Raja's sole intent appeared to be to gain time, Nightingall resolved to attack him at dawn on 7th June. First, though, he sent an ultimatum, informing the Raja that he had ten hours to agree to terms, otherwise hostilities would commence. The Raja's reply was evasive, and so the 59th and 78th formed a column of attack before daylight, under the command of Lieutenant-Colonel McLeod, and set off at precisely the time notified to the Raja. The *Regimental Record* tells the story:

'The column moved from Fort Rotterdam by the road leading through the town, along the beach. The Commander of the Forces saw us move off, and gave his final instructions to Lieutenant Colonel McLeod, who put himself at the head of this small party and proceeded to attack the enemy, who were posted behind the stockade already mentioned and were about 4,000 or 4,500 in number, armed with muskets and blunderbusses in very good order, and some with spears and krisses only, but very few were without firearms.

'These kept up a heavy fire for a very short time, from rear and both flanks of the column, under complete cover on the right by the houses, and on the left by several boats hauled up on the beach. Captain [Francis] Fuller, who commanded the Rear Guard, consisting of 30 Europeans (59th) and two guns, dispersed the attack from the rear with the loss of his sergeant killed and three men wounded; and Lieutenant [John Pyne] Pennefather, with a section of the Grenadiers [59th], cleared the boats on the left flank. The Rifle Company moved to the right and extended among the houses: the march of the little column was not impeded.

'The Raja made no stand; but from the crowd around his palace the loss of the enemy was considerable for the short time they remained. They carried off all their wounded, and only 60 or 65 dead persons were found on the ground. Our loss was one sergeant killed and 17 wounded, most of whom afterwards died of lockjaw.[902]

'Orders were previously been given by General Nightingall to burn the palace and the town, and it was done accordingly, with all their valuable effects. The Raja had an immense accumulation of European and China clothes, services of table glass, valuable telescopes, &c, and every house in the town contained webs of the Bhoogies tartan, so prized in the East; for the Wajeb merchants who inhabit this town are all weavers as well as traders and pirates. These two last professions are always united here. The 59th were ordered to remain until all the houses were set on fire. They returned to Fort Rotterdam about midday.'

James Chadwick, Adjutant of the 59th, left his own impressions of the march of McLeod's column on 7th June:

'As we passed along there were a number of armed people drawn up on each side of the street. We were told they were our friends, and they all salaamed to us very quietly and seemingly with great respect. No sooner had we got clear of them than they fired after us and rushed in on the rear of the column. This was quite

---

[902] Private John McDonald of the 59th, a veteran of the 73rd and 94th who had served at the storming of Seringapatam in 1799 and in the Mahratta Wars of 1803-5, was listed as killed in action on 7th June 1814, and Privates Benjamin Spatton and Brian Dunn died of their wounds on 14th and 18th June respectively.

unexpected. The action then became general, but they soon found that it was not those despicable wretches the Dutch they were now fighting with, for our men very soon took ample vengeance on them for the nineteen poor fellows that fell in the first onset. As we moved on we were completely hemmed up by the enemy, who kept up an irregular fire on us.

'They fled directly that we had taken possession of the palace, and finding it ineffectual to follow [them], the place was given up to plunder for a short time, and then the whole town, &c, set on fire.'

The following General Order was issued by General Nightingall at Macassar on 7th June 1814:

'The Commander of the Forces congratulates the troops on the success of the assault which took place at daylight this morning on the town and residence of the Raja of Boni. The rapid advance through the several barriers, and the gallantry displayed by every officer and soldier in the attack, is highly creditable and is an additional proof that nothing can withstand the bravery and discipline of British troops when led by distinguished officers. To Lieutenant Colonel McLeod, who commanded and led the column, the Major General is particularly indebted; not only for his able and officer-like conduct during the action, but also for the valuable advice, and friendly assistance which he has so handsomely offered throughout this service, and which the Major General will recollect with the utmost satisfaction. The conduct of every officer engaged has been so eminently conspicuous that it is impossible to particularise any individual by name.'

However, the Order goes on to 'particularise' as follows:

'The gallant and spirited manner in which H.M.'s 59th Regt., the Light Battalion and the detachment of Bengal Volunteers were led into action by Lt. Col. McGregor of H.M.'s 59th Foot, Capt. Cameron of the 78th Regt., and Lt. Watson of the 6th Volunteer Battalion is so highly creditable to those officers as to call for the particular approbation of the Commander of the Forces… Nor can the Major General omit to record his entire approbation of the conduct of Captain Fuller of the 59th Regt., in command of the Reserve, who by his judicious and spirited conduct checked the advance of a party which had got in rear of the column.'

That night the troops were turned out to extinguish the fires they had lit in the morning, which had spread to the vicinity of the Dutch town.

The Raja escaped in disguise and fled into the interior. His followers had retreated to the north and north-east, and their track as far as the eye could see was marked for two days by burning villages. There was no immediate pursuit, but on the 9th, Lieutenant-Colonels McLeod and McGregor were sent in search of the Raja with four hundred of the 59th and 78th, as recalled by James Chadwick:

'About eleven o'clock on the 9th [we] received orders to be in readiness to march in an hour, which we did, and embarked on board prows of various kinds and sizes, in which we went up the river [Kaimba] for some distance, and disembarked on the right bank of it at half past four in the evening. Marched about twelve miles, and halted in the midst of paddy fields, where we bivouacked until one o'clock next morning when we commenced a most tiresome and disagreeable march through paddy grounds, in which we were sometimes above the knee. We continued this kind of marching until nine o'clock next morning, at which time we arrived at Fort Maros[903] and heard that the report which had been spread about the Raja of Boni were false, as he had not been near that part of the country. The men were much fatigued.[904]

Next day McLeod's force marched out five miles to the Raja's country palace, which was much larger than the one at Macassar, but the place was deserted and the villages were on fire in every direction. The German commandant of Fort Maros[905] could offer no information about the Raja, so on 12th June McLeod abandoned the fruitless pursuit and returned to Fort Rotterdam, gliding down-river all the way to the sea, then coasting back to Macassar.

---

[903] *The Regimental Record* notes, with some irritation, that 'the fort is built close to the bank, about twelve miles from the mouth of the river, up which we might have come all the way in our boats if Captain Phillips, the Resident [at Macassar], who accompanied us, had any information respecting the country or the enemy.'

[904] There may have been some opposition, for Sergeant William Wilson was recorded as wounded in the left arm at the taking of Fort Maros, 8th (sic) June 1814. Enlisted into the 59th in 1790, he was a veteran of the Carib War on St. Vincent.

[905] The garrison of this outpost, which was in a ruinous state, consisted of 20 Amboynese commanded by a German, who had been taken prisoner by the British in Java, having been taken before that by the French in the Tyrol, where he had been a corporal in the Austrian Army.

'This trip being without the smallest service to our cause, was likely to prove very alarming to our Regiment,' wrote James Chadwick, 'as both men and officers were daily going into the sick report, and from thirteen sick (the number landed with) it was increased to ninety-three in four days.'

On the 30th of June, a force of some four hundred men under Captain Cameron, 78th, including the Light and Rifle Companies of the 59th, sailed south against the Raja of Balicombo. They landed at Balicombo on 4th July and, according to *The Regimental Record*, 'After a most fatiguing march of two days through swamps, jungles and every other natural impediment, they succeeded in capturing the Raja and the whole of his force.' Subsequently, 'the Raja and one of his principal chiefs were put to death in attempting to murder the sentry placed over them during the night,' The detachment returned on 11th July to Macassar, where Captain David Graham of the 59th and his two companies were highly praised in Brigade Orders.

The 59th embarked for Java on 16th July, and Lieutenant and Adjutant James Chadwick was heartily glad to depart:

'We were indeed rejoiced to quit Celebes, where we had nothing but constant sickness amongst men and officers. There was one large ship in which all the sick were sent, and though the ship I was in did not take one sick man on board, three days after we sailed we had twenty-two in the sick report, and almost every man in the ship complained.'

On their return to Java, the 1st/59th landed at Samarang and marched eight miles up a very steep ascent to a new cantonment at Serondol, where they were quartered until their return to India in 1815. The cantonment was delightfully situated, but the 59th continued very sickly as a result of the Macassar expedition.

'During the first three months after our arrival,' wrote James Chadwick, 'the Regiment lost upwards of sixty men, not including twenty invalids,' while twenty officers were dangerously ill at Macassar or later, most with fever and dysentery, and Chadwick was one of only three officers who remained fit for duty throughout. On Christmas Day 1814 the Battalion numbered 37 sergeants, 21 drummers and 674 rank and file, 99 men having died in the course of the year. Only seven men were received from England that year, for the 2nd/59th were heavily engaged in Spain.

Alexander McLeod returned to Batavia to command the Western Division of the Army in Java, but went home in December to recover his health, much to the regret of both the regiment and his superior officers. A General Order was issued at Weltevreden on 10th December 1814:

'Major General Nightingall most sincerely laments, both on public and private grounds, that ill health has obliged Lt. Col. McLeod to return to England. He cannot allow that gallant and distinguished officer to leave a Colony where his services are so well known and appreciated without once more publicly recording the high sense he will ever entertain of the able assistance he has uniformly derived from his talents and experience, and although the Major General has repeatedly attempted to do justice to his merits on various occasions, he will not fail to embrace the first opportunity of again drawing the attention of His Excellency the Right Honourable the Commander in Chief to the truly valuable services which he has so often rendered in this Colony and its dependencies, where his name will ever be remembered with pride and pleasure by every soldier who had had the happiness to serve under him.'

It is sad to relate that despite this fulsome recommendation for promotion, and his frequent active service commands at brigade level, it was 12th August 1819 before Alexander McLeod belatedly received the brevet rank of Colonel, in which rank he died at Dinapore, India, still in command of the 59th, on 27th March 1821.

George McGregor was also absent, in command of the Eastern Division of Java, so Brevet-Lieutenant-Colonel Matthew Shawe, a very experienced officer, formerly of the 74th, who had joined from England on 24th July 1814, took over the 59th for the last few months of their tour on the island of Java[906]. James Chadwick,

---

[906] Matthew Shawe had joined the 59th from the 74th (Highland) Regiment in June 1813 on promotion to major. He had served as a young subaltern in the First Mahratta War, 1803-05, seeing action at Ahmednuggur, Assaye, Argaum, Gawilghur and Chandore, and then as a captain in the Peninsula 1810-12, serving at Busaco, the pursuit of Massena, Fuentes d'Onoro, El Bodon, Ciudad Rodrigo and Badajoz, where he was seriously wounded leading a detachment at the storming of Fort Picurina, 26th March 1812, for which he was mentioned in Wellington's dispatch and appointed CB. He did not remain long with the 59th, and indeed his biographical note in *The Royal Military Calendar, 1820* is completely silent about his period of command in Java. In April 1817 he was promoted to a substantive lieutenant-colonelcy in the 84th Foot, and he died in Burma on 11th April 1826 in command of the 87th Regiment.

promoted to captain on his return from Macassar, also left the Battalion when, on 24th January 1815, he was appointed aide-de-camp to Sir Miles Nightingall. He departed with mixed feelings:

'I took leave of my dear friends and brother officers of the 59th – a regiment which, so help me God, nothing would have induced me to quit but the idea of getting from under the command of an upstart tyrant who made it his whole study to annoy the officers of that Corps, which but a few years before was the envied and crack Corps of India; envied for having two such officers as Gibbs and McLeod at its head, and with them what Corps could not be brought to the highest state of discipline and brotherly regard.'

In July 1815, the 1st/59th embarked for Calcutta. The following is an extract from a letter, dated Weltevreden, 22nd June 1815, addressed to Lieutenant-Colonel McGregor:

'On the approaching departure of H.M. 59th Regiment the Commander of the Forces conceives it to be due to that distinguished Corps to record the sense he entertains of its conduct and services. The high reputation that accompanied it to India has been uniformly and gallantly sustained, but the glory it has acquired in this colony is alone sufficient to secure a distinguished place for H.M. 59th Regiment in the annals of the British Army.'

Lieutenant-Colonel Alexander Hamilton CB, Commanding Officer 30th 1812-1829 wounded at Quatre Bras

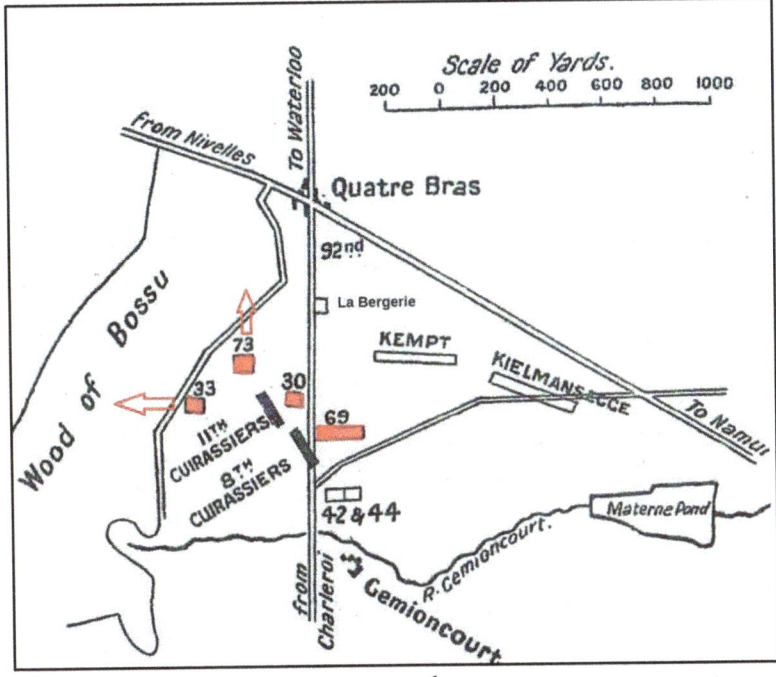

Quatre Bras at about 7 pm 16th June 1815 showing the attack of Kellerman's Cuirassiers on Halkett's brigade when the 69th were broken & the 33rd & 73rd retired into the Bois de Bossu while the 30th stood firm

Major Morris William Bailey commanded the 30th at Waterloo

James Elkington, Surgeon to the 30th at Quatre Bras & Waterloo

Lieutenant Purefoy 'Bombproof' Lockwood, 30th a Peninsula veteran, severely wounded at Quatre Bras

Left: Gemioncourt Farm, captured by the 30th at the end of the Battle of Quatre Bras

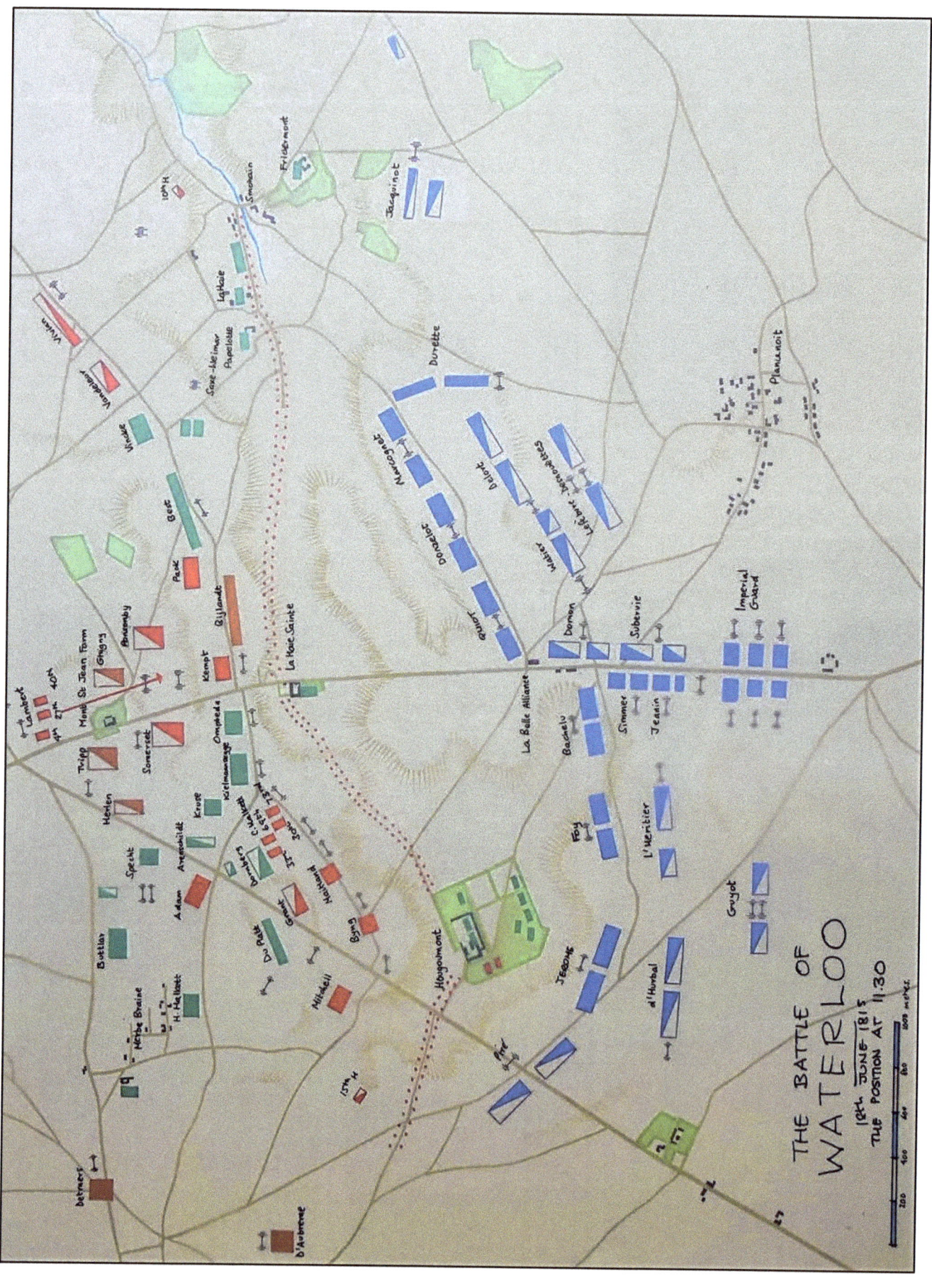

THE BATTLE OF WATERLOO

18th JUNE 1815
THE POSITION AT 11.30

Showing positions of the 30th & 40th Regiments at the start of the battle

French cavalry attack on the 30th & & 73rd square, Waterloo
(73rd incorrectly depicted in highland dress)

Officer & Private 30th Foot, 1815

Major Thomas Chambers, 30th

Sergeant
Grenadier
Company
40th, 1815

Major Edward Macready
(ensign 30th at Waterloo)

Captain Robert Howard, 30th

Major Arthur Heyland, 40th

Left: Contemporary view of the field of Waterloo looking towards the French lines from the position occupied by the 30th Regiment towards the evening of 18th June 1815. This was the ground over which the Imperial Guard advanced from the hollow (centre left) beyond La Haie Sainte and which was later occupied by Donzelot's Division

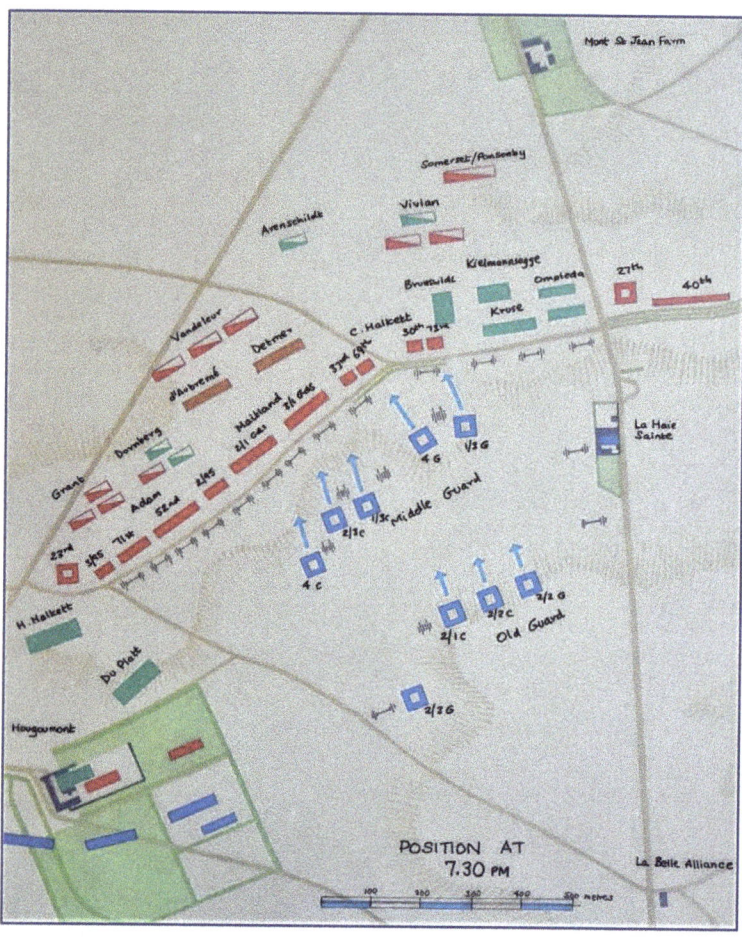

WATERLOO Advance of the Imperial Guard, of which the first and largest Grenadier column (1st/3rd), led by Marshal Ney, was routed by the 30th and 73rd Regiments

View towards Hougoumont (in woods) from Wellington's right centre – near where the 30th stood towards the evening of the 18th – showimg (right) the 'Lion' spur

View towards La Haie Sainte from the final position of the 40th Foot who were engaged with French infantry on the rising ground to the left of the road, then took part in the capture of the farm during Wellington's final advance to La Belle Alliance (building in the background)

Chapter XI:
The Waterloo Campaign

Mobilisation & Concentration (30th, 40th, 59th & 81st) – 'an Infamous Army' – Battle of Quatre Bras (30th) – Withdrawal to Waterloo (30th) & Halle (59th) – 40th March to Waterloo – the Field of Waterloo – Opening Moves (30th & 40th) – French Cavalry Attack (30th & 40th) – Crisis in the Centre (30th & 40th) – Defeat of the Imperial Guard (30th) – General Allied Advance (30th & 40th) – After the Battle – Advance on Paris (30th, 40th & 59th) & Storming of Cambrai (59th)

Buonaparte Returns

The 2nd Battalions of the 30th and 81st Regiments were still in garrison at Antwerp, in daily expectation of orders for disbandment, when on 9th March 1815 they heard that Napoleon Buonaparte had escaped from Elba and, having landed near Cannes on the 1st of that month, was making a triumphant progress to Paris. To Ensign Edward Macready of the 30th, aged sixteen and anticipating a premature end to his military career, the news was not unwelcome.

'We soon after heard of Ney's treachery, and subsequently of the unimpeded flight of the sacred eagle from steeple to steeple till it rested on the turrets of Notre Dame… It strikes me that Napoleon's return must have been an arranged plan, and fully expected by a great portion of the French Army. The saying of *'la violette, elle reparaitra au printemps,'* the movements among the military, many of whom appeared at Antwerp in full uniform, and vanished some days before we knew the cause, together with other according circumstances, confirm my opinion. However, the effect was too agreeable to allow me to trouble my head about the cause, as it again opened the path that leads to the goal of a soldier's ambition – promotion or a turf pillow.'

Surgeon James Elkington of the 30th, an experienced campaigner who had also noted the Buonapartist sentiments of the French troops, made some profitable predictions: 'I laid two wagers of £5 each, one with Colonel Bailey and one with Captain Howard; that Napoleon would reach Paris without firing a shot, and secondly, that in six months the Allied armies would be in Paris.'[907]

'The military were all bustle,' wrote Macready. 'We had inlying and outlying pickets, fatigue parties loading stores for the frontiers, guards at every turn, guns and tumbrils rattling through the streets, and all the fuss and confusion of a commencing campaign. The officers were three nights in a week on duty, and the men had hardly a night in bed. Orders were given to fire on loiterers about the ramparts, and to apprehend all suspicious-looking personages, many of whom were sent off daily. The Citadel was provisioned for a year and, on account of the scarcity of artillerymen, one hundred flankers from each British corps were exercised at the guns. [Lieutenant Thomas] Moneypenny and I volunteered the command of our quarter. In fact, we were very soon in a very respectable state of defence, and old Crawford's[908] eyes used to glisten as he stalked about the works and watched our progress.

'Our only wish now was to be ordered forward, which we constantly expected, as the Regiment had appeared in orders as a part of Sir C[olin] Halkett's brigade, then in the Walloon [country]. The Duke of Cambridge passed through Antwerp and reviewed the garrison, and soon after our Corps was minutely inspected by Sir H[enry]. Clinton. The report of the latter, together with the repeated applications of Halkett, caused the wished-for order to appear, and we marched on the 8th April.

'Under other circumstances we should have left Antwerp with regret. Many had formed attachments and were sincerely loved by the Anversoises. Poor creatures, it was pitiable to see several of them, far advanced in

---

[907] Extracts from Journal of Surgeon James Goodall Elkington in the *XXX Journal*, June 1911, p. 12.
[908] Colonel Robert Crawford, late 73rd Foot, was appointed Commandant of the Citadel of Antwerp on 2 September 1814, remaining there throughout the Waterloo campaign when the citadel became the principal supply depot for Wellington's army.

their pregnancies, following our rascals and weeping over the reprobates, who either laughed at their nonsense (as they called it) or replied to their tears by a joking compliment [to] their beauty. The girls cried, their relatives swore, and our comrades of the 81st gave us three cheers as we defiled over the drawbridge.'[909]

The 30th marched to Malines that day, and on through their old billet at Vilvorde, where 'our old friends received us with shouts of congratulation,' and on the 10th reached Brussels, where the Duke of Wellington had arrived five days earlier to assume command of what, in one of his unguarded remarks, he harshly dismissed on 8th May as 'an infamous army.'

There was indeed some justice in his characteristically pithy and acerbic summary. He had taken over an Anglo-Netherlands force which, in terms of both numbers and capability, fell well short of his assessed need and of his old Peninsula army. Consisting of British, Dutch and Belgians, and of Germans from Brunswick, Nassau and Hanover, by June some 45% of this force was German-speaking and only 36% British. A majority of the Dutch/Belgian and German units, regular, militia and landwehr, were comparatively recently raised, and there were doubts over their morale and state of training. Many of the Belgians had formerly marched with Napoleon, and their loyalty was understandably suspect.

The reliable backbone of the Allied army would be twenty-six thousand British troops and nearly seven thousand of the King's German Legion, part of the British Army since 1803, but even the British units were of variable experience. Whilst all nine of the light cavalry regiments had been with Wellington in the Peninsula, only one of the seven heavies (the 1st Royal Dragoons) had seen recent active service. All but four of the twenty-one British line infantry and rifle battalions who fought at Waterloo had served in the Peninsula, the exceptions being the 3rd/14th, 33rd, 2nd/69th and 2nd/73rd, but only one of the four Guards battalions (the 2nd Coldstream) had participated as a complete unit in Wellington's Peninsula campaigns.

In Brussels, Macready observed that Belgian support for the Allies was somewhat equivocal: 'Corps of Dutch and Belgian troops were every day passing thro' the city. The former bodies seemed animated with a favorable feeling to the Allied cause, but the latter neither admired their king nor relished the idea of fighting their old comrades. *"La brave jeunesse Belge"*, as the proclamations called these gentry, deserted constantly, and when speaking of the French assured us *"qu'ils se battirent comme des demons."*'

Whilst in Brussels, the 30th received a final reinforcement on 13th April when Lieutenant Francis Tincombe's draft joined with Ensigns John James and James Bullen, both fated to die at Waterloo, two drummers, two corporals and 27 privates, completing the Battalion, almost[910], to the strength of 44 officers and 615 rank and file with which it entered the campaign. This total included all men in the country, but the number present and fit for duty on 25th May was 34 sergeants, 14 drummers and 570 rank and file. On taking the field, an officers' guard under Lieutenant John Roe (1) was left to look after regimental baggage, and the men in charge of transport, ammunition and stores would not have been in the ranks, while Lieutenant Nevill was attached to the Engineers. The 30th, therefore, cannot have taken the field with more than the 42 other officers, 36 staff-sergeants and sergeants, 36 corporals, 13 drummers and 533 privates listed on the Waterloo Medal Roll. According to Macready the number of rank and file was about 510, and he must have had good reason for saying so.

After three weeks in Brussels, the 30th marched on 26th April to Halle, where they joined Major-General Sir Colin Halkett's brigade, part of Lieutenant-General Count Charles Alten's 3rd Division.[911] Apart from the 30th, this brigade consisted of three of the youngest and least experienced British battalions, the 33rd, 2nd/69th and 2nd/73rd. All three had most recently campaigned with Graham in Holland, where the 33rd and 69th had been

---

[909] Captain Richard Machell of the 30th remained as Town Major at Antwerp, where Lieutenant Andrew Baillie was also on the staff, while Ensign Joseph Berrige was on duty at Ostend, the principal port on the army's lines of communication.

[910] One officer was still absent: Captain James Finucane had visited France during the peace and had nearly become a prisoner of war on the return of Napoleon. It was impossible to reach the Regiment by crossing the Belgian frontier, but he managed to find a ship sailing from Bordeaux to Ostend and was able to rejoin on 17th May.

[911] Alten, a veteran of the King's German Legion, was the only Hanoverian to command a British division, and had led the Light Division in the Peninsula. His selection to command the 3rd 'British' Division was a good choice, for two out of its three brigades were German (King's German Legion and Hanoverian). Halkett, too, was particularly suited to this formation: although a Scot, his service had almost exclusively been with the King's German Legion, with whom he did good service in Spain.

involved in the debacle at Bergen-op-Zoom and the 73rd had fought well at Ghorde and Merxem, but none of them had served in the Peninsula.

The 2nd/30th, by contrast, was by any measure a veteran battalion: the average private soldier was aged 27 with five years in the ranks, most of which would have been spent on active service.[912] The October 1815 Inspection Return records that 412 of the 2nd/30th soldiers then had more than five years' service, and none had served for less than two years, while some two-thirds of the Battalion's Waterloo casualties were owed prize money for actions in the Peninsula in 1812. The average height of the Battalion in 1815 was five foot seven inches, exactly the same as their successors of The Lancashire Regiment 150 years later. Such men would form the backbone of Wellington's army in the Waterloo campaign, and he fully appreciated their worth. Walking one day in the Park, Brussels, he drew attention to a British infantryman gawping at the statuary, saying, 'There – it all depends on that article whether we do the business or not. Give me enough of it and I am sure.'

In command of the 30th was Alexander Hamilton, a much-respected old campaigner who had first faced Buonaparte at Toulon in 1793. Since then, he had served with distinction under Abercromby, Nelson, Wellington and Graham. A sound trainer and much-respected commander, Hamilton took good care of his men, and he was well supported by experienced officers, including four of field rank, and by battle-hardened non-commissioned officers.

Macready was delighted to return to the Light Company, an unusual honour for an ensign. Following the arrival of Tincombe's draft, the company was completed to sixty, 'as handsome and active fellows as ever stepped.'

'As we marched them to and from parade, every one stopped to admire them, and there was quite a murmur of '*Ils sont des chasseurs, jolis garçons, nets, sveltes.*' They were the prettiest company I ever looked at. "Ashes to ashes; dust to dust" – poor fellows! A few years have left little of this gallant band but recollections so dear and deep that time only renders them more indelible.'

The 30th were quartered from 27th April until 4th May in the villages of Petit Roeulx and Steinkirk, just north of Soignies, in the 3rd Division concentration area. It was at Steinkirk, where their predecessors of Castleton's Regiment had seen action in 1692, that Macready witnessed an extraordinary scene:

'As some of us were passing the door of the Burgomaster's on the day of our arrival, we were surprised to hear an infernal uproar and, as we listened to the noise, could plainly distinguish the voice of our French Bandmaster overwhelming the terrified magistrate with his eloquence. '*Ventre bleu – chez un cordonnier! Sacre nom! Mettre un homme avec un habit comme ceci chez un cordonnier! Mon Colonel vous écrasera!*' At this moment he sprang down the steps, saluted us with a smile, and walked over to one of the best houses in the village. He had learned this style of conversation in Germany and Prussia.'

On 4th May the 30th were present near Lens for an inspection of the 1st Corps by Prince William of Orange, otherwise known as 'Slender Billy,' titular second-in-command of the Allied army, and were then quartered in the hamlet of Montignies-lez-Lens. On the 10th the 2nd/30th, together with the 33rd, moved to the town of Soignies, on the high road from Mons to Brussels, which was seen as a likely French line of advance.

Training up to division and even corps level took place twice a week on Casteau Heath, near Mons, to reach which the 30th marched down the road which on August 1914 rang with the British Army's first shots of the Great War. Macready complained that they were 'drilled out of all patience':

'These parades, with our return to quarters, often lasted from three in the morning to six in the afternoon. Our men sometimes fainted, and more frequently pretended to faint, from heat and fatigue; so much so that it became a standing trick, if I may be allowed the expression, for some old hand to drop as the Prince passed the line. This had always a good effect, and we soon marched home.

We used to be much diverted by the activity and perseverance of the little beggar boys, who accompanied us in swarms to these exercises and would run for miles, turning over and over before us. They were almost naked,

---

[912] By way of comparison, the 28th, another acknowledged 'Old Spanish Army' battalion, had 371 soldiers with more than five years' service, while the newly-raised 3rd/14th included 14 officers and 300 men under the age of twenty.

and between every somersault would roar out '*Vivent les Anglais! – Vive le Roi de France! – Donnez-moi un sou, Monsieur – Jacques, regardez le joli officier! – Vive le Prince d'Orange! – Vive les Hanoveriens! – Ah, qu'il est beau – Sacre nom, Messieurs le Francais, vous serez joliment étrillés! – Vive les Anglais! – un sou, Monsieur!*' We generally put a stop to their good wishes for every legitimate sovereign and every nation in the alliance by making them unanimously shout '*Vive l'Empereur*' and pitching a franc amongst fifty of them.'

Some of the officers, including Elkington and Macready, found time on the 28th to attend a grand review of the British cavalry at Grammont, while young Macready rode over to Horrues to pay court to Fanny, the sixteen-year-old daughter of his relative, Major Lewis Watson of the 69th.

When the 30th were quarteed at Montignies, a hamlet between Soignies and Lens, the Light Company subalterns, Macready, Pratt and Rumley, were billeted on a rich and simple farmer, with a beautiful daughter who rebuffed their advances. 'I was rather sceptical as to the invincibility of her virtue,' young Macready confided to his Journal, 'and found out that Pratt had his doubts as we jostled each other at her bedroom door one night; but neither of us were made happy.'

Among the next to take the field were the 2nd/59th, veterans of Vitoria, San Sebastian and the Nive, who were at Warrenpoint, near Newry, when the news broke of Buonaparte's escape from Elba. Sailing from Carlingford Lough, the Battalion landed at Deal on 17th April, under the command of Lieutenant- Colonel Henry Austen, and were immediately re-embarked for Ostend, where they landed on the 3rd of May. From that port the 59th boarded large open barges and were towed up the canal through Bruges to Ghent, from where they marched to Oudenarde. There they joined Major-General Johnstone's Brigade of Sir Charles Colville's 4th Division with 35 officers, 40 staff-sergeants and sergeants, 37 corporals, 12 drummers and 408 privates.

It was late April before the 2nd/81st left Antwerp for Brussels, where on 21st May they were transferred to Major-General Sir John Lambert's 10th Brigade, of which the other battalions – 1st/4th, 1st/40th and 1st/27th – had not yet landed in Belgium from America.

The veteran 40th were in fact well on their way. After provisioning at Havana, they had enjoyed a fast passage in pleasant weather, in the course of which they heard from a passing frigate the news of Buonaparte's return.

'It caused no amount of stir aboard,' recalled Sergeant William Lawrence, 'for the young officers, who were looking ravenously forward to promotion, were so rejoiced at the news that they treated all the men to an extra glass of grog, to make everybody as lively as themselves.' The convoy anchored off Spithead on 15th May.

'A signal was raised,' reminisced Lawrence, 'and we fell in on the quarantine ground, hoisting a yellow flag for a doctor to inspect us on board. When he came he found all on board our ship to be in very good condition, which was reported to the general, and the very next morning he signalled to us to weigh anchor and proceed to Flanders; so without setting foot on English ground we again went on our way to meet our common enemy... I left Portsmouth this time with a good deal lighter heart than I had last, being now more used to war and hardships than to peace and plenty, though perhaps I would rather have landed than proceed on this errand; and, indeed, there were many of us who had left wife and children at home who went off with a sad heart.'[913]

The 40th landed at Ostend on 23rd May and, like the 59th, travelled inland by canal barge, arriving on the morning of the 25th at Ghent, where the fugitive King Louis XVIII of France held court. Lieutenant Colonel Henry Thornton did not accompany the Regiment, being required to give evidence at a general court martial in London, so command devolved on Major Fielding Browne. On June 1st, Lieutenant George Hibbert wrote from Ghent to his father in Manchester:

'I wrote to you from Portsmouth Harbour, which letter I presume you have received. We did not disembark there, but proceeded the day after to Ostend, where we arrived after a voyage of about thirty-six hours. We disembarked the day after, and the whole of the regiment was immediately put into large boats and conveyed up the canal to this place. We were landed and sent about six miles off to a small village, on the road to Brussels,

---

[913] On 16th May the 40th were directed by telegraph despatch to proceed to Ostend, to which port the transports sailed on the 18th under convoy of HMS *Bermuda* gun brig. They arrived next day, but disembarkation was delayed by boisterous weather until the 23rd.

called Zeerberghem [Zevergem], but, owing to the regiment wanting refitting with clothing, etc., we were marched back to this place, where we are likely to remain a fortnight. I never saw a more delightful country. This town is one of the best I ever saw; and the country is now like a large garden.

'I never in all my life met with so much hospitality as from the inhabitants. On Sunday last I witnessed as grand a sight as possibly there can be, a procession of the Host. It was owing to some great holiday amongst the Catholics which had been suppressed by Buonaparte, and was revived, for the first time that day. I afterwards went to the Mass, and was within a foot of Louis the 18th and the Duchesse d'Angouleme. He is quite an old, worn-out man; she is very interesting. As you or my brother Sam often have some little excursion in the summer, I think one of you could not have a pleasanter than to cross over from Dover to Ostend, and come and see me here; if not here, we shall not be far off either at Brussels or the neighbourhood. Lord Wellington's army itself will be worth coming to see.

'Since writing this letter I have been induced to unseal it, to inform you of the arrival of the Duke of Wellington in this town, and of the flattering observation he made of our regiment. He spoke to the officer of the guard of the King's palace (Lieutenant [James] Anthony) in a familiar manner, saying, "I am very happy to have the old 40th with me again"; and turning about to the Duke de Grammont, observed to him that the 40th was one of his favourite regiments.

'There is no news here; all is as yet quiet. They say Buonaparte is making great preparations at Paris by fortifying the town.'

Apart from providing the King's Guard, and finding working parties on the fortifications, duties were light at Ghent, and, having excellent quarters, all ranks of the 40th thoroughly enjoyed their stay in the town. On 28th May a detachment consisting of two sergeants and 77 rank and file, under Major Arthur Rowley Heyland, joined from the 2nd Battalion 40th, and as Major Heyland was the senior, he assumed command [914]. Later arrivals at Ghent were Sir John Lambert, on 11th June, and Captain Harry Smith, who had been appointed Lambert's brigade major:

'When we reached Ghent,' recalled Harry Smith, 'we found Sir John Lambert had reached it the day before. Louis XVIII was there, his Court and idlers, and Ghent was in as great a state of excitement as if the Duke of Marlborough was again approaching. I found our Brigade were all New Orleans Regiments – three of the best regiments of the old Army of the Peninsula, the 4th, 27th, and 40th, and the 81st in garrison at Brussels. We were ordered to be in perfect readiness to take the field with the warning we had been so many years accustomed to. During our stay at Ghent we had Brigade parades almost every day, and my General, an ex-Adjutant of the Guards, was most particular in all guard mountings, sentries, and all the correct minutiae of garrison. The three regiments were in beautiful fighting trim.'

The Allied strategic plan was to make a coordinated advance into France with over three quarters of a million men once some two hundred thousand Austrians, followed by a similar number of Russians, had reached the Rhine. Until the arrival of these armies from the east, the smaller Allied armies forming in Belgium would be vulnerable to a pre-emptive French strike. Well aware of this possibility, but uncertain of its direction, Wellington's polyglot army and Marshal Blucher's Prussians occupied widely scattered cantonments along the frontier. The 130,000 Prussians were quartered around Charleroi, Namur and Liège, from where their supply lines ran back to the Rhine, and Wellington's 112,000 troops were stationed from Brussels, Nivelles and Mons in the south and west to Ghent in the north, with lines of communication through Ostend and Antwerp. The Allies maintained an outpost line on the French frontier, but their posture was essentially defensive, waiting and watching.

---

[914] Major Arthur Heyland, a married man aged 33, had rejoined from half-pay for the campaign. Because of high officer casualties in the Peninsula (a total of 75 in the 40th), he had been one of several captains to command the Regiment in action, and had twice been wounded. He also had the distinction, as a young ensign, of having had his first commanding officer, in the 14th Foot, tried by court-martial for high-handed brutality to a soldier.

Wellington was throughout the campaign concerned that Napoleon might attempt to turn his right flank, cutting his supply line to the Channel ports: after all, as in the Peninsula he had charge of Britain's only field army. But he was also determined to maintain close co-operation with the Prussians, and to that end he met with Marshal Blucher in early May, when it was agreed that if Napoleon invaded Belgium the two armies must combine to defeat, him and, on the assumption that the French would attack Wellington first, that the Prussians would march to his assistance.

The Battle of Quatre Bras, 16th June 1815

By 14th June, Napoleon Buonaparte, with 123,000 men of the Armée du Nord, was poised on the French frontier with his centre of gravity opposite Charleroi and just south of the junction between the two Allied armies. He appreciated that a quick victory in Belgium was his only realistic chance of survival through a negotiated peace. Showing for the last time his old organisational and strategic flair, he had seized the initiative with remarkable speed and secrecy, and in classic Napoleonic style had occupied the interior lines. The French Emperor's plan was to penetrate between his adversaries, defeat them separately and capture Brussels. Defeat of the British, his most constant adversaries and paymasters of the Allied coalition, was of prime importance; but contrary to expectations, the weight of his first attack fell on the Prussians.

One of the very first British soldiers to come under fire during the Waterloo campaign, and almost certainly the first infantryman, was Lieutenant Park Percy Nevill of the 30th Foot. Seconded once more to the engineer department, by 10th June he was deployed with the Allied outpost line on the frontier, where Blucher's Prussians were assembling:

'About this time,' he recalled, 'a despatch had arrived from the Duke's headquarters... to say that the Duke expected the enemy would soon advance and attack the Prussian position at Charleroi, and directing us to remain in observation to the last moment.'

'On the 14th of June some French cavalry were seen reconnoitering the Prussian outposts, and on the 15th the Prussians were driven back, crossed the Sambre and Meuse, and occupied Charleroi in force. The French advanced, also crossed those rivers, and skirmished with the Prussians. About 11 a.m. the enemy came on in force, and drove back the Prussians through Charleroi. The Engineer officers were on some high ground, watching the advance of the enemy; they had sent their baggage to the rear on the 14th, and only retained their horses, bridle in hand. Some French Chasseurs had got to our rear, and it was now quite time to be off. We were well mounted, and galloped past them within shot. They called upon us to halt, but we had something else to think of, so heeded them not. They then fired at us, but we were soon out of sight, along with a patrol of the 1st Hussars King's German Legion, who directed us to a road to the extreme right of the British army, on our way to Halle.'[915]

Between 6 and 7 on the evening of the 15th Wellington gave orders for his troops to assemble at the headquarters of their respective divisions and to hold themselves in immediate readiness to march. In Brussels, as recalled by Private Wilcox of the 81st, 'when we was all in bed the news came to the Duke Wellington, when he and a great many of the officers were at a ball the same time, that the French were drawing near, so he ordered the ball to dismiss, and ordered all the bugles and drums in the town to beat to arms, and to be formed in one place by 2 o'clock in the morning, and our Regiment was the first on the ground appointed for the Regiments to assemble. At 4 o'clock they began to march off, and our Regiment was ordered to stop to do the duty of the town and attend the sick and wounded.' Wellington had indeed ordered the 81st, together with Picton's 5th Division and the Hanoverian Brigade of the 6th Division, 'to be in readiness to march from Bruxelles at a moment's notice.'

At Soignies, the 30th were, in Macready's words, 'all in a charming state of anxiety.' Having heard that morning that the Prussian advanced posts had been driven in, they anticipated an early move.

'As a group of us were standing in the square at Soignies discussing the probable events of the approaching campaign, about four o'clock on the evening of the 15th of June, a rumour got afoot that the French had crossed

[915] *Some Recollections in the Life of Lieut.-Col. P. P. Nevill*, p,p. 40-42.

the frontier. We were looking at each other with a sort of half-incredulous and half-apprehensive kind of smile, when General Halkett galloped up, and called out, "Are any Light Infantry officers among you?" "Yes, Sir," said I. "Parade your company in ten minutes on this spot," was his reply, and away I went to arouse the men. I ordered my servant to put the baggage, and a box of light infantry appointments that had just arrived, on my pony, and by the time specified, Rumley, Pratt, and I were on the ground with the Company.

'Lieutenant Colonel Vigoureux[916] was ordered to plant us on picket at a village called Naast, about a league from Soignies. As we marched to our post we met several regiments of our division hurrying to the town; it was evident that the game was afoot. We placed our Company in a large barn, and threw out advanced pickets on the Rouelx and Nivelle roads, communicating by patrols with our old friends the [Hanoverian] Jägers von Kielmansegg[e]. A corporal came in from headquarters about nine o'clock, and told us that the French had certainly advanced and were pressing the Prussians considerably; also that our whole division had entered the town of Soignies, and occupied the Church and other buildings. The night passed quietly.'

Halkett's 5th Brigade had concentrated in Soignies by early evening on the 15th, and when they were joined by the Hanoverians of their division the little town was crowded with some nine thousand troops. The church bell was striking midnight when the drummers beat the *General* preparatory to marching and, according to both Surgeon Elkington and Lieutenant Tincombe, the main body of the 30th Foot marched at 2 a.m. Such was the haste that their detached Light Company had not been called in from Naast.

The 30th was the last battalion of Halkett's Brigade to leave Soignies, and early morning sunshine lit the column as they marched into Braine-le-Comte, from where the regimental baggage was ordered to continue north to Halle. Lieutenant Pattison of the 33rd described the high spirits of the soldiers:

'As the sun began to appear above the horizon, and as we marched through a beautiful and highly cultivated country, everything inspired the troops with life and animation, and the songs of the men, caught up by one company after another, expressed the feelings of a party going to a banquet [rather] than of soldiers marching to a field of blood.'[917]

Tradition has it that the regimental band of the 30th struck up a jaunty marching song, *The Young May Moon*:

Then awake! The heavens look bright, my dear,
'tis never too late for delight, my dear,
and the best of all ways
to lengthen our days
is to steal a few hours from the night, my dear.

By the time the 3rd Division reached Braine-le-Comte they had received orders to march on south to Nivelles. By mid-afternoon the men were sweltering in oppressive heat, their woollen tunics soaked in sweat.

'We commenced our march on the road to Braine-le-Comte, on the Brussels road, and from thence took the road to Nivelles, where we arrived about 1 p.m., and proceeded to a small stream near Houtain-le-Val. Here the men were ordered to cook, but before they had half finished they were ordered forward. There was heavy firing to our front, [and] shortly after the men were put into double quick to keep up with the artillery, that was much wanted. Shortly after 4 p.m. we reached the north of the wood of Bossu [at Quatre Bras]. The men had now been fourteen hours marching.'[918]

Having followed the 30th on their march to Quatre Bras, we must set the scene there with a brief description of the action up to the time of their arrival. Having crossed the frontier on 15th June and pushed the Prussians out of Charleroi, Napoleon had advanced with his main force through Fleurus against the Prussians at Ligny, sending Marshal Ney with two corps and a strong force of cavalry to secure Quatre Bras on the main road from Charleroi

---

[916] Lieutenant-Colonel Charles Vigoureux of the 30th commanded the Light Companies of Halkett's brigade.
[917] *Personal Recollections of the Waterloo Campaign* by Lieutenant Frederick Hope Pattison, printed in the *XXX Journal*, September 1905, p. 6.
[918] Diary of Surgeon James Goodall Elkington, printed in the *XXX Journal*, June 1911, p. 12.

to Brussels. Napoleon's orders to Ney were sketchy and incomplete, imparting little sense of urgency and giving ample scope for future misunderstanding.

The hamlet of Quatre Bras was the designated alarm post for the Nassau-Usingen brigade of Perponcher's 2nd Netherlands Division, the left-hand formation of Wellington's army, and thanks to the prompt anticipatory action of their commander, Prince Bernard of Saxe-Weimar, it was occupied on the afternoon of the 15th by the 2nd Nassau Regiment, whose 2nd Battalion clashed with the Poles of the Imperial Guard Cavalry at Frasnes before falling back half-way to the hamlet. Ney did not pursue, and throughout that night just 4,300 Nassauers and sixteen Dutch guns held the future battlefield as 42,000 Frenchmen assembled to their front.

Quatre Bras is, as the name implies, a cross-roads, where the Charleroi-Brussels chaussée is crossed by that from Nivelles to Namur. Whilst of strategic importance as a main road link between the Allied armies, it was not a natural defensive position. The surrounding country is gently rolling, with a series of low ridges running across the battlefield in an east-north-easterly direction. These conceal much dead ground, while in June 1815 the woods and high crops of ripening rye also hid much movement. The north-south Charleroi chaussée was the French axis of advance. To the west of that road was the extensive Bois de Bossu, since felled, which touched the Nivelles road at its north end and extended south from there for some 2,000 yards, the distance from wood to road widening from 200 yards near Quatre Bras to 500 yards. Moving south down the Charleroi chaussée from the hamlet of Quatre Bras, after 300 yards the farm of La Bergerie is passed on the left, and at half a mile the road cuts through the low ridge of Bati Saint-Bernard, which runs across the centre of the battle area. From there, the ground falls away to a wood-lined stream in a shallow valley, beyond which on the left lies the walled farm of Gémioncourt, 1,200 yards from the cross-roads, and then the heights of the same name and another ridge, the heights of Lairalle. The Namur road runs south-east from Soignies and through Quatre Bras towards the battlefield of Ligny, some 6-8 miles away. At 1,500 yards from Quatre Bras, and just beyond where the Namur road crosses the end of the Bati Saint-Bernard ridge, lay the Bois des Censes and the village of Thyle, forward of which were the farm and hamlet of Piraumont. Finally, between Piraumont and Gémioncourt movement was restricted by the Materne Lake, which in 1815 was larger than more recently.

Wellington rode out from Brussels early on the morning of 16th June, reaching Quatre Bras by 10 a.m. By that time the 2nd Netherlands Division was there in strength, holding a line on the Gémioncourt ridge. There was little evidence of French activity to their front, and so, having made a reconnaissance and approved of the Dutch-Belgian dispositions, the Duke rode on to meet with Blucher near Brye.

Marshal Ney, normally bold to the point of recklessness, had been uncharacteristically indecisive and dilatory in bringing forward and concentrating his troops on the evening of the 15th and morning of the 16th, and had thereby forfeited his best opportunity of a prompt capture of the vital cross-roads. The reasons for this delay remain controversial and uncertain, but Ney's apparently excessive caution may have been in large part caused by Napoleon's imprecise direction and by consequent lack of understanding by Ney of the Emperor's intentions, all compounded by inadequate staff-work.[919] Suffice to say that lack of timely direction resulted in tactical errors on the 16th which contributed in no small measure to French strategic failure.

Even so, when Ney launched his attack at 2 p.m. with just over 10,000 infantry, nearly 2,000 cavalry and thirty guns, he had a very good chance of taking the vital cross-roads from the 7,500 infantry and sixteen guns of the 2nd Netherlands Division before they could be reinforced. The outnumbered Dutch-Belgians fought well but were steadily borne back. The French captured Gémioncourt and Piraumont and started to clear the Bois de Bossu.

By the time Wellington returned from his meeting with Blucher, at around 2.30 to 3 p.m., the situation was critical. Ney had some 20,000 infantry, over 2,500 cavalry and fifty guns to wrest Quatre Bras from the exhausted remnant of Perponcher's division. 'By God,' the Duke later remarked, 'if I had come up five minutes later the battle was lost.'

---

[919] It was only on the evening of the 16th, by which time the battles of Quatre Bras and Ligny were all but over, that the Emperor clearly explained to Ney that his battle at Quatre Bras was of secondary importance to the decisive defeat of the Prussians at Ligny. It was by then too late.

The Allied position was saved by the timely arrival of Picton's 5th Division with the British brigades of Kempt and Pack, and Best's Hanoverians, together with the Duke of Brunswick's contingent and some Dutch/Belgian cavalry. There followed a hard-fought defensive action which, had it not been overshadowed by the battle of Waterloo, would be counted among the British Army's most famous engagements.

Nevertheless, by 5 p.m., a combination of artillery, cavalry and skirmishers had taken a heavy toll on the outnumbered Allies, whose ammunition was running low. Several British squares had been savaged by the French lancers, the Duke of Brunswick had been killed rallying his men, and Ney's infantry had pressed forward through the Bois de Bossu to take the farm of La Bergerie, only to be expelled in a sacrificial charge by the 92nd Highlanders. Both flanks of the Allied line were under severe pressure, while in the centre, Picton's depleted battalions were very exposed. Pack's battered 42nd and 44th, deployed in a combined square on the Bati Saint-Bernard ridge, overlooking Gémioncourt and just to the left of the Charleroi chaussée, were particularly vulnerable. Their left flank was supported by the 28th and Royals of Kempt's brigade, but their right was in the air.

Such, in outline, was the precarious situation of the Allies when Sir Charles Alten's 3rd Division marched up from Houtain-le-Val, their bands playing *The British Grenadiers*. 'We soon came near the place of action,' wrote Lieutenant Francis Tincombe of the 30th, 'and met a great number of Belgic and Dutch cavalry wounded and going to the rear. Our Regiment was in great spirits.'

The men of the 30th, unaware of the stand made by Perponcher's division, viewed with contempt the large numbers of disorganised Dutch-Belgian units and stragglers apparently leaving the battlefield. Macready was later told that 'As our Regiment entered the action, an order was brought to Hamilton to leave his Light Infantry to stop those rascals. Poor Hamilton, in the warmth of his feelings, shouted, "My Light Company is detached, so I can't leave it; but damn them, let them run, we want no cowards here." This was carried to the Prince of Orange, and Hamilton lost the Order of Wilhelm of the Netherlands.'

Surgeon Elkington was soon treating his first casualty of the day: 'As we passed the wood of Bossu a staff officer, whom I had known in the Peninsula[920], came out of it wounded in the foot. The firing was sharp in the wood, and some of the balls came whizzing over our heads, so he would not dismount and I bandaged him up on his horse. The Regiment passed Quatre Bras and proceeded some way down the Namur road and entered the cornfields. It was certainly 5 o'clock now.'[921]

Alten's two brigades were immediately deployed. Wellington took Kielmansegge's Hanoverian brigade to bolster the left flank, while Halkett's 5th brigade, some two thousand strong, was ordered from the Quatre Bras cross-roads into the open ground between the Charleroi road and the Bois de Bossu, where the Brunswickers were still in action, with orders from Sir Thomas Picton, according to Halkett, 'to move through the wood, and if possible to fall upon the left of the French Army.' It was at this point that Halkett received an urgent appeal from Pack to support the hard-pressed and exposed 42nd and 44th, who were almost out of ammunition. The 69th, Halkett's leading battalion, was ordered to move out to the left of the brigade and deploy as requested. This brought that battalion into low ground to the left of the Charleroi road and some 200 yards in rear of the Bati Saint-Bernard ridge, behind the 42nd and 44th.

In compliance with his original orders, the balance of Halkett's brigade, led by the 30th, moved up astride the Charleroi road from Quatre Bras, where Lieutenant James Hope of the 92nd Highlanders saw them pass near La Bergerie:

'As the troops passed us on the road, we cheered them. Tears of joy bade them welcome to share our perils and our glory. Our feelings on this occasion were very acute, but they were the feelings of men and of soldiers. We prayed for blessings to be showered down on our friends as they passed and our best wishes followed them, too many of them to their last and silent abode.'

---

[920] This was Major John Jessop, 44th Foot, Assistant Quartermaster-General of the 3rd Division. His replacement, who would have a significant influence at Waterloo, was Captain James Shaw, who as General Sir James Shaw-Kennedy became Colonel of the 47th Regiment 1854-65.
[921] Elkington, in the *XXX Journal*, June 1911, p. 12.

Once clear of the Bois de Bossu, Halkett's battalions 'brought their left shoulders up' and deployed in succession onto the open ground to their right [922], covered by the light companies of the brigade under Lieutenant-Colonel Vigoureux. In the absence of the Light Company 30th, the Grenadier Company of that battalion replaced it in the skirmishing line. The brigade deployed in open column of companies, preserving their distances so as to deploy into line when required. On the right, close to the wood, Lieutenant Pattison of the Grenadier Company 33rd noted that the undulating ground was 'in full crop of rye,' hindering observation.' Lieutenant Francis Tincombe of the 30th described the 5th Brigade's arrival on the field of battle and its initial deployment:

'We (the British Brigade 30th, 33rd, 69th, 73rd) were ordered by poor Sir T. Picton to remain with him and the remainder of the Division moved on. We were then ordered down a little valley and formed in open column, before which was performed we lost several men. We were then formed into squares of Regiments and the Light Companies sent out to skirmish.[923]

The 30th halted on a swell in the ground where the road cuts through a low spur half-way between La Bergerie and the west end of the Bati Saint-Bernard ridge[924], with the 69th in the hollow ground some three hundred yards to their left front, while the 33rd and 73rd moved to their right in support of the battered remnants of four battalions of Brunswickers, who could be seen closely engaged with French light troops near to the edge of the Bois de Bossu.

The immediate crisis appeared to have been dealt with, but neither Wellington nor Ney had sufficient fresh troops to take offensive action without reinforcement, which both commanders were expecting. Wellington knew that Cooke's Guards Division must shortly arrive, while Ney impatiently anticipated the arrival of D'Erlon's 1st Corps, with which he would make his final victorious advance on Quatre Bras. However, shortly after 5 p.m. Ney's plans were dashed when he received new orders from the Emperor, directing him to march against the Prussian rear, and learned that Buonaparte had already diverted D'Erlon towards St. Amand to attack the Prussian right flank. Ney's anger and frustration at this turn of events, which left him with no infantry reserve, may be understood [925], but they led him to issue two irrational orders. He rashly ordered D'Erlon's corps to return to him, which caused them to counter-march without appearing on either battlefield that day, and he equally impetuously committed his last available reserve, a cavalry brigade, in a desperately quixotic charge against the Allied right.

There was some controversy as to what then happened, but it appears that as the 5th Brigade completed its deployment Halkett rode forward and saw French cavalry approaching the Gémioncourt stream. They were Guiton's heavy cavalry brigade, the 8th and 11th Cuirassiers, led by Lieutenant-General Kellerman, who had been ordered by Ney to charge the Allied right wing.[926] Kellerman could see that the charge would be suicidal, and objected that the eight hundred cuirassiers immediately available were insufficient for the task, but Ney was adamant: 'It's not important. Charge with what you have, trample them underfoot. I will make all the cavalry

---

[922] There is some evidence that the 33rd moved through the eastern edge of the Bois de Bossu to reach its position on Halkett's right flank, and the 73rd may also have done so; the 30th apparently did not, but moved straight down the Charleroi road.

[923] Francis Tincombe's letter to his brother dated Bivouac near Paris (8 miles off), July 5th-15th. In the *XXX Journal*, September 1911, p. 2.

[924] Macready, writing to Siborne in 1845: 'I am sure our Regt (conspicuous by its white trousers) was on the swell of the knoll so distinctly shown on your plan by the cutting of the road thro' it, as I should guess about 500-600 yards from Quatre Bras'. This is consistent with Surgeon Elkington having a clear view of the 30th, on the rise through which the cutting ran, from his viewpoint on the Namur road, noting in his Journal that, 'I had the regiment in view, knowing it more particularly by the Adjutant, Andrews, having a white horse.' The 30th were probably on the right of the road, opposite to where the monument to the Duke of Brunswick now stands. Ensign Thain, Adjutant of the 33rd, also noted the 30th halted close to the Charleroi road.

[925] Ney wrote on 26th June that 'Our victory [at Quatre Bras] was not in doubt, when at the moment when I was going to advance the 1st Corps, which until then had been left by me in reserve at Frasnes, I learnt that the General [Buonaparte] had deployed it without warning me, as well as Girard's division of the 2nd Corps, towards St Amand to support the right wing that was committed to action against the Prussians. The blow this struck me was terrible; having only three divisions under my orders, instead of the eight on which I had counted, I was obliged to let victory escape and despite all my efforts, despite the devotion of my troops, I was then just able to maintain my position until the end of the day.'

[926] Ney's desperate order, according to Kellerman, was as follows: *'Mon cher General, il s'agit du salut de la France. Il faut un effort extraordinaire. Prenez votre cavalerie, jetez-vous au milieu des Anglais. Ecrasez-les. Passez-leur sur le ventre!'*

present follow you. Go, but go quickly!' Kellerman moved forward over the Gémioncourt stream to the west of the Charleroi chaussée, with the 8th Cuirassiers on the right and the 11th on the left, while the French guns increased their rate of fire in support. Kellerman ordered, 'Charge, at full gallop, forward, charge!'

Seeing this menacing cavalry advance, Halkett ordered the 5th Brigade from column into square[927], and the 30th and 69th were accordingly changing formation when the Prince of Orange came up and, denying that there was a cavalry threat, ordered them to form line. Colonel Morice of the 69th reluctantly obeyed, but Hamilton, observing the approach of cavalry, disregarded the Prince and rapidly formed the 30th in square. Vigoureux' composite light battalion, which appears to have deployed to the left front of the brigade, fell back to join the 30th, their addition altering its 'square' into a thickened irregular oblong.

The leading squadron of the 8th Cuirassiers apparently saw that the 30th were prepared to receive them but that the 69th were in disorder 'dans un vallon' on the far side of the chaussée. Veering to their right, and brushing past the 42nd and 44th, the armoured horsemen rushed down on the unfortunate 69th. That corps, stationed as they were in hollow ground and surrounded by high crops, were not aware of the approaching cuirassiers until thundering hooves in rear of their right flank, and within thirty yards, were all too obvious. The 69th then made a belated attempt to re-form square, but two companies faced about and fired ineffectually as they wheeled back, and the incomplete square was ridden down and scattered, losing a Colour and 174 men killed and wounded. Their casualties would have been even higher but for Allied artillery fire and volleys from a nearby British battalion in white trousers, the 30th.

On the left, it appears that the 11th Cuirassiers were initially engaged by the unbroken squares of the Brunswick battalions and by the 33rd, causing the cavalry to swerve to their right. The leading squadron then charged the 30th. That battalion, having formed square with remarkable rapidity, reserved their fire until the very last moment and easily beat off the Cuirassiers with loss. The steady performance of the 30th undoubtedly owed much to the example of its veteran commander, and Bannatyne[928] reports a regimental story which, even if embellished in the telling, shows that Alexander Hamilton was regarded by his men as an exceptionally cool and resolute officer:

'Colonel Hamilton, like most old campaigners, chewed tobacco, and tradition says that in action it was his custom when he thought he saw any sign of nervousness or impatience in the ranks to ask audibly if anyone had any tobacco. Half a dozen brass boxes were of course offered to the great man, who, with all eyes fixed on him, would select one and cutting a convenient quid, insert it in his cheek, nor until he had it comfortably under weigh would he deign to notice the enemy. He thought a 30-yard range was quite long enough.'

Captain Joseph Harty of the Light Company 33rd, who was present, later recalled that 'the firm conduct of the [30th] square called forth the unqualified approbation of the late Sir Thomas Picton, who was an eye-witness, and galloped up; and, calling for the commanding officer, told Colonel Hamilton that he would report their gallant conduct to the Duke.' Picton was heard to say that if he lived the 30th should be done justice. Harty added, in reply to Macready's 1845 questionnaire: 'It so happens that I know personally much more about your gallant little battalion on 16th June than of my own, having been detached, as you may recollect, with the light companies immediately after entering the field. Three times in the course of the day I took refuge from the cavalry in the square of the 30th, and had the heartfelt gratification of witnessing the determined charges of the cuirassiers repulsed in splendid style.' Another of Macready's correspondents, a brother-officer of the 30th, recalled that 'I am nearly certain we were thanked by five General Officers that day.[929] One said we were a noble set of fellows, but that we made a noise like devils – he feared there were no officers with us.'

The 33rd, meanwhile, found themselves exposed on a ridge near the wood to heavy fire at short range from two French batteries. Taking casualties in their close-packed square, they were ordered into line to reduce further loss. It appears that the second squadron of the 11th Cuirassiers then approached the 33rd through the tall rye, and

[927] Surgeon James Elkington took the opportunity to fall back, with his hospital sergeant and a bat horse carrying his instruments and medicine, to the Namur road where he set up his aid post.

[928] *History of the 30th Regiment*, p. 316.

[929] The Prince of Orange and Generals Picton, Alten, Halkett and Kielmansegge.

a shout of 'cavalry' was enough to panic the already shaken battalion, which broke and rushed into the Bossu wood, on the far side of which they were re-formed. The cuirassiers then rode on, close enough to the 73rd to prompt a number of its men to break ranks and run to the perceived safety of the nearby wood, though the majority remained in square.[930] At least some of the cuirassiers then continued as far as the Quatre Bras crossroads, but then, with horses blown and much reduced in numbers,[931] they fell back, in Kellerman's words, 'in the disorder usual in such circumstances.' Kellerman himself was unhorsed, so did not see that at least some of his cuirassiers had rallied and, reinforced by Piré's lancers, were preparing to renew their gallant assault.

Meanwhile Vigoureux' skirmishers, including Lieutenant Richard Heaviside's No. 8 Company of the 30th, went out to engage the French *tirailleurs*, and Major Tom Chambers formed the 30th into a more regular square. It was then that, according to Macready, Heaviside's men 'suffered cruelly from the *tirailleurs* while endeavouring to skirmish before the Light Company came up,' losing two serjeants and near twenty rank and file killed and wounded.

Shortly after the first attack of the cuirassiers, Alexander Hamilton was seriously wounded in circumstances described by his obituarist:

'After waiting some time for their return, considering it probable they were watching for an opportunity in an adjacent field, Colonel Hamilton, with that generous solicitude he always evinced for his officers and men, but forgetful that his duties as commanding officer demanded that he should not expose himself, ordered the battalion to stand fast while he singly approached the hedge to reconnoitre. The cavalry were not visible, but two *tirailleurs* who had posted themselves in a tree both fired at the Colonel: one of them hit him in the left leg,' Fortunately, Hamilton's horse was uninjured[932], and the wounded officer regained his square before riding back towards the regimental aid post at Quatre Bras. As he did so, he met his Light Company hastening to the battle.

It will be recalled that the Light Company 30th had inadvertently been left behind on outpost at Naast when the Regiment marched, and on the morning of the 16th, young Edward Macready rode into Soignies:

'About eight o'clock next morning, it was agreed that I should ride over to the Regiment to order out a few necessaries; and accordingly away I went. I cantered on without thinking, and pulled up in the market-place. I was thunderstruck. Not a soul was stirring. The silence of the tomb reigned here where I had expected to have met 10,000 men. The breath left my body as if extracted by an air pump. I ran into a house, and asked "Where were the troops?" "They marched at two this morning", was the chilling reply. "By what road?" "Towards Braine le Compte", was all I said or heard, when, jumping on my pony's back, I endeavoured, by sympathetic heel, to convey the rapidity of my ideas into his carcass. But vain were my efforts – Gil Blas' ass was lightning compared to him; Soignies was his home, and his obstinacy invincible. So, getting off, I thrashed him in the face till my knuckles ran blood, and made the best of my way on foot, lugging him by the bridle.

'On reaching Naast, I found Rumley[933] and Pratt in deep consultation with the burgomaster, who had informed them that the French had crossed the Sambre and occupied Charleroi; that the Prussians were falling back, and our troops hastening up to support them. Our patrols had examined the country on every side, and not

---

[930] Sergeant Tom Morris was one of the 73rd who headed for the woods: 'The ground, for a considerable distance, being covered with rye, and of an extraordinary height, some of it measuring seven feet, prevented us from seeing much of the enemy; but, though we could not see them, they were observing us. We continuing to advance, the glittering of the tops of our bayonets guided towards us a large body of the enemy's cuirassiers, who, coming so unexpectedly upon us, threw us in the utmost confusion. Having no time to form a square, we were compelled to retire, or rather to run, to the wood through which we had advanced.' *The Recollections of Sergeant Morris*, p. 68.

[931] The eventual loss of the two regiments of cuirassiers was some three hundred men out of under eight hundred.

[932] Dalton's *Waterloo Roll Call*, p. 143-444, tells an amusing anecdote about Hamiliton's charger, which was apparently very valuable: 'Knowing that if it was shot in the battle he would only get the Government price of £20 for another charger, he exchanged horses before going into action at Quatre Bras with his steady old quartermaster [John Williamson], who, being a non-combatant, was to remain in the rear. The quartermaster's horse was what is called a "safe convenience", but the Colonel's charger was very high-spirited and fresh. Unaccustomed to the quietude of his position in the rear of the army, he fretted and fumed at being kept back from the excitement going on in front. His rider had a bad time of it, and was a source of much amusement to the idlers and "non-effectives" in the rearward.'

[933] Lieutenant John Rumley commanded the Light Company, with John Pratt and Edward Macready as his subalterns.

a soldier to be seen. We were most unpleasantly situated; ignorant whether we were left here by mistake or design, and dreading equally the consequences of quitting our post without orders, or the Division being engaged in our absence. Our commissions were safe by remaining where we were; but (as Mr. Egan said, "Ireland for ever, and damn Kilmainham") we determined to risk them, and all the hopes of young ambition, rather than be absent from the field of glory.

'Away we marched towards Braine le Compte. There we learnt that the troops had struck off to Nivelles, and we followed their route. We soon got among the baggage of the army, passed it, and quickened our pace on hearing a noise like distant peals of thunder. "The Dutch artillery are practising", said a young soldier, in a tremulously inquisitive tone. "They've redder targets than your cheeks, my boy, that fire those guns", replied a swarthy veteran, who had learned this music in Spain. In a few minutes, regular discharges could be distinguished. They came from the Prussians and French at Ligny.

'We redoubled our speed, and entering Nivelles, found considerable difficulty in forcing our way thro' the crowds of baggage animals, commissaries, quartermasters, and women, who thronged the streets. Some of our regimental wives came up, blessed us, and kissed their husbands, many for the last time. Such memories agitate the hearts even of soldiers' wives, the most callous and insensible creatures in existence. They told us the Division had halted at Nivelles, and marched again, about an hour before, towards Quatre Bras, where the enemy were said to be. We met our stores, and, seizing them, took out an allowance of spirits for every man. The repeated "God in Heaven bless you, my dear child" of a poor woman who was choking in a ditch, and who shared my gin, was a better renovator than the spirits. Thus reinspired, our boys started double quick, for the firing increased. It was now past three o'clock.

'We passed the Division of Guards. Rumley had some words with a staff officer about crossing their line of march, and our fellows began to laugh and jeer them. They had some cause, for I never saw such numbers of men knocked up in my life. "Shall I carry your honour on my pack?" said one of ours to a Grenadier Guardsman, as he was sitting down. "Haven't you some gruel for that young gentleman?" shouted another, and continued, "It's a cruel shame to send gentleman's sons on such business. You see they don't like it; they've had quite enough at Bergy-my-Zoon." High words arose; but we stop'd our men, who, however, took leave of them saying, "Good-bye to ye, young gentlemen. Pray don't hurry yourselves – we'll do your work, never fear."

'We continued our double-quick, and struck across the fields. Our men had now marched about eighteen miles, and run six. They began to faint very fast, but not a soldier fell out till he drop't, black in the face and senseless. Many of them reeled while replying to our encouragements, "Never fear, sir, I'll keep up." We cut their pack-straps, took off their stocks, and left them gasping.

At length we had a confused view of the field, with our troops and the enemy firing away under their sulphurous canopy. Clouds of birds were flying and squealing above the smoke. We loosened our ammunition, and pushed on for it. Hedges, streams, and ditches were passed like thought. After scrambling thro' a thick, thorny plantation, we found ourselves close to a body of men with whose uniform we were unacquainted. Not above twenty of our Company were present.

'We advanced to these people, and found them to belong to the Nassau Usingen contingent. They had just been driven from the wood of Bossu, which was in front of us, and between ourselves and the army. We made for it, and came up with Sir George Berkeley, Adjutant-General to the Prince's corps, who had just escaped from the Lancers. He told us our Regiment had entered the field about a quarter of an hour before, and that they were on the other side of the wood, which we must pass on the left, near Quatre Bras, as the enemy occupied the whole of it. This we were convinced of by numerous round shot coming from it, one of which splashed dirt and mud over the whole Company. "Close your files, and hould up your heads, my lads", roared an old campaigner, named Terry O'Neil[934]. One feels a thrill at these moments.

'We soon reached Quatre Bras, where the Brunswickers and some of Picton's people were in square; and on turning the end of the wood, found ourselves in the hurly-burly of the battle. The roaring of great guns and

---

[934] Corporal Terence O'Neil survived Quatre Bras and Waterloo unscathed.

musquetry, the bursting of shells, and shouts of the combatants raised an infernal and indescribable din; while the galloping of horses, the mingled crowds of wounded and fugitives (Belgians), the volumes of smoke, and flashing of fire, struck out a scene which accorded admirably with the music.

'As we passed a spot where the 44th, our old chums, had suffered considerably, the poor wounded fellows raised themselves up and welcomed us with faint shouts: "Push on, old Thirtieth – pay 'em off for the poor 44th. You're much wanted, my boys. Success to ye, my darlings." Here we met our old Colonel riding out of the field, shot through the leg. The [92nd] Highlanders were crossed like the marks of their plaid in some spots.[935]

'I don't know what might have been my sensations on entering this field coolly, but as it was, I was so fagged and choked with running, and was pressed so suddenly into the very thick of the business, that I can't recollect anything at all, except that the Highlanders (over whom I stumbled almost every step) were most provokingly distributed.

'Hamilton showed us our Regiment, and we reached it just as a body of Lancers and Cuirassiers had enveloped two faces of its square. We formed up to the left and fired away. The tremendous volley our square (which, in the hurry of formation, was six deep on the two sides attacked) gave them, sent off these fellows with the loss of a number of men, and their commanding officer. He was a gallant soul; he fell while crying to his men, '*Avancez, mes enfans! Courage! Encore une fois, Français!*'[936]

Lieutenant Francis Tincombe described the two attacks of the French cavalry to his brother:

'The enemy's Cavalry and Lancers drove everything in on our right, and then charged the 69th square which they penetrated and cut up most dreadfully, then wheeled off and served the 33rd Regiment the same, after which they charged our square, but our brave fellows, who were cool and steady, took good aim at their opponents and killed and wounded numbers and made the remainder run in great disorder. This was the time we wanted our Cavalry, which was in the rear. They rallied and charged. A second time we served the gentlemen as badly, only one of them got on our bayonets, who was of course killed. We were immediately thanked on the ground by Sir T. Picton and every General near us.' [937]

'On the repulse of the cavalry,' agreed Macready, 'Sir Thomas Picton rode up and thanked us warmly, as this body had cut up two or three regiments. I think the men I saw dead belonged chiefly to the 11th Cuirassiers. They were savage looking fellows – fine subjects for Bonaparte or Salvator.[938]

'The Light Bobs were ordered to pursue the rest of them, so we dashed out and followed them firing, until we were brought up by a line of *tirailleurs*, with whom we kept up a brisk fire. [Lieutenant Purefoy] Lockwood, of our Grenadiers, came out with us, and dropped with a shot in his head as he was speaking to me. He was a noble fellow, and as he was led by the Regiment his last words were an exhortation to his company to do their duty.'

It was now around 6 p.m., and Maitland's brigade of Guards had arrived, together with additional artillery batteries. These reinforcements gave Wellington a sufficient numerical advantage to launch an offensive across the field. The Guards entered the Bois de Bossu, and for the next two hours, they cleared through the wood from north to south in close fighting, which cost their two battalions a fearful 547 casualties. To the right rear of the 30th, the 73rd also resumed their advance, while Kielmansegge's Hanoverians relieved Picton's battered battalions to the east of the Charleroi chaussée, their light troops coming up in line with Vigoureux' companies. Macready painted the scene:

---

[935] The 92nd Highlanders had suffered severe losses when retaking the farm of La Bergerie on the Charleroi road.

[936] This second charge on the 30th was made by Piré's 5th and 6th Lancers, who had rather belatedly come forward to support Kellerman, together with rallied elements of the 11th Cuirassiers.

[937] Letter dated Bivouac near Paris, July 5th-15th 1815.

[938] This account from Macready was written up in 1816, but in a letter to his father, dated Paris on 7th July 1815, he wrote, 'Poor Picton commanded us on the 16th and sent his Aide-de-Camp to thank our Regiment which was nearly the only one not rode through by the French cavalry that day. The 69th, 33rd, 92nd, 44th and nearly all the Scotch Regiments were rode through before they could form. We had luckily formed square and gave a great peeling, killed their colonel and dropped lots of them.'

'The cannonade and skirmishing were lively on both sides. Our broken columns and their cavalry were re-forming, while the heavy fire from the woods in our rear showed that the Guards and the enemy were nobly disputing it. On the left of our company were some Hanoverian Jägers, one of whom covered a soldier of ours named Tracy[939]. A tirailleur dashed out from their line and shot the German thro' the head; upon which Tracy ran over to him, and before he could get off blew his skull to pieces. This enraptured their officers; who, to say the truth, were marvellously distempered with drink or choler, and they were lauding us with praises, such as *"Engleesh and Hanover fiell good for the Franceosens – Franceosens à la monde capoote, etc."* when the advance of the enemy's cavalry obliged us all to retire to our columns.

'They made a faint charge on ours[940] and some other battalions, but being uniformly repulsed, retired, and we occupied our former ground. We now descended a slope towards our right in the direction of a deep ravine [the Gémioncourt stream], across which the Royal Scots and ourselves drove a heavy body of infantry after a severe fire.[941] The enemy was retiring from the wood, and the Guards pressing them very closely. A retrograde movement was perceptible along their whole line, and it was performed in beautiful style; their columns and skirmishers kept their alignment and distances as if on a parade. The dimness of the evening made the firing doubly livid, and above its roar, one occasionally heard German bugles sounding the "Advance and fire". We had no cavalry to spoil this spectacle, but the light troops pushed rapidly from hedge to hedge.

'Major Chambers, of ours, was pushing on with two companies towards a house [the walled farm of Gémioncourt] in our front, and I joined him with as many of the Light Infantry as I could collect. We rushed into the courtyard, but were repulsed. He re-formed us in the orchard, directed the men how to attack, and it was carried in an instant by battering open the doors and ramming the muskets into the windows. We found 140 wounded and some excellent beer in the house.

'This was the extent of our advance. A useless fire of musketry, with occasional volleys of grape and some shelling, continued till near ten o'clock. The enemy on the whole did not lose ground in this action; in fact they took more in the early part from the foreigners than we had daylight to recover.'

'Our Regiment piled arms about ten o'clock at night, and laid down to sleep, covered by the ravine in our front. The dead and dying were around us, but no one slept the worse. Military men know this, but it appears incredible to the uninitiated that a few hours of glory should give the heart such a stoical insensibility. [Lieutenant William] Warren and I pig'd together under a cuirassier's cloak, and Jack Rumley made a pillow of my buttock.'

Considering that it was late in the day before the Allies overtook the French in point of numbers, their losses were remarkably closely balanced. French casualties totaled about 4,200, and those of the Allies around 4,523 including 2,275 British. The loss of the British fell chiefly on Picton's division, the Guards, who found very tough work in the woods, and those regiments of Halkett's brigade who did not keep out the cuirassiers.

Before leaving the action at Quatre Bras, it is necessary to dispose of the idea, initially accepted by William Siborne, that the whole of Halkett's brigade was either overrun or driven into the Bois de Bossu by Kellerman's cuirassiers. In relation to the 30th, this error was comprehensively refuted by Major Edward Macready in an article in the *United Service Magazine*,[942] but since the error has been perpetuated in some more recent studies of the Waterloo campaign, his evidence clearly requires repetition. Five officers of the 30th, in addition to Macready, and Captain Harty of the 33rd, all strongly maintained that the 30th never entered the Bois de Bossu. A few of their comments should suffice to settle the matter:

'I can state most positively, and am willing to swear to it, if necessary, that the 30th Regt. never entered any wood from the moment they were first engaged at Quatre Bras'; 'The 30th *never* entered the wood of Bossu.

---

[939] Private Thomas Tracey was among the few of the Light Company 30th to survive the campaign unscathed.

[940] This indicates that the 30th beat off a total of three cavalry charges at Quatre Bras, as confirmed by Captain Harty of the 33rd. Macready commented in 1845 that 'The latter advances of the French cavalry were very tame and lukewarm, and apparently (as stated by their own historians) only intended to put a decent face on their retreat.'

[941] This accords with an 1845 statement by one of Macready's correspondents, an officer of the 30th: 'Towards evening we moved to the right. We were formed in column when some French troops crossed to our right, Our grenadiers fired, and they returned it to our cost.'

[942] *United Service Magazine*, March 1845.

The Regiment *never* retired at Quatre Bras. Their movement was always in advance until the termination of the battle'; 'My decided impression is *it never did* [enter the wood] at any period of the day'; 'I declare that I have no recollection of our corps having ever been driven into the wood; and more, I have not the slightest remembrance of our having *entered into it at all*: in fact, I never before heard it even supposed so.'

The loss of the 30th at Quatre Bras was comparatively moderate: One sergeant, a corporal and three privates were killed[943], while four officers[944], two sergeants and 27 rank and file were wounded and five men missing, of whom two rejoined the following day. The small loss was due to the fact that, except for the skirmishers, the Battalion was not engaged in any serious musketry exchange and never came under effective artillery fire.[945]

Lieutenant-Colonel Hamilton was seriously wounded and nearly lost his leg. His obituary in 1832 recalls that 'the tourniquet had thrice encircled his leg preparatory to amputation,' but each time the surgeons were diverted elsewhere, and the limb escaped to join the dancing at the Waterloo Ball held by the 30th at Limerick in 1816.

James Elkington, who had established his dressing station on the Namur road, left an interesting account of his work as regimental surgeon that day:

'On the road I received Colonel Hamilton of the Regiment wounded in the leg. He did not dismount while I dressed him. I also received Lieutenant Lockwood with a wound of a musket ball in the frontal sinus. I sent him to the farm at Quatre Bras. Whilst here I saw the artillery on my right open fire on the advance of cavalry up the Charleroi road. Shortly after the repulse of the cavalry I was ordered up to the front to some wounded of the Regiment. I attempted to pass down the high road but my horse would not pass the numerous dead men and horses of the French that lay in the road, and I entered the fields on my left and dressed some men at a farm-house [La Bergerie]. I then returned to Quatre Bras and extracted the ball (as I thought) from Lieutenant Lockwood's frontal bone, but three weeks after a portion of it was found in the sinus and the trephine was used to extract it.'[946]

Purefoy Lockwood's head wound was assumed to be mortal, and little hope was entertained of his recovery. The story goes that the vicar's son from County Tipperary was being taken to a grave-pit when a nun intervened to save him; if so, it was a just reward for an incident at the storming of Badajoz when young Lockwood chivalrously saved a distressed nun and restored her safely to her parents. Lockwood survived his dangerous wound, and the hole in his head was covered with a silver plate on which was engraved 'Bombproof,' which he carried with him until his death 44 years later. As Captain of Invalids at Kilmainham, he became something of a celebrity, and when King George IV visited Dublin, he insisted on meeting the man with the 'bomb proof' skull.

Away from the field of Quatre Bras, on 16th June the 40th and 59th were on the march, while in Brussels the 81st anxiously awaited the order to move.

'The drums beat at midnight,' recalled Sergeant Lawrence of the Grenadier Company 40th, 'and we arrayed ourselves as quickly as possible. The landlord of the house where I was staying had got up, and would kindly insist on filling our canteens – that is a capacity of about three pints – with gin, giving us as well some bread and meat each, and warning us to look out, for he knew the French were coming. All having assembled at the rendezvous, orders were given to march on Brussels immediately.'[947]

Lambert's brigade marched from Ghent within the hour, halting that afternoon at Asche after a forced march of some thirty miles. As Brigade Major, Harry Smith expected at any moment an order to move on: 'The

---

[943] Sergeant John Suttle, a Londoner, Corporal John Gadborough from Nottingham, and Privates John Leslie, Francis McGlinn and John O'Brien were killed at Quatre Bras. Macready states that about 45 men were *hors de combat*, but this slight discrepancy may include some few who were slightly wounded and would not be included in the casualty report.

[944] Lieutenant-Colonel Alexander Hamilton and Lieutenant Purefoy Lockwood were severely wounded, and Lieutenants Richard Harrison and John Roe 2nd (there were two officers of this name in the 2nd/30th) slightly, the latter earning the distinction of being wounded at both Quatre Bras and Waterloo.

[945] Captain Robert Howard stated, in a letter to Macready, 'With respect to us suffering from artillery . . . as I was with the Regiment until the French had retreated I can positively assert that the 30th did not lose a man from that arm.'

[946] Elkington, in the *XXX Journal*, June 1911, p. 12.

[947] Lawrence, p.p. 202-03.

rapid and continuous firing at Quatre Bras, as audible as if we were in the fight, put us in mind of old times, as well as on the *qui vive...* We believed the firing to be at Fleurus.'

The 2nd/81st had been warned on 15th June to be in readiness to march at 4 a.m. the following morning, but as the rest of Lambert's brigade was still at Ghent, the Battalion was instead ordered to take over essential duties in Brussels, which included attending the sick and wounded, and taking charge of the military chest. Consequently, by the time Lambert marched through the city on the afternoon of the 17th the whole of the 81st were committed, on guards or on duty at the hospitals. The following morning the commanding officer, Lieutenant-Colonel Henry Milling, earnestly entreated General Lambert to permit his battalion to accompany the brigade, but the hospitals were already filling with the wounded of Quatre Bras, and so the 81st could not be relieved. However, it seems that a subaltern's detachment of the Regiment may have been present on or near the battlefield.[948]

The 2nd/59th had also moved forward, with Colville's Division, on the 16th, marching that morning from Oudenarde to Grammont and Enghien[949]. The next day, they were ordered to march on Nivelles, but having reached Braine-le-Compte they were ordered back early on the morning of the 18th to take up a position near Tubize, about three and a half miles in front of Halle, covering the Mons-Brussels road on Wellington's right flank. There they would remain until the 19th.

Withdrawal to Waterloo, 17th June 1815

On the battlefield of Quatre Bras, both sides were very considerably reinforced during the night of the 16th June. On the return of d'Erlon, Ney had some 35,000 men in hand facing Wellington, who had some ten thousand more by morning, but neither commander made a move as both waited for news of the outcome of the battle of Ligny; and meanwhile, both were concerned that their opponent might attack again.

The 30th had bivouacked overnight in the low ground to the north of Gémioncourt, but despite his fatigue, Ensign Edward Macready had a disturbed sleep:

'I was ordered up in the middle of the night to reconnoitre some figures moving in our front; they were Brunswickers. About two in the morning I was woke by a heavy fire, and seeing flashes all around me I started up and found that some one had raised a false report of the enemy's advance; it was a mere joke, but no joke to us poor *caçadores*, who were ordered to the front to support the picquets in case of an attack. We extended between the captured farm-house and the wood, and at daybreak the enemy showed a line of *tirailleurs* opposite to us.

'The outposts on both sides stood looking at each other at daylight, and neither party seemed inclined to commence an unprofitable fire, till a Brunswick officer rode up so close to the enemy's advance that they were obliged to slap at him. He was either a fool or a rogue, and I really think he wanted to desert. As these shots came whistling about our ears, we returned the compliment, and a lively tiraillade was the consequence. In about half an hour it slackened as if by mutual consent, and at length ceased entirely. Our men were employed in rummaging the dead Frenchmen, and we in reading their letters and memorandums. This work, occasionally interrupted by a few stray shots on both sides, amused us till late in the morning, when we were led to expect more serious occupation by receiving an order "to hold the farm-house to the last man." A reinforcement of [95th] Riflemen came up to us, and we saw frequent groups of French officers come to the front as if reconnoitring.'

---

[948] One subaltern, a sergeant and fifteen rank and file of the 81st were listed as entitled to shares in the Waterloo Prize Money. Bearing in mind the nature of their Regiment's duties in Brussels, it may be conjectured that this detachment was pushed forward to assist in the field hospital at Mont St. Jean or in evacuating the wounded.

[949] It may have been at Enghien that a curious reminder of the Waterloo campaign occurred in 1919 when 2nd Battalion The East Lancashire Regiment, the old 59th Foot, were preparing to take part in the World War I victory parade through Brussels. It was customary to put up wooden billeting boards, marked with the number of men each property could accommodate, and the Battalion's boards still carried their old '59th' sign, a white fleur-de-lys. When the boards went up in Enghien, they excited considerable interest and a crowd of local people gathered. Eventually an old lady went into her house and returned with an almost identical board, apparently left behind by the 59th Foot in 1815.

Lieutenant John Rumley, commanding the Light Company 30th, painted a picture of the front line that morning, with the opposing light troops within half a musket shot of each other:

'The heights in our front, which I believe are the heights of Frasne, were covered with troops, and column succeeded column in quick succession, arriving from the Army which had been engaged with the Prussians the day before… The outposts, altho' in such close contact, did not molest each other, except when a solitary individual attempted to pass towards the front, beyond a sort of imaginary line which appeared to have been tacitly agreed to. Looking back towards our own position, not a soldier could be seen, but as the ground was greatly broken, and covered with crops, we concluded that they were concealed from view, but did not doubt that they were there… About 9 a.m. I have a distinct recollection of the Major General commanding our brigade [Halkett] coming to the outposts, giving us instructions how to defend ourselves when attacked, and expressing his conviction that a great conflict would take place on the same ground which was so hardly contested the day before.'

No such battle took place, for shortly after daybreak Wellington had learned of the Prussian defeat at Ligny when Colonel Gordon returned from a liaison visit. Turning to a companion, the Duke observed, 'Old Blucher has had a damned good licking and gone back to Wavre, eighteen miles. As he has gone back, we must go too. I suppose in England they will say we have been licked. I can't help it; as they are gone back, we must go too.' He immediately issued orders for a retirement.

It was not until about 9 a.m. in the morning that Ney received peremptory orders from the Emperor's headquarters expressing surprise that the Marshal did not know about the French victory at Ligny and delivering a stinging rebuke:

'The Emperor is disappointed that you did not concentrate your divisions yesterday; they acted individually and so you suffered casualties.'

Having belatedly sent Marshal Grouchy in pursuit of the defeated Prussians, Buonaparte announced that he was advancing down the Namur road against Wellington's left flank and that he expected Ney to make a frontal attack on Quatre Bras. Whether from pique or the knowledge that he was now outnumbered, Ney took no action, and by the time Napoleon approached it was too late: Wellington had executed a timely withdrawal.

'We were every moment expecting an attack,' Macready recalled, 'when, about ten o'clock, we were ordered to withdraw as quietly as possible, and our place was occupied by Jägers. We joined the Regiment, and, while looking for something eatable, I fell in with Major Watson, 69th, who appeared dreadfully chagrined. He told me that his corps had been dreadfully cut up, and had lost their King's colour, and then devoutly damned the Prince of Orange.'

At about 11 a.m., having ascertained the full extent of Blucher's defeat at Ligny, Wellington ordered the main body of his army to retire through Genappe, covered by Alten's 3rd Division, which was then to withdraw by a country road parallel to and east of the main Brussels chaussée. Captain Arthur Gore of the Grenadier Company 30th described the rearguard's deceptive movements:

'This division fell back on Quatre Bras from the position it had occupied during the night… and re-advanced in the direction of Namur as far as the cabaret [tavern] called Le Paradis, in the village of Thyle, in front of the right of the French position. This admirable manoeuvre completely deceived Marshal Ney, who threw back the right wing of his army upon the wood of Delhutte in order to be prepared to repel this attack, at the same time that he expected his left wing to be engaged by a force which he fancied lay concealed in the wood of Bossu. On the contrary, the Third Division, having occupied the village for an hour, defiled to the rear of Le Paradis in the direction of Genappe, covered by the houses and adjoining wood [the Bois de Censes]; nor did Marshal Ney discover, for some time, the error into which he had fallen.'[950]

Leap-frogging back by brigades, the 3rd Division made a text-book clean break. The light troops of the Division retired a little before noon 'in a manner evincing admirable skill, steadiness and regularity,' moving to

---

[950] *An Historical Account of The Battle of Waterloo*, Captain Arthur Gore, 30th Regiment, London 1817.

their left along the Chemin de Bati St.-Bernard and crossing the Namur road to reach the village of Sart-Dames-Avelines.

'We passed over the ground that Picton's division had so gallantly defended,' wrote Macready, 'and crossing one road, came to a second, down which we proceeded for half a mile, and halted at a village. We thought we were going to join the Prussians in forcing the enemy's right. I slept here, nearly an hour, on a fine soft dunghill, tho' the firing between the Jägers and the French was very heavy. Numbers of our wounded were carried thro' the yard we were in, and, before we marched, balls repeatedly whizzed thro' it. This shewed our friends were losing ground. We again stood up, and turned into a narrow road which branched off to the left. On entering a wood, we found parties of Hussars scattered here and there to cover the retreat. These groups, some of whom were sleeping, bridle in hand, others smoking their German pipes, a few cleaning their horses, and the rest irregularly idling about amongst the trees, had a very picturesque appearance.'

'Everyone now said that the heights of Genappe would be the scene of action, and this report acquired credit from our halting near a village for a considerable time; but this delay was merely occasioned by the passage of troops on the high road, as we were destined to be the rear division of the army.

'As we re-commenced our march, at about three or four o'clock, a most furious storm arose. The rain came down in torrents, and in a moment we were drenched to the skin. The thunder rolled awfully above our heads, and the lightning glistened among the bayonets. The enemy's artillery, pushing on closer every minute, mingled its roar with this hubbub of the elements. These things look and feel ominous to a retreating army. As we descended a steep declivity, our men rolled head over heels from top to bottom, and the road in the low ground for a quarter of a mile was knee-deep.'[951]

Early that morning James Elkington had sent off his wounded, and when the retirement started he and his medical staff kept to the high road: 'On the road side I found Bailey, who had been on leave of absence to Brussels in plain clothes. I lent him my sword and coat and he borrowed a cocked hat from [Assistant Surgeon] Deane.' Brevet Lieutenant-Colonel Morris William Bailey then went off to find the Battalion and assume command.

The route followed by the 30th from Sart-Dames-Avelines, no more than a country track, crossed the river Dyle at Bassy-Ways, after which the going became so difficult that the 3rd Division was obliged to joined the main Brussels chaussée where it rose to the north of Genappe[952], just in time to witness the British cavalry fight a rearguard action which their commander, Lord Uxbridge, described as 'the prettiest field day of cavalry and horse artillery that I ever witnessed.'

'About half-past five,' recalled Macready, 'we came on the Charleroi chaussée as the covering division. Our Jägers and the Brunswicks were busy on the flanks, the cannonade was brisk, and report said that the enemy had captured two of our guns. At this time the 7th Hussars charged some Red Lancers near Genappe, and were sadly beaten. The Life Guards then came up and fully revenged them. I saw a regiment of heavy Dragoons deploy to support the Household if necessary; they had on their red cloaks, and looked like giants. Numbers of the Hussars galloped by us, so covered with mud that their uniforms could not be distinguished; from counter to tail, and from spur to plume, horse and man were one cake of dirt. They must have had pretty rolling or running. The rain continued unabated, and night drew on.'[953]

The retirement continued on the Brussels chaussée until the Allies reached Wellington's selected battlefield, the famous field of Waterloo. Then, passing the farm of La Haie Sainte, the troops filed left and right at a ridge-top crossroads, since known as the Elm Tree Crossroads, to reach their respective positions. Alten's 3rd

---

[951] Sergeant Morris of the 73rd agreed, recalling 'The rain descended literally in torrents . . . and the rapidly accumulating water came down with such inconceivable force, that it was with the utmost difficulty we could keep our feet.'

[952] Captain James Shaw, who was acting as Assistant Quartermaster-General to the 3rd Division, said that the division's move onto the main road was 'without orders from headquarters, but by obvious necessity.'

[953] Sergeant Morris of the 73rd witnessed the same action as Macready: 'On emerging from this obscure road to the main road to Brussels, at the village of Genappe, the scene was grand, but of the most fearful description. On our right was the rear of our troops, on their way to Waterloo. On the hills to the left, the main body of the French were rapidly advancing; in Genappe was a body of the enemy's cuirassiers, whose advance the 7th British Hussars vainly endeavoured to check, when the Earl of Uxbridge brought up the Oxford Blues [Royal Horse Guards] and the Life Guards, and drove the cuirassiers back.' (Morris, p. 73).

Division moved to the left, and Halkett's 5th Brigade halted about midway between La Haie Sainte and the chateau of Hougoumont. The withdrawal had been a model operation.

'So orderly and so perfect were all the arrangements connected with this retreat, from its commencement to its close, that the movements partook more of the appearance of a Field Day upon a large scale than of an operation executed in the actual presence of the enemy.'[954]

'It must have been near eight o'clock,' recalled Macready, 'when we formed in contiguous columns on the heights of Waterloo. The enemy opened on our part of the position from some light guns, and knocked over a few men of the 73rd, but were soon silenced by old Cleve's nine-pounders.[955] The loss of the army on this day did not exceed 200 men. Our Corps had only one man killed[956], three wounded, and eight missing.'

'The whole of the ground was covered with corn,' recalled Sergeant Tom Morris, 'and the soil of so loose a nature that, owing to the heavy rain, which continued to fall, we were literally knee-deep in mud… To lie down was out of the question, and to stand up was almost equally so. We endeavoured to light some fires, but the rain soon put them out, and the only plan we could adopt was to gather arms-full of the standing corn and, rolling it together, made a sort of mat, on which we placed our knapsack; and sitting on that, each man holding his blanket over his head to keep off the rain, which was almost needless as we were so thoroughly drenched.'[957]

Even James Elkington, a seasoned campaigner, decided that 'a more severe night was never experienced by the British Army, who were lying out in cornfields up to their knees in mire. Colonel Vigoreaux and myself lay together, having my hospital panniers to windward, our only shelter.'

'The rain still continued,' recalled Macready, 'and we found great difficulty in lighting our fires. Fortunately, we occupied ground from which the Guards had been ordered rather hastily, and they had left a good deal of wood and some biscuits. Rumley, Pratt, and I, shared a fowl, which we roasted, or rather warmed, on a ramrod; and the third of this animal, with an onion at Genappe, some beer at the captured farmhouse, and a couple of biscuits, was all that exhilarated my inward man on the 16th, 17th, and 18th June.[958] We lay down on the mud around our fires, and the rain continued pouring on us all night.'

'In the morning we were almost petrified with cold, many could not stand, and some were quite stupified. Poor Pratt, who had fainted the day before at Genappe, set off (at our earnest entreaty, and promise to call him when things looked serious) towards Mont St. Jean, and shortly after we found him at our fire, unconscious of where he had been or what he was about. I had occasion to pull open the buttons of my cloaths about 9 o'clock on the night of [the] 17th, and was not able to re-button them till eleven this morning. It was a miserable night; however, motion brought us about in some degree, and we began to gape and stroll about the field. The rain had ceased, and our soldiers were busily employed in firing off and cleaning their pieces in case of accidents.'

Elkington painted a similar picture: 'Early in the morn it began to clear. The men and officers were actually benumbed, being so saturated with the wet. After a little running about, wringing their blankets, and the issue of some spirits, the circulation returned, and by 10 o'clock the muskets were all in good order.'[959]

The 40th Regiment spent the 17th marching in the opposite direction, towards the front. Late on the evening of the 16th Wellington had sent orders for Lambert's brigade to march from Asche to Genappe, but as they approached Brussels they were met with new orders directing them on to Quatre Bras.

---

[954] William Siborne, *The Waterloo Campaign 1815*, 5th Edition, 1900, p. 284.

[955] Picton ordered Cleeve's and Lloyd's batteries of the 3rd Division to engage the French guns. Sergeant Tom Morris reckoned that 'one of their large shot killed two of our [73rd] Light Company'.

[956] Private George Smith of the 30th was killed on the 17th of June.

[957] Morris, p.p. 73-4.

[958] The 3rd Division should have been fed at Genappe but, according to Lieutenant Pattison of the 33rd, 'From the cowardice of the Commissariat – whose duty it was to make provision for the troops, but who, in a panic, fled – no refreshment could be obtained there, except what was got by the men individually here and there.' The offending Commissary was later court-martialed.

[959] Elkington's Journal, in the *XXX Journal*, June 1911, p. 13.

'We marched through Brussels,' reminisced Sergeant Lawrence, 'amid the joy of the inhabitants, who brought us out all manner of refreshments. I heard some remarks from them to the effect that we were all going to be slaughtered like bullocks, but we only laughed at this, telling them that this was nothing new to us.'[960]

That afternoon, south of Brussels, they found a scene of confusion, with baggage, wounded and stragglers all falling back. The brigade was ordered to halt at the village of Épinay, on the northern side of the forest of Soignies, following a false report that the enemy's cavalry was threatening the army's communication with Brussels. The troops were in a continued state of excitement, and when fleeing Hanoverians of the Cumberland Hussars galloped in, declaring they were pursued by the French, bugles sounded and the troops ran to their alarm-posts in front of the village until Sir John Lambert coolly dismissed the scare and went back to his dinner, a turbot brought out from Brussels by his butler.

That afternoon and evening, while Lambert's brigade stood fast at Épinay, the 40th were drenched by the same thunderstorm as the troops further south. 'That night,' recalled Lawrence, 'we crept into any holes we could find, cowsheds, cart-houses, and all kinds of farmstead buildings, for shelter, and I never remember a worse night in the Peninsular war, for the rain descended in torrents, mixed with fearful thunder and lightning, and seeming to foretell the fate of the following day, the 18th.'

Major Arthur Heyland, commanding the 40th, wrote a fond farewell letter to his wife and children, of which the following are extracts:

'My darling Mary, I must tell you again how tranquilly I shall die, should it be my fate to fall. We cannot, my own love, die together – one or other must witness the loss of what we love most. Let my children console you, my love.'

'My children, may you all be happy and may the reflection that your father never in his life swerved from the truth and always acted from the dictates of his conscience preserve you virtuous and happy, for without virtue there can be no happiness.'

'The hazards of military life are considerable, but still it has its pleasures, and it appears to me of no consequence whether a man dies old or young, provided he is employed in fulfilling the duties of the situation he is placed in in this world... I have no desponding ideas on entering the field, but I cannot help thinking it almost impossible I should escape either wounds or death.'

There was little opportunity for rest, for in the course of that night Lambert's Brigade was ordered forward to Wellington's chosen position south of the Forest of Soignies. Their march was very much impeded by upset wagons and baggage, which choked the vital Brussels chaussée north of the village of Waterloo.

'All that night was one continuous clamour,' recalled Sergeant Lawrence, 'for thousands of camp followers were on their retreat to Brussels, fearful of sticking to the army after the Quatre Bras affair. It was indeed a sight, for owing to the rain and continued traffic the roads were almost impassible, and the people were sometimes completely stuck in the mud: and besides these a continual stream of baggage-wagons was kept up through the night.'[961]

The Duke sent Sir George Scovell back to ensure the rear was unblocked, and at around 6 a.m. Lambert's brigade was ordered to clear the road before they moved on. According to Lieutenant Edward Drewe of the 27th, '[we] were occupied some time in clearing the road of provision carts containing bread, forage, and spirits that had been left on the road by the peasantry taking their animals from the carts, and concealing themselves in the wood.'[962] The troops were not impressed, as Harry Smith recorded:

'Our men were on fire at the idea of having to remain and clear a road when an attack was momentarily expected, and an hour would bring us to the position. The wand of a magician, with all his spells and incantations, could not have effected a clear course sooner than our three thousand soldiers of the old school.'

Nevertheless, as a result of this diversion, it was between 10 and 11 a.m. on the 18th before the 40th reached the field of Waterloo.

---

[960] Lawrence, p.p. 204-05.
[961] Lawrence, p. 206.
[962] *Waterloo Letters*, edited by Major-General H. T. Siborne, London, 1891, No. 174.

The Field of Waterloo

Weeks before the opening of hostilities, the Duke of Wellington had noted the tactical potential of the ridges astride the chaussée south of the Forest of Soignies if he should have to fight a defensive battle in front of Brussels, and on the morning of the 17th he sent Colonel De Lancey, his Quartermaster-General (chief of staff) to carry out a rear reconnaissance of that area. De Lancey confirmed the suitability of the position at Mont St. Jean, and on his return to Wellington, then at Genappe, the decision to withdraw to the future field of Waterloo was taken. The Duke's resolve to stand and fight there was made on the assumption that Blucher would march from Wavre to his support on the 18th. This would involve a ten-mile advance across difficult country to attack Buonaparte's right rear.

The battlefield of Waterloo is remarkably small, with most of the fighting confined to an area hardly more than two miles square. It is centred on a shallow, gently rolling valley bounded to north and south by low ridges, running from south-west to north-east, and crossed by two main roads, both of which in 1815 were broad highways with paved centres. The Genappe and Nivelles chaussées converged near the farm of Mont St. Jean, half a mile behind the northern ridge, then ran on towards Brussels.

The northern, or Mont St. Jean Ridge (also known as Wellington's Ridge) rises by no more than one hundred feet from the valley. It is centred on the Elm Tree Crossroads, where the Charleroi-Genappe-Brussels chaussée bisects the crest-line. From this crossroads a minor road, or cart-track, from Wavre ran along the crest of the ridge, which for over two miles would form the Allied front line. For some two hundred yards to the south and west of the crossroads both roads were sunk in cuttings, some ten feet deep in places and significant obstacles to cavalry, while the minor lateral road was bounded for much of its length by low banks and hedges. Behind the crest, a classic reverse slope position gave complete cover from view, a measure of protection from fire, and security for manoeuvre of reserves. During the battle the 30th were frequently obliged to advance and hold the crest, sometimes for considerable periods, but they were withdrawn under cover whenever possible.

Substantial walled farms on the forward slope became redoubts around which to disrupt enemy advances. The right flank of the position was anchored on the chateau and grounds of Hougoumont, and the left flank lay on the village of Smohain, the farms of Papelotte and Frichermont, and surrounding deep lanes and close country. In the centre, to the west of the Genappe-Brussels chaussée stood the walled farm of La Haie Sainte, with its garden and orchard, a bastion some two hundred yards in front of the vital Elm Tree Crossroads, additionally strengthened by a sandpit and knoll on the far side of the road to its left rear.

Across the valley from the Mont St. Jean Ridge, the chaussée rose to the inn of La Belle Alliance, which was the central point of the southern, or La Belle Alliance Ridge, which would be occupied by the French. The two ridges were some 1,400 yards apart in the centre, but closed to around four hundred yards on both flanks. Almost half-way between the two main ridges, and mostly to the east of the chaussée, lay a further bare height running north-east for some thousand yards. From its role in the battle this became known as the Grand Battery Ridge.

One final point must be made about the shape of the ground to the west of the Genappe-Brussels chaussée. In 1815 the crest from the Elm Tree Crossroads towards Hougoumont rose gradually until, some five hundred yards from the chaussée, it had gained about fifty feet. At that point the track forked, one branch running north-west towards Braine l'Alleud, the other continuing along the crest-line. The whole ridge was considerably lowered and reshaped in 1823-26 to provide soil for the Lion Monument (*Butte de Lion*) which today disfigures that part of the ridge. Before the erection of that great mound, the ridge-top was effectively divided in two by a steep and prominent spur, or tongue of ground, jutting out and rising to a dominating plateau-like summit, slightly higher than the main ridge and some two hundred yards south of the track junction. The subsequent removal of this dominating feature, and the adjacent ridge-top, by the Dutch altered the lie of that part of the field to the extent that Lieutenant John Pratt, visiting the field in about 1833, 'tried in vain for several hours to place myself in the exact position occupied by the 30th Regt on that day… the crest of that part of the position has been lowered and

I very much doubt if a regiment lying down in the position occupied by the 30th in square during that day would now – in the actual state of the ground – receive much shelter from the fire of the enemy batteries.'

The Emperor brought some 53,400 infantry, 15,600 cavalry and 246 guns to the field, while Wellington mustered 53,850 infantry, 13,350 cavalry and 157 guns, with a further 15,000 infantry, 1,200 cavalry and 22 guns detached at Halle, ten miles to the west. Apart from artillery, and to a lesser degree cavalry, the opposing armies were nearly matched numerically, but numbers alone can be very deceptive.

Whereas the French had a homogeneous army composed very largely of highly motivated veterans, Wellington had a disparate polyglot force including units of variable morale, training and experience, and some contingents of doubtful loyalty and willingness to fight. He could only completely rely on his 33,600 British and King's German Legion troops (21,100 infantry, 8,700 cavalry and 95 guns). The consequence was that the Duke's defensive disposition was an untidy but carefully blended multinational patchwork, with less dependable and inexperienced contingents interspersed and stiffened with British and King's German troops, while many of the least reliable, largely Dutch-Belgian units, were held in reserve.

At daybreak on 18th June the 30th found themselves in the middle of the centre right of Wellington's ridge, which was held by Alten's 3rd Division from the Elm Tree Crossroads to just beyond the 'Lion Spur,' from where Cooke's Guards Division continued the front line to Hougoumont. Halkett's 5th Brigade were on the right of the 3rd Division, with the Hanoverian and King's German Legion brigades of Kielmansegge and Ompteda to their left, supported by Kruse's Nassauers. The 2nd Light Battalion of the King's German Legion held La Haie Sainte, with the 1st/95th holding the roadside sandpit and knoll in support. On the far side of the chaussée, beyond the crossroads, stood Picton's 5th Division, with Perponcher's 2nd Netherlands Division to their left around Smohain, Papelotte and Frichermont. The Allied cavalry stood in support further down the reverse slope, as did Wellington's infantry reserves, including Clinton's 2nd British Division, the Brunswick Contingent and, out on the extreme right at Braine l'Alleud, Chassé's 3rd Netherlands Division. Almost all these infantry reserves were initially stationed to the west of the Nivelle chaussée, a reflection of Wellington's concern for his right flank.

There was a significant exception to the generally westward deployment of the British infantry reserves, and that was Sir John Lambert's 10th Brigade of Peninsula veterans, who, after a march of 54 miles in two days, approached Mont St. Jean that morning between 10 and 11 a.m. General Lambert sent his brigade major, Harry Smith to Wellington for orders.

'I was to find the Duke himself, and receive orders from no other person. About 11 o'clock I found his Grace and all his staff near Hougoumont. The day was beautiful after the storm, although the country was very heavy. When I rode up, he said, "Hallo, Smith, where are you from last?"

"From General Lambert's Brigade, and they from America."

"What have you got?"

"The 4th, the 27th, and the 40th; the 81st remain in Brussels."

"Ah, I know, I know; but the others, are they in good order?"

"Excellent, my lord, and very strong."

"That's all right, for I shall soon want every man."

One of his staff said, "I do not think they will attack today." "Nonsense," said the Duke. "The columns are already forming, and I think I have discerned where the weight of the attack will be made. I shall be attacked before an hour. Do you know anything of my position, Smith?"

"Nothing, my lord, beyond what I see – the general line, and right and left."

"Go back and halt Lambert's Brigade at the junction of the two great roads from Genappe and Nivelles. Did you observe their junction as you rode up?"

"Particularly, my lord."

"Having halted the head of the Brigade and told Lambert what I desire, ride to the left of the position. On the extreme left is the Nassau Brigade, those fellows who came over to us at Arbonne, you recollect. Between them and Picton's Division (now the 5th) I shall most probably require Lambert. There is already there a Brigade of newly-raised Hanoverians, which Lambert will give orders to, as they and your Brigade form the 6th Division.

You are the only British Staff Officer with it. Find out, therefore, the best and shortest road from where Lambert is now halted to the left of Picton and the right of the Nassau troops. Do you understand?"

"Perfectly, my Lord." I had barely turned from his Grace when he called me back. "Now, clearly understand that when Lambert is ordered to move from the fork of the two roads, where he is now halted, you are prepared to conduct him to Picton's left." I had hardly got back to Lambert, after reconnoitring the country and preparing myself to conduct the troops, when the Battle of Waterloo commenced.'

It had been intended that Lambert's 10th Brigade, with Best's 4th Hanoverian Brigade should form the 6th Division under Sir Lowry Cole, but the latter was absent on his honeymoon and so, on arrival at Mont St. Jean, Lambert took over that division while Lieutenant-Colonel Francis Brooke of the 4th (King's Own) assumed command of the brigade.

The 40th halted in column of companies on the left of the road near the farm of Mont St. Jean and the junction of the Genappe and Nivelles chaussées. Having piled arms, the exhausted men lay down and, oblivious of the battle that was shortly raging to their front, and artillery 'overs' which occasionally ploughed through their ranks, many slept until called forward several hours later. Lieutenant James Mill's diary suggests that their officers went forward to examine the ground.

The strength of the 40th, according to the Adjutant-General's return for 18th June 1815, was 43 officers, 57 sergeants, 17 drummers and 747 rank and file, totaling 864 all ranks, but the Waterloo Medal Roll, which is probably more accurate as regards presence on the battlefield, lists only 42 officers and 748 other ranks.[963]

Meanwhile, the 30th prepared for battle in the most advanced and exposed position of Wellington's front line. Their total strength, allowing for the casualties at Quatre Bras and on the 17th, was probably close to the 615 quoted by Siborne, though Macready stated that 'from the number of sick, and on detached duties, they did not enter the field above 460 bayonets' (i.e. rank and file), and he may be right. Based on their Waterloo Medal Roll, less the casualties on the 16th and 17th June, the 2nd/30th should have brought a total of 618 all ranks to the field: 40 officers, 38 staff-sergeants and sergeants, 13 drummers and 527 rank and file.

The medal roll, entitling those listed to the coveted medal, prize money and two years extra service or seniority, should have been absolutely accurate, but it is not infallible. In 1878, Sergeant John Goddard, who had served with the 30th from 1829 to 1836 when many 'Waterloo Men' were still present, wrote to the then sergeant-major of the Regiment. He mentioned a number of anomalies. He told of how Private Thomas Smith, a Yorkshire man who was in hospital in Brussels when the 30th marched to Waterloo, scaled the walls and joined his company, fought all day and got back into hospital before the roll was called. His name was not put forward for the medal, but despite several applications when he was later serving in India, it was not until Smith's discharge that Edward Macready, then a captain commanding the Regimental Depot, managed to obtain for him the much-prized medal. Even more bizarre was the case of Private Mulhally, who in jest had picked up and put on a French cuirass: this was apparently construed as an act of cowardice, and he was not allowed his medal, extra years' service or prize money. On the other hand, Private (later Colour-Sergeant) Frank Curtis, who was Orderly Room Clerk at Brussels and whose duty was to make out the roll, apparently added his own name and wore the medal despite being nowhere near the field of battle.[964]

Halkett's brigade, consisting of the 30th, 33rd, 69th and 73rd, stood on the right of Sir Charles Alten's 3rd Division, with Kielmansegge's Hanoverians to their left and Maitland's brigade of Guards to their right, and were initially stationed just to the west of the present Lion Mound and some hundred yards west of the track junction mentioned above, behind the summit of the spur. They were at first lying down in column on the reverse slope of the ridge, with a bank and sparse beech hedge on the lateral lane immediately to their front. Macready observed that the slope was 'covered with grain higher than our heads.'

---

[963] It is reasonable to assume that not all those 'on the strength' were present at Waterloo. Captain Richard Turton is known to have been left behind at Ghent or on the line of march, there would have been a baggage escort, some sick, and no doubt a few men fell out on the forced march from Ghent.

[964] *Reminiscences of an Old Comrade*, published in *The XXX* regimental journal, October and November 1885.

The layout of the 3rd Division was delegated by Sir Charles Alten to Captain James Shaw, who, noting the strength of the French cavalry and artillery, laid the units out so that they had the necessary deploying intervals to move rapidly from line into square and back again, depending on the threat. When in squares, or 'oblongs' as Shaw rather pedantically described them, the Division was to assume a chequer-board formation in two lines, five squares in the first line and four in the second line, which covered the intervals in the first line. The stronger battalions were to form their own squares, while the numerically weaker ones were combined. In Halkett's brigade, the 30th and 73rd would form a single square in the first line, with the 33rd and 69th, also acting together, in second line some hundred yards to the right rear. Lieutenant Frederick Hope Pattison of the 33rd, in his *Personal Recollections of the Waterloo Campaign*, gave a rather more detailed description of this initial brigade deployment:

'The 73rd and 30th Regiments formed contiguous columns of companies at quarter distance, the former right, and the latter left, in front. The 33rd and 69th were also formed in contiguous columns of companies at quarter distance, in second line to the right of the 73rd and 30th Regiments, they being at an intermediate distance to the rear, of from 80 to 100 paces, intersected by the Wavre Road, each brigade preserving its relative distance so as to deploy into line in case of a simultaneous advance, which actually took place at the crisis.'

To the left of the 30th and 73rd, the Bremen and Verden battalions of Kielmansegge's brigade, also acting as one corps, were deployed close to the track junction, while a Nassau battalion in the second line covered the deploying interval between the Bremen and Verden square and that of the 30th and 73rd. To the right stood the 3rd/1st Guards, the left flank battalion of Maitland's brigade.

In front of the crest-line were posted Lloyd's and Cleeves' batteries of 9-pounders, Lloyd to the right of the 30th and Cleeves to the left. Behind Halkett and Kielmansegge were the predominantly Hanoverian cavalry brigades of Dornberg and Arenschildt respectively, while Lord Edward Somerset's brigade of Household Cavalry stood beside the Charleroi road in support of Ompteda.

In marked contrast to Wellington's patchwork deployment, the French layout on La Belle Alliance Ridge was remarkably uniform and symmetrical. D'Erlon's Ist Corps deployed to the right of the Charleroi chaussée, and Reille's IInd Corps to the left, with Kellerman's and Milhaud's Cavalry Corps respectively behind them, and Jacquinot's and Piré's light cavalry divisions on the right and left flanks. Lobau's VIth Corps and the Imperial Guard stood in reserve astride the Charleroi chaussée. Whilst almost all the Allied troops were screened by their reverse slope deployment, the imposing French array was paraded in full view of its opponents.

'About ½ past ten o'clock,' recalled Macready, 'the enemy began moving his forces, and displayed strong columns of infantry and cavalry opposite every part of our position. A superb line of red Lancers stretched from their left, far beyond our right flank, but from the nature of the ground and the disposition of Clinton's division they were not much feared. Thus, at near eleven o'clock, stood the contending armies… We (I mean the multitude) were not aware that Blucher could afford us any assistance, as we heard that he was completely beaten and hotly pursued; but no British soldier could dread the result when Wellington commanded. Our poor fellows looked wretchedly, but the joke and laugh was bandied between them, heartily and thoughtlessly as in their happiest hours.

'About eleven o'clock some rations and spirits came up; the latter was immediately served out to the men, but I dared not drink on my empty stomach. I had just stuck a ramrod thro' a noble slice of bull beef, and was fixing it on the fire, when an aide de camp galloped up, and roared out, "Stand to your arms." We were in line in an instant.'

Opening Moves

It was late morning before the battle opened: the heavy downpour did not ease up until just before dawn, leaving the fields sodden and tracks little better. Movement of horses, guns and wagons was slowed by clinging clay and muddy puddles, and this in particular delayed the deployment of Buonaparte's artillery. In addition, many of the French bivouacs were some considerable distance from the field, and there was only one good approach road. Consequently, his army was far from ready for the Emperor's originally intended 9 a.m. attack.

Buonaparte eventually issued his orders at 11 a.m. Despite the advice of Peninsula veterans among his generals, he was brusquely dismissive of his enemy: 'Because you have been beaten by Wellington,' he told Soult, his Chief of Staff, 'you consider him a great general. And now I tell you that Wellington is a bad general, that the English are bad troops, and that this affair is nothing more serious than eating one's breakfast.' In consequence of these arrogant assumptions, his battle plan was brutally simplistic. His intention, disregarding any possibility of a Prussian advance, was to smash the centre of Wellington's line with concentrated artillery fire and then launch his two leading corps in a massive frontal assault to take Mont St. Jean and push on to Brussels.

Ensign Edward Macready of the Light Company, 30th, aged just seventeen, watched as the French moved to their battle positions:

'Considerable movements were perceptible among the enemy's columns, and from the number of mounted officers riding to and from one group of horsemen, I should think Napoleon was there, issuing his decrees. Our artillery arrived full gallop, and the guns were disposed on the most favourable ground in front of their respective divisions. The regiments formed column and marched a little to the rear, under cover of the brow of the hill; our company and the 73rd Grenadiers were ordered as coverers to Cleve's and Lloyd's brigades of guns. The men were in great measure covered by the crest of the hill, but the whole French army, with the exception of its reserve, was exposed to our artillery. There was a pause for some minutes, and I imagined there were few of the many thousands assembled that did not experience a sort of chill, and rising sensation in their breasts. It was indeed a spirit-stirring sight – the chivalry of two mighty nations in grand and deadly rivalry.'

The Emperor's simple plan was almost immediately modified, possibly as he lost patience with the delay, for by about 11.30 a.m. he committed Reille to what was almost certainly intended as a limited diversionary attack against the loopholed chateau of Hougoumont to draw Wellington's reserves away from the centre. In the event, this move proved to be a major diversion for the French, who became bogged down in successive attacks on Hougoumont throughout the day, involving nearly a quarter of their infantry, whilst Wellington economically fed in just sufficient reserves to hold the place.

Standing with the 30th 'Light Bobs' on the forward slope by the guns, Edward Macready prepared for battle:

'At length the enemy's left appeared in motion towards Hougomont, and old Cleve slapped away at them. When the first shot was fired [by Cleeves' Battery] I threw off a wet blanket I had wrap'd around me, gave myself a shake, and… considered all as clear gain that I might bring out of the battle. Cleve's guns, which told most gloriously on the columns as they approached the orchard, were unanswered for some minutes, but we soon saw the enemy's artillery trotting down the hill, and at once they opened from above two hundred pieces. The cannonade extended along the whole line, and the musketry commenced in thundering volleys at Hougomont.'

Halkett's flankers were soon ordered down the slope to protect the Allied guns, and, extending his men to twelve paces between files, Lieutenant-Colonel Charles Vigoureux joined a line of skirmishers extending from the rear of the Hougoumont grounds to La Haie Sainte. On their right, in Hougoumont orchard, were the two light companies of the 1st Guards under Lord Saltoun, while to their left Kielmansegge's Hanoverian 2nd Feldjäger Company and Ompteda's light troops continued the line to La Haie Sainte. Lieutenant John Pratt of the Light Company 30th, who acted as Vigoureux's adjutant, preserved Halkett's orders to his Light Battalion, which were:

'To cover and protect our batteries. To establish ourselves at all times as much in advance as might be compatible with prudence. To preserve considerable intervals between our extended files for greater security from the fire of the enemy's batteries. To show obstinate resistance against Infantry of the same description, but to attempt no formation or offer useless opposition to charges of Cavalry, but to retire in time upon the squares in our rear, moving in a direct line without any reference to Regiments or Nations. When the charge was repulsed, to resume our ground.'[965]

---

[965] Letter by Major John Pratt to Siborne, dated London 23rd March 1835 (*Waterloo Letters*, No. 138).

From this skirmishing line, Edward Macready had a clear view of the first, and fiercest, of the assaults on Hougoumont:

'The obstinacy of the assailants was only exceeded by the gallantry of their opponents. For an hour and a half they were muzzle to muzzle and bayonet to bayonet. Fresh bodies were poured in incessantly by the enemy, and the Guards repeatedly reinforced their comrades. I saw them amid the flames of the trees and outhouses, to which the French had set fire, alternately advancing and retiring, first the red and then the blue jackets prevailing. Around single trees whole companies lay dead. At length the overwhelming force of the enemy enabled him to establish himself in the orchard and gardens, and the building itself became the point of attack. From its doors and windows our gallant Guardsmen poured an unceasing shower of bullets, and the enemy fell dead in heaps around them. Repeated and successful sallies astonished the Frenchmen, and convinced them of the inutility of their perseverance. After two hours of most determined exertion they retired from this spot, leaving it covered with the bodies of their countrymen. The conduct of the Guards was most glorious.

'On the retreat of the enemy, the firing still continued at this point; but it was no longer considered as an attack, merely occupation for both parties. The artillery on both sides, covered by their respective light troops, who kept up a brisk fire, were dealing destruction around them; and the only bodies in motion were the groups of staff officers, who attracted the fire of the enemy and the curses of their friends wherever they appeared.'

Whilst combat raged around Hougoumont, only the light troops of Halkett's brigade were engaged, and his battalions remained in contiguous columns of companies at quarter distance[966] in dead ground, 'lying at length under the hill to shelter themselves as much as possible from the showers of shot and shell which were tearing up every part of the field.' The 30th were on the left of the 73rd.

'We were under the brow of a hill,' wrote Lieutenant Francis Tincombe, 'but they soon found us out, and then shot and shell did great execution among our squares.'

It was about 1 p.m. when the French, having at length hauled sixty guns and twenty howitzers onto the Grand Battery Ridge, opened their preliminary bombardment, at a range of six to eight hundred yards, upon the centre and centre-left of Wellington's front line. Thanks to the Duke's use of the reverse slope to protect almost all his troops, leaving few exposed in the target area, and the deadening effect of the soft ground, the noise and apparent intensity of this massed artillery belied its negligible effect. It failed to smash the anticipated hole in Wellington's line, and only the Dutch/Belgians of Bijlandt's brigade, initially exposed on the forward slope, were 'softened up'.

At around 1.30 p.m. the Emperor launched what was intended to be his decisive blow, a deliberate attack on Wellington's left, from Papelotte to La Haie Sainte. This massed assault, on a frontage of over one thousand yards was made by the twenty thousand men of d'Erlon's I[st] Corps, additionally supported on their left by Dubois' 1st Cuirassier Brigade. It was Buonaparte's best chance of victory, and the outcome was for a few minutes in doubt; indeed, some historians have termed it the crisis of the whole battle. Suffice to say that the main effort, to the east of the Charleroi road, was eventually checked by Kempt's and Pack's brigades of Picton's 5th Division and then routed by Sir William Ponsonby's Union Brigade with a perfectly timed counter-stroke. The British heavy cavalry took some three thousand prisoners and two eagles, and then rode on through the French Grand Battery, cutting down gunners, before they were themselves counter-attacked from the front and left flank by 2,400 French lancers and chasseurs. Their horses blown, the elated troopers out of hand, and regiments disorganised, the British heavies were driven back with severe loss.

The initial French attack was rather more successful at La Haie Sainte, where Quiot's division captured the garden and orchard around the farm and drove the 1st/95th from the sandpit, almost isolating the defenders. Wellington sent Kielmansegge's newly-raised Lüneburg Light Battalion down the hill to reinforce La Haie Sainte, As they approached the farm, around which there was considerable smoke and confusion, the untried Hanoverians met the Allied skirmish line falling back, and then, to their horror, saw hundreds of French cuirassiers breasting

---

[966] A battalion in column at quarter distance, the standard formation for battlefield movement, would have a frontage of about twenty yards and a depth of fifty yards.

a rise less than two hundred yards to their front. These were the 1st and 4th Cuirassiers of Dubois' brigade, 780 heavy cavalry. The Hanoverians attempted to regain the heights, but were caught and sabred, as were some of Alten's skirmishers. Edward Macready described the scene:

'Our company and the 73rd Grenadiers, after a pretty long skirmish, had pushed our opponents close under their guns, and our shot began to whistle among the artillerymen, when we perceived a body of cavalry coming down on us at a gallop. We were too far extended to effect any formation, and the ground was quite open, so Colonel Vigoureux gave the word to us to make off, and away we went at score. Pratt, with some men, reached an Hanoverian square;[967] Rumley, one of Nassau's; and I, with about a dozen men, made our own. The rest of our men were dispersed into La Haye Sainte and various squares, and some few of them cut down. Our rapid retreat was peculiarly dangerous, as we had to run thro' high corn towards our own guns, which opened with grape on the enemy's cavalry.

'Kielmansegg's jägers, who were on our left, trusting to their numbers and the nature of their ground, stood, and were annihilated. After cutting them to pieces, the cavalry galloped up the slope, sabred the greater part of Lloyd's artillerymen, and charged an Hanoverian square. They were repulsed, and before they could effect their retreat, totally destroyed by a squadron of our Life Guards. These ruffians laughed at us as we scudded from their uplifted sabres, but as their own proverb says, *"il rit bien qui rit le dernier."* I could not help grinning at some of '*les bons sabreurs*,' tho' certainly they made noble-looking corpses.'

The British counter-attack west of the Charleroi road, by Lord Somerset's Household Cavalry, was simultaneous, at about 2.20 p.m., with that of Ponsonby's Union Brigade to their left, and resulted in the only heavy cavalry melee of the day, when 840 Life Guards and Horse Guards advanced between the King's German Legion and Hanoverian squares to meet Dubois' Cuirassiers on the crest. After a short sharp hand-to-hand struggle, the cuirassiers turned to flee, pursued by excited British horsemen, many of whom were then caught up in the attack on the French gun lines.

Although D'Erlon's attack was heavily defeated, it had caused significant loss to Wellington's left centre, which was in any case the weakest part of his line. Picton was killed at the head of his division, Bijlandt's brigade had retired in disorder, and the brigades of Kempt and Pack, already thinned by heavy casualties at Quatre Bras, had suffered further loss. Moreover, the Union Brigade was almost a spent force, its commander among the dead[968], and the Household Cavalry little better. Accordingly, at about 3 p.m., the Duke ordered forward Lambert's brigade to bolster his centre, a move anticipated by Harry Smith:

'We soon saw that where we should be moved to, the weight of the attack on Picton would be resisted by none but British soldiers. For a few seconds, while every regiment was forming square, and the charge of Ponsonby's Brigade going on (which the rising ground in our front prevented us seeing), it looked as if the formation was preparatory to a retreat. Many of the rabble of Dutch troops were flying towards us, and, to add to the confusion, soon after came a party of dragoons, bringing with them three (*sic*) eagles and some prisoners. I said to General Lambert, "We shall have a proper brush immediately, for it looks as if our left will be immediately turned, and the brunt of the charge will fall on us." At this moment we were ordered to move to the very spot where the Duke, early in the morning, had expected we should be required. Picton had been killed, Sir James Kempt commanded on the left of the road to Genappe, near La Haye Sainte; his Division had been already severely handled, and we took their position.'

As Lambert's brigade of Peninsula veterans marched forward from Mont St. Jean the band of the 4th King's Own struck up the *Marseillaise*, which was greeted with ironic cheers.

---

[967] In his own account of Waterloo, John Pratt confirmed that 'Throughout the whole day, and during my frequent advances and retreats, I only once, or at most twice, entered my own square, the line on which I had to direct myself usually leading me on a German or Hanoverian square.'

[968] Sir William Ponsonby, commanding the Union Brigade, lost his life when his horse became stuck in a heavy ploughed field and was unable to extricate itself before its rider was killed, apparently by a lancer. On the evening after Quatre Bras, the story goes, Ponsonby had sent his ADC to Colonel Hamilton of the 30th offering to buy the latter's fine charger, Hamilton being wounded; but for some reason the bargain was not concluded and Ponsonby lost his life next day from being badly mounted.

'During this movement,' wrote Sergeant William Lawrence of the Grenadier Company 40th, 'a shell from the enemy cut our deputy-sergeant major in two, and having passed on to take the head off one of my company of grenadiers, named William Hooper, exploded in the rear – not more than one yard from me, hurling me at least two yards into the air; but fortunately doing me but little injury beyond the shaking and carrying a small bit of skin off the side of my face. It was indeed another narrow escape, for it burned the tail of my sash completely off, and turned the handle of my sword perfectly black. I remember remarking to a sergeant who was standing close by me when I fell, "This is sharp work to begin with, I hope it will end better." [969]

Lambert's brigade was to occupy what was in effect Wellington's 'vital ground,' the angle north-east of the Elm Tree Crossroads, with the Charleroi-Brussels chaussée to their right and, on the ridge-top to their front, the sunken lane to Wavre, described by Lieutenant James Mill as a 'ravine'[970], with hedges. Beyond this was rising ground and, some 250 yards away to the right front, the farm of La Haie Sainte, still held by Major Baring's 2nd Light Battalion King's German Legion. The battered 5th Division had closed to their left to fill the gap left by Bijlandt's brigade. Major Fielding Browne, 40th, tells us that Lambert's battalions frequently changed their positions throughout the day, but initially they were drawn up facing the Charleroi chaussée on their right, ready to counter any attempt at a breakthrough along that road. In this position, their left flank was exposed to the French artillery, and shortly after moving into position, Lambert's brigade, and in particular the 27th Inniskillings on their right, suffered severely from what James Mill described as 'a very tremendous cannonade':

'We lay down in square to escape as far as possible its destructive effects. Half the 27th Inniskillings were mowed down in a similar position, without having the power or opportunity to return a shot. At one time the officer commanding the 27th Regiment, when there was a temporary cessation of fire from artillery, rode up to our major and announced the fact of having barely an officer left to command each company. Major Browne offered to lend him some from the 40th. This, however, was imperatively declined. The sergeants of the regiment, he said, liked to command the companies, and he would be loth to deprive them of the honour.'[971]

Returning to the 30th, after the defeat of Dubois' cuirassiers, the Light Company reassembled at Cleeve's Battery and lay down among the guns until ordered back down the slope to engage advancing *tirailleurs*. According to Cotton, 'the entire space between La Haye Sainte and Hougoumont was up to this time defended by Alten's skirmishers, commanded by Colonel Vigoureux (30th Regiment).'[972]

Shortly afterwards, at about 3 p.m., Vigoureux's flankers took part in the repulse of the leading brigade of Bachelu's 5th Division which had advanced across the valley to their front and wheeled to its left in an attempt to envelop Hougoumont through its orchard. Vigoureux hung upon the French column's flank and plied it with musketry, and when Cleeve's guns joined in the brigade was driven back in disorder to the position from which it had started. The skill with which the flank battalion was handled was much admired. Halkett's Light Bobs had now almost run their independent course, but the greatest trials for the 30th were yet ahead.

The French Cavalry Attack

Following the defeat of d'Erlon's attack, there was a very perceptible lull, during which French movements were watched with anxiety as Allied commanders tried to work out what the Emperor's next move might be. The answer, when it came, at about 4 p.m., was a surprise: Buonaparte launched his magnificent heavy cavalry in a massed assault on the unbroken infantry of Wellington's centre and right, a move which left seasoned soldiers on both sides shaking their heads in disbelief, none more so than those French officers who had experienced in the Peninsula the tenacity of British infantry in defence.

It appears that the Emperor, peering through the smoke, had mistaken the rearward movement of wounded and prisoners on the ridge to his front, and of units ordered back to the protection of the reverse slope, for the start

---

[969] Lawrence, p.p. 206-07.
[970] The term 'ravine' in the early nineteenth century meant something rather less dramatic than it does today.
[971] Mill, quoted in *Historical Records of the 40th Regiment*, p. 190.
[972] Sergeant-Major Edward Cotton, *A Voice from Waterloo*, p. 70.

of an Allied retirement. Having misread the battle, he intended to exploit the supposed retreat by launching his heavy cavalry. To prepare for this attack, he deployed the 12-pounder guns of the Imperial Guard, his 'beautiful daughters,' to the west of the chaussée, and pushed forward lighter batteries on his left under cover of a dense line of skirmishers.

In command of the French cavalry assault was Marshal Ney, who eventually committed some nine thousand horsemen: 67 squadrons in twenty regiments of cuirassiers, dragoons, horse grenadiers, carabineers, lancers and chasseurs, of whom over sixty percent were armoured, accompanied by six horse artillery batteries. It would be the most concentrated, prolonged, gallant, and utterly futile cavalry attack in the whole of the Napoleonic Wars.

General Alten and his 3rd Division staff watched the French deployments from near where the Lion Mound now stands, and in front of where the 30th lay concealed. Among the staff who perceived the French intention with mounting incredulity was Captain James Shaw:

'At about four o'clock the cannonade became violent in the extreme, probably as much as has been witnessed in any open field of battle. This was evidently the prelude to some serious attack. To our surprise we saw that it was the prelude to an attack of cavalry upon a grand scale. Such an attack we had fully anticipated would take place at some period of the day; but we had no idea that it would be made upon our line standing in its regular order of battle, and that line as yet unshaken by any previous attack by infantry. The moment that it was observed that the movement of the great masses of the French heavy cavalry was directed towards his division, General Alten passed the order to form oblongs, into which formation the division rapidly passed.'

'The formation and advance of that magnificent and highly disciplined cavalry had, as a spectacle, a very grand effect. These splendid horsemen were enthusiastic in the cause of Napoleon – full of confidence in him and in themselves – thirsting to revenge the reverses which had been suffered by the French armies – led by most experienced and able cavalry commanders – and they submitted to a rigid discipline. Their advance to the attack was splendid and interesting in the extreme. Our surprise at being so soon attacked by this great and magnificent force of cavalry was accompanied with the opinion that the attack was premature, and that we were perfectly prepared and secure against its effects, so far as any military operation can be calculated upon.'[973]

Wellington's line was indeed well prepared to meet such an attack with a combination of artillery, infantry in square, and cavalry in support. As the French squadrons advanced they were first engaged by the Allied guns, stationed forward of the crest-line and firing cannister until the horsemen were almost upon them. The gunners then ran back to the shelter of the nearest infantry squares. Remarkably, although the French cavalry repeatedly overran the Allied batteries there was no attempt to spike or otherwise disable the guns, so that whenever the cavalry passed on the batteries were manned again and resumed firing.

The cavalry then advanced on the squares, the front faces of which opened fire at a range of about thirty yards as described by Sergeant Tom Morris, who stood in the same square as the 30th:

'Our rear ranks poured into them a well-directed fire, which put them into confusion, and they retired; the two front ranks, kneeling, then discharged their pieces at them.'[974]

This caused the attacking horsemen to swerve to the right and left, passing through the intervals of the front line of squares, only to receive the fire of the squares in second line. Whilst the cavalry could not force themselves, or rather their horses, onto the bayonets of the infantry, they made every other effort to enter the squares by firing into them, cutting at the front ranks, and circling round, looking in increasing frustration for a gap in the hedge of bayonets. Despite great gallantry and obstinacy, most authorities agree that all their efforts failed and not one square was broken, or even penetrated.[975]

---

[973] *Notes on the Battle of Waterloo*, General Sir James Shaw Kennedy KCB, 1865, p.p. 114-15.

[974] Morris, p. 77.

[975] However, Sergeant Morris of the 73rd maintained that during the first cavalry attack, 'the square next to us [the 33rd and 69th] was charged at the same time, and were unfortunately broken into and retired in confusion, followed by the cuirassiers; but the Life Guards coming up, the French in their turn were obliged to retrograde, and the 33rd and 69th resumed their position in square, on our right.' (Morris, p. 78).

Their ranks thinned and disorganised by fruitless manoeuvres up to and around the infantry squares, the French horsemen then became vulnerable to counter-attacks by Allied cavalry waiting on the reverse slope, who, although inferior in numbers, were able to drive back their exhausted opponents in a series of limited charges.

The first impact of the renewed French assault was experienced by the light troops skirmishing in the valley, including Ensign Edward Macready:

'Before the commencement of this attack, our company and the Grenadiers of the 73rd were skirmishing briskly in the low ground, covering our guns and annoying those of the enemy. The line of *tirailleurs* opposed to us was not stronger than our own, but on a sudden they were reinforced by numerous bodies, and several guns began playing on us with canister. Our poor fellows drop'd very fast, and Colonel Vigoureux, Rumley, and Pratt[976] were carried off badly wounded in about two minutes. I was now commander of our company.

'We stood under this hurricane of small shot till Halkett sent to order us in, and I brought away about a third of the Light Bobs; the rest were killed or wounded, and I really wonder how one of them escaped. As our bugler was killed [977], I shouted and made signals to move by the left, in order to avoid the fire of our guns and to put as good a face on the business as possible.

'When I reached Lloyd's abandoned guns, I stood near them for about a minute to contemplate the scene: it was grand beyond description. Hougoumont and its wood sent up a broad sheet of flame thro' the dark masses of smoke that overhung the field. Beneath this cloud, the French were indistinctly visible. Here a waving mass of long red feathers could be seen; there, gleams as from a sheet of steel showed that the Cuirassiers were moving. Four hundred cannon were belching forth fire and death on every side. The roaring and shouting were indistinguishably commixed – together they gave me the idea of a labouring volcano.

'Bodies of infantry and cavalry were pouring down on us, and it was time to cut contemplation, so I moved towards our columns, which were standing up in square. Our Regiment and 73rd formed one, and 33rd and 69th another. To our right, beyond them, were the Guards, and on our left the Hanoverians and German Legion of our division.'

'As I entered the rear face of our square I had to step over a body, and looking down, recognised Harry Beere, an officer of our Grenadiers, who about an hour before had shook hands with me, laughing, as I left the column. I was on the usual terms of military intimacy with poor Harry, *i.e.*, if either of us had died a natural death, the other would have pitied him as a good fellow, and smiled at his neighbour as he congratulated him on the step; but seeing his herculean frame and animated countenance thus suddenly stiff and motionless before me (I know not whence the feeling could originate, for I had just seen my dearest friends drop almost with indifference), the tears started in my eyes as I chucked up my head and sighed out, "Poor Harry!" The tear was not dry on my cheek when poor Harry was no longer thought of.

'A few minutes after, the enemy's cavalry galloped up and crowned the crest of our position. Our guns were abandoned, and they formed between the two brigades, about an hundred paces in our front. Their first charge was magnificent. As soon as they quickened their trot into a gallop the Cuirassiers bent their heads, so that the peaks of their helmets looked like vizors, and they seemed cased in armour from the plume to the saddle.

'Not a shot was fired till they were within thirty yards, when the word was given, and our boys peppered away at them. The effect was magical. Thro' the smoke we could see helmets falling, cavaliers starting from their seats with convulsive springs as they received our balls, horses plunging and rearing in the agonies of fright and pain, and crowds of the soldiery dismounted; part of the squadrons in retreat, but the more daring remainder hacking their horses to force them on our bayonets. Our fire soon disposed of these gentlemen.[978]

'The main body re-formed in our front, were reinforced, and rapidly and gallantly repeated their attacks. In fact, from this time (about four o'clock) till near six, we had a constant repetition of these brave but unavailing

---

[976] According to his own account Pratt was not wounded until much later in the day, about 7 p.m.

[977] Drummer Thomas Elliott of the Light Company was killed at Waterloo.

[978] Next morning, on rejoining the 30th, Lieutenant Nevill was informed that some of the wounded horses and cuirassiers had rolled headlong into the squares.

467

charges. There was no difficulty in repulsing them, but our ammunition decreased alarmingly. At length an artillery wagon galloped up, emptied two or three casks of cartridges into the square, and we were all comfortable.

'The best cavalry is contemptible to a steady and well-supplied infantry regiment. Even our men saw this, and began to pity the useless perseverance of their assailants, and as they advanced would growl out "Here come these damned fools again!" One of their superior officers tried a *ruse de guerre* by advancing and dropping his sword, as tho' he surrendered. Some of us were deceived by him, but Halkett ordered the men to fire, and he coolly retired, saluting us.[979]

'Their devotion was invincible. One officer whom we had taken prisoner was asked what force Napoleon might have in the field, and replied, with a smile of mingled derision and threatening, '*Vous verrez bientot sa force, Messieurs.*'

This was the adjutant of the 6th Cuirassiers, brought into the square by Lieutenant Robert Hughes. Captain Arthur Gore tells how Hughes saved him from the bayonets raised to kill him, and taking him by the hand drew him into the square, and for further safety made the young Frenchman take his arm. For three hours they stood arm in arm until the Imperial Guard formed up for attack, when the adjutant implored Hughes to send him to the rear that he might not be killed by his friends. Hughes pointed out that his life would not be worth a minute's purchase if he left the square, but in a moment of confusion they were separated and in all likelihood the young Frenchman was killed.[980]

'A private Cuirassier was wounded and drag'd into the square; his only cry was, '*Tuez, donc, tuez, tuez moi, soldats!*' and as one of our men drop't dead close to him, he seized his bayonet, and forced it into his own neck; but this not despatching him, he raised up his cuirass, plunged it into his stomach, and kept working it about till he ceased to breathe.[981]

'Tho' we constantly thrashed our steel-clad opponents, we found more troublesome customers in the round shot and grape which all this time played on us with terrible effect, and fully avenged the Cuirassiers. Often, as the volleys created openings in our square, would the cavalry dash on, but they were uniformly unsuccessful.[982] A regiment on our right [the 33rd] seemed sadly disconcerted, and at one moment were in considerable confusion. Halkett rode out, and seizing their snow-white colour, waved it over his head, and restored them to something like order, tho' not before his horse was shot under him.[983] At the height of their unsteadiness we got the order 'Right face,' to move to their assistance. Some of the men mistook it for 'Right about,' and faced accordingly, when old Major M'Laine, 73rd, called out, "No, my boys, it's 'right face'; you'll never hear the right about as long as a French bayonet's in front of you!' In a few moments he was mortally wounded. We would willingly have charged these guns, but had we deployed the cavalry that flanked them would have made an example of us.'

'A regiment of Light Dragoons, by their facings either 16th or 23rd, came up on our left and charged the Cuirassiers.[984] We cheered each other as they passed us. They did all they could, but were obliged to retire after a very few minutes at the sabre. A body of Belgian cavalry advanced for the same purpose, but, on passing our square, they stop'd short. Our noble Halkett rode out to them and offered to charge at their head. It was of no use. The Prince of Orange came up and exhorted them to do their duty, but in vain. They hesitated till a few shots whizzed through them, when they turned about and galloped like fury, or, rather, like fear. As they passed the right

---

[979] This incident is also mentioned by Captain Arthur Gore.

[980] Years later Macready amplified his account, saying, 'I was near him soon after that gallant fellow Hughes, wounded as he was, had brought him in a prisoner, when some of ours told me to speak to him, and on my blundering out '*Bonaparte quel force a-t-il?*' he replied with an angry smile, offended I suppose at my omission of Napoleon's title, '*Vous verrez sa force bientôt, Messieurs*'.

[981] This incident is also mentioned by Sergeant Tom Morris of the 73rd, at whom the cuirassier had made a cut.

[982] According to Dalton's *Waterloo Roll Call*, p. 186, 'Once, and once only, during the dreadful carnage at Waterloo did the stern 73rd fail to fill up a gap which the relentless iron had torn in their square. Their Colonel [Harris], at once pushing his horse lengthways across the space, said, with a smile, "Well, my lads, if you won't, I must." Immediately his horse was led back to its proper place and the ranks closed up by men still more devoted than before'.

[983] 'The other square (33rd and 69th) was in our rear rather to the right', wrote Francis Tincombe. 'They were ordered up but I am sorry to say did not behave as well as we could have wished.'

[984] It was the 23rd Light Dragoons of Dornberg's 3rd Cavalry Brigade, which was posted in rear of Halkett's brigade.

face of our square the men, irritated by their rascally conduct, unanimously took up their pieces and poured in a volley among them, and 'many a good tall fellow was destroyed so cowardly.'

This body of cavalry must have been part of Tripp's Dutch/Belgian Heavy Cavalry Brigade, who had fought well at first but then refused to charge and fled. An account by Lieutenant Pattison of the 33rd is consistent with Macready's observation:

'As they passed near the 73rd Regiment, then in square, Sir Colin Halkett… commanded them to halt. Then he earnestly addressed them, and proposed that they should charge a menacing body of French cavalry to his right. He drew his sword to lead the charge; but they hesitated, and in spite of his noble example and earnest exhortations, nothing could induce them to follow him. Soon after this, the leading troops went threes about, and, followed by the whole regiment, galloped off the field, pursued by the indignant execrations, hissings and hootings of our brigade.' Tincombe of the 30th, too, stated that 'The Belgian cavalry ordered to support us ran away.'

Commenting on Macready's account of the French cavalry action, Major Bailey wrote, 'I remember four or five consecutive charges from the Cuirassiers and Imperial Guards [Cavalry]. Do you remember a Captain of the latter body being mortally wounded, when some of us tried to rally his spirits, and we either tried or did get him into our square?'

Regarding the Allied cavalry counter-attacks in their part of the field, and in particular the actions of the British hussars and Belgian heavy cavalry, in 1844 Major Macready asked his correspondents, 'Did you see these incidents? And did you see any other of our cavalry charge by us during the time the French horsemen held the ground in front of us? I certainly did not, between the Life Guard charge in the early part of the day and the passage of the German hussars to our right at night.' Bailey responded, 'It was the 23rd [Light Dragoons] that made the charge alluded to, & our boys, thinking the regt. was the runaway Belgian regt. from having [*illegible*] the same uniform, continued to fire on them whilst retreating, & I could only prevent this by going personally in front. I saw no other cavalry regt. charge.'

At some point during the cavalry attacks, it appears that Wellington ordered the infantry squares over the ridge-top to give some protection to the artillery batteries, as described by Lieutenant Francis Tincombe:

'We were moved forward to support our guns, which [the cavalry] had charged and taken five out of six of our brigade belonging to the division, but fortunately when they saw us they left the guns and charged. We could not fire before the artillerymen were clear of us, many of whom came into our square for protection. At length the moment came. We gave them a terrible fire which no troops could withstand. They ran, formed again and charged – off again – charged several times but could not come near us.'

From their exposed forward position, the 30th and 73rd were at the very heart of the storm throughout the attacks of the French cavalry. Captain Arthur Gore of the Grenadier Company 30th reckoned that 'the square formed by the 30th and 73rd British regiments, somewhat in advance, immediately under the command… of Major-General Sir Colin Halkett, was charged eleven times by the lancers of the guard and cuirassiers,' and Colonel Harris of the 73rd in a letter to Cotton wrote that, 'My impression is that the gallant and enduring stand made by the 30th and 73rd Regiments against *thirteen* charges of cuirassiers and an unceasing discharge of artillery for seven hours, besides the fact of successfully driving the French cavalry away by a charge in square, has not been done sufficient justice by historians of the battle.'

The 40th also faced alternating cavalry and artillery attacks, with the addition of clouds of skirmishers, and, towards the end of the day, close assaults of infantry in column. Whilst Lambert's battalions did not face the full force of the cavalry onslaught, for much of their time in the front line they were in more or less close contact with French infantry around La Haie Sainte, and they were well within round shot range of the French guns on Grand Battery Ridge.

Most of their regimental accounts were written twenty years later or more, in response to Siborne's circular, and are rich in anecdote but less helpful as regards the sequence of events. The only contemporary accounts from the 40th are from the diary of Lieutenant Hugh Wray and the letters of Lieutenant James Mill. The latter described the ground beyond the hollow lane to their front:

469

'A spacious tract of smooth and open country was exhibited to the eye, comprising the left and left centre of the British position, which, sweeping down from the ridge in a gradual descent for the distance of half a mile to the base of the valley, stretched itself lengthwise in the contrary direction for nearly twice that distance, thus including at the extremity the farmsteads and brick-wall enclosures of La Haye Sainte, situated down towards the valley on our right. This smooth, open extent of land, though an incline, together with the valley down below of a larger and much wider expanse, was fitted peculiarly for cavalry, and it was chiefly to the resistance of this arm, and to the endurance of the fire of artillery that was both numerous and of the heaviest calibre, that our efforts were exercised throughout the day.'[985]

Most accounts of the Battle of Waterloo entirely ignore the cavalry attacks east of the Brussels-Charleroi chaussée. They most certainly occurred, but seem to have been confined to Lambert's brigade, for whilst Kempt's battalions formed square, there is no suggestion that they were actually assaulted. Indeed, it is hard to see how cavalry could have attacked Lambert's brigade position from their front or immediate right as these approaches were protected by deep cuttings, and it seems more probable that such attacks as came their way, all apparently consisting of cuirassiers, came from across the chaussée from the right rear and involved horsemen who had already run the gauntlet of Alten's squares, and who may well have been pushed back in that direction by Allied cavalry. This would be consistent with the narrative of Sergeant Lawrence, which suggests that in his part of the field, the French horsemen encountered Allied cavalry both before and after closing with the infantry squares:

'We endured some heavy work throughout the day, having constantly to be first forming square to receive the repeated attacks of their cavalry, and then line to meet their infantry, charge after charge being made upon us, but with very little success... On the turnpike road was placed a brigade of German cavalry with light horses and men.[986] When Buonaparte's Bodyguards came up they charged these, making fearful havoc amongst their number; they were routed and obliged to retreat, but the Life Guards and Scotch Greys fortunately making their appearance immediately, some close handwork took place, and the Bodyguards at last finding their match, or even more, were in turn compelled to fall back before the charge of our cavalry, numbers of them being cut to pieces.

'Still nothing daunted, they formed again, and this time ascended at us; but of the two, they met with a worse reception than before, for we instantly threw ourselves into three squares with our artillery in the centre; and the word having been given not to fire at the men, who wore armour, but at the horses, which was obeyed to the very letter, as soon as they arrived at close quarters we opened a deadly fire, and very few of them wholly escaped. They managed... at first to capture our guns, but they were again recovered by the fire of our three squares, and it was a most laughable sight to see these guards – in their chimney armour – trying to run away after their horses had been shot from under them – being able to make very little progress, and many of them being taken prisoners by those of our light companies who were out skirmishing.'[987]

Lieutenant James Mill described how the 40th were 'surrounded and beset by hordes of horsemen, who were slashing and cutting at our kneeling ranks. The file-firing of our standing ranks, being constant and concentrated, was very effectual against their attacks, and both horse and rider were to be constantly discerned rolling over onto the plain, and the remainder flying backward in disorder to their own lines in very diminished numbers, leaving the ground near and around us thickly strewed with their comrades' bodies. This would take place after they had expended their pistol shots, ardour, and determination in the first onset of the charge... and this having been ineffectual, the troopers would encompass us with fierce gesticulations and angry scowls, in which a display of incisors became very apparent to all.'[988]

---

[985] Mill, quoted in *Historical Records of the 40th Regiment*, p. 189-90.
[986] There were no German cavalry in that area. These were almost certainly Dutch/Belgians. Major Fielding Browne, 40th, mentions that 'there were some Belgian troops (particularly cavalry with yellow jackets) in our neighbourhood, and in the rear of our flanks.' No Allied cavalry wore yellow jackets, but the 3rd Dutch Carabiniers had yellow turnbacks and the 5th Belgian Light Dragoons wore yellow facings. Both these regiments were in the Netherlands Cavalry Division which was deployed on either side of the Brussels road close to Mont St. Jean, and was heavily engaged with French cavalry in the afternoon.
[987] Lawrence, p.p. 208-09.
[988] Mill, quoted in *Historical Records of the 40th Regiment*, p. 191.

So amused were the 40th by this display that, according to Major Fielding Browne, when he issued the command to 'Prepare for Cavalry,' his officers would shout 'Now, men, make faces!'

Lieutenant Hugh Wray wrote that, 'Nothing could exceed the determination with which the French fought, particularly the cuirassiers, who came up to our old regiment four times during the action, as if determined to *swallow* us, but they found us too steady.'[989]

James Mill agreed that 'The enemy, indeed, fought with a resolution and persistency that appeared desperate,' which he contrasted with the 'coolness, equanimity, and even good humour' of his own soldiers, saying that:

'It would be difficult to over-extol or over-estimate the conduct of our men, or to too highly eulogise their untiring constancy and unshaken courage on receiving wounds of a mortal kind, or such terrible injuries as could not but carry into their minds a sense of helplessness and of despair. For instance, a grenadier of our company, whose face as it seemed to me had been cleft asunder and so slashed by a sabre cut that it rested partly on his shoulder, I beheld walk with a firm step without any assistance off the ground. I knew the man well, and it was a shocking spectacle, and I do not remember any incident throughout this day, or any former one, that affected me so powerfully as this sight.'[990]

Brevet-Major Sempronius Stretton, who commanded the left wing of the 40th at Waterloo, described how 'the field immediately about the 40th was thickly scattered with horses and men of the French cavalry, who repeatedly charged our squares (without making any impression) and who passing and returning through the squares of the 40th, 27th and 4th Regiments, suffered severely from the fire of each.'

It is clear from several 40th accounts that attacks from cavalry and infantry followed in quick succession that afternoon. Lawrence again:

'That affair [the cuirassier attack], however, had only passed off a very few minutes before their infantry advanced, and we had again to form line ready to meet them. We in our usual style let the infantry get well within our musket-shot before the order was given to fire, so that our volley proved to be of fearful success; and then immediately charging them we gave them a good start back again, but not without a loss on our side as well as on theirs. And no sooner had they disappeared than another charge of cavalry was made, so that we had again to throw ourselves into square on our old ground. These cavalry had no doubt expected to appear amongst us before we could accomplish this, but fortunately they were mistaken, and our persistent fire soon turned them.

'We did not lose a single inch of ground the whole day, though after these successive charges our numbers were fearfully thinned; and even during the short interval between each charge the enemy's cannon had been doing some mischief among our ranks besides. The men in their tired state were beginning to despair, but the officers cheered them on continually throughout the day with the cry of "Keep your ground, my men!" It is a mystery to me how it was accomplished, for at last so few were left that there were scarcely enough to form square.'[991]

The 40th frequently changed formation from square into column, and occasionally into line, and back again, and as James Mill observed:

'From these repetitions of attacks, and trampling of horses, the plunging of shots from artillery, and other descriptions of missiles, the position on which we stood became so broken up and miry that at one time we were almost knee-deep in mud. We were, besides, slightly and insensibly retrograding from our original ground owing to the reiterated onslaughts, the imperative restriction that we were not to advance a step, and the natural results of this uniform system of defence.'[992]

'About four o'clock,' recalled Sergeant Lawrence, 'I was ordered to the Colours. This, though I was used to warfare as much as any, was a job I did not at all like, but still I went as boldly to work as I could. There had

[989] Wray's diary entry for 22nd June 1815, the first day after the battle he was able to write, quoted in *Historical Records of the 40th Regiment*, p. 188.

[990] Mill, quoted in *Historical Records of the 40th Regiment*, p. 191.

[991] Lawrence, p.p. 209-10.

[992] Mill, op. cit., p. 192.

been before me that day fourteen sergeants already killed and wounded while in charge of those colours, with officers in proportion, and the staff and colours were almost cut to pieces. This job will never be blotted from my memory; although I am now an old man, I remember it as if it had been yesterday.

'I had not been there more than a quarter of an hour when a cannon shot came and took the captain's head clean off. This was again close to me, for my left side was touching the poor captain's right, and I was spattered all over with his blood. One of his company who was close by at the time, cried out, "Hullo, there goes my best friend", which caused a lieutenant, who quickly stepped forward to take his place, to say to the man, "Never mind, I will be as good a friend to you as the captain." The man replied, "I hope not, sir", the officer not having rightly understood his meaning, the late captain [William Fisher][993] having been particularly hard on him for his dirtiness, giving him extra duty and suchlike as punishment. This man, whose name was Marten, was a notorious character in the regiment, and I was myself tolerably well acquainted with him, for he had once been in my company; but on account of the same thing, dirtiness in his person, he had been transferred to this, the Fifth Company, where neither this poor captain had been able to reform him, try however hard he might. Still, he was for all this an excellent soldier in the field.'[994]

Lieutenant Hugh Wray may well have been the officer who misunderstood Marten's remark, for when writing up his diary on 22nd June he described the effect of the French artillery, with entirely pardonable exaggeration, as 'the most destructive fire that ever was felt':

'During this time we had three companies almost cut to pieces. One shot killed and wounded twenty-two of the 4th Company, another of the same kind (round shot) killed poor Fisher (my captain) and eighteen of our company (the 5th), and another took the 8th, and killed and wounded twenty-three. This all happened by our being in open column of quarter distance and the shot took us in flank. At the same time poor Fisher was hit, I was speaking to him, and I got all over his brains. His head was blown to atoms.'[995]

Major Sempronius Stretton told a similar story: 'Towards the evening, whilst the Regiment was in open column, a round shot from the enemy took the head off a Captain (Fisher) near me, and striking his company on the left flank, put hors de combat more than twenty-five men. This was the most destructive shot I ever witnessed during a long period of service.'[996]

Shortly after this, the French cavalry made what was, according to Sergeant Lawrence, their last attack on Lambert's brigade:

'Few as we were, when we saw it coming we formed squares and awaited it. Then we poured volley after volley into them, doing fearful execution, and they had to retire at last before the strong dose we administered; not, however, without our losing more men and so becoming even weaker than before. We were dreading another charge, but all the help we got was the cry of "Keep your ground, my men, reinforcements are coming!"'[997]

By around 6 p.m. the magnificent French heavy cavalry was an exhausted and largely spent force, and for all their gallantry they had achieved almost nothing, though their supporting guns had inflicted significant casualties on Wellington's front line. D'Erlon's corps, though still battling to take La Haie Sainte, had suffered heavy losses, Reille's corps had been frittered away in protracted but vain attempts to take Hougoumont, and both Lobau's corps and the Young Guard had been committed to holding back the Prussians, who had reached the village of Plancenoit in the right rear of the French army.

---

[993] Captain William Fisher had served with the 40th for over ten years. In the Peninsula, where he also served with the 24th Portuguese, he had been present at Roliça, Vimeiro, Talavera, Busaco, Burgos, Bidassoa, Nivelle, Nive, Orthez and Toulouse, and he was also with the 40th in North America.
[994] Lawrence, p.p. 210-11.
[995] Wray's diary entry for 22nd June 1815, quoted in *Historical Records of the 40th Regiment*, p. 187.
[996] Colonel Sempronius Stretton, letter to Siborne dated Lenten Priory, Notts, 7th February 1837 (*Waterloo Letters*, No. 177).
[997] Lawrence, p. 211.

Crisis in the Centre

For those in the centre of the Allied line, the situation took a turn for the worse at about 6.30 p.m. when La Haie Sainte fell to the 2nd Légère of Donzelot's 2nd Division after an heroic five-hour defence by its greatly outnumbered King's German Legion garrison, who were forced to abandon the farm when they ran out of ammunition. An ill-judged counter-attack ordered by the Prince of Orange only resulted in the destruction of the 5th King's German Legion and the death of its brigade commander, Colonel Ompteda.

The capture of this bastion, together with the adjacent sandpit and knoll, enabled the French to advance infantry and guns to within sixty yards of the Elm Tree cross-roads, Wellington's vital ground and Buonaparte's initial objective. From there they were able to engage Alten's left, Lambert and Kempt at short range. Ney saw that the elusive break-through at last appeared possible, and he sent to the Emperor for fresh infantry to exploit this opportunity.

Buonaparte, however, now had almost no reserves but his Imperial Guard, and he was not yet desperate enough to play this last card. '*Ou voulez-vous que j'en prenne?,*' he stormed, '*Voulez-vous que j'en fusse?*' Despite the Emperor's failure to take advantage of the capture of La Haie Sainte, the situation on the left of Alten's 3rd Division was, for a time, critical, as seen by Captain James Shaw:

'Ompteda's brigade was nearly annihilated, and Kielmansegge's so thinned, that those two brigades could not hold their position. That part of the field of battle, therefore, which was between Halkett's left and Kempt's [and Lambert's] right was unprotected; and being the very centre of the Duke's line of battle, was consequently that point, above all others, which the enemy wished to gain. The danger was imminent; and at no other period of the act was the result so precarious as at this moment.'[998]

Alten and other senior officers had fallen, and so Shaw took it on himself to gallop direct to the Duke, and inform him of the gap in his line.

'This very startling information he received with a degree of coolness, and replied to in an instant with such precision and energy as to prove the most complete self-possession: "I shall order the Brunswick troops to the spot, and other troops besides; go you and get all the German troops of the division to the spot that you can, and all the guns that you can find".'[999]

Wellington then went to the threatened sector and put himself at the head of the reinforcements, Brunswickers and Nassauers, while Kielmansegge rallied the remnant of his Hanoverians, more guns were brought up, and Vivian's brigade of light cavalry were brought in from the left wing to stand in support of the infantry. Even so, the line remained thin, fragile and vulnerable.

Halkett's brigade was less directly threatened by the French position around La Haie Sainte, but the end of the massed cavalry assaults left the front line infantry exposed to artillery, and none were more vulnerable than those in the square of the 30th and 73rd. As William Siborne rightly observed:

'The most exposed to the fierce onslaught of the French cavalry and to the continuous cannonade of their artillery, were the two British squares posted during a very great portion of the battle in advance – at times, considerably so – of the narrow road which ran along the crest of the Duke's position. They consisted of the 3rd Battalion of the 1st Guards, belonging to Maitland's brigade; and of the 30th and 73rd Regiments... belonging to Halkett's brigade. It was upon these troops, also, that the French gunners seldom neglected to pour their destructive missiles, so long as they continued to constitute, by their exposed position, such prominent marks for their fire.'[1000]

'The enemy's cavalry were by this time well sobered,' wrote Macready, 'and as they had discovered the inutility of their charges, what were left of them commenced annoying us by occasional shots from their carbines, which they advanced singly and bravely to fire, and which we were directed not to reply to. After this had lasted some time, some French artillery trotted up our hill, which I knew by their caps to belong to the Imperial

[998] Shaw-Kennedy, p. 127.
[999] Ibid, p. 128.
[1000] Siborne, p. 484.

Guard;[1001] and I had scarcely mentioned this to a brother officer when two guns unlimbered at a cruelly short distance, down went the portfires and slap came their grape into the square. They immediately reloaded and kept up a most destructive fire.

'It was noble to see our fellows fill up the gaps after each discharge. I had ordered up three of my Light Bobs, and they had hardly taken their places when two falling sadly wounded, one of them (named Anderson[1002]) looked up in my face, uttering a sort of reproachful groan, when I involuntarily said, "By God! I couldn't help it." I suppose we could not charge these guns for fear of the cavalry that flanked them. It had now become what I more than once heard the smothered muttering from the ranks declare it, "Bloody thundering work", and it was to be seen which side had most bottom, and could stand killing longest.'

'Never shall I forget those two guns,' recalled Ensign Robert Rogers of the 30th. 'Every discharge made a regular gap in the square. It surprised me with what coolness our men and the 73rd closed them up. Our men were saying it was bloody murdering work, and growling much at not being allowed to charge.'

Lieutenant-Colonel Bailey had indeed to restrain his men from charging the guns: 'It was, I think, poor Pratt who wished me to permit him to undertake the capture or dislodgement of these destructive neighbours. I mentioned this noble offer to Sir Colin Halkett, but Sir Colin replied it could not be sanctioned without reference to the Duke.'

'This was a murderous time of the day,' said Captain Robert Howard. 'It *was* glorious to see fellows fill up the gaps; no urging of the officers necessary, and it appeared to me that the more desperate the fight became, the more determined the gallant fellows were to keep their ground.'

'The Duke visited us frequently at this momentous period,' wrote Edward Macready. 'He was coolness personified. As he crossed the rear face of our square, a shell fell amongst our Grenadiers, and he checked his horse to see its effect. Some men were blown to pieces by the explosion, and he merely stirred the rein of his charger, apparently as little concerned at their fate as his own danger. Wherever he appeared, a murmur of "Silence – stand to your front – here's the Duke", was heard thro' the column, and then all was steady as on a parade. His Aides de Camp, Colonels Canning and Gordon, fell near our square, and the former died within it.[1003]

'As he came near us late in the evening, Halkett rode out to him and represented our weak state, begging his Grace to afford us a little support. "It's impossible, Halkett", said he, and our General replied, "If so, Sir, you may depend on the brigade to a man!" Bailey adds that the Duke told Halkett that 'There must not even be a symptom of retreat.'[1004]

'Sir C. Halkett certainly was delighted at the pluck of our lads,' wrote Bailey, 'and *entre nous* in doing so said he wished some other regiments of the brigade would profit by the example (the 33rd & poor Elphinstone to wit).'

It appears that at some time after the fall of La Haie Sainte the whole of Halkett's brigade shifted its ground some 200 yards along the ridge to its left to cover some of the ground abandoned by Kielmansegge's much reduced brigade, and Maitland's Guards made a commensurate move in the same direction. It appears that

---

[1001] One quite recent account of the final hours of the battle constructs a scenario around these guns being in support of the final advance of the Imperial Guard infantry, but this occurred more than an hour later. The guns referred to here were Old Guard Horse Artillery, part of one of the Imperial Guard Cavalry divisions, and most probably the Light Cavalry Division, elements of which we know charged the 30th/73rd square late that afternoon.

[1002] Private William Anderson of the Light Company was indeed wounded, but survived.

[1003] Sir Alexander Gordon was evacuated to the Field Hospital at Mont St. Jean by Sergeant-Major Woods of the 30th, and died there, while Captain Arthur Gore of the 30th held the dying Canning's hand. Gore stated that 'The majority of the staff of the Duke of Wellington were killed or wounded upon the right and rear of the advanced square of General Halkett's brigade (i.e. that formed by the 30th and 73rd), His Grace being frequently with it during the action.' Lieutenant Tincombe's near-contemporary account confirms that 'Lord Wellington was frequently with us and was very anxious for our position which was the centre. Two of his ADC.s were killed within our square.'

[1004] Sergeant Morris has a similar account: 'The Duke of Wellington riding by, again addressed our general with, "Well Halkett, how do you get on?" The general replied, "My Lord, we are dreadfully cut up; can you not relieve us for a little while?" "Impossible", said the Duke. "Very well, my Lord", said the general; "We'll stand until the last man falls".' (Morris, p. 79).

they vacated the exposed position, forward of the ridge-top lane, where they had formed square to meet the cavalry and had suffered loss from the French guns. This change of position, according to Bailey, 'was mainly effected by bringing up our right shoulders and not by any great change of ground'; but however it was accomplished this adjustment appears to have brought Halkett's left-hand square, the 30th and 73rd, close to the track junction and to the left rear of the high point of the crest where the Lion Mount now stands.

It was probably around this time that Wellington sent Colonel Gordon to Halkett to enquire what square of his was lying down so much in advance, and was informed that it was the heaped casualties on the position from which the 30th and 73rd had just moved. Bailey rather confirmed this when, in a letter to Macready, he explained that 'any other changes [of position] during the day were for the purpose of freeing ourselves from the inconvenience of the dead & wounded.'

'Our Colours were ordered to the rear,' recalled Macready. 'This measure has been reprobated by many, but I know I never in my life felt such joy, or looked at danger with so light a heart, as when I saw our dear old rags in safety. Our brigade did not stand 800 men, and how could they be expected to protect four stand of Colours from the most dreaded troops in Europe, approaching with an awful superiority of numbers?'

When the French cavalry fell back, the skirmishers of Halkett's brigade once more descended the slope, and with them was Lieutenant John Pratt:

'Towards the close of the day I found myself for the last time near the bottom of the slope with the few light troops that were remaining. The firing on the left had slackened or ceased, and the enemy's position in our immediate front was being covered with infantry. Their artillery also had taken up a position much in advance, and was firing, chiefly grape, amongst the scattered light troops, which were gradually retiring before the overwhelming force opposed to them. La Haye Sainte being in possession of the enemy, our left was necessarily much thrown back, so as to place us nearly in echelon with the crest of the position. It was at this period that I was wounded and, of course, I ceased to be an eye-witness of what took place afterwards.'[1005]

Beyond the Elm Tree Crossroads, Lambert's brigade faced close attack by infantry and artillery following the fall of La Haie Sainte. According to Sir John Lambert, the 4th Regiment (together with the 1st/95th, who had been pushed back from the sandpit and knoll) held the front edge of the lane to Wavre, while the 40th were extended behind the embankment hedge on the rear side of that lane, with Kempt's brigade to their left. The long-suffering 27th remained in square to their right, in the angle formed by the chaussée and the lane, ready to pour a flanking fire onto any French troops attempting to force the position along the line of the highway. In 1835, Major Fielding Browne, 40th, recollected in some detail the situation at that point:

'The 40th Regiment, which had previously, and mostly throughout the day, been in square against cavalry, were formed in line, and thus quickly advanced to the brow of the hill, where there was a low and somewhat broken-down hedge, short of which we halted and over which we fired. There were a few large trees here and there, particularly on our side of it, the branches of which were much cut and lopt by cannon shot; but of what description the trees were I cannot now recollect.'

'A heavy column of French Infantry was advancing; at the moment I observed them they were rather in front of the farmhouse of La Haie Sainte by, I believe, the left of it as we faced the house, they having then crossed the road. The divisions of the column appeared to me to be at about quarter distances. The 40th was formed rather facing the house, the latter being a little to the right of the Regiment, but more in front of us. There were several other similar columns advancing at the same time upon different points of our position, both to the right and left of the house; and much cavalry were congregating or re-forming in... that part of the enemy's position which artists would term the middle distance.'

'To the right of the house and near it, was a bank or small hill, which was occupied by the head of a French column, halted, but not very regularly formed. I think they had been driven back from their attempt to ascend the hill, partly by our fire, and partly by that of the troops on our right; but the cloud of smoke in which we were almost constantly enveloped prevented me from discovering their object in remaining there thus exposed, which

---

[1005] Pratt, letter to Siborne dated 23rd March 1835 (*Waterloo Letters*, No. 138).

they did in the most dauntless and daring manner; as fast as they fell their places were supplied with fresh troops, until the general advance of the British, when they retired.

'Whilst we were in this situation, boxes of ammunition were placed at intervals along our rear, from about fifty to one hundred paces from us, so that the men could help themselves when they required it.'[1006]

Colonel Sempronius Stretton of the 40th, writing to Siborne in 1837, added the information that 'the formation of the enemy's force immediately in our front was a double line of *tirailleurs*, supported by a heavy column of infantry; the former had possession of a rising ground on the opposite side of the road to the farm of La Haye Sainte, who, whilst lying down, appeared to select their targets with great precision. It appeared to me that this force formed the French line which, supported as above, charged our front that evening, as some of them were bayoneted *close* to our front rank.'[1007] He accompanied his letter with a sketch map which shows the line of tirailleurs extending over the rising ground to the east of the sandpit, and three French columns, of which the most advanced appears to have advanced through their light troops to the east of the rising ground and (assuming his sketch is roughly to scale) approached the British line in the sunken lane some two to three hundred yards east of the crossroads. The other two columns were to the south of the rising ground, with their heads abreast of La Haie Sainte.

Finally, it is worth noting the account of Captain Jonathan Leach of the 1st/95th, whose battalion was forced back from the sandpit and knoll to the sunken lane when the French captured La Haie Sainte. He stated that from that time until the General Advance:

'The mode of attack and defence was remarkable for its *sameness*,' and the musketry contest was in his opinion 'the closest and most protracted almost ever witnessed... It consisted of one uninterrupted fire of musketry (the distance between the hostile lines I imagine to have been rather more than one hundred yards) between Kempt's and some of Lambert's regiments posted along the thorn hedge and the French infantry lining the knoll and the crest of the hill near it. Several times the French officers made desperate attempts to induce their men to charge Kempt's line, and I saw more than once parties of the French in our front spring up from their kneeling position and advance some yards towards the thorn hedge, headed by their officers with vehement gestures, but our fire was so very hot and deadly that they almost instantly ran back behind the crest of the hill, always leaving a great many killed or disabled behind them.'[1008]

Attack of the Imperial Guard

Historians of the Waterloo campaign are greatly indebted to Captain William Siborne of the 47th (Lancashire) Regiment. Siborne, then serving with the 9th Foot, was not present at Waterloo but made it his life's work to record the battle in detail. Commissioned in 1830 to construct a model of the historic battle, he carried out an accurate topographical survey and wrote a circular to surviving Waterloo officers, principally to ascertain the position of troops at the time of what has become known as 'the crisis,' around 7 p.m. The replies to his ground-breaking circular, and the subsequent correspondence, amount to an unique mass of primary source material. This archive enabled Siborne to complete his model by 1838 and then to make much-needed commercial use of the material by publishing, in 1844, the first edition of his classic *History of the War in France and Belgium in 1815*. This work and the supporting letters remain of fundamental value to any historian of the campaign, but as might be expected there are inconsistencies between accounts, gaps in Siborne's information, and some obvious subjectivity at least partially related to his pressing need to obtain subscribers for his work.

Consequently, when Major Edward Macready read Siborne's first edition he was surprised to find some major inaccuracies with regard to Halkett's 5th Brigade at Quatre Bras, as noticed above, and during the repulse of the Imperial Guard, when its involvement was completely ignored. 'Captain Siborne,' he wrote, 'represents that at Waterloo the attacks of both the columns of the French Imperial Guard in the evening were made

[1006] Fielding Browne, letter to Siborne dated 6th May 1835 (*Waterloo Letters*, No. 176).
[1007] Sempronius Stretton, letter to Siborne dated 7th February 1837 (*Waterloo Letters*, No. 177).,
[1008] Leach, letter to Siborne dated 22nd November 1840 (*Waterloo Letters*, No. 160).,

exclusively on the ground held by General Maitland's Brigade of Guards; whereas I affirm that a portion of one of these attacks (the first) was directed against, and defeated by, the 30th and 73rd Regiments.' Macready took it upon himself to correct these errors and, although characteristically passionate in his advocacy, he determined to fill the gaps in Siborne's correspondence honestly and objectively by collecting additional evidence from surviving officers of 'The Old Three Tens.' This he did by circulating an edited version of his own near-contemporary journal and asking for constructive comment:

'I will thank you to return the paper to me with your marginal comments on it stating with what you coincide, wherein you differ from me, what you did see, what you did not. Wherein you think I am deceived. In short, anything that may assist me to come at the actual truth & to lay it before Captain Siborne.'

The result was an analytical article in the March 1845 *United Services Magazine*[1009] in which Macready exposed Siborne's errors point by point. His efforts were not in vain, for when the 3rd edition of Siborne's history appeared in 1848 the offending passages were substantially re-written to conform with Macready's well-supported account.[1010]

There is no episode of the battle of Waterloo more controversial in almost every detail than the final French attack by Napoleon's Imperial Guard, often styled 'the crisis.' It was the last throw of an incorrigible gambler, using his last reserve, but had it been well directed it might just have been sufficiently successful to save the day, if not the campaign, for the French. As it turned out, excessive delegation of vital tactical decisions, in particular to the impulsive Ney, and the weak overall control which marked the Emperor's style of command throughout the day of Waterloo, doomed this last attack to failure.

Napoleon was already too well aware that the black columns closing in increasing numbers on his right flank were Prussians, but to motivate his troops for a final effort, he deliberately spread the false news that the approaching troops were French reinforcements led by Grouchy. This particularly incensed Marshal Ney and fed his growing sense of personal grievance:

'About seven o'clock in the evening, after the most frightful carnage which I have ever witnessed, General [de la Bédoyère] came to me with a message from the Emperor, that Marshal Grouchy had arrived on our right, and attacked the left of the English and Prussians united. This general officer, in riding along the lines, spread this intelligence among the soldiers, whose courage and devotion remained unshaken, and who gave new proofs of them at that moment, in spite of the fatigue which they experienced. Immediately after, what was my astonishment, I should rather say indignation, when I learned that so far from Marshal Grouchy having arrived to support us, as the whole army had been assured, between forty and fifty thousand Prussians attacked our extreme right and forced it to retire!'[1011]

The final French attack was spearheaded by five battalions of the Middle (Moyenne) Guard supported by three battalions of the Old Guard. Although a general advance was ordered, in the event the assault was confined to the left of the Elm Tree Crossroads, while to its right the French engaged in more tentative advances and inconclusive fire fights between La Haie Sainte and Smohain .

At about 7.30 p.m. the Imperial Guard stepped off from La Belle Alliance and marched forward by the left of the Genappe road, led by their band playing the tunes that had heralded French victories on battlefields across Europe. The Emperor himself, with his staff, led his Guard down the slope to their line of departure in the hollow ground south of La Haie Sainte; but there he handed over just five battalions (some 3,000 men) to Marshal

---

[1009] *Colburn's United Service Magazine*, 1845, Vol I, p.p. 392- 403.

[1010] Over the thirty years after the battle Macready wrote several accounts of what he saw at Waterloo. All are consistent, but some introduce additional detail. His first, very brief, account of the battle is in a letter to his father sent from Paris on 7th July 1815. His next, and most complete narrative, is in his Journal, which he wrote up at Limerick from February 1816. Then there is a letter to George Gawler, drafted but not sent in 1836, giving some additional detail. In 1844 Macready sent to surviving officers of the 30th a circular which is essentially an edited and partially expanded version of his Journal entries. On the basis of this, and the replies, he produced the March 1845 *United Service Magazine* article mentioned above. There are other significant details in a letter to Siborne dated 23rd April 1846. In this present chapter, the 1816 Journal narrative will be quoted unless otherwise stated.

[1011] Extract from a letter, dated Paris 26th June 1815, from Marshal Ney to Joseph Fouché, Duke of Otranto, Buonaparte's Minister of Police.

Ney with an expansive but insufficiently explanatory gesture towards Wellington's Ridge, and retired. He held back a further six battalions of his elite troops.

It appears that Napoleon intended the Imperial Guard to make a massed attack from La Haie Sainte to break Wellington's line at or close to the Elm Tree Crossroads, but that is not what happened. Someone, most probably Ney, altered the point of attack. There has to be a reason for this, and the most likely explanation is that the direct line of advance to the ridge was already congested. Donzelot's 2nd Infantry Division, which had taken La Haie Sainte, was still there, with Quiot's 1st Division coming up on its right, while from a position to the west of the farm a French artillery battery was engaging such Allied troops as were still visible on the ridge. We do not know with any certainty, but it would be consistent with Ney's impulsive nature and his irritation with Buonaparte's duplicity that he took it upon himself to change the direction of advance, giving himself more room for manoeuvre. After all, what could go wrong? So far as he could see, few troops remained on the Allied right of Wellington's Ridge.

The Emperor blamed Ney for this divergence from his intended line of advance, as became apparent to Colonel Crabbe, the Marshal's senior aide-de-camp, who was summoned to headquarters as the Guards' attack commenced:

'I reached the rise near the farm of La Belle Alliance where the Emperor was located… Slumped in his chair, he appeared to me both exhausted and angry. One of the ADCs informed him of my arrival. Without even turning to me, he said out of the blue, "Ney has acted stupidly again. He has cost us the day! He has destroyed my cavalry and is ready to destroy my Guard. He manoeuvres like a good-for-nothing. He attacks the plateau obliquely instead of assaulting at the centre. Go at best speed and order him to modify his march and to pierce the centre of the English position in a compact mass."'

It was, however, too late, for the Guard was already committed. There is some doubt as to the formation adopted by the five assaulting battalions, for most British observers maintained that they advanced in close columns, as had invariably been their practice in the Peninsula, but most French witnesses more persuasively state that they formed and advanced in battalion squares, and in view of the rough handling of D'Erlon's Corps by the British cavalry earlier that day this would have been a likely precaution.[1012] It seems that there was no skirmishing line, but that each square was directed by officers marching in front and was propelled up the slope to the ridge by drummers within the square beating the *pas de charge*. Sections of 6-pounder guns moved in the intervals between the squares.

These squares advanced obliquely from behind La Haie Sainte towards the Allied right centre, the battalions staggered in echelon from right to left so that each square was both behind and to the left of the preceding one. The senior battalion, 1st/3rd Grenadiers à Pied, led on the right, then the 4th Grenadiers, followed on the left by three battalions of Chasseurs, which had the furthest to advance before reaching the ridge and consequently approached it last. The effect of this formation was inevitably that instead of a massed attack on the crossroads, as the Emperor had apparently intended, the attack was dissipated along the ridge over a front of some 600 yards, piecemeal and uncoordinated.

To understand this part of the action, it must be remembered that the approaches to Wellington's right centre were effectively divided by the prominent spur running down into the valley from where the Lion Monument now stands. The Allied deployment, in particular to their left of this spur, was very thin: Ompteda's brigade was all but destroyed, Kielmansegge's Hanoverians were about to pull back to rally at Mont St. Jean, the young soldiers of the Brunswick and Nassau contingents were with difficulty kept in place behind the ridge, and the guns of Cleeves' and Lloyd's batteries were out of ammunition. The only reliable infantry between the spur and the crossroads were the battered, reduced and exhausted battalions of Halkett's brigade. To the right of the 'Lion' spur the situation was considerably better, for Adam's strong brigade (52nd, 71st and 2nd/95th) had been brought into the front line to the right of Maitland's brigade, the 2nd and 3rd Battalions of the 1st Foot Guards, and there were still effective British artillery batteries.

[1012]The biographer of Lieutenant-General Count Friant (his son) describes the formation as *formés en colonne par echelons*.

478

In outline, primary source evidence shows that the attack and defeat of the Imperial Guard then developed as follows, the whole sequence taking as little as 15-20 minutes:

The first battalion to approach the ridge was the 1st/3rd Grenadiers à Pied, about 580 all ranks, led by Marshal Ney, described as '*démonté, à pied, en tête de ce bataillon, l'épée à la main*,'[1013] and by Generals Friant and Poret de Morvan. They were closely followed, to their left rear, by the 4th Grenadiers.

The 1st/3rd Grenadiers, moving to their right (east) of the spur, were met and repulsed by the 30th and 73rd with a single volley and bayonet charge, their rout being completed by the guns of Krahmer's Netherlands battery, which fortuitously arrived from reserve at that critical time.

The 4th Grenadiers, 520 all ranks, moving to the west of the 'Lion' spur, were then defeated by Maitland's 3rd/1st Guards, with support on their left flank from the 33rd and 69th, brought forward by Halkett from their 'covering interval' between the 30th/73rd and the Guards. This was the moment highlighted, with such mythical embellishments as Wellington's supposed cry of 'Up Guards, and at 'em,' in popular histories of the battle, though there is no doubt that the 3rd/1st Guards eventually won the fire fight, albeit with help from the 33rd and 69th.

Halkett's brigade and the 3rd/1st Guards then advanced some hundred yards onto the forward slope to complete their rout of the Imperial Grenadiers, but the retirement of the latter left Halkett's and Maitland's men exposed to French guns, firing cannister at close range, and to hovering cavalry, and they were in consequence ordered to retire in square to their original positions behind the ridge. This retirement under fire caused considerable confusion among the 33rd and 69th, who lost heavily and retired, Halkett being among the casualties, and in the 3rd/1st Guards, who fell back to the ridge in disorder. The retiring 33rd/69th square then ran into that of the 30th and 73rd, and for a few minutes, the whole of Halkett's brigade became a struggling mob, passing the ridge-top hedge before they were able to rally.

Within minutes of the repulse of the Imperial Grenadiers, what is sometimes referred to as the second column, but was in fact the third, comprising three fairly contiguous battalions of Chasseurs of the Guard – the 1st/3rd, 2nd/3rd and 4th, with a combined strength of about 1,900 all ranks, approached the ground held by Maitland. It is uncertain whether the 1st Guards were actually engaged with the Chasseurs to their front, but there is no doubt that the decisive blow was delivered by Adam's brigade, over 2,000 strong, and in particular by Colborne's 52nd, which wheeled to attack the left flank of the advancing battalions.

Meanwhile, Halkett's 5th Brigade, having quickly recovered from its confusion, were engaged in a desultory fight to their left front with Donzelot's division, which, suddenly and unexpectedly, ended when Adam's brigade swept obliquely across the battlefield and all gave way.

Having sketched this outline of events, which does not entirely agree with accounts given by other historians, and even by some participants in the battle, it is necessary to substantiate it point by point, starting with the account in Macready's near-contemporary journal:

'It was near seven o'clock, and our front had sustained three attacks from fresh troops, when the Imperial Guard were seen ascending our position, in as correct order as at a review. As they rose step by step before us, and crossed the ridge, their red epaulettes and cross belts, put on over their blue greatcoats, gave them a gigantic appearance, which was increased by their high hairy caps and long red feathers, which waved with the nod of their heads as they kept time to the drums in the centre of their column. "Now for a clawing", I muttered; and I confess, when I saw the imposing advance of these men, and thought of the character they had gained, I looked for nothing but a bayonet in my body, and I half breathed a confident sort of wish that it might not touch my vitals.

'While they were moving up the slope, Halkett, as well as the noise permitted us to hear him, addressed us, and said, "My boys, you have done everything I could have wished, and more than I could expect, but much remains to be done; at this moment we have nothing for it but a charge." Our brave fellows replied by three cheers.[1014]

[1013] According to *Vie Militaire de Lieutenant-Général Comte Friant* by his son, Comte Friant, Paris 1857.

[1014] In his letter from Paris to his father, dated 7th July 1815, Macready wrote of Halkett, 'A finer fellow never stepped. He made an elegant speech to us in the middle of the action which was answered by the reiterated cries of our brave fellows, "Let's charge your

'Our square was ordered to open out from its rear face, and wheel up right and left into line four deep… I know that we were called to silence, and told we were to fire one volley by word of command, and then to port our arms.'

'The enemy halted, carried arms about forty paces from us, and fired a volley. We returned it, and giving our 'Hurra!' brought down the bayonets. Our surprise was inexpressible when, pushing thro' the clearing smoke, we saw the backs of the Imperial Grenadiers. We halted, and stared at each other as if mistrusting our eyesight. Some nine-pounders from the rear of our right [Krahmer's battery] poured in the grape amongst them, and the slaughter was dreadful. In no part of the field did I see carcases so heaped upon each other. I could not account for their flight, nor did I ever hear an admissible reason assigned for it. It was a most providential panic. We could not pursue on account of their cavalry, and their artillery was still shockingly destructive.'

Macready subsequently added some significant detail about this first attack of the Imperial Guard. In his 1836 letter, he wrote that:

'I saw no troops of the Guard to the French right of that column which advanced on us (30th and 73rd), and which, though it came over the hill in beautiful order, was an inconceivable short time before us, turning and flying to a man at the single volley we fired, and the hurrah that followed it. Having expected great things from them, we were astonished at their conduct, and we young soldiers almost fancied there was some "ruse" in it.'

In his 1844 circular, Macready adds that as the Imperial Guard advanced, their officers were 'looking to their alignment,' and that he thought they fired badly; while in a footnote about Krahmer's guns, he says, 'Craan's plan represents these guns to be Mr. Van der Smissen's. Whosoever they were, they were served most gloriously, and their grand metallic bang, bang, bang, bang, with the rushing showers of grape that followed, were the most welcome sounds that ever struck my ears – until I married.'

In his April 1846 letter to Siborne, Macready states that he is sure that 'we fixed & brought down our bayonets immediately before Van der Smissen [Krahmer] opened fire,' indicating that it was the single volley of musketry that rolled back the 3rd/1st Grenadiers, who were then raked as they fell back by the timely addition of Krahmer's 9-pounders.

Macready also maintained, in his *United Services Magazine* article, that the column, which was met by the 30th and 73rd, could have suffered little or no loss from Allied artillery as it advanced:

'I assert with no fear of contradiction that in front of Halkett's brigade no single gun or skirmisher was in advance of or on the ridge to interfere with it, and Captain Siborne shows how thoroughly Kielmansegge's and Ompteda's brigades were occupied with Donzelot's people, declaring that "the artillery on the allied right of the high road in front of these brigades was at this moment completely disabled." It is therefore evident that the only fire that could touch the mass was that of Napier's or other guns on the right of the brigade of Guards, from which Captain Siborne states they became sheltered "as the column neared the rise of ground which constituted the highest point of the ridge" [i.e. the 'Lion' spur]… To my thinking, no body of the French army could have passed over to our front so little molested as the Imperial Guard.'

Macready's accounts were fully supported by all the surviving Waterloo officers of the 30th, to whom he had sent the modified version of his journal entry for comment.

Lieutenant-Colonel Bailey replied, 'I have so perfect a recollection of the gentry you mention that at this very moment I fancy I can see their grim mustachios under their hairy hats, as also hear the rat-a-tat-tat of the drummers.' As for the 'providential panic,' his surmise was that the Grenadiers 'were in possession of some unpleasant news from their Emperor's entourage,' the inference being that word of Buonaparte's *Voilà Grouchy* trickery had spread.

Captain Robert Howard, who was all too familiar with the French army from his eight years' imprisonment at Verdun, wrote, 'Quite correct. I remember the advance of this column of the Imperial Guard, for such we were

---

honour. We'll stick it into them." He told us our conduct forced him to make the most favourable report of us in the power of a general officer.'

told they were by more than one of the *French* army. I have no doubt of it, as I had had many opportunities of seeing the whole of the Imperial Guard. They did come in admirable order, with (I think) supported arms.'

Ensign Robert Rogers observed, 'The square now formed a line four deep. Almost at the same moment we saw the hairy caps over the rise of ground. It was a column of the Imperial Guard, I know for two reasons: 1st, their dress, which was large hairy caps, blue great coats, red epaulettes, their accoutrements over the great coat; 2nd, some time after, one of them crawled into our square. I had a flask of water, and gave him some – he blessed me for it. I asked him to what corps he belonged – he stroked his moustache, and said "*Garde Imperiale.*" This column came over the hill as if marching on a parade. I saw an officer a pace or two in front, as if regulating the time. I distinctly saw them carry arms as they halted, and then pour in their fire. We fired, cheered, and came to the charge. Just at the time when I supposed we were closing with them, for we were on the ground they'd stood on, I was thunderstruck to hear our men damning their eyes for not waiting till they had their revenge for what the artillery had done.'

Lieutenant Robert Hughes, a veteran of many Peninsula battles, responded, 'On the 18th, the column with the bearskin caps, which advanced on us late on that eventful evening, was the leading column of the Grenadiers of the Guard, and was stopped by ours and the 73rd, where we had pretty sharp practice, as you may well remember. We did our duty, and so said the French officer of the 6th Cuirassiers, when hanging on my arm during that struggle for victory. You must recollect him.'

Of the other officers of the 30th questioned by Macready, Lieutenant Edward Drake answered, 'I perfectly recollect the advance of the Imperial Guard late in the evening of the 18th, and the way we got rid of them was by the charge of the bayonet.' A second (unnamed) officer replied: 'Till the receipt of your letter I was ignorant that any doubt had been thrown on the fact of our having been attacked by the Imperial Guard. I think I could adduce the testimony of French officers to the fact. I perfectly remember the circumstance, and what you mention of our formation to meet the advancing enemy.'

Lieutenant Francis Tincombe, in his brief account of the battle written less than one month later, said that 'They then brought up a great number of Imperial Guards (foot)... The infantry looked at us, gave us a volley, and then retired, not however without leaving a number on the ground.' Tincombe was wounded by the Guard's volley.

Many years later, in 1852, Captain Arthur Gore, who had commanded the Grenadiers of the 30th at Waterloo, published an account of 'the crisis' which has been wrongly attributed to Macready.[1015] The following statement may be extracted from Gore's hyperbole-laden article:

'On the near approach of the Imperial column, directly on our front, our flanks were thrown forward to resist its attack. On it moved, protected by a tremendous cannonade, whose effects were severely felt by the troops destined to dispute the palm of victory with those far-famed warriors... On they came, the *pas de charge* their step, their arms *aux bras*, guns in the centre and on their flanks, and severally loaded with round-shot and grape. Arrived within about eighty paces of us... they halted, and, for a moment, stood as if amazed at our effrontary in offering opposition to their onward movement; then, saluting us, they commenced that work of death so often narrated, when our thinned ranks told but too well with what precision their fire was given.'

There is further evidence of this attack from Hanoverian officers. Major Julius von Schkopp, commanding the combined Bremen and Verden light infantry battalions to the immediate left of the 30th and 73rd, recalled, 'I observed a strong column of enemy infantry coming directly towards us. I asked and received permission from General Alten to attack in square with the bayonet. But before this could happen, the enemy column moved to the left towards the square commanded by General Sir Colin Halkett, which was to our right, who received the enemy with a murderous fire delivered at a very short distance, which of course stopped the enemy.' Captain Carl von Scriba of the Bremen battalion described how 'I saw a strong column of enemy infantry moving at the pas de charge and with beating drums towards the English brigade of Major General Sir Colin Halkett. General Halkett

---

[1015] *The Crisis of Waterloo, by a Soldier of the Fifth Brigade*, in *Colburn's United Service Magazine*, 1852, Part II, p.p. 51-52. Many passages in this article are repeated verbatim from Gore's 1817 commentary on Craan's map of the battle.

advanced against them and very calmly met them with levelled bayonets and brought them into such disorder that they made off singly in full flight.'[1016]

It is clear from the letters of General Kielmansegge, Captain von Scriba and Lieutenant Wilhelm von Tschirschnitz that the Hanoverians, exhausted and almost out of ammunition, then withdrew in some disorder to Mont St. Jean, where they were with difficulty rallied but took no further part in the battle. The Nassauers had already fallen back behind the ridge.

We are fortunate in having the most authoritative possible French account of this clash, from Major Guillemin, commanding the 1st/3rd Grenadiers à Pied, who wrote in 1835:

'Arriving on the plateau that dominated the battlefield… we opened fire in two ranks. We remained in this position for some time, always losing many men… A battery of the Guard was a little ahead and to the left of this square. A little time afterwards, the battery was dismounted, the horses and the gunners killed or put *hors de combat*… Marshal Ney came into my square and said to General de Morvan [Commander, 3rd Grenadier Regiment], "General, it is necessary to die here!" We remained for some time, but the musketry and case shot vomited death from all sides and, in an instant, the square was no longer.' Major Guillemin and Generals Friant and Poret de Morvan were all wounded.

There are, perhaps understandably, discrepancies over the range at which volleys were exchanged. In his July 1815 letter to his father Macready claimed twenty paces, which in his 1816 Journal he amended to forty, but when on the morning after the battle Arthur Gore measured the distance between the two lines of dead he made it eighty paces.

Whatever the range, the mathematics of relative firepower were with 30th and 73rd, whose front two ranks may have been able to bring some two hundred muskets to bear against fewer than one hundred in the front two ranks of the 1st/3rd Grenadiers square.

There is, incidentally, no credible evidence, or indeed any eye-witness account, to support the theory that the 1st/3rd Grenadiers rallied and made a second advance on the 30th and 73rd, which was supposedly also repulsed, still less the idea that they actually pushed back the 30th and 73rd. Not one of the nine surviving officers of the 30th who recalled the Imperial Guard attack made any mention of a second assault, or of a reverse at their hands. Both these inventions can conclusively be dismissed.

'All I heard and all I read of these events soon after their occurrence,' wrote Macready in the *United Service Magazine*, 'would, equally with what I saw, lead me to conclude that the first attack of the Imperial Guard came in contact with the British front line in an echelon or line (and not in a mass) of columns – something as represented in Craan's plan, published in 1816.[1017] There can be no doubt, I suppose, that of this attack one column led against the Guards. I hope there will be none that another came against the 30th and 73rd Regts.'

Again in his letter to Siborne on 23rd April 1846, Macready writes, 'As to a separate body of the Guard coming against us, God knows I am sure of it as that I live, and it is well to bear in mind that of my testimonies in favour of it, myself, Rogers, Drake and Moneypenny were none of them more than 17 or 18 years old, & consequently that their recollection (backing up my statement of 1816) must be supposed to be clearer & more satisfactory than that of men then 40 & now 70 years of age.'

Replying on the 27th of that month, Siborne accepted that it was 'a point fully established by your own evidence and by that of others' that a separate body of the Guards advanced against the 30th and 73rd.' Siborne was, however, wrestling with other, influential but rather less substantiated or credible, accounts. 'As to the formation of the remainder of the Guard,' he wrote, 'that is another affair. Your column appears to have been a battalion-column, whilst our Guards are very positive that the two columns which came against them were in

[1016] *Waterloo Hanoverian Correspondence*, John Franklin, Ulverston 2010, p. 130, and *Waterloo Archive: German Sources*, Gareth Glover, 2010, p. 109.

[1017] Macready, in his letter to Siborne on 23rd April 1846, says that 'I never had any – the slightest – doubt of the general correctness of Craan's description of the mode of the French advance on our part of the line. Our people all thought it capital & it came out in a year or so after the battle. So far as we could judge & as far as we could see it looked exactly as the real thing had appeared to us.'

mass and amounting to from 4 to 5,000 men <u>each</u>.' It is not difficult to appreciate poor Siborne's dilemma as he attempted to square well-supported historical truth with his urgent need for patronage and financial support.

Turning our attention, then, to the 4th Grenadiers, this second 'column,' or perhaps square, marched up the slope some 250 yards to the left of the 1st/3rd, emerging just to the west of the plateau on which the Lion Mound now stands. Sir Colin Halkett, when interviewed by Colonel Bailey, in 1846, reckoned that this second 'column' was about fifty yards behind the first.[1018] Moving up on the right of this battalion were two guns. Facing this second body of Grenadiers, concealed behind the bank and in the ditch of the ridge-top cart track, lay the left-hand battalion of Maitland's brigade, the largely inexperienced 3rd/1st Guards[1019], behind whom might be seen a mounted figure, the Duke of Wellington.

The Duke was not the only senior officer observing the approaching Guard battalion: Sir Colin Halkett, who had brought all four of his battalions up into four-deep line, left the 30th and 73rd to deal with the 1st/3rd Grenadiers while he personally led his two weaker battalions, the 33rd and 69th, to support Maitland. It appears that he advanced to the right of and a little beyond the 30th and 73rd and then wheeled right, so as to bring a flanking fire onto the second body of Imperial Grenadiers, most probably from the dip in the ground which then linked the 'Lion' plateau to the main ridge. Unfortunately, this exposed the left flank of his battalions at close range to the fire of at least one of the French guns which accompanied the Guard, from which they suffered severely. Although not mentioned in 1st Guards accounts of the clash, it is well attested by those present that the 33rd and 69th exchanged fire with the 4th Grenadiers, and suffered severely.

Gore's narrative confirmed that the second column of Imperial Guards, 'passing the 33rd and 69th Regiments diagonally,' attacked Maitland's Guards. His article appears largely intent on eulogising Halkett, to whom in later years he was apparently close:

'When General Halkett first observed the dark mass moving on the heights parallel to our position, he took the precaution of advancing the 33rd and 69th Regiments a little to our front and right, in order to fill up the chasm which existed between us and the British Guards, and in an instant this fearless and devoted officer was seen effecting this important movement, waving in his hand one of the Colours of the former corps.'

To the right of the 33rd and 69th, the 3rd/1st Guards were lying down in line four deep until the 4th Grenadiers appeared, when Wellington apparently took charge of the tactical battle, ordering, 'Now, Maitland, now's your time!' and then, 'Stand up, Guards. Make ready – present – fire!' The first volley caused the Imperial Grenadiers to stagger, but it took a fairy lengthy fire-fight, in which the 33rd and 69th gave flanking support, before their opponents wavered and fell back before the Guards' charge. It was a creditable performance by inexperienced troops who had stood all day in the front line, though some of the more extravagant claims of their officers, particularly regarding their opponents' strength (not eight to ten thousand as imagined, but in reality about 520), must be heavily discounted.

Unfortunately, the advance of Halkett's brigade and the 3rd/1st Guards onto the forward slope, and the rout of the Imperial Grenadiers, left the victorious British battalions exposed to enemy artillery crossfire and to the hovering remnants of French cavalry, while the 3rd/1st Guards were additionally threatened to their right front by the approaching Chasseurs of the Imperial Guard. The result was an acute but mercifully short-lived confusion. It appears that having advanced some hundred yards the Guards, 'thinking they were to form square, got into confusion and retired hastily over the crest of the position and beyond it on the reverse slope'[1020], where they rallied on the orders, 'Halt, front, form up.' The 33rd and 69th, raked by cannister from their left flank at close range, suffered heavy casualties including General Halkett and Colonel Morice of the 69th, and fell back obliquely towards their original ground. This withdrawal carried those two battalions in a direction which converged with a concurrent movement back to the ridge by the 30th and 73rd.

[1018] Letter from Bailey to Macready, dated Army & Navy Club 22nd April 1846.
[1019] Ensign Robert Batty of the 3rd/1st Guards said of his men that 'the very largest part . . . were very young soldiers and volunteers from the militia, who had never been exposed to the fire of an enemy, or witnessed its effect.' The contrast with the veterans of the 30th, 40th, 59th and other Peninsula battalions was obvious.
[1020] Lord Saltoun (*Waterloo Letters*, No. 106), and Leeke of the 52nd, the latter quoting the Sergeant-Major of the 3rd/1st Guards.

We return now to examine how this 'great falling back' affected the 30th and 73rd. In his journal, Macready explained their difficult situation after defeating the Imperial Grenadiers: 'We could not pursue on account of their cavalry, and their artillery was still shockingly destructive.' He amplified this in his 1845 article, saying 'Directly after they [the Imperial Guard] had fled there was an alarm of cavalry, and we hastily re-formed square, and again began to suffer from their artillery.'

In his April 1846 letter to Siborne, Macready wrote, 'I remember us doing this [forming square], hurriedly wheeling back from our four deep line, & I well recollect feeling excited at the length of time the rear left angle took to close. I think at the time there were scattered French horsemen very near to the left of our front.' He recalled that the 30th and 73rd had casualties of the Imperial Guard about them when they formed square: he spoke to several wounded and one unwounded man, who told him that they were *Moyenne Garde*.

Then, in his 1836 letter to George Gawler, he recalled, 'The French had brought up two guns to the crest of our position, which fired grape into our square... with very deadly effect. Someone in authority must have thought that the bank of a hedge which ran a very short distance in our rear would afford us some cover, and in an evil moment we received the commands to about face and march down to it.'

Macready produced three accounts of what happened next, all consistent, the latter two being amplifications of the first. Here is the entry from his 1816 Journal:

'There was a hedge in our rear, to which we were ordered to move as some cover from the fire. As we descended the declivity, the enemy thought we were flying, and, according to their invariable custom, turned a trebly furious cannonade upon us. Shot, shell, and grape came like a hurricane thro' the square, and the hurly burly of these moments can never be erased from my memory. A shriek from forty or fifty men burst forth amid the thunder and hissing of the shot. I was knocked off my legs, by the fall of a brother officer, and, just as I recovered my feet, an intimate friend, in the delirium of agony occasioned by five wounds, seized me by the collar, screaming, 'Is it deep, Mac, is it deep!' Another officer [Lieutenant Edmund Prendergast] was seen to halt, as if paralyzed, and stare upon a burning fuze, till it fired the powder and shattered him to pieces.

'At this instant the two regiments who were on our right rushed amongst us in frightful confusion, and our men passed the hedge at an accelerated pace. The exertions of the officers were rendered of no avail by the irresistible pressure, and as, crying with rage and shame, they seized individuals to halt them, they were hurried on by the current. At this moment, some one huzzaed, we all joined, and the men halted.

'Major Chambers ordered me to dash out with our Light Bobs and Grenadiers while the Regiments marched up to the hedge and re-formed. The whole brigade was within an ace of ruin. Our men were steady as rocks till the others came amongst them, when the disorder was extreme. The officers did wonders, but the shout alone saved us. I never could discover who raised it, nor can I conceive what the enemy was about during our confusion. Fifty Cuirassiers would have annihilated our brigade.'

In his draft 1836 letter, Macready begged Gawler to 'consider what follows to a certain extent as private, for I should be loth to offend any of my old friends by causing a public allusion to an awkward circumstance, of which I really know nothing but its alarming consequences.' He then described the withdrawal, under artillery fire, of the 30th/73rd square to the ridge-top hedge:

'You may readily conceive that fire would not slacken on a body effecting such a movement; but though suffering sadly, and disordered by our poor wounded fellows clinging to their comrades thinking they were being abandoned, our little square retained its formation, and we had all but reached the hedge when a body of men (British) rushed in amongst us, turned us altogether into a mere mob, and created a scene of frightful confusion. Fortunately the enemy took no advantage of it.

'Nothing could be more gratifying than the conduct of our people at this disastrous period. While men and officers were jammed together and carried along by the pressure from without, many of the latter, some cursing, others literally crying with rage and shame, were seizing the soldiers and calling on them to halt, while these admirable fellows, good-humouredly laughing at their excitement, were struggling to get out of the melee, or exclaiming, "By G-d, I'll stop, Sir, but I'm off my legs."'

Macready's 1845 *United Services Magazine* article also varies in detail, and in particular gives more information about the officer casualties at that time:

'The momentary confusion of our Guards after their first repulse of the French ones… and the hurried cry of "Form square", being passed along the line, coincides curiously with that in Halkett's brigade at the same moment. As it may not be unacceptable to military readers to know the leading particulars of this confusion in Halkett's brigade, I will proceed to detail them.

'There was a hedge in our rear, to which it was deemed expedient to move us, I suppose, for shelter from the guns. We faced about by word of command, and stepped off in perfect order. As we descended the declivity the fire thickened tremendously, and the cries of men struck down, as well as from the numerous wounded on all sides of us, who thought themselves abandoned, were terrible. An extraordinary number of men and officers of both regiments went down almost in no time. Prendergast of ours was shattered to pieces by a shell; [Captain Alexander] McNab killed by grape-shot, and [Ensigns John] James and [James] Bullen lost all their legs by round-shot during this retreat, or in the cannonade immediately preceding it. As I recovered my feet from a tumble, a friend knocked up against me, seized me by the stock, and almost choked me, screaming (half-maddened by his five wounds and the sad scene going on), "Is it deep, Mac, is it deep?"

'At this instant we found ourselves commingled with the 33rd and 69th Regiments; all order was lost, and the column (now a mere mob) passed the hedge at an accelerated pace. I imagine the 33rd and 69th must have received a similar order to ourselves, and that the two bodies clashed from bad leading on one or both parts, the officers, from the nature of our formation, being inoperative within the squares. The exertions of the officers, added to the glorious struggling of lots of the men to halt and face about, were rendered of no avail by the irresistible pressure, and as many, crying with rage and shame, seized individuals to halt them, they were themselves jammed up against them and hurried on with the current, literally for many yards not touching the ground. At this moment, some one huzzaed, we all joined, and the men halted.'

'I cannot conceive what the enemy were about during our confusion. Fifty Cuirassiers would have annihilated our brigade; they must, however, have been quick about it, for terrible as this occurrence was, I suppose five minutes would have included it all from first to last. The officers did wonders, but the shout alone saved us. I never could learn who raised it.'

Macready submitted his account of the 'confusion' to his brother officers, three of whom remarked on it as follows:

Lieutenant-Colonel Bailey said only, 'I quite agree with you as to the sad slaughter that preceded our movement to the hedge.'

Captain Howard was a little more forthcoming, agreeing with Macready's narrative and adding that 'I always considered this (our retirement) the most critical period of the day. I remember the shout well, accompanied with the words "Prepare to receive cavalry", which had the effect of righting everything like magic.'

Lieutenant Rogers offered that 'I never could learn exactly what caused the confusion we got into when ordered to retire; certainly there had been a murdering fire of artillery on us, and I well recollect Major [Matthew] Ryan and I being between the other men and ours, and doing all we could to keep them from mixing, and Ens. [William] Bartlett, of the 69th, was doing the same. I recollect an huzza – the men instantly turned round. I thought it was the enemy's cavalry, and the men had turned round to meet them. At this time I was much exhausted from fatigue, hunger, and the dreadful squeezing I got trying to prevent confusion and rally the men.'

The most circumstantial account of the 'confusion,' apart from Macready's, is in Captain Arthur Gore's rather sycophantic 1852 account of 'the crisis':

'Exposed, as well as ourselves, to the concentrated fire of the artillery from the neighbouring heights, the conflict with [the 33rd and 69th] appeared to be even more terrible than with us. I can never forget the fearful slaughter which then took place in the ranks of the 33rd and 69th Regiments, animated, as they were, by our beloved commander, still waving in his hand the King's Colour of the 33rd, nor the apprehensive cry which arose almost simultaneously from our men, "See where the General is – between two fires, he cannot escape! He will certainly be killed!"

'The 33rd and 69th… which had so long been exposed to a concentrated fire, unable any more to endure it, falling back, carried us with them for some paces to the rear… This desperate confusion was, however, of short duration. Suddenly a cry was raised of "The cavalry are coming!" and a few shots being fired, we soon re-formed as one corps, and continued to hold that position which His Grace the Duke of Wellington had ordered us to "maintain whilst a man remained." At length, severely wounded, our gallant and enthusiastic general was compelled to leave the field.'

There is very little detail of this 'confusion' from letter-writers and diarists of the 33rd and 69th. Lieutenant-Colonel Elphinstone, commanding the 33rd, is among those who do not mention it, and nor does Lieutenant Pattison. Ensign George Ainslie of the 69th is unusually guarded:

'Some heavy bodies of French infantry approached us, and the fire of grape and musketry increased to a degree that would soon have put us all *hors de combat* and which compelled us slowly to give way. In the space of a few minutes all our mounted officers were killed. Colonel Morris [Morice] was first severely wounded, and almost immediately afterwards struck by a grape shot on the temple… This severe fire obliged us to give way, which we did slowly step by step; still keeping our front to the enemy, and every one calling "Halt" and continuing to recede. The impulse once given, it was impossible to restrain it.'

Macready gleaned some additional information from the 69th, albeit at second-hand, which he passed to Siborne: '[Lieutenant Henry] Anderson… was in them & wounded by a shot from the Imperial Guard. Whether he would or could tell in which shape they came against his Regt & 33rd I know not. I think – of course this is <u>most controversial</u> – the morale of both these Regts was shook by what happened to each of them on the 16th & by neither of them having first rate commanding officers. I saw Halkett at one time with the white Colour of the 33rd, waving it over his head, & they seemed shook then, and that was certainly not the time when they came bodily into us & made our unit a mob, so that of course it is not easy to get particulars out of those of them who had their eyes about them at the time. Col. Muttlebury' [Major & Brevet Lieutenant-Colonel of the 69th at Waterloo] 'distinctly told me that the fire of the Imperial Guard knocked in the front face of his square & caused the confusion to which I have last alluded.'

Wellington, present as ever at the critical point, was passing the rear of the 5th Brigade with officers of his staff when he saw the confusion and, without directing himself to anyone in particular, said, 'See what's wrong there.' Major Dawson Kelly[1021] of the 73rd rode up to Sir Colin Halkett, who at that instant was wounded in the face and was obliged to retire to the rear. This left the brave but ineffective Lieutenant-Colonel Elphinstone of the 33rd in command of the brigade but paralysed by responsibility and calling out, 'What is to be done? What would you do?' Kelly told him. Lieutenant-Colonel Bailey of the 30th, who was wounded soon after, had a blunter exchange: 'It was at this time that Elphinstone and his cowardly major were running about asking what was to be done. I told the former "Do your duty."' As for the latter, Bailey later commented to Macready that 'It is really disgusting to think of that fellow Parkinson of the 33rd. Poor Knight [a captain of the 33rd] would not sit in the same room with him, & Halkett has often lamented bitterly that he was not able to accompany his brigade to Paris, in which case he would have shown up the gentleman & commented rather severely on one or two others of a similar taste.'[1022]

There is some doubt as to who, if anyone, was actually in command of the brigade at that time. Macready maintained that Chambers was the only effective chief, but with Halkett, Bailey of the 30th and Harris of the 73rd all wounded, and the Brigade Major and Morice of the 69th both dead, Dawson Kelly seems to have felt an obligation to bolster, if not supplant, the incompetent Elphinstone: 'Having observed that the different battalions

---

[1021] Dawson Kelly was commissioned into the 47th Regiment in 1800 and obtained a majority in the 73rd in 1811. His account of joining Halkett's brigade, dated 26th November 1834, is in *Waterloo Letters*, No. 145.

[1022] Elphinstone and Parkinson not only escaped censure for their conduct at Waterloo but were richly rewarded. William Elphinstone rose to become a major-general and Commander-in-Chief in Bengal. His incompetence and vacillation in the First Afghan War were in large measure responsible for the disastrous 1842 retreat from Kabul. Edward Parkinson, who was described by Bailey as a 'poltroon' (underlined five times!), was made brevet lieutenant-colonel for his services at Waterloo, and became a lieutenant-general and Colonel of the 93rd Highlanders. Charles Knight later commanded the 33rd Regiment.

of the brigade had got intermixed from the frequent formation of squares, I advised Colonel Elphinstone to order both officers and men to resume their respective stations, to form as extended a front as possible, directing them to cover themselves as well as they could by lying down, to renew or check their flints, and to fresh prime, so as to meet the next attack with the best means left us. This he instantly directed.' Whilst he was talking to Elphinstone, some sergeants of the 73rd came up and told him they had no officers left to command them, which was very close to the truth. 'I therefore considered it my duty to remain with them, and upon my saying so, they cheered and instantly returned to their several posts.'

Macready, as the only Light Company officer still on his feet, had meanwhile been ordered by Major Chambers to dash out as far as he dared and form a skirmish line. This he did, gathering up his fourteen remaining Light Bobs and a few others including several Grenadiers, reinforced shortly by Lieutenant John Roe's company and some men under (he thought) Lieutenant Charles Ingle of the 69th.

'The enemy's columns were within one hundred and fifty yards of us,' he recalled, 'and yet neither party advanced. I lost some men while covering the Regiment, but the dead horses and soldiers formed capital shelter for both sides.'

Under cover of the skirmishers, deployed up to fifty yards to its front, the brigade resumed a four deep formation at the hedge, and according to some accounts the 33rd and 69th soon afterwards took ground to their right and front. Macready estimated the brigade strength at that time as six hundred men at most.

It will be recollected that the withdrawal of Kielmansegge's Hanoverians and the Nassauers had left a dangerous gap in the line to the left of the 5th Brigade. However, Wellington's centre right was then reinforced by troops of the Brunswick contingent, who, according to Macready, fell back at nearly the same time as Halkett's brigade, but then rallied:

'While things were looking badly, some Brunswickers had marched up to our left. They gave way once bodily just as they reached the crashing line of fire, but were rallied, and afterwards stood well, throwing out light troops to the left of our skirmishers.'

In his letter to Gawler, Macready remarked that, 'If I am not deceived, Captain Hughes… (then a lieutenant of the 30th) and, if I may be permitted to say so, a *most* gallant officer, received a wound while assisting to rally them.' Bailey recalled that the Brunswickers came up just as he retired wounded.

Once the 5th Brigade and the Brunswickers had re-established their hold on the ridge, which they did without interference, there appears to have been a stand-off with Donzelot's columns, and Macready sensed that an 'apathetic listlessness' possessed the exhausted troops on both sides:

'A sort of lull now took place, close skirmishing with heavy columns in grey great-coats formed to the left of our front being all our work. Our Regiment and 73rd were in line four deep behind the hedge, and the enemy's columns two or three hundred yards from them, but neither party advanced. All at once the fire of musquetry thickened so as to tell on our skirmishers, who were crouched behind dead horses, and to cause many casualties in the line… There was a strange hurly-burly on all sides – firing, and shouting, and movement, and it lasted several minutes. Our grey great-coated opponents disappeared as if the ground had swallowed them.[1023]

Dawson Kelly's recollection of this episode, nearly twenty years or so after the event, are entirely consistent with Macready's 1816 account of a lull, followed by an outburst of activity from French columns, and lastly their sudden and unexplained disappearance, though he makes rather more of Donzelot's rather half-hearted final attack, perhaps because he was then in effective command of the brigade:

'We remained for a short time inactive, when the *last attacking column* made its appearance through the fog and smoke, which throughout the day lay thick on the ground. Their advance was as usual with the French, very noisy and evidently reluctant, the officers being in advance some yards cheering their men on. They however kept up a confused and running fire, which we did not reply to until they reached nearly on a level with us, when

---

[1023] French line infantry wore grey greatcoats, whereas those of the Imperial Guard were, as noted by Macready and Rogers, blue. In a draft letter to Sir Colin Halkett dated 11th January 1845, Macready speaks of 'masses of grey greatcoated troops what [*sic*] fired obliquely on us from the left', further proof that these were of Donzelot's division.

a well-directed volley put them into confusion [from] which they did not appear to recover, but after a short interval of musketry on both sides, they turned about to a man and fled.'

Similarly, Macready stated that 'Our opponents rapidly and unexpectedly disappeared.'

The capture by the 30th of a drum of the French 105th Ligne, who were in Bourgeois' brigade of Quiot's 1st Infantry Division suggests that at least some of that division may have deployed west of La Haie Sainte, together with Donzelot, to support the advance of the Imperial Guard.[1024]

In a slightly later letter[1025], Kelly owns that 'whether [the last column] were of the Imperial Guard or of D'Erlon's Corps we had no opportunity of judging. I should rather think the latter, for after some firing between us the enemy retreated without any *very apparent cause*. I presume it might have been about this time that some of our troops had got to the rear or flank of the enemy, which caused their sudden retreat."

He was quite right. Whilst the 5th Brigade skirmished inconclusively with Donzelot's men, a final decisive clash had occurred some five hundred yards to their right and well to the west of the 'Lion' spur. Three battalions of Chasseurs of the Imperial Guard had approached the ridge, their battalion squares heading for the right flank of Maitland's brigade. There is some controversy as to what followed, but it is quite clear that the main role in defeating the Chasseurs was played by Adam's brigade, and in particular by Colborne's 52nd which wheeled to attack the left flank of the advancing column, routed it, and then pursued the Imperial Guards obliquely across the battlefield to cross the Genappe chaussée south of La Haie Sainte.

The evidence rather suggests that neither battalion of the 1st Guards fired into the head of the third column. Indeed, the 2nd/1st Guards had run out of ammunition. Lord Saltoun, then commanding the 3rd/1st Guards, hesitantly suggested that his battalion might, perhaps, have fired on the Chasseurs, but with no great conviction: 'We advanced against the second [actually third] column of the Imperial Guards, but which body was defeated by General Adam's brigade before we reached it, although we got near enough to fire if we had been ordered so to do; and as far as I can recollect at this distance of time we did fire into that column.'[1026]

James Shaw had no doubt that 'The effect of the defeat of the... Imperial Guard, and Colborne's diagonal march, was electrical on Donzelot's division, which was in fact compromised by the advance of Adam's brigade. Its attack, which had up to that time been violently severe on Alten's division, was at once slackened and very soon suspended, and a retreat commenced.'[1027]

By chance, Lieutenant Nevill of the 30th took part in the advance of Adams' brigade. Having completed his engineer reconnaissance tasks, he was at Halle by the 16th, and there 'I now had leisure to think of my corps, the 2nd Battalion of the 30th Regiment, to which I was much attached. We were like brothers, so friendly did we feel towards each other, and much I wished to be with them.' On the morning of the 18th, he handed over his reports and sketches, bought a pony, and set off alone to find the 30th.

'As I had not the least idea where my regiment was, the thought occurred to me to make for the right of the army, and thence along its line until I fell in with my corps; but little did I think of the difficulty of doing this, amidst fire, smoke, death, and the confusion of so great a battle. I persevered, however; but it was not until late in the day that I got to the right of the army, and where I received no information. As I struggled along as well as

---

[1024] This 'Waterloo Drum', which is now in the Regimental Museum, was for many years carried by the Corps of Drums of the 30th. Neil Bannatyne, the historian of the 30th, related the following story: 'Among the victors was Private Lawrence Carroll of the Light Company of the 30th, an old Peninsular man. It certainly was an eventful day in the Carroll family, for not only was he wounded in the great battle, but on or almost on the battlefield his wife was delivered of a son. The boy was christened William, and was known all his life as 'Waterloo Bill', He accompanied his parents to India, and at twelve years of age was allowed to enlist as a boy Very soon afterwards he was appointed Drummer . . . When the custom began no one knows, but for a great part of Waterloo Bill's life in the Regiment one of his duties was to march into the Officers' Mess on Waterloo night carrying the French drum and there perform all the beats and flourishes he knew. General Sir Mark Walker, V.C., when Adjutant of the Depot in 1853, was present at one of those performances and says Bill was given so many glasses of wine that he ended by believing he had captured the drum himself.'
[1025] *Waterloo Letters*, No. 146 dated 14th October 1835.
[1026] Ibid., No. 106 dated 29th January 1838. Lieutenant Maule of Rogers' Battery RA said that the French Guards came 'nearly to our Guards' before being taken in flank by Adams' brigade and Rogers' guns.
[1027] Shaw-Kennedy, p.p. 147-48.

I could, amidst artillery, cavalry, and cannon-balls flying past me in abundance, I was determined to join any regiment I could. At this moment a cannon-shot struck my pony, knocking us both over, and killing him instantly.

'I now made my way to the front line, where I fell in with the 95th Rifles. Here I met with a kind friend, Captain Logan[1028]; but everyone here was too busy to mind anybody, until, during one of the lulls in the French cannonade, a large column of the Imperial Guard approached our front. We were ready for them; and it was about this time that another column of the same Guard was seen approaching us on the left. At this moment a strong regiment of ours [the 52nd] advanced from the front and met this left column in the most undaunted manner, preserving a beautiful line, shoulder to shoulder, not firing a shot until close to them; then, after one most effective volley, they charged and defeated the enemy… The column coming on in front of our Guards and the 95th were charged by those regiments in the most gallant manner, and defeated; as were also other columns of the Imperial Guard which had attacked the right centre of our army.'[1029]

General Allied Advance

The last rays of the setting sun pierced the enveloping smoke of battle to show the Duke of Wellington on the rise where the Lion Mount now stands, as he raised his hat as a signal for the whole line to advance. Cheers rolled from right to left along the ridge as the Duke rode towards the Elm Tree Crossroads.

The 5th Brigade did not take part in this general advance. 'We could hardly walk with fatigue,' Macready told his father, though the young ensign reckoned that if Halkett had still been in command, his brigade would have moved forward.

'A regiment of German hussars passed to our right,' he later wrote, 'stopping to breathe their horses, or align themselves just even with us, and saying they would pay 'em off for us. I suppose this was the final charge.[1030] We marched obliquely to our right to near the crest of the hill, but just before we moved a stray round-shot carried off the four men it encountered, close to our Commanding Officer, and this was the last of our casualties.'

'A heavy column of Dutch infantry (the first we had seen) passed, drumming and shouting like mad, with their chakos on the top of their bayonets, near enough to our right for us to see and laugh at them, and after this the noise went rapidly away from us. Soon after we piled our arms and lay down to rest.'

This was the first appearance in the front line of Detmers' Dutch-Belgian brigade which some revisionist, not to say inventive authors have credited on very flimsy and insubstantial evidence with having defeated an element of the Imperial Guard, whereas the extent of their involvement was to join in the pursuit of an already defeated and fleeing enemy, a belated and chaotic participant in the general advance. Neither Detmers himself nor any of his subordinates claimed to have exchanged fire or crossed bayonets with a formed body of the Imperial Guard, which was perhaps fortunate as many of their troops were inebriated. Their superior, Lieutenant-General Chassé (formerly an officer of Napoleon's army) attempted to associate his 3rd Netherlands Division with the defeat of the Guard, but avoided an outright untruth by such obfuscatory statements as 'I had the pleasure to witness the Garde Impériale retire from the confrontation with our brigade.'[1031]

By 1836 Chassé had embellished his memory with deliberate misrepresentations, such as: 'I saw the Garde Impériale advancing, while the English troops were leaving the plateau en masse and moving in the direction of Waterloo.' Had Chassé verified this observation he would have known that what he was seeing was the withdrawal of Kielmansegge's Hanoverians (who wore British red coats) to regroup at Mont St. Jean. On the basis of such falsehoods, a myth has arisen that the Moyenne Garde threw back Halkett's brigade and that Detmers' Dutch-

---

[1028] Captain Joseph Logan was with the 2nd/95th of Adams' brigade, which was at that time in the front line with the 52nd on their right and the 2nd/1st Guards on their left. At the time of the final advance Logan had assumed command of his battalion.

[1029] Nevill, p.p. 43-5.

[1030] Lieutenant Rogers confirmed, in his reply to Macready's circular, that 'it was almost at the end of the day that the German Hussars came up to us and halted.' They were probably the 1st Hussars, King's German Legion, in Sir Hussey Vivian's brigade.

[1031] Report of Lieutenant-General Chassé, commanding 3rd Netherlands Infantry Division to the Prince of Orange dated 4th July 1815.

Belgians arrived just in time to restore the situation with a bayonet charge and to pursue the Imperial Guard some time before the general advance. This scenario is not supported by any contemporary eye-witness accounts. Colonel Detmers himself speaks only of having 'pursued the enemy in a lively manner,' while Major-General Constant-Rebècque, Quartermaster-General and Chief of Staff of the Netherlands Army, who was in the thick of the action throughout, makes no mention of Detmers' brigade when he describes the defeat of the Imperial Guard, noticing them only as having joined in the advance of 'the whole line,' which he says 'had just been reinforced by the 1st Brigade [Detmers'] of the 3rd Netherlands Division, and which advanced in closed columns at attack pace towards the enemy.'[1032]

The outcome of the final confrontation with the Imperial Guard was anxiously awaited by Lambert's brigade. 'Late in the day,' wrote Harry Smith, 'when the enemy had made his last great effort on our centre, the field was so enveloped in smoke that nothing was discernible. The firing ceased on both sides, and we on the left knew that one party or the other was beaten. This was the most anxious moment of my life. In a few seconds we saw the red-coats in the centre, as stiff as rocks, and the French columns retiring rapidly, and there was such a British shout as rent the air. We all felt then to whom the day belonged…

'At this moment I saw the Duke, with only one Staff officer remaining, galloping furiously to the left. I rode on to meet him. "Who commands here?" "Generals Kempt and Lambert, my lord." "Desire them to get into a column of companies of Battalions, and move on immediately." I said, "In which direction, my lord?" "Right ahead, to be sure." I never saw his Grace so animated.'

Lieutenant Hugh Wray of the 40th told a similar story from a regimental viewpoint: 'About eight in the evening Lord Wellington came up waving his hat and hurraing, and ordered us to charge a column that was forming to cover their retreat, which we did, first giving them a volley (which they returned), and then charged, but they did not stand.'[1033]

Major Fielding Browne was now in command, for Arthur Heyland was dead. According to his son, Heyland was killed by a ball in the neck during this final advance, though some evidence from those present indicates that he may have fallen a little earlier during the intense duel of musketry mentioned above. His sword had previously been shattered, his horse wounded, and for the greater part of the day he had been riding bare-headed, his cap having probably been shot away.

Captain Peter Bishop of the 40th recalled, in 1835, 'I think about seven o'clock on the evening of the 18th, the 40th Regiment had formed into line, having just charged the enemy, in which we lost several officers and men, and amongst them Major Heyland (our then Commanding Officer). The Duke of Wellington came up to us at the moment, and we gave him three hearty cheers.'[1034]

In the earliest history of the 40th, a manuscript compiled by Captain Frederick Hibbert Nelson, the author states that the Regiment 'was particularly engaged in receiving and repulsing the last attack of the enemy, on the left centre of the British position, and in driving them into a gravel pit at the point of the bayonet. In following up this success the right of the Regiment retook La Haye Sainte, on which occasion the Commanding Officer, Major Heyland, was killed and the command of the Regiment devolved on Major Fielding Browne.' This account is not derived from the *Record of Service*, so it is most likely to have been obtained from regimental veterans of the battle known to Captain Nelson.

Sergeant Lawrence said that Heyland was no longer present when Wellington came up to the 40th and asked who was in command: 'On being told it was Captain Brown [Major Browne], he gave the order to advance which we received with three cheers, and off we set as if renewed with fresh vigour.'[1035]

Captain (later Colonel) Sempronius Stretton described the advance: 'When the British line moved forward, the 40th drove the *tirailleurs* from the rising ground in its front, and occupied it; at the same time the

---

[1032] See *Waterloo Netherlands Correspondence*, John Franklin, 2010.
[1033] Wray's diary, quoted in *Historical Records of the 40th Regiment*, p.p. 187-88.
[1034] *Waterloo Letters*, No. 178.
[1035] Lawrence, p. 212.

27th, with Grenadiers of the 40th, took possession of the farm of La Haie Sainte, where they made prisoners of a general officer and a party of the enemy.'

There appears to have been little serious resistance to this final advance of the British left. Sir John Lambert recalled that, 'When the General Advance was ordered, at half-past seven, I do not recollect that the enemy made any stand at the Haye Sainte; all that could get away retired, leaving it full of wounded, and many prisoners were made there.'

Major Jonathan Leach, then commanding the $1^{st}/95^{th}$ in the hollow lane, confirmed this, stating that a few minutes before the General Advance, 'the French suddenly evacuated the farmhouse of La Haye Sainte and the ground near it, and retreated in haste; and this, I conclude, was in consequence of the total repulse of the Imperial Guards, and the forward movement of a part of the Duke of Wellington's right wing.'[1036]

Indeed, the oblique advance of Adam's brigade across the field was about to cut off the retreat of d'Erlon's men from around La Haie Sainte, while at much the same time Zeiten's Prussian corps advanced diagonally across the eastern half of the field from Smohain to La Belle Alliance. 'We were indeed glad to see the arrival of these Prussians,' recalled William Lawrence, 'who now coming up in two columns on our left flank, advanced on the enemy's right.'

After the Battle

As the tide of battle rolled away from them, the 30th remained on the ridge, exhausted. 'After the battle was over,' Macready told his father, 'I fell down on the ground and slept till the bugle sounded the "advance" next morning.' 'I remember, as long as I remained awake,' he recalled in his journal, 'I was thinking on the day's work, and considering whether it would be called an action or a battle. I certainly considered we had 'spilt blood enough to make our title good' to the latter honour; but I fancied that, so far as we were concerned, some grand bayoneting charge, some concluding *coup de théatre*, or rather *coup de grace*, was wanting to entitle us to it.'

Having secured La Haie Sainte, Lambert's brigade continued their advance onto the Belle Alliance Ridge, where they halted for the night near the Charleroi chaussée.

'We were so fatigued,' recalled Lieutenant Hugh Wray of the 40th, 'as not to be able to pass the French position, where we halted that night amongst their dead and wounded. During the night of the 18th, when the Prussian heavy troops came up, they halted close to us, and their soldiers and officers came up to us, tapping us on the backs, saying, "*brave Anglois*,' and giving us lots of brandy to drink, of which we much wanted, as we were all wet. Their bands played *God Save the King*, and every one of them saluted us as they passed next morning. Marshal Blucher and our noble commander met at a farmhouse just in our front and where I got some clean straw to lie on that night.'[1037] Next morning, Wray observed, the soldiers of the 40th were using French cuirasses as frying pans to cook their beef steaks.

Sergeant William Lawrence described how the 40th, having followed the retreating French for about a mile, 'encamped on the enemy's ground':

'If ever there was a hungry and tired tribe of men, we were that after that memorable day of the 18th of June. Then the first thing to be thought of was to get a fire and cook some food, which was not so easy, as wood was scarce and what there was wet through.'

The search for fuel resulted in a fatal accident, the last casualty of the 40th on the battlefield of Waterloo:

'One of our [Grenadier] company, named Rouse, who went out in search of sticks, came across one of the enemy's powder-wagons that we had taken in the battle... and immediately commenced cutting the cover up for fuel; but his hook coming in contact with a nail or some other piece of iron and striking fire, as a natural consequence the remains of the powder in the wagon exploded and lifted the poor fellow to a considerable height in the air. The most remarkable thing was that he was still alive when he came down and able to speak, though

---

[1036] *Waterloo Letters*, No. 171.
[1037] Lieutenant Hugh Wray's Journal, entry for 22nd June 1815, at Bavay, quoted in *Historical Record of the 40th Regiment*, p. 188.

everything had been blown from him except one of his shoes. He was a perfect blackguard, for although he was in a most dangerous state he did not refrain from cursing his eyes, which happened, as it was, to be both gone, and saying what a fool he must have been. He was that night conveyed to Brussels Hospital with the rest of the many wounded, and died in a few days, raving mad.'[1038]

Lawrence himself was very much more fortunate in his foraging. He happened that night to be Brigade Orderly Sergeant, and as such, he reported to Sir John Lambert, who he found sitting on a gun-carriage, bridle in hand. The General asked him to find some corn for his horse:

'Off I went accordingly, and found two bushels or so in a sack which had evidently been left by the enemy, as it was on one of their cannon. When I opened the sack I found to my great surprise that it likewise contained a large ham and two fowls, so I asked the General if he would accept them; he, however, declined, saying he would take the corn, but that I might keep the meat for myself, advising me, however, to keep it out of sight of the Prussians, who were a slippery set of men and very likely to steal it if they saw it. I prepared the hanger for the pot as quickly as possible, putting cross-sticks over the fire at a sufficient distance to prevent them igniting; but before I had finished doing this a quantity of these same Prussians whom the General had been watching and warned me against passed by; and two of them coming to my fire to light their pipes noticed the ham and remarked that it looked good. I thought it best to take my sword and immediately cut them off a piece each, and they relieved my fears by going off seemingly quite satisfied.'[1039]

Lawrence was soon joined by two other duty sergeants, and the three of them, having 'enjoyed our mess as much as men ever did,' retired to rest on some straw they found under a French cannon.

'I was too tired to go to sleep for a long time,' recalled Lawrence, 'and lay contemplating the scenes of the day. I was merely scratched on the face myself during the whole day, besides being a little shaken by the bursting of the shell I mentioned; but this scratch had been terribly aggravated by a private who had been standing next to me having overprimed his musket, with the consequence that when he fired, my face being so close, the powder flew up and caught my wound, which although originally a slight one soon made me dance for a time without a fiddle.'[1040]

The field of battle that night was a place of horror, haunted by marauders, as experienced by Lieutenant-Colonel Frederick Ponsonby of the 12th Light Dragoons. He was wounded in the early afternoon cavalry melee and then lanced as he lay on the ground, where he was plundered by French and Prussians, and trapped beneath a dying man.

'An hour before midnight, I saw a man in an English uniform coming towards me; he was, I suspected, on the same errand. I spoke instantly, telling him who I was: he belonged to the 40th, and had missed his regiment. He released me from the dying soldier, took up a sword, and stood over me as sentinel.' Day broke, and at 6 a.m. help was summoned.

As the Duke of Wellington rode slowly back across the battlefield from La Belle Alliance to his Waterloo headquarters he was unable to contain his tears as he contemplated the terrible cost of victory. Some 13,700 of his army lay dead or wounded, including 6,344 British, together with some 7,000 Prussians and 31,000 Frenchmen.

Surgeon Elkington's diary states that over the three days fighting the 30th had six officers and 51 other ranks killed in action, fifteen officers and 208 other ranks wounded, and 27 men missing, a total of 280 killed and wounded (45.5% of their strength). Macready reckoned the total casualties of the 30th at 279 killed and wounded, a figure he may well have obtained from the surgeon.

The number of killed was indeed at first given officially as six officers and 51 other ranks, but the latter figure was later amended to 36, clearly not including men who died later of their wounds.[1041]

[1038]Lawrence, p. 213.

[1039]Ibid., p. 214.

[1040]Ibid., p.p. 215-16.

[1041] The 2nd/30th lost the following killed on 18th June: Major Thomas Walker Chambers, Captain Alexander Macnab, Lieutenants Henry Beere and Edward Prendergast, Ensign John James, Sergeants Thomas Catlin, Pat Gunning and John Wilkinson, Drummer Thomas

Elkington's figure for the wounded may be accepted as accurate for those he sent to general hospital, though there would almost certainly have been others, lightly wounded, who remained with the Regiment and accompanied the advance. They would not be included in the totals. Macready was himself slightly wounded but did not give in his name because, as he wrote to his father, '21 is enough for one regiment.' Several of his brother-officers had lucky escapes: Captain Howard and Lieutenant John Gowan were both shot through their shakos, and Lieutenant Rogers' cap was shot off.[1042]

There are three quite different accounts of the death of Major Tom Chambers, of which by far the most credible is that of Lieutenant Frederick Hope Pattison of the 33rd, who was present:

'On halting, a number of little coteries were formed to discuss the proceedings of the day... The officers composing my circle were Colonel Elphinstone, Captain Gore and Major Chambers. Major Chambers, having commanded the 30th Regiment for some time previous to the termination of the battle, was in high spirits, and had just remarked that, having been in command, he would, no doubt, be gazetted a Lieut.-Colonel at once. We all acquiesced in this, and congratulated him on his anticipated promotion. While engaged in this social conversation, our attention was directed to some desultory firing going on in front. A few shots having passed close by us (in passing they made a sharp whistling noise), I quitted my friends, saying, "I will go and see what those fellows are about." On getting to a rising ground close to the circle I had just quitted, I saw a few straggling skirmishers firing towards the Brigade. On a shot passing close to my left, I involuntarily turned round, when I saw poor Chambers leave his friends, advance towards me, put his hand to his breast, lay himself down close to me, and immediately expire. This sad event was the cause of great regret, as Chambers was much liked and respected in his regiment, and by all who knew him. He was, I think, the last man – certainly the last officer – killed in our brigade at Waterloo.'[1043]

Captain Arthur Gore confirms this account of Chambers' death: 'At the moment he was declaring "that he had hitherto escaped unhurt, and that he was too small to be hit", he received a ball through the heart from a *tirailleur* of the Guards, and instantly expired.'[1044]

Elliott, and Privates John Ashby, Thomas Bailey, William Brewitt, William Brien, James Campbell, Ben Colley, William Eaden, Thomas Freeney, John Goodchild, John Grady, William Hopeful, William Hughes, Thomas Jones, Richard King, John Lister, Henry Lynch, Timothy Maher, Pat McGrath, Henry Miller, Thomas Miskill, Pat Morton, Charles Norfolk, John Parker, John Raysdale, Ben Siddons, Francis Smith, Robert Sparrow, Samuel Tyers, Garret Vizer and George Webb. Died of wounds: Ensign James Bullen, Colour-Sergeant Christopher Barnewell, Sergeant Charles Kilmartin, Corporal Richard Brown, and Privates John Addy, William Cranaway, Henry Day, John Fletcher, Thomas Freeman, Thomas Harker, John Hilton, Joseph Jordan, Richard Keys, Michael Lahey, Nicholas Lumsden, William Moran, Richard Morrisey, John Niell, William Perchender, James Pick, William Pryor, John Sharp, Richard Snodden, Charles Storer, and John Towey.

[1042] Wounded of the 2nd/30th on the 18th included Brevet-Lieutenant-Colonel Charles Albert Vigoureux, Major Morris William Bailey, Captain Arthur Gore, Lieutenant and Adjutant Matthias Andrews, Lieutenants Robert Daniel, Richard Charles Elliott, Robert Hughes, Richard Mayne, Thomas Moneypenny John Pratt, John Roe (2nd), John Rumley (seriously), and Charles Ouseley Warren (dangerously), Quartermaster-Sergeant Joshua Harrington, Drum-Major Thomas Poole, Paymaster-Sergeant Thomas Cuthbert, Colour-Sergeant Joseph Scotton, Sergeants Isaac Burrows, John Carroll, Jonathan Cart, Ben Detheridge, William Frohock, George Sheridan, and John Smith, Corporals Joseph Andrews, Charles Cooke, Thomas Dobbs, John Flinn, Sam Lumsden, Denis Moran, Patrick Murphy and Joseph Saville, Drummer John Brice and 124 Privates. Although Colonel Vigoureux served on until 1839, a bullet had lodged near his spine and could not be extracted, causing him great suffering for the rest of his life. Captain John Garland of the 73rd, who had been Adjutant of the 30th in the Peninsula, lost his leg serving beside his old regiment, and was so seriously injured that he was said to have been the last of the British wounded to leave Brussels. His obituary was prematurely printed in *The Gentleman's Magazine*, but he died in 1851 a lieutenant-colonel.

[1043] Macready thought that Chambers died a little earlier, but he was not a witness as he was out skirmishing.

[1044] The least credible account was given to Mr John Chambers, who wrote from Lowestoft on 15th August: 'I was sent for to the hospital at Yarmouth. There I found seven of the 30th Regiment, one of which told me he was not more than two yards from the Major when he fell. Before this he had two horses shot from under him, the other which was a beautiful mare got away from poor Tom as he [was] trying all possible means to gain the square to save himself from the French cavalry. Just as he came to the square a ball struck him on the left breast and poor Thomas fell without a word.' This was supposed to have happened at 3.30 p.m., but Chambers was clearly active at least four hours later.

Gore paid a tribute to 'my friend and companion in arms': 'He was an active, zealous, and intelligent officer, and a great loss to his regiment, both as a soldier, and a gentleman. His character was not less to be admitted as a private member of society; and by his death, some amiable young females have to regret a sincere friend, and affectionate brother.'

When Chambers fell, Lieutenant Benjamin Nicholson, a close friend from their time with the 1st Battalion in India, threw himself on the body and sobbed aloud, 'My friend – my friend!'

Macready had incurred Chambers' displeasure when serving as a Light Company volunteer, but, according to the younger man's tactful account, the two appear to have effected a battlefield reconciliation. 'It is only in and after a battle,' he reflected, 'that men act without dissimulation. Their common danger makes them forget, and their pride tells them to despise, the thousand petty disguises and acts of general society. Two of our officers were not on terms: the one saw the other behaving gallantly; he ran up to him, and cried, "Shake hands, and forgive all that has passed; you're a noble fellow".'

'Poor young Bullen was much regretted,' recalled Macready. 'He had left his home contrary to the wishes of a fond mother, and had only been with us three weeks. His legs were both terribly shattered.[1045] Just before the amputation of one of them, he was smiling and saying he must now return to his mamma, and he thought £150 per annum (his half-pay and two pensions) would make her more comfortable. He bore the operation nobly, but as soon as it was ended, exclaimed, "Gentlemen, you have done for me!" and breathed his last.'

'As Harrison was standing near me in our square, a poor fellow, his servant, came up and said, "My dear master, I am wounded and must go away; but I wished to say good bye to you, for I know I shall never see you again." The words were hardly out of his mouth, when a round shot dashed his head to pieces, and covered us with his blood and brains.'

Lieutenant Richard Harrison's servant was not the only man of the 30th with a premonition of death. On the night before the battle Captain Alexander Macnab, having taken snuff with his friend Arthur Gore, confided to Bailey that he felt certain he would be killed, requesting the Colonel to think of his nieces, which he did, getting them pensions.

Macnab was described by Captain Arthur Gore as 'popular with the officers and men of his regiment... brave and steady in time of danger... patient and God-fearing in fulfilling his obligations in camp or the battlefield.' A Virginian-born United Empire Loyalist, he was the only Canadian known to have been killed at Waterloo.[1046]

Lieutenant Nevill, who had passed the day of battle with the 2nd/95th, was shocked when late on the following morning he found the 30th: 'On joining them, what a wreck did I see! – the field officers all struck down, and Major Chambers killed. Of the captains, all were killed or wounded save one, who then commanded the Regiment – Captain Howard; in short, six officers were killed on the spot, sixteen officers wounded, and half the battalion *hors de combat*.[1047]

The 40th suffered a total of 223 all ranks killed and wounded (28.25% of their strength). Three officers, seven sergeants and 42 rank and file were killed, and 15 officers, 12 sergeants and 147 rank and file were wounded, of whom 24 subsequently died of their wounds.[1048]

[1045] Sergeant Tom Morris of the 73rd recalled the quip of one of his men, when quartered near Soignies, that a certain officer of the 30th 'would be a decent-sized fellow if his legs were taken off'. 'I thought of the remark when I saw the officer lying with both legs broke, just below the knees, by a cannon ball. He requested me to cut off his legs, but I had not the heart to do it, though it would have been an act of mercy; for when I saw him next morning, he was in the same situation, having had no assistance.' This unfortunate officer must have been either James Bullen or John James, the other Colour ensign, who also lost both his legs.

[1046] Alexander Macnab's M.I. in the crypt of St Paul's Cathedral perpetuates the apocryphal tale that Macnab was acting as an additional ADC to Sir Thomas Picton when he fell mortally wounded, aged 42. However, Macready's rather more circumstantial account records that he was killed by cannister. As he lay dying he instructed his servant to convey his watch, ring, sword and regimental sash, together with some messages, to his family in Scotland and Canada.

[1047] Nevill, p.p. 45-46.

[1048] Major Arthur Rowley Heyland, Captain William Fisher and Lieutenant Frederick Ford were killed, Captain John Henry Barnett, Lieutenants James Anthony, the Honourable Michael Browne, Andrew Eugene Glynne, James Mill and Robert Moore, Ensigns William

'Poor Major Heyland… was shot through the heart,' wrote James Mill in a contemporary note, 'and poor Ford was shot thro' the spine of his back, but did not die for a short time after he was carried away. Poor Clarke lost his left arm and I am much afraid [the Hon. Michael] Browne will lose his leg, he is shot thro' the upper part of his thigh and the bone terribly shattered. There are eight more of our officers wounded, but all doing well except little Thornhill, who was wounded thro' the head. Anthony here got his eighth wound and is doing well.' Mill was himself struck by a spent musket ball in his right eye.

That night, the 30th had only 160 men in line.[1049] Edward Macready, aged just seventeen, commanded what was left of the 30th 'Light Bobs':

'Our Light Company marched into the field three officers and fifty-one men; of these two officers, one sergeant, one bugler, and thirty-seven rank and file were killed or wounded; six more were away assisting them, and we stood at night, one commissioned, two non-commissioned officers, and eight privates. When we formed four deep, and the poor Light Bobs could only muster a front of two men, I really didn't know whether I should laugh or cry.'

The Advance on Paris

The 59th Foot had passed the day of battle quietly near Tubize, though menaced at a distance by French cavalry; indeed, Sir Charles Colville, commanding the 4th Division, stated that not a shot was heard all day. Although they were less than ten miles from the field of Waterloo, the noise of conflict was apparently deadened by intervening woods. Consequently, the 4th Division piled arms and spent the time collecting forage.[1050] On 19th June, the 59th advanced with Colville's relatively intact 4th Division at the head of Wellington's army, occupying Nivelles that evening.

When Edward Macready woke on the morning of the 19th he had no idea that the victory was so complete. Indeed, on 7th July he wrote to his father that, 'So little did we know of it next morning, as we fought till dark, that I assure you I expected to see the enemy on the heights opposite us.' He recorded his impressions of the battlefield in his journal:

'The field in the morning presented a most distressing spectacle. It was covered with caps, cartridge-boxes, guns, tumbrils, belts, books, and arms of all kinds, and lacerated and mangled carcases. The poor wounded chargers, looking patience in their misery, were nibbling the trampled grain round the spot they lay upon, while our wounded were bitterly reviling us and calling for assistance which we had not in our power to give. I spoke to numbers of the Frenchmen; they were not very communicative, but a common phrase among them was, 'Monsieur, nous sommes joliment foutus.' I went to look for our poor fellows who had fallen while skirmishing, but every one was dispatched; the sabre had settled their worldly affairs. My remaining eight Lights stole me a capital breakfast, after which, about ten o'clock, we left this glorious spot, encumbered with thousands of the dead and dying.'

At least some of the 30th were buried near where they fell, as discovered by Major-General Campbell, late of that Regiment, when he visited the battlefield in 1893. Entering the small museum attached to the Hotel du Musée, close behind the Lion mound, he walked up to a table on which were displayed numerous skulls. Picking up one of these macabre exhibits at random, to his surprise he found it marked as *The Skull of a Soldier of the*

Aldworth Clarke, Henry Hemsley, and Volunteer Richard Thornhill were seriously wounded, and Captain Conyngham Ellis, and Lieutenants Thomas Campbell and Hay Robb were slightly wounded.

[1049] This is consistent with the statement of Sergeant Morris, 73rd, that on the morning of the 19th the four regiments of Halkett's brigade did not muster more than six hundred men.

[1050] Among the relatively few valid criticisms of Wellington's conduct of the battle on the 18th is that he should have remained in touch with his outlying force at Halle and Tubize, and, once it was clear that Buonaparte was not turning his right, he might to considerable advantage have ordered the detached sixteen thousand men to advance against the Emperor's left flank. Sir Charles Colville, commanding the troops at Halle, did apparently send a staff officer to Wellington on the evening of the 17th June to ask him whether the force at Halle should join the main army, but the suggestion only reached Waterloo a few hours before the battle commenced.

XXXth whose skeleton, identified by his uniform buttons, had been discovered when digging out the foundations of the hotel.[1051]

Before moving off on the morning of the 19th, Captain Arthur Gore tried to help some of the wounded:

'As I slowly moved along... a feeble cry reached my ear, which seemed to proceed from someone just expiring: it was the voice of a wounded Frenchman, and murmured the touching petition, "*De l'eau, pour l'amour de Dieu!*" Alas! I felt that he entreated in vain, for no water was available in the vicinity; but filled with pity... I opened my canteen and administered to the wounded man a few drops of brandy and water, which I had fortunately reserved for a case of urgent necessity. Somewhat revived, he bent on me a look of intense gratefulness which long dwelt in my memory.

'As I proceeded, regretting that I could render him no further service, a similar petition was repeated by a brother officer who lay near him. That petition was acutely distressing, for having parted with my scanty supply to the first applicant, I was aware that I had no means wherewith to slake the dying thirst of this hapless sufferer. Bending over him, I endeavoured to explain this in the gentlest manner, but darting on me a reproachful glance, he exclaimed in a tone of bitter agony, "*Ah! c'est parceque je suis un enemi!*" "Good God!" I replied, "Can you think me so inhuman? In such a situation no one is my enemy!" To convince him of my sincerity, I set out upon a search for water; but the search proved ineffectual. On my return to make this sad communication, he still reiterated (gazing at my canteen) the painful petition, "*Donnez moi à boire aussi!*" At his request, I put the canteen into his hands, and never can I forget the agonized energy with which he strained it to his lips, in the hopes of eliciting a single drop. It was in vain.'

There was a happy sequel to this painful battlefield encounter, for in December 1816, Gore and a friend were dining at a restaurant in Dunkirk when two French officers entered the room. A few questions revealed that they were the badly wounded men who Gore had tried to aid on the field of Waterloo. The reunion was, as may be imagined, enthusiastically cordial.

The 30th marched on the 19th to Nivelles, where they were in bivouac, and on the 20th were billeted at Binche. Nerves were still taut after three days of fighting with little sleep and less food, and whilst at Binche Macready observed a curious 'affair of honour' with a fortunate outcome:

'Soldiers during a campaign disregard the punctilios of civil society and seem to acquire a slight tinge of the brigand. They act more from impulse. An odd circumstance which verifies this conjecture occurred to us near Binch[e]. Two officers were talking of the second battle, and one remarked that at a particular period the other ought to have taken charge of the King's Colour. "Excuse me", replied his friend, "it was your duty as junior Lieutenant." "By God, Sir, if you say so I'll run you through the body!" was the rejoinder, and "By God, Sir, I do say so!" the retort. Out flew their swords, and by a simultaneous movement out came every sword in company. Seeing us all brandishing our weapons, Howard rode up and put the aggressor under arrest. We then burst into a fit of laughter and sheathed our spits. Frenchmen would have let our two heroes pink each other and looked on with indifference, but an Englishman can't see a row without thinking himself bound to increase the confusion.'[1052]

As he had in the South of France, Wellington was at great pains to assure the people of France that his army came as friends and as allies of their legitimate sovereign, King Louis XVIII, and so on the 20th he issued a timely General Order to that effect, though the more historically aware of the French may not have been entirely impressed that it was issued from the field of Malplaquet.

'On the 21st we crossed the frontier,' wrote Macready, 'and loosened our ammunition on hearing a heavy but irregular fire in front of us. A commissary met us, riding like John Gilpin and swearing he did not turn his

---

[1051] Campbell's letter about his visit, sent from Brussels to the Regiment, then in India, was reported in *The XXX*, Vol. IX, No. 6, May 1889. The Hotel du Musée, since demolished, was on the site of the present interpretation centre.

[1052] Ensigns James and Bullen, who should have been carrying the Colours at the start of the battle, were both killed, and Macready, the only other ensign, was detached with the Light Company. The junior lieutenant was Edward Drake, so he was almost certainly one of the protagonists in this quarrel. We know that the next in seniority, Robert Rogers, did carry one of the Colours, so the other protagonist may well have been David Latouche, the next senior, of whose performance at Waterloo Macready had a low opinion.

back till his pistol ammunition was expended. In half-an-hour we reached the field of action, and found the Hanoverians hard at work cleaning their pieces. We halted near Bavai [Bavay], a neat town, abandoned by its inhabitants.'

In passing the fortified town of Mons, Captain James Finucane of the 30th was detached to act as commandant of that fortress.

Surgeon James Elkington of the 30th had remained at Mont St. Jean, presumably working from the farm where the army's Main Dressing Station was established, until 21st June, by which time he had sent off all the regimental wounded to Brussels.

'I rode over the field to report on the number of the French wounded still to be removed. At La Haie Sainte I found a number of badly wounded. Those able to walk made the best of their way to Brussels. The transport was not sufficient to move the British, [so] the different pieces of French artillery, as they were brought to the rear, were loaded as well as possible with these unfortunate beings. A day or two after a general action is the period to gain a fine idea of the miseries of war.

'The inhabitants were now returning to collect what little remained of their household property, for friends and foe had made free with everything they wanted. Their houses were so full of wounded there was no room or shelter for them. The bodies of the dead began to be offensive, and the whole air was contaminated from the numerous carcasses of men and horses. Peasants were employed to collect the bodies of the men to burn, and bury the horses, having their nostrils covered with handkerchiefs to mitigate the stench.'

'June 21st: About 3 p.m. I left Mount St. Jean by the Nivelles road, passed Nivelles and halted at Seneffe, where I was gladly received by a farmer, whom the enormous number of Prussians, Belgians and English stragglers had greatly alarmed by repeatedly firing and demanding rations. He was about to leave his house when I arrived and promised protection for the night. This I was able to do having collected a good many of the 30th Regiment and kept them with me.

'June 22nd: I reached Mons by 10 a.m., and hearing the headquarters was at Bavay I again started and reached Bavay at 8 a.m., [and] got into a farmhouse that had been completely pillaged.

'June 23rd: Early in the morn I marched and joined my Regiment in bivouac about one league in front of Bavay.'[1053]

The 40th were also at Bavay on the 22nd, having remained on the field of battle for at least the morning of the 19th, when it appears they may have provided fatigue parties to clear the road for the artillery. Major Fielding Browne and Lieutenant Hugh Wray rode over the whole Waterloo position that morning, when they saw the captured cannon and eagles. 'Good God!' wrote Wray on the 22nd, 'what a scene of carnage – men, horses and carriages upset and groaning.' Lieutenant George Hibbert wrote on 2nd July that 'I crossed the field two days after the action; you could not walk three yards without crossing over a body, even though the country people had been employed to bury them the intervening time.'

Before they left the field of battle, the 40th also had the sad duty of burying Arthur Heyland, one of only two British infantry commanding officers killed at Waterloo (the other being Morice of the 69th). He was laid to rest in a garden at Mont St. Jean, where his wife later placed the tomb which may now be seen in the yard of Wellington's headquarters in Waterloo village.

The 81st, reluctantly left out of battle on the 18th, remained in Brussels until 15th July, attending the wounded of all nations in the crowded hospitals and escorting the French prisoners to Ghent for embarkation to England.

On 23rd June, most of the army rested to enable stragglers to catch up, together with ammunition and baggage. The exception was the 4th Division, which had reached Le Cateau by the 22nd. Before the Allied armies could march on Paris it was prudent to secure the border fortresses, and so General Sir Charles Colville marched from Le Cateau to Cambrai with Grant's Hussar Brigade, Lyon's Hanoverian Brigade, three batteries of artillery and a letter from Wellington to the governor summoning him to surrender. The summons was refused, and early

---

1053 Elkington's Diary, in the *XXX*, June 1911, p. 13.

on the morning of the 24th, Wellington ordered the two British brigades of the 4th Division, then at Le Cateau, to reinforce Colville. Johnstone's Brigade, with the 59th, marched up the Roman road to Cambrai, which, nearly a century later, would be trodden by their East Lancashire successors when it marked the British II Corps battle line on 26th August 1914.

Cambrai was, or should have been, one of the strongest fortresses in French Flanders, but its defences had been neglected. Although it boasted scarps from 40 to 70 feet high where the ditch was dry, and 30 to 40 feet high where it was wet, they had not been maintained, and the ditch near the Paris gate was full of mud and weed. Moreover, the garrison was quite inadequate for the extent of the fortifications. In view of these weaknesses, on the arrival of Johnstone's and Mitchell's brigades Colville decided to dispense with a formal siege and take the place by escalade without delay that evening.

Three columns of attack were formed. Johnstone's brigade, including the 59th, was to escalade the curtain wall by the Valenciennes Gate and a large ravelin near the Amiens road, while Mitchell's brigade was to force the outer gate of the *couvre port* in the hornwork and, passing both ditches by means of the rails of the drawbridges, was to take the main Paris Gate. The walls were stormed with minimal loss, including Corporal James Gannon and four men of the 59th wounded.[1054]

Lieutenant Lewis Carmichael of the 59th, who had already distinguished himself at the storming of San Sebastian in 1813 and would do so again at the storming of Bhurtpore in 1826, was again to the fore and was Mentioned in Despatches. The garrison withdrew to the citadel, where on the 25th the Governor surrendered to King Louis XVIII.

The 30th had halted for the day on the 23rd in the wood of Crevecoeur[1055], about three miles beyond Bavay, a rest which was most welcome to Edward Macready:

'My boots, which had been on my feet since the morning of the 15th, had become hardened by the mud and turned on one side, so as to cut me dreadfully, and during the last march I was obliged to support myself by [Lieutenant Richard] Heaviside's stirrup leather, walking on the sides of the soles. I had them cut off my legs here, and procured a good pair of shoes from the Light Bobs. These fellows furnished me with everything. When they could not find wine for my dinner, I have known them to go and buy it from the sutlers at five francs a bottle, and bring it to me, declaring that they [had] made (i.e. stolen) it, lest my delicacy should prevent my accepting it.'

The 30th were in bivouac near Le Cateau on the 24th, at Prémont on the 25th, and at Caulaincourt, west of St. Quentin, on the day following.

'We had most strict orders against plundering of any description,' wrote Macready, 'and all marauders taken by the Provost Marshals were to be immediately executed. Two of our men had been taken, but the Duke released them, as his note expressed, "in consequence of the excellent behaviour of our corps." However, neither compliments nor commands can fill empty stomachs, and as our Commissariat only served out three rations in twenty days, our men were obliged to forage or starve. I had myself mounted [Captain Matthew] Ryan's horse, and was reconnoitring the neighbourhood of Caulaincourt, when I heard a confused noise of pigs squeaking and men swearing behind a hedge very near me. I rode up, and discovered four soldiers of the 33rd cutting the throats of an old sow and her litter. "Hallo!" said I, "what are you gentlemen about? Don't you know that if the Provost sees you, you'll swing for this?" "Yes, Sir," answered the spokesman, "we do, but then there's no rations and – perhaps your honor would like a pig." "Why, as the pigs are killed, I have no objection; but I assure you, my good fellows, this is a very serious business, and I wish I could have prevented it. I'll thank you for that pig on the left. Good morning." I galloped off with my prize, and the ramrod was through him immediately.'

The 40th, having halted at Bavay since the 22nd, marched again on the 24th, and arrived on the 26th at Ham. The French had been expected to contest the Somme crossing there, but the town and its fortress surrendered, and the Regiment encamped about a mile outside.

[1054] Private Denis Whonahon of the 59th, who died of wounds on 27th July 1815, was probably one of the Cambrai casualties.
[1055] Not identified, but probably part of the Forêt de Mormal.

On the evening of the 27th of June, the 40th bivouacked near the town of Roye. Here, according to Hugh Wray, a demonstration was made by the ladies of the place, young and old, who met the Regiment carrying white lilies in their hands and crying 'Vivent les Anglais! Vive le Roi!' At 5 a.m. the next morning the Regiment was on the march again, but owing to the heat of the weather advanced only seven leagues, and again bivouacked. Six more marches, of which the last two were spent more in manoeuvring than advancing, brought the 40th to within one or two leagues of Paris.

The weather was hot, and the commissariat was still not functioning properly, but Wellington was determined to reach Paris without delay, and so the army advanced by forced marches, along much of the same route that the regimental successors of the 30th were to take in August 1914.

The 30th marched on by Cressy, near Nesle, where Macready learned that all his baggage had been stolen, and on through Roye, Boulogne-la-Grasse, Estrées-St. Denis, Pont St. Maxence and Senlis to La Chappelle en Serval, near Luzarches, on 30th June.

'On this day's march,' wrote Elkington in his diary for the last date, 'we fell in with the route the Prussians had advanced by. We found the villages completely plundered, there was nothing to be got but vegetables and pigeons, that still remained about the houses.' Lieutenant-Colonel Bailey rejoined the 30th that day.

On 1st July, the 30th halted near Aulnay-sous-Bois, a small village within seven miles of Paris and in sight of Montmartre. Their brigade was on the left of the Anglo-Allied army, which had relieved the Prussians, and that same day Ensign Macready was sent with an outlying picquet[1056] near the chateau of a Baron de Schonen, whose letters of nobility, he admitted, 'we disposed of most irreverently.' 'It was a beautiful seat, but the Prussians had destroyed every thing except the books and some peacocks. We had fine fun chasing these birds, but they were insufferably tough.'

Surgeon Elkington was also billetted in Aulnay, probably in the same chateau, and in his diary entry for 1st July wrote, 'There was some nice villas here. The one I occupied had been beautifully furnished, but the Prussians had broken everything; the most beautiful pier glasses were destroyed. The garden was full of fine fruit, and the grounds well laid out. We sent a picquet to the bridge.' Next day he wrote, 'Returned to Aulnay. Being on the alert we threw the nice bedding out on the lawn, and slept soundly that night. We expected the French position at Le Villette would be attacked next day. During the day we received news of the Capitulation of Paris.'[1057]

The 59th saw some final action on 1st July when Colville's light companies took over from the Prussians in contact with the French at Aubervilliers. At least half of this village, an advanced post of the outer defence line of Paris, which ran along the St. Denis Canal, was held by the French. The British light troops determined to capture the entire village. Having first taken two or three of the highest houses, they broke through partition walls from the top of these into some that were lower, and so mouse-holed their way down the street to take the greater part of the village. The French commander, who had offered only weak resistance, then asked for a truce.

The Prussians, meanwhile, had circled round to the north of Paris to reach Versailles. Macready recalled that, 'On the evening of the 2nd a heavy cannonade was heard to our right and was kept up briskly for some hours. We were under arms and expected every minute to be ordered forward. Montmartre frowned in our front and we looked for serious occupation. The firing proceeded from Versailles, whence the French were driven after hard fighting and pursued thro' St. Cloud to the heights which overlook Paris on the south-west side.'

The capture of the suburb of Issy by the Prussians was the last action before a military convention and suspension of hostilities was agreed on 3rd July, under which the French army was to evacuate Paris and the Allies would take possession of the capital on the 7th. Lieutenant George Hibbert of the 40th proudly added a postscript to a letter to his brother from 'Camp outside Paris':

'We have just had the intelligence that Paris has surrendered. Repeated huzzas in the camp seem to confirm the news. The firing in front also has ceased, which was very heavy, which seems to confirm the report.'[1058]

[1056] The 30th provided a picquet at a bridge over the Ourcq Canal, part of the advanced line of defence of Paris.

[1057] Elkington's Diary, in the *XXX*, June 1911, p. 13.

[1058] While negotiations were under way sporadic musket shots continued across the St. Denis Canal, and according to Adrian Lewis (*The Lilywhite 59th*, 1985) a sentry of the 59th was among those killed. We have been unable to validate this claim.

Lieutenant Hugh Wray, also of the 40th, made the following entry in his diary on July 6th:

'This day appears a day of great joy to the Parisians, who are in great numbers at this moment in our camp, waving white handkerchiefs, flags, and lilies to us all. There are about three hundred carriages, lots of the National Guard, and people of all sorts here waiting the arrival of the King, who passes by here in a couple of hours on his way to St. Denis, which is only half a mile from our camp and three and a half miles from Paris. The French army left Paris this morning, and Lord Wellington and Marshal Blucher entered at the head of our hussars and Prussian Guards in triumph.

'5 o'clock: The King has just passed with all his guards, going at an easy walk. He was received by us in line, and all the people with loud and frequent shouts of "*Vive le Roi! Vivent les Bourbons!*"'[1059]

As Sergeant Lawrence recalled, the triumphant veterans of the 40th could not resist the opportunity for teasing banter:

'We used to aggravate the people not a little, on our march into the city, by singing, "God save Buonaparte, who has fled and given himself up to the 'Billy Ruff'uns' [the crew of HMS *Bellerophon*, to whom the Emperor had surrendered], in opposition to their cry of "God save the King"; thousands of them having come out with white cockades in their hats to welcome the King. They even wanted to take the horses out of his carriage and draw him into the city, but Lord Wellington would not allow this, knowing well their changeable disposition, and fearing they might make their king a head shorter by the morning. The King therefore slept that night at St. Denis.'[1060]

That same day, the 3rd Division marched through La Villette to the northern suburb of La Chapelle, close to Montmartre and the barrier of Paris, where they bivouacked. Crowds of Parisians came out to see them.

'As our Grenadiers were in front,' wrote Macready, 'they all agreed that England had picked her finest men to beat them. They laughed at our ragged colours, and called our riflemen, whose clothes were discolored, *des ramoneurs de chéminée*. Nothing is too high or too low for the laughter of a Frenchman.'

Among the crowd who watched the British troops enter Paris was young Victor Hugo, who wrote:

'Paris was full of the victors, and I full of woe. But to describe what one felt a day later as I watched that victorious vagabond army march into the City is beyond perception. One can accept, and even admire, those tall and soldierly Prussian or Russian guardsmen, who look so grand in their well cut tunics with epaulettes and buttons of gleaming gold, and stand up to the cut of a sabre wielded by a proud Silesian or Hungarian hussar on their great stallions of war. But to stand and watch this English army march past, in those ridiculous little black caps, and red tunics which hung about their shoulders like so many wet blankets, with grey drab trousers enclosing their knock knees, and shoes and boots of all manners; but then one gradually noticed also the sparkle of their faces and the fresh vigour about their stature. And as I watched, of the many hundreds that passed that day, not one breast contained the bric-a-brac of campaigning that other nations bestow on their warriors: only occasionally did one see the red ribbon of good conduct on an officer's tunic. No, these English need no baubles of war, no proof of the courage and tenacity for which they are so renowned. No, it is the love of old Albion, that inborn pride of country, that makes them the most formidable soldiers of all.'

It is hardly surprising that on July 2nd Wellington had issued an order urging his officers to 'be dressed uniformly, and if possible according to the King's Orders.' A vain hope indeed, for the 30th and 40th were among the many who had lost all their baggage. Young Edward Macready's appearance, described in his 7th July letter to his father, would certainly not have excited a tailor's or drill sergeant's admiration:

'Having lost my baggage, my dress is rather ludicrous: a pair of shoes belonging to a French Grenadier, a pair of blue trousers taken off a dead officer, shirt taken out of a portmanteau on the field; for the rest, it's pretty good it holds together but is black with blood [and] powder, which with my burnt hands and face, long hair and moustache, and half my sabre scabbard taken off, makes me rather a respectable figure.'

[1059] Wray's Diary, in *Historical Records of the 40th Regiment*, p. 201.
[1060] Lawrence, p. 219.

On 7th July, the 30th and 59th marched round the walls of Paris and into the Bois de Boulogne, where they encamped.[1061] The 40th escorted Louis XVIII into the city, then encamped in the beautiful grounds of Neuilly Park, previously the residence of Princess Pauline Borghese, Buonaparte's sister and wife of Marshal Murat, King of Naples. William Lawrence described the entry into Paris:

'About three thousand men with cannon and cavalry were ordered to convey [the King] into the city, amongst whom was myself. We started at about eleven or twelve o'clock, still not knowing how we should be welcomed, which was the reason for this large force being thought necessary; but as we met with no opposition at the entrance, the bands of each regiment soon struck up, and on proceeding through the streets we found flags from endless windows, and the cry, "God save the King!" resounding everywhere. Our destination was of course the palace, where the King was again placed on his throne, with a strong guard to protect his person.'[1062]

That same day, Macready wrote dutifully from camp to his father, then at Lancaster, with an account of the battle of Waterloo, and gave his first impressions of Paris:

'I yesterday had a good laugh in my own mind at the 'Grande Nation' on looking over the famous Champs de Mars where the scaffolding yet remains whence the Corsican a few weeks ago assured them of Freedom and Victory. I felt for weakness of human nature on seeing the grass worn off the ground where the same Imperial Guard marched over, swearing to conquer or die, who on hearing our Huzza, and seeing our bayonets levelled, a few days after ran like sheep.'

'I was yesterday in Paris, saw the Hotel des Invalides, the dome of which is beautifully covered with gilt. The maimed relics of Jena, Austerlitz and Leipsic regarded us with a coldness which sufficiently explained their feelings. But our late Waterloo friends saluted us very cordially, but will not be persuaded that we had not a million of men in the field. We expect to march into the city today, or tomorrow.'

'Here we are victors at Paris, a thing never heard of since the days of Edward and Henry. They say we are to get medals. I hope so.'

For the men who took part in the Waterloo campaign, there were indeed rewards. All ranks, including the dead, were granted a silver Waterloo Medal, while surviving officers who had succeeded to command of their battalions received the Companionship of the Bath (CB).[1063]

The 1st Foot Guards were renamed the Grenadier Guards in the erroneous belief that they alone, or principally, had defeated the Grenadiers of the Imperial Guard, but no such honour was granted to the 30th and 73rd, who had defeated the first, senior and larger of the two assaulting Grenadier battalions.

The non-commissioned officers and men were entered in the musters and pay lists as 'Waterloo Men' and were granted two years' service towards an increase of pay and pension. All subalterns present were also granted two years' service towards increased pay, which gave them an additional shilling a day after five instead of seven years' service as lieutenants. Major Fielding Browne of the 40th was promoted to brevet lieutenant-colonel, and Captains Robert Howard of the 30th and Conyngham Ellis of the 40th to brevet major.

There were other rewards, albeit delayed until July 1817, when Waterloo prize money for captured artillery was paid out: £2-11s-4d a head for the rank and file, £19-4s-4d for sergeants, £34-14s-9½d for subalterns, £90-7-3¾d for captains, and £433-2s-4½d for field officers.[1064]

The 30th and 40th Regiments were awarded with the Battle Honour 'WATERLOO,' and for their steadfastness and discipline on that day were additionally permitted to encircle their badges with a laurel wreath. The battle is commemorated annually with a parade at which the Colours are decorated with wreaths of laurel,

---

[1061] The bivouac of the 30th was by the farm of La Minette, close to Passy.

[1062] Lawrence, p. 219.

[1063] The Waterloo Medal was awarded to 597 all ranks of the 30th, 790 of the 40th and 520 of the 59th. The CB was awarded to Lieutenant-Colonel Hamilton, Major Bailey and Captain Howard of the 30th, and to Major Fielding Browne of the 40th.

[1064] The often-repeated contention that Wellington's officers were well-funded scions of the aristocracy and gentry rarely applied to the line infantry. Several dependents of the regimental officers killed at Waterloo were fortunate to receive an annual allowance from the Royal Bounty. Captain Alexander Macnab's sister Mary was granted an allowance of £50 per annum, 'in consideration of her age, infirmities and destitute situation', while the mother of Lieutenant Frederick Ford, 40th, was awarded £40 per annum, 'she being left thereby in distressed circumstances.'

whilst all ranks of the Regiment are given a laurel leaf each, to be worn behind the cap badge for the remainder of the day, and a citation outlining the activities of the Regiment at Waterloo is read aloud on parade by the junior subaltern.[1065]

The occupation of Paris marked not only the end of the campaign, but of the long war which, with two short intermissions, had pitted Britain against Revolutionary and Napoleonic France for 22 years. This was truly a world war, in the course of which the forebears of The Queen's Lancashire Regiment fought on five continents and on seas and oceans throughout the world. In the course of this conflict, they earned twenty Battle Honours, representing just a few of the 140 separate actions they fought, from set-piece land battles and bloody sieges to smaller 'affairs,' and from fleet actions to large-scale amphibious operations and ship-to-ship engagements. Their opponents ranged from the imperial armies of France and her satellites, including Dutch, German, Polish, Irish, Italian, Spanish, and Swiss soldiers, to Arab pirates, Bantu tribesmen, Danes, Maroons, and assorted East Indian rajahs and sultans, not to mention Americans, north and south. Their allies were equally diverse.

The sustained regimental achievement over this long period was by any standard remarkable, but was entirely consistent with the traditional British foreign policy of opposing the domination of Europe by a centralising continental superpower while building influence and commercial opportunities worldwide. On the battlefields of Europe, they had repeatedly met and worsted the vaunted legions of Napoleon Buonaparte, thwarting his overweening imperial ambitions and bringing peace to most of the continent for a generation. Their involvement in projecting British power and influence beyond Europe helped set the scene for a global expansion in western liberal values, education, scientific advances, and free trade, together with particularly British ideas of freedom under the law and freedom of the seas. These, together with widespread use of the English language, have shaped the world to the present day.

[1065] I had the honour, as junior subaltern. of reading the Waterloo Citation in Swaziland at a memorable parade on the 150th anniversary of the battle. (EJD)

Index to Volume II

A

Barnard, Andrew, Col, 141, 143, 147-48.

Barnett, John Henry, Capt, 40th, later Maj, 286, 332, 350, 354, 494.

+ Barnewell, Christopher, C-Sgt, 30th, 493.

Baroda, 403-04.

+ Barrett, John, Pte, 59th, 418.

Barrosa, Battle, 143-50.

Barrouillet. Plateau & Mayor's House, Basses Pyrenées, 333-40, 343.

Batavia (now Jakarta), Java, 390, 409-12, 414, 420, 424-25, 427, 431.

Bati Sant-Bernard Ridge, Quatre Bras, 444-46, 455.

Battle Barracks, Sussex, 3, 9.

Battle Honours: 'Cape of Good Hope 1806,' 15; 'Maida,' 25; 'Monte Video,' 42; 'Rolica,' 65; 'Vimiera,' 65; 'Corunna,' 89; 'Talavera,' 113; 'Tarifa,' 186; 'Badajoz,' 211; 'Salamanca,' 230; 'Vittoria,' 287; 'Pyrenees,' 308; 'St Sebastian,' 324; 'Nivelle,' 332; 'Nive,' 340; 'Orthes,' 348; 'Toulouse,' 355; 'Peninsula,' 362; 'Niagara,' 364, 'Java,' 418; 'Waterloo,' 501.

Batty, Robert, Ensign, 3rd/1st Guards, 327, 332, 338, 483.

Bavay, 497-98.

Baylen, Battle, 56.

Bayonne, 267, 289, 232-35, 338-40, 344, 349, 355-58, 361.

Bearhaven, Bantry Bay, 365-66.

Beaumont, John Percival, Capt, 30th, 393.

+ Beere, Harry, Ensign, 30th, 231, 243, 467, 492.

Belem, Lisbon, 66, 69, 136.

Belfast, 10, 117.

Bembibre, Leon, 71-72, 76,

Benavente, Leon, 75-76.

+ Bennett, Thomas, Ensign, 47th, 322.

Bentinck, Lord William, 30, 82, 84, 237, 267, 271, 325, 358.

Beresford, Sir William Carr, later Lord Beresford, Lt-Gen (Portuguese Marshal), 15, 35-36, 48, 101, 128, 151, 153, 162-65, 167-68, 288, 329, 340, 345-46, 348-51, 353, 355.

Bergen-op-Zoom, 374-77, 379, 439, 449.

Bermuda, 4.

+ Berrige, Joseph, Ensign (from C-Sgt), later Lt, 438.

Berwick, 370.

Betanzos, Galicia, 70, 80-81.

+ Bethel, J., Lt & Adjt, 40th, 230.

Bevan, Charles, Lt-Col, 4th King's Own, 161-62, 172.

Bexhill Barracks, near Hastings, 9, 36, 370.

Biarritz, 334, 358, 361.

Bidart, near Bayonne, 332-33, 335-36.

Bidassoa, River, 289, 309-10, 314, 324-25, 326-28, 358.

+ Bigland, Thomas, Pte, 59th, 417.

Bingham, George Ridout, Capt 81st, Maj 82nd, Lt-Col 53rd, later Maj-Gen Sir George, 106, 108, 231, 282, 285, 289, 294-95, 304, 329-30.

Bircham, Samuel, Maj, 30th, later Lt-Col, 3, 399, 407.

Bishop, Peter, Capt, 40th, 332, 490.

Blaauwberg, battle, Cape of Good Hope, 14-15.

+ Blakeney, Morgan, Pte, 30th, 243.

Blakeney, Robert, Lt, 28th, 123, 141-48, 197-98, 209.

+ Blakewell (?), Ensign, 47th, 322.

+ Bland, Humphrey Dalrymple, Maj, later Lt-Col, 47th, 118, 123-24, 404-05.

Blanquefort Camp, Bordeaux, 361, 364.

Blayney, Lord, Maj-Gen, 126-27.

Blessington, Lady Marguerite, 10.

Constant-Rebeque, Baron J. V., Maj-Gen, 470.
Conyers, Charles Edward, Lt-Col, 82nd, 348.
+ Cook, William, Pte, 30th, 211.
Cooke, Charles, Cpl, 30th, 493.
Cooke, George, Maj-Gen, 174, 177-78, 185-86, 233-34, 377, 446, 459.
Cooper, John, Sgt, 7th, 109, 346.
Cooper, Noah, Pte, 40th, 172.
Coote, Sir Eyre, Gen, former Maj, 47th, 95, 98.
Copenhagen, 31-33.
Copons, Don Francisco de Copons y Navia, Gen, 175, 178, 180-81, 184, 270-71, 358.
+ Corbet, Samuel, Lt, 81st, 88.
Cork, 10-11, 14, 16, 30, 35, 54-55, 70, 117, 361, 364, 366, 387.
Cornelis Lines (Meester Cornelis), Java, 409-10, 412-19.
Corrale del Miserere, Buenos Aires, 46-49.
Corunna, 70, 73, 76, 81-90, 93-94, 101, 117, 252, 267.
Cove of Cork, 2, 30, 50, 55, 364, 366.
Cowell, wife of Sgt, 47th, 248.
Cowes, 36, 258, 371.
Cowper, John, Ensign, 59th, 88.
Cradock, Sir John, Gen, 68, 75, 99-102.
Craig, James Henry, Lt-Gen, previously 30th & 47th, later Gen, 7, 9, 17-19, 27.
+ Cranaway, William, Pte, 30th, 493.
+ Crann, William, Pte, 59th, 417.
Craufurd, Robert, Maj-Gen, 17, 45-48, 111-12, 130, 160 194-96.
Crawley, Thomas, Ensign & Adjt, 59th, 313.
Creighton, Joseph, Capt, later Maj, 59th, 427, 429.
Creighton, William, Pte, 59th, 336.
+ Crigan, Charles, Maj, 81st, 88.
+ Croft, Thomas, Pte, 59th, 418.
Croix Dorado Bridge, Toulouse, 350-51
+ Crompton, George, Capt, 40th, 367.
Crowe, Charles, Lt, 27th, 272, 274, 283-85, 294-96, 346-47, 352-53, 361.
Crowhurst Park, 9.
Cuesta, Gregorio, Spanish Gen, 68, 100, 102, 104-06, 111-12.
Cullinan, Anthony, Pte, 30th, 196.
Cuming, James, Lt-Col, 47th, later Lt-Gen, 394.
Cureton, Charles Robert, Pte, 14th Light Dragoons, Ensign, 40th, later Brig-Gen, 344.
Curragh, the, Co. Kildare, 7-8, 10, 30, 70, 117.
+ Curry, John, Maj, 30th, 408.
Curtis, Frank, Pte, later C-Sgt, 30th, 460.
Cuthbert, Kingston, Lt, 82nd, 332.
Cuthbert, Thomas, Paymaster-Sgt, 30th, 493.
Cuxhaven, 15.
Cuyler, Jacob Glen, Capt, 59th, later Col, 16.

D

D'Aguilar, Charles George, Capt, 81st, later Maj-Gen Sir George, 269.
Dalhousie, Lord, Lt-Gen, 267, 276, 279-82, 291, 304-0, 308, 311, 348.
Dalrymple, Sir Hew Whiteford, Lt-Gen, 27, 53-4, 59, 66-67.
+ Dalrymple, John, Maj, 40th, 39-41.
Daman, Portuguese Colony, India, 394.
Daniell (or Daniel), Robert, Ensign, later Lt, 30th, 137, 28, 372-73, 383, 493.

Drummond, Gordon, Lt-Gen, 362-63.

Drummond, John McGregor, Lt, later Capt, 82nd, 348.

Dublin, 6-7, 9-10, 17, 30, 36, 117, 235, 365, 452; George St. Barracks, 7; Royal Barracks, 8, 116; Royal Hospital Kilmainham, 88, 452.

Du Maurier, Daphne, 69.

Duncan, Alexander, Maj, RA, 141, 146-47.

Duncan, Edward, Lt, 59th, 322.

Dundalk, Co. Louth, 70.

Dungeness, Kent, 12.

Dunlop, James Wallace of that Ilk, Lt-Col, 59th, later Lt-Gen, 13, 137, 139, 151, 155, 159-60, 162, 189.

+ Dunn, Brian, Pte, 59th, 429.

Durham, 3, 405.

Dutch Ships: Ceres, 391; *Kortenaar*, 391; *Pluto*, 391; *Resolutie*, 390; *Revolutie*, 391; *Rustloff*, 391; *Scipio*, 390.

Dyer, Moses, Pte, 30th, 196.

E

+ Eaden, William, Pte, 30th, 493.

Eagles, French: 22nd Ligne, 226; 34th Légère, 307.

Eastbourne, 370.

East India Company (HEIC), 388, 393-95, 397, 401.

East India Company Armies:

       Bengal Army: Governor-General's Bodyguard, 409; Bengal Europeans, 393, 423, 429; 6th Bengal NI, 409.
       Bombay Army: 2nd Bombay NI, 395-96.
       Madras Army: 5th Madras Cavalry, 399-400; 6th Madras Cavalry, 398-99; Madras Europeans, 398; 3rd Madras NI, 399, 406; 5th Madras NI, 406; 8th Madras NI, 399; 9th Madras NI, 406; 13th Madras NI, 398; 14th Madras NI, 408; 15th Madras NI, 399, 406; 16th Madras NI, 399; 19th Madras NI, 398; 24th Madras NI, 398.

East India Company Ships: *Ariel*, 395; *Aurora*, 395; *Fury*, 395; *Mercury*, 395; *Mornington*, 394-95; *Nautilus*, 395; *Prince of Wales*, 395; *Stromboli*, 395: *Sylph*, 395; *Teignmouth*, 394; *Ternate*, 395.

Edwards, Wright, Ensign, 59th, 322.

El Bodon, combat, near Ciudad Rodrigo, 189-90.

Elche, Alicante, 237.

Elkington, James Goodall, Surgeon, 30th, 370-71, 373, 384, 437, 440, 443, 445-47, 452, 455-56, 492-93, 497, 499.

Elliott, Richard Charles, Lt, 30th, 493.

+ Elliott, Thomas, Drummer, 30th, 467, 492-93.

Ellis, Conyngham, Lt, later Capt (Brevet Maj), 40th, 68, 99, 286, 495, 501.

Elm Tree Crossroads, Waterloo, 455, 458-59, 465, 473, 475, 477-78, 489.

Elphinstone, William Keith, Lt-Col, 33rd, later Maj-Gen, 486-87, 493.

Elrington, Richard George, Capt, later Lt-Col, 47th, 45.

Elvas, Portugal, 67-68, 99-100, 113-14, 128, 153, 163-64, 166-67, 171, 192, 197, 214-15, 248.

Elviña, village, near Corunna, 82-86.

Emery, Henry Gresley, Staff Surgeon attached 5th Division, 191.

Enghein, Belgium, 382, 453.

Enniskillen, 10, 117.

Ensenada de Barragon, Bay, near Buenos Aires, 45.

Enxara dos Cavaleiros, Lines of Torres Vedras, 136-37.

Erskine, Sir William, Maj-Gen, 151, 155, 161-62.

Escorial Palace, 232-33, 235, 243.

Esla River, 73-75.

Estremoz, Portugal, 128, 172, 187, 214, 231-32.

+ Evans, John, Assistant-Surgeon, 30th, 191-92, 196, 208.

Evans, John, son of Cpl Evans, 81st, first student at Royal Military Asylum, later Duke of York's Royal Military School, 5.

Ewing, James, Ensign, 47th, 336.

Eyre, Henry Samuel, Maj, 82nd, later Lt-Col, 52, 65-66, 69.

F

Fair, David, Lt, 81st, 88, 239.
Fairfield, Richard, Capt, 59th, 8.
Fairlight Camp, near Hastings, 3, 9.
Falmouth, 14, 37, 53, 70, 88, 118, 372, 387.
+ Fane, Charles, Lt-Col, 59th, 69-70, 81, 85-86, 88-89, 95, 98, 267, 277-78, 288.
+ Fane, George, Lt, 59th, 322.
Farmer, Maurice St. Leger, Capt, 47th, 9-10.
Faro, Sicily, 20, 27, 29-30.
Farrer, James, Maj, later Lt-Col, 81st, later HP Maj-Gen, 237, 269, 364.
Faunce, Alured, Lt-Col, 4th King's Own, 226.
Faversham, 17.
Featherstone, Francis, Capt, 47th, 118, 141, 150.
Fenton, William, Lt, 81st, 239.
Ferdinand, King of the Two Sicilies, 18-19, 30.
Ferguson, Sir Ronald Crawfurd, Lt-Gen, 14, 56-58, 60-63.
Fermoy, Co. Cork, 55, 117, 364.
Filer, Charles, Pte, 40th, 203.
Finucane, James, Capt, 30th, 438, 497.
Firman, Brook, Capt, 82nd, 292
+ Fisher, William, Capt, 40th, 367, 472, 494.
Fitzgerald, Charles John, Lt, 82nd, 281.
Fitzgerald, William Edward, Maj, 82nd, 291-92, 306.
Fitzpatrick, Right Hon Richard, MP, Gen, Col 47th 1807-13, 10-11.
+ FitzPatrick, Timothy, Lt, 40th, 39.
+ Flanagan, Edward, Pte, 30th, 230
+ Flanagan, Valentine, Pte, 30th, 211.
Fleming, Thomas, Capt (Brevet Maj), 30th, 16-17.
+ Fletcher, Elijah, Pte, 30th, 211.
+ Fletcher, John, Pte, 30th, 493.
Fletcher, Sir Richard, RE, 134, 165, 312.
Flinn, John, Cpl, 30th, 493.
Flockhart, Robert, Pte, 81st, 4.
Flushing (Vlissingen), Walcheren, 92-98.
+ Ford, Frederick, lt, 40th, 494-95, 501.
+ Fordyce, Alexander, Capt, 81st, 106.
Forrest, George, Lt, 59th, 422.
Fort Batz, South Beverland, 92, 97, 374-75.
Fort Bowyer, Mobile, 368-69.
Fort Concepcion, near Almeida, 159-60.
Fort Cumberland, Portsmouth, 17.
Fort Erie, Niagara, 362-64.
Fort Frederick, Lillo, near Antwerp, 92, 374, 376-79.
Fort Knocke, Cape Town, 15.
Fort Mackinac, Lake Michigan, 364.
Fort Maros, Celebes, 430.
Fort Puntales, Cadiz, 125.
Fort Ricasoli, Malta, 18.
Fort Rotterdam, Macassar, Celebes, 428-30.
Fort St. Angelo, Cannanore, Malabar Coast, 406.

Hay, Andrew Leith, Lt, later Lt-Col, 73-74, 79-81, 83, 86-87, 137-39, 205-06, 210, 215, 217-21, 224-26, 317-18, 321-22, 327.

Hay, William, Lt, later Capt, 47th, 278.

+ Hayton, Thomas, Pte, 59th, 418.

+ Heath, Thomas, Pte, 59th, 418.

Heatley, Tade, Lt, 47th, 40, 45, 49..

Heaviside, Richard, Lt, 30th, 120, 448, 498.

Helvoetsluis, Holland, 373.

Hemsley, Henry, Ensign, 40th, 495.

Hendaye, Basse Pyrenées, 324, 327.

Hennen, John, Surgeon 30th, later Deputy Inspector of Military Hospitals, 160-61.

HM Ships:
>*Achille*, 93; *Alceste*, 369; *Akbar*, 408; *Alfred*, 87; *Apollo*, 20; *Ardent*, 37; *Aurora*, 4; *Bellepoule*, 369; *Bellerophon*, 500; *Bermuda*, 440; *Blenheim*, 389-90; *Bulwark*, 364; *Camilla*, 4; *Caroline*, 389-91, 395; *Cephalus*, 238; *Crescent*, 366; *Culloden*, 391; *Daphne*, 37; *Delight*, 39; *Déterminée*, 4; *Druid*, 176; *Encounter*, 39; *Endymion*, 82; *Ennis*, 2-3; *Fame*, 28, 238; *Fox*, 391; *Greyhound*, 389; *Haerlem*, 2; *Halcyon*, 27; *Hussar*, 423; *Illustrious*, 408; *Imogene*, 4; *Indefatigable*, 56; *Jaseur*, 391; *La Chiffone*, 395; *La Sybille*, 4; *Lion*, 388-89; *Macassar*; 389; *Modeste*, 408; *Orpheus*, 4, 17; *Phaeton*, 408; *Phoenix*, 422; *Piedmontaise*, 398; *Plantagenet*, 364; *Pompée*, 20, 26; *Powerfull*, 391; *Psyche*, 390; *Redwing*, 237; *Regulus*, 173; *Rinaldo*, 373; *Rodney*, 87, 126-28; *Royal Oak*, 369; *Samarang* (former *Scipio*), 391; *Seaflower*, 391; *Shamrock*, 366; *Spartiate*, 29; *Stately*, 176-77; *Sultan*, 364-67; *Surveillante*, 313; *Swiftsure*, 126; *Topaze*, 126; *Undine*, 4; *Victoria*, 391; *Victorious*, 4; *Victory*, 87; *Volage*, 423.

Hermandad, Vitoria, 280-82.

+ Heyland, Arthur Rowley, Capt, later Maj, 40th, 109, 165, 267, 288, 296, 355, 441, 457, 490, 494-95, 497.

+ Heywood, John, Pte, 59th, 418.

Hibbert, George, Ensign, later Lt-Col, 40th, 359, 369, 440-41, 497, 499.

+ Hibbert, William, Lt, 40th, 8-9, 42, 55, 57-58, 63, 67-68.

High Wycombe, 6.

+ Hill, George, Lt, 47th, 278.

+ Hill, James, Capt, 59th, 420.

Hill, John, Lt, 47th, 184.

Hill, John, Pte, 30th, 150.

Hill, John (2), Pte, 30th, 196.

Hill, Sir Rowland, Gen, 16, 106-07, 128, 153, 186, 215, 234, 243-44, 250, 266-67, 273, 276, 282, 289-93, 303, 329, 340, 344-45, 349-50.

Hill, William Henry, Ensign, 59th, 335.

Hilsea Barracks, Portsmouth, 3, 17, 36, 387.

+ Hilton, John, Pte, 30th, 493.

Hitchen, John, Capt, 30th, 121, 140, 211, 231, 243.

+ Hoblyn, Francis, Capt, 40th, 112.

+ Hodge, John, Pte, 30th, 211.

+ Hodges, William Arthur, Capt, 47th, 278, 322.

Hoghton, Daniel, formerly 82nd, Maj-Gen, 122-23, 168, 170.

Holdsworth, Samuel, Lt & Adjt, 82nd, 306.

Holy Island, or Lindisfarne, 370.

+ Hooper, William, Pte, 40th, 465.

Hope, Sir Alexander, Lt-Gen, Col 47th 1813-35, 381.

Hope, James, Lt, 92nd, 445.

Hope, Sir John, Lt-Gen, 72, 76, 82-83, 85-87, 329, 331, 334, 336, 339, 355-57.

+ Hopeful, William, Pte, 30th, 493.

Hopkins, Ellers, Lt, 4th King's Own, 205-07, 240, 242.

Horner, Thomas, Pte, 30th, 123.

Horsham Barracks, Sussex, 11, 54.

Louis XIV Redoubt, Nivelle, 330-31.
Louis XVIII, King of France, 440-41, 496, 498, 500-01.
Ludlam, Christopher, Pte, 59th, 80-81, 88.
Lugo, Galicia, 71-73, 76, 78-80, 88, 90.
+ Lumsden, Nicholas, Pte, 30th, 493.
Lumsden, Sam, Cpl, 30th, 493.
Lutman, John, Lt (later Capt) & Adjt, 81st, 88, 93.
Lutman, John Adrian, Volunteer, 81st, 88.
Luxton, William, Sgt, 40th, 39.
+ Lynch, Henry, Pte, 30th, 493.
Lynch, Robert Blake, Capt, later Maj, 30th, 121, 139.

M

Macartney, Lawrence, Lt, 81st, 88.
Macassar, Celebes, 428-31.
Macau, 393.
Macdonnell, Randolph, Lt, 47th, 336.
MacGregor, James, Lt, 59th, 278.
Machel (or Machell), Richard, Capt, 30th, 122, 140, 206, 211, 379, 438.
+ Mackay, John, Ensign, later Lt-Col, 82nd, 31, 150, 306.
+ Macken, Pat, Pte, 30th, 211.
Mackenzie, John, Maj-Gen, 70-71, 268-69, 270-71.
+ Mackenzie, Lewis, Lt-Col, 81st, 4-5.
Maclean, Archibald John, Maj, 73rd, 468.
+ Macnab (also variously McNabb & M'Nabb), Alexander, Capt, 30th, 485, 492, 494, 501.
Macpherson (or McPherson), Aeneus McIntosh, Lt, 59th, 322, 338.
+ Macpherson (or McPherson), Alexander, Lt, 59th, 15, 278.
+ Macpherson (or McPherson), Evan, Lt, then Capt, 59th, 413-15, 418.
Macready, Edward Nevil, Volunteer & Ensign, later Maj, 30th, 374-84, 437-40, 442-43, 446-56, 460-64, 467-69, 473-77, 479-89, 491-99, 500-01.
Madden, George, Ensign, 30th, 243.
Madeira, 14, 387, 398.
Madras, 15, 49, 387-92, 398-99, 401, 408,
Madrid, 72, 99, 104-05, 111, 230, 232-33, 235, 238, 243-44, 246-48, 256.
Maguire (or Macguire), Francis, Lt, 4th King's Own, 226, 315-16.
+ Maher, Timothy, Pte, 30th, 493.
Mahon, Anthony, Lt, 47th, 336.
Mahon, Thomas, Col, 45-46, 48-49.
Mahrattas, 388.
Maida, battle, 20-25.
Maida Tortoise, 25.
Maitland, Frederick, Lt-Gen, 237.
Maitland, Peregrine, Maj-Gen, later Gen Sir Peregrine, 450, 460-61, 473-74, 476, 479, 483, 488.
Malacca, 391, 408-09.
Malaga, 126.
Maldonaldo, 35-38.
+ Malet, Elias, Capt, 30th, 121-23, 153, 324.
Malines, 381-82, 437.
+ Malone, Anthony, Lt, 40th, 296-97.
Mallow, Co. Cork, 365.
Malta, 2-3, 5, 18-19, 30.
Manchester, 55, 118.

Mermet, Julian Augustin Joseph, French Gen, 84, 151.

Messina, Sicily, 19-20, 26-27, 29, 53, 237.

+ Metcalfe, George, Sgt, 30th, 211.

Meullenacre, Joseph, Lt & Porte-Aigle, 22nd Ligne, 226.

Middelburg, Walcheren, 94, 98.

Milazzo, Sicily, 19-20, 28-30.

Mill, James, Lt, later Maj, 40th, 262, 272, 274-75, 283, 286, 294, 296-303, 307-08, 331, 344, 346-47, 350-52, 354-55, 361, 460, 465, 469-71, 494-95.

+ Millady, Michael, Pte, 59th, 417.

Millbay Barracks, Pymouth, 11.

Miller, Henry, Lt, 40th, 210.

+ Miller, Henry, Pte, 30th, 493.

Milling, Henry, Maj, later Lt-Col, 81st, 70, 88-89, 370, 453.

Milman, Francis, Capt, Coldstream Guards, later Lt-Gen, Col 82nd 1850-56, 111.

Minet, William, Lt-Col, 30th, later Gen, 8, 116-17, 119-20, 123, 137, 139, 188.

Minorca, 2-3, 174, 237.

Minto, Lord, Governor-Gen of India, 408-09, 411, 417.

+ Miskill, Thomas, Pte, 30th, 493.

Mississippi River, 366-68.

Moate, Co. West Meath, 7.

+ Mobbs, Thomas, Pte, 30th, 211.

Mondego Bay, Portugal, 56.

Mondego River & Valley, 125, 128, 130-31, 151-2, 154, 190, 192.

Moneypenny, Thomas Gybbon, Ensign, then Lt, 30th, later Lt-Col, MP & DL, 384, 437, 482, 493.

Monkstown, Co. Cork, 70, 364-65.

Mons, 370, 439, 441, 497.

Monsanto Camp, Lisbon, 67.

Monte Agraça Great Redoubt, Lines of Torres Vedras, 135-37.

Monte Mero Ridge, Corunna, 82-86.

Monte Video, 35, 38-42, 45, 49, 105.

+ Montfort, Lewis, Lt, 47th, 118, 120.

Montgomery, Knox, Lt, 81st, 95.

Montignies-lez-Lens, SW France, 439-40.

Mont Orgueille Castle, Jersey, 371.

Montreal, Canada, 364.

Montreal de Gers, SW France, 360-61.

Mont St. Jean, Waterloo, 433, 456, 458-60, 462, 464, 470, 474, 478, 482, 489, 497.

+ Moody, John, Pte, 59th, 417.

Moore, Sir John, Lt-Gen, 12-13, 19, 26-28, 52, 67-70, 72-87, 89-90, 99-102, 155, 208.

Moore, Robert, Lt, 40th, 200, 494.

Moran, Denis, Cpl, 30th, 493.

+ Moran, William, Pte, 30th, 493.

Morice, Charles, Lt-Col, 69th, 447, 483, 486, 497.

Morris, Tom, Sgt, 73rd, 379, 448, 455-56, 466, 468, 474, 494.

+ Morrisey, Richard, Pte, 30th, 493.

Mortimer, Charles, Lt, 82nd, 332.

+ Morton, Pat, Pte, 30th, 493.

Moulin à Poudre, Mauritius, 402.

Mountain, Robert George, Ensign, 47th, 246.

Mulhally, Pte, 30th, 460.

Mullingar, Co. Westmeath, 7, 30, 70.

Murat, Joachim, Marshal, 28-29.

Murphy, Patrick, Cpl, 30th, 493.

40th (2nd Somersetshire) Regiment of Foot (later **1st South Lancashire**):

1st Bn, 2, 8-9, 13, 36-50, 52, 54-59, 61-68, 99-101, 103-06, 108-10, 112-14, 128-39, 150-53, 162-67, 169-72, 187-90, 192-95, 197-99, 201-03, 208-11, 213-14, 216-22, 227-33, 243, 248-50, 256, 259-62, 267, 276, 282-88, 292-303, 306-11, 315, 323-25, 330-32, 340, 343-44, 346, 348-55, 359-62, 364-70, 440-41, 452, 456-57, 459-60, 46, 469-72, 475, 483, 490-92, 494-95, 497-501.

2nd Bn, 2, 8-9, 13, 36, 42, 54, 187, 216, 233, 359, 364-65, 441.

47th (Lancashire) Regiment of Foot (later **1st Loyal North Lancashire**):

1st Bn, 4, 9-10, 13, 17, 33, 35-36, 38, 41, 44-45, 47, 49, 93, 387-88, 393-97, 403-05.

2nd Bn, 6, 9-10, 13, 117-24, 141, 144, 146-47, 149-50, 173-86, 233-34, 248-54, 256-58, 267, 272-74, 276-78, 287-88, 311-22, 324, 327-28, 331-33, 336, 338, 340, 343, 355-57, 361-62, 380-81.

59th (2nd Nottinghamshire) Regiment of Foot (later **2nd East Lancashire**):

1st Bn, 3, 12-13, 14-15, 34, 387-90, 398-403, 408-32.

2nd Bn, 13, 69-73, 78-82, 85-89, 93-98, 101, 107, 234, 257-58, 267, 272-74, 276-78, 287-88, 311, 313-17, 319-24, 327-28, 331-32, 334-40, 343, 355-57, 361-62, 389, 427, 440, 452-53, 483, 495, 498-99, 501.

81st (Loyal Lincoln Volunnteers) (later **2nd Loyal North Lancashire**):

1st Bn, 4-5, 11, 13, 17-30, 70-71, 106, 237-39, 267-70, 325-26, 358-59, 361-62, 364, 370, 403.

2nd Bn, 1113, 27-28, 30, 69-76, 81-82, 85, 87-89, 93-96, 98-99, 101, 370, 372-76, 380-81, 383, 437-38, 441-42, 452-53, 459, 497.

82nd (Prince of Wales's Volunteers) (later **2nd South Lancashire**),

1st Bn, 3, 13, 27, 30-33, 52-54, 6-68, 75-78, 81, 83-84, 87-89, 93-9, 97-99, 101, 109-10, 113, 122, 125-28, 141-42, 144, 150, 174, 176, 178-80, 184-86, 229, 231-33, 243-44, 246, 248-52, 254-57, 29, 261-62, 267, 272-74, 276, 279-82, 287-89, 291-93, 304-06, 308, 311, 324-25, 331-32, 334, 340, 343-44, 346-49, 359, 361-62, 403.

2nd Bn, 11-13, 30, 33, 52, 89, 150, 304, 364, 371.

Royal Horse Guards, 455, 464; **Life Guards**, 455, 464, 466, 469-70; **1st Royal Dragoons**, 438; **2nd Dragoon Guards (Scots Greys)**, 470; **3rd Dragoon Guards**, 226, 260; **4th Dragoon Guards**, 226; **5th Dragoon Guards**, 226; **7th Hussars**, 455; **9th Light Dragoons**, 45; **11th Light Dragoons**, 217, 250; **12th Light Dragoons**, 492; **13th Light Dragoons**, 130, 163-64; **14th Light Dragoons**, 69, 344; **15th Hussars**, 72, 282; **16th Light Dragoons**, 339; **18th Hussars**, 350; **19th Light Dragoons**, 389; **20th Light Dragoons**, 14, 17, 6, 268, 326; **22nd Light Dragoons**, 409, 413, 415, 417; **23rd Light Dragoons**, 468-69; **25th Light Dragoons**, 399-400; **1st Hussars King's German Legion**, 442, 489; **2nd Hussars King's German Legion**, 141-42, 149, 174-75, 233-34.

1st Foot Guards, 84-85, 141, 147, 234, 361-62, 473, 478-79, 483, 488-89, 01; **Coldstream Guards**, 141, 148-49, 438; **3rd Foot Guards**, 141, 147, 245.

1st Royals, later Royal Scots, 70-71, 85, 137, 206, 225, 241-42, 313, 336, 377, 398, 445, 451, 464; **3rd Buffs**, 13, 102, 168, 293, 301; **4th King's Own**, later King's Own Royal Regt (Lancaster), 12, 84, 137, 140, 161-62, 186, 205-06, 214, 225-26, 240-42, 257, 267, 273, 277, 314-15, 327-28, 336, 440-41, 49, 471, 475; **5th (Northumberland)**, later Royal Northumberland Fusiliers, 47, 58; **6th (1st Warwickshire)**, later Royal Warwickshire, 291, 346, 363, 371; **7th Royal Fusiliers**, 106, 108-09, 169, 294-95, 307, 368; **8th King's**, 363; **9th (East Norfolk)**, later Norfolk, 16, 54, 8, 121, 137, 141, 184, 206, 225, 235, 240-42, 274, 278, 328, 336, 476; **10th (North Lincolnshire)**, later Lincolnshire, 237, 267, 269-70, 326; **11th (North Devonshire)**, later Devonshire, 174, 176-79; **12th (East Suffolk)**, later Suffolk, 12, 402;, **14th (Buckinghamshire**, later Prince of Wales's Own West Yorkshire, 9, 93, 408-09, 414, 425-26, 438-39; **20th (East Devonshire)**, later Lancashire Fusiliers, 20-21, 24, 294-95; **22nd (Cheshire)**, 4; **23rd (Royal Welch Fusiliers)**, 93, 169, 294-95; **24th (2nd Warwickshire)**, later South Wales Borderers, 14, 109, 160, 235, 257; **25th (King's Own Borderers)**, later King's Own Scottish Borderers, 383; **26th (Cameronians)**, 70, 93, 186; **27th (Inniskilling)**, 20-21, 24-25, 167, 214, 218-20, 223, 267-69, 272, 283, 294-95, 299, 306, 326, 330, 346, 32, 361, 440-41, 459, 465, 471, 475, 491; **28th (North Gloucestershire)**, later 1st Gloucestershire, 121-22, 141, 148-49, 168, 290, 439, 445; **29th (Worcestershire)**, later 1st Worcestershire, 52, 56, 58, 64, 106-07, 117, 168; **31st (Huntingdonshire)**, later 1st East Surrey, 109, 168; **32nd (Cornwall)**, later 1st Duke of Cornwall's Light Infantry, 31-32, 52, 98; **33rd (1st West Riding)**, later 1st Duke of Wellington's, 377, 427, 438-39, 446-48, 450, 460-61, 466, 468, 479, 483, 485-87, 498; **34th (Cumberland)**, later 1st Border, 4, 268, 290; **35th (Sussex)**, later 1st Royal Sussex, 21, 46, 375; **36th (Herefordshire)**, later 2nd Worcestershire, 46-48, 55-56, 62, 64, 161-62; **37th (North Hampshire)**, later 1st Royal

S

Uxbridge, Lord Henry Paget, later _{Field Marshal} & Marquess of Anglesey, 455.

V

Valencia, 236-38, 271, 325.
Valencia-de-Leon, 73-74.
Valenciennes, 16, 333.
Valladolid, 70, 72, 216, 231, 235, 240, 256, 267.
Valletta, Malta, 2, 18.
Valls, north of Tarragona, Catalonia, 326, 358.
Vandermaesen, Edmé-Martin, French Gen, 298-99, 305-06, 309, 324-25, 402.
+ Van Strawbenzie, George, Lt, 40th, 166.
+ Vassal, Spencer Thomas, Lt-Col, 38th (previously 59th), 35, 41.
Vaughan, Edward, Lt, 47th, 246.
Vaumorel, Philip Choet de, Lt-Col, 30th, 7, 390, 392, 399, 405-08.
Veere, Walcheren, 94-95.
Vellore Fort, Madras, 389-90.
Venta de Urroz, Combat, 308.
Ventosa (near Vimeiro), 59-60, 62, 64.
Vera, Pyrenees, Combat, 324-25.
Verdun, 16, 123, 154, 222-3, 245, 480.
Vere, Charles Broke, Maj, 204, 218, 228-29.
+ Vevers, Charles Nicholas, Lt, 59th, 322.
+ Vice, Robert, Pte, 59th, 417.
Victor, Claude, Duke of Belluno, Marshal, 102-03, 105-07, 110, 120-21, 140, 142-44, 148-49, 174-75, 184.
Vigo, 78, 81.
Vigoureux, Charles Albert, Maj, 38th, later Lt-Col, 30th, 130, 372-73, 379, 382, 443, 446-48, 450, 456, 462, 464-65, 467, 493.
Villafranca del Bierzo, Leon, 72, 76, 78, 88.
Villamuriel, Combat, 240-43, 248.
Villatte, Eugene Casimir, Comte d'Oultremont, French Gen, 143-44, 289, 314, 335, 348, 351.
Vimeiro, Battle, Portugal, 59-65.
Vincent, William, Capt, later Maj, 82nd, 184, 332, 348, 362.
+ Vipond, Thomas, Drum-Maj, 30th, 378-79
Vitoria, Battle, etc., 267, 274-288, 305, 307.
+ Vizer, Garret, Pte, 30th, 493.

W

+ Wade, John, Lt, 30th, 408.
+ Wadsworth, James, Cpl, 30th, 211.
Wainwright, Henry Maxwell, Lt, later Capt, 47th, 124, 141,
Wainwright, John, Commodore, 395-97.
Wakefield, 6, 123.
Walahjabad Cantonment, Madras, 389-90.
Walcheren, Campaign, 92-99, 125, 234, 370.
Walcheren Fever, 92, 96, 98-99, 125, 231, 233, 148, 255.
+ Walker, George Henry, Lt, 59th, 278.
Walker, George Townsend, Maj-Gen, 191, 205-06, 214, 257, 346.
Wallace, Charles, Lt, 40th, 332.
+ Wallace, Hugh, Lt, 40th, 41.
Wallace, Peter, Sgt-Maj, 30th, 3.
Wall, Adam, Capt, RA, 70-72.

Walmsley, John, Maj, 82nd, 322.

Ward, John, Sgt, later Quartermaster, 30th, 227.

Wardrobe, William, Lt-Col, 47th, 10, 17-18.

Wardropp, John Murdoch, Capt, 81st, 364.

+ Waring, William, Lt, 59th, 417.

War of 1812, 362-70.

Warren, Charles Ouseley, Ensign, then Lt, 30th, 384, 451, 493.

Warrenpoint, Co. Down, 440.

+ Waterhouse, Peter, Capt (later Brevet Lt-Col), 47th, 25, 238-39.

Waterloo, Battle, 15, 370, 438, 445, 452-53, 455, 458-497, 501-02.

+ Waters, James, Pte, 30th, 16, 123, 372.

Waters, William Hamilton, Ensign, 59th, 418.

+ Watson, Charles, Sgt, 30th, 137.

+ Watson, C. S., Lt, 30th, 390-92.

+ Watson, Lawrence, Ensign, 59th, 316, 322.

Watson, Lewis, Brevet Maj, 69th, 374, 440, 454.

+ Watts, Thomas, Capt, 59th, 411, 413-14, 420.

Wavre, Belgium, 454, 458.

+ Webb, George, Pte, 30th, 493.

Weeley Barracks, Essex, 69, 89, 98.

+ Weir, John Laing, Brevet Lt-Col, 59th, 278.

+ Weld, Standish, Lt, 47th, 396.

Wellesley, Sir Arthur, Duke of Wellington, 55-61, 63, 65-67, 90, 99-100, 102-06, 108, 110-14, 116-17, 122, 128-40, 150-56, 159-62, 164-67. 171-72, 178, 185-89, 191-95, 197-99, 203-04, 207, 209, 213-15, 217-18, 220-25, 227-33, 235-43, 248-51, 254-57, 261-62, 266-67, 269-70, 272-74, 276-77, 279-80, 288-89, 292, 296, 298-305, 307-11, 314, 324-29, 331, 333-36, 338-40, 344-46, 348-51, 355, 358-59, 361, 368, 438, 441-42, 446, 450, 454-59, 461, 463, 465-67, 469, 473-74, 479, 483, 486, 489-90, 492, 495-500.

+ Welstead, Benjamin, Lt, 82nd, 177, 179, 325.

Weltevreden, near Batavia, 410, 412-14, 426, 431-32.

Werlé, François-Jean, French General, 167-69.

Weser, expedition, 16-17.

+ West, John, Pte, 59th, 418.

West Indies, 2, 17, 45.

Wetherall, Frederick Augustus, former Lt-Col 82nd, Maj-Gen, 406-07, 409-12..

Whalley, Henry, Lt, 47th, 252.

Wheeler, William, Cpl, 51st, 94, 280-81, 305-06, 311, 361-62.

Whetham, John, Lt, 40th, later Maj-Gen, 41.

+ White, George, Pte, 59th, 417.

White, John Lorraine, Lt, 30th, 196.

+ White, James, Pte, 30th, 211.

Whitelocke, John, Lt-Gen, 43-50.

White Mutiny, Madras Army, Madras Army, 397-401.

Whittaker, Richard, Ensign, 82nd, 332.

Whittingham, Samuel Ford, Capt, later Lt-Gen Sir Samuel, 49, 144-45, 267-29.

+ Whonahon, Denis, Pte, 59th, 498.

Widenham, Joseph A., Volunteer, 40th, 210.

Wilcox, Pte, 81st, 442.

Willemstadt, Holland, 374-75.

+ Wilkinson, John, Sgt, 30th, 492.

Wilkinson, William, Lt-Col, 30th, later Gen Sir William, 6, 392, 398-99, 405.

Wilkinson, William, Capt, 59th, 374, 336, 340.

Williams, Edmund, Keynton, Capt, 81st, Lt-Col Portuguese Army, 102, 132, 336, 340.

Williams, William, Maj, 40th, then 81st, later Maj-Gen Sir William, 71, 88-89, 93, 159-60.

+ Denotes Regimental officers and men died in service.